Scorched Earth

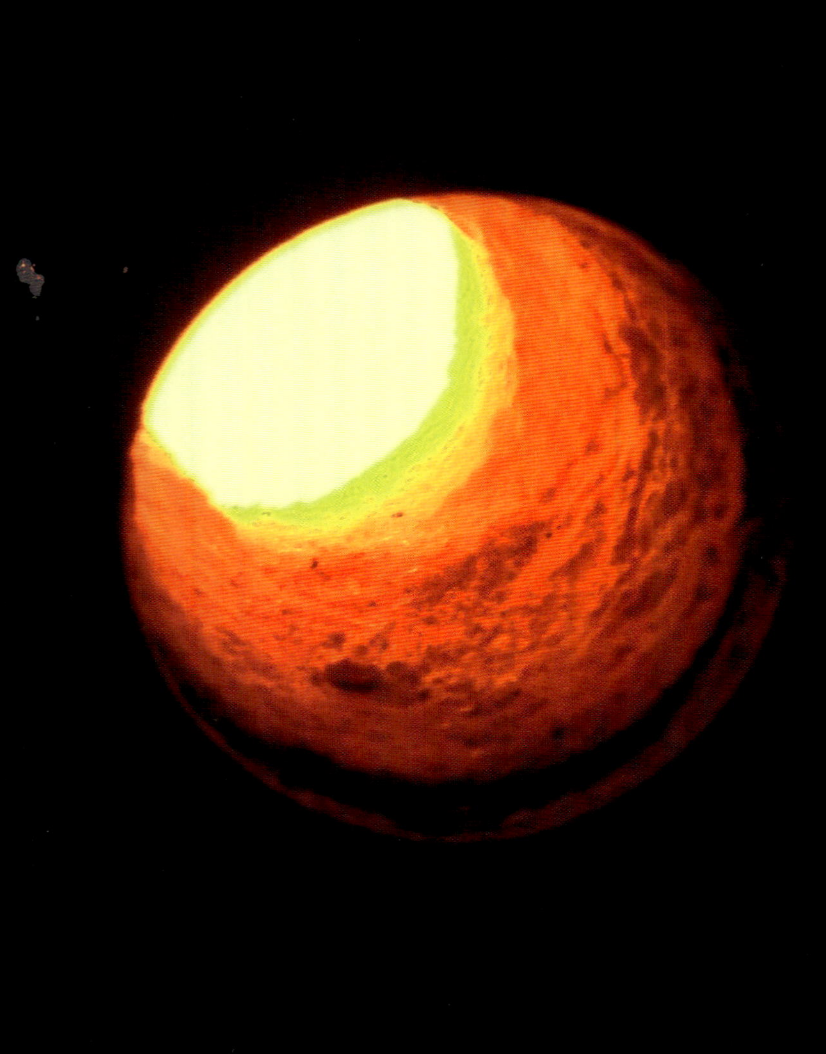

Scorched Earth

100 Years of Southern African Potteries

Wendy Gers

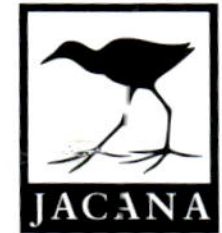
JACANA

This book is dedicated to my family – Mathieu, Noah and Gabriel. I also thank my parents and parents-in-law who have graciously supported my research over the years.

Structure of the book

Potteries are listed alphabetically, with the exception of the Conrand group of potteries, which are listed chronologically. Conrad stands for Consolidated Rand Brick, Pottery and Lime Company.

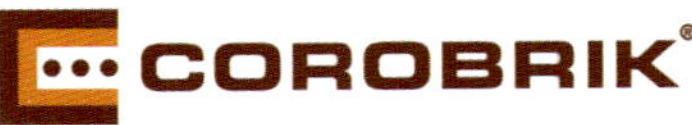

First published by Jacana Media (Pty) Ltd in 2015

10 Orange Street
Sunnyside
Auckland Park 2092
South Africa

ISBN 978-1-4314-2126-8

Set in FrescoSans Std Light 10/13.5pt
Printed and bound by Imago
Job no. 002313

Also available as an e-book:
d-PDF 978-1-4314-2127-5

See a complete list of Jacana titles at www.jacana.co.za

FRONT COVER: Kalahari | Charger | Woman with yellow dread-locks | 184x45mm | Provenance: Wendy Gers | Marks: hand-painted black glaze marking, 'Kalahari' | Photograph by Damien Artus

BACK COVER: Dykor | Jug with pale blue interior and exterior | 178x125x97x55mm | Provenance: TAG | 2436/06 | Marks: glazed blue-grey base with incised 'dykor' mark beneath the glaze | Additional information: evidence of multiple glaze layers | Photograph by Natalie Field

Contents

PREVIOUS PAGE LEFT: Untitled | Detail of kiln peephole during firing | Photograph by Laura du Toit

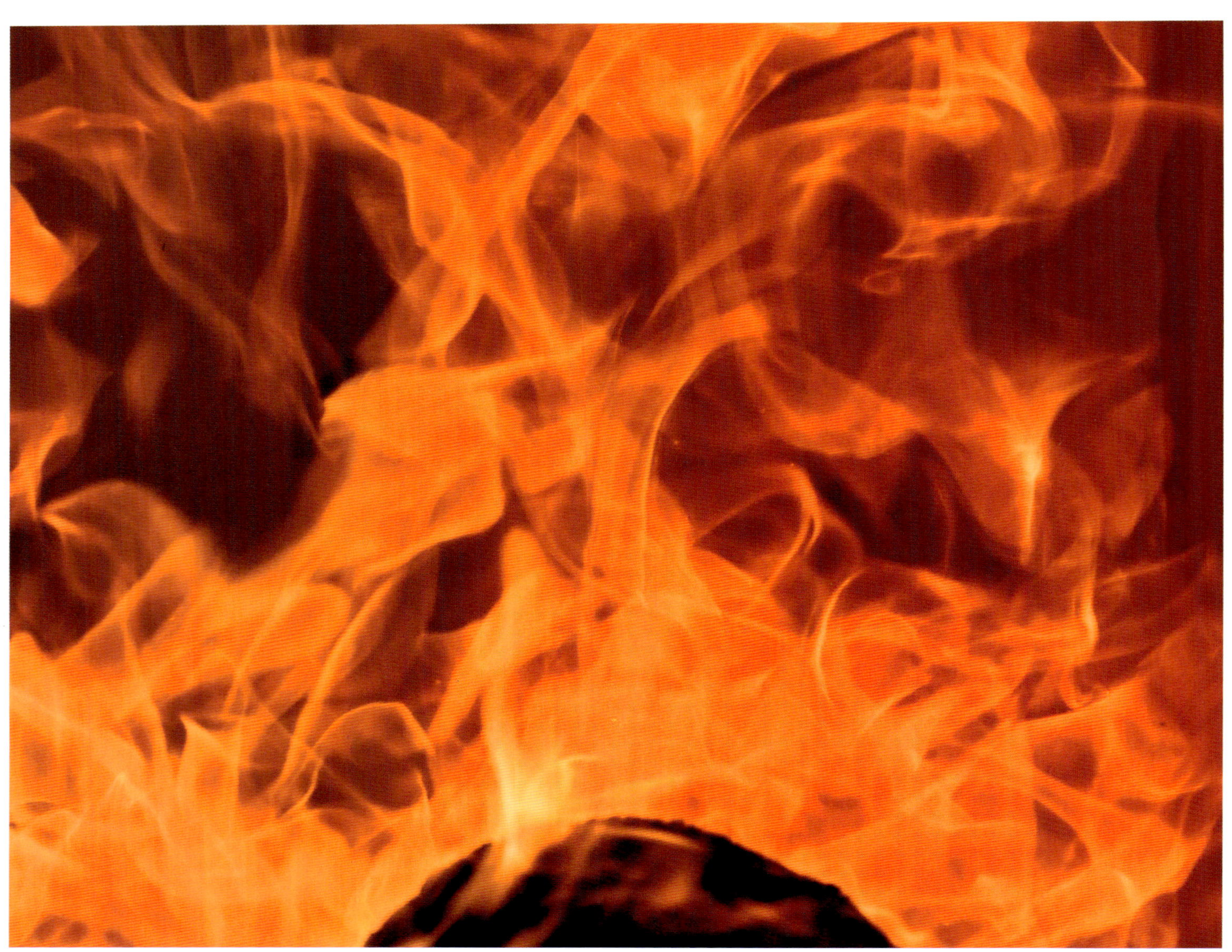

Untitled | Detail of kiln interior during firing | Photograph by Richard Yates

Abbreviations

ADF	African Development Foundation
aka	Also known as
APSA	Association of Potters of South Africa
BEP	Boksburg East Potteries
CCDI	Cape Craft and Design Institute
CED	Community Economic Development Enterprise
CUSO	Canadian University Services Overseas
Conrand	Consolidated Rand Brick, Pottery and Lime Company
CSIR	Council for Scientific and Industrial Research
DAG	Durban Art Gallery
DNMCH	Ditsong National Museum of Cultural History, Pretoria
EDESA	Economical Development Bank for Equatorial and Southern Africa
ILO	International Labour Organisation
JAG	Johannesburg Art Gallery
LNDC	Lesotho National Development Corporation
NA UP	Nilant Archives, University of Pretoria
NMMAM	Nelson Mandela Metropolitan Art Museum, Port Elizabeth (formerly the King George VI Art Gallery)
NSA	National Society of the Arts
SAG	South African Glazing Company
SANG	South African National Gallery, Isiko Museums of Cape Town
SEDCO	Small Enterprises Development Company
SHC Iziko	Social History Collection, Iziko Museums of Cape Town
TAG	Tatham Art Gallery, Pietermaritzburg
TNDC	Transkei National Development Corporation
TOJ	The Old Jar Pottery
UNDP	United Nations Development Project
UNISA	University of South Africa, Pretoria
VBTC	Vereeniging Brick, Tile and Lime Company
WHAG	William Humphreys Art Gallery, Kimberley

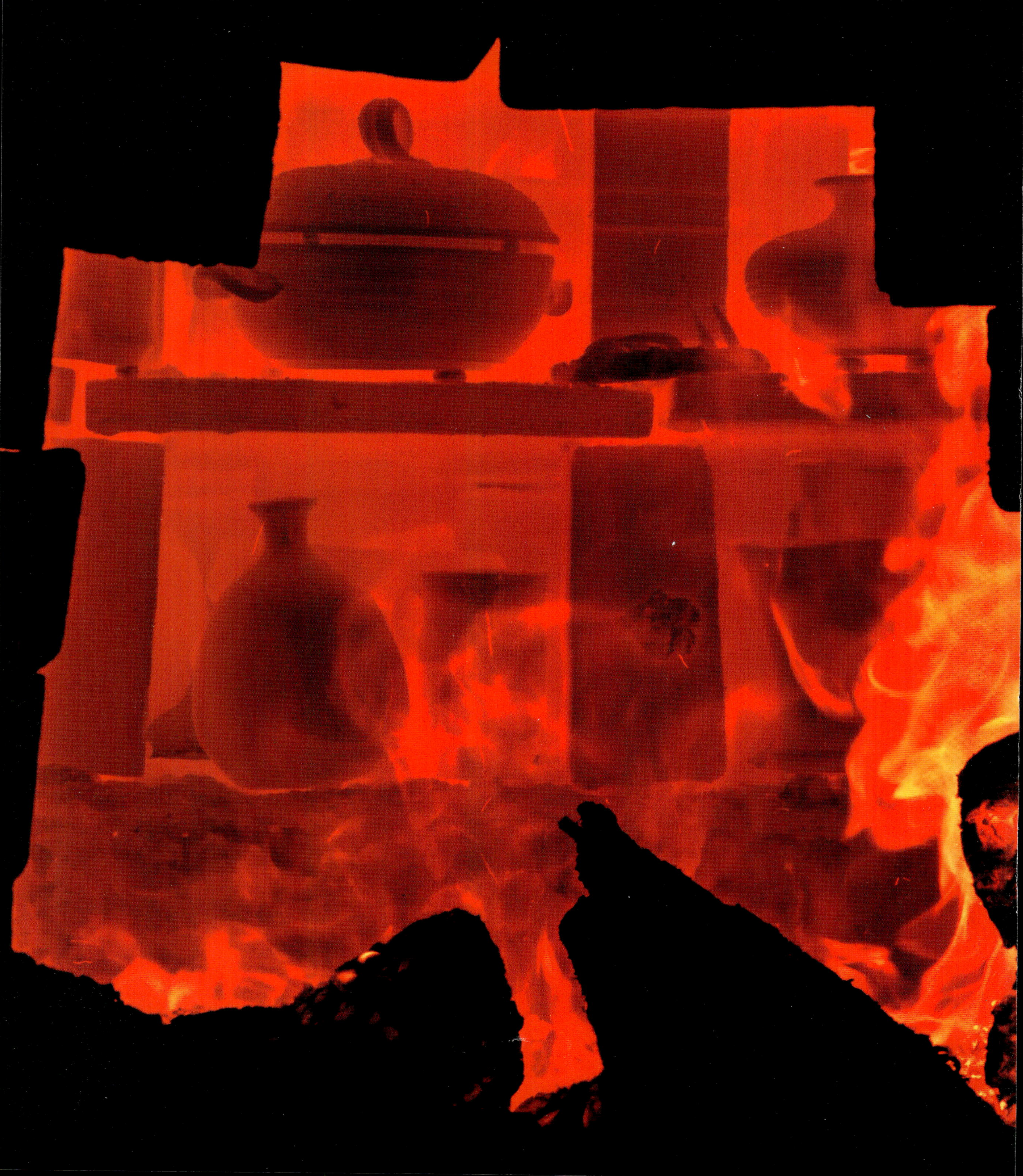

Introduction

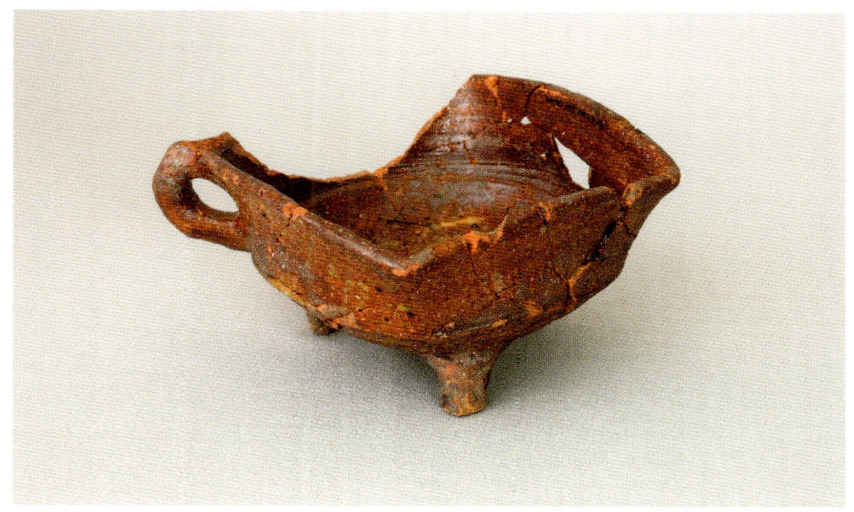

> In Europe the factory in which an object has been made is an eminently important consideration when people choose porcelain or earthenware. People feel proud to have in their possession a piece made in some world-famous pottery or other. In South Africa the circumstances are quite different. People are not only indifferent to, but quite unaware of, the various potteries in existence (Nilant 1963:71).

The title, *Scorched Earth*[1] alludes to the union of two primal elements – fire and earth – which under certain conditions produce a marvellous commodity, pottery.[2] This metaphor also describes the cyclic nature of the southern African ceramics industry; potteries are born, grow, mature and die as new potteries rise from their ashes.

In 1963 Professor F G E Nilant, then head of the Department of History of Art and Fine Arts at the University of Pretoria, made this poignant remark. Over 50 years later, his sentiments still ring true, the primary reason being a resounding lack of research on local craft and design history by both heritage institutions (including art and cultural history museums) and humanities faculties of universities. Pottery in general is saddled with a perceived stigma of being a craft, commodity or material culture, and not an art. The question of utility that is associated with most ceramics marginalises it in terms of its status in the Western pantheon of arts. Furthermore, commercial or production potteries face the additional stigma of producing 'debased' wares because of their perceived industrial mode of production. Many potters that I interviewed confirmed the existence of these hierarchies of perception. Often they attempted to side-step these hierarchies by embracing 'other' identities, such as that of 'crafter' (Sammy and Mary Liebermann of Liebermann Pottery and Tiles), 'entrepreneur' (I A Perold of Dykor), 'designer' (France Marot and Hester Locke of Grahamstown Pottery) or artists (Aleksanders Klopcanovs and Elma Vestman of the Kalahari Pottery).

The marginalisation of ceramics is also historically associated with the rise of modernism in Western art. In the latter half of the nineteenth century and the first half of the twentieth century numerous critics, theorists, artists and architects trivialised the perceived 'decorative' or 'domestic' aspects of applied arts. Finally, in the post-war years Pop Art radically revised those notions, and

ABOVE: DEIC Pottery | Coarse red earthenware | 18th century | The Castle (M90) | Source: University of Cape Town, Archaeology Department | Photograph by Natalie Field

LEFT: Untitled | Detail of kiln interior during firing | Photograph by Richard Yates

drew attention to the decorative nature of art and its links to craft. This opened the door to ceramic production, among other crafts, which had hitherto been somewhat excommunicated from the realm of fine arts.

Yet, these advances are still unheeded by the majority of art museums internationally, which are too set in their ways to change collecting practices, and argue that cultural history, design and local history museums are better suited to fulfil this mission. In southern Africa, the vast majority of art and cultural history museums have failed to collect and exhibit locally produced production pottery, thereby denying the significance of this unique aspect of our cultural heritage, which is profoundly democratic and surpasses the classic binary cleavages of white and black, rich and poor, urban and rural.

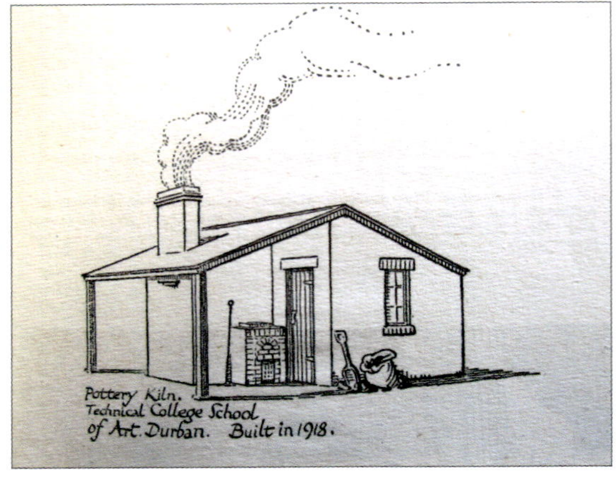

Pottery Kiln, Natal Technical College, School of Art, Durban (1918) | Scan by Anthony Starkey

Scope

What

The book focuses on the products, histories and personnel of a selection of southern African, twentieth-century, small- and medium-sized artistic and production potteries. These potteries produced both utilitarian wares (dinner services, vases, tiles) and decorative items (sculptures, ornaments, chargers, artistic[3] and fancy goods). They produced wares for different markets, including 'the man on the street', tourists (souvenirs) and commercial wares (promotional objects). The terms industrial artware and production ware[4] describe the majority of these diverse wares. Most of these potteries employed between five and 50 staff members, including potters (who hand-built or threw articles on a potter's wheel), designers, various skilled workers, administrators, managers, and sales and marketing staff. This book excludes individual studio potters,[5] who became increasingly prominent from the 1960s. Similarly, potteries that primarily manufactured industrial tiles,[6] bricks,[7] sanitary whiteware,[8] industrial ceramics,[9] electrical elements and insulators,[10] unglazed planters,[11] and industrial storage vessels (such as stock and gallon jars)[12] and commercial tiles[13] have been excluded from the book.

This personal research project was initially envisaged as encyclopaedic in its scope. However, as the vast size of the ceramics industry became apparent, I realised that it was beyond the scope of an individual, and so have tried to focus on potteries that I feel are historically significant or representative of a sector of the industry. The scope of my research was also influenced by financial and physical constraints as well as by the willingness of potters, former potters and their families to assist with this endeavour. Finally, when it came to publishing, my research had to be restructured to respond to the current economic realities of the publishing industry and the needs of the reading public. The end result is a somewhat partial and eclectic selection of potteries.[14]

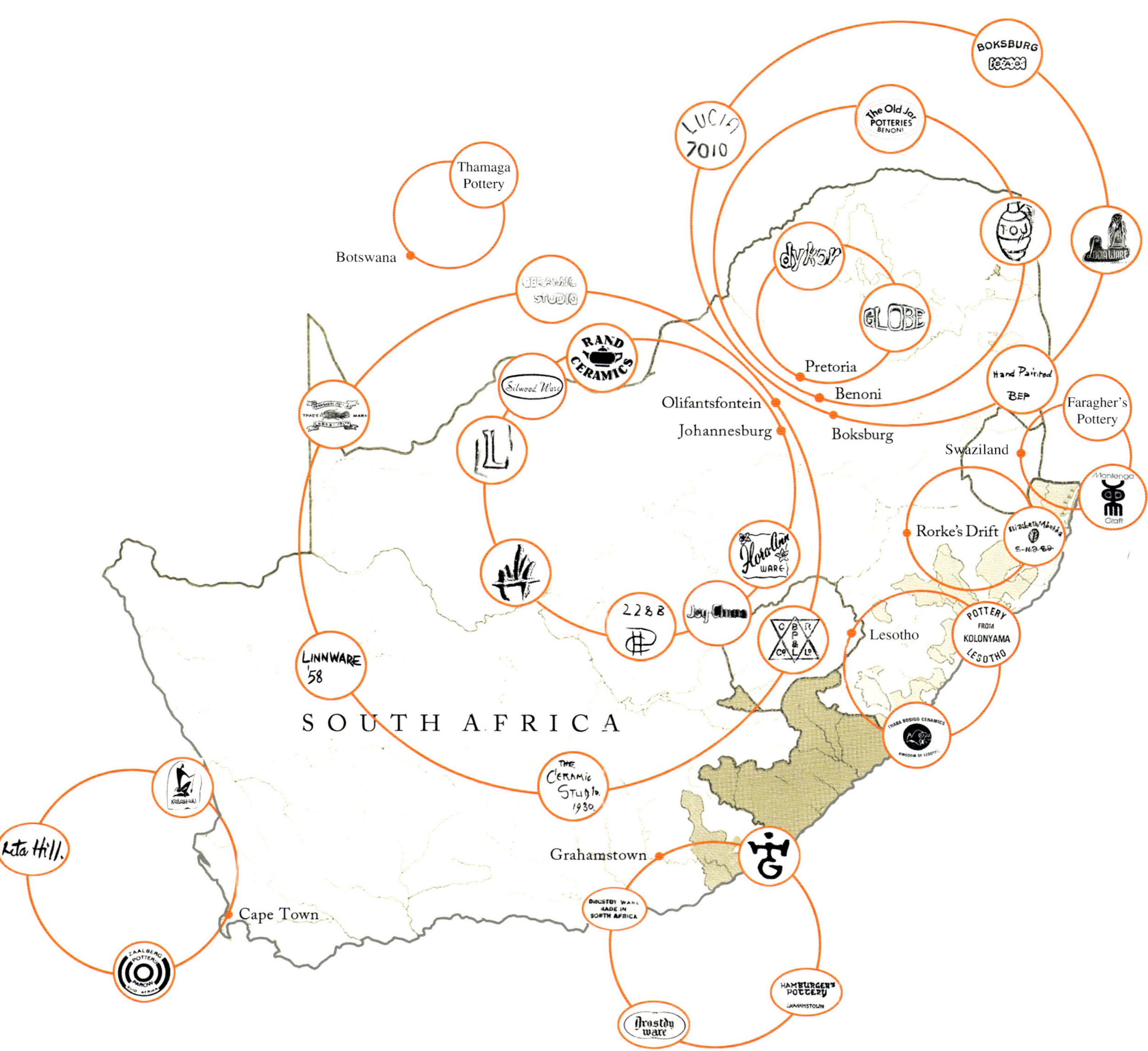

Map of major potteries in southern Africa and some of their maker's marks

Where

The decade I have spent researching southern African potteries has convinced me of the importance of a southern African vision of ceramics production. During the period 1880 to 1980, the national economies of South Africa, Botswana, Swaziland, Lesotho, Zimbabwe, Mozambique and Namibia were interwoven on both macro and micro levels. Furthermore, the potteries of South Africa's neighbouring states, many of which are geographically landlocked, were (and still are) frequently dependent on South Africa. Essential raw materials, technical expertise and retail markets were only obtainable in South Africa. Furthermore, cultural tourism from South Africa sustained many potteries.

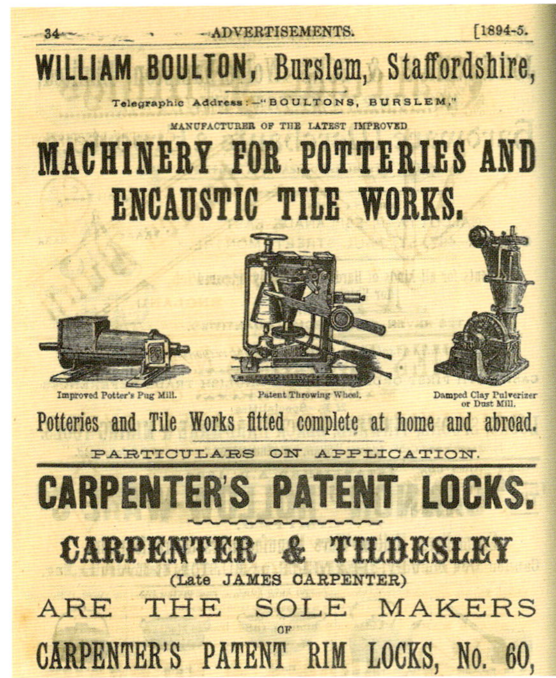

Advert for British pottery plant machinery | Provenance: Edwards, D (1895) *The General Directory of South Africa for 1894–95*. Cape Town: Dennis Edwards p. 34 | Scan by William Martinson

When

The book begins with the establishment of the South African art and production pottery industry during a period of immigration and industrial growth spurned by mineral discoveries on the subcontinent. It culminates in the 1980s, a period marked by apartheid oppression, escalating armed resistance and international economic sanctions, which crippled the South African economy and resulted in the decline and demise of many potteries. The late 1980s and early 1990s are marked by important changes at all levels of society, as the winds of change swept away many entrenched political and cultural regimes.

Aims

Art and production pottery has been historically stigmatised with various negative associations as a result of modernist canons of high and low art. Art historians have only relatively recently become aware of the centrality of these monolithic modernist canons and begun challenging them (Preziosi 1998). This book is a revisionist project that challenges modern art canons in southern Africa. It is rooted in a long-term commitment to enlarging our understanding of modern southern African artistic production and design.

Scorched Earth documents and celebrates the creative pioneers of the southern African pottery industry. It attests to the essential contribution of decades of unknown African artists and artisans – both able-bodied and handicapped. Extensive biographical sections detail the professional lives of the founders, managers, decorators, designers and artists of over 30 major potteries. The establishment and consolidation of the ceramics industry was facilitated by access to cheap labour and these anonymous workers deserve recognition.

The promotion of southern African ceramics is what has motivated this project, which operates on multiple levels. On a purely technical level, South Africa has all the raw materials required to make and decorate quality wares,[15] and has been exporting china clay and other raw materials from the turn of the twentieth century, if not earlier.[16] But southern African raw materials lack sophisticated processing that facilitates ceramic production and experimentation. This is in contrast to some northern European nations, which, despite a lack of essential raw materials, manufacture internationally renowned ceramics, due to the availability of imported high-quality clay bodies.[17]

On a more political level, southern African art and production pottery of the twentieth century is a highly mobile and democratic commodity. In both the manufacturing processes and in consumption practices, it transcends the classic binary cleavages of white and black, rich and poor, urban and rural. Whether received as a gift or personally acquired, these artefacts are loaded with dense histories of emotional and affective charge. They speak of the status and personality of the owner, the giver and the exchange. Furthermore, utilitarian wares frame dining practices and the social rituals associated with consuming tea, coffee or even, in certain instances, beer! Via their design, dinner services may determine the size of a portion, the number of courses, what accompanies a meal, how food is presented, what is served[18] and the ambience of the table setting – stark or rustic, sober or casual, homely or contemporary, exotic or classic, elegant or creative, or infused with African, Western or Asian ambience.

The southern African pottery industry is struggling in an increasingly global market. Like so many other nations internationally, the region is experiencing the Chinese 'onslaught' in ceramics and in many other manufacturing sectors. If the southern African ceramics sector is to fulfil its potential, it needs a sense of its historical legacy, and must embrace new markets, technologies, dining and décor trends. *Scorched Earth* details the historical roots of the southern African art and production potteries sector and serves as a reference text aimed at promoting both vernacular connoisseurship and further scholarship. It is also a reference tool that the ceramics sector can use to chart its future.

Advert for Cullinan Refractories and Insulators | Source: Donaldson, K (ed.) (1955) *South African Who's Who*. Johannesburg: Ken Donaldson. p. 170 | Scan by William Martinson

1000 BC–1880: Historical Context

Khoikhoi/Khoekhoen and 'Bantu' traditions

While this book focuses on industrial artware and production pottery, it is important to contextualise this alongside indigenous low-fired, unglazed earthenware. From 1000 BC indigenous Khoikhoi/Khoekhoen produced simple vessels for cooking and storage of wet and dry foodstuffs. Other communities, including the San and the various later groups of African immigrants (Bantu-language speakers), also made ceramic vessels and objects. These African immigrants used clay as a building material, to make beads, pipes, moulds for casting glass, fertility figurines, body decoration and, no doubt, for medicinal purposes. Religious artefacts, including masks, and human and animal figurines, are relatively rare in archaeological digs, but the exceptional Lydenberg Heads (ca.500–AD 800) testify to the incredible creativity of these artists. African women continue to produce unglazed 'traditional' and tourist pottery (including beer vessels, figurines and other forms) in southern Africa.

Early colonial glazed pottery

In the early years of colonial settlement, settlers experienced a dire shortage of domestic pottery, cooking pots and cutlery, which severely compromised their

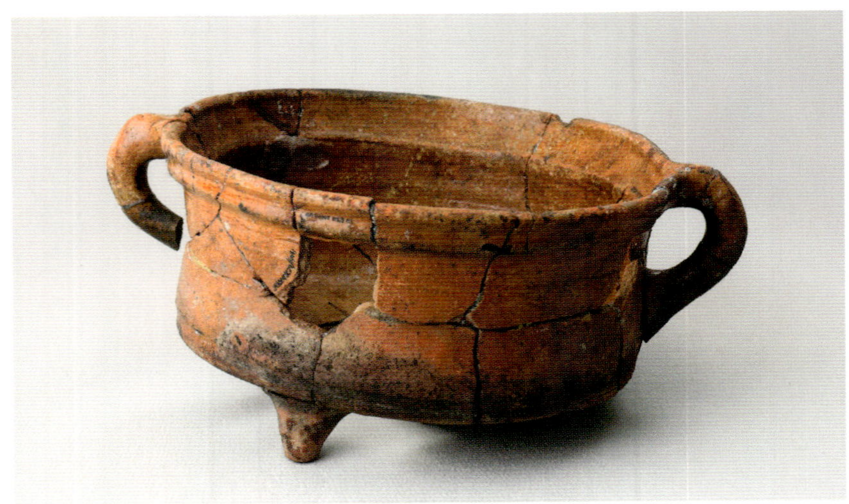

LEFT: DEIC Pottery | Coarse red earthenware | 18th century | The Castle (M90) | Source: University of Cape Town, Archaeology Department | Photograph by Natalie Field

eating and drinking habits. This horrified Van Riebeeck's successor, Zacharias Wagenaer, who compared these settlers to swine. A sample of Cape white clay was sent to Batavia in 1661 to investigate the possibility of establishing a local pottery. It was found to be suitable for ceramic production and Wagenaer petitioned the Dutch East India Company (DEIC) for potters to be sent to the Cape, but was unsuccessful. After Wagenaer submitted a second petition to the Company in 1663, two slave potters were sent on a passing ship in 1664, and in September 1665 Wagenaer reported the successful manufacture of glazed ceramics at the Cape. This coarse, lead-glazed earthenware crockery, included cooking and serving vessels, was similar to contemporary wares from Bergen-op-Zoom and Sommelsdijk in the Netherlands. A variety of different colour glazes were used – yellow, black, brown, orange and dark green, the latter two colours being predominant. Examples have been reconstructed from archaeological digs. Within a relatively short period the local needs were met and wares were produced for export to the interior and brick production was prioritised. Over time, ceramic production became more professional and by 1710, the tiles,[19] bricks and pottery made at the Cape were, according to the governor-general, equal to any imported items. The fate of DEIC Cape pottery production is unclear at the end of the DEIC period, ca.1795.

In the late eighteenth century it appears that local enterprises continued to ensure a local supply for certain domestic ware and building materials. Archival records refer to three Cape-based eighteenth-century potteries. In 1785 the surgeon Mr P J Claude established a pottery near Cape Town to manufacture tiles, bricks, wine-jars and jars for preserving fish and salted meat. In that same year other potteries were established by Surgeon Condee of the mercenary Regiment Meuron in Tamboerskloof, Cape Town and in Saldanha Bay (Laidler 1927). Sadly, there is no information about the fates of these three potteries. The advent of British rule in 1795 coincided with the peak of English ceramic production, and hence the arrival of mass-produced

British ceramics, including bone china (English porcelain) and industrial white-bodied wares (cream-coloured, white- and pearlware) (Malan and Klose 2003:194–6). As in the seventeenth century, South Africa was a pawn in the global economy, which was created and controlled by the colonial powers. The country was 'flooded' with imported English domestic ware and the fortunes of local pottery operations waned.

During the Second British Occupation (1806–1910) potteries were established in the Fish River area of the Eastern Cape, which produced lead-glazed earthenware pots in yellow that were fired in pits in the ground, using dung as fuel. The only named potter is James Hancock, a British settler and former Staffordshire china-painter, who started a pottery at Salem, near Grahamstown, in 1822. Hancock claimed that a company had been formed by some Staffordshire potters, but disagreements led to closing of the company before the commencement of commercial production. Hancock's Salem pottery overcame many hardships, including devastating floods, and he produced bricks and a limited amount of domestic ware before he relocated to Port Elizabeth in 1827, where he re-established himself as a builder and potter. Hancock sold quarry tiles and bricks, and soon received orders from Cape Town for garden pots, domestic crockery, bed pans, jars, dishes and covers, cheese pans and covers, pipkins, milk pans and roof tiles. His relocation to an urban area and his production of building materials was indicative of a growing urbanisation and an urgent need for building materials. Sadly, there are currently no positively identified examples of his wares.

By the closing years of the nineteenth century, the pattern of mass importation was slowly reversed as the urban colonial population increased and transport infrastructure improved. Brick and tile yards became an important industry, and by 1901 there were 69 brick and tile enterprises in the KwaZulu-Natal region. Brickfields are intricately associated with many of the first potteries, including Groenkloof Brick, Tile and Pottery Works, Grahamstown Pottery, Transvaal Pottery and Vereeniging Brick and Tile Company.

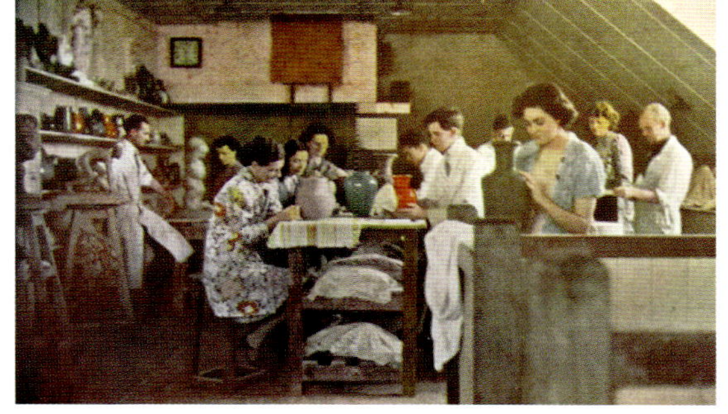

Students at work in the Pottery Room, Natal Technical College | Source: *Common Room* magazine. Durban Art School (June 1938) p. 30 | Scan by Anthony Starkey

1880–1940: Pioneer Potters

In 1905 ceramic engineer and Pietermaritzburg resident E R C Most[20] explained that:

> A gentleman who has been connected with several local ventures, particularly clay and pottery works, gave as his opinion the reason why they had not hitherto been a success, [was] that the people would rather pay considerably more to import an article no better in quality than one from Home.[21]

A decade later, the pioneer ceramics teacher John Adams (1882–1953) noted:

> In Natal we have several well equipped brick and roofing-tile works that are

making goods of an excellent quality. They have instituted machinery and kilns of the latest types. The manufacture of such building materials is naturally an early feature in the progress of the colony ... But until the population increases, bringing about a higher standard of life, there will be less scope for local endeavours in the direction of the finer kinds of pottery (1916:1).

These two quotations illustrate a complex economic and psychological dependency on Britain at the time (also known as 'colonial cringe'[22]), with the easy availability of imported British china playing a seminal role in countering the establishment of the South African ceramics industry. This dependency continued until the 1950s, when a vibrant local industry was established – a situation that has parallels in various other local industries, including the glass industry, which was dependent on imported glass bottles for beverages (alcoholic and non-alcoholic, carbonated and still), medical compounds, chemicals and certain foods. While the first known South African glass bottles were produced by Woods and Sons, Durban in 1918, this fulfilled a fraction of domestic needs and the nation depended on imported ceramics and glass wares until after World War II.[23]

In the late nineteenth and early twentieth century, pioneer potters fell into three groups: university lecturers, wealthy industrialists and immigrant entrepreneurs. Lecturers were associated with early art schools, such as John[24] and Truda Adams of the School of Art, Durban[25] and Frederick William Armstrong (1875–1969)[26] of the Grahamstown School of Art, who, with his wife Ruth Beatrice Armstrong, established Grahamstown Pottery and pioneered art pottery production in the Eastern Cape. Randlord industrialists like Sammy Marks (who established the Vereeniging Pottery) and Sir Thomas M Cullinan (founder of Transvaal Pottery) were often associated with brick works. The final group of immigrant entrepreneurs consists of British and Indian potters, whose oeuvre is exclusively known through archival references.

Indian potters of Natal

An exciting discovery of this project was the archival references in the National Art Library, London to the earliest known formal potteries in what is now Natal, which were operated by Indian immigrants who had arrived from the 1860s onwards to work as indentured labourers on sugar cane plantations. John Adams (see note 24) reported on numerous small family-run potteries operated by Indian potters from Madras in the Mayfair area of Durban. Seated on the ground in their back gardens, the potters used foot-operated horizontal flywheels to make flower pots and items for special occasions, including wedding and funeral vessels. They may also have made cooking utensils, storage vessels and pots for the local Indian community. It is likely that these vessels were unglazed, but some items were decorated with a wash of bright red ochre that came from India. As with so many earlier potteries, positively identified examples of these wares are unknown (Adams 1916).

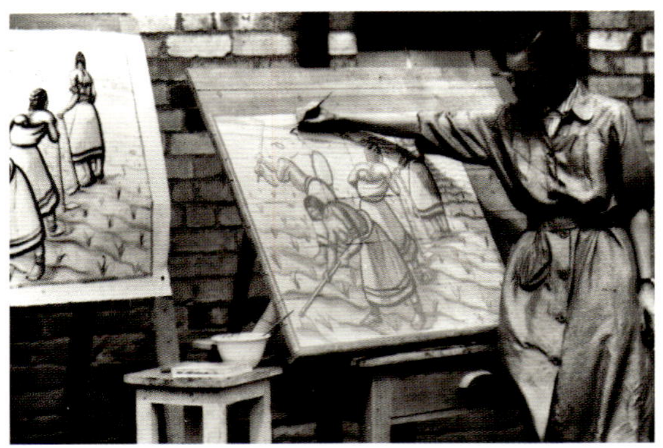

Joan Methley Quembe Post Office tile panel (1937) | Source: Heymans, J A (1989) 'Potterbakkerswerk in Suid-Afrika met spesifieke verwysing na die werk wat vanaf 1925 tot 1952 by Olifantsfontein gedoen is'. MA thesis, University of Pretoria. Vol 2, Catalogue A, p. 6 | Scan by Douglas van der Horst

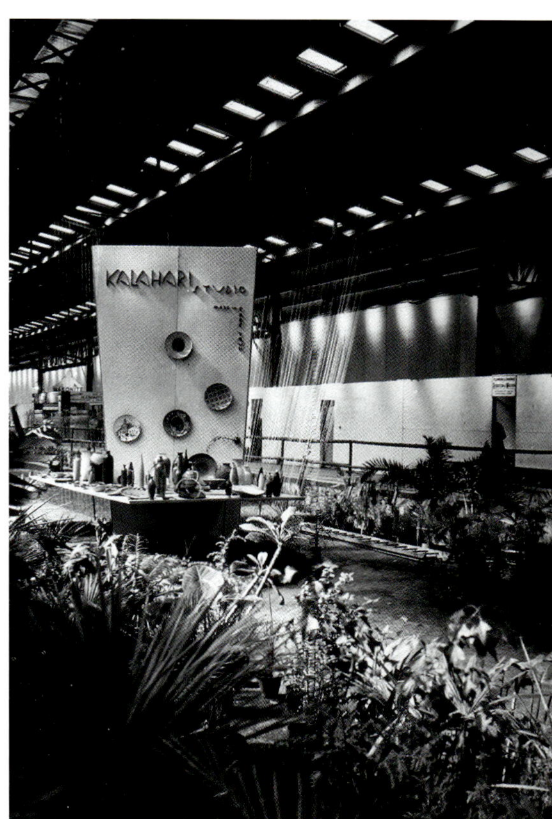

Kalahari Studio Stand at the Van Riebeeck Tercentenary Festival, Cape Town | Provenance: SHC Iziko | Scan by Nicole Piriou

1940–1965: Modern ceramics

Rapid economic growth and urbanisation characterised the post-war years in South Africa. The aftermath of World War II saw the influx of numerous talented British and European migrant artists, craftsmen and art dealers into South Africa. The pottery industry was further boosted by expatriate South African potters who trained in England and returned in the 1950s. These include Sammy Liebermann, Sophy Bodenstein and Esias Bosch. These immigrant and expatriate potters brought fresh ideas, energy and talent to the local pottery scene and established numerous potteries in the late 1940s and 1950s. The table below lists some of the most important immigrant potters and their origins.

Some prominent immigrant potters of the late 1940s and early 1950s

Germany	Albrecht Schließler of Crescent Potteries Jürgen Hamburger of Hamburger Pottery
Great Britain	Albert Brown of Crescent Potteries Donald Turgel of Marrakesh Ware Denis Morgan Blewett of Marrakesh Ware Mary Liebermann of Liebermann Pottery and Tiles Norman Steele-Gray of Grahamstown Pottery Alfred Adams of Grahamstown Pottery John Edwards of Grahamstown Pottery and Lucky Bean Farm Leila P Simpson of Grahamstown Pottery J B Livesey of Silwood Ceramics (see endnote 221) G H B Lovell of Silwood Ceramics (see endnote 221)
Holland	Herry Duys of The Old Jar Henk W M Jacobs of The Old Jar Leslie Lulofs of SA Glazing Maarten Zaalberg of Zaalberg Potterij
Italy	S Varanini of National Ceramics Industries Nicola Canosa of Zaalberg Potterij
Sweden	Aleksanders Klopcanovs (b. Uzbekistan) and Elma Vestman (b. Latvia) of the Kalahari Studio

Ceramics and post-war consumer society

The post-war years saw a gradual rebirth of Western economies and consumer society. The monopoly maintained by foreign ceramic producers in South Africa, particularly English potteries, was challenged during the post-war years, with the establishment of over 40 potteries. This period was a golden age of regional ceramic development, and was characterised by various different articulations of Art Nouveau, Anglo-Orientalism and the New Look or Contemporary Style.

The flourishing of the South African pottery industry was facilitated by two key factors. Firstly, in the 1950s, potteries in Britain, Western Europe,

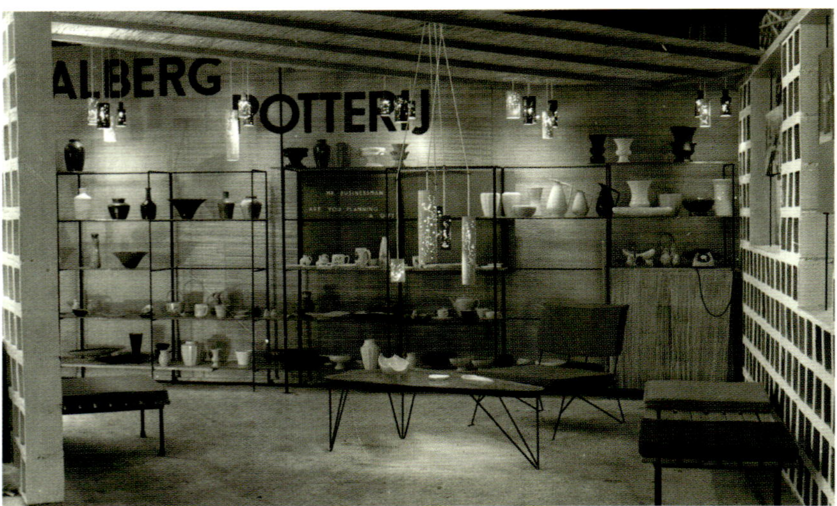

Zaalberg Potterij exhibition stand at the Goodwood Show (1967) | Provenance: Zaalberg Archives, SHC, Iziko | Scan by Lailah Hisham

the USA and South Africa increasingly produced luxury wares in addition to their customary crockery sets. These luxury items responded to new fashions in gift giving, home decorating, informal dining and entertainment. New forms included lamps, candle holders, smoking accessories, snack bowls, cocktail platters and sets for Danish pastries, among other articles (Bogaers 1988:53,56.). This plethora of new consumer products, as well as the more traditional ceramic staples of tableware, vases and wall-plates (also known as chargers) boosted the ceramics industry. Secondly, flower-arranging was considered an important skill for middle- and upper-class white women in southern Africa.[27] This involved collecting a variety of vases that would complement floral arrangements. As vase sales were a significant source of revenue, some potteries, including Grahamstown Pottery, employed demonstrators to travel throughout South Africa and Rhodesia (now Zimbabwe) to teach the uses of various vases.[28] Flower-arranging was such a popular artistic activity that even the illustrious Professor Nilant of the University of Pretoria became involved in a public debate on this subject. In 1963 he bemoaned the fickle nature of flower-arrangers, who abandoned large-necked vases in favour of vases with narrow necks, '... Any other types [of vases] are no longer in demand at the kilns. And that is what happens in South Africa with its abundance of flowers!' (Nilant 1963:99, 100).

Decline of the pottery industry in the late 1950s

Despite a robust economic context within South Africa, the industry began to collapse from approximately 1957 as a result of the deregulation of government import tariffs, quotas and protective legislation, and a 'dumping' of cheap ceramics from Japan and America. It is important to note that South Africa was not alone in dealing with this problem. In the late 1950s and early 1960s Dutch potteries also struggled against inexpensive mass-produced wares from Eastern Europe and Japan (Bogaers 1988:72). Many South African firms did not survive this flood of cheap domestic ware. Failed potteries include Linnware (which finally closed around 1962), Globe Potteries (closed 1958), Grahamstown Pottery (liquidated in 1965) and Rand Ceramics Industries (closed in 1955). Ailing smaller potteries were taken over by larger potteries, including Silwood Ceramics. Other potteries restructured production, for example, National Ceramic Industries focused on tiles and Dykor focused on ceramic tiles and concrete. The local ceramic sector was in peril by 1965. Potteries that survived this period included The Old Jar, Crescent Potteries, Liebermann Pottery and Tiles and the Kalahari Studio. Their wares somehow fitted into niche markets and they were able to remain buoyant in the rising tide of imported wares.

1965–1980 Social turmoil and upliftment potteries

'The wind of change is blowing ...'[29] The social context of the 1960s and 1970s

From the 1950s South Africa slid deep into the apartheid state's rigid control over political, economic and social structures. In 1960 Harold Macmillan prophesied that South Africa and the African continent were on the eve of a new dispensation. Newly formed African states emerged from the shackles of colonial rule. From 1964, many southern African states entered into a vortex of internal and regional conflicts, including Zimbabwe,[30] Mozambique,[31] Namibia[32] and Angola.[33]

As an attempt to treat some of the 'symptoms' of the regional woes in the 1960s and 1970s, various international aid organisations,[34] religious fraternities[35] and local development authorities[36] established community economic development enterprises (CEDs), including craft projects, throughout southern Africa. These projects aimed to host political exiles and refugees as well as to try to develop skills and jobs among locals in poor and rural communities, and frequently prioritised women. Craft projects, including textile, weaving, jewellery and ceramic workshops mushroomed throughout the region. The relatively stable 'peace-havens' of Lesotho,[37] Swaziland[38] and Botswana[39] attracted various pottery CEDs. Within South Africa, most potteries established between 1965 and 1980 had a strong humanitarian focus, and were located in rural regions or within former homelands. These potteries included Ikwezi Lokusa, Mthatha, Transkei; Izandla, Mthatha, Transkei; and the Rorke's Drift Pottery, KwaZulu-Natal.

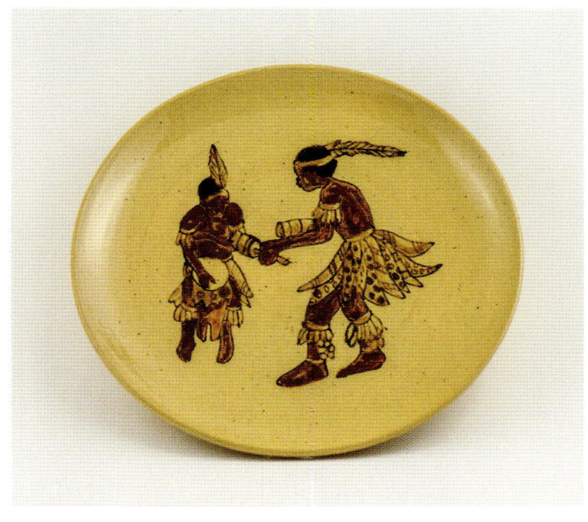

Mzilikazi Art and Craft Centre, Bulawayo, Zimbabwe | Small plate depicting a pair of African dancers | 131x15mm | Provenance: Wendy Gers | Marks: base glazed with transparent glaze, round gold sticker 'Mzilikazi Pottery' with elephant logo, sgraffito marks 'NP / 15' and brown hand-painted glaze marks 'AM' | Photograph by Damien Artus

On a purely technical level, the emergence of the ceramic industry in South Africa from the doldrums was facilitated by an improvement in the availability of reliable information concerning local raw materials. Between 1958 and 1969, Renier Oelof Heckroodt (b.1936), then Chief Research Officer in the Ceramics Unit of the National Building Research Institute, CSIR, regularly published studies on ceramic raw materials in South Africa.[40] These publications alerted potters to what was locally available, and were widely consulted. They significantly facilitated the work of potteries, which previously had to rely on personal research and word of mouth to locate and obtain various essential raw materials used in clay and glaze bodies.

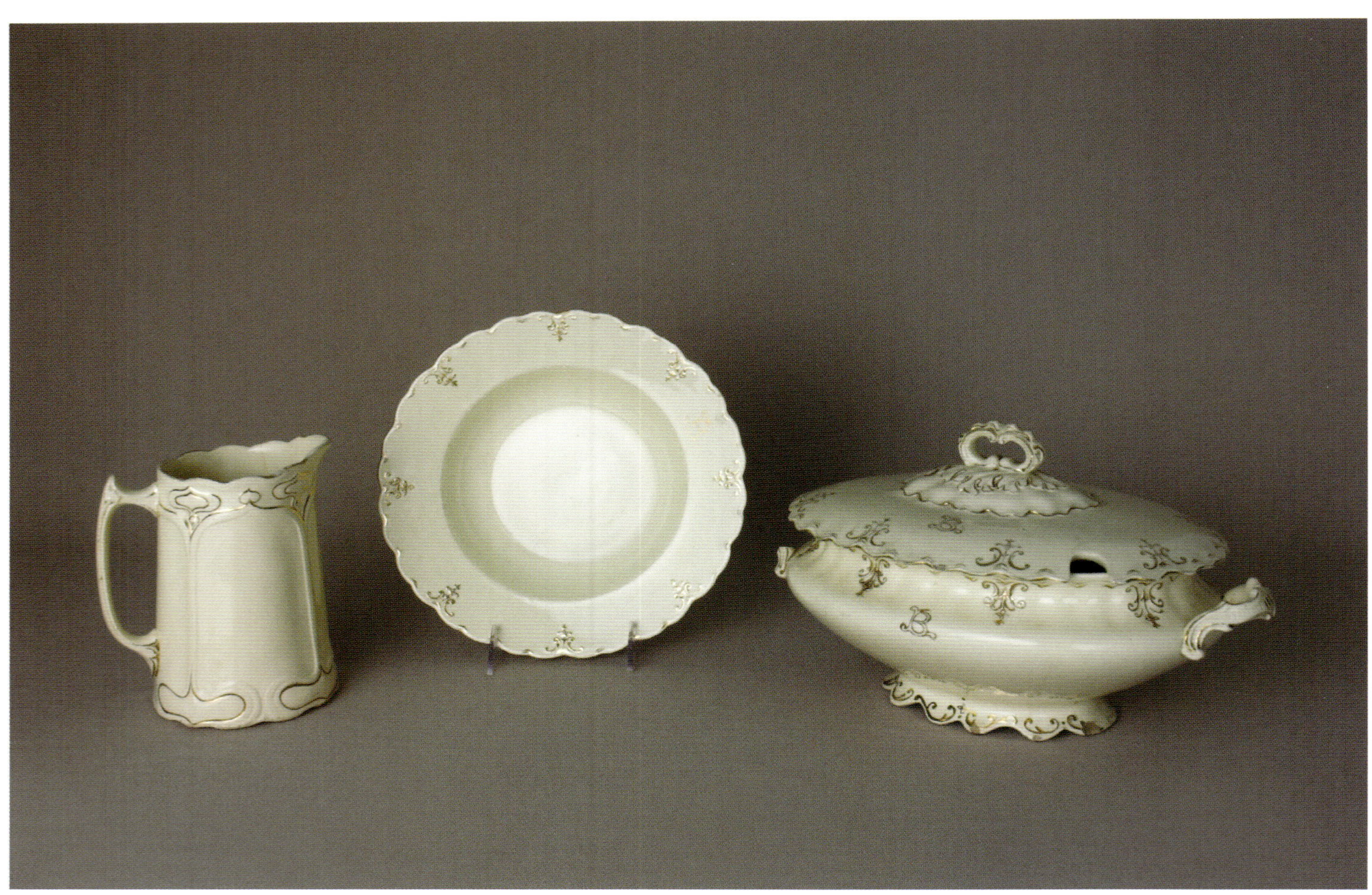

Transvaal Pottery | Jug, tureen and plate from dinner service of the Prime Minister, General Louis Botha (1908) | Jug: 180x107x112mm; plate 255x40mm; tureen 200x300x220mm | Provenance: DNMCH | HG 8144/2 tureen 8144/1 | Marks: base of jug, inscribed marks in transparent glazed base 'R. Je 6-10-08 P'; stamp in the form of a star of David containing the initial C.R. B. P. and L. Co. Ld; plate, same stamp on back, LB insignia on front; tureen, same stamp on back, LB insignia on front | Photograph by Natalie Field

Conrand: Transvaal Pottery (1908–1915)

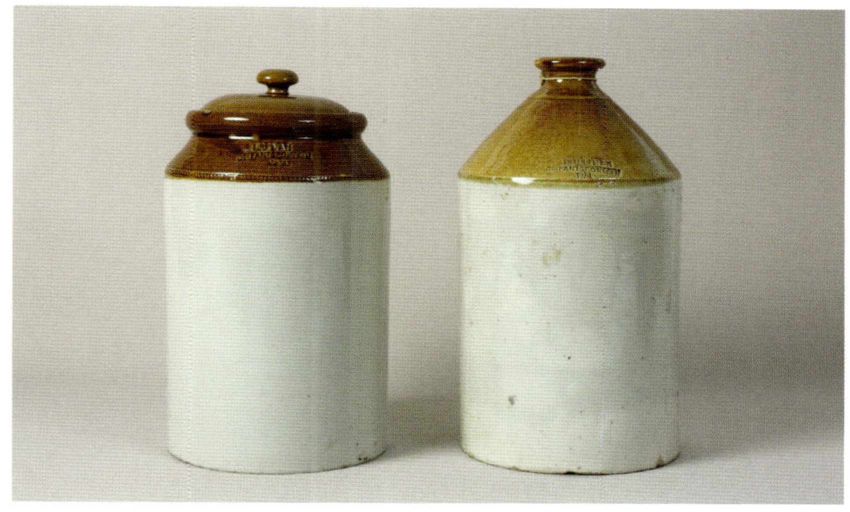

ABOVE: Transvaal Pottery | Stock jar and gallon jar | Stock jar 305x140x170mm; gallon jar 320x55x175mm | Provenance: Ditsong SACHM | stock jar CS 2704; gallon jar HG 14280 | Marks: both jars have impressed stamp marking on their shoulders, 'Olifantsfontein, TVL', cream glazed bases with no marks | Photograph by Natalie Field

Location and founder

Transvaal Pottery (also called Transvaal Potteries), located on the premises of the Consolidated Rand Brick, Pottery and Lime Company (Conrand)[41] in Olifantsfontein, was established by Sir Thomas M Cullinan (1862–1936),[42] an eminent Randlord, upon the discovery of a seam of white-firing clay below the brick clay.

Wares manufactured

Conrand produced slip-cast creamware crockery derived from English and continental originals, in addition to various domestic goods such as wash jug and basin sets, food storage jars, vases and promotional wares. Various domestic goods and promotional wares feature decorative (monochrome) transfers and (multi-coloured) decals of motifs including rosebuds, dogs, children playing, a hen and chicks, etc. Transvaal Pottery also produced terracotta flowerpots and glazed acid-resistant bottles, jars and containers of various sizes, primarily for chemicals associated with mining activities.

Brief history of the pottery

In 1907 Cullinan invited Harold Emery, a ceramic engineer from Stoke-on-Trent, to investigate clay samples, and appointed him Works Manager of the pottery. In June of that year the erection of a factory and accommodation was put to tender, but work was delayed due to Emery's prolonged fever and hospitalisation. Cullinan also sent his son Roland to Stoke-on-Trent to study ceramics. Transvaal Pottery (or 'The New Pottery Works' as it was often called) was inaugurated in 1908, with the full-scale production of industrial pottery and creamware. Emery had brought approximately 30 English potters, technicians and management staff, and their families, from Stoke-on-Trent, who were bound to an initial contract of three years.[43] Conrand also employed approximately 80 Boer children from the Potchefstroom Orphanage from 1909 as indentured apprentices. The staff was housed on the premises, and the workers' village included a cricket oval and sports club.

The earliest known example of Transvaal Pottery creamware is a large dinner service[44] from 1908, which was presented to Louis Botha (1862–1919), the first prime minister of the Union of South Africa (1910–1919). Realising the need to get the support of contemporary political leaders and prominent personalities if his pottery was to survive, Cullinan regularly invited dignitaries to visit the pottery and offered his guests complementary gifts of crockery.[45]

In 1912 Cullinan secured his first corporate customers, who ordered personalised wares (vases, mugs and tankards) as Christmas presents. These articles are marked with the Transvaal Pottery logo that features a maize cob.[46] The shift from the star logo to the maize cob is significant. One is tempted to speculate that Cullinan changed the logo to woo Afrikaans customers and was aware of anti-Semitic sentiments among certain sectors of this community. However, the variety of marks on Transvaal Pottery's industrial stoneware (stock and gallons jars) and the lack of confirmed dates of production of these items would tend to discourage any simplistic generalisations about Cullinan's personal ambitions as well as his perception of the market.

Despite Cullinan's huge personal and financial investments, the pottery made a loss from its outset. The clay was unsuitable and the English staff was unmotivated, undoubtedly suffering from acute homesickness. Cullinan persevered as he believed that there was a great potential for the industry. In 1913, he declared that the venture was *finally* profitable and ventured that its produce was 'equal to anything of imported value' (Rosenthal [1960]). Despite this brief reprieve, the pottery made a loss in the following year, and in a final attempt to save the enterprise Cullinan personally petitioned Parliament for assistance. His petition was unsuccessful and Transvaal Pottery closed in May 1915. Most of the English staff was repatriated and the studios and potters' village were abandoned.

Transvaal Pottery's closure resulted from a variety of factors, including the absence of Tariff Protection, which resulted in uncontrolled competition from German and English ceramics. Furthermore, the pottery was uncompetitive as its market was confined to the Transvaal and Orange Free State as a result of a lack of transport infrastructure. Similarly, Cullinan's policy of employing white labour also had an adverse effect on the per capita labour costs. The tragedy of the pottery's closure was magnified by the start of World War I, as crockery was practically unobtainable by the middle of 1915. Disillusioned by his past experiences, Cullinan refused to reopen the pottery for many years.

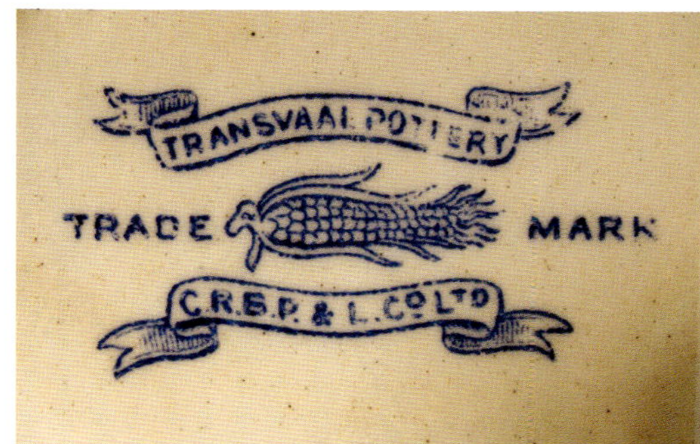

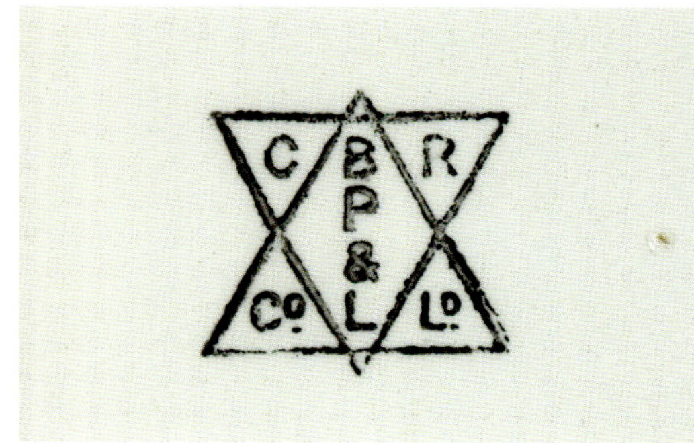

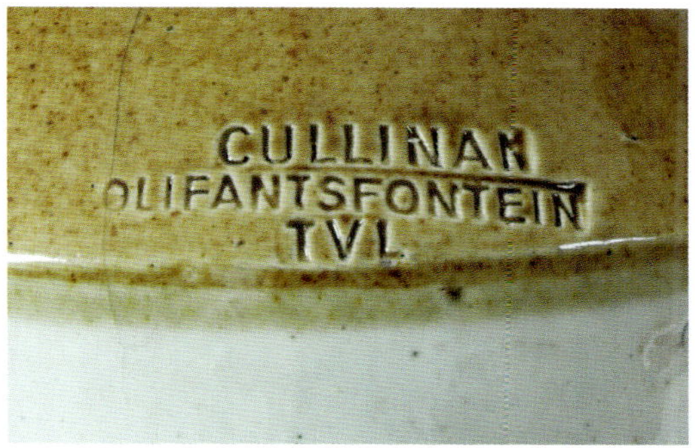

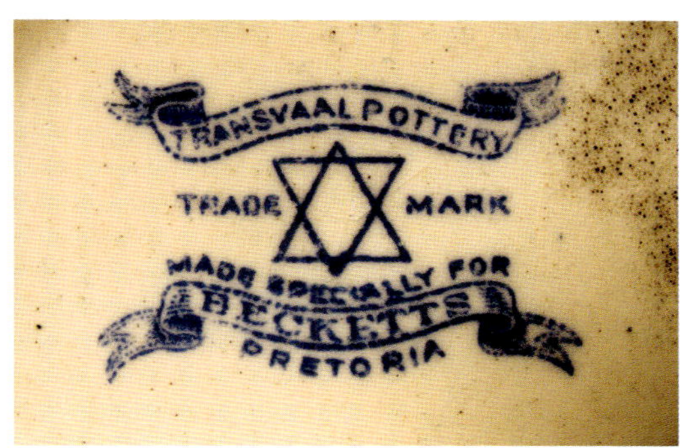

TOP LEFT: Transvaal Potteries | Maker's mark | Blue transfer, maize cob between two banners, 'Transvaal Pottery, Trade Mark, C.R.B.P. & L. Co Ltd' | Photograph by Natalie Field

TOP RIGHT: Transvaal Potteries | Maker's mark | Black glaze stamp of star incorporating initials, 'C.R.B.P. & L. Co Ld' | Photograph by Natalie Field

BOTTOM LEFT: Transvaal Potteries | Maker's mark | Impressed stamp on neck of gallon jar, 'Cullinan Olifantsfontein TVL' | Photograph by Natalie Field

BOTTOM RIGHT: Transvaal Potteries | Maker's mark | Blue transfer, star between two banners, 'Transvaal Pottery, Trade Mark, Made Specially for Becketts, Pretoria' | Photograph by Natalie Field

Marks

- Most creamware is marked with a glaze stamp bearing a logo of a star (which may be considered to resemble the Star of David) and contains the initials 'C.R B.P. & L. Co. Ltd.'.
- Some creamware is marked with a maize cob trademark between two ribbons containing the words 'Transvaal Pottery' and 'C.R.B.P. & L. Co. Ltd.'.
- Some creamware has a glaze stamp mark in the form of a star and additional handwritten marks inscribed under the transparent glaze of the base. These additional marks contained a date and an alpha-numeric code, which possibly included the initials of the decorator, e.g. 'R. Je 6-10-08 P.'.[47]
- Commercial wares have additional inscriptions. For example, a tobacco jar with domed cover and pierced finial has a transfer that indicated it was produced for 'Van Erkom's; Celebrated Magaliesberg Tobacco; Pretoria; Old Governments Buildings P.O. Box 309'.
- The various glazed acid-resistant bottles, jars and containers are frequently marked with an impressed stamp in the form of a star, containing the initials 'C.R.B.P. & L. Co. Ltd.'.

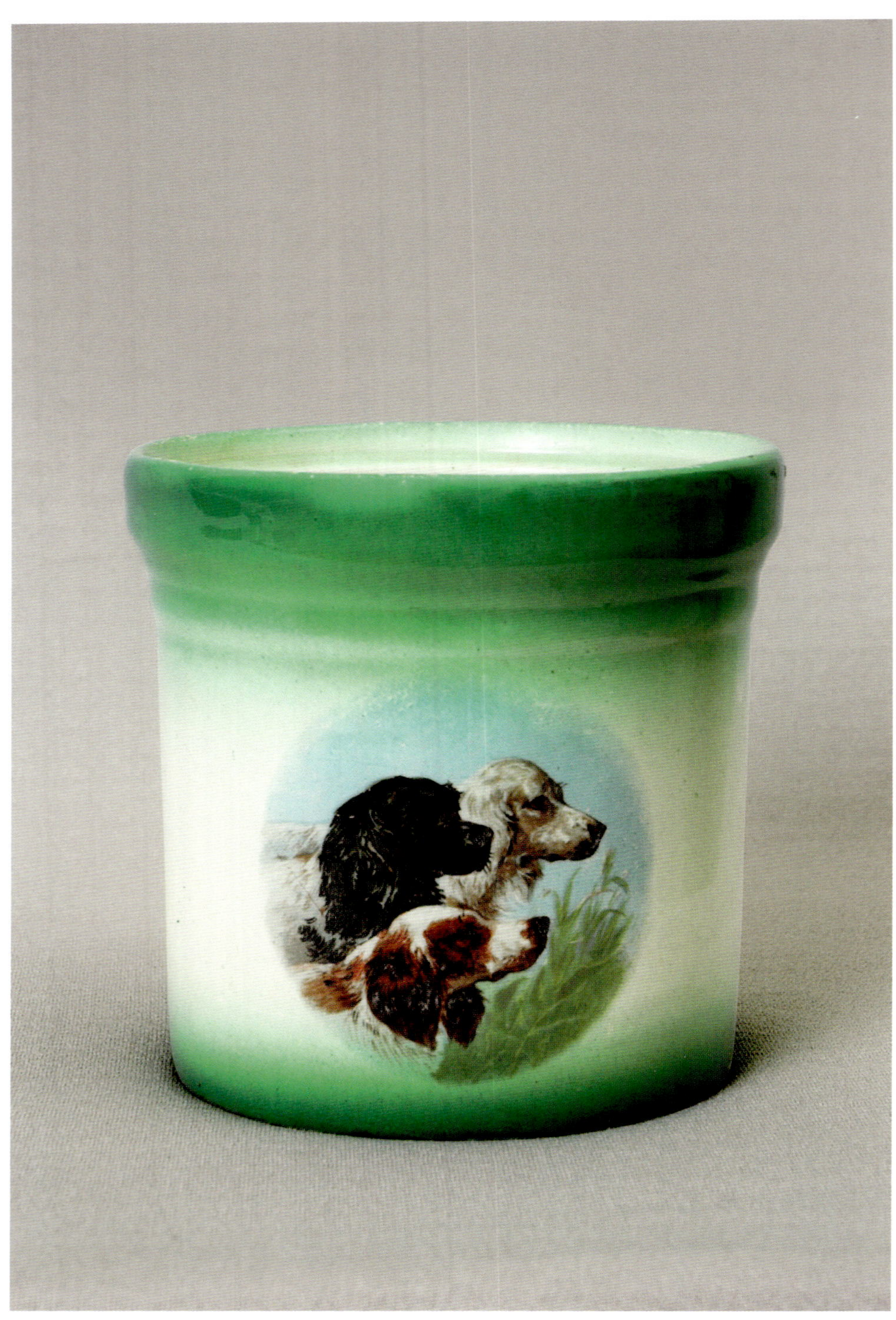

Transvaal Pottery | Jar, green sprayed glaze around rim and base, decorative image of three dogs and advert, 'With the Compliments of Worthington Bros, Cleveland, Xmas 1912, P.O. Box 16.Tel. 5', | 158x150x130mm | Provenance: De Kamper and Welman Collection | Marks: cream base with a transfer | Photograph by Natalie Field

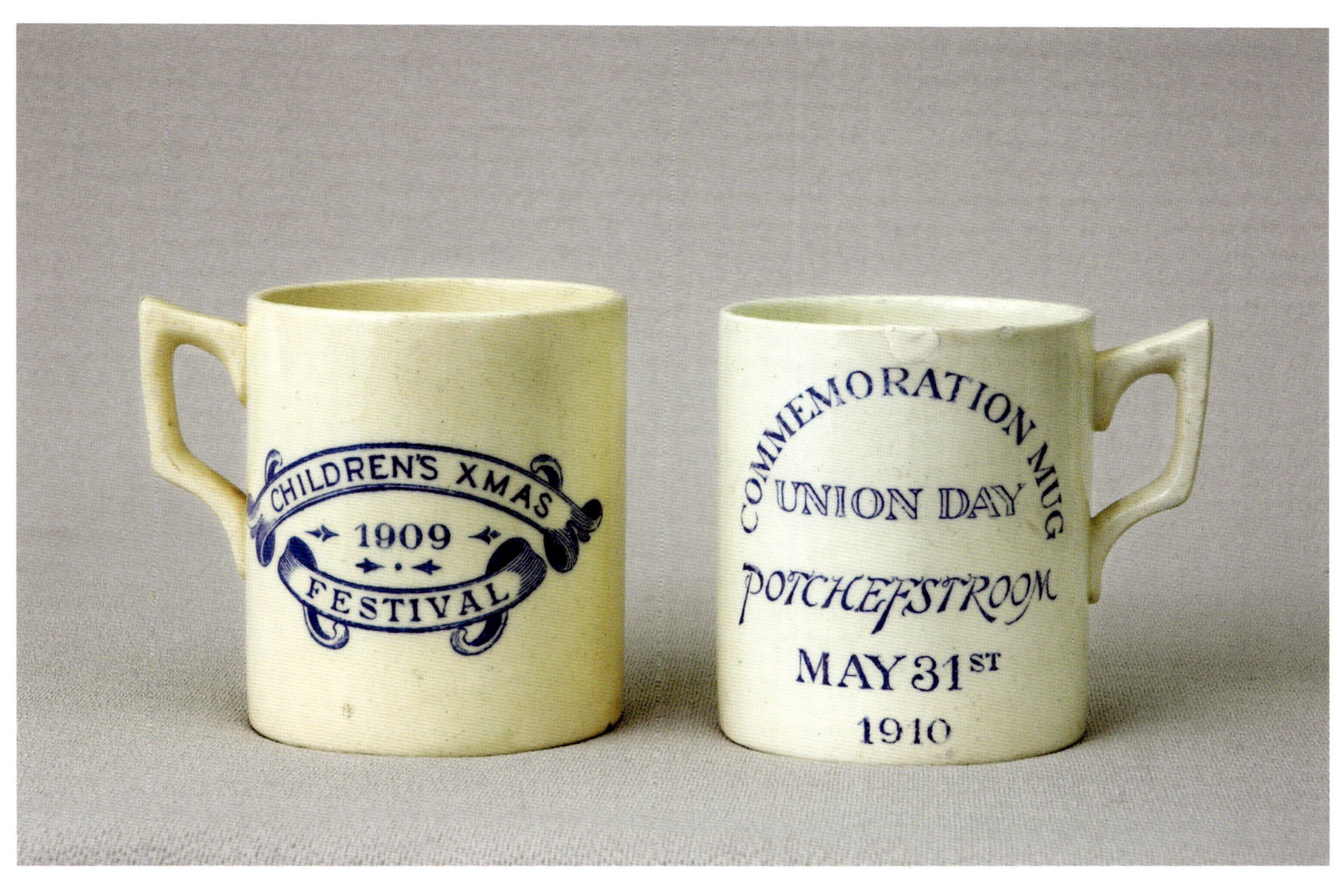

Transvaal Pottery | Two mugs: left mug: Children's Xmas Festival, 1909, and South African coat of arms on back; right mug: Commemoration mug, Union Day, Potchefstroom, May 31st 1910 | 85x87x87mm; 85x87x87mm | Provenance: De Kamper and Welman Collection | Marks: left mug transfer, blue star between two banners, 'Transvaal Pottery, Trade Mark, Made Specially for Becketts, Pretoria'; right mug blue transfer, maize cob between two banners, 'Transvaal Pottery, Trade Mark, C.R.B.P. & L. Co Ltd' | Photograph by Natalie Field

Conrand: The Ceramic Studio (1925–1942)

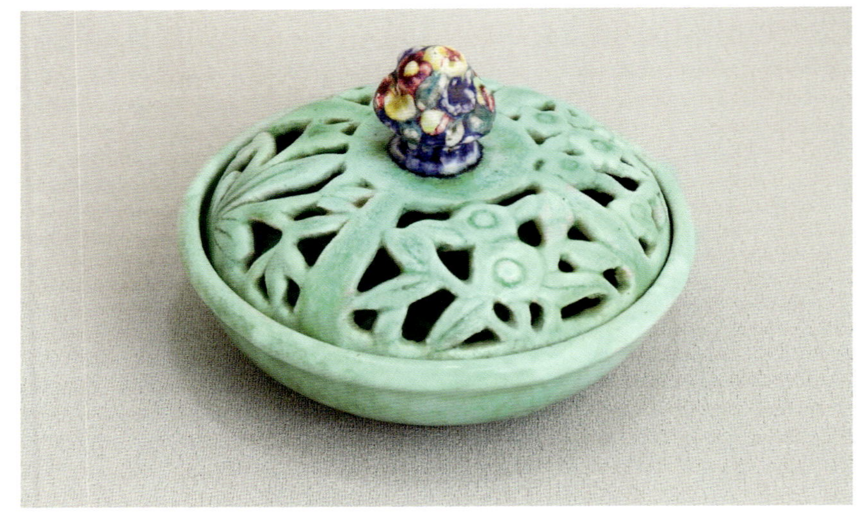

The Ceramic Studio | Potpourri bowl with incised lid | Green glazed body with multi-coloured floral knob | 80x140x30mm | Provenance: The Alphen Collection | Marks: base signed, 'THE CERAMIC STUDIO 1927 JFM' | Photograph by Natalie Field

Founders

Gladys Short and Marjorie Johnstone founded the Ceramic Studio when they rented workshop premises from Cullinan's company.

Staff

The Ceramic Studio and later Linnware employed many trained artists who were former students of the Natal Technical College, Art School. Accounts vary as to who was responsible for the revival of the pottery, but the co-founders were Gladys Short and Joan Methley. Significant artists included Audrey Frank, Marjorie Johnstone and Thelma Currie (née Newlands). Mary Stainbank designed many significant works in the early years.[48] The studio had various short-term employees and commissioned outside artists to design artworks for the studio, including Eric Byrd, Isa Cameron, Yolande Friend, Rosa Somerville Hope, Erich Mayer, Joyce Ordbrown, Florence Vann-Hall and Alfred Palmer. Other temporary artists included Jan Juta, R J Pope Fincken, E Quails and Allen Yates.[49] George Mace, one of Cullinan's original Staffordshire employees, was employed as the chemist for the pottery. Throwers and technical assistants included Guilio (Frank) and Joseph Agliotti, James and Sam Cromie, Bettie Prinsloo, Hans Ouwenkamp, G Scott and A Storm. An unnamed African woman was employed to decorate certain large planters with white or cream slip.

Wares manufactured

The Ceramic Studio produced five categories of wares:

- The original intention was to focus on the production of architectural faience decorated in the Della Robbia style, but this ambition was relatively short-lived.

- The majority of its products consisted of earthenware[50] crockery (jugs, vases, bowls, platters, beer mugs, chalices, ashtrays and dinner services) and planters. These articles were usually glazed with either a single colour or hand-painted in one or more colours.
- Tiles and domestic ware depicted a variety of Africana motifs (such as native studies, indigenous flowers, ships that called at the Cape, Cape-Dutch houses, Voortrekkers, historical views of Durban and Algoa Bay and images derived from books on San parietal art) as well as characters from English nursery rhyme.
- It made a small range of sculptures.
- It also produced various utilitarian objects such as decorative air bricks, wall fountains, light-switch plates and matching door furniture items (including finger plates, door knobs and keyhole escutcheons).

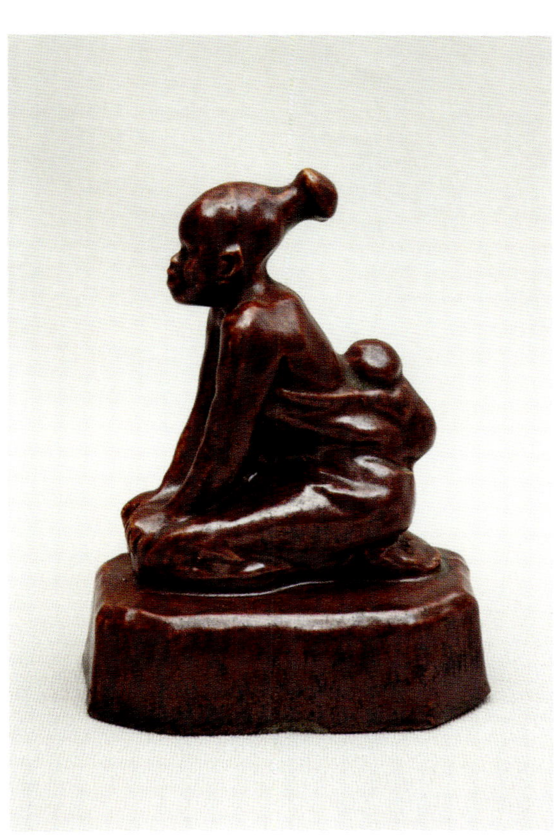

The Ceramic Studio | Figurine of a kneeling African woman | 125x90mm | Provenance: Douglas van der Horst | Marks: unmarked, identified by means of archival photographs | Additional information: this item is probably a part of a side-line of African figurines produced by Audrey Frank (Hillebrand 1991:23) | Photograph by Natalie Field

Production methods

- Crockery and planters were hand-thrown on the potter's wheel.
- Some planters and vases were made from assembled slabs.
- In the early years the Ceramic Studio slip-cast white and cream tiles.[51] During the 1940s and 1950s, industrial blanks were hand-decorated using the pouncing technique.
- Most sculptures and door furniture was slip-cast.
- Some sculptures, fountains and other special commissions were hand-built.
- A few sculptures, such as Mary Stainbank's book-ends, were press-moulded.

Brief history of the pottery

Gladys Short and Marjorie Johnstone, both dynamic young pottery graduates of the School of Art of the Durban Technical College, established The Ceramic Studio. Johnstone was friendly with the Cullinan family and obtained permission to rent workshop premises and accommodation within the abandoned Transvaal Pottery factory complex. Joan Methley, who had studied with Short in Durban and London, was invited to join them. In 1926 Johnstone married into the Cullinan family and left the pottery. Audrey Frank, another recent graduate of the Durban School of Art joined and was soon followed by Thelma Currie in 1928. These five women established a pottery that was legendary for being almost entirely staffed by women decorators, designers and artists. Until the 1940s, the only men involved in the operation were one or two potters who operated the kick wheels and some unskilled assistants.

The Ceramic Studio aimed to produce artistic pottery that 'reflect[ed] the personality of South Africa and [was] not merely a soulless imitation of that which originates in other countries' (Methley 1926:24). Thus the women of Olifantsfontein decorated tiles and, to a lesser extent, domestic ware with images of local history, flora, fauna and San parietal art. Their

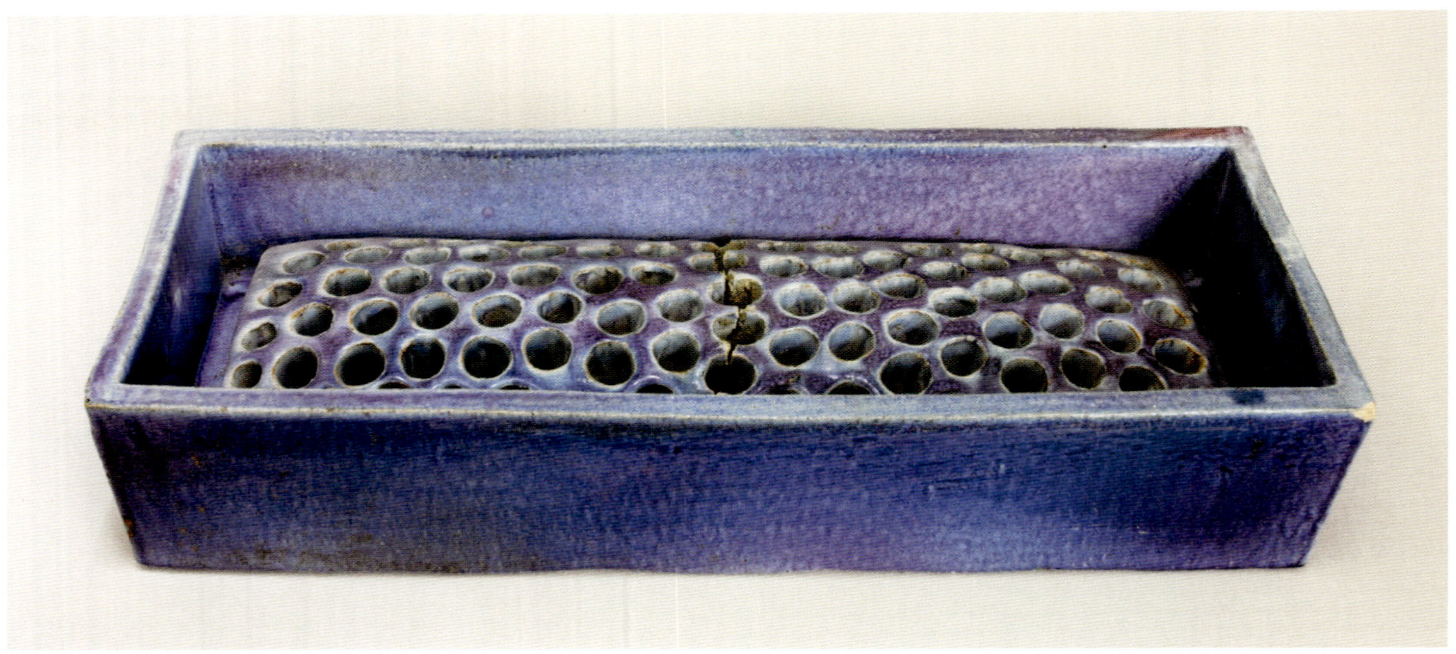

The Ceramic Studio | Large, long, blue-mauve 'trough' vase | 615x230x130mm | Provenance: The Alphen Collection | Marks: hand-painted marks, 'The Ceramic Studio 1939' on the base | Photograph by Natalie Field

preoccupation with indigenous themes had significant parallels with the contemporary architectural scene, where there was an attempt to develop a South African style, and numerous new public buildings consequently required embellishment with local motifs. As a result of the friendship between Cullinan and John Stockwin Clelland (1879–1950), chief architect of the Public Works Department of the Union of South Africa from 1920 to 1939, the company received many public commissions, the most prestigious being for the Union Buildings in Pretoria. Another major public commission was 11 000 hand-painted tiles to decorate the Johannesburg railway station. The studio completed more than 100 public commissions between 1927 and 1941 for hospitals, post offices, police stations, schools, railway stations and muncipal buildings. Private commissions for homes, bars and hotels were not just for tiles but included massive carved concrete facades, fireplace border tiles, urns, planters and various other architectural elements. The subject matter and styles of execution were as diverse as their clients and included detailed portraits of famous leaders, narrative reconstructions of historical scenes, pseudo-Delft Africana motifs, Spanish Moorish tiles, and modernist figurative compositions.

Despite its relatively prolific output, the Ceramic Studio was never profitable, their aesthetic and ethical rigour being the main reason. The artists were concerned with the authenticity of the local imagery they designed. Research was given priority and regular field trips were undertaken to study and reproduce 'authentic' motifs. For example, Frank and Currie spent an entire

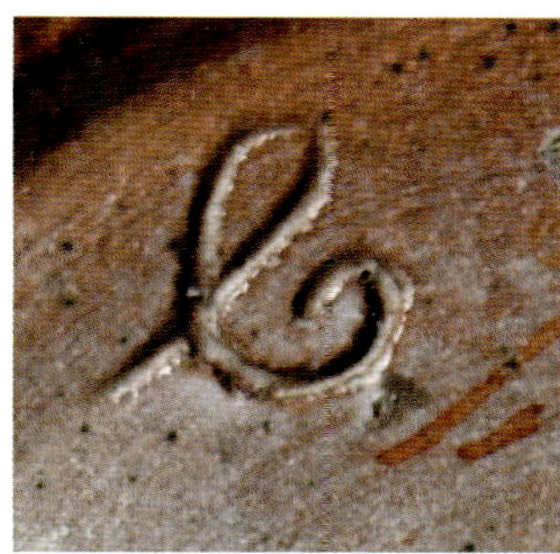

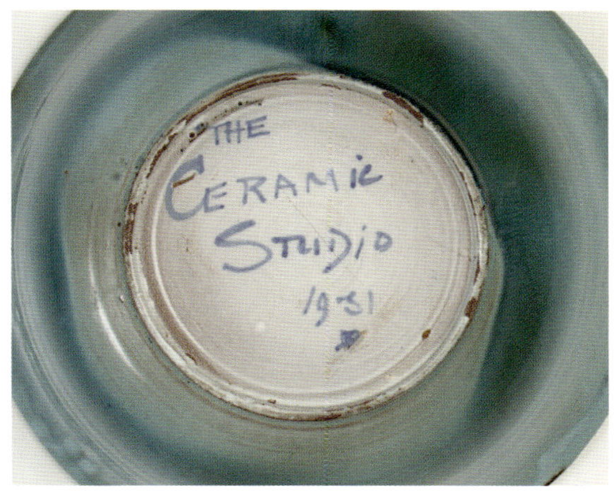

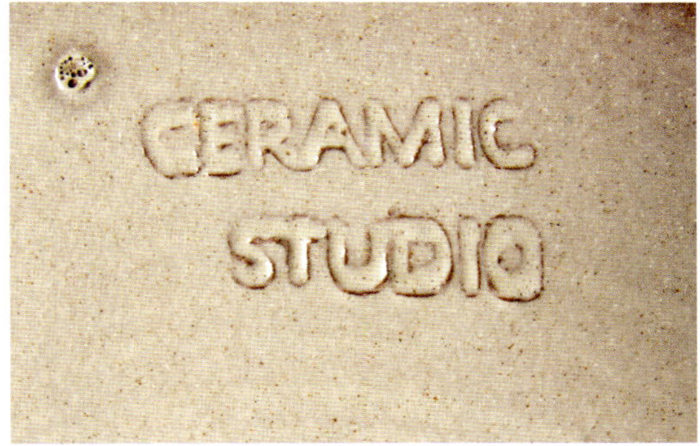

TOP: The Ceramic Studio | Maker's mark | Detail of relief 'C' on hand marked 'Ceramic Studio' vessel | Photograph by Natalie Field

MIDDLE: The Ceramic Studio | Maker's mark | Hand-painted glaze maker's mark, 'The Ceramic Studio' | Photograph by Natalie Field

BOTTOM: The Ceramic Studio | Maker's mark | Stamped 'The Ceramic Studio' | Photograph by Natalie Field

year researching and painting the tiles for the Johannesburg railway station. Similarly, Currie visited isolated villages in the Orange Free State to study Basotho architecture and costume for the tile panels of the Fouriesburg post office.

During World War II the Ceramic Studio suffered a dire shortage of English glaze components and was faced with closure. However, in February 1843, the benevolent Cullinan family bought the pottery and made changes to the company's staff and focus. The pottery, which was renamed Linnware, continued some of the Ceramic Studio products, while developing new lines.

The Ceramic Studio is renowned for the consistent quality of its ceramics. The walls of most of its hand-thrown vessels are generally fine. While many of the hand-decorated wares now seem quaint and dated; they are, however, a lasting legacy of the sutdio's high standard of design. The Ceramic Studio is unique in its structure and physical location – a small artistic women-run studio operating within a large industrial factory. The works of the Ceramic Studio bear testimony to the pioneering endeavours of a group of women working in harsh and isolated conditions. Despite their relative isolation, the artists were highly respected and attracted many VIPs. The studio diary includes visits by General Smuts's family, Princess Alice, Countess of Athlone (1883–1981), Dame Gracie Fields (1898–1979) the English-born actress, singer and comedienne, and the wife of the Governor General, who commissioned tiles with South African scenes for Kensington Palace (Van der Horst 1996:35). The women of the Ceramic Studio and Linnware certainly rose above difficult circumstances and created an important cultural landmark by which other potters measured themselves for many years. Their contribution to domestic, decorative, architectural and artistic pottery in South Africa during the first half of the twentieth century is resolutely unique.

Marks

Various marks were used to identify the Ceramic Studio, including:

- Domestic and fancy ware was usually hand-marked on the base in blue (cobalt oxide) with the studio name, the artist's name or initials and a date.
- During the late 1930s and early 1940s a studio stamp impressed into the wet clay bore the wording 'Ceramic Studio', sometimes with a year, as in 'Ceramic Studio 1939' (Illus. Kerrod 2010:117).
- Some tiles were marked on their verso – either with a hand-painted mark ('The Ceramic Studio 1929 AF'), which indicated the decorator, Audrey Frank, or with a stencil ('Ceramic Studio Olifantsfontein'). Other Ceramic Studio tiles are unmarked.
- Tile panels frequently contain marks in a lower corner, e.g. the Kalk Bay post office tile panel is marked 'IC The Ceramic Studio 1936' (IC are the initials of Isa Cameron).

Select exhibitions

1927	Industrial Craft Exhibition, Johannesburg
1927	Industrial Show, Pretoria
1927	Eastern Province Society of Arts and Crafts, Port Elizabeth
1928	Natal Society of Artists, Durban
1928	Industrial Show, Pretoria Town Hall
1928	Eastern Province Society of Arts and Crafts, Port Elizabeth
1929	Natal Society of Artists, Durban
1929	Eastern Province Society of Arts and Crafts, Port Elizabeth
1930	Natal Society of Artists, Durban
1930	Eastern Province Society of Arts and Crafts, Port Elizabeth
1931	Industrial Exhibition, Johannesburg
1931	S A Academy, Johannesburg
1931	Natal Society of Artists, Durban
1931	S A Institute of Art, Johannesburg
1931	Pretoria Women's Club
1933	S A Academy, Johannesburg
1933	Everywoman's exhibition, Johannesburg
1934	Ideal Homes Exhibition, Pretoria
1935	Kenilworth Craft Guild, Kenilworth
1936	Exhibition, Government House, Cape Town
1936	S A Academy, Johannesburg
1937	S A Academy, Johannesburg
1938	Empire Exhibition, Glasgow
1939	Henwood's, Durban

Select commissions for tile panels

Hospitals	Groote Schuur Hospital, Cape Town (the children's wards and playrooms); Addington Hospital, Durban; Pretoria Hospital (the children's playrooms).
Post Offices	Muizenberg, Kalk Bay, Noordhoek, Gordon's Bay, St James and Table Bay in the Western Cape; Balfour, Burgersdorp, Dordrecht and Tsomo in the Eastern Cape; Irene, Halfway House, Alberton, Heidelberg, Randfontein and Springs in Gauteng; Fouriesburg and Parys in the Free State; Balfour and Sabie in Mpumalanga; Calvinia, Petrusville in the Northern Cape; and Umhlali in KwaZulu-Natal.
Public Buildings	The Union Buildings, Pretoria; South Africa House, London; The Old Port Elizabeth Law Courts, Port Elizabeth; the former Bantu Affairs Building, Pretoria; the Germiston Law Courts; and the Pretoria zoo.

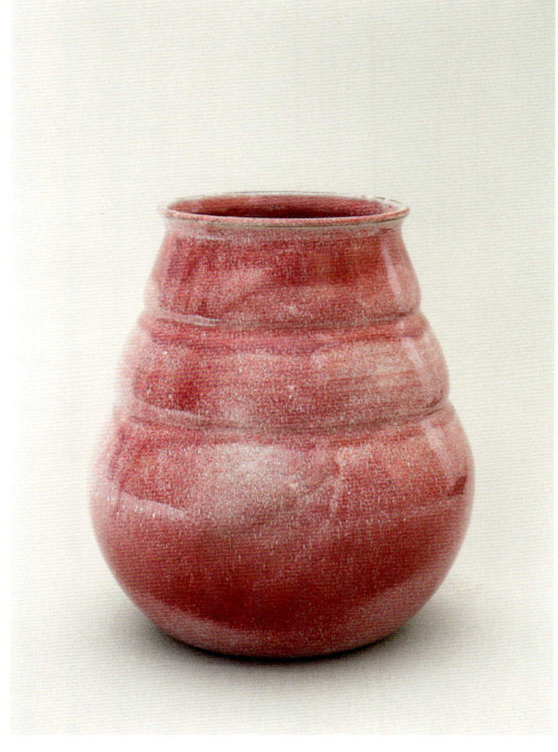

The Ceramic Studio | Vase with sprayed red glaze decoration | 305x162x145mm | Provenance: DNCHM | MJ 74. 232 | Marks: white glazed base with impressed stamp, 'Ceramic Studio' | Photograph by Natalie Field

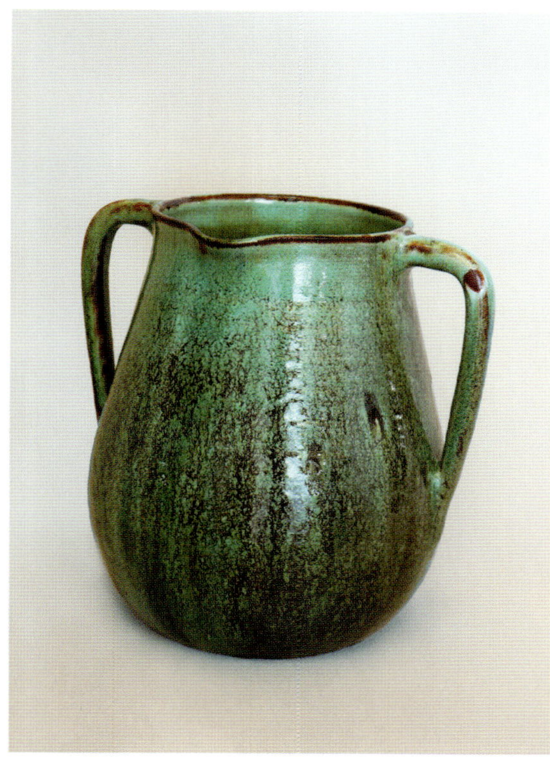

The Ceramic Studio | Vase in the form of a jug | 272x171x144mm | Provenance: SHC Iziko | 98/177 | Marks: 'Ceramic Studio' (stamp) | Photograph by Natalie Field

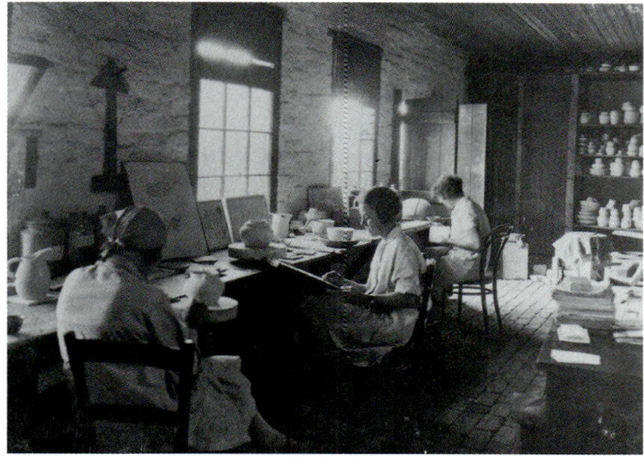

Ceramic Studio | Joan Methley, Gladys Short and Marjorie Johnstone, Olifantsfontein, 1926 | Scan by Douglas van der Horst

Private Buildings	Home of R Cullinan, 'Sunlawns', Irene; and the Alphen Hotel, Cape Town.
Schools	King Edward's School, Johannesburg; Roedean School, Johannesburg; and Sarel Cilliers High School, Johannesburg.
Train Stations	Park Station, Johannesburg (including the ladies bar and tea room); and many small Cape Town train stations, including Muizenburg and Simonstown.

Biographies

FRANK, Audrey (1905–1990)

Born in Durban, Frank studied at The School of Art, Durban under Joan Methley from 1916 to 1918, and in London at the Reimann Art School (1938). Upon her return to South Africa, Frank briefly taught pottery at the Durban Technical College.

She was employed at the Ceramic Studio in 1927, upon Johnstone's departure. Between 1932 and 1936 she taught at the Durban School of Art. In the late 1920s Frank worked with Gladys Short and Joan Methley at Olifantsfontein, where she helped with the tile panels for the Umhlali Post Office, the Johannesburg station tea room (1928), and those for the childrens' ward of Groote Schuur Hospital. Among other designs, she was responsible for the set of tiles, 'Ships that called at the Cape' and 'Nursery rhymes'.

Frank also taught pottery in Johannesburg, Port Elizabeth, Pietermaritzburg and at the Bloemfontein Technical College. Frank served as principal of the Frank Joubert Art Centre, Rondebosch, Cape Town from 1945 to 1956.

JOHNSTONE, Marjorie Lucy (Mrs Reginald Cullinan) (b.1904)

Born in Johannesburg, Johnstone was a graduate of the School of Art of the Durban Technical College (1921–1924), where she won various scholarships. Together with Gladys Short, she co-founded The Ceramic Studio in 1925. Johnstone departed in October 1926 to marry Reginald Cullinan and returned briefly in 1931 to produce fittings for the Cullinan house 'Sunlawns'.

METHLEY, Joan Foster (1898–1975)

Born in Pietermaritzburg, Joan Methley was a student of John Adams at the School of Art, Durban (1916–1918). She and Gladys Short studied pottery at the Royal College of Art, London (1919–1921), and the Camberwell School of Art. Upon her return to Durban, Methley was appointed as a lecturer at the School of Art. In 1922 she participated in a pottery exhibition at the Durban Technical College. Methley taught until the winter of 1926, when she departed to join her former classmates at Olifantsfontein. Methley was the manager of Linnware until 1952, playing an integral role as designer, potter and decorator, and was in charge of the public relations of the studio.

NEWLANDS, Thelma (1903–1990) (Mrs Gifford-Gayton, Mrs Tilton, Mrs van Schalkwyk, Mrs Newlands-Currie)

Newlands was born in Durban, and trained at the Durban School of Art and the Royal College of Art, London. She travelled in Europe before returning to South Africa in 1928 to work at the Ceramic Studio as a designer and decorator. The artist signed works with the various surnames associated with her multiple husbands, one of whom was Francois van Schalkwyk, works manager at Conrand from the mid-1920s. Newlands was responsible for tile panels for the Pretoria Hospital children's playroom (Peter Pan and the pirates; Robinson Crusoe; Game reserve); Pretoria zoo (1929); Native Affairs Department, Pretoria ('bushman' paintings) (1932); Groote Schuur children's ward (How Table Mountain got its cloud; Old Malay ditty); the Table Bay post office (1934–1935); the Fouriesburg post office (Basotho scenes) (1937); the Gordon's Bay post office (Table Bay scenes) (1938); individual tiles for the Johannesburg railway station, among many others. She later taught art at St Mary's Diocesan School for Girls, in Pretoria, where she died.

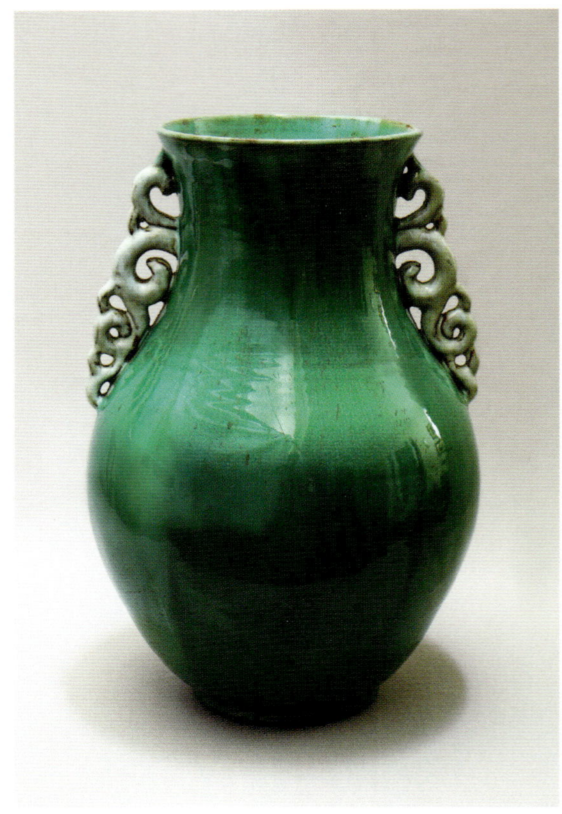

The Ceramic Studio | Large vase with elaborate white handles | 440x182mm | Provenance: The Alphen Collection | Marks: glazed marking on base, 'The Ceramic Studio' | Photograph by Natalie Field

ORDBROWN, Joyce (1894–1974)

Born in Port Shepstone, Ordbrown trained at the Westminster, and Lambeth Art School, London from 1909 to 1911, the Johannesburg Art School in 1914, and the Michaelis School of Fine Art in Cape Town. She taught art in Johannesburg and Pretoria. She was responsible for various Ceramic Studio tile panels, including the Kalk Bay post office (1936); the Noordhoek post office (1937); the Gordon's Bay post office (1937); the St James post office (1937); the Dordrecht post office (1938); the Balfour post office, Eastern Cape (1938) and the Petrusville post office, Northern Cape (1939). She died in East London.

STAINBANK, Mary Agnes (1899–1996)

Born near Durban, Stainbank enrolled in 1916 at the Durban School of Art to study fine art under the renowned ceramicist, John Adams, before being awarded a scholarship to the Royal College of Art, London, in 1922. During this period she also attended classes in bronze foundry techniques at an engineering school. In 1925 she returned to South Africa and established a studio at Coedmore, Bellair, Durban.

Stainbank was awarded numerous architectural commissions, including the decoration of the children's hospital at Addington, the government offices on Aliwal Street, Durban and the Port Elizabeth Magistrate's Court. These commissions were not enough to sustain her financially and in 1926 she was obliged to return to teaching at the Durban School of Art. Stainbank worked with the Ceramic Studio from 1929 to 1934.

Between 1939 and 1945 Stainbank undertook war service in a military drawing office in Johannesburg. In 1945 she returned to the Durban School of Art, where she was employed as a lecturer in sculpture until her retirement in 1957.

In the late 1980s a large travelling retrospective exhibition, accompanied by a catalogue, formalised her important contribution to South African art.

Her studio and its contents were bequeathed to the Voortrekker Museum, Pietermaritzburg, where Dr Estelle Liebenberg-Barkhuizen (1998, 2002, 2003) has researched Stainbank's oeuvre.

SHORT, Gladys Constance (1892–1974)
Born in Durban, Short was a student of John Adams from 1916 to 1918. She and Joan Methley studied pottery at the Royal College of Art, London (1919–1921), and at the Camberwell School of Art. Upon her return, she established a small pottery studio in Durban, near the School of Art and used the school's kiln facilities to fire her works. Marjorie Johnstone assisted her in the studio. In 1922 she participated in a pottery exhibition at the Durban Technical College.

Needing a larger studio, she was invited by Roland Cullinan to work at Olifantsfontein. In 1925 Short and Johnstone co-founded the Ceramic Studio. Short threw items as well as designing decorated wares. Later she managed the studio, and was responsible for its bookkeeping. She regularly visited architects who commissioned tile panels and garden wares and was responsible for marketing and sales. She retired in about 1943 as a result of failing health and a lack of enthusiasm for the commercial orientation of the newly formed Linnware enterprise.

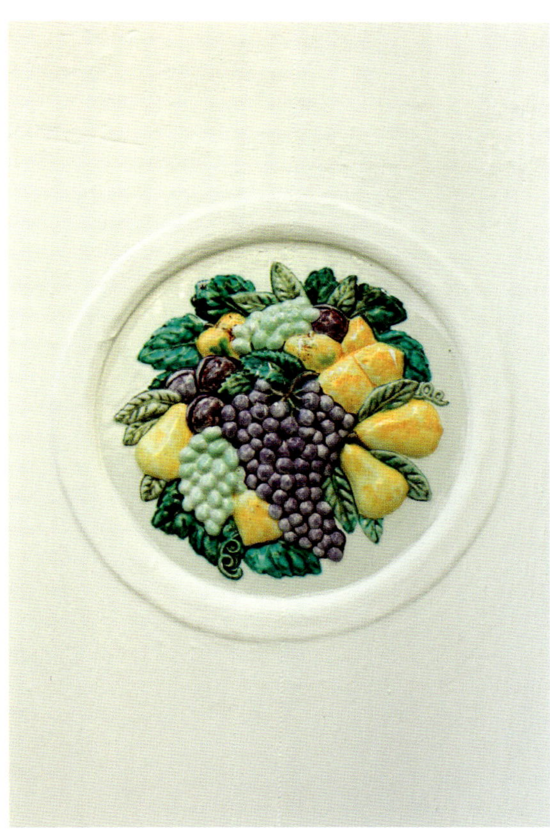

The Ceramic Studio | Roundels with grapes and other fruit | Provenance: The Alphen Collection | Additional information: made between 1950 and 1950 for the Farm Store; moved to their current location in c.1985 | Photograph by Natalie Field

Freelance artists and designers, decorators, potters and technical assistants

ADDISON, Daphne
Addison was a graduate of the Durban School of Art, and worked at the Ceramic Studio in 1934.

AGLIOTTI, Guilio (aka Frank)
Born in Italy, he was employed by Conrand. A capable potter, Agliotti could throw large planters taller than an average man. He took over throwing from Gladys Short in approximately 1926. Agliotti trained James Cromie, who eventually succeeded him upon his retirement. In the 1920s he bought land in Kempton Park, a small town with excellent clay deposits, where later he started his own pottery.

AGLIOTTI, Joseph
Joseph Agliotti was probably the son of Guilio Agliotti, and worked at the Ceramic Studio and Linnware from 1940 to 1952.

BYRD, Eric B (1905–1983)
Born in Durban, Byrd lived in Britain from 1906 to 1935, studying at the Cardiff School of Art, Wales and the Hornsey School of Art, London. In 1927 Byrd was appointed art master at Hornsey County School. He lectured at the Durban School of Art from ca.1935 to 1937 and at the University of Natal, Pietermaritzburg in 1938. From 1938 to 1943 he was a lecturer in the

Department of Fine Arts of the Johannesburg Technical College, where he was acting head of department from 1940 to 1943 and taught students such as Carl Büchner, Hennie Potgieter, Eben Leibbrandt and Douglas Portway.

Between 1943 and 1950, Eric Byrd taught at the Natal Technical College. He was a renowned painter and actively participated in Durban's art life, serving as a council member of the NSA, Durban. During this interlude, Byrd designed the tile panel of the Groblershoop post office (1938).

In 1950, he immigrated to Canada. He taught in Montreal, Quebec and in 1953 was briefly affiliated to the art faculty of the Banff School of Fine Arts. In 1954 he was employed by the School of Art at the Sir George Williams University, Montreal, Canada. Byrd retired in 1965 and in subsequent years visited and exhibited in South Africa.[52]

CAMERON, Isa

Born in Pietermaritzburg, she studied in London at the Royal College of Art and Chelsea School of Art, London, and in Paris in the late 1920s. She returned to South Africa in 1929, and established herself as a painter and sculptor. She exhibited at the Empire Exhibition in Johannesburg in 1936. Cameron designed tile panels for the Ceramic Studio including the Muizenberg (1934) and Kalk Bay (1936) post offices, Western Cape; the Tsomo (1934) and Lusikisiki (1936) post offices, Eastern Cape (1934); the Tzaneen post office (1934), Limpopo; and the Balfour post office (1937), Mpumalanga. Cameron subsequently relocated to Durban.

COETZER, Willem Hermanus (1900–1983)

Coetzer studied art in London and, upon his return to South Africa, devoted much of his career to the portrayal of patriotic Afrikaner images, particularly of the Voortrekker period. His commissions included the design of the marble friezes and tapestries for the Voortrekker Monument, Pretoria, and the historical mural in the Transvaal administration buildings, Pretoria. While Coetzer did extensive research to ensure the accuracy of his images, his interpretation of events was, inevitably, that of an Afrikaner male. Coetzer designed Voortrekker and similar images for Linnware.

CROMIE, Sam

Sam, James Cromie's son, started working at the Ceramic Studio as a schoolboy. He was there from 1929 to 1939, and returned in 1951 as the Linnware foreman.

CROMIE, James (aka Jim)

Cromie worked at the Ceramic Studio from 1927–1929, and part-time until 1942.

FRIEND, Yolande

Friend worked as a freelance designer for The Ceramic Studio, and designed the tile panel of the Halfway House post office (1939).

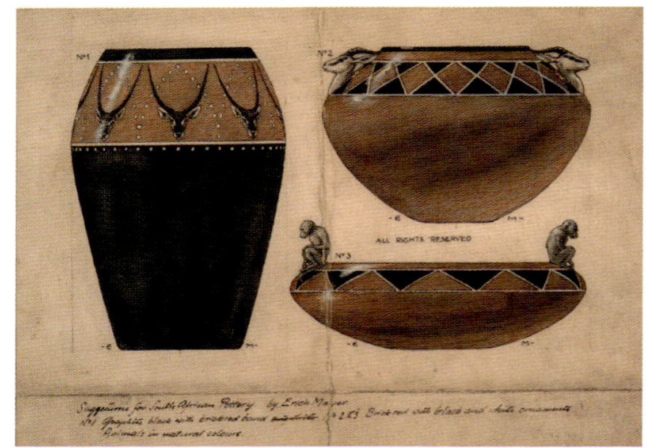

Sketch by Erich Mayer for The Ceramic Studio | Provenance: University of Pretoria Art Collection | 407725 | Photograph courtesy of University of Pretoria Art Collection

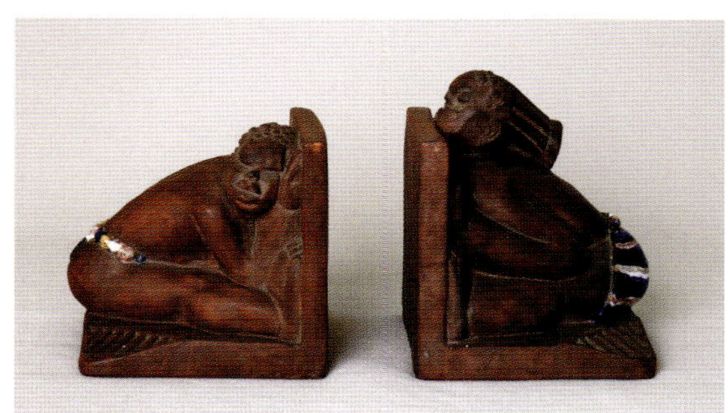

The Ceramic Studio | Pair of book-ends | From left: 140x140x135mm; 170x150x150mm | Provenance: TAG | From left: 1671/1; 1671/2 | Marks: both items contain painted marks in the interior, 'The Ceramic Studio, 1932' | Photograph by Natalie Field

HOPE, Rosa Somerville (1902–1972)
Born in Manchester, Hope studied at the Slade School of Fine Art and the Central School of Arts and Crafts in London. In 1926 she was a finalist for the Prix de Rome. In 1935 she came to South Africa as a lecturer at the Michaelis School of Fine Art in Cape Town, where she founded the Department of Engraving. From 1938 to 1957 she was a senior lecturer in fine arts at the University of Natal, Pietermaritzburg. She was responsible for designing the Irene post office Voortrekker tile panel (1940). She died in Kokstad in 1972.

MAYER, Erich (1876–1960)
Mayer, a German-born artist, produced images of San parietal art that were used on tiles by the Ceramic Studio, including tiles for the 1934 Native Commissioner's Building, Pretoria.[53] A patriotic nationalist, he argued for the creation of an indigenous national style, and created designs for pottery decorated with geometric friezes and a variety of wildlife including kudu, lion, rhinoceros, buffalo and springbok.[54]

OUWENKAMP, Hans
Ouwenkamp worked as a technical assistant at The Ceramic Studio from 1937 to 1941.

PALMER, Alfred (1877–1951)
Born in London, Palmer trained at the Royal Academy and in 1899 studied in Paris under Marcel Barchet and Jean-Paul Laurens. He was primarily a painter of figures, including native studies, which abound with homo-erotic nuances. Palmer designed for Linnware, including the 1934 tile panel for the Eshowe post office, KwaZulu-Natal.

POPE FINCKEN, R J
Fincken was a freelance artist who collaborated with the Ceramic Studio, including the designs for the Sabie post office.

PRINSLOO, Bettie
Prinsloo worked as a technical assistant from 1929 to 1933 and 1934 to 1942.

ROUILLARD, Germaine
Rouillard visited the Ceramic Studio regularly while undertaking her studies at the Durban School of Art. She subsequently worked there in 1931 as a decorator.

SCOTT, G
Scott worked as a potter for the Ceramic Studio from 1928 to 1929.

STORM, A
Storm worked for the Ceramic Studio from 1929 to 1934.

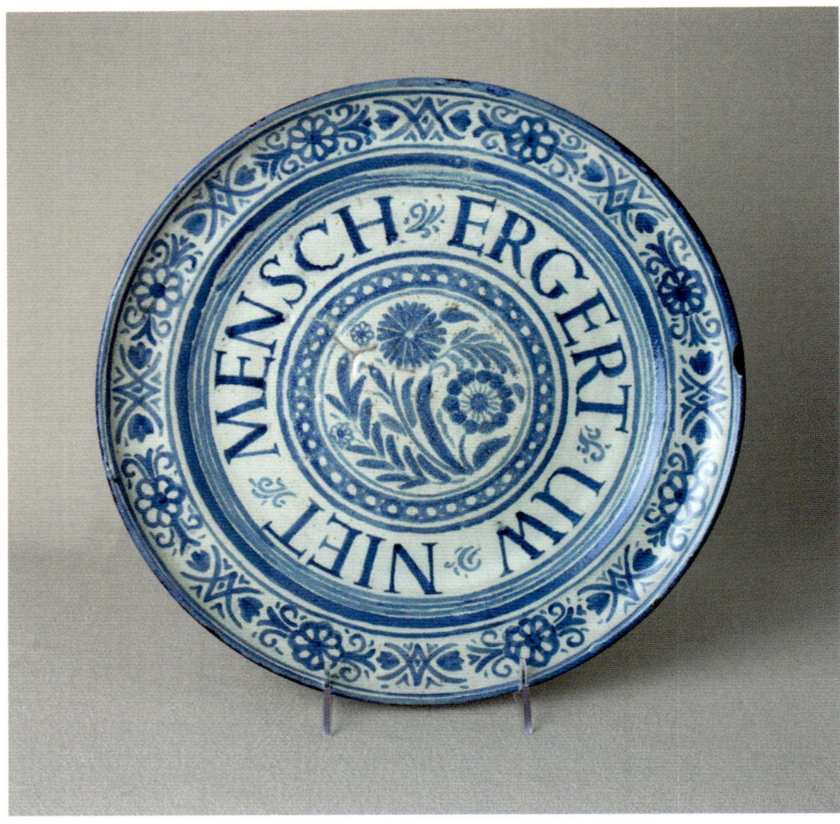

The Ceramic Studio | Charger, blue-and-white decoration with proverb, 'Ergert uw niet mensch' | 310x35mm | Provenace: DNMCH | HG 34860 | Marks: white glazed base, blue glaze marks, 'The Ceramic Studio, L.M. 1942' | Photograph by Natalie Field

VANN-HALL, Florence Wilgeforde Agnes (1894–1981) (aka Wilgy)
Vann-Hall was born in Leicester[55] and trained at the Liverpool School of Art and the Royal College of Art, London, in 1921. She studied stained-glass painting and book illustration, qualified as an art teacher in Liverpool, gained associateship of the RCA in design in 1924, and obtained an RCA Scholarship for a teaching diploma with distinction, in 1926. Her friendship with Stainbank resulted in her immigration to South Africa in 1926. Together they established the Ezayo Studio at Coedmore, Durban, where they worked together on a variety of commissions and on their own private work.

Vann-Hall undertook numerous commissions, including stained-glass windows and mural paintings for public buildings. She designed several Ceramic Studio tile panels, including for the New Law Courts, Port Elizabeth (1933), the children's ward of Groote Schuur Hospital, Cape Town (1934), the Burgersdorp post office (1934), and the Parys post office (1936). She died in Durban.

VISICK, Rosamund (Mrs Shephard)
Visick was a graduate of the Durban School of Art, and worked at the Ceramic Studio from February to May 1931.

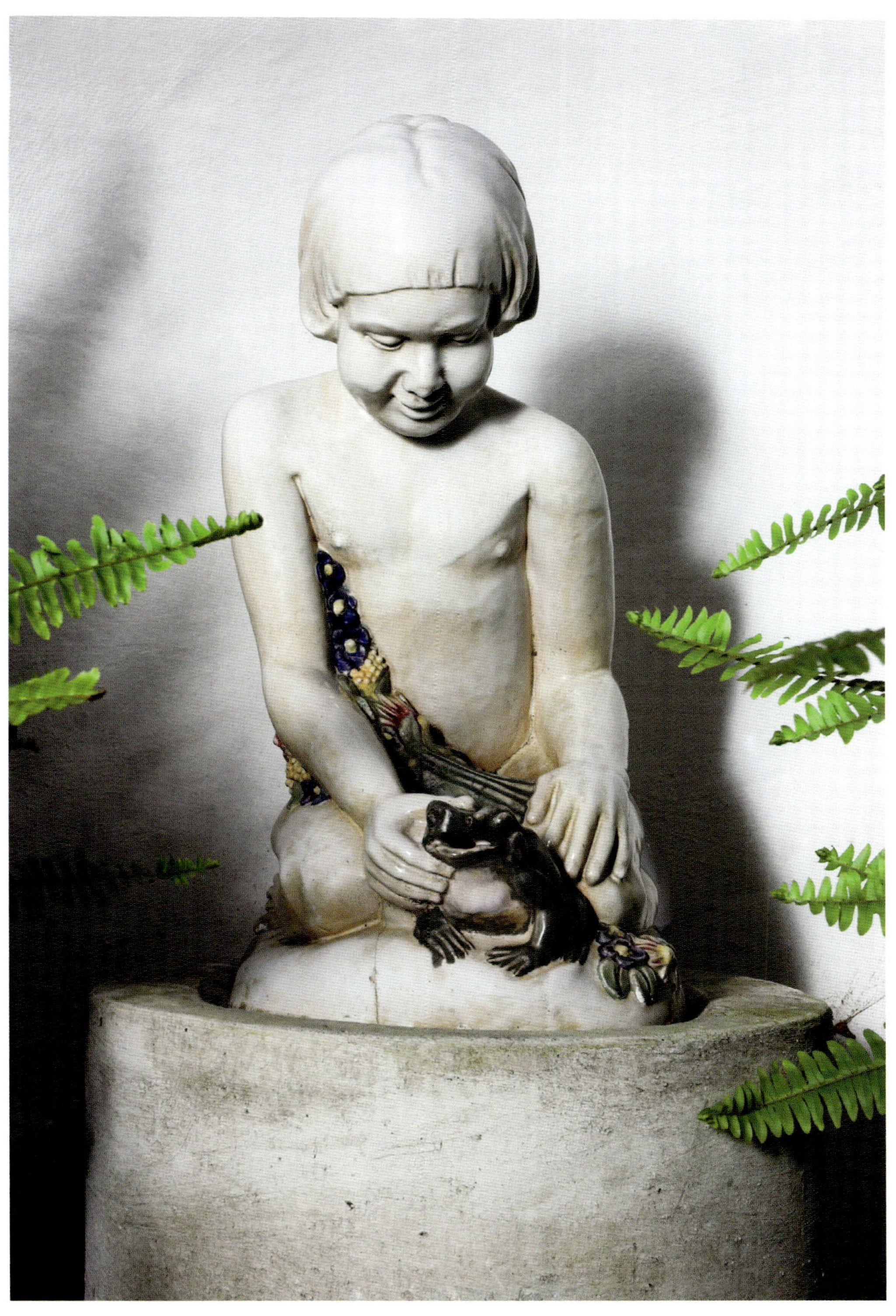

The Ceramic Studio | Sculpture of a girl with a frog | 600x400mm | Provenance: The Alphen Collection | Marks: unmarked; identified by means of archival photographs | Photograph by Natalie Field

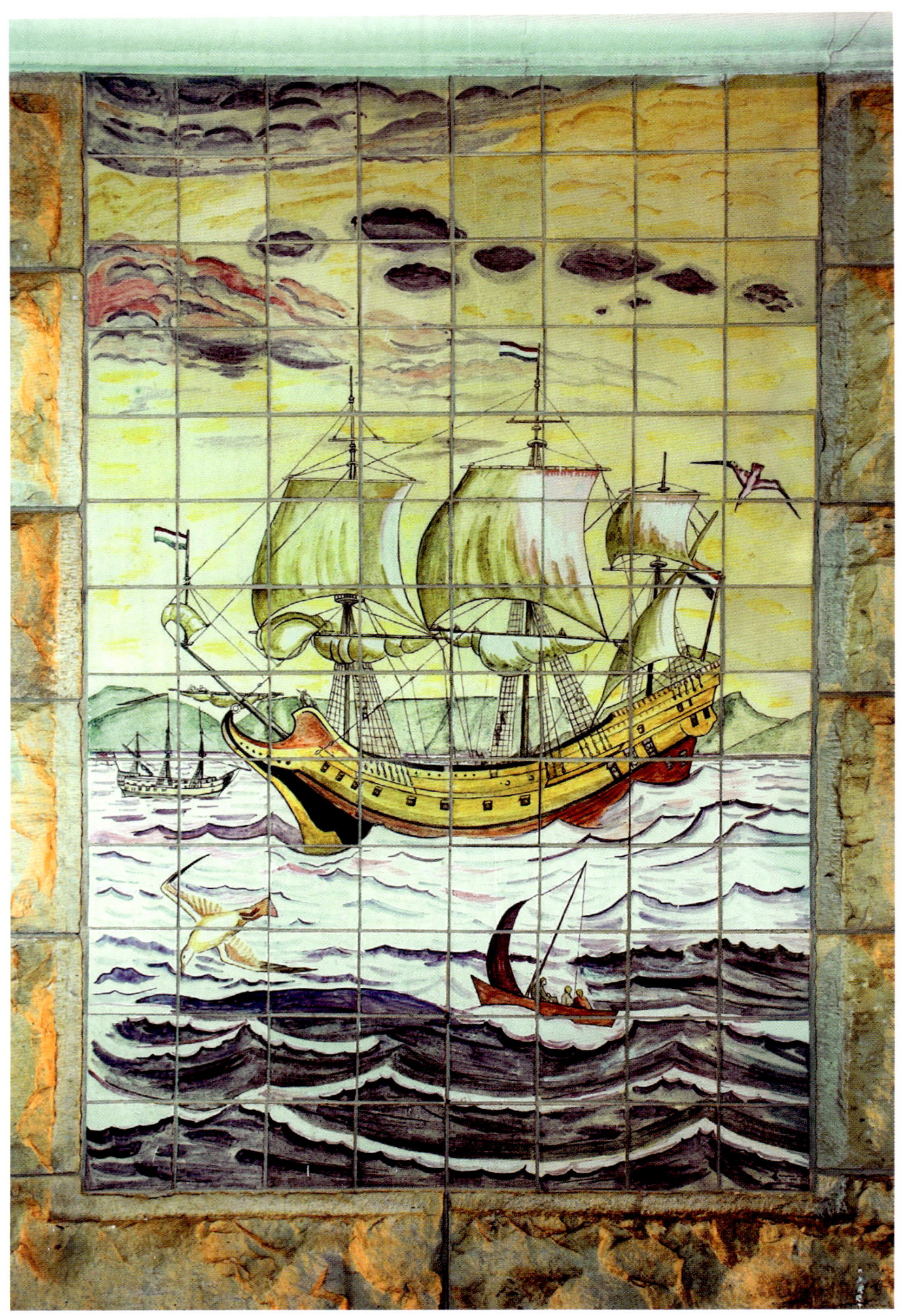

The Ceramic Studio | Tile panel depicting a large galleon | 2x1.22m | Old Post Office, 153 Main Road, Muizenberg, Cape Town | Marks: unmarked | Photograph by Natalie Field

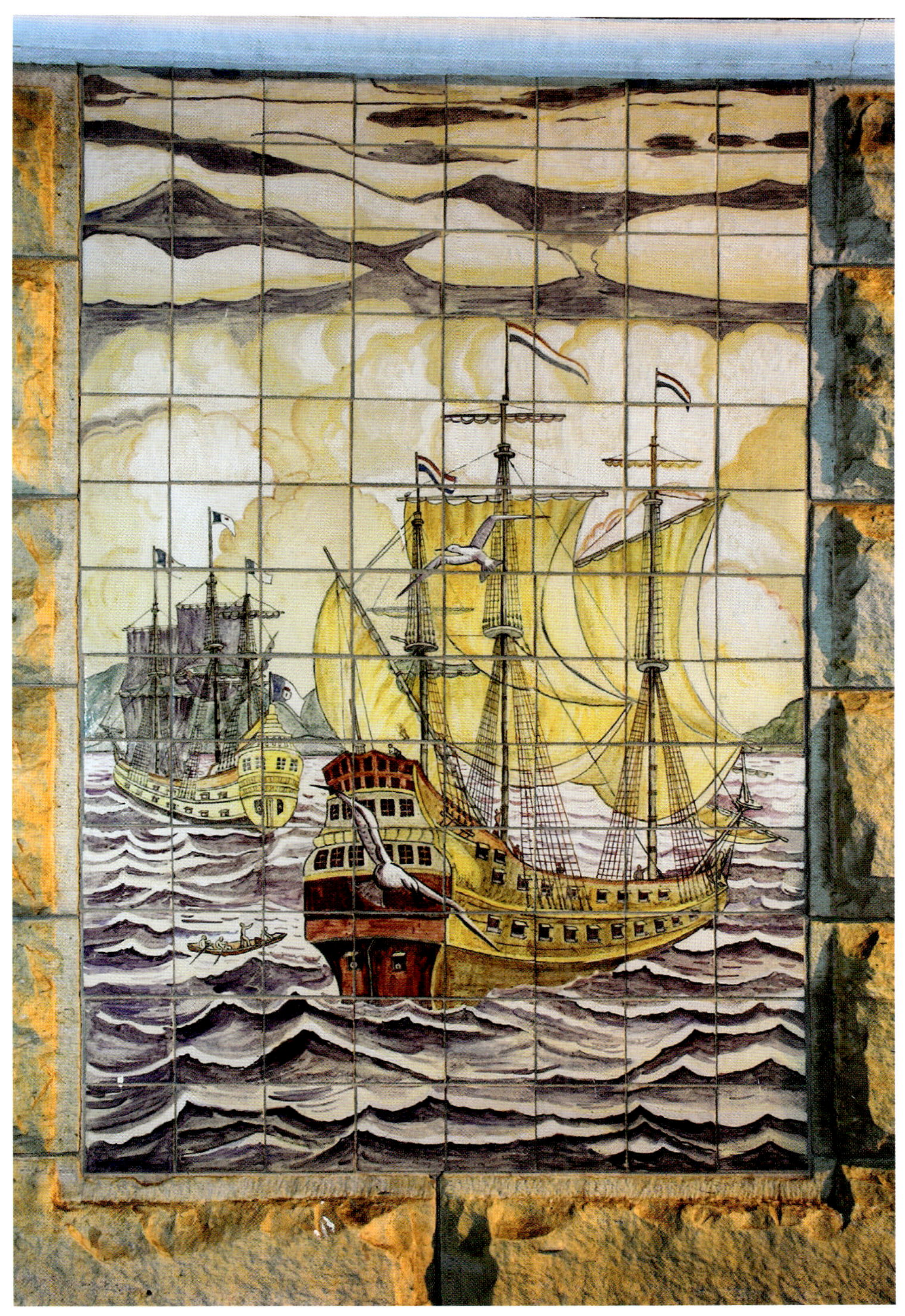

The Ceramic Studio | Tile panel depicting two large galleons | 1.99x1.23m | Old Post Office, 153 Main Road, Muizenberg, Cape Town | Marks: unmarked | Photograph by Natalie Field

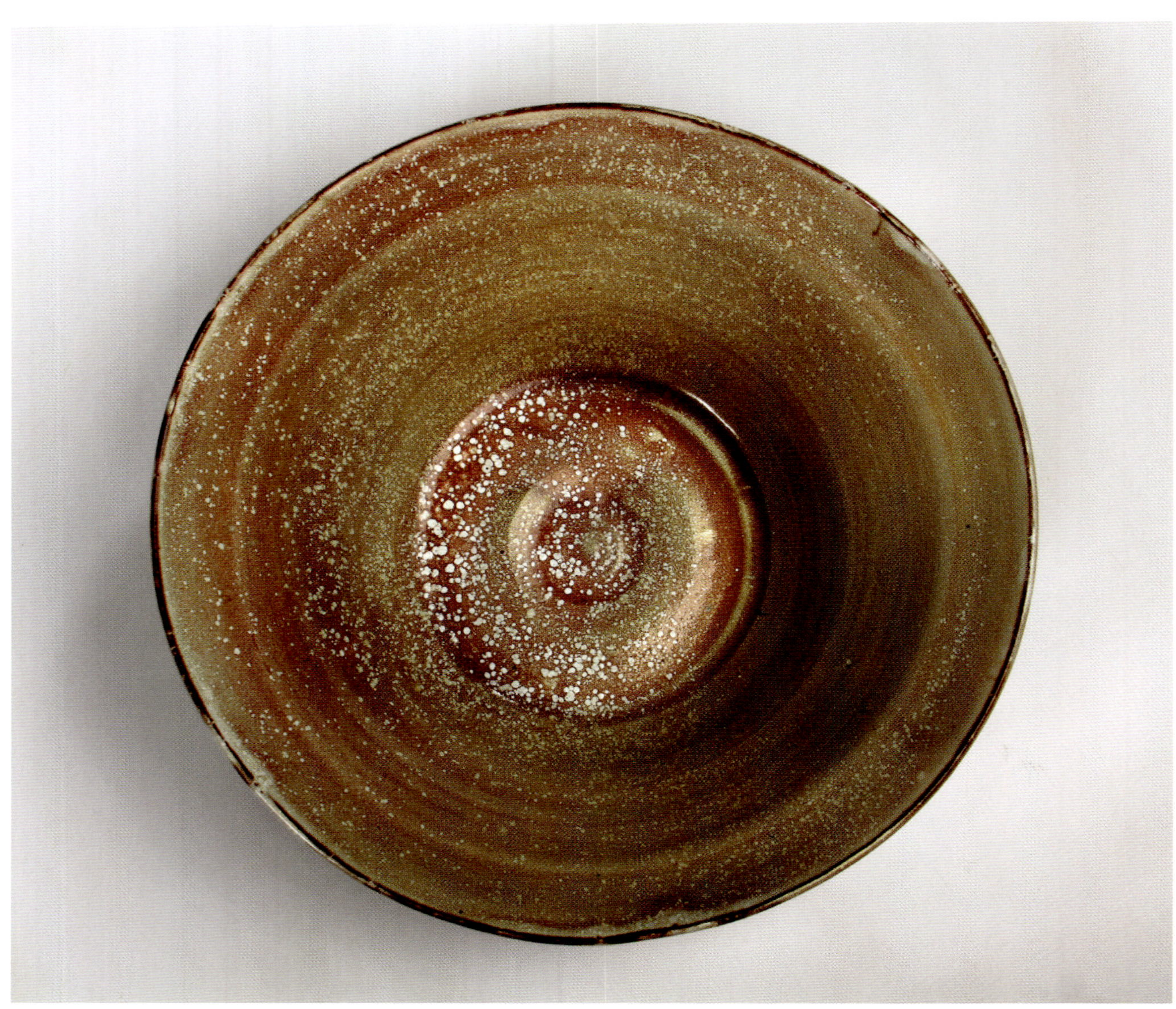

The Ceramic Studio | Bowl with stepped sides, sprayed with ochre, pink and white glaze decoration | 125x360x360 mm | Marked with CERAMIC STUDIO 1930 stamp. Provenance: Wilhelm van Rensburg | Marks: white glazed base with impressed stamp, 'Ceramic Studio 1930'| Photograph by Micha Birch Hannemann

Conrand: Linnware (1943–ca.1962)

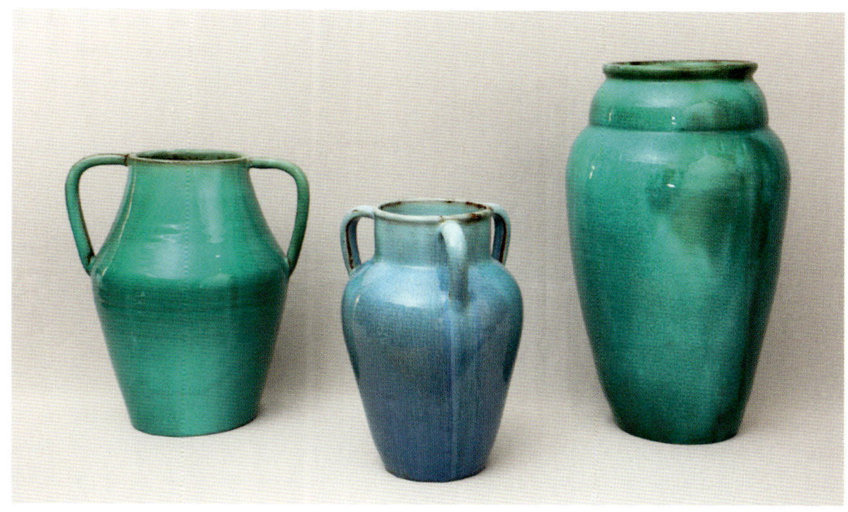

Linnware | Group of three vases | Left vase: 305x125x127mm; central vase: 272x1[illegible]3x97mm; right vase: 415x158x127mm | Provenance: Clive Newman | Marks: left vase: two stamps with LW in a circle; central vase: hand-written, 'Linn ware'; right vase: hand-written, 'Linn ware' | Photograph by Natalie Field

Founder

Sir Thomas M Cullinan (See Transvaal Pottery and the Ceramic Studio)

Staff

When the Ceramic Studio became Linnware many of the original staff remained. One notable exception was Gladys Short, who retired in 1943 as a result of failing health and a lack of enthusiasm for the more commercial orientation of the pottery. Those who stayed included Joan Methley, Audrey Frank and Thelma Newlands. Over the years there were many changes to the staff body, with various temporary potters and decorators, including Barbara Dorrington (née Kelly) (1908–1967),[56] A Gunn, Innes Reich and Inez Sprenger de Rover. Elma Vestman and Aleksanders Klopcanovs (Kalahari Studio) had a brief sojourn at Linnware in the late 1940s. In the early 1950s, the prominent English potter Michael Gill (Izandla) stayed briefly and produced porcelain wares and experimented with various new glazes (Grice 1951:304). Archival records claim that in 1951 the pottery was run by Methley, four (unidentified) decorators, a secretarial assistant, Sam Cromie, four trained throwers, an apprentice thrower and 19 'non-Europeans' (Rosenthal [1960]). Unidentified decorators include 'MV', 'R' and 'C'.

Wares manufactured

- Linnware pottery is characterised by a dark red earthenware body.
- Linnware primarily manufactured earthenware crockery that was sold in a complete set (12 settings) or a half set.[57] Its monochrome tableware was largely based on Ceramic Studio prototypes. Most crockery was decorated with the trademark Linnware deep turquoise glaze, but the pottery also manufactured wares with pale grey, pale yellow, mauve and rich mulberry glazes. These glazes, which display a wonderful depth and luminosity, were

achieved by means of a technique known as double-glazing.

- The pottery also produced polychrome decorated chargers and other vessels, including jugs, beer mugs and vases. Some of these items were commemorative wares, others were decorated with children's motifs, while yet others bore colourful maiolica floral motifs.
- Linnware manufactured fancy goods (such as candelabra and candlesticks, lamp bases, trinket boxes and ashtrays).
- It also produced a limited quantity of small sculptures (including a lioness paperweight and an antelope).

Production methods

- Vases, chalices and large planters were hand-thrown on a potter's wheel.
- Saucers and plates were slip-cast.

Brief history of the pottery

From the outset, Linnware (sometimes spelt Linn Ware, Lynnware) was operated on a more commercial basis than the Ceramic Studio, with less time and energy devoted to artistic wares. The reorientation of the pottery bore fruits, and by the end of 1943 showed a profit of £833. By the end of 1944 Linnware showed a profit of £1 098.

Despite this new orientation, production dwindled between 1952 and 1955 due to an influx of cheap Asian ceramics that flooded the local market as a result of the relaxation of import control tariffs. Also, while the pottery tried to introduce a couple of new shapes in the late 1950s, the bulk of its forms and glazes were outdated.

The final closure of Linnware occurred between 1958 and early 1962. In 1958 Conrand participated with Cecil Michaelis and Rosenthal Porzellan in the loan of £70 000 to Brackenware for the production of quality crockery, which was sold under the name of 'Continental'. Similarly, in 1960 Conrand participated in a loan to Pilkington Tiles SA (Pty) Ltd. The granting of these loans reveals that Cullinan clearly no longer envisaged any form of revival of tile departments or the reorientation of Linnware. Furthermore, Cullinan's electrical insulators that were made on site were highly successful and overshadowed the dwindling fortunes of Linnware.

The Linnware enterprise is renowned for the consistent quality of its ceramics, and is almost synonymous with deep, rich and sumptuous green and turquoise glazed wares. The works of Linnware, like those of the Ceramic Studio, bear testimony to the creative vision of a group of women working in harsh and isolated conditions. For two decades these women championed the cause of handmade pottery. Their original vision set the standard for domestic and decorative pottery in South Africa in the mid-twentieth century. Linnware paved the way for subsequent potteries, such as Liebermann Pottery, which picked up the baton of craftsmanship and led a new generation of potters in the quest to articulate a contemporary South African pottery canon.

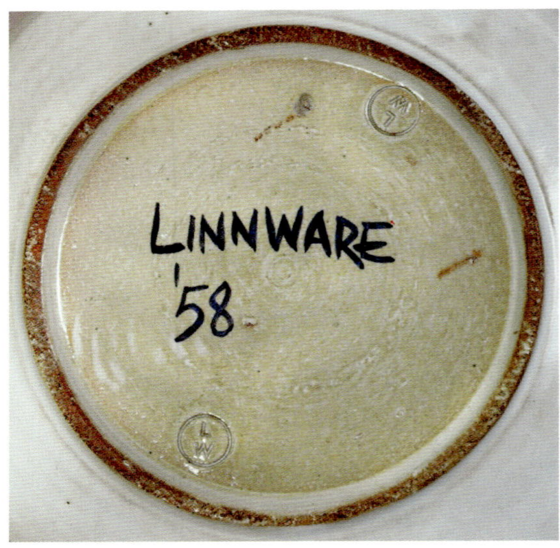

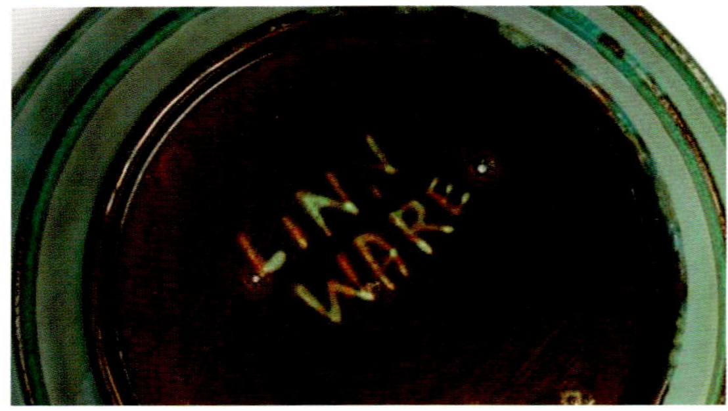

TOP: Linnware | Maker's mark | Hand-written glaze marking, 'Linnware '58', two 'LW' stamped marks | Photograph by Natalie Field

BOTTOM: Linnware | Maker's mark | Hand-written glaze marking, 'Linnware' and a 'bowl and lid' stamped mark | Photograph by Micha Birch Hannemann

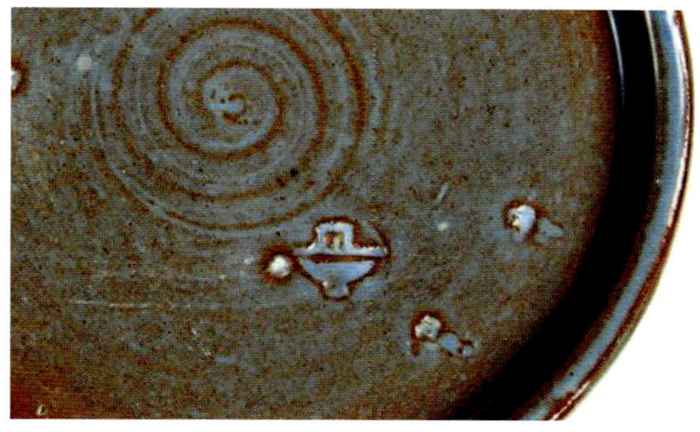

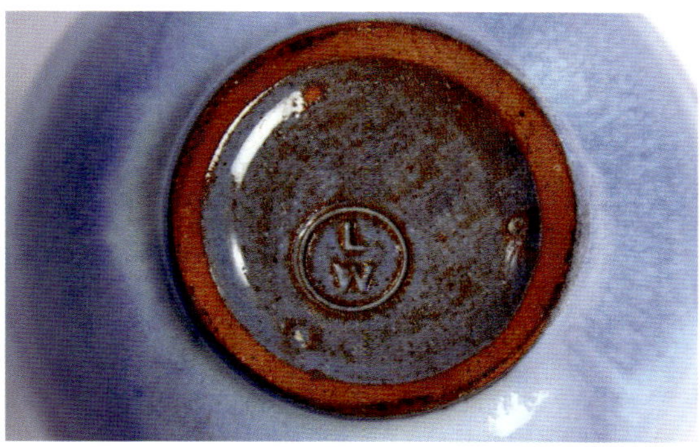

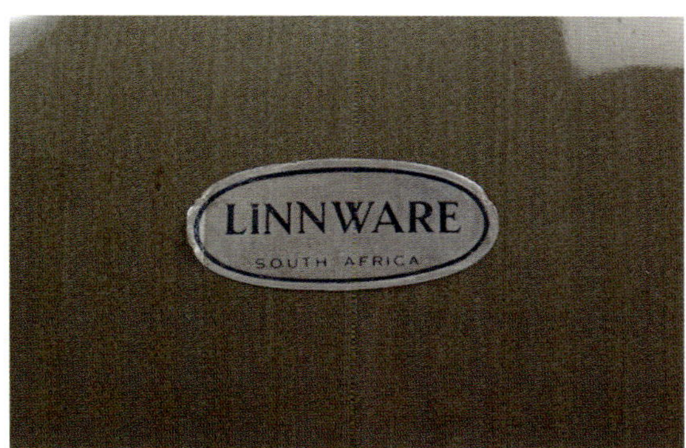

TOP: Linnware | Maker's mark | 'Bowl and lid' stamp and indistinct hand-written 'Linn Ware' glaze marking | Photograph by Micha Birch Hannemann

MIDDLE: Linnware | Maker's mark | 'LW' circular stamp | Photograph by Micha Birch Hannemann

BOTTOM: Oval silver sticker with blue markings, Linnware, South Africa | Photograph by Micha Birch Hannemann

Marks

- Hand-painted marks include 'LINN WARE', 'LINNWARE' and 'L.W'. This is sometimes accompanied by 'SA', the artist's name or initials and a date.
- Linnware also used at least two different studio impressed marks. One mark superficially resembles an African hut, but actually represents a profile view of a dish with a lid. A second consists of a circle containing an L above a W.
- Some wares have an oval gilt sticker containing 'Linnware'.

Biographies

In addition to many of the artists in the biographical listing of Conrand: The Ceramic Studio, the following artists worked at Linnware.

BABER, Ruth and Rhoda

In the late 1940s and 1950s the Baber sisters decorated domestic ware at Linnware.

GUNN, A

Gunn decorated works for Linnware from 1945 into the 1950s.

REICH, Innes

Reich worked as a decorator in the late 1940s.

SPRENGER DE ROVER, Inez (née Morrison) (1924–2012)

Born in Pretoria to John William Morrison (1888–1969) and Nora Morrison (née Vorster) (1897–1949), Inez chose to attend Meisies Hoerskool, Pretoria because the well-known artist Bettie Cilliers Barnard (1914–2010) taught there. She studied at the Rand Afrikaans University, Johannesburg and also took classes at the University of the Witwatersrand, Johannesburg. In 1948 Inez decided to join her then best friend, Bettie Cilliers Barnard, as well as the sculptors Laurika Postma and Hennie Potgieter for further studies overseas at the University of Den Haag.

In Dordrecht, Holland she met her husband Louis Hendrik Sprenger de Rover (b.1925). They returned to Pretoria, married and moved to Olifantsfontein in 1950 where Louis was employed by Cullinan Refractories.

Inez Sprenger de Rover worked at Linnware from 1957 to 1958, decorating tiles and chargers. Among her tile designs are recipes for cocktails, stylised images of African women, and studies of fish and vegetables. Her tableware was signed ISdR [58]

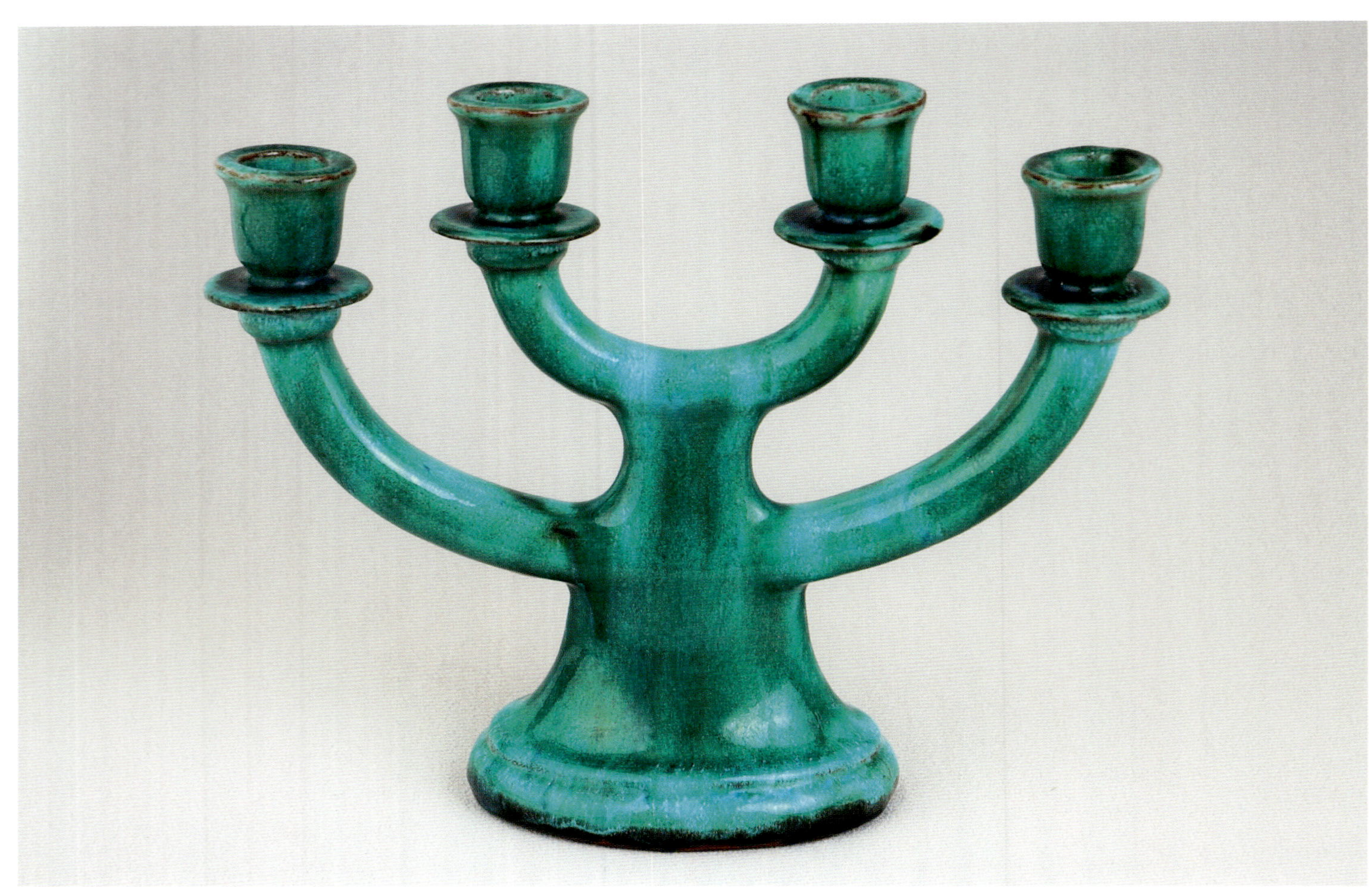

Linnware | Candelebra | 135x282x40mm | Provenance: SHC Iziko | 89/183 | Marks: Hand-painted marks, 'Linn Ware' | Photograph by Natalie Field

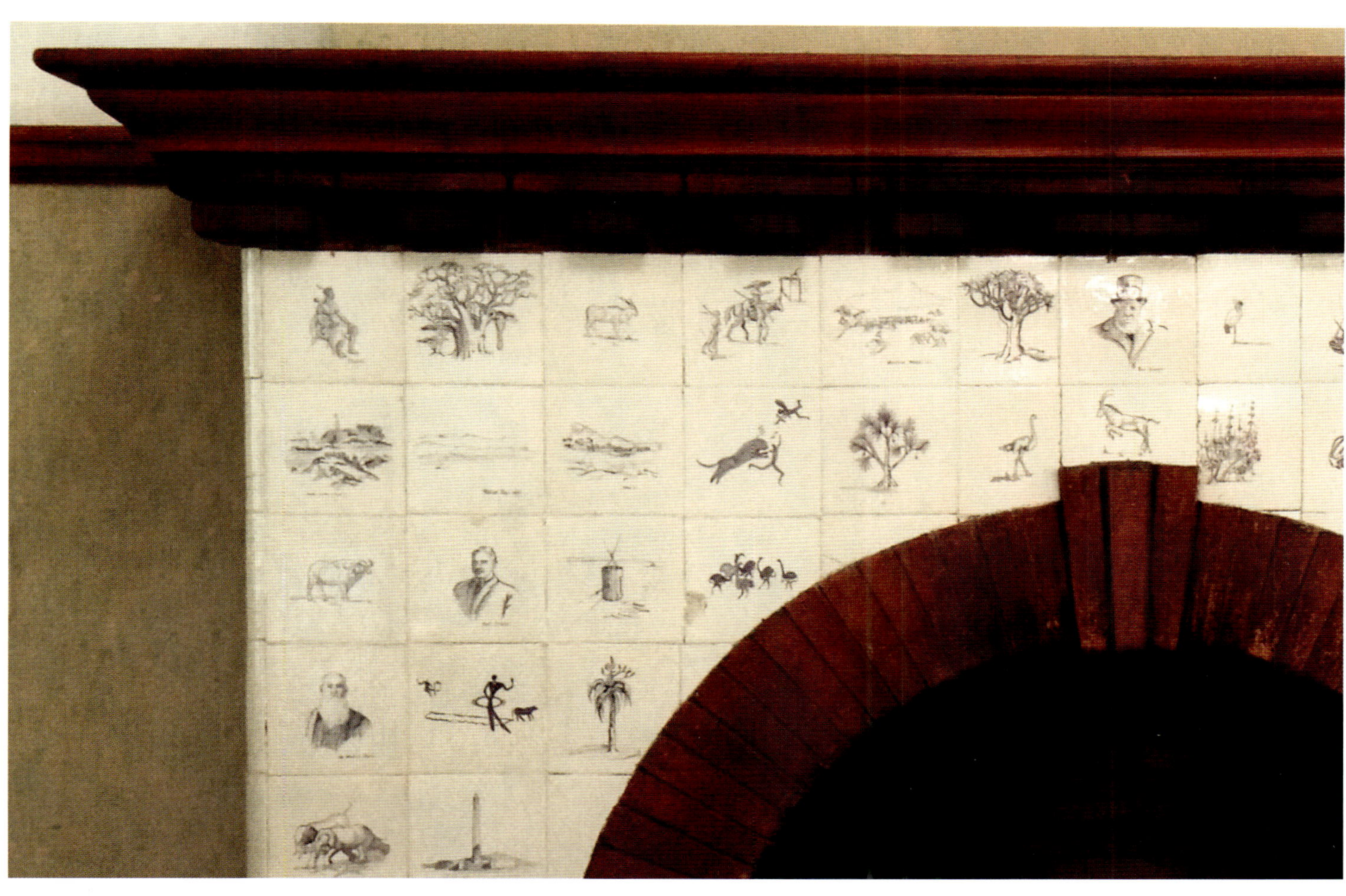

The Ceramic Studio | Hand-painted blue-and-white tiles for the Club Hall, University of Pretoria (1936) | Architect: Gerard Moerdyk | Photograph by Kyle Rath

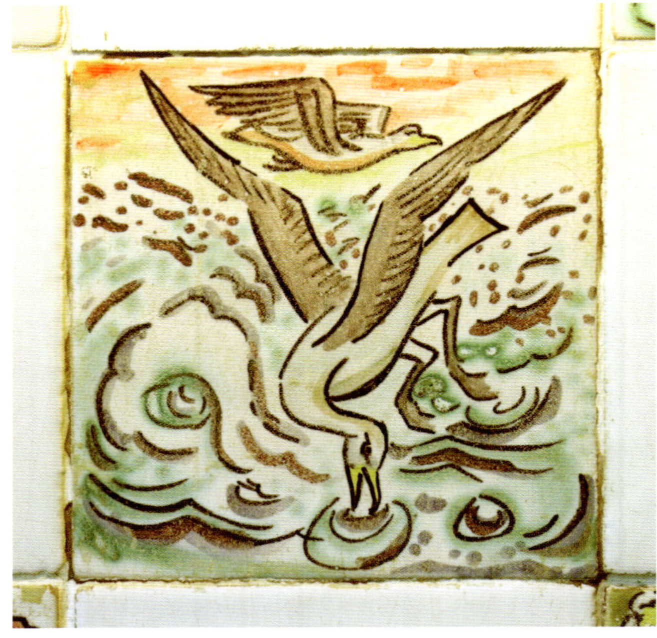

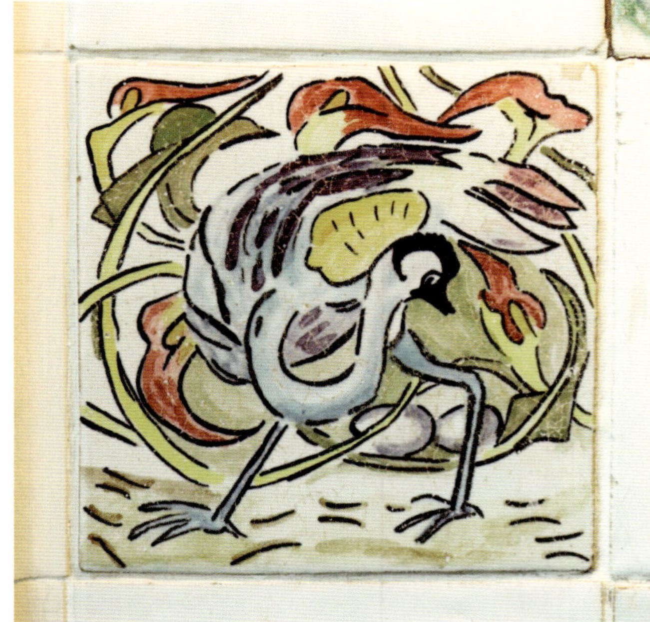

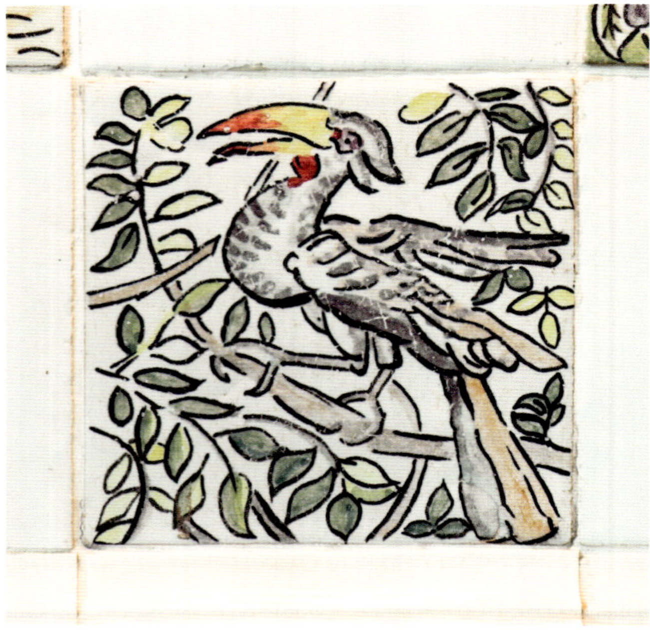

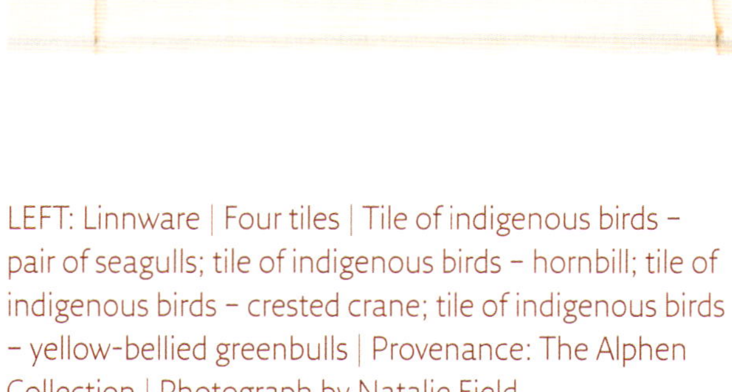

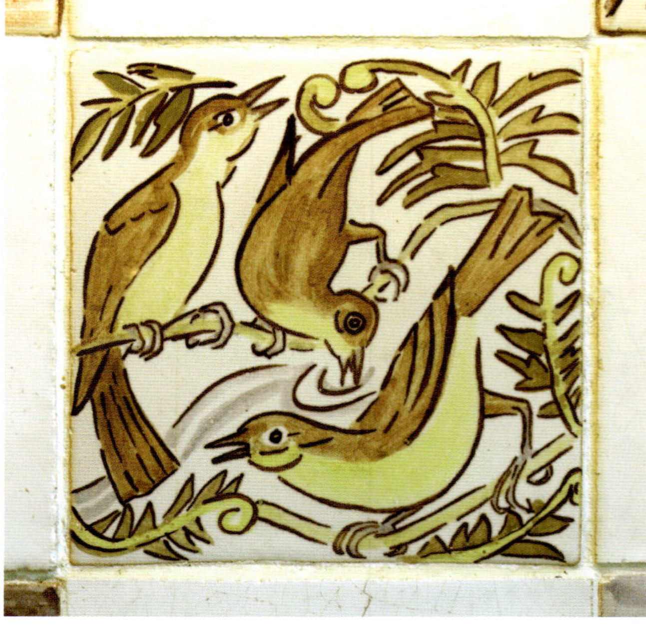

LEFT: Linnware | Four tiles | Tile of indigenous birds – pair of seagulls; tile of indigenous birds – hornbill; tile of indigenous birds – crested crane; tile of indigenous birds – yellow-bellied greenbulls | Provenance: The Alphen Collection | Photograph by Natalie Field

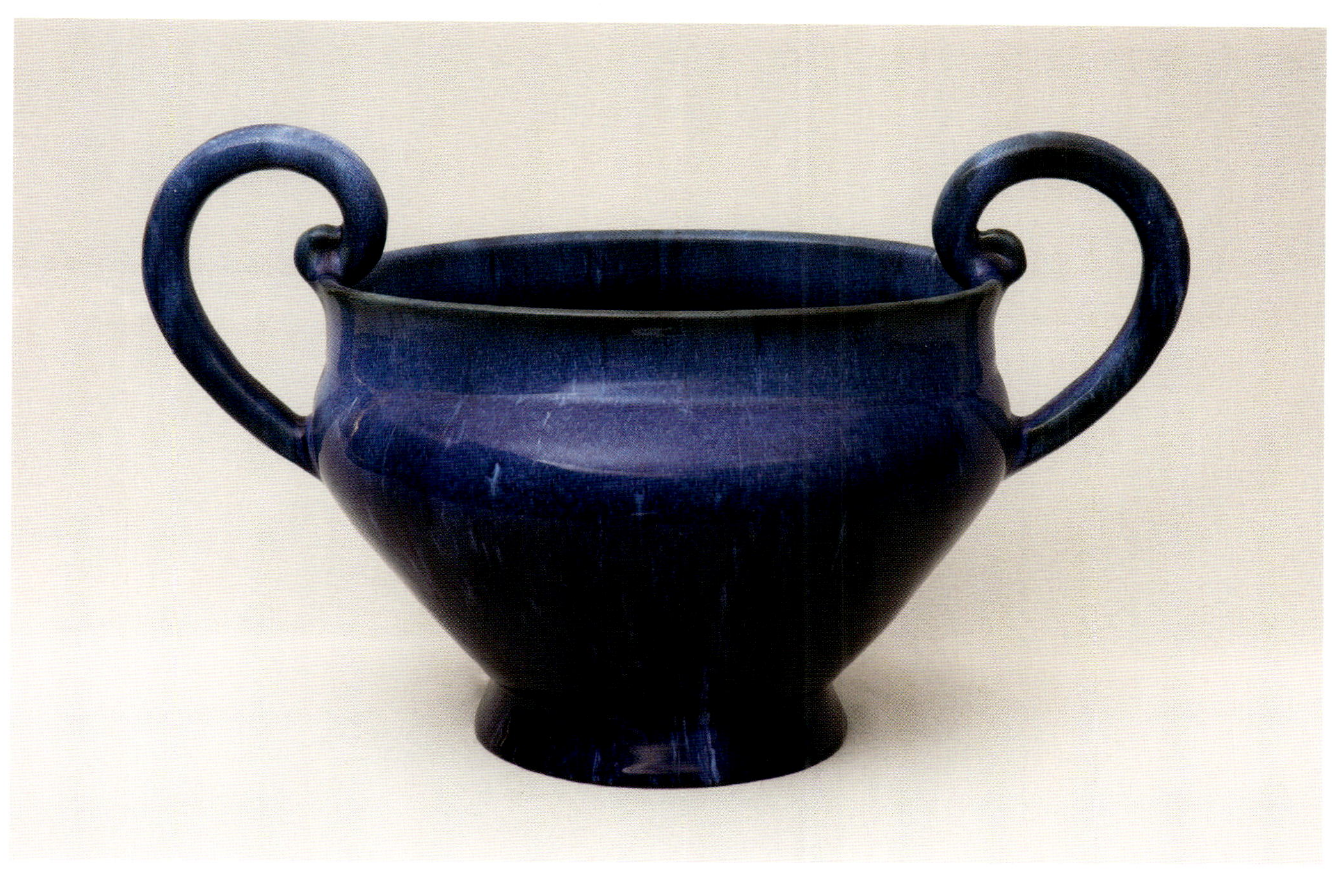

Linnware | Large blue vessel with elaborate scrolled handles | 203x400x150mm | Provenance: Clive Newman | Marks: black glazed base with two impressed stamps of LW in a circle | Photograph by Natalie Field

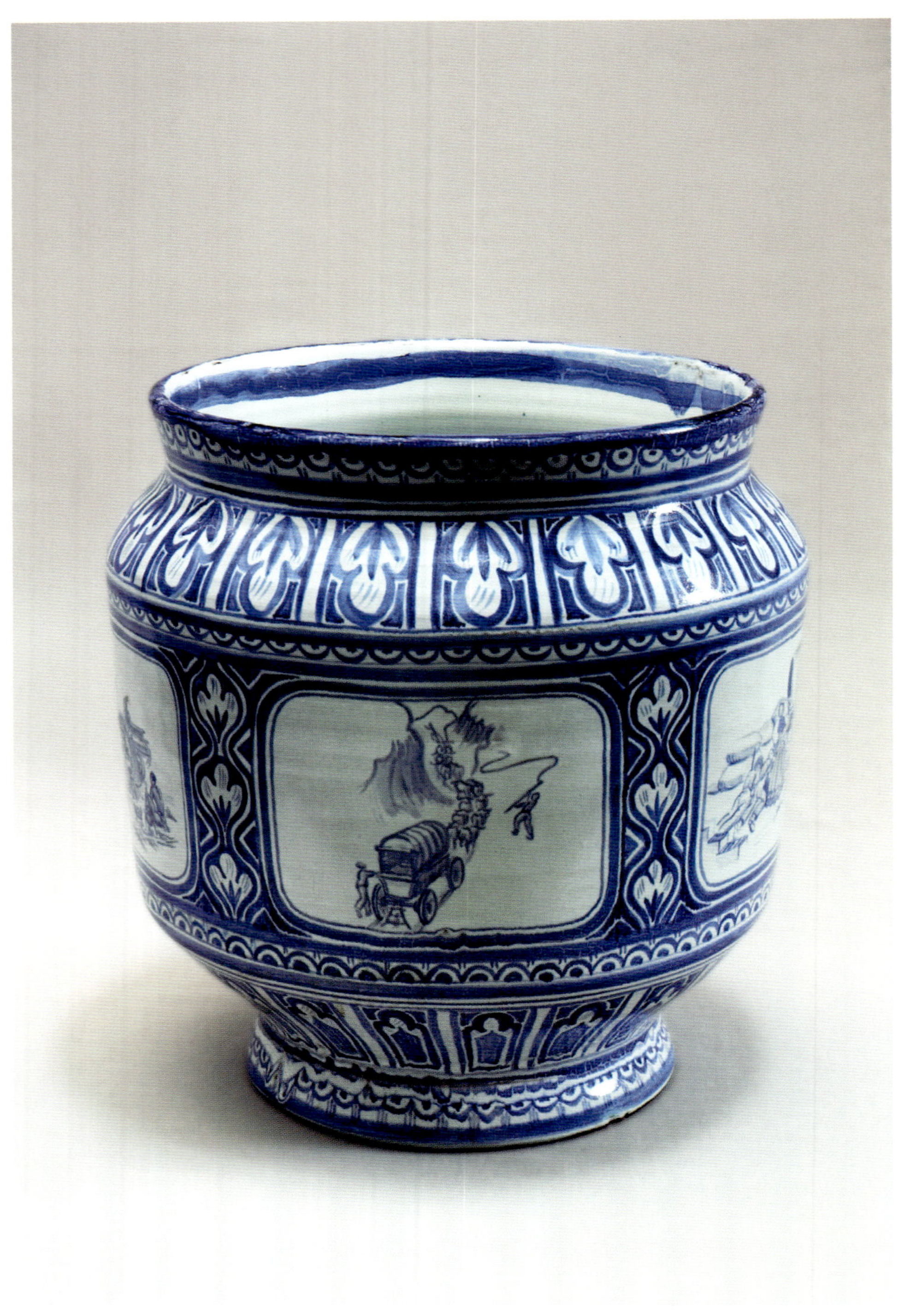

Linnware | Jar decorated with vignettes of Voortrekkers (lid missing) | 320x280x280mm | Provenance: The Alphen Collection | Marks: base signed, 'LINN WARE 1946 GUNN', impressed dish stamp | Photograph by Natalie Field

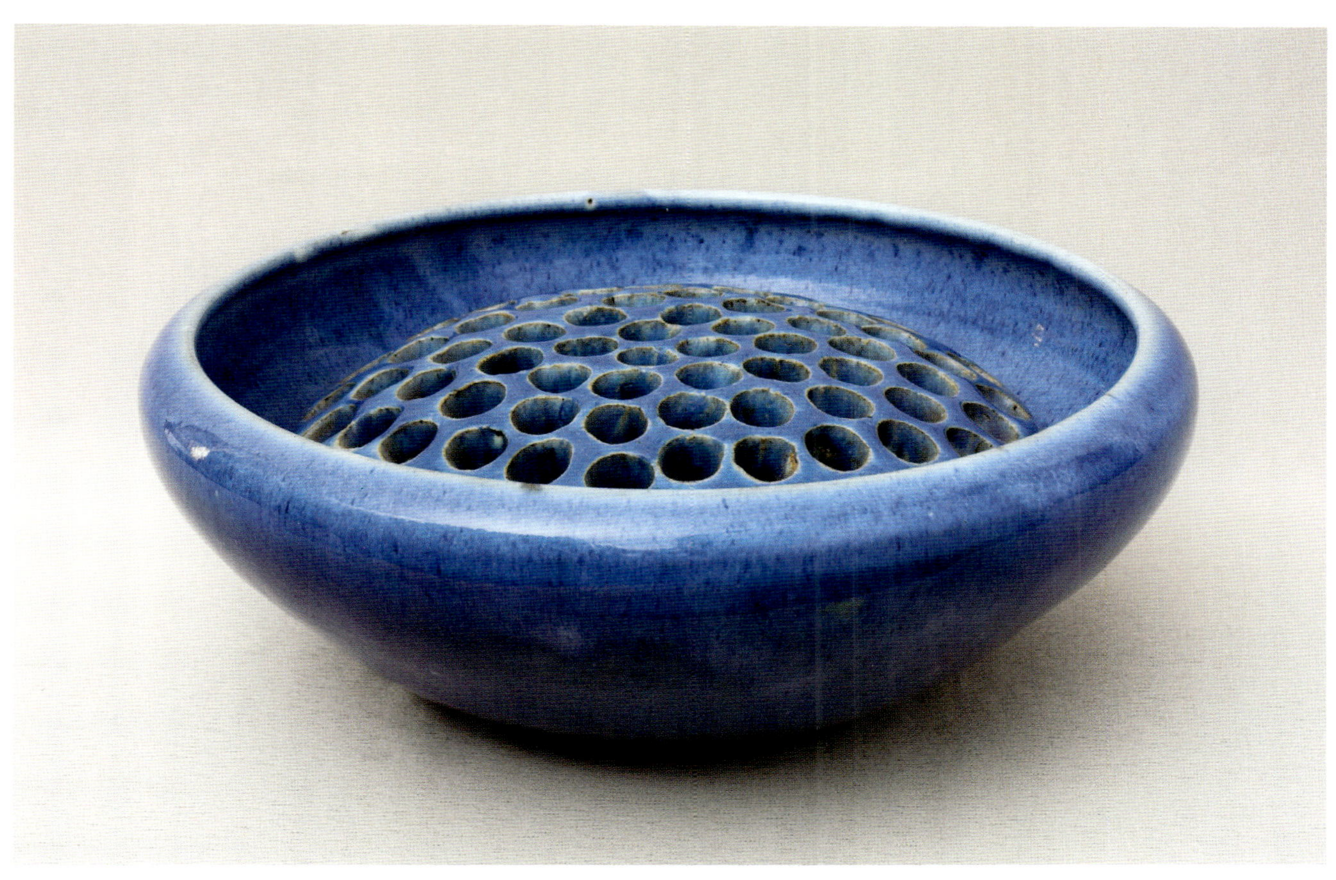

Linnware | Large, open, light-blue bowl with flower rose | 133x136x165mm | Provenance: Clive Newman | Marks: glazed blue base with impressed Linnware stamp of lidded pot | Photograph by Natalie Field

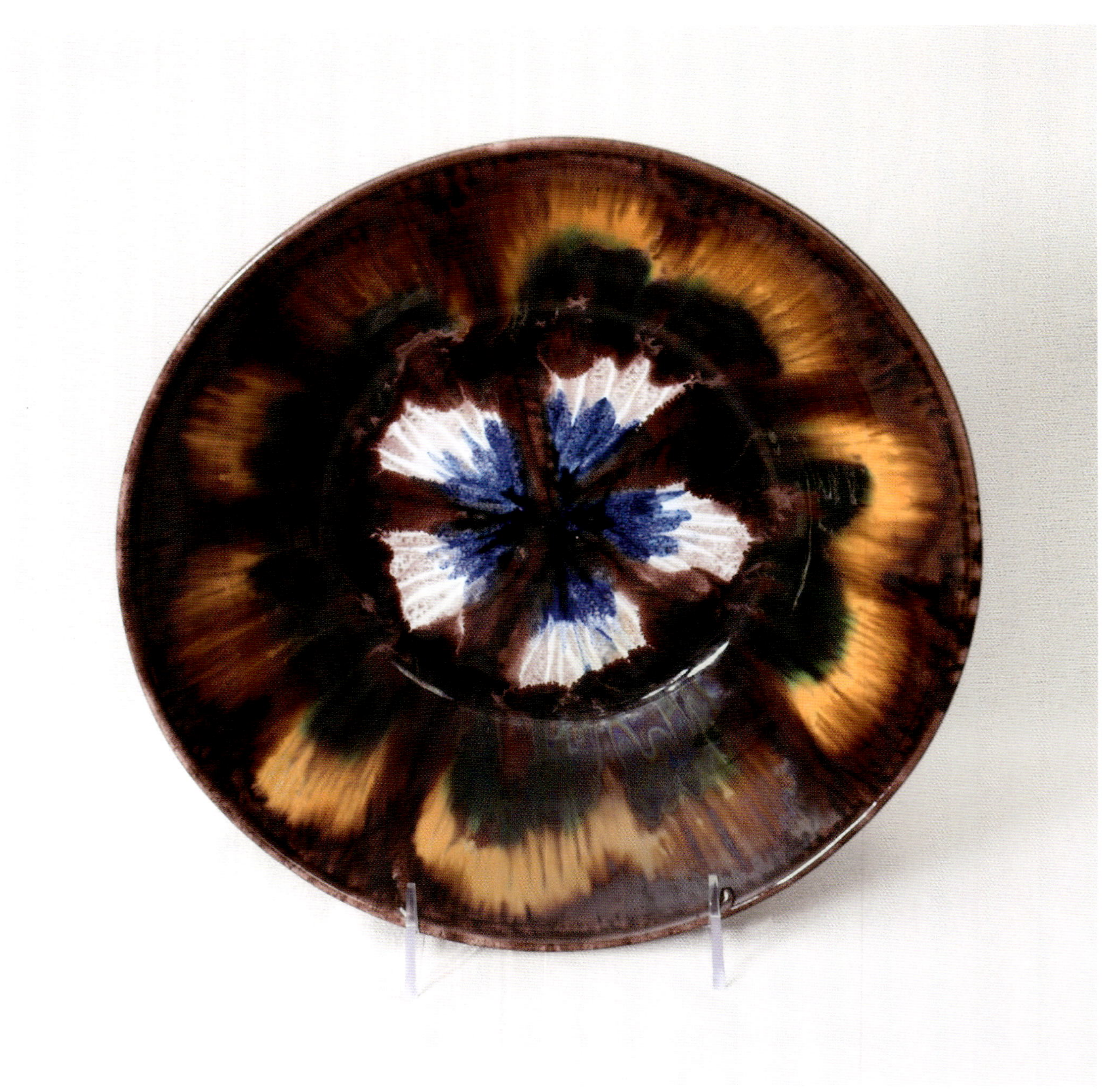

Linnware | Bowl with abstract floral design in brown, blue and white | 70x262x158mm | Provenance: Clive Newman | Photograph by Natalie Field

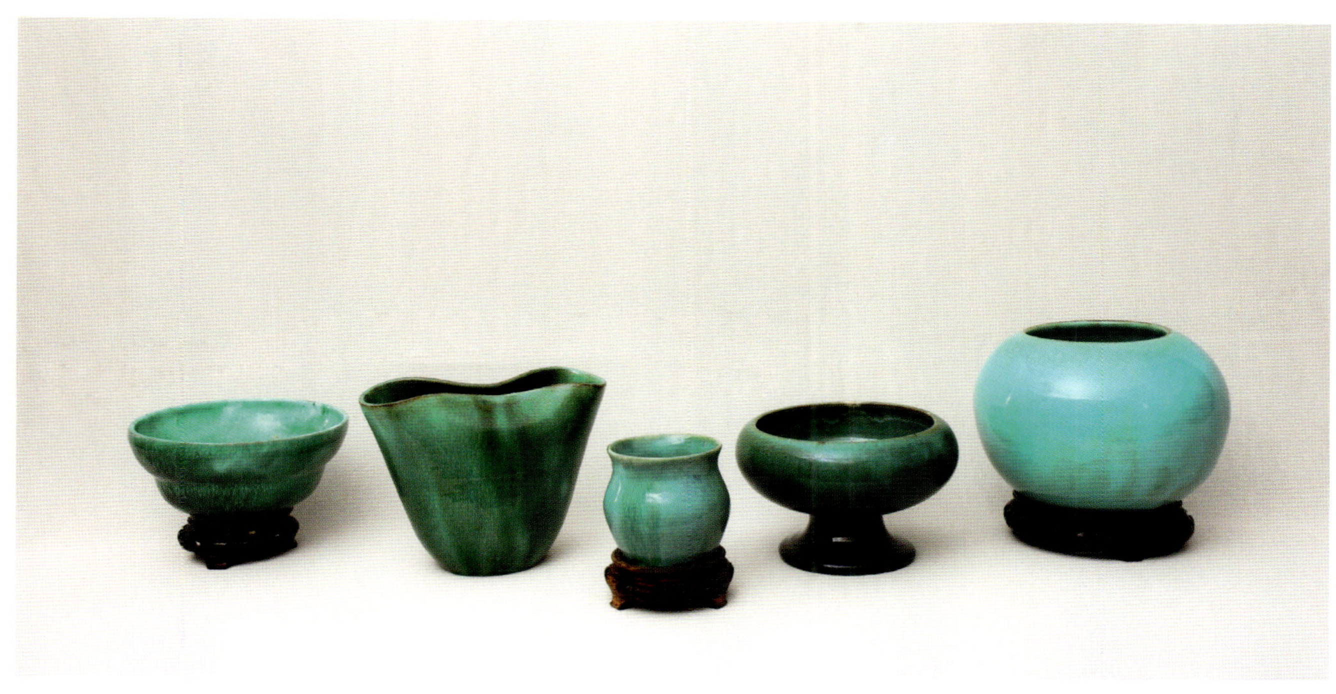

Linnware | Group of five vases | From left: 87x160x80mm; 152x192x78mm; 87x82x67mm; 111x135x104mm; 133x95x111mm | Provenance: Clive Newman | Marks: from left: marks not visible due to base; glazed base with stamp mark, LW in a circle; white glazed base, sgraffito initials, M.J. Blue glaze mark, 'The Ceramic Studio, 1930'; green glazed base with stamped mark, LW in a circle; turquoise glazed base with painted mark, 'Linn Ware' | Photograph by Natalie Field

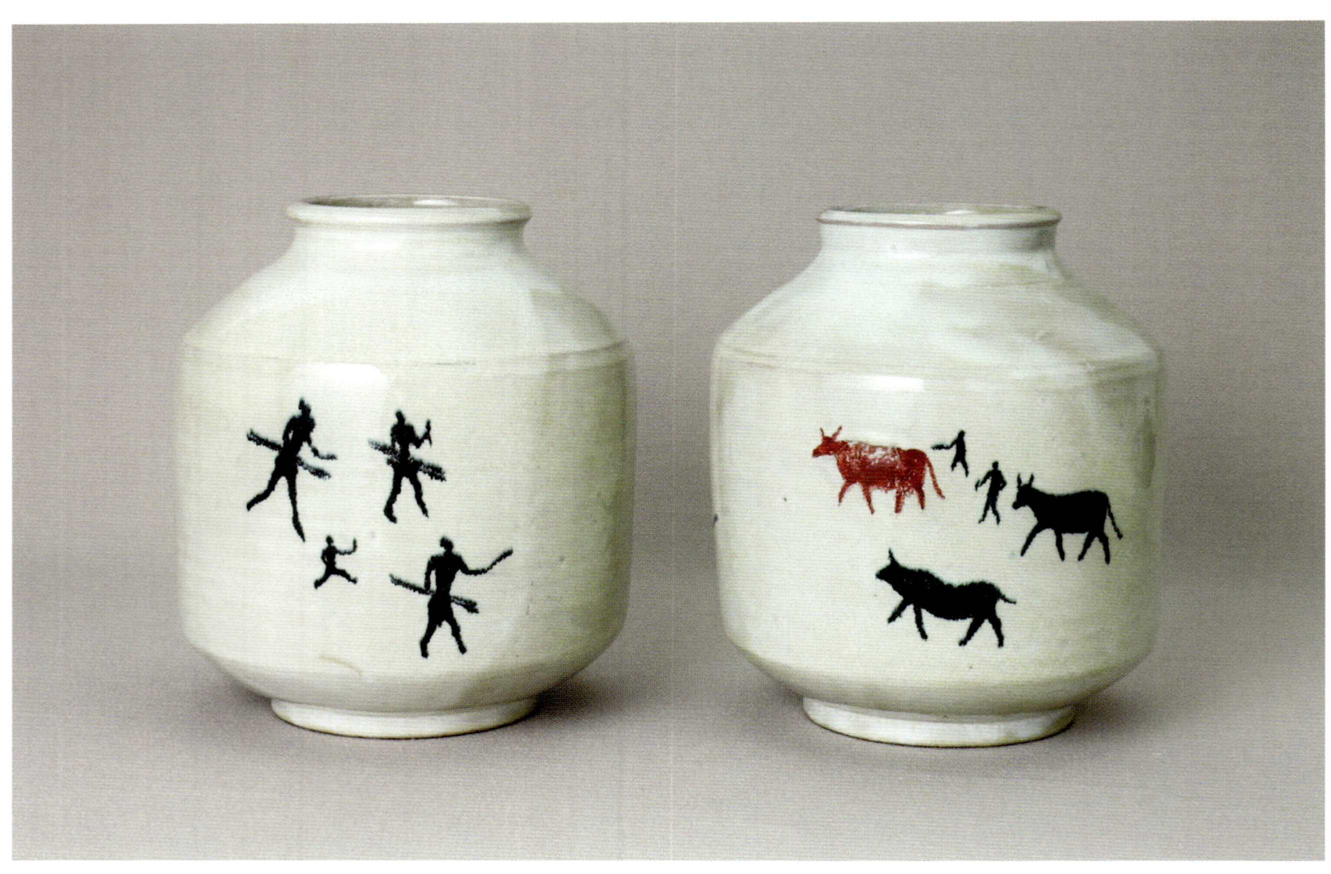

Linnware | Pair of vases painted with Bushman images | 225x105x115mm | Provenance: DNMCH | MJ 74/459 | Marks: brown glazed base, 'Linn Ware 55' | Photograph by Natalie Field

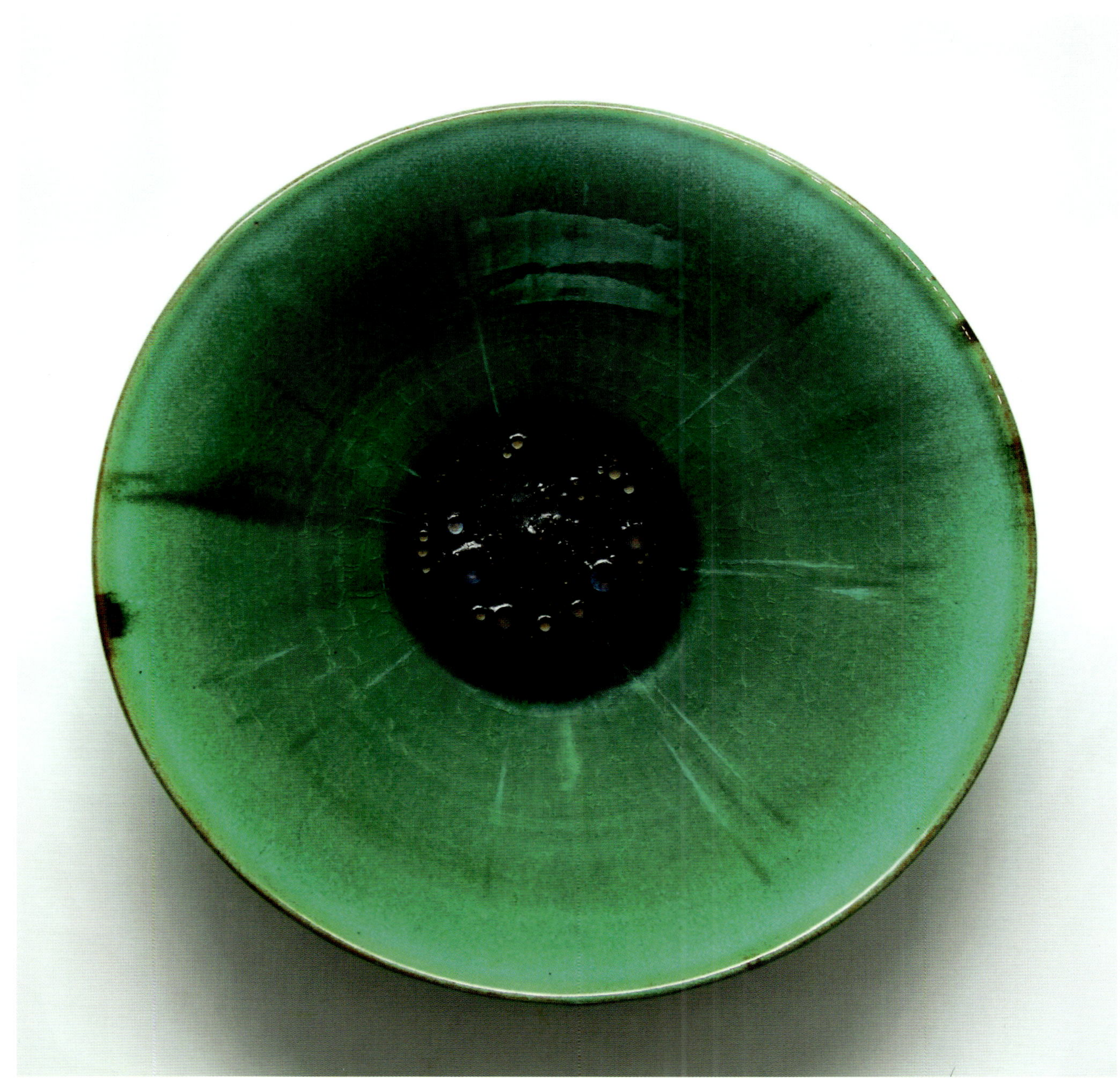

Linnware | Charger with green glaze and a pool of bubbling 'volcanic' glaze in the centre | 302x94mm | Provenance: Micha Birch Hannemann | Marks: brown glazed base, hand-written glaze marking, 'Linnware' and a 'bowl and lid' stamped mark | Photograph by Micha Birch Hannemann

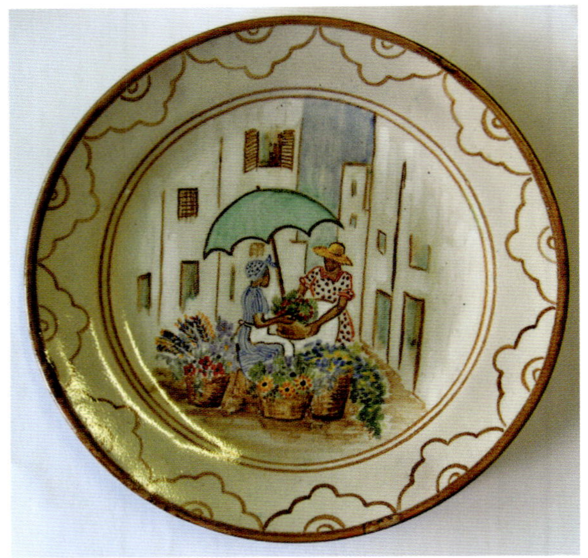

LEFT: Linnware | Charger decorated with image of flower seller and assistant | 210x35mm | Provenance: Antiques and Things, East London | Marks: glaze marks, 'Linn Ware' | Photograph by William Martinson

LEFT BOTTOM: Linnware | Charger depicting two sun birds and flowers | 200x25mm | Provenance: Flo Bird | Marks: cream glazed base with painted brown marks, 'Linn Ware '56 AL' | Photograph by William Martinson

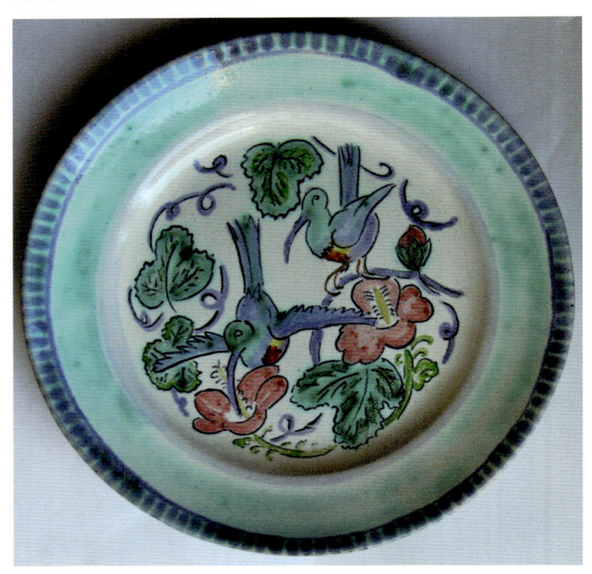

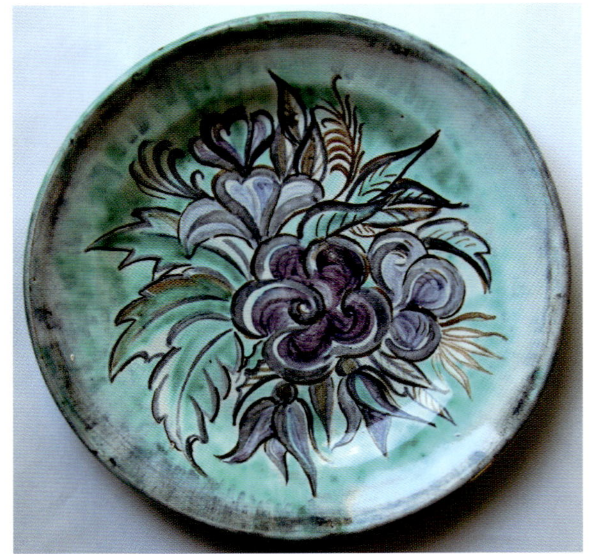

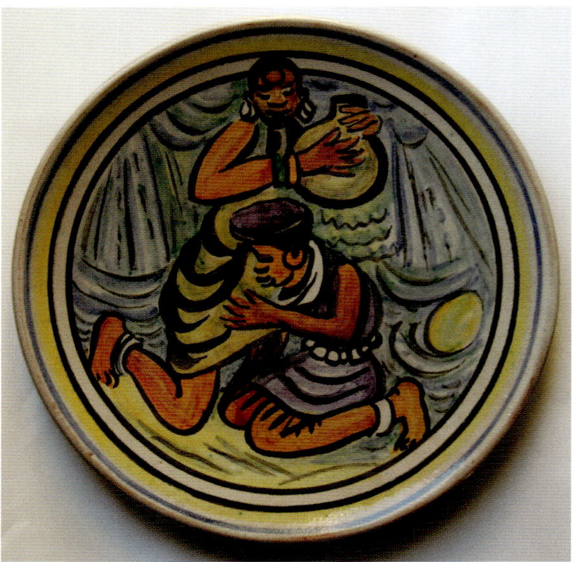

RIGHT TOP: Linnware | Charger decorated with foliate imagery | ca.250x35mm | Provenance: Flo Bird | Marks: glazed base, blue hand-painted glaze marks, 'LINN WARE 49 RhB' | Photograph by William Martinson

RIGHT: Linnware | Charger decorated with image of two African women, one bearing a clay pot | ca.250x35mm | Provenance Flo Bird | Marks: glazed base, black hand-painted glaze marks, LINN WARE '52 MV' | Photograph by William Martinson

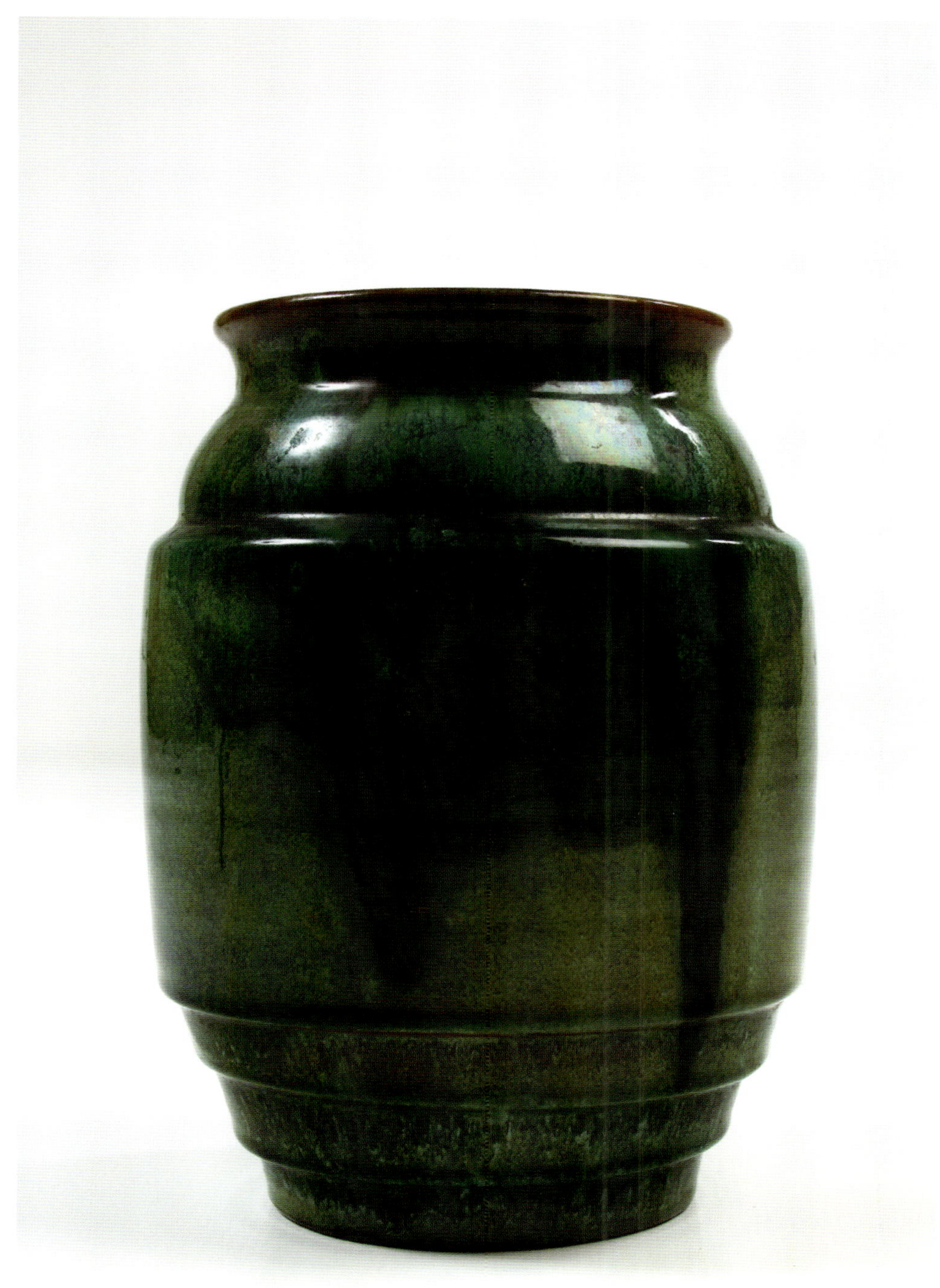

Linnware | Tall, stepped base and neck vase, dark mottled green | 225x160x160mm | Provenance: Wilhelm Van Rensburg | Marks: hand-marked in green glaze: LINN WARE | Photograph by Micha Birch Hannemann

Crescent Potteries (1952–1992)

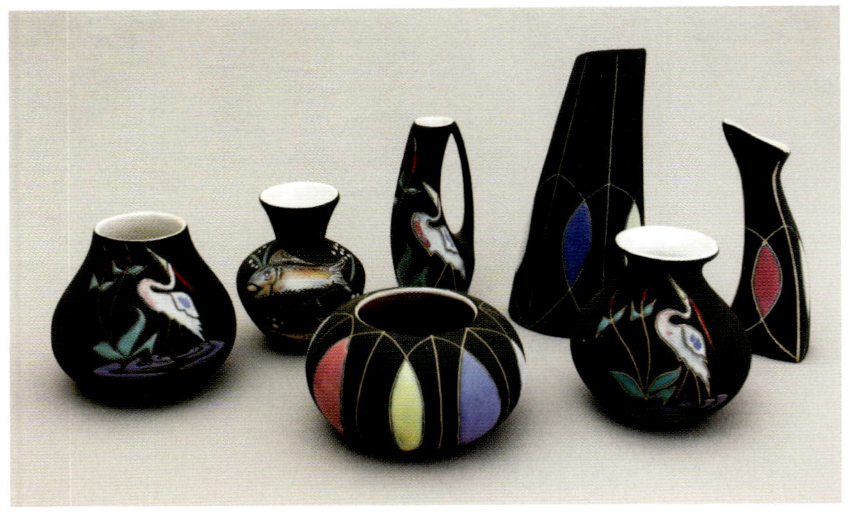

Crescent Potteries | Vases | 170x60mm | Provenance: Douglas van der Horst | Marks: various items marked with holiday resort names; bases with various marks, from left front, '229 Hand Painted Crescent'; front row, second vase, 228B incised CP monogram; front row, right vase, 226, Port Shepstone under crane; back row, from left '227 Hand Painted Crescent'; 'Jim Fouche-Oord' on the back; 'M21 Hand Painted Crescent', Margate on side; back row, third vase from left, 214 B Crescent monogram; last vase on left, Crescent monogram 211B | Photograph by Natalie Field

Location

Luipaardsvlei, near Krugersdorp

Founders and directors

Crescent Potteries took over South African Artistic Potteries in 1952. The original director and designer was Albert Brown. Morrie Shain and his brother Harry Shain purchased the pottery from Brown in 1958. Morrie was responsible for the financial management of the business, as well as sales and marketing; while Harry was a sleeping partner and did not actively participate. Albrecht Schließler joined Crescent Potteries in approximately 1954 as a 'boy Friday', responsible for menial chores and the technical aspects of production. Two years later he was promoted to the position of joint director with Morrie Shain, Harry Shain and Albert Brown. As the operations director, Schließler was in charge of the entire production cycle, including design and supervision of the designers and painters, mould-making, modelling, glazing and firing. However, a personality clash between Brown and Schließler resulted in Brown leaving the firm in 1958. In 1963 Morrie Shain bought his brother's shares in the business, and he and Schließler remained joint directors until the pottery closed down.

Staff

Durant Sihlali, 'Stompie' Ernest Manana, Isaac Witkin, Nicodemus (Darius) Molefi, Isaac Sello and Memling Morningstar Motaung.

Wares manufactured

Crescent produced a diverse range of domestic ware (jugs, plates, vases, bowls, mugs, tankards, sugar bowls, egg cups, ashtrays and condiment sets) and decorative items (wall plaques, masks, ornaments, lamp bases, smokers' stands and planters). Initially, most wares were decorated by hand, but with the loss of numerous key painters and designers, including Durant Sihlali in the mid-1960s, the pottery turned to the use of imported transfers from England and Germany.

Crescent Potteries is perhaps most well-known for its souvenir African wares, decorated with sgraffito motifs of Africans and wildlife. African figures were depicted in a variety of stereotypical activities, including dancing, drinking, beating drums, cooking and nursing infants, on glazed bowls, mugs, small snack plates, ashtrays and vases. Later souvenir wares featuring African animals were decorated with a transferred image.[59] On many wares bearing wildlife, the name of a heritage institution was either incised into the body of the item (under the decorative image) on the base or printed as part of the transfer.[60] From the mid-1950s to early 1980s, Crescent Potteries produced souvenir wares for almost every game park and wildlife reserve in South Africa, and for various local museums and oceanaria.

Its wall masks reflected a synthesis of various western and central African models, and were named after the indigenous people of South Africa, such as 'Zulu Boy'. Isaac Witkin designed a series of African totemic figurines that resembled ritual and fetish objects from west and central Africa.

It also produced a range of vessels, predominantly vases, that were almost the complete antithesis of the African series. The modernist 'free-form' range of vases are characterised by their chocolate-brown or charcoal-coloured matt-glazed bodies, decorated with colourful glaze and sgraffito decorations of modernist 'abstract' imagery. In terms of their depictions of biomorphic forms and their calligraphic and linear qualities, these modernist 'abstract' designs recall the work of Joan Miró (1893–1983), Jean Arp (1887–1966) and Paul Klee (1879–1940). Imagery from Miró, Arp and Klee was extensively appropriated and recycled by European and American designers in the 1950s and early 1960s.

An extremely popular modernist range from the late 1950s and early 1960s was called 'Uranium City'. Wares were decorated with a matt black engobe onto which yellow glaze (possibly an enamel) was applied, a common practice in contemporary European decorative pottery from the 1950s.[61]

In the 1950s, Crescent Potteries made two series of flowerpots with matching trays – one with a rounded foot and the other with a straight foot. Both series were decorated with polka dots of contrasting colour, evoking Suzie Cooper's 'Polka Dot' series of dinner services and tea and coffee wares, which were imported into South Africa from the 1950s until the 1970s.[62]

In the 1950s it manufactured ashtrays, smokers' stands and planters mounted in tall elegant metal stands. These ashtrays are notable for their freeform shape, which characterised international design trends of the 1950s. The planters were somewhat more conventional and did not feature any innovative designs or decorative features.

During the same decade it made various zoomorphic ornaments. These included a horse, a fawn (which resembles the Walt Disney cartoon character

Bambi), a large bear, a bear cub on its back (this ornament functioned as an ashtray), a pig, a kangaroo, a giraffe, a camel and an elephant. The vast majority of these ornaments were copies of items made by foreign manufacturers.

Crescent Potteries also made commemorative wares, many in the form of beer tankards, including one for the 1987 Australian cricket tour of South Africa, and promotional items for corporate customers. Annually, for 24 years, Albrecht Schließler designed a different promotional beer tankard for the *Sunday Times* with a miniaturised front page of the newspaper on the body of the vessel.

In the late 1970s and through the 1980s, there was a shift in public taste concerning decorative imagery on pottery. The public no longer wanted to acquire ceramic wares that depicted African people, probably due to changes in the political environment. A massive emotional jolt experienced by white society as a result of the Soweto Riots of 1976. Thus, floral motifs became the vogue – the 'Lady Di' range, the 'Delft' range, the 'Antoinette' range, the 'Kirstenbosch' range of the early 1980s and the 'Harlequin' range of 1987 – all decorated with transfers. The standard of design and draughtsmanship of the floral transfers and the vessels was considerably inferior to previous designs. These mass-produced wares were sold through contemporary department stores such as Dion, Makro and Greatermans. Crescent also sold to the retail industry at trade shows, such as the 1987 Pharmaceutical Show in Johannesburg.

From about 1965 Crescent Potteries commissioned Robert (Bob) James Connolly (1907–1981), a cartoonist for the *Rand Daily Mail*, to design cartoons to be applied to mugs and tankards. The cartoons are generally in poor taste, e.g. the 'Sabrina and friends' series, which depicts a blonde-haired woman with large exposed breasts. Connolly also created a range of cartoons for the Kruger National Park, including a mug called 'Trunk call', which depicts a man speaking down an elephant's trunk. The cartoon range was commercially successful.

Production methods

Crescent ware was mechanically produced on jiggers or jolleys, or slip-cast in moulds.

Brief history of the pottery

The pottery was named after Crescent Potteries, Stoke-on-Trent, a large conglomerate that operationed between 1907 and 1962 producing dinnerware with gold printed and powdered decorative friezes, as well as elaborate enamelled transfers on plates with embossed edges.[63] The link, if any, between the two potteries is unknown, but possibly Albert Brown had dealings or past experience with this pottery. While the Stoke pottery aimed at the higher end

OPPOSITE TOP: Crescent Potteries | Maker's mark | Sgraffito marks on the base '227 Hand Painted CRESCENT', 'Transfer marking, 'Jim Fouche – Oord' near base | Photograph by Natalie Field

OPPOSITE MIDDLE: Crescent Potteries | Maker's mark | Sgraffito mark, 'CP [logo] 228B.' ca.1950s–70s | Photograph by Natalie Field

OPPOSITE BOTTOM: Crescent Potteries | Maker's mark | Gold transfer, 'Crescent Potteries. Rose Ware', with logo of a rose and gold painted marks '213' | Photograph by Damien Artus

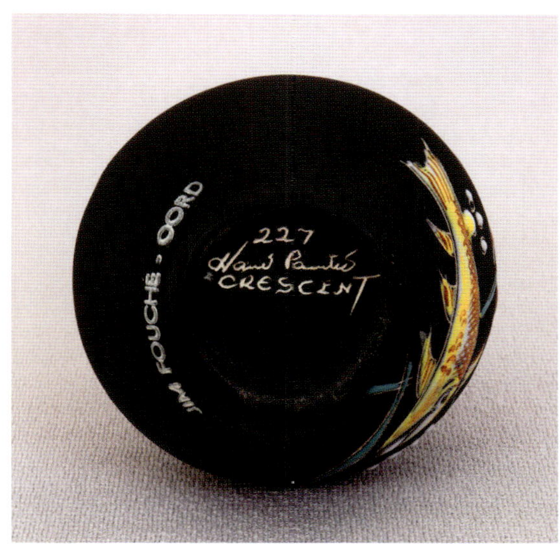

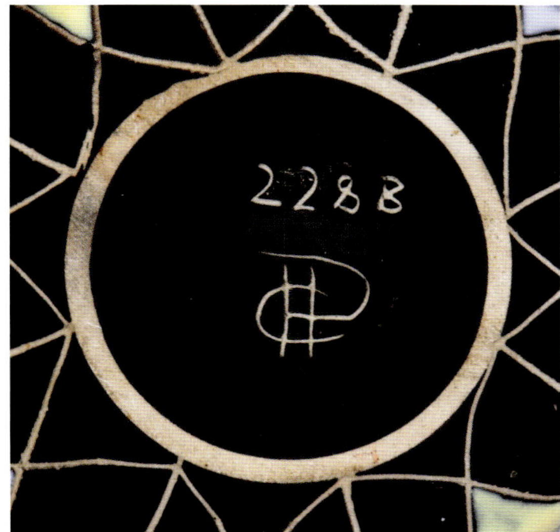

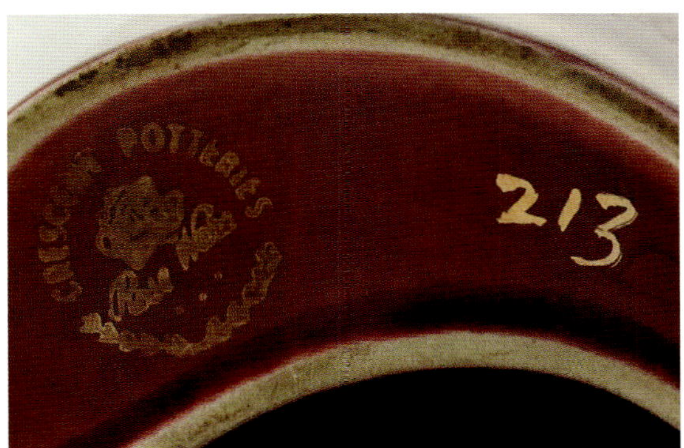

of the market, Crescent Potteries, Luipaardsvlei positioned itself as a mass producer of popular pottery and tourist wares.

With its large range of wares decorated with African figures, wildlife and 'primitive' masks. Crescent Potteries was the primary local producer of 'African' souvenir wares. While these popular items may seem supremely kitsch by contemporary standards, they answered a real need for a cheap, 'authentic' modern souvenir or memento, which could serve as an item of everyday crockery after the holiday. In short, they provided a sophisticated mediation of an essentialised primitive Africa or a mythical pristine environment, which had been domesticated and transformed into a useful commodity.

While most well-known for its tourist and souvenir wares, Crescent Potteries probably produced the most diverse range of utilitarian and decorative wares yet manufactured by a single South African pottery. Among numerous other examples, its lines include sophisticated wares that reflect contemporary popular interest in atomic developments, and a fascination with abstract art, as exemplified by the oeuvre of Joan Miró, Jean Arp and Paul Klee, while later wares reflect popular taste for pottery with cartoon decorations and floral transfers. Perhaps its ability to manufacture such a diverse range of wares enabled the studio to weather the trials and tribulations associated with the removal of import controls that brought down many contemporary potteries in the late 1950s and the mid-1960s.

Some of the Crescent designers and decorators subsequently received national and international acclaim, including Isaac Witkin, Durant Sihlali and Memling Morningstar Motaung. Crescent Potteries is also recognised as rather unique in that, from 1957, it almost exclusively employed African staff in its design, production and decoration departments. While this was largely for economic reasons, it remains a pioneer among South African commercial potteries.

Marks

Wares manufactured by Crescent Potteries were marked by various means:

- Frequently, Crescent pottery was unmarked.
- From the 1950s to the 1970s many articles excluded the name of the pottery, but featured a transfer or stencil mark of a game reserve or heritage venue, e.g. 'Royal Natal National Park Hotel'.
- In the 1950s and 1960s some wares feature a moulded mark, 'Crescent Ware', that was sometimes accompanied with a number, e.g. '962'.
- From the 1950s to the 1970s most wares had a sgraffito mark on their bases of an interwoven 'CP'. Some wares have an additional element such as numerical and alpha-numerical marks, e.g. 'A70 Hand Painted. Crescent'.
- Other wares have a transfer mark that displayed the studio's name in black on the base.

- An oval, black-and-gold foil sticker, 'Crescent Potteries Est. 1952' was used in the 1980s.
- In the 1980s 'Roseware' is indicated by a gold transfer on the base or by a sticker.

Biographies

BROWN, Albert (d. ca.1960)

Albert Brown was born in England and was trained and employed as a 'public modeller', making 'clay-sketch' prototypes for mass production. He furthered his studies in the evenings and was later employed in the modelling section of the Royal Crown Derby Porcelain Company. He then joined a large continental firm that produced a variety of sanitary, domestic and fancy ceramics. Brown emigrated from England to South Africa and became a lecturer at the Johannesburg Technical College (Nilant 1963:48, 49).

Brown joined Crescent Potteries in 1952 and was one of the original directors, as well as the designer and mould-maker. Isaac Witkin succeeded him as designer in 1955. Brown left the pottery in 1958 due to a personality clash with Schließler.[64] He died in Johannesburg.

KUMPF, Hans

Kumpf worked as a freelance designer of images of wildlife for transfers produced by both Crescent Potteries and Drostdy Ware. Some of his transfers contain his signature in the lower right corner.

MANANA, 'Stompie' Ernest

'Stompie' Ernest Manana was employed as a painter, but was soon promoted to designer status. He supervised the decorating department and was responsible for designing various caricatures of African faces, cartoon-like images that depicted rural African scenes, and images that were used in the 'African' series, e.g. the fisherman and an image of a woman carrying a water pot on her head. Manana subsequently changed careers and worked as a jazz trumpeter.

MOLEFI, Nicodemus (Darius)

Nicodemus Molefi was one of the first employees of Crescent Potteries. He joined in 1952 and left the firm when it closed down. He was responsible for the manufacture of slips and glazes and assisted in all aspects of production. He presently lives in Johannesburg and has silicosis, a lung disease frequently experienced by people employed in the ceramics industry.

MOTAUNG, Memling Morningstar (1935–1985)

Motaung, born in Germiston in 1935, was a painter of township scenes, figures and portraits, and worked predominantly in watercolour and oil paint. He studied briefly under Cecil Skotnes (1926–2009) and was a founder member

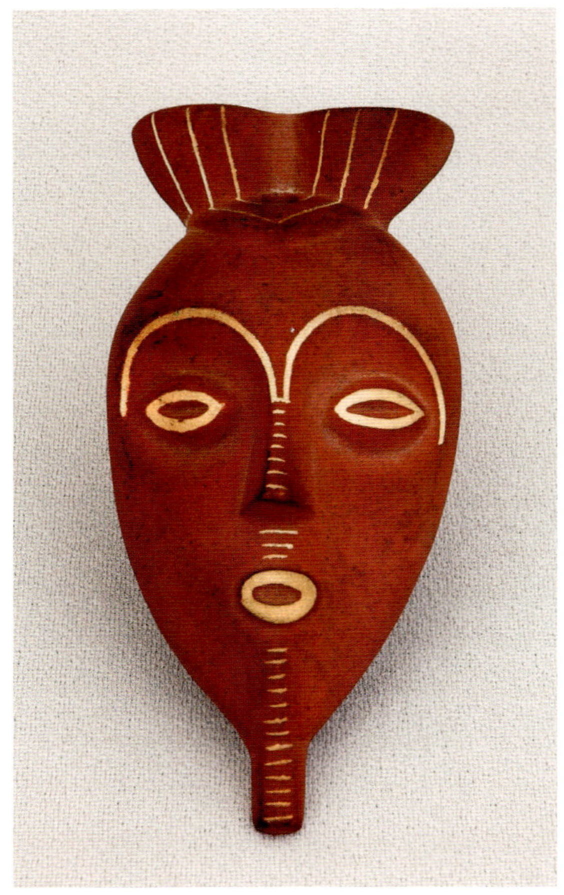

Crescent Potteries | African mask wall ornament | 140x64x20mm | Provenance: Douglas van der Horst | Marks: A11, incised CP Monogram | Photograph by Natalie Field

and past chairman of the Katlehong Art Society in the early 1960s. Together with the sculptor Stanley Nkosi, and other stalwarts, the association applied for sponsorship to the East Rand Administrative Board. The society was granted the use of a disused dairy barn, and kilns and a vehicle were donated by private sponsors.

Crescent Potteries employed Motaung from the late 1960s until 1985. In the 1970s Motaung designed wares that depicted African animals and other wares that featured a bas-relief image of African animals. Motaung exhibited his personal works in South Africa, the United Kingdom, America and the former West Germany. Motaung died in prison in Johannesburg in 1985.

SCHLIEßLER, Albrecht (b.1924)

Born in Germany in 1924, he was the son of sculptor Otto Schließler (1885–1964).[65] a professor of Fine Arts at Karlsruhe Academy. His education was disrupted by World War II, after which he trained as an apprentice at the Mosbacher Majolika Fabrik in Mosbach from 1947 to 1950. The factory manufactured a diverse range of products, including tile ovens, vases, ashtrays and figurines. Upon completion of his apprenticeship, he was engaged by Kurpfalz Keramik in Mannheim. In 1951, Schließler was employed as a production assistant and designer at the ceramic factory, Schriessheimer Keramik Manufaktur, in southern Germany. Schließler also undertook contract work for various art galleries, including the Rheinisches Museum, reproducing sculptural pieces.

In 1952 Schließler came to South Africa to study the feasibility of establishing a factory in South Africa, commissioned by the widow of Philip Rosenthal, of Rosenthal Ceramics, Germany. He worked in a laboratory in Rivonia, Johannesburg, for one year, testing local clay specimens. In 1954 he joined Crescent Potteries as a 'boy Friday'. Two years later Schließler was made a joint director with Shain, and was responsible for production, including supervision of the designers and painters, mould-making, modelling, glazing and firing. Schließler was responsible for design before Isaac Witkin arrived and again for a period when Witkin left. He worked at Crescent until 1960, when he returned to Germany, working as a freelance pottery designer and in the production of 'trick films'. In 1962 he returned to South Africa and was offered his previous position at Crescent Potteries and a senior position at Grahamstown Pottery, but chose to return to Crescent.

Shain described Albrecht Schließler as 'the master potter' and 'Mr Crescent'. Schließler designed over 100 items, including vases, ashtrays, bowls, figurines, jug-and-basin sets, tankards, condiment sets and wall plaques. The pottery was sold in May 1992, upon Schließler's retirement.

Crescent Potteries | Mask | 260x145x60mm | Provenance: TAG | 2453/c6 | Marks: terracotta base, with sgraffito mark, 'CP [logo] S. Africa' | Photograph by Natalie Field

SHAIN, Morrie (1922–2008)

Born in Johannesburg, he attended evening classes in commercial art and fine art at the Johannesburg Technical College from 1854 to 1956 under Maurice van Essche (1906–1977). Before joining Crescent Potteries, Shain worked as a sales representative for Sax Toys, Krugersdorp. Shain was responsible for the financial management, sales and marketing of Crescent Potteries.[66]

SIHLALI, Durant Basi (1935–2004)

Durant Sihlali was born in Germiston in 1935. He did not finish high school, due to financial constraints following the death of his parents, and entered the commercial art market. During this period he painted souvenirs, scarves and clay-casts with 'African' images. Sihlali studied at the school of art of Alpheus Kubeka (b.1927) at the Chiawelo Art Centre in Moroka, Transvaal, from 1950 to 1953; the Polly Street Art Centre, Johannesburg from 1953 to 1958; and under Sydney Goldblatt (1919–1979) from 1955 to 1958.

In the 1950s and early 1960s, for a period of eleven years, Sihlali designed jewellery and painted curios (souvenir wooden plaques, ceramics, mother-of-pearl coasters and lampshades) for Atlanta Wholesalers.[67] From 1955 to 1958 Sihlali also painted souvenirs for Baroness von Treskow, who assisted in the organisation of some of Sihlali's earliest exhibitions of paintings. The souvenirs he produced included hand-painted landscapes, animals and indigenous scenes on bone china plates that were imported from Rosenthal, Germany.

Sihlali worked full-time at Crescent Potteries from 1960 to 1962 and from 1962 to 1964 in a freelance capacity. Shain used to transport Sihlali from his home to the pottery. Sometimes, a batch of 200 to 700 items would be delivered to Sihlali's home and he would decorate them there. During this period he also worked for Maiolica Pottery and studied under Ulrich Schwanecke (1932–2007) from 1965 to 1966. During 1965 and 1966 Sihlali and Ulrich Schwanecke undertook watercolour painting tours. In 1978 he started teaching in the FUBA Outreach Programmes and participated in a 1981 European tour organised by the National Art Society. Sihlali commenced the production of sculpture in 1981, and held his first exhibition of sculpture that year. He was head of Fine Arts at FUBA from 1983 to 1988 and was awarded a French government travel scholarship to attend the Villa Arson Art School, Nice in 1985. Sihlali also participated in the Thupelo workshops. In his last decades he produced paintings and multimedia works made from paper pulp and fibres.[68]

From 1952 Sihlali participated in numerous solo and group exhibitions in South Africa, the former West Germany, Israel, Greece, the United Kingdom, America, France, Australia, Botswana and Sicily. His works are represented in numerous public and private collections. A large collection of his works, intended for a personal museum, is at the centre of a legal dispute (De Wet 2012).

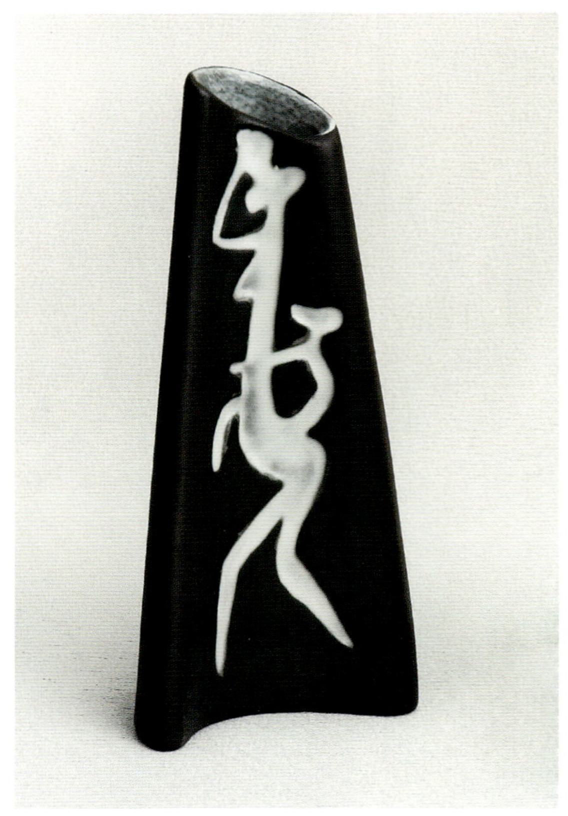

Crescent Potteries | Vase with white glazed incised stylised figures | 165x37x75mm, 18mm depth lip, 30mm depth base | Provenance: Clive Newman | Marks: glazed base with 'A18' marked in red pencil | Photograph by Natalie Field

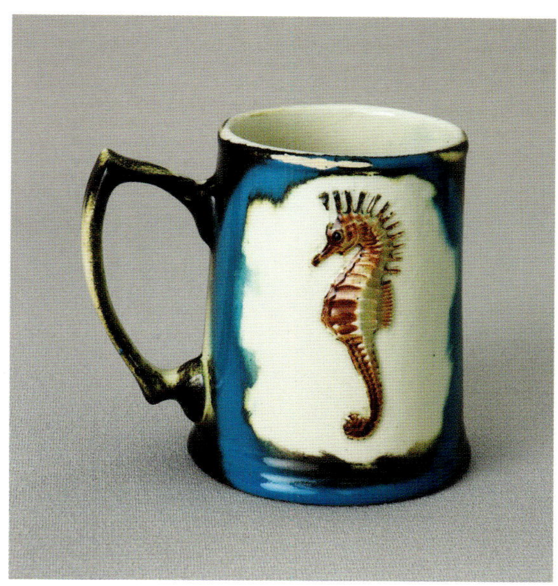

Crescent Potteries | Mug with moulded seahorse decoration | 111x175x90mm | Provenance: Jan Middlejans | Marks: base glazed with characteristic cream and dark brown sprayed glaze; incised marks, 'Hand Made S.A 0930/41'; 'Tsitsikamma Park' marked in white marker on glazed surface | Photograph by Natalie Field

WITKIN, Isaac (1936–2006)

Isaac Witkin was born in Johannesburg in 1936. A graduate of the Johannesburg Technical College, Witkin worked as an assistant to the sculptor Herman Wald (1906–1970)[69] in Johannesburg for a year. Witkin worked as a designer for Crescent from 1955 to 1957 despite a lack of formal training in ceramics.

Witkin claimed that he 'was given free reign as far as design was concerned so long as it had an African motif'.[70] He designed terracotta 'African' masks, which reflected a synthesis of various west and central African masks, and are named after local 'tribes', such as *Zulu Boy*. Witkin also designed a series of African totemic figurines that resembled ritual and fetish objects from West and Central Africa. In addition, Witkin designed various wares that were decorated with 'abstract' motifs. Nilant declared that Witkin had 'a flair for abstract designs, and all designs in this category, which make up about half of the output of Crescent Potteries, are his' (1963:49).

In 1957 Witkin immigrated to England, where he studied at St Martin's School of Art in London under Anthony Caro (1924–) from 1957 to 1960, and worked as an assistant to Henry Moore (1898–1986) from 1961 to 1963. He taught at Maidstone and St Martin's Schools of Art from 1963 to 1965. In the 1960s, Witkin gained a reputation as a significant constructivist sculptor.

Witkin moved to America, where he was appointed Artist in Residence at Bennington College, Vermont in 1965. He taught sculpture there for the next 13 years, and simultaneously taught at the Parsons School for Design in New York City. In 1981 he won a Guggenheim Fellowship.

Witkin has exhibited internationally in numerous group and solo exhibitions and has undertaken seven major public commissions. His works are in numerous public collections, including the Tate Gallery (London), San Francisco Museum of Modern Art, Fine Arts Museum (Sydney), National Museum of American Art (Washington DC), and the Israel Museum (Jerusalem). In 1981 he visited the University of the Witwatersrand and lectured on his work.

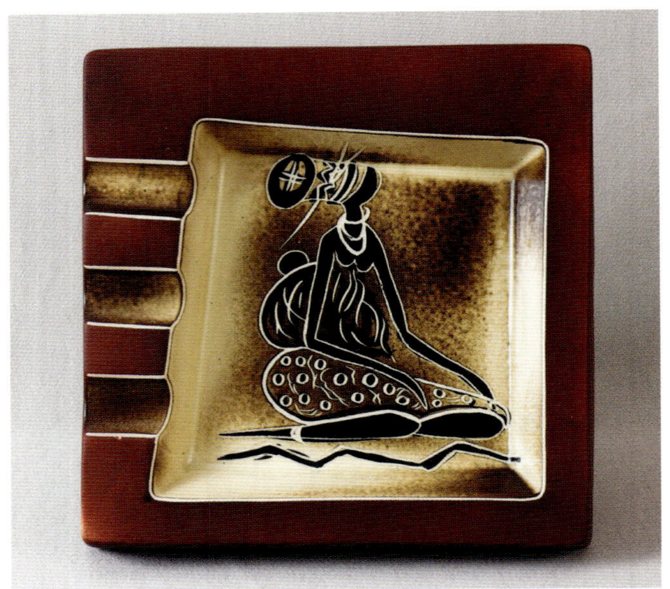

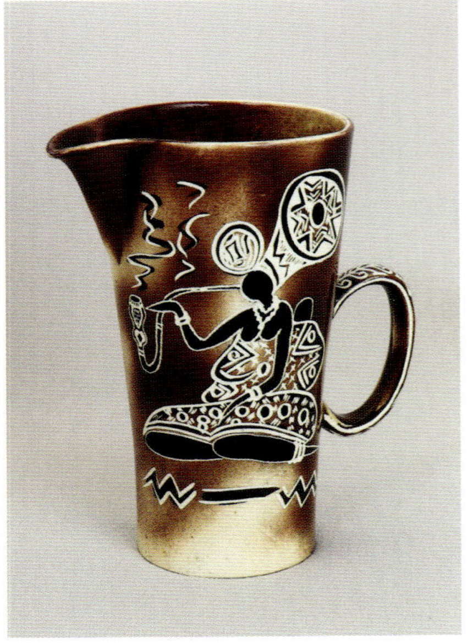

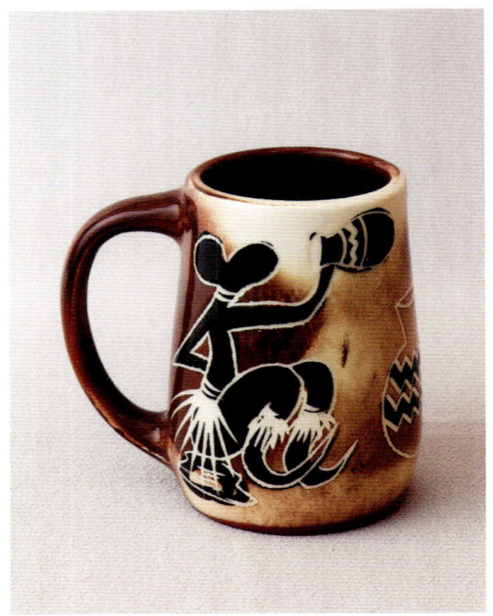

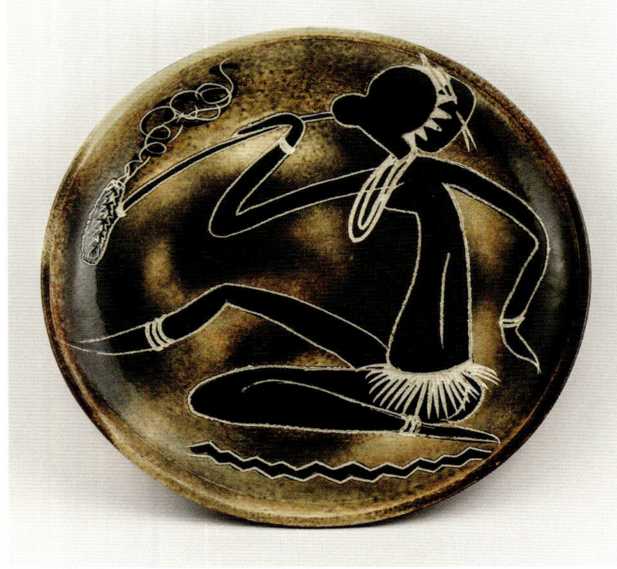

TOP LEFT: Crescent Potteries | African series, large ashtray, broad matt terracotta rim with glazed interior, sgraffito image of seated African woman with baby on her back | 237x235x43mm | Provenance: Professor Mark Watson | 2457/06 | Marks: sgraffito marks, 'A115 Hand painted Crescent' | Photograph by Natalie Field

TOP RIGHT: Crescent Potteries | Pitcher, African series, sgraffito decoration of a seated African women smoking | 237x160x95mm | Provenance: TAG | Marks: terracotta base with sgraffito marks, 'A70 Hand Painted Crescent' | Photograph by Natalie Field

BOTTOM LEFT: Crescent Potteries | Mug | 157x65x67mm | Provenance: Professor Mark Watson | Marks: unglazed terracotta base with sgraffito marks, 'A27, Hand Painted, Crescent', 'Swaziland' written in white ink | Photograph by Natalie Field

BOTTOM RIGHT: Crescent Potteries | Charger, African series, sgraffito decoration of a seated African women smoking | 270x2mm | Provenance: Wendy Gers | Marks: brown matt base with transfer or stamped mark, 'Royal National Park Hotel' | Photograph by Damien Artus

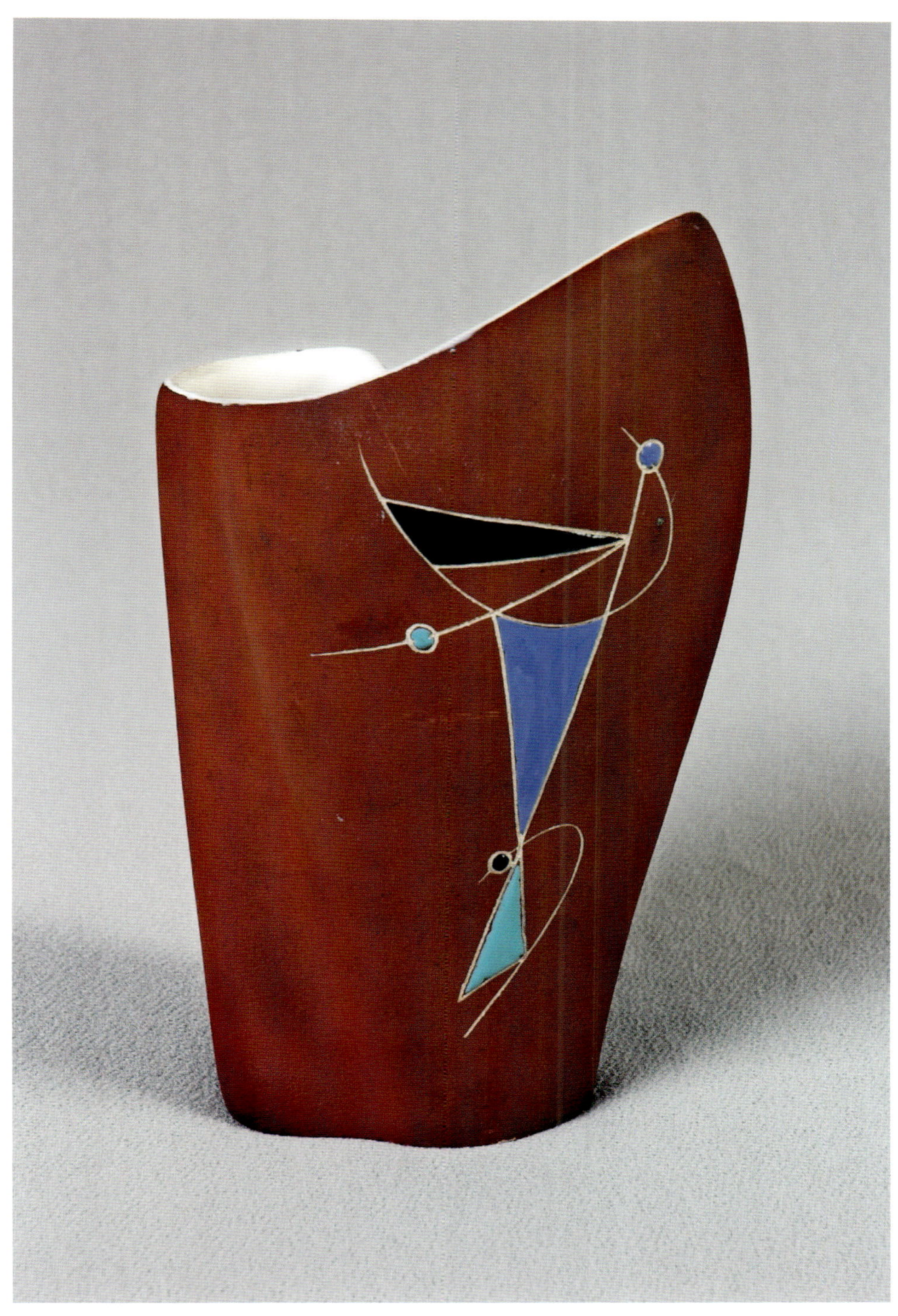

Crescent Potteries | Free-form terracotta vase with abstracted, linear decoration | 190x104x65mm | Provenance: TAG | 2438/06 | Marks: terracotta base, with sgraffitto mark, 'CP [logo] 201' | Photograph by Natalie Field

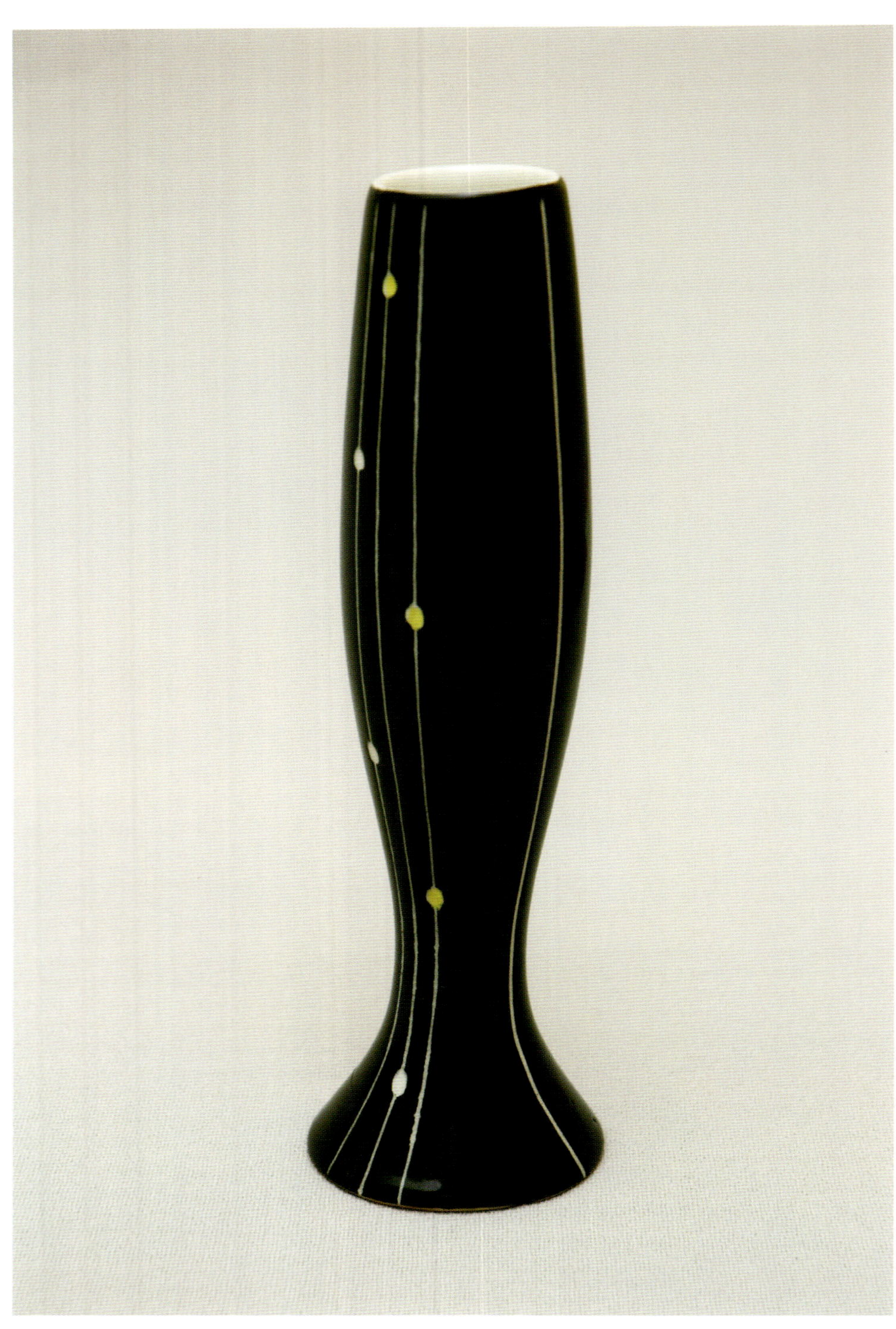

Crescent Potteries | Vase | 207x37x60mm | Provenance: Jan Middeljans | Marks: black glazed base with sgraffito marks, 'CP 208 A' | Photograph by Natalie Field

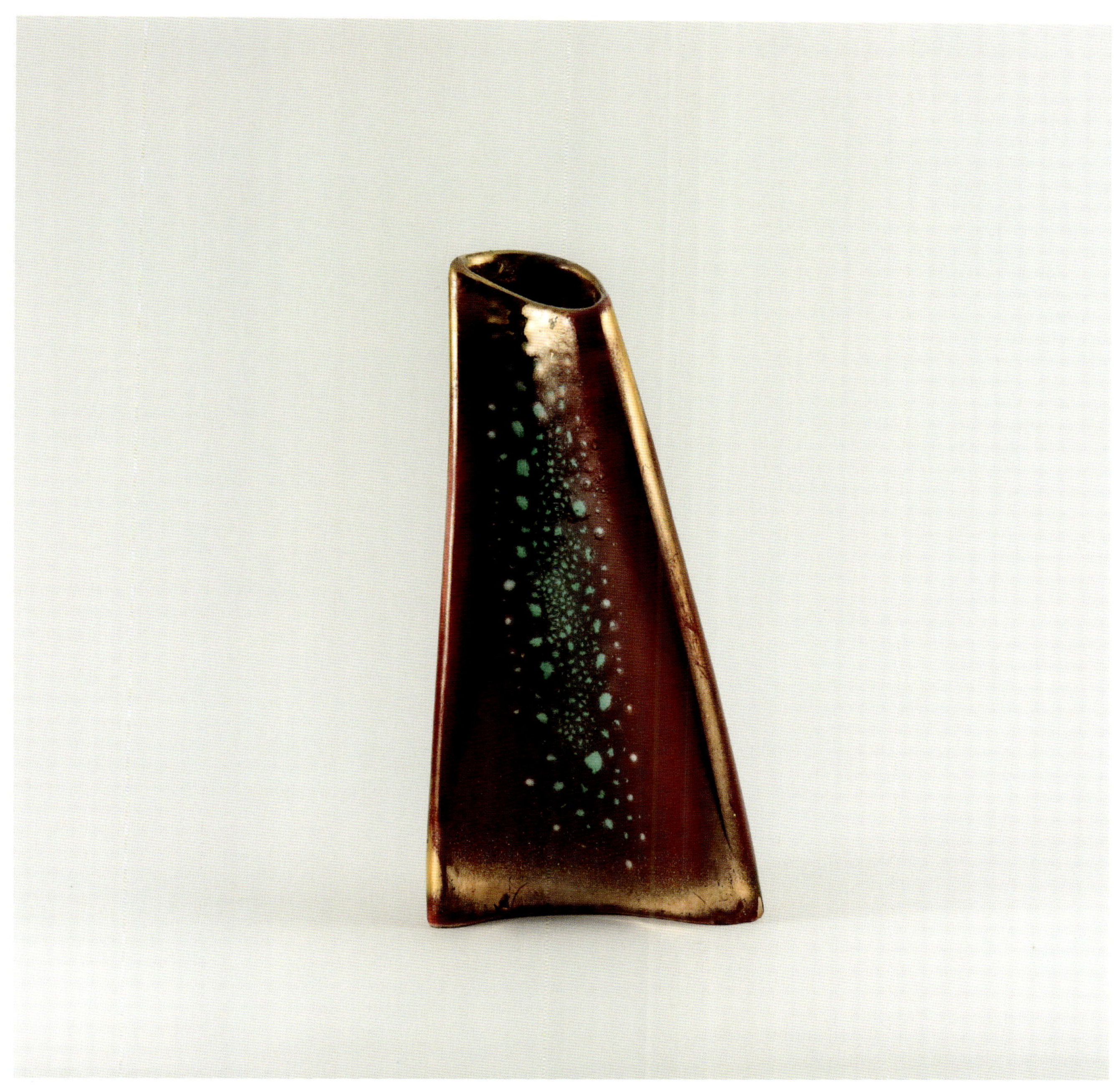

Crescent Potteries | Rose ware vase | 175x40x85mm | Provenance: Wendy Gers | Marks: gold transfer, 'Crescent Potteries. Rose Ware', with logo of a rose | Photograph by Damien Artus

Dykor Ceramic Studio (1952–1959)

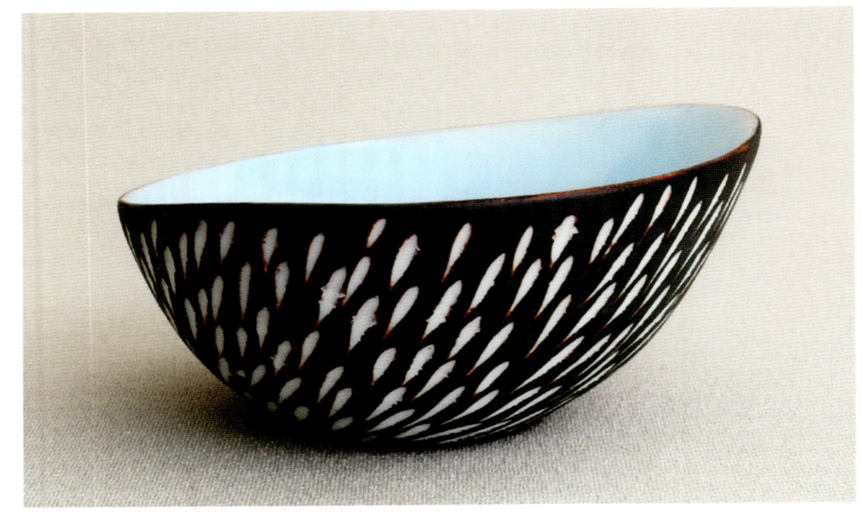

Dykor | Bowl with light blue glazed interior and very dark brown matt exterior with incised glaze-filled decoration | 138x120x62mm | Provenance: Douglas van der Horst | Marks: Dykor impressed stamp | Photograph by Natalie Field

Location

Dykor was established in 1952 in the backyard of Izak A Perold's home in Menlo Park, Pretoria. In 1957 it relocated to a former tailor's workshop in the Indian trading zone on Church Street, Pretoria. In 1959 it ceased production of domestic ware, and focused on ceramic tiles and concrete. Dykor is still operational but no longer produces ceramics; it just sells remaining tile stock and undertakes mosaic commissions.[71]

Name

The name 'Dykor' was chosen because of its phonetic similarity to the word 'décor', when pronounced by a person with an Afrikaans accent (as Perold had).

Founder

Izak Abraham Perold

Staff

Perold was the original thrower, designer and glazer, assisted by his first wife, Anna Margaretha Susanna Perold (née Kok), known as Rita. Louis Wilsenach, then a schoolboy, worked part-time as the artist from approximately 1957 to 1959. William Thabane also decorated wares. Kansamy (aka Robert or Bob) Chetty and his brother worked at Dykor as throwers. In the 1950s the studio had seven African employees including Johannes Themba and Jeremiah Skhosana. Abram Thage joined in the 1960s. Key staff members employed in the 1970s and 1980s include Ben Bonani, Timothy Mabena and Beauty Magandlela. Perold's fourth wife, Marie-Josee Perold, worked in the pottery in the 1980s until the early 1990s, and continues to undertake mosaic commissions.

Wares manufactured

- Initially, Dykor made vases and troughs for gift shops and florists.
- In the mid-1950s Dykor manufactured a wide variety of large, bold, colourful plates, elongated platters, bowls and ashtrays.
- From 1957 to 1959 it produced decorative plates featuring colourful, stylised images of African women.
- From 1958 Dykor produced small mosaic tiles and other architectural elements.

Production methods

Initially, Perold and the Chetty brothers threw wares on the wheel. Later the majority of the wares were slip-cast. A jigger was employed to make plates and ashtrays. Jolleys were not used.

Brief history of the pottery

Perold was a self-trained ceramicist who learnt his trade as manager of Globe Potteries. In 1949, after acquiring a new kiln,[72] Perold established Dykor. Between 1952 and 1953 Perold's first wife, Rita, was responsible for glazing. Aware of current tendencies in Scandinavian pottery, and of the colourful fusion of Nordic and African traditions in the wares of the Kalahari Studio, Perold decided to branch out in a similar vein. Dykor initially made vases and troughs that were sold in florists, gift shops and in the upmarket chain-store Greatermans. Like the clients of Drostdy Ware, Dykor clients benefited from floral arrangement classes offered by associated suppliers. In keeping with practices learned at Globe, Perold did not make full crockery sets, which he considered 'too fiddly',[73] and avoided marketing the pottery at exhibitions or trade fairs.[74]

From humble origins, Dykor progressed steadily in terms of quality and output. In the mid-1950s it manufactured a wide variety of large, bold, colourful plates, elongated platters, bowls (including soup bowls and aperitif bowls) and ashtrays. These Scandinavian-inspired wares often feature bright primary-coloured streaks of glaze that melt into a darker base glaze. Perold realised that the pottery market was less and less viable and thus diversified in 1958 to the production of architectural ceramics (large rustic wall tiles and door knobs), concrete bricks, ceramic channelled tiles and small glazed earthenware mosaic tiles. By 1959 Dykor had stopped making ceramic vessels, and focused on tile production. In the 1960s, the heyday of mosaic-tile production, Dykor employed approximately 70 workers. Dykor was, according to Perold, the first and only pottery to manufacture earthenware mosaic tiles in South Africa. Its range was varied and included walls, floors, outdoors, kitchens, bathrooms and swimming pools.[75]

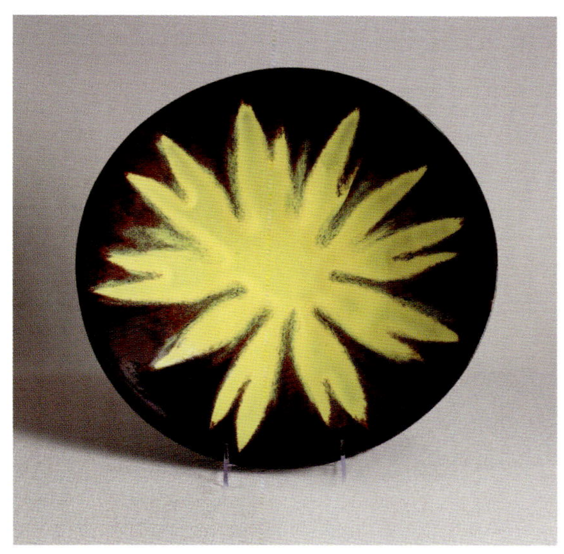

Dykor | Platter, dark brown glaze with yellow starburst in centre; no footring, three feet | 360x60mm | Provenance: SHC Iziko | 90/767 | Marks: glazed base with inscribed mark, 'dykor' | Photograph by Natalie Field

In the 1960s Dykor's production of cast concrete bricks increased rapidly. In 1967 it was renamed Dykor Ceramics and Concrete and moved to a Perold-designed factory, built in a new industrial area, Silverton. The building was such a landmark that the municipality renamed the road, Dykor Street. Perold now concentrated on concrete architectural elements to the detriment of ceramic-tile production. The company, a shell of its former self, continues to use this name and operates from the Silverton location as a tile merchant.

Perold is significant as he overcame his lack of formal artistic or technical education and through Dykor produced some extremely sophisticated wares. While his ceramic production was sadly short-lived, he applied his aesthetic vision, creativity and problem-solving ability to numerous other domains. Perold was part of the artistic avant-garde of Pretoria, and his friendships with prominent artists and architects (J H Pierneef, Norman Eaton and Oscar Hirsch) resulted in his collaboration in the creation of many diverse products during his lifetime. Pierneef and Eaton championed the development of an indigenous artistic vernacular; Perold, too, played his part in developing an aesthetic that was contemporary and modern yet distinctly African. In doing so, Perold left an indelible mark on the architectural landscape of Pretoria and other cities. Dykor's legacy to South African ceramics is observed in its diverse and experimental oeuvre. The company was always responsive to changes in local and international pottery, and produced interesting interpretations of avant-garde European wares. For a brief moment in the 1950s Dykor offered a radically unique product in South Africa. It is indeed a shame that Perold's commitment to international modernist glazed pottery was so short-lived.

Marks

Dykor used a variety of methods of marking the base of wares including:

- A stamped impression, 'dykor'.
- A raised cast-maker's mark, 'dykor'.
- Sgraffito maker's mark etched under the glaze, 'dykor'.
- An elaborate (wax-resist) stencilled terracotta shape of the national boundaries of South Africa. The landmass contains a black-glazed handwritten mark, 'dykor S.A.'.

Dykor's characteristic angular lettering, which was intended to resemble runic script,[76] is common to all mark methods. Runic script was used from the first century to the Middle Ages by various northern European groups, and is steeped in spiritual significance. The visual similarity between Dykor's typography and runic script was intended to enhance a mystical or mythical quality in the wares.

Commissions

Dykor's small mosaic wall-tiles decorated the facades and interiors of numerous public and private buildings in Pretoria. Dykor tiles were included in the original Jan Smuts Airport, Johannesburg, and Dykor's architectural elements adorned Polley's Arcade Shopping Centre, Pretoria.[77] Perold was especially proud of certain glazes that he developed, including 'gun-barrel

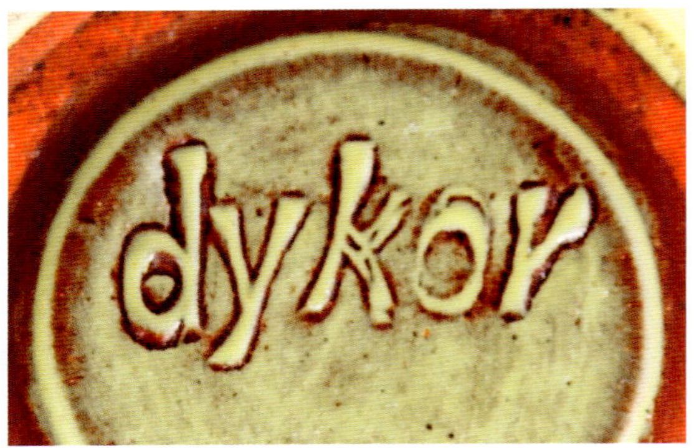

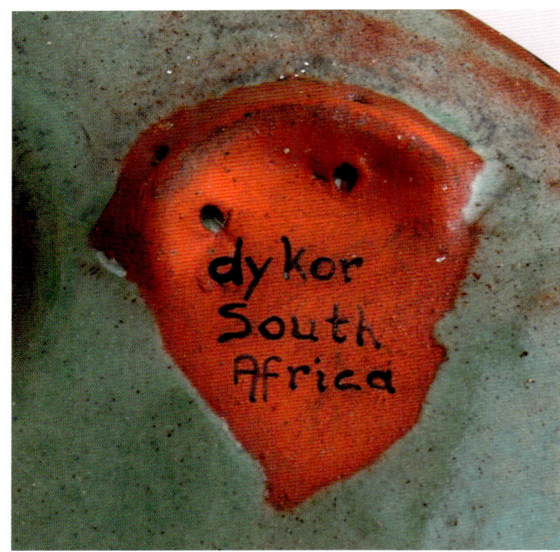

TOP: Dykor | Maker's mark | Stamp 'dykor' | Photograph by Natalie Field

BOTTOM: Dykor | Maker's mark | Hand-painted glaze marking 'dykor South Africa' within a shape that resembles the borders of South Africa | Photograph by Natalie Field

black' and a primary orange that he called 'airways orange' and used in the Jan Smuts Airport tile commission. In conjunction with Norman Eaton (1902–1966), Perold produced wares decorated with large knobs that may recall the *amasumpa* decorative 'warts' of Zulu pottery. These bowls were the size of a standard baking measure, the *kommetjie*.[78]

Biographies

BONANI, Ben

One of the longest-serving employees, Bonani was responsible for firing tiles.

MABENA, Timothy

Mabena was employed in 1988 in the sales department. He currently works in this capacity.

MAGANDLELA, Beauty

Magandlela was employed as the tea lady in 1975. From 1978 to 2004 she sorted tiles, and cut clay for mosaics. She currently works at Dykor as the tea lady and general assistant.

PEROLD, Izak Abraham (aka Pierre) (1929–2006)

Perold was born in Somerset West, Cape Province. Orphaned as an infant, he was raised by an aunt. After matriculation he worked with the Roads Department, supervising construction crews in the Eastern Cape, Transkei and KwaZulu-Natal He then joined the Roads Department laboratories in Pretoria, which was located next door to Globe Pottery. Here he studied soil chemistry, but soon joined Globe as a manager.

A variety of factors converged to facilitate the establishment of Dykor in 1952. Perold was frustrated by the technical limitations of the down-draught, coal-fired kilns at Globe, the limited glaze palette, and the high rate of rejects. He was also deeply disappointed when, in 1949, the director of Globe, Mr Hoather, devalued the stock of that company. Later, he unexpectedly inherited some money from a deceased friend and used this to buy a kiln, which arrived a year later. Mr Hattingh of Globe Potteries offered Perold pottery tuition. He privately experimented with new forms and colours and later resigned from Globe and established Dykor in his home.

In the early years Perold was assisted by his first wife,[79] Rita, who was a wedding-dress maker. From 1952, Perold rented a small factory and set up a pottery in Church Street, with supplied clay from a quarry on a plot he owned in the Willows, Pretoria. Despite the relative commercial success of the pottery, it was never financially lucrative.

In the late 1950s Perold met the architect Oscar Hirsch, who introduced him to other architects who might be inclined to include his tiles in their buildings.[80] In 1959 he decided to concentrate on earthenware mosaic tiles and discontinued the production of domestic pottery. He built a factory, showroom

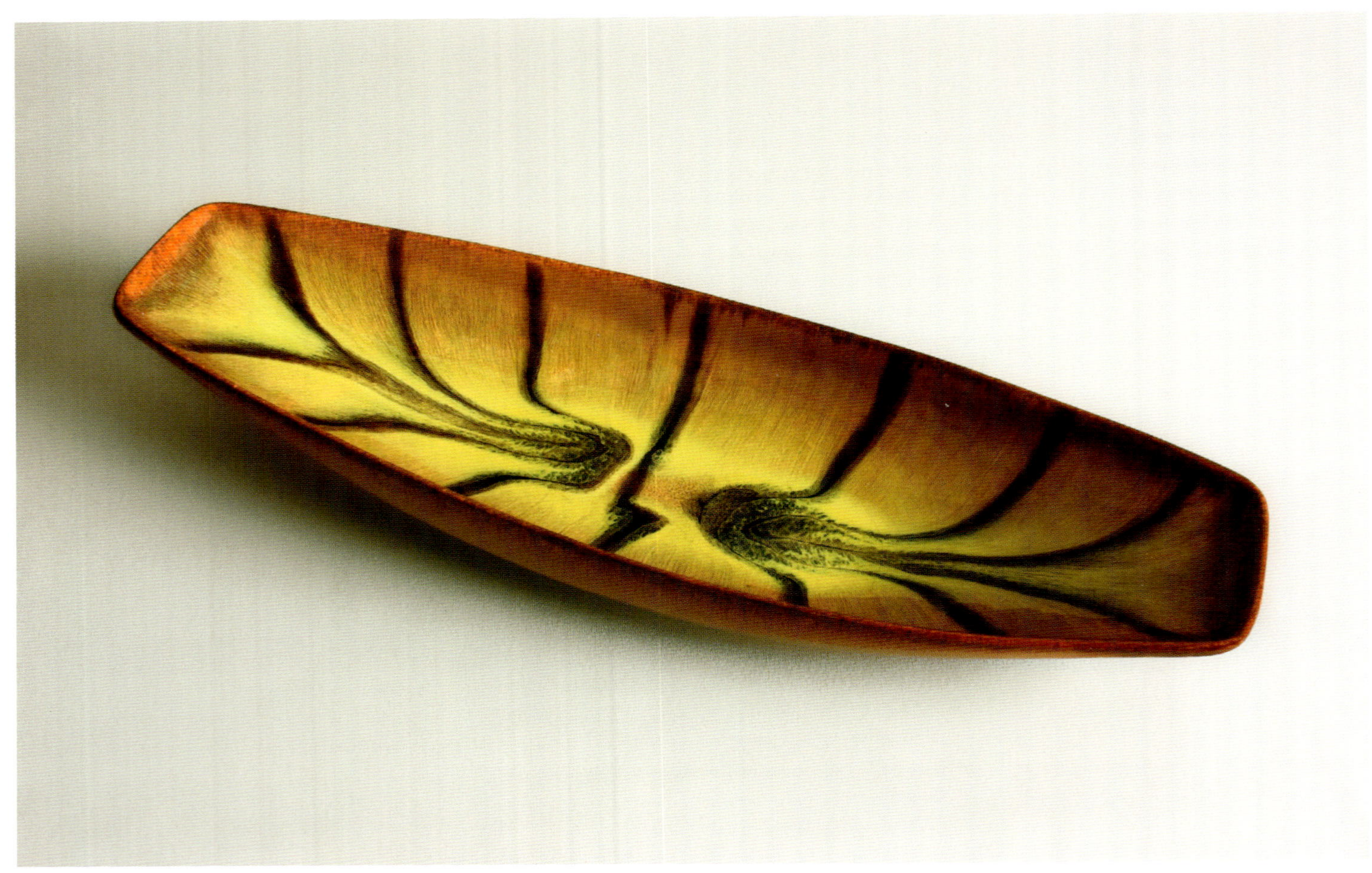

Dykor | Elongated, boat-shaped dish; interior has yellow ochre, burnt-orange, and reddish brown glaze decoration; exterior has thick mustard glaze that stops short of foot-ring | 143x422x50mm | Provenance: SHC Iziko | 91/259 | Marks: glazed base with inscribed mark, 'dykor' | Photograph by Natalie Field

and offices for Dykor in Silverton, Pretoria, in 1961, for his mosaic-tile factory. Clay was obtained from Garsfontein and was dried, crushed and reconstituted at Perold's home in the Willows. Perold also had a factory in Church Street, Pretoria West, where he had kilns and manufactured mosaic tiles.

In the 1950s Perold met and briefly dated Marita Pierneef, the daughter of the celebrated artist J H Pierneef (1886–1957). This relationship led to his discovery of 'Elangeni', Pierneef's unique home in the adjacent suburb of Brummeria. Pierneef and Perold struck up a special friendship and Pierneef later gave him a watercolour sketch of his kraals and home and a photo of himself doing that sketch. Pierneef collaborated with important contemporary artists and architects to build and decorate his home, including Norman Eaton who designed and extended the 'kraals'. Perold and Eaton became close friends and their friendship resulted in Perold befriending other leading Pretoria architects such as Aziz Tayob. Over time these friendships generated various commissions for architectural elements, such as door knobs, stained-glass windows, floor tiles and wall mosaics. One of the most important Eaton commissions that Perold worked on was the Nedbank Building, Durban, in 1961.

In 1967 the company changed and became Dykor Ceramics and Concrete, under which name it presently operates. In 1969, upon the death of Pierneef's wife, Elangeni was sold to the architects Wynand and Eleonor Smit, with whom Perold was also friendly. Smit, the architect of the former Jan Smuts Airport in Johannesburg, invited Perold to create wall murals for the building. For this project Perold formulated his signature 'airlines orange' glaze. Construction works started in 1948 and the airport was inaugurated in 1952.

Perold intended the concrete bricks he manufactured to create the impression of a sandcastle. Perold was fascinated by 'primitive' architecture, including the Xhosa and Zulu settlements he encountered on his road construction job, Turkish architecture, or the Great Zimbabwe ruins. He avoided sophisticated tools and aimed to simplify the production in his factory so that, in his absence, the workers could continue operating.

In 1982 he married his fourth and last wife Marie-Josee de Wit (b.1959). Around this time all the major South African tile producers discontinued their production of standard 15-cm square tiles. The couple realised that there was a niche in the market for bands of tiles to be used in kitchens and bathrooms. Dykor thus changed focus and started producing tile mosaic friezes for builders' merchants. The mosaics were all in the standard dimensions of 45 or 60cm, to fit between the kitchen counter and wall cabinets, or above a basin. The mosaic friezes were made from old Dykor tiles, as well as new imported tiles, some of which were cut to size. Some tiles were also cut into triangles. In the 1980s long, thin bisque-fired earthenware tiles were imported from Italy and then glazed and fired by Dykor.

In 2006 upon the death of Perold, Dykor was bought by its current owner, Hansie Prinslco, a developer who loved the buildings and intended to use them for his headquarters.

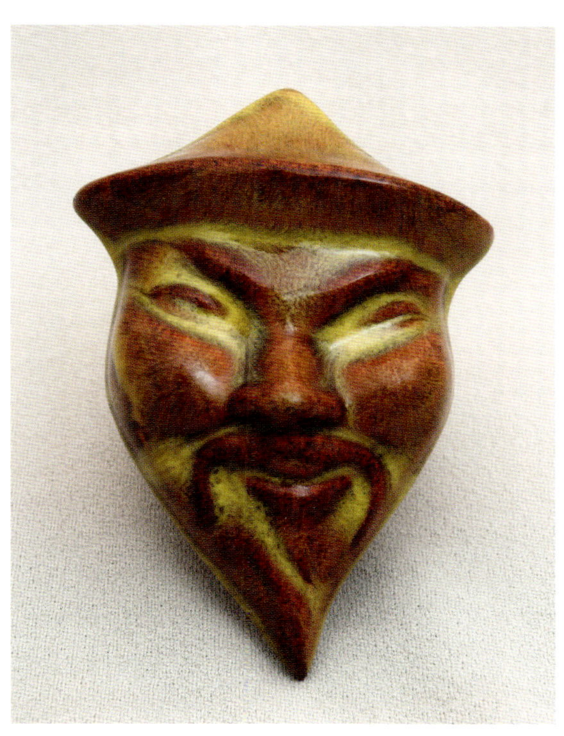

Dykor | Mask of laughing Asian male face | 127x87x37mm | Provenance: Douglas van der Horst | Marks: Dykor impressed stamp | Photograph by Natalie Field

PEROLD, Marie-Josee (née De Wit) (b.1959)

Married to I A Perold in 1982, she worked in the pottery from the 1980s until the early 1990s, producing tile mosaic friezes for kitchens and bathrooms.[81]

SKHOSANA, Jeremiah (d.2004)

Skhosana was employed in production. He was responsible for building the Dykor factory and showrooms in Silverton.

THAGE, Abram (b.1947)

Thage was employed in 1964 and initially worked as a kiln-packer and later in the production of mosaics. He cut tiles in wet clay and then, when glazed, would make tile mosaics by arranging and pasting different coloured tiles onto sheets of brown paper. In the 1980s and 1990s Thage was the foreman of the mosaic section, where he ensured there was sufficient clay, mixed the mosaics, and supervised the female workers. He then made sure that they were bundled and packed. He still works for the company.[82]

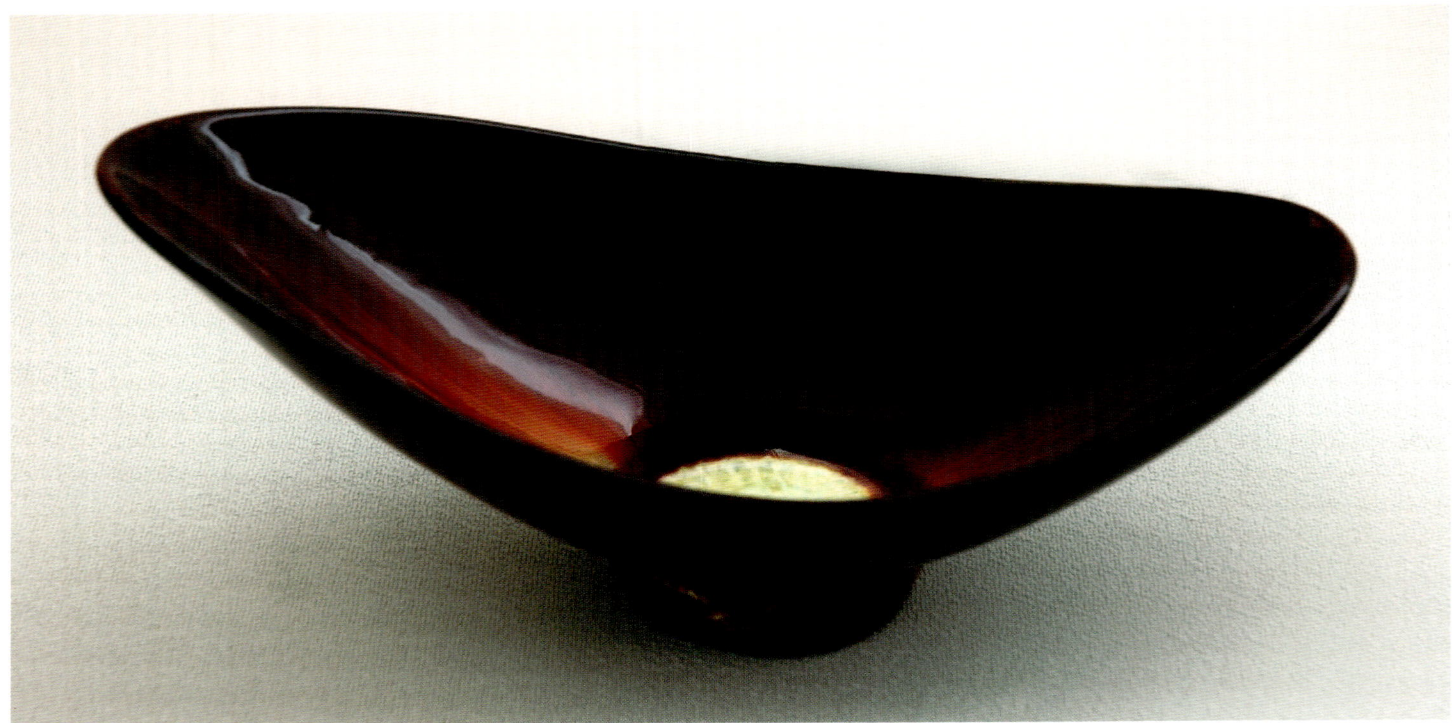

Dykor | Oval-shaped bowl with one side higher than the other; rust-coloured glaze with yellowish streaks in the interior | 125x230x98mm | Provenance: SHC Iziko | 91/618 | Marks: glazed base with inscribed mark, 'dykor' | Photograph by Natalie Field

THEMBA, Johannes (d.2005)
Themba was one of the longest-serving employees. He worked in production and was, at different periods, responsible for spraying the tiles and mosaics and for firing the tiles.

WILSENACH, Louis (b.1940)
Wilsenach was born in Pretoria and grew up on a mission station in the north-eastern Transvaal. In 1956 or 1957 he worked at Dykor while studying at the Pretoria Art School, designing and decorating wares after school and on weekends. He specialised in images of African women, and in later years he assisted Perold with sand-cast cement blocks. Wilsenach studied architecture and graphic design at the University of Pretoria. He graduated at the end of 1961 and worked for Perold until 1962. Wilsenach then worked in the advertising industry, directing the firm Louis Wilsenach and Associates, Johannesburg. He participated in a team of advisors who formulated the concept of a 'New South Africa' for President F W de Klerk. The phrase caught the imagination of the cabinet and crystallised an overwhelming desire for change. Wilsenach is now retired and lives in Muldersdrift.[83]

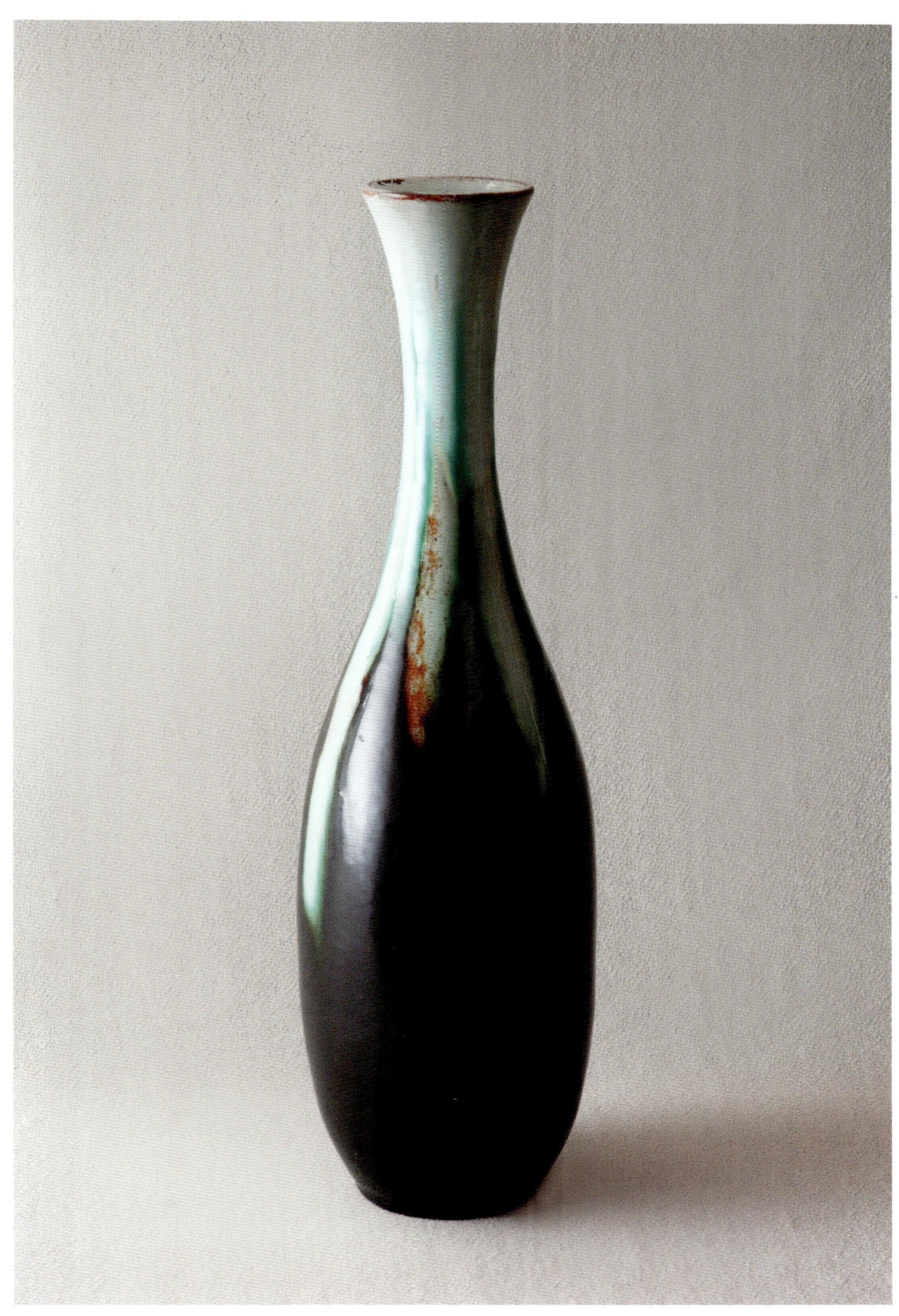

Dykor | Tapering vase with green and black glaze trail | 359x55x63mm | Provenance: Wendy Gers | Marks: glazed base with impressed stamp, 'Dykor' | Photograph by Natalie Field

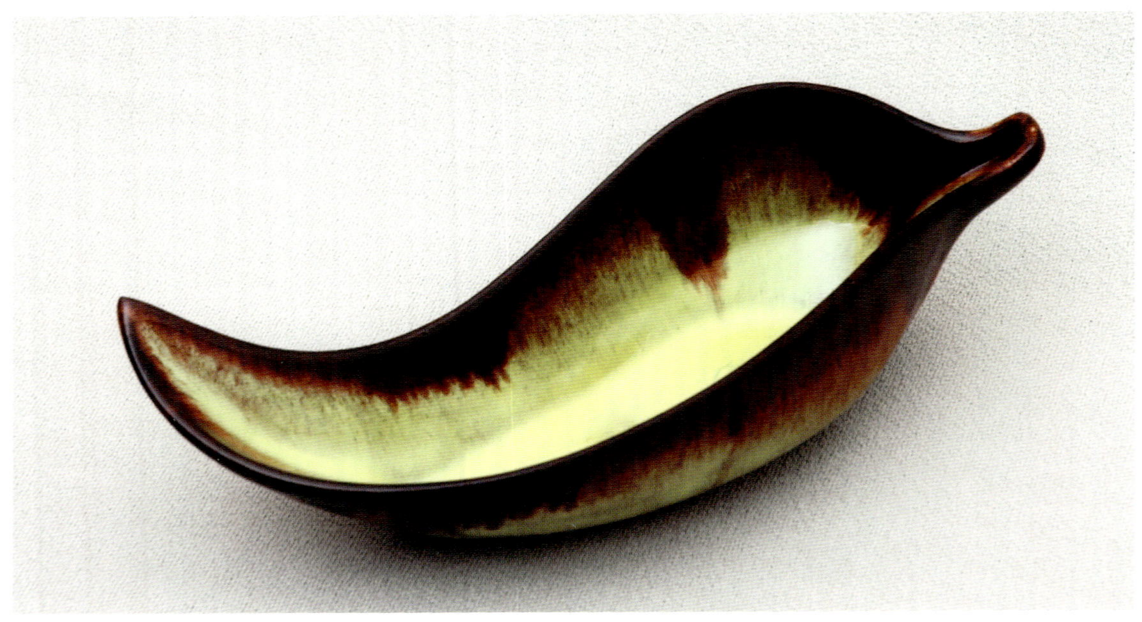

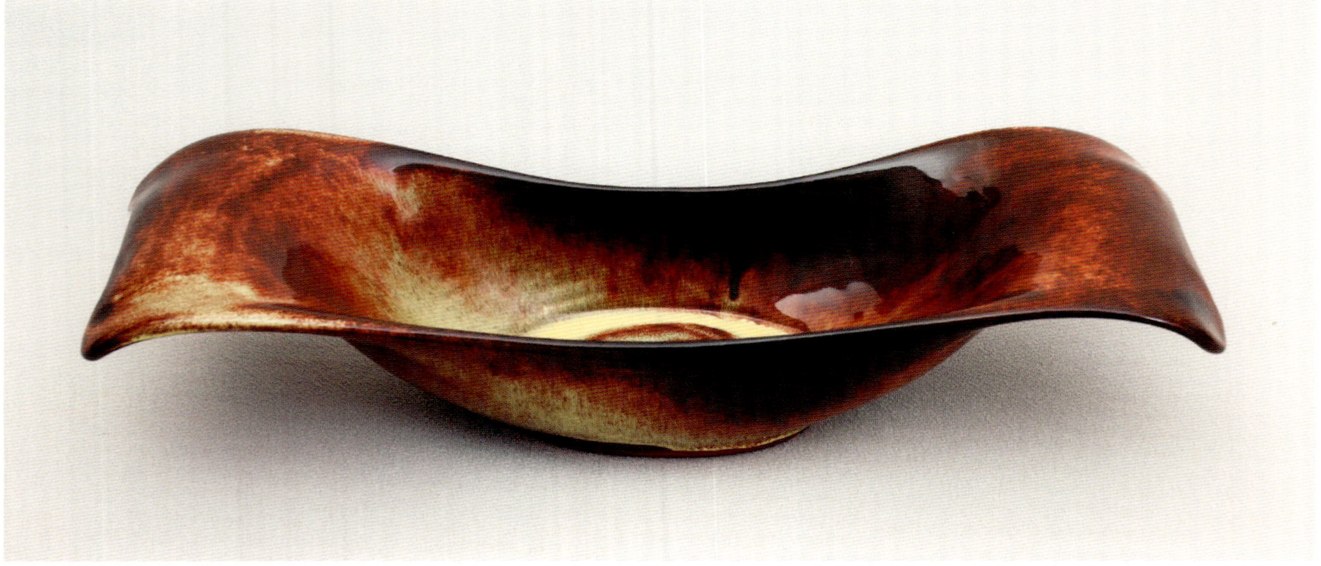

TOP: Dykor | Small yellow leaf-shaped bowl | 84x66x50mm | Provenance: Douglas van der Horst | Marks: Dykor impressed stamp | Photograph by Natalie Field

BOTTOM: Dykor | Elongated bowl with rust-coloured glazed exterior and rust interior with yellow glaze ring in centre | 94x135x420mm | Provenance: Douglas van der Horst | Marks: Dykor impressed stamp | Photograph by Natalie Field

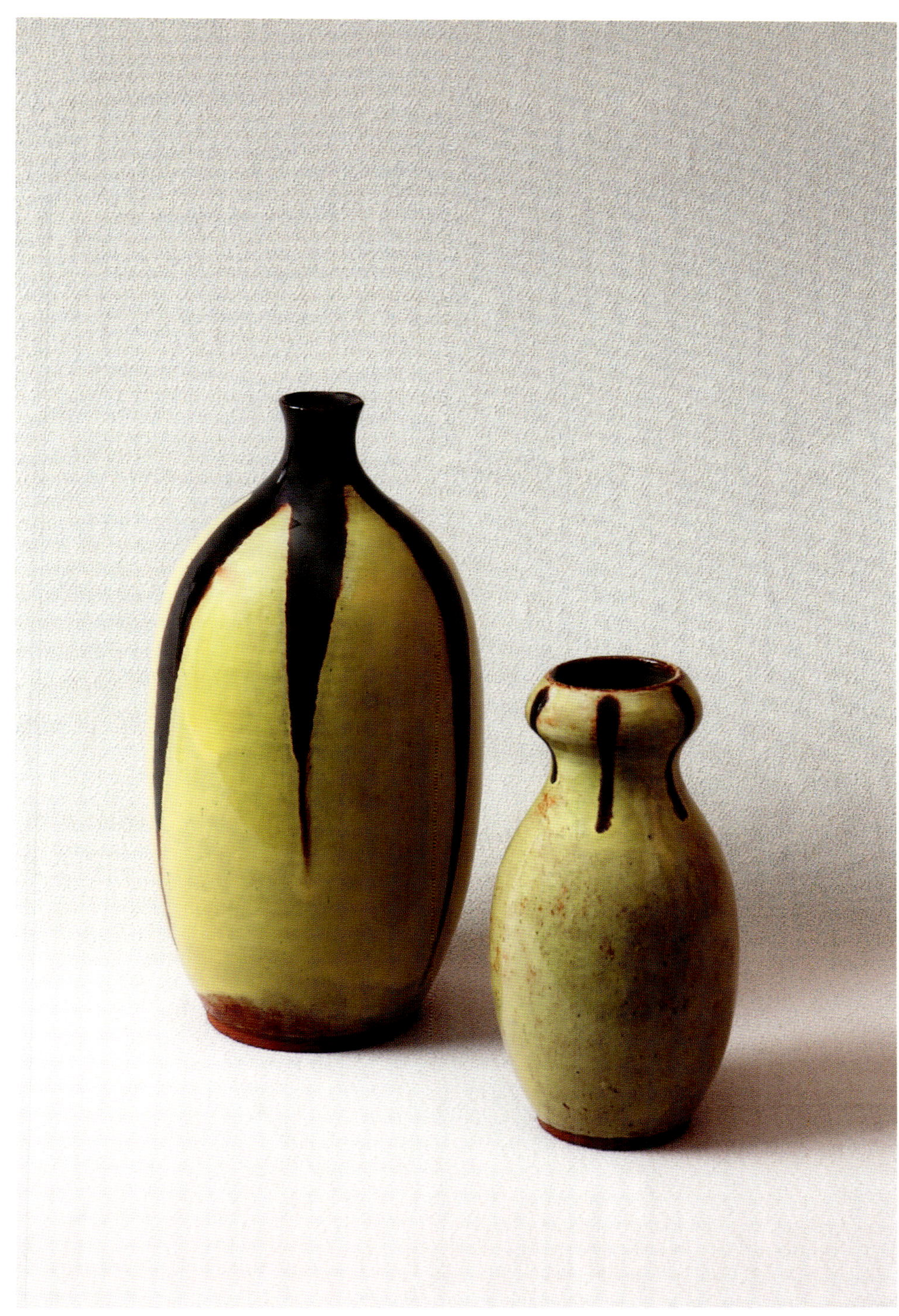

Dykor | Two vases, glazed with ochre and brown glazes | Left vase: ca.300mm; right vase: ca.200mm | Provenance: Wendy Gers | Marks: impressed stamp, 'Dykor' | Photograph by Natalie Field

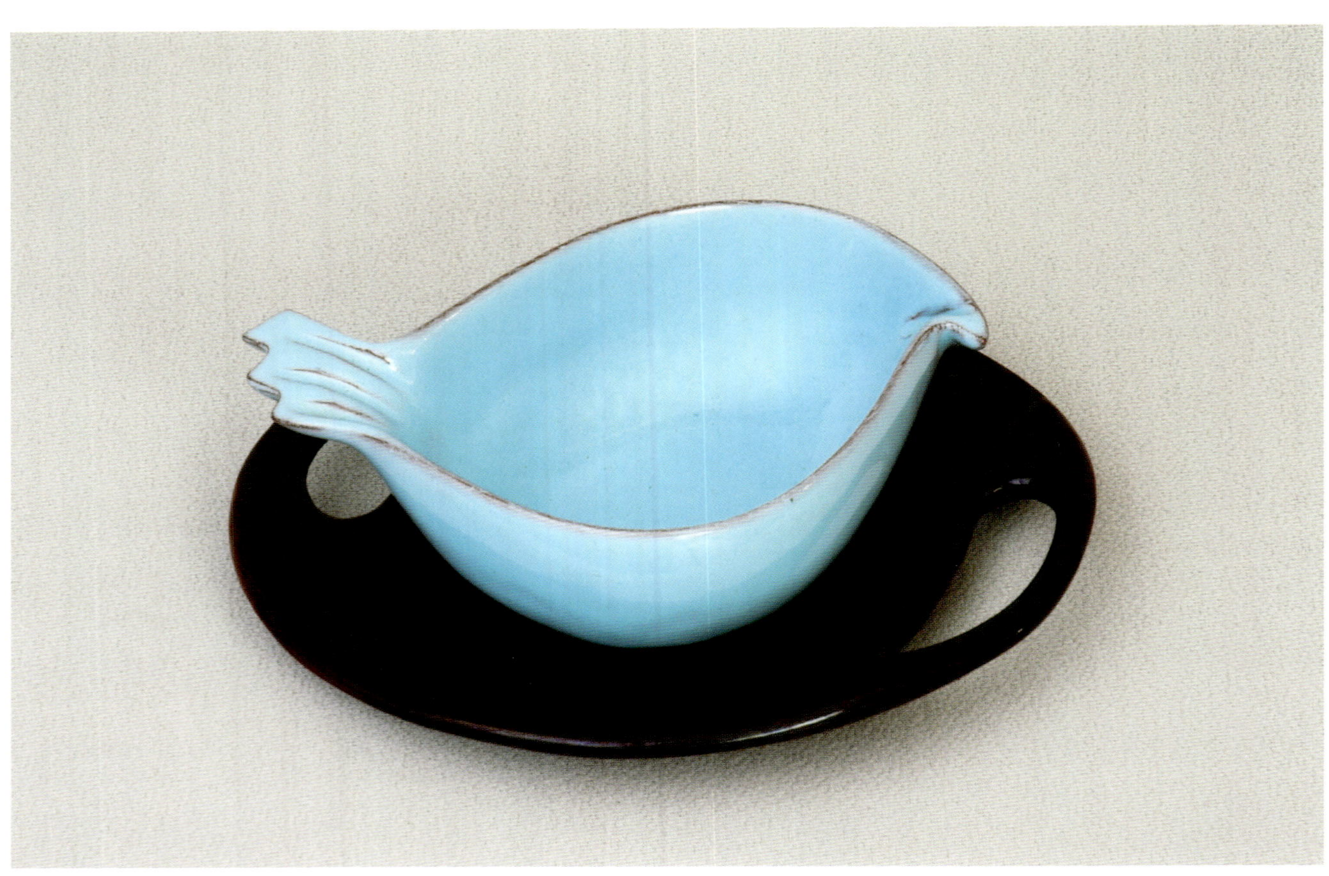

Dykor | Bird bowl and saucer | Bird bowl: 105x145x50mm; saucer: 145x175x20mm | Provenance Wendy Gers | Marks: bowl unmarked; saucer: impressed stamp, 'Dykor' visible under glaze | Additional information: part of a set of multicoloured bird bowls; other bowls marked with Dykor stamp | Photograph by Natalie Field

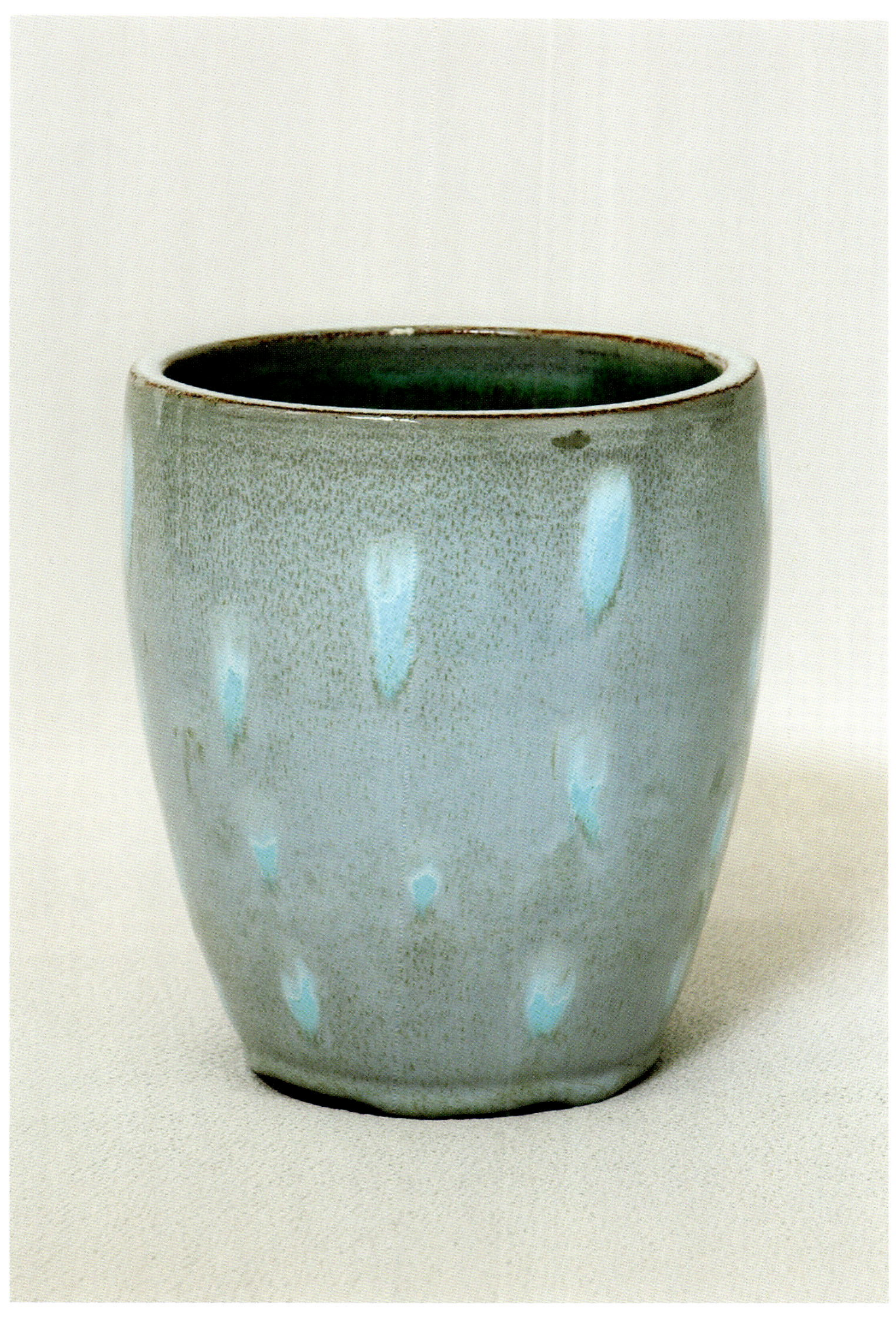

Dykor | Vase, pale grey-blue glazed exterior, with decorative lines of pale blue glaze spots; interior grey turquoise, with darker centre | 132x112x74mm | Provenance: TAG | 2414/06 | Marks: glazed blue-grey base with impressed 'dykor' stamp mark beneath the glaze | Additional information: evidence of multiple glaze layers | Photograph by Natalie Field

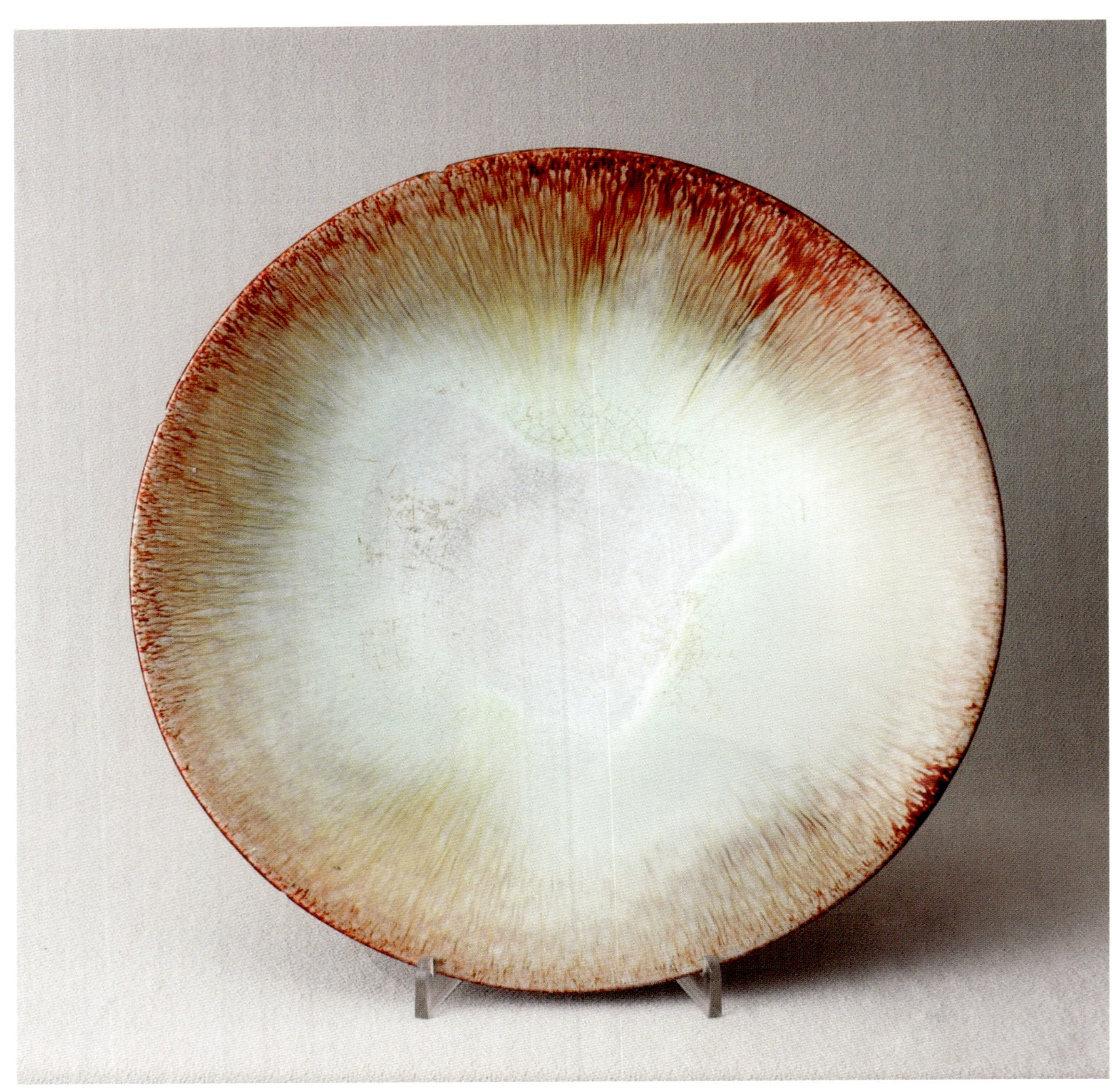

Dykor | Platter decorated with beige and rust-coloured glazes | 307x55mm | Provenance: Wendy Gers | Marks: impressed stamp, 'Dykor' | Additional information: three small rounded conical feet on base | Photograph by Natalie Field

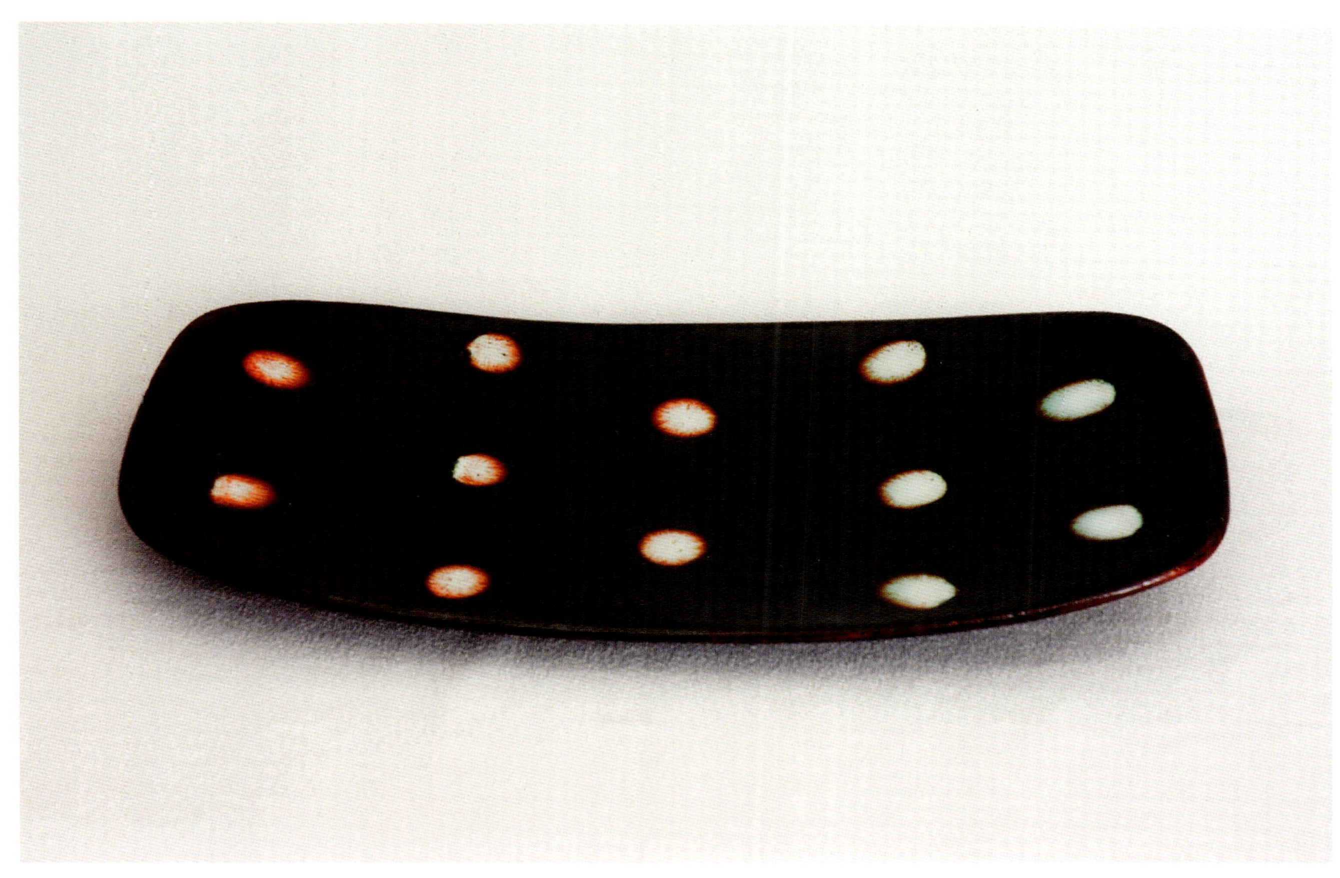

Dykor | Curved rectangular platter with rounded corners and light glaze dots | 332x75x39mm | Provenance: Douglas van der Horst | Marks: Dykor impressed stamp | Photograph by Natalie Field

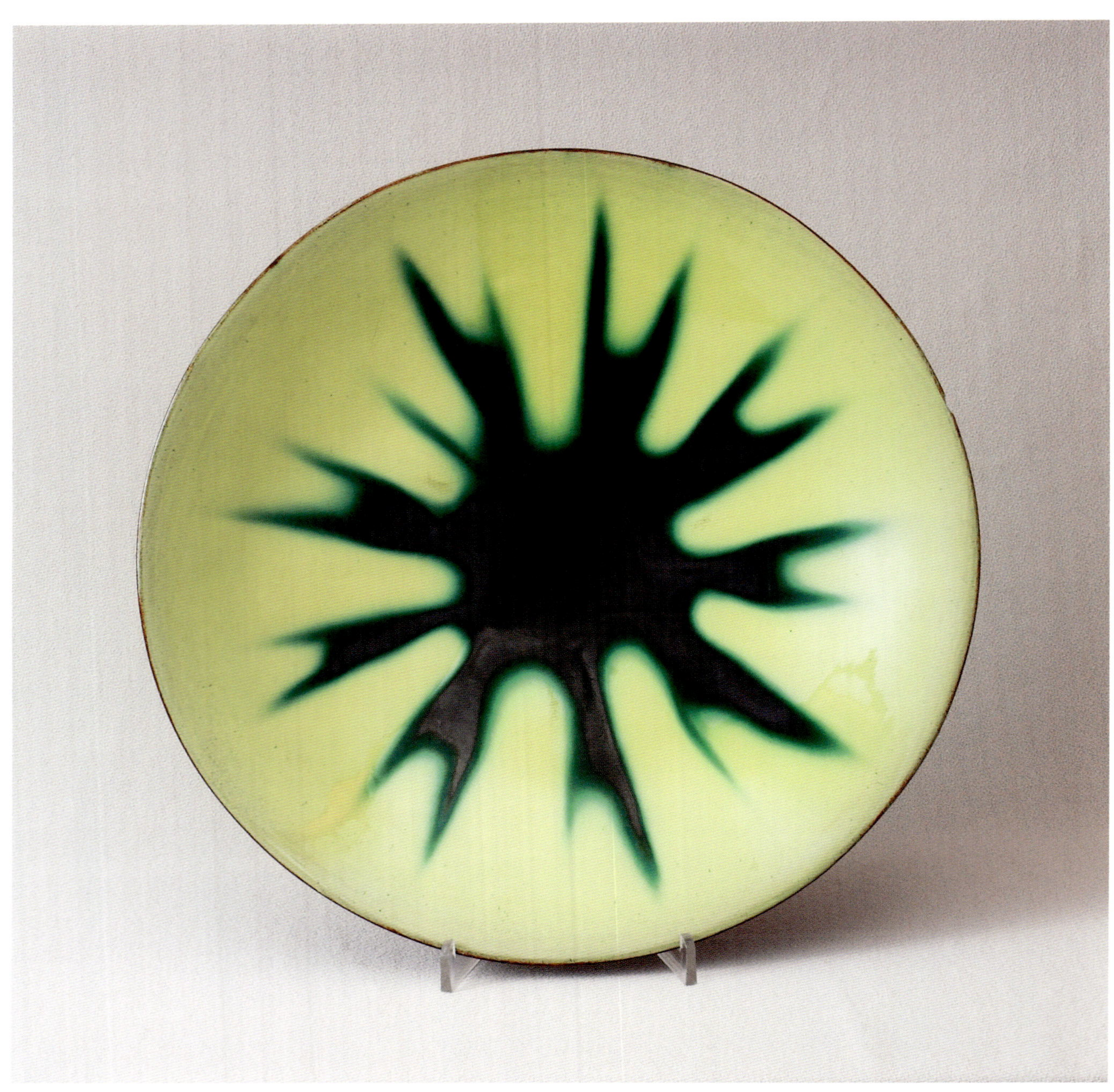

Dykor | Platter, yellow glazed background with green star-burst in centre | 355x60mm | Provenance: Wendy Gers | Marks: impressed stamp, 'Dykor' | Additional information: three small rounded conical feet on base | Photograph by Natalie Field

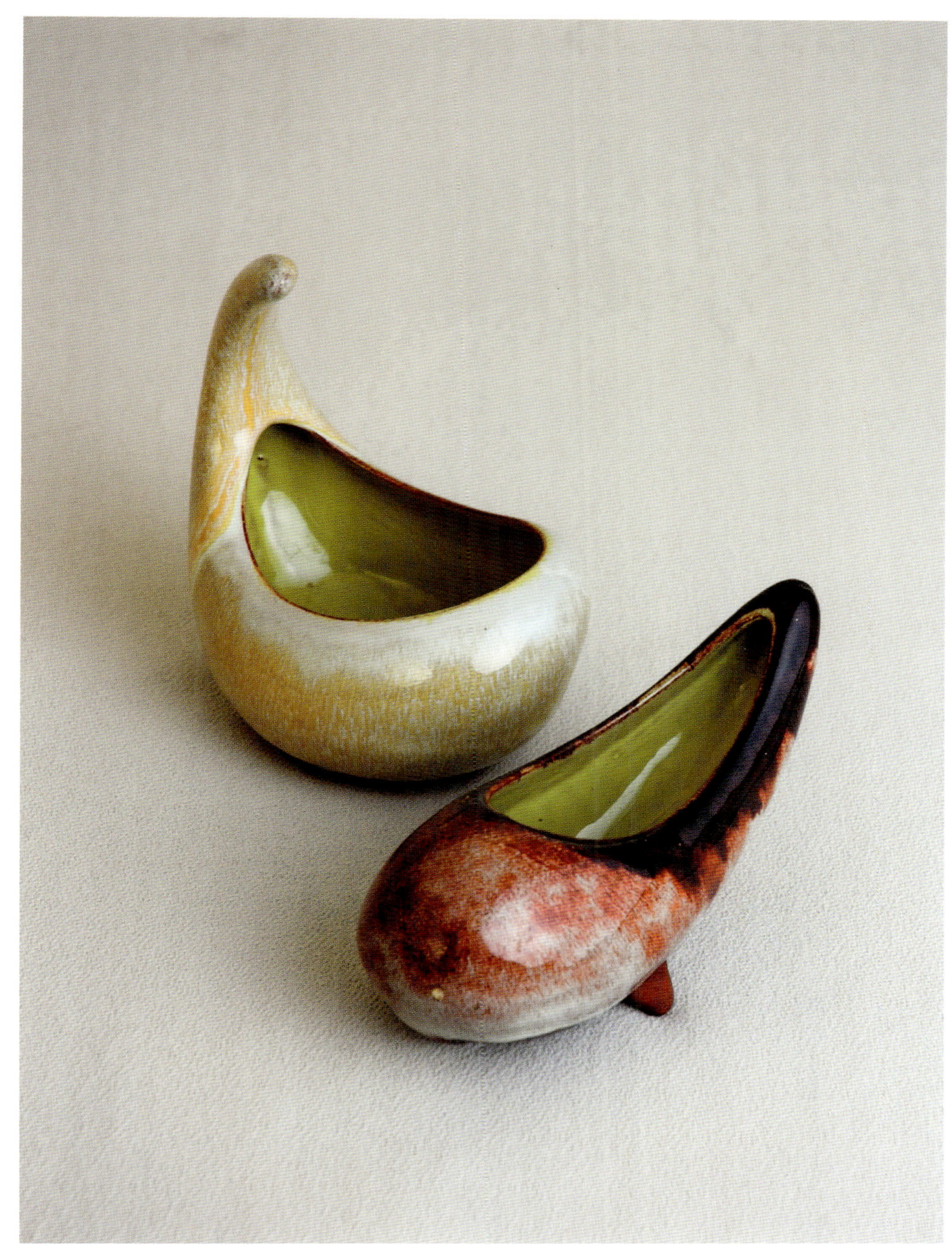

Dykor | Two vessels in the form of stylised calabashes | Rust-coloured vessel 100x165x73mm; cream-coloured vessel 162x147x79mm | Provenance: TAG | rust 2432/06; cream 2437/06 | Marks: dark brown glazed base with impressed mould mark, 'Dykor'; cream-coloured glazed base with incised mark, 'Dykor' | Photograph by Natalie Field

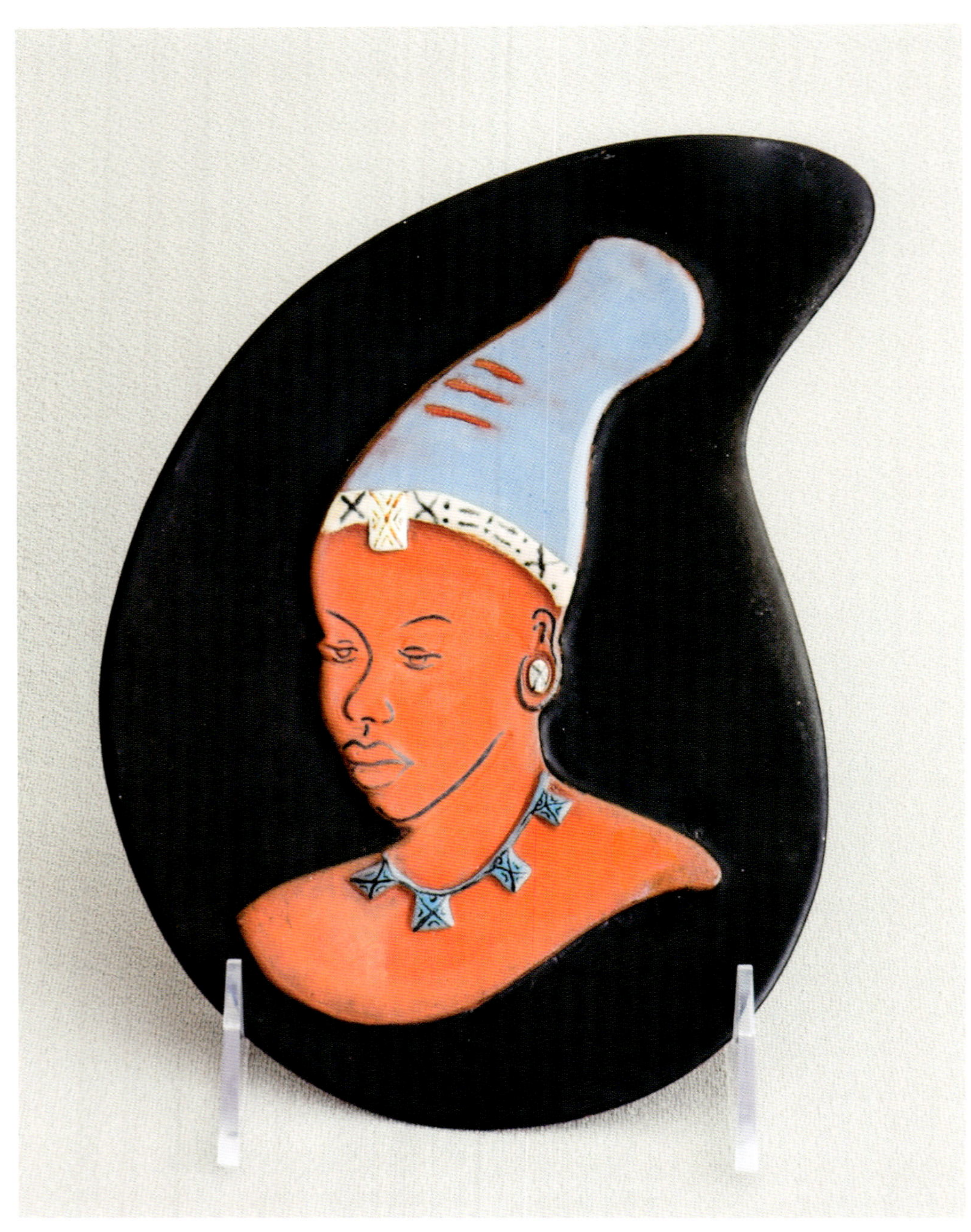

Dykor | Wall plaque with image of African woman | 205x140x20mm | Provenance: Douglas van der Horst | Marks: glazed base with resist earthenware motif of southern Africa and painted mark 'dykor South Africa' | Photograph by Natalie Field

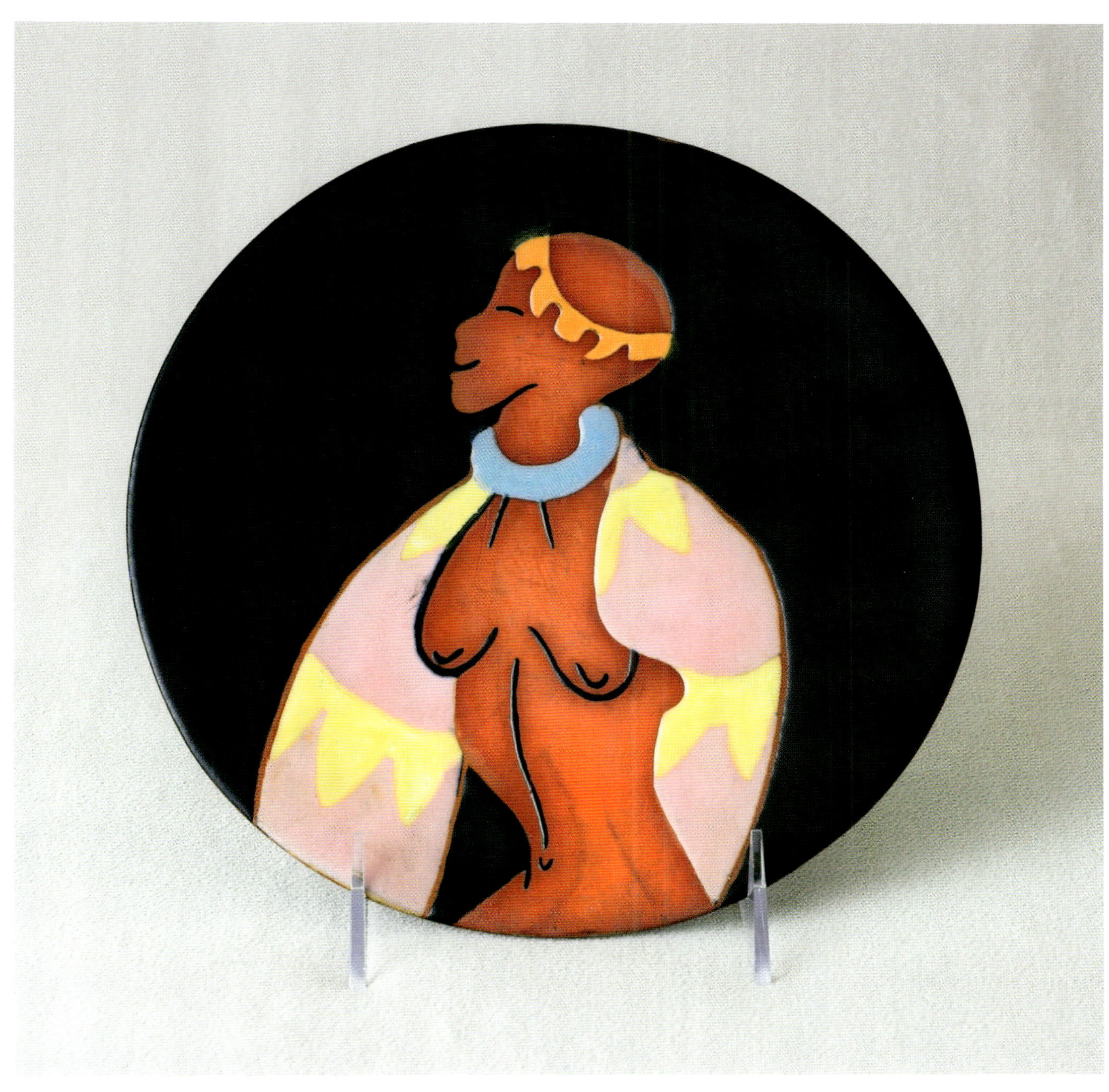

Dykor | Charger with portrait of an African woman | 205x16mm | Provenance: TAG | 2435/06 | Marks: green glazed base with resist terracotta map of southern Africa, 'dykor S.A.' painted in black in the map | Photograph by Natalie Field

Faragher's Pottery, Swaziland (1970–1976)

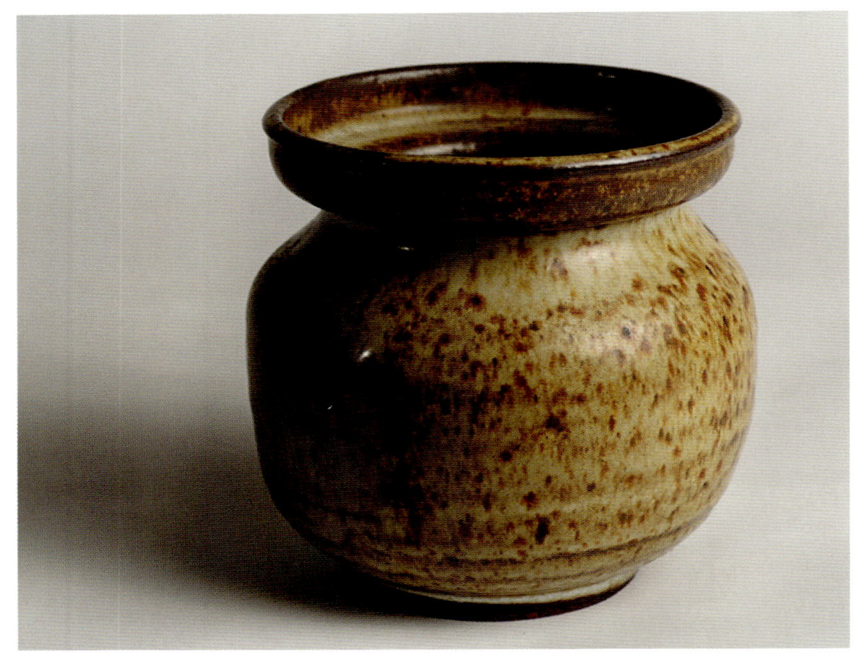

Faragher's Pottery | Jar | 105x110x90mm | Provenance: Tamsin Faragher | Marks: unmarked | Photograph by Alan Millar

Location

Mbabane, Swaziland

Founders

Joe Faragher and his wife Lynette Faragher (née Murray) established Faragher's Pottery.

Designers and decorators

David Fakuduze, Joe Faragher, Balunzi Masuku, Meshack Masuku, Petros Masuku, Jobe Mavuso and Timothy (surname unknown)

Wares manufactured

- The main wares manufactured were utilitarian tableware like dinner services, teacups and saucers, teapots, wine carafes and goblets, casseroles, round butter dishes with a strap handle, flatware (including pizza, pasta and lasagne dishes), and casserole sets that were glazed and decorated in the Anglo-Oriental tradition.
- Glazed, decorated planters.
- Unglazed terracotta capsular roasting dishes for chickens (known as 'chicken bricks').
- Sculptural wares including masks, small ornamental animals, totemic creations and *tokoloshes*, and undertook architectural commissions for murals.
- Local herd-boys worked in the pottery after school making animals.

- Faragher experimented with the manufacture of porcelain wares, and was assisted in this endeavour by the well-known porcelain expert, Thelma Marcuscn (1919–2009).
- Faragher's stoneware articles are characterised by a very dark brown body that is incredibly strong as they were fired to 1 350°C.[84]

Production methods

All wares were hand-built or thrown on one of the five potter's wheels. Stoneware c ay was mined nearby at Mahlana, and porcelain was made from clay mined near Piet Retief. Clay was ground and mixed in a pugmill made by Joe s father. The clay was filtered in a filter-press bought from Sammy Liebermann. Wares were fired in a large, 200-cubic-metre, oil-fired kiln. A second Catenary arch kiln was built later. The two kilns were fired simultaneously, the latter operating on the heat from the former.

Brief history of the pottery

When a loan from the United Nations Development Project (UNDP) did not materialise to start the pottery, Faragher and his wife Lynette invested their teachers' salaries into setting up this enterprise. The pottery employed seven staff members, including three or four potters. The rest of the staff were responsible for making animals, preparing clay, packing the kilns, etc. Almost all the equipment was made by Faragher and his father, assisted by the staff. Lynette Faragher provided organisational skills as well as labour when needed.

In the early years the pottery experienced many disastrous firings and lost great quantities of stock as a result. In 1971, upon accepting an important commission for a baptismal font and lights for the All Saints Church in Mbabane, the Faraghers requested an exorcism of the kiln by the local priest. This ritual was performed during the firing of the ecclesiastic commission. Miraculously, the pottery never again experienced any similar technical problems!

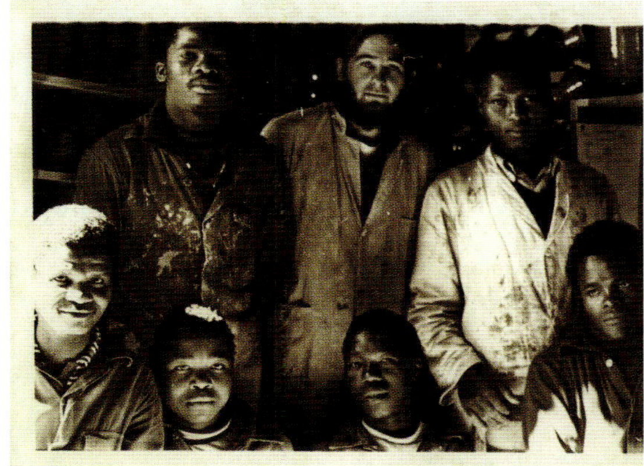

Faragher's Pottery | Staff 1970 | Top row from left: Meshack Masuku, Joe Faragher and unidentified staff member; front row: Jobe Mavuso, Balunzi Masuku and two unidentified staff members | Provenance: Ruth, Mary, Tamsin and Lynette Faragher | Photograph courtesy of Joe and Lynette Faragher

Despite its relative isolation, the pottery had lots of passing trade and wares were primarily sold from an onsite showroom. However, it also supplied some galleries and craft shops in neighbouring South Africa, including Helen de Leeuw's Craftsman's Market, Johannesburg, the Potter's Shop, Hyde Park, Johannesburg and Lion Bridge Nursery, Pretoria. The couple tried unsuccessfully to sell the operation and in 1976 they packed up the machinery, Joe demolished the kilns and they left. Lynette Faragher recalls the event: 'It was a completely devastating waste of a good plant'.[85]

While Faragher's Pottery was a relatively small and short-lived operation, it had a significant impact on local art and craft developments. Its existence spurned the creation of similar projects, such as the SEDCO Pottery Development Centre, which was set up across the road from Faragher's, and the Mantenga Craft Centre. Faragher's Pottery is testament to what one motivated couple can achieve, without virtually any capital. For a brief moment, this small pottery competed with other large, professional, well-financed potteries operating in the Anglo-Oriental style, such as Kolonyama. Faragher's Pottery was also responsible for the training of Meshack Masuku, who has become an important teacher and artist, a stalwart of contemporary South African ceramics.

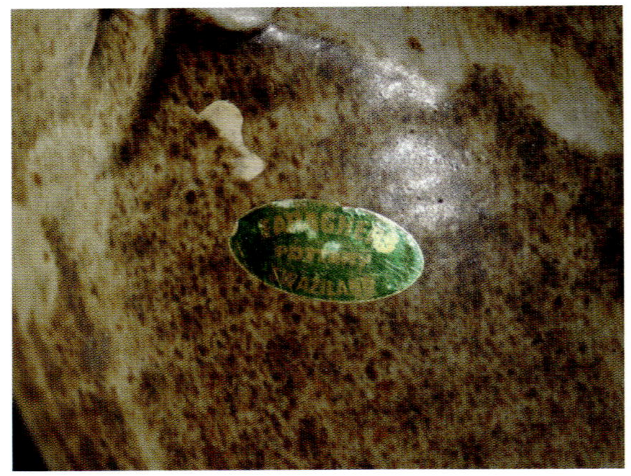

Faragher's Pottery | Maker's mark | Green and gold sticker

Marks

Wares were not marked, but were sold with a gold-and-green sticker marked 'Faragher's Pottery'. Personal wares made by Faragher were marked with a stamp, bearing a curvilinear F.[86]

Select exhibitions and commissions

- 1976 Faragher's Pottery exhibited at the Fourth National Ceramics Exhibition (called MUD), Hilton College, Natal.
- 1975 Faragher's Pottery exhibited at the SA Association of Arts Gallery, Pretoria.
- 1973 Commission for a three-storey mural for the Standard Bank head office in Mbabane, Swaziland.
- 1973 SA Association of Arts Gallery Pretoria – exhibition of handmade stoneware and decorative items.
- 1971 Commission for a baptismal light and an octagonal font for All Saints Church, Mbabane, Swaziland.

The Pottery also exhibited at the Goodman Gallery and Helen De Leeuw, Johannesburg.

Biographies

FAKUDUZE, David

Fakuduze was the second employee of Faragher's Pottery, joining in 1970 and departing in 1973. He was extremely talented and specialised in huge masks and *tokoloshes*. The masks, which were shaped over galvanised poles, were inspired by Native American masks and totems, which he had viewed in the home of Peter Simpkin, the UNDP administrator, who had formerly lived in Argentina and had a collection of masks and totems.

FARAGHER, Joseph (aka Joe) (1943–2009)

Faragher was born in Roodepoort and on completion of his military service in 1962 he joined the Union Corporation mining company, and enlisted in a training course for officials in mine engineering. He left in 1965 and started studying industrial design at the Johannesburg Art School in 1966. He soon changed to pottery and as a student assisted with the teaching of art history. Faragher's mentors included Joyce Lennard, Spies Venter (b.1935) and Tim Morris. The artist and author Gavin Younge was a student with Joe at the art school. Politically engaged, Faragher was elected president of the Students'

Representat ve Council at the art school. He completed his studies in 1968.

In 1969 he married Lynette Murray (b.1946, Johannesburg) and they got involved with a pottery therapy project for the rehabilitation of drug-dependent adolescents n Phoenix House, Johannesburg. The numerous setbacks of this project led them to depart for Swaziland a year later. In 1970 the couple established Faragher's Pottery, while working as teachers – Joe for the Waterford Kamhlaba, a well-known, private, non-racial school, and Lynette at St Francis Secondary School. The pottery was a profitable venture, and it was Faragher's intention to sell it and restart a similar venture elsewhere. However, the United Nations had established a pottery across the road in the SEDCO site, and this rendered the sale impossible. As a result of the Swazi authorities' crack-down on foreign workers, the pottery was raided and Faragher arrested as he was not in possession of his work permit. Faragher was soon released from detention, but the climate of political and personal insecurity resulted in the decision to close the pottery and destroy the kilns. The couple left Swaziland in June 1976.

Faragher then joined Ikhwezi Lokusa School and established a pottery workshop for physically and mentally challenged adults, managing it from 1976 to 1984. The workshop facilities included a darkroom, and during this period Faragher experimented with photographic images on tiles and vessels. Most of these images were of Africans, and had been taken by his wife, Lynette, who was an amateur photographer.

In 1985 and 1986, Faragher established a similar pottery rehabilitation project at Camphill Village, an institution located near Hermanus in the Western Cape, which provides care and employment for adults with intellectual disabilities.

In 1987 he moved to Potgietersrus where he managed a tile plant, a subsidiary of the Weenen Brick Works, which had been awarded a commission to reproduce tiles required in the restoration of the Cape Town Castle. He was commissioned to resolve the technical problems they were experiencing and was involved in the design of murals for the Lost City. During this period he also worked with local African women potters, who made and decorated large coiled pots. He departed at the end of 1988 after a serious car accident.

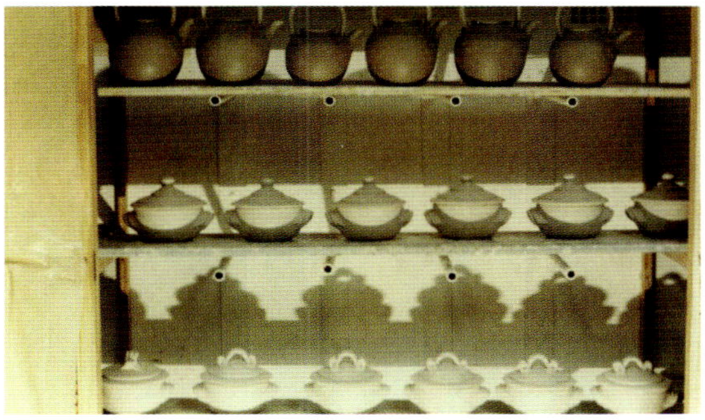

In 1989 Faragher relocated to Cape Town where he was employed by the Quaker community to provide skills training to unemployed township youth. The training location was not an appropriate setting for the project and was closed down after about six months. He was a founder member of The Clayman, a company that produced clay bodies, porcelains, glazes, bisqueware and casting slip in Retreat, Cape Town.

In Cape Town, Faragher renewed his interest in the application of photographic transfers to ceramic bodies. In the 2000s, he was involved in various community projects, and produced ceramic wares with photographic images of Mandela, Robben Island and the South African War (1899–1902). Faragher continued to work closely with members of the community who were mentally or physically disabled. He conducted workshops, trained numerous economically disadvantaged potters and helped establish several studios.

Faragher's Pottery | Wares drying 1970 | Provenance: Ruth, Mary, Tamsin and Lynette Faragher | Photograph courtesy of Joe and Lynette Faragher

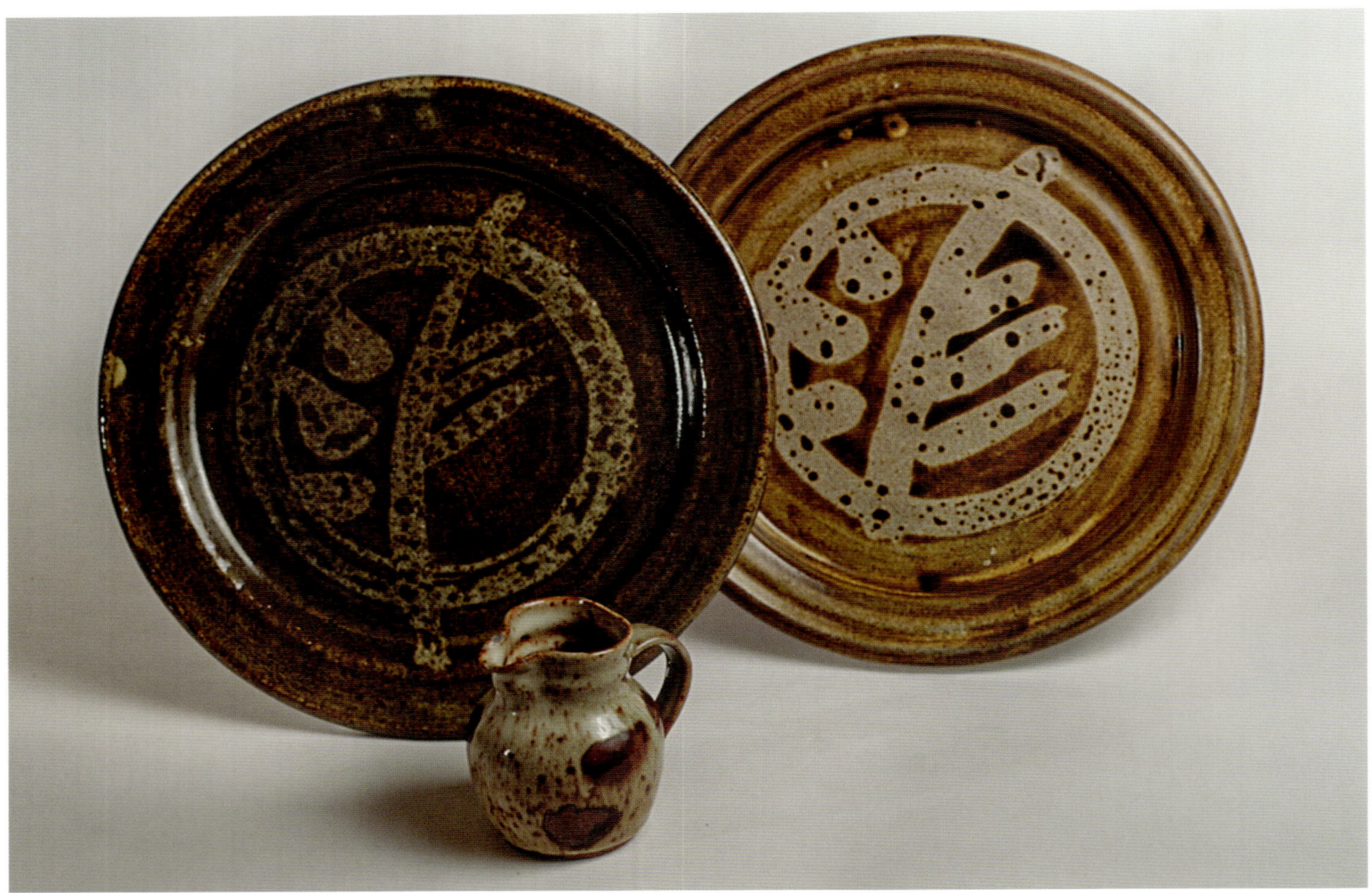

Faragher's Pottery | Two platters and a jug | Platters: 30x270mm; jug: 85x75x50mm | Provenance: Tamsin Faragher | Marks: unmarked | Photograph by Alan Millar

Faragher is frequently described as an alchemist. His last works are redundant kiln shelves that feature collages of photographs documenting aspects of the South African War. Images were sourced from photographic archives, including Museum Africa. His grandfathers fought on both the English and the Boer sides and the multi-layered images are frequently blurred and distorted, a metaphor for the processes of creating and documenting history. His works are allegories of the archival process, where fairly random information is recorded and 'fossilised' in the ceramic firing processes. Shortly before his death, his work was honoured with a memorial exhibition at the Irma Stern Museum, University of Cape Town.

Faragher's works are in many public and private collections, including NMMAM, SANG and JAG. Faragher was a loyal member of APSA. He wrote for, and was featured in, the *Ceramic Review* magazine, the *Ceramic Review Clay* magazine and *Glaze Book* (1977, 1981, 1984), the *Ceramic Monthly* magazine and *Sgraffiti* (an APSA publication).

Commissions

A ceramic door for the General Mining Corporation offices in Johannesburg was done in 1968. It was relocated to Gallery Elysia, a small art gallery in Braamfontein, owned by Eleanor Anderson.

Exhibitions

2008 'Deadly Semantics', Irma Stern Museum, University of Cape Town.

2008 'Capturing the Colonial', group exhibition, The Thompson Gallery, Johannesburg.

1995 'Hand-coloured Photos in Ceramic Frames: A Collaboration between Photographer and Ceramicist', Cape Gallery, Cape Town. Exhibition of collaborative works by Faragher and photographer Chris Ledochowski.

MASUKU, Balunzi

Trained by Meshack Masuku, he was the general assistant at Faragher's Pottery and was a highly talented modeller of animal figurines, especially warthogs. He also made ornamental oxen, horses and lions. He was a chief and was assassinated.

MASUKU, Meshack Lembelele (b.1954)

Born in Swaziland, Masuku was employed by Faragher's Pottery as a general labourer and assistant, where he worked in the garden, did cleaning, made clay animals, prepared clay and packed kilns. He departed in about 1971 for a year to finish his primary school education and returned in 1972. After working hours, Masuku taught himself how to throw, and was soon invited to work as a potter.

In 1977 he left Swaziland and moved to South Africa. Between 1978 and 1988 he was employed by Canosa Pottery near Hammanskraal, Gauteng and at Ceramex at Isithebe, KwaZulu-Natal. He worked in design, training, quality control and management. From 1989 Masuku joined the Alexandra Art Centre in Johannesburg, where he initiated and coordinated their ceramics department. From 1990 until 1993, Masuku worked as a studio potter with David Schlapobersky and Felicity Potter, and from 1993 was guest potter at numerous APSA 'Clay Day' workshops. In 1994 he registered for a National Diploma in Ceramic Design at the Port Elizabeth Technikon, and from 1995 he undertook various lecturing duties while doing his diploma. In 2000 Masuku was appointed a lecturer at the Port Elizabeth Technikon. Masuku has exhibited extensively, and won various ceramics and leadership awards. He presented papers at various conferences in the mid-1990s, including the Ilitha Educational Conference in Grahamstown and the Growth Strategy Conference of the Department of Arts and Culture in Grahamstown.[87]

Guest Artist

2004 The Potters' Association of Namibia's Second National Ceramics Biennale. Masuku was invited to be the selector, award judge, guest exhibitor and workshop host.

2000 APSA Eastern Cape Regional Exhibition, NMMAM.

1998 APSA National Exhibition, Sandton Civic Centre, Johannesburg.

1993 'CraftArt', Standard Bank Festival for the Arts, Grahamstown.

Collections

Masuku has exhibited extensively locally and internationally, and his works are in many public and private collections, including NMMAM and the TAG, Pietermaritzburg.

Select exhibitions

2000 – 'Fire and Fibre', Bayside Gallery, Durban

1994 – ca.2006 – APSA Eastern Cape Regional Exhibition, NMMAM

1998 – 'People, Places and Perspectives', NMMAM

1978–1980 – APSA Northern Transvaal Regional Exhibition

1982, 1983 – APSA Natal Regional Exhibition

MASUKU, Petros (d.1985)

Petros Masuku formerly worked in a bakery and was a competent wedger. He was the third employee of Faragher's Pottery. He was a very strong man, and was a consistent thrower. Masuku, a distant cousin of Meshack Masuku, was foreman for approximately four years at Faragher's Pottery. Upon his departure from the pottery, he worked at Messina Potteries in the Northern Province, South Africa, before returning to Swaziland in 1983. He later worked for a pottery near Springs.

MAVUSO, Jobe

Jobe Mavuso was the first employee of Faragher's Pottery. He was a former soapstone carver who made interesting structural sculptures and huge wheel-thrown casseroles with straight sides. Many of Mavuso's casseroles feature handles in the forms of animals, including lizards and crocodiles. Mavuso left Faragher's Pottery when it closed down and joined Mantenga Craft Pottery.

[Surname unknown], Timothy

Timothy was born in Mbila, a small rural town in eastern Swaziland. He made slab bottles and murals and is presently a truck driver. According to Meshack Masuku, he was extremely talented but did not take his talent seriously.

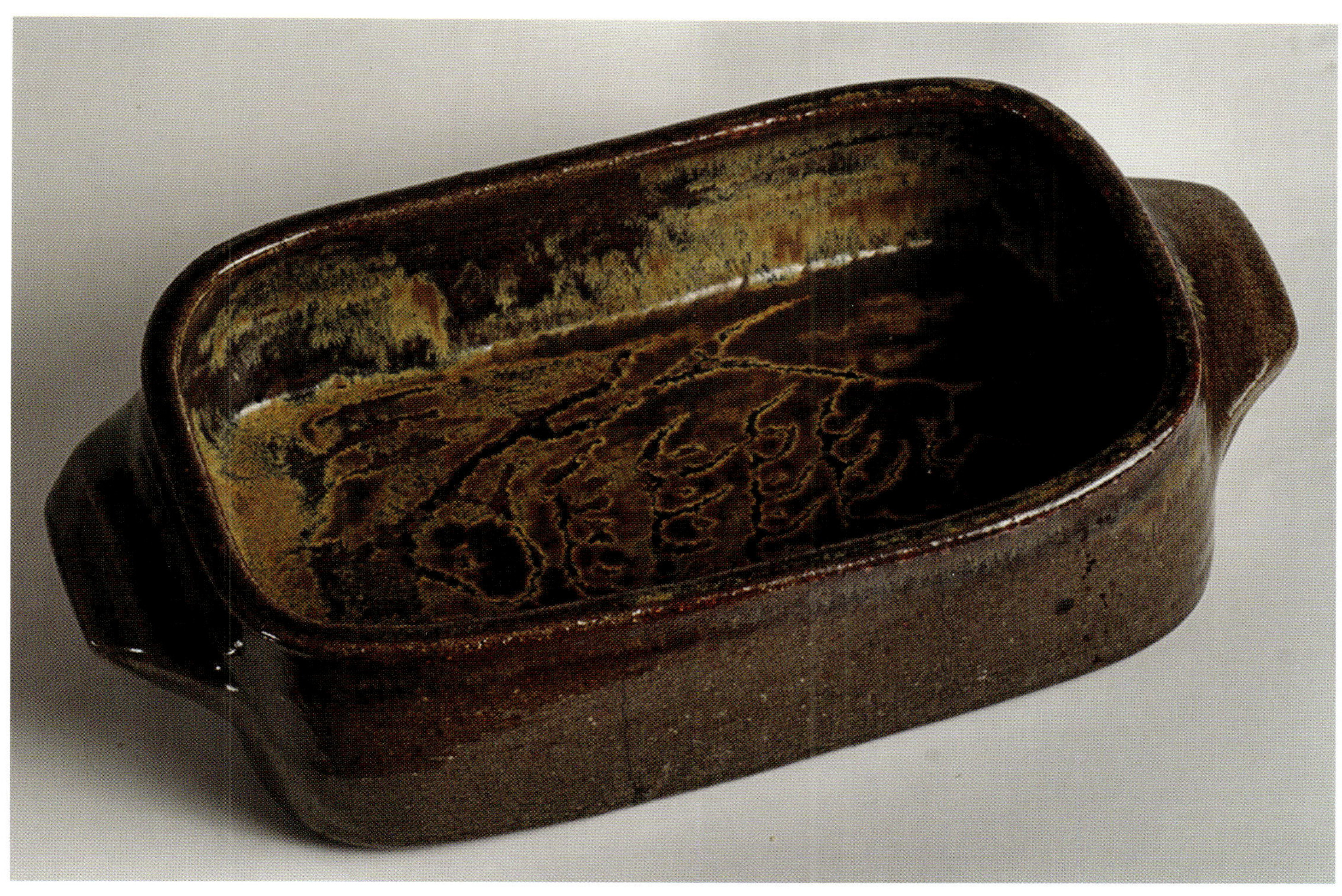

Faragher's Pottery | Casserole, interior decorated with a fish | 340x180x80mm | Provenance: Tamsin Faragher | Marks: unmarked | Photograph by Alan Millar

Flora Ann (1951–1972)

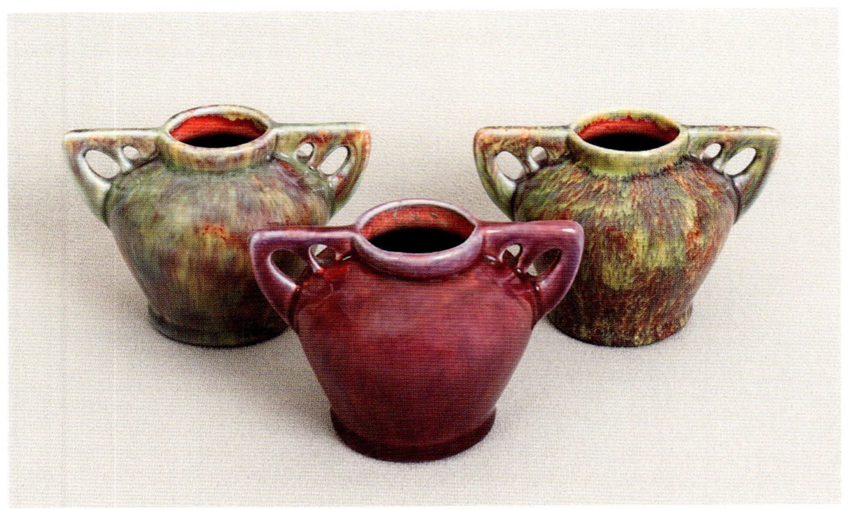

Flora Ann Ware | Three ornamental vases | 82x40x53mm | Provenance: Douglas van der Horst | Marks: outer vases have silver 'Flora Ann Ware' stickers | Additional information: Flora Ann spelled with or without hyphen | Photograph by Natalie Field

Location

Robertsham, Johannesburg

Founders

Flora Ann was established by R R Verity.

Wares manufactured

Vases, ashtrays, ornaments and promotional wares were produced by Flora Ann. Most of these were small and extremely well crafted, meticulously designed with sophisticated lustrous glazes. Numerous wares are glazed in shades of turquoise, pink, blue and green. Some articles, such as cruet and condiment sets, feature metal fittings.

Production method

Slip-cast earthenware

Brief history of the pottery

The history of Flora Ann is somewhat enigmatic. Its designer was G Woolley and it employed 30 African staff. The company was acquired by Silwood Ceramics in 1962, which was subsequently purchased by Liebermann Pottery and Tiles. Archival records suggest that Flora Ann appears to have out-lived the demise of Silwood, as it was embroiled in a legal dispute with Terme Investments and Finance Company in 1972.

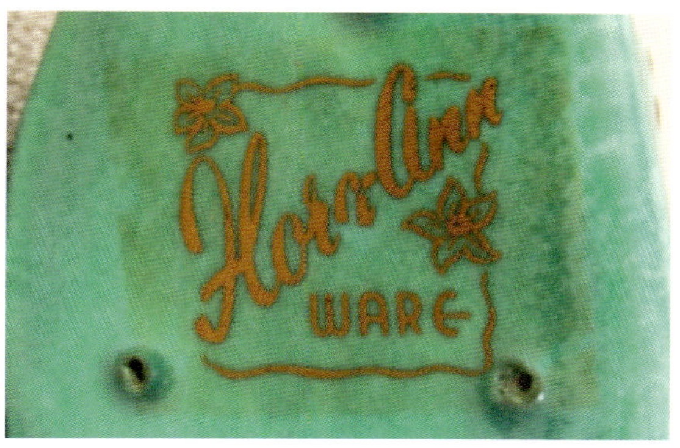

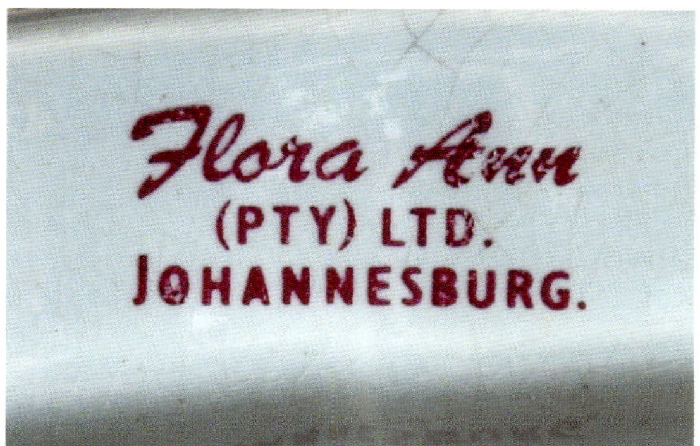

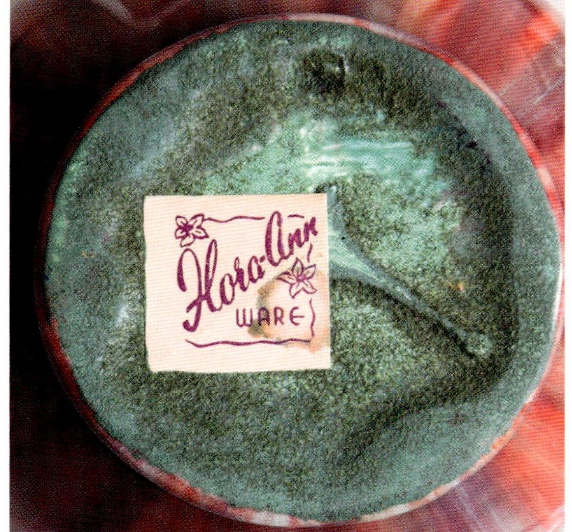

Marks

A variety of marks were applied:

- All wares have a distinctive green baize-like finish on the base.
- Items often have a sticker on the base. Three stickers were used: a beige one is marked 'Flora Ann'; a gold one bears these same marks; another features the studio's name and '(Pty) Ltd, Johannesburg'.
- Some wares have a raised moulded mark, 'Flora Ann', and a mould number, e.g. '299'.
- Some wares are marked with a transfer, 'Flora Ann (Pty) Ltd, Johannesburg'.

TOP: Flora Ann | Maker's mark | Gold transfer, 'Flora-Ann Ware' | Photograph by Natalie Field

MIDDLE: Flora Ann | Maker's mark | Transfer with magenta logo, 'Flora-Ann. (Pty) Ltd Johannesburg' | Photograph by Natalie Field

BOTTOM: Flora Ann | Maker's mark | Cream sticker with magenta logo, 'Flora-Ann Ware' | Photograph by Natalie Field

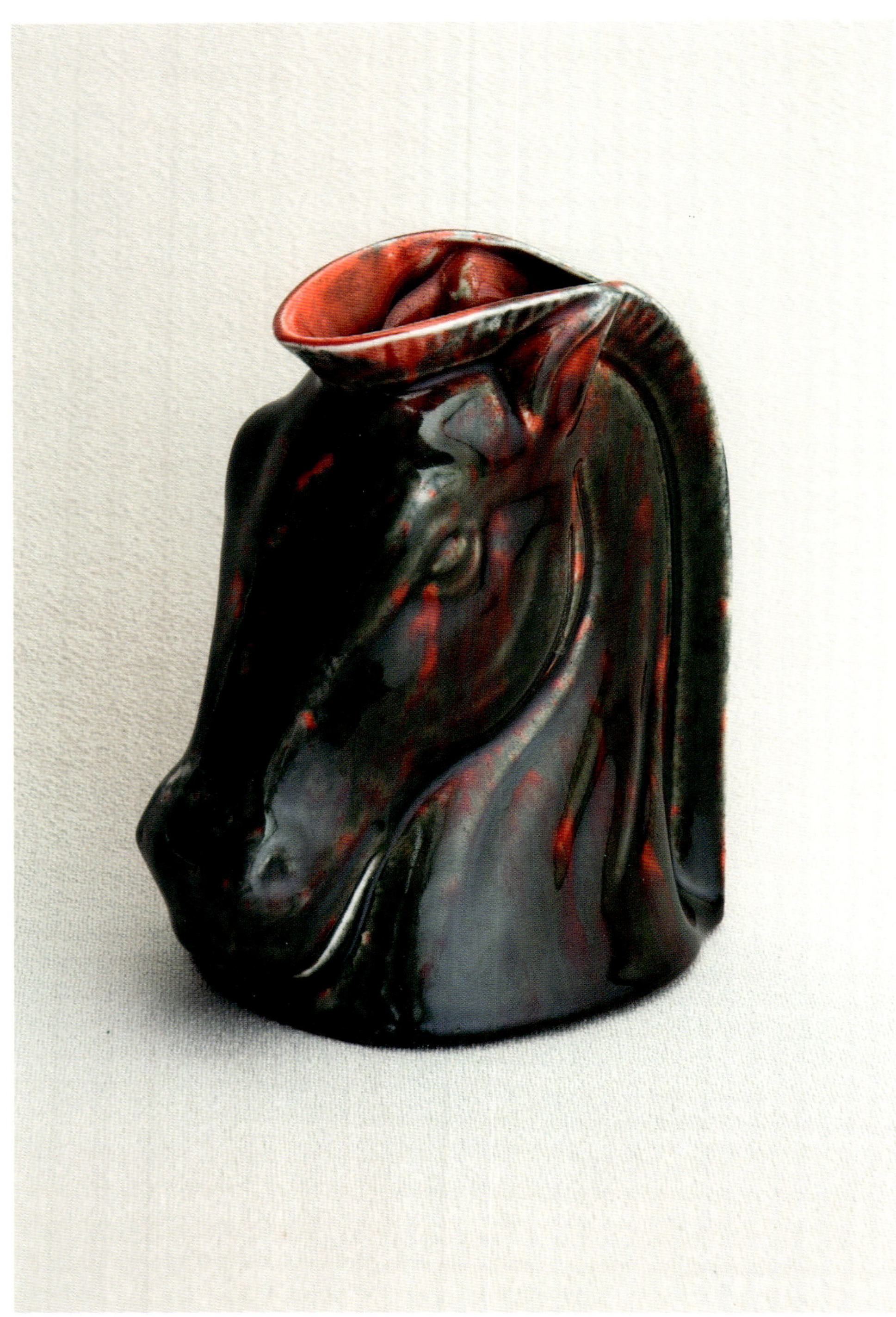

Flora Ann Ware | Vase in the form of a horse head | 136x115x47mm | Provenance: Douglas van der Horst | Marks: gold lettering on cream sticker, 'Flora Ann Ware' on base | Photograph by Natalie Field

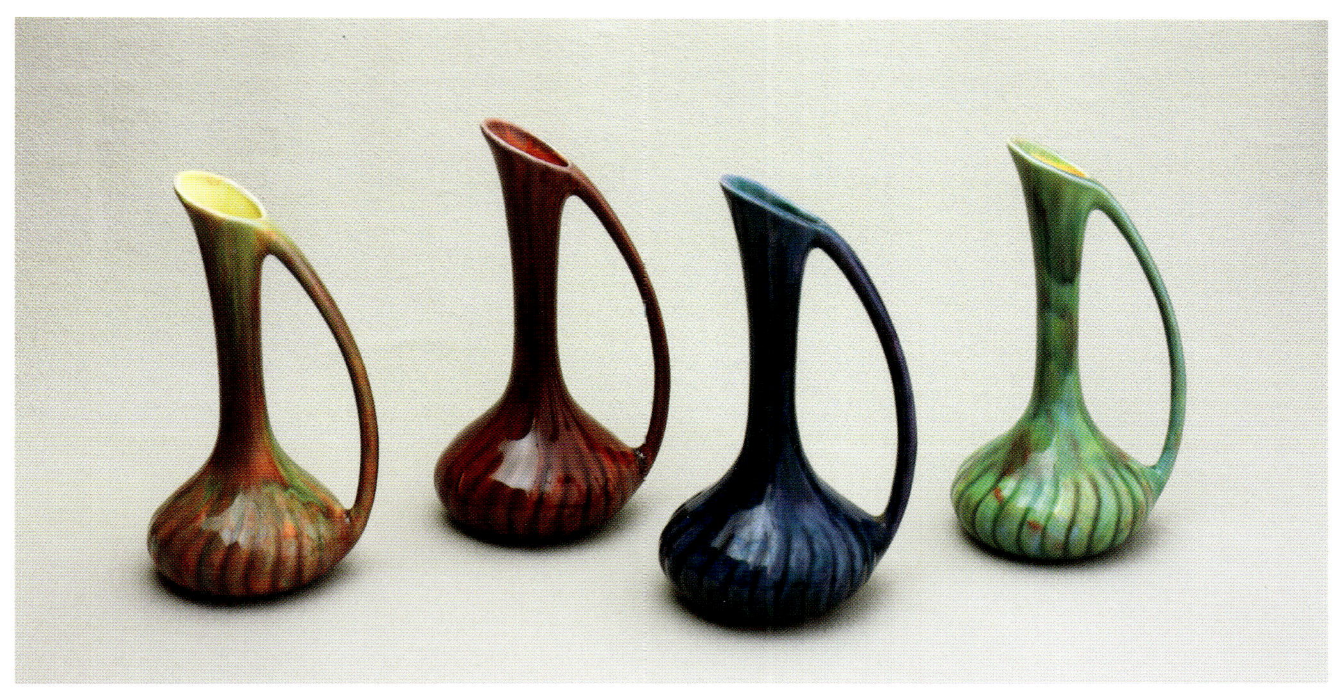

Flora Ann Ware | Four slim elongated vases with handles | 67x33x58mm | Provenance: Douglas van der Horst | Marks: sticker and green baize-like paint on the base | Photograph by Natalie Field

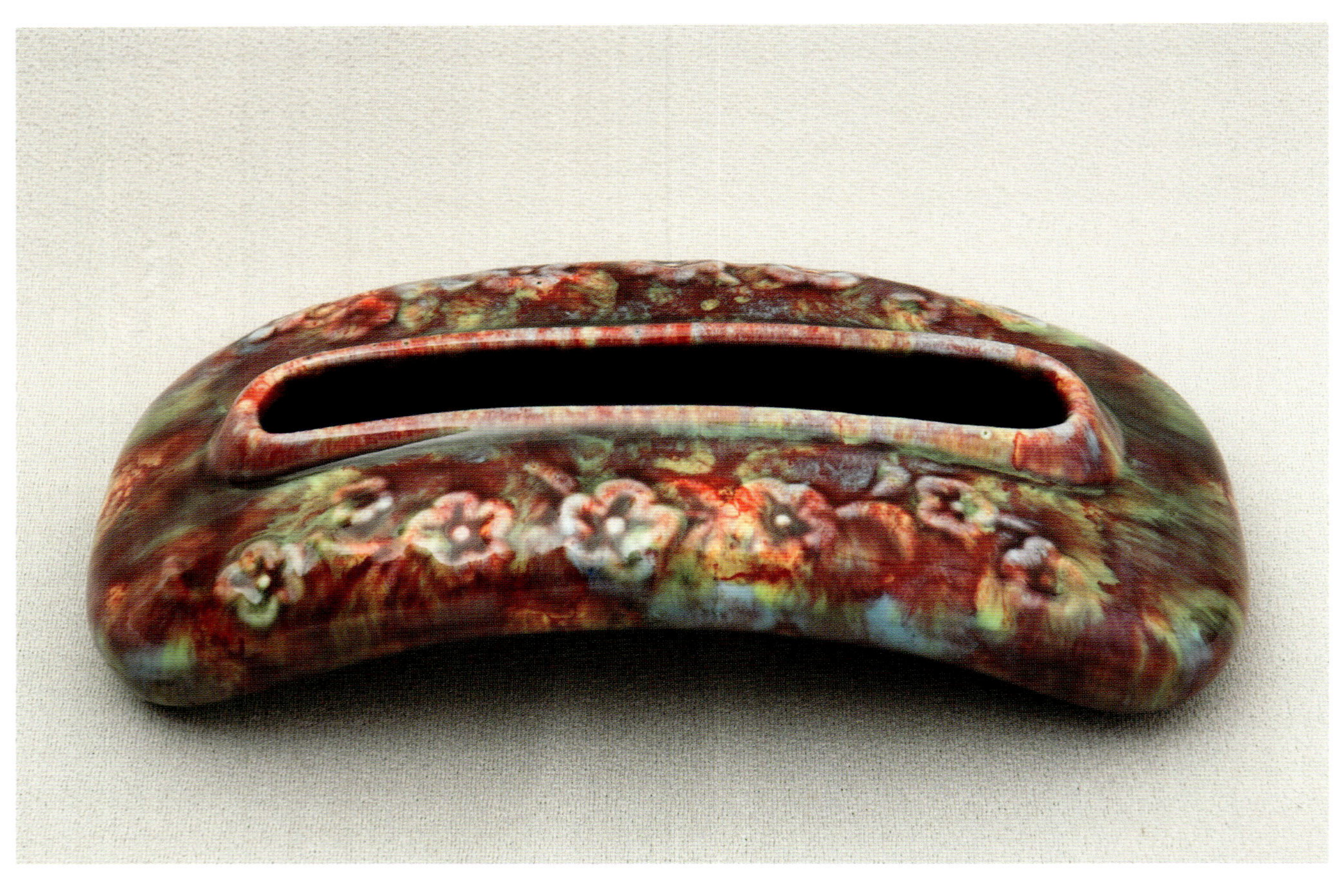

Flora Ann Ware | Vase, form recalls a tissue box | 215x95x60mm | Provenance: Douglas van der Horst | Marks: unmarked, with green baize | Photograph by Natalie Field

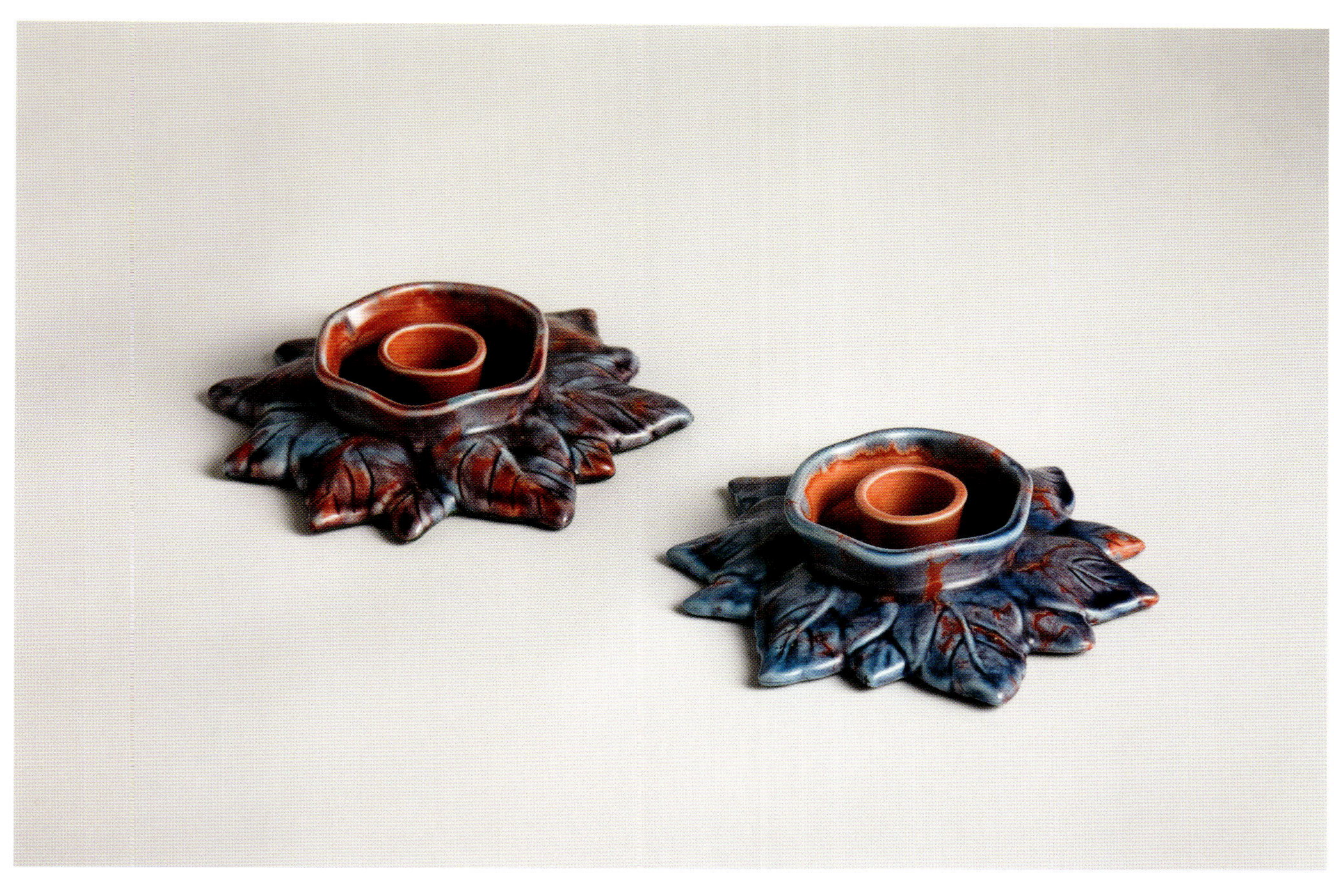

Flora Ann Ware | Pair of candle holders | 36x78x150mm | Provenance: Wendy Gers | 2402/06 | Marks: pair: green baize-like finish on the base and faded pale brown sticker, 'Flo-a-Ann Ware' | Photograph by Damien Artus

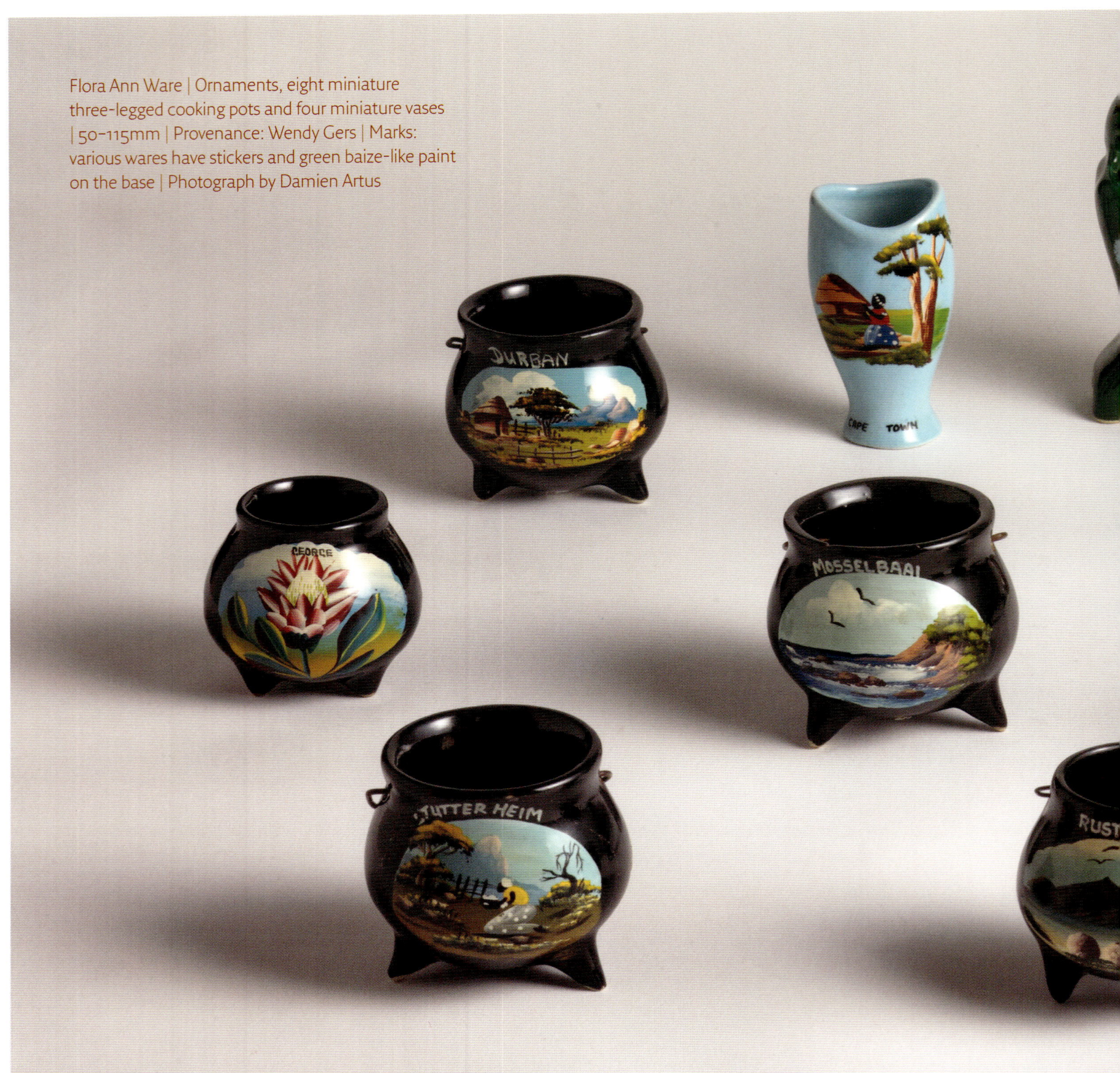

Flora Ann Ware | Ornaments, eight miniature three-legged cooking pots and four miniature vases | 50–115mm | Provenance: Wendy Gers | Marks: various wares have stickers and green baize-like paint on the base | Photograph by Damien Artus

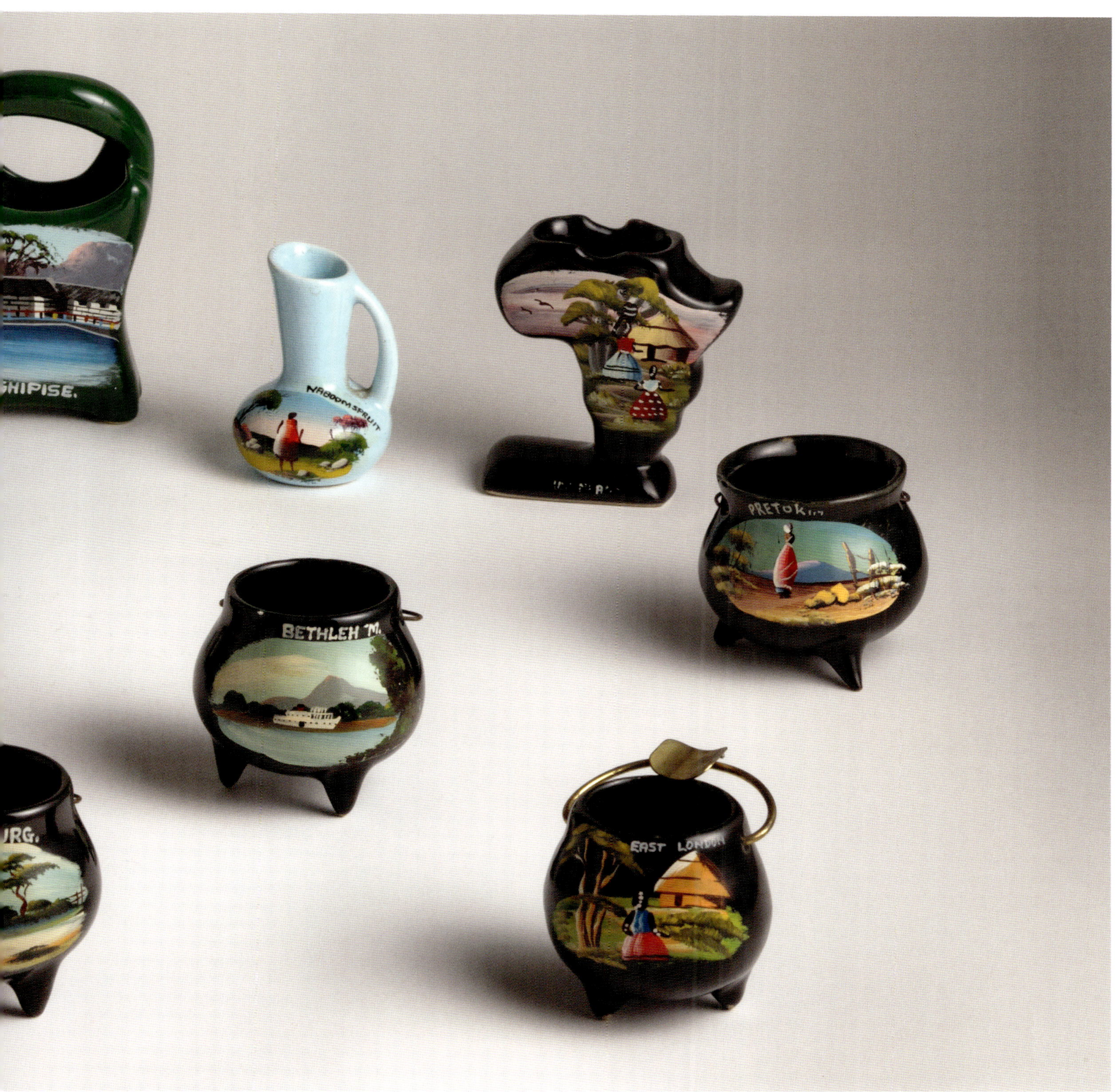
NABOOMSPRUIT
BETHLEH M.
EAST

Globe Potteries (ca.1920–1957)

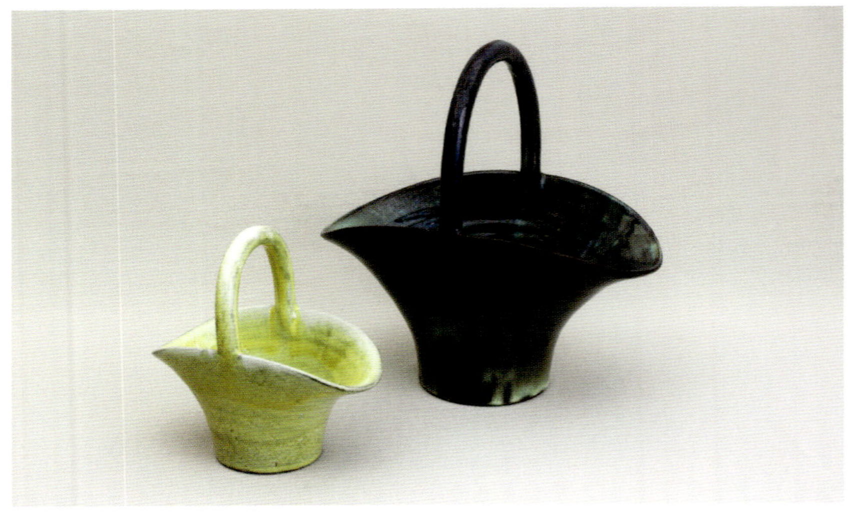

Globe | Pair of two vases in the forms of baskets | tall basket 300x260x100mm; smaller basket 160x165x70mm | Provenance: Douglas van der Horst | 93/554 | Marks: white glazed base with impressed Globe stamp visible under glaze; ochre glazed base with impressed Globe stamp visible under glaze | Photograph by Natalie Field

Location

Globe Potteries was located in New Muckleneuk, Pretoria on the site of the current Austin Roberts Bird Sanctuary.

Founders and managers

Information concerning the early years of Globe is sketchy. Globe was established by the brothers Albert and J Walker, from England, in the first decades of the twentieth century prior to the establishment of the Ceramic Studio. Robert Leggat, a renowned local builder, bought Globe from the Walker brothers in the early 1940s.[88] George Elson originally managed the pottery on behalf of the Walker family, succeeded by a Mr Fourie and Izak A Perold, who managed Globe between 1949 and 1952. Mr Hoather was the director of Globe in the early 1950s. Hoather and Perold had a disagreement over management strategies and as a result Perold departed and established his own pottery, Dykor.[89] In the late 1950s the director of Globe Potteries was C J Reid.

Staff

Elsa Cameron (b.1903) worked as a decorator between 1949 and 1952. Douglas Portway (1922–1993) worked there between 1949 and 1950 on a part-time basis. Potters included Jan de Beer, Stoffel de Beer, Mr Aukamp and Kansamy (aka Robert or Bob) Chetty. Chetty started in about 1950. Mr Hattingh was responsible for glazing. Chetty and Aukamp left Globe in the early 1950s and later joined Perold at Dykor. Between September 1952 and January 1953, Esias Bosch worked as a decorator at Globe, painting 'bushman' motifs on ashtrays, vases and ornaments (Bosch & De Waal 1988:22).

Wares manufactured

Globe Potteries produced domestic wares, including vases, jugs, honey pots with lids, mugs and tankards, cups and saucers, gallon jars, condiment sets, teapots, platters and florist's items such as small baskets, bowls and troughs. It also made sets of flying swallows that could be attached to walls or similar flat surfaces.

An advert from 1925 indicates that at this period Globe had a very limited range of products, all of which were plain, undecorated, basic glazed kitchenware, e.g. monochrome-brown and brown-and-white lidded jars and pots in a variety of sizes, including half-gallon, three-quarter gallon, one gallon and two gallon pots. The wares featured a restrained glaze palette, and only used white, cream, Van Dyk brown and light and dark blue. Brown/white and brown/cream glaze combinations were frequently used on lidded wares.

In 1951 Globe was commissioned to produce shaving mugs for the Seagram Company. In the 1950s wares were glazed in green, blue-black and brown. By the mid-1950s, Globe had completely abandoned its signature gallon jars and teapots in favour of more contemporary forms and colours as well as hand-decorated wares. The pottery also produced souvenir vases, ornaments and crockery decorated with indigenous motifs, such as stylised renditions of San art. During this period Globe produced a highly stylised ornamental jug with a large exaggerated spout in various colours, among them a subtle black lustre glaze. Both the glaze and the form appear to prefigure wares produced by Perold at Dykor, notably in the use of a reflective pewter-like 'gun-metal black' glaze, and in terms of an exaggerated spout and stylised form. Globe also produced a beautiful stylised boat-like vessel (probably a vase) that was frequently glazed in a mildly speckled, liquid-blue or turquoise colour. These boat-shaped pieces are among the most successful of the wares created.

Globe Potteries is frequently criticised for copying Linnware's hallmark turquoise glaze. However, the extent of this 'copying' must not be exaggerated. Perold claimed that Globe's standard ware in the early 1950s was brown teapots, and not turquoise domestic ware,[90] and Esias Bosch recalls 'hundreds of tear-drop-shaped vases in a shrill copper-green, which sold like hot cakes in those days!' (Bosch & De Waal 1988:22).

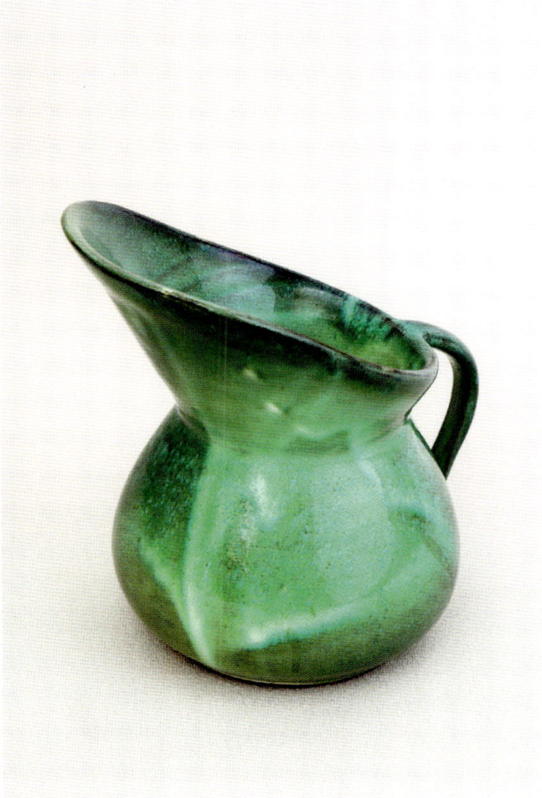

Globe | Vase in the shape of a jug | 165x155x87mm | Provenance: SHC Iziko | 93/691 | Marks: impressed Globe mark | Photograph by Natalie Field

Production methods

Initially most wares were hand-thrown using clay obtained from the nearby Pretoria Bird Park. As time progressed, an increasing percentage of wares were slip-cast, and under Perold a jigger was employed. Globe experienced many technical problems as a result of its old-fashioned, down-draught kilns.[91]

Brief history of the pottery

Globe Potteries remains something of a mystery and it seems as if it operated just below the radar of public opinion. This lack of information is particularly odd, given its longevity. It appears that Globe's isolation was entrenched by a complete lack of desire to engage with the media and other marketing structures, as well as its lack of participation in exhibitions and commercial fairs.[92]

As Globe operated for almost the same length of time and within a relatively close geographical proximity to Conrand (site of the Ceramic Studio and later Linnware), the relationship between the two potteries appears to have been terse. In 1926 Joan Methley described Globe's wares as 'a good type of cheap commercial ware' (Methley 1926:21). This statement comes hot on the heels of Globe winning a Gold Medal at the Pretoria Show in 1923 and 1924. In 1954, three decades later, in a similarly terse statement, the Linnware staff acknowledged Globe Potteries as a major national enterprise (South African Association of the Arts, 1954). One of the reasons for the difficult relationship between the two potteries is that of plagiarism. Globe copied Linnware's distinctive turquoise glazes. The pottery also copied Zaalberg Potterij's sgraffito 'bushman' motifs.

Like Linnware, Globe failed to stay ahead and public taste evolved fast among post-war, décor-conscious baby-boomers. In addition, Globe's management had failed to revamp antiquated fabrication methods and production was compromised by unreliable down-draught kilns. The final restructuring of their production in 1956 was hopelessly too late. In 1957 Globe was sold and amalgamated with Elwood Pottery.

Marks

A variety of marks were applied to the base, which was coated in a white or transparent glaze:

- The bases of wares usually had a mark with the company's name, 'Globe'.
- A raised moulded mark 'Globe' appears on some cast wares.
- Certain industrial wares were marked with an impressed stamp, 'Globe Potteries, Pretoria'.
- Some wares were unmarked.

Biographies

BOSCH, Esias (1923–2010)

One of the most important studio potters in South Africa (Bosch & De Waal 1988), Bosch was trained as an art teacher at the Art School, Johannesburg, and was awarded a bursary to study pottery at the Central School of Art, London. Bosch worked for six months at Winchcombe in 1952 before his return to South Africa in September of that year. Working as a decorator at Globe between September 1952 and January 1953 at Globe, he painted 'bushman' motifs on ashtrays, vases and ornaments. He subsequently taught for a few years before opening his own studio in White River, where he spent most of his life. His work is collected nationally and internationally. Among other important commissions, Bosch is well-known for his large mural that was commissioned for the former Jan Smuts Airport, Johannesburg.

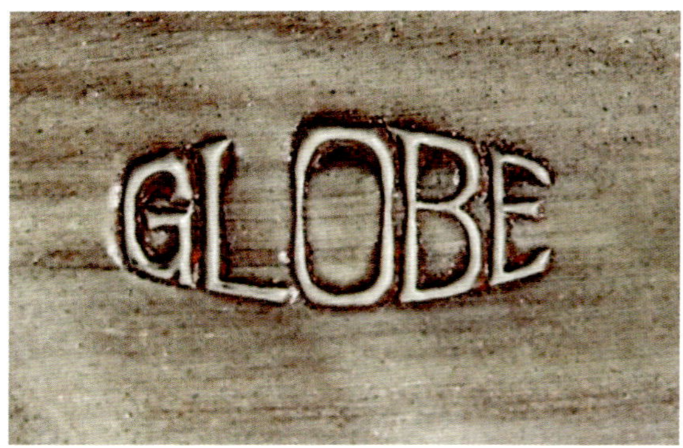

Globe | Maker's mark | Oval stamp, 'Globe' | Photograph by Natalie Field

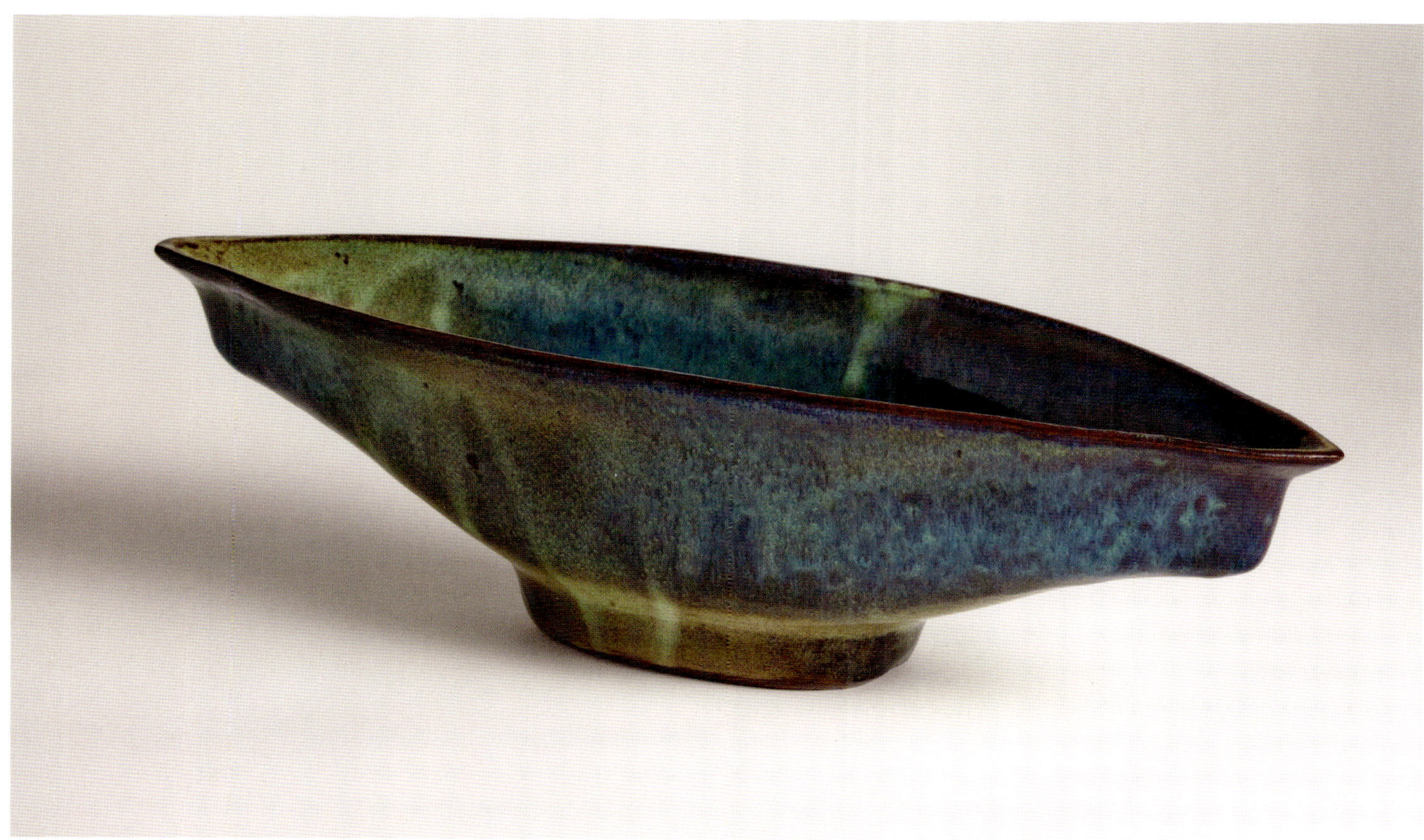

Globe | Bowl in the form of a stylised boat | 93x355x155mm | Provenance: Wendy Gers | Marks: unglazed foot-ring, white glazed base, impressed mark, 'Globe' | Photograph by Damien Artus

PORTWAY, Douglas (1922–1993)
Born in Johannesburg, Portway attended art school in the 1940s and taught at the University of the Witwatersrand. Portway worked for Globe between 1949 and 1950 as a decorator on a part-time basis. After his first solo exhibition in 1945, Portway was the first South African recipient of a travel grant from the Institute of International Education. In subsequent years the artist travelled in the USA, the UK and Europe, and ultimately settled in St Ives where he was associated with artists involved in the British Abstract movement of the 1950s and 1960s. Portway's work is to be found in international public collections, including the Tate Gallery, London; the Victoria and Albert Museum, London; and the Scottish Gallery of Modern Art, Edinburgh.

Globe | Coffee set | Coffee pot and lid (measured together) 163x193x116mm; milk jug 93x115x79mm; cups (6) all approximately 56x82x71mm; saucers (6) all approximately 20x132x50mm | Provenance: TAG | 2953/7/11 (1 – 15) | Marks: coffee pot and lid, unmarked; milk jug, inscription on base: GLOBE (incised/imprinted); cups, inscription on base: 4 cups have GLOBE (incised/imprinted) two 2 cups are unmarked; saucers, unmarked | Photograph by Justin James | © TAG

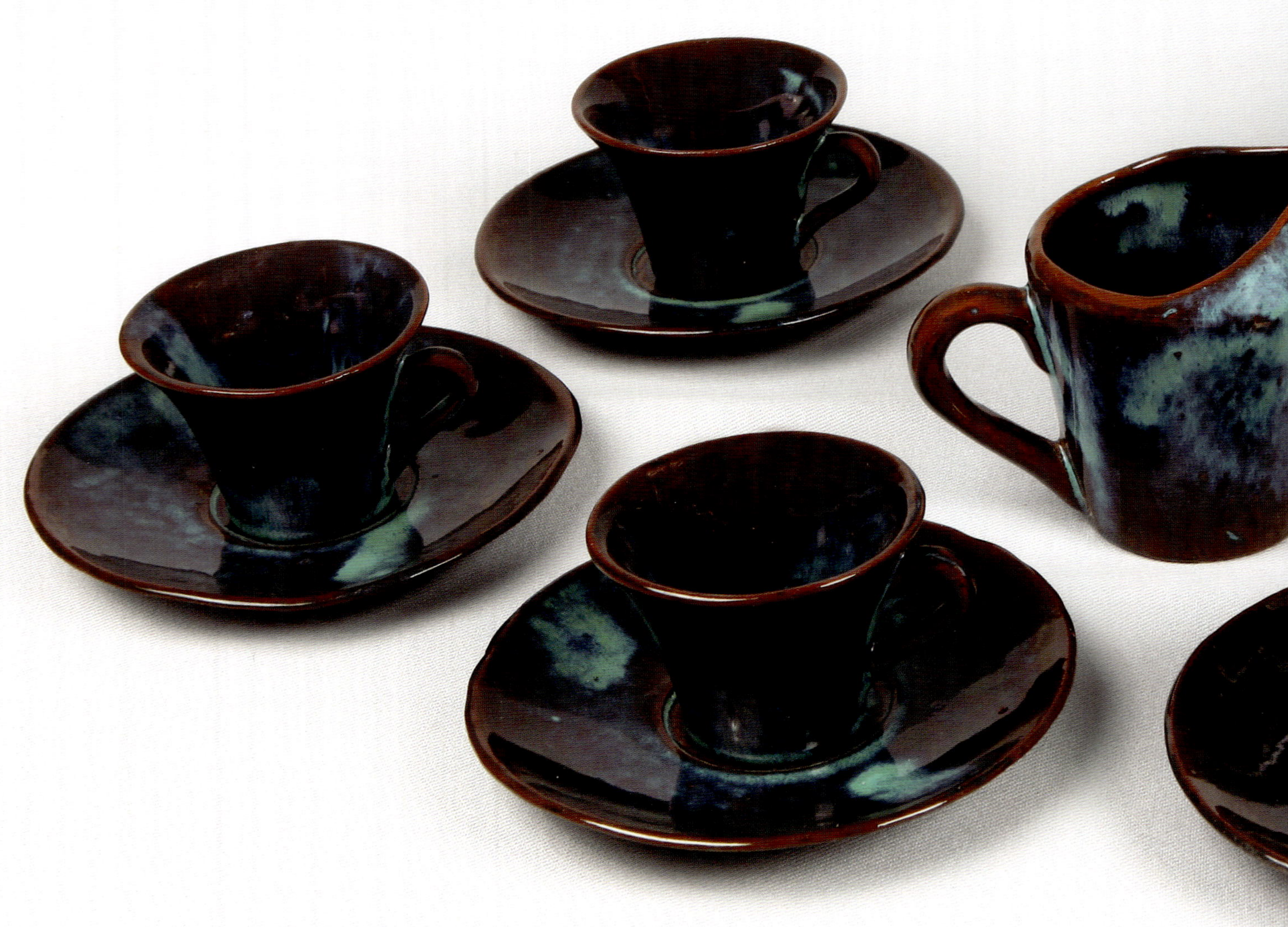

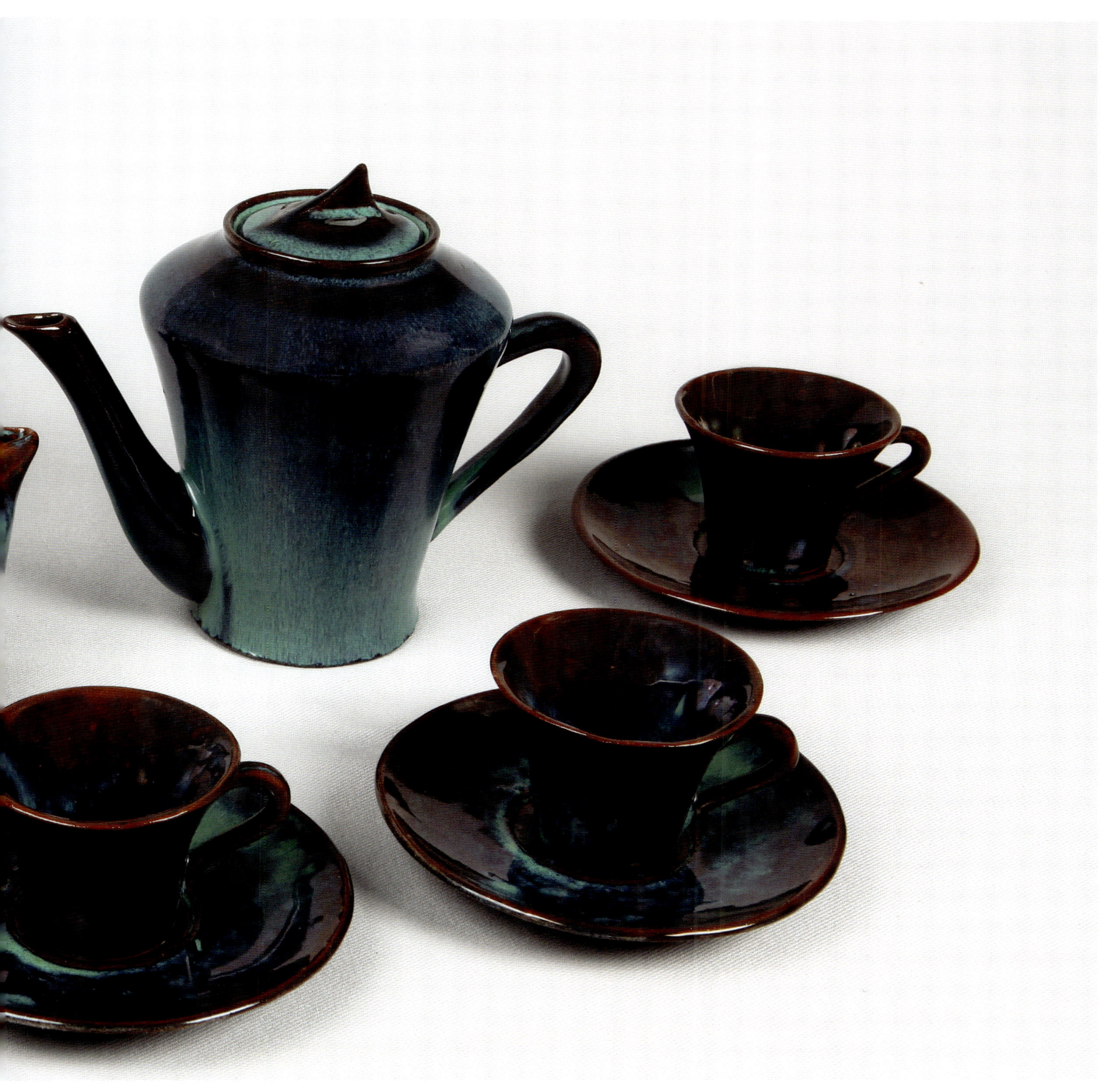

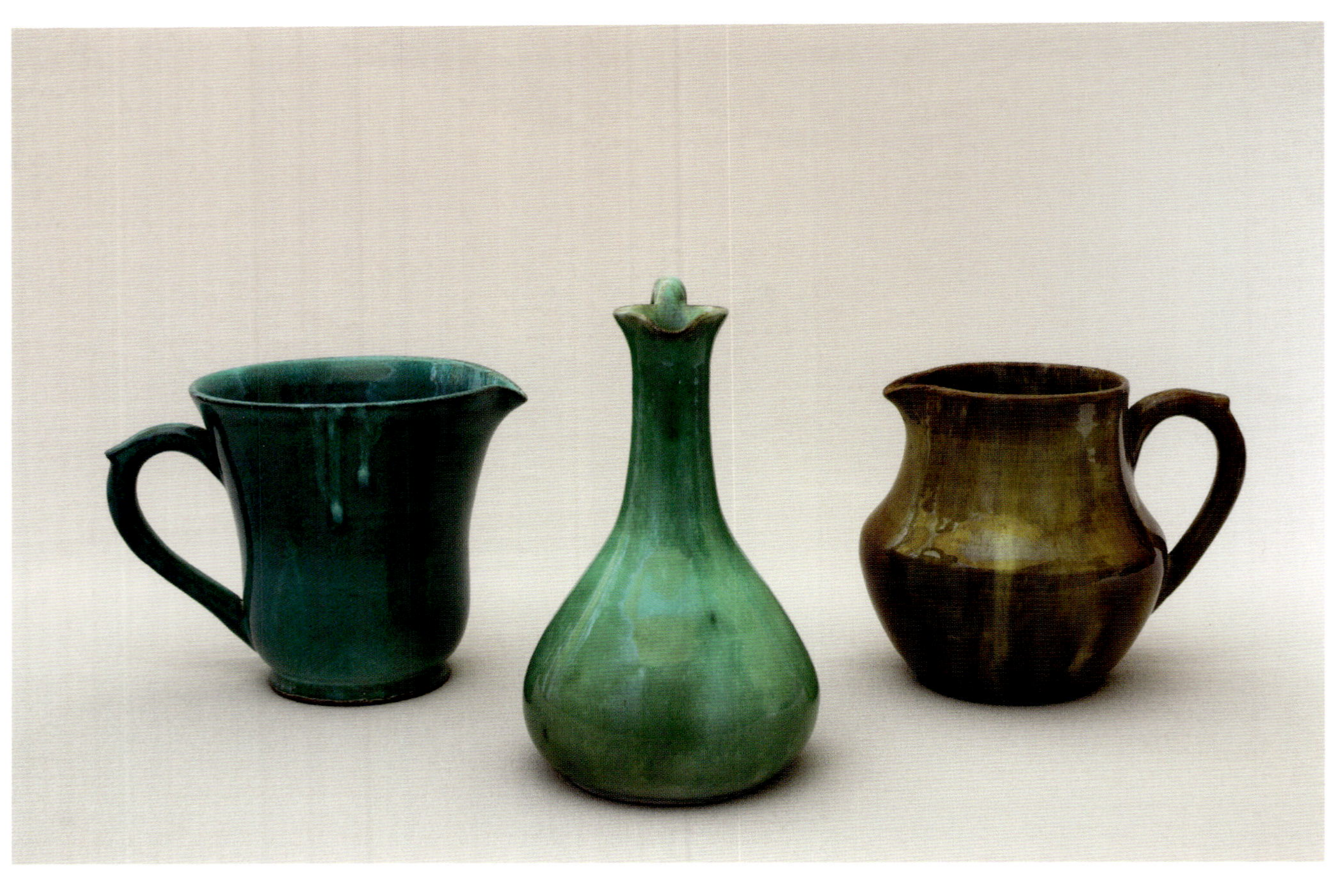

Globe | Two pitchers and one bulbous jug | From left: 180x163x100mm; 250x50x100mm; 180x110x100mm | Provenance: Tatham Art Gallery | 2439/06; 2345/06; 2416/06 | Marks: white glazed base with impressed Globe stamp visible under glaze; white glazed base with impressed Globe stamp visible under glaze; ochre glazed base with impressed Globe stamp visible under glaze | Photograph by Natalie Field

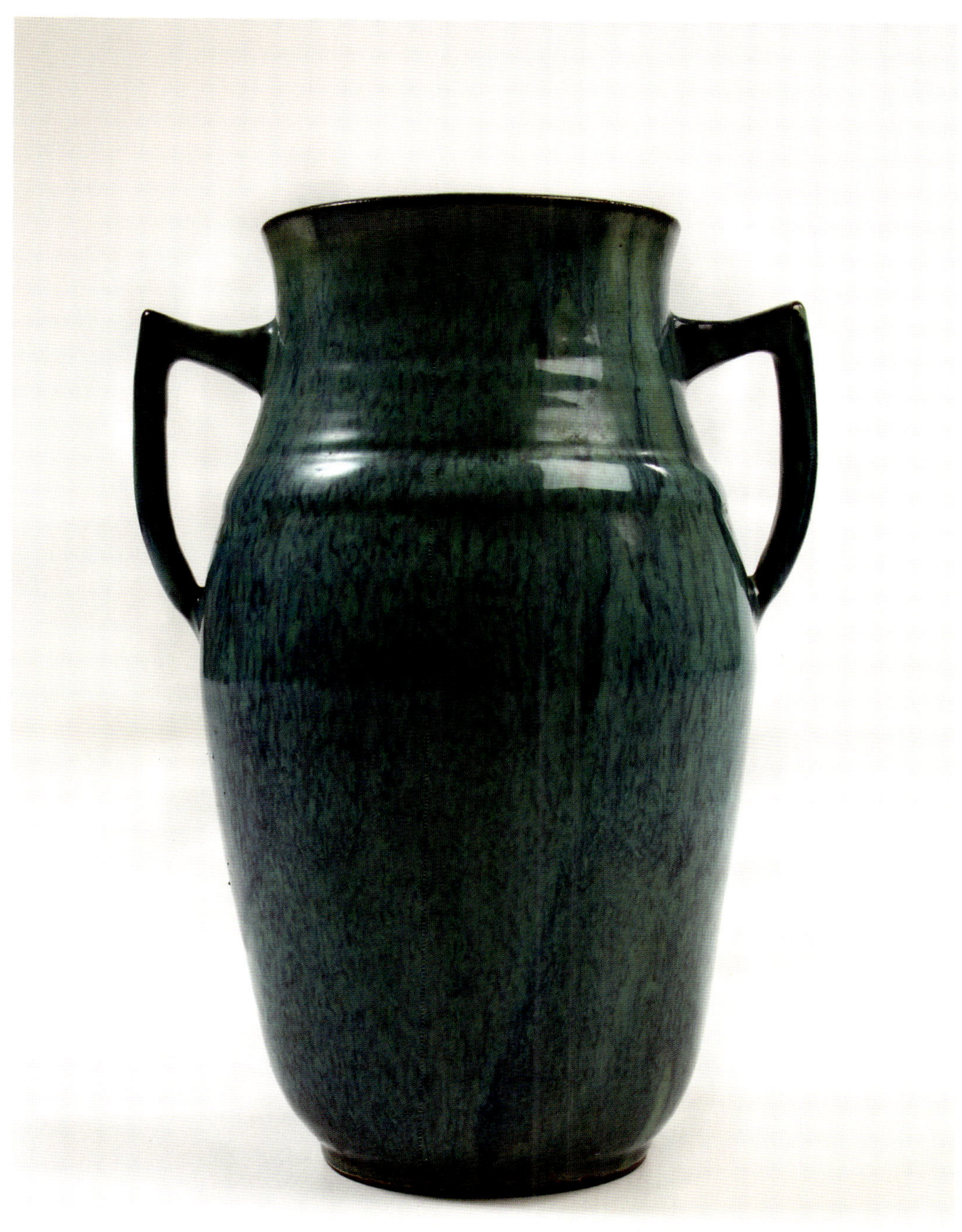

Globe | Tall urn-shaped vase with pointed handles, mottled blue | 290x190x150mm | Provenance: Wilhelm Van Rensburg | Marks: GLOBE stamp | Photograph by Micha Birch Hannemann

Grahamstown Pottery (1922–1965, 1968–1985); Drostdy Ware (1948–1965, 1968–1985)

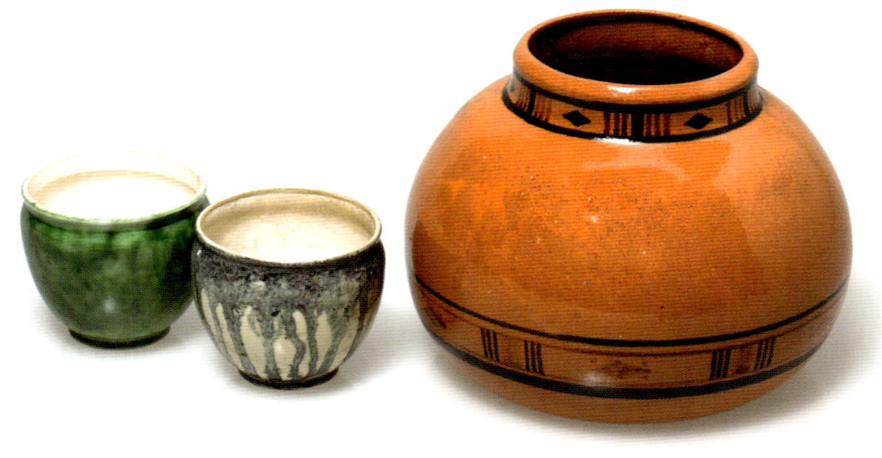

F W Armstrong | Group of three vases | From left: small vase with exterior glazed leaf green and unglazed pale cream interior; small vase with grey-blue drip glaze decoration on exterior and unglazed pale cream interior; pot-bellied vase, decorated with black parallel lines, black diamonds within orange/brown vertical lines, design echoed near base at broad part, terracotta body with clear glaze | From left: 65x75mm; 65x75mm; 137x95x126mm | Provenance: Museum Africa, Johannesburg | MA 1972-4162; MA 1952-1500; MA 1972-4164 | Marks: from left: signed in black on centre of the base 'F.W. Armstrong' and to the side of the base 'FWA GT 1922'; signed on base in black 'F.W Armstrong' and to side 'FWA GT 1926'; signed in black on base 'F W Armstrong' and at edge 'FW GT 1923', incised initials in base 'FW' | Photograph courtesy of Museum Africa, Johannesburg

Location

The pottery was initially located in the home of Frederick William and Ruth Armstrong in Grahamstown, but later moved to industrial premises.

Founder

Professor Frederick William Armstrong (1875–1969)

Directors

1922–1938 – Frederick William Armstrong and his wife Ruth Beatrice Armstrong
1938–1948 – Jürgen Hamburger
1948–ca.1965 – Norman Steele-Gray
1965–1985 – Alwyn Murray

Staff

Under Steele-Gray, France Marot was the main designer and the superintendent of the art department was Hester Locke. Drostdy Ware primarily employed women as decorators,[93] including Sylvia Baxter, Patricia Butterworth, Kay Cope-Christy, Susan Douglas, Jane Krone, Rosalie Levinsohn, Margaret Scott, Leila P Simpson and Annette Southey. Male decorators included Anthony Tarr and Allan Butterworth. Unidentified decorators include AEB, CB, CPRS, DMT, EBT, EMGS, GB, GdeB, GLC, JB, JF, JPC, LMS, MP, ON, PAG, PRG, SP and SLC. The pottery commissioned images from various freelance illustrators and cartoonists such as Robert (Bob) Connolly and Gerard de Witt. Wilfred Pryce-Lewis was a mouldmaker in the 1950s. Titch Butterworth and Norman Walters worked in production. Alfred Adams and Sam Bloor were employed as works managers and John Edwards (Lucky Bean Farm) and Ludos de Pian as chemists.

Wares manufactured

Under Armstrong the pottery produced small decorative wares, including vases and bowls as well as vases autographed by famous people, including H R H Edward, the Earl of Athlone and Dr D F Malan. The range of wares produced expanded considerably under Steele-Gray, and the pottery produced commercial and artistic ceramics, including figurines, chargers, individual decorated tiles and tile panels, as well as promotional and commemorative wares.

Production methods

Under Armstrong wares were hand-thrown using local clay and were initially fired in the kilns of the local brickfield. Under Steele-Gray the wares were slip-cast or made with jiggers and jolleys. Methods used to apply decorative motifs to wares evolved over time and included sgraffito, hand-painting,[94] hand-coloured transfers,[95] homemade glaze pastels, homemade screen-printed transfers[96] and imported commercially manufactured, screen-printed-on glaze transfers.[97]

Brief history of the pottery

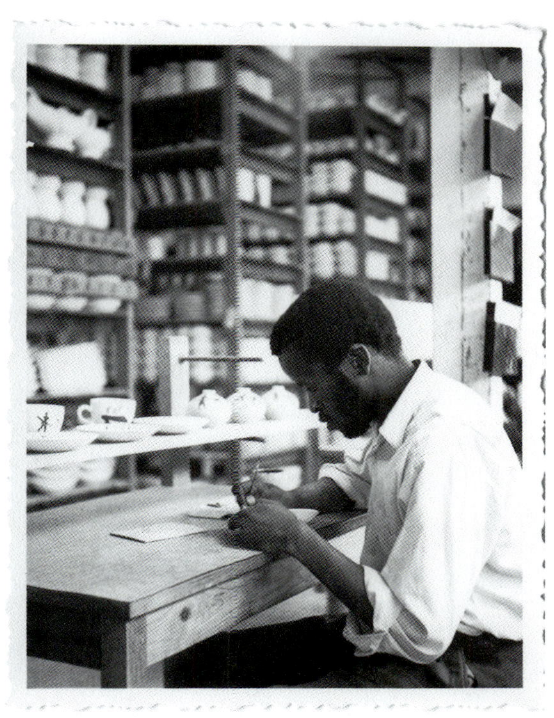

Grahamstown Pottery | Unidentified decorator | Provenance: Wendy Gers, ex Hester Locke | Photograph by Hester Locke

In 1909 Armstrong discovered some deposits of pure white clay in the Grahamstown brickfields. Disregarding negative responses from his friends in England, Armstrong and his wife Ruth pioneered the production of art pottery in Grahamstown. While the exact date of the establishment of Grahamstown Pottery is unclear, in 1922 Armstrong signed a lease with the Grahamstown Municipality for ten acres of clay-bearing land for 30 years, and officially founded the business. Despite basic facilities, Armstrong was awarded a gold medal the following year at the Pretoria Society of Agriculture and Industries show. Armstrong received similar awards from the Central Agricultural Society, Bloemfontein in 1922 and from the Port Elizabeth Agricultural Society Show in 1923. Armstrong exhibited about 100 pieces of pottery at the 1934 British Empire Exhibition and was awarded a gold medal.

In 1925 Armstrong, in association with the Grahamstown Chamber of Commerce, presented an illuminated address and submitted a petition to H R H Edward, the Prince of Wales, who was then touring South Africa. Armstrong requested permission for Grahamstown Pottery to use the prefix 'Royal' and rename the pottery 'The Royal Grahamstown Pottery'. Despite Armstrong's earnest lobbying, this authorisation was denied in 1932.[98] Theories abound regarding the size and level of commercial success of the original Grahamstown Pottery. According to Leta Hill, Armstrong produced 'good, decorative pottery on a commercial scale'.[99]

In 1938 Armstrong sold the pottery to Jürgen Hamburger, who operated the pottery under the name of Grahamstown Pottery until 1948, when he sold his interests in the company to Norman Steele-Gray. Very little is known about the pottery's history under Hamburger, except that he entered into a partnership

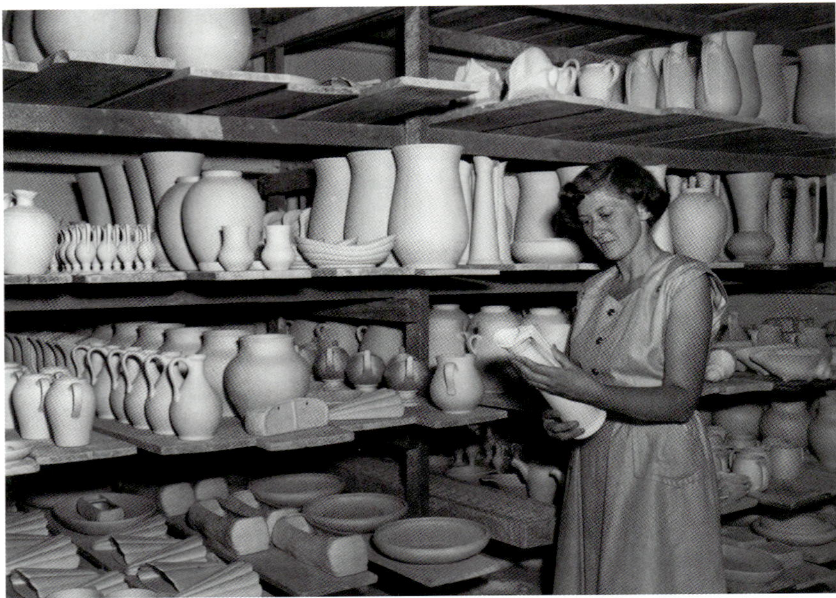

Grahamstown Pottery | Hester Locke | Provenance: Wendy Gers, ex Hester Locke | Photograph courtesy of Hester Locke

with Mr Cornforth, who provided capital for the construction of an industrial tunnel kiln in 1940. According to Steele-Gray, under Hamburger the pottery's management was disorganised and the company's production methods were inefficient.

Steele-Gray began new lines: industrial porcelain for electrical components, Cookery Nook Kitchenware (inexpensive monochrome functional 'oven-to-table' crockery, including coffee and early morning tea sets, soup and hors d'oeuvres sets, mugs and jugs), promotional pottery and Drostdy Ware utilitarian and decorative ceramics decorated with distinctly South African imagery (including decorative masks, wall vases, vases, 'native' figurines, 'bushman' wares, tiles, chargers and animal ornaments). These changes soon paid dividends: when Steele-Gray took over in 1948 the company had between 20 and 30 staff; between 1948 and 1955 its output increased 40 times and employed a staff of 200.

In the late 1940s Drostdy Ware produced its finest range of images, the 'Sgraffito' series, which displayed strength of design and elegant sgraffito renditions of diverse images. The range included images of South African wildlife (such as springbok, impala, elephant and giraffe), native studies, an image of three tropical fish and a rose). According to Locke, the variety of Drostdy's sgraffito decoration allowed customers to 'mix and match' images that appealed to them. This 'mix and match' sensibility was current in contemporary interior decor trends. Drostdy Ware also manufactured decorative tiles bearing motifs derived from San parietal art, native studies, indigenous flora and African wildlife. Most of these tiles were commercial blanks manufactured by Pilkington.[100]

In the early 1950s Drostdy Ware was extensively exhibited at festivals, trade and gift fairs, such as the 1953 Rhodes Centenary Festival in Bulawayo, Rhodesia, and the South African Association of Arts Exhibition, Cape Town in February 1950. From 1952 to 1955, Drostdy Ware won three consecutive gold medals for its stand at the Rand Easter Show in Johannesburg.

In the late 1940s and early 1950s Grahamstown Pottery's largest categories of corporate customers were the various independent beer breweries.[101] But in 1956 South African Breweries (SAB) attained monopoly with various mergers, closed down all its tied houses,[102] and cut its advertising budget for promotional pottery by 30 per cent. This move had a dire effect on Grahamstown Pottery as it could not survive financially without the business of the various independent breweries, forcing it to diversify its output. It thus began producing oven-to-table ware and simple, inexpensive kitchenware and teaware, known as 'Cookery Nook Kitchenware', with a loan from the South African Industrial Development Corporation to finance this diversification.[103]

A decade later, in 1965, the business went into provisional liquidation, unable to compete with inexpensive imports from America, China and Japan. In 1968 Continental China purchased the firm and restructured it, keeping the original name. The new management cut down the range of wares and produced cheap, popular coffee mugs, teacups and saucers, and side plates along with wood coasters and paper plates. In the early 1970s it employed approximately 250 individuals, the majority of whom were female. However, the company's financial situation was bleak and Continental China closed down their operations in Grahamstown in 1985.[104]

Over the decades Grahamstown Pottery has manufactured an extremely large diversity of wares, including industrial cookware, electrical components, household ornaments, decorated tiles, advertising wares, special commissions and artistic wares. The pottery is significant because of the considerable flexibility the staff displayed when faced with various financial and aesthetic problems. They repeatedly re-invented themselves, and restructured their production in response to changes in the market.

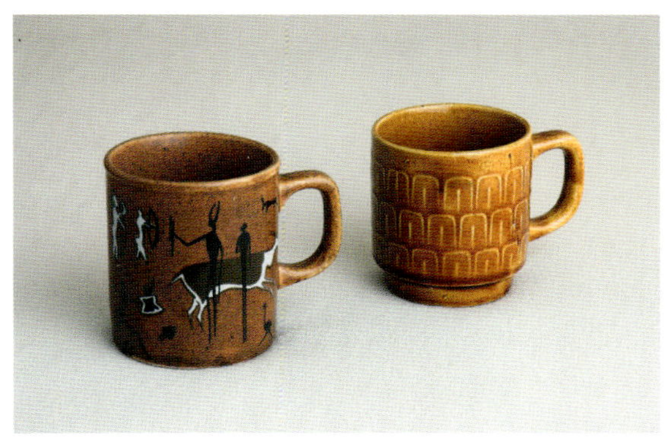

Grahamstown Potteries | Two coffee cups | 90x75x70mm | Provenance: TAG | 2333/6 | Marks: brown glazed bases with Grahamstown Potteries, RSA | Photograph by Natalie Field

The application of industrial technology after 1968 allied it with the large production factories in Britain. However, the Drostdy decorators were constantly striving to improve the quality of their hand-decorated wares and their productivity. Furthermore, Drostdy's designers and decorators avoided adopting a single generic design formula and rather produced hundreds of diverse, frequently intricate, competent and interesting images and forms. Drostdy Ware's early sgraffito Africana series is among their most significant. The native studies in this series speak lyrically and eloquently of the 1950s perceptions and concerns of liberal white middle-class women, in an isolated settler town, located on the cusp of the independent Xhosa state of the Ciskei.[105] Various works depicted romanticised images of African women engaged in domestic pursuits, while a limited number of wares depicted spectacularised views of African males. However, clichéd representations were not all-pervasive in the oeuvre of the studio. The wares decorated by Leila Simpson attested to contemporary realities and the domestic drudgery experienced by the majority of contemporary African women, thereby subverting the dominant paradigm. Finally, Drostdy's various series of wares depicting indigenous flora, fauna, ichthyology and San parietal art tell a heartwarming tale of wonder in respect to their local cultural heritage and celebrate national biodiversity.

Marks

1922–1938

Wares bear dark hand-painted glaze marks on the base with two sets of interwoven initials 'F W A' and 'G T' and a date. This is accompanied by the signature, 'F.W. Armstrong'.

1938–1948

Works made under Hamburger do not feature distinctive maker's marks, but some had inscriptions, e.g. a set of three hand-thrown turquoise glazed mugs that were commissioned as trophies by the Grahamstown Lawn Tennis Club in 1939 and 1940. They are marked 'G.L.T.C MENS DOUBLES HANDICAP 1940 M. DOLD'; 'G.L.T.C MENS DOUBLES 1939 M. DOLD' and 'MIXED DOUBLES 1940 M. DOLD' that commemorated the achievements of the late Melvin Dold.

1948–ca.1965

Many different maker's marks were applied, and often various marking methods were applied simultaneuosly.

Hand-painted

Elaborate hand-painted titles describe various early artistic wares such as the sgraffito African series, San parietal art series, indigenous flower series, and other artistic wares that feature detailed hand-decoration. These titles are used in conjunction with a transfer mark and a moulded mark. For example, a charger with sgraffito decoration depicting a Xhosa woman and five huts is marked with an impressed stamp, 'Drostdy' and has hand-painted marks: 'Kay Duncan. Hand decorated – Xhosa woman – No 1000 NX. Y. Drostdy Ware, Made in South Africa'.

Glaze stamps

Glaze stamp mark include 'Drostdy Ware, Made in South Africa. Grahamstown Potteries Ltd.'; 'Drostdy Ware, Made in South Africa' and 'Drostdy Ware'.

Sgraffito

Sgraffito marks include 'Drostdy Hand Decorated South Africa' and 'Drostdy Ware. Made in South Africa'.

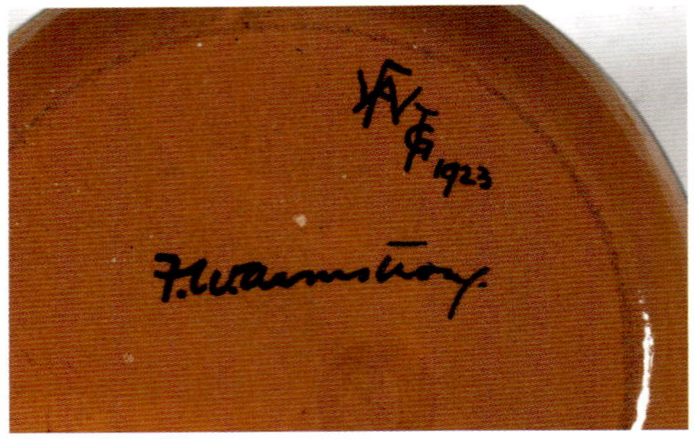

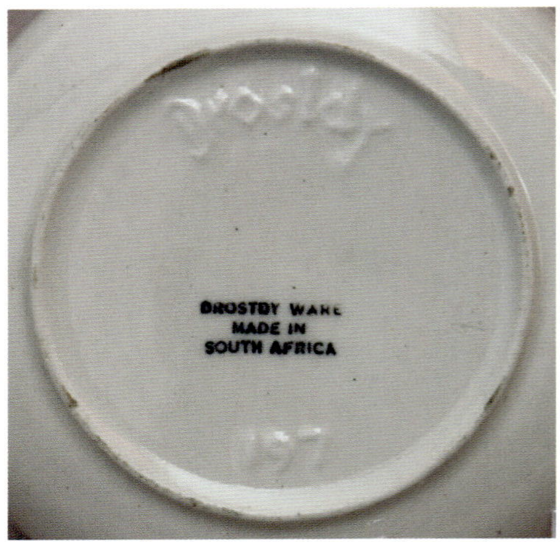

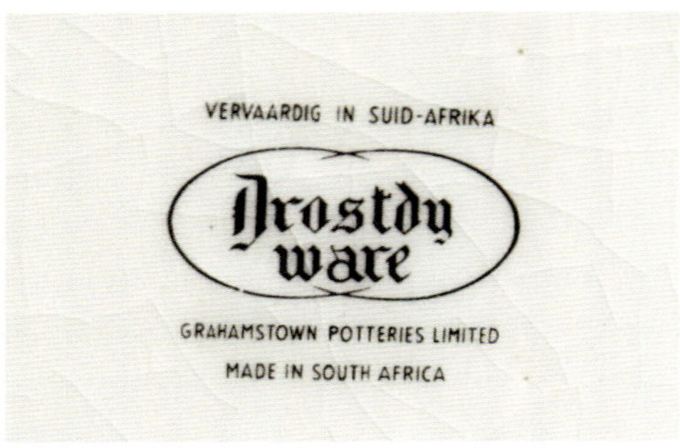

TOP: Grahamstown Pottery | Maker's mark | Hand-painted glaze mark with two sets of interwoven initials 'F W A' and 'G T' and '1923' | F W Armstrong | Photograph courtesy of Museum Africa, Johannesburg

MIDDLE: Grahamstown Pottery, Drostdy Ware | Maker's mark | Glaze stamp, 'Drostdy Ware Made in South Africa' | Photograph by Natalie Field

BOTTOM: Grahamstown Pottery, Drostdy Ware | Maker's mark | Transfer, 'Vervaardin in Suid-Afrika, Drostdy Ware, Grahamstown Potteries Limited, Made in South Africa' | Photograph by Natalie Field

Transfers

Transfer marks include 'Grahamstown Pottery'; 'Grahamstown Drostdy Ware'; 'Grahamstown Potteries, RSA'; 'Vervaardig in Suid-Afrika, Drostdy Ware, Grahamstown Potteries Limited, Made in South Africa' and 'Made in South Africa. Grahamstown Potteries Ltd.'.

Cast marks

Raised as well as relief cast marks include 'Drostdy' and 'GP Ltd', which were sometimes accompanied by a numerical or alpha-numerical code, e.g. '337' or '168c'.

Stickers

A variety of stickers were used. A silver-and-black foil sticker in the form of an inverted triangle, containing 'Drostdy Ware' was used on some early wares. The pottery also used two oval-shaped stickers with undulating borders, 'Grahamstown Potteries Limited, Drostdy Ware, Grahamstown CP'. One of these stickers was made of green-and-gold foil, the other consisted of black-and-gold foil. 'Cookery Nook' ware was marked with a foil sticker in the form of a rolling pin, 'Cookery Nook Kitchen Ware' (Illus. Kerrod 2010:64).

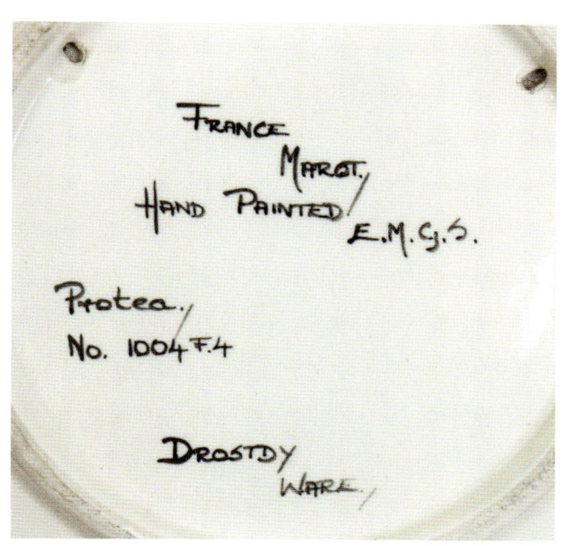

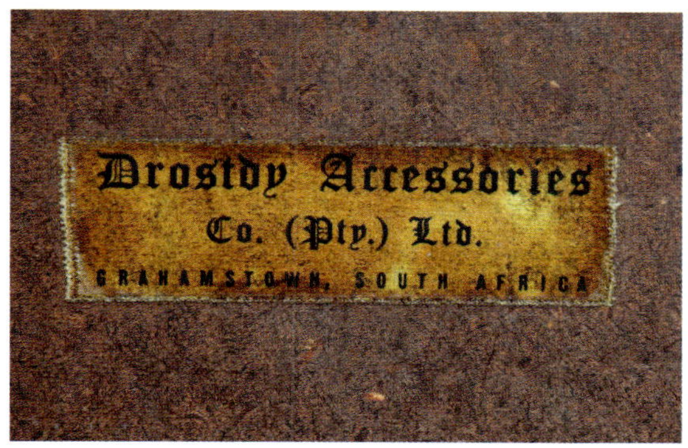

TOP: Drostdy Ware | Maker's mark | Painted glaze marks, 'France Marot.' | Hand painted E.M.G.S. Protea No 1004. F4. Drostdy Ware' | Photograph by Natalie Field

BOTTOM: Grahamstown Pottery, Drostdy Ware | Maker's mark | Adhesive tape, 'Drostdy Accessories Co. (Pty.) Ltd. Grahamstown, South Africa' | Photograph by Natalie Field

1968–1985

Cast marks

Under Continental, Grahamstown Pottery used a raised cast mark, 'GP'.

Adhesive tape

Customised adhesive tape marked with 'Drostdy Accessories, Co. [Pty.] Ltd. Grahamstown South Africa'.

Transfers

In the 1980s, a double circle transfer mark, 'Drostdy Stonecraft', was used, often accompanied by the SABS logo and 'Dishwasher proof, oven proof, hand decorated, made in SA'.

Select commissions

Commemorative wares include a *kommetjie* for the German Settlers Centenary Committee (1958), a plate for Selborne College's golden jubilee (1957), and a mug for the Friends of Rhodesia Association.[106] In 1953 a limited edition of 50 coronation orbs, resembling ladies' powder containers, was produced. This was sent to Queen Elizabeth II and to prominent local and national politicians and museums.[107]

Grahamstown Pottery's largest corporate customers were the various independent southern African beer breweries for whom it produced promotional wares such as tankards, jugs and ashtrays. Some of these tankards are wonderfully whimsical, such as stag, tusker and castle rendered in caricature. Drostdy Ware also produced some very basic promotional wares for other liquor companies, including a pitcher for 'Queen Anne, Rare Scotch Whisky' and a tankard for 'Green, Limosin Brandy'.

Other promotional wares included ashtrays depicting 'The Big Hole, De Beers Diamond Mines, Kimberley'; and a series of small plates entitled 'Landmarks of Grahamstown'. In the late 1950s and early 1960s Drostdy Ware produced ashtrays and bowls depicting landmark modern buildings in Port Elizabeth.[108] It also produced promotional ware for institutions including South African Airways, the Kruger National Park, the municipalities of Mossel Bay and George, Delta Motors, Potchefstroom University, the Ichthyology Department at Rhodes University,[109] the South African Rock Lobster Association (1958), the 'South African Legion Congress, Port Elizabeth' and the South African Motor Assemblers and Distributors (SAMAD).[110]

Biographies

ADAMS, Alfred

Adams was employed as works manager at Grahamstown Pottery from 1948–1953. Adams was previously employed for 23 years as a potter at Bullers, Minton, England.

ARMSTRONG, Frederick William (1875–1969)

Armstrong was born in 1875 in Sunderland, Durham, England into a large family of draughtsmen, art masters and artists, and was apprenticed in 1890 as an art pupil in Bath Lane School (now Rutherford College), Newcastle-on-Tyne. After gaining an art teacher's and then an art master's certificate, he was appointed art master at Bede School. In 1898 he was awarded a scholarship for the Royal College of Art, London. He graduated with distinction and won national awards, including a silver medal, a bronze medal, five book prizes and three Queen's prizes.

Armstrong was posted to South Africa in 1904, where he was appointed headmaster of the Grahamstown School of Art, the first South African tertiary art school. He taught there until 1923, when the school was incorporated into Rhodes University College, and was awarded a professorship by the University of South Africa. He later became head of the Department of Fine Arts at Rhodes University. After retirement, from 1928 to 1933, Armstrong was principal of the art school at the Johannesburg Technical College and also the president of the South African Institute of Art.

Armstrong was a multi-talented artist, well-known for his oil and water-colour landscape paintings and sculptures. In 1913 he produced stained-glass windows of the Grahamstown Settlers Memorial, the first to be made in South Africa, for the Greathead Memorial Church, Grahamstown; the chancel screen in St Bartholomew's Church, Grahamstown and memorial plaques in

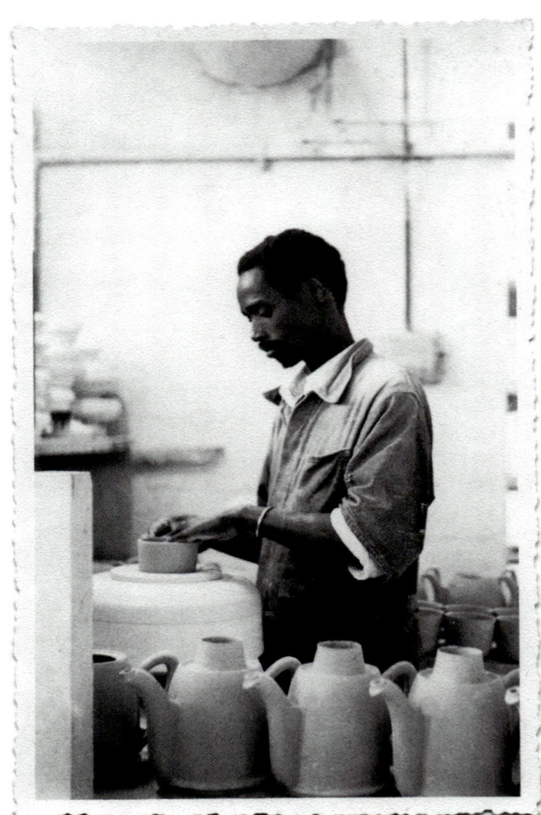

Grahamstown Pottery, Drostdy Ware | Unidentified worker in the slip-casting division | Provenance: Wendy Gers, ex Hester Locke | Photograph by Hester Locke

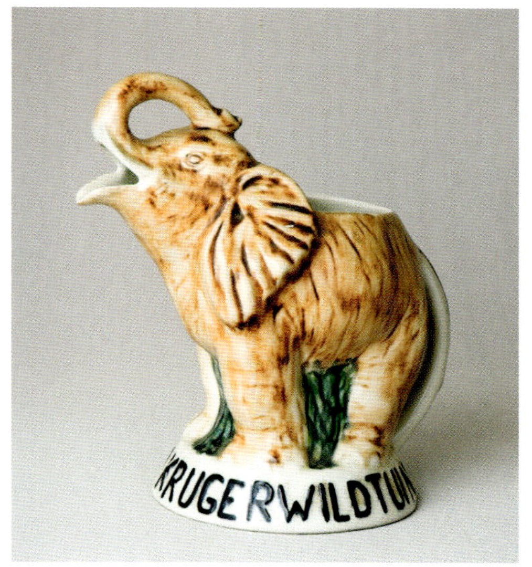

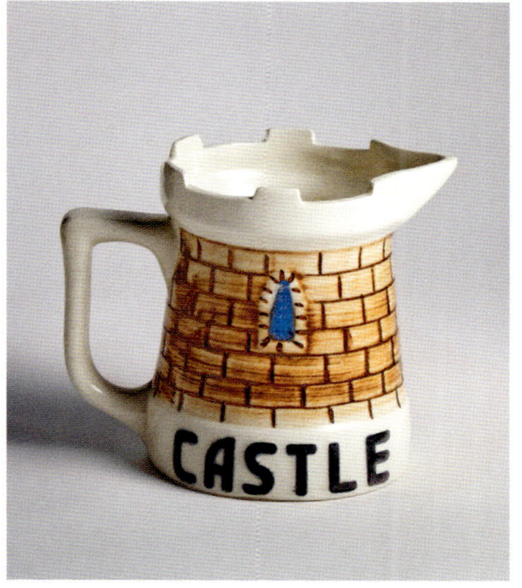

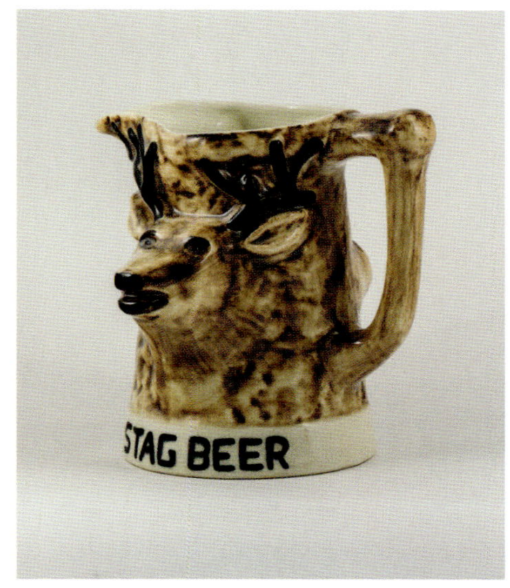

ABOVE: Grahamstown Pottery, Drostdy Ware | Pitcher in the form of an elephant | 230x200x100mm [measurements of form, not lip] | Provenance: TAG | 2333/06 | Marks: base glazed with a transparent glaze, black glaze stamp, 'Drosty Ware, made in South Africa', separate black glaze stamp, 'Krugerwild / Kruger P' | Photograph by Natalie Field

MIDDLE: Grahamstown Pottery, Drostdy Ware | Pitcher in the form of a castle | 127x185x127mm | Provenance: Wendy Gers | Marks: glaze stamp marking, 'Drostdy Ware, Made in South Africa. Grahamstown Potteries Ltd' | Photograph by Damien Artus

RIGHT: Grahamstown Pottery, Drostdy Ware | Pitcher in the form of a stag | 190x190x125mm | Provenance: Wendy Gers | Marks: glaze stamp marking, 'Drostdy Ware, Made in South Africa. Grahamstown Potteries Ltd' | Photograph by Damien Artus

St Andrew's College Chapel, Grahamstown. Other public commissions include a bronze relief panel of Cecil John Rhodes for the Bulawayo Town Hall and a bust of Sir William Hoy for the Johannesburg railway station foyer in 1932. He exhibited his paintings in Grahamstown, Springs and Bulawayo. He designed the Grahamstown School of Art and the Victoria Falls and Zimbabwe exhibits at the Empire Exhibition, Johannesburg in 1936. The Grahamstown Corporation commissioned Armstrong to produce an illuminated souvenir of the Declaration of Peace of World War I. Other commissions included addresses for the Royal Family on their visit in 1947 and for the Grahamstown Centenary. Armstrong produced the first AA maps of the Eastern Province.

Upon his 80th birthday Armstrong mused, 'You know. I wish I could have concentrated on pottery. I think I might have become quite good at it.'[111] His works are in various public and private collections including the Grahamstown Council Chamber, the Albany Museum and Art Gallery, Grahamstown and Museum Africa, Johannesburg.

BLOOR, Sam

Bloor was a graduate of, and part-time lecturer at, the North Staffordshire Technical College. He was employed as works manager at the Spode Works, Staffordshire, England before becoming works manager at Grahamstown Pottery.

CONNOLLY, Robert (aka Bob) James (1907–1981)

Bob Connolly,[112] a freelance illustrator and cartoonist for *Rand Daily Mail*, designed cartoons for Crescent Potteries from approximately 1965 to 1973. Several of his cartoons were made into transfers and applied to beer mugs, like the 'Sabrina and friends' series.

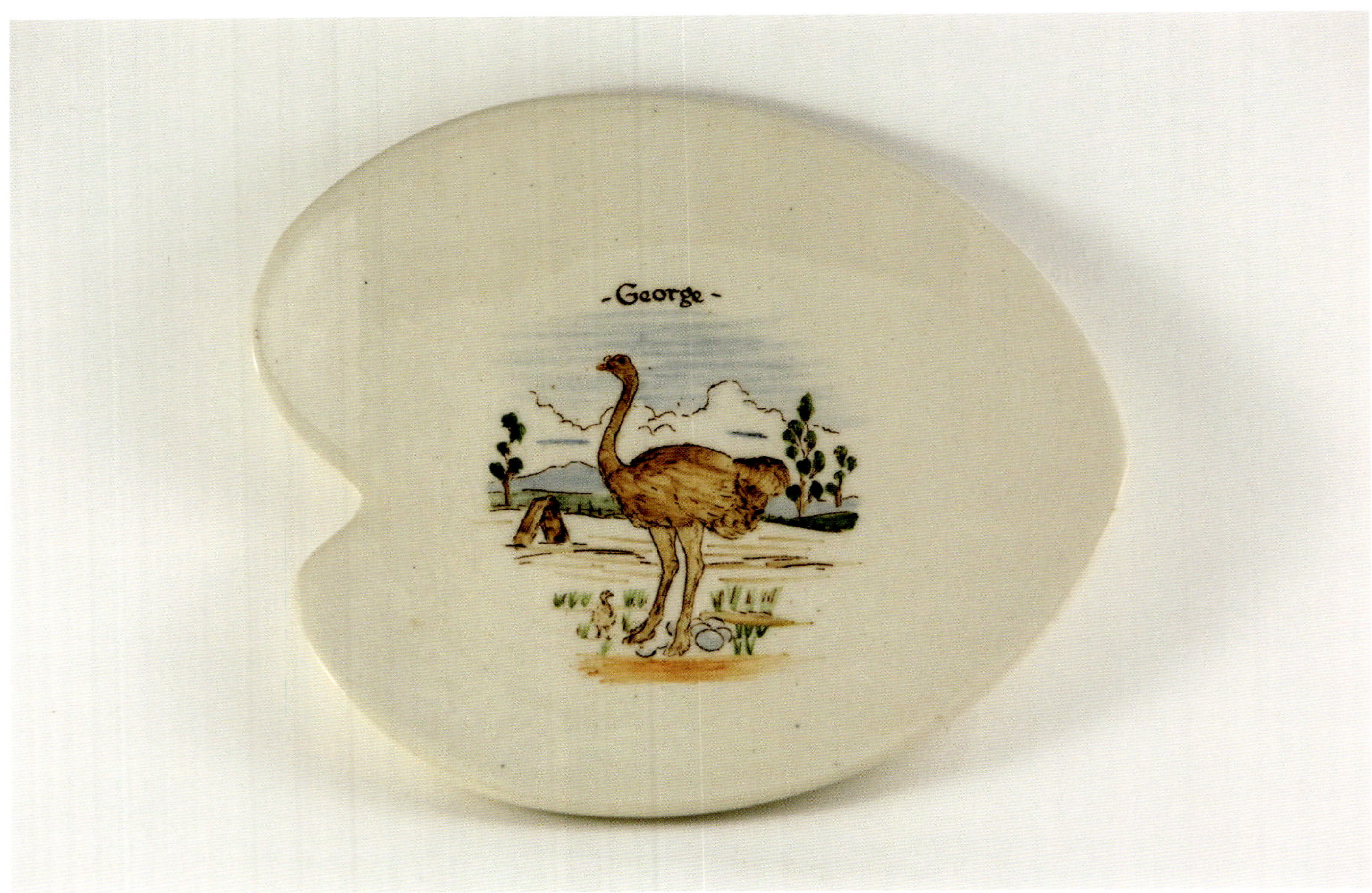

Grahamstown Pottery, Drostdy Ware | Palette-shaped plate decorated with an ostrich and 'George' | 155x175x20mm | Provenance: Wendy Gers | Marks: impressed stamp, 'DROSTDY', stamped glaze marks, 'Drostdy Ware, Made in South Africa' | Photograph by Damien Artus

COPE-CHRISTY, Kay
Kay Cope-Christy worked as a paintress for Drostdy Ware, decorating numerous wares in the 'bushman' series and initialling them with KCC on the base.

DE PIAN, Ludos
Ludos de Pian was employed as a chemist at Grahamstown Pottery after the departure of John Edwards.

DE WITT, Gerard
A freelance artist, Gerard de Witt designed transfers for Grahamstown Pottery.

DUNCAN, Kay A
Kay Duncan was a graduate of the Department of Fine Arts at Rhodes University. She was initially employed by the South African Department of Education. According to Nilant, she was a superintendent of Grahamstown Pottery's art department along with Hester Locke. This is refuted by the former

staff of Drostdy Ware, who claimed that Duncan was merely a paintress and not employed as long as Locke.

KRONE, Jane (née van der Riet)

Jane van der Riet, the daughter of Justice Ernest van der Riet, worked as a paintress for Drostdy Ware while studying at Rhodes University. She decorated numerous of the 'bushman' wares. Her initials, JvdR, appear on the bases of wares that she decorated.

LEVINSOHN, Rosalie (née Wood)

Born in Fort Brown, she used to work at Grahamstown Potteries as a decorator in the 1950s and early 1960s.

LOCKE, Hester W (née Dreyer) (1920–1996)

Locke was born in Adelaide, Cape Province. She graduated with teaching certificates in primary and infant school teaching, and was employed to train African teachers at the Healdtown Methodist Mission, where she met her future husband who was training teachers in sports instruction. Locke then worked at the Teacher Training College in King William's Town. In 1945 she moved to Grahamstown where the renowned ichthyologist Dr J L B Smith commissioned her to work as an illustrator for his first publication. Locke and other illustrators accompanied Smith to Mozambique where they spent the winter of 1946 near Lourenço Marques (now Maputo) and on Inhaca Island. She worked for Smith until the publication of *The Sea Fishes of Southern Africa* in 1949. The first edition contained approximately 12 of Locke's sketches.

In 1949 Locke and her husband travelled in Europe for six months. In Scandinavia she visited internationally renowned potteries, weaving studios and designers who were to influence her designs in terms of the incorporation of organic decorative motifs and forms. Later that year Locke was employed as a paintress at Grahamstown Pottery, initially part-time, but was soon promoted to full-time employment. She was later appointed superintendent of the art department, where she was responsible for all the hand-decorated wares. After the pottery closed in 1965, Locke studied psychology, but worked on a voluntary basis, never professionally. Upon her retirement, she ran a small bed and breakfast from her home in Port Alfred.

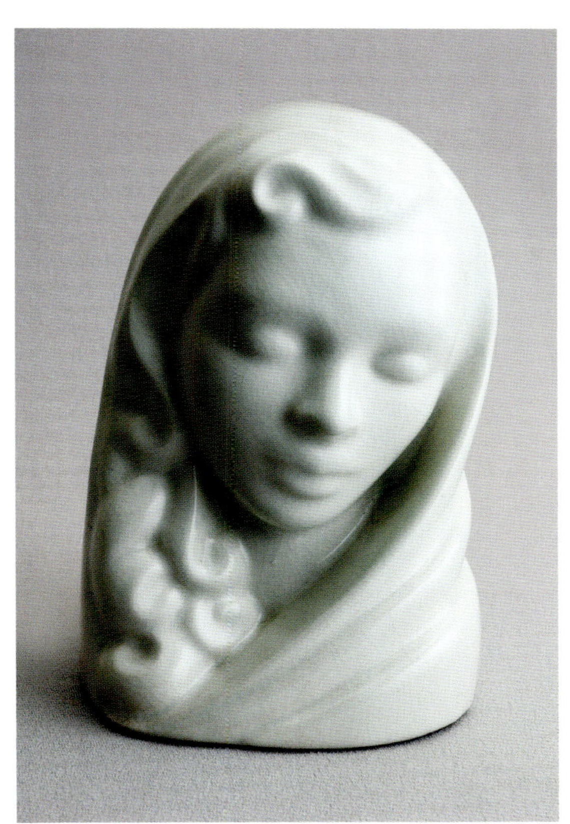

Grahamstown Pottery, Drostdy Ware | Sculptural vase of woman's head and shoulders | 200x125mm | Provenance: Douglas van der Horst | Marks: faint Drostdy impressed mark, and remains of Drostdy sticker | Photograph by Natalie Field

MAROT, France (b.1921)

France Marot was born in Tongaat, Natal to French-Mauritian parents. After completing a Bachelor of Commerce degree, she studied for a Higher National Diploma in Education, specialising in the teaching of commercial subjects, after which she taught for three years at Warner Beach in KwaZulu-Natal.

Dissatisfied with teaching, Marot enrolled in a pottery course at the Natal Technical Art School, where she was taught by Sylvia Baxter, Nils Andersen

(1897–1972),[113] and Ernest and Sylvia Fincher. Marot attended additional evening drawing classes conducted by Mary Stainbank (1899–1997) (see page 12). On graduating, she joined the college as a pottery 'instructress' for 18 months, before being recruited by Steele-Gray to head the design department of Grahamstown Pottery. In 1952 and 1956 Marot travelled in England and Europe, and upon her return in 1956 worked on a freelance basis for Grahamstown Pottery. She spent prolonged periods in Durban to tend to her ill mother, but worked for the pottery until its liquidation in 1965.[114]

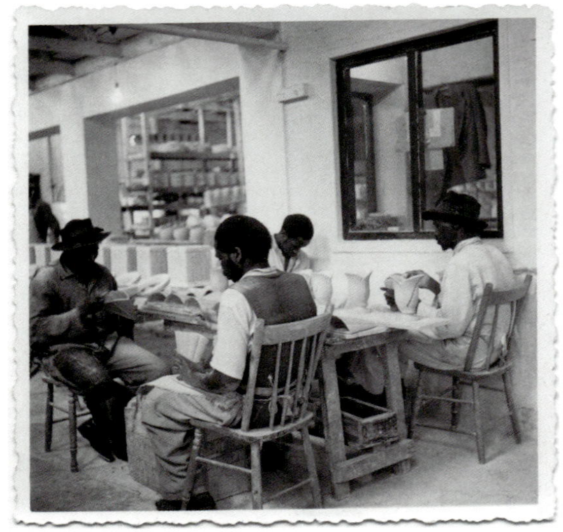

Grahamstown Pottery | Unidentified workers | Provenance: Wendy Gers, ex Hester Locke | Additional information: Some of the vases are depicted on page 102 | Photograph by Hester Locke

SCOTT, Margaret

Margaret Scott, from Swaziland, worked as a paintress for Drostdy Ware. The wares that she decorated are identifiable by her initials, MS, on the base of various wares.

SIMPSON, Leila Patricia (1931–1959)

Leila Patricia Simpson was born in Hull, England. A sculptor by profession, she was employed as a paintress and a designer at Drostdy Ware. She died tragically on 16 October 1959 in Grahamstown from a sleeping pill overdose. Simpson was an 'outsider' to the discriminatory politics and practices that were pervasive in South Africa in the 1950s. Locke described Simpson as a free-spirited woman who cared for all – 'years ahead of her time'.[115] As she used to go dancing in the local townships with African friends, she was shunned by many of the white Grahamstown locals, and those who accepted her did so hesitantly.

Simpson was responsible for designing transfers that depicted African people as individuals rather than Drostdy's generalised, nostalgic and picturesque images of rural African women that characterised the dominant tradition of the white designers at the studio. Simpson designed a transfer that depicted a mature African woman, an adolescent and a child carrying large loads of dietary staples, including water and vegetables. It is argued that Simpson's sensitivity to the plight of African people in South Africa during the 1950s was informed by her friendships with locals from a near-by township. While her social engagement may be viewed as oppositional to the dominant traditions, it is noted that she was not perceived to be subversive or threatening by Steele-Gray, Locke or Marot.

SOUTHEY, Annette

Annette Southey worked as a paintress for Drostdy Ware. She decorated numerous 'bushman' wares, which are identifiable by her initials, AS, on the base of various wares.

Grahamstown Pottery, Drostdy Ware | Charger depicting a pair of a zebra | 265x28mm | Provenance: Douglas van der Horst | Marks: hand-painted black glaze marks, 'STOX. Hand painted A.E.B. Zebras. No. 1010 A9. Drostdy Ware, Made in South Africa', two impressed 'Drostdy' stamps | Photograph by Natalie Field

STEELE-GRAY, Norman (1916–2004)

Born in England, Steele-Gray came to South Africa in 1936 when he was offered a position at National Ceramic Industries, Johannesburg, a firm that primarily manufactured salt-glazed industrial and sanitary ware. He was then employed at the Cullinan Refractories, Olifantsfontein, as the technical manager, and later as the general manager of the refractory. While there, he was responsible for £1 750 000 worth of extensions.

In 1948 the board of J R Howie of Scotland invited Steele-Gray to direct the reconstruction of their ceramic plant, destroyed by the war. Steele-Gray rebuilt the sanitaryware plant and put it into operation, but the unfavourable climate and the election of a Labour government resulted in his returning to South Africa. In 1949 Steele-Gray, in partnership with Charles Berry, formed a consulting company called Gray-Berry. While on a visit, Steele-Gray was approached for assistance by the management of Grahamstown Pottery, as the company was experiencing financial problems. Steele-Gray returned to Johannesburg, raised capital and bought a controlling interest in the business. In the 1950s he lobbied, unsuccessfully, to obtain significant government protection for the local ceramics industry. In 1957 Steele-Gray was appointed a Fellow of the Institute of Ceramics, England. He also served as chairman of the Ceramics Industries Association of South Africa.[116]

TARR, Anthony (b.1936)

Born near Port Elizabeth, Tarr attended Graeme College High School for Boys, Grahamstown, and took extra-curricular art classes at Carinus Art School. He loved art, and from approximately 1953 to 1958, while studying at Rhodes University, Tarr worked as a decorator at Drostdy Ware. Paid 3/6 p hour, Tarr specialised in applying delicate gold on-glaze lettering to Coronation Orbs and beer mugs. In addition, he painted 'Bushman' motifs on tiles for trays, indigenous birdlife, South African scenes and African costumes and headdresses inspired by Barbara Tyrrell's books. Tarr also decorated sgraffito plates and Delft-ware. The latter involved freehand drawings with blue chalk. Tarr recalls he was sent to the Albany Museum to study the stripe patterns on Burchell's zebras and spots on giraffes, as prior to this 'the zebras looked like Western Province rugby players!' This series was a special commission for a South African Delegation to the United Nations.

Tarr became a chemist and later worked as the Chief Theatre Technician (1820 National Monument Theatre, Grahamstown) and Theatre Manager (SWAPAC, Windhoek, Namibia). He is presently retired and lives in Port Alfred.

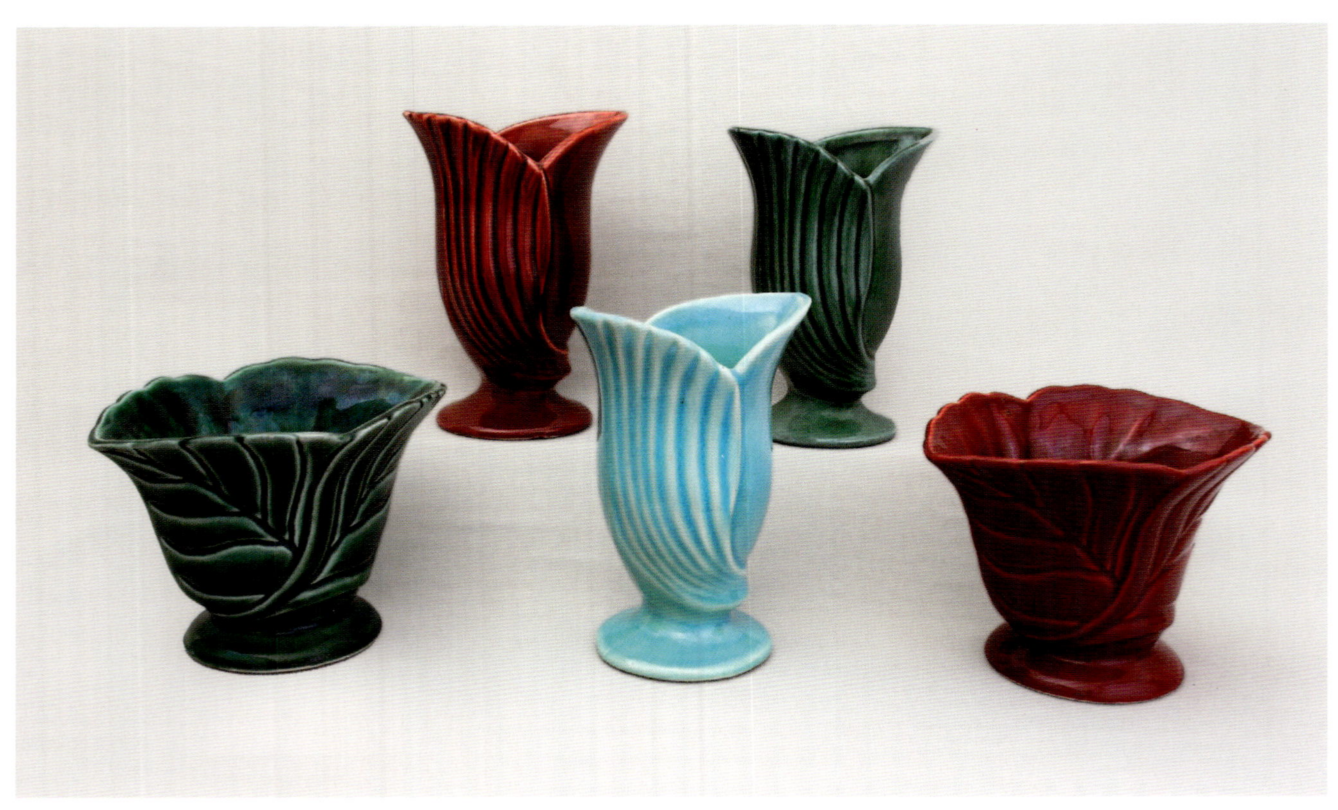

Drostdy Ware | Group of five different vases | Smaller vases 123x175x90mm; taller vase 182x135x90mm | Provenance: Douglas van der Horst | Marks: red taller vase has impressed mark, 'Drostdy 155'; green smaller vase has impressed mould mark, 'Drostdy 157' | Photograph by Natalie Field

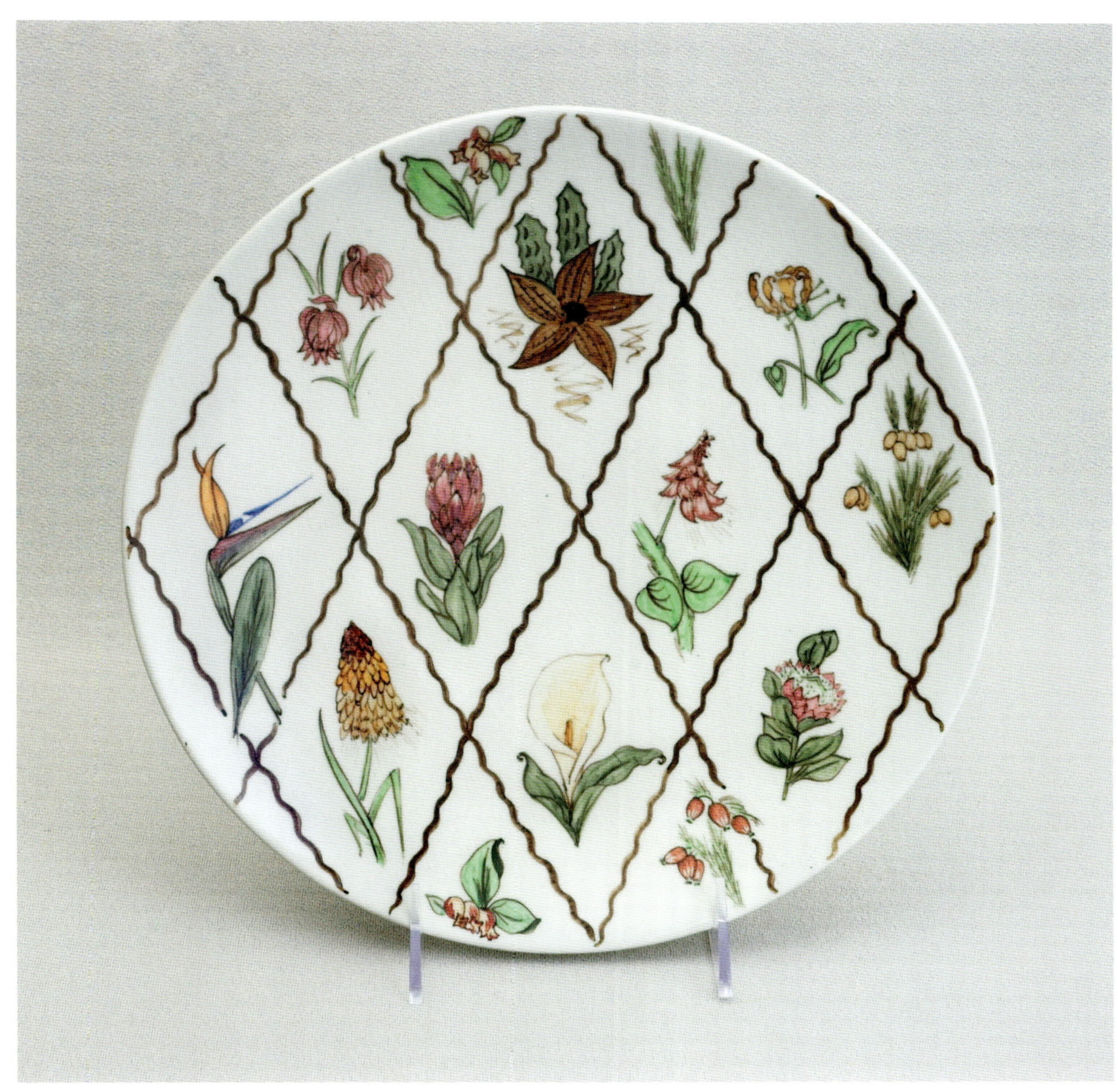

Grahamstown Pottery, Drostdy Ware | Charger depicting South African wildflowers | 265x28mm | Provenance: Douglas van der Horst | Marks: base glazed with a transparent glaze, painted glaze marks, 'France Marot. Hand painted M.L.S. S.A. Wild Flowers. NO. 1003.A03. Drostdy Ware Made in South Africa' | Photograph by Natalie Field

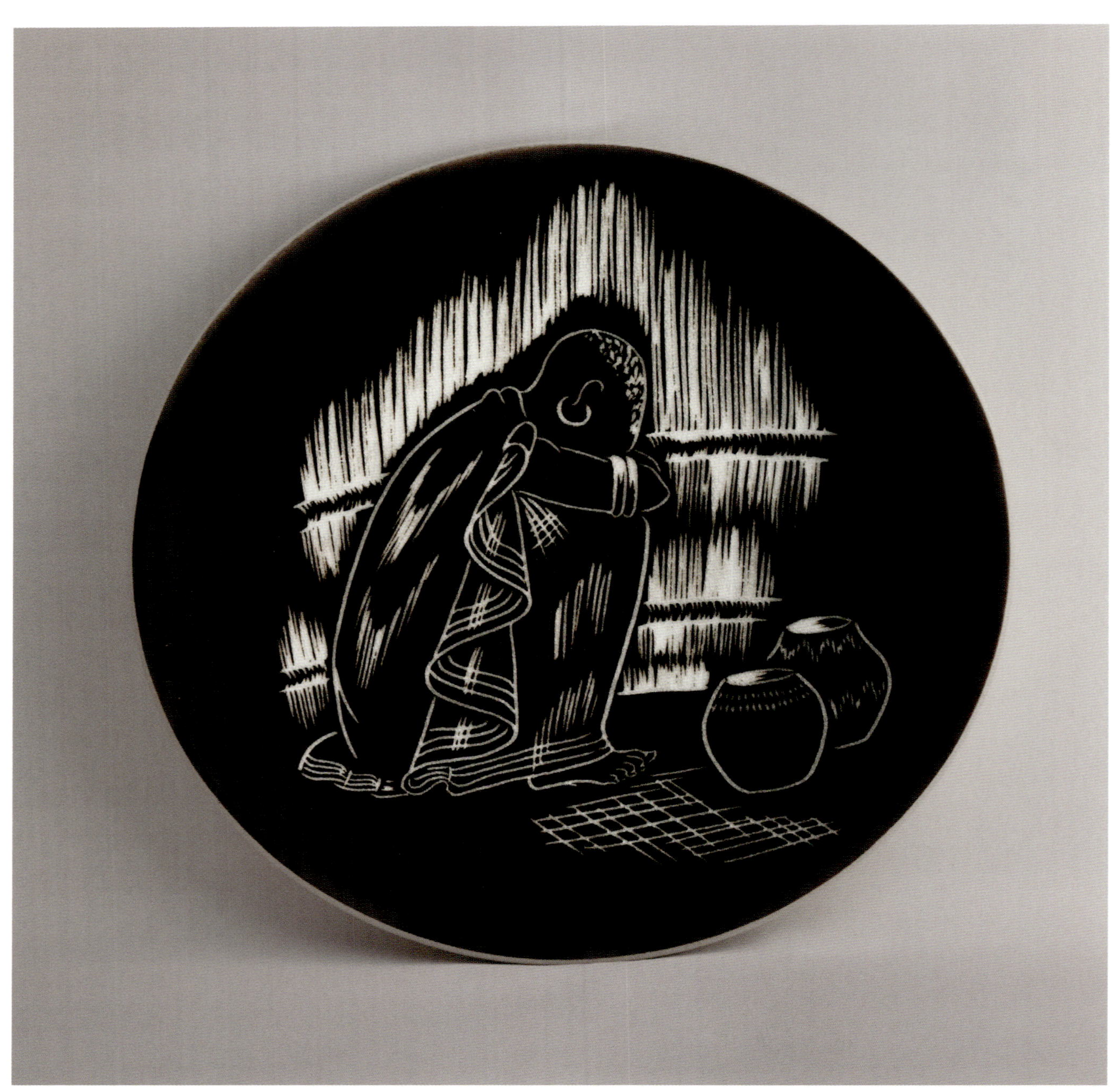

Grahamstown Pottery, Drostdy Ware | Charger with sgraffito decoration of an African man seated in hut | 264x30mm | Provenance: Wendy Gers | Marks: hand-painted black glaze marks, 'France Marot. Hand decorated E.M.G.S. Inqilika.' Drostdy glaze stamp, 'Drostdy Ware, Made in South Africa by Grahamstown' | Photograph by Damien Artus

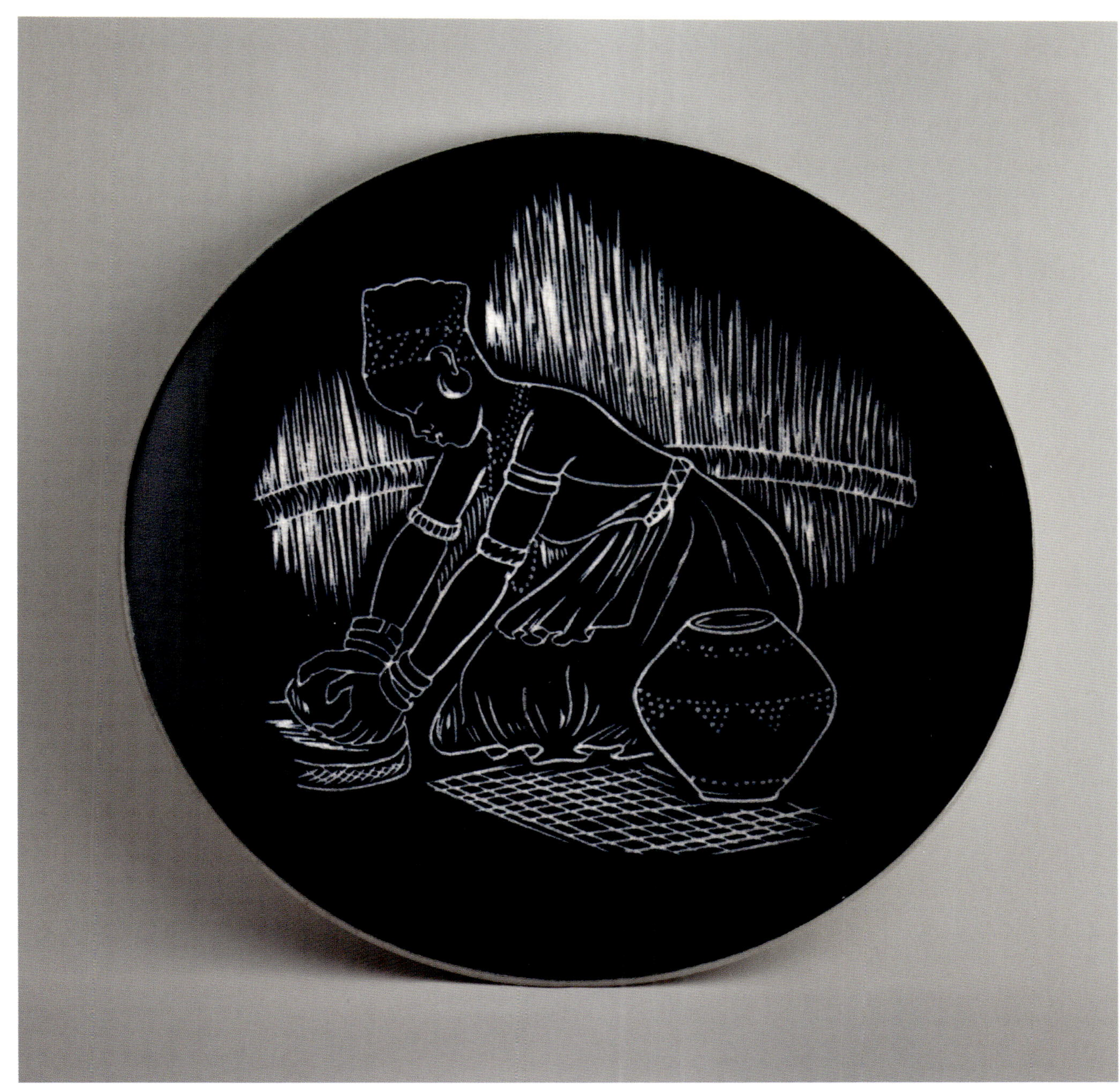

Grahamstown Pottery, Drostdy Ware | Charger with sgraffito decoration depicting a Zulu woman grinding corn | 263x34mm | Provenance: Wendy Gers | Marks: impressed stamp, 'Drostdy. Hand-painted, France Marot. Hand decorated EBT. Zulu woman grinding corn. No 1007. N2. Drostdy Ware, Made in South Africa' | Photograph by Damien Artus

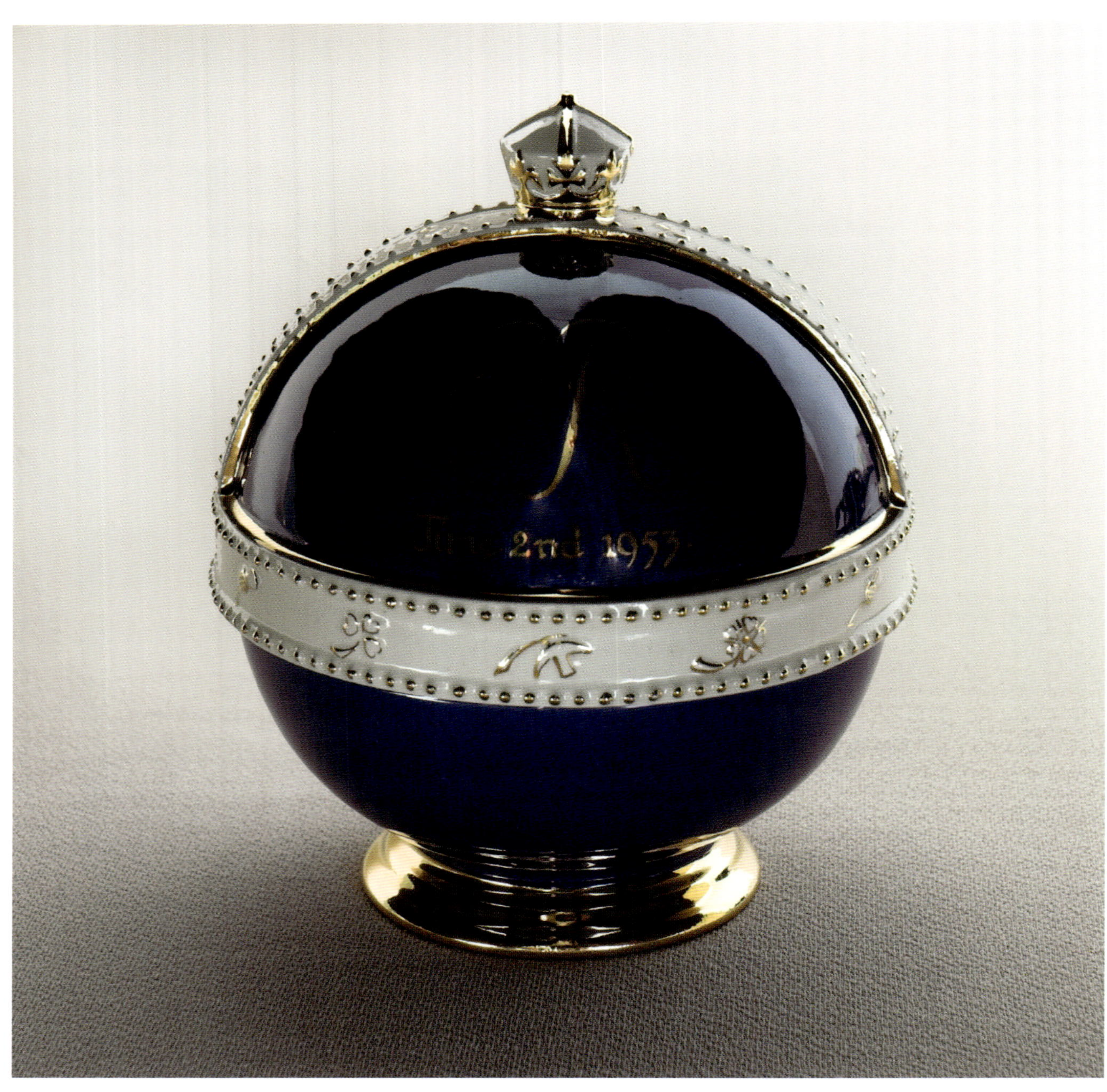

Grahamstown Pottery, Drostdy Ware | Coronation Orb | 160x105x75mm | Provenance: DNMCH | HG 12199 | Marks: Blue glazed base with gold marks, 'Drostdy Ware. No 16 of a limited issue of 50. E.M.G.S. Grahamstown Potteries LTD. South Africa' | Additional information: Orb accompanied by Certificate, 'Presented to His Excellency, the Governor General, Dr. The Honourable E.G. Jansen. This bowl, made to commemorate the Coronation of Her Majesty – Queen Elizabeth II – on June 2nd 1953, is one of a limited number of fifty only, made in Drostdy Ware by Grahamstown Potteries Limited of South Africa. [signature Steele Gray] Managing Director. Certificate for Orb Bowl No. 16.' | Photograph by Natalie Field

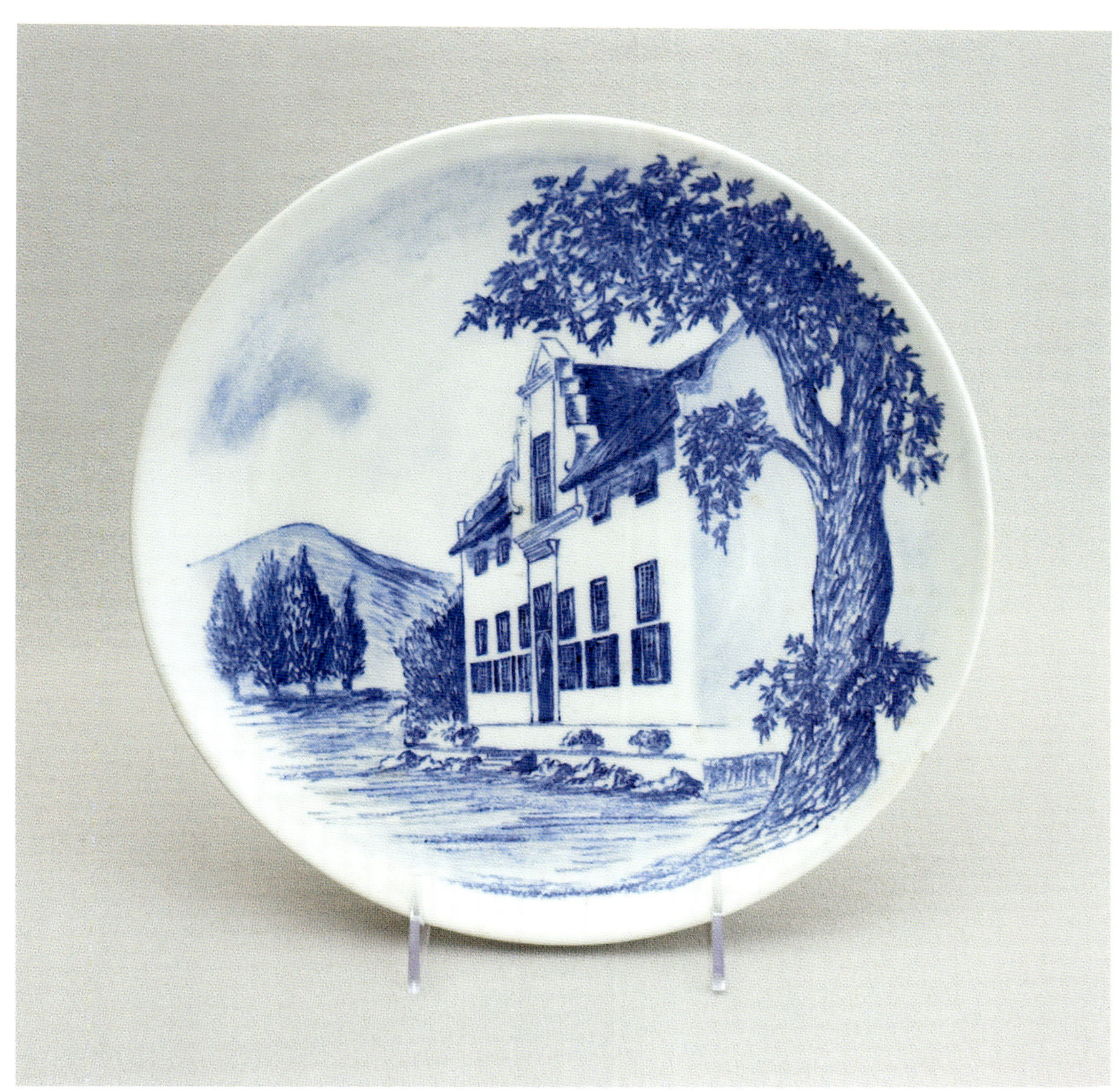

Grahamstown Pottery, Drostdy Ware | Imitation Delft image of 'Old Dutch Homestead' | 265x30mm | Provenance: Douglas van der Horst | Marks: Drostdy impressed mark and painted info, 'France Marot hand decorated P.A.G. 012L3, Drostdy Ware. Made in South Africa' | Photograph by Natalie Field

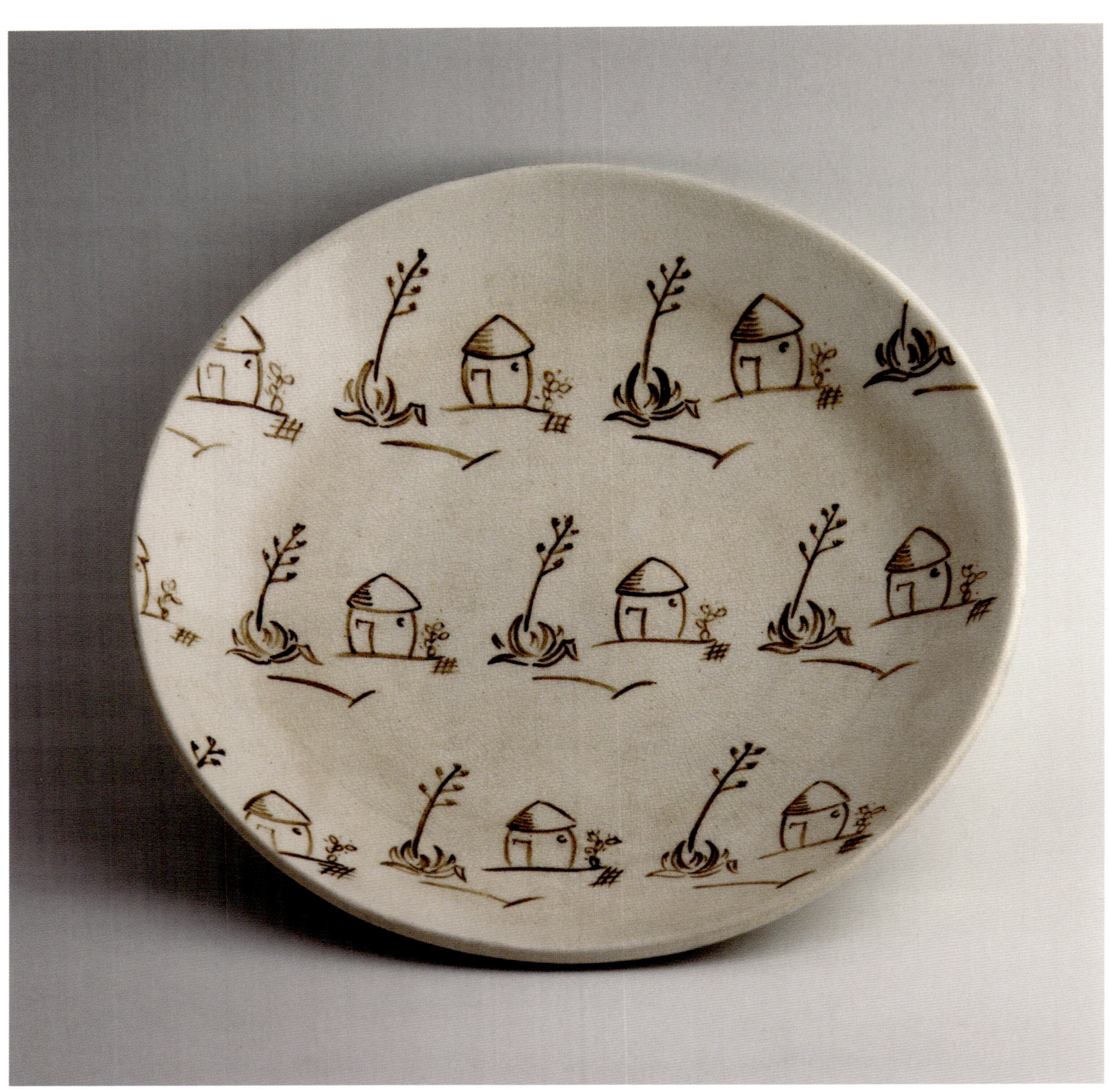

Grahamstown Pottery, Drostdy Ware | Charger, repeat pattern of huts and aloes | 210x35mm | Provenance: Wendy Gers | Marks: stamped glaze marks, 'Drostdy Ware, Made in South Africa Grahamstown Potteries LTD' | Additional information: This design was a prototype, and never went into production | Photograph by Damien Artus

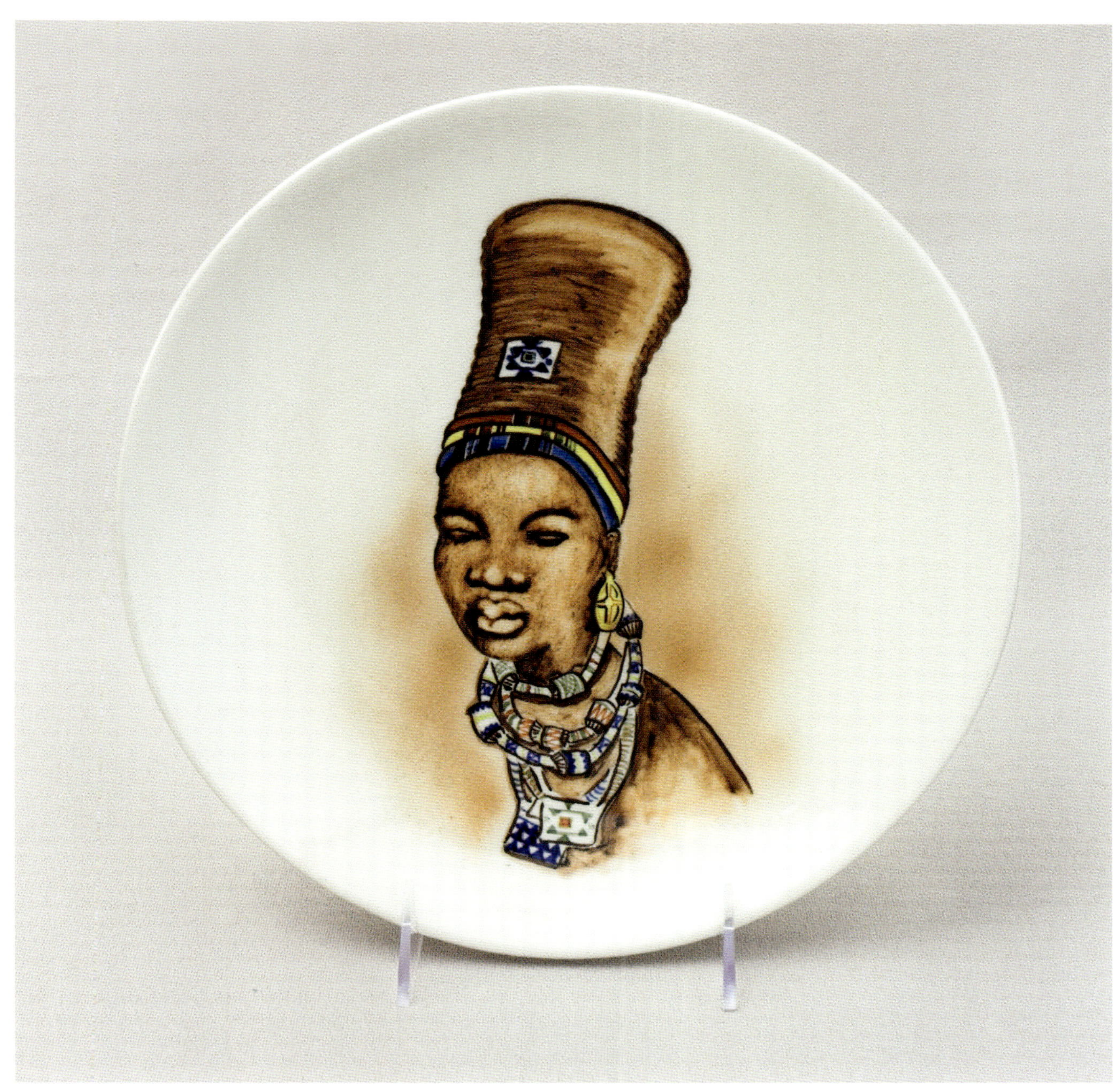

Grahamstown Pottery, Drostdy Ware | Charger, portrait of a Zulu woman | 265x28mm | Provenance: Douglas van der Horst | Marks: impressed stamp, 'Drostdy', hand-painted glaze marks, 'France Marot. Hand painted. S.P. Zulu woman grinding corn. No 1019 N8. Nasionale Krugerwildtuin Kruger National Park. Drostdy Ware, Made in South Africa' | Photograph by Natalie Field

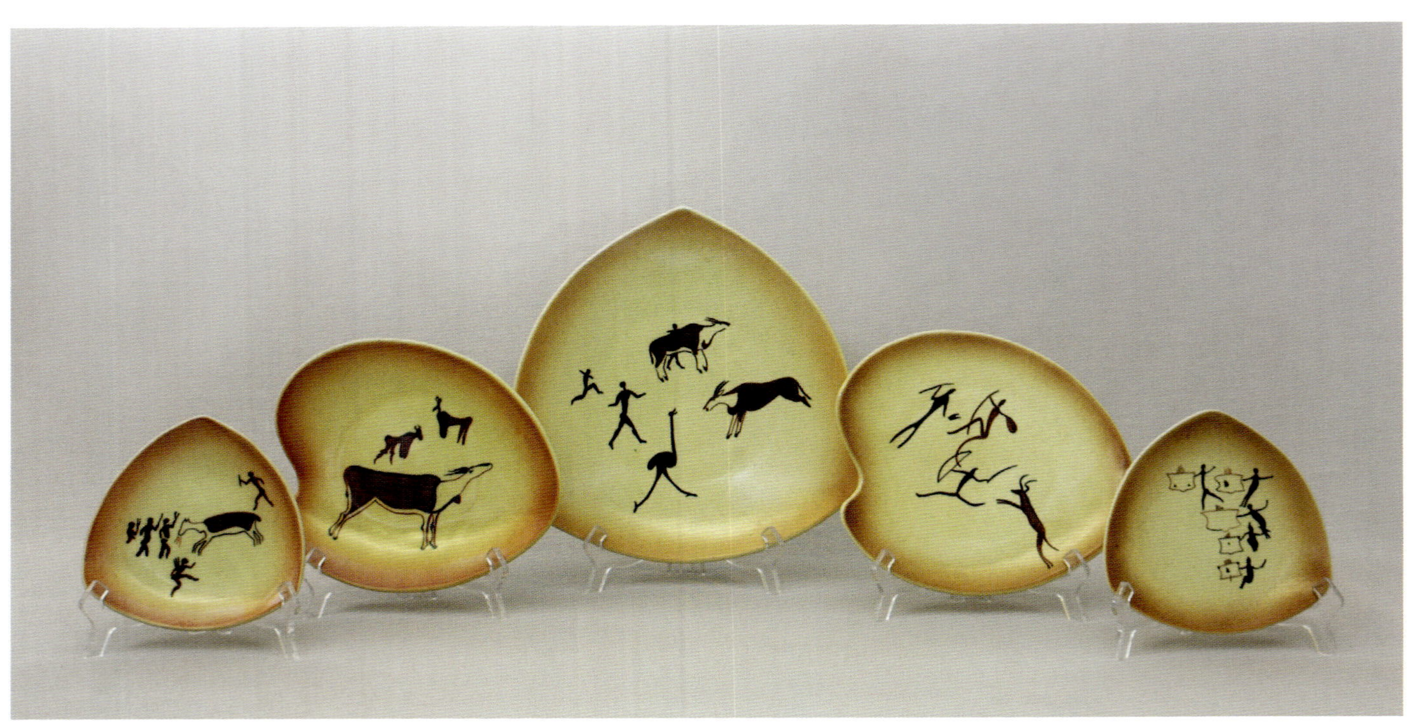

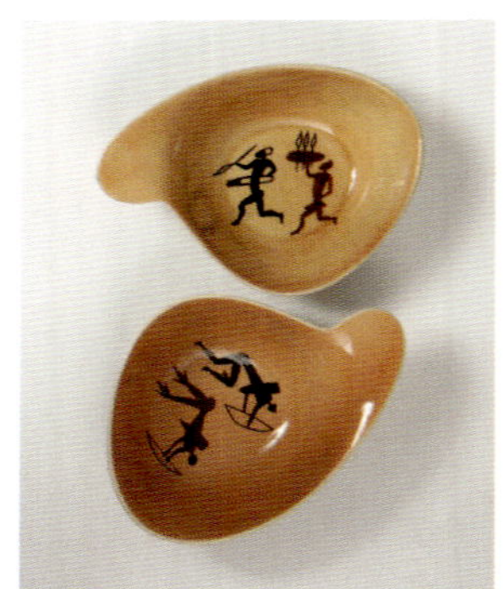

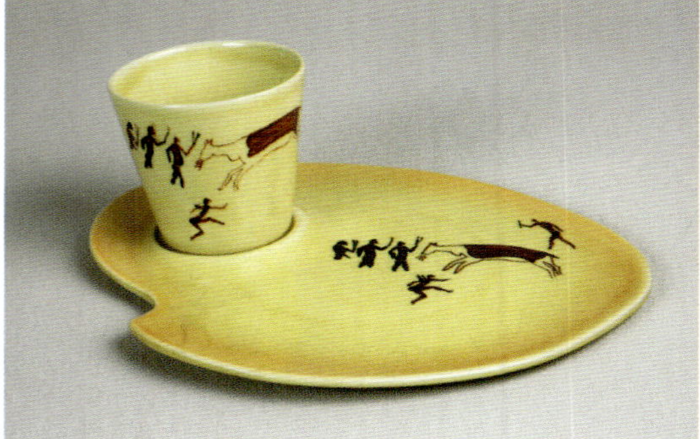

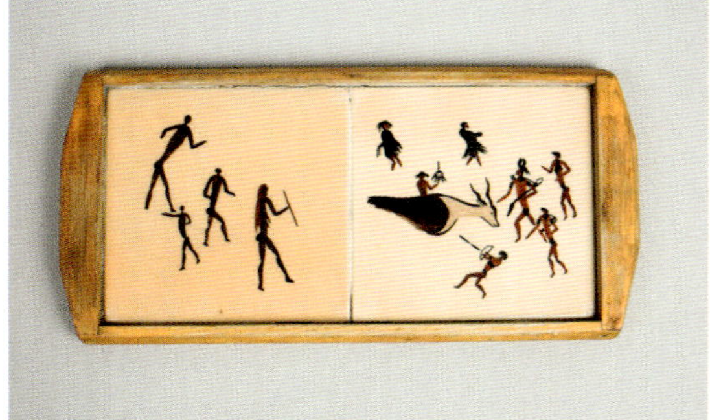

TOP: Grahamstown Pottery, Drostdy Ware | Group of plates decorated with images derived from illustrations of San parietal art | From left front 160x160x20mm; second plate 210x240x20mm; third plate 300x280x45mm; fourth plate 210x245x20mm; fifth plate 167x163x20mm | Provenance: TAG | First plate 2365/06; second plate 2367/06; third plate 2370/06; fourth plate 2369/06; fifth plate 2366/06 | Marks: first plate pale yellow, transparent glaze on base, impressed stamp, 'Drostdy', black glaze marks, 'Hand Painted, L.M.S. Reproduction. Bushman Rock Painting', black glaze stamp, 'Drostdy Ware, Made in South Africa'; second plate, pale yellow, transparent glaze on base, impressed stamp, 'Drostdy', black glaze marks, 'Hand Painted Reproduction, G. de B. Bushman Rock Painting', black glaze stamp, 'Drostdy Ware in Suid-Afrika vervaardig'; third plate, pale yellow, transparent glaze on base, impressed stamp, 'Drostdy', black glaze marks, 'Bushman Rock Painting. Hand Painted Reproduction, MP. Drostdy Ware Made in South Africa'; fourth plate, pale yellow, transparent glaze on base, impressed stamp, 'Drostdy', black glaze marks, 'Hand Painted Reproduction, JF. 'Bushman Rock Painting. Drostdy Ware Made in South Africa'; fifth plate, pale yellow, transparent glaze on base, black glaze marks, 'Hand Painted Reproduction G.B. Bushman Rock Painting. Drostdy Ware. Made in South Africa. E' | Photograph by Natalie Field

BOTTOM LEFT: Drostdy Ware | Pair of bowls decorated with San art | Provenance: Wendy Gers | Photograph by Damien Artus

BOTTOM MIDDLE: Drostdy Ware | Plate and cup decorated with San art | cup 77x81mm; plate 15x242x210mm | Provenance: Nelson Mandela Metropolitan Art Museum | 1436/2005/01-02 | Marks: hand-painted GdeB / Reproduction bushman rock painting | Photograph by Natalie Field

BOTTOM RIGHT: Drostdy Ware | Tile panel decorated with images of San art | Each tile 150mm^2; tray 190x360mm | Provenance: Nelson Mandela Metropolitan Art Museum | 1068/2000 | Marks: no marks | Additional information: glazed earthenware tiles mounted in a wooden tray | Photograph by Natalie Field

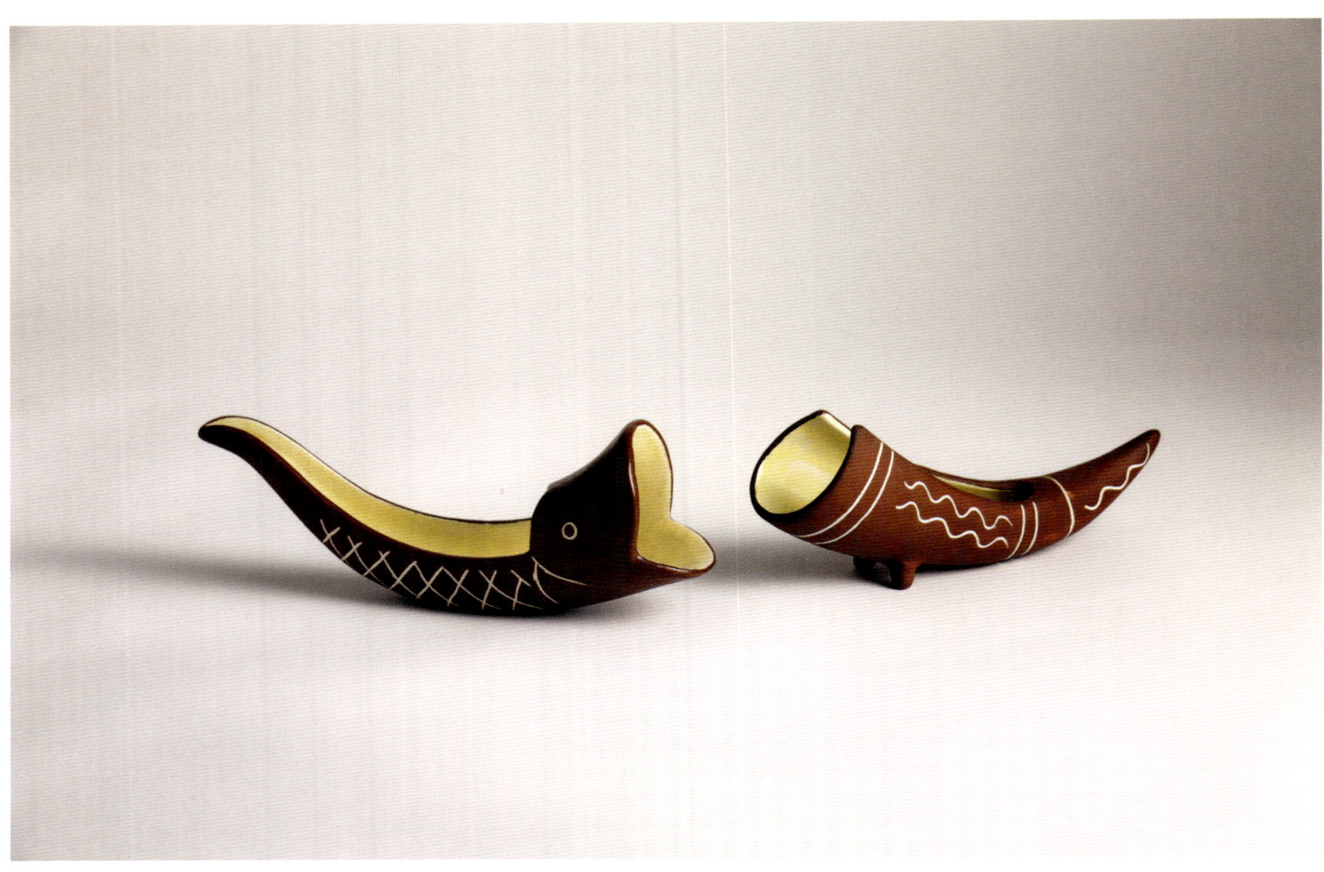

Grahamstown Pottery, Drostdy Ware | Pipe ashtrays | Fish 80x200x60mm; horn 75x195x50mm | Provenance: Wendy Gers | Marks: pair: sgraffitto marks, 'Drostdy Ware. Made in South Africa' | Photograph by Damien Artus

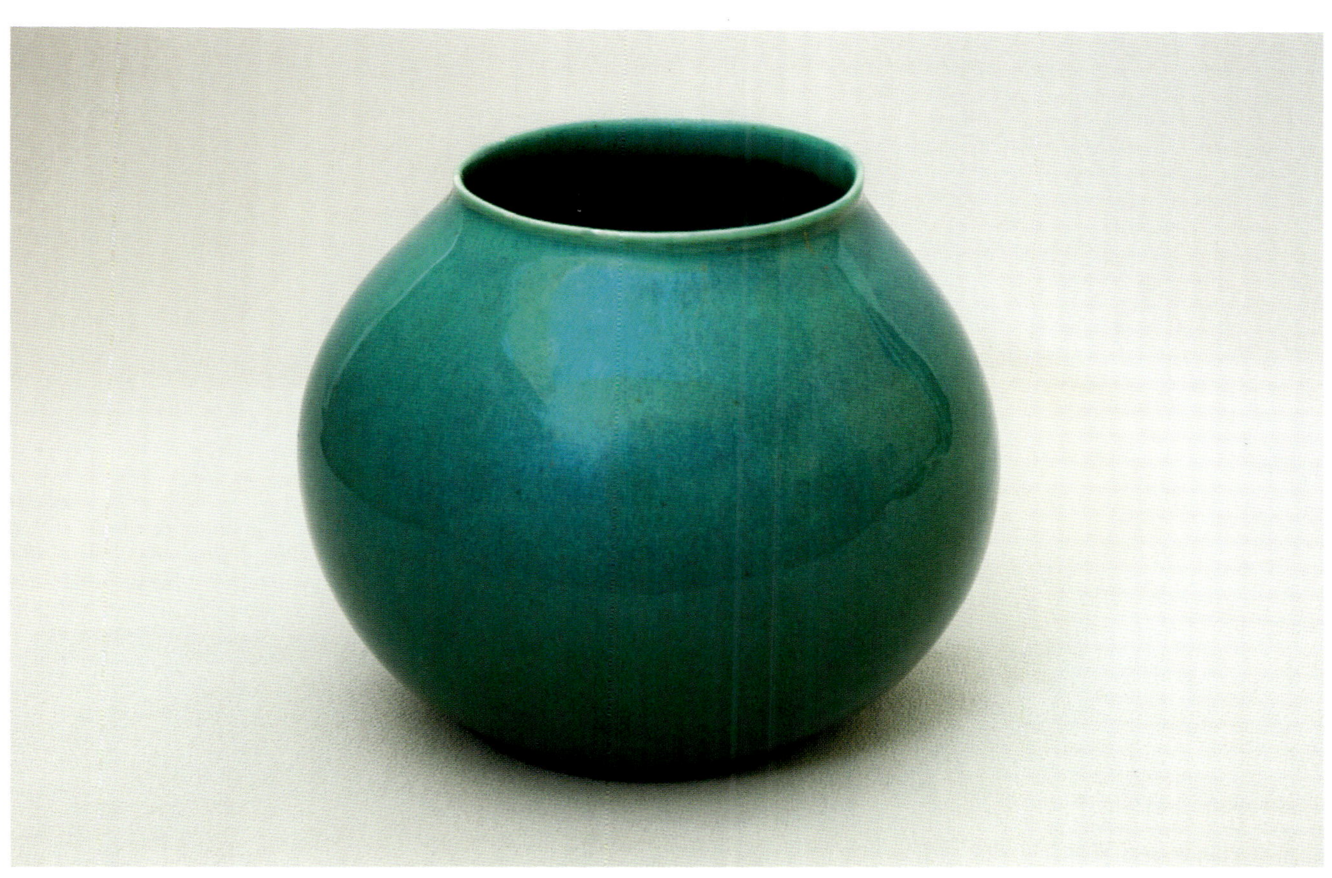

Drostdy Ware | Large rounded vase resembling a traditional Xhosa *Ukhamba* | 200x129x120mm | Provenance: TAG | 2332/06 | Marks: Damaged Drostdy Ware sticker on base | Photograph by Natalie Field

Groenkloof Brick, Tile and Pottery Works (1880–ca.1958)

In 1880 John Johnston Kirkness (1857–1939)[117] established the Groenkloof Brick, Tile and Pottery Works in Pretoria, which produced bricks, roof tiles, floor tiles and unglazed decorative garden ceramics, including ornate terracotta flowerpots and decorative garden edging tiles. He became a highly successful building contractor and was awarded numerous commissions for local buildings, including the Raadsaal Building, Church Square, Pretoria. In 1924 Kirkness was succeeded by his sons, T G and J N Kirkness.

Archival records are vague with claims of a 'comprehensive range of pottery' ranging in colour from 'a light cherry copper red to a deep mottled copper bronze' (Macmillan ca.1935:374), which probably refers to the clay body with a transparent glaze. During the 1950s, the pottery was managed by Mr Aukamp, who originally worked at Globe Potteries and subsequently at Dykor.[118] While there are no known examples of its wares, Groenkloof Brick, Tile and Pottery Works is significant in that it is possibly the earliest pottery in South Africa with a discerning eye and a concern for artistry.

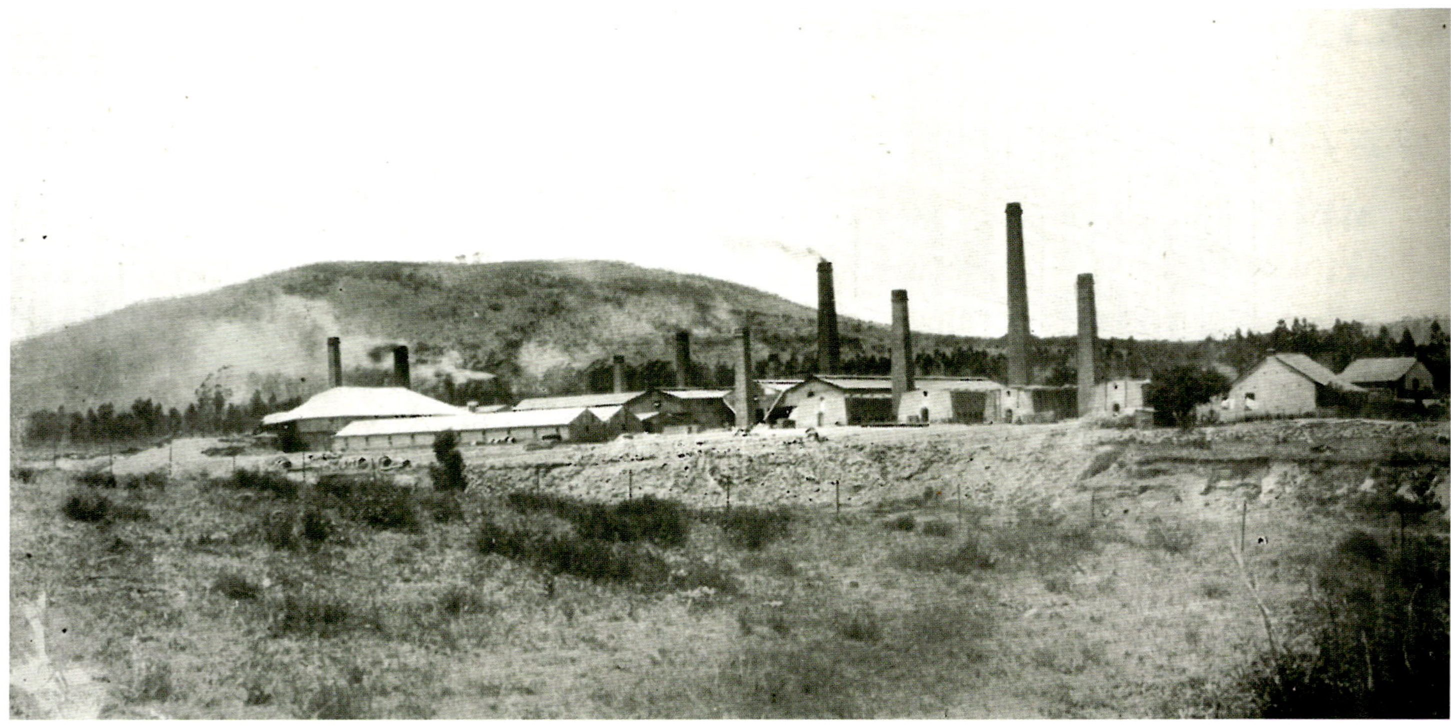

Groenkloof Pottery, Pretoria | Donaldson, K. (ed.) (1926) *South African Who's Who (Social and Business) 1925–1926*. Cape Town: Ken Donaldson | Scan by William Martinson

Hamburger's Pottery (1947–1986)

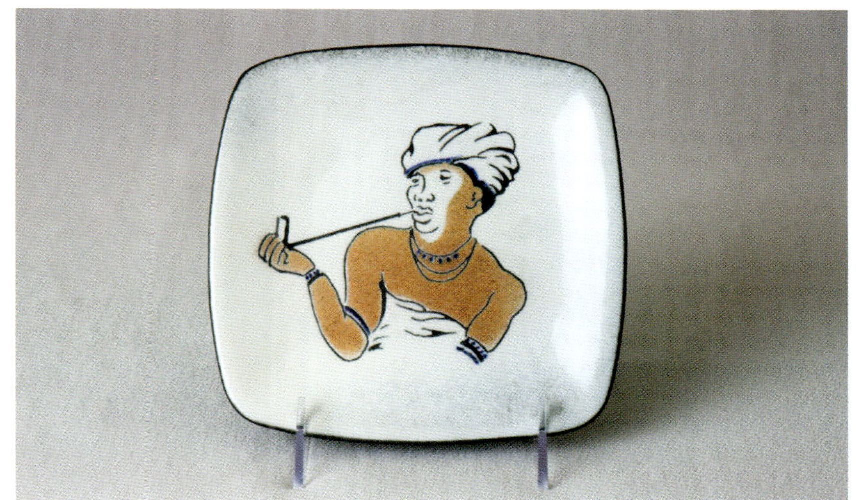

Hamburger's Pottery | Plaque, Xhosa woman smoking a pipe | 165x19mm | Provenance: TAG | 2372/06 | Marks: Hamburger logo | Photograph by Natalie Field

Location

Grahamstown

Name

The pottery was originally called 'Graham-Kiln: J. Hamburger's Pottery'. In the small community of Grahamstown, where Hamburger was well-known for his eccentricity and poor grasp of the English language, the studio was known as Hamburger's Pottery. Eventually, in 1962, Hamburger officially changed the studio's name to Hamburger's Pottery. In 1986 the pottery was renamed Koch Pottery.

Owners

1947–1977 Jürgen Hamburger
1977–1986 Richard and Margreet Koch

Staff

Jürgen Hamburger and his parents were the original designers and decorators. With the exception of N Bates, other employees are unknown.

Marks

The wares feature at least two of the studio's distinctive cast mark. The earlier mark consists of a diminutive H straddling a large G and is accompanied by a relatively small number.[119] The later and more common one consists of a logo containing H, G and I, the splayed H resembling a crown-like form, also sometimes accompanied by a number. Some exceptional wares that feature the earlier logo have an additional impressed mark, such as 'N. Bates'.[120] In later years the pottery used a rectangular gold sticker with black text, 'Hamburger's

Pottery, Grahamstown'. From 1986 wares were marked with a circular gold foil sticker with blue text, 'Koch Ceramics, Grahamstown'.

Wares manufactured

Hamburger's Pottery primarily manufactured crockery and domestic ware characterised by restrained decoration.[121] Fancy ware, including chargers and bowls that were skilfully decorated with sgraffito or slip-trailed images, were an important line of production with chickens and cockerels, children, indigenous flora and native studies, among other motifs.

Production methods

In the early years, all wares were produced and decorated by hand. From 1957 the studio used two electrical and one manual potter's wheel. In later years, Hamburger purchased a jigger and jolley machine, and began to slip-cast wares. Hamburger's pottery features both matt and gloss glazes, sgraffito and wax-resistance decoration.

Brief history of the pottery

Hamburger's lack of siblings and descendants, as well as his outsider status,[122] have resulted in an extreme dearth of information about him and his pottery. It is clear that from his arrival in South Africa, Hamburger had a burning passion for ceramics. In 1940, with capital from Mr Cornforth, he built Grahamstown Pottery's first tunnel kiln. His failed attempts to operate the pottery between 1939 and 1948 no doubt reinforced the need for moral and financial assistance. Thus, with his newly immigrated parents' assistance, Hamburger established the Graham-Kiln: J. Hamburger's Pottery, which operated from his home in Cobden Street, Grahamstown. The pottery was renamed Hamburger's Pottery in 1962.

In the early years Hamburger's Pottery produced abstract figurines and small ornamental sculptures of animals. However, these were not commercially successful and were soon discontinued. Many early clients were his university students and colleagues. However, gradually Hamburger sold his wares through craft and gift shops, craft exhibitions (such as the South African Association of the Arts, Arts and Crafts Exhibition 1954). He generally avoided large department stores and commercial trade shows.

Hamburger's oeuvre was rich, varied and complex, and was grounded in northern European modernist ceramic design traditions articulated by the Bauhaus and characterised by minimal forms and an earthy palette. Hamburger's hallmark tea, coffee and dinner services with simple geometric decorative motifs recall the oeuvre of the renowned Jewish Austrian/English potter, Lucy Rie (1902–1995).[123] It is important to note that like many other contemporary South African potteries, Hamburger could not survive by exclusively producing wares in earthy tones. He also produced his modernist sgraffito decorated wares with a bright blue-turquoise glaze.

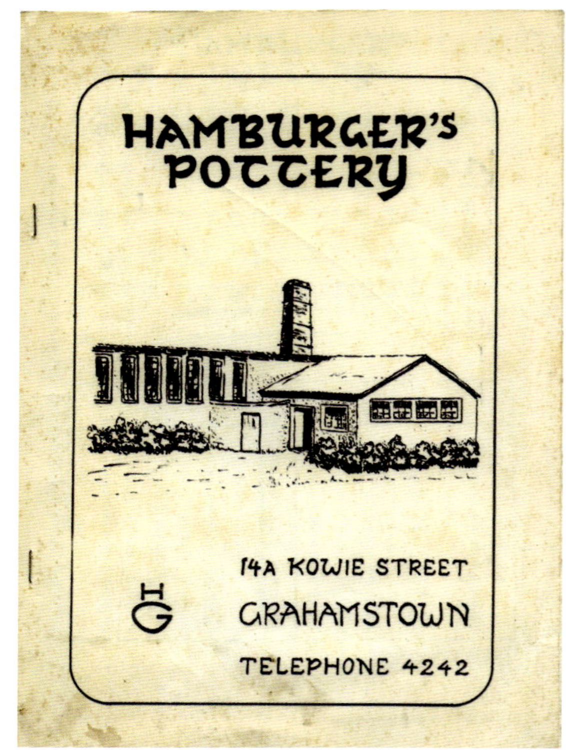

Hamburger's Pottery | Catalogue March 1985 | Provenance: Wendy Gers, ex Richard Koch | Scan by Nicole Piriou

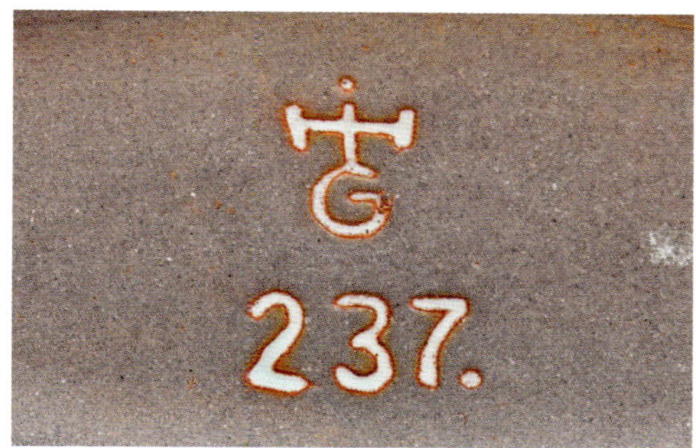

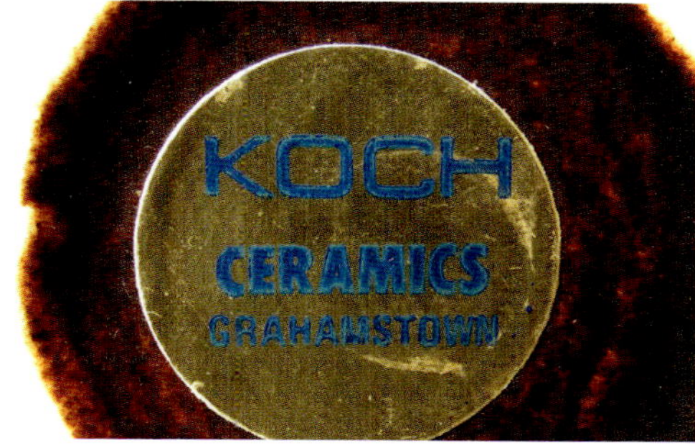

TOP: Hamburger's Pottery | Maker's mark | Relief moulded logo of entwined 'HG' and '237' | Photograph by Natalie Field

ABOVE BOTTOM: Koch Ceramics, Grahamstown | Maker's mark | Gold foil sticker with blue text, 'Koch Ceramics, Grahamstown' | Photograph by Natalie Field

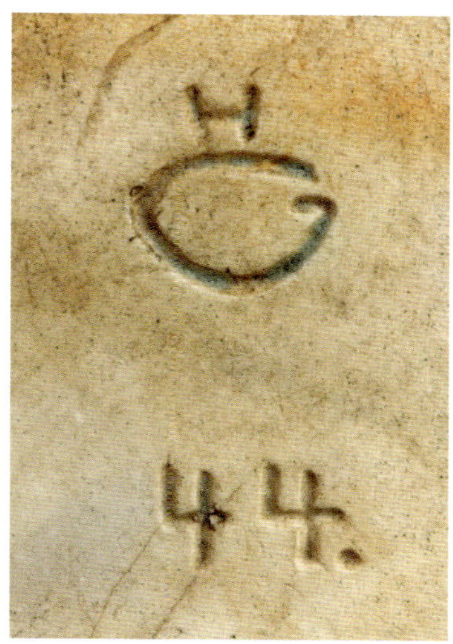

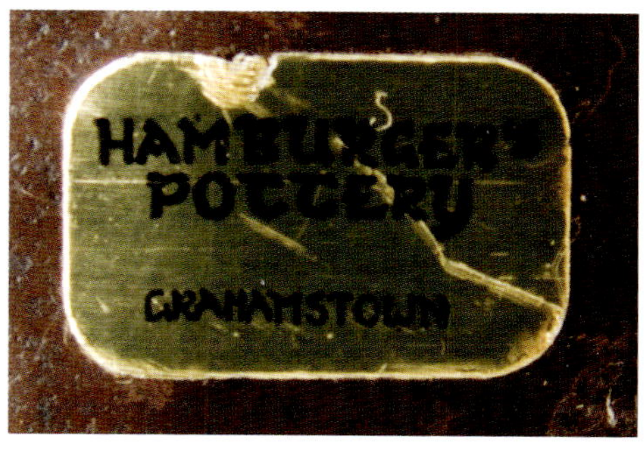

ABOVE: Hamburger's Pottery | Maker's mark | Gold foil sticker with black text, 'Hamburger's Pottery, Grahamstown' | Photograph by Natalie Field

LEFT: Hamburger's Pottery | Maker's mark | Relief moulded logo, 'HG' and '44' | Photograph by Natalie Field

Hamburger's work, like that of his world-renowned teacher Marguèrite Wildenhain (1896–1985), refers to leaves and flowers they would have found on daily rambles. For example, Hamburger produced original stylised vases whose forms resemble those of the prickly pear and pineapple, both fruit cultivated in the Albany region. He also created chargers depicting protea species. Indeed, stylised organic abstractions of leaves, flowers and fruit are among the most successful of Hamburger's wares. He also incorporated references to local Xhosa material culture, designing at least one charger that depicted a Xhosa man in traditional garb, smoking a distinctive slender, elongated pipe. In addition he produced subtle, refined glazed wares that are shaped like *iphiso* and other traditional African pottery forms. It is noteworthy that Drostdy Ware produced some similar forms. Hamburger also manufactured charming flatware that was skilfully decorated with sgraffito images of chickens and cockerels, children, indigenous flora and native studies, among other motifs. These are among his finest designs.

In 1977 Hamburger sold the studio to Richard and Margreet Koch. For approximately a year or two the pottery continued to produce wares pioneered by Hamburger. However, public taste had evolved and there was a demand for less austere wares. Over the next few years Margreet Koch (a graduate of the pottery department at the Port Elizabeth Technikon) introduced new shapes and lighter and brighter colours into the Hamburger palette, including red, pink and blue. She also introduced floral decoration, e.g. the pansy range featured pansies against a matt speckled beige background, and later against a gloss white glaze background.

In approximately 1986 the Kochs renamed the enterprise Koch Pottery. They changed the focus of the business, from craft pottery to commercial ceramics expanded operations considerably, mechanised the production and decoration departments, added new kilns, and significantly increased

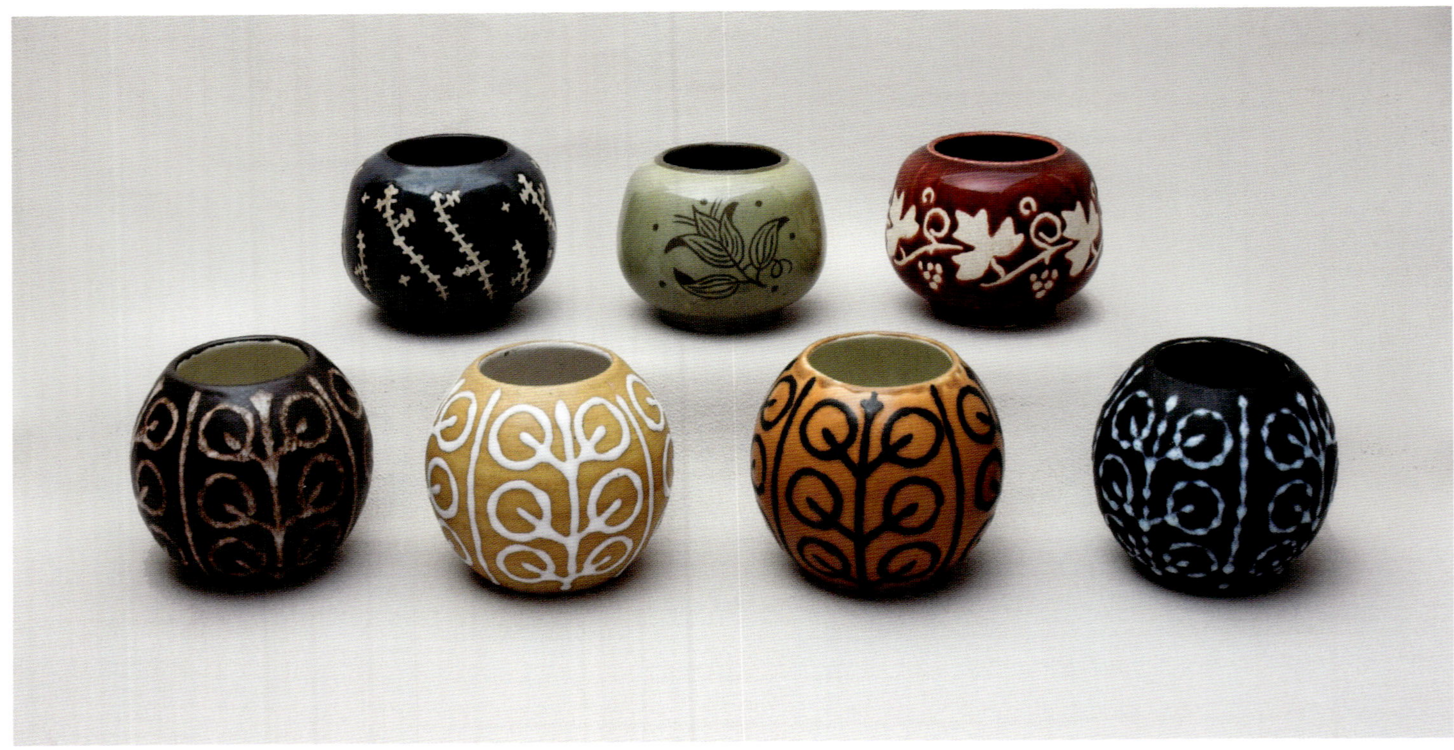

Hamburger's Pottery | Seven vases with wax resist, and slip trailed decoration | front row ca.100x70mm; back row: ca.80x65x70mm | Provenance: Douglas van der Horst | Marks: front row Hamburger logo; back row Hamburger logo, '209' | Photograph by Natalie Field

the output. At the peak of its success, the pottery employed approximately 40 staff. Koch Potteries also sold potter's tools and supplies and, for a while, manufactured place mats. Wares were exclusively sold through Houseware, a sales agency that employed travelling salesmen. In approximately 1995 Houseware was declared insolvent, an event that proved fatal for the pottery, which closed in 1997.

Biography

HAMBURGER, Jürgen (d.1995)

Jürgen Hamburger was born in Germany, where he trained as a pottery apprentice and later studied ceramics under Marguèrite Wildenhain.[124] He worked in various German ceramic studios before opening his own pottery near Berlin. In 1938 Hamburger and his two sisters left Germany due to increasing Semitic persecution. A British humanitarian organisation that aided Jewish emigration from Germany assisted with his appointment as pottery instructor at the Grahamstown Art School that same year. In 1938 Professor F W Armstrong sold Grahamstown Pottery to Hamburger.

Grahamstown Pottery was not financially successful and Hamburger sold the business to Norman Steele-Gray in 1948. He subsequently established Hamburger's Pottery, which was briefly known as the Graham Kiln, and sold it in 1977 to Richard and Margreet Koch. In the last years of his life Hamburger worked two mornings a week for the entomology department of the Albany Museum, making cardboard unit-trays for their collections. He was a member of the Diaz Cross Bird Club from 1978 and died in Grahamstown in 1995.

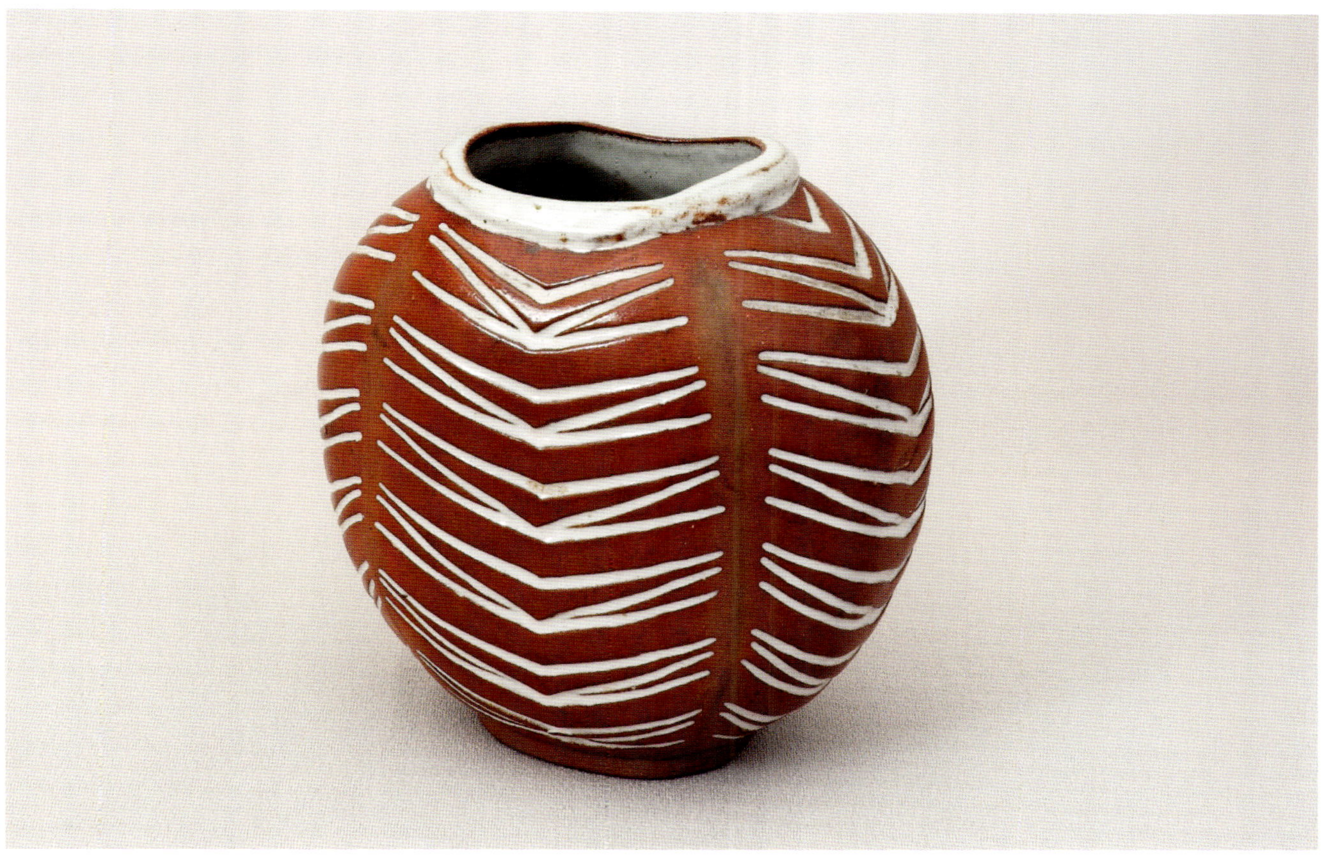

Hamburger's Pottery | Vase, slip-cast with incised decoration | 170x90x75mm | Provenance: Douglas van der Horst | Marks: Hamburger logo, '593' | Photograph by Natalie Field

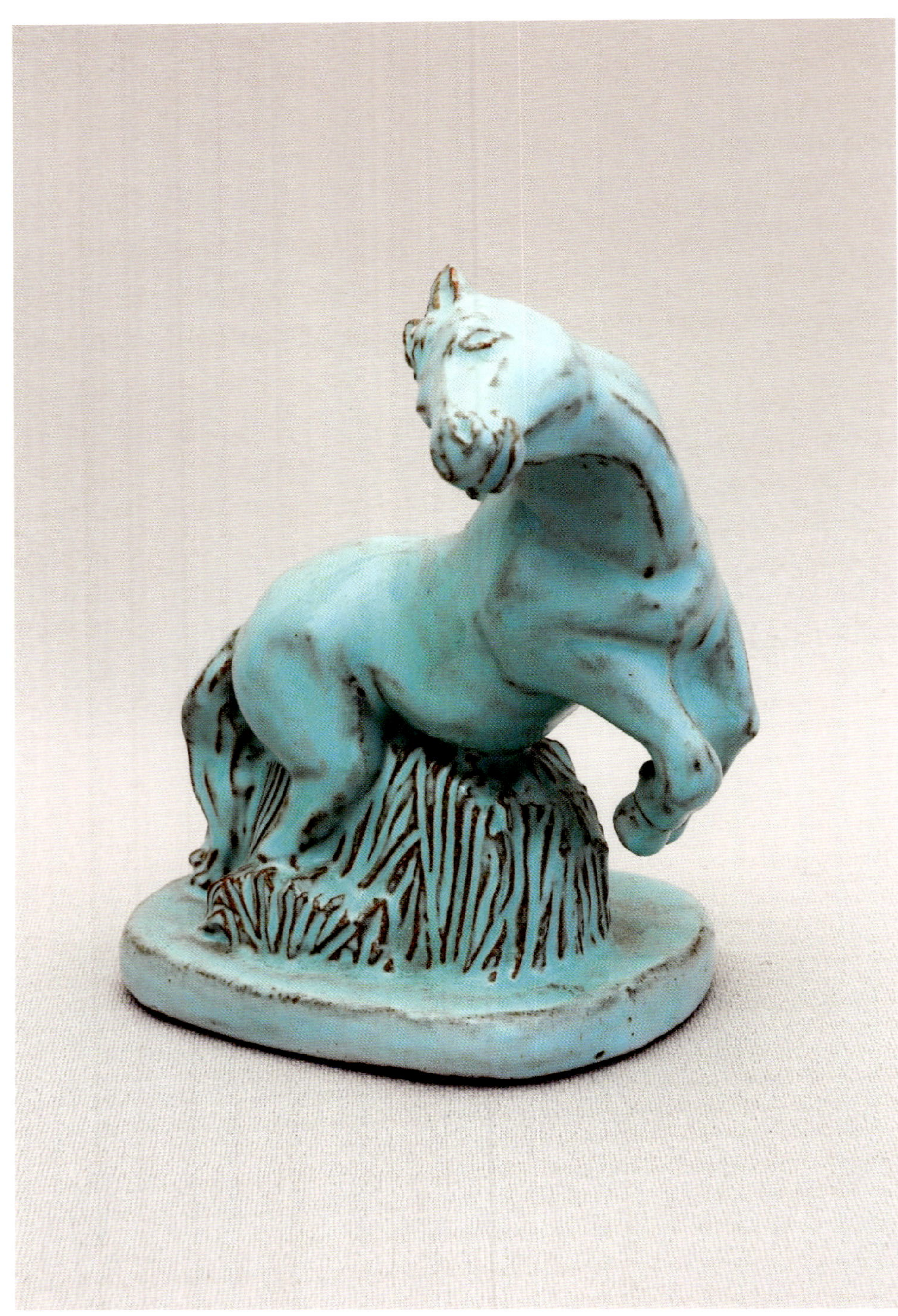

Hamburger's Pottery | Ornament, light blue rampant horse | 160x130mm | Provenance: Douglas van der Horst | Marks: Hamburger logo | Photograph by Natalie Field

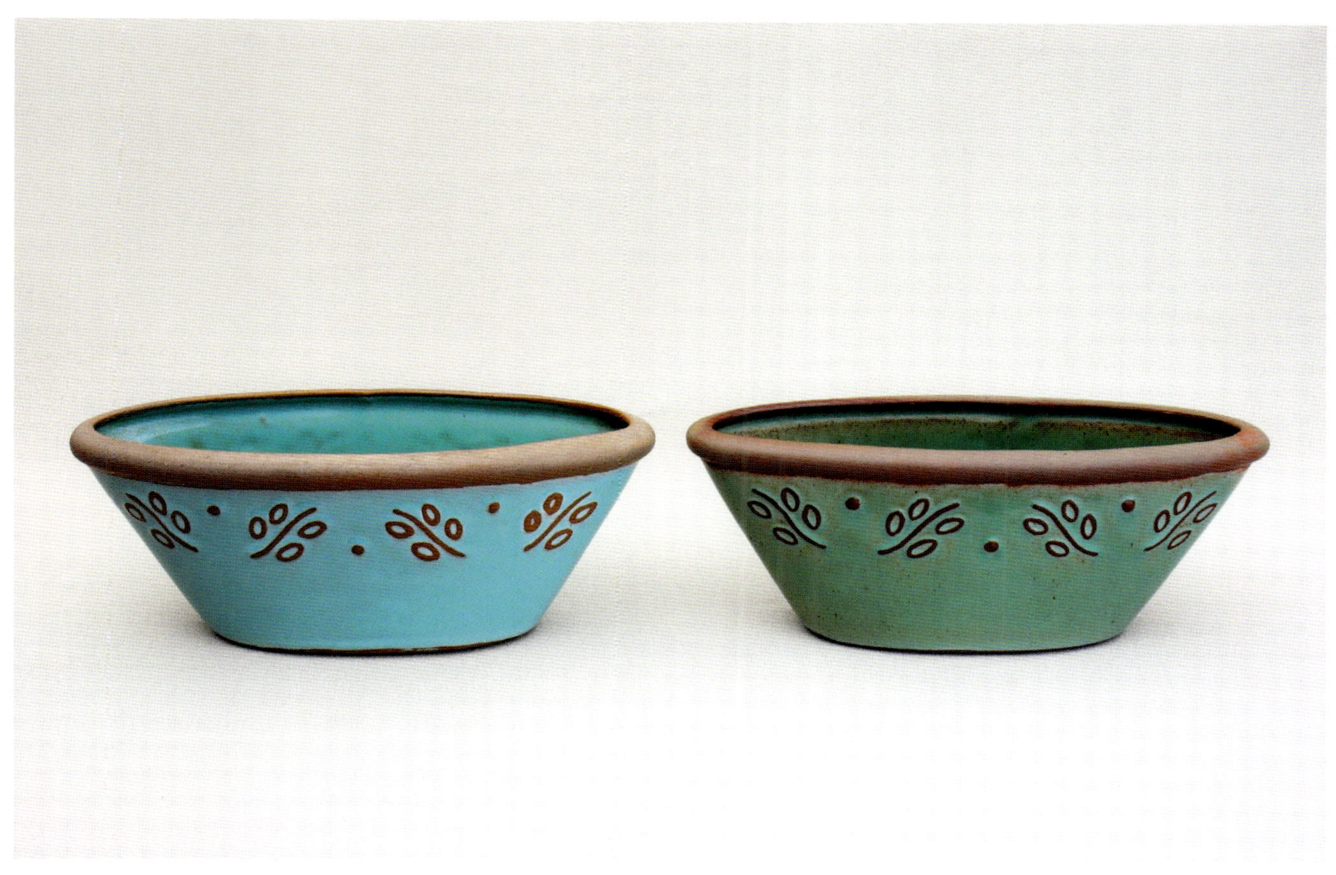

Hamburger's Pottery | Two trough vases, with moulded floral motif below unglazed rim | 110x280x100mm | Provenance: Douglas van der Horst | Marks: left vase unmarked; right vase Hamburger logo, '237' | Photograph by Natalie Field

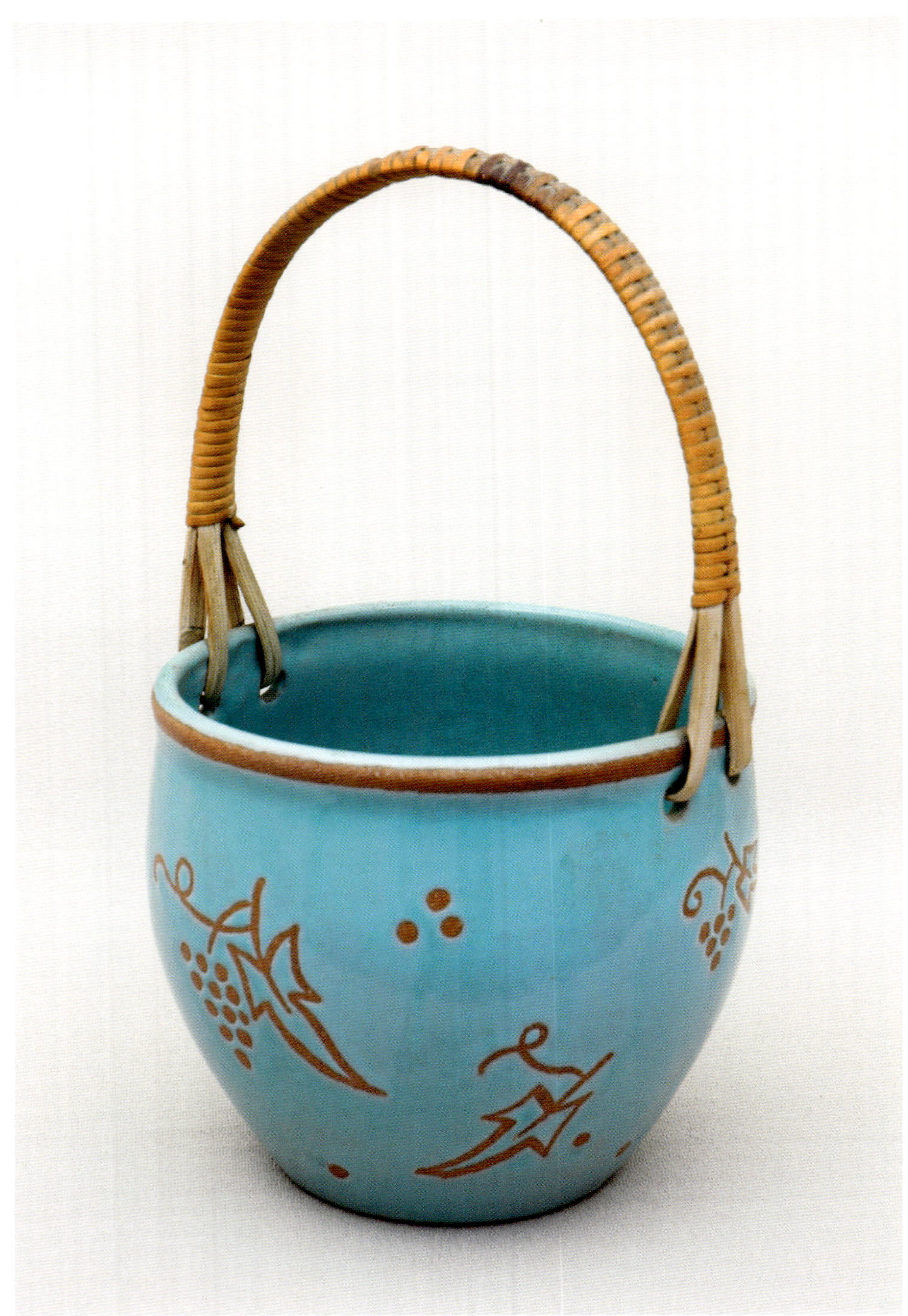

Hamburger's Pottery | Light blue vase with terracotta spots | 140x155x90mm | Provenance: Douglas van der Horst | Marks: Hamburger logo, and partially visible '26' | Photograph by Natalie Field

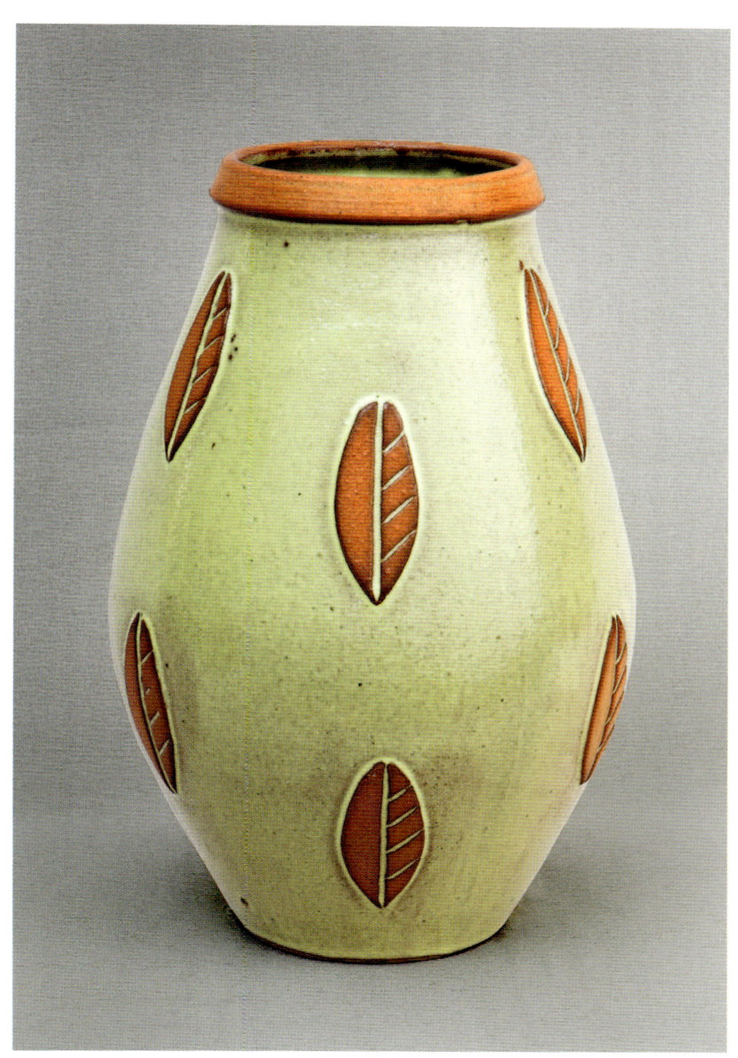

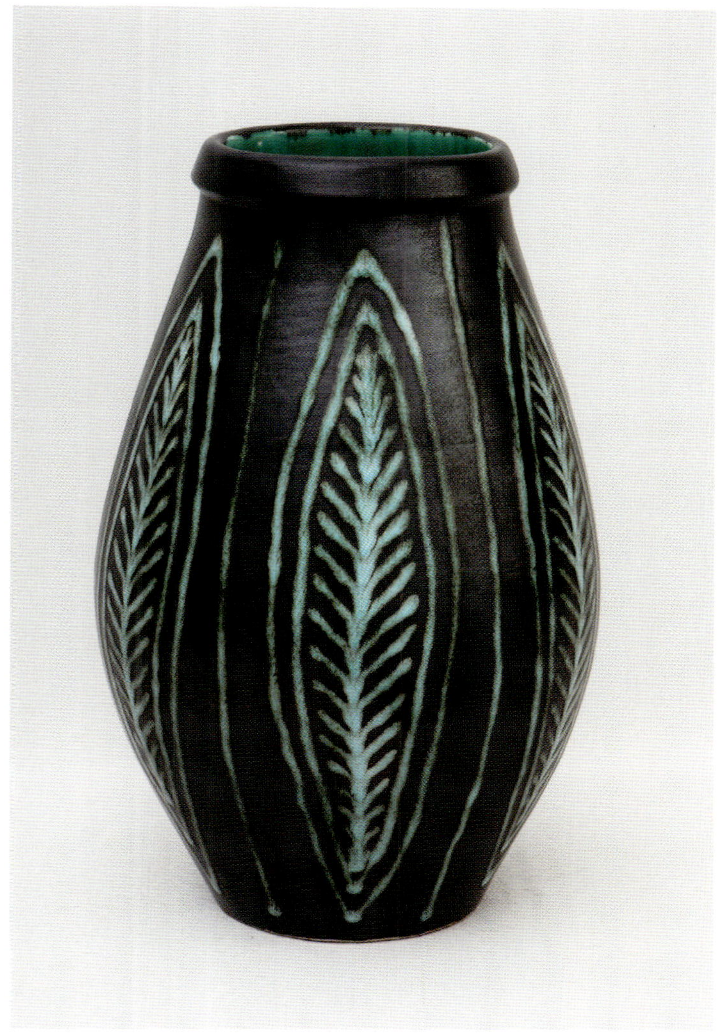

Hamburger's Pottery Vase, yellow-beige glazed body with terracotta leaves | 299x111x100mm | Provenance: Clive Newman | Marks: Hamburger logo, '276' | Photograph by Natalie Field

Hamburger's Pottery | Vase, black glazed body with green slip-trailed leaf motifs | 299x111x100mm | Provenance: Clive Newman | Marks: faint 'GH' | Photograph by Natalie Field

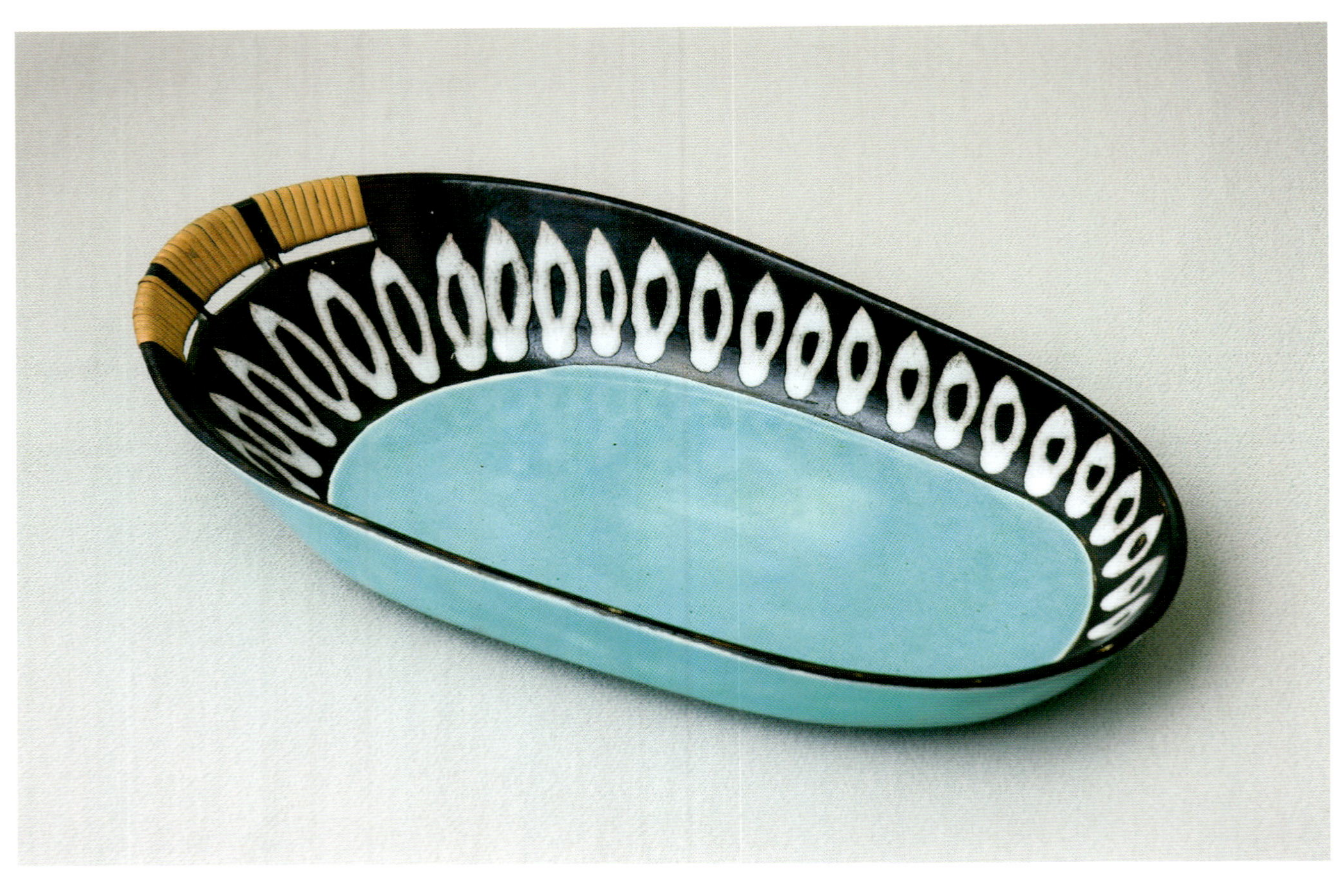

Hamburger's Pottery | Bowl, slip-trailed decorative geometric motifs, cane wrapped on handle | 65x315x180mm | Provenance: TAG | 2487/06 | Marks: Hamburger logo | Photograph by Natalie Field

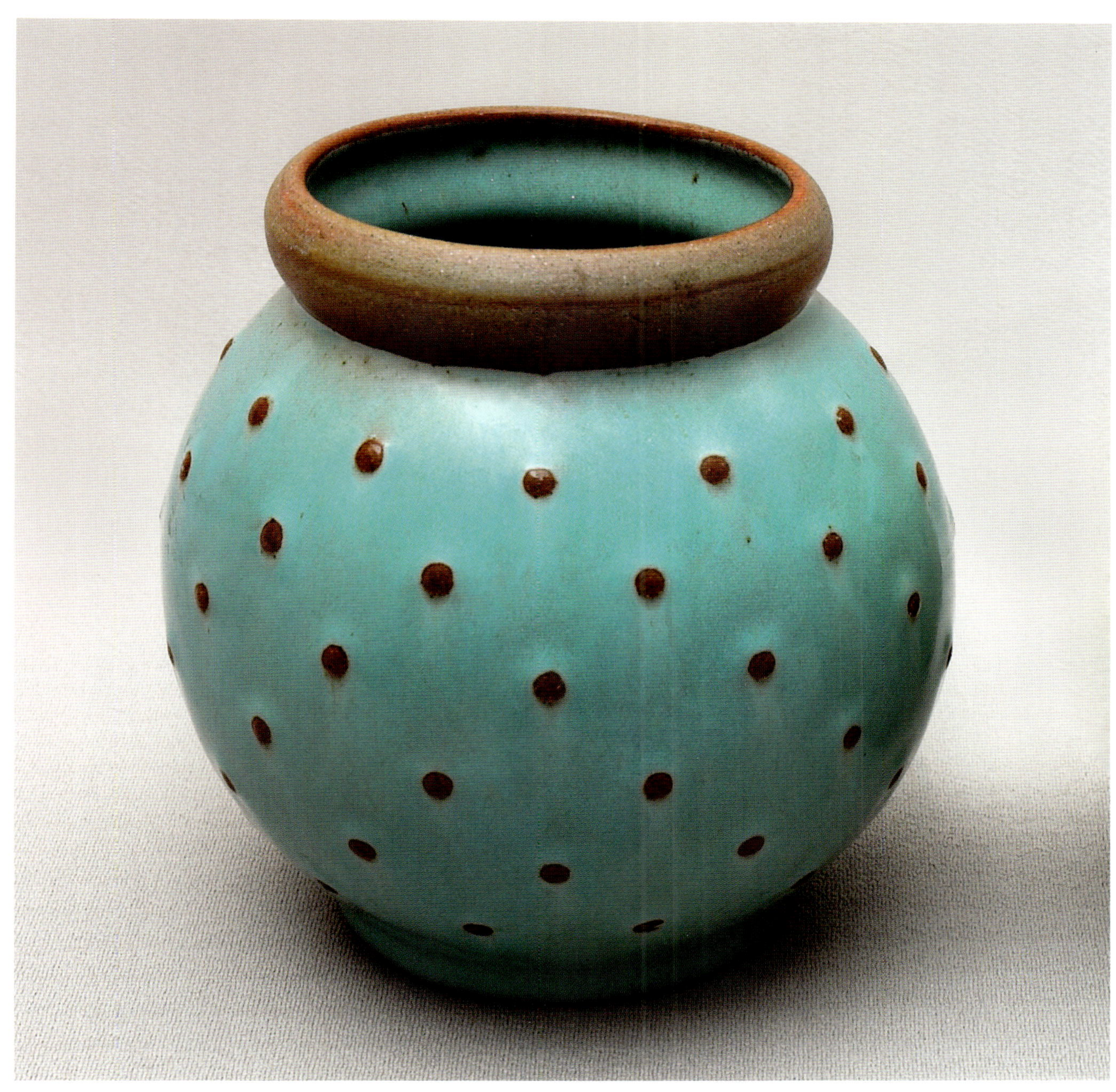

Hamburger's Pottery | Light blue vase with dots | 155x105x90mm | Provenance: Douglas van der Horst | Marks: Hamburger logo, '204' | Photograph by Natalie Field

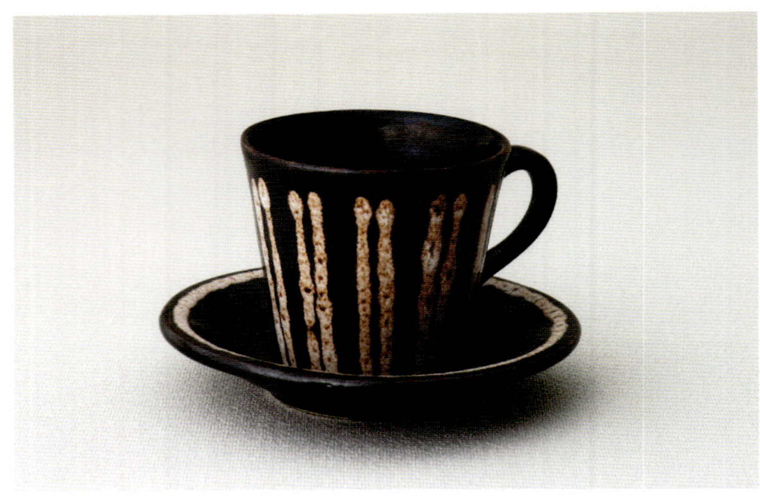

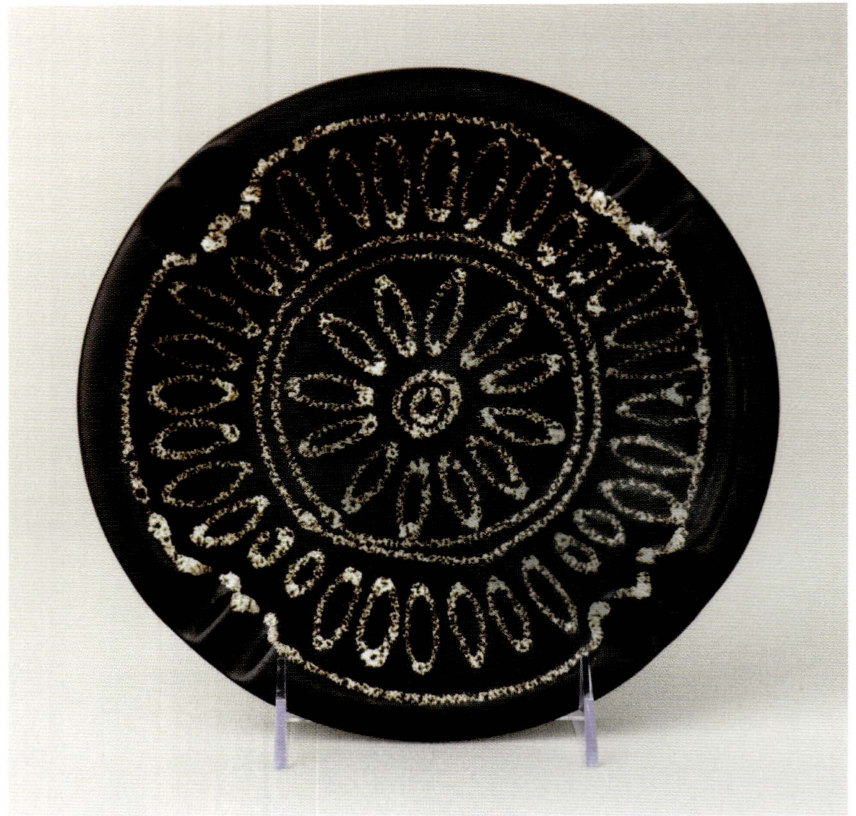

TOP: Hamburger's Pottery | Coffee cup and saucer, dark brown glazed body with off-white striped, slip-trailed decoration | Cup 70x72x47mm; saucer 115x25mm | Provenance: Dr J. van Schalkwyk | Marks: pale grey stoneware clay, gold and blue sticker, 'Koch Ceramics, Grahamstown' | Photograph by Natalie Field

ABOVE BOTTOM: Hamburger's Pottery | Ashtray, dark brown glazed body with slip-trailed floral motif | 215x40mm | Provenance: Jan Middlejans | Marks: base glazed with dark brown glaze, pale grey base clay foot rim, gold-and-black sticker, 'Hamburger's Pottery, Grahamstown' | Photograph by Natalie Field

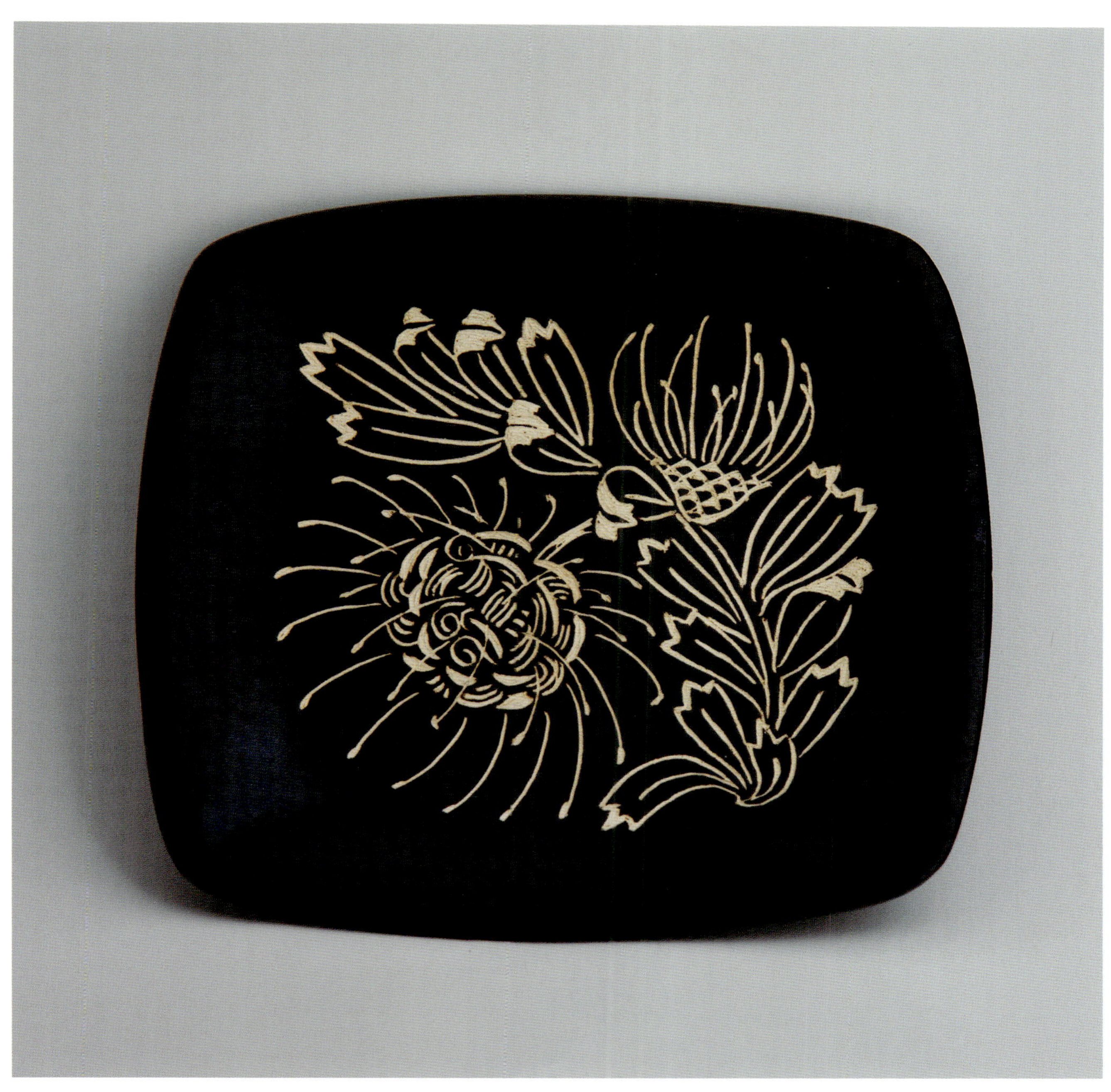

Hamburger's Pottery | Plaque, sgraffito decoration of a pin-cushion protea | 165x25mm | Provenance: Wendy Gers | Marks: Hamburger logo | Photograph by Damien Artus

Ikhwezi Lokusa Pottery (1972–2000, 2002–present)

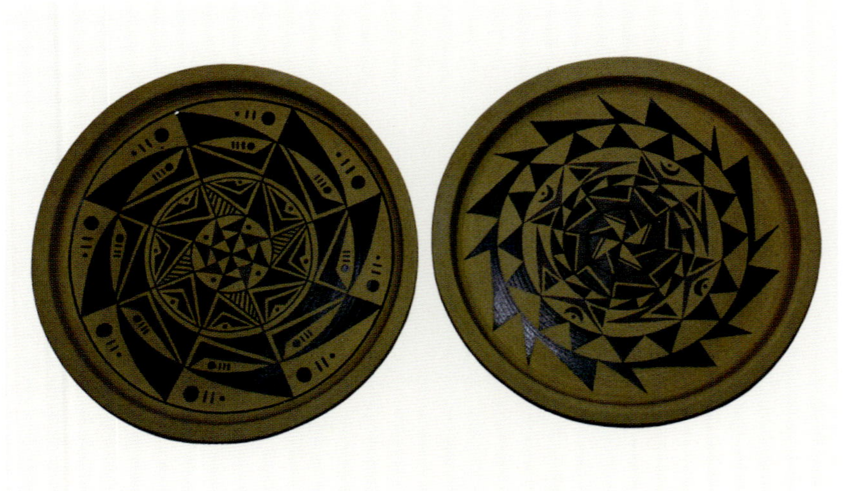

Ikhwezi Lokusa Pottery | Two large platters | ca.350mm | Provenance: Ihkwezi Lokusa Pottery | Unknown photographer

Location

The pottery, located within the grounds of the Ikhwezi Lokusa Rehabilitation and Development Society, is located five kilometres outside Mthatha, Eastern Cape.

Name

The name Ikhwezi Lokusa means Morning Star in Xhosa, a symbol of dawning hope, a pertinent image for the staff and students.

Founders

Ikhwezi Lokusa was established in 1958 by Catholic nuns of the Missionary Sisters of the Precious Blood as a residential school for cerebral palsied and orthopedically handicapped children, who were frequently abandoned at the convent. Over the years this institution has grown and transformed substantially and includes a nursery, primary and high school classrooms, sports facilities and various occupational workshops, including tailoring and jewellery making. The pottery was founded in 1972 by Sr Dolorata van Vijfeijken (1925–1998), and established with the technical and artistic guidance of Sr Maria Corda.

Managers

1976–1984	Joe Faragher
1984–1992	John Steele
1992–ca.2000	Onke Ntantiso
2002–ca.2006	Marius and Leanne Nel
2006–2009	D J Nditha
2009–present	Mathemba Ncoyini

Staff

- The pottery employed approximately 13 to 25 adults per year.
- The longest serving and most talented were David Velaphi, Eric Mtswane, Columbus Soshwebe, Kenilworth Peter and Jim Ngxabazi.
- Other potters, sculptors and assistants included Michelle Barnard, Lunga Bunywana, Simbongile Cutshela, Moses Dimane, Mr N Gubangca, Nqobile Gugushe, Nteda Makwenkodwa, Xolile Maliphale, Bongoza Mathemba, Nceba Mazoko, Nkosivumile Mchunu, Zakade Mtshulana, Mncedisi Mzileni, Bonga Mzomba, Novulile Ndabangaye Thandeka (aka Ria) Nkohla, Zanele Raraza Phindile Sihele, Zipho Sihlali, Michael Sityalweni, Sibongile Sotyalweni, Andile Tshali and Agnes Xhasa.
- Missionary Sisters of the Precious Blood included Sr Maria Michaele Renate Koch, Sr M. Bernadette and Sr Herman Joseph.
- Unidentified staff include Clovis, Khulalakeli, Linda, Lubalalo, Nonceba and Rogers.

Wares manufactured

Early wares included simple handmade crosses, plates and ashtrays with melted crushed glass used for the glazes, producing reduction glaze effects. As the pottery became more professional, it produced utilitarian wares (including thrown tea and coffee sets, casseroles, platters, sugar bowls, milk jugs, plates, pitchers, goblets, pie dishes, and salad bowls) and unique vessels and sculptural works. It also produced slip-cast ornaments (including candlesticks, a frog, dog, monkey and rhinoceros), decorative tiles, water features for homes and gardens, and items for florists such as moulded vases. In the mid-1990s the pottery manufactured necklaces.

Production methods

Faragher constructed an extruder to produce coils for hand-built vessels, and there was also a slab roller. Sculptural wares were hand-built; votive sculptures and ornaments were slip-cast. Salt and raku firings were occasionally undertaken, and earthenware and porcelain bodies were also used.

Brief history of the pottery

In 1969 on a visit to Ikhwezi Lokusa, Sr Maria Corder together with Sr Maria Ignatia Schausberger made some clay objects as a recreational activity. When the centre's director Sr Dolorata heard about this, she transferred Sr Corda to the Ikhwezi Lokusa School for the Handicapped with the idea of establishing a ceramic therapy programme for physically and mentally challenged children. In 1972 Sr Dolorata requested Sr Corda to draw plans for a pottery workshop. In September that year, the pottery workshop was built, equipped and operational.

The clay exercises had a significant therapeutic value for the children. They helped to stabilise those with cerebral palsy, so that they could then

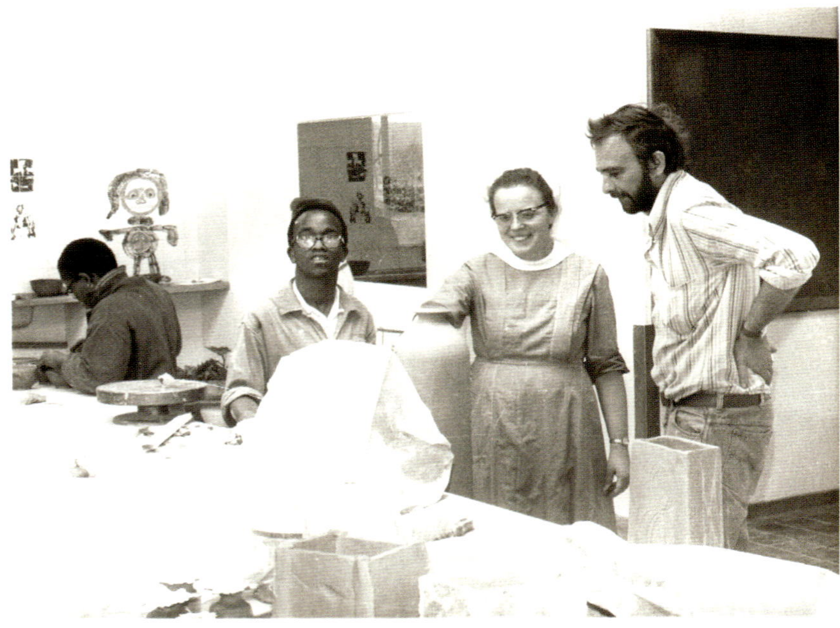

Joe Faragher, Sipho Sihlali and Sr Michaele Koch | Provenance: Ruth, Mary, Tamsin and Lynette Faragher | Photograph courtesy of Joe and Lynette Faragher | Scan by Mary, Ruth and Tamsin Faragher

use typewriters, either with a stylus in the hands or with their feet, to do their schoolwork. All materials were locally procured – clay from the Mthatha brickfields and empty glass bottles, especially blue milk of magnesia bottles from chemists for glazes. These bottles were put into a bag and crushed with crutches to get rid of the frustrations experienced by students. Soon some of the more severely handicapped learners, asked to be allowed to do full-time pottery, rather than continue with academic learning. Other students, who had completed their education at the school, but could not be reintegrated into the community, came for further training and assistance. The therapeutic workshops continued and the pottery workshop evolved into a larger project for sheltered employment.

Joe Faragher was employed as the first professional manager, working there from 1976 to 1984.[125] He was succeeded by John Steele who managed Ikhwezi Lokusa Pottery from 1984 to 1992. Onke Ntantiso succeeded Steele, leaving in approximately 2000, when the pottery finally closed after a protracted unproductive period characterised by chronic internal problems. Ntantiso was involved in local politics and had neglected the management of the pottery. In 2002 Marius and Leanne Nel leased the pottery from the nuns, intending to establish a new pottery called Kwanobuntu.[126] They were succeeded by D J Nditha (2006–2009) and Mathemba Ncoyini, who currently manages the pottery.[127]

One of the success factors behind this enterprise was its ability to create a variety of products. Wares ranged from highly original art works and sculptures to mass-produced kitsch replicas. With regard to the more original wares,

Steele claimed that he gave the staff no models and little guidance. The sculptors were discouraged to refer to the 'real', and Steele referred them to images of wood carving for inspiration. The studio notice boards also had photocopies of Esie stone figurines from Nigeria, American Indian pottery from the Southern plains, and details of fretwork. Steele claimed they had regular meetings that stressed what worked and what failed aesthetically.[128]

Ikhwezi Lokusa Pottery had an ambitious exhibition programme, won various national prizes and also undertook various challenging public commissions. The pottery was especially significant in that it was the only such pottery in southern Africa that offered sheltered employment for handicapped Africans. It was a place of immense personal growth and happiness, and gave disadvantaged and disabled people skills, an occupation and a small income. This is no small feat in the Eastern Cape, where over 26 per cent of disabled persons have no schooling, 7.5 per cent have completed school, and only 0.09 per cent are employed (Riddle 2006). The location and success of this pottery, in such an isolated and impoverished region, deserves special recognition.

Marks

Wares were not consistently marked. Stickers marked 'Ikhwezi Lokusa Pottery' and 'Ikhwezi Lokusa, Mthatha' were used. In some instances the maker's name was engraved on wares.

Select exhibitions, commissions and awards

1990 Eastern Cape Ceramics, Monument Art Gallery, Grahamstown.
1989 12th Annual Association of Potters of SA (APSA), Regional Exhibition, NMMAM.
1988 Ikhwezi artists completed a 20m² sculpted tile mural for Magwa Tea Corporation headquarters, Mthatha.
1988 Works from Ikhwezi Lokusa received highly commended awards at the 11th Annual APSA Regional Exhibition, NMMAM.
1988 David Velaphi and Eric Mtswane jointly won the Durban Art Gallery Award at the Corobrik National Ceramics Exhibition.
1987 One of David Velaphi's pots gained a highly commended award at the APSA Eastern Cape Regional Exhibition, NMMAM.
1986 Columbus Soshwebe won a prestigious bursary at the 24th Sanlam New Artists' Exhibition.
1983 Murals for the outdoor theatre of Walter Sisulu University, Mthatha.
1981 Mural on crèche in Ngangelizwe Township, Mthatha produced in collaboration with architect Peter Hoskin.

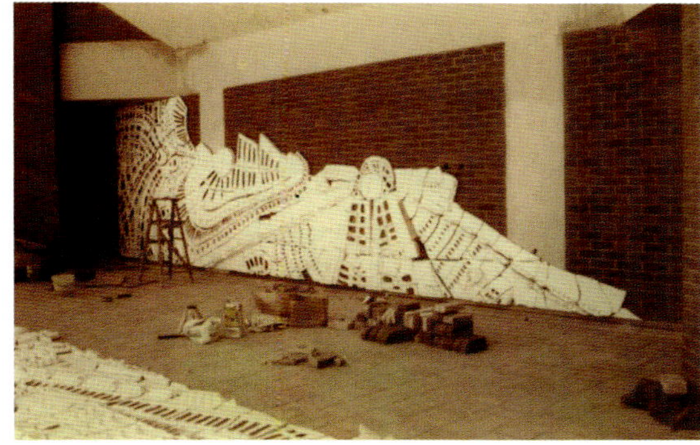

Installation of murals for the outdoor theatre, Walter Sisulu University, Mthatha, 1993 | Provenance: Joe Faragher | Photograph by Joe Faragher

Faragher claimed that the pottery won gold medals for three consecutive years at the Rand Easter Show.[129]

Biographies

BUNYWANA, Lunga

Bunywana worked briefly at Ikhwezi Lokusa Pottery in 1997.

CORDA, Sr Maria CPS (b.1940)

Born in Puchkirchen, Austria, she was the fourth of eight children. Inspired by a local church youth leader, she entered the Missionary Sisters of the Precious Blood in 1956. After taking her first vows in 1960 she was sent to Germany, where the congregation had opened an Oxford Education Centre, then to Digby Stuart College, London to qualify as a maths teacher. Sr Corda chose pottery as a practical subject, and studied under Mr String, a reputed potter. She came to St Francis College in Mariannhill in March 1969 as a maths teacher.

Sr Corda visited the convent in Mthatha, and with Sr Maria Ignatia Schausberger made some clay objects for fun. When the director heard about this, she transferred Sr Corda to Ikhwezi Lokusa School for the Handicapped with the idea of establishing a ceramic therapy programme for the children. In 1972 Sr Corda drew plans for a pottery workshop and a pottery was built, equipped and became operational. Sr Corda worked alongside the various pottery managers, assisting the adults. In 1980 health issues led to her retirement and her return to Mariannhill to teach maths part-time at St Francis College.

CUTSHELA, Simbongile

Cutshela worked at Ikhwezi Lokusa in 1997 and 1998.

DIMANE, Moses

Dimane worked at Ikhwezi Lokusa briefly in the late 1990s.

GUGUSHE, Nqobile

Gugushe worked briefly at Ikhwezi Lokusa in 1997.

GUBANGCA, N

The elderly Mr Gubangca made slabbed vessels at Ikhwezi Lokusa.

KOCH, Sr Maria Michaele Renate CPS (aka Sr Michaele Koch) (b.1940)

Born in Wasserlosen, Germany, she was sent to Glen Avent Convent in Mthatha in 1964. She joined the Ikhwezi Lokusa School when it opened in 1966, and worked with orthopaedically handicapped children, doing occupational therapy and producing useful craft articles in wool, mosaic and seeds. When pottery was introduced, she immediately showed great interest and Faragher trained her as a ceramicist. She also did arts and crafts teaching in the then higher primary school at Ikhwezi Lokusa. When Sr Maria Corda left Ikhwezi Lokusa, Sr Michaele Koch assisted Faragher in the aftercare section.

In 1981 she exhibited at the APSA National Exhibition, held at the Rand Afrikaans University. In 1986 she officially qualified as an occupational therapy technical instructor. She was subsequently employed by the King George V Hospital as the head of the occupational therapy section for long-term TB patients from 1987 to 2000. A letter from the hospital commends the sister on her exemplary employment record. She was absent for approximately 12 days in 13 years, spent her lunch breaks with patients, worked overtime and gave freely of her remaining personal time. Sr Michaele Koch is now based at Mariannhill Convent.

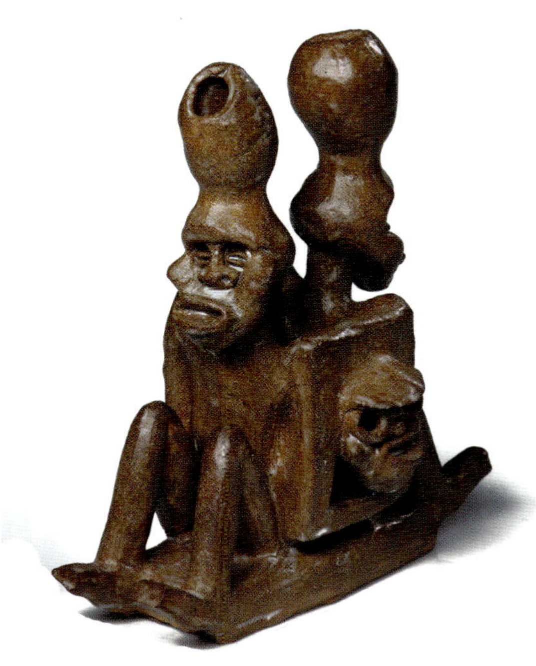

Ikhwezi Lokusa Pottery | Columbus SOSHWEBE, two figures (seated back to back) | 240x130x270mm | Provenance: Ann Bryant Art Gallery, East London | 363 | Marks: signed: Soshwebe (at base) in iron oxide | Additional information: Acquired 31 January 1990, donated by the Border Association of Potters of Southern Africa | Photograph by Jean Paul Photography, East London | Copyright Jean Paul Photography, East London

MAKWENKODWA, Nteda
Makwenkodwa worked at Ikhwezi Lokusa from 1996 until 1999.

MALIPHALE, Xolile
Maliphale worked at Ikhwezi Lokusa from 1996 until 1999.

MATHEMBA, Bongoza
Mathemba worked at Ikhwezi Lokusa from 1996 until 1999.

MAZOKO, Nceba
Mazoko worked at Ikhwezi Lokusa from 1996 until 1999.

MCHUNU, Nkosivumile
Mchunu worked at Ikhwezi Lokusa from 1997 until early 1999.

MTSHULANA, Zakade
Mtshulana worked infrequently at Ikhwezi Lokusa in 1997. His name appears on attendance registers in 1998, but he never appeared to be present.

MTSWANE, Eric
Mtswane made magnificent, large, hand-built coiled pots and large slab bottles at Ikhwezi Lokusa. He was squint and partially blind, with a deformed hand and feet. He worked with Faragher and Steele. David Velaphi frequently decorated his pots. Two of his large pots were selected in 1989 for the 12th Annual APSA Regional Exhibition, NMMAM.

MZILENI, Mncedisi
Mzileni made pots and small objects. He worked at the pottery from 1997 to 1999.

MZOMBA, Bonga
Mzomba worked at Ikhwezi Lokusa from February 1999.

NDABANGAYE, Novulile
Ndabangaye worked at Ikhwezi Lokusa from 1991 until 1999.

NGXABAZI, Jim
Ngxabazi, a deaf-mute sculptor, worked under John Steele. The last mention of him is in the attendance registers of 1989. Ngxabazi made naturalistic sculptures. One of his works is in the permanent collection of the Ann Bryant Museum, East London.

NKOHLA, Thandeka (aka Ria)
Born in Qumbu, Nkohla was a potter at Izandla, and was responsible for throwing goblets, casseroles and lidded pots. She was retrenched from Izandla, and subsequently worked at Ikhwezi Lokusa. She currently works for a cleaning firm in Mthatha.

RARAZA, Zanele
Raraza worked briefly at Ikhwezi Lokusa in 1997.

SIHELE, Phindile
Sihele was a thrower at Ikhwezi Lokusa until 1999.

SIHLALI, Zipho
Sihlali was a slab-maker at Ikhwezi Lokusa from 1979 until 1999.

SITYALWENI, Michael
An extremely versatile and talented potter and organiser, Sityalweni was the toolmaker and foreman at Ikhwezi Lokusa. He made large, complex slab vessels that were decorated by David Velaphi or John Steele. He also made slab tiles with Steele, and undertook most of the work for the huge sculpted tile mural for Magwa Tea Corporation headquarters, Mthatha. When he worked as a tractor driver for the Transkei Development Corporation, an industrial accident limited the use of his hands and arms. He worked at the pottery from 1978–1999.

SOSHWEBE, Columbus (deceased)
Soshwebe made votive items and other sculptures at Ikhwezi Lokusa. Possibly the most talented and creative artist at the centre, he talked about dreaming and visions, which he expressed in an astounding variety of unique and monumental figurative sculptures. Many of these works are meditations on his suffering from a degenerative form of spinal tuberculosis.

In June 1986 he won a prestigious bursary at the 24th Sanlam New Artists Competition. In 1989 his sculpture entitled 'What's Up' was selected for exhibition at the 12th Annual APSA Regional Exhibition, NMMAM and for the subsequent APSA National Exhibition in Johannesburg. One of his works is also in the permanent collection of the Ann Bryant Art Gallery, East London.

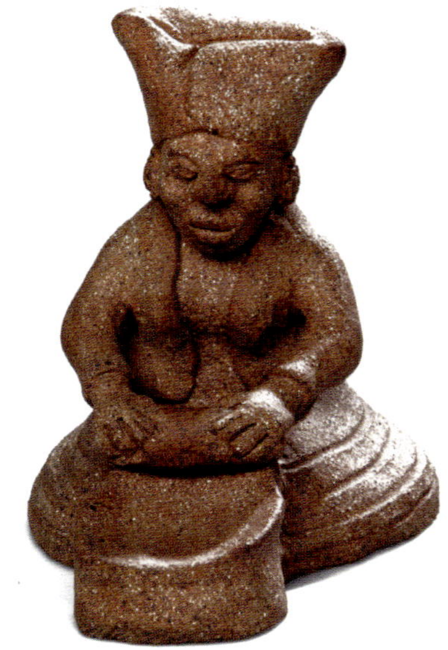

Ikhwezi Lokusa Pottery | Jim NGXABAZI, kneeling woman | 210x140x210mm | Provenance: Ann Bryant Art Gallery, East London | 364 | Marks: unmarked | Additional information: Acquired 31 January 1990, donated by the Border Association of Potters of Southern Africa | Photograph by Jean Paul Photography, East London | Copyright Jean Paul Photography, East London

SOTYALWENI, Sibongile
Sotyalweni worked briefly at Ikhwezi Lokusa in 1997. She was literate.

STEELE, John (b.1954)
Steele was born in Pretoria and obtained a BA at Rhodes University, then honours and masters in art history at UNISA. He was taught basic pottery skills by Gundi Weinek at the Doornfontein Recreation Club in Johannesburg. From approximately 1970 to 1980, Steele worked as a studio potter at Tintern Pottery in Grahamstown. Being without electricity, he used a kick wheel and reduction fired his utility ware in a kiln that used engine oil as feul. During this period Lindsay Scott (Izandla Pottery), David Schlapobersky and Felicity Potter (Cresset House Pottery) were his mentors.

In 1984 Steele took up the position of manager at the Ikhwezi Lokusa Pottery, recently vacated by Faragher. During this period the emphasis at Ikhwezi Lokusa moved from utility ware to 'one off' sculptural pieces. One such work by Eric Mswane and David Velaphi won the Durban Art Gallery Award at the 1988 Corobrik National Ceramic Exhibition. Steele was responsible for trebling the turnover of the pottery ([No author] 1988).

In 1992 Steele moved to East London and began teaching pottery and art theory from his home studio, and at the Belgravia Art Centre. He is currently employed as head of the Department of Fine Art, Walter Sisulu University, East London.

Steele has exhibited regularly in various group exhibitions. His works are in private collections as well as in the Ann Bryant Art Gallery, East London. He has presented various papers at conferences, including the 2001 12th ACASA Triennial Symposium on African Art, St Thomas, US Virgin Islands, and at the 1999, 2002, 2004, 2005 and 2006 conferences of the South African Association of Art Historians. In 2005 he was a guest lecturer at the Sir J J School of Art, Mumbai University, India.

TSHALI, Andile
Tshali worked at Ikhwezi Lokusa in 1998 and 1999.

VAN VIJFEIJKEN, Sr Dolorata CPS (1925–1998)
Sr Dolorata was born into a large family in Deume, Holland. In 1945 she joined the Missionary Sisters of the Precious Blood and in 1948 was transferred to South Africa. In 1967 she was assigned to the Transkei as deputy-principal of Ikhwezi Lokusa. She became the director of the Ikhwezi Lokusa Special School and the Ikhwezi Lokusa Rehabilitation and Development Centre in 1969, a post she held until she retired in 1993. From then to her death, she served as director of the Ikhwezi Lokusa Rehabilitation and Development Centre. She was responsible for all the initial fundraising and for importing the equipment from England to establish the pottery.

Sr Dolorata was an active member of the greater Mthatha community. She assisted in the establishment of various other institutions for the handicapped, including the Khanyisa Special School, the Thembisa Special School, the Vukuzenzele Special School and the Mpumalanga Special School. She was also involved in mentoring two Cheshire Homes: Camama Cheshire Home for disabled adults and the Mount Fletcher Cheshire Home for mentally and physically disabled children. She served on the management committee of the Mthatha Child and Family Welfare Society. Sr Dolorata died of cancer in Durban's St Augestine's Hospital in 1998.

VELAPHI, David (b.1963)

Known as Bongo-Bongo, Velaphi was a decorator at Ikhwezi Lokusa. He was particularly renowned for his diamond and other geometric patterns applied to coiled pots made by Eric Mswane. The decoration was applied in iron or cobalt pigment. Occasionally he incorporated sgraffito elements into his decoration. In 1997 one of his pots gained a highly commended award at the APSA Eastern Cape Regional Exhibition, NMMAM. Velaphi also experimented with tile production. His tiles were decorated with impressed designs, obtained by using a slab roller and a stencil cut-out. In addition to pottery production, in the late 1980s, Velaphi and his trainee Agnes Xhasa were responsible for administration, including pricing, cataloguing, stocktaking and sales.

A polio victim who suffered from spina bifida, Velaphi was wheelchair bound. He worked with Faragher and Steele and was last mentioned in 1989.

XHASA, Agnes

Xhasa was responsible for administration, the showroom and customer relations. She worked at Ikhwezi Lokusa from 1986 until 1999. She currently works in the sewing department.

Unidentified staff

[Surname unknown], Clovis

He made interesting sculptures and reproduced key works.

[Surname unknown], Khulalakeli (deceased)

Khulalakeli made porcelain and stoneware figurines at Ikhwezi Lokusa, mostly of Xhosa women in traditional garb.

[Surname unknown], Linda

Linda was responsible for clay preparation at Ikhwezi Lokusa.

[Surname unknown], Lubabalo

Lubalalo worked at Ikhwezi Lokusa in 1999.

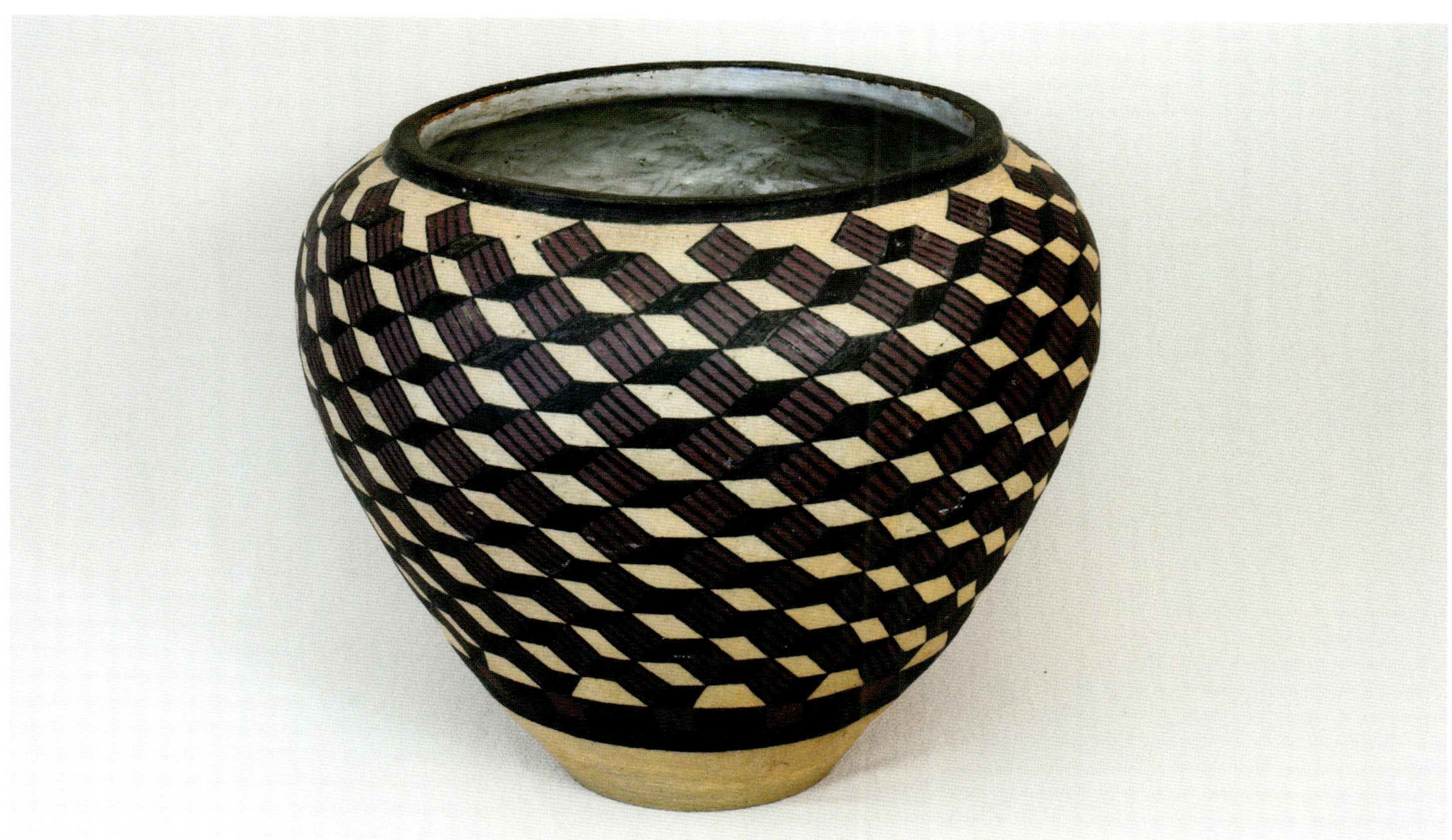

Ikhwezi Lokusa Pottery | Large pot | 285x240x115mm | Provenance: Professor Mark Watson | Marks: sticker, 'Ikhwezi Lokusa, Umtata, H.W. R165.00' | Photograph by Natalie Field

[Surname unknown], Nonceba
Nonceba was a thrower at Ikhwezi Lokusa. She also did handling and made teapots.

[Surname unknown], Sr Herman Joseph
While Faragher was manager, Sr Herman Joseph assisted at Ikhwezi Lokusa. She later left to help the school children with therapeutic clay work.

[Surname unknown], Sr M Bernadette
Sr Bernadette was responsible for the administration of Ikhwezi Lokusa.

[Surname unknown], Rogers
Rogers was responsible for clay production and rolling slabs at Ikhwezi Lokusa. He was mentally handicapped, but was incredibly strong and would carry the raw materials.

Izandla Pottery (1977–1996, 2001–ca.2010)

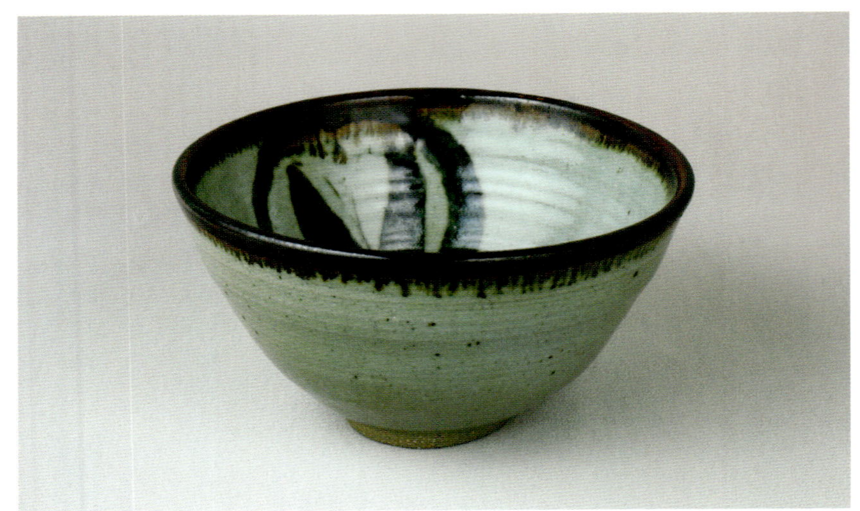

Izandla | Bowl, speckled oatmeal glaze with brown band along lip and leaf motifs in interior | ca.550x170mm | Provenance: Clive & Ann Berlyn | Marks: unmarked | Photograph by Natalie Field

Location

For approximately a year, the pottery was temporarily housed in factory facilities belonging to the Transkei Development Corporation (TDC). A new factory was soon built on Thornhill farm, Mthatha, adjacent to another TDC employment project, the Wonkomntu Weavers. The Izandla premises included a shop.

Name

Izandla means hands in Xhosa and Zulu.

Founders and managers

Izandla Pottery was essentially a development project, founded and funded by the former TDC. The managers included:

1977–1979	Angelique and Stephen Kirk
1979–1984	Lindsay Scott
1984–ca.1989	Michael Gill
1989	Faan Kruger
1989	John Sachs
1989	Aneas Quinta
1989–1991	Wonga Tuswa
1992–1993	George Coo
2001–ca.2010	Bongani Mzantsi

Staff

The Kirks predominantly recruited rural, less-educated Transkeian women. This employment profile persisted under subsequent managers. Staff included Nozulu Dondi, Buyiswa Dudumashe, Thandekile Faya-Mafanya, Ntombi

Gcaba, Constance Gwala, Florence Jara, Elsie Thembeka Jumbile, Rahaba Kakudi, Elaine Kark, Nozityilelo Langa, Keslina Madosini, Vivian Madosini, Vusiwe Mahogana, Leonie Malherbe, Grace Mase, Zuziwe Mathokazi, Leslie Mbelekana, Peter Mbi, Ndileka Mbobana, Gerda Meershoek, Cynthia Mjacu, Soslina Mlala, Faniswa Mnakaniso, Nokuzola Moyakhe, Fundi Mpayipheli, Lawrence Makwazewa Mvokwe, Nonzwakazi Mzazela, Keslina Ndabeni, Miriam Lumka Ndabeni, Beatrice Ngaleka, Cynthia Ngubo, Keslina Matuzana Ngubo, Thandeka (aka Ria) Nkohla, Lindiwe (aka Lindie) Nyoni, Aeneas Quinta, Judy Radlof, Khawuleza Sakwe and Florida Xintolo. Unidentified staff included Eslina, Khulukazi, Mavis, Msotho, Nokwandia, Nomute, Nomvula and Patience.

Wares manufactured

Izandla primarily produced reduced stoneware utilitarian items, including bowls, casseroles, vases and lidded jars. Under Angelique Kirk it produced figurines of Xhosa women in traditional costume, and whistles in the form of an ox. Some casseroles had sharply inclined lids resembling traditional Transkeian homesteads; others had handles with oxen heads. The wares featured reduction glazes, with grey, blue and white glaze decoration. Initially Kirk did all the decoration with oxides, painting loose gestural impressions of organic forms such as wheat, flowers and grass. Later, colour slips and sgraffito decoration, depicting figurative motifs and geometric patterns and lines, were introduced.[130]

Scott phased out all hand-building and focused on dinner services, platters, bowls, casseroles and mugs. Scott also phased out vases and tall jars in favour of more classical casseroles. He discontinued the use of blue and grey glazes and floral motifs and introduced a new range of celadon glazes and a new type of decoration using iron red/brown slips. Under Scott, Izandla initially used either a celadon glaze or a matt oatmeal-coloured glaze with decoration in a light terracotta (iron) slip, but later switched to a green glazed body featuring intense red combed patterns (produced by slip with a high iron content). Items such as jugs frequently featured very simple bands of red slip on the body and a single line of slip around the rim. Under Scott, the bases of wares were turned but did not have a foot ring, and teapots had handles made of local cane bound with garden twine.[131]

The Izandla repertoire expanded under Gill, and included ten-litre, celadon-glazed wine jugs that were fitted with a wooden tap and cork stopper. The pottery made numerous large bowls, including a 40-cm bowl that was finished with a matt glaze and a 42-cm celadon platter. Gill introduced sets of six 'nesting' casseroles and sets of four unglazed lidded dishes. He was also responsible for the production of tenmoku tea sets, which were finished with imported Japanese bamboo and cane handles. Other items produced during this period include trays, celadon blue trinket jars, 26-cm bottles and cider jars with taps imported from France.[132]

Production methods

Wares were thrown on the potter's wheel and others were hand-built. The bases of the wares were turned but did not have a foot ring. Izandla wares are characterised by their strong, coarse, pale grey clay body.[133]

Brief history of the pottery

The founding of Izandla needs to be understood within the historical context of the Transkei and the TDC. It was part of a broader scheme that aimed to establish local industries and create employment in the Transkei. The TDC offered generous concessions in terms of credit, tax relief and transport. Trade unions were banned from 1977, and salaries were incredibly low compared to nearby South African factories (Rich 1996:205). The TDC was essentially run by the Corporation for Economic Development in Pretoria and its long-term aim was for these businesses to be taken over by local professionals.[134]

In 1977 the TDC granted Kirk R80 000 for equipment and one year's worth of salaries. In exchange, the TDC insisted that Izandla focus on mass production of utilitarian wares, rather than the production of individual artistic pieces, which may have been more difficult to market. The undertaking was required to generate income from the outset. The relationship with the TDC was strained, and in 1979 Izandla had to downscale its staff, from 35 to 20 employees. It took Kirk almost three years to train the staff in the basic skills involved in pottery production ([No author] 1970s).

Lindsay Scott visited Izandla when it was in the process of being closed down by the TDC. He pleaded with them to allow him six months to improve its financial status and he ran the pottery from September 1979 to the beginning of 1984. Izandla was soon awarded many large orders. Under Scott wares were marketed to hotels in the region, which each had a display case from which tourists could order. Izandla also supplied some large department stores, but these orders were not sustained. It sold large quantities through their showroom to locals and passing trade and participated in a few exhibitions.

Scott reorganised the staff, trained them and assigned new tasks. He instituted new products, glazes and decoration styles. Ngubo was the only staff member who could decorate in the style that pleased Scott, so she was made a decorator and ceased being a thrower. He also instituted basic improvements that boosted staff morale, like heating the factory in winter and allowing the throwers to use warm water to lubricate pots during the throwing process.

During this period, Faan Kruger was responsible for marketing Izandla's wares. In the 1970s and early 1980s the TDC senior manager for operations responsible for Izandla was Nick van Rensburg. He, together with numerous other managers, was fired by Chief Kaiser Matanzima (1915–2003) in October 1984. Van Rensburg was replaced by Wilberforce Nyati. There was a lack of understanding between Nyati and Scott, which led to Scott's resignation.

After Scott's departure, Michael Gill was appointed manager in 1984.

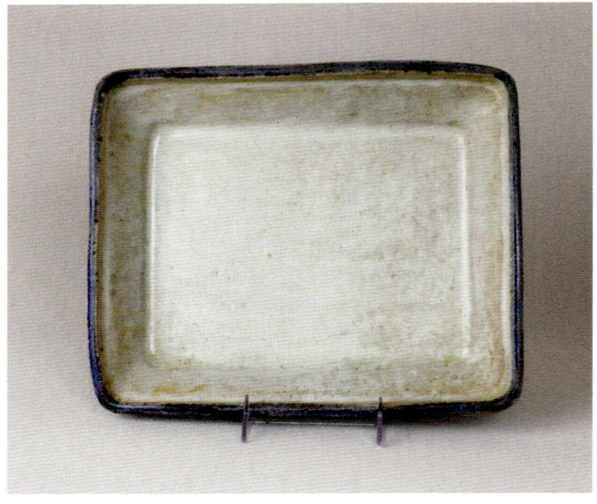

Izandla | Square bowl made from slabs | Provenance: Clive and Ann Berlyn | Marks: unmarked | Photograph by Natalie Field

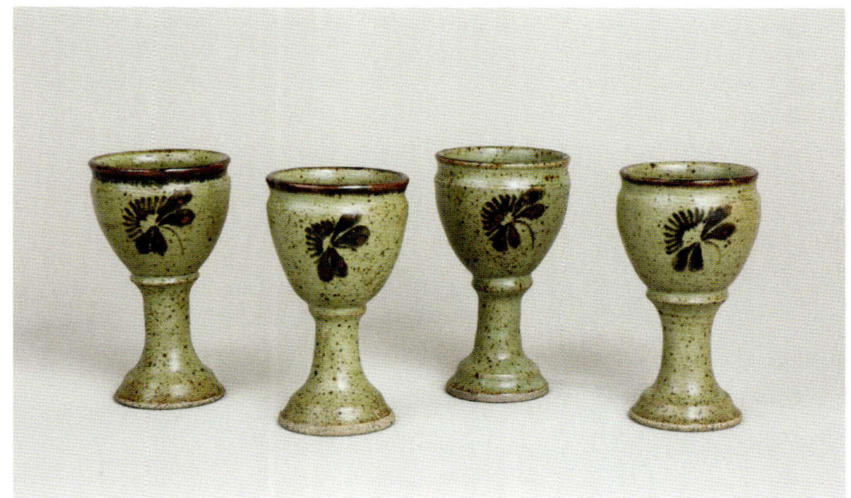

Izandla | Wine goblets, stoneware decorated with stylised floral decorative motif | Provenance: Clive and Ann Berlyn | Marks: unmarked | Photograph by Natalie Field

Gill made various sweeping changes to the pottery, which had been operating at a loss for some years. He reorganised the staff and retrained them in various tasks, especially decoration styles. Gill negotiated salary raises for the staff and introduced a system of payment by the piece. He designed new smaller boxes and other specialised packaging material for transporting wares. The 'sale of return' policy was stopped. Gill requisitioned wares used as decoration in hotels and department stores. He favoured rail transport and discontinued freight by road, which had resulted in over 30 per cent breakage. Gill also instituted firm stock control procedures after the discovery of significant pilfering by the staff. According to Gill, most wares were sold from their shop to visiting holidaymakers. The pottery made a profit in the 1984 financial year and prospects were good. However, the international economic boycott of South Africa caused the cancellation of large international orders, and soon thereafter, the pottery began to struggle.

Gill's honeymoon period was cut short in February 1986 when Matanzima was forced to retire as Transkei's president. He was succeeded by his brother George, who made radical staff changes at the TDC. Gill's relationship with his new superiors was strained as they made sweeping changes to the pottery's administration, increasing the rent significantly and failing to undertake essential maintenance work on the buildings. The TDC also failed to pay contractors such as electricians for their services. Realising that the pottery was in financial and 'political' difficulty, Gill encouraged his staff to embark on night studies, and many retrained as nurses. Gill was requested to present a five-year development plan for Izandla to his new superiors; it failed to meet their expectations and he was dismissed.

Under Kirk, Scott and Gill, the pottery, despite not always meeting the financial expectations of the TDC, was an extremely joyful and productive enterprise. In fact, it was known for the excellence of its singers and dancers.

Faan Kruger, an administrator with no pottery skills, succeeded Gill, but did not stay long, departing in 1986. John Sachs replaced Kruger. A crippling blow was dealt to the pottery when approximately 125 boxes of wares for the Rand Easter Show were allegedly stolen. Izandla never recovered financially and Sachs was replaced by an administrative clerk and driver, Mr Aneas Quinta. Under Quinta, Izandla continued to make the same products as instituted by Gill. Quinta was shortly thereafter promoted to the TDC head office.

Wonga Tuswa succeeded Quinta as manager from 1989 to 1991 after which the pottery was closed by Nyati. Tuswa, like Quinta, had no pottery skills and little understanding of the business. The pottery experienced numerous kiln problems and there were production delays while waiting for experts from the Transvaal to repair their kilns. During this period the Transkei went through a period of extreme political, social and economic instability. In 1989 Stella Sigcau usurped the Matanzima dynasty and ruled for 88 days. She was replaced by a military coup led by Bantu Holomisa, which heralded a new period of civil disorder. This climate of political instability undermined the local economy, and Izandla, like so many other businesses, suffered.

In 1992 George Coo, a Ghanaian art teacher and potter was hired by the TDC to manage Izandla. He repaired the kiln and introduced some new designs, many of which were similar to Gill's. However, the TDC did not renew his work contract and in 1993 Coo departed. The TDC sold Izandla as a private company, but it did not survive six months under its new owners and was finally closed at the end of 1996. After several years of closure, the much-neglected pottery was reopened in 2001 and was semi-operational under the direction of Bongani Mzantsi. The kiln no longer functioned and the company made small ornaments and sculptures that were painted with acrylic paint and varnish.[135]

The fate of Izandla was integrally linked to that of the TDC and its personalities and politics. Unfortunately most of Izandla's talented managers were mistreated or misled by their TDC superiors. Amazingly, Izandla survived almost three decades of continual blundering by the TDC. It is in no small part due to the loyalty of the staff and the devotion of the managers that the undertaking managed to eke out an existence over such a long period. Its products were innovative, and their interesting contemporary forms, colours and decorations won a loyal clientele. Creative marketing consolidated Izandla's presence in this isolated region and further afield. Finally, it was the building and its facilities that ground Izandla to a halt. The lack of maintenance and renewal, especially of the kiln, the heart of a pottery, sealed Izandla's fate. In 2010 Izandla was struck off the register of South African companies.[136]

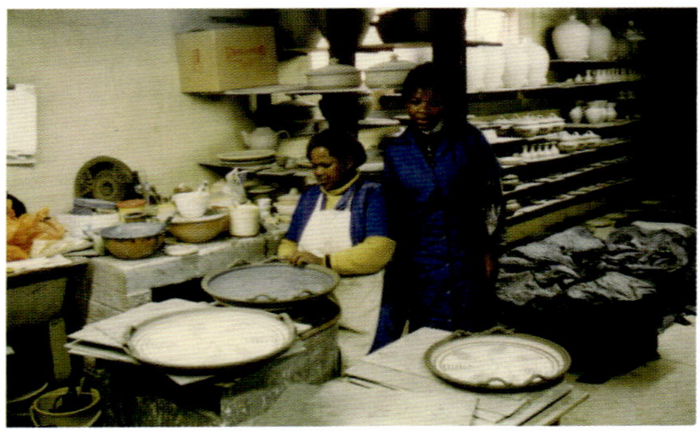

Izandla | Keslina Ngubo seated and unnamed staff members (ca.1989) | Provenance: Keslina Ngubo | Photograph by Michael Gill

Marks

Under Kirk, some wares were marked with a stamp, 'Izandla Pottery'. Under Scott and Gill works were not marked. Stickers were also used and were marked, 'UMthatha/Izandla Pottery'.

Select exhibitions

1985 APSA Corobrik Regional Ceramics Exhibition, NMMAM. Five items were selected for the APSA National Exhibition, Genkor Gallery, Rand Afrikaans University, Johannesburg.

1981 APSA National Exhibition, Genkor Gallery, Rand Afrikaans University, Johannesburg. The pottery submitted a set of goblets, a celadon platter and an 18-piece dinner set. Scott received a highly commended award for his raku-fired bowl with lid.

1977–1979 Izandla exhibited on the Transkei Government Stand at the Rand Easter Show.

Biographies

COO, George

Born in Ghana, Coo was an art teacher, kiln technician and ceramicist, who managed Izandla from 1992 to 1993. When he left Izandla he went to Bophuthatswana and currently lives in Swaziland.

DONDI, Nozulu

Born in Mthatha, Dondi was responsible for firing the kiln.

DUDUMASHE, Buyiswa

Born in Engcobo, Dudumashe was initially employed as a wedger but was subsequently trained as a thrower.

FAYA-MAFANYA, Thandekile

Born in Mthatha, Faya-Mafanya was initially trained as a waxer, and subsequently as a decorator by Keslina Ngubo. She was later transferred to the glazing department. She currently lives in Butterworth, where she runs a small shop.

GCABA, Ntombi

Gcaba was one of the original throwers employed by Izandla. After many years, she was retrenched.

GILL, Michael (b.1927)

Gill was born in London and studied at Bryanston, England, where he was introduced to pottery by Donald Potter in 1941. As a scholar he became an enthusiastic potter and exhibited at the first Heals School Exhibition. Gill worked at Leach Pottery in 1943 with the renowned English ceramicist Michael Cardew. He then continued his studies in Chemistry at Princeton University and upon his return to England in 1949 Gill taught pottery at the Central Art School with Dora Billington (1890–1968) and Lucy Rie.

Between 1950 and 1956 Gill undertook an extensive 'round the world' trip, which included sojourns in Denmark, Finland, Uganda, northern Kenya, Australia, New Zealand and Israel. During this period he worked in Copenhagen and Helsinki and started a pottery in the Kibbutz Sasa, Israel. Gill also travelled to South Africa, arriving in late 1952 on a motorcycle from Uganda. He met Audrey Frank in Cape Town, and was invited to join Linnware in order to assist with the development of porcelain and stoneware. Gill spent a brief month at Olifantsfontein, at the beginning of 1953, largely developing glazes for porcelain and stoneware bodies, including a synthetic wood ash glaze.[137] Unknown to Gill, after his departure a small exhibition of his work at Olifantsfontein was mounted in Johannesburg, under the name of Gillimeads Stoneware. His work was also included in a 1953 exhibition at the S A Association of the Arts, Cape Town, which included wares by Methley and Van Schalkwyk.

In 1954 Gill visited Ivan McMeekin, a pioneer potter who had trained and worked with Michael Cardew at Wenford Bridge Pottery, and who was working in Sturt, Australia. He then visited and worked in New Zealand, where another pioneer potter, Helen Mason (b.1915) described him as the 'first bearded, sandalled potter to arrive in this country [New Zealand] with a post-war outlook and a new set of values'.[138] From 1956 to 1966 Gill worked for the Ugandan Development Corporation, and set up a pottery and craft centre with local potters. Upon his return to England, Gill taught pottery part-time.

Gill later returned to South Africa upon the recommendation of Hyme Rabinowitz, and at the invitation of Lindsay Scott managed Izandla Pottery from 1984 to 1989. During Gill's first six months, the Transkei was a stable, peaceful haven. However, the military coup by Kaiser Matanzima resulted in radical staff changes at the TDC. Gill's relationship with his new superiors was strained and he was ultimately dismissed. Gill returned to England and taught chemistry and physics. He retired in 1990 but continued to make pottery from his studio in Dorset.[139] In 2005 he moved to Australia.

GWALA, Constance

Born in Mount Frere, Gwala was a potter and glazer under Scott. Under Gill she worked as a waxer. She was also the lead chorister in the Izandla dance group.

JARA, Florence

Born in Qumbu, Jara worked as a thrower and specialised in small items, such as jugs. While working at Izandla she completed her high school studies through a local night school, and was subsequently employed by the post office.

JUMBILE, Elsie Thembeka

Born in Lusikisiki, Transkei, Jumbile was initially a thrower but, being literate, she was promoted to the sales department, where she was responsible for packing. She was a general sales assistant under Kirk, Scott and Gill, and was also a driver for the factory.

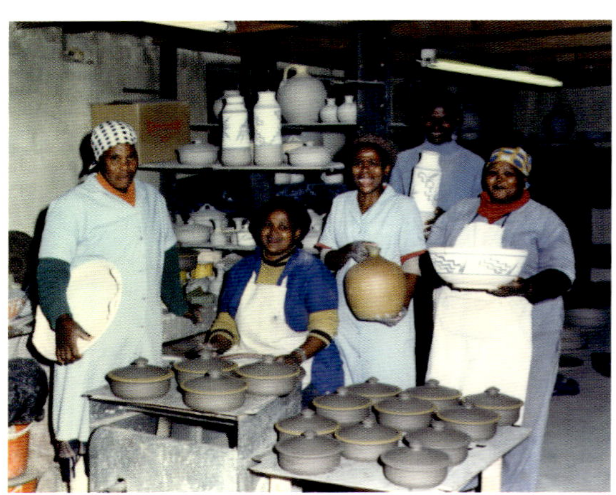

Izandla | Keslina Ngubo seated and unnamed staff member (ca.1989) | Provenance: Keslina Ngubo | Photograph by Michael Gill

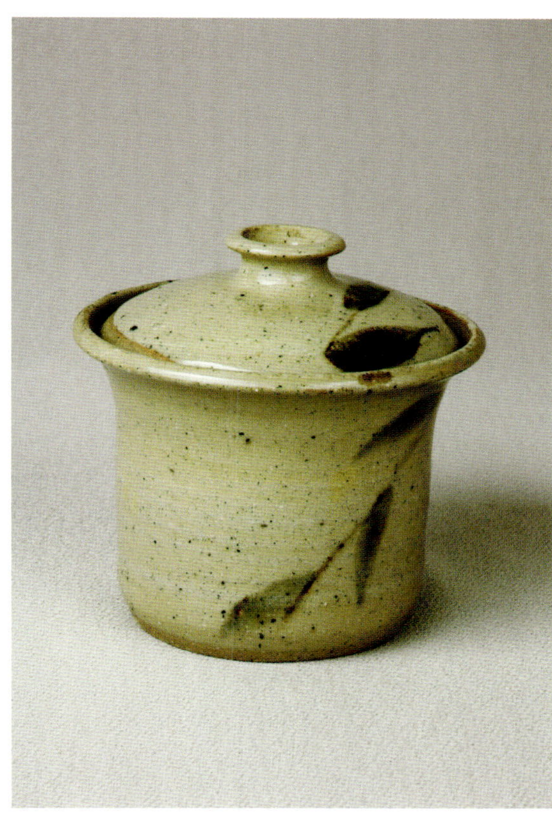

Izandla | Pot with lid, speckled beige oatmeal glaze with leaf motifs on lid and pot | ca.170x120mm | Provenance: Clive and Ann Berlyn | Marks: unmarked | Photograph by Natalie Field

KAKUDI, Rahaba

Born in Sterkspruit, Kakudi was recruited and trained by Scott in 1979 and worked at Izandla as a thrower. She was also a talented singer.

KARK, Elaine (deceased)

Kark was responsible for marketing and public relations.

KIRK, Angelique (b.1953)

Born in Pietermaritzburg, Kirk studied sculpture at the Durban Technical College from 1972 to 1974 and took extramural pottery classes with Barbara Simpson and had a brief apprenticeship with Bryan Everard Haden in 1975. With her husband, Stephen Kirk, she opened a pottery school and studio in Claremont, Cape Town.

In August 1977 the couple set up Izandla Pottery near Mthatha. Kirk's contract was terminated in 1979 by the TDC when she fell pregnant. Kirk recalls that there was a wonderful spirit among the workers, who voluntarily worked on weekends and were always singing. In 1979 the Kirks moved to Emithini, near Port Edward and in 1980 they established the Old Pont Pottery.

From 1986 to 1992 she taught pottery part-time at Northdale Technical College, Pietermaritzburg, and ran her own home-based production studio. In the 1990s Kirk worked with unemployed women in Khayelitsha, in a pottery project called Umfoleni.

She has won numerous awards, including the regional Corobrik Awards in 1989, 1990, 1991 and 1994. Kirk has participated in the International Exhibition of Ceramic Art at the National Museum of History, Taipei, Taiwan. Her works are found in the permanent collections of numerous art museums, including the Tatham Art Gallery, Pietermaritzburg; the Durban Art Gallery; the Pretoria Art Museum; and the SANG, Cape Town.

KIRK, Stephen Dale (b.1952)

Born in Durban, Kirk trained as an electrical engineer at the University of Natal, Durban, but never completed his degree. He briefly trained in pottery in 1974 and 1975 with Bryan Everard Haden. Kirk assisted his wife in their various pottery undertakings. At Izandla he built a trolley kiln and taught staff firing skills. He currently lives in Germany.

LANGA, Nozityilelo

Born in Port St John's, Langa was a wedger and then a thrower. She now works in a supermarket.

MADOSINI, Keslina

Madosini was the head decorator at Izandla.

MADOSINI, Vivian (deceased)
Born in Mthatha, Masosini was a wedger and was responsible for carrying the clay from the storage area to the wedging tables.

MAHOGANA, Vusiwe
Mahogana was employed as a clerk. She presently works for Standard Bank, Mthatha.

MALHERBE, Leonie (b.1942)
Malherbe was born in Cape Town. She was an art teacher in Mthatha, prior to being hired by the TDC to assist Scott at Izandla in 1981. She was initially responsible for secretarial duties, pottery sales, the gallery and various displays that were housed at each of the TDC hotels on the Transkei coast. Malherbe designed the Izandla logo for the letterhead, business cards and packing materials. Malherbe, a highly creative person, was frustrated with her essentially administrative post and thus swapped posts with the thrower, Grace Mase. The change in profile involved a significant financial shift – Malherbe received R150 per month as a thrower, as opposed to R500 as a manager. She worked as a production thrower from 1982 to 1984. Her duties, in addition to throwing a daily quota of pots, included training new throwers, organising production quotas for co-workers, and doing clay body and glaze tests. Malherbe submitted various production ware designs to the pottery including storage jars of 1kg and 4kg.

Malherbe and Scott left Izandla and set up Hillfold Pottery on the Midlands Meander. In 1986 she moved to Durban, where she operated her children's art school for ten years. In the 1990s, Malherbe became involved in fabric and fibre arts, and has participated in various quilting and fabric art exhibitions, both locally and abroad. She is also a freelance writer and has published many articles about various crafts in *Your Family* magazine. Since the 1990s she has worked part-time for the African Art Centre, Durban.[140]

MASE, Grace
The sister of Florence Jara, Mase was born in Encobo and was originally a thrower. Both Mase and Malherbe were unhappy in their respective roles at the pottery and swapped jobs. Mase thus became the showroom manager and continued to manage sales and stock under Gill.

MATHOKAZI, Zuziwe
Born in Matatiele, Mathokazi was a thrower at Izandla. She is now a traditional healer.

MBELEKANA, Leslie
Born in Tsomo, Mbelekana was a potter at Izandla. She specialised in platters, trays, lidded pots and other large wares. Under Gill, she was responsible for throwing sets of six 'nesting' casseroles. She retired shortly after Gill's departure.

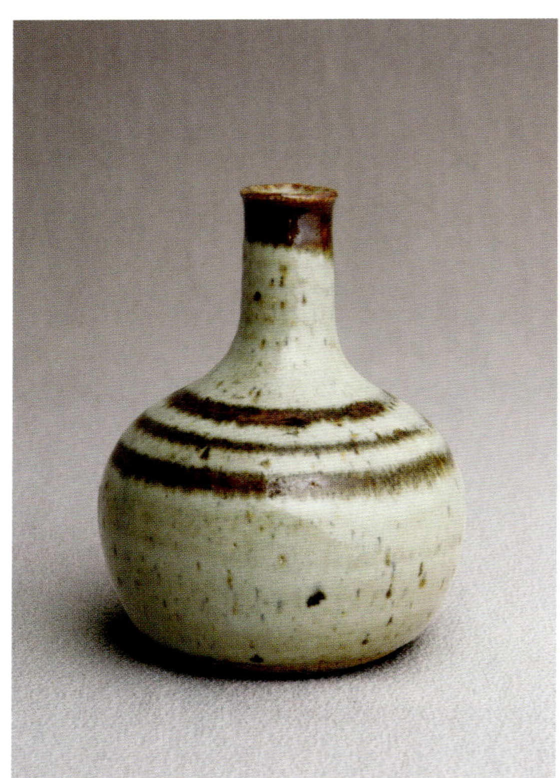

Izandla | Small tapering vase, speckled oatmeal glaze with three brown bands of glaze decoration and a brown lip | ca.250x200mm | Provenance: Clive and Ann Berlyn | Marks: unmarked | Photograph by Natalie Field

MBI, Peter
Born in Elliotdale, Mbi threw large wares and assisted with the firing of the kiln.

MBOBANA, Ndileka
Born in Mqanduli, Mbobana worked in the sales department.

MEERSHOEK, Gerda
Meershoek worked at Ikwesi Lokusa with Joe Faragher and then with Scott from 1980 to 1987. She worked in the showroom.

MJACU, Cynthia
Born in Port St John's, Mjacu was a glazer and attached handles to trays. She presently works in a supermarket in Mthatha.

MLALA, Soslina
Born in Mount Frere, Mlala mixed and wedged clay with Vivian Madosini.

MNAKANISO, Faniswa
Born in Libode, Mnakaniso was employed as a wedger and then worked as a glazer.

MOYAKHE, Nokuzola
Moyakhe was born in Mthatha and worked in the sales department. She left before Izandla was closed.

MPAYIPHELI, Fundi
Born in Ngqeleni, Mpayipheli was a thrower. He was deaf and had previously received training at a special school.

MVOKWE, Lawrence Makwazewa (deceased)
Born in Qumbu, Mvokwe was Hyme Rabinowitz's assistant before he went to work for Izandla, where he was responsible for packing and firing the kiln. He also served as a glaze assistant and was the general handyman. He was badly injured while firing the kiln, and was forced to take an early retirement.

MZAZELA, Nonzwakazi
Mzazela was born in the Mount Frere Ayliff region and was a wedger. She is currently employed as a consultant by the African Bank.

NDABENI, Keslina
Ndabeni was a decorator at Izandla.

NDABENI, Miriam Lumka

Born in Port St John's, Ndabeni was a potter, responsible for throwing medium-sized wares. She served under Kirk, Scott and Gill. An accomplished thrower, she was renowned for her fine goblets and even won a prize at an exhibition. She presently runs a small food business.

NGALEKA, Beatrice

Born in Engcobo, Ngaleka was an accomplished potter, capable of making a number of different products. Under Gill she produced trays that were finished with macramé handles, made by the Wonkomntu Weavers. She took an early retirement.

NGUBO, Cynthia

One of the few original employees who were literate, Ngubo was a potter and was the forewoman at Izandla under the Kirks and Scott.

NGUBO, Keslina Matuzana (b.1938)

Born in Matatiele, Ngubo attended St Columba's Junior Secondary School. She never finished high school as a result of financial problems and the death of her mother. After the death of both parents, in 1954 and 1956 respectively, Ngubo and her siblings were placed under the guardianship of their paternal grandparents. Her grandmother was a potter and passed on her specialist knowledge to Ngubo.

In 1968 Ngubo departed for Mthatha to seek employment. She worked as a domestic worker until 1975, when she started sewing for a living. In 1977 she heard about the establishment of Izandla. She made a horse and a bull out of local clay and waited at the gate for the arrival of the Kirks. She was immediately employed and progressed swiftly from hand-building birds and large vases to waxing and then to the wheel. Ngubo was responsible for the application of tenmoku glaze as well as the light blue and white wares under Gill. She has retired and presently lives in Mthatha.[141]

NKOHLA, Thandeka (aka Ria)

Born in Qumbu, Nkohla was a potter, and was responsible for throwing goblets, casseroles and lidded pots. She was retrenched from Izandla and subsequently worked at Ikhwezi Lokusa Pottery. She currently works for a cleaning firm in Mthatha.

NTLOKWANA, Lungisa (deceased)

Ntlokwana was born in Mthatha. She was a glazer and opened a small business when Izandla closed.

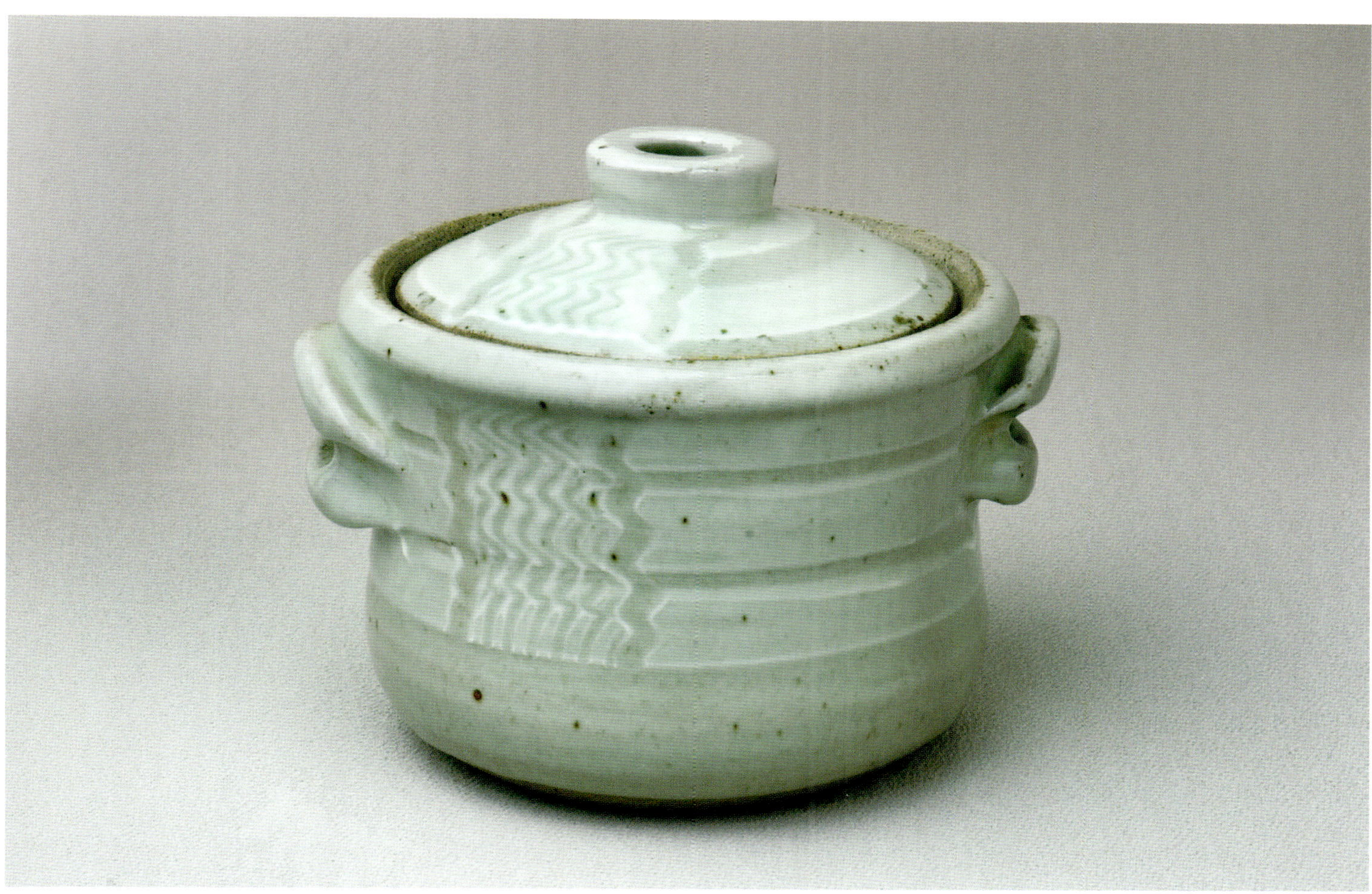

Izandla | Casserole with lid, celadon glaze with combed decorative motifs | Provenance: Clive and Ann Berlyn | Marks: unmarked | Photograph by Natalie Field

NYONI, Lindiwe (aka Lindie)
Born in Swaziland, Nyoni was employed as a clerk and assisted with sales. She left and worked for various companies. She is presently employed as a secretary in the Department of Public Safety within the Mthatha municipality.

QUINTA, Aeneas
Quinta was the bookkeeper, office manager and driver. He briefly managed Izandla in 1991, before being promoted to a position at the TDC head office.

RADLOF, Judy
Radlof was the first sales manager. She was employed briefly in 1980.

SAKWE, Khawuleza
Born in Mthatha, Sakwe was employed as a thrower of medium-sized wares, including goblets.

SCOTT, Lindsay (b.1947)
Scott matriculated from Christian Brothers College, Boksburg in 1964 and graduated from Seattle University and Portland State University in 1970.

Scott managed Izandla Pottery from September 1979 to March 1983. He replaced the trolley kiln built by Stephen Kirk with a huge eight-burner, oil-fired kiln, and in 1983 also built a wood-fired kiln for salt firings. Scott phased out animals and Xhosa figurines, and focused on dinner services and platters decorated with iron slips and combing. While at Izandla Scott made production wares and, after hours, he made his own distinctive wares, such as bowls, plates, casseroles and mugs. Many of these wares were signed and feature distinct turning on their bases. Some of them were decorated with a grass ash glaze; others with a (red) iron slip over a speckled green glaze.

Scott currently operates Hillfold Pottery on the Midlands Meander, KwaZulu-Natal.

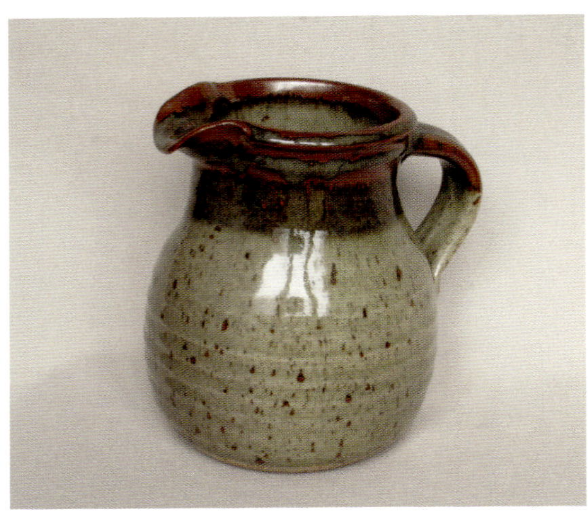

Izandla | Jug | 190x170x115x140mm | Provenance: Chris Hartley-Wiley | Marks: unmarked | Purchased from Izandla in the 1980s | Photograph by Wendy Gers

XINTOLO, Florida
Born in Engcobo, Xintolo was an accomplished potter and was the head thrower under Kirk, Scott and Gill. She was responsible for throwing many of the more complex forms, including wine jugs, casseroles, butter dishes, jugs, trays and flat bowls. In the early 1980s she went to night school and matriculated. She then attended a nursing training college, and was employed as a nurse and midwife at the Mthatha General Hospital.

Unidentified staff

[Surname unknown], Eslina
Born in Mt Frere, and employed under Scott and Gill, Eslina was a glaze assistant, fettler and hand-builder.

[Surname unknown], Khulukazi
Born in Mount Ayliff, Khulukazi was employed as a glazer. She presently works at the Walter Sisulu University of Science and Technology, Transkei.

[Surname unknown], Mavis
Mavis was born in Qumbu and was employed as a wedger and cleaner.

[Surname unknown], Msotho (deceased)
Born in Mthatha, Msotho was Lawrence Mvokwe's assistant. He packed the kiln and made clay.

[Surname unknown], Nokwandia (deceased)
Born in Ngqeleni, Nokwandia undertook many different tasks as a wedger, modeling small animals, and cleaning in the afternoons.

[Surname unknown], Nomute
Born in Idutywa, Nomute was a wedger and cleaner.

[Surname unknown], Nomvula
Nomvula was born in Sterkspruit and was a wedger. She subsequently left for Johannesburg.

[Surname unknown], Patience
Born in Engcobo, Patience was a thrower who specialised in teapots.

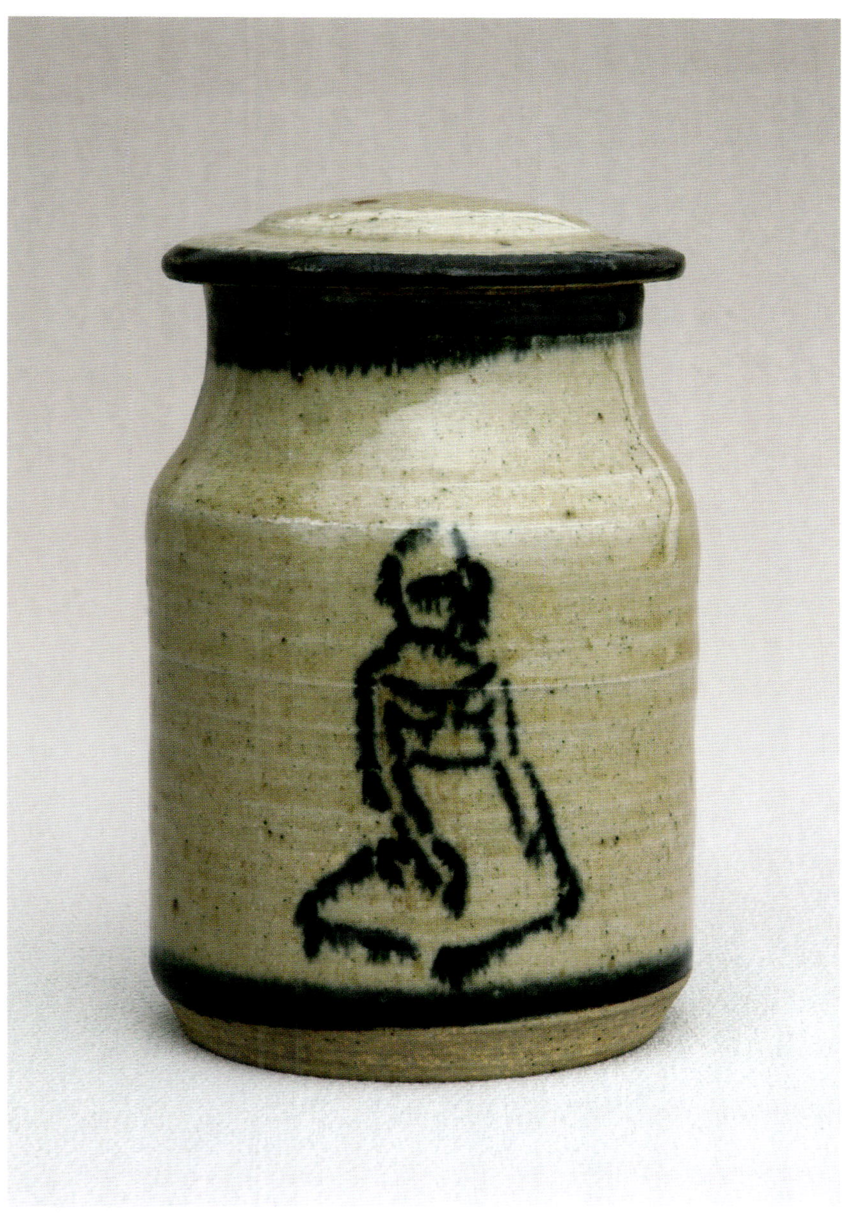

RIGHT: Izandla | Tea caddy with illustration of seated Xhosa woman | Provenance: Clive and Ann Berlyn | Marks: hand-painted glaze marks, 'MAGWA TEA TRANSKEI' | Photograph by Natalie Field

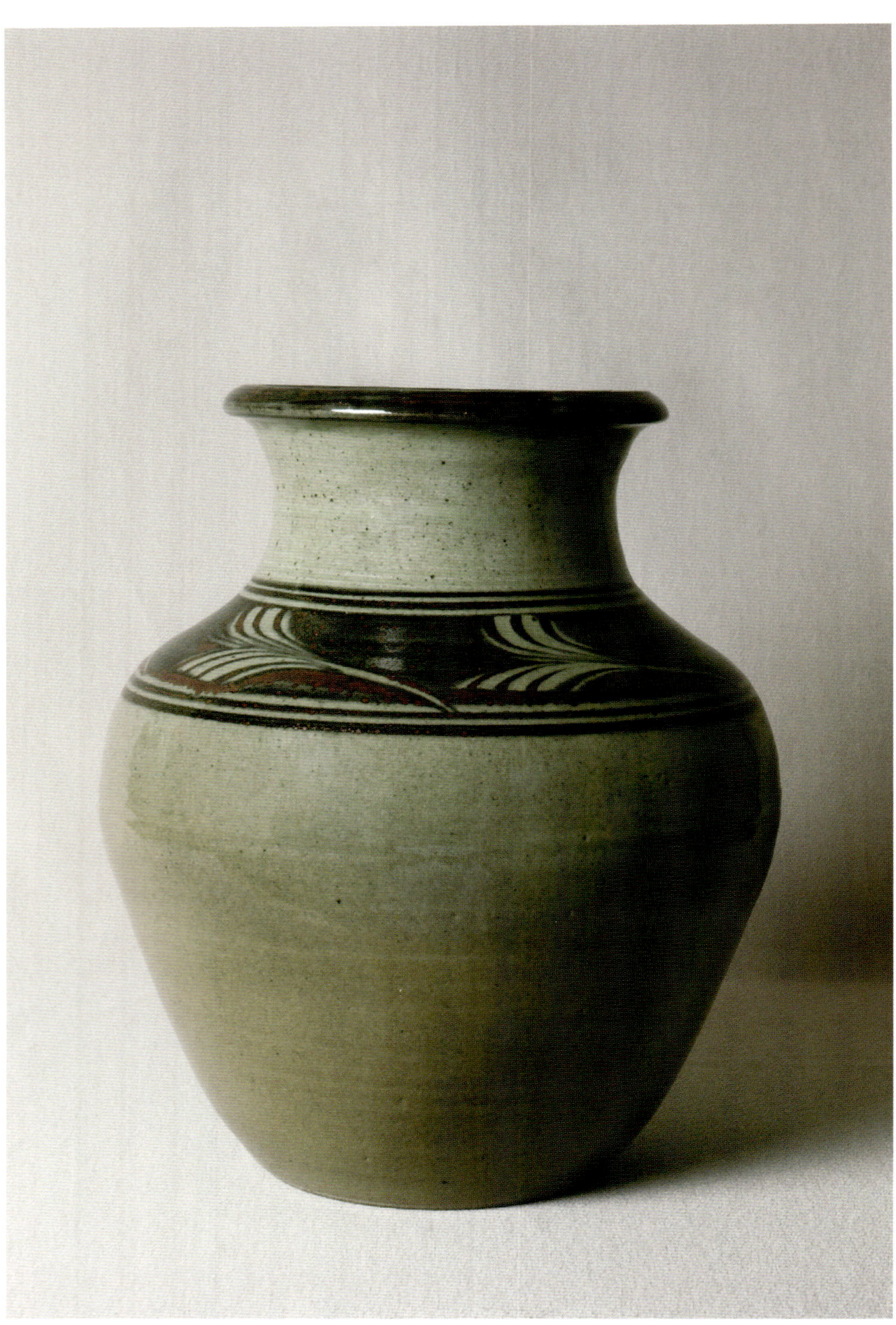

Izandla | Large vase, oatmeal glaze with narrow brown band on lip and wide band on shoulder featuring combed decorative motifs | ca.400x200mm | Provenance: Clive and Ann Berlyn | Marks: unmarked | Photograph by Natalie Field

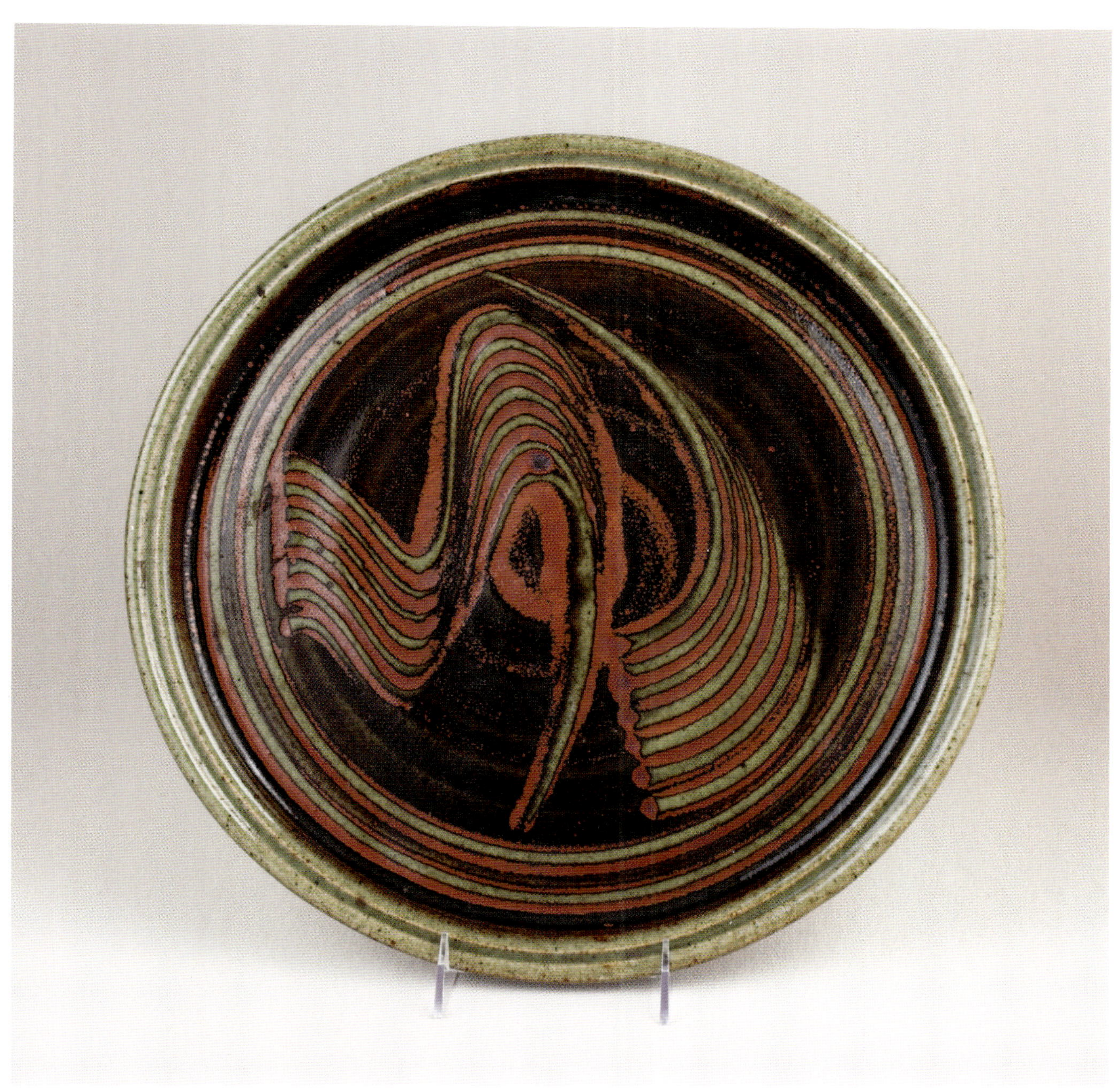

Izandla | Large platter, combed decoration | ca.450x50mm | Provenance: Clive and Ann Berlyn | Marks: unmarked | Photograph by Natalie Field

Kalahari Studio (1948–1973)

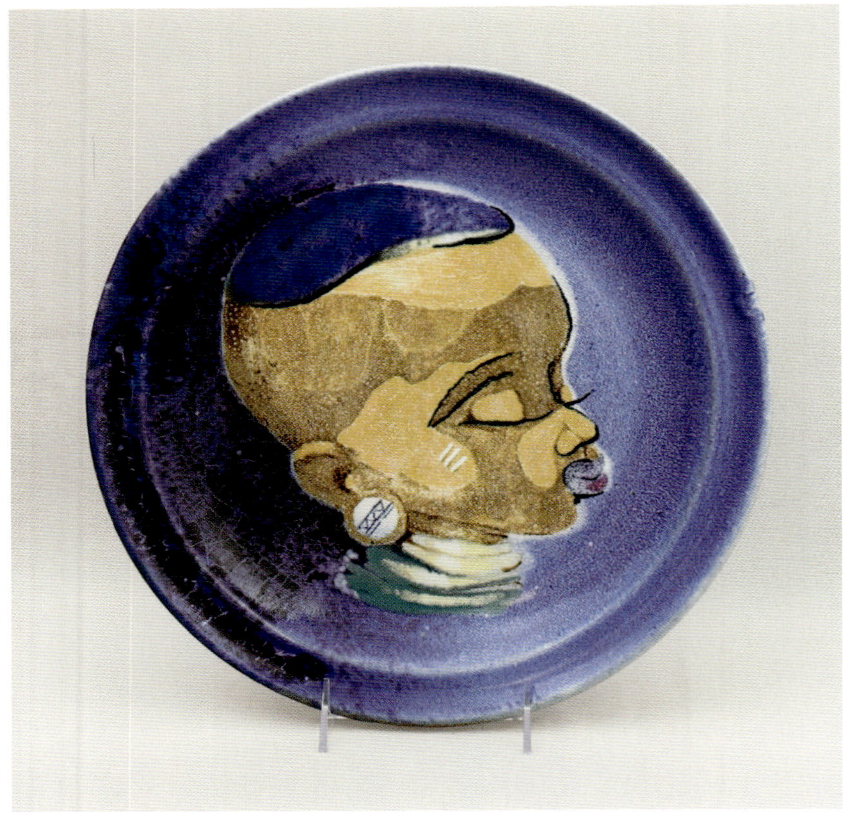

Linnware | Plate, painted image of boy with ear plug | 317x43mm | Provenance: Clive Newman | Marks: glazed white base with blue painted marks, 'Linn Ware, AK, – 48' | Additional information: This plate predates the establishment of the Kalahari Studio and clearly illustrates the style and interest of Aleksanders Klopcanovs | Photograph by Natalie Field

Location

Originally set up in Bramley, Johannesburg, the studio relocated to Cape Town in July 1950. The pottery was subsequently briefly re-established in Franschhoek.

Name

The name Kalahari was chosen as the word evoked both the desert tones and the terracotta colour of the earthenware clay that they used. While the name had associations with the vast African desert that stretches from the North West Province in South Africa to northern Namibia and through Botswana, for Vestman and the Klopcanovs it also had Scandinavian links. Klopcanovs's pronunciation of the words 'Kalahari' and 'Arabia' stressed the individual syllables (i.e., Kal-a-har-i and A-ra-bi-a), and both words thus sounded similar, especially in terms of the repetition of vowels. The Scandinavian links are also reinforced by the fact that Arabia produced items that display earthy tones and qualities. Arabian stoneware was very popular in the period under consideration, and many 'seconds' were imported into South Africa.[142] In addition, the the word Kalahari is composed of angular letters, that are relatively easy to apply with a stylus or paint brush.

Founders

Elma Vestman (1914–1991) and Aleksanders (Sacha) Klopcanovs (1912–1997) were joint directors of the Kalahari Studio. While the couple shared many aspects of the administration and production, Vestman was responsible for the production processes, quality control, glaze testing and product development, as well as the design of most of the wares. Klopcanovs was also a painter, and directed much of his energy in this domain.

Staff

Klopcanovs and Vestman were solely responsible for the design and decoration of wares. The Kalahari Studio employed a small non-professional staff complement of about 10 to 12 coloured women to assist with the menial aspects of ceramic production. Anna Grivainis, a fellow Latvian, was employed by the studio from 1955 to 1956 as an assistant.[143]

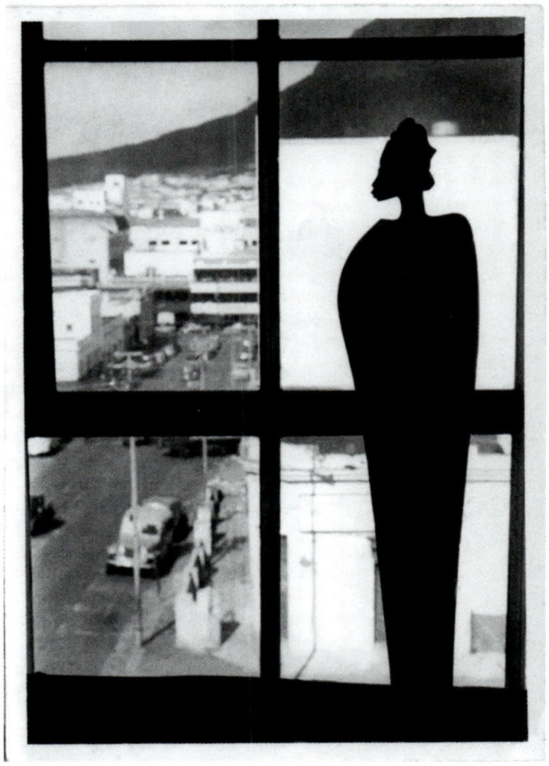

View from the Kalahari Studio window with profile of African figurine, Cape Town, 1950s | Provenance: Private collection | Unknown photographer

Wares manufactured

The Kalahari Studio manufactured a variety of products, including sculptures, dinner services, ashtrays, jugs, platters, candelabra, egg cups, vases and wall plaques. However, the most common wares appeared to be bowls, platters and wall plaques. In many instances these were multi-functional – they could be used as utilitarian kitchenware or as decorative wall plaques. The majority of the decorative wares have small holes in the back, which were threaded with a short length of string or gut so they could be hung on a wall.

The studio also produced some individual decorated tiles and large composite tile panels including the large panel inspired by Southern San parietal art in the foyer of Garmor House, Plein Street, Cape Town. It produced a limited number of promotional items, including ashtrays for Safmarine, the KWV[144] and the Kruger National Park.

The wares of the Kalahari Studio were decorated with a variety of figurative motifs as well as geometric patterns. The majority of wall plates depict synthesised geometric designs that are derived from either Nguni material culture or Scandinavian sources. Some of the motifs appear to resemble Zulu beadwork and Zulu earplugs of the 1950s. Other motifs recall Latvian folk embroidery, needlework design elements or Scandinavian weaving. The studio also produced wares decorated with images of flora (tulips, peaches, protea, banana-palm leaves, husks of wheat and fern fronds) and fauna (lion, penguin, springbok doe and fawn and a seagull). Images of Africans also decorate some of the wares.

Production methods

Wares were hand-thrown, slip-cast or press-moulded. A variety of clays were used, including red-, yellow- and white-bodied clays. Coloured glazes and slips were used to decorate the wares. It was claimed that their pottery was 97.5 per cent South African, the remaining 2.5 per cent consisting of imported materials.

Brief history of the pottery

Much of the history of the pottery is bound up in the life histories of the founders, Elma Vestman and Aleksanders Klopcanovs, whose exotic origins, Scandinavian training and international careers framed this endeavour. The duo, and more particularly Vestman, was responsible for introducing contemporary international modernism to South African ceramics and revolutionising local ceramic design.

The pottery participated in numerous international exhibitions, received many important awards, and may be viewed as the pre-eminent pottery in South Africa in the 1950s for numerous reasons. The most obvious is the quality of both the design and the production methods. Vestman contributed to the technical development of ceramics in South Africa, in terms of her highly skilled handling of multi-coloured glazes and multiple firings, and the application of refined and sophisticated designs. Under her guidance, the Kalahari Studio was the first, and arguably the only, local pottery to successfully synthesise an indigenised South African content with international modernist design trends of the 1950s. Attempts by other contemporary studios and factories, such as Crescent and Dykor, to combine South African content with aspects of international modernism, were aesthetically less successful and in a few instances wares by Dykor appear to be plagiarised versions of Kalahari products.

Marks

- The majority of wares have 'KALAHARI' or 'Kalahari, Made in S. Africa' painted on their bases in black or a dark tone. Occasionally the initials 'K' or 'KP' appear on the bases of smaller items such as ashtrays and egg cups. Some wares were marked 'EAK' and 'EV AK'.
- Some wares have a sgraffito mark, 'Kalahari', on the base under the glaze.
- Two seals were used, sometimes in conjunction with painted marks, sometimes independently. One depicts a seated figure that resembles a 'bushman' holding an erect arrow. This seal indicates that the item was produced after 1954, when the Kalahari Studio registered their 'Bushman' trademark.[145] Another seal contains the wording 'Kalahari' above the seated figure, and 'RTM' (Registered Trade Mark) below the figure.

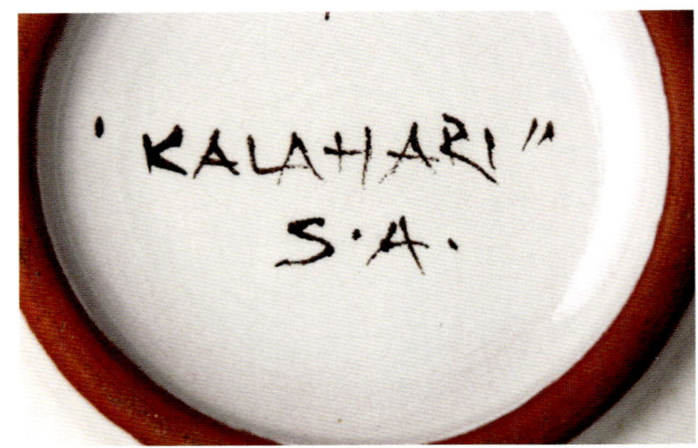

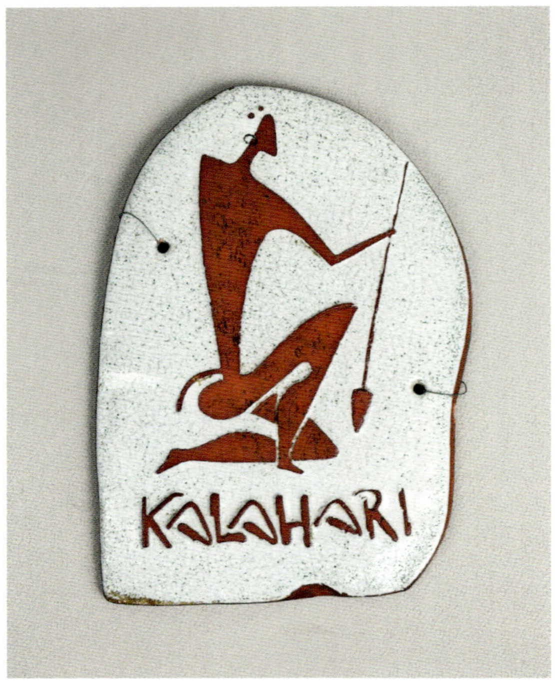

TOP: Kalahari | Maker's mark | Painted marking in black glaze, 'Kalahari S.A.' | Photograph by Natalie Field

ABOVE BOTTOM: Kalahari | Plaque | 228x148x14mm | Provenance: NMMAM | 0991/1999 | Marks: no marks | Additional information: Purchased from the estate of the late A Klopcanovs, June 1999 | Photograph by Natalie Field

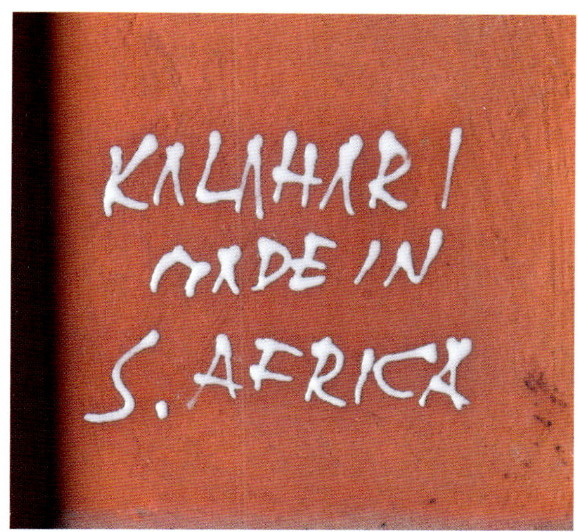

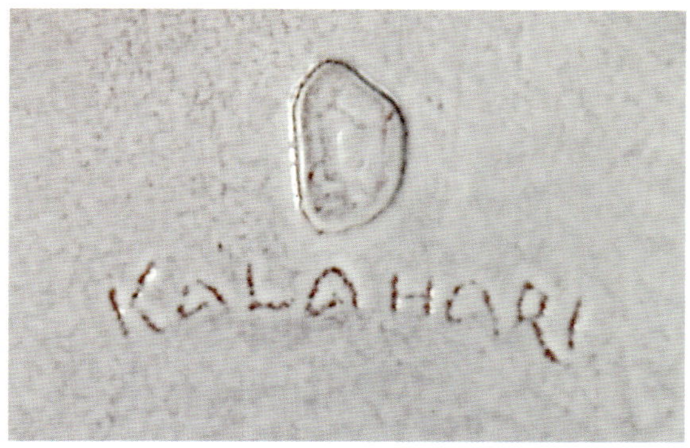

TOP: Kalahari | Maker's mark | Painted marking in white glaze, 'Kalahari, Made in S. Africa' | Photograph by Natalie Field

ABOVE BOTTOM: Kalahari | Maker's mark | Cast logo and 'Kalahari' | Photograph by Natalie Field

Select exhibitions, commissions and awards

1950 SA Industries Exhibition (now known as the Rand Easter Show), hosted by the Witwatersrand Agricultural Society, Johannesburg. The Kalahari Studio was awarded a gold medal and was acknowledged by General Jan C Smuts, 'who was so impressed with the work that he stopped and made an impromptu speech in which he extolled the importance of allowing such talented immigrants into South Africa' ([No author] 1962). Klopcanovs then presented Smuts with two pieces of Kalahari ware.

1952 Van Riebeeck Tercentenary Festival Fair, Cape Town.

1953 Fourth International Exhibition of Ceramic Arts, Washington DC. This exhibition also featured other ceramicists of international stature such as Peter Voulkos. The South African exhibit attracted widespread attention and, of the 26 countries taking part, was most favourably reviewed by the Washington Press, as well as being singled out in a television broadcast.

1953 Central African Rhodes Centenary Festival Fair, Bulawayo, Rhodesia (now Zimbabwe).

1954 The Kiln Club of Washington, Fifth International Exhibition of Ceramic Arts, Washington DC.

1954 South African Association of the Arts, Arts and Crafts Exhibition, Cape Town.

1955 'Buy South African' campaign banquet, Cape Town.

1955 Centenary Exhibition of SA Crafts [SA Association of the Arts, Pretoria].

1955 *Exposition Internationale des Chefs-d'œuvres de la Céramique Moderne*, Cannes, France. The Kalahari studio won three awards, including a gold medal.

ca.1956 Fifth International Exhibition of Ceramic Arts, The Kiln Club of Washington DC, USA. An undated newspaper article claimed that, 'This show has such status that anything exhibited on it is automatically displayed at the Smithsonian Institute'.[146]

1956 International Hobbies and Handicrafts Fair, London.

The Kalahari Studio also executed a large tile panel for the former Security Police headquarters (now known as the Provincial Protection and Security Services, Western Cape), Garmor House, Plein Street, Cape Town. The date of this commission is unknown.

Biographies

KLOPCANOVS, Aleksanders (1912–1997)

Aleksanders Klopcanovs was born in 1912 in Tashkent, Uzbekistan. In 1930 and 1931 he undertook his compulsory military service in the navy, then travelled to Finland, where he 'discovered' Arabia pottery. Upon his return, Klopcanovs entered the Academy of Fine Arts in Riga, Latvia, to study figurative painting,

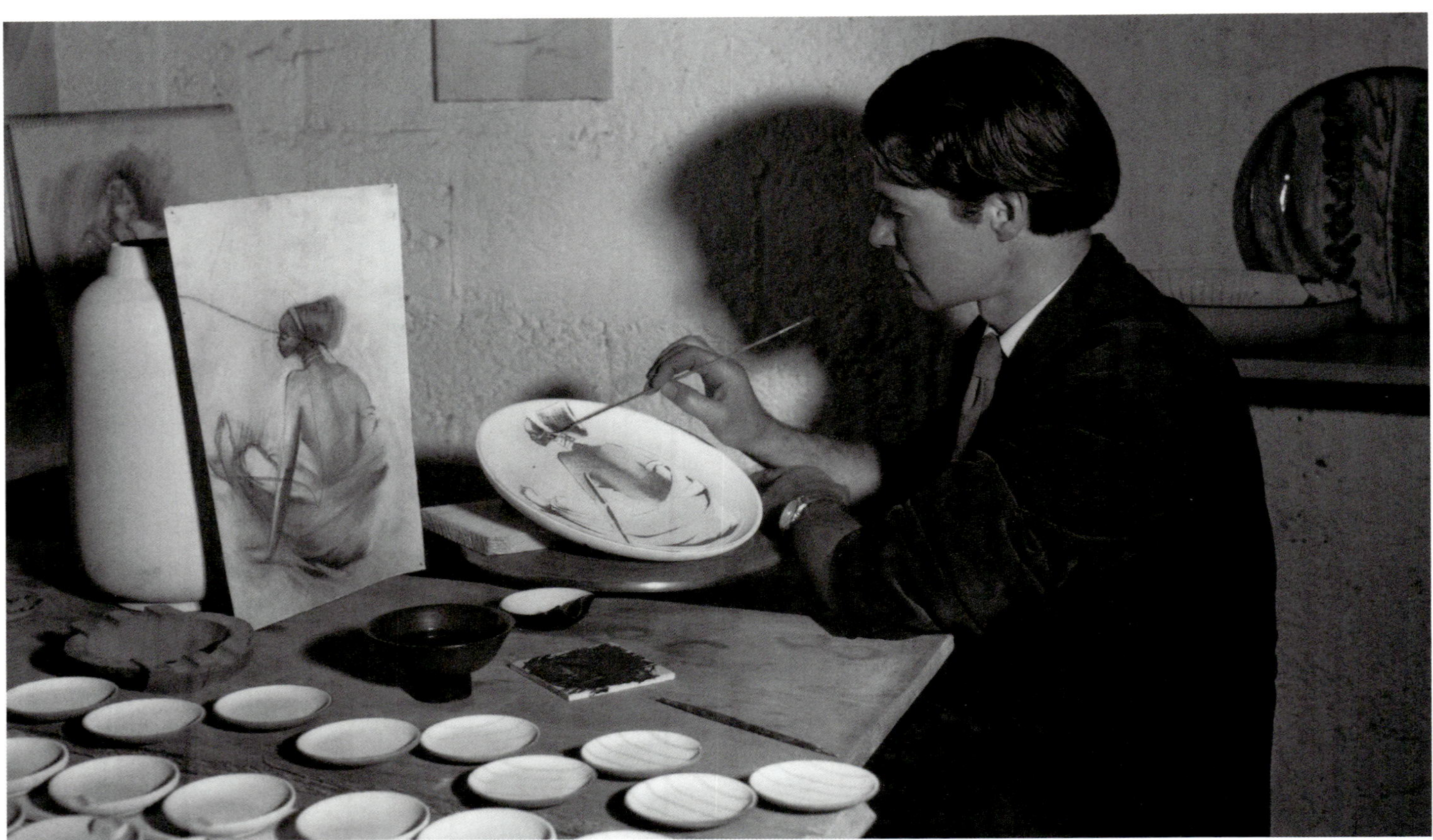

Aleksanders Klopcanovs, Kalahari Studio, 1950s | Provenance: Private collection | Unknown photographer

mural painting and sculpture. In Riga, he met Elma Vestman in the late 1930s or early 1940s, and married her in 1968 in South Africa. Due to the tumultuous political upheavals in the continent between 1939 and 1944, the couple had fled across the Baltic to Sweden in a dilapidated fishing boat on 2 November 1944. Klopcanovs specialised in figurative painting at the Royal Academy in Stockholm and followed Vestman to Linnware, Olifantsfontein, in February 1948, where she had been working since 1947.

Apart from his assistance with the Kalahari Studio, Klopcanovs – whose primary interest was oil painting – participated in numerous solo and group exhibitions in South Africa between 1961 and 1973. His oil paintings of the 1950s and 1960s are primarily figurative, although landscapes were also undertaken. His large canvases usually depicted seated, supine, naked and scantily clad women, often in a single pastel tone. Klopcanovs's early landscapes depict romantic European landscapes featuring castles and panoramic views. Later landscapes were decidedly influenced by his colleague J H Pierneef, in terms of their ideological romanticisation of an uninhabited rural landscape and their pastel palettes.

Between 1969 and 1977 Klopcanovs travelled frequently to Western Europe to promote and sell their ceramics and paintings, with Switzerland being their largest market. In 1973 the couple immigrated to Switzerland, but encountered major financial problems and were obliged to return to South Africa in 1976. Their problems continued, however, and they sank into further debt when they decided to re-establish the Kalahari Studio. Klopcanovs built a new electric kiln, designed new machinery for preparing clay, purchased new glazes and manufactured about six different cast resin sculptures of the heads of African women. These sculptures were not commercially successful, as there had been a shift in the taste and sensibilities of the South African public.

Financial difficulties continued to plague the couple and in 1989 they retired to Franschhoek, where they intended to teach art to supplement their income. These attempts were unsuccessful as the town was too small to provide an adequate number of art pupils. Elma died in 1991 and Klopcanovs died intestate in Franschhoek in 1997. His decomposed body was discovered a month later by a neighbour.

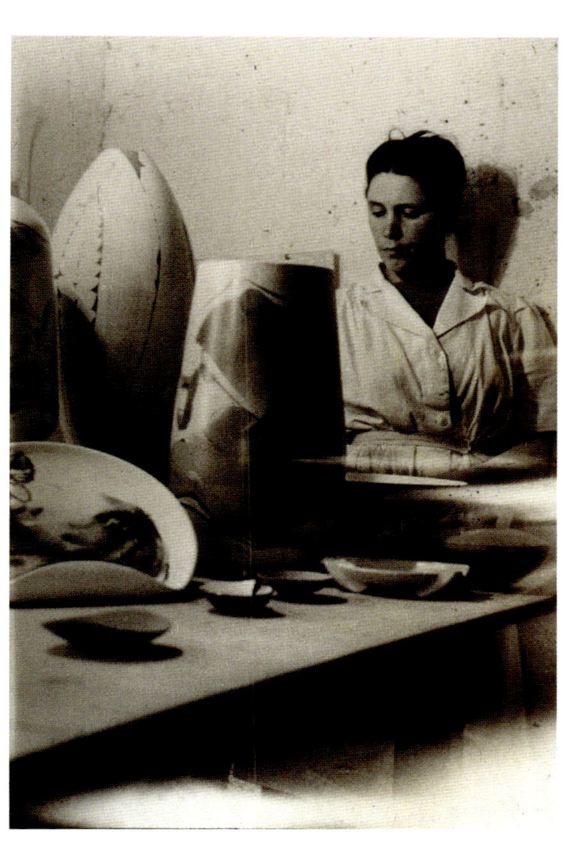

Elma Vestman, Kalahari Studio, 1950s | Provenance: Private collection | Unknown photographer

VESTMAN, Elma (1914–1991)

Elma Aleksandra Vestman was born in 1914 in Lubana, Latvia into a family of peasant farmers. She majored in ceramics at the Academy of Fine Arts in Riga and met Aleksanders Klopcanovs, whom she married on 6 March 1968 in South Africa. In 1944 the couple fled to Sweden, where she continued her studies at the Royal Academy of Arts in Stockholm under Professor Berys and worked and studied with the acclaimed ceramicist Professor Wilhelm Kåge,[147] at the Gustavsberg Ceramic Factory. She also worked in a production-ware factory at Upsala-Ekeby in Uppsala.

In 1947 Vestman was employed by Linnware at Olifanstfontein on a six-month contract.[148] The couple had good relationships with the staff and respected their skills, but felt that many of the studio's designs were too Victorian, and so left Linnware in 1948 and set up the Kalahari Studio in Bramley, Johannesburg on a two-acre plot that was formerly a mushroom farm. In July 1950, the couple relocated the studio to Cape Town, despite their ceramicist friends in Johannesburg strongly discouraging the move, claiming that the clay from the Cape Province was inferior to Transvaal clay. They laboured relentlessly to build their business, working seven days a week without any holidays for the first seven years. The couple retired from commercial pottery in the 1960s, but Vestman continued to make ceramic wares from their home. In 1973 they immigrated to Switzerland but returned to South Africa 1976. She attempted to re-establish the Kalahari Studio. While some new wares were produced, many of these designs echoed prototypes from the 1950s.

Vestman died in the Paarl Hospital on 6 July 1991, after a protracted struggle with cancer.

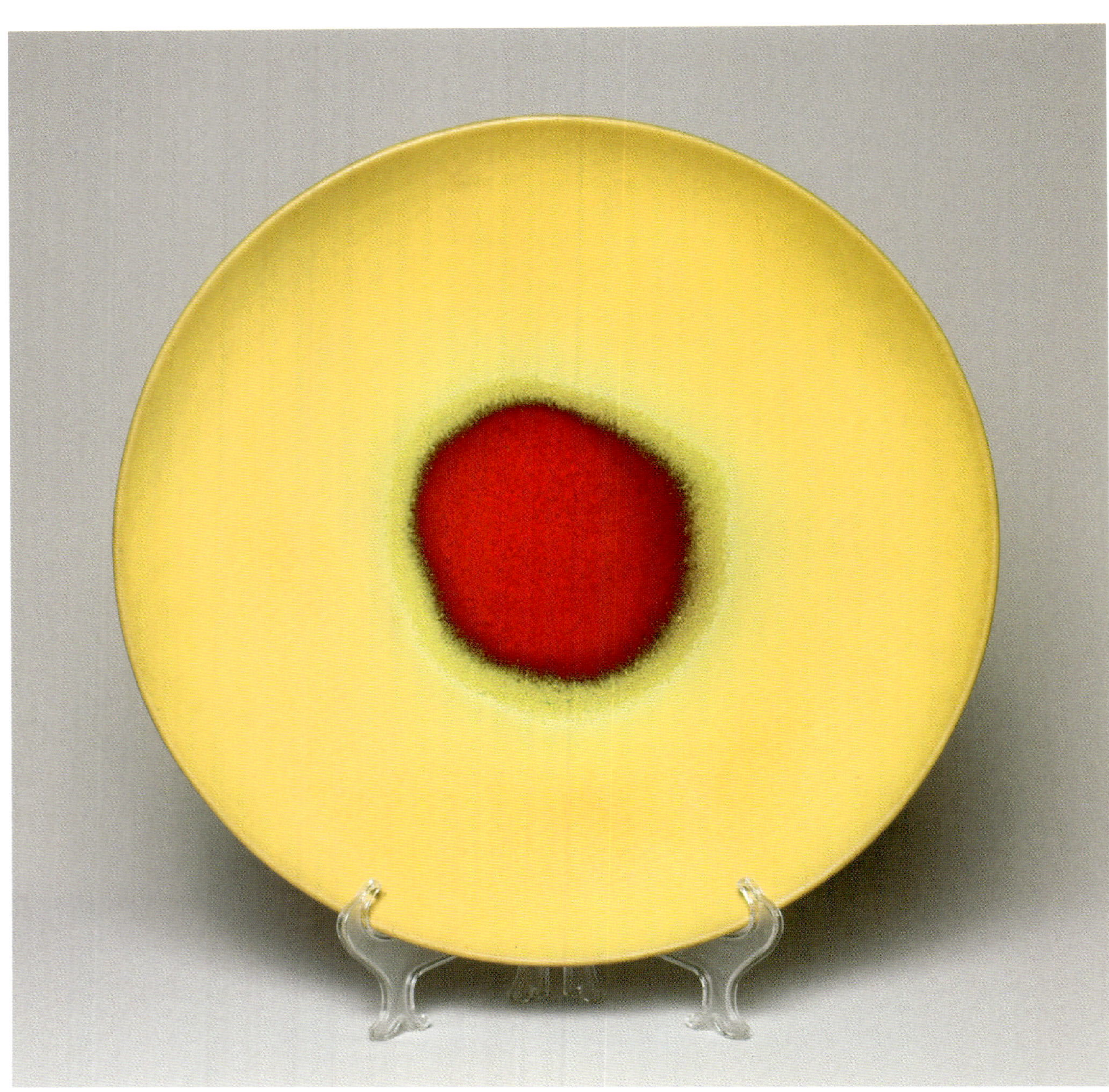

Kalahari | Charger, yellow glaze decoration with red central spot | 445x70mm | Provenance: NMMAM | 0993/1999 | Marks: hand-painted black glaze marking, 'Kalahari' and impressed stamp | Additional information: Purchased from the estate of the late A Klopcanovs, June 1999 | Photograph by Natalie Field

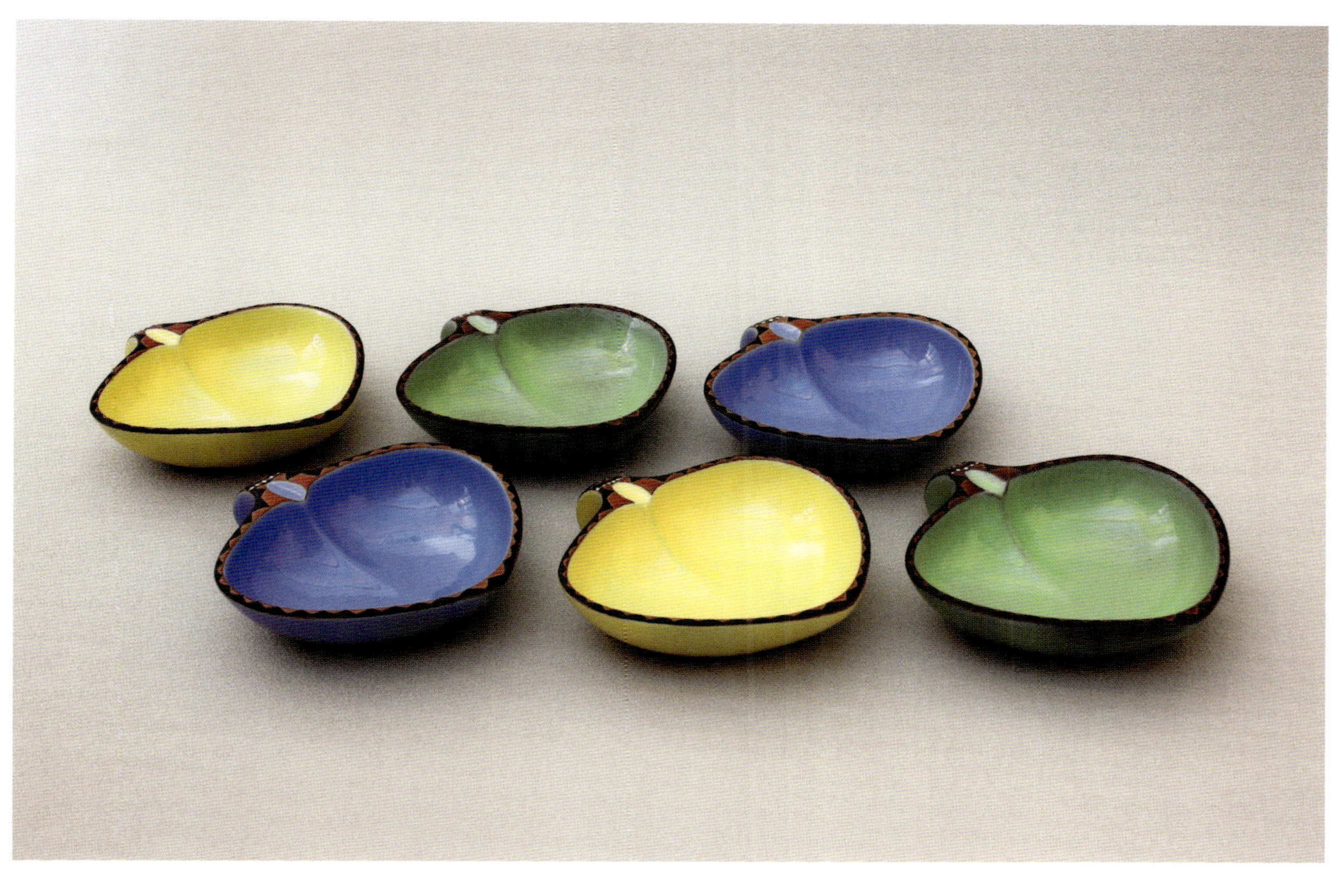

Kalahari | Group of six heart-shaped bowls | 45x163x140mm | Provenance: TAG | 1707/5/93 1707/3/93; 1707/1/93; 1707/4/93; 1707/2/93; 1707/6/93 | Marks: glazed base that corresponds to individual item, dark brown painted marking, 'Kalahari' | Photograph by Natalie Field

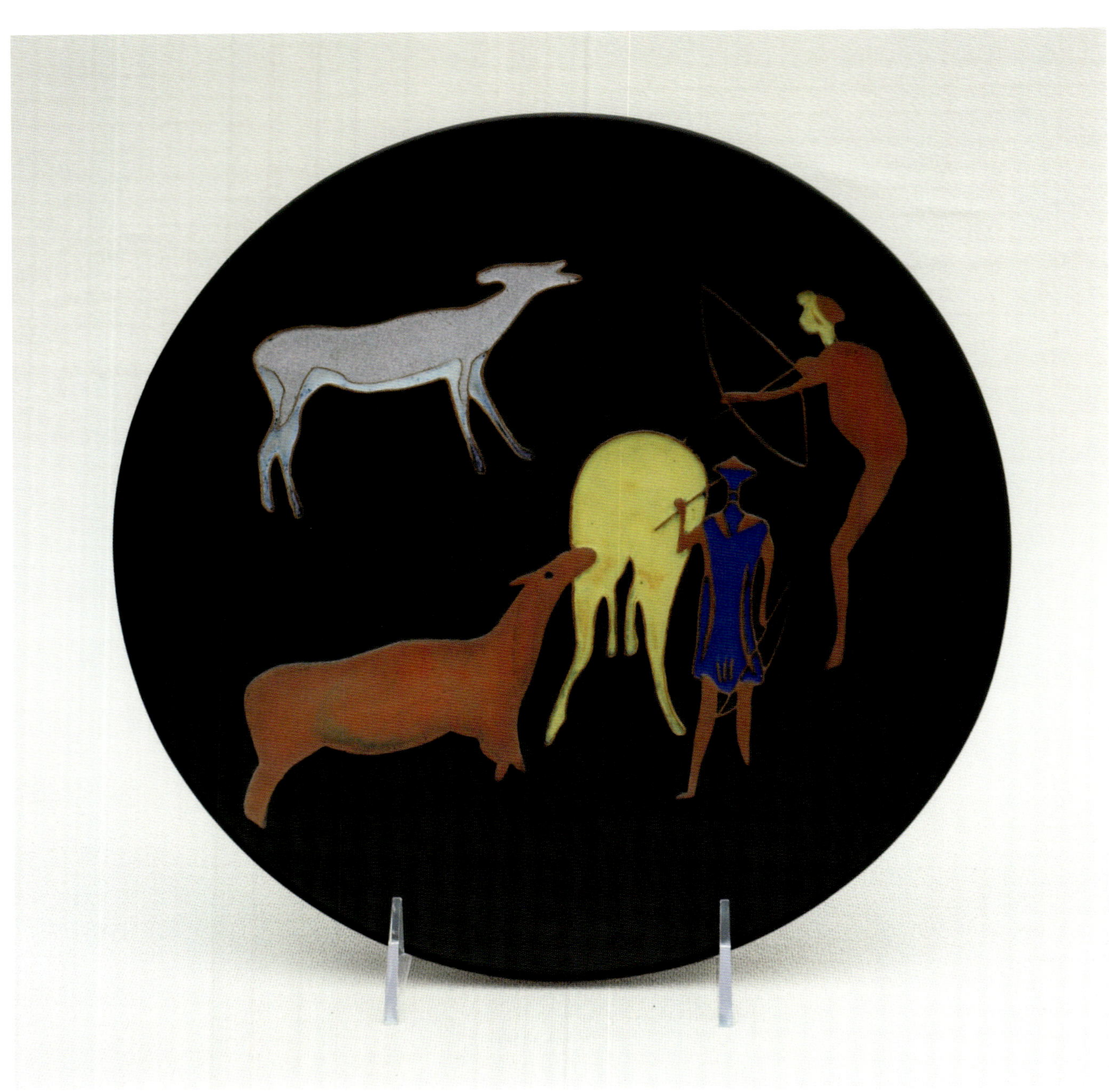

Kalahari | Black charger with San images | 251x44mm | Provenance: DNMCH | HG16922 | Marks: black glazed base with incised 'Kalahari' evident under glaze | Photograph by Natalie Field

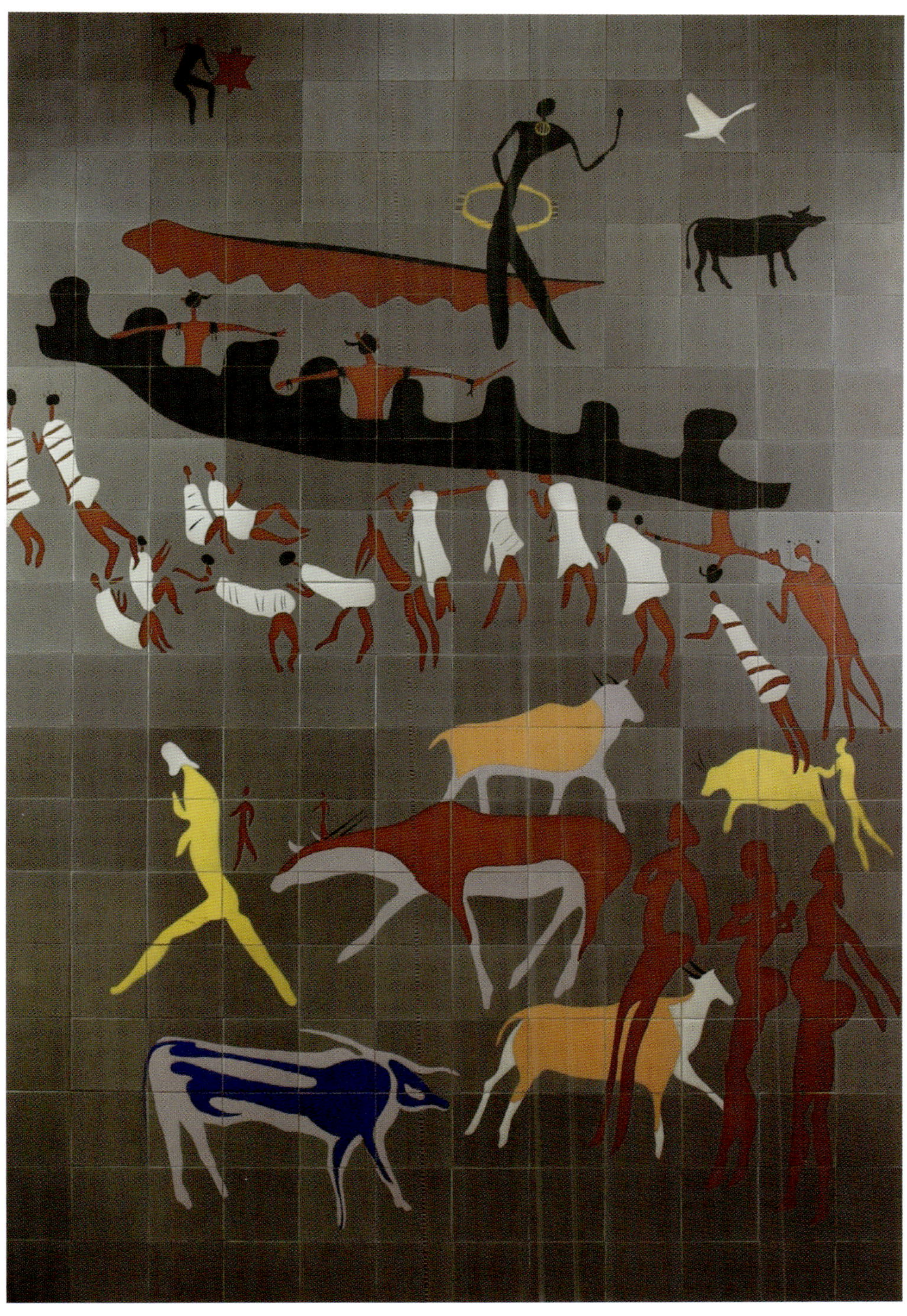

Kalahari | Tile panel | 2.78x1.81m | Provenance: Provincial Protection and Security Services, Western Cape, Garmor House, Plein Street, Cape Town | Marks: painted signature, 'Kalahari SA' in top left corner | Additional information: tiles square, 15cm each | Photograph by Natalie Field

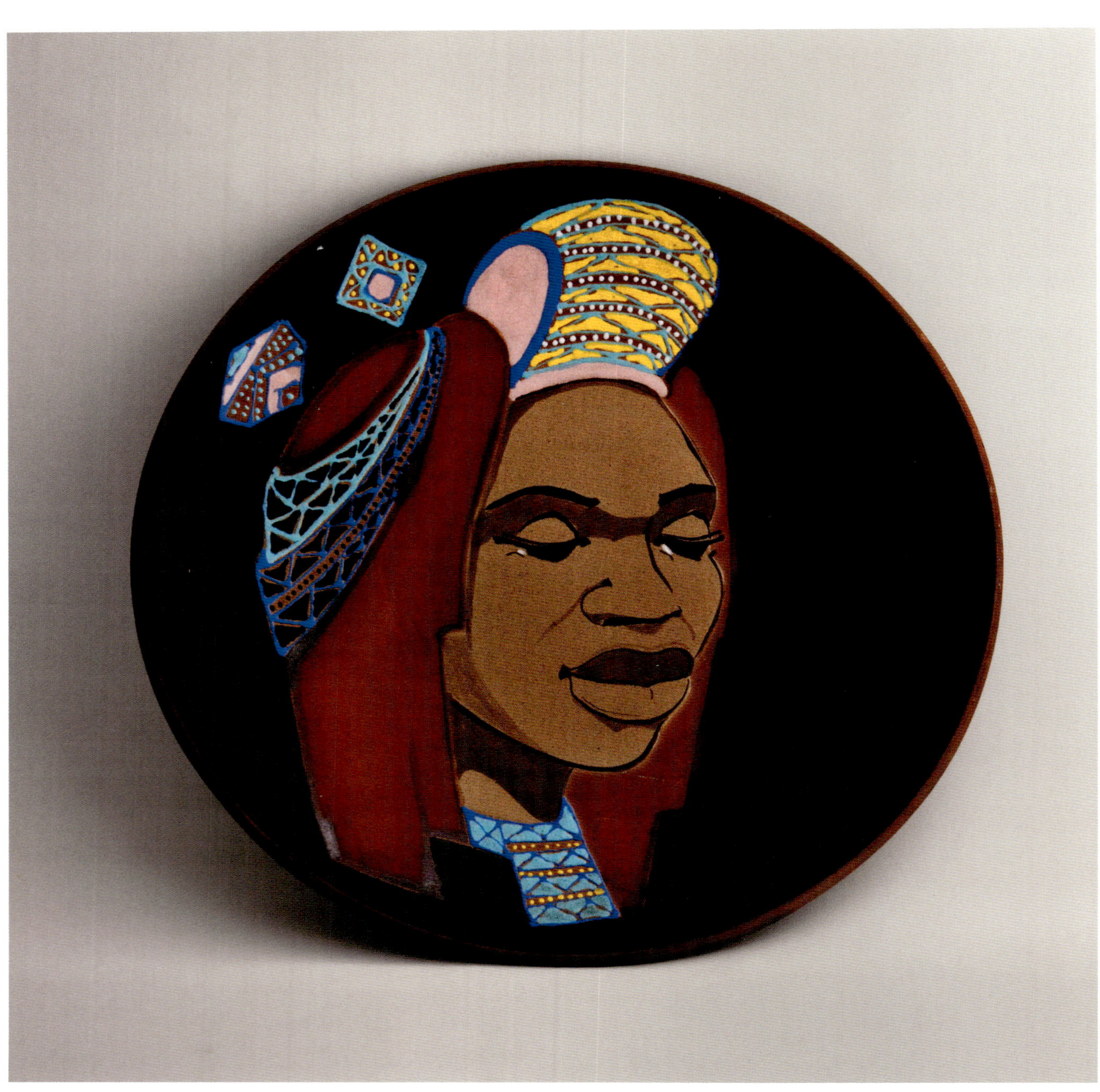

Kalahari | African with large headdress | 260x40mm | Provenance: Wendy Gers | Marks: incised marking beneath glaze, 'Kalahari' | Photograph by Damien Artus

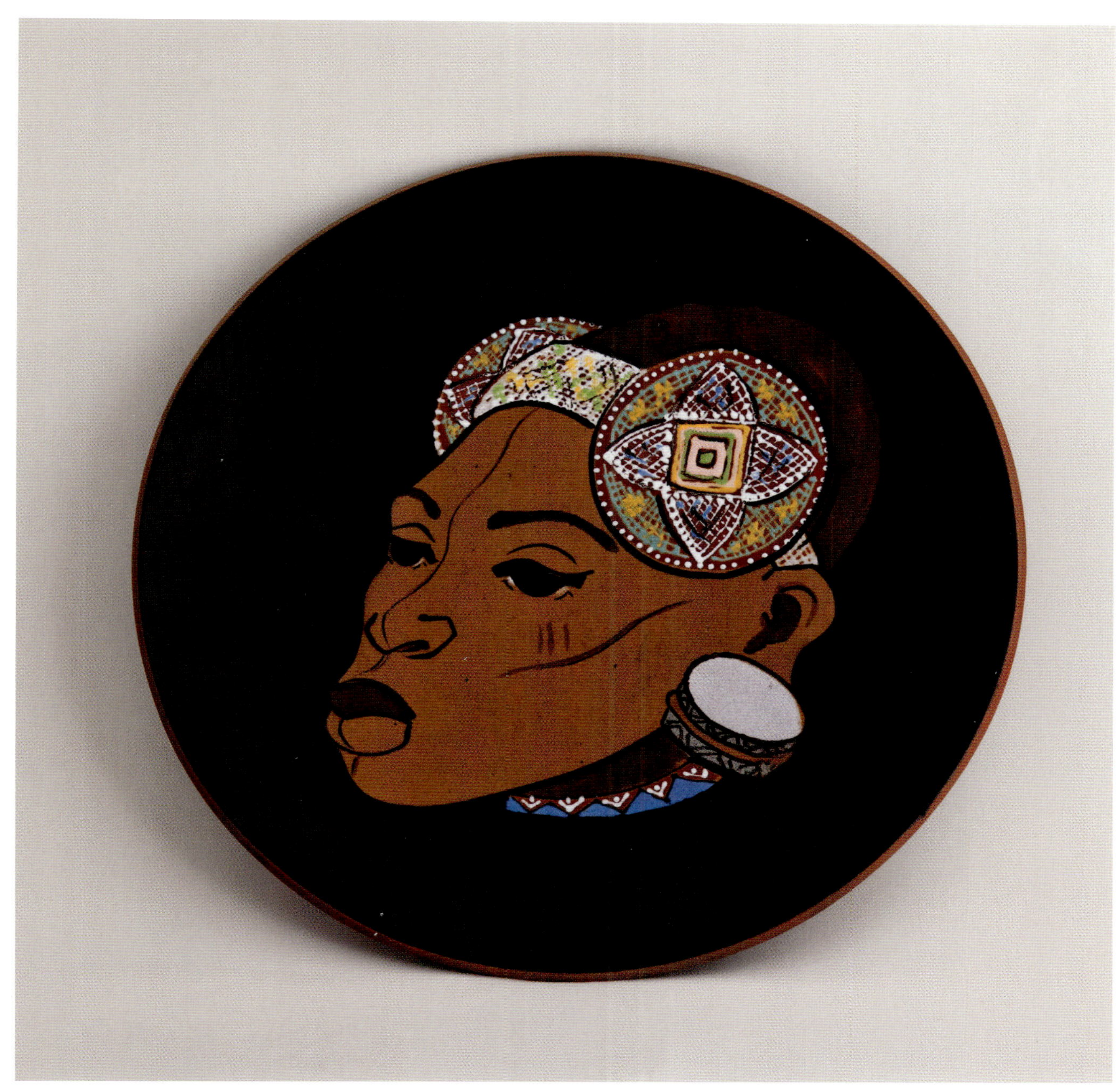

Kalahari | Charger, African boy with an earplug | 258x40mm | Provenance: Wendy Gers | Marks: incised marking beneath glaze, 'Kalahari' | Photograph by Damien Artus

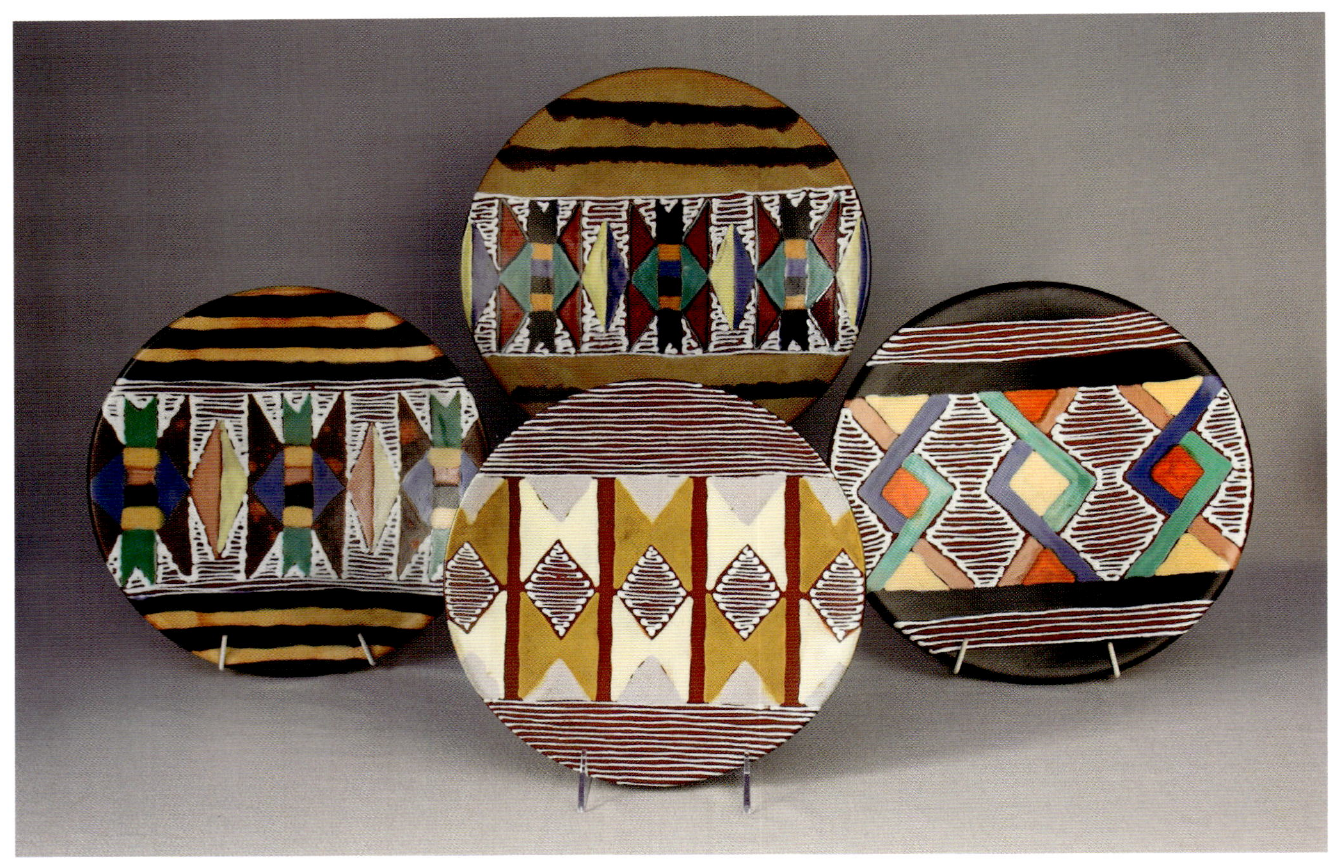

Kalahari | Group of four decorative wall chargers with applied geometric designs | Front 245x35mm; middle two 290x45mm; rear 350x50mm | Provenance: Gordon Radowsky | Marks: front and middle: hand-painted marking, 'Kalahari' and impressed Kalahari stamp; rear: hand-painted marking, 'Kalahari' | Additional information: polychrome slip-trailing recalling Ndebele mural motifs | Photograph by Natalie Field

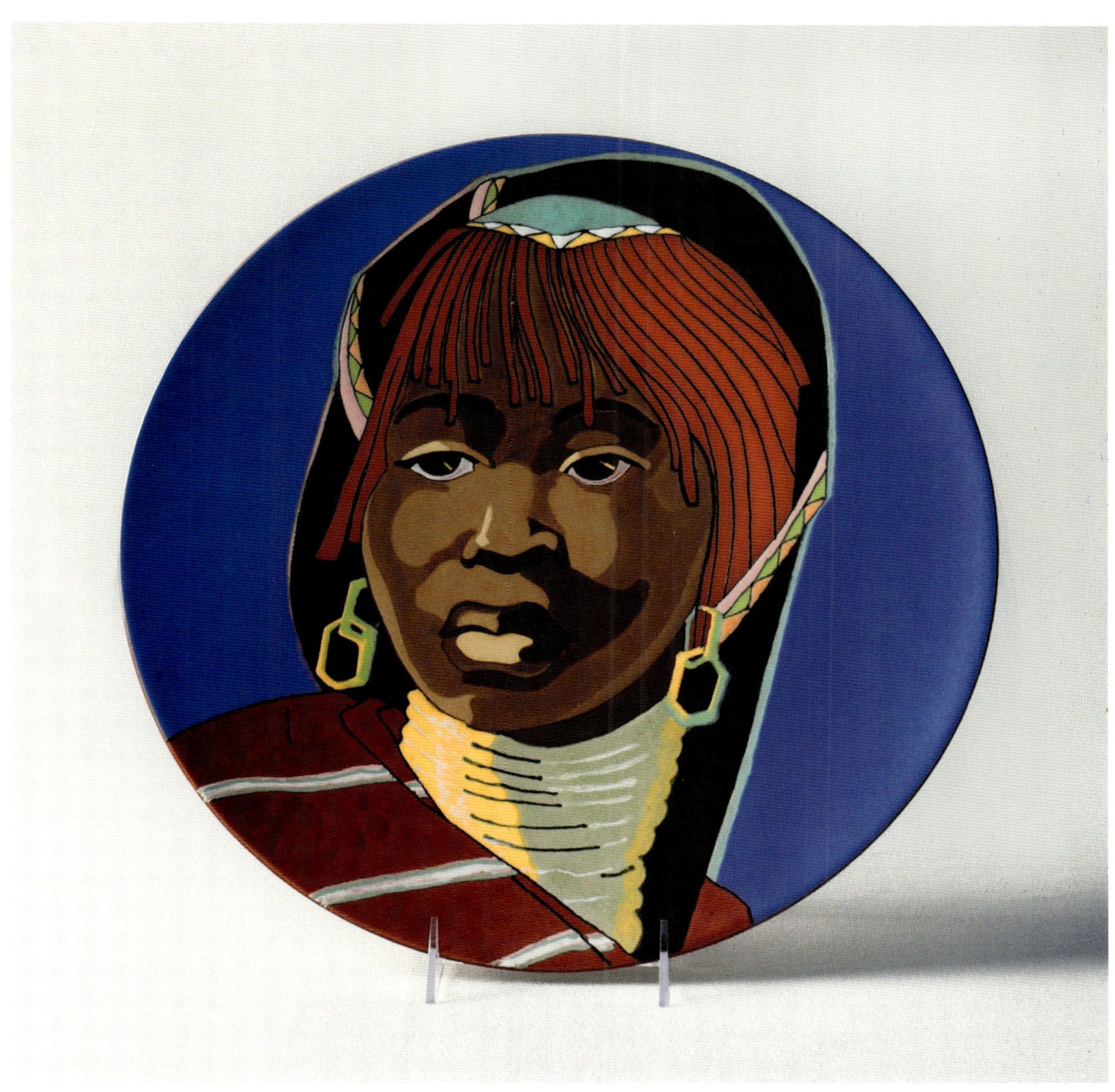

Kalahari | Portrait charger with Ndebele woman in headdress and jewellery | 566x50mm | Provenance: Collection Gordon Radowsky, Cape Town | Marks: painted marking, 'Kalahari. Made in S. Africa' | Photograph by Natalie Field

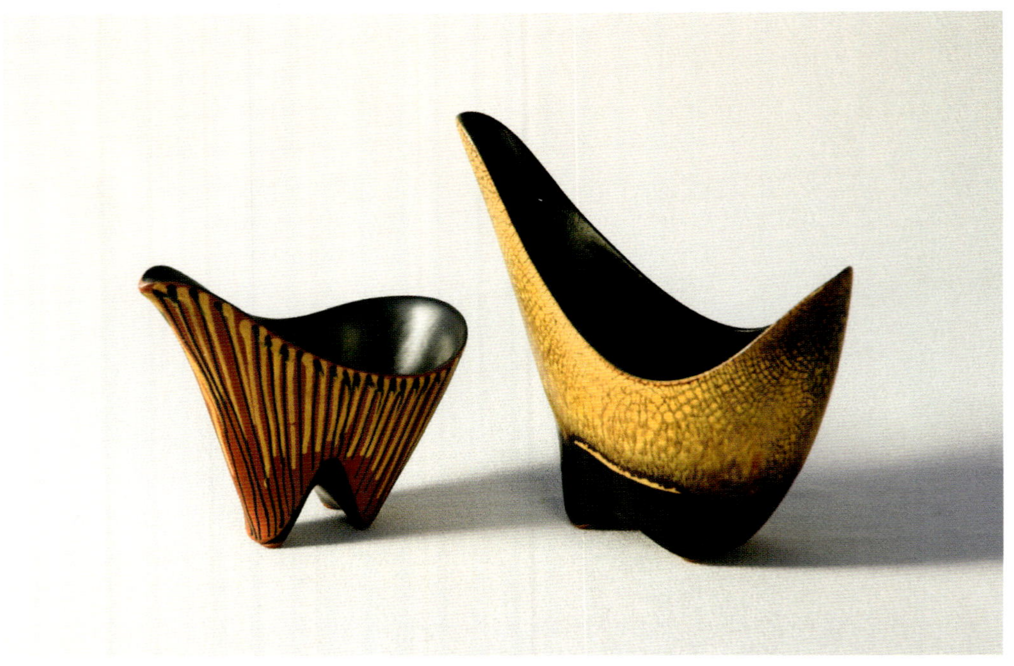

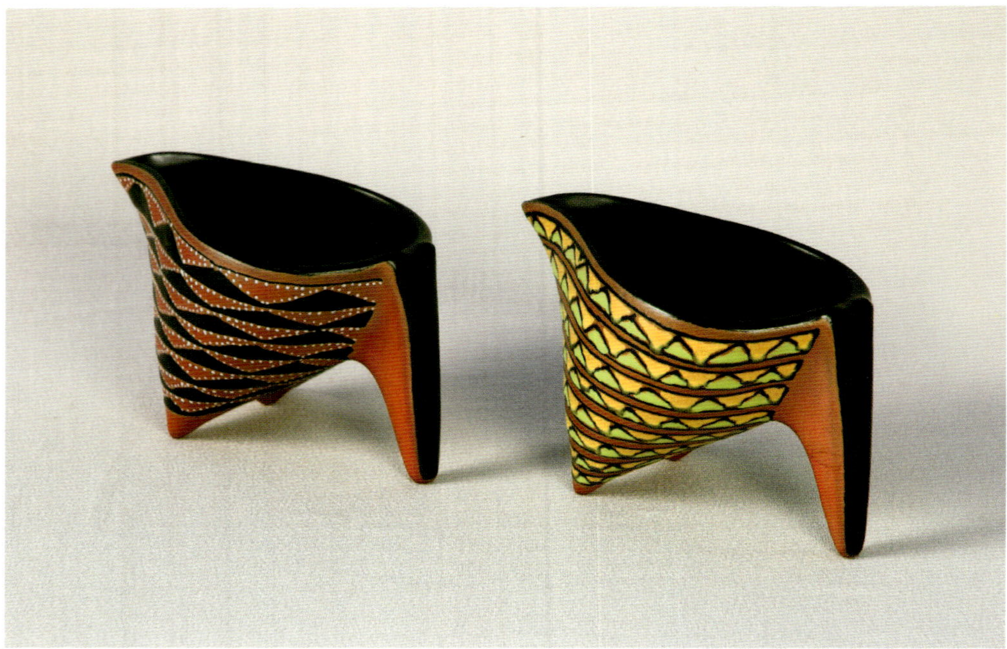

TOP: Kalahari | Two sculptural forms, probably pipe ashtrays | From left: 150x170x80mm; 190x190x85mm | Provenance: Gordon Radowsky | Marks: faint Kalahari incised marking beneath glazed bases | Photograph by Natalie Field

ABOVE BOTTOM: Kalahari | Pair of jugs decorated with slip-trailed geometric surface pattern | 104x155x95mm | Provenance: Gordon Radowsky | Marks: hand-painted black glaze marking, 'Kalahari' | Photograph by Natalie Field

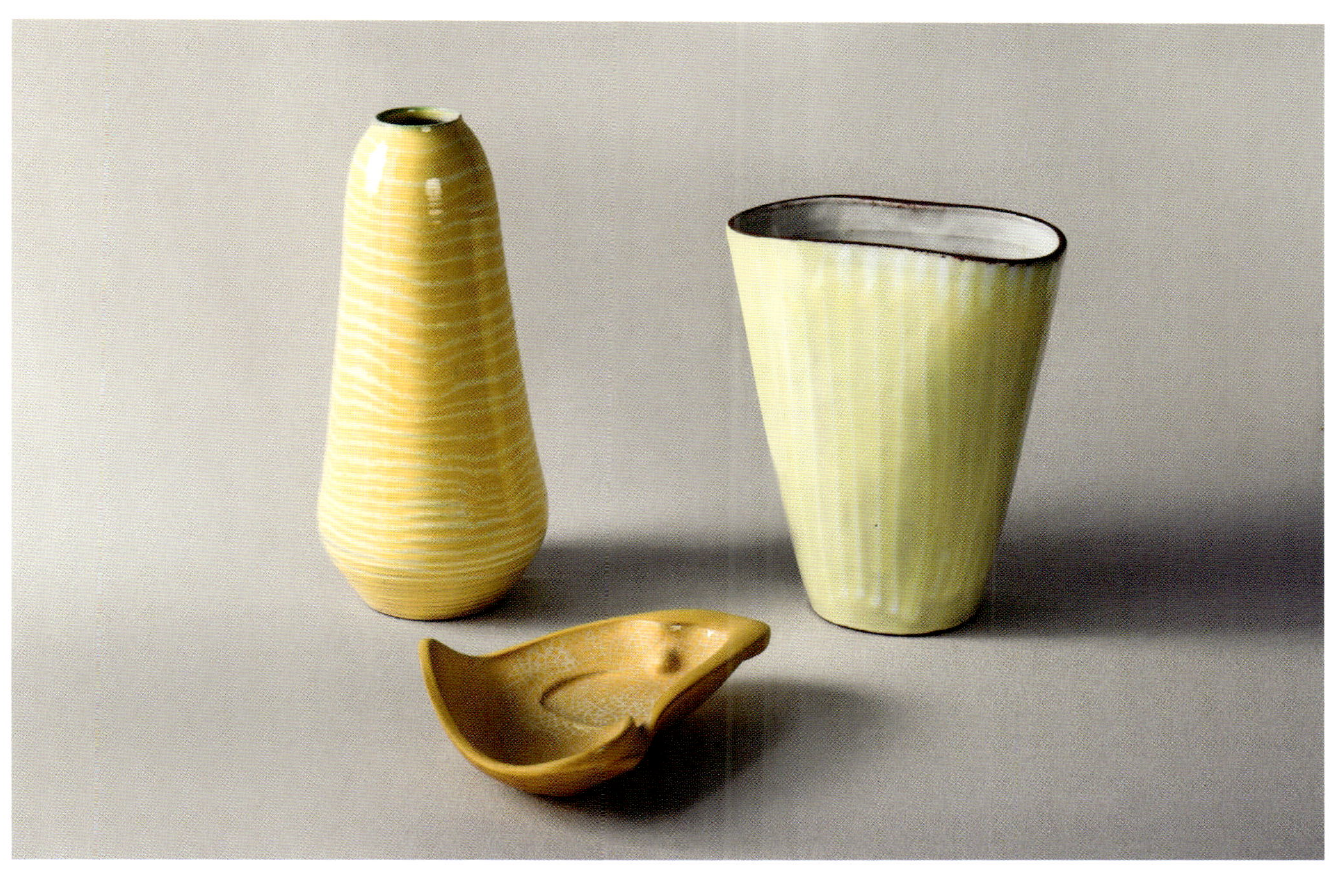

Kalahari | Two yellow vases and a bonbonnière | From left: 285x50x85mm; 185x135x65mm; 220x185x90mm | Provenance: Gordon Radowsky | Marks: from left: incised Kalahari; painted Kalahari; painted Kalahari | Photograph by Natalie Field

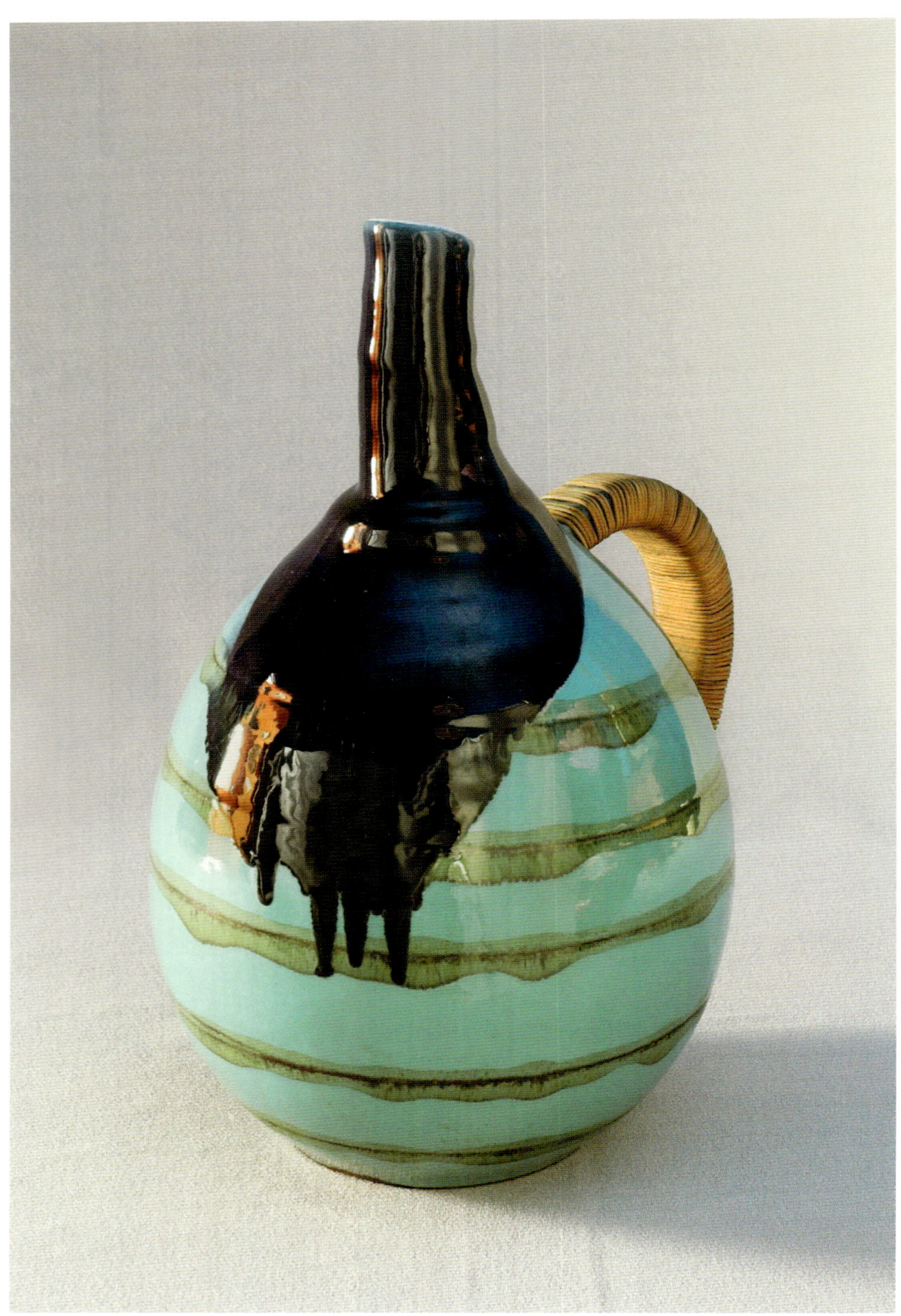

Kalahari | Ovoid bottle with eccentric neck, and woven cane handle | 365x40x120mm | Provenance: Gordon Radowsky | Marks: painted marking, 'Kalahari' | Photograph by Natalie Field

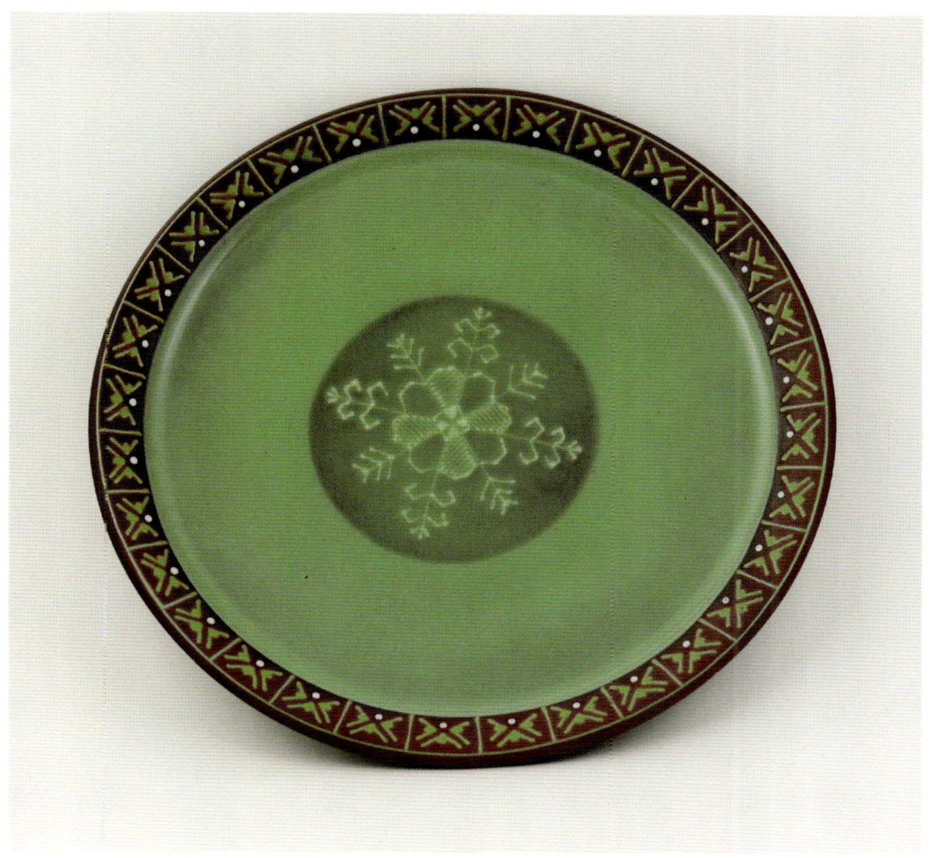

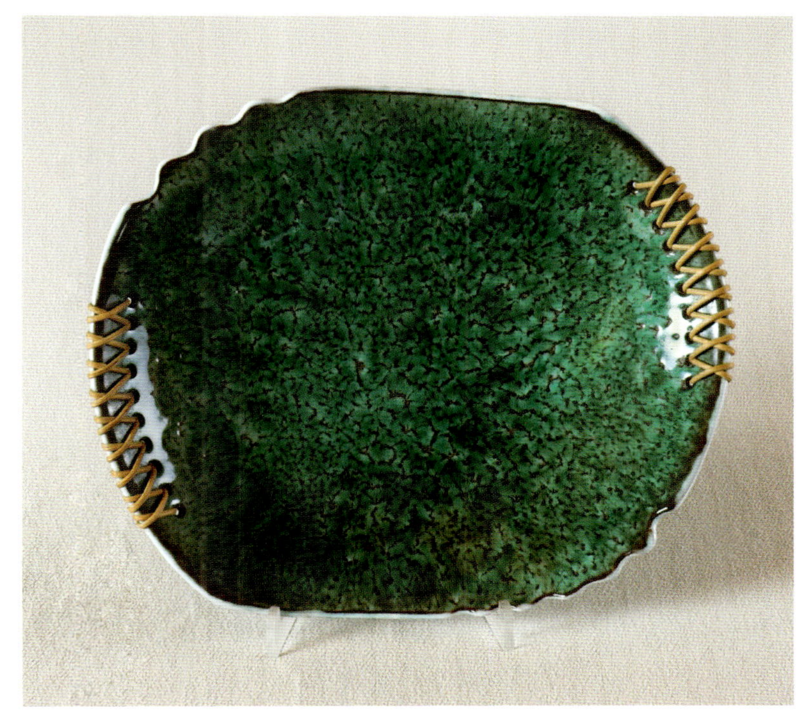

ABOVE: Kalahari | Charger, celadon glaze with ornamental geometric frieze along rim and roundel with floral motif inspired by Eastern European vernacular embroidery | 255x20mm | Provenance: Wendy Gers | Marks: green glazed base with black hand-painted glaze marks, 'Kalahari' | Photograph by Damien Artus

RIGHT: Kalahari | Plate with wicker decoration | 233x270x51mm | Provenance: SHC Iziko | 90/768 | Marks: painted marking, 'Kalahari' | Photograph by Natalie Field

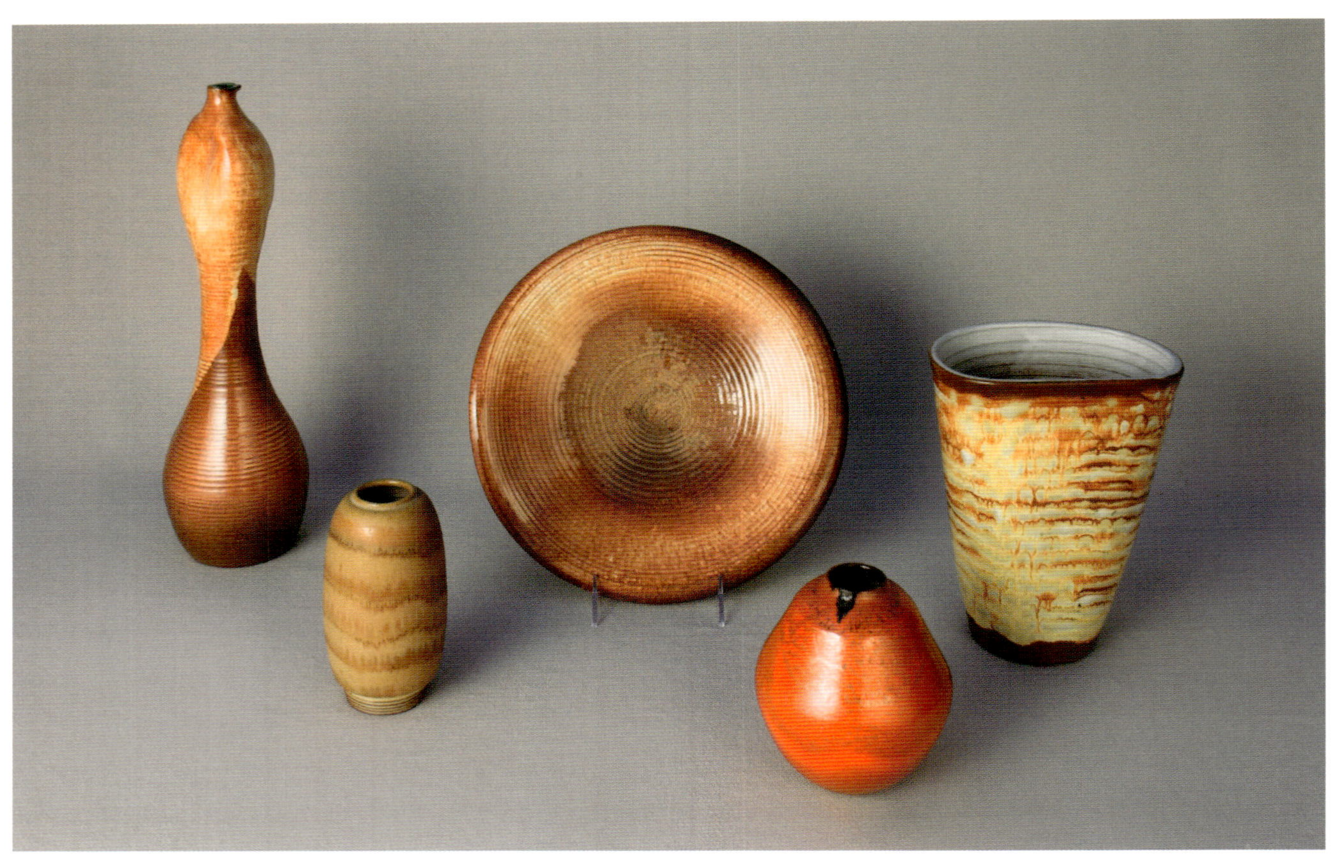

Kalahari | Group of varied organic terracotta forms | From left: 390x30x85mm; 155x40x52mm; 290x50mm; 150x8x50mm; 220x178x90mm | Provenance: Gordon Radowsky | Marks: from left: painted marking, 'Kalahari'; incised marking beneath glaze, 'Kalahari'; incised marking beneath glaze, 'Kalahari' and impressed stamp; incised marking beneath glaze, 'Kalahari'; painted Kalahari | Additional information: 2 and 4 Prov. Auction of the estate of the late A Klopcanovs, Stephan Welz and Co. in association with Sotheby's, Cape Town, 20 October 1998 | Photograph by Natalie Field

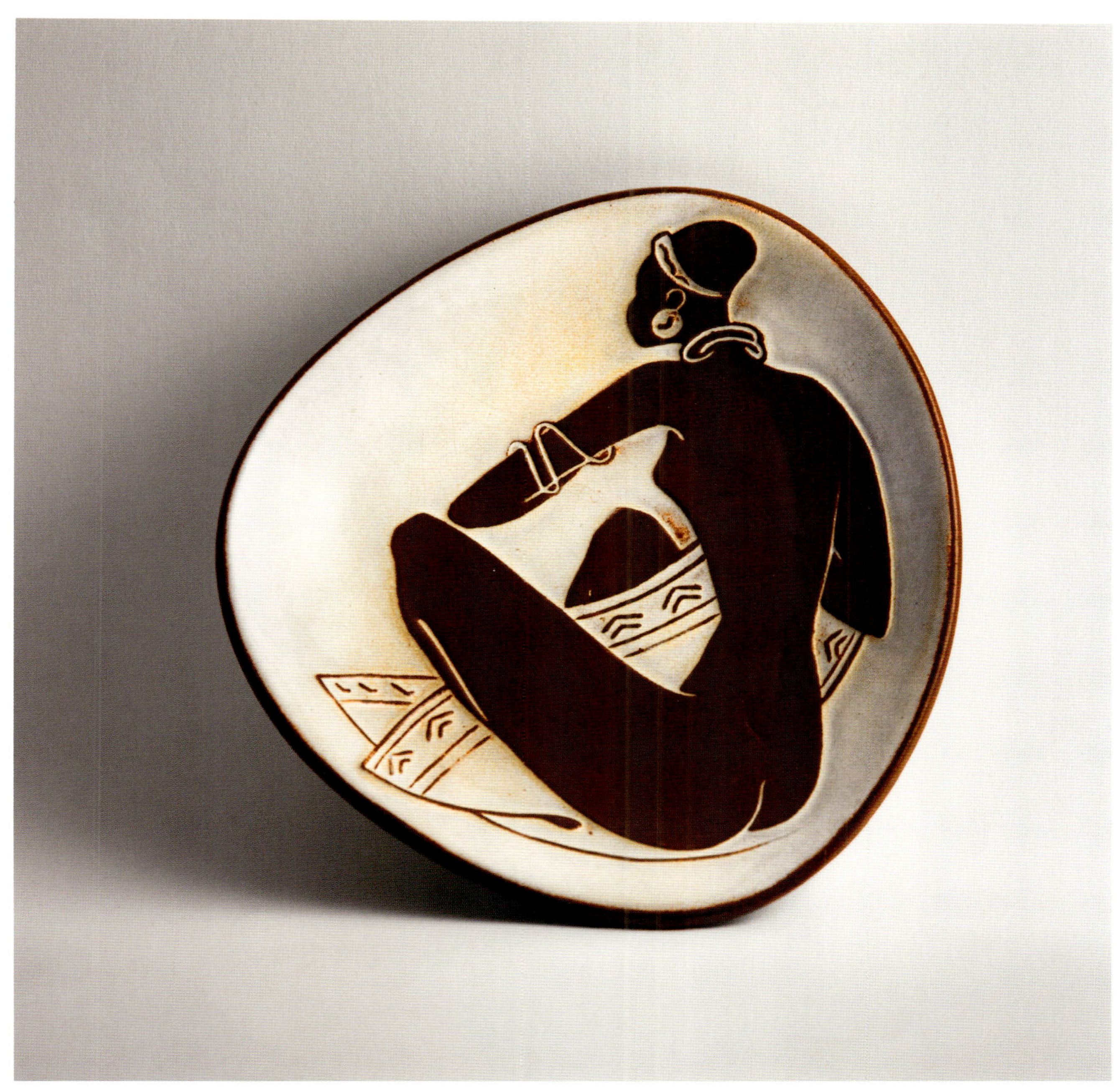

Kalahari | Ovoid charger depicting a seated woman | 160x145x30mm | Provenance: Wendy Gers | Marks: hand-painted brown glaze marking, 'Kalahari' | Photograph by Damien Artus

Kolonyama Pottery, Lesotho (1968–1994)

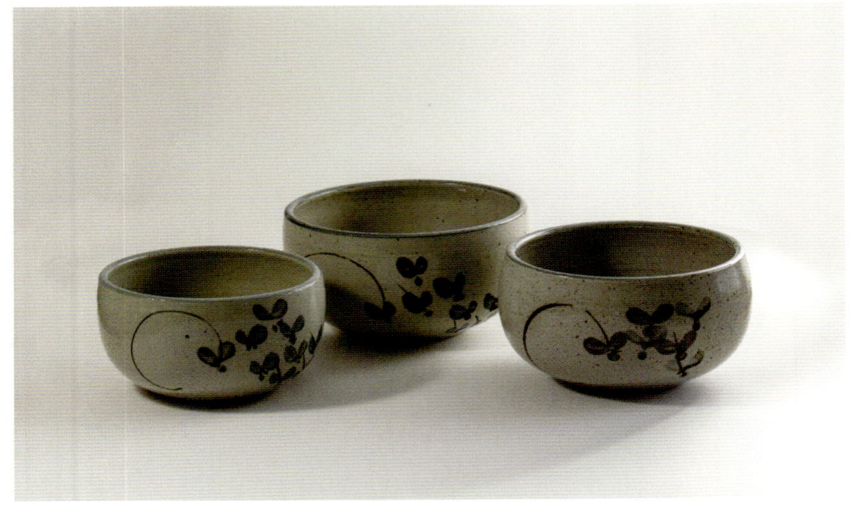

Kolonyama Pottery | Three nesting bowls | From left: 160x90mm; 175x100mm; 190x105mm | Provenance: Wendy Gers | Marks: impressed 'KP' mark | Photograph by Damien Artus

Location

The pottery was nestled at the foot of the Kolonyama Mountain near Teyateyaneng, Lesotho between Ficksburg and Maseru.

Name

The exact meaning of the word 'Kolonyama' is contested, but there is a degree of consensus on the notion of plenitude. *Kolonyama* is derived from the Sesotho word for 'mountain of meat' as in times of raids all the cattle were driven to the summit of the mountain during raids.

Founder and managers

Kolonyama Pottery was founded and financially managed by Lesotho businessman Ian T H D Dare and funded by the Lesotho National Development Corporation. Trudi and Joe Finch set up the workshop, built the kiln and other equipment, trained staff and made most of the early pots. Various British-trained potters managed the pottery at Kolonyama, many of whom later became renowned ceramicists and were directly or indirectly connected with the Finch family of Winchcombe Pottery,[149] England. The first English 'import' to Lesotho was Joe Finch, the son of Raymond Finch of Winchcombe Pottery. Joe and his wife Trudi worked at Kolonyama from May 1969 to November 1970. When Joe Finch returned to England, his father, Raymond Finch, arrived to expand the operation and was there from November 1970 to April 1971. Back in England, Joe Finch recruited Malcolm Bandtock in early 1971 to manage the pottery, train staff and expand production. Bandtock assisted Ray Finch for a brief period and continued to manage the pottery until early 1973.

Bill van Gilder, a young American potter who was connected to Winchcombe while training, managed the pottery from 1973 to 1976. Toff

Milway, also formerly of Winchcombe, arrived at Kolonyama in 1974 and worked as an assistant manager under Van Gilder until the latter left. Milway subsequently managed the pottery until 1977, when Jim Webster, also formerly of Winchcombe, assumed this role until early 1980. Graham and Lynda Taylor, who had been working at Joe Finch's Appin Pottery in Scotland, took over the management of Kolonyama in early 1980. The Taylors subsequently bought the pottery from Dare. Dave Wilson, who was also from Winchcombe Pottery, was Taylor's assistant manager until 1982. Upon Wilsons' departure, Malcolm Dare, the son of Ian Dare, replaced Wilson as a trainee manager until 1983. The Taylors continued to manage the pottery until its closure in 1994.

Staff

Malcolm Bandtock, Lissa Claassens, Yvonne Dare, Trudi Finch (née Pickford), Christopher (aka Chris) Green, Peter Grub, Anita Hutchings, Julia Khalane, Philemon Koloko, Frank Mahope, Sina (Alice) Mantala, Florina (Tamati) Matala, Moto Matsa, Tsitso Mohapi, Florina Molebelefi, Alex Moshoeshoe, Amelia Moshoeshoe, Lesole Motanyane, Evodia Nena, Mathabo Nthako, Jeanette Ramatola, Patrick Rorke, Masebete Sebete, Emmanuel Setsabi, Julia Setsabi, Setsabi Setsabi, Lynda Taylor, Theboho Wrenford Tloome, Stella Webster, and Dave Wilson. Staff whose surnames are not recalled include Joseph, Josephina, Majolani, Malefi, Mathabiso and Rosaline.

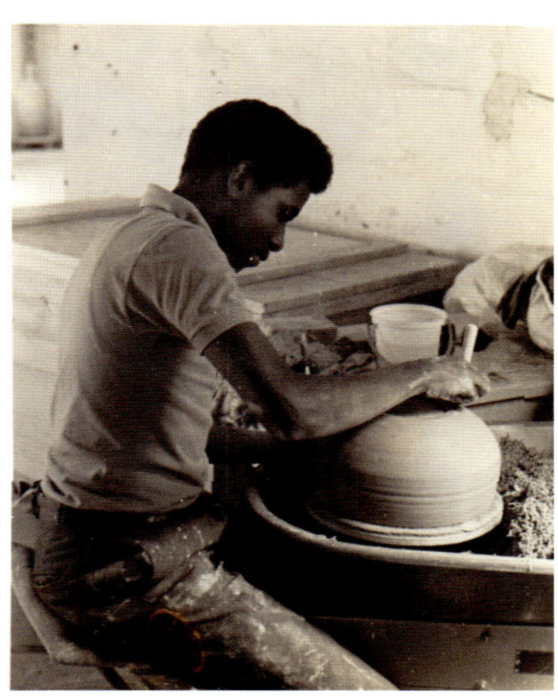
Kolonyama Pottery | Joseph (surname unknown) turning | Provenance: Joe Finch | Photograph by Joe Finch

Wares manufactured

Kolonyama's wares followed the general designs and production practices of Winchcombe Pottery. The pottery almost exclusively made reduction-fired stoneware of household crockery sets, goblets, storage jars, domestic pots, slab-built pots, table lamps and individual pieces. The skills of its potters were evident in many of the larger items, such as 9- and 12-pint (4–5½ litres) casseroles, 16-inch (40cm) wall-plates, large jugs and bowls. While the majority of its wares were made on the wheel, Kolonyama produced slab and press-moulded platters and plates. A limited number of small sculptures were also produced.

The managers tended to make more complex and sophisticated pieces, such as goblets, while Basotho staff made production ware. Many of the English and American potters' wares were individual exhibition pieces, sold via art exhibitions, exclusive craft shops and galleries. The less artistic wares were regarded as stock dinnerware and were sold in the Kolonyama shop or at other outlets. This is not to say that the Basotho staff were not skilled – indeed, many of the Basotho throwers were highly skilled. Frank Mahope, for example, who was renowned for large thrown pots, also made cider jars, bread crocks, casseroles and large jugs. Similarly, Julia Setsabi was an excellent thrower of small items. She is remembered for her consistency, as she could be relied upon to produce long runs of identical pieces.

Decoration

Initially two principal glazes were used, a black tenmoku and an oatmeal glaze, but these were soon supplemented by a glassy green glaze and a foggy white ash glaze. Joe Finch introduced a white zirconium glaze over which a blue glaze was applied. Milway introduced a green matt glaze, which was discontinued in 1979. The standard lidded storage jars were decorated with a semi-matt saturated iron-red glaze. Celadon green glaze with red iron decoration was used on certain wares. Glaze recipes were generally developed by Ray Finch.

More decorated wares were produced after Trudi Finch's arrival and by 1979 almost all wares were decorated, usually with coloured slips. Trudi developed the hallmark blue leaf design. Milway decorated some pots using the paper relief method, but these were commercially not very popular. Often simple organic motifs or 'loose' brushwork in the Anglo-Oriental tradition were applied. Yvonne Dare tended to apply elaborate floral motifs in the late 1970s. Lynda Taylor painted cosmos daisies and leaf motifs. The wares from the Webster period feature more 'brushy' glaze decoration. Certain potters, such as Van Gilder, mainly decorated using the Winchcombe style of slip-combing or slip-poured patterns with over-glazing.

Other forms of glaze decoration include salt-glazing and the random decorative effects of smoke-fired wares. A salt-glazing kiln was built by Van Gilder in late 1974 and slip-decorated; salt-glazed wares were produced from approximately 1975 to 1979.

Lissa Claassens noted the following when she worked at Kolonyama in 1981:

> The standard decorations that were made for stock and to order were: 'Cosmos', 'Wheat and Cosmos', and 'Blue' and 'Brown' Leaf. When I was a decorator at Kolonyama all the Cosmos was painted by Dave Wilson, the Wheat and Cosmos by Lynda Taylor and the Blue and Brown Leaf by myself. The look of each person's interpretation of a design was completely different so serious collectors could recognise who had painted a particular design by the style. For instance, my Blue Leaf looked different to Stella Webster's and when Lynda took over when I left it was completely different. I often wonder how people felt about these different styles being mixed into their dinner services! Lynda introduced a variety of new decorations to the standard range. Her style was very bold and big.[150]

Graham Taylor introduced a range of wood-fired wares, however problems of fuel scarcity constrained this range's development. Taylor extended Kolonyama's range of domestic ware and introduced a series that was intended to convey an African flair, called the 'Litema' range.

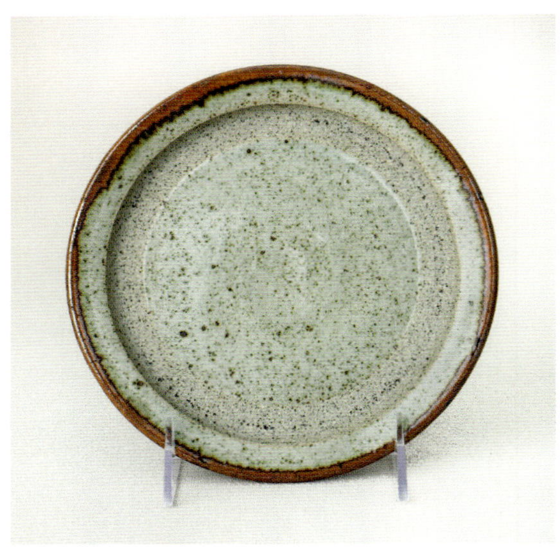

Kolonyama Pottery | Side plate | 177x180mm | Provenance: Jan Middlejans | Marks: impressed 'KP' mark and gold sticker | Photograph by Natalie Field

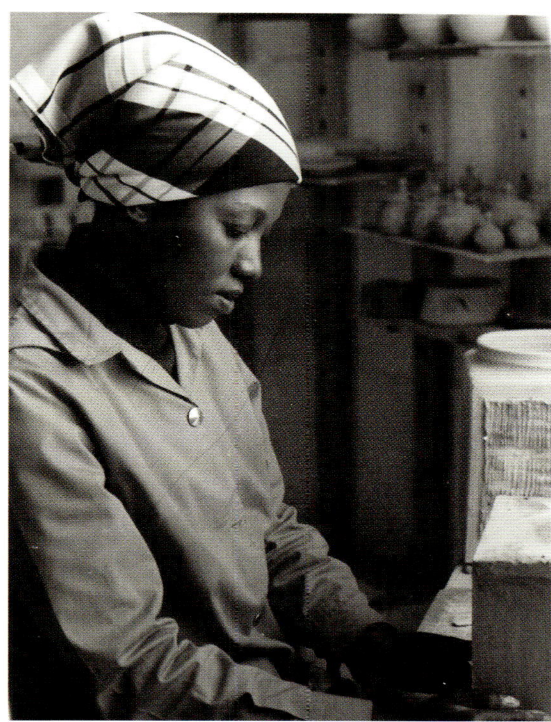

Kolonyama Pottery | Evodia Nena making a slab pot | Provenance: Joe Finch | Photograph by Joe Finch

Production methods

Kolonyama produced its own clay.[151] The clay was transformed into domestic and decorative wares and sculpted by hand or via the potter's wheel. In addition, hand-built wares were coiled while others were assembled from slabs.

Brief history of the pottery

While the pottery was the brainchild of the Dare family, the fundamental connection with Winchcombe pottery can be traced to a doyen of South African pottery, Esias Bosch. A good friend of Ray Finch, with whom he had worked (1951–1952), Bosch invited Joe to stay with him at White River when at the age of 21 he wished to travel. Bosch had suggested that Swaziland or Lesotho might be interested in having help with their ceramics as they had contacted him but nothing had been arranged.[152] Joe Finch travelled to Lesotho and tried to arrange finance for a pottery venture. Growing impatient with the constant delays, Joe lamented about his precarious situation to Yvonne and Ian Dare, new acquaintances whom he had just met at the opening of a carpet factory in Maseru. The Dares were enthralled by this charming young man and invited Joe to set up a pottery in the unused empty grain silos located on their farm at Kolonyama. Within a week of this fortuitous meeting, Kolonyama Pottery was established. Joe and his future wife Trudi spent the following 18 months building the pottery, doing clay-and glaze-testing and training local staff.

An elderly Ray Finch recalls:

> [Joe] took on about half a dozen local people, women and men, and on the whole the men took to the wheel and the women did the hand building ... Trudi, his wife, before they were married, went out there to help him and she taught them to make slab pots, you know, and they made those. I think there were about 6 or 8 working when he finished. But in the end, after about, I think, 3 years [sic], he wanted to come home, he wanted to get married so they had to find somebody else and in the interim I said I'd go out there for 6 months. So in 1970, I think it was, I went out there and took over from Joe and went on, I think it ended up with about twelve working there, local people ... It went well because the South Africans used to come into Lesotho for holidays, you know, and they were the market, and we used to send pots to Johannesburg and so on (Hale 1994:59,60).

The pottery and shop were located in six disused grain silos on the Dare farm. These buildings were modified and subsequently extended. The production was arranged in linear progression, commencing with the clay-processing shed, and finishing with the stock rooms and showroom.[153] Joe Finch was technically competent and resourceful and personally constructed much of the original equipment or had it made locally.[154] Kolonyama initially had five potters' wheels[155] and produced mostly domestic ware. Kolonyama held three major exhibitions under Joe and Trudi Finch.

Each subsequent manager left his fingerprint on the pottery, by upgrading facilities, training new staff, and changing glazes and production forms.[156] In 1976 the pottery employed 15 Basothos. This number waxed and waned over the years. In the 1980s the pottery employed a staff of approximately 30.

Kolonyama, via its shop, helped to develop and market the work of independent Basotho artists, crafters and herd-boys. Two local artists of significance include MéAlice Mantala, who made a wide variety of traditional pots and Tsitso Mohapi, who made incredibly skilled figurative sculptures of traditional rural scenes. Until the late 1970s, local herd-boys made cattle, horses and other figurines that were glazed and sold in the shop.

In the early years, Kolonyama paralleled Winchcombe and Liebermann in its hospitable, convivial and fraternal approach to pottery training and production. Glaze recipes were freely shared and Kolonyama hosted many residential workshops for potters from around southern Africa. The pottery was a stalwart supporter of APSA exhibitions, and Van Gilder contributed articles to their journal, *Sgraffiti* (including volumes 2 and 3). Staff also afforded technical and logistical assistance to other potteries, such as Thamaga in Botswana and Mantenga in Swaziland.

In the 1970s Kolonyama participated in various APSA exhibitions including the First APSA National Exhibition at the Association of Arts Gallery, Pretoria, in 1973, and the fourth APSA National Exhibition (called MUD) at Hilton College, KwaZulu-Natal.[157] At this exhibition both undecorated pieces made by Basotho potters and more refined items by the managers were displayed. Kolonyama wares were sold through numerous private galleries and at various trade fairs.[158]

Despite its significant network of sales points, Kolonyama sold a substantial percentage of wares from its own shop. In 1979 the pottery ceased to make a profit, largely because the marketing of its products was neglected as Ian Dare's business interests became increasingly diverted to KwaZulu-Natal. Furthermore, Lesotho's social and economic environment had changed in the decade since its establishment, and political instability scared away many potential tourists. In addition, the recently established Lesotho casino (which hosted cinemas screening pornographic films and gambling facilities) brought a new type of tourist to Lesotho. Most casino tourists were not interested in venturing off the beaten track to explore the country's artistic heritage. However, with careful nurturing the pottery regained its foothold in the market.

In the early 1980s the Taylors bought a controlling share from Dare[159] and significantly changed various aspects of the pottery's operations. Kolonyama's association with APSA ceased under the Taylors, who focused on local sales and exhibitions. Graham Taylor renovated the showroom, making it more like a gallery and ran several exhibitions each year. He also organised regular exhibitions in Maseru, where he taught, and was well-known within the artistic community. This period of stabilisation was short as a result of economic

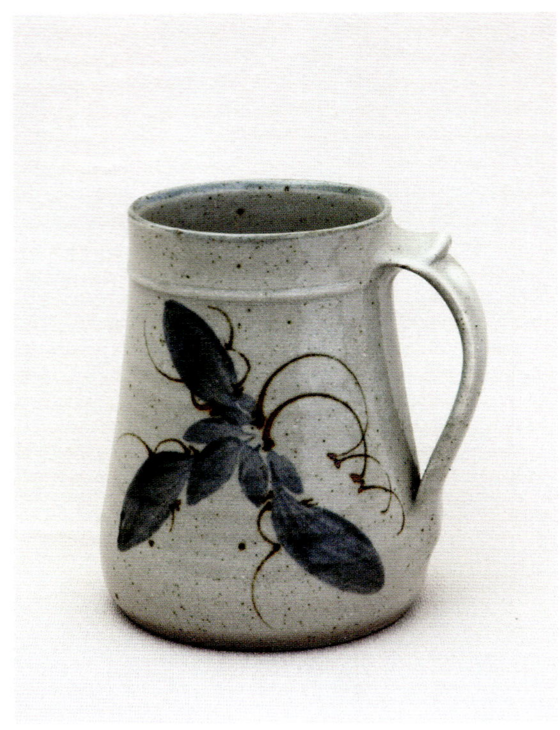

Kolonyama Pottery | Tankard | 140x185x100mm | Provenance: Douglas van der Horst | Marks: impressed 'KP' mark | Photograph by Natalie Field

troubles caused by the relocation of many important aid and diplomatic agencies from Maseru to Pretoria in the 1990s. The subsequent drain of capital from Lesotho, combined with an unstable market for luxury goods in South Africa, resulted in the ultimate demise of Kolonyama. In an attempt to salvage the business, Graham Taylor introduced a range of new wares, produced a new catalogue and tried to get assistance from aid agencies, but to no avail. Kolonyama finally ceased its activities in 1994.

Marks

Early wares have a small stamp, usually on the foot or near the base, bearing the initials KP. From the late 1970s a round gold sticker was attached to the products. This stated 'Pottery from Kolonyama Lesotho' or 'Kolonyama Pottery Lesotho' (together with the KP mark).

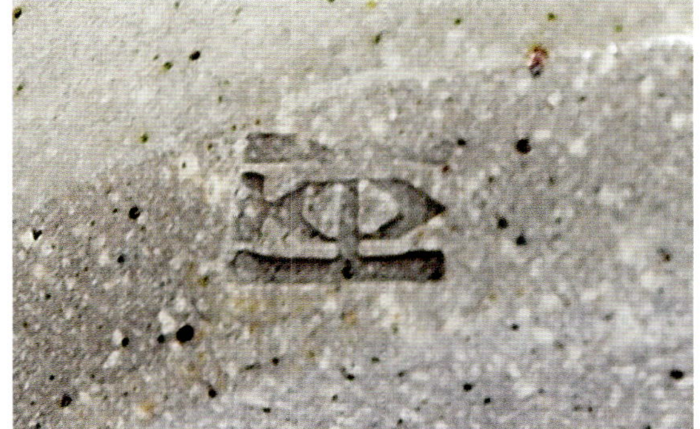

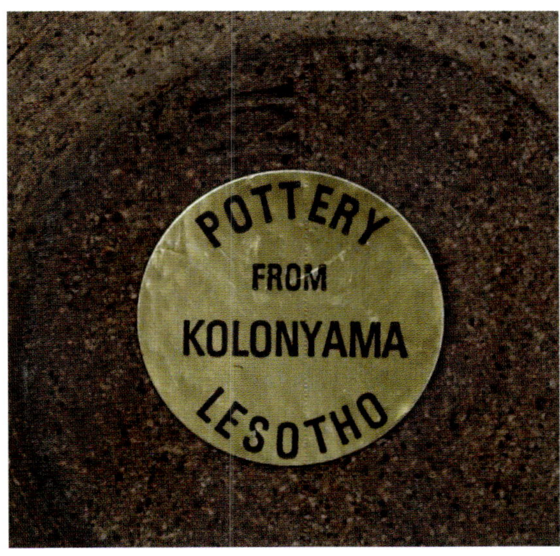

TOP: Kolonyama Pottery | Maker's mark | Stamp. 'KP' | Photograph by Natalie Field

ABOVE BOTTOM: Kolonyama Pottery | Maker's mark | Gold foil sticker with black text, 'Pottery from Kolonyama lesotho' | Photograph by Natalie Field

Biographies

BANDTOCK, Malcolm (1941–1988)

Born in London, Bandtock was employed by Kolonyama between 1971 and 1973. He visited the pottery again in the late 1970s and early 1980s, and worked there for a short period at the end of 1981. Subsequently, Bandtock set up his own pottery in Norfolk, which he ran until the mid-1980s. In 1986 he spent a year working for the UNHCR in Cyprus, running two pottery ventures.[160]

CLAASSENS, Lissa (b.1959)

Born in Pretoria, Claassens obtained a degree in African languages and social anthropology from the University of Cape Town in 1979. She studied pottery under Rika Meijer, Leslie-Ann Hoets and Margie Chilton-Malan. Claassens worked at Kolonyama from 1980 to 1981 and at Mapepe Craft, Henley-on-Klip from 1981–1982. She subsequently studied ceramic science at the Witwatersrand Technikon under Karin Boyum. From 1983 to 1985 she worked in Johannesburg before returning to Cape Town in 1987. In 1990 Claassens returned to Pretoria to assist her mother, Val Claassens, in her pottery studio. In 1995 she returned to Cape Town from where she continues to work as a professional potter, teaching adults and children while pursuing production throwing and supplying various South African homeware stores. Since 2005 Claassens has been exploring sculptural work using paper-clay. Since August 2011 she has been technical and artistic adviser to Art in the Forest, Cape Town. More recently she has been training their ceramic artists to be teachers and running outreach programmes for orphaned and vulnerable children from the Cape Flats.

DARE, Ian T H D (1935–1998)

Born in Mapoteng, Lesotho, Ian Dare was awarded a BA from Rhodes University, Grahamstown in 1959. Upon graduation he returned to his family

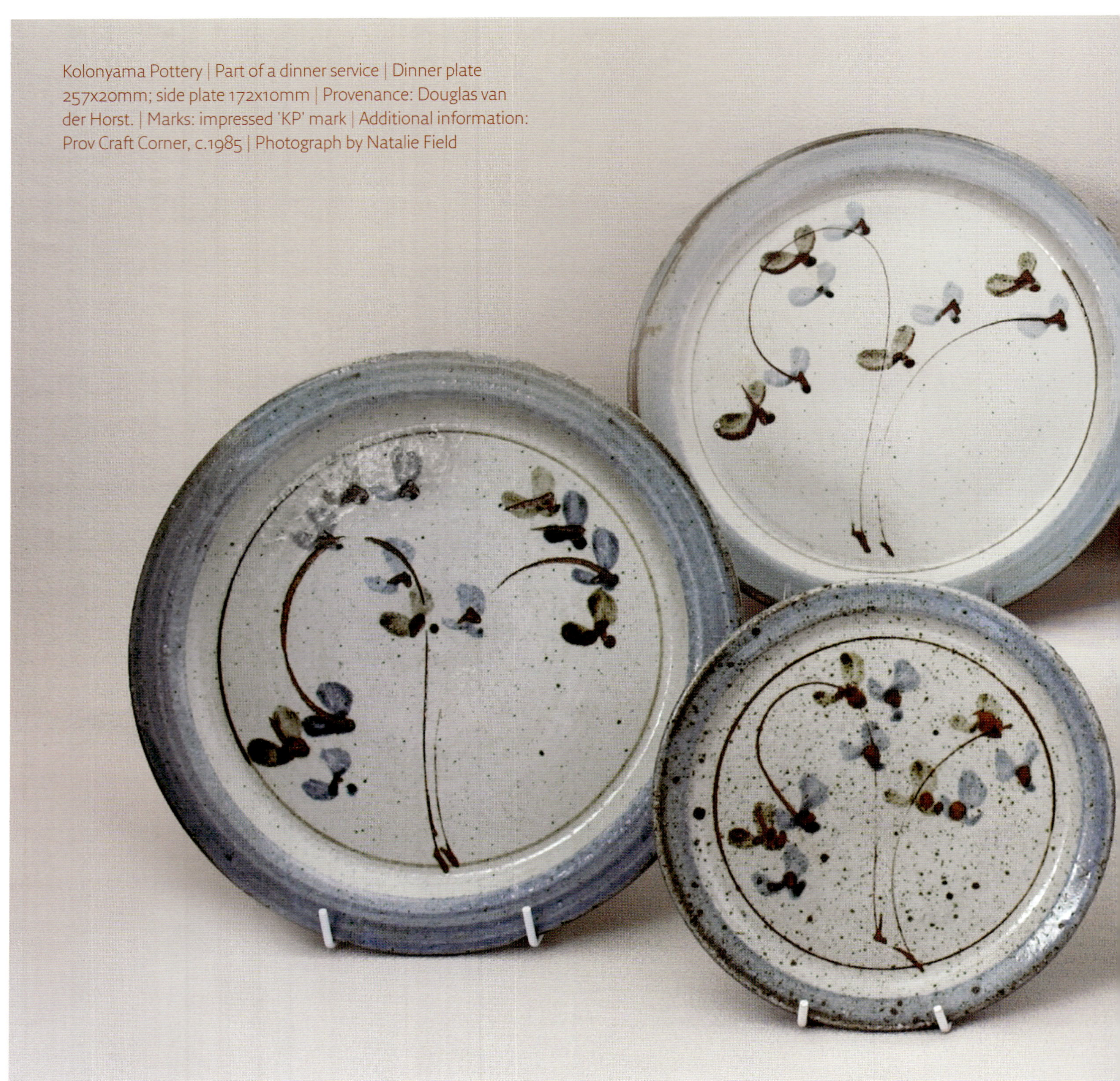
Kolonyama Pottery | Part of a dinner service | Dinner plate 257x20mm; side plate 172x10mm | Provenance: Douglas van der Horst. | Marks: impressed 'KP' mark | Additional information: Prov Craft Corner, c.1985 | Photograph by Natalie Field

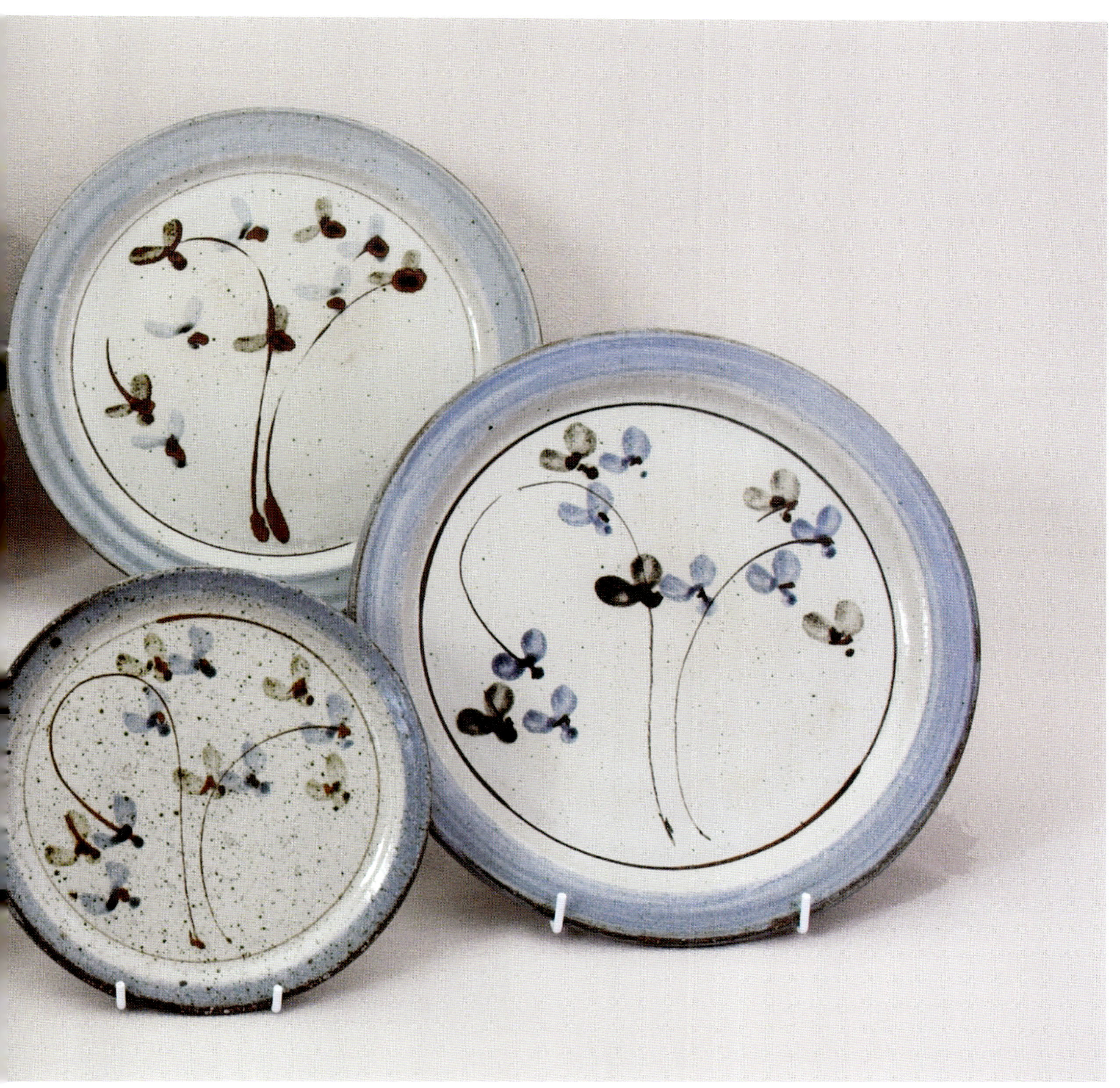

farm in Lesotho. Legislation at the time decreed that only the Basotho could farm, and Dare subsequently entered into various entrepreneurial ventures. He founded Kolonyama and was responsible for the construction of the pottery on his farm. Dare did all the administrative duties and, in the early years, the marketing of the wares. He later sold the pottery to Graham Taylor.[161]

DARE, Yvonne (b.1938)

Born in Leribe, Lesotho, Yvonne trained as a nurse in Cape Town and married Ian Dare in 1960. Yvonne started to train as a thrower but found that the spinning wheel made her nauseous as she was pregnant, so Trudi Finch taught her how to do brushwork decoration. She worked as a decorator from approximately 1969 to 1979. Dare lived in Lesotho until 1980, when she retired to Cape Town.

FINCH, Joseph (aka Joe) (b.1947)

Born in Winchcombe, Finch was apprenticed to his father at Winchcombe Pottery from 1964 to 1968. In 1969 he established Kolonyama Pottery, Lesotho's first studio pottery, with the financial backing of Ian Dare.

In 1970 he married Trudi Pickford and returned to Winchcombe. In 1973 the young couple moved to Appin, Scotland, to establish their own pottery. They retained Appin as their base until 1984, but periodically worked abroad. During the Scottish winters of 1975 and 1977, they worked at Kolonyama and in 1979 they spent three months at Gellibrand Pottery, Australia. In 1980 Finch co-managed the Dartington Pottery Training Workshop for six months. Between 1986 and 1989 he operated a small studio pottery in Powys, Wales. In October 1998 and April 1999 Finch participated in an aid programme to improve the wood-fired kilns of potters in Rajasthan, India. Since 1990 he and his wife have been involved with their pottery and gallery, 'Joe and Trudi Finch, Pottery and Paintings', in Cardigan, Wales. Paisley and Stoke City Museums own works by Finch. He won an award for 'The best ceramic piece' at Ceramica Cymru in 2003.[162]

FINCH, Michael (aka Mike) (b.1946)

Born at Winchcombe, the first-born son of Ray Finch, Mike worked at Winchcombe Pottery from 1968 to 1972. He travelled overland to Lesotho with a band of musicians and worked for six months at Kolonyama, commencing in June 1973. When he returned to England he rejoined Winchcombe, where he presently works as a potter and manager.[163]

FINCH, Alfred Raymond (aka Ray) (1914–2012)

Born in London, Finch attended the Central School of Art, London, under Dora Billington in 1935. The following year he worked at Winchcombe under Michael Cardew and began managing it when Cardew moved to Wales in 1939. In 1943 he joined the National Fire Service. Finch purchased Winchcombe Pottery from Cardew and restarted production in 1946. In 1960 Finch held his first exhibition

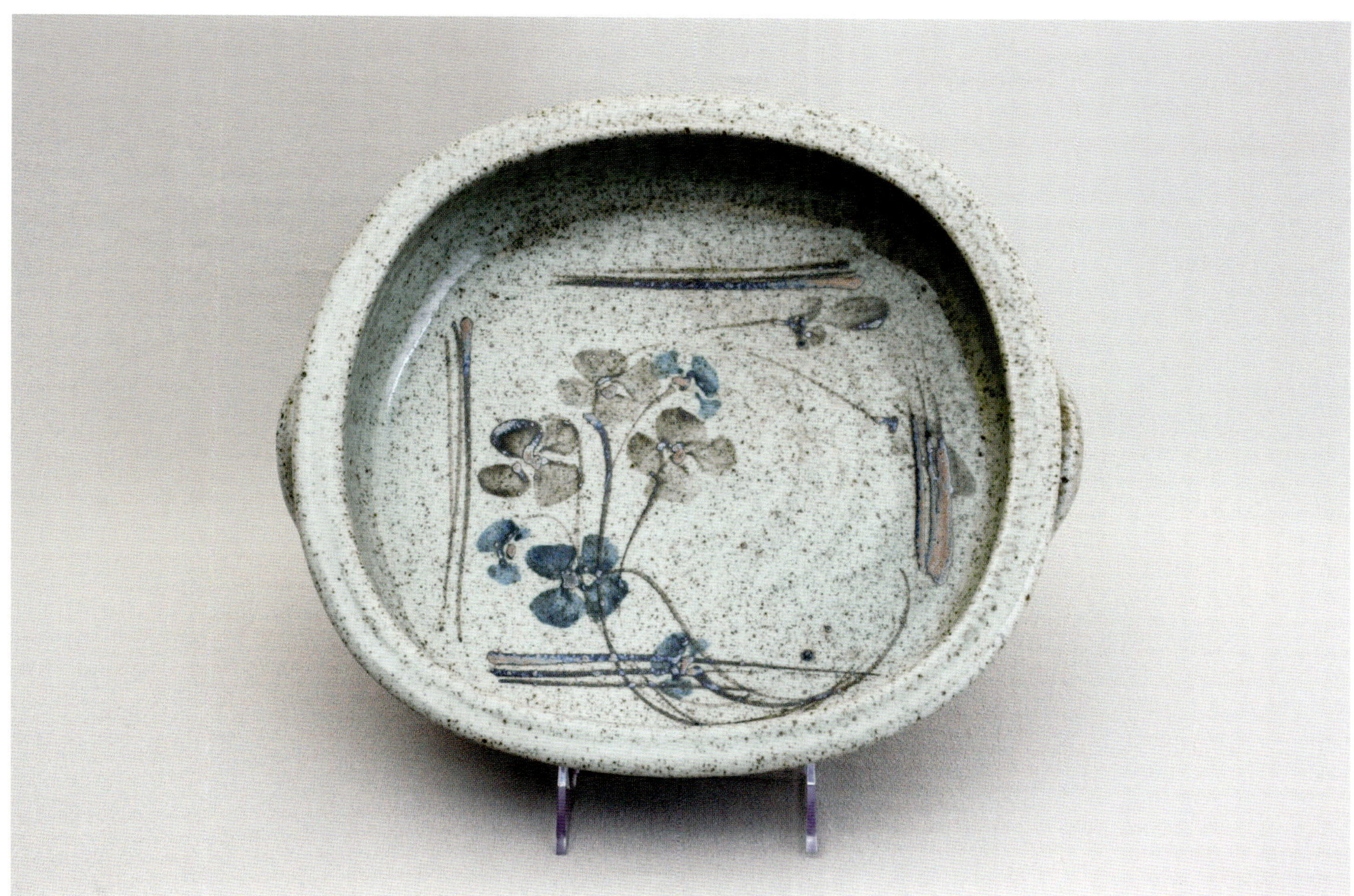

Kolonyama Pottery | Baking Dish | 280x290x60mm | Provenance: Douglas van der Horst | Marks: impressed 'KP' mark | Photograph by Natalie Field

at the new Craftsmen Potters Association shop and gallery. In the following year he received an important commission from the reputed vegetarian restaurant, Cranks. Between November 1970 and April 1971 he managed Kolonyama Pottery, before returning to Winchombe. Finch, who describes himself as a 75 per cent 'country potter' and 25 per cent studio potter (because he was forced to make commissions and special wares) (Hale 1994:61), passionately believed in the functional value of his wares:

> ... we still try to keep them reasonable, because we want people to use them, and that seems to work because we get people coming back after 20 years and saying they've had pots for 20 years and they want to replace them and that sort of thing. I mean that happens quite frequently, surprisingly frequently ... (Hale 1994:62).

In 1979 he retired from the management of Winchcombe, and the following year was awarded an MBE. Winchcombe is an internationally renowned studio and still continues to make pots in the Anglo-Oriental tradition. Ray is the father of Joe and Michael Finch.[164]

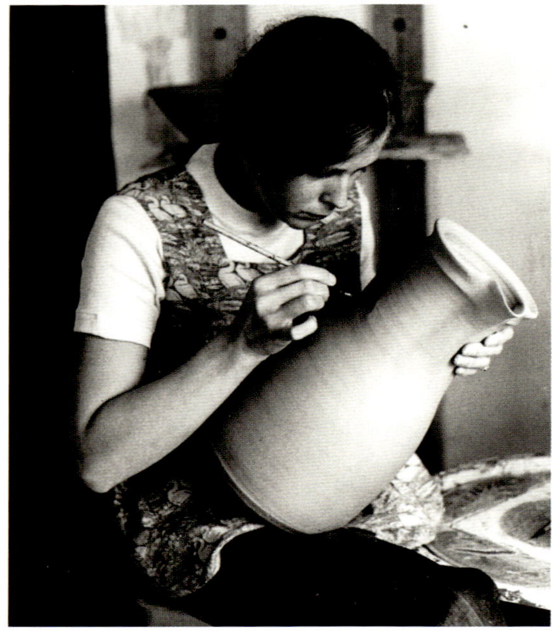

Kolonyama Pottery | Trudi Finch decorating a large jug| Provenance: Joe Finch | Photograph by Joe Finch

FINCH, Trudi (née Pickford) (b.1947)
Born in Tewkesbury, Gloucestershire, Finch studied Fine Art at Cheltenham College of Art from 1964 to 1965, and subsequently completed a diploma in art and design (ceramics), Farnham (1965–1968). Upon graduation she worked in a pottery in Suffolk producing slipware, and in 1965 she spent three months during the summer at Winchcombe Pottery, where she met Joe.

Together they established Kolonyama Pottery and worked there from 1969 to 1970, when they got married and returned to Winchcombe. Together they worked in Africa and Australia and eventually set up their own pottery, Appin, in the Scottish highlands. The birth of her daughter resulted in less time for working on the wheel. She initially concentrated on pottery decorating and later gave up pottery in favour of pastels, watercolours and dry-point etchings, which she printed on her own handmade paper. Finch had many solo and group exhibitions as a painter. She produced a large range of cards and prints and illustrated a book by Jeanine McMullen.

GRUB, Peter (deceased)
Grub worked at Kolonyama with Van Gilder for approximately three months in 1976. He had previously spent two years working at Serowe Pottery in Botswana.

KHALANE, Julia
Taylor trained his former domestic employee, Julia, as a decorator.

KOLOKO, Philemon
Koloko was trained by Joe Finch in clay preparation, but he soon progressed to an assistant kiln firer. He was also responsible for collecting ashes for glazes. He became chief kiln operator when Lesole Montanye left. Under Graham Taylor, Koloko trained Theboho Tloome who succeeded him upon his departure.

MAHOPE, Frank
Under Joe and Trudi Finch, Mahope worked as manager of the candle factory (next to the pottery). He occasionally made beautiful clay animals for Kolonyama. Later, he joined Kolonyama and was trained by Van Gilder as an expert thrower. According to Taylor, he had a real eye for form and was capable of throwing very large pots. He also made cider jars, bread crocks, casseroles and large jugs. He often worked with another thrower, Moto Matsa.

MANTALA, Sina (aka Alice or MéAlice) (deceased)
An elderly Basotho lady, Sina used to make traditional pots – some were glazed, and others were fired and left plain. She died in approximately 1980.

MATALA, Florina (aka Tamati)
The sister of Frank Mahope, Matala was trained as a thrower by Milway. She worked for many years at the pottery and Taylor recalled that she made excellent jugs and bowls. She acquired her nickname, Tamati, the Afrikaans word for tomato, as a result of her round reddish face.

MATSA, Moto
Matsa was a good production thrower, making plates and vegetable dishes. He was trained by Frank Mahope and worked under Taylor.

MILWAY, Christopher John (aka Toff) (b.1949)
Milway was born in Preston, Lancashire and educated at Campbell College in Northern Ireland. His first experience of pottery was in 1968 working for Christa Reichel, a German sculptress, followed by West Cork Pottery in 1969 and Glencraig Pottery from 1967 to 1970. He then spent a year working as the manager of a production workshop for Camphill Village Trust. From 1970 to 1972 Milway studied for a diploma in Pottery at the Harrow College of Technology and Art. In 1973 he joined Joe Finch at Appin Pottery, Scotland. He also worked at Winchombe pottery that year. From 1974 until 1977 Milway worked at Kolonyama Pottery, initially as the assistant manager, then as manager. During this period he acted as a consultant for Thamaga Pottery, Botswana and the Mantenga Craft Centre in Swaziland.

In 1978 Milway worked with Bill van Gilder at Stoney Hollow Pottery, USA. He subsequently returned to England and worked at Winchcombe Pottery from 1978 to 1983. From 1983 to 1984 he worked as a technical adviser on handcrafts in Kenya, and in 1985 established his own studio workshop and gallery, Conderton Pottery in Worcestershire, where he presently works. Milway is an active member of the Gloucestershire Guild of Craftsmen and is a Fellow of the Craft Potters Association.[165]

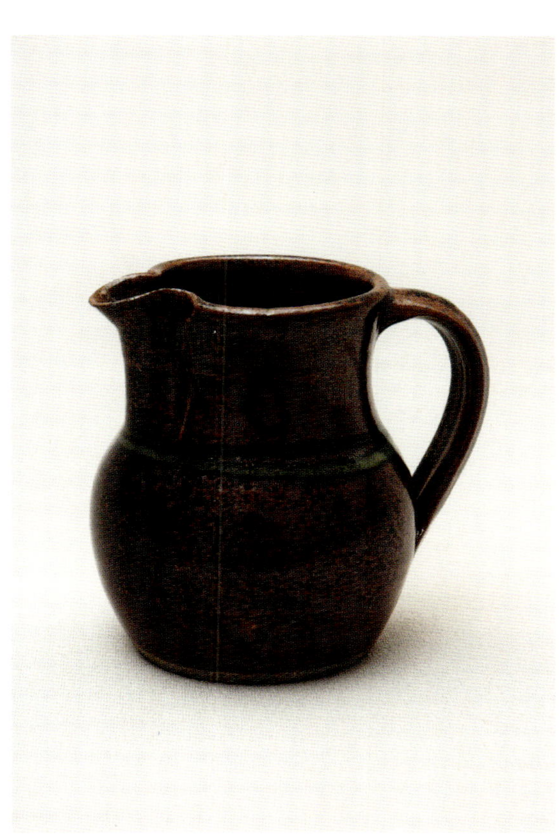
Kolonyama Pottery | Jug with iron glaze | 280x90x78mm | Provenance: Douglas van der Horst | Marks: impressed 'KP' mark | Photograph by Natalie Field

MOHAPI, Tsitso
Mohapi was associated directly and indirectly with Kolonyama. Under Joe Finch, Toff Milway and Graham Taylor he used to buy clay from the pottery, which they used to fire and buy the finished work. He produced extremely delicate figurative sculptures. His refined dioramas of Basotho figures reflect a masterful skill in the rendering of human anatomy with no formal art training. He worked in both terracotta and with high-fired stoneware. During the 1980s he became increasingly involved in running his own garage and did less and less sculpture.

MOSHOESHOE, Alex
A brickmaker by profession, Moshoeshoe was the official clay maker at Kolonyama. Moshoeshoe was employed by Kolonyama between 1971 and the late 1980s. He was related to Julia Setsabi and possibly to Philemon Koloko.

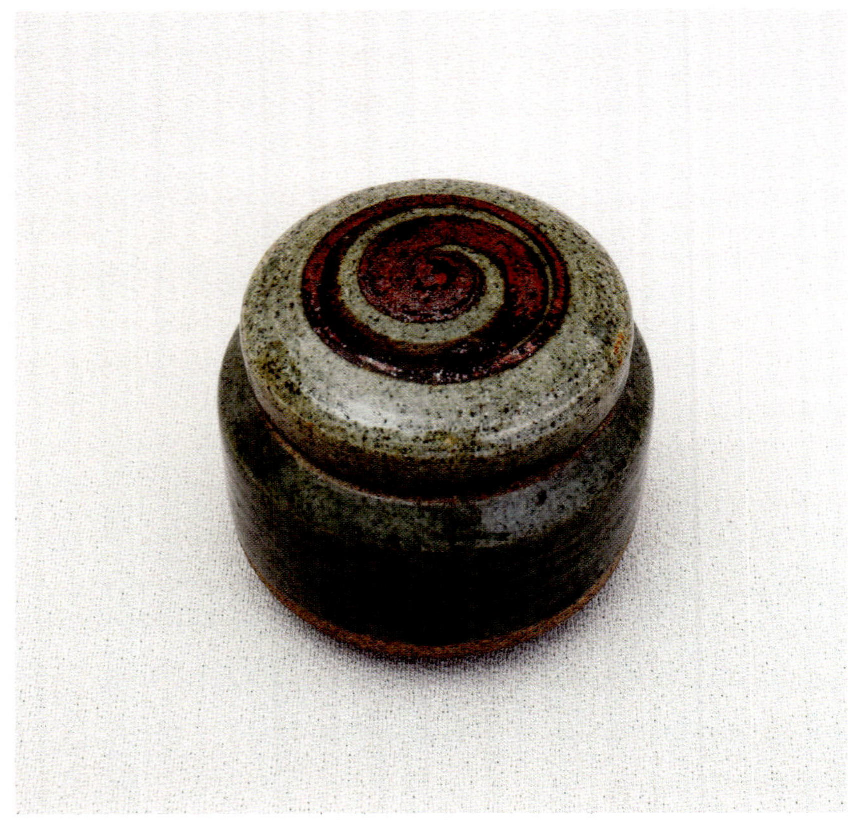

Kolonyama Pottery | Small lidded jar | 74x75x54mm | Provenance: Douglas van der Horst | Marks: impressed 'KP' mark and gold sticker | Photograph by Natalie Field

MOSHOESHOE, Amelia
A long-serving employee, Moshoeshoe was a general glazing assistant and was responsible for the showroom, helping to organise orders. She spoke perfect English and six other languages, and often translated for staff who weren't anglophone. She left to pursue her higher education at Roma University.

MOTANYANE, Lesole
One of the longest-serving employees of Kolonyama, Montanyane was employed as a clay worker under Joe Finch. He lost the end of one of his fingers while working with the filter press. He progressed to kiln-packer and firer. He was Ray Finch's general assistant, and was responsible for general maintenance, setting the kiln and the electricity generator. Under Taylor he became chief kiln-firer in charge of glaze firings.

NENA, Evodia (aka Forty)
Nena was a general glazing assistant.

NTHAKO, Mathabo (b.1954)
Born in Lekokoaneg Ha Kubere, Lesotho, Nthako was a school teacher until 1988. Her interest in pottery began in the 1960s, but it wasn't until 1990

that she began producing enchanting clay figures and animals in clay. With a rudimentary home-built kiln to fire her works based on traditional African firing techniques, Mathabo developed her very personal style of working. Hand-painted with enamels, her figures blend religious, historical and everyday imagery with a delightful understated sense of humour. Between 1990 and 1994 she sold her wares through the Kolonyama shop.

RAMATOLA, Jeanette

Ramatola ran the showroom in the early 1970s. She joined under Milway and worked there until the day it closed, after which she managed the art centre Graham and Lynda Taylor established at Machabeng College in Maseru. She is remembered as a very intelligent and dignified lady, with an excellent command of English.

RORKE, Patrick (b.1953)

Born in Morija, Lesotho, Rorke matriculated in 1971 at the Belgravia Art Centre, East London. From 1980 to 1989 he returned to Lesotho for political reasons, and worked briefly at Kolonyama Pottery. From 1989 to 1994 Rorke taught art and pottery at the Alexandra Art Centre, Johannesburg. He now works as an independent painter and mosaic artist.

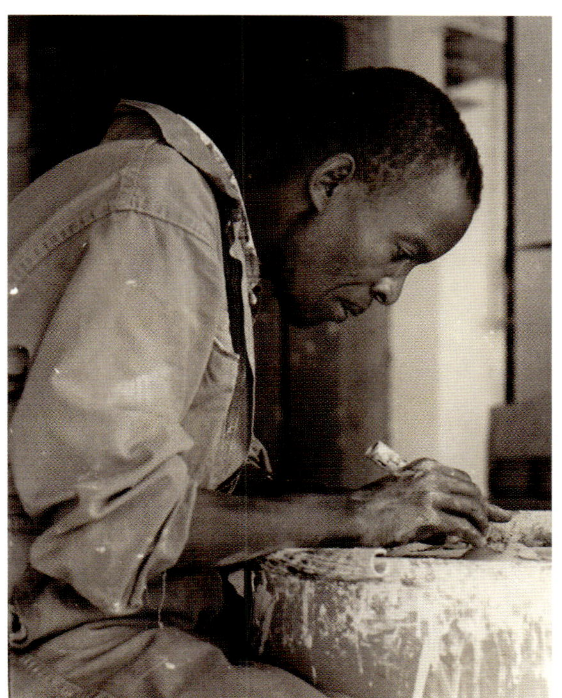

Kolonyama Pottery | Emmanuel Setsabi turning | Provenance: Joe Finch | Photograph by Joe Finch

SETSABI, Emmanuel

Julia Setsabi's husband, Emmanuel, joined as a clay worker and progressed to become a thrower.

SETSABI, Julia

Julia was the first Basotho thrower trained by Joe Finch at Kolonyama. She generally made small items and was an excellent thrower, noted for her consistancy – she could be relied upon to produce long runs of identical pieces. She remained as a thrower until the pottery closed. According to Taylor, she always claimed to speak no English but understood everything that was said to her.

TAYLOR, Graham (b.1954)

Taylor studied at the Newcastle School of Art and Design, and the Manchester Polytechnic from 1974 to 1977, completing a BA Honours degree in ceramics and glass. He subsequently worked as an apprentice to Joe Finch at Appin Pottery (1977–1980). On Finch's recommendation Taylor managed Kolonyama Pottery and Studio from 1980 until 1994. Taylor was responsible for the administration and workshop production. While at Kolonyama he and his wife, Lynda, exhibited and conducted workshops throughout southern Africa.

Upon the closure of Kolonyama, Taylor was employed as the head of creative arts and director of Selibeng Arts & Cultural Centre at Machabeng College, Lesotho, from 1993 to 2000. In 2001 he returned to England, where he established the Crown Studio, from where he and Lynda work and exhibit.

Taylor has participated in numerous exhibitions, including the Hexham Moothall and Gallery (2003), Selibeng Arts & Cultural Centre (1996–1999), Maseru Arts Festival (1994), Grahamstown Festival, South Africa (1988–1991) and The Potters Gallery Johannesburg (1984). He has been awarded numerous commissions including a contemporary vessel for the NNPA Ingram Visitor Centre, a centenary memorial plaque for the Saltwell Masonic Lodge, reproductions of Samian ware and Roman pottery for the Museum of Antiquities, Newcastle upon Tyne.[166] He has works in various private collections including that of the Prince of Wales.

TAYLOR, Lynda

Taylor studied art at the Newcastle School of Art and Manchester Metropolitan University where she specialised in ceramics and jewellery. In 1977 she and her husband Graham went to work with Joe and Trudi Finch at Appin Pottery. Taylor and her husband managed Kolonyama Pottery from 1980 to 1994. At Kolonyama she was the chief decorator and organised the orders.

Lynda briefly taught art and design at Machabeng College, Lesotho. In 1996 one of her paintings was included in the SASOL New Signatures Exhibition in Pretoria. In June 1999 Lynda became the first recipient of the Darracott Prize for the best five annotated essays submitted to the Open College of the Arts. Her work was exhibited at The Bankside Gallery, the gallery of the Royal Watercolour Society in London in 1999.

TLOOME, Theboho Wrenford

Tloome was trained by Philemon Koloko and succeeded Koloke as chief kiln-firer when he left.

VAN GILDER, Bill (b.1951)

See Mantenga Craft Pottery, Swaziland p.247.

WEBSTER, Jim

Formerly from Winchcombe Pottery, Webster also worked at Appin Pottery from 1975 to 1976. Webster managed Kolonyama Pottery from 1977 until early 1980. On his return to England he rejoined Winchcombe Pottery, before immigrating to Australia. Webster is the brother-in-law of Toff Milway.

WEBSTER, Stella (née Geech)

A ceramics graduate from the University of Natal, Pietermaritzburg, Geech assisted Jim Webster at Kolonyama Pottery from 1977 to 1980. Geech and Webster subsequently married and left Kolonyana in early 1980.

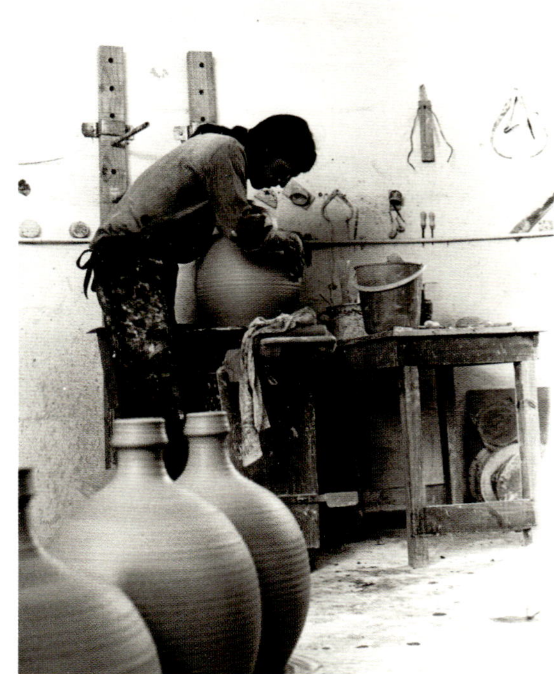

Kolonyama Pottery | Bill van Gilder applying handles, 1976 | Provenance: Toff Milway | Photograph by Toff Milway

Cuisine des familles

La cuisine française

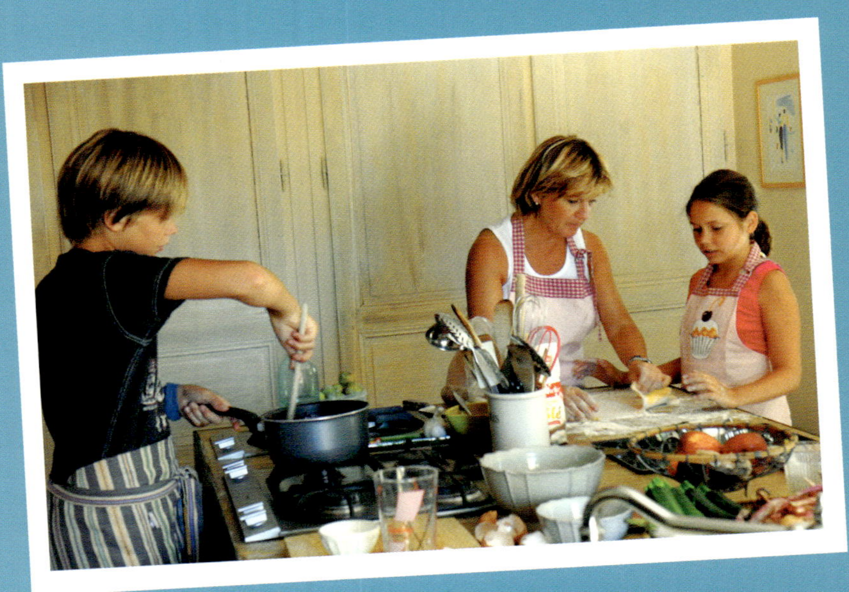

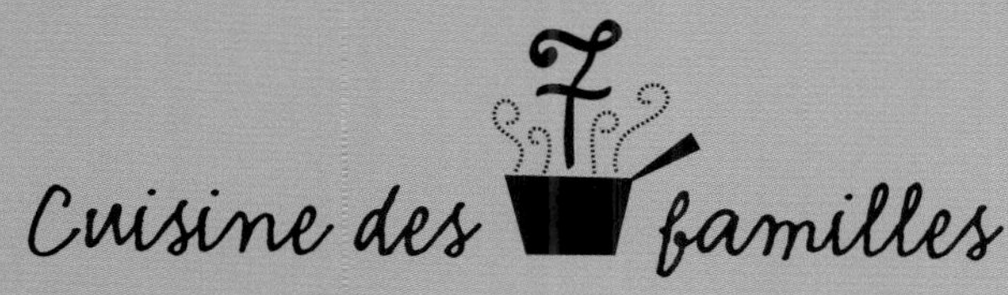

La cuisine française

Véronique Cauvin

Reportage photo

Jean-Marc Wullschleger

Photographies des recettes

Valéry Guedes

Stylisme des recettes

Natacha Arnoult

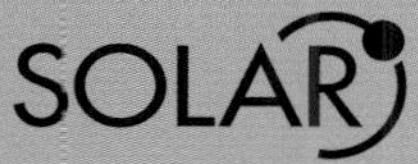

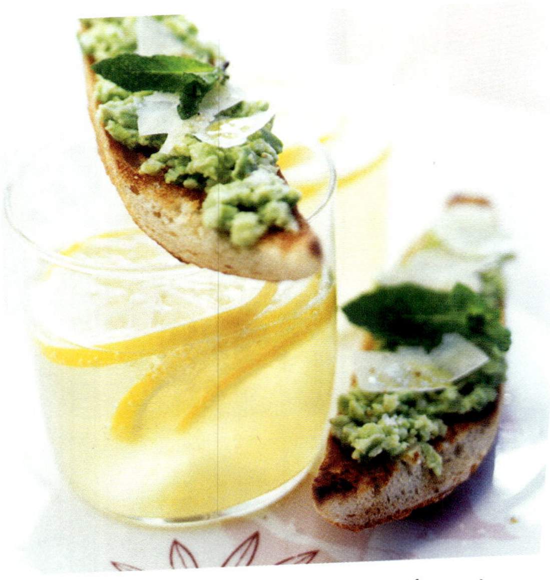

Les petites tartines de Véronique
p. 20

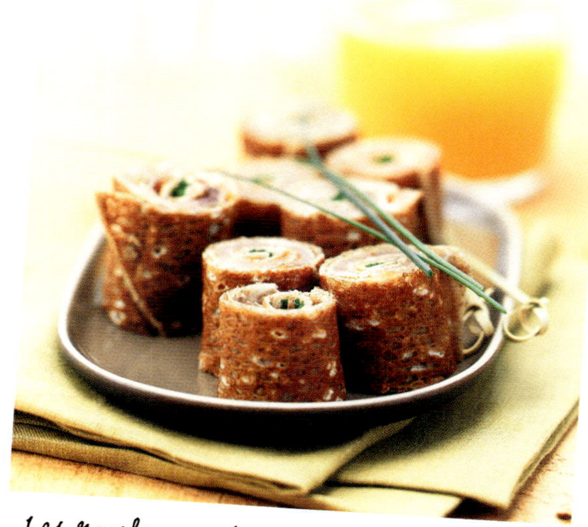

Les rouleaux de saumon de Patrick
p. 46

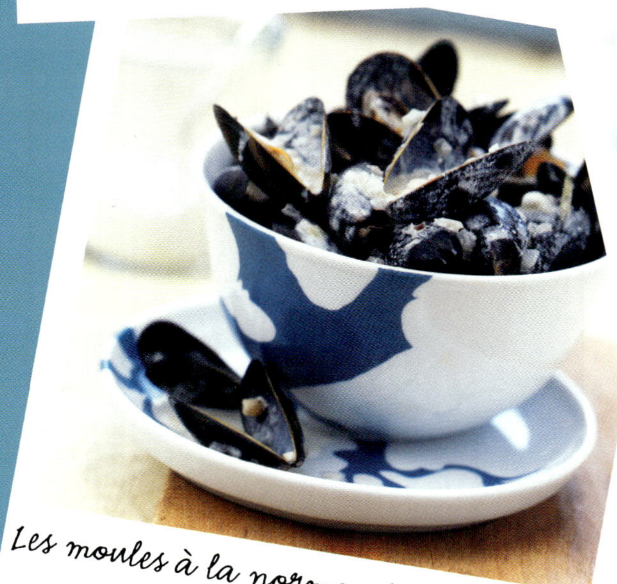

Les moules à la normande de Zoé p. 62

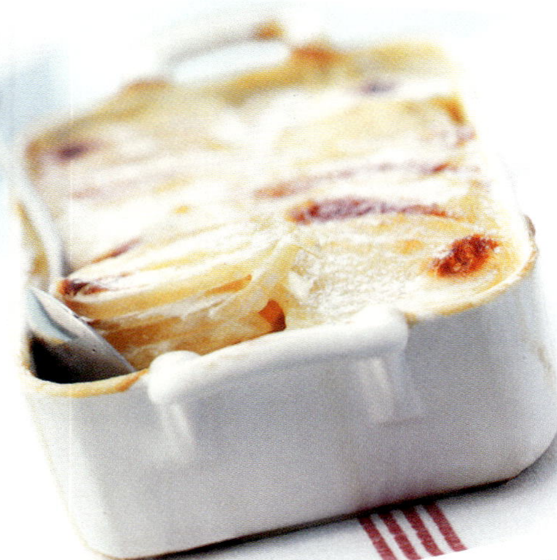

Le gratin dauphinois d'Arthur p. 80

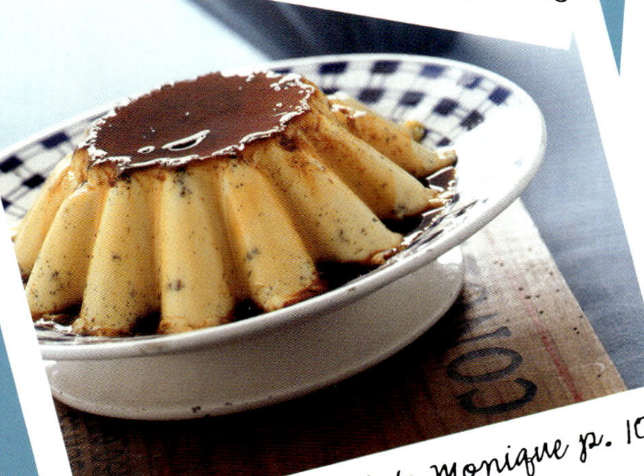

La crème caramel de Monique p. 108

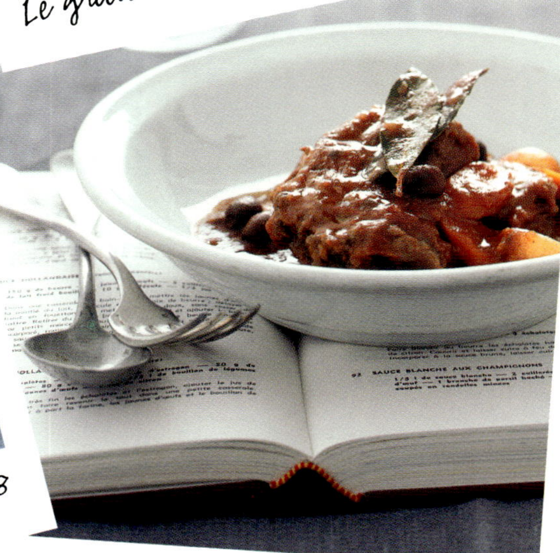

La daube provençale de Jean-Paul
p. 118

Sommaire

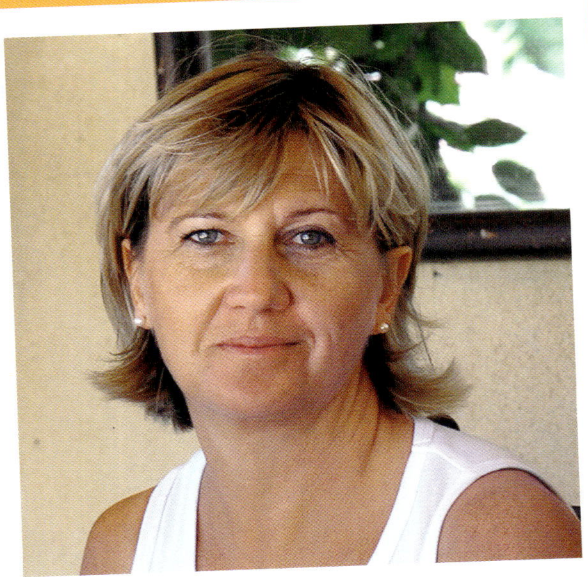

Véronique, la mère

Mon nom est Véronique. Ma passion pour la cuisine date de mes premières expériences de mousse au chocolat, à 7 ans. Adulte, j'ai suivi une carrière dans la vente et le management. Il y a deux ans, j'ai passé mon CAP de cuisinier. J'ai alors organisé des réceptions et tenu un stand de cuisine dans un grand magasin parisien. Aujourd'hui, je donne des cours de cuisine « sur mesure » à mon domicile. Chez nous, à Saint-Germain-en-Laye, à l'ouest de Paris, tout est prétexte à se mettre au fourneau ; la cuisine est notre lieu de vie et d'échanges.

Patrick, mon mari, a son propre répertoire culinaire et ses spécialités. Avec ses airs de chef devant le barbecue ou la plaque de cuisson, il cuisine avec méthode, suivant pas à pas le déroulement des recettes qu'il affectionne, comme sa fameuse fondue savoyarde. Il devient alors le chef d'orchestre, et je deviens petite main pour éplucher l'ail, couper les dés de fromage… Il faut bien l'avouer, le résultat vaut la peine, même si un certain désordre règne après son passage…

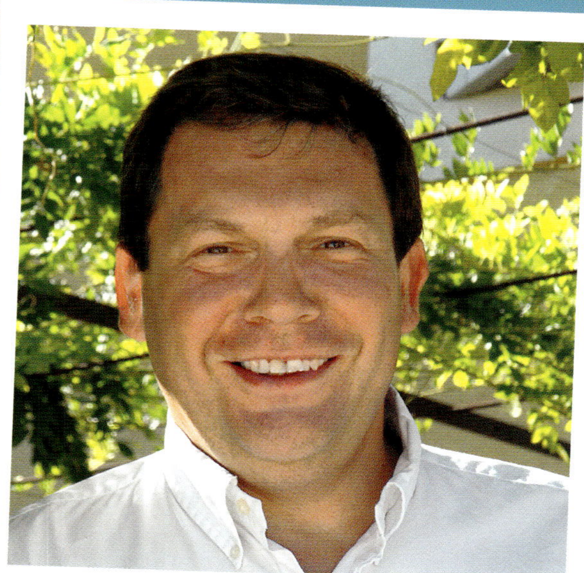

Patrick, le père

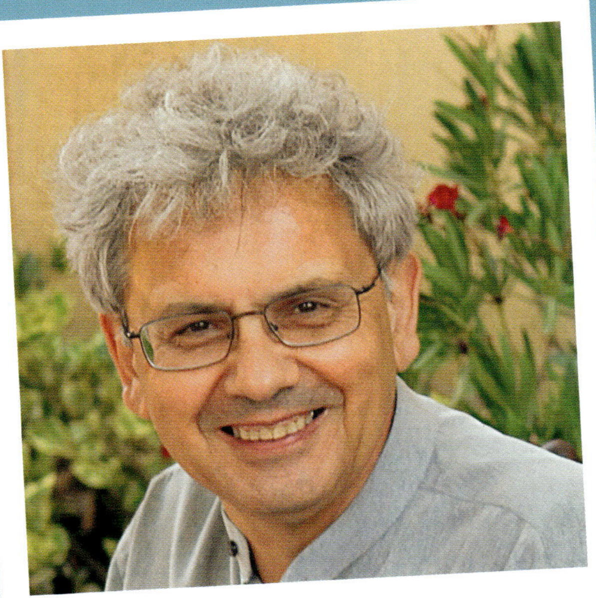

Jean-Paul, le grand-père

Grand'Pa (Jean-Paul) est né en Provence, où il a conservé la maison familiale dans laquelle nous nous rendons l'été. Sa cuisine est parfumée et colorée comme la garrigue. Chaque année, quand la lavande est en fleur, nous passons quelques jours près de lui. Il nous conduit au marché agricole de Velleron et nous présente à ses petits producteurs favoris. En quelques minutes et à un moindre coût, nous remplissons notre panier de magnifiques fruits et légumes.

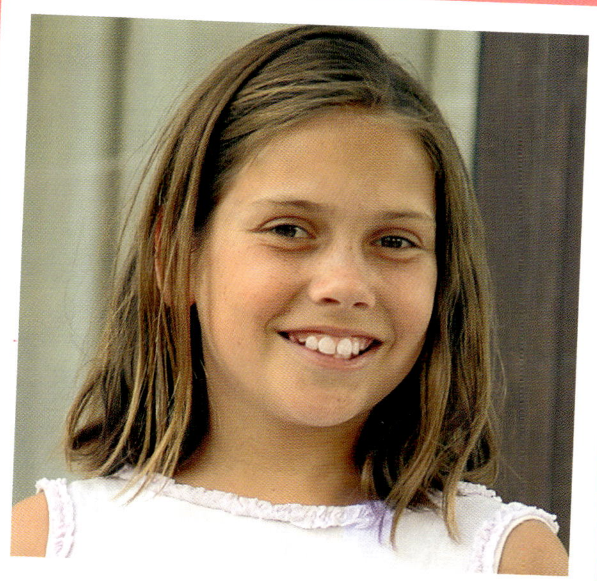
Zoé, la fille

Arthur et Zoé manient la cuillère en bois et le fouet depuis l'âge de 2 ans. Je suis très heureuse de leur avoir donné le goût des bonnes choses et ce plaisir de cuisiner. Ils sont créatifs, curieux et gourmands. Leurs gestes sont précis, et ils sont très organisés. Ils gagnent leur argent de poche en faisant des desserts pour mes copines qui ne savent pas très bien cuisiner. Vous l'aurez compris, ils sont ma fierté, mon bonheur, même si, pendant qu'ils officient, ma cuisine ressemble souvent à un laboratoire expérimental...

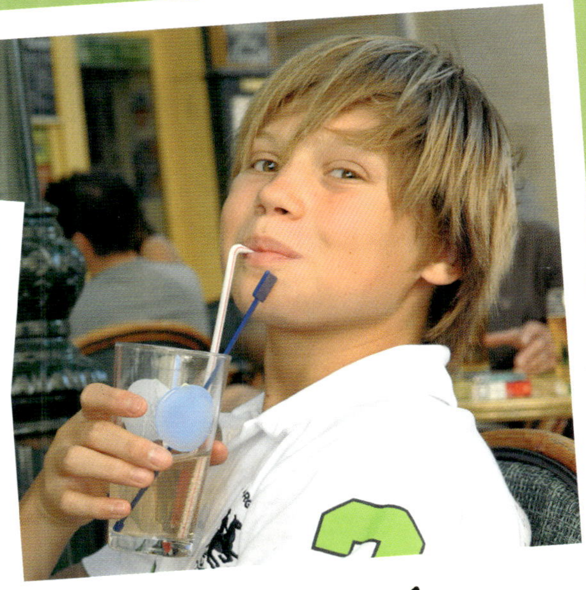
Arthur, le fils

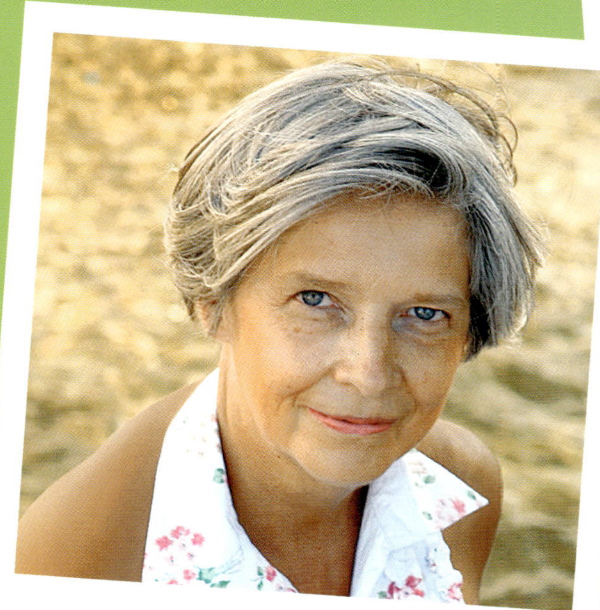
Monique, la grand-mère

Mam (Monique) vit avec Grand'Pa en Basse-Normandie, là où la cuisine s'enrichit souvent de crème fraîche onctueuse et de beurre. C'est dans sa jolie maison familiale à colombages, près d'une petite rivière, que mes parents nous accueillent pour des week-ends 100 % campagne. Le dimanche matin, nous faisons le marché à Honfleur ou à Trouville, où de beaux étals de poissons frais, de crustacés et de coquillages font notre bonheur à tous. Rares sont les repas sans un fromage affiné de la région, accompagné d'un bon cidre brut fermier.

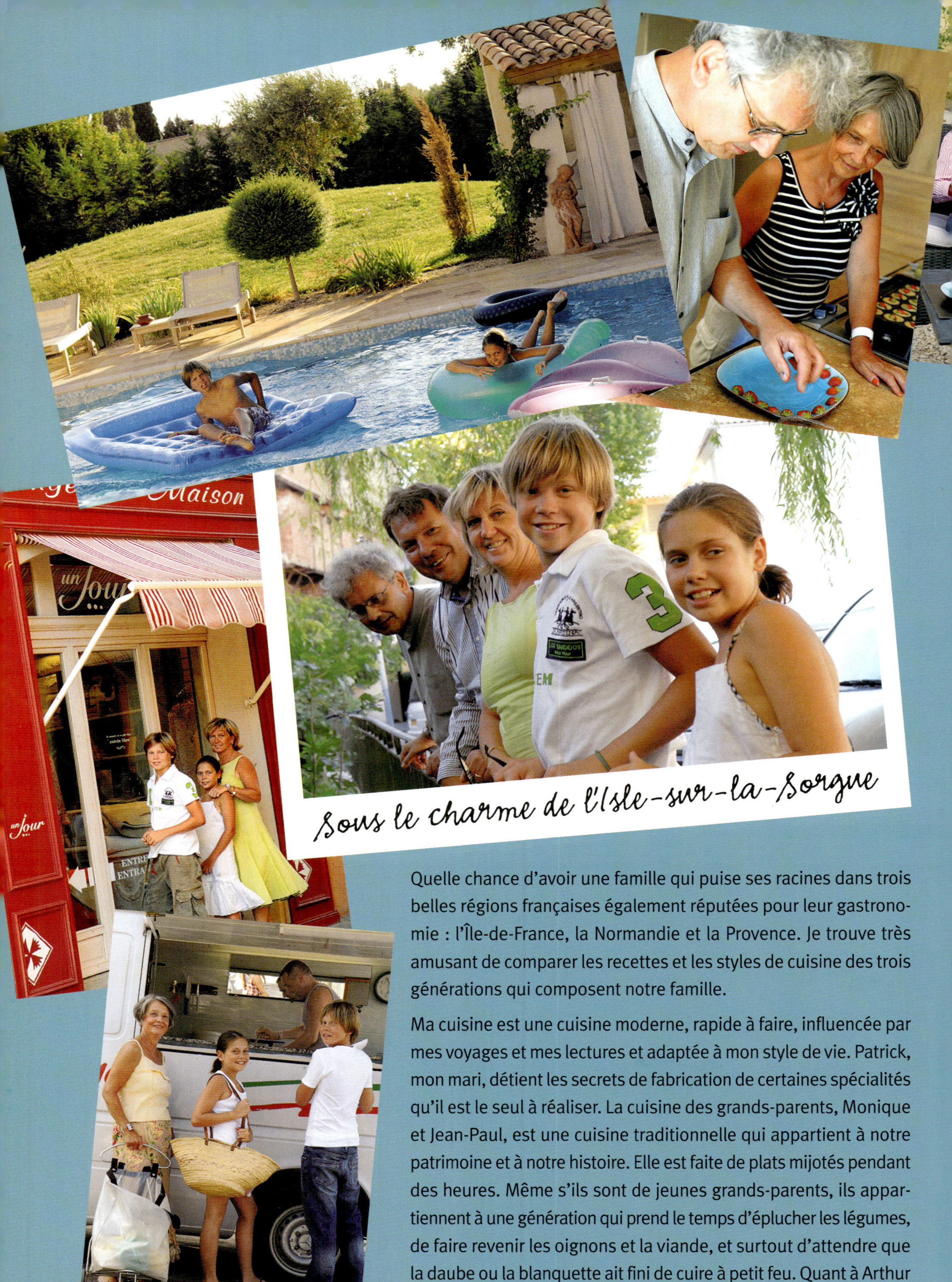

Sous le charme de l'Isle-sur-la-Sorgue

Quelle chance d'avoir une famille qui puise ses racines dans trois belles régions françaises également réputées pour leur gastronomie : l'Île-de-France, la Normandie et la Provence. Je trouve très amusant de comparer les recettes et les styles de cuisine des trois générations qui composent notre famille.

Ma cuisine est une cuisine moderne, rapide à faire, influencée par mes voyages et mes lectures et adaptée à mon style de vie. Patrick, mon mari, détient les secrets de fabrication de certaines spécialités qu'il est le seul à réaliser. La cuisine des grands-parents, Monique et Jean-Paul, est une cuisine traditionnelle qui appartient à notre patrimoine et à notre histoire. Elle est faite de plats mijotés pendant des heures. Même s'ils sont de jeunes grands-parents, ils appartiennent à une génération qui prend le temps d'éplucher les légumes, de faire revenir les oignons et la viande, et surtout d'attendre que la daube ou la blanquette ait fini de cuire à petit feu. Quant à Arthur et Zoé, ils mélangent desserts et bonbons, préfèrent la purée de pomme de terre aux épinards et la viande au poisson.

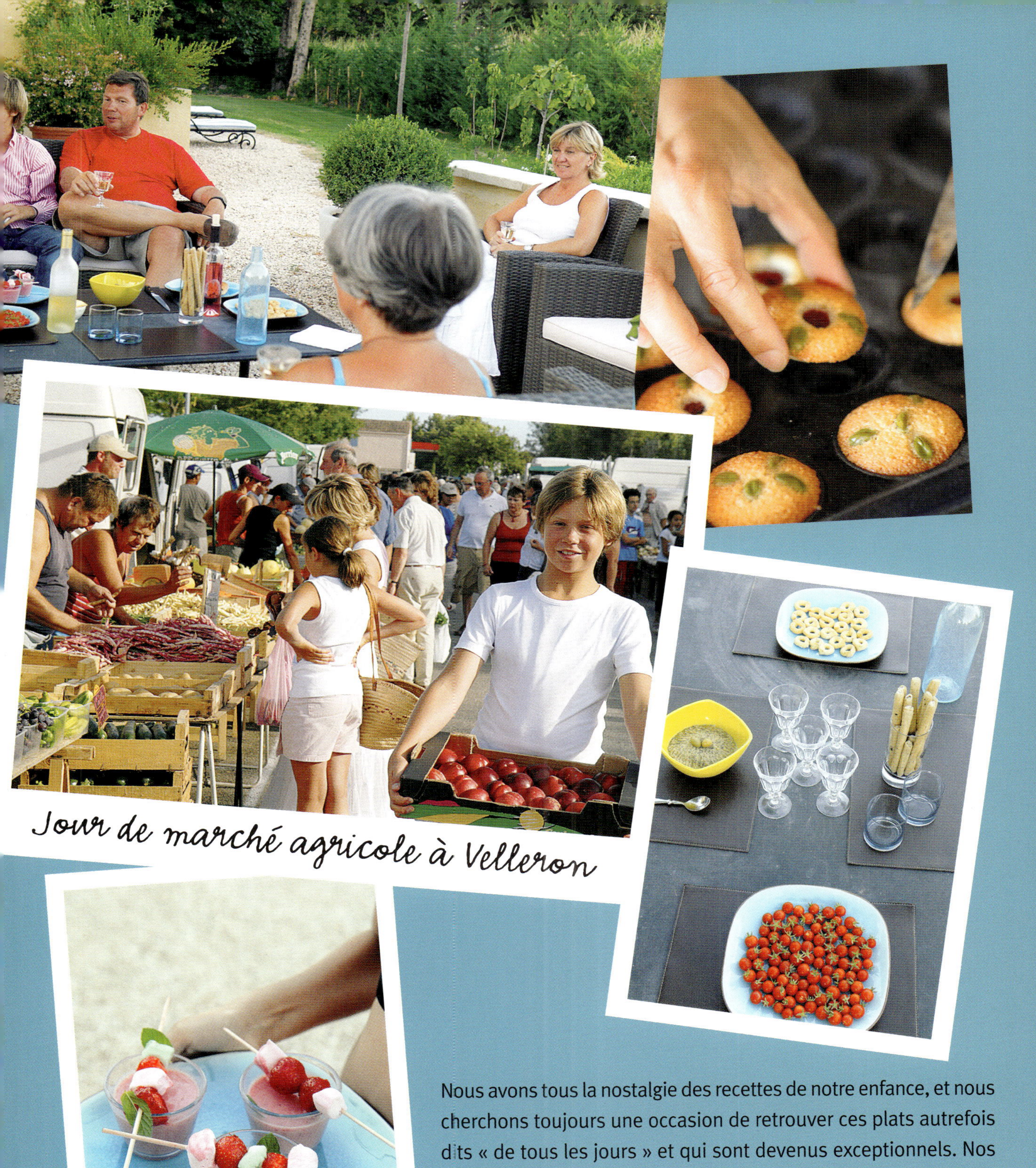

Nous avons tous la nostalgie des recettes de notre enfance, et nous cherchons toujours une occasion de retrouver ces plats autrefois dits « de tous les jours » et qui sont devenus exceptionnels. Nos placards débordent de produits que nous ramenons de vacances. Nous aimons partir à la conquête des marchés de France. Nous parcourons leurs allées, nous nous exclamons devant les nouveaux produits et repartons les sacs pleins à craquer d'innombrables souvenirs gourmands.

Dans notre ville de Saint-Germain-en-Laye, il y a un marché cinq fois par semaine. Nous nous y rendons tous les quatre le dimanche. Nous garnissons notre panier de produits qui varient selon les saisons et nos envies. Les commerçants connaissent nos exigences et nous conseillent sur nos achats.

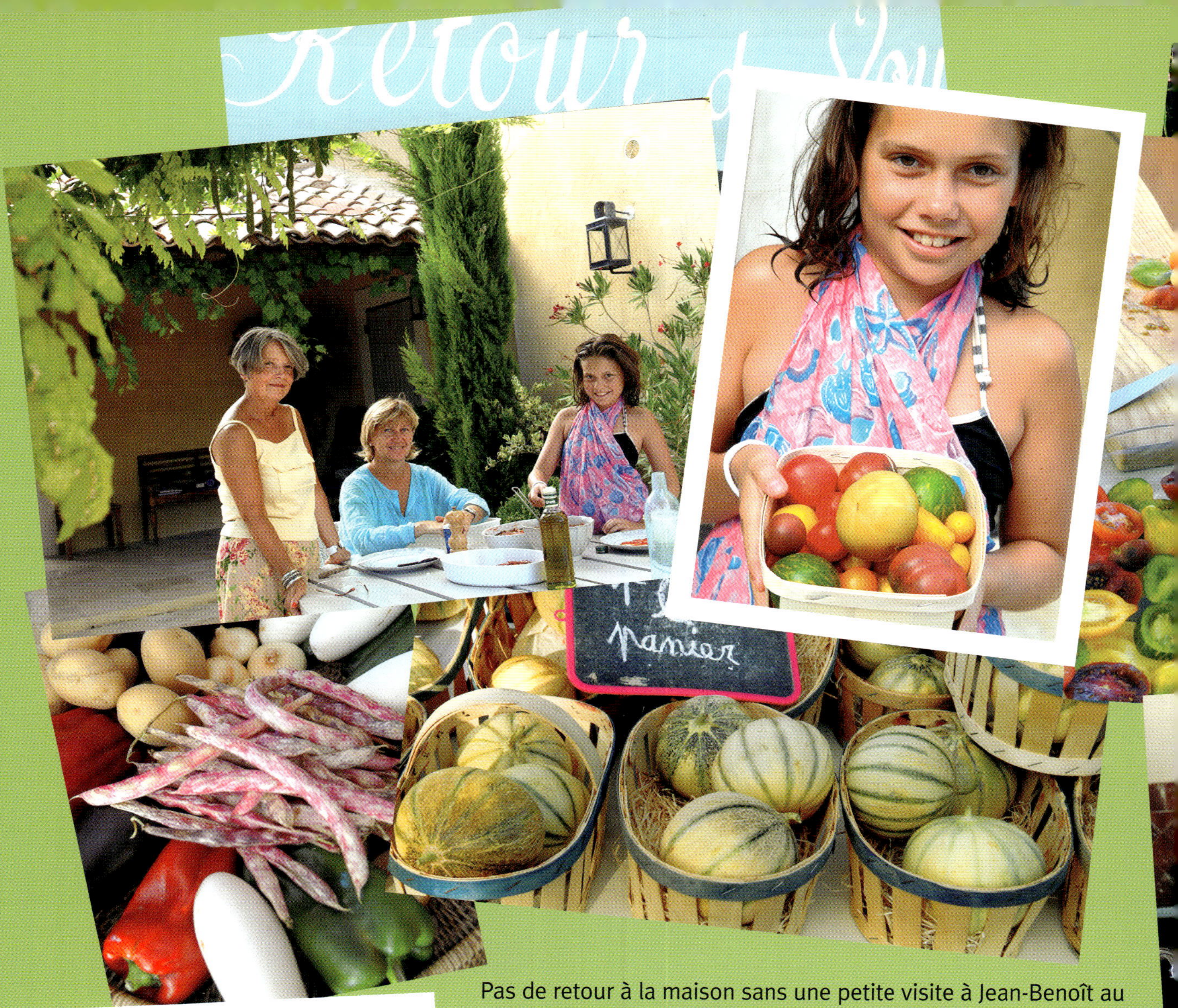

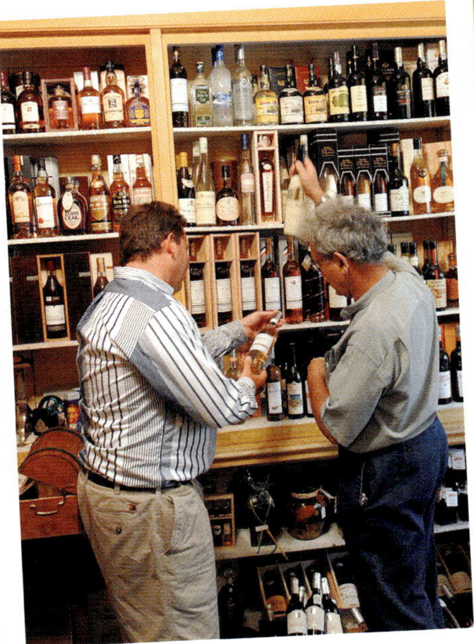

Pas de retour à la maison sans une petite visite à Jean-Benoît au Repaire de Bacchus. Chaque dimanche, il propose aux membres du Club des dégustations de vin (à consommer avec modération). Sa bonne humeur et son rire sont légendaires. Homme avisé et connaisseur, il appartient à ce genre d'épicurien intarissable sur la bonne chère et le vin. Si un jour vous passez par là, vous nous trouverez au fond de sa boutique en train de profiter de l'un de ces moments si conviviaux.

Quand nous sommes en week-end en Normandie chez les grands-parents, la journée commence par un petit déjeuner composé de croissants tièdes et de pain frais croustillant. Dans un grand bol de chocolat chaud, onctueux et épais, les enfants trempent leur tartine beurrée couverte de confiture « maison » à la framboise. Après cela, direction le marché local ! La liste de courses est prête, le menu établi… mais comment ne pas changer d'avis face à une montagne de coquilles Saint-Jacques ! Nous repartons avec nos 10 kilos de coquillages. La saison est courte, le prix attractif, et l'envie plus forte que la raison. Certes, nous passerons un peu de temps à les préparer en vue de les congeler, mais quand la saison sera terminée, nous continuerons de les déguster avec plaisir. Nous en profitons pour faire le plein de crème fraîche fermière, de

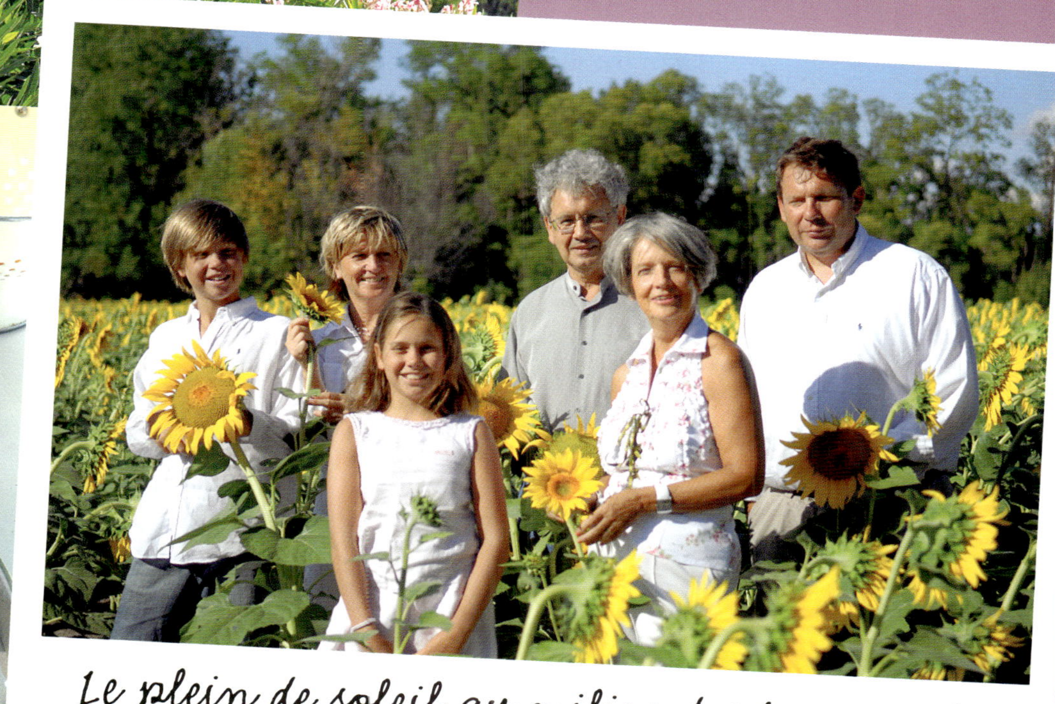

Le plein de soleil au milieu des tournesols

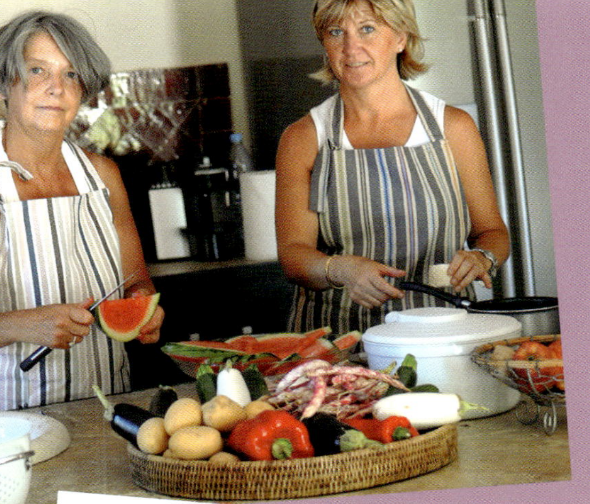

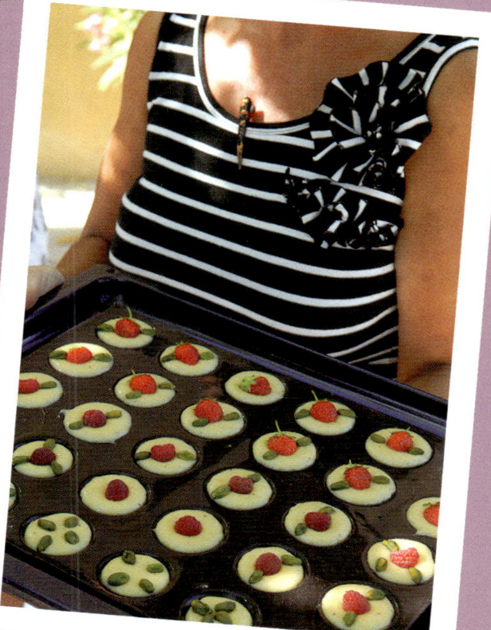

beurre, d'œufs et de fromages régionaux dont Arthur raffole. Un camembert et un pont-l'évêque « à point » font toujours l'unanimité. Une bouteille de cidre brut termine généralement la liste des achats pour le repas dominical.

En revanche, dans la maison familiale de Grand'Pa en Provence, les fruits et les légumes constituent la base de notre alimentation. Le marché agricole situé à quelques kilomètres est notre source d'approvisionnement. Il faut dire que les prix pratiqués sont les meilleurs de la région, et les petits producteurs fournissent des produits de qualité gorgés de soleil. Au menu : fougasse aux olives ou aux lardons et tapenade à l'apéritif, salades mélangées selon l'inspiration du jour au déjeuner, viandes ou poissons grillés à la plancha par Patrick ou Jean-Paul. En dessert, au dîner, nous optons souvent pour une tarte aux nectarines ou une simple salade de fruits. Curieuse de nature, je suis toujours en quête de produits méconnus ou insolites qui apportent une saveur originale. Ainsi, j'aime égayer et enrichir les plats avec de l'huile d'olive à la mandarine ou à la menthe, aux noix ou au basilic.

Passage obligatoire pour Arthur et Zoé : le marchand de bonbons, pendant que je patiente dans la file d'attente du fleuriste et que Patrick achète le journal. Qui fera la queue à la boulangerie ? Zoé se dévoue. À peine sortie de la boutique, elle attaque allègrement le croûton de l'une des baguettes toutes chaudes. Cela valait la peine d'attendre. L'odeur du pain attise notre appétit et, à ce rythme-là, il n'y en aura bientôt plus pour le déjeuner... Allez, il est temps de rentrer à la maison, nous sommes tous affamés !

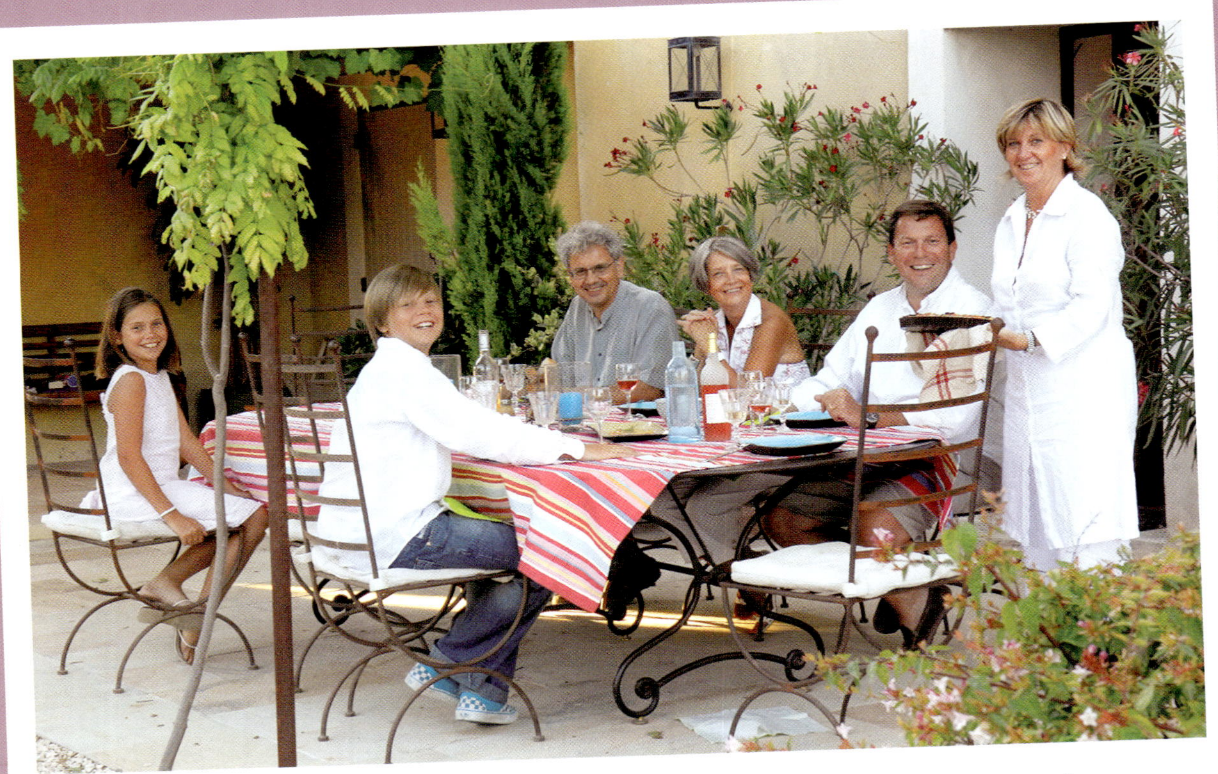

La famille au complet pour un repas de fête

Pendant que nous rangeons les courses et préparons le repas, les enfants mettent la table sur la terrasse et proposent, pour patienter, une boisson accompagnée de petites gourmandises. Ils disposent avec goût les verres et les assiettes, et ajoutent une touche décorative personnelle : une feuille de lierre sur laquelle ils écrivent nos noms, de jolies serviettes de couleur, des fleurs... tout concourt à donner à notre déjeuner un air de fête, une jolie table étant propice à un bon repas. De bonnes odeurs parviennent de la cuisine et nous chatouillent les narines, le déjeuner est enfin prêt, à table, il est 14 heures...

C'est dimanche,
nous avons tout notre temps...

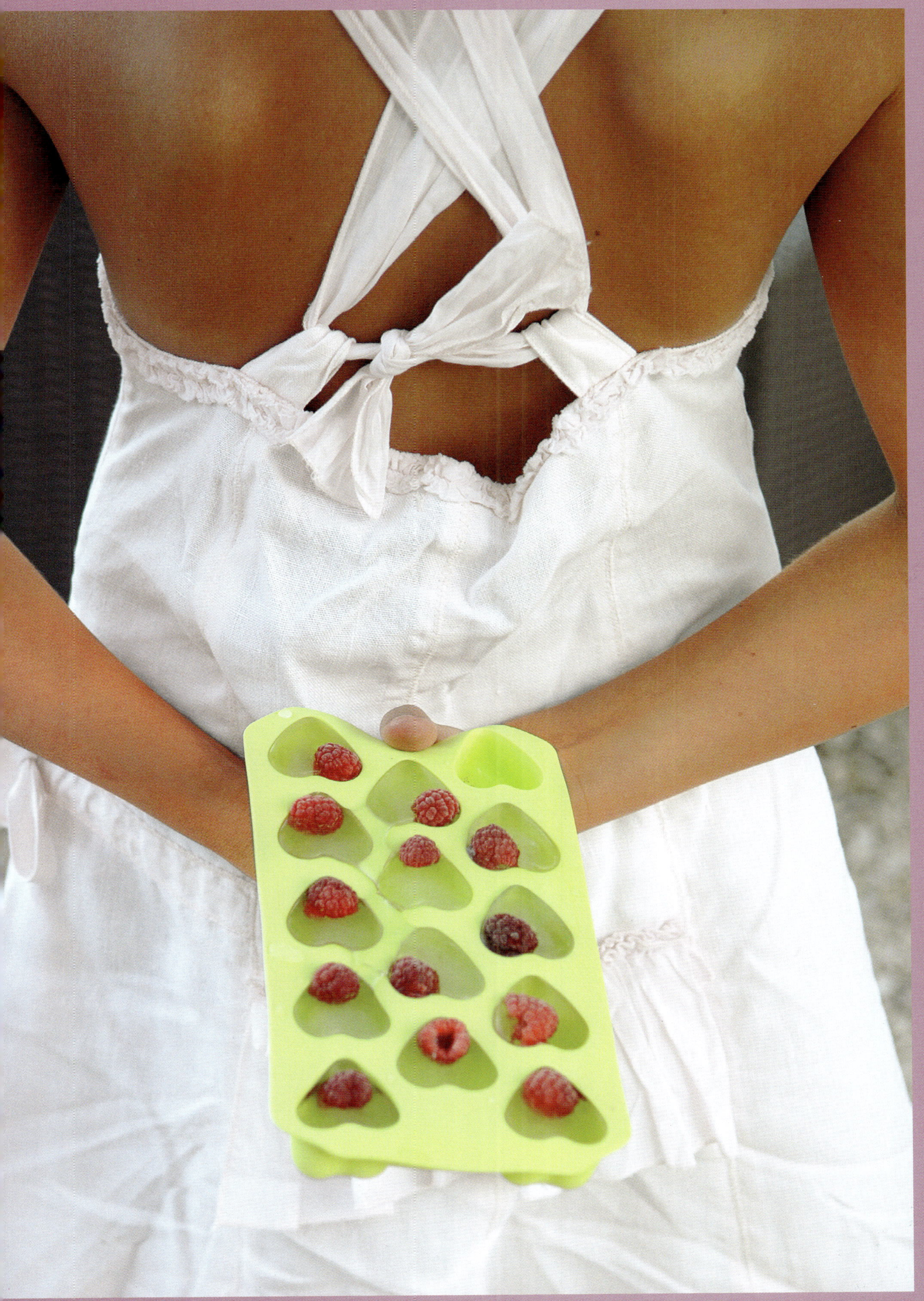

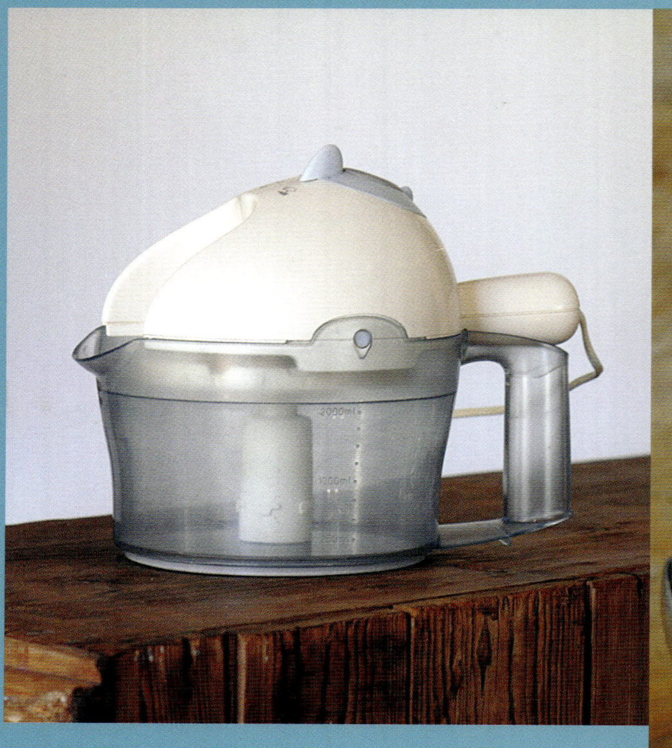

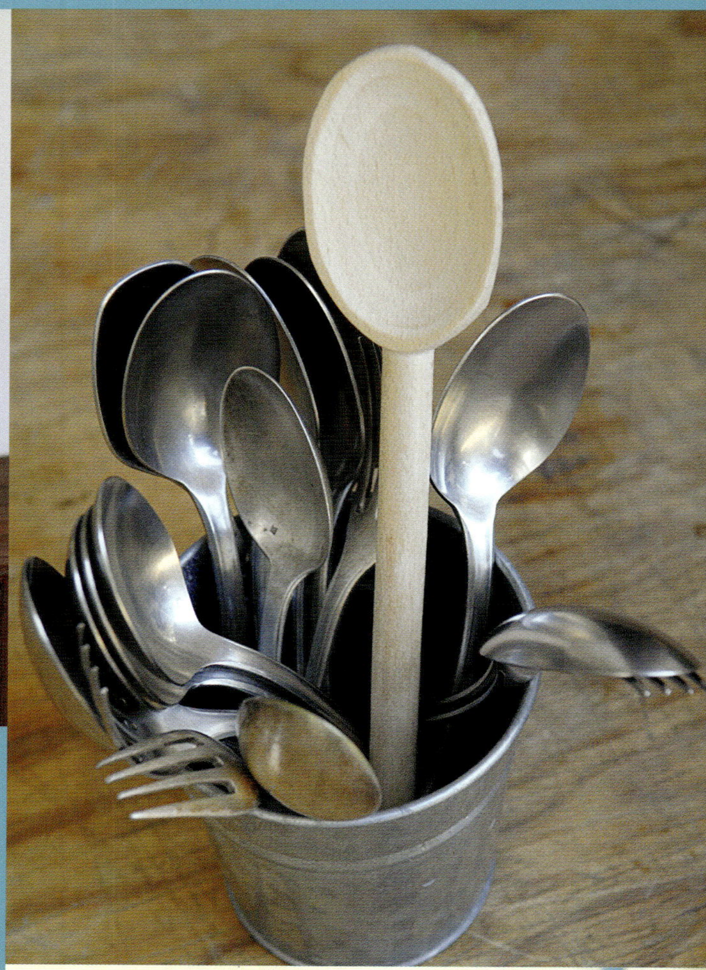

Les 6 ustensiles de la cuisine française

Le robot et le hachoir

Deux accessoires dont on ne peut se passer ! Le robot coupe, réduit en miettes, écrase, mixe, mélange. Petit ou grand, il occupe une place de choix dans la cuisine, au même titre que son petit frère le hachoir, qui s'occupe du persil et des oignons.

La cuillère en bois

Inusable et incassable, la cuillère en bois est notre meilleure alliée pour tourner la crème anglaise ou mélanger la pâte à choux. Elle ne donne pas de goût aux aliments, traverse la mode et le temps ! C'est un ustensile simple et indispensable.

La cocotte de grand-mère

Ronde ou ovale, elle est incontournable et indispensable pour la réalisation des plats mijotés. En général en fonte, elle est munie d'un couvercle que l'on soulève avec délicatesse et gourmandise, afin de humer tous les parfums qu'elle conserve jalousement.

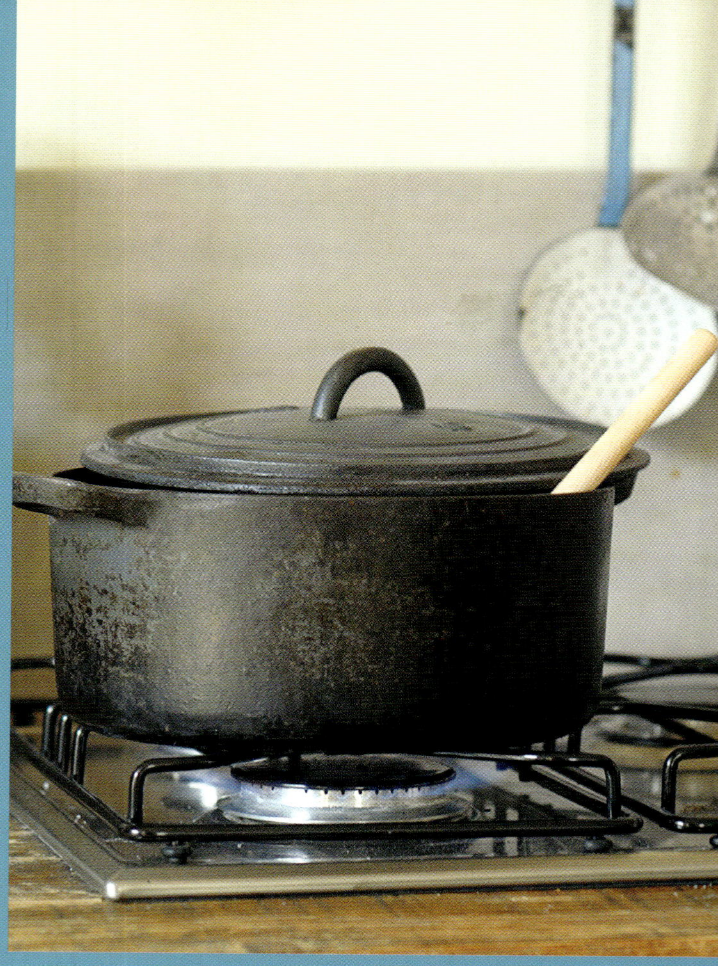

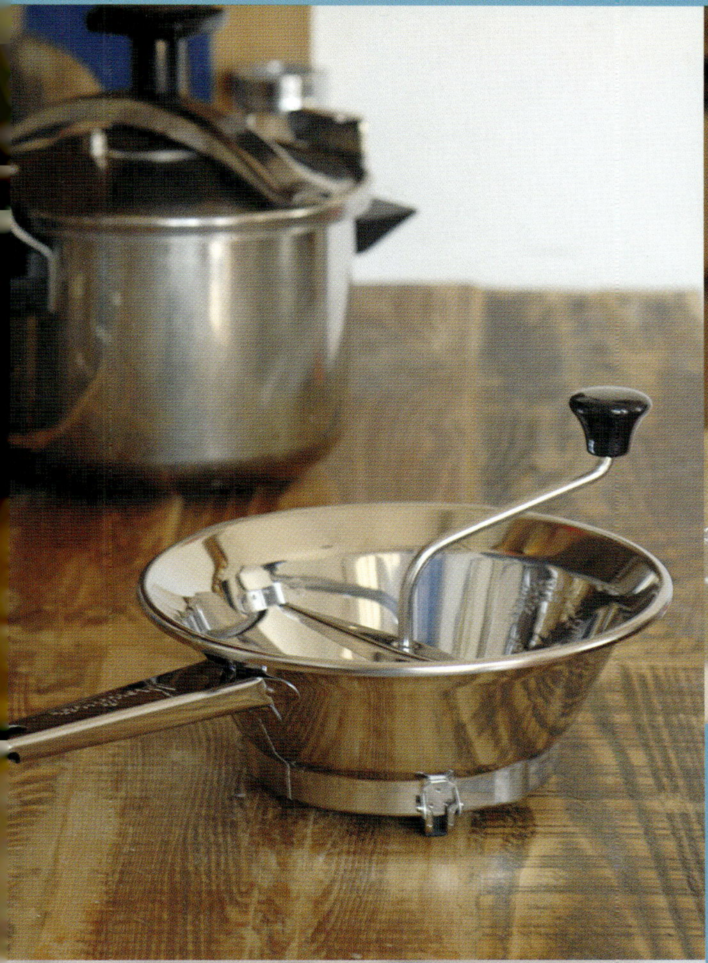

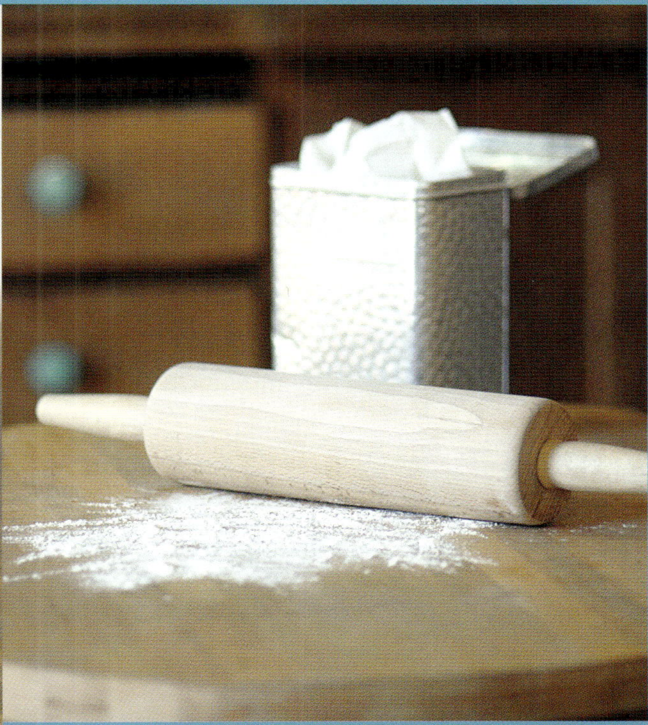

Le presse-purée ou moulin à légumes

Il était en voie de disparition, mais le presse-purée revient en force pour préparer les délicieuses purées de pommes de terre maison. Relooké par des créateurs, il est devenu très « design ». Les enfants adorent tourner le moulin, tandis que les adultes retrouvent leurs souvenirs d'enfance grâce à cet ustensile.

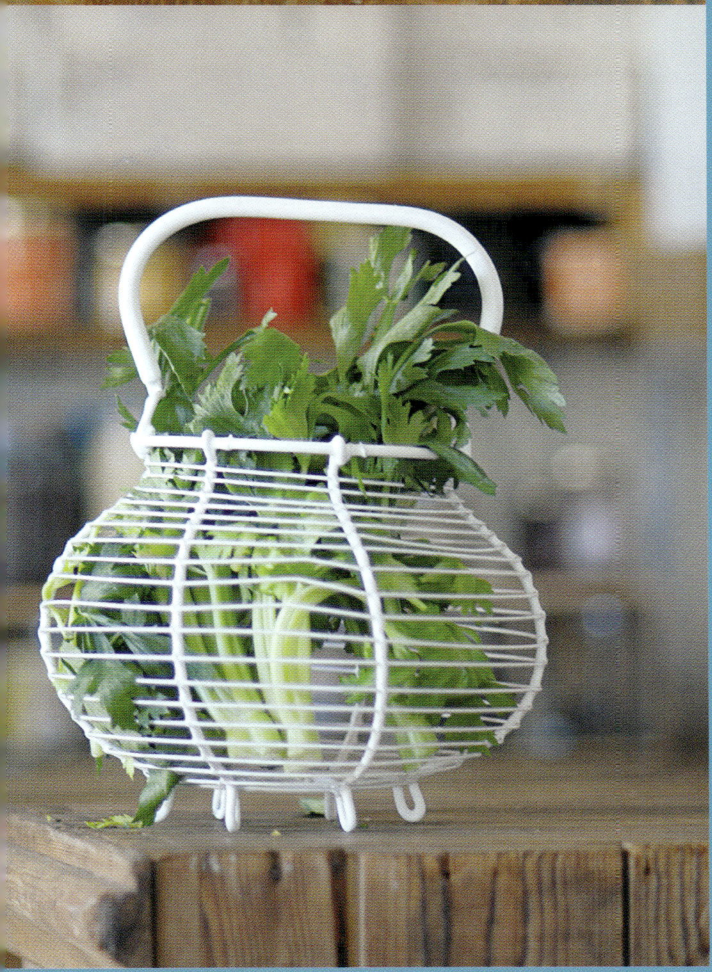

Le panier à salade et l'essoreuse

Le panier à salade ne se trouvera bientôt plus que dans les brocantes, remplacé dans nos cuisines par l'essoreuse à salade, mieux adaptée à la vie moderne. Mais certains gardent un souvenir nostalgique du temps où leur grand-mère ou leur mère tenait le panier à salade à bout de bras et le secouait sur l'herbe du jardin.

Le rouleau à pâtisserie

Symbole éculé de la ménagère qui attend le retour de son mari en retard, le rouleau à pâtisserie est un ustensile de base de la pâtisserie. Il est généralement en bois et comporte deux poignées plus effilées. On trouve maintenant des rouleaux en matière antiadhésive.

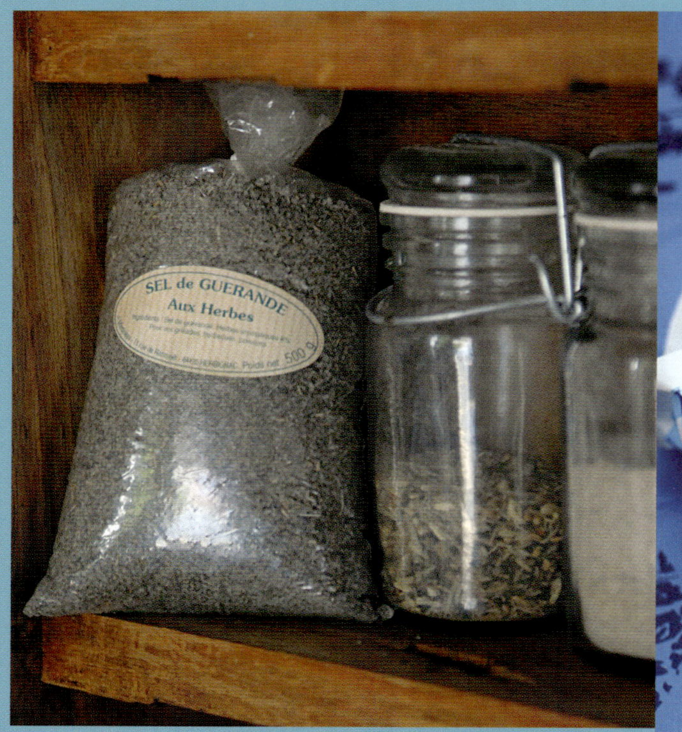

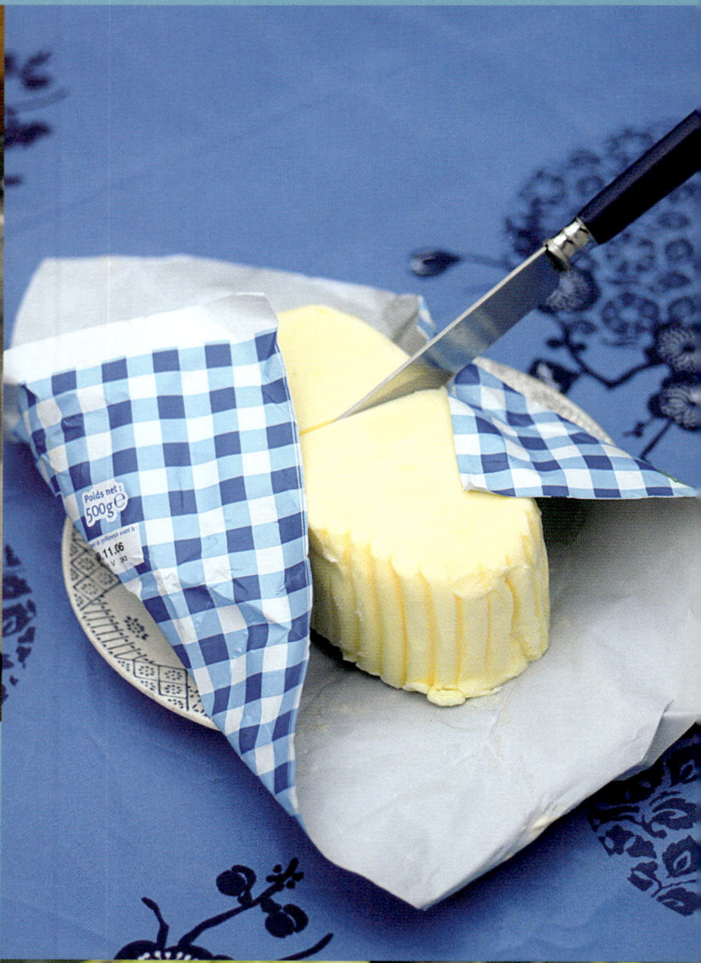

Les 6 ingrédients de la cuisine française

Le sel de Guérande

Il est tendre et savoureux, avec un parfum de violette. Sans amertume, il sublime la saveur originelle des aliments. Il faut le saupoudrer du bout des doigts et le conserver au sec dans une petite boîte.

La crème et le beurre de Normandie

Indissociables, puisque le beurre est fabriqué à partir de la crème, qui elle-même provient du lait... Un très grand merci à toutes ces belles vaches normandes qui broutent consciencieusement et paisiblement une herbe verte et grasse et qui contribuent à la réussite de nos recettes. Ces produits se conservent au réfrigérateur, à une température de 5 à 6 °C.

L'huile d'olive de Provence

Il existe une grande variété d'huiles d'olive. Demandez à les goûter pour apprécier leur qualité et apprenez à les utiliser selon vos recettes. Nature ou aromatisées, pour les salades ou pour la cuisson, avec des fruits ou des légumes, des viandes ou des poissons, découvrez-les comme on goûte un vin.

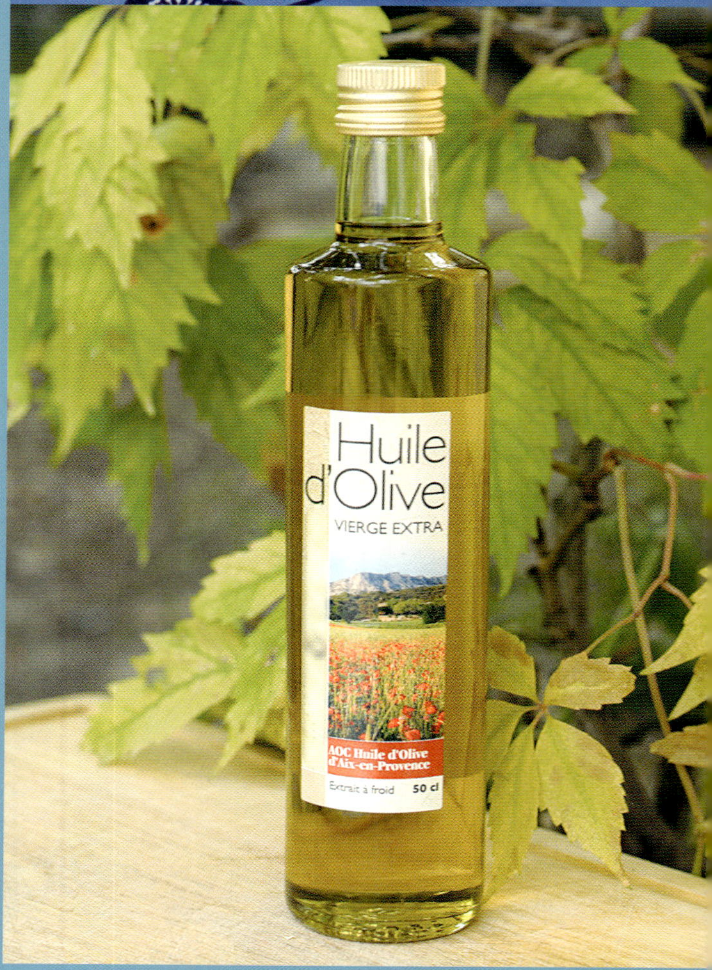

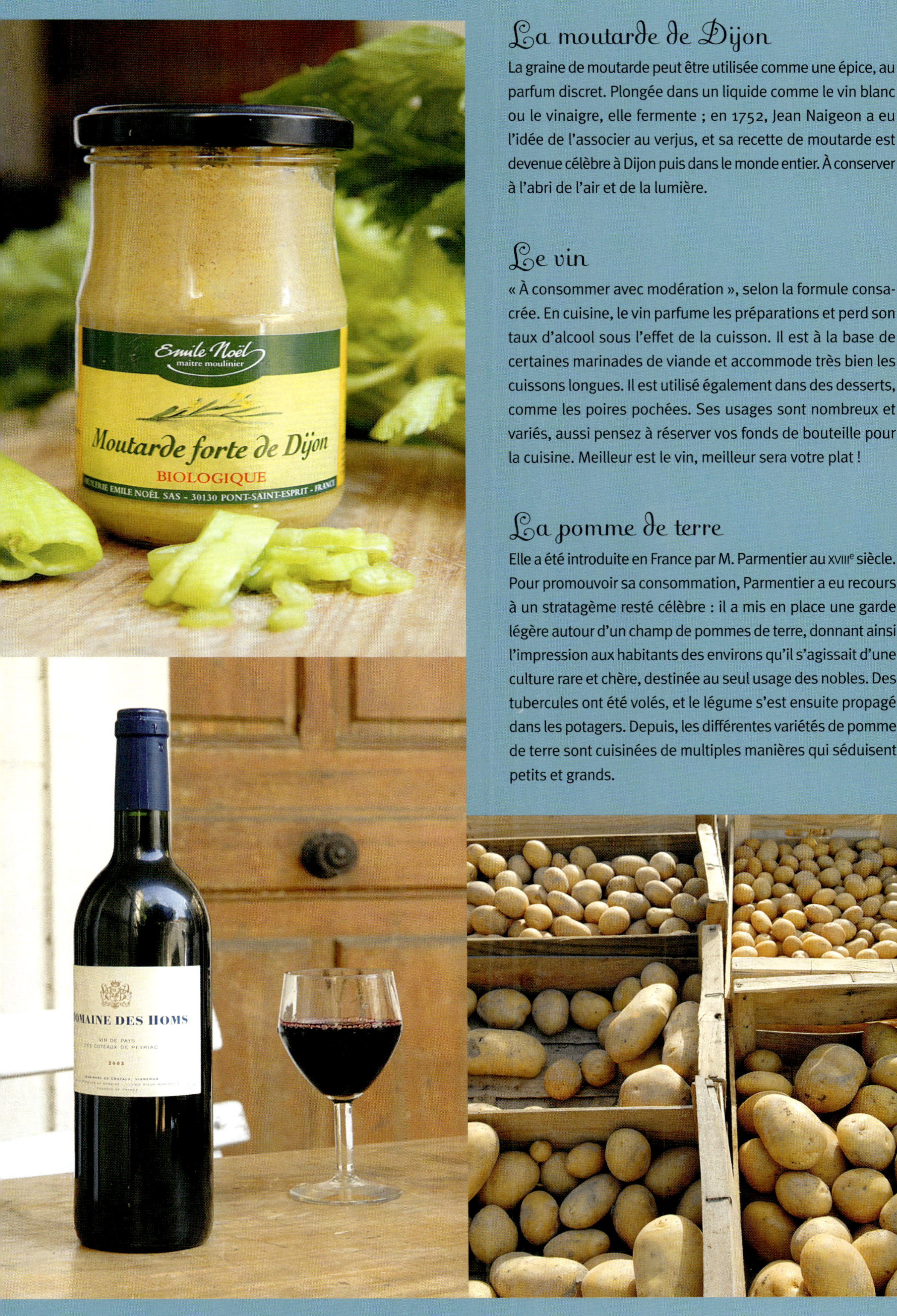

La moutarde de Dijon

La graine de moutarde peut être utilisée comme une épice, au parfum discret. Plongée dans un liquide comme le vin blanc ou le vinaigre, elle fermente ; en 1752, Jean Naigeon a eu l'idée de l'associer au verjus, et sa recette de moutarde est devenue célèbre à Dijon puis dans le monde entier. À conserver à l'abri de l'air et de la lumière.

Le vin

« À consommer avec modération », selon la formule consacrée. En cuisine, le vin parfume les préparations et perd son taux d'alcool sous l'effet de la cuisson. Il est à la base de certaines marinades de viande et accommode très bien les cuissons longues. Il est utilisé également dans des desserts, comme les poires pochées. Ses usages sont nombreux et variés, aussi pensez à réserver vos fonds de bouteille pour la cuisine. Meilleur est le vin, meilleur sera votre plat !

La pomme de terre

Elle a été introduite en France par M. Parmentier au XVIIIe siècle. Pour promouvoir sa consommation, Parmentier a eu recours à un stratagème resté célèbre : il a mis en place une garde légère autour d'un champ de pommes de terre, donnant ainsi l'impression aux habitants des environs qu'il s'agissait d'une culture rare et chère, destinée au seul usage des nobles. Des tubercules ont été volés, et le légume s'est ensuite propagé dans les potagers. Depuis, les différentes variétés de pomme de terre sont cuisinées de multiples manières qui séduisent petits et grands.

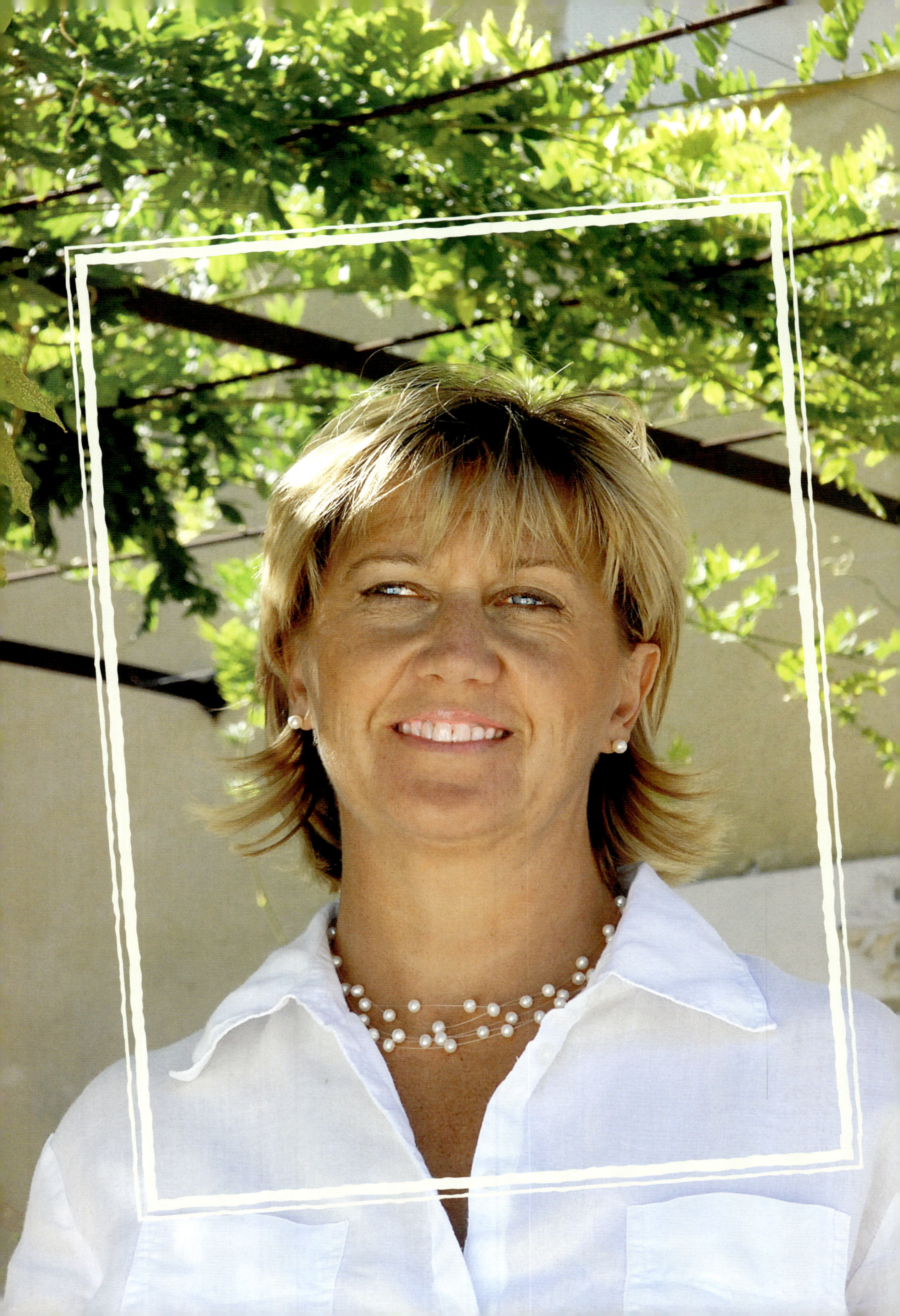

Véronique
La mère

Si j'étais… une couleur,

je serais celle du caramel pour sa teinte ambrée, dorée,
comme ces roudoudous que je « léchais » pendant des heures à la sortie de l'école.

Si j'étais… une odeur,

je serais celle que répand le café le matin et qui me réveille doucement.

Si j'étais… une saveur,

je serais celle de la confiture de fraises, en souvenir des grosses tartines de pain de campagne
de mon enfance, recouvertes de fruits rouges gorgés de sucre et de soleil.

Si j'étais… un ustensile,

je serais un robot multi-fonctions bien utile à une maman multi-tâches…
qui ne doit jamais tomber en panne !

Si j'étais… un souvenir gourmand,

je serais une brioche à la crème de lait
que mon arrière-grand-mère fabriquait dans sa cuisine le dimanche matin.

Si j'étais… un péché mignon,

je serais une tablette de chocolat au lait, car depuis plus de 40 ans,
je reste fidèle à la petite vache violette à laquelle je n'ai jamais su résister.

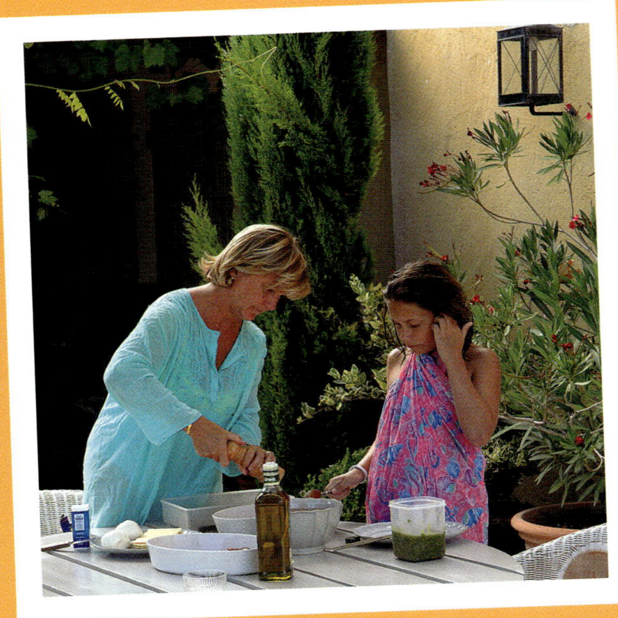

J'aime cuisiner les fèves fraîches, car elles me font penser au célèbre conte « Jacques et le haricot magique ». La saison des fèves fraîches étant courte (d'avril à début juin), on peut utiliser des fèves surgelées pour préparer cette recette.

Petites tartines aux haricots magiques

Préparation : 30 minutes Cuisson : 5 minutes Pour 8 personnes

300 g de fèves fraîches écossées (environ 1 kg avec les cosses) ou surgelées
100 g de parmesan râpé
3 cuillerées à soupe de crème fraîche
le jus de 1/2 citron
1 gousse d'ail épluchée et hachée
2 grandes cuillerées à soupe d'huile d'olive
5 feuilles de menthe ou de basilic hachées, plus quelques feuilles entières pour la décoration
6 tranches de pain de campagne ou 1 baguette
sel, poivre du moulin, gros sel

- Amenez une casserole d'eau salée à ébullition, versez les fèves et laissez-les cuire 5 minutes : elles doivent rester croquantes. Égouttez-les, laissez-les refroidir, puis ôtez la grosse peau qui les entoure.
- Écrasez grossièrement les fèves à la fourchette ou à l'aide d'un mixeur. Ajoutez le parmesan râpé, la crème fraîche, le jus de citron, l'ail, l'huile d'olive et les feuilles de basilic ou de menthe hachées ; mélangez l'ensemble tout en conservant une texture granuleuse contenant des morceaux de fèves. Salez et poivrez. Conservez au frais.
- Tartinez sur du pain grillé et décorez de feuilles de basilic ou de menthe.

Vous pouvez remplacer les fèves par des petits pois frais ou surgelés, et la crème fraîche par du chèvre frais ou du fromage à tartiner.

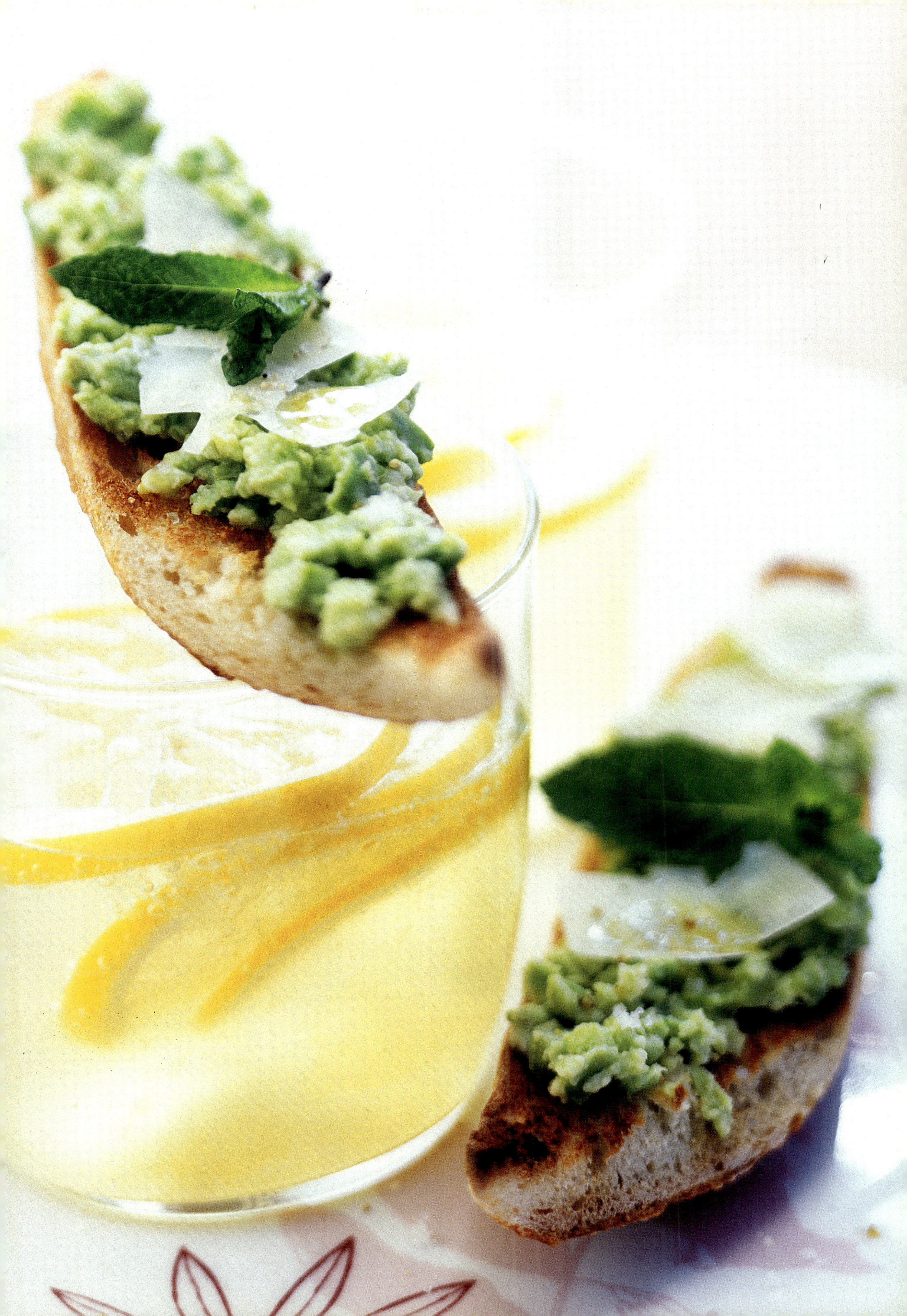

Symbole de fête et de luxe, produit authentique de notre terroir, le foie gras est une matière beaucoup plus facile à cuisiner qu'on ne le croit. Et puisque le foie gras frais est bien plus abordable que le foie gras mi-cuit ou en conserve, cela permet d'en manger plus souvent.

Foie gras poêlé à la mangue

Préparation : 30 minutes Cuisson : 2 minutes Pour 4 personnes

1 foie gras de canard cru entier prêt à l'usage (de 800 g à 1 kg)
1 grosse mangue fraîche, bien mûre
sel de Guérande, poivre

- Épluchez la mangue et coupez de belles tranches. Mettez au frais.
- Préparez le foie gras : séparez les deux lobes à la main, dégagez le nerf principal et tirez-le : il entraînera les autres nerfs. Éliminez en grattant avec la pointe d'un couteau les petites pointes de sang. Coupez des tranches d'environ 1,5 cm d'épaisseur. Poivrez et salez sur toutes les faces. Cette préparation peut être réalisée à l'avance, à condition de bien protéger le foie gras dans un film alimentaire et de le conserver au frais, afin qu'il ne sèche pas.
- Répartissez les tranches de mangue sur les assiettes.
- Faites chauffer une poêle antiadhésive ; quand elle est bien chaude, posez-y les tranches de foie gras les unes à côté des autres, laissez-les se colorer pendant 1 minute, retournez-les, faites-les dorer 1 minute sur l'autre face. Posez les tranches de foie gras sur les tranches de mangue. Saupoudrez d'une pincée de sel de Guérande et servez immédiatement.

Choisissez un foie gras de qualité, qui rendra peu de graisse (les tranches ne perdront pas plus de 15 % de leur poids initial). Conservez la graisse rendue à la cuisson pour préparer des pommes de terre sautées.

Vous pouvez fariner légèrement les tranches de foie gras avant cuisson. Au-delà de six convives, cette recette est déconseillée, car la cuisson n'est pas facile à gérer.

Boissons conseillées : Sauternes, Jurançon, Saussignac.

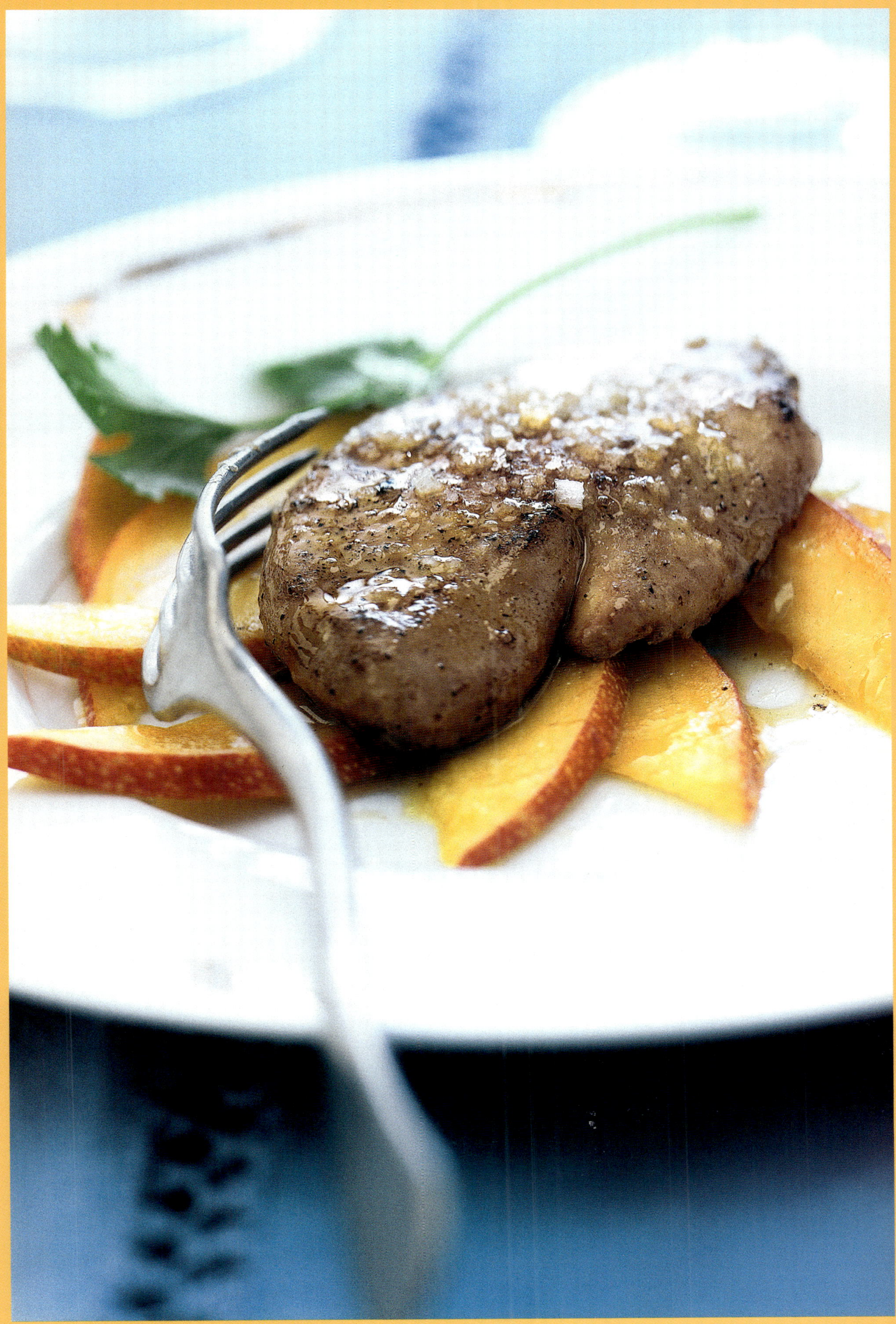

J'aime rester à table avec mes invités, c'est pourquoi j'essaie toujours de trouver des recettes à faire à l'avance, comme cette jolie et délicieuse tarte que l'on peut servir chaude ou tiède.

Tarte du jardin de Monsieur Seguin

Préparation : 20 minutes Cuisson : 40 minutes Réfrigération : 1 heure Pour 4-6 personnes

1 botte d'asperges vertes fraîches
(à défaut, des surgelées)
300 g de chèvre frais
300 g de crème fraîche épaisse
4 œufs
beurre
sel, poivre

Pour la pâte brisée
250 g de farine
5 g de sel
125 g de beurre
1 jaune d'œuf
5 cl d'eau

- Réalisez la pâte brisée selon la recette de la page 28 (étape 1). Mettez-la au frais pendant 1 heure au moins.
- Pendant ce temps, coupez la base des tiges des asperges et lavez-les (les asperges vertes ne se pèlent pas), ficelez-les en botte et plongez celle-ci dans un récipient d'eau salée bouillante. Faites cuire 10 à 12 minutes (les asperges doivent rester un peu fermes), égouttez sur un linge propre et laissez refroidir.
- Préchauffez le four à 180 °C. Dans un récipient, mélangez le fromage de chèvre, la crème, les œufs, le poivre et le sel.
- Beurrez un moule à tarte. Avec un rouleau à pâtisserie, étalez la pâte aux dimensions de votre moule. Déposez la pâte dans le moule, piquez-la avec une fourchette, versez la préparation. Disposez dessus les asperges, les unes à côté des autres. Enfournez pendant 30 minutes.
- Sortez du four et laissez tiédir ou refroidir.

Remplacez les asperges par d'autres légumes au fil des saisons. Vous pouvez aussi remplacer le chèvre frais par un sainte-maure assez fait si vous préférez un goût plus prononcé.

Boisson conseillée : Viogner.

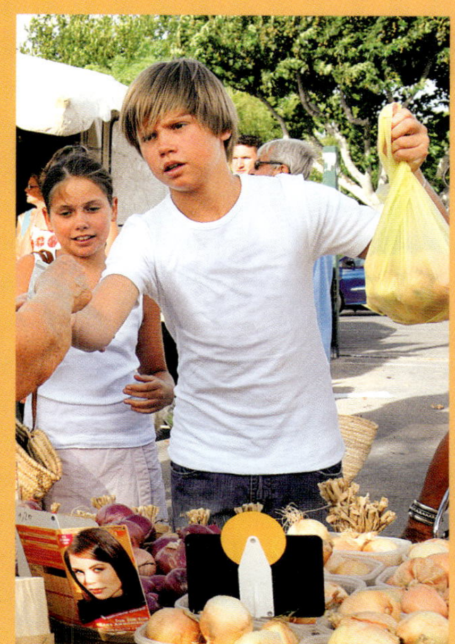

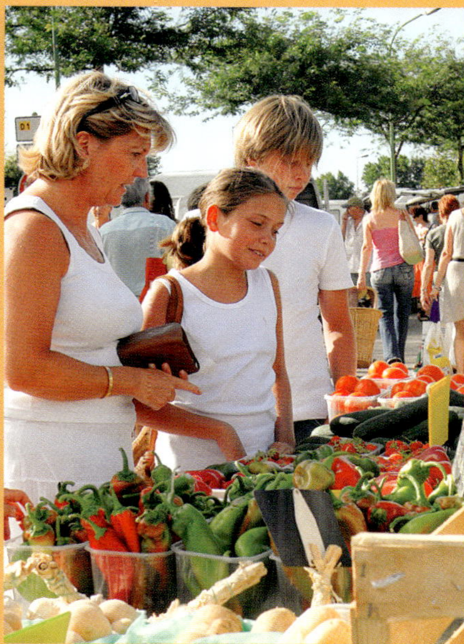

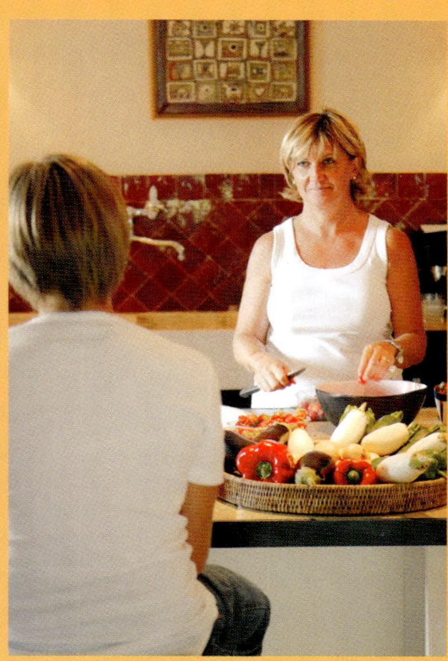

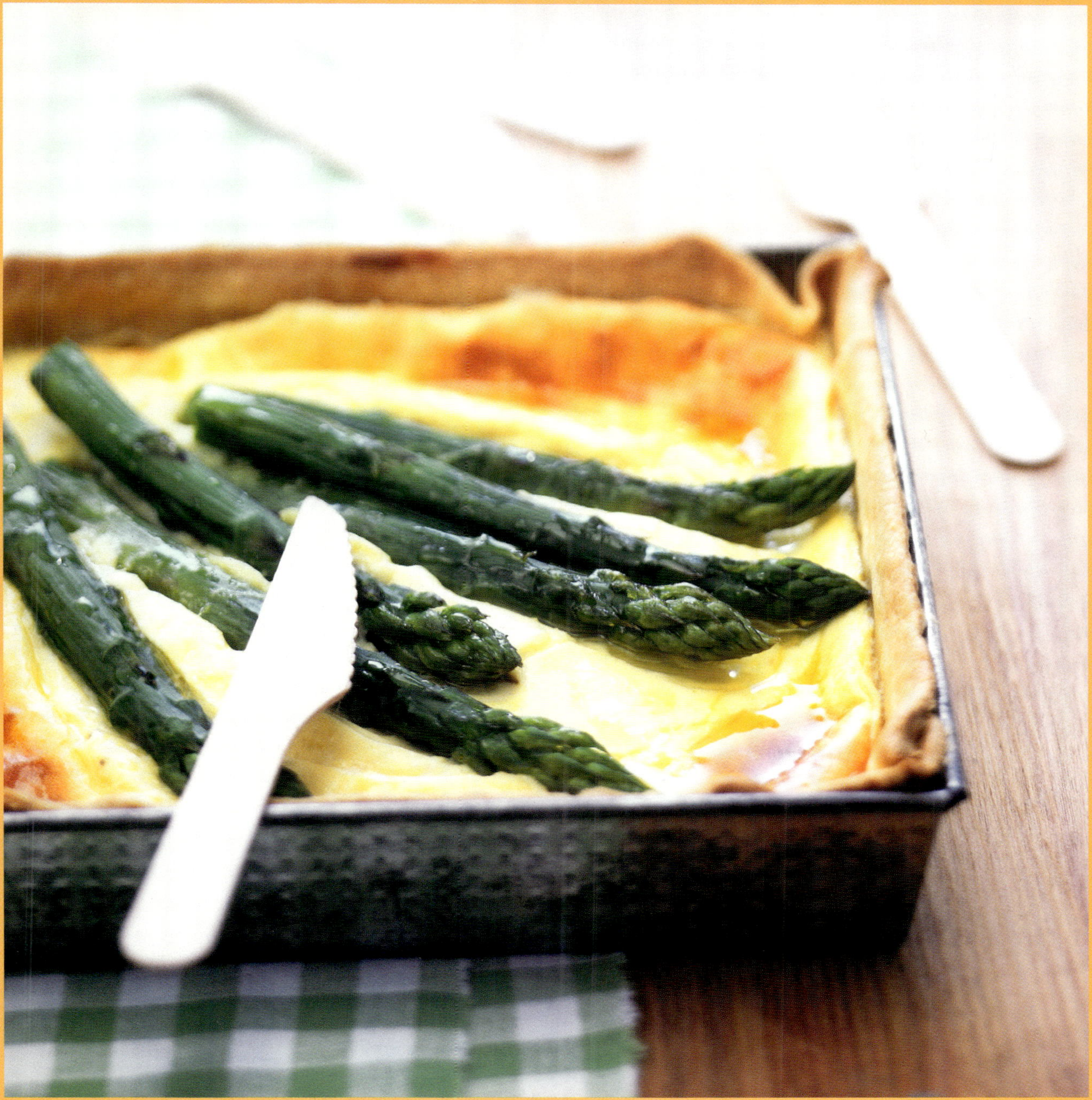

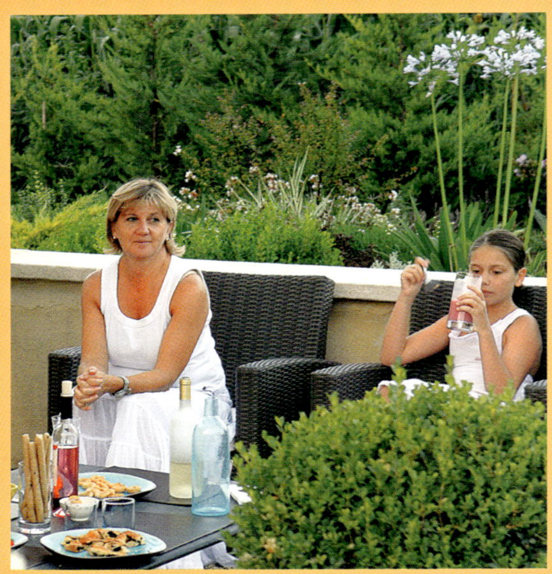

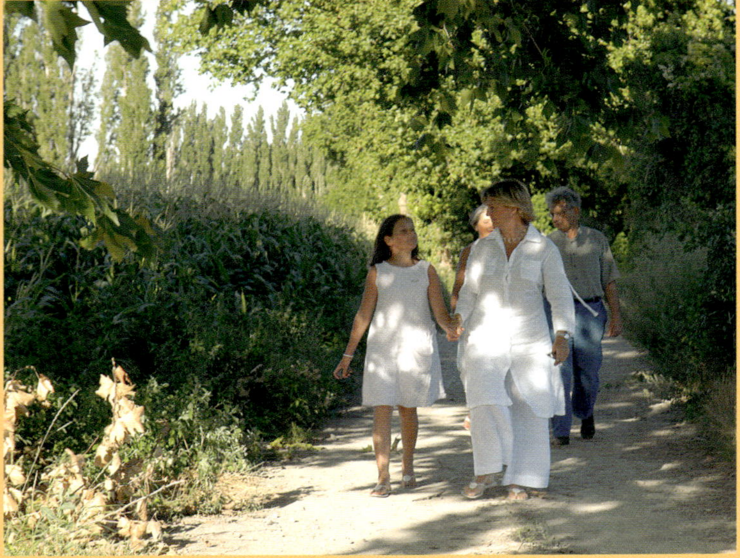

Ces œufs sont cuits au four dans un bain-marie : le blanc est à peine pris, le jaune est juste chaud et crémeux. À déguster avec des mouillettes de pain frais ou grillé.

Œufs « cot cot »

Préparation : 5 minutes

Cuisson : 15 minutes

Pour 4 personnes

8 œufs extra-frais
20 g de beurre
20 cl de crème fraîche épaisse
ciboulette
sel de Guérande, poivre blanc

- Préchauffez le four à 180 °C. Beurrez quatre ou huit petits ramequins en porcelaine (selon leur taille). À défaut, utilisez des tasses à café ou de petits verres supportant la chaleur du four. Saupoudrez légèrement l'intérieur de sel et de poivre.
- Cassez 1 ou 2 œufs dans chaque ramequin, sans briser les jaunes.
- Posez une feuille de papier sulfurisé sur le fond d'un plat à rôtir (cela évitera à l'eau du bain-marie de monter), placez dessus les ramequins et versez de l'eau bouillante dans le plat, jusqu'à la moitié de la hauteur des « cocottes ». Faites cuire au four pendant 15 minutes environ, selon l'épaisseur des cocottes. Surveillez attentivement la cuisson : le blanc doit juste cuire et prendre une belle couleur blanche, le jaune de l'œuf doit rester crémeux.
- Pendant ce temps, versez la crème dans une petite casserole, ajoutez un peu de sel et de poivre blanc. Laissez réduire d'un tiers. Sortez les cocottes du four, essuyez l'extérieur, versez la crème sur les œufs, parsemez de ciboulette ciselée. Servez immédiatement avec des mouillettes beurrées.

En faisant cuire la crème à part, vous pouvez surveiller la cuisson des œufs, ce qui est plus difficile quand ils sont recouverts de crème dès la mise au four.

Vous pouvez accompagner de mouillettes originales, en tartinant celles-ci de beurre enrichi d'œufs de saumon ou d'œufs de lump, voire de caviar les jours de fête…

S'il me reste un fond de ratatouille ou d'épinards cuits, j'en dépose une couche au fond des ramequins.

Boissons conseillées : Viogner, Rolle.

Fondue de la mer à la mode de Bécassine

Préparation : 40 minutes Cuisson : 15 minutes Pour 8 personnes

1 kg de grosses crevettes cuites décortiquées avec la queue, (surgelées)
16 noix de coquilles Saint-Jacques
1 kg de filet de saumon sans peau
1 l de soupe de poisson
1 tête de brocoli
1 carotte
40 cl de crème fleurette
1 bouquet de coriandre
1 gousse d'ail
1 pincée de piment d'Espelette
1 pincée de piment de Cayenne
1 noix de gingembre frais
1 cuillerée à soupe d'huile d'arachide
sel, poivre

- Découpez les filets de saumon en dés de 1 cm. Lavez les noix de coquilles Saint-Jacques et coupez-les en deux. Épongez les crevettes sur du papier absorbant après décongélation. Réservez l'ensemble au frais.
- Lavez et essuyez le brocoli, détaillez-le en petits bouquets. Épluchez, lavez et coupez la carotte en rondelles. Réservez au frais. Pelez et râpez le gingembre.
- Dans une cocotte, un poêlon à fondue ou un wok, faites revenir dans l'huile le gingembre râpé, l'ail écrasé et les piments. Versez la soupe de poisson, la crème fleurette, portez à ébullition et maintenez à frémissement pendant 10 minutes.
- Hors du feu, rectifiez l'assaisonnement, ajoutez la coriandre ciselée et placez le récipient sur la table. Chaque invité piquera avec une fourchette à fondue un morceau de poisson, une demi-noix de saint-jacques, une crevette, un brocoli ou une rondelle de carotte, et les plongera dans la fondue pendant quelques secondes.

Je sers généralement cette fondue avec un beurre blanc ou un beurre à l'orange (mélangez du beurre mou avec du jus d'orange, du zeste d'orange râpé et une pointe de curry).

Boissons conseillées : rosé de Bandol, Muscadet.

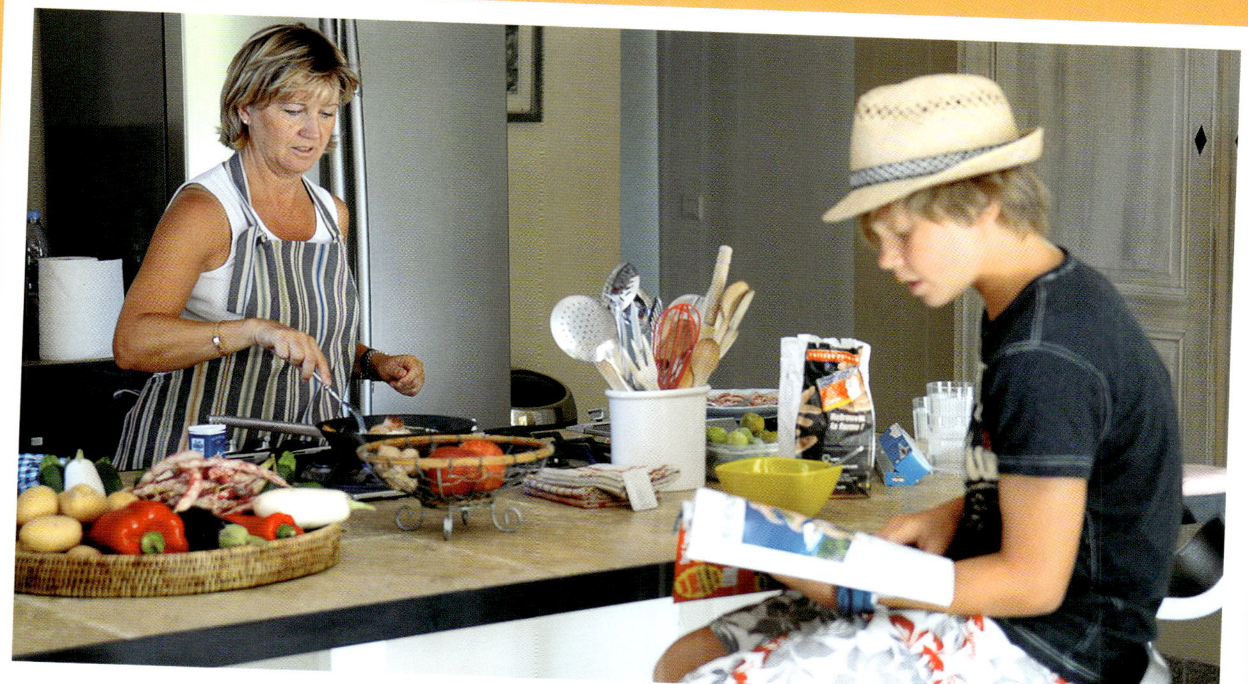

Un plat unique et complet à base de produits de la mer à déguster entre copains.

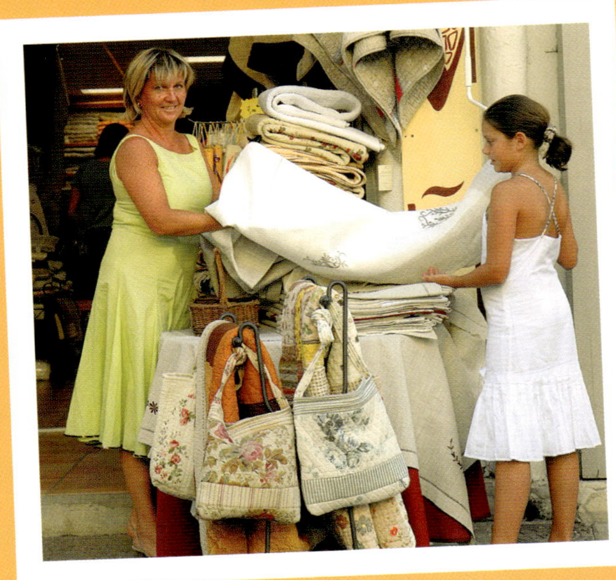

J'ai dégusté ce plat pour la première fois lors d'un déjeuner entre filles : ma copine Agnès, qui est une excellente cuisinière, avait associé les endives à du foie gras frais poêlé. Quelques jours plus tard, j'ai repris sa recette, mais avec des coquilles Saint-Jacques, et le résultat a été également très bon. Essayez les deux...

Tatin aux chicons caramélisés et noix de saint-jacques

Préparation : 30 minutes Cuisson : 15 minutes Réfrigération : 1 heure Pour 4 personnes

2 kg de chicons (endives)
20 g de sucre
80 g de beurre
8 noix de coquilles Saint-Jacques fraîches ou surgelées
quelques feuilles de coriandre ou de cerfeuil pour la décoration

Pour la pâte brisée
250 g de farine
5 g de sel
125 g de beurre
1 jaune d'œuf
5 cl d'eau

- Versez la farine dans un récipient, ajoutez le sel, le beurre en morceaux, le jaune d'œuf et l'eau. Mélangez du bout des doigts, jusqu'à obtenir une boule de pâte. Mettez-la au frais pendant au moins 1 heure.
- Nettoyez les noix de coquilles Saint-Jacques sous l'eau froide, enlevez le boyau noir sur le côté, puis essuyez les noix. Mettez-les au frais dans une boîte fermée.
- Retirez les feuilles abîmées des endives et le cône amer à la base. Coupez les endives en quatre dans le sens de la longueur.
- Faites fondre 40 g de beurre dans une grande sauteuse, déposez-y les endives. Saupoudrez de sucre et faites cuire en mélangeant pendant 15 à 20 minutes.
- Préchauffez le four à 180 °C. Abaissez la pâte au rouleau. Beurrez un moule à manqué, répartissez les endives sur le fond, recouvrez de la pâte, en enfonçant l'excédent à l'intérieur, tout le long du bord. Faites cuire 30 minutes au four. Environ 10 minutes avant la fin de la cuisson de la Tatin, mettez 30 g de beurre à fondre dans une petite poêle, faites-y dorer les coquilles 2 minutes sur chaque face.
- Démoulez la Tatin sur un plat, disposez les coquilles Saint-Jacques sur le dessus, décorez de coriandre ou de cerfeuil ciselés et servez immédiatement.

Boisson conseillée : Chablis.

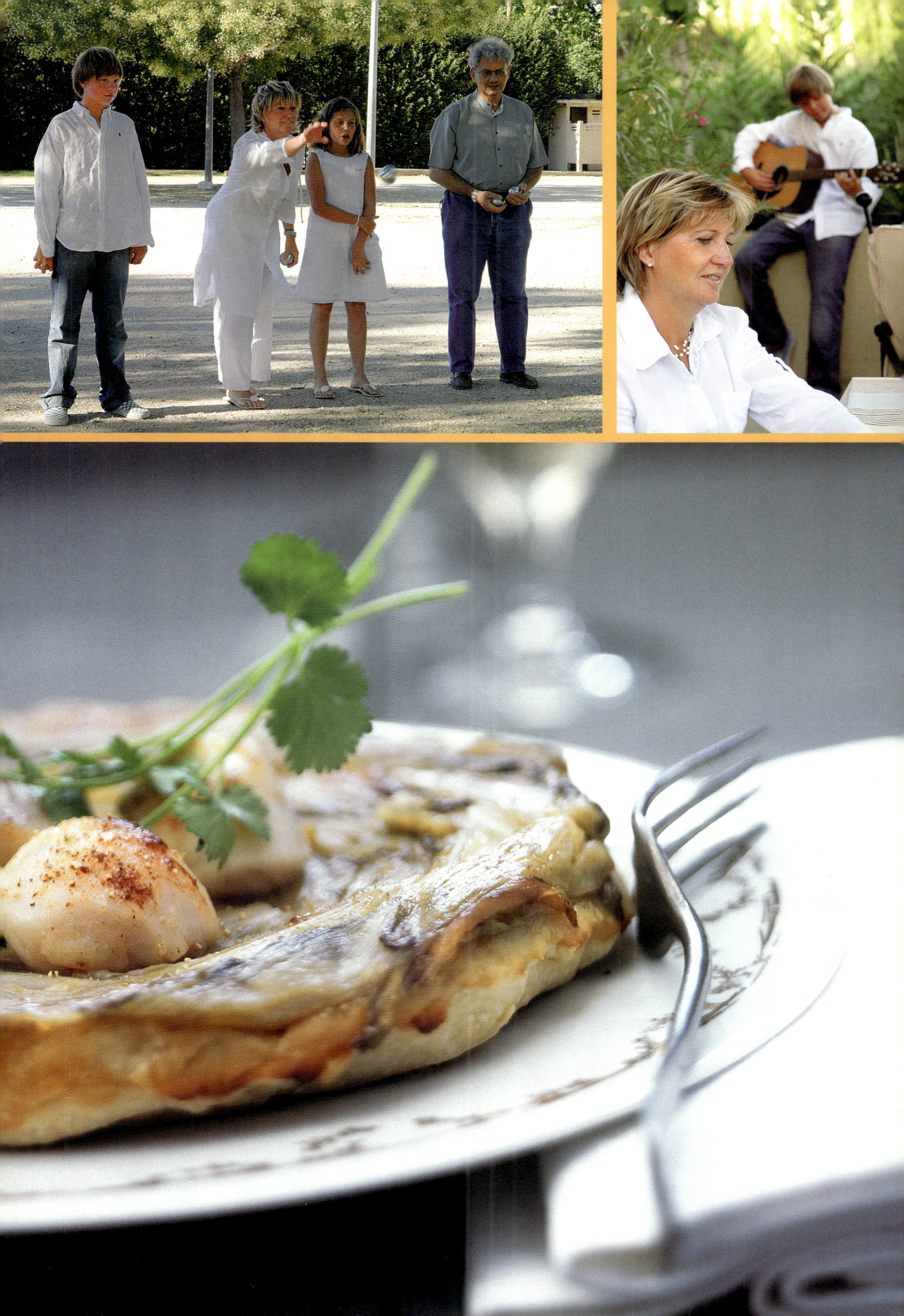

Si vous cherchez une recette à base de poisson, qui se confectionne à l'avance, se cuit facilement, présente bien et mélange agréablement les saveurs... Vous l'avez trouvée...

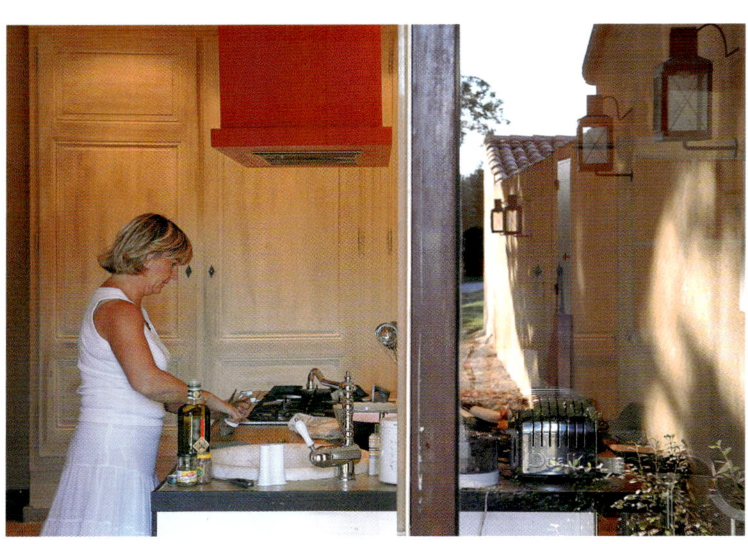

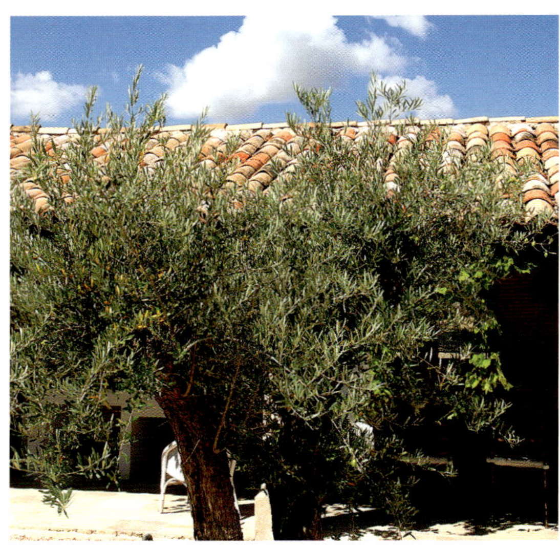

Filets de bar farcis aux tomates confites, aux pignons et au basilic

Préparation : 15 minutes Cuisson : 40 minutes Pour 6 personnes

les filets de 6 bars « portions »
avec peau (écaillée)
100 g de pignons de pin
1 bouquet de basilic
300 g de tomates confites à l'huile
1 tranche de pain de mie
1 gousse d'ail pelée
6 cuillerées à soupe d'huile d'olive
6 tranches de poitrine fraîche
très fines
sel, poivre

- Préparez la farce. Dans le bol d'un robot, versez les pignons de pin, les feuilles de basilic, 200 g de tomates confites à l'huile, le pain de mie, la gousse d'ail, du sel, du poivre et 2 cuillerées à soupe d'huile d'olive. Mixez grossièrement.
- Préchauffez le four à 180 °C. Étalez 6 filets de bar bien à plat, peau en dessous, salez-les et poivrez-les légèrement, puis recouvrez-les de farce. Posez les autres filets dessus, peau vers le haut. Recouvrez avec 1 fine tranche de poitrine fraîche.
- Ficelez, sans serrer, les filets de bar à trois endroits (aux deux extrémités et au milieu). Déposez-les dans un plat à rôtir légèrement huilé. Répartissez le reste de la farce dans le plat, ainsi que le reste des tomates confites ; arrosez de 2 cuillerées à soupe d'huile d'olive. Cuisez au four environ 40 minutes.

Remplacez éventuellement le bar par du saumon.

Servez dans le plat de cuisson, accompagné d'une purée de pomme de terre à l'huile d'olive et aux olives noires hachées.

Boisson conseillée : Hermitage blanc.

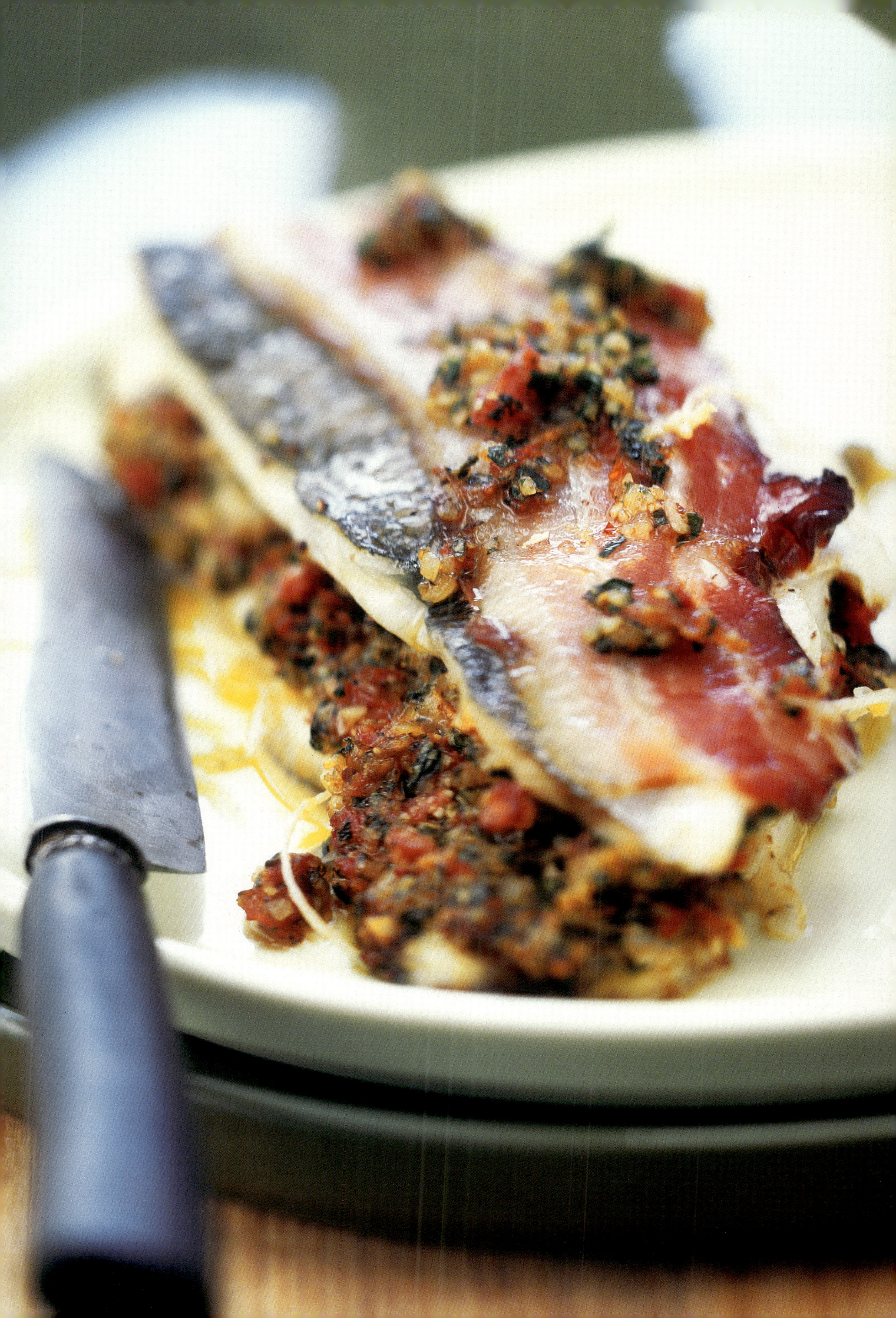

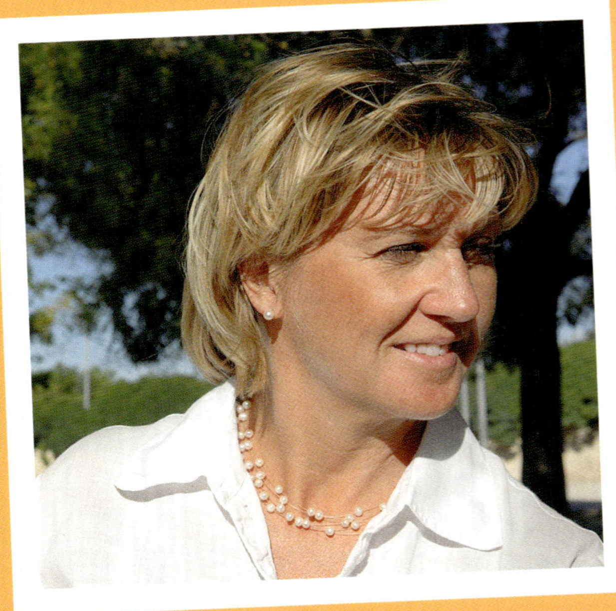

Dès que les petits légumes nouveaux pointent le bout de leur fane sur les marchés, je prépare cette recette. Un vrai tableau gourmand que l'on admire avec les yeux avant de déguster avec bonheur.

Navarin d'agneau aux légumes de printemps

Préparation : 30 minutes Cuisson : 1 h 30 Pour 6 personnes

1,600 kg d'épaule d'agneau désossée et coupée en morceaux
1 botte de carottes nouvelles
1 botte de navets nouveaux
1 botte d'oignons blancs nouveaux
400 g de haricots verts
400 g de petits pois écossés frais ou surgelés
1 grosse tomate bien mûre épépinée et coupée en dés
2 gousses d'ail
2 cuillerées à soupe d'huile d'olive
1 cuillerée à soupe de sucre
1 cuillerée à soupe de farine
25 cl de vin blanc
3 branches de thym
1 feuille de laurier
40 g de beurre
1 bouquet de coriandre pour la décoration
sel, poivre

- Dans une grande cocotte, faites chauffer l'huile d'olive et mettez-y les morceaux de viande à revenir ; la viande doit être bien dorée sur toutes les faces.
- Saupoudrez le sucre et la farine, mélangez et faites cuire environ 2 minutes, pour que la viande prenne une jolie couleur brillante. Versez le vin, ajoutez le sel et le poivre, la tomate, l'ail pelé, le thym et le laurier ; couvrez d'eau juste à hauteur de la viande et laissez mijoter pendant 50 minutes à feu très doux.
- Pendant ce temps, épluchez et lavez les carottes, les navets et les oignons blancs. Gardez un peu des fanes pour une plus jolie présentation.
- Dans une grande sauteuse, faites fondre le beurre. Ajoutez les carottes, les navets et les oignons blancs, laissez-les colorer pendant environ 10 minutes.
- Versez le mélange de légumes dans la cocotte contenant la viande et prolongez la cuisson de 20 minutes à feu très doux.
- En parallèle, mettez à cuire, environ 12 à 15 minutes, les haricots verts dans une casserole d'eau bouillante salée. Cuisez de la même manière les petits pois. Égouttez les haricots verts et les petits pois, plongez-les dans de l'eau froide pour les garder bien verts.
- Mettez les haricots verts et les petits pois dans la cocotte, salez et poivrez, parsemez de coriandre ciselée, faites cuire 5 minutes et servez sans attendre.

Si vous n'aimez pas l'agneau, remplacez-le par du veau.

Boissons conseillées : Gevrey-Chambertin, Pauillac, Côtes-du-Rhône (Côte-Rôtie).

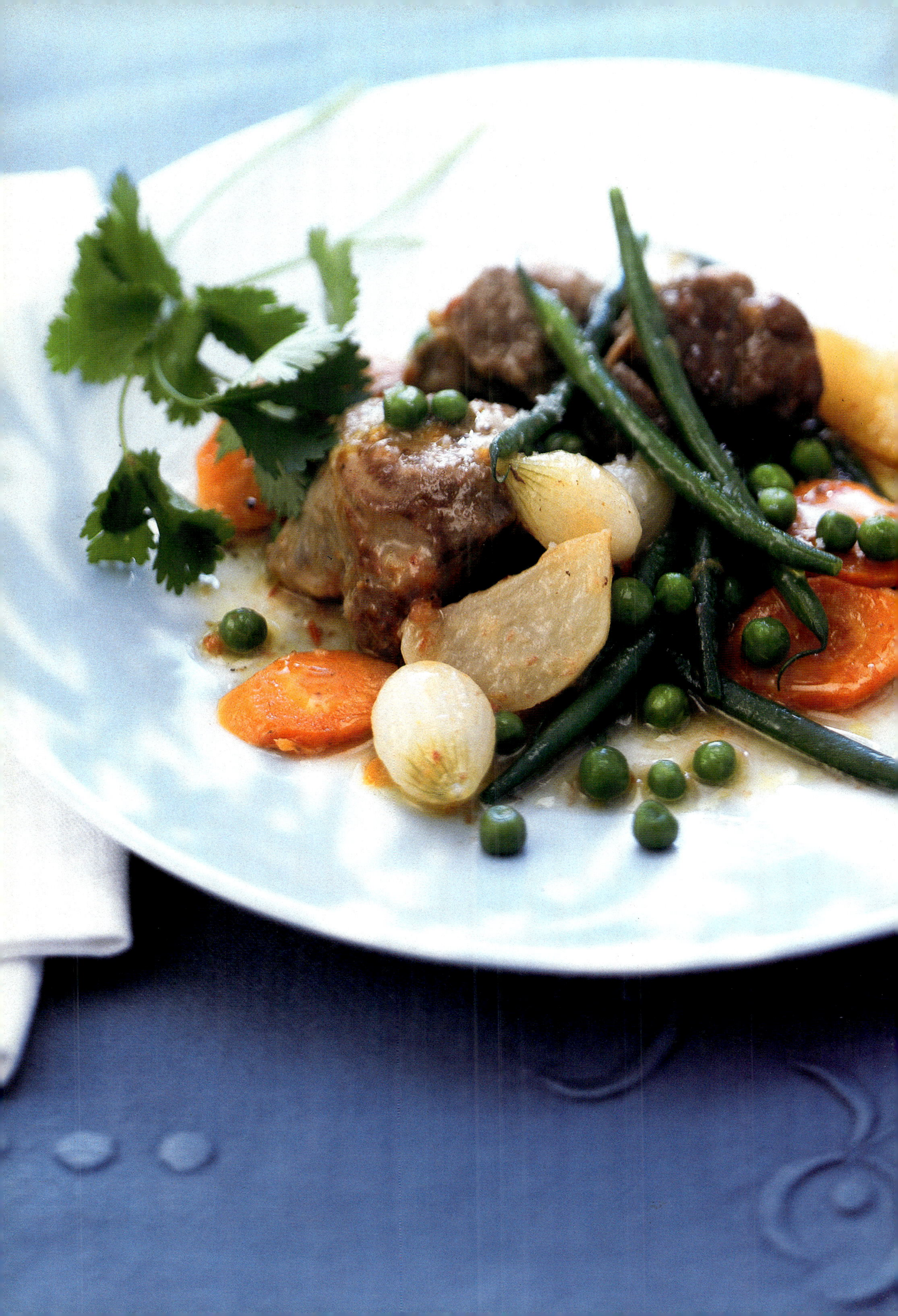

Vous n'avez que 10 minutes devant vous et vous voulez étonner vos convives... alors cette recette est pour vous !

Mon brie truffé

Préparation : 10 minutes Réfrigération : 24 heures Pour 6 personnes

1 morceau de brie équivalant à 2 parts
1 petit pot de crème fraîche
1 belle truffe de Bourgogne
ou du Périgord (fraîche si possible)
poivre

- Ouvrez le brie en deux dans l'épaisseur, poivrez légèrement l'intérieur des deux moitiés, tartinez de crème fraîche. Posez des lamelles de truffe sur l'une des moitiés et recouvrez avec l'autre moitié. Enveloppez l'ensemble dans du film alimentaire, placez dans une boîte hermétique et laissez 24 ou 48 heures au réfrigérateur, pour que la truffe imprègne le brie de son parfum.
- Sortez du réfrigérateur 20 minutes avant de servir.

La truffe de Bourgogne (Tuber uncinatum chatin) *est tout aussi savoureuse mais moins chère que la truffe du Périgord. Elle se congèle très bien. À défaut de truffe fraîche, utilisez de la conserve.*

L'été, je remplace les truffes par des framboises écrasées... Le résultat n'a évidemment rien à voir, mais c'est quand même délicieux.

Boissons conseillées : Saint-Julien, Nuits-Saint-Georges.

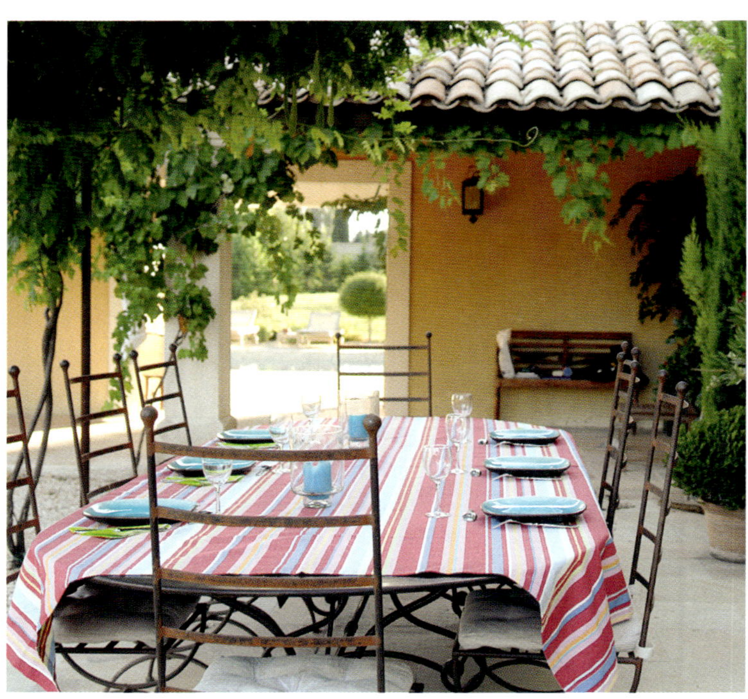

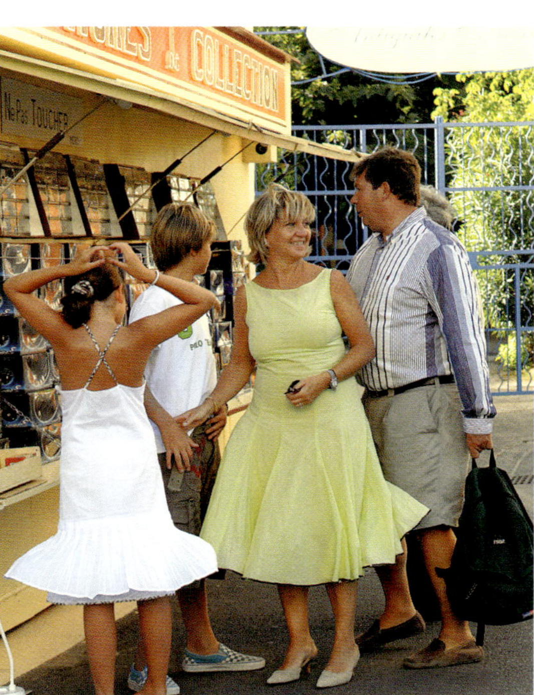

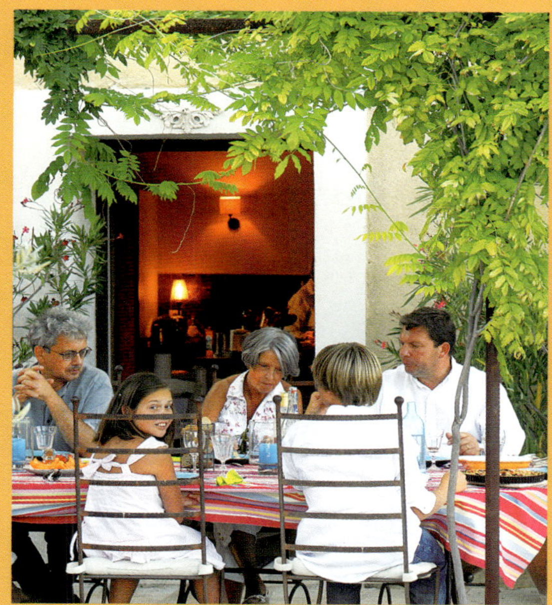

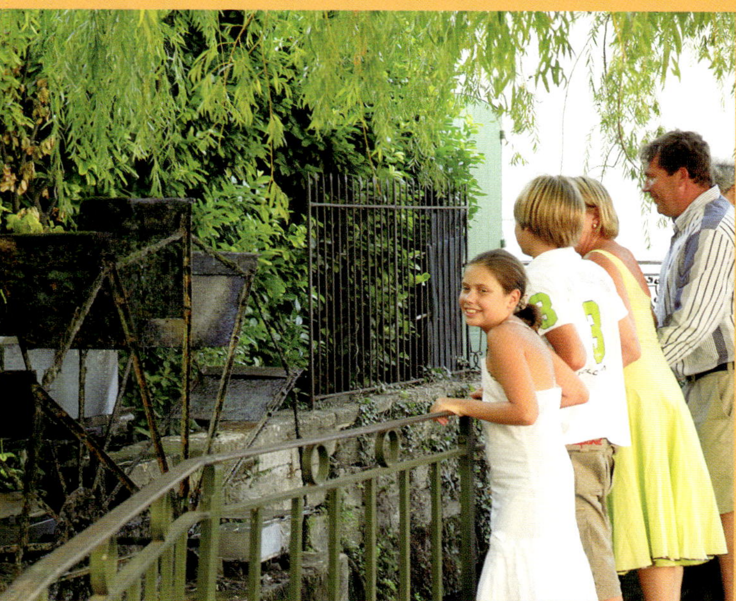

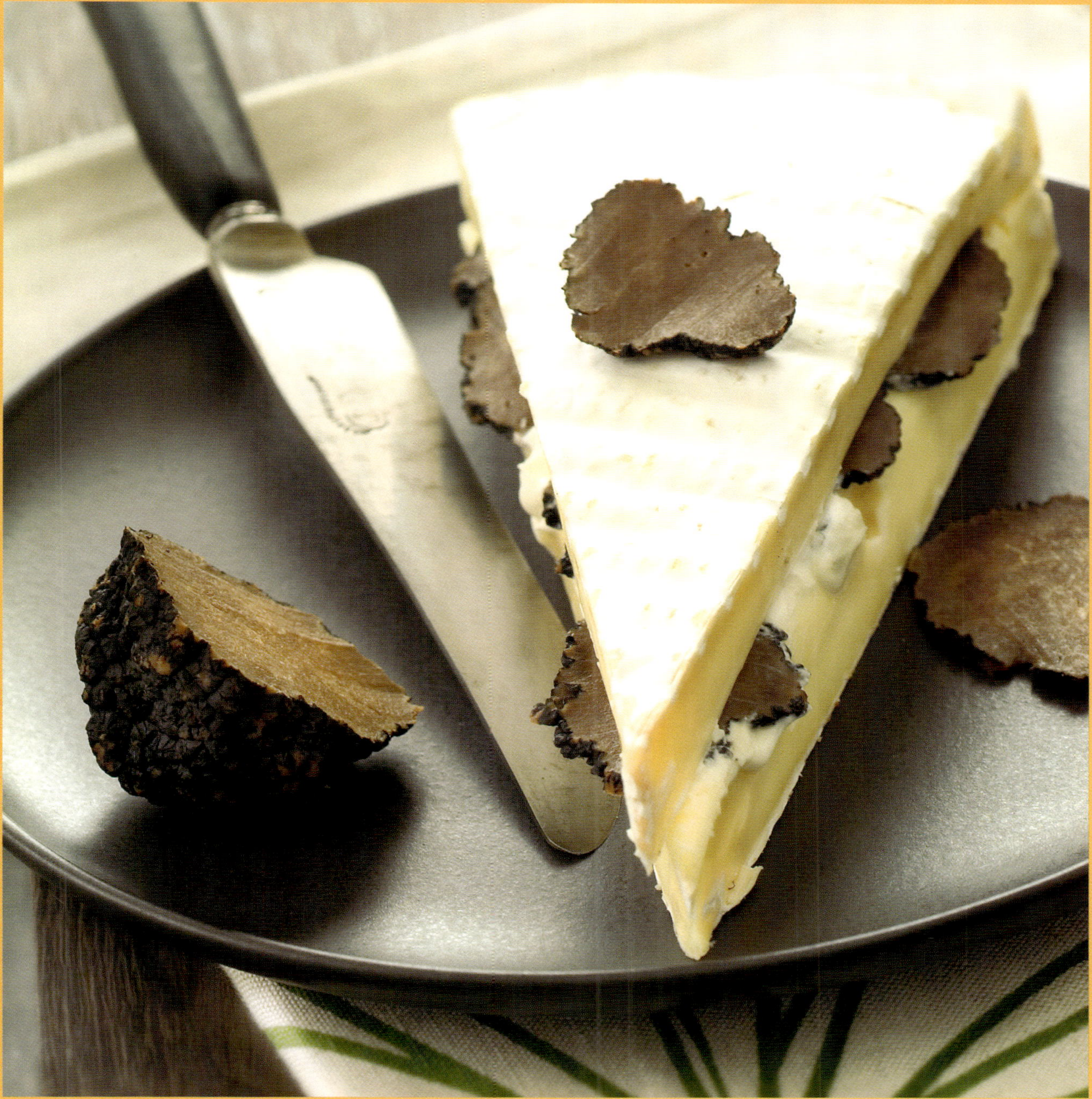

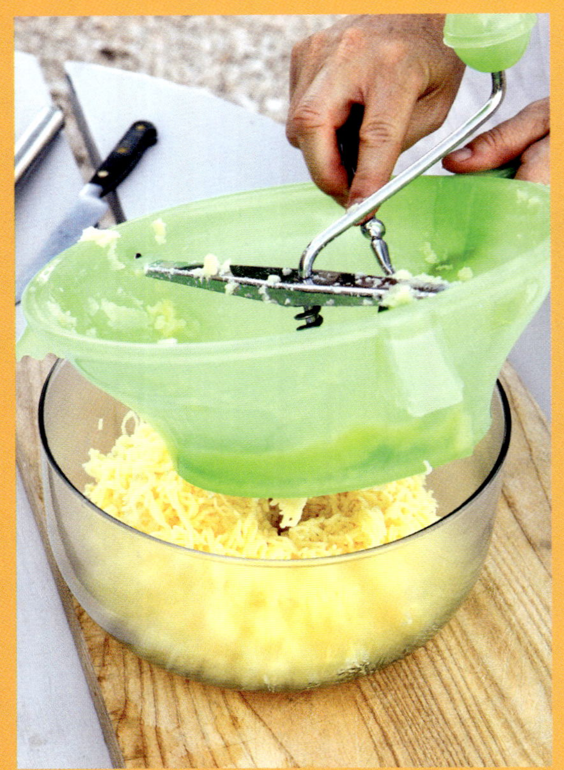

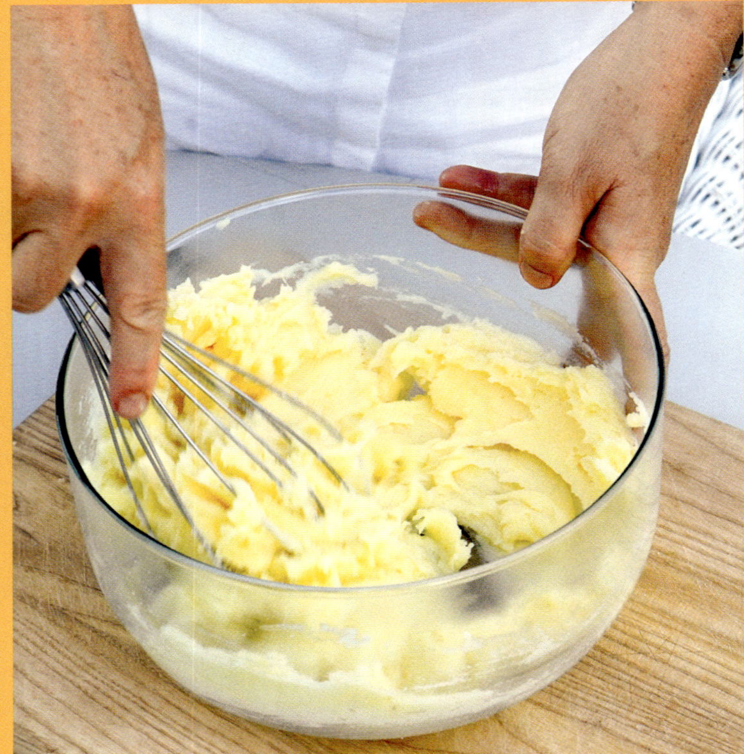

Je suis née dans la ville de M. Parmentier, célèbre pour avoir importé en France la fameuse pomme de terre. Cette version inhabituelle du hachis Parmentier associe la pomme de terre du Nord de mon enfance et la tomate du Sud.

Hachis Parmentier aux tomates confites

Préparation : 35 minutes Cuisson : 2 h 10 Pour 6 personnes

800 g de viande d'agneau
ou de veau cuite, hachée
1 kg de pomme de terre à purée
6 tomates
10 gousses d'ail
80 g de beurre
15 cl de lait
2 cl d'huile d'olive
1 cuillerée à soupe de sucre
100 g de gruyère râpé
sel de Guérande, poivre

- Préchauffez le four à 150 °C. Pelez l'ail et hachez-le. Coupez les tomates en deux, ôtez les pépins, déposez-les dans un plat, saupoudrez de fleur de sel, de poivre, d'ail, de sucre et d'huile d'olive. Faites cuire au four pendant 1 h 30, jusqu'à ce qu'elles soient confites.
- Pendant ce temps, préparez la purée de pomme de terre. Épluchez et lavez les pommes de terre, faites-les cuire 30 minutes à l'eau bouillante salée, écrasez-les au presse-purée ou au moulin à légumes. Incorporez le lait et 50 g de beurre mou en morceaux.
- Beurrez un moule à gratin, déposez-y la viande hachée, recouvrez de tomates confites, puis de purée. Étalez le fromage râpé et parsemez de noisettes de beurre. Passez au four à 180 °C pendant 20 minutes pour réchauffer et gratiner.

Utilisez des restes de viande cuite pour cette recette. Vous pouvez d'ailleurs remplacer la viande par du jambon passé à la moulinette, surtout si vous cuisinez pour des enfants.

Boissons conseillées : Madiran, Côtes du Roussillon.

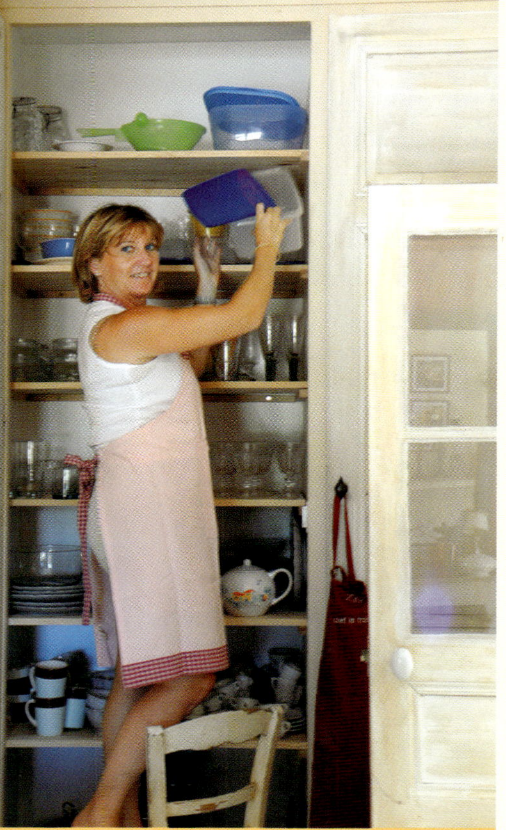

La cerise sur le gâteau

Des cerises juteuses, cuites dans une pâte légèrement sucrée et recouvertes d'une crème onctueuse, font de ce dessert un régal de saveurs et de couleurs.

Préparation : 30 minutes
Cuisson : 45 minutes
Pour 8 personnes

farine
beurre
1 jaune d'œuf
sucre en poudre

Pour la pâte

150 g de farine
3 cuillerées à soupe de sucre en poudre
80 g de beurre froid
1 pincée de sel
1 verre d'eau froide

Pour la garniture

2 œufs
8 cuillerées à soupe de crème fraîche
1 kg de cerises
100 g de sucre
20 g de beurre mou
30 g de farine

Pour la crème

3 cuillerées à soupe de crème fraîche
1 cuillerée à soupe de kirsch
1 cuillerée à café de sucre

- Préparez la pâte. Mettez la farine, le beurre coupé en morceaux, le sucre et le sel dans le bol d'un robot et mixez jusqu'à obtention d'une semoule fine. Ajoutez l'eau pour amalgamer et obtenir une boule de pâte. Couvrez et mettez au réfrigérateur.
- Préparez la garniture. Dénoyautez les cerises et mettez-les dans un récipient avec le beurre mou en morceaux, le sucre et la farine. Battez dans un bol les œufs et la crème fraîche, ajoutez à la préparation précédente.
- Préchauffez le four à 180 °C. Étalez finement la pâte sur le plan de travail fariné, piquez-la avec une fourchette et déposez-la dans un moule à manqué beurré et fariné. Versez la préparation aux cerises et ramenez les bords de la pâte vers le centre du moule.
- Battez le jaune d'œuf, badigeonnez-en la pâte avec un pinceau. Faites cuire environ 45 minutes. Saupoudrez de sucre en poudre.
- Mélangez les ingrédients de la crème dans un bol et servez avec la tourte tiède ou froide.

En automne, je remplace les cerises par des mirabelles ou des prunes, et le kirsch de la crème par une liqueur de mirabelle ou de prune.

Boissons conseillées : kirsch, sherry.

La tarte au citron est indémodable et intemporelle, et vous avez certainement eu l'opportunité de tester d'autres recettes. Je vous propose une version avec une pâte croustillante faite à base de petits gâteaux écrasés, très facile à réaliser.

Tarte au citron rapide

Préparation : 30 minutes Cuisson : 10 minutes Pour 6 personnes

Pour la pâte
150 g de biscuits Thé brun
120 g de beurre fondu
3 cuillerées à soupe de sucre brun

Pour la crème au citron
200 g de sucre
40 g de farine
50 g de Maïzena
1 pincée de sel
40 cl d'eau
3 jaunes d'œufs
5 citrons verts non traités
1 cuillerée à soupe de crème fleurette ou de beurre

- Préchauffez le four à 180 °C. Dans le bol d'un robot, mixez les biscuits pour les réduire en miettes, puis ajoutez le beurre fondu et le sucre. Mélangez pour obtenir une pâte d'une jolie couleur brune. Tapissez-en le fond (sur 1 cm d'épaisseur) et les côtés d'un moule à fond amovible, en tassant bien. Faire cuire 10 minutes au four.
- Râpez le zeste des citrons et pressez leur jus.
- Mélangez dans une casserole le sucre, la farine, la Maïzena et la pincée de sel, ajoutez l'eau et portez à ébullition, en tournant constamment jusqu'à épaississement. Ôtez du feu, incorporez les jaunes d'œuf, ajoutez le jus et le zeste des citrons, mélangez, versez 1 cuillerée à soupe de crème fleurette ou de beurre. Répartissez ce mélange sur le fond de pâte et laissez refroidir.
- Dégustez ce dessert bien froid. Attention, la pâte est très friable… Ne démoulez qu'au moment de servir !

Je remplace parfois les citrons verts par des citrons jaunes, mais aussi par des oranges ! Dans ce dernier cas, utilisez seulement le jus de 3 oranges.

Boisson conseillée : caïpirina (rhum blanc, sirop de canne et citron vert).

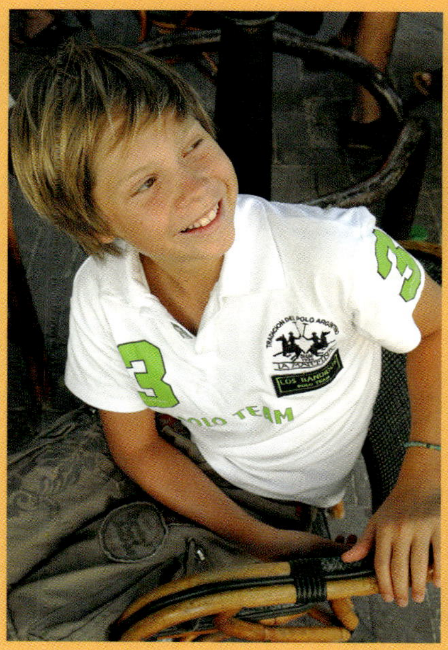

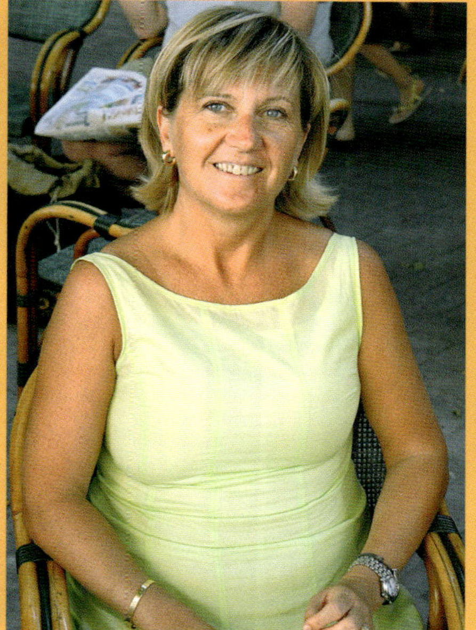

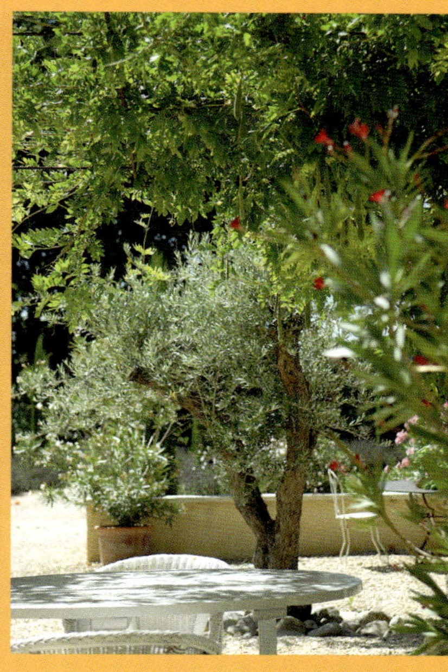

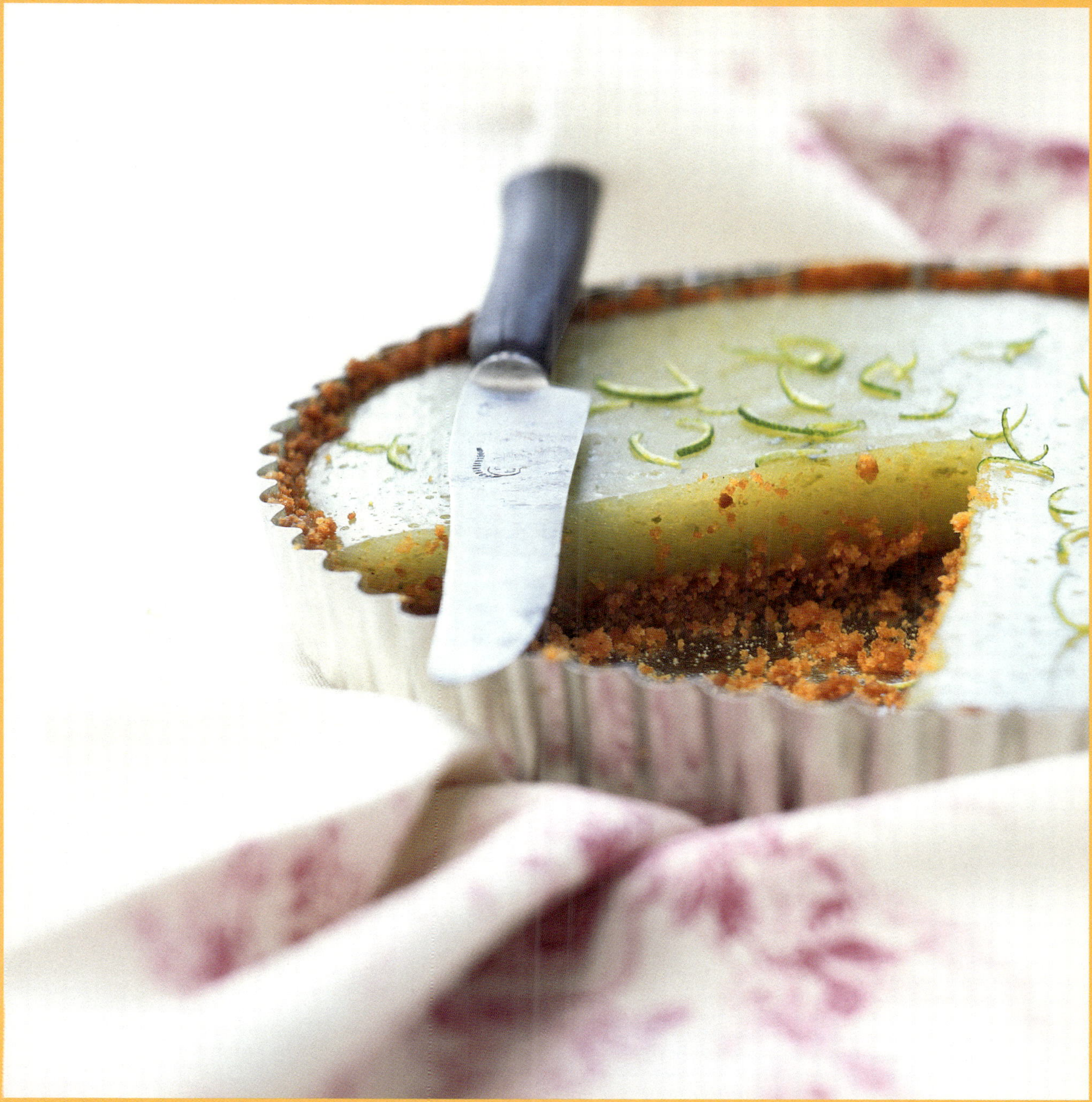

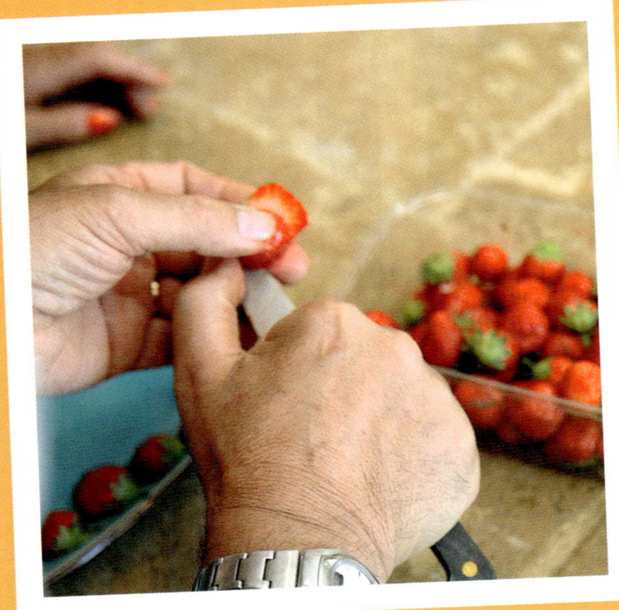

Ce dessert porte le nom d'un plat à four, carré ou rectangulaire, en terre vernissée ou non, utilisé dans la cuisine provençale. Il sert à cuisiner des gratins de légumes, qui prennent également le nom de « tians ». Je vous propose une version sucrée très sympathique.

Tian de fraises au basilic

Préparation : 40 minutes Pour 6 personnes

1 kg de fraises
10 biscuits à la cuillère
8 jaunes d'œufs
20 g de Maïzena
75 g de sucre en poudre
50 cl de lait entier
15 belles feuilles de basilic frais
30 g de beurre

- Lavez, essuyez, équeutez les fraises ; réservez-en quelques-unes entières et coupez les autres en deux. Faites fondre le beurre dans une poêle, ajoutez les demi-fraises, mélangez doucement sur le feu pendant 1 minute. Versez dans un plat et parsemez de feuilles de basilic lavées, séchées et ciselées (réservez 2 feuilles entières pour la décoration).
- Faites chauffer le lait. Mélangez dans un saladier les jaunes d'œufs avec le sucre, ajoutez la Maïzena, puis délayez avec le lait bouillant. Portez le mélange à ébullition et remuez avec un fouet sans arrêt, afin d'éviter la formation de grumeaux. Versez la crème sur les fraises et laissez refroidir, puis mettez au frais.
- Émiettez les biscuits dans un bol. Environ 10 minutes avant de servir, recouvrez la crème avec les biscuits émiettés. Passez 1 ou 2 minutes sous le gril du four à 220 °C, en surveillant très attentivement, car les biscuits peuvent brûler très vite.
- Décorez des fraises entières et des feuilles de basilic réservées. Servez immédiatement.

En refroidissant, une peau se forme sur la crème. Afin de l'éviter, couvrez la crème de film alimentaire, en plaçant ce film au contact direct de la crème.

Vous pouvez remplacer le basilic par de la menthe.

Boissons conseillées : vin de vendanges tardives, vin de paille.

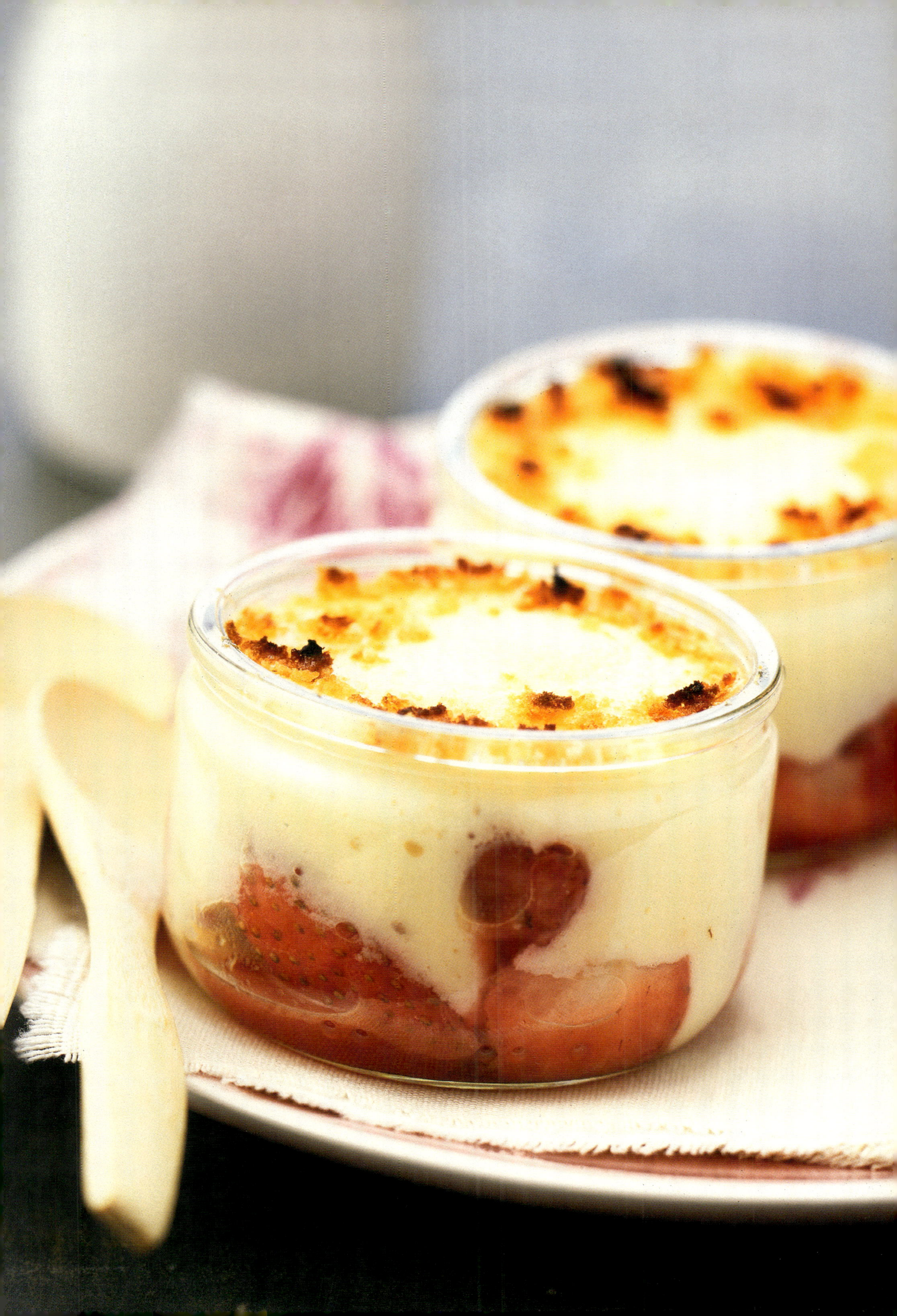

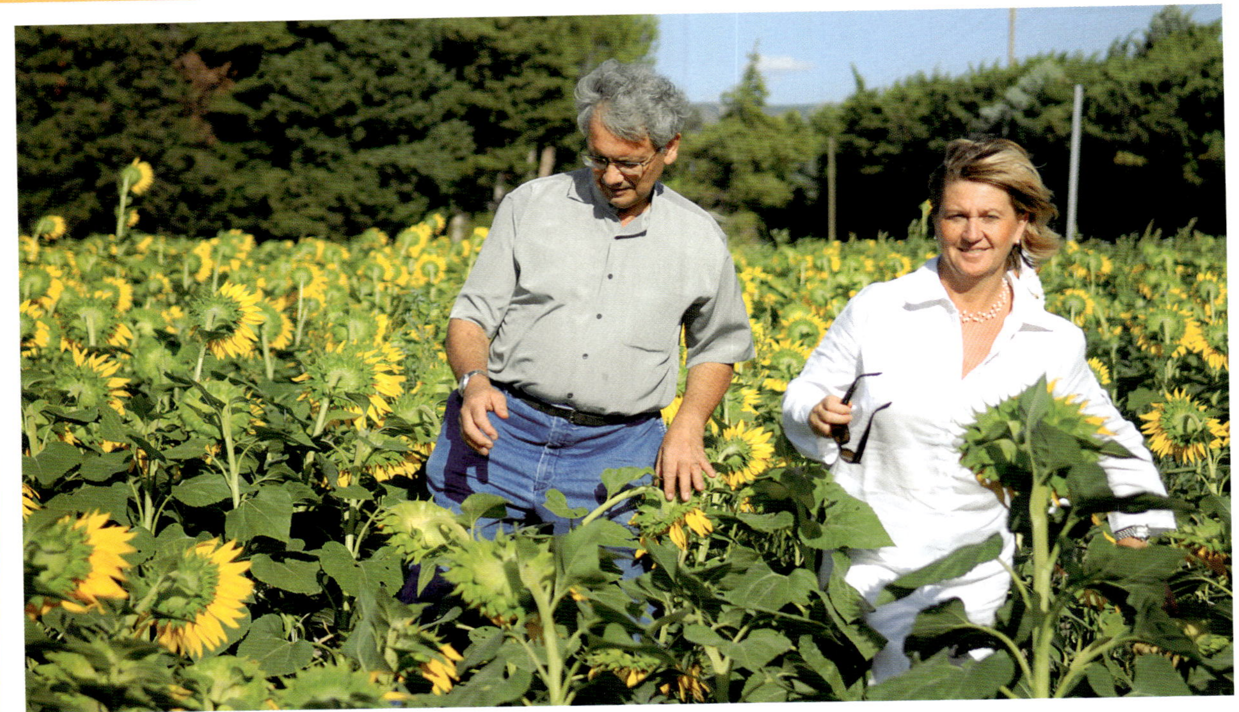

Quel mistral… le jour de cette promenade dans les tournesols !

Pour mettre en valeur la soupe de fraises, accompagnez-la de petits gâteaux qui se préparent rapidement avec seulement 3 ingrédients.

Soupe de fraises et petits moelleux à la crème

Préparation : 15 minutes Cuisson : 20 minutes Pour 6 personnes

Pour la soupe de fraises
1 kg de fraises parfumées (gariguettes, fraises du Périgord, maras des bois…)
3 cuillerées à soupe de sucre en poudre ou de sirop de canne
quelques feuilles de menthe pour la décoration

Pour les petits moelleux
100 g de crème fraîche épaisse
100 g de farine
100 g de sucre en poudre

- Préparez la soupe de fraises. Passez les fraises sous l'eau et essuyez-les délicatement. Réservez 6 fraises pour la décoration et équeutez les autres. Mixez 250 g de fraises (les moins belles) avec le sucre ou le sirop.
- Dans un joli plat de présentation, coupez en lamelles le reste des fraises, recouvrez de coulis de fraise et placez au frais. Au moment de servir, vous décorerez de fraises entières et de feuilles de menthe.
- Préparez les petits moelleux. Préchauffez le four à 180 °C. Mélangez la crème et le sucre en poudre, ajoutez la farine. Versez 1 cm de pâte dans des petits moules à muffins ou à tartelettes, faites cuire pendant 20 minutes au four. Démoulez et laissez refroidir.

En vacances, si vous ne disposez pas de balance, utilisez une tasse pour doser les ingrédients des moelleux : 1 tasse de crème, 1 tasse de sucre, 1 tasse de farine.

Vous pouvez remplacer la menthe par le basilic.

Boissons conseillées : champagne rosé, eau-de-vie blanche (abricot).

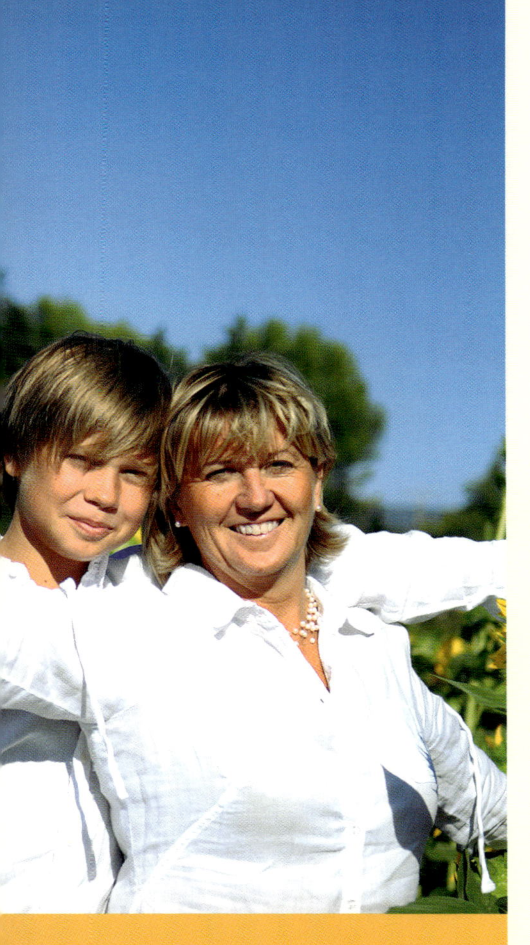

Crèmes brûlées à la vanille

Il y a 20 ans, j'ai fait croire au cuisinier d'un grand restaurant que j'étais journaliste gastronomique dans un quotidien national ; c'est ainsi que je lui ai soutiré la recette de ce dessert. J'espère qu'il me pardonnera de lui avoir menti et de partager avec vous son délicieux secret !

Préparation : 15 minutes
Cuisson : 35 minutes
Pour 4 personnes

25 cl de lait
25 cl de crème fleurette
6 jaunes d'œufs
100 g de sucre semoule
1 gousse de vanille
sucre roux

- Préchauffez le four à 170 °C. Faites bouillir le lait et la crème avec la gousse de vanille fendue en deux. Éteignez le feu, laissez infuser, puis grattez l'intérieur de la gousse avec la pointe d'un couteau, afin de récupérer les petites graines, et ajoutez celles-ci au mélange.
- Fouettez les jaunes d'œufs avec le sucre, versez progressivement dans le mélange précédent : puis versez la préparation dans des plats à crème brûlée. Cuisez au four durant une trentaine de minutes.
- Retirez du four, laissez refroidir, mettez au frais.
- Un peu avant de servir, préchauffez le gril du four à 220 °C. Saupoudrez le dessus des crèmes avec du sucre roux et passez sous le gril pour faire caraméliser. Servez aussitôt.

Si vous préparez souvent des crèmes brûlées, cela vaut la peine d'investir dans un petit chalumeau à gaz, grâce auquel vous pourrez caraméliser les crèmes sans pour autant les réchauffer.

Remplacez éventuellement la vanille par de la cannelle, du gingembre, du citron, de la menthe, de la lavande...

Boissons conseillées : Banyuls blanc, Beaumes-de-Venise blanc.

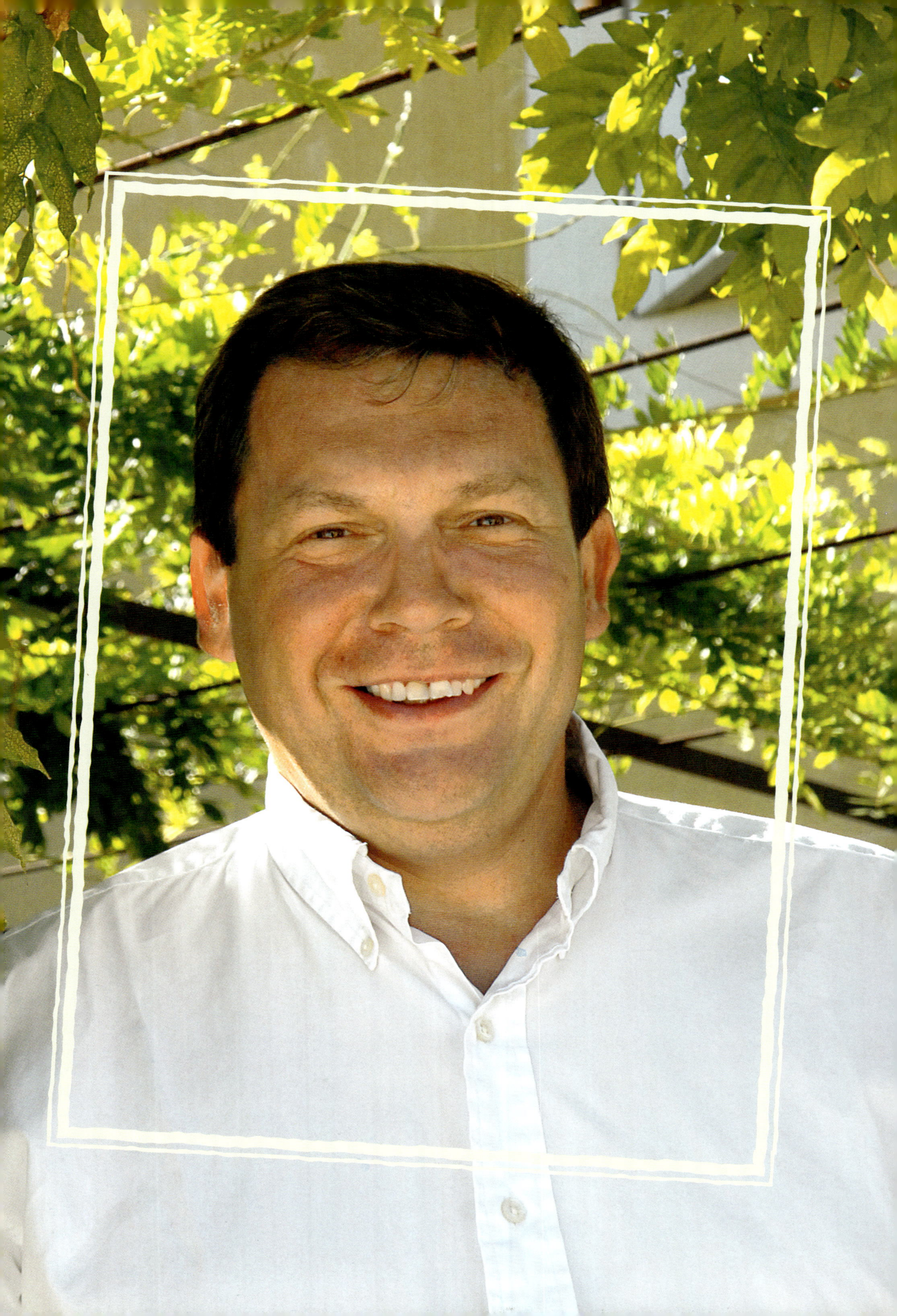

Patrick

Le père

Si j'étais... une couleur,

je serais le rouge, symbole de l'appétit, de la chaleur et de la vie.

Si j'étais... une odeur,

je serais celle que dégage un bon pain grillé,
comme celui qui m'aide à attaquer la journée du bon pied.

Si j'étais... une saveur,

je serais celle de la cannelle avec son parfum d'exotisme
et son goût singulièrement doux, chaud et agréable.

Si j'étais... un ustensile,

je serais un batteur électrique qui, en quelques minutes, rend homogène une préparation
et donne du volume à tous les ingrédients qu'il mélange.

Si j'étais... un souvenir gourmand,

je serais une bûche au moka, dessert familial préparé par ma grand-mère,
puis par ma mère au moment des fêtes de fin d'année.

Si j'étais... un péché mignon,

je serais de la frangipane associée à de la pâte feuilletée,
pour son odeur d'amandes, son fondant et son goût sucré.

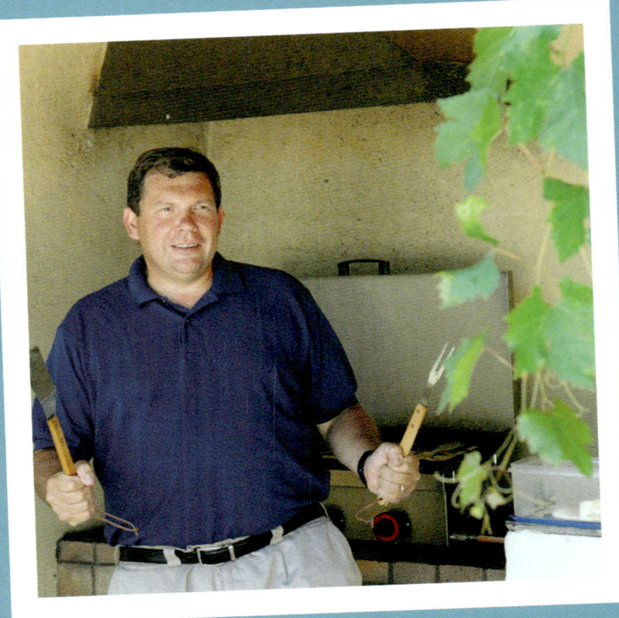

Une recette à réaliser pour l'apéritif entre amis. La présentation est jolie et le mariage du blé noir et du saumon est apréciable au goût.

Rouleaux de saumon

Préparation : 10 minutes Cuisson : 2 heures Pour 4 personnes

4 galettes de blé noir
2 cuillerées à soupe de crème fraîche épaisse
4 à 6 grandes tranches de saumon fumé
1 bouquet de ciboulette

- Posez un grand morceau de film alimentaire sur le plan de travail. Placez dessus (avec précaution, car elle est très fragile) une galette de blé noir et couvrez aux trois quarts de saumon fumé. Tartinez de crème fraîche.
- Déposez 10 tiges de ciboulette sur le bord de la galette qui se trouve devant vous. Roulez délicatement la galette sur elle-même : la ciboulette va se retrouver au centre du rouleau. Enroulez le film autour de la galette, en serrant un peu. Procédez ainsi avec les autres rouleaux. Mettez au frais pendant au moins 2 heures.
- Au moment de servir, retirez le film. Coupez en biais des tranches de 2 cm et posez sur les assiettes, à la manière des sushis.

Vous pouvez remplacer le saumon par tout autre poisson fumé : thon, anguille...

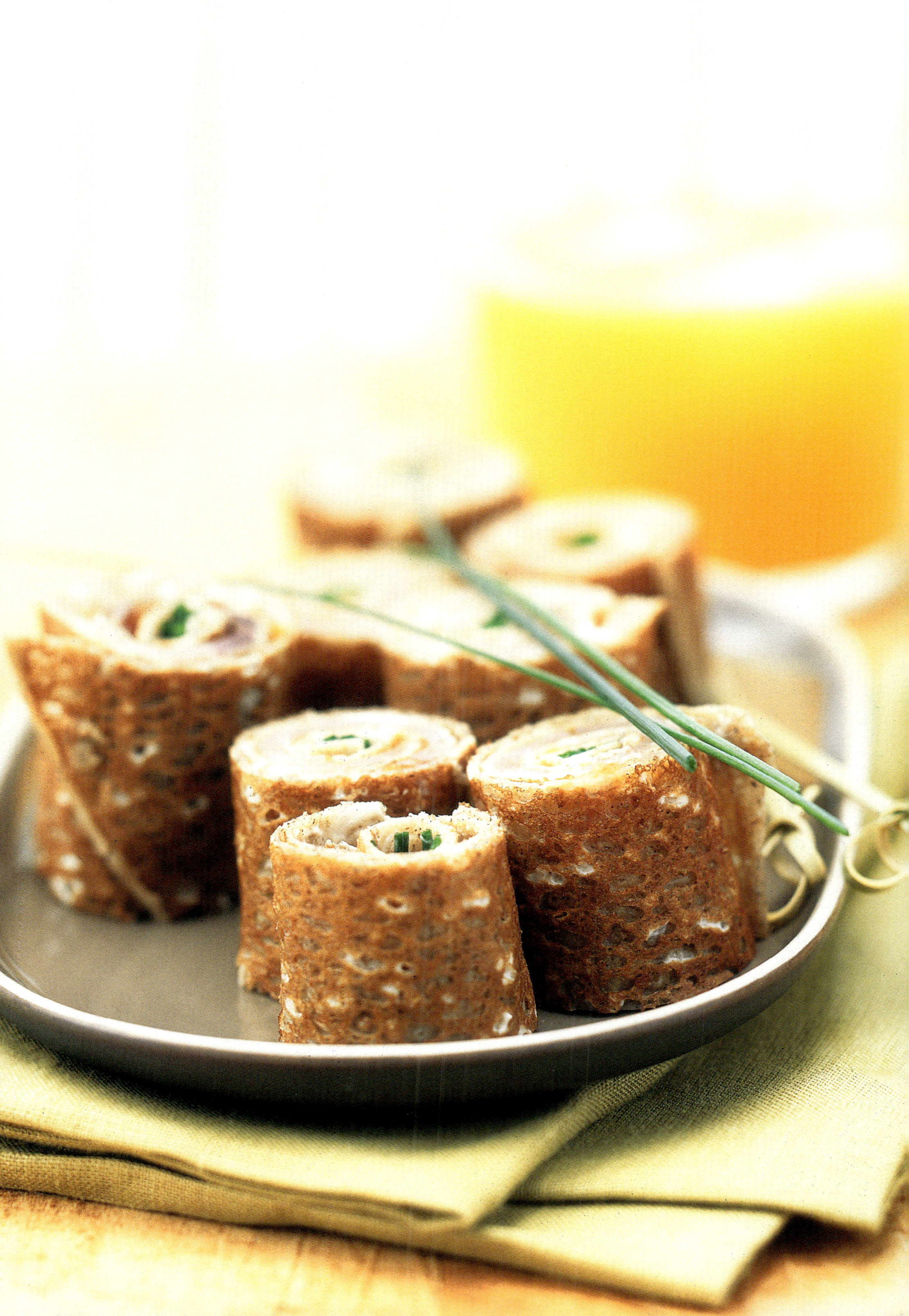

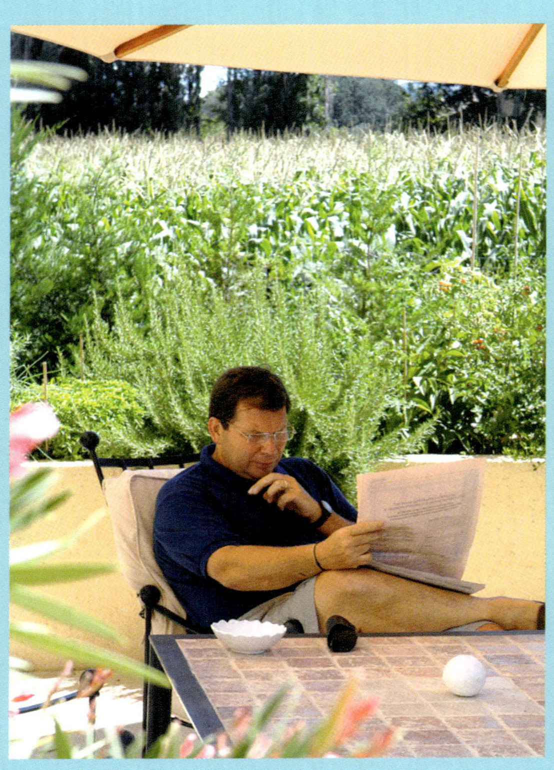

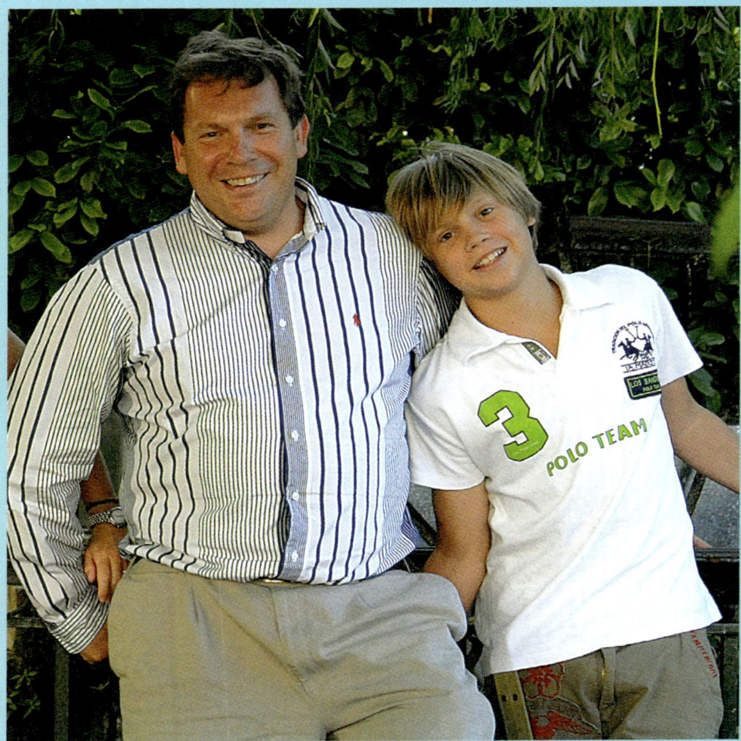

Cette recette, très facile à faire et offrant un résultat proche du foie gras, est parfaite pour tartiner à l'apéritif ou pour servir en entrée, accompagnée d'une salade de feuille de chêne et de bon pain grillé.

Foie gras de volaille truffé

Préparation : 15 minutes Cuisson : 5 minutes Réfrigération : 6 heures Pour 6-8 personnes

1 kg de foies de volaille
1 petite truffe fraîche ou sous vide (10 g)
50 cl de vin blanc sec
4 cuillerées à soupe de porto
400 g de beurre
1 pincée de quatre-épices
sel, poivre

- Faites bouillir le vin blanc, plongez-y les foies. À la reprise de l'ébullition, comptez 3 minutes, puis sortez les foies à l'aide d'une écumoire. Égouttez et laissez refroidir.
- Mixez la truffe. Ajoutez les foies dans le bol du mixeur et mixez rapidement en incorporant progressivement le beurre ramolli. Incorporez le porto, salez, poivrez, ajoutez le quatre-épices.
- Versez dans une terrine en tassant bien. Recouvrez d'une feuille d'aluminium et mettez au frais au moins 6 heures.
- Servez avec du pain grillé, un peu de fleur de sel et du poivre. Ne conservez pas votre foie gras plus de 3 jours.

Boissons conseillées : vieux porto, vieux Banyuls, vieux Rivesaltes.

Petits escargots de mer sautés à l'ail

Préparation : 15 minutes Cuisson : 5 minutes Pour 4 personnes

1 kg de bulots cuits
2 gousses d'ail
quelques feuilles de basilic
40 g de beurre
sel, poivre

- Décoquillez les bulots à l'aide d'une pique. Rincez-les à l'eau froide, essuyez-les.
- Hachez le basilic. Pelez et hachez l'ail.
- Faites fondre le beurre dans une poêle, ajoutez les bulots et l'ail ; laissez cuire à feu vif pendant 5 minutes, en remuant régulièrement pour ne pas laisser l'ail brûler. Saupoudrez de basilic et servez aussitôt dans de petits bols ou ramequins.

Remplacez le basilic par du persil plat.

Boissons conseillées : Quincy, Bergerac blanc sec, Bourgogne aligoté.

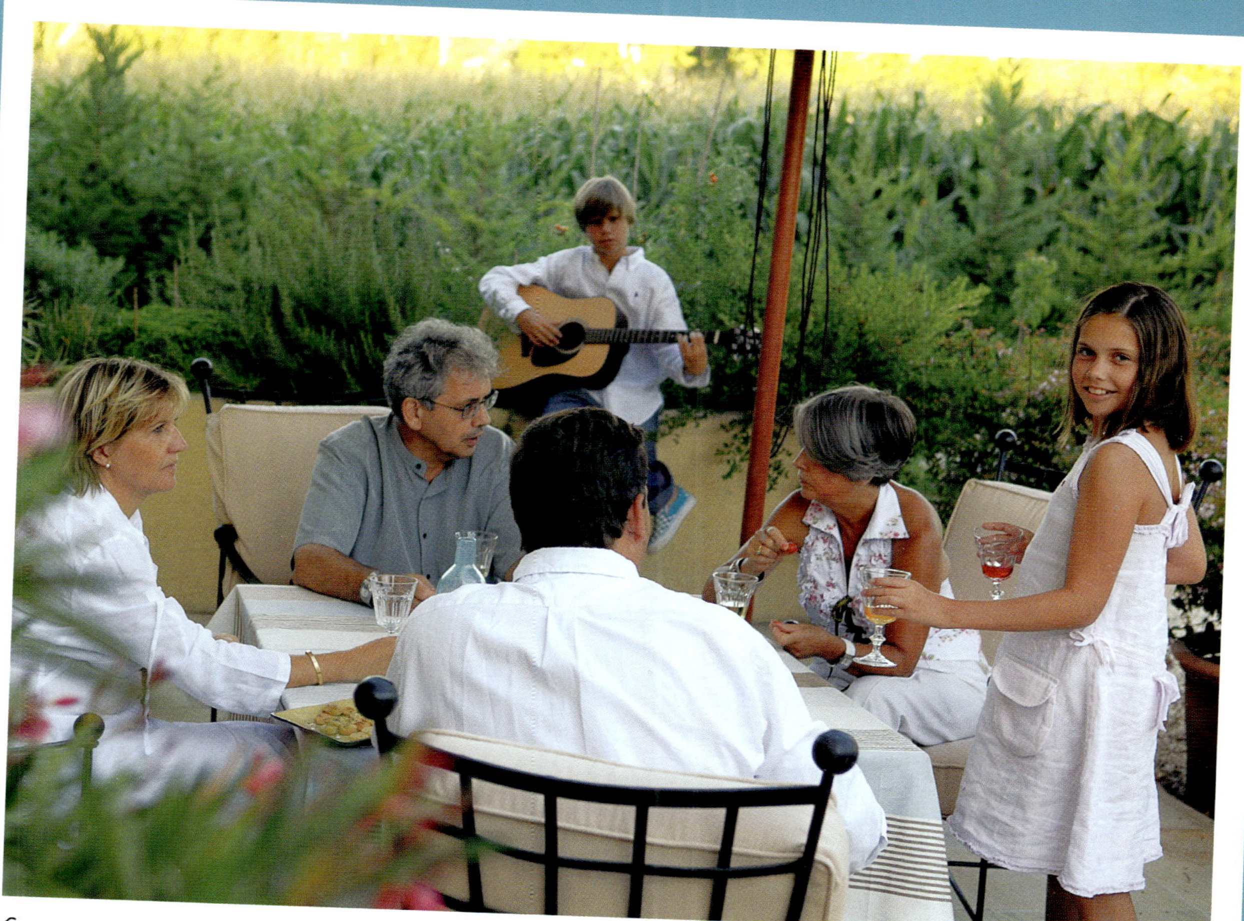

En souvenir de nos vacances en Bretagne avec les copains et pour changer du traditionnel bulots-mayonnaise, nous dégustons volontiers chauds ces « tapas » bretons, accompagnés d'un verre de vin blanc bien frais…

Le homard est le plus gros, le plus recherché et le plus cher des crustacés. Mon préféré est le homard de Chausey. Il est bleu marine comme l'eau de cet archipel de 365 îlots, situé en face de Granville ; sa chair est légèrement rosée, et son goût est unique. Malheureusement, il se vend exclusivement sur son île ; vous le remplacerez donc par des homards de Bretagne, d'Europe ou du Canada. À accompagner de beurre pimenté, vanillé ou citronné...

Homards grillés au beurre aromatisé

Congélation : 1 heure Préparation : 15 minutes Cuisson : 20-30 minutes Pour 4 personnes

4 homards portions (environ 500 g)
100 g de beurre
poivre en grains
sel de Guérande, poivre

Pour le beurre pimenté
1 pincée de piment de Cayenne
1 pincée de piment en poudre
1 gousse d'ail hachée

Pour le beurre vanillé
les graines de 2 bâtons de vanille

Pour le beurre au citron vert
le zeste de 2 citrons verts
le jus de 1 citron vert

- Placez les homards pendant 1 heure au congélateur pour les endormir et les insensibiliser avant de les découper.
- Préparez le beurre aromatisé de votre choix. Prenez du beurre mou, salez-le et poivrez-le, ajoutez les ingrédients de la version choisie. Remplissez un petit pot et placez au frais.
- Posez un homard sur le ventre sur une planche à découper (assurez-vous que ces pinces sont attachées). Tout en le maintenant fermement, enfoncez la pointe du couteau à découper au centre de la marque en croix qu'il a sur le dos ; incisez de la tête vers la queue, pour obtenir deux moitiés égales. Le homard est tué instantanément, même si des contractions nerveuses se produisent. Divisez de la même manière les autres homards.
- Posez les demi-homards sur la carapace, afin de conserver l'eau qu'ils retiennent. Donnez un léger coup de marteau sur les pinces, posez-les tête-bêche sur la grille du barbecue, dos contre la grille. Salez et poivrez. Faites cuire 20 à 30 minutes selon la taille des homards (ils sont cuits quand la chair se détache de la carapace). Servez immédiatement, avec le beurre aromatisé découpé en rondelles, à faire fondre sur la chair des homards.

Si vous avez peur d'ouvrir les homards vivants, plongez-les au préalable dans de l'eau bouillante salée pendant 4 minutes.

Boissons conseillées : Chassagne-Montrachet, Pessac-Léognan blanc.

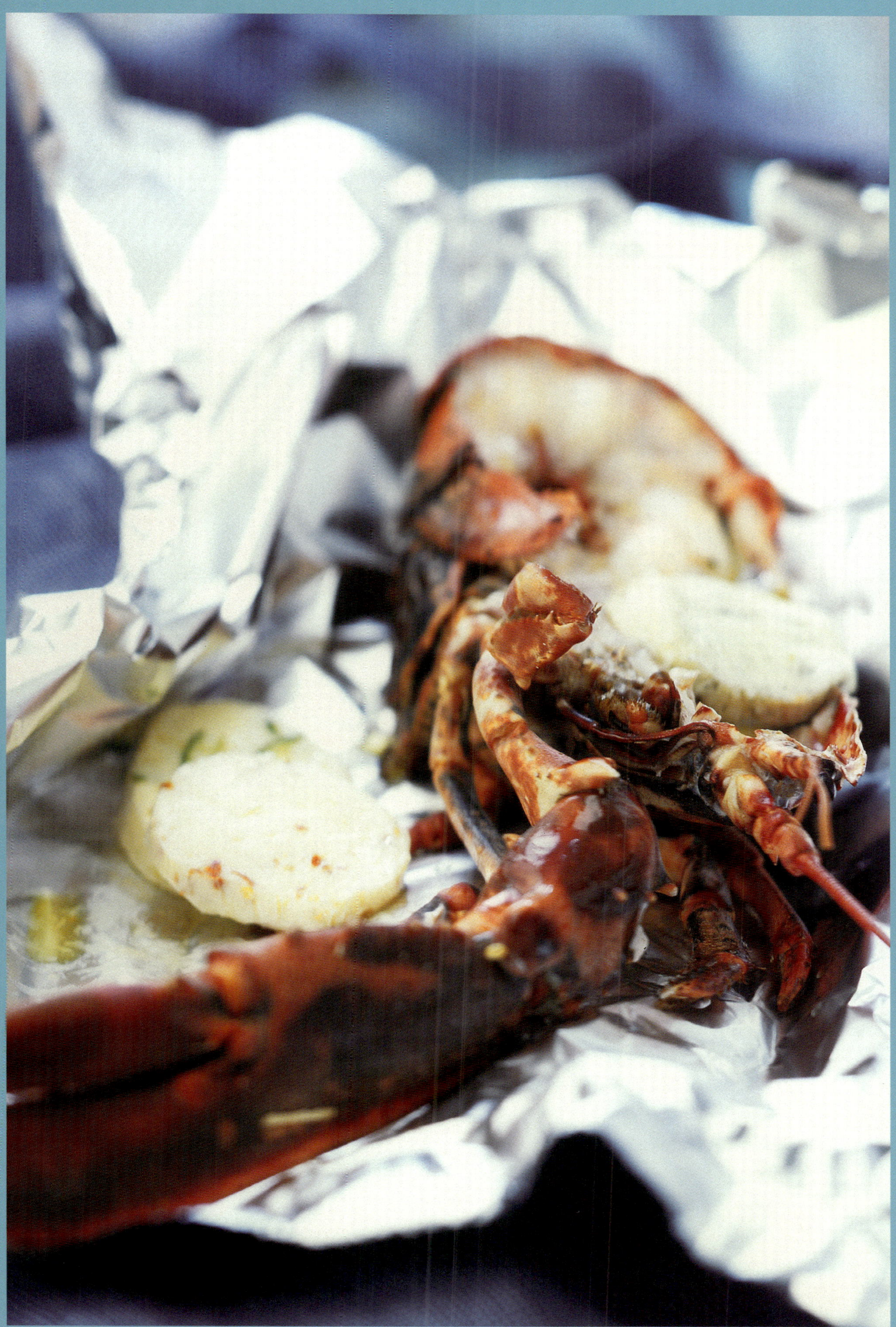

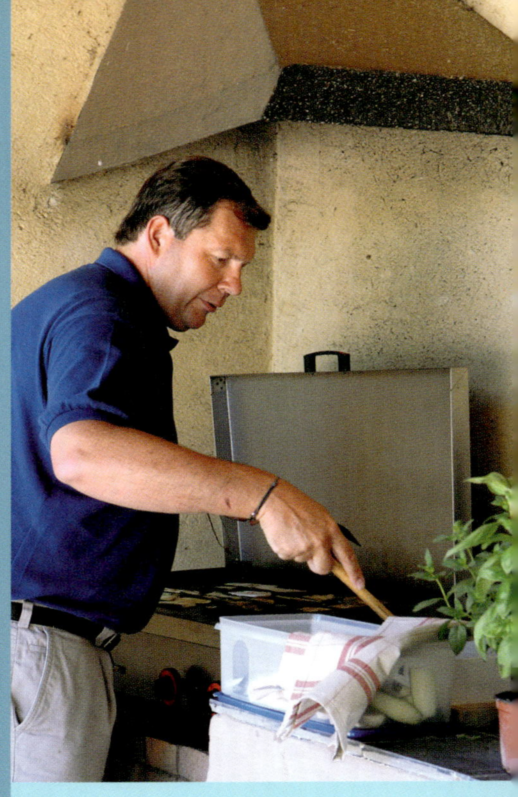

Côte de bœuf sauce béarnaise

Avec les beaux jours vient souvent le temps de la braise et des barbecues. C'est alors moi qui joue les grands chefs du dimanche. Je choisis une viande de qualité, tendre et goûteuse, et je l'accompagne d'une sauce béarnaise « maison ».

Préparation : 20 minutes

Cuisson : 30 minutes

Pour 4 personnes

1 côte de bœuf de 1 kg
sel de Guérande, poivre

Pour la sauce béarnaise
2 échalotes
4 cuillerées à soupe de vinaigre d'alcool
4 cuillerées à soupe de vin blanc
11 branches de cerfeuil
8 branches d'estragon
2 jaunes d'œufs
125 g de beurre demi-sel fondu et refroidi sans le petit lait
poivre

- Préparez la réduction de la béarnaise. Épluchez, lavez, et hachez finement les échalotes. Hachez le cerfeuil et l'estragon. Réunissez dans une petite casserole les échalotes, les trois quarts de l'estragon et du cerfeuil, le vinaigre et le vin blanc ; laissez réduire jusqu'à ce qu'il reste l'équivalent de 1 cuillerée à café de liquide. Filtrez au travers d'un chinois (petite passoire très fine) placé au-dessus d'un petit bol, afin de recueillir le jus, pressez pour récupérer tous les parfums.
- Faites cuire la côte de bœuf sur les braises du barbecue (15 minutes par livre, soit 30 minutes), en la retournant à mi-cuisson. Salez et poivrez.
- Environ 10 minutes avant la fin de la cuisson de la côte de bœuf, préparez la béarnaise. Dans une petite casserole, mélangez les jaunes d'œufs à la réduction filtrée, ajoutez 1 cuillerée à soupe d'eau froide et fouettez énergiquement sur feu très doux, en faisant des « 8 » avec le fouet. Lorsque la consistance est mousseuse et que vous apercevez le fond de la casserole à chaque mouvement de fouet, incorporez progressivement le beurre fondu. Fouettez l'ensemble pour obtenir une sauce onctueuse et consistante. Rectifiez l'assaisonnement et ajoutez le reste de l'estragon et du cerfeuil hachés.

Pour ne pas être stressé au dernier moment, préparez la réduction de la béarnaise bien à l'avance. Si la sauce est trop liquide ou si elle tourne, ajoutez 1 cuillerée d'eau froide ou un glaçon, et fouettez avec vigueur.

En remplaçant l'estragon et le cerfeuil par de la menthe, vous obtiendrez une sauce paloise qui accompagnera des brochettes d'agneau grillées ou du poisson.

Boissons conseillées : Pomerol, Corton, Hermitage rouge.

Préparation : 20 minutes

Cuisson : 15 minutes

Pour 4 personnes

300 g de comté
300 g de beaufort
300 g d'emmenthal français
45 cl de vin blanc de Savoie
1 cuillerée à soupe de jus de citron
3 cuillerées à café de Maïzena
1 gousse d'ail
10 cl de kirsch
1 bonne pincée de noix muscade râpée
2 baguettes de pain, bien cuites
poivre

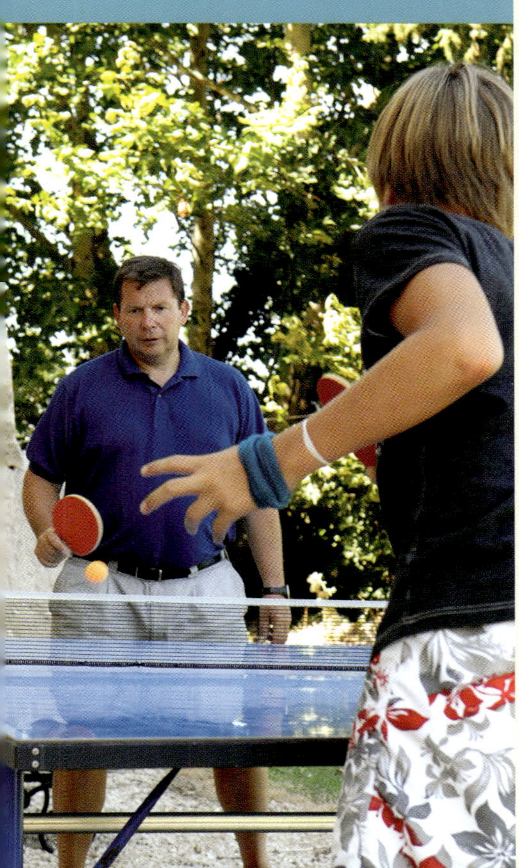

Fondue aux trois fromages

Choisissez de bons fromages et surtout ne les râpez pas : détaillez-les en petits dés, ils fondront plus lentement et s'amalgameront mieux.

- Coupez le pain en morceaux en veillant à ce que chacun d'eux ait un peu de croûte. Déposez-les dans une panière.
- Écroûtez les morceaux de fromage et coupez-les en petits dés.
- Pelez la gousse d'ail et frottez-en les parois et le fond du poêlon à fondue. Hachez le reste et mettez-le dans le poêlon. Ajoutez le vin blanc.
- Dans un verre, mélangez rapidement 3 cuillerées à soupe d'eau et la Maïzena, versez dans le poêlon. Commencez à faire chauffer à feu très doux.
- Déposez progressivement dans le caquelon les dés de fromage et mélangez régulièrement à la spatule en bois, jusqu'à ce que le fromage soit complètement fondu et constitue une masse homogène et onctueuse. Ajoutez la noix muscade, du poivre, le jus de citron et le kirsch. Laissez mijoter encore quelques minutes.
- Posez le caquelon sur le réchaud à fondue placé au centre de la table. Maintenez le feu aussi bas que possible. Chaque convive embrochera solidement un morceau de pain sur sa pique et le plongera dans la préparation, en faisant des « 8 » pour bien mélanger le fromage.

À la fin, cassez un œuf dans le fond du poêlon et mélangez pour récupérer les restes de fromage. Délicieux ! Accompagnez la fondue d'une salade verte. Vous pouvez aussi proposer du jambon de Savoie coupé très finement.

Vous pouvez remplacer le pain par des tomates-cerises ou de petits légumes pré-cuits.

Boissons conseillées : vin blanc de Savoie (type Apremont ou Roussette). Bien souvent, nous réservons l'Apremont à la préparation de la fondue et débouchons un Fendant suisse pour l'accompagner.

Ce dessert est toujours apprécié. Vous pouvez le servir accompagné d'une crème anglaise ou d'un coulis de fruits rouges.

Charlotte aux fraises

Préparation : 30 minutes Réfrigération : 5 heures Pour 6-8 personnes

36 biscuits à la cuillère
(les plus larges)
500 g de fraises (maras des bois)
40 cl de crème fraîche
15 cl de rhum brun ou blanc
2 blancs d'œufs
1 pincée de sel
3 cuillerées à soupe de sucre en poudre
3 cuillerées à soupe de confiture
de fraises sans morceaux
beurre
sucre cristallisé

• Commencez par confectionner la garniture de la charlotte. Équeutez, rincez et séchez les fraises ; réservez-en une douzaine (les plus belles) pour la décoration et coupez les autres en deux ou en quatre selon leur grosseur. Réservez-les.

• Montez les blancs en neige avec le sel. Fouettez la crème fraîche, puis ajoutez le sucre et la confiture de fraises ; mélangez. Incorporez délicatement les blancs en neige et les morceaux de fraises.

• Pour faciliter le démoulage ultérieur, beurrez légèrement l'intérieur du moule et saupoudrez les parois de sucre cristallisé. Jetez l'excédent de sucre.

• Dans une assiette à soupe, mélangez un fond d'eau tiède avec 1 cuillerée à soupe de rhum. Renouvelez ce mélange autant de fois que nécessaire.

• Trempez rapidement les biscuits sans les imbiber dans le liquide et tapissez-en le bord du moule à charlotte, en rapprochant bien les biscuits, côté bombé vers l'extérieur. Tapissez ensuite le fond du moule avec 2 couches de biscuits, en inversant le positionnement des biscuits sur la deuxième couche (comme un quadrillage) ; comblez les espaces vides par des morceaux de biscuits préalablement trempés dans le mélange eau-rhum.

• Versez la moitié de la garniture, couvrez d'une nouvelle couche de biscuits trempés, versez le reste de la garniture et terminez par une couche de biscuits. Posez une assiette à dessert sur le moule à charlotte et un poids (une boîte de conserve, par exemple) par-dessus, de manière à tasser le contenu. Placez au réfrigérateur pendant au moins 5 heures.

• Au moment de servir, placez le fond du moule dans de l'eau chaude pendant 2 minutes ; démoulez ensuite la charlotte sur le plat de service et décorez-la avec les fraises réservées.

Mieux encore... mélangez des framboises aux fraises et servez la charlotte avec un coulis de fruits rouges, ou bien remplacez la garniture aux fruits par une mousse au chocolat et ajoutez une crème anglaise.

Boisson conseillée : champagne.

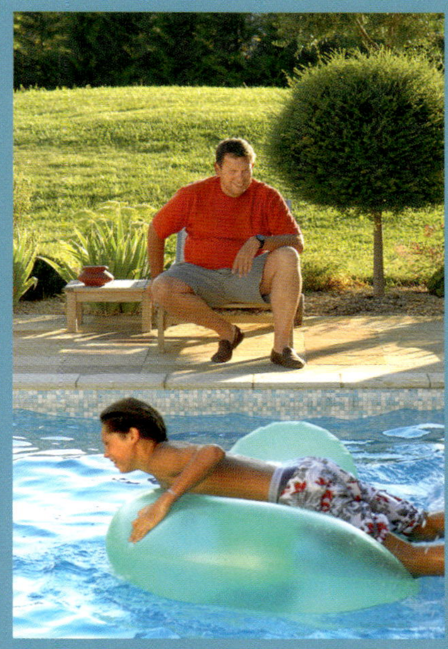
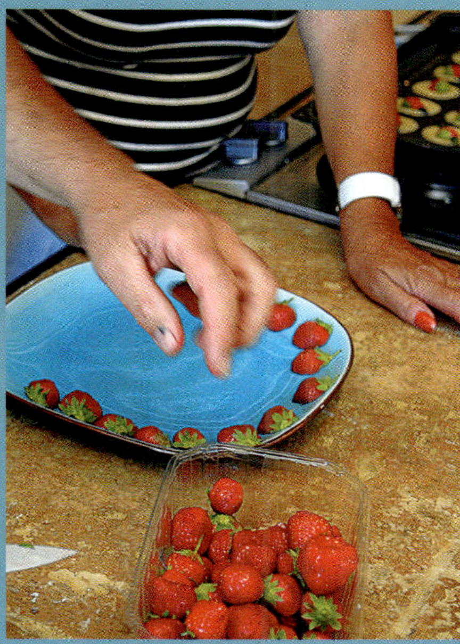
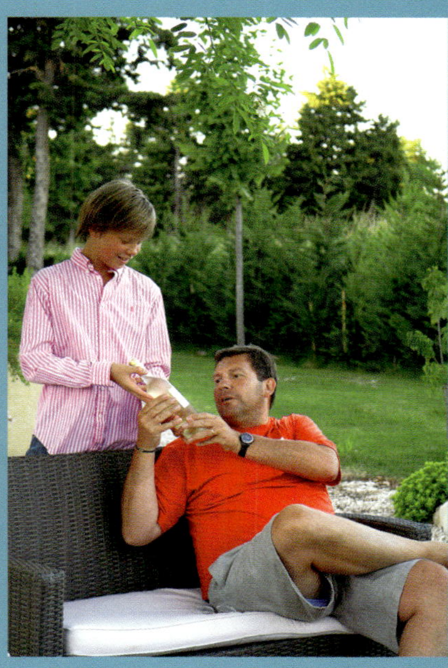

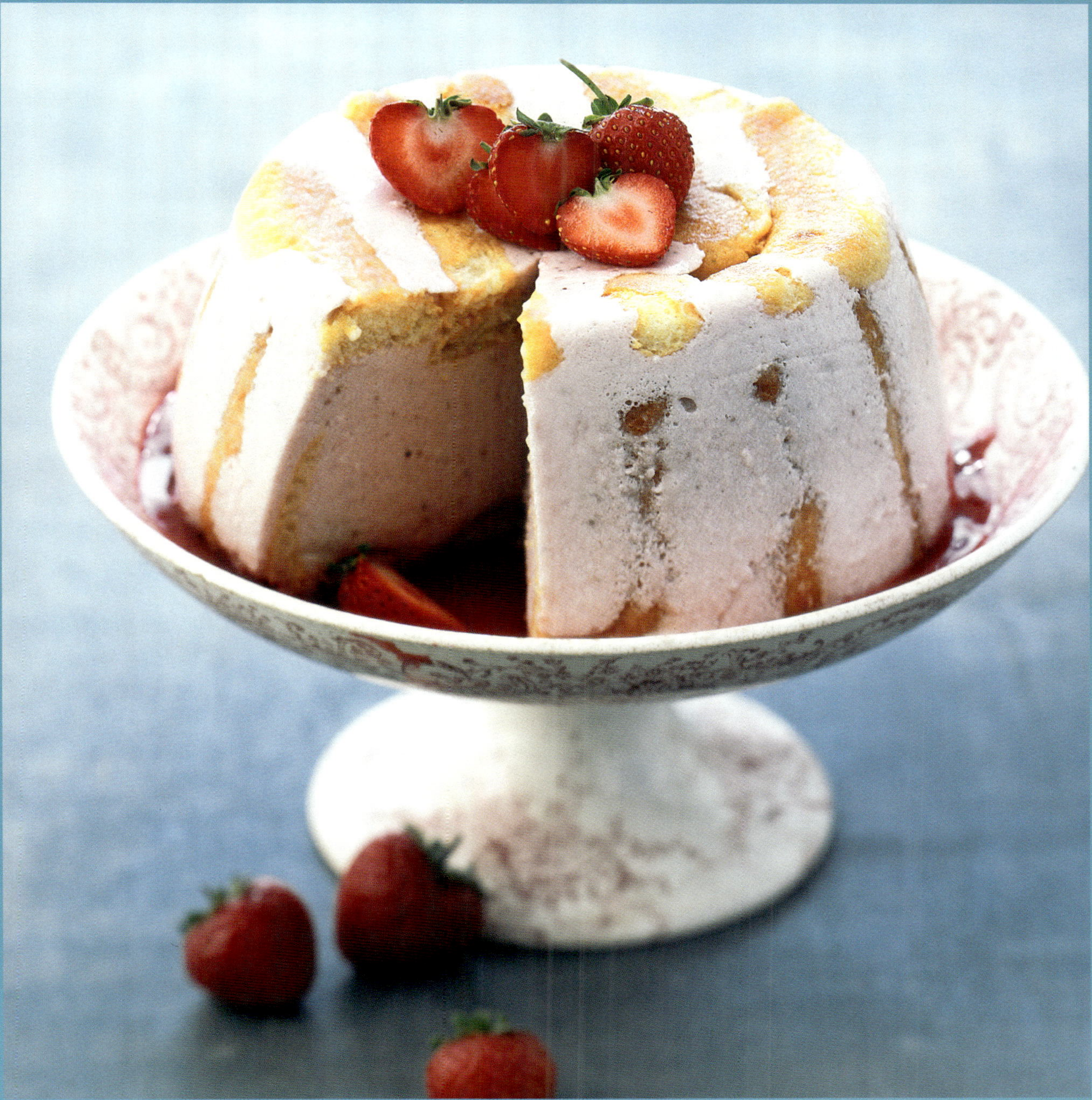

Nous aimons tous le riz au lait... aussi en avons-nous plusieurs versions. Essayez-les toutes et choisissez celle que vous préférez !

Trois versions d'un riz au lait maison

Préparation : 20 minutes Cuisson : 30 minutes Pour 6 personnes

150 g de riz rond
1 l de lait entier
3 jaunes d'œufs
60 g de sucre en poudre
1 gousse de vanille

Pour le riz au lait au chocolat blanc et aux pralines roses
100 g de chocolat blanc (chocolatier)
10 cl de crème fleurette
quelques miettes de pralines roses

Pour le riz au lait au caramel
200 g de sucre blanc

Pour le riz au lait à la crème de caramel
200 g de sucre blanc
10 cl de crème fleurette

- Lavez soigneusement le riz et égouttez-le. Mettez-le dans un récipient d'eau froide et portez-le à ébullition pendant 1 minute pour enlever l'amidon, puis rafraîchissez-le sous l'eau froide et égouttez-le.
- Fendez la gousse de vanille en deux et grattez l'intérieur pour récupérer les petites graines noires ; mettrez-les à infuser dans le lait avec la gousse. Portez à ébullition, puis ajoutez le riz et baissez le feu. Faites cuire environ 30 minutes en mélangeant régulièrement, afin que le riz ne colle pas au fond de la casserole. Le riz est cuit quand il est tendre (goûtez pour apprécier sa cuisson).
- Dans un bol, mélangez au batteur les jaunes d'œufs et le sucre. Vous obtenez une crème mousseuse jaune pâle. Hors du feu, ajoutez cette crème au riz, mélangez et versez dans de petits verres transparents ou de jolies tasses.
- *Pour le riz au chocolat blanc et aux pralines roses* : faites fondre le chocolat avec la crème fleurette. Versez au fond des verres, couvrez de riz au lait et décorez de miettes de pralines roses.
- *Pour le riz au lait au caramel :* préparez un caramel en faisant fondre le sucre dans 10 cl d'eau et laissez cuire jusqu'à obtention d'une jolie couleur caramel. Versez dans le fond des tasses ou d'une jatte et couvrez avec le riz au lait.
- *Pour le riz au lait à la crème de caramel :* préparez un caramel comme précédemment. Puis ajoutez-y la crème fleurette hors du feu et incorporez au riz au lait. Versez dans des verres ou des tasses.

Boisson conseillée : Sauternes.

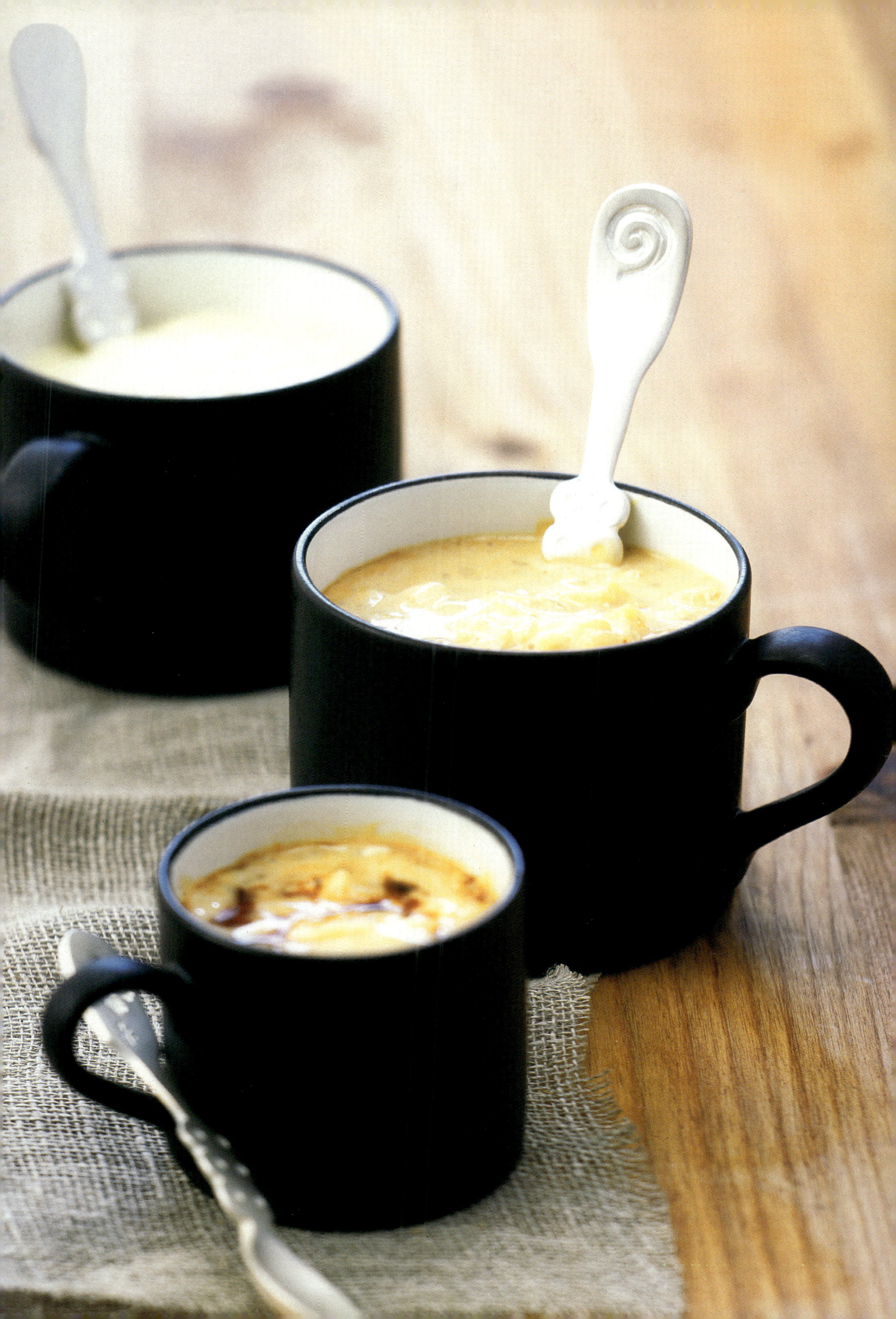

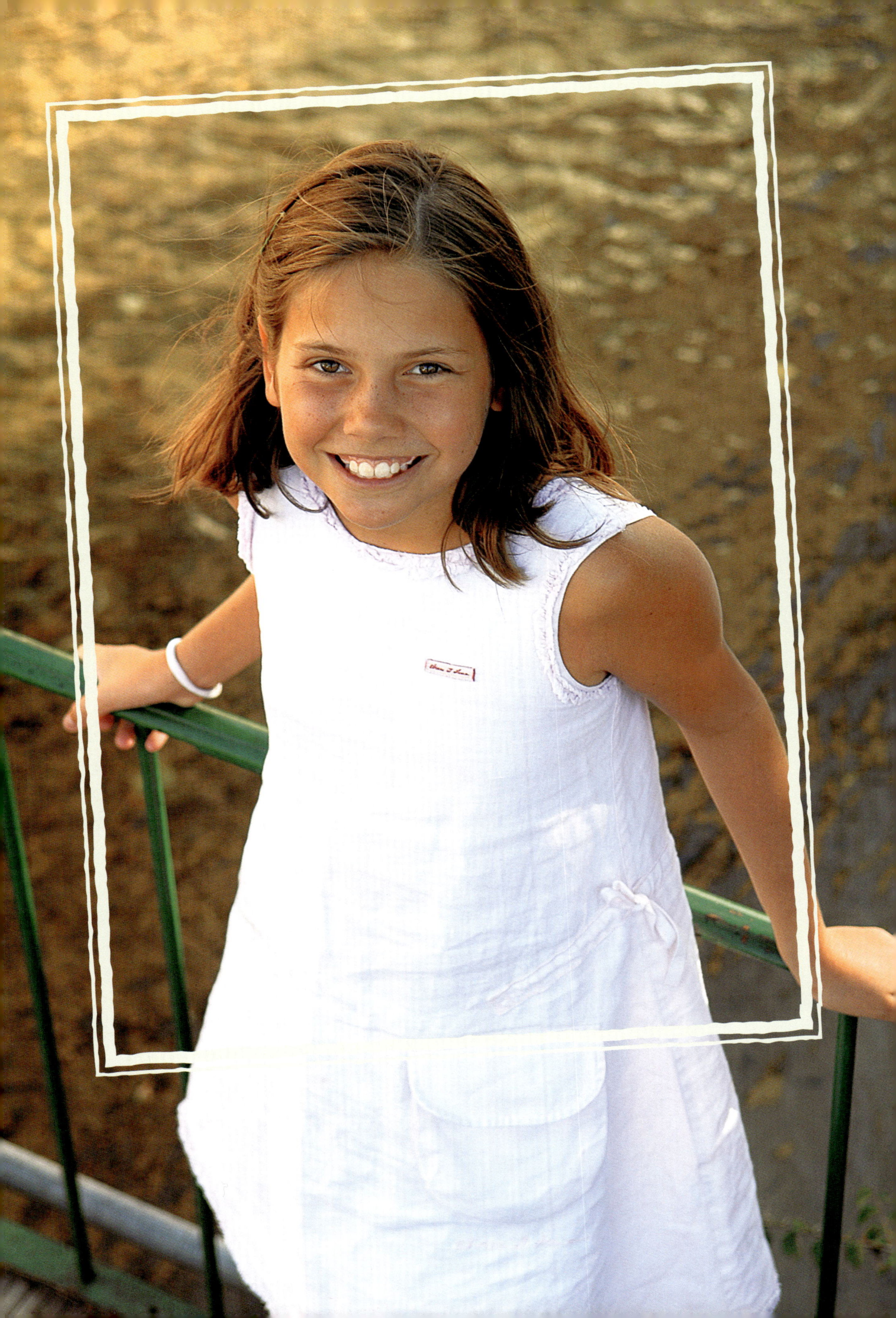

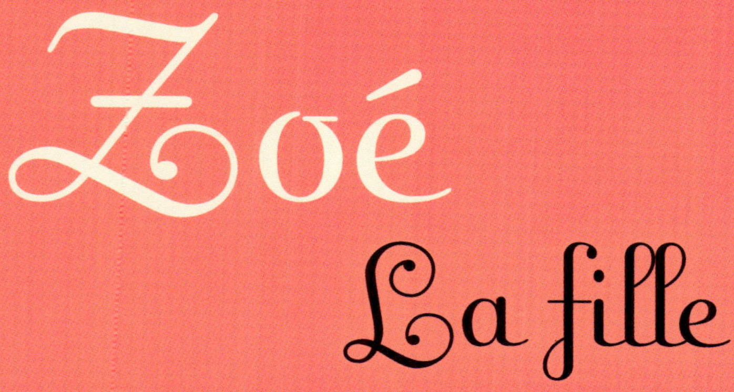

Si j'étais... une couleur,

je serais celle du chocolat comme les murs de ma nouvelle chambre,
moitié chocolat blanc et moitié chocolat au lait.

Si j'étais... une odeur,

je serais celle de la vanille qui rappelle mes meilleures vacances à l'Île de la Réunion,
mais également l'odeur de la crème anglaise.

Si j'étais... une saveur,

je serais celle de la crème chantilly, je remplirais une bombe
et je ferais une bataille avec mes cousines et mon frère dans le jardin.

Si j'étais... un ustensile,

je serais une poche à douille, avec laquelle je peux fabriquer avec précision
de jolies meringues aux formes amusantes.

Si j'étais... un souvenir gourmand,

je serais un chou garni de crème chantilly ;
le premier que j'ai mangé était si gros que j'en avais jusque sur le bout de mon nez ...

Si j'étais... un péché mignon,

je serais un financier, ma pâtisserie préférée depuis que je suis bébé.

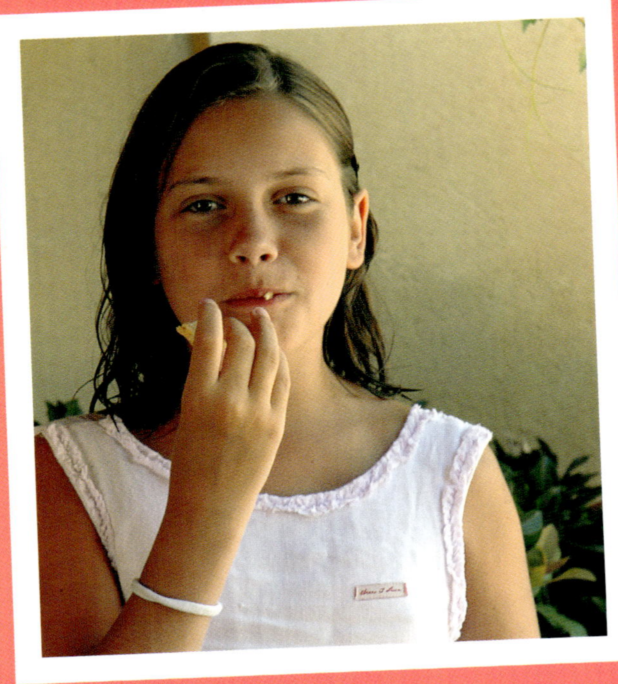

Je suis gourmande et j'aime préparer ces petites madeleines que je déguste à la sortie du four. Je les confectionne dans des mini-moules ; c'est plus joli et j'en ai plus pour moi.

Madeleines aux olives

Préparation : 15 minutes Cuisson : 12-15 minutes Repos : 1 heure Pour 4 personnes

180 g de farine
180 g de beurre
2 œufs
10 cl de lait
100 g d'olives noires et vertes, dénoyautées et hachées
1 cuillerée à café de levure chimique
1 pincée de sucre
1/2 cuillerée à café de poivre du moulin
1 pincée de sel

• Faites fondre le beurre et laissez-le refroidir. Fouettez les œufs dans un saladier avec le sel, le poivre et le sucre ; versez le lait, puis la farine et la levure. Incorporez le beurre, mélangez et ajoutez les olives. Laissez reposer 1 heure au frais.

• Préchauffez le four à 180 °C. Remplissez de pâte les moules à madeleines aux trois quarts. Cuisez dans le four pendant 12 à 15 minutes. Sortez les madeleines dès qu'elles ont une jolie couleur dorée et qu'elles sont bien gonflées.

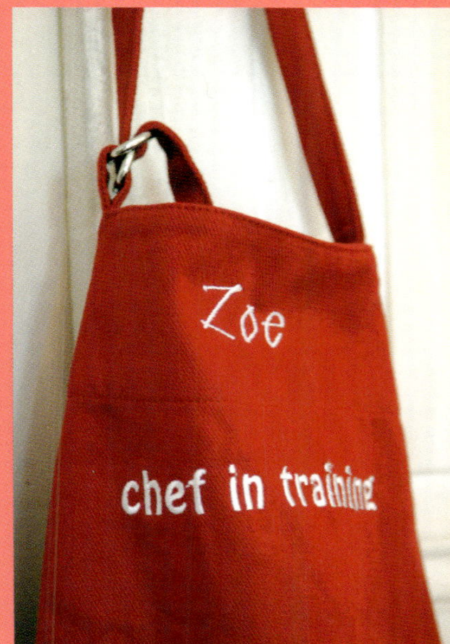
Zoe
chef in training

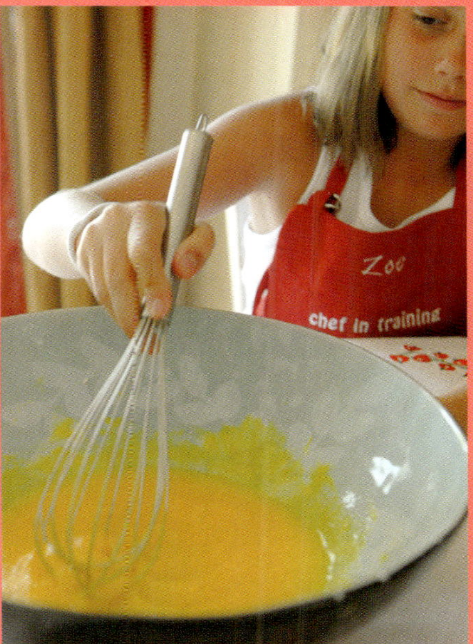
Zoe
chef in training

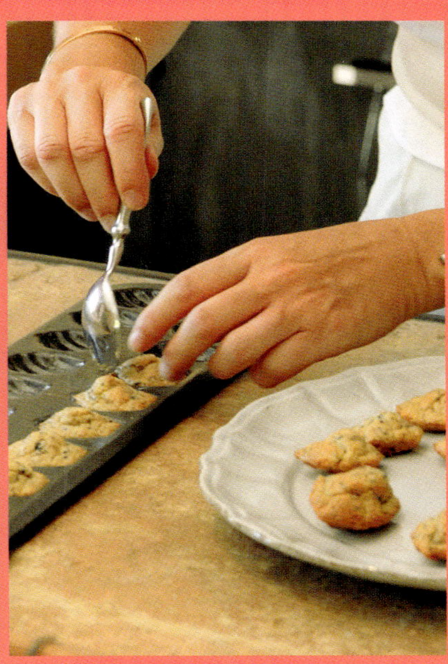

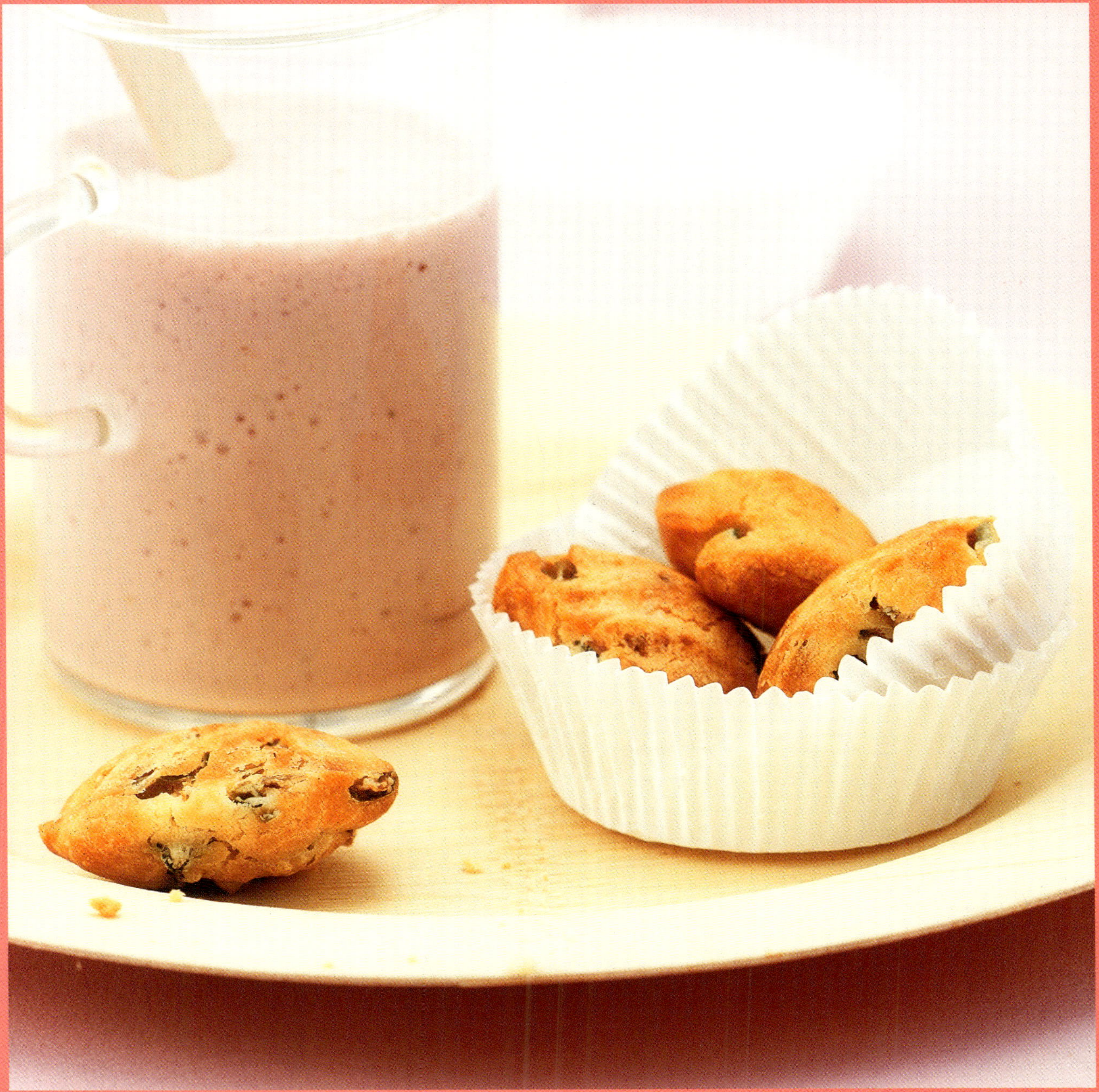

La période idéale pour manger des moules se situe entre juillet et janvier. Celles que je préfère sont les moules de bouchot. Achetées vivantes, elles doivent être fermées, et il faut les cuisiner dans les deux jours qui suivent l'achat. Elles sont vendues au litre, et l'on compte 1 l de moules par personne.

Moules à la normande

Préparation : 15 minutes Cuisson : 12-15 minutes Pour 4 personnes

4 l de moules
30 g de beurre
1 gros oignon
1 échalote
5 grosses cuillerées à soupe de crème fraîche épaisse
poivre

• Nettoyez les moules et lavez-les à l'eau froide. Pelez et hachez l'oignon et l'échalote. Faites fondre le beurre dans une grande marmite ou un faitout, ajoutez l'oignon et l'échalote, laissez revenir 1 minute.

• Ajoutez les moules, poivrez, remuez, couvrez. Secouez le faitout deux ou trois fois et remuez avec une cuillerée en bois. Lorsque toutes les moules sont ouvertes, ajoutez la crème fraîche, mélangez, laissez réduire la sauce quelques minutes. Servez immédiatement dans des assiettes à soupe.

S'il vous reste quelques moules, décoquillez-les, mixez-les avec le jus de cuisson, ajoutez un peu de crème fleurette ; vous obtiendrez ainsi une merveilleuse soupe de moules.

Remplacez la crème par du vin blanc pour confectionner des moules marinières. Vous pouvez aussi ajouter à la crème quelques pistils de safran ou une pincée de curry pour une recette plus exotique.

Boisson conseillée (pour les adultes) : muscadet.

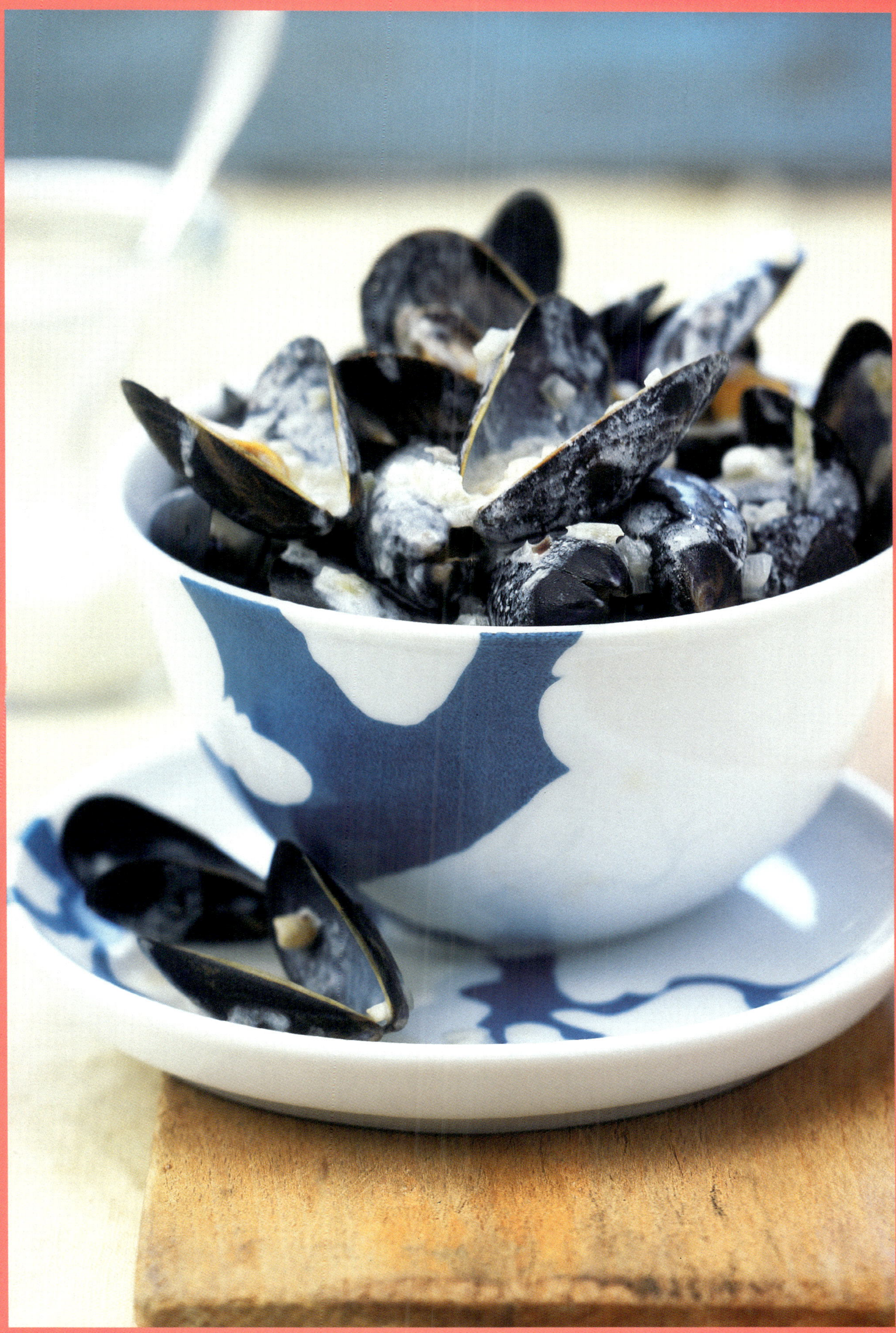

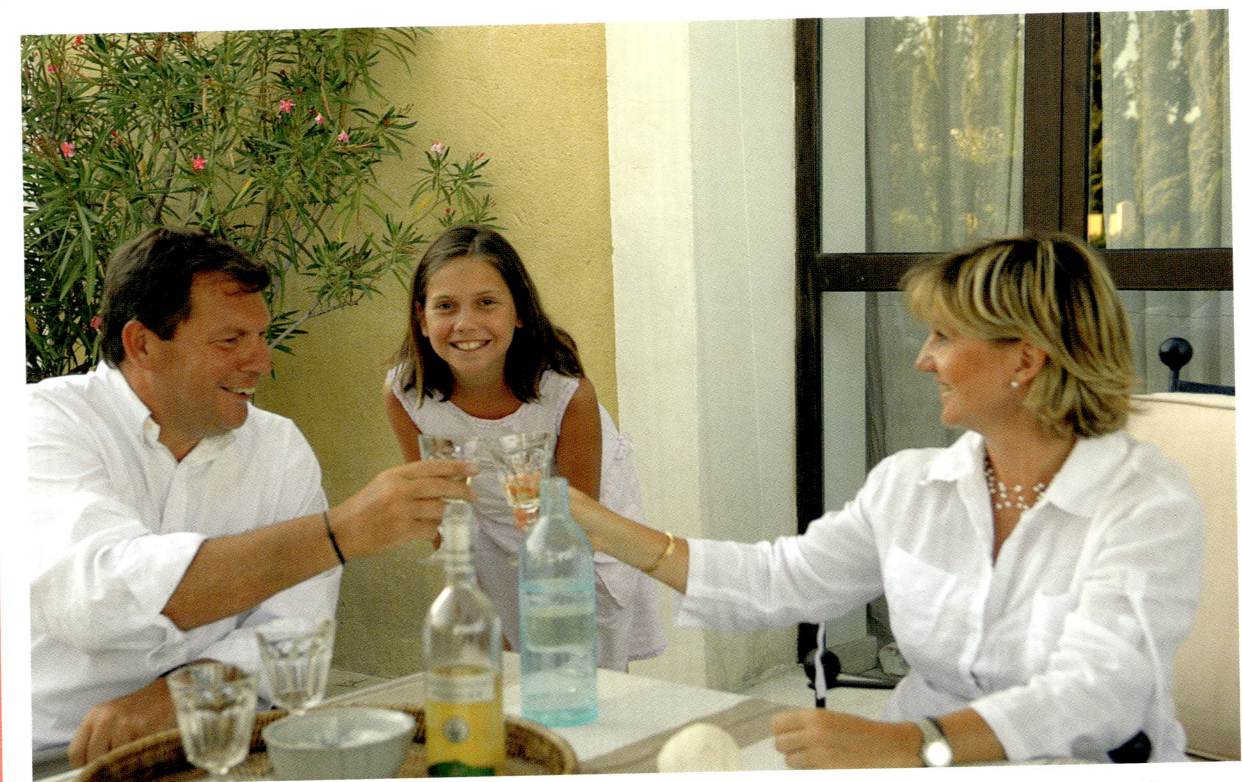

C'est mon plat préféré, et je demande à Maman de me le préparer chaque année pour mon anniversaire. Maman m'a donné sa recette, et comme finalement elle n'est pas bien compliquée, je crois que je vais les préparer moi-même pour en manger plus souvent.

Escalopes à la crème

Préparation : 20 minutes Cuisson : 20 minutes Pour 4 personnes

4 escalopes de veau
400 g de champignons
4 cuillerées à soupe de crème fraîche épaisse fermière
40 g de beurre
calvados pour les adultes (facultatif)
sel, poivre

- Épluchez les champignons en ôtant le bout terreux, lavez-les, séchez-les et coupez-les en lamelles. Faites fondre 20 g de beurre dans une poêle et faites-y revenir les champignons jusqu'à ce qu'ils soient bien dorés.
- Pendant ce temps, faites fondre le reste du beurre et mettez-y à cuire les escalopes salées et poivrées, jusqu'à ce qu'elles se colorent légèrement. Ajoutez les champignons, la crème fraîche, grattez le fond de la poêle pour décoller les sucs et laissez réduire la sauce pendant 2 minutes. Rectifiez l'assaisonnement en sel et poivre et servez aussitôt.

Servez avec la purée à tomber par terre de Zoé (voir recette page 65) !

Flambez les escalopes avec un peu de calvados, juste avant de mettre la crème.

Boisson conseillée (pour les adultes) : Satellite Saint-Émilion.

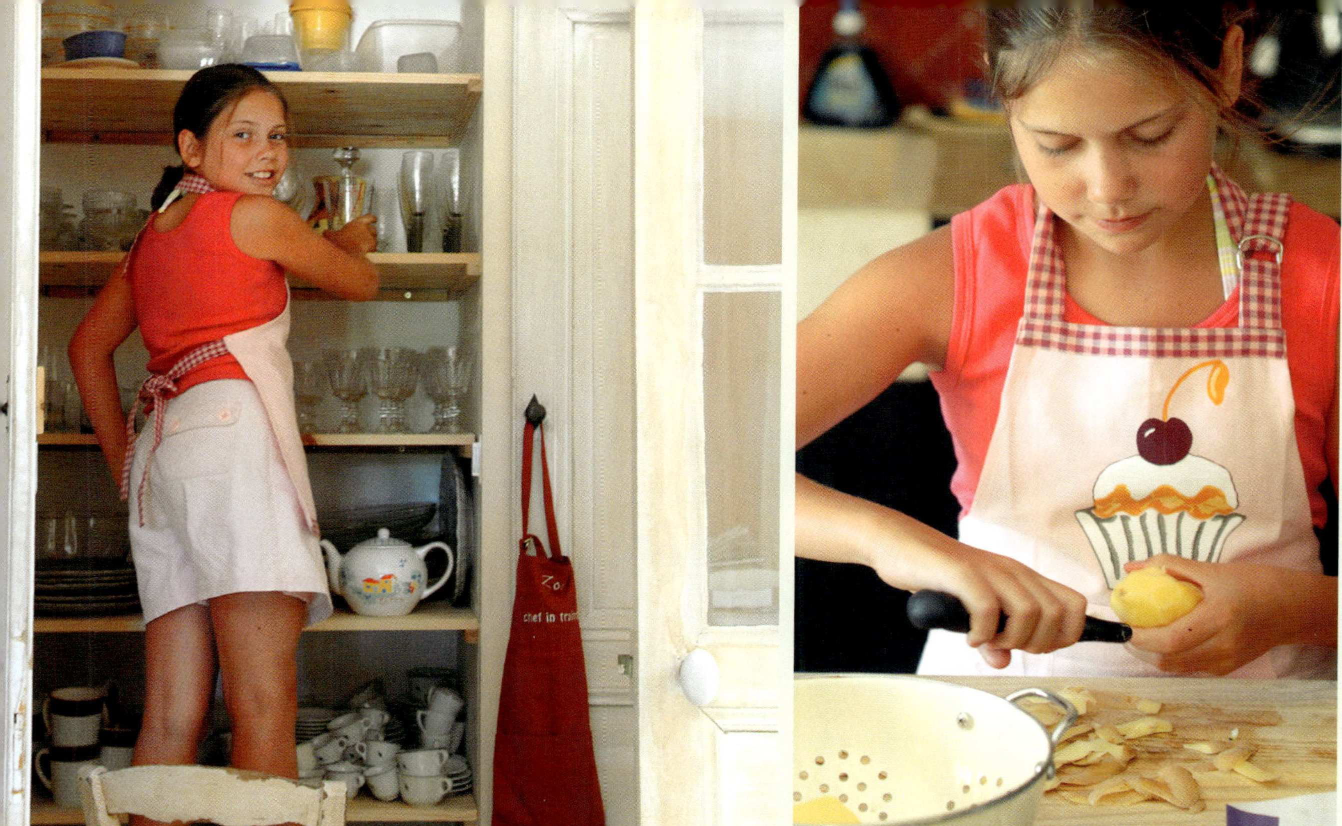

Préparation : 15 minutes

Cuisson : 30 minutes

Pour 4 personnes

1 kg de pommes de terre à purée
300 g de beurre coupé en morceaux
15 cl de lait
sel, poivre

Purée à tomber par terre

Je l'ai baptisée ainsi parce qu'elle est extraordinairement bonne. Mais si vous annoncez la quantité de beurre utilisée à vos invités, eux aussi risquent de tomber par terre !

- Épluchez et lavez les pommes de terre, coupez-les en dés, mettez-les dans une casserole d'eau froide salée et laissez-les cuire 20 à 25 minutes. Vérifiez avec la pointe d'un couteau qu'elles sont cuites.
- Chauffez le lait. Égouttez les pommes de terre, écrasez-les, encore chaudes, au presse-purée ou au moulin à légumes. Reversez dans la casserole, ajoutez la moitié du lait, mélangez au fouet, incorporez les parcelles de beurre en deux fois. Si la purée est trop épaisse, ajoutez du lait jusqu'à la consistance désirée.
- Salez et poivrez. Mélangez énergiquement avec un fouet pour incorporer de l'air. L'association air et beurre est le secret de la réussite de cette purée à la consistance si légère.

Si vous ne consommez pas la purée tout de suite, faites fondre un petit morceau de beurre à la surface et couvrez d'un film alimentaire en mettant celui-ci en contact avec la purée ; cela évitera à celle-ci de sécher. Donnez un ultime coup de fouet juste avant de servir.

J'adore le croustillant de la panure ! En plus, ces aiguillettes sont rapides à faire et sont bien meilleures quand on les mange avec les doigts...

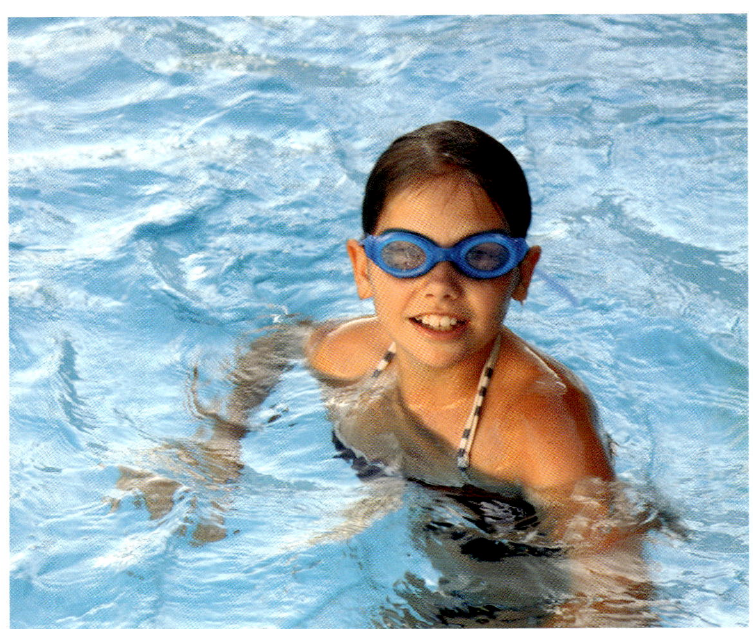

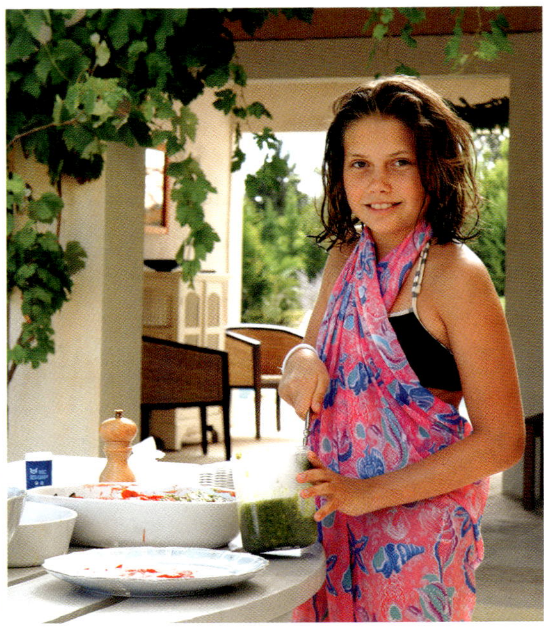

Aiguillettes de poulet pané

Préparation : 10 minutes Cuisson : 10 minutes Pour 4 personnes

12 aiguillettes de poulet
40 g de beurre
2 cuillerées à soupe d'huile
80 g de farine
2 œufs
300 g de chapelure
1 citron

- Dans une assiette, battez les œufs en omelette avec 1 cuillerée à soupe d'huile. Dans une autre assiette, mettez la farine. Dans une troisième assiette, versez la chapelure.
- Passez successivement les aiguillettes de poulet dans la farine, dans les œufs battus et dans la chapelure ; posez-les sur un plat.
- Faites fondre le beurre avec le reste de l'huile ; faites-y dorer les aiguillettes en surveillant bien la cuisson, car la chapelure se colore rapidement. Retournez la viande et faites cuire l'autre face. Assaisonnez en sel et poivre et servez avec des quartiers de citron.

Vous pouvez remplacer les aiguillettes de poulet par des escalopes de veau ou des filets de poisson.

Boissons conseillées (pour les adultes) : Mercurey, Pinot noir.

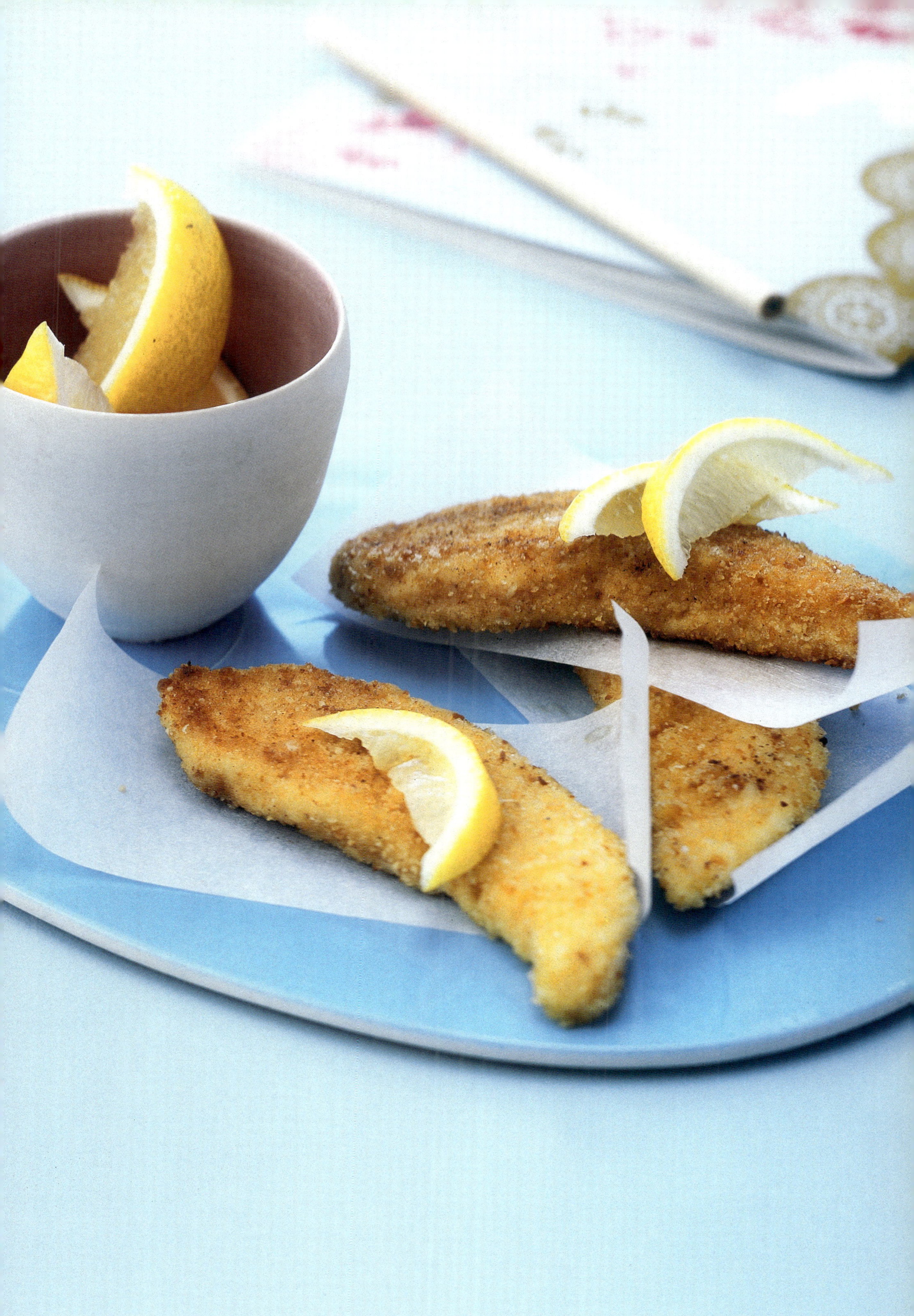

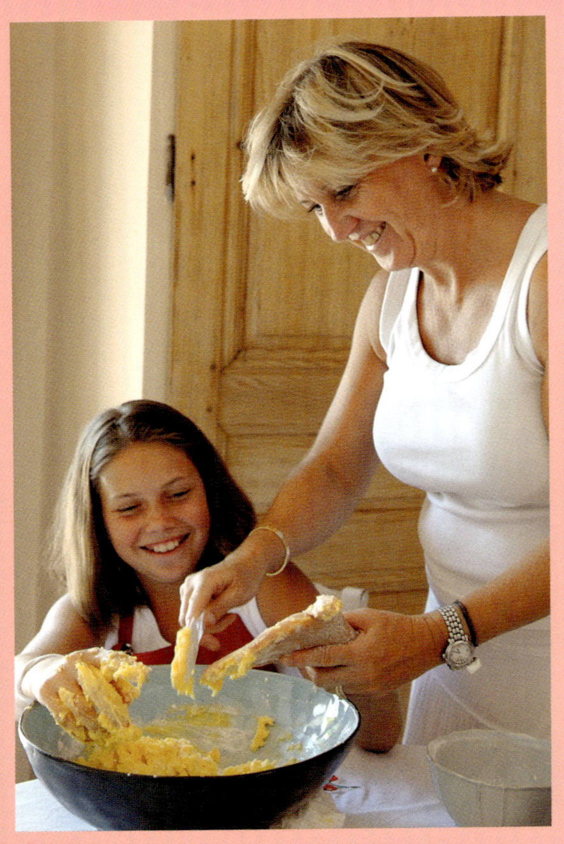

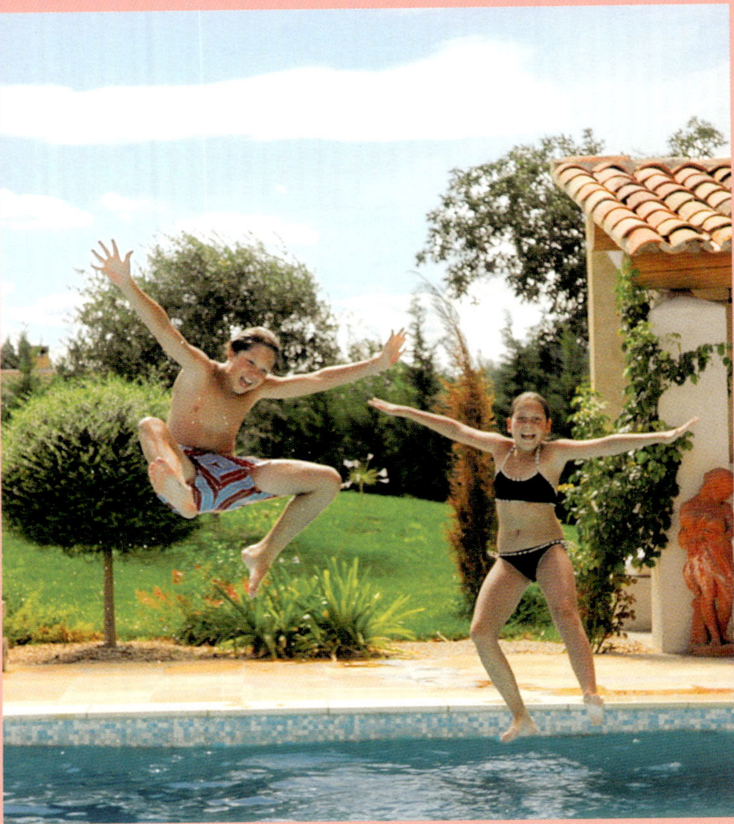

Nous utilisons beaucoup de jaunes d'œufs en cuisine, mais que faire des blancs ? À la maison, nous les congelons, et lorsqu'un goûter se profile à l'horizon, je les fais décongeler et prépare ces adorables meringues.

Mini-meringues

Préparation : 10 minutes Cuisson : 45 minutes Pour 6 personnes

3 blancs d'œufs
1 pincée de sel
175 g de sucre en poudre
20 g de farine
1/2 cuillerée à café de vinaigre

Pour la décoration
1 bombe de chantilly
1 barquette de framboises
quelques feuilles de menthe

- Montez les blancs en neige avec la pincée de sel, en ajoutant 110 g de sucre à mi-parcours. Lorsque les blancs sont bien montés, incorporez le reste du sucre, puis la farine et le vinaigre.
- Préchauffez le four à 180 °C. Posez un papier sulfurisé sur la plaque à pâtisserie. À l'aide d'une poche à douille (à défaut, utilisez une cuillère à café), déposez sur la plaque de petits tas réguliers de la préparation.
- Baissez la température à 150 °C et enfournez. Faites cuire 45 minutes.
- Laissez refroidir les meringues hors du four, puis décollez-les délicatement à l'aide d'une spatule. Déposez un peu de chantilly sur chaque meringue ; décorez avec une framboise et une petite feuille de menthe.

On peut aussi fabriquer une meringue géante (cuisson : 1 heure) et la recouvrir de la même manière de chantilly et de framboises.

Boissons conseillées (pour les adultes) : Minervois, Beaumes-de-Venise.

Petits sablés aux fraises et à la glace Tagada

Préparation : 10 minutes Repos : 2 heures Congélation : 2 heures Cuisson : 12-15 minutes Pour 6 personnes

250 g de fraises lavées et équeutées

Pour la glace Tagada
20 fraises Tagada
20 cl de crème fleurette

Pour les sablés
125 g de farine,
plus 20 g pour le plan de travail
125 g de beurre,
plus 20 g pour la plaque
125 g de sucre
5 jaunes d'œufs

- Préparez la glace. Faites fondre les bonbons dans 15 cl de crème fleurette. Laissez refroidir et versez dans 6 tout petits verres. Mettez au congélateur pendant 2 heures.
- Préparez la pâte à sablés. Mélangez le sucre et 4 jaunes d'œufs, ajoutez le beurre ramolli et la farine. Amalgamez, roulez en boule et laissez reposer pendant 2 heures.
- Préchauffez le four à 180 °C. Sur un plan de travail fariné, aplatissez la pâte sur 5 mm d'épaisseur environ. Découpez-y des formes à l'aide d'emporte-pièces amusants ou tout simplement d'un verre. Posez les sablés sur la plaque à pâtisserie beurrée.
- Dans un petit bol, mélangez le dernier jaune d'œuf à la fourchette. Badigeonnez-en les sablés avec un pinceau. Enfournez 12 à 15 minutes. Surveillez la cuisson.
- Sortez les sablés du four ; ils vont durcir en refroidissant. Décorez-les de fraises et dégustez avec la glace Tagada.

Boissons conseillées : liqueur de fraise des bois (pour les adultes), grenadine (pour les enfants).

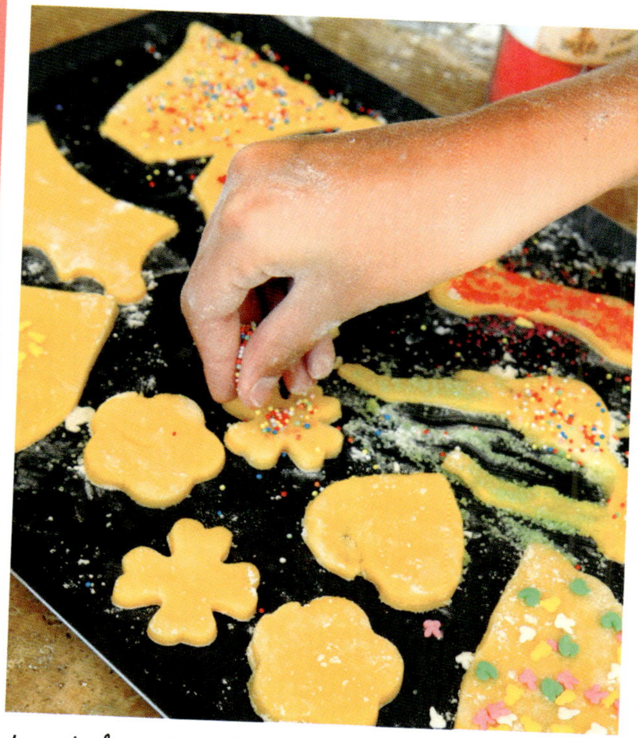

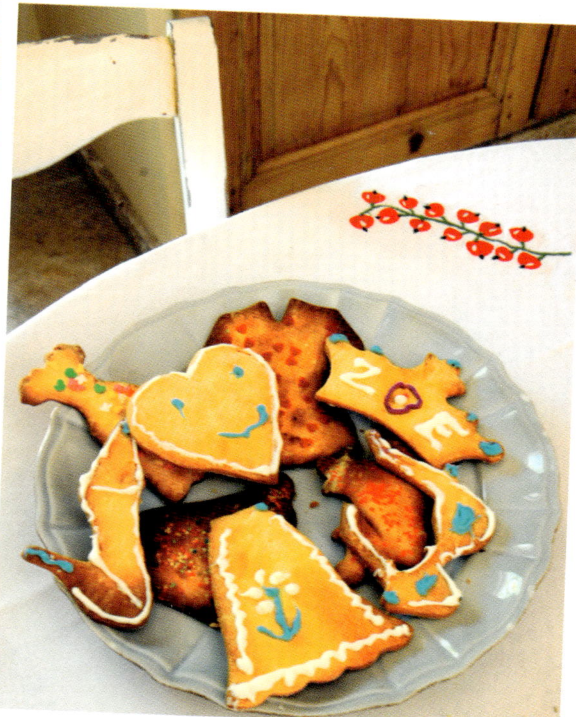

Je suis la reine des sablés, et toutes les occasions sont bonnes pour fabriquer ces petits gâteaux au goût de beurre, que j'adore manger avec de la glace aux fraises Tagada. On peut leur ajouter quelques bonbons pour en faire des bonshommes rigolos.

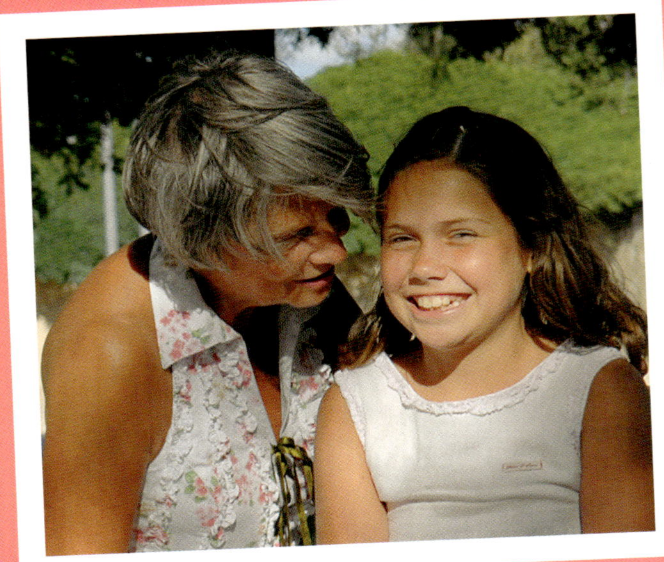

Ne soyez pas découragé par la longueur de la recette… Le résultat vaut vraiment la peine !

Chouchoux chantilly

Préparation : 1 heure Cuisson : 30 minutes Pour 8 personnes

beurre pour la plaque
1 œuf pour la dorure
sucre glace pour la finition

Pour la pâte à choux
25 cl d'eau
5 g de sel
10 g de sucre semoule
80 g de beurre
125 g de farine
4 œufs

Pour la chantilly à la vanille
60 cl de crème liquide froide
40 g de sucre glace
quelques gouttes d'extrait de vanille

- Préparez la pâte à choux. Dans une casserole, réunissez l'eau, le sel, le sucre et le beurre découpé en parcelles. Portez à ébullition pour faire fondre le beurre. Hors du feu, ajoutez la farine en une fois. Mélangez vigoureusement avec une cuillère en bois. Reposez la casserole sur le feu et laissez dessécher la pâte quelques secondes, jusqu'à ce qu'elle n'adhère plus à la casserole. Retirez du feu, versez dans un saladier et ajoutez les œufs un par un.
- Préchauffez le four à 200 °C. Beurrez légèrement une plaque de cuisson. Avec une poche à douille (à défaut, utilisez deux petites cuillères), déposez sur la plaque de petits tas de pâte en quinconce. Espacez-les suffisamment pour laisser aux choux la place de gonfler correctement. Égalisez le dessus des choux, en appuyant légèrement avec le dos d'une fourchette trempée dans de l'eau, puis badigeonnez-les d'œuf battu à l'aide d'un pinceau. Faites-les cuire au four 25 à 30 minutes, puis déposez-les sur une grille pour qu'ils refroidissent.
- Pendant ce temps, confectionnez la chantilly. Versez la crème dans un récipient froid. Ajoutez quelques gouttes d'extrait de vanille. Fouettez jusqu'à ce que le mélange soit consistant, ajoutez le sucre glace et fouettez à nouveau pendant quelques secondes.
- Coupez un chapeau aux choux refroidis, remplissez ceux-ci de chantilly à l'aide d'une poche à douille cannelée, en faisant légèrement déborder la crème. Replacez les chapeaux, saupoudrez de sucre glace. Conservez dans une pièce fraîche en attendant de déguster.

La pâte à chou doit être utilisée immédiatement ; ne la préparez pas trop longtemps à l'avance. Ces choux sont encore plus délicieux nappés de quelques gouttes de caramel au beurre salé…

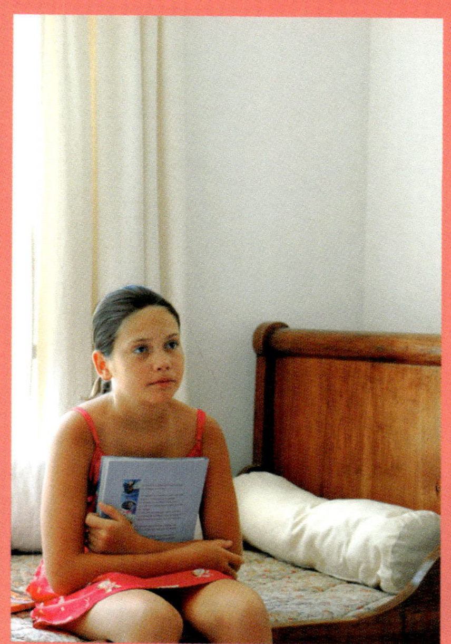

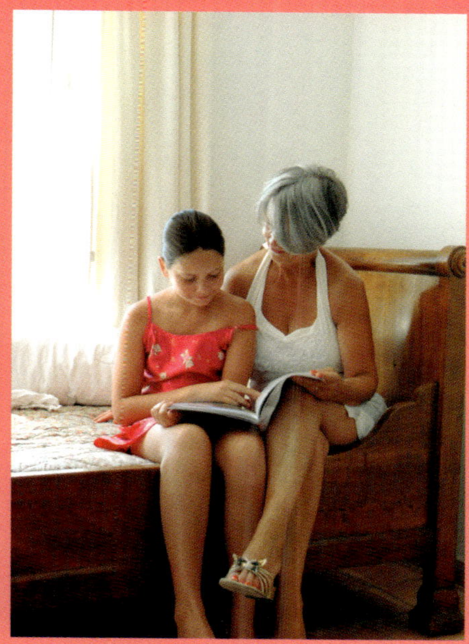

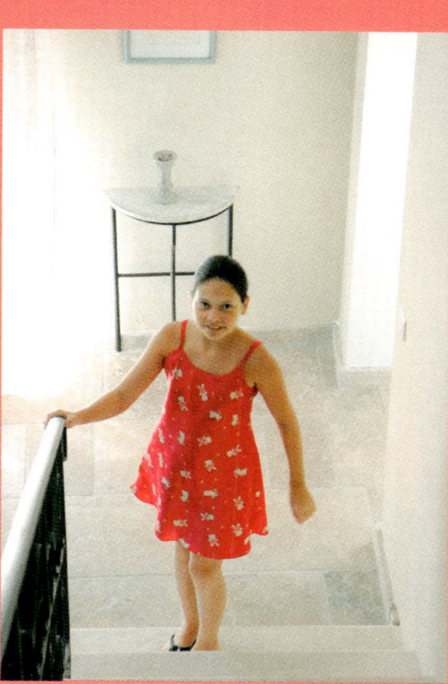

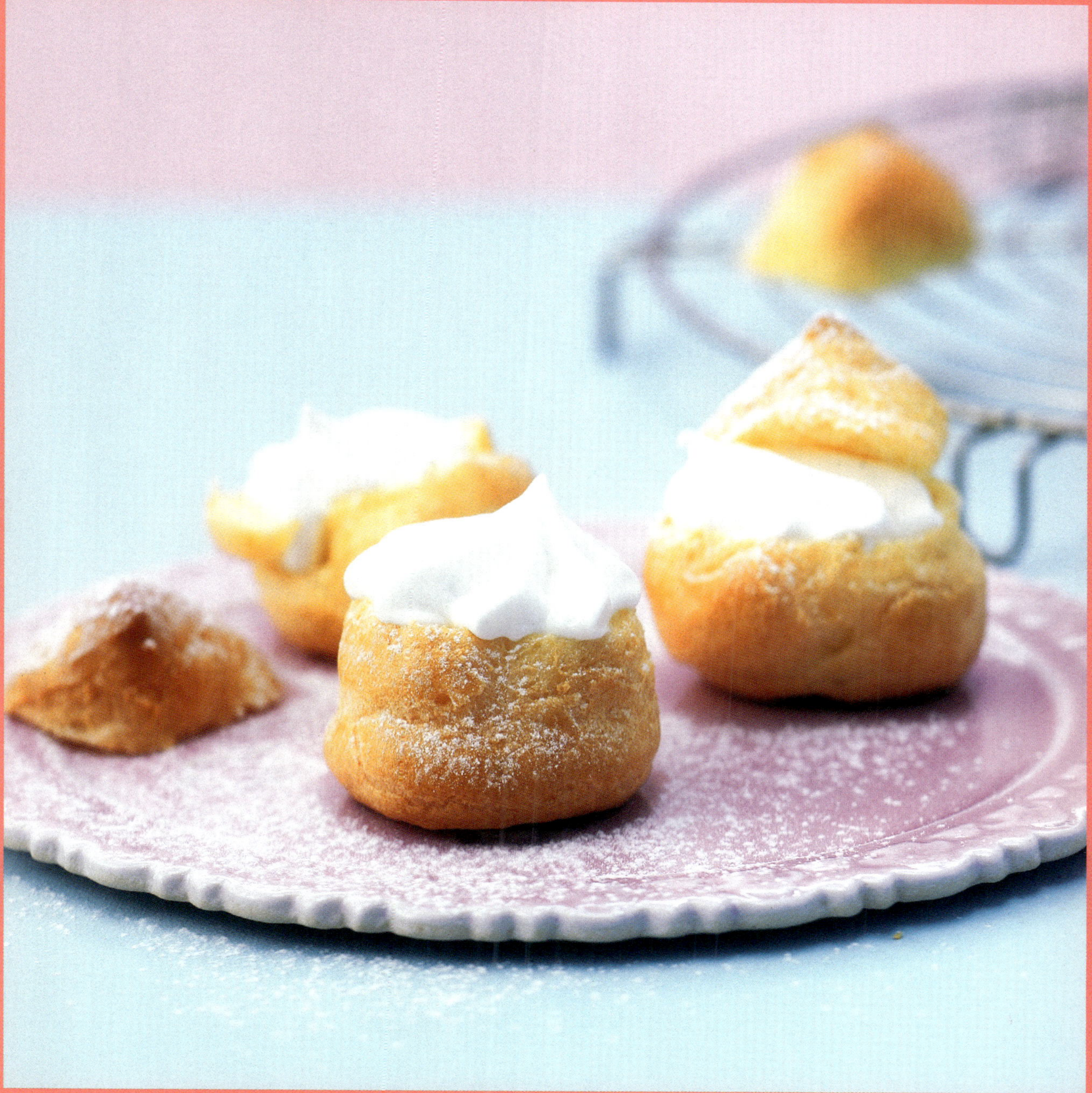

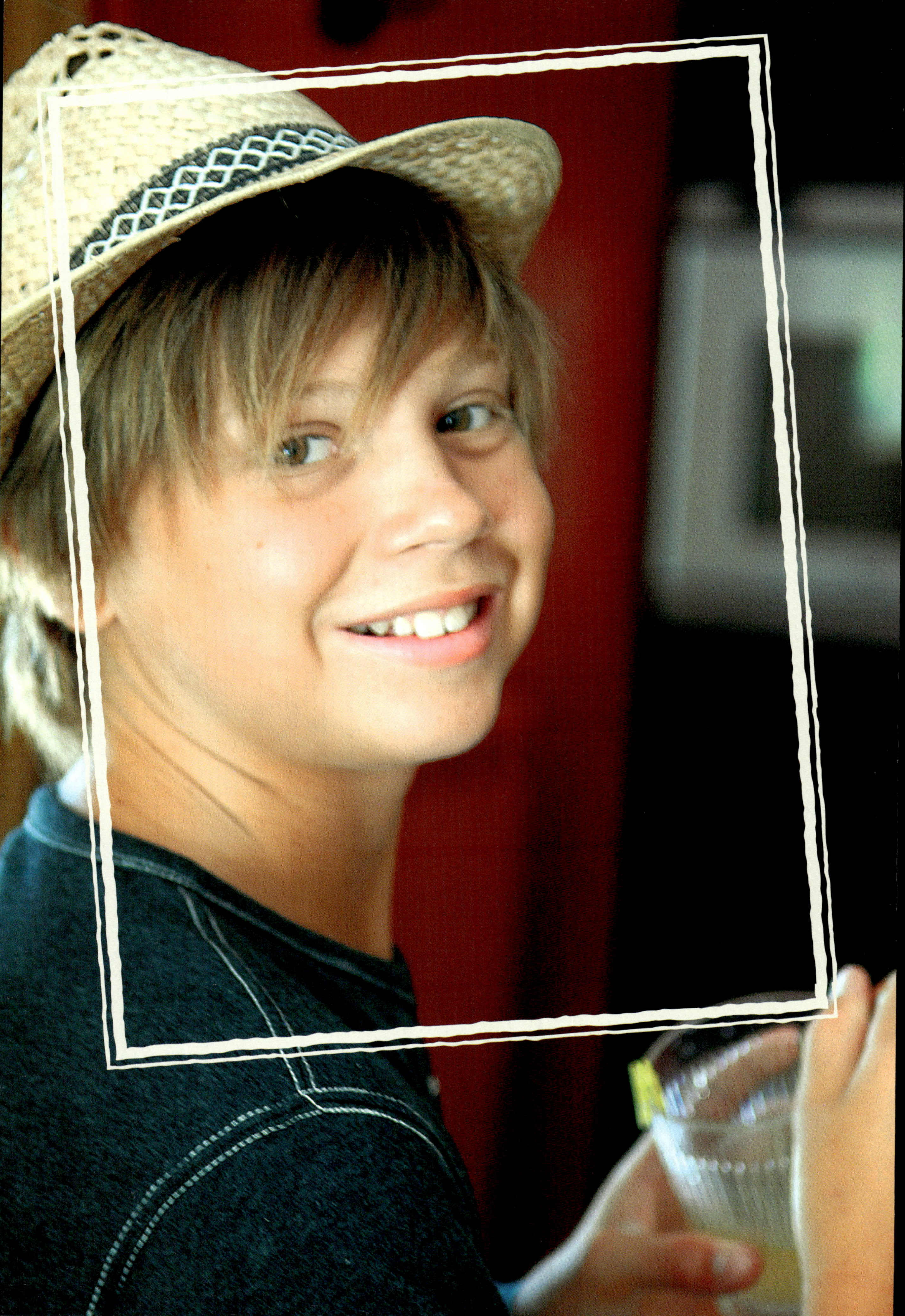

Arthur

Le fils

Si j'étais... une couleur,

je serais celle du citron comme les citronnades dont je raffole, avec de la limonade ou de l'eau.

Si j'étais... une odeur,

je serais celle d'un moelleux au chocolat chaud à la croûte fine et craquante sur le dessus et tout moelleux à l'intérieur.

Si j'étais... une saveur,

je serais celle d'un carré de chocolat, à cause de Maman qui m'a communiqué son faible pour la vache violette !

Si j'étais... un ustensile,

je serais une Cocotte-minute. Comme elle je suis plein d'énergie, je m'énerve rapidement, je deviens tout rouge, et la vapeur me sort par les oreilles...

Si j'étais... un souvenir gourmand,

je serais un plat de crevettes roses. J'adore en décortiquer plusieurs à l'avance, avant de les engloutir sur une tartine de pain et de beurre salé.

Si j'étais... un péché mignon,

je serais du fromage et je me glisserais dans l'assiette de ma sœur, juste pour l'embêter car elle déteste ça... alors que moi j'adore !

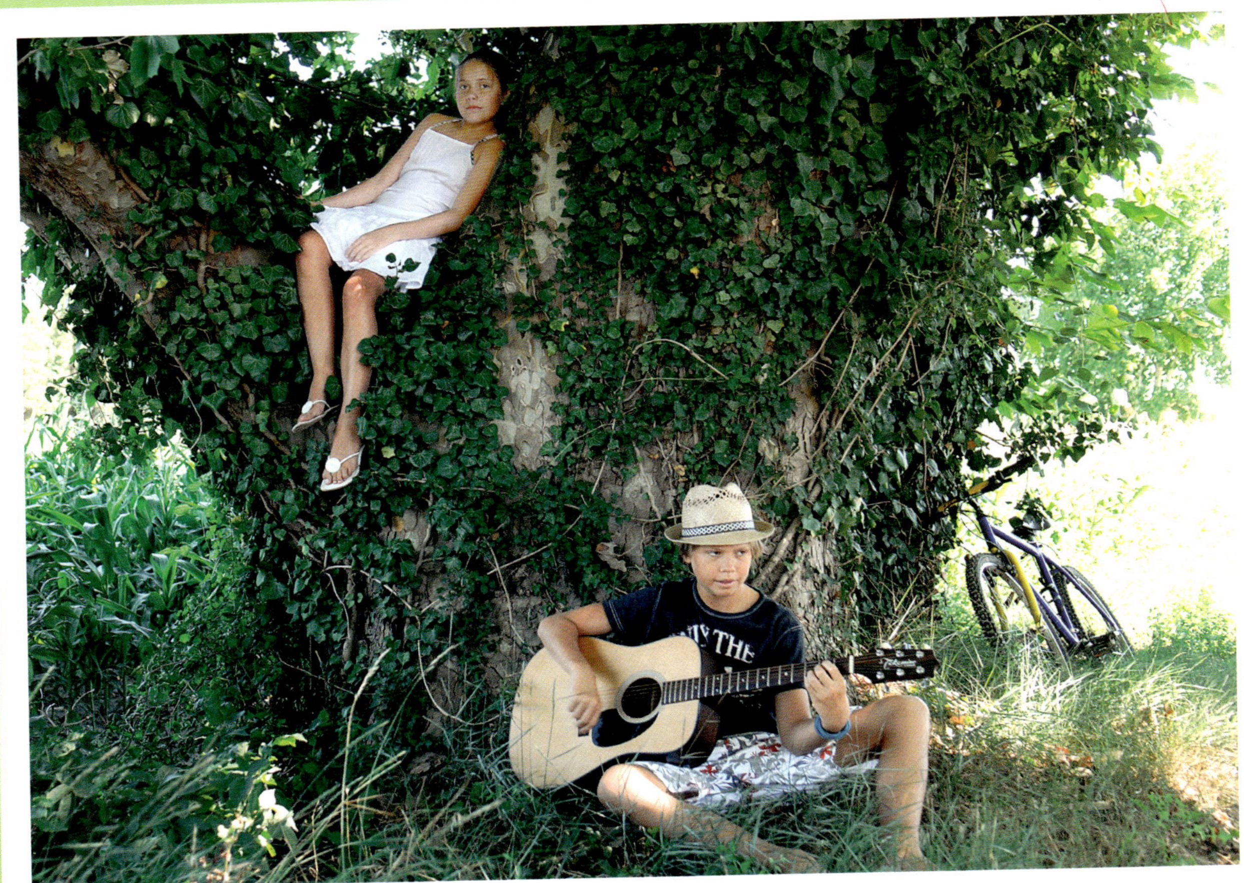

J'ai 14 ans... l'âge des boums et des dîners de copains de classe. Pour changer des pizzas quand on se réunit entre ados, ces mini-cakes sont super sympas !

Mini-cakes au jambon

Préparation : 30 minutes Cuisson : 30-40 minutes Pour 6 personnes

4 œufs
180 g de farine
1 sachet de levure
1 verre de lait chaud
1 verre de vin blanc
150 g de gruyère râpé
4 ou 5 tranches de jambon blanc
100 g de lardons allumettes fumés
100 g d'olives noires ou vertes dénoyautées
sel, poivre

- Préchauffez le four à 200 °C. Coupez le jambon en petits morceaux et hachez les olives. Passez les lardons 5 minutes à la poêle avec 1 cuillerée à soupe de vin blanc.
- Dans une jatte, mélangez avec un fouet les œufs, la farine et la levure. Ajoutez progressivement le lait chaud et le reste du vin blanc. Terminez par le gruyère râpé, le jambon, les lardons et les olives, salez et poivrez.
- Versez dans des mini-moules à cake et faites cuire au four pendant 30 à 40 minutes. Démoulez et laissez refroidir avant de couper en tranches.

Vous pouvez confectionner toutes sortes de mini-cakes à partir de la même base, en y mettant ce qui vous tombe sous la main : cheddar, chèvre ou mozzarella, poulet, chorizo, estragon, basilic, tomates confites, pesto...

Quiche lorraine

Préparation : 45 minutes
Cuisson : 30 minutes
Pour 6 personnes

1 abaisse de pâte brisée maison (voir recette page 28)
ou une pâte toute prête
beurre pour le moule

Pour la garniture
250 g de lardons fumés
10 cl de vin blanc
200 g d'emmenthal râpé
2 œufs entiers
2 jaunes d'œufs
25 cl de lait
25 cl de crème fleurette
sel, poivre
1 pointe de piment de Cayenne

Quand je dois apporter un plat pour un buffet chez des copains, je préfère que ce soit une quiche lorraine plutôt que le traditionnel gâteau au chocolat.

- Mettez les lardons et le vin blanc dans une casserole, laissez cuire 10 à 12 minutes, égouttez les lardons.
- Préchauffez le four à 180 °C. Dans une jatte, mélangez les œufs entiers et les jaunes avec la crème et le lait, assaisonnez en sel, poivre et piment de Cayenne.
- Beurrez votre moule à tarte. Avec un rouleau à pâtisserie, étalez la pâte aux dimensions du moule. Déposez la pâte dans le moule, piquez-la avec une fourchette. Répartissez les lardons dessus, ajoutez le fromage râpé, puis versez la préparation aux œufs. Enfournez pendant 30 minutes.

Vous pouvez remplacer les lardons par des dés de jambon blanc.

Boissons conseillées (pour les adultes) : Saint-Nicolas de Bourgueil, Marange rouge.

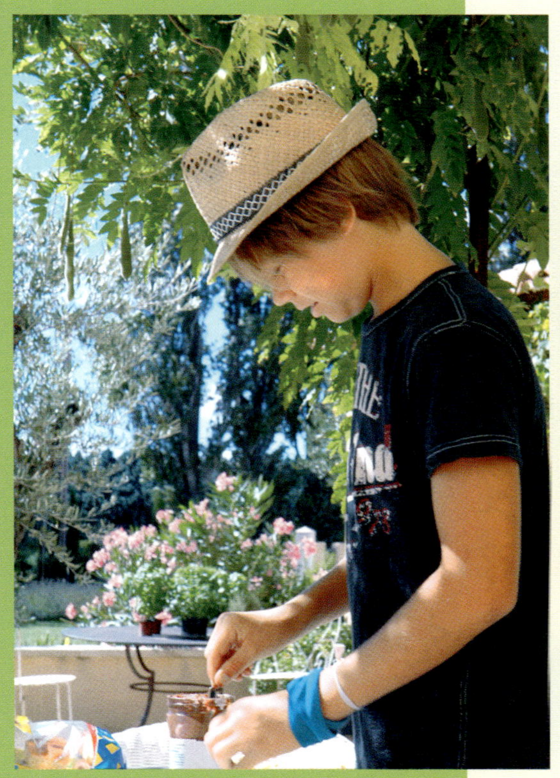

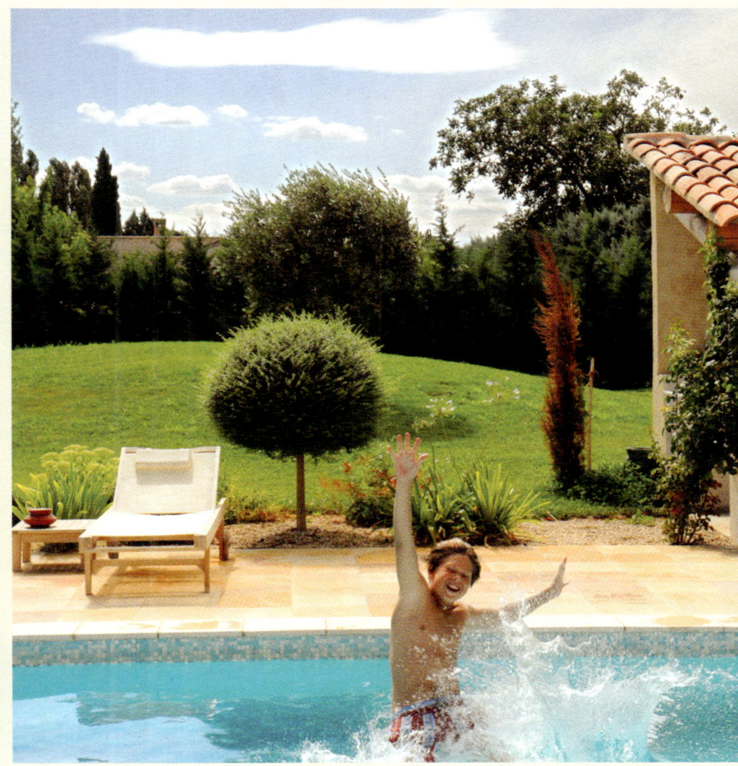

C'est mon plat préféré, et je vous livre ici mon secret de fabrication. Il n'y en a jamais assez… et mes parents doivent se battre pour que je leur en laisse un peu.

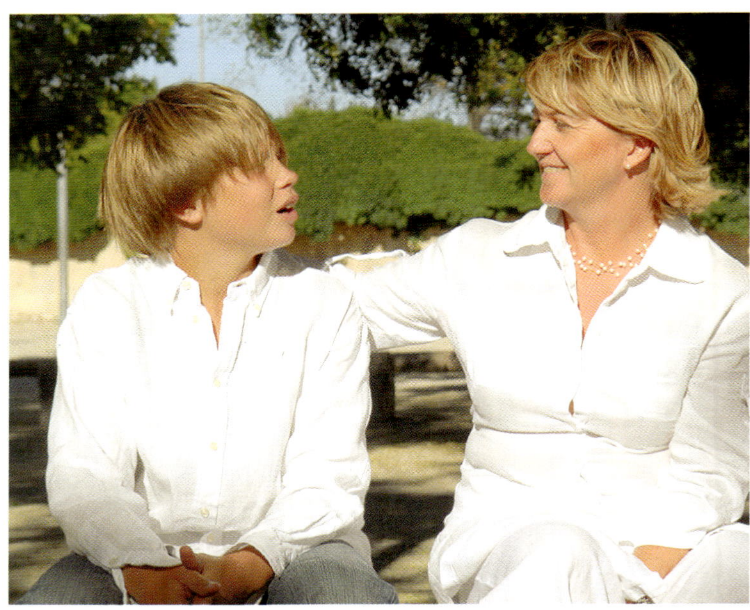

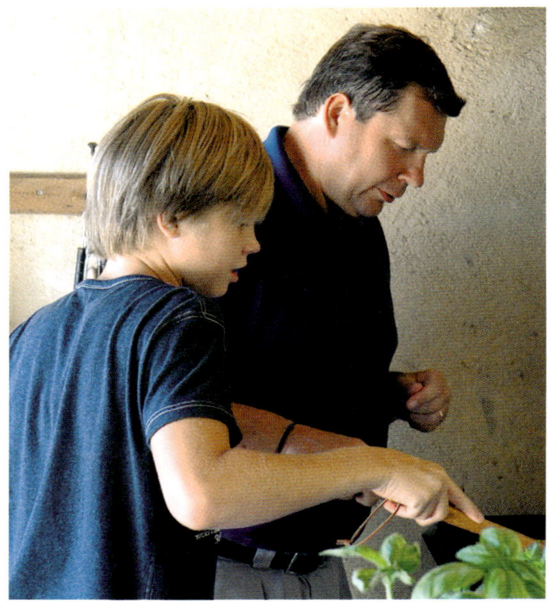

Coquillages farcis

Préparation : 30 minutes Cuisson : 20 minutes Pour 6 personnes

36 praires
ou 18 coquilles Saint-Jacques
48 pétoncles ou 60 palourdes
24 moules d'Espagne
1 à 2 cuillerées à soupe de chapelure

Pour la farce

2 échalotes
2 gousses d'ail
1 bouquet de persil plat
250 g de beurre demi-sel ramolli
poivre

- Pelez l'échalote et l'ail. Hachez-les avec le persil équeuté. Mélangez avec le beurre ramolli, poivrez.
- Lavez les coquillages à l'eau courante pour enlever toute trace de sable. Posez praires, palourdes et moules dans un plat à gratin, mettez-les au four à 200 °C pendant 5 minutes pour les faire bâiller. Ouvrez les coquillages avec un couteau et laissez les mollusques dans une demi-coquille.
- Préchauffez le four à 180 °C. Répartissez la farce sur les coquillages, saupoudrez légèrement de chapelure et enfournez 15 à 20 minutes. Dégustez de suite.

Vous pouvez préparer vos coquillages quelques heures à l'avance pour n'avoir qu'à les faire cuire au dernier moment ; dans ce cas, protégez-les avec un film alimentaire et conservez-les au frais.

Ajoutez des amandes, des noix ou des pistaches hachées pour donner un peu de croustillant à vos coquillages farcis.

Boissons conseillées (pour les adultes) : cidre brut ou doux, Muscadet-sur-lie.

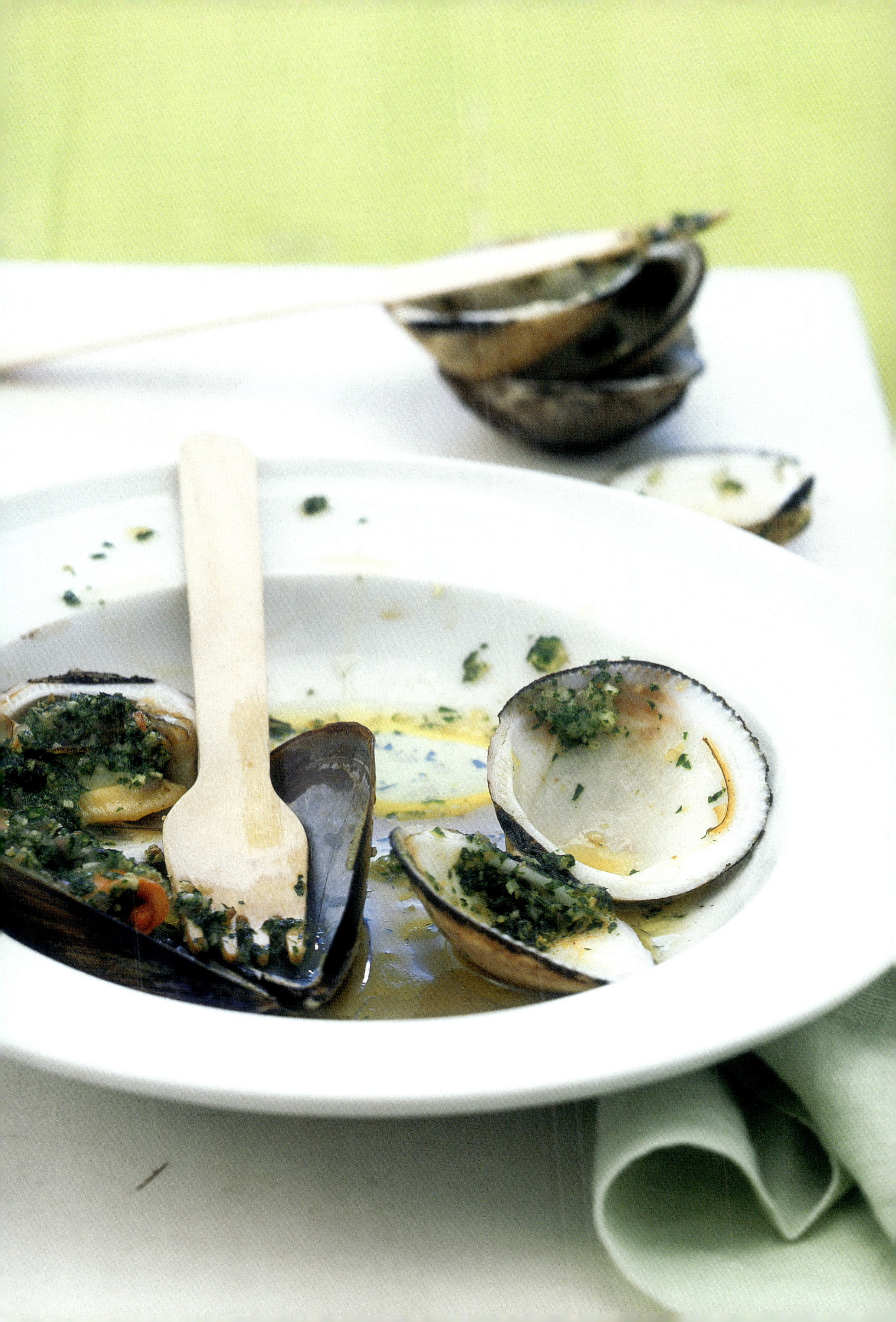

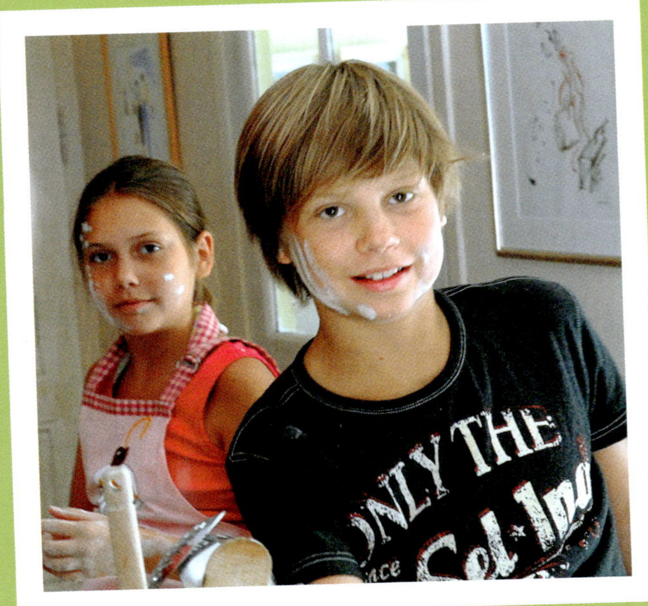

J'aime tellement le fromage que j'essaie d'en mettre dans tous les plats. Ma dernière invention est cette entrecôte au brie...

Entrecôte à la crème de brie

Préparation : 15 minutes Cuisson : 5 minutes Pour 4 personnes

4 entrecôtes
20 g de beurre
1 part de brie fermier à point
1 cuillerée à soupe de crème fraîche
sel, poivre

- Ôtez la croûte du brie et coupez-le en morceaux. Mettez-le dans une petite casserole avec la crème fraîche, laissez fondre à feu doux en mélangeant de temps en temps, salez et poivrez.
- Quand la sauce est prête, faites fondre le beurre dans une poêle et mettez-y à cuire la viande sur les deux faces comme vous l'aimez : bleue, saignante, à point ou bien cuite.
- Nappez les entrecôtes de crème de brie ou servez la sauce à part.

Accompagnez de pâtes fraîches.

Remplacez éventuellement le brie par le fromage de votre choix : bleu, cantal, saint-nectaire, reblochon, camembert...

Boissons conseillées (pour les adultes) : Madiran, Bandol rouge, Gigondas.

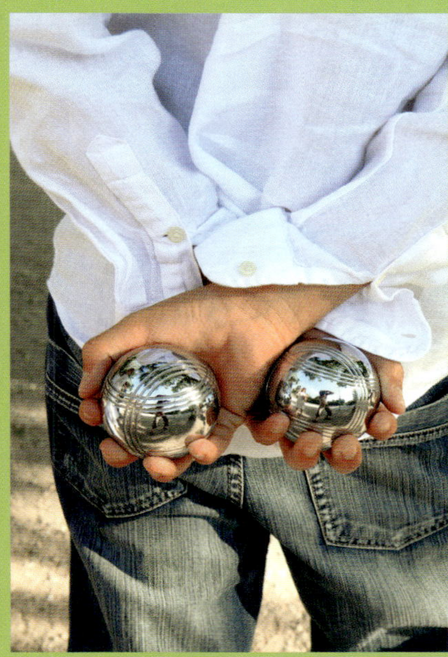
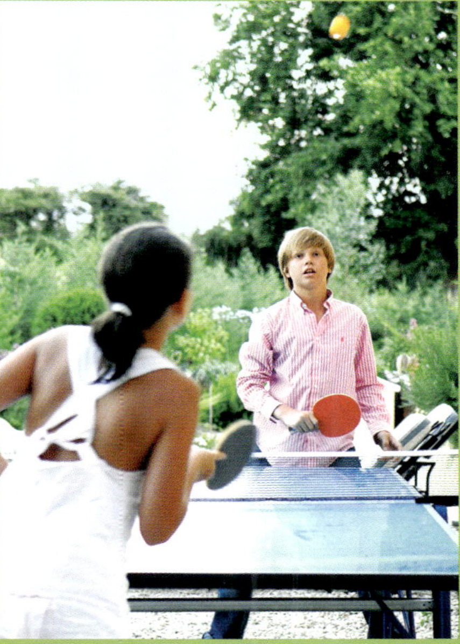
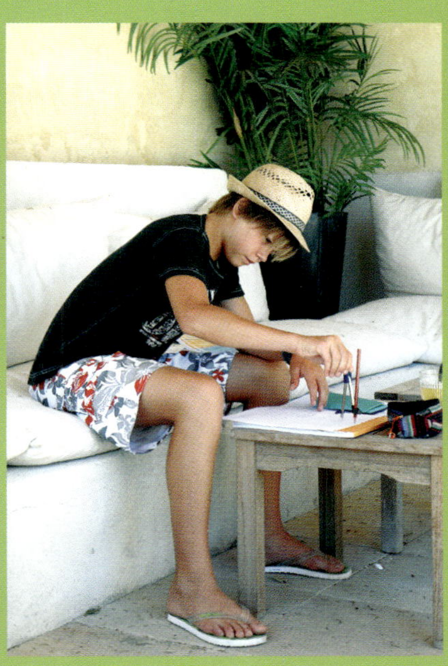

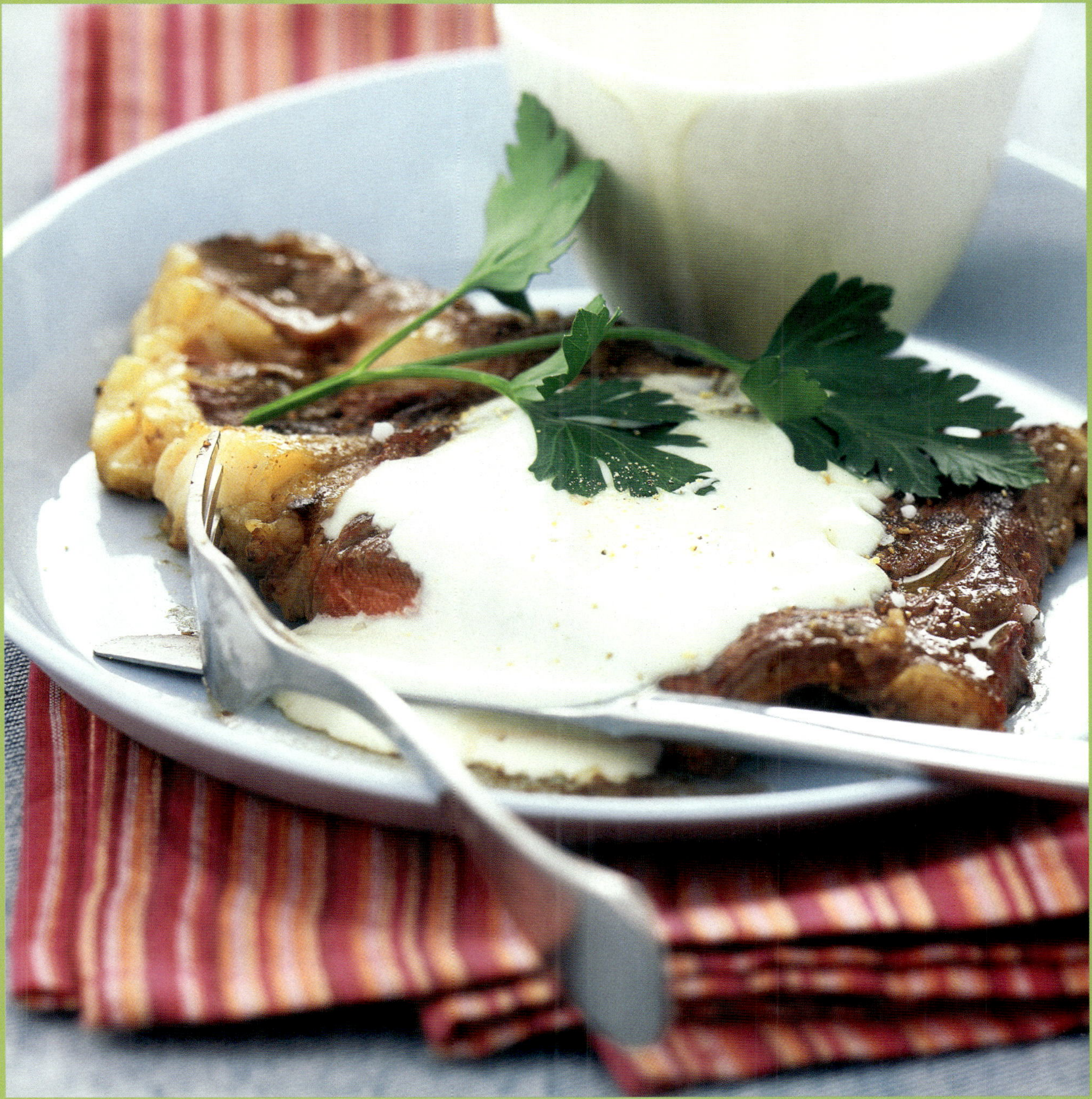

Après un bon match de hockey sur gazon, je reprends des forces avec ce gratin de pommes de terre...

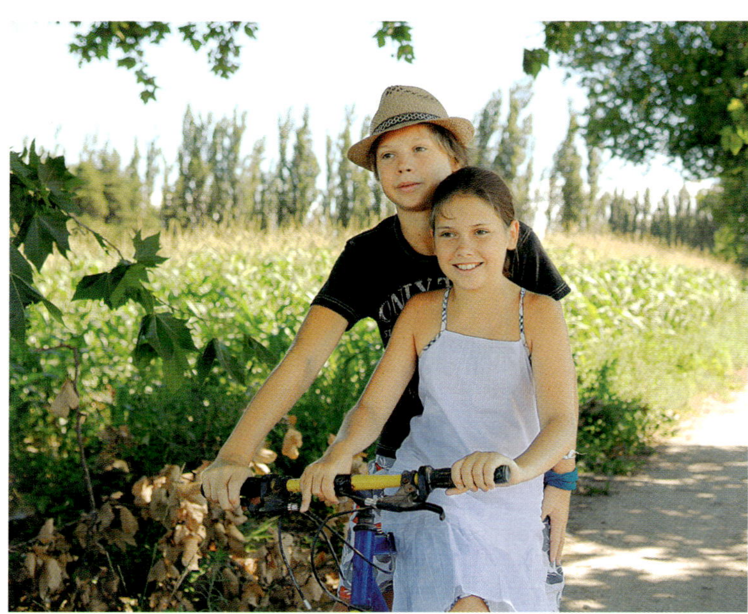
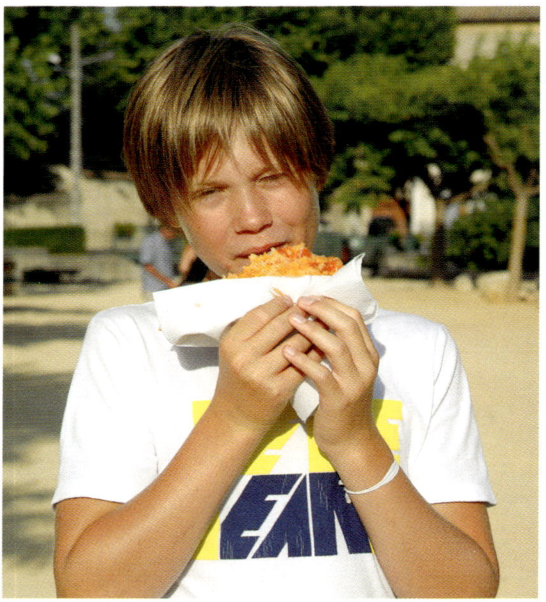

Gratin dauphinois

Préparation : 30 minutes Cuisson : 1 h 20 Pour 8 personnes

2 kg de pommes de terre à chair ferme
2 gousses d'ail
50 cl de crème
30 cl de lait
noix muscade
beurre
sel, poivre

- Épluchez et lavez les pommes de terres, épongez-les soigneusement. Coupez-les en rondelles. Ne les faîtes pas tremper afin de préserver leur fécule naturelle qui assurera la prise du gratin.
- Préchauffez le four à 160 °C. Épluchez les gousses d'ail et coupez-les en deux. Frottez-en l'intérieur d'un grand plat à gratin. Beurrez copieusement le fond et le bord du plat. Mélangez la crème et le lait dans une jatte, salez et poivrez.
- Rangez les pommes de terre par couches successives dans le plat, en les assaisonnant de sel et de poivre et de quelques râpures de noix muscade entre chaque couche. Versez le mélange lait/crème sur chaque couche de pommes de terre. Le liquide doit arriver à hauteur des pommes de terre.
- Parsemez de petites parcelles de beurre sur la dernière couche. Placez le gratin dans le four et laissez cuire pendant environ 1 h 20.

Certains ajoutent du fromage râpé entre les couches de pommes de terre et sur le dessus du plat...

Boisson conseillée (pour les adultes) : Crozes-Hermitage blanc.

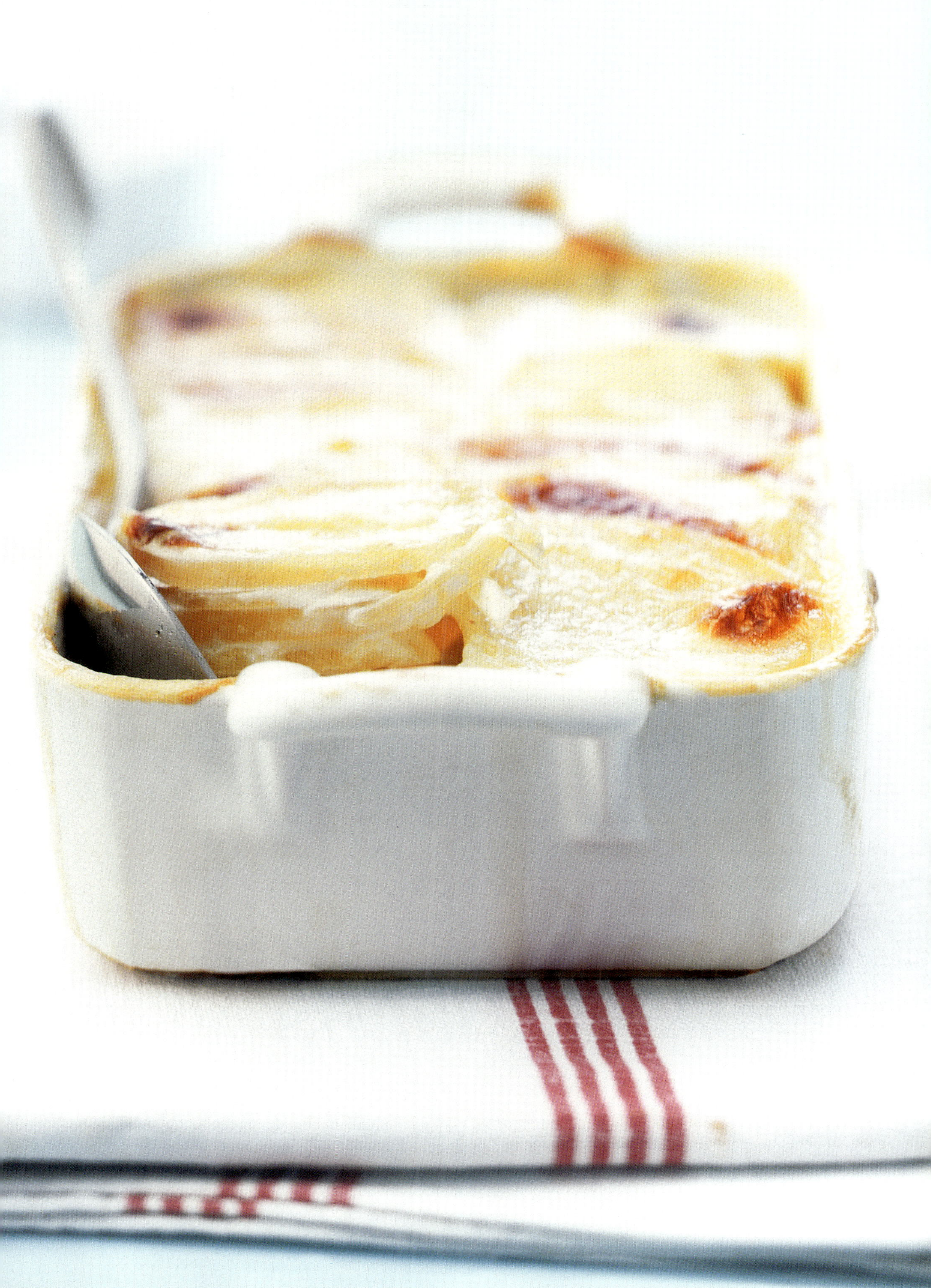

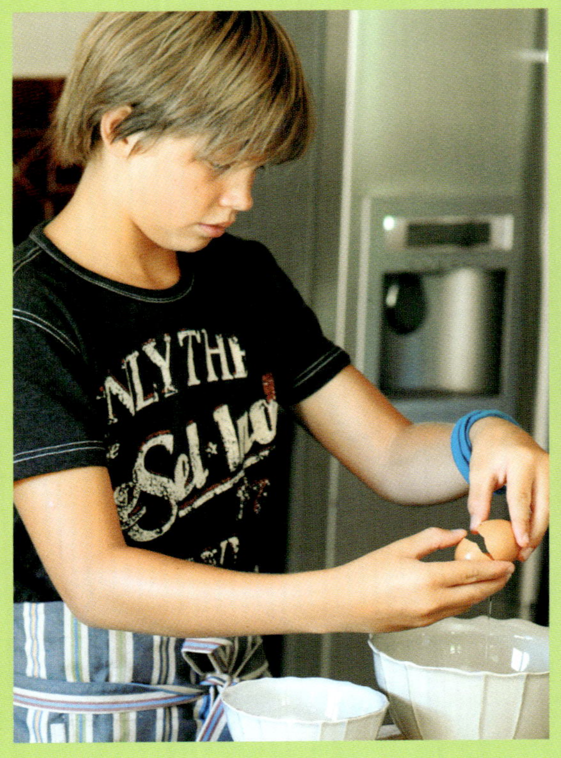

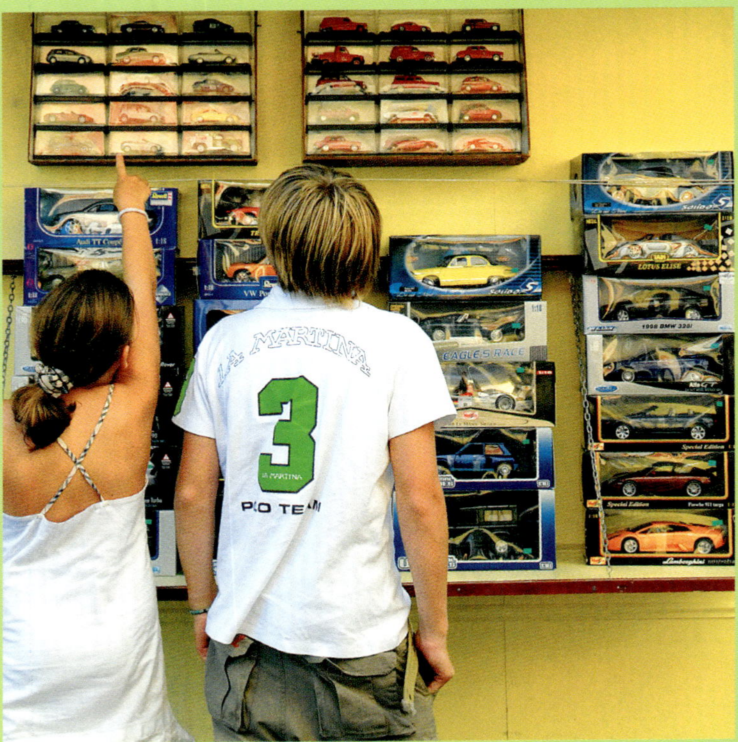

J'aime bien cuisiner. Même si les plats que je prépare ne sont pas très compliqués, je les apprécie encore plus quand c'est moi qui les ai réalisés.

Coquillettes aux lardons

Préparation : 30 minutes Cuisson : 15 minutes Pour 4 personnes

250 g de coquillettes
1 pincée de gros sel
1 barquette de lardons
10 cl de vin blanc
2 cuillerées à soupe de crème fraîche
1 jaune d'œuf
fromage râpé
sel, poivre

- Faites cuire les pâtes dans de l'eau bouillante salée selon le temps indiqué sur l'emballage.
- Pendant ce temps, faites cuire les lardons dans une petite casserole avec le vin blanc.
- Égouttez les pâtes quand elles sont cuites, remettez-les dans la casserole, ajoutez les lardons et leur jus de cuisson, la crème fraîche, mélangez l'ensemble, réchauffez à feu doux, salez et poivrez.
- Juste avant de servir, retirez la casserole du feu, ajoutez le jaune d'œuf et mélangez. Servez accompagné de fromage râpé.

Vous pouvez remplacer les coquillettes par les pâtes de votre choix, rondes ou longues, petites ou grosses, natures ou aromatisées.
Boissons conseillées (pour les adultes) : Moulin-à-vent, Fleury.

Gâteau choc'noisettes au yaourt

Préparation : 15 minutes Cuisson : 30 minutes Pour 6 personnes

1 yaourt nature en pot de verre
3 œufs
2 pots à yaourt de sucre
3 pots à yaourt de farine
1/2 pot à yaourt d'huile
1 sachet de sucre vanillé
1/2 sachet de levure chimique
beurre
1 pot de pâte à tartiner
aux noisettes et au chocolat

• Préchauffez le four à 180 °C. Dans un saladier, battez ensemble les œufs et le yaourt. Lavez le pot de yaourt et servez-vous en comme verre doseur pour mesurer les autres ingrédients. Ajoutez en mélangeant régulièrement le sucre, la farine, l'huile ; terminez par la levure chimique et le sucre vanillé.

• Versez la pâte dans un moule beurré et mettez à cuire au four pendant 30 minutes environ. Vérifiez la cuisson en piquant le cœur du gâteau avec une pointe de couteau ; si elle ressort sèche, c'est que le gâteau est cuit ; sinon, prolongez la cuisson de quelques minutes. Démoulez et laissez refroidir sur une grille.

• Coupez le gâteau en deux dans le sens de l'épaisseur. À l'aide d'une spatule ou d'une grosse cuillère, recouvrez l'intérieur d'une des moitiés de pâte à tartiner, puis reposez l'autre moitié du gâteau par-dessus. Vous pouvez également tartiner le dessus du gâteau et le décorer de friandises.

Vous pouvez remplacer la pâte à tartiner par de la confiture ou déguster tout simplement ce gâteau nature.

Boisson conseillée (pour les adultes) : Coteaux du Layon.

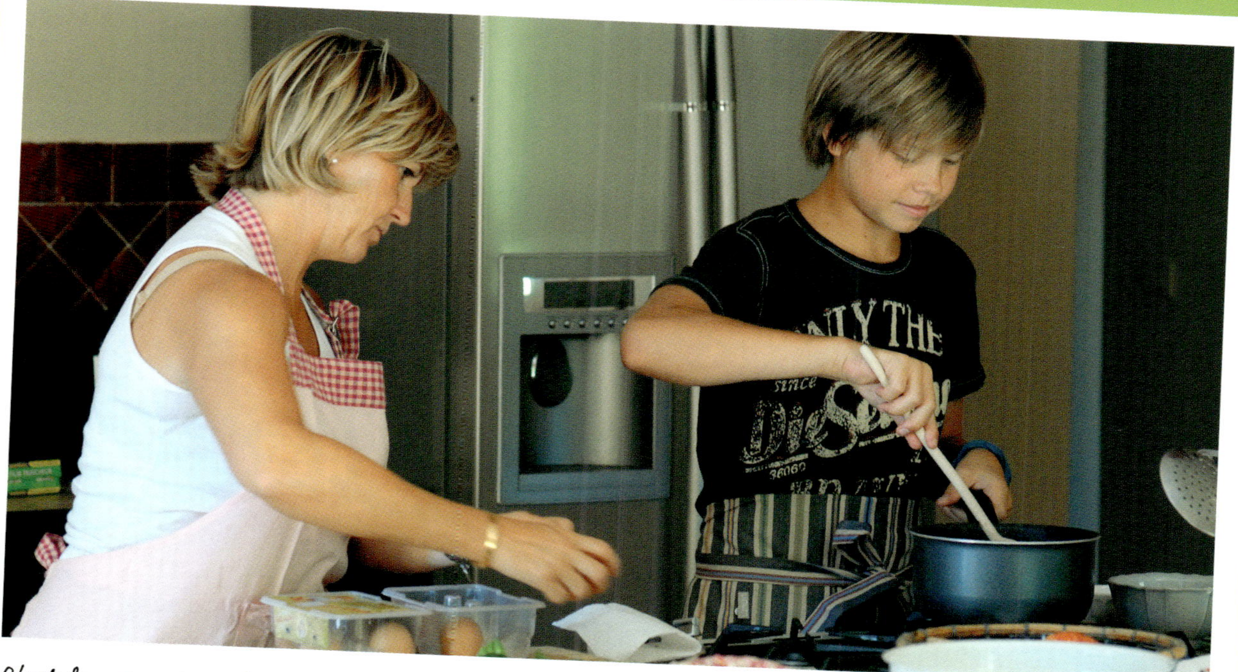

C'est le premier gâteau que j'ai fait (avec l'aide de Maman, bien sûr) : j'avais 2 ans ! C'est un classique gâteau au yaourt, recouvert d'une épaisse couche de pâte à tartiner aux noisettes.

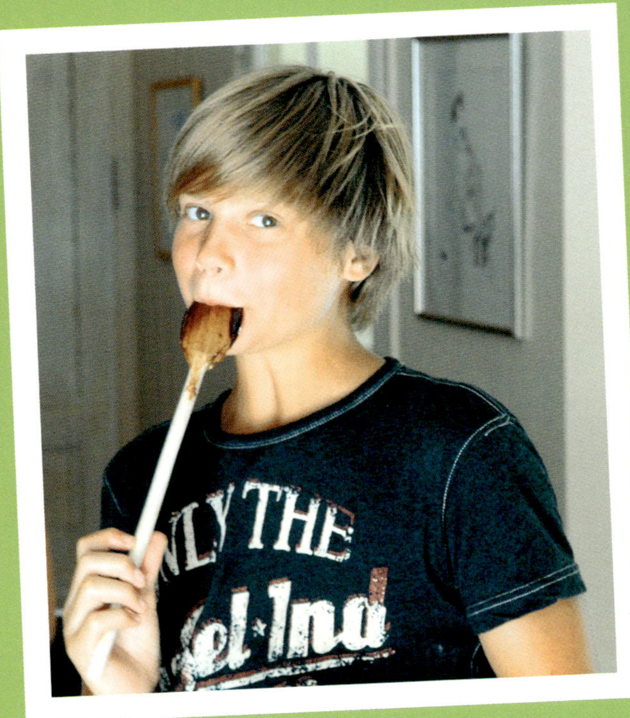

Un incontournable que j'ai amélioré en y associant chocolat noir et chocolat au lait. J'y ajoute des friandises au chocolat. Mes parents trouvent qu'il y a beaucoup de chocolat et de sucre, mais ils sont les premiers à se jeter dessus.

Mousse aux chocolats

Préparation : 20 minutes Réfrigération : 2 heures Pour 6 personnes

150 g de chocolat noir
100 g de chocolat au lait
100 g de beurre
4 jaunes d'œufs
6 blancs d'œufs
50 g de sucre semoule
1 paquet de bonbons Maltesers ou Kit Kat Ball
1 paquet de pépites Crunch

- Cassez le chocolat noir et le chocolat au lait dans une casserole ; mettez-les à fondre à feu très doux avec le beurre en parcelles. Mélangez jusqu'à obtenir une crème lisse et brillante.
- Hors du feu, ajoutez les jaunes d'œufs un par un, mélangez rapidement.
- Montez les blancs d'œufs en neige avec un batteur. Lorsqu'ils sont bien fermes, ajoutez le sucre semoule et battez l'ensemble.
- Versez le chocolat dans un plat creux, ajoutez 1 cuillerée à soupe de blanc en neige pour assouplir le chocolat, puis incorporez le reste des blancs en mélangeant délicatement avec une spatule pour ne pas casser la neige (le mélange se fait de bas en haut, tout en tournant le plat sur lui-même). Versez la mousse dans de petits pots ou un joli récipient transparent. Couvrez de film alimentaire et placez au réfrigérateur pendant au moins 2 heures.
- Décorez la mousse avec les friandises au chocolat ou proposez celles-ci à part.

Vous pouvez utiliser exclusivement du chocolat noir et supprimer le sucre pour un goût plus fort en cacao.

Boissons conseillées (pour les adultes) : Banyuls, porto vintage.

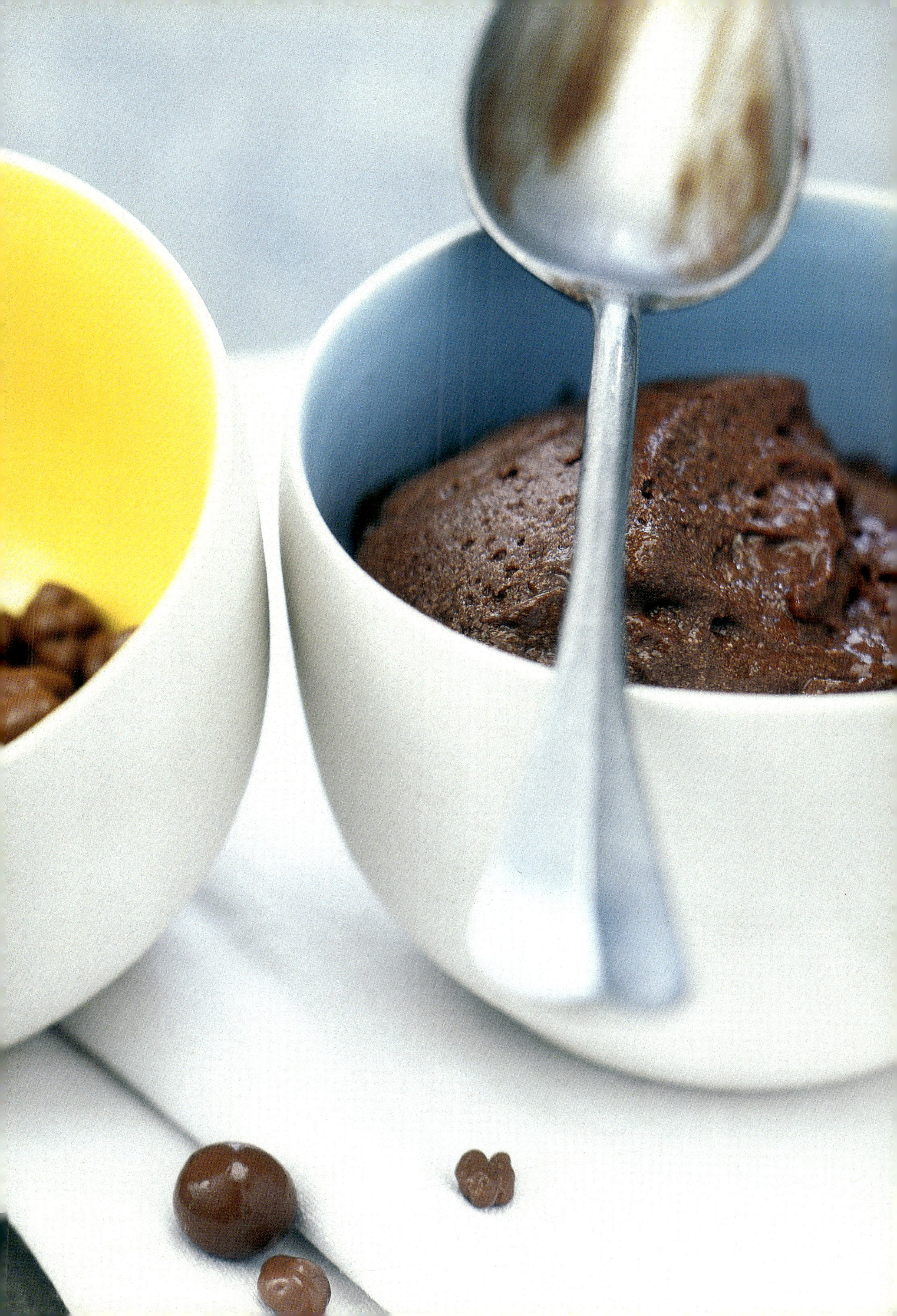

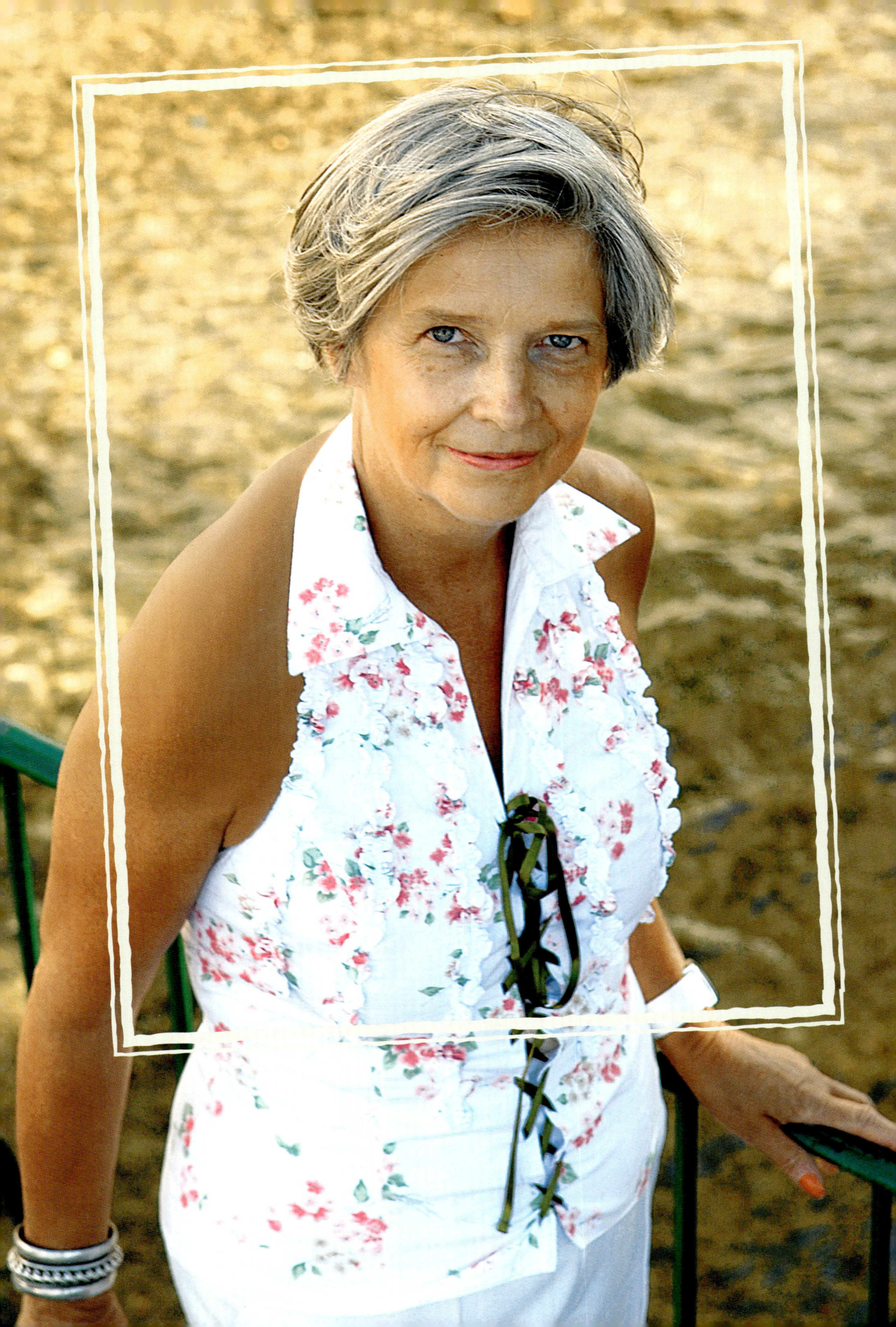

Monique
La grand-mère

Si j'étais... une couleur,

je serais le rose pastel d'une meringue à la fraise.

Si j'étais... une odeur,

je serais celle de la rose pour ses senteurs fruitées et épicées.

Si j'étais... une saveur,

je serais celle d'une framboise, la star de mon jardin, au goût inimitable pour la préparation des confitures, coulis et pâtes de fruits.

Si j'étais... un ustensile,

je serais un moule à gâteau, indispensable pour réaliser de délicieuses recettes sucrées et salées à partager en famille ou entre amis.

Si j'étais... un souvenir gourmand,

je serais les petits pots de crème dessert de mon enfance.

Si j'étais... un péché mignon,

je serais un macaron, craquant et fondant à la fois.

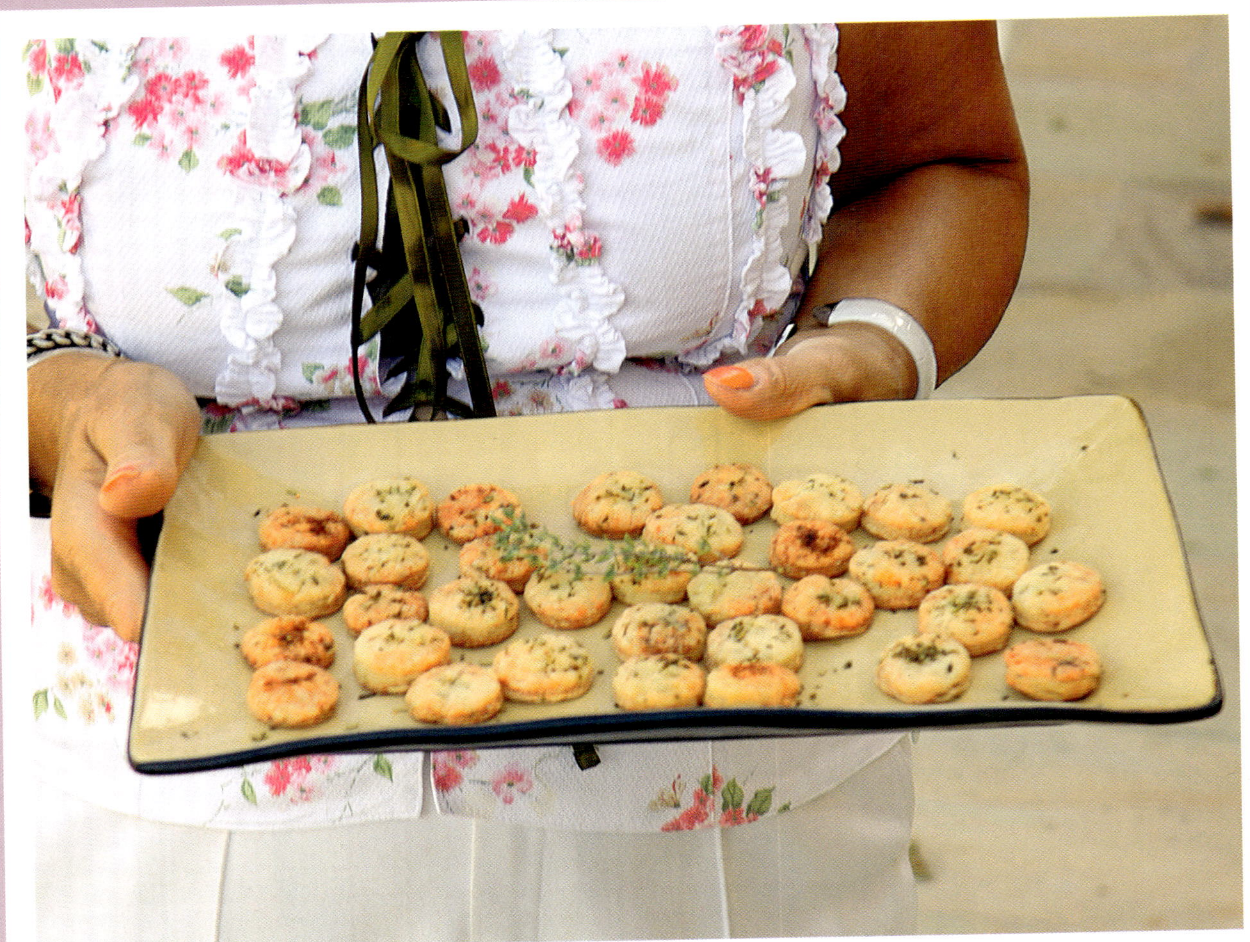

En souvenir d'une petite chèvre dont l'abondant lait permettait de faire de bons fromages, nous avons adapté une ancienne recette à base de parmesan en remplaçant celui-ci par du fromage de chèvre.

Petits sablés de Dame Biquette

Préparation : 10 minutes Repos : 2 heures Cuisson : 15 minutes Pour 6 personnes

100 g de fromage sainte-maure
200 g de farine,
plus 20 g pour le plan de travail
120 g de beurre mou,
plus 20 g pour la plaque
50 g de sucre
thym et romarin
1 pincée de sel

- Écrasez le fromage de chèvre. Mélangez-le avec la farine, le beurre, le sucre et le sel. Aplatissez la boule de pâte obtenue pour lui donner l'aspect d'une grosse galette épaisse (cela permettra de l'étaler plus facilement ensuite). Recouvrez-la de film alimentaire et laissez-la reposer au frais pendant 2 heures.
- Préchauffez le four à 180 °C. Sur le plan de travail fariné, étalez la pâte sur 0,5 cm d'épaisseur. Découpez-y des ronds avec un verre. Parsemez de thym et de romarin effeuillés. Faites cuire 15 minutes au four sur une plaque beurrée. Laissez refroidir et dégustez avec l'apéritif.

Essayer, un jour, de remplacer le chèvre par du parmesan.

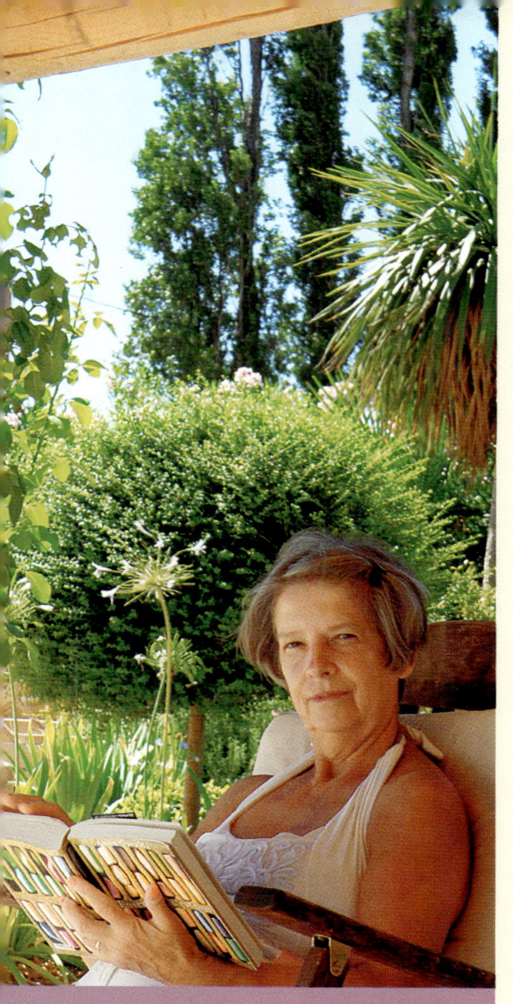

Huîtres gratinées aux oignons doux

À l'époque des fêtes de fin d'année, on sert souvent des huîtres crues. Malheureusement pour moi, je n'ai jamais aimé cela, et pendant des années, j'ai regardé les autres se régaler. Jusqu'à ce que j'aie l'idée de les cuisiner au four... Depuis, ce sont les autres qui me regardent déguster sans retenue ce petit délice !

Préparation : 15 minutes

Cuisson : 15 minutes

Pour 4 personnes

24 huîtres
2 gros oignons doux des Cévennes
20 cl de crème fraîche
60 g de gruyère râpé
8 cl d'huile

- Pelez et émincez les oignons, faites-les revenir dans l'huile, laissez-les dorer légèrement, puis faites mijoter à feu doux environ 10 minutes. Égouttez sur du papier absorbant.
- Mettez les oignons dans une casserole et ajoutez la crème. Laissez mijoter. Ajoutez du poivre et très peu de sel (les huîtres sont déjà naturellement salées).
- Lavez et brossez les huîtres, rangez-les dans un plat à gratin et faites-les ouvrir au four à 240 °C.
- Laissez refroidir les huîtres, puis enlevez la coquille du dessus et videz l'eau. Remettez-les dans le plat (calez-les éventuellement avec du gros sel pour les maintenir bien horizontales). Mettez 1 cuillerée de préparation aux oignons sur chaque demi-huître. Saupoudrez une pincée de gruyère râpé et passez sous le gril à 220 °C pendant 3 minutes pour faire gratiner. Servez immédiatement.

Tous les coquillages peuvent être cuisinés de cette façon.

Boissons conseillées : Pouilly Fumé, Entre-Deux-Mers.

Parfois, nous arrivons assez tard dans notre maison familiale en Normandie... Nous sommes alors bien contents de n'avoir rien à préparer pour le dîner : j'emporte cette terrine que j'ai préparée la veille, et nous attendons sereinement l'arrivée des enfants. Nous la dégustons chaude en hiver et froide en été, avec de la mayonnaise aromatisée au citron ou une sauce cocktail (mayonnaise, ketchup, 1 goutte de cognac).

Terrine de saumon aux poireaux et aux noisettes

Préparation : 30 minutes Cuisson : 1 heure Réfrigération : 4 heures Pour 6 personnes

400 g de filet de saumon en morceaux épais de 2 cm
1 kg de poireaux avec le vert
125 g de noisettes entières
3 œufs
20 cl de crème fraîche
1 cuillerée à soupe d'œufs de saumon
50 g de beurre,
plus 15 g pour le moule
2 tranches de pain de mie finement émiettées
sel, poivre

- Épluchez les poireaux, séparez le blanc du vert, lavez-les soigneusement. Émincez les blancs et faites-les revenir 15 minutes avec 50 g de beurre, une pincée de sel et de poivre. Laissez refroidir.
- Faites cuire le vert des poireaux environ 5 minutes dans une casserole d'eau bouillante salée. Plongez-les quelques instants dans de l'eau glacée (pour conserver la couleur verte), puis posez-les à plat sur un linge ou du papier absorbant pour les égoutter.
- Beurrez un moule à cake. Garnissez-le fond et les côtés de vert de poireau, en laissant dépasser légèrement à l'extérieur.
- Mixez grossièrement les noisettes. Faites-les dorer à feu vif dans une poêle antiadhésive, jusqu'à ce qu'elles dégagent une bonne odeur de grillé (attention à ne pas les faire brûler !).
- Préchauffez le four à 180 °C. Battez les œufs en omelette. Incorporez la crème fraîche, les noisettes grillées, la mie de pain émiettée et les œufs de saumon. Ajoutez les blancs de poireau, mélangez le tout et rectifiez l'assaisonnement.
- Remplissez le moule en alternant des couches de filet de saumon et de crème de poireau. Rabattez ensuite le vert des poireaux pour recouvrir la garniture, puis faites cuire au four dans un bain-marie pendant 45 minutes.
- Laissez refroidir la terrine et réservez-la au réfrigérateur pendant au moins 4 heures avant de la démouler.

Boissons conseillées : Smith Haut Lafitte blanc, Rully.

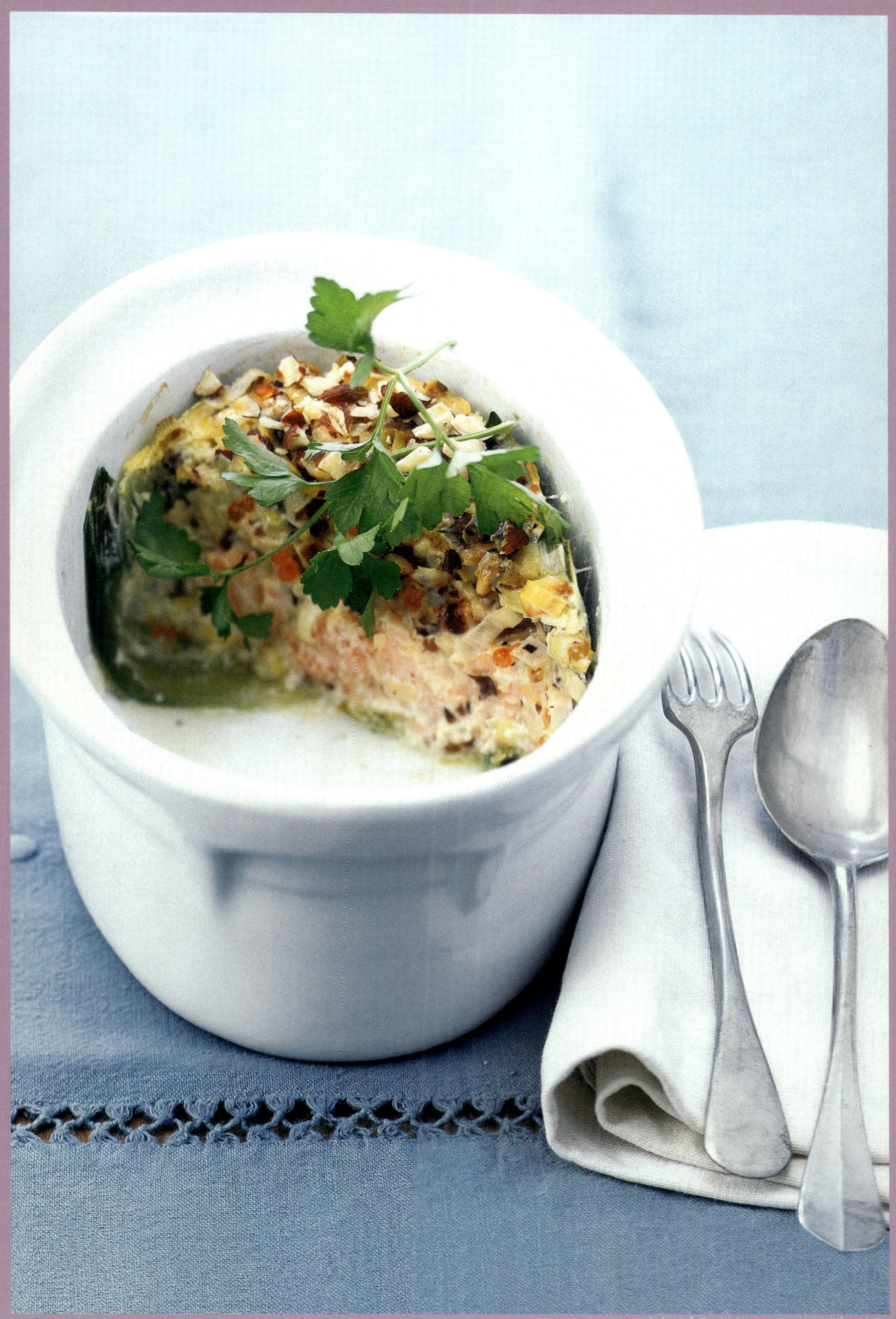

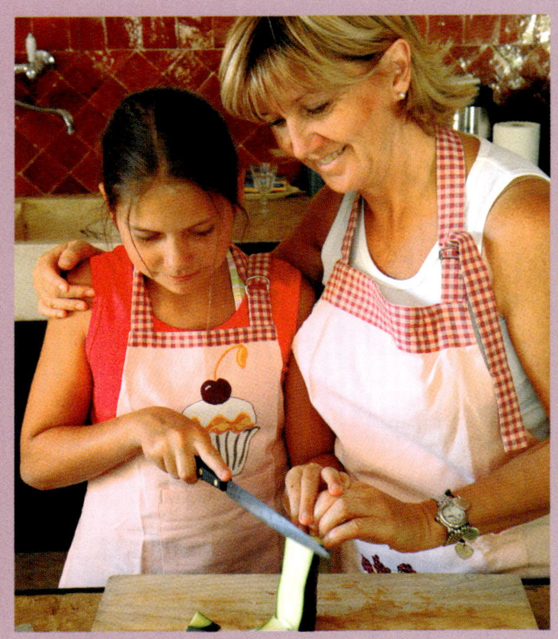

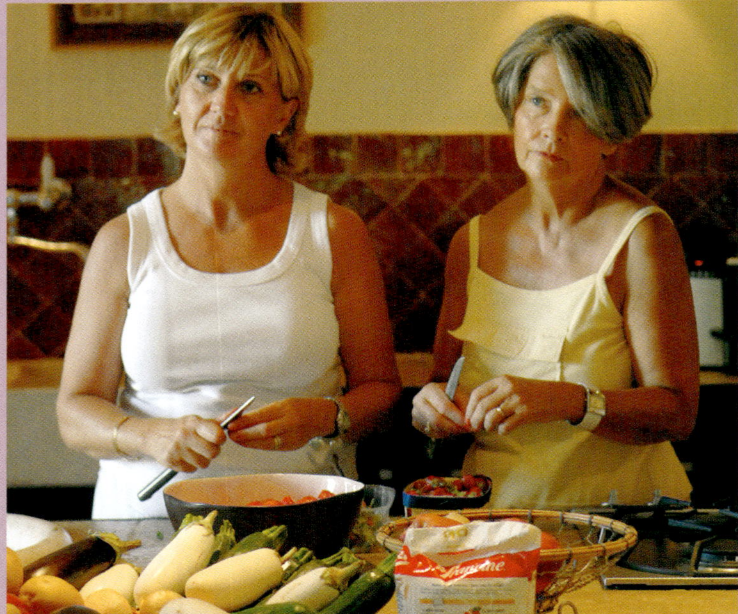

Ce plat peut se préparer à l'avance. L'important est d'acheter des produits de qualité. L'association sucré/salé est agréable, et les produits normands (pommes, andouillette, calvados...) se complètent parfaitement.

Millefeuilles de pommes à l'andouillette

Préparation : 20 minutes Cuisson : 10 minutes Pour 4 personnes

4 pommes reinettes
2 andouillettes
30 g de beurre
2 cuillerées à soupe de calvados
2 cuillerées à soupe de crème fraîche
roquette
sel, poivre

- Lavez les pommes entières et évidez-les. Coupez-les en rondelles de 1 cm d'épaisseur et faites-les revenir à la poêle dans 20 g de beurre, jusqu'à l'obtention d'une belle coloration dorée (environ 3 à 4 minutes, les pommes devant rester légèrement fermes). Laissez refroidir dans une assiette.
- Dans la même poêle, mettez à fondre le reste du beurre et faites-y dorer rapidement de chaque côté les andouillettes coupées en rondelles.
- Préchauffez le four à 160 °C. Dans un plat à gratin, superposez à deux reprises une rondelle de pomme et une rondelle d'andouillette, en terminant par une rondelle de pomme ; maintenez avec une petite pique en bois et enfournez environ 10 minutes.
- Dans une casserole, faites chauffer le calvados, flambez avec précaution, ajoutez la crème et laissez réduire 2 minutes ; salez et poivrez.
- Dressez dans l'assiette, sur quelques feuilles de roquette, assaisonné d'un peu de crème au calvados.

Remplacez l'andouillette par des rondelles de boudin blanc ou noir (ou les deux) ; pour une version plus festive, essayez des tranches de foie gras poêlées, qui se marieront parfaitement avec les pommes.

Boissons conseillées : cidre, Bergerac rouge.

Crêpes au jambon

Préparation : 15 minutes Repos : 1 heure Cuisson : 40 minutes Pour 8 personnes

beurre ou huile pour la cuisson

Pour la pâte à crêpes
250 g de farine
3 gros œufs
50 cl de lait
2 pincées de sel fin
20 g de beurre fondu demi-sel

Pour la garniture
16 fines tranches de jambon
20 cl de crème fraîche épaisse
100 g de gruyère râpé

- Préparez la pâte à crêpes. Versez la farine en fontaine dans un saladier, ajoutez le sel, les œufs entiers. Mélangez délicatement avec un fouet et versez progressivement le lait, en remuant sans cesse, afin d'éviter la formation de grumeaux et obtenir une pâte bien lisse. Versez le beurre fondu et mélangez. Laissez reposer au frais pendant 1 heure.
- Faites chauffer une poêle légèrement graissée avec du beurre ou de l'huile. Versez-y une petite louche de pâte à crêpes et répartissez sur toute la surface de la poêle. Faites cuire environ 20 secondes sur chaque face. Confectionnez ainsi 16 crêpes.
- Préchauffez le four à 180 °C. Déposez sur chaque crêpe une tranche de jambon et roulez la crêpe sur elle-même. Déposez les rouleaux les uns à côté des autres dans un plat à gratin préalablement beurré. Versez la crème fraîche et recouvrez de fromage râpé. Faites cuire au four environ 20 minutes, puis passez 3 minutes sous le gril à 220 °C.

Boissons conseillées : Menetou rouge, Chinon.

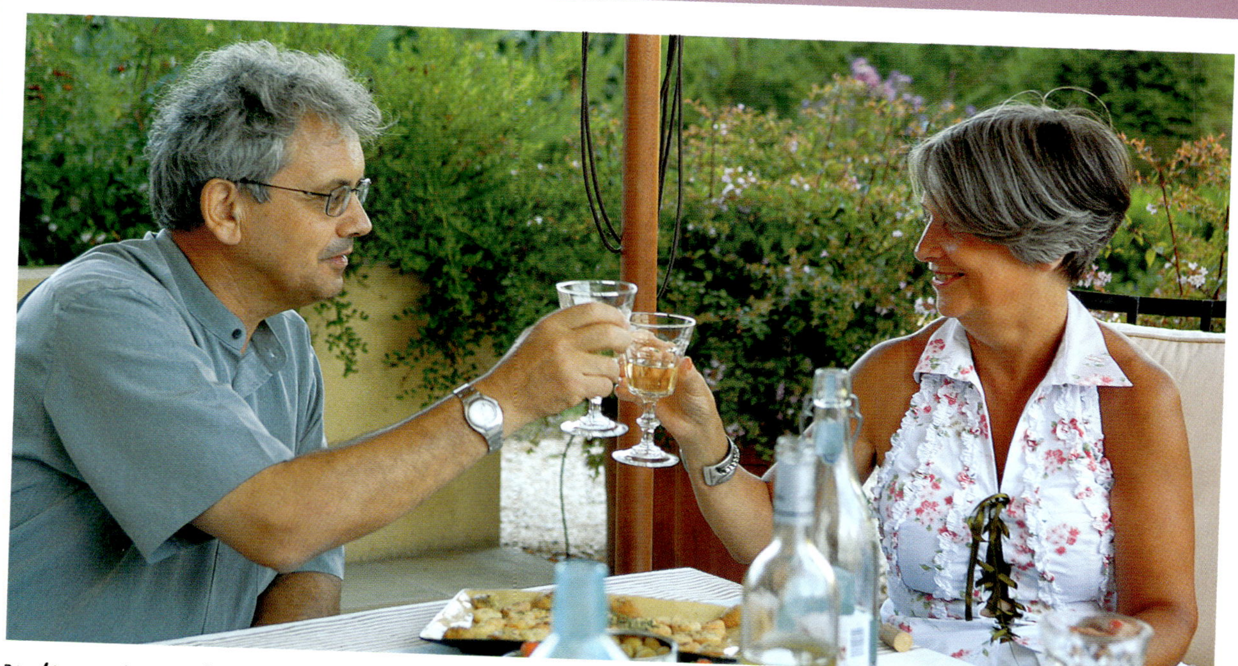

Notre saison des crêpes démarre le 15 octobre et s'achève le 14... octobre de l'année suivante. Vous l'aurez compris, chez nous, les crêpes, c'est toute l'année... Salées ou sucrées, elles font le bonheur de toute la famille.

La saison des mirabelles est très courte, aussi achetez-les en saison, dénoyautez-les et mettez-les au congélateur pour pouvoir en disposer toute l'année ; ces petites prunes sont parfaites pour accompagner le porc.

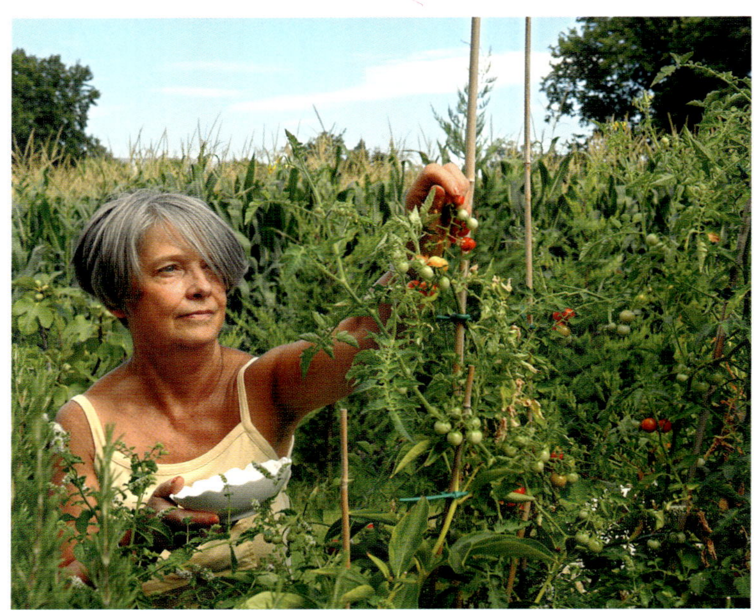

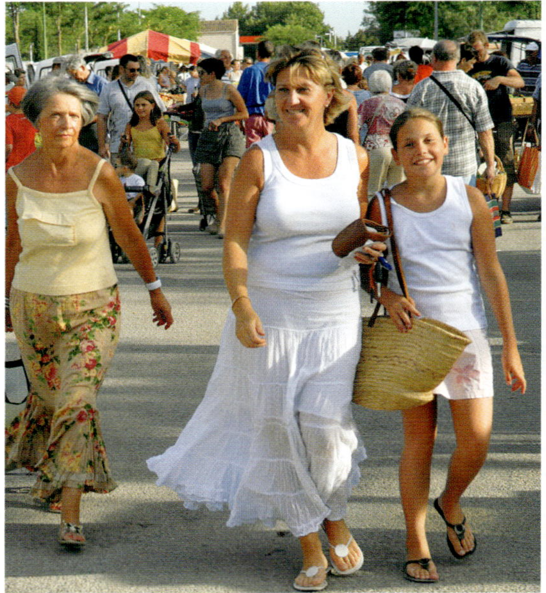

Filets mignons farcis et compote de mirabelles

Préparation : 20 minutes Cuisson : 1 heure Pour 4 à 6 personnes

2 filets mignons de porc
800 g de mirabelles
1 échalote
1 bouquet de persil plat
1 tranche de pain de mie
8 cuillerées à soupe d'huile d'olive
20 g de beurre
1 cuillerée à café de miel
1 verre de muscat

• Dans le bol d'un robot, mixez l'échalote pelée, la mie de pain et le persil. Faites revenir ce mélange quelques minutes dans 4 cuillerées à soupe d'huile d'olive.

• Préchauffez le four à 200 °C. Entaillez profondément les filets mignons dans le sens de la longueur, farcissez-les avec le mélange et mettez-les dans un plat à rôtir ; arrosez avec le reste de l'huile d'olive et faites cuire au four pendant 1 heure, en retournant les rôtis à mi-cuisson et en les arrosant fréquemment (ajoutez 2 ou 3 cuillerées à soupe d'eau dans le plat si le jus réduit trop).

• Pendant ce temps, dénoyautez les mirabelles, faites-les revenir dans une casserole avec le beurre, le miel et le muscat pour obtenir une compote. Servez avec les filets mignons.

Vous pouvez remplacer les mirabelles par des quetsches ou des prunes.

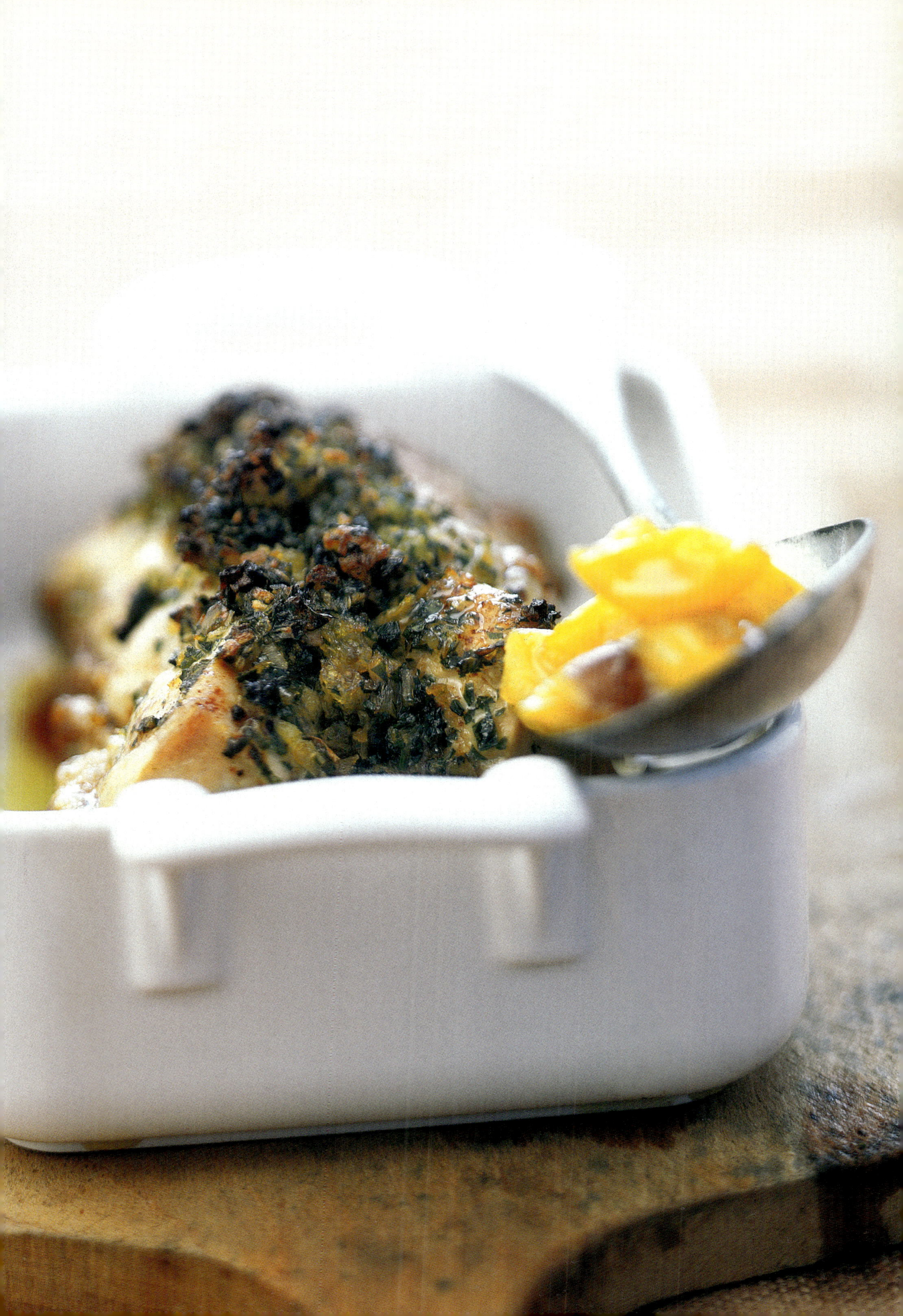

Ces petits farcis sont une recette traditionnelle, un peu oubliée comme beaucoup des délicieuses spécialités que préparaient nos grands-mères avec trois fois rien…

Petits farcis aux gésiers de canard confits

Préparation : 45 minutes Cuisson : 15 minutes Pour 8 personnes

1 bocal de gésiers de canard confits
1 chou vert
2 échalotes
4 gousses d'ail
50 g de beurre
2 tranches de pain de mie
2 cuillerées à soupe de lait
1 œuf
3 cuillerées à soupe de persil plat haché
100 g de fromage râpé
sel, poivre

- Détachez 16 grandes feuilles de chou, plongez-les dans de l'eau bouillante pendant 3 minutes, puis passez-les sous l'eau froide, afin de préserver leur couleur verte. Égouttez-les et essuyez-les bien.
- Lavez le reste du chou, coupez-le en deux, supprimez son trognon et coupez-le en lanières. Faites blanchir ces lanières 3 minutes dans de l'eau bouillante , égouttez-les et réservez un peu de leur eau de cuisson.
- Pelez et hachez les échalotes. Pelez et hachez l'ail. Coupez les gésiers confits en petit dés.
- Dans une sauteuse, faites revenir les gésiers avec la moitié des échalotes hachées. Réservez dans une assiette.
- Dans la même sauteuse, faites fondre 40 g de beurre avec le reste des échalotes, l'ail, le persil et les lanières de chou. Faites cuire environ 15 minutes, salez et poivrez.
- Dans un saladier, mélangez l'œuf avec la mie de pain trempée dans le lait. Ajoutez les dés de gésiers et la fondue de chou. Mélangez intimement et assaisonnez cette farce.
- Déposez sur chaque grande feuille de chou 1 cuillerée à soupe de farce, couvrez avec une autre feuille de chou en pressant bien, rabattez les bords vers le haut et maintenez avec de la ficelle de cuisine comme un paquet-cadeau.
- Préchauffez le four à 180 °C. Déposez les petits farcis dans un plat à gratin beurré, arrosez avec 4 cuillerées à soupe de jus de cuisson du chou. Faites cuire 15 minutes au four.
- Saupoudrez un peu de fromage râpé sur les petits farcis et faites gratiner sous le gril du four. Ôtez la ficelle avant de servir.

Boissons conseillées : Saint-Estèphe, Châteauneuf-du-Pape.

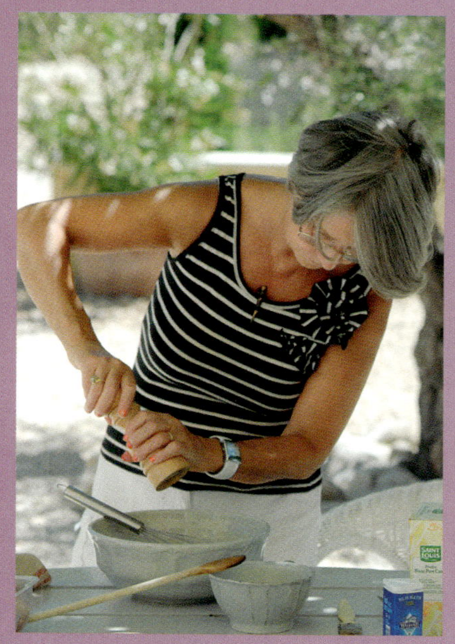

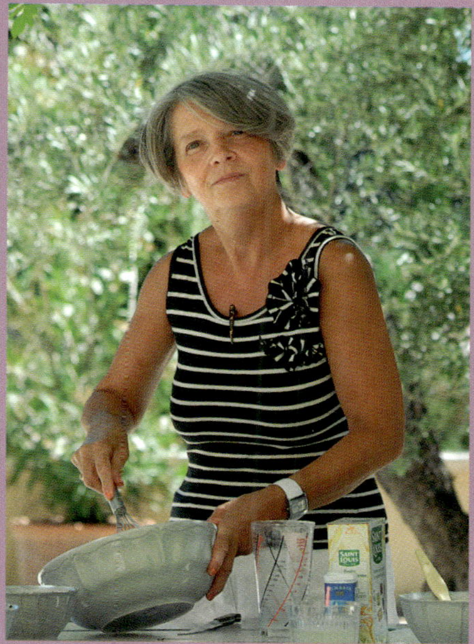

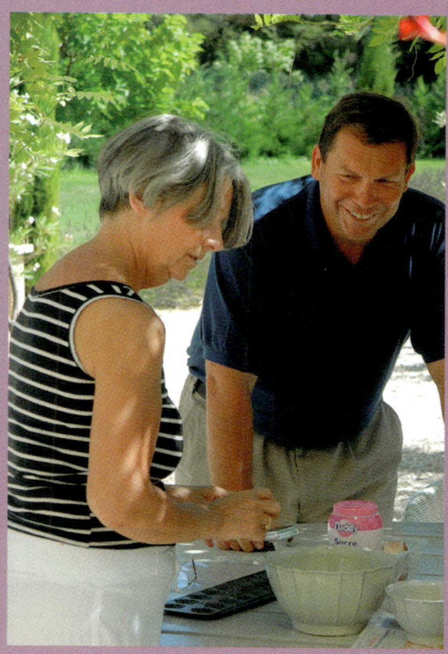

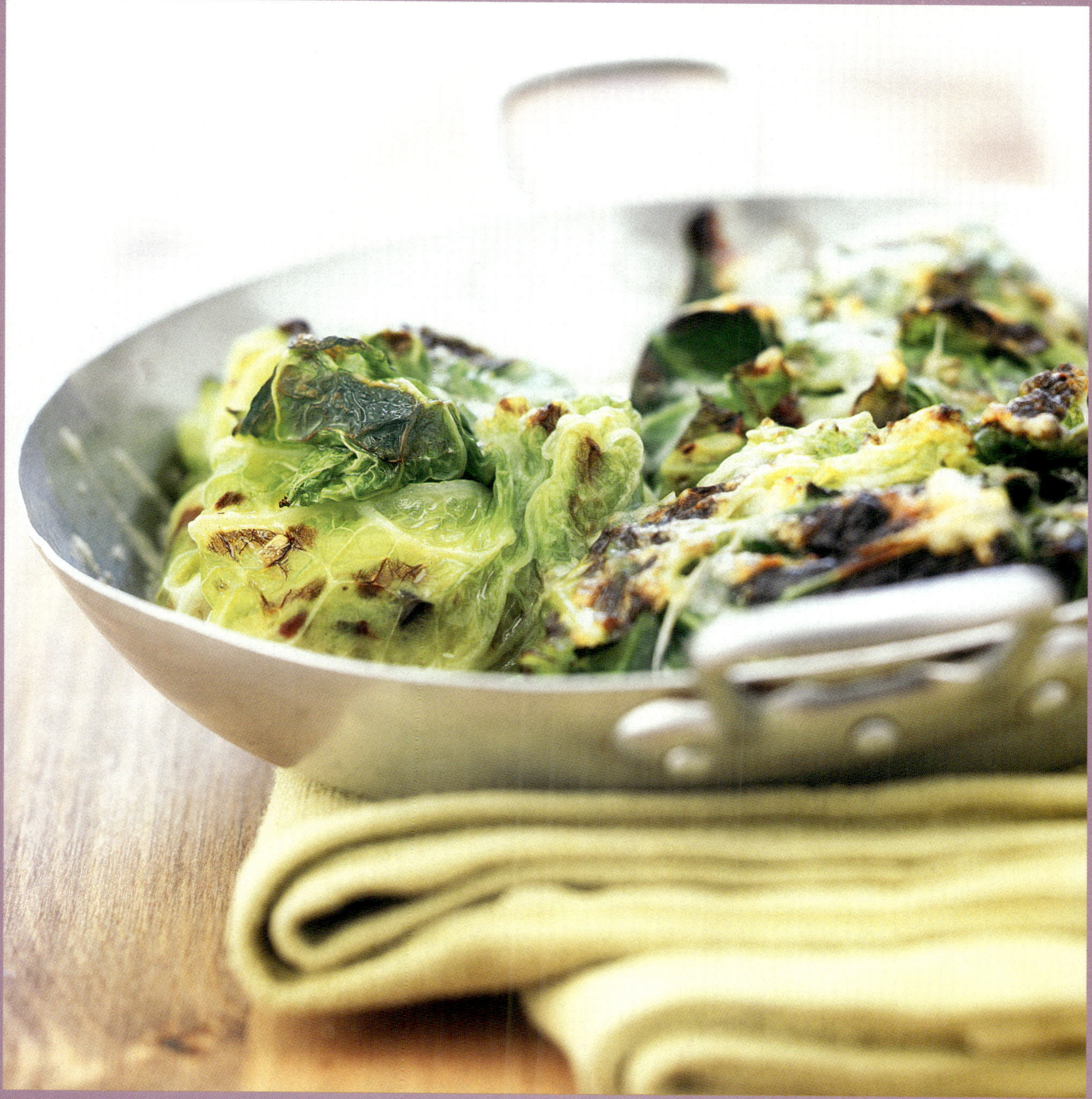

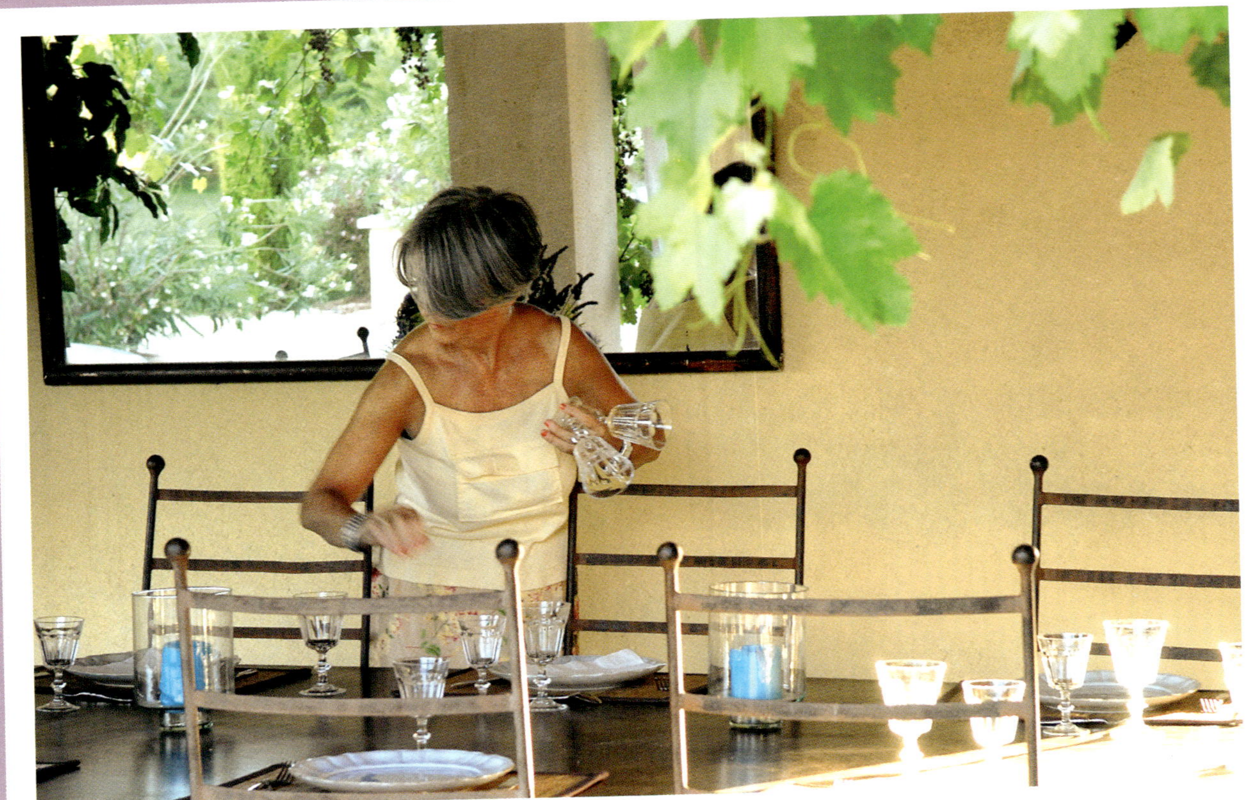

Cette recette me vient de ma propre grand-mère. La joue de boeuf est un excellent morceau de viande, très économique de surcroît, mais les gens ont souvent un a priori contre elle. Longuement mijotée, elle en surprendra pourtant plus d'un...

Confit de joue de bœuf

Préparation : 10 minutes Cuisson : 3 heures Pour 6 personnes

800 g de joues de bœuf coupées en morceaux
2 gousses d'ail
6 feuilles de sauge
2 carottes
1 branche de céleri
6 cuillerées à soupe de graisse de canard
2 branches de thym frais
15 cl de bouillon
1 os à moelle (facultatif)
sel, poivre

- Épluchez les gousses d'ail et coupez-les en trois. Lavez et essuyez les feuilles de sauge et coupez-les en deux. Épluchez les carottes et coupez-les en rondelles épaisses. Effilez le céleri et émincez-le.
- Faites fondre la graisse de canard dans une cocotte en fonte ou à fond épais. Posez les morceaux de joue et faites-les revenir sur toutes les faces. Répartissez l'ail, les feuilles de sauge, le thym effeuillé, le céleri et les rondelles de carotte. Salez et poivrez. Mouillez avec le bouillon à hauteur. Ajoutez éventuellement l'os à moelle.
- Fermez hermétiquement en intercalant une feuille de papier aluminium entre la cocotte et son couvercle. Faites cuire 3 heures à feu très doux, en remuant de temps en temps. Si nécessaire, rajoutez du bouillon en cours de cuisson.

Accompagnez de morceaux de légumes (carottes, panais, oignons rouges, pommes de terre, navets...) rôtis au four à 180 °C pendant 45 minutes avec des lardons, du thym, du romarin et de l'huile d'olive.

Boissons conseillées : Madiran, Côte de Provence rouge.

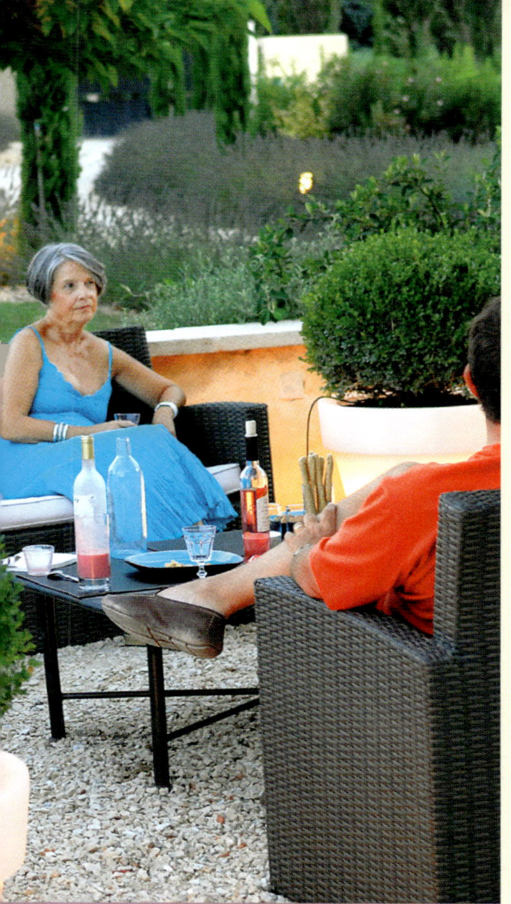

Lotte à l'américaine

Savez-vous pourquoi on ne voit jamais sur l'étal du poissonnier une lotte entière ? Tout simplement parce que la tête de ce poisson est hideuse et ferait fuir les clients ! Mais débarrassée de sa vilaine « gueule », la lotte, appelée aussi baudroie, est un poisson raffiné dont vous apprécierez la chair délicate.

Préparation : 20 minutes

Cuisson : 25 minutes

Pour 4 personnes

1 kg de lotte en morceaux
8 langoustines
500 g de tomates
quelques brins de cerfeuil, de persil et d'estragon
3 échalotes
3 gousses d'ail
100 g de beurre ramolli
2 cuillerées à soupe de farine
10 cl de vin blanc sec
5 cl de cognac
10 cl d'huile
sel, poivre de Cayenne

- Mettez la farine dans un sac en plastique, puis insérez les morceaux de lotte, secouez le sac, posez les morceaux de lotte farinés sur une assiette.
- Épluchez et hachez l'ail. Coupez les tomates en deux, épépinez-les et coupez leur chair en gros dés.
- Faites chauffer l'huile dans une cocotte. Faites-y dorer les morceaux de lotte avec l'ail et l'échalote. Flambez avec le cognac. Ajoutez les tomates, le vin blanc, une pincée de sel et une pincée de poivre de Cayenne. Laissez cuire à feu doux, cocotte ouverte, pendant 20 minutes.
- Faites cuire les langoustines dans de l'eau bouillante salée pendant 5 minutes. Laissez-les refroidir, puis décortiquez 4 d'entre elles. Dans le bol d'un mixeur, mettez les herbes, la chair des 4 langoustines, le beurre mou ; salez et poivrez légèrement, puis mixez l'ensemble.
- Déposez les morceaux de lotte dans un plat et maintenez au chaud dans le four. Faites réduire le jus de cuisson 5 minutes sur feu vif. Ajoutez le beurre aromatisé, fouettez quelques secondes à feu très doux en évitant l'ébullition, versez sur la lotte. Décorez avec les 4 langoustines restantes et servez aussitôt, accompagné de riz safrané ou de pommes de terre vapeur.

Boissons conseillées : Chablis, Châteauneuf blanc.

La blanquette de veau fait partie du patrimoine culinaire français. Cuisinée dans de nombreuses régions, elle convient particulièrement bien à la Normandie, pays de la crème, des œufs et du beurre. Vous l'apprécierez plutôt en hiver, accompagnée tout simplement de riz blanc.

Blanquette de veau à l'ancienne

Préparation : 30 minutes Cuisson : 1 h 20 Pour 6 personnes

1,500 kg de tendrons, de flanchet et d'épaule de veau désossée, en morceaux
2 carottes
1 branche de céleri
1 oignon
2 branches de thym
1 feuille de laurier
3 brins de persil
1 poignée de gros sel et de grains de poivre
1 clou de girofle
50 g de beurre
2 cuillerées à soupe d'huile d'arachide

Pour la sauce
2 jaunes d'œufs
250 g de crème fraîche
le zeste et le jus de 1/2 citron
70 cl de bouillon de cuisson de la blanquette

Pour la garniture
80 g de beurre
18 petits oignons grelots
300 g de champignons frais
sel, poivre

• Épluchez les carottes et l'oignon, piquez ce dernier avec le clou de girofle. Coupez les carottes en fines rondelles. Préparez un bouquet garni en ficelant ensemble la branche de céleri coupée en trois, les queues de persil, le thym et le laurier.

• Chauffez le beurre et l'huile dans une cocotte. Faites-y dorer les morceaux de veau sur toutes les faces, par petites quantités.

• Remettez tous les morceaux dans la cocotte ; ajoutez les carottes, l'oignon, le bouquet garni, le gros sel et les grains de poivre. Couvrez avec suffisamment d'eau pour recouvrir la viande de 1 cm. Portez à ébullition, puis baissez le feu et laissez mijoter tout doucement à couvert pendant 1 heure. Piquez avec une fourchette pour vérifier la cuisson de la viande, prolongez celle-ci si nécessaire.

• Pendant ce temps, préparez la garniture. Épluchez les oignons. Lavez et séchez les champignons, coupez-les en quatre. Faites dorer les champignons à la poêle dans 40 g de beurre, salez et poivrez. Faites cuire de la même manière les oignons grelots dans 40 g de beurre. Mélangez avec les champignons et maintenez l'ensemble au chaud.

• Prélevez 70 cl de bouillon de cuisson de la viande dans la cocotte. Dans une grande casserole, mélangez les jaunes d'œufs avec le zeste et le jus de citron ; ajoutez la crème. Délayez avec le bouillon.

• Retirez les morceaux de viande et les carottes, mettez-les dans un plat creux. Ajoutez les champignons et les oignons, et réservez au chaud.

• Mettez la casserole sur feu doux et faites cuire sans cesser de fouetter, en ajoutant si nécessaire un peu de bouillon. Versez sur la viande et servez immédiatement.

Attention ! la sauce ne doit absolument pas bouillir, car les œufs coaguleraient, et elle aurait une allure de lait tourné. Il est possible de préparer la blanquette à l'avance, mais la sauce doit être réalisée à la dernière minute, car elle ne peut être réchauffée.

Boissons conseillées : Saint-Émilion, Côte de Beaune.

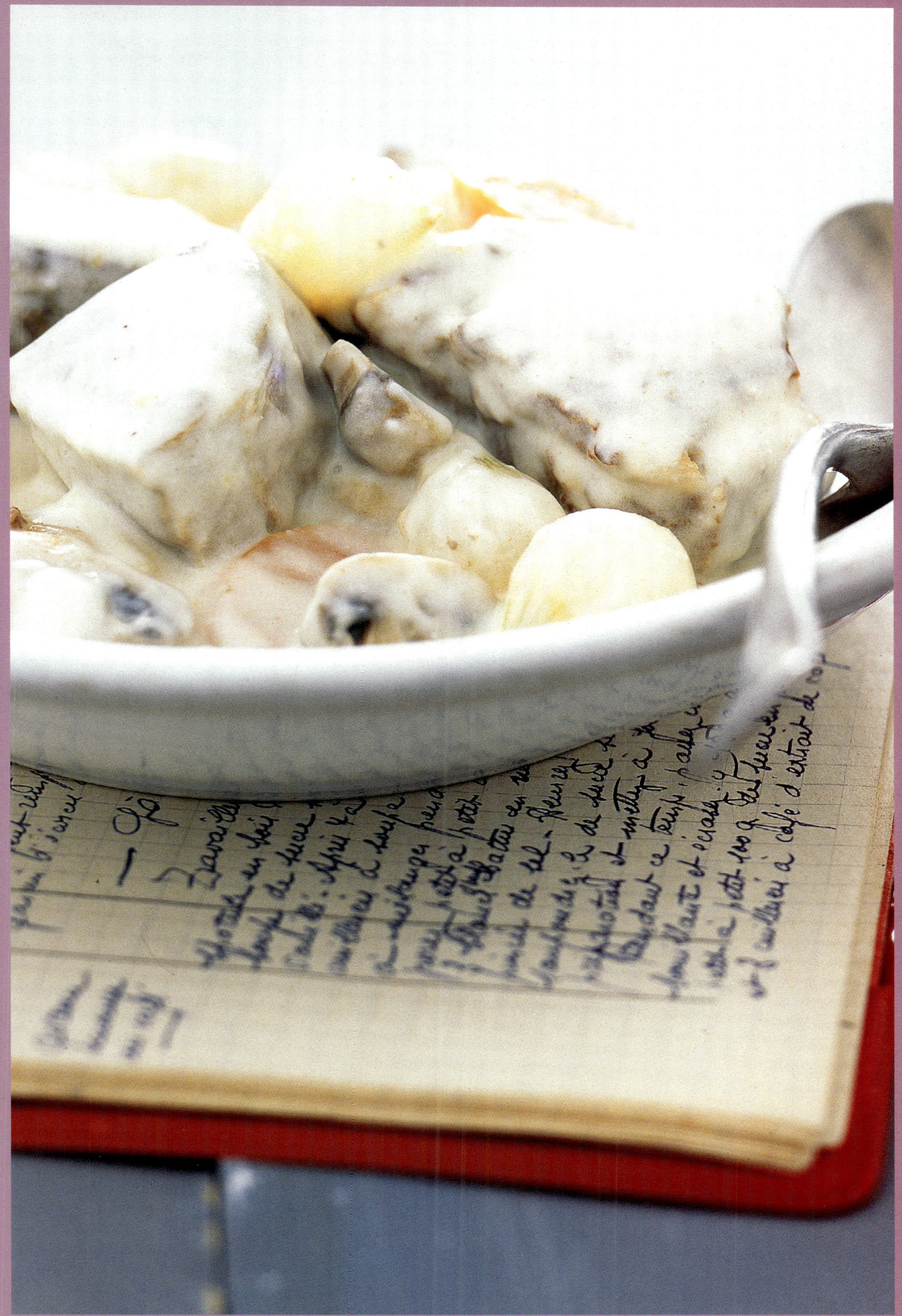

Des touristes américains visitant la Normandie en vélo à la recherche d'un lieu typique sont tombés amoureux de notre chaumière. Ils cherchaient une cuisinière prête à leur faire découvrir les produits régionaux pendant une pause déjeuner. C'est à cette occasion que la terrine aux pommes et au Camembert a vu le jour !

Terrine aux pommes et au camembert

Préparation : 20 minutes Réfrigération : 12 heures Pour 4 personnes

1 camembert à point
1 boîte de crème de camembert (facultatif)
2 belles pommes golden
2 cuillerées à soupe de calvados
35 g de beurre

• Épluchez les pommes, supprimez leur trognon et coupez-les en tranches. Faites-les revenir au beurre dans une poêle sur feu vif, en remuant avec précaution, pendant 3 minutes. Flambez avec le calvados. Laissez refroidir.

• Pendant ce temps, ôtez la croûte sur le pourtour du camembert et grattez celles du dessus et du dessous avec la pointe d'un couteau. Coupez le camembert en fines tranches.

• Mouillez l'intérieur d'une petite terrine en porcelaine ou d'un petit moule à cake et déposez-y un grand morceau de film alimentaire. Tapissez le fond du moule d'une première couche de pommes, recouvrez avec des tranches de camembert, tartinez avec de la crème de camembert, remettez une couche de pommes, une autre de camembert et une autre de crème de camembert, et terminez par une couche de pommes. Rabattez le film alimentaire pour recouvrir la terrine, tassez avec la paume de la main, posez un poids sur le dessus et mettez au réfrigérateur pendant une nuit.

Servez à la place du traditionnel plateau de fromages, accompagné d'une salade verte croquante au vinaigre de cidre, parsemée de pommes séchées et de noix concassées.

Remplacez éventuellement le camembert par du bleu d'Auvergne, et les pommes par des poires.

Boissons conseillées : cidre, calvados.

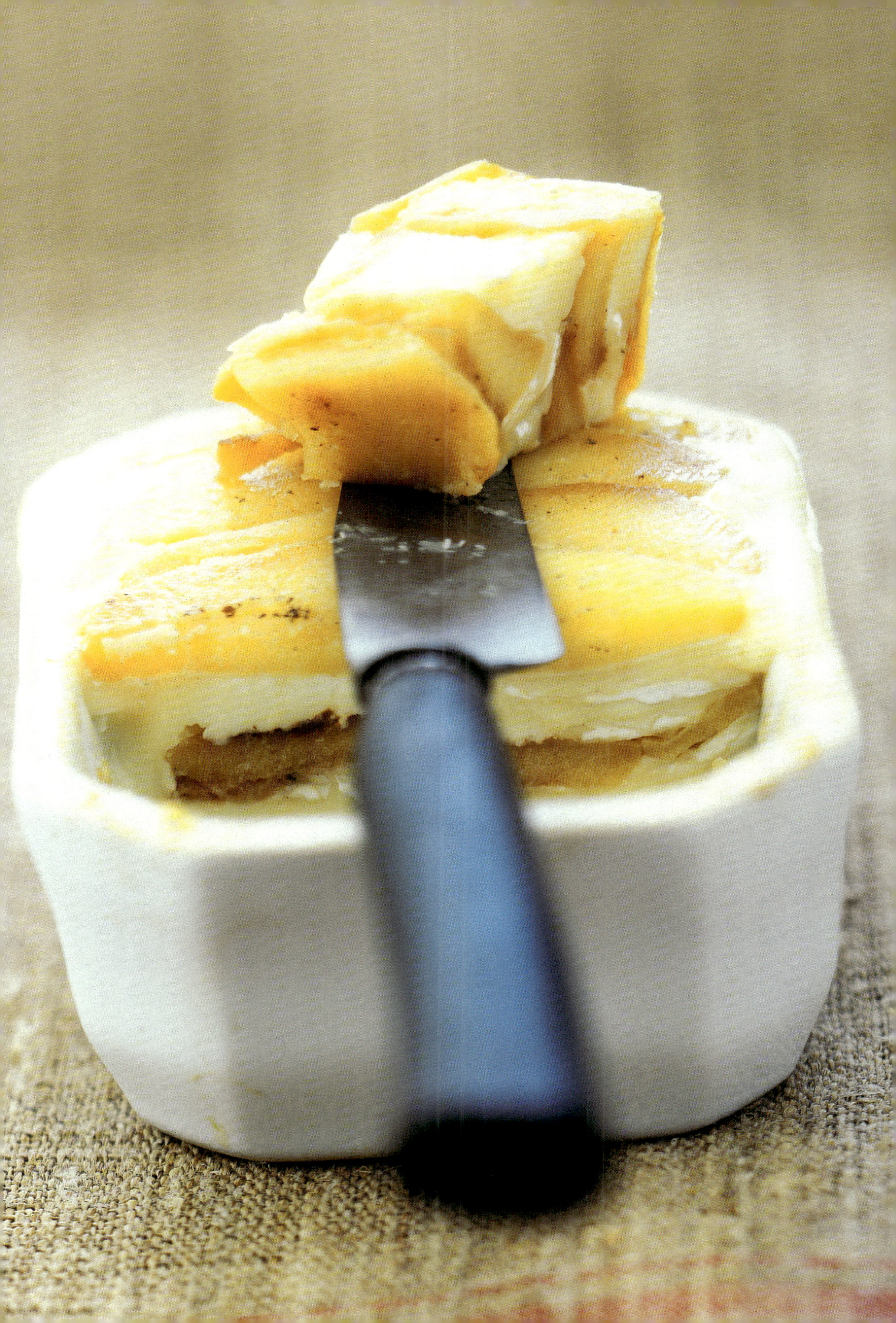

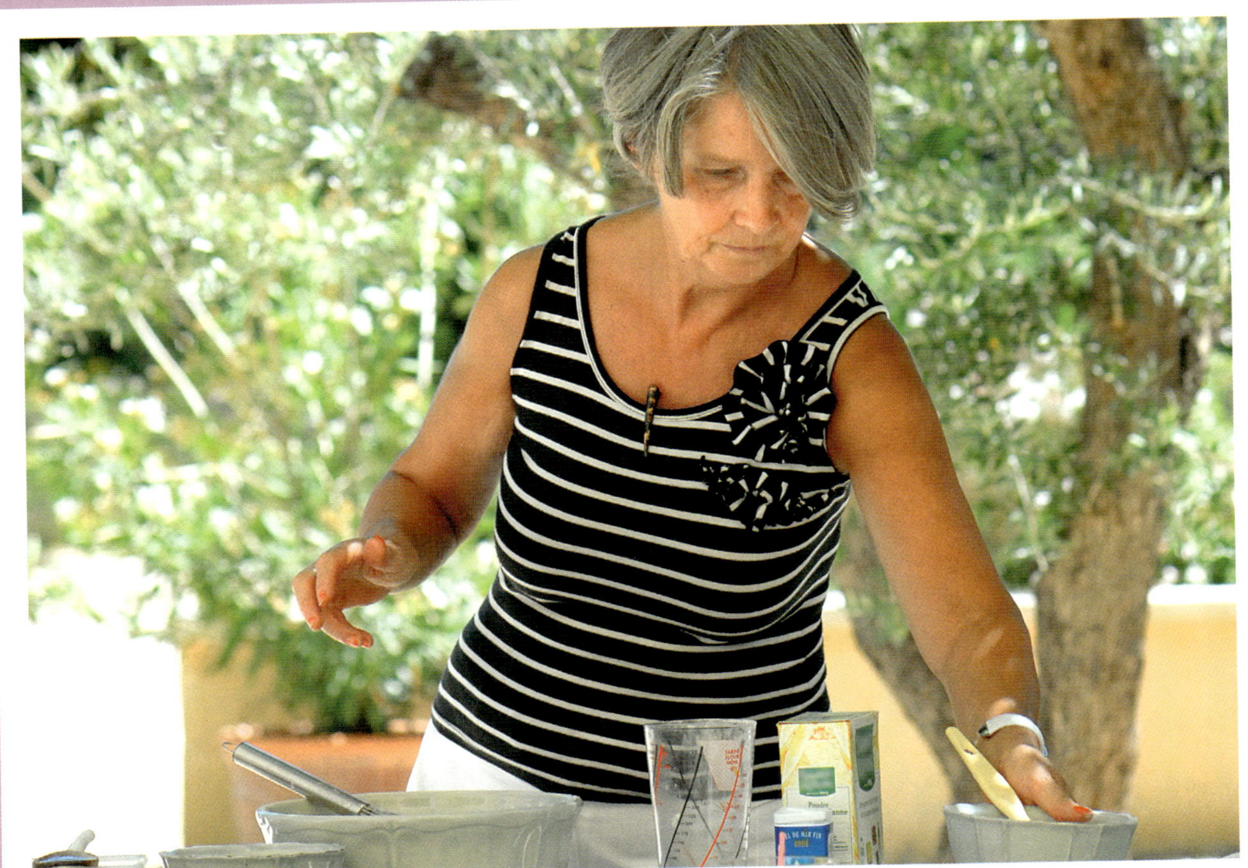

Celui qui ne connaît pas ces petits gâteaux au goût d'amande passe à côté de quelque chose... Chez nous, on aime bien poser des fruits sur les financiers pour les décorer.

Financiers aux fruits d'été

Préparation : 15 minutes Cuisson : 15 minutes Pour 24 financiers

200 g de beurre
250 g de sucre glace
5 blancs d'œufs
135 g d'amandes en poudre
55 g de farine
6 framboises
6 fraises
6 cerises
6 groseilles

- Préchauffez le four à 180 °C. Faites fondre 170 g de beurre dans une casserole jusqu'à l'obtention d'une couleur noisette.
- Dans un saladier, mélangez le sucre, la poudre d'amande et la farine, incorporez les blancs d'œufs, versez le beurre noisette, mélangez.
- Versez la pâte dans de petits moules à financiers beurrés ou de petits moules ronds. Déposez un fruit sur chaque financier, laissez les queues des cerises et des groseilles. Laissez cuire 15 minutes environ. Démoulez et laissez refroidir.

Boissons conseillées : thé, café.

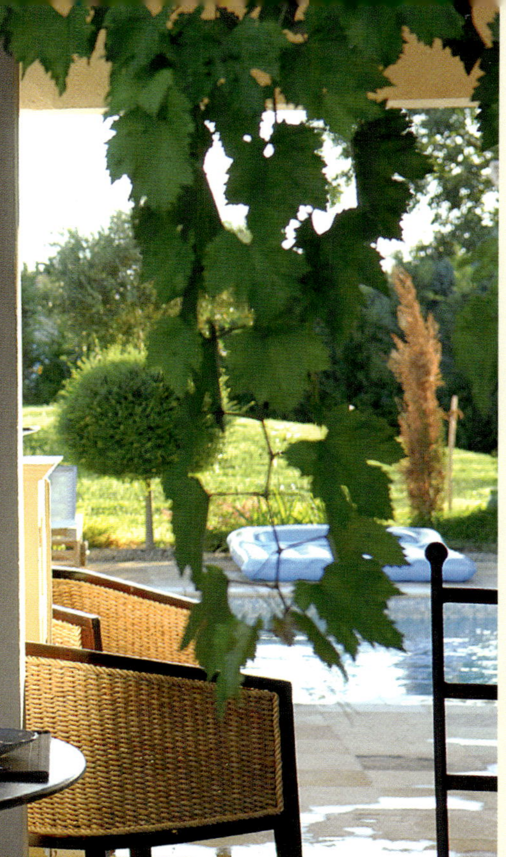

Clafoutis aux abricots et aux amandes

Dès que les premiers abricots font leur apparition, je prépare ce dessert ; c'est le préféré d'Arthur, qui le finit souvent le lendemain matin, au petit déjeuner…

Préparation : 10 minutes
Cuisson : 35-40 minutes
Pour 6 personnes

500 g d'abricots
50 g de beurre
200 g de sucre semoule
2 œufs entiers
2 jaunes d'œufs
60 g de Maïzena
25 cl de lait
25 cl de crème liquide
50 g d'amandes entière émondées

- Préchauffez le four à 180 °C. Ouvrez les abricots en deux et retirez le noyau. Faites fondre 40 g de beurre dans une poêle, ajoutez les abricots et 50 g de sucre, cuisez à feu vif pendant 5 minutes.
- Beurrez un moule en verre ou en porcelaine, saupoudrez 20 g de sucre dans le fond du plat, déposez les abricots.
- Faites griller les amandes dans une poêle avec 1 cuillerée à café de sucre pour leur donner un goût légèrement caramélisé.
- Délayez la Maïzena dans le lait froid. Fouettez les œufs entiers et les jaunes d'œufs dans un saladier avec 100 g de sucre. Ajoutez le mélange lait/Maïzena. Versez la pâte sur les abricots et enfournez 30 minutes.
- Parsemez les amandes et faites cuire encore 5 à 10 minutes. Sortez du four et saupoudrez un peu de sucre en poudre.

Remplacez les abricots par des cerises, des prunes, des mirabelles, des pruneaux… en fonction des saisons ; remplacez les amandes par des pistaches ou des pignons. Les enfants adorent aussi ajouter de petits morceaux de nougat de Montélimar aux abricots (20 g).

Boissons conseillées : muscat de Rivesaltes, muscat corse.

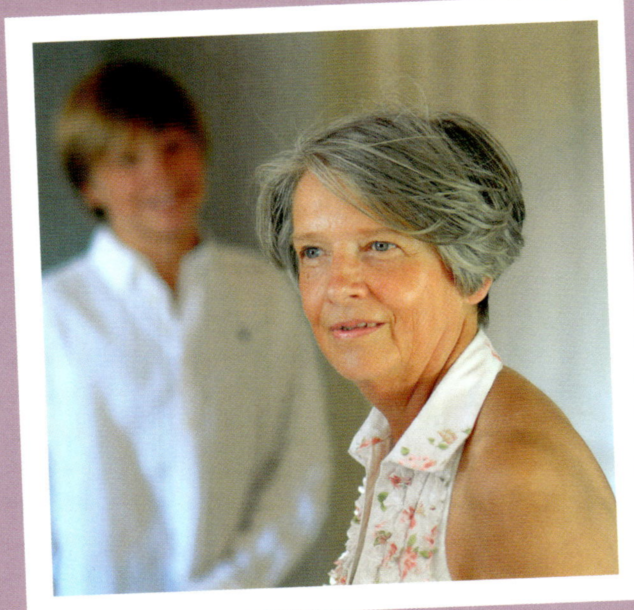

J'ai toujours vu ma grand-mère préparer ce dessert de cette manière. Je ne connais pas de meilleure recette, et je suis toujours déçue au restaurant quand je me laisse tenter par une Tatin, car elle ne ressemble pas à la nôtre, qui reste pour moi la meilleure du monde.

Tarte Tatin à notre façon et son petit pot de crème

Préparation : 40 minutes Réfrigération : 1 heure Cuisson : 40 minutes Pour 6 personnes

1 pot de crème fraîche épaisse

Pour la pâte
250 g de farine
125 g de sucre
100 g de beurre mou
2 cuillerées à soupe de lait

Pour le caramel
100 g de sucre
10 cl d'eau

Pour la garniture
1,500 kg à 2 kg de pommes
50 g de beurre

- Commencez par préparer la pâte. Dans un saladier, mélangez du bout des doigts la farine, le beurre coupé en morceaux, le sucre et le lait ; ramassez la pâte en boule, puis aplatissez-la légèrement. Mettez-la au frais pour 1 heure.
- Préparez le caramel en faisant chauffer le sucre et l'eau dans une casserole jusqu'à obtenir une jolie couleur brune. Versez dans un moule à manqué et répartissez-le au fond du moule.
- Épluchez les pommes et coupez-les en quartiers. Dans une poêle, faites fondre le beurre, mettez-y les pommes à dorer sur chaque face, puis déposez-les sur le caramel. Comblez tous les espaces et n'hésitez pas à superposer les morceaux si nécessaire ; à la cuisson, les pommes vont se tasser.
- Préchauffez le four à 180 °C. Étalez la pâte à la dimension de votre moule, recouvrez-en les pommes et rentrez l'excédent de pâte à l'intérieur du moule le long du bord. Faites cuire au four pendant 35 à 40 minutes.
- Démoulez sur un grand plat et servez tiède, accompagné d'un pot de crème fraîche épaisse.

Boissons conseillées : vin doux naturel, bourbon.

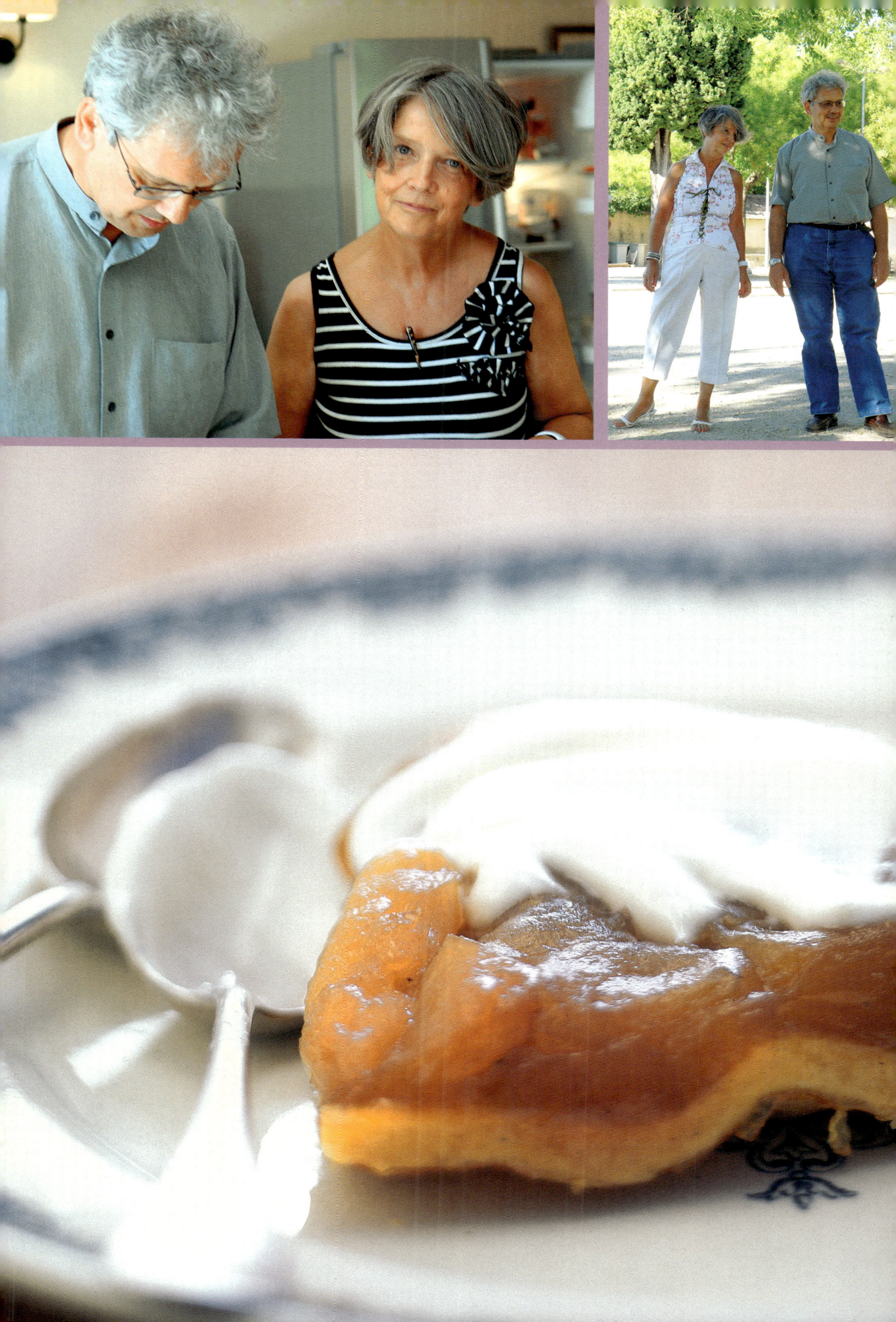

La crème renversée est le dessert des grands-mères par excellence. Je tiens de ma chère Maman cette recette au goût de vanille et de caramel ; nul doute que, comme à moi, elle vous rappellera votre enfance…

Crème renversante au caramel

Préparation : 30 minutes Cuisson : 50 minutes Réfrigération : 2 heures Pour 8 personnes

Pour la crème

1 l de lait entier
6 œufs
200 g de sucre semoule
1 gousse de vanille

Pour le caramel

140 g de sucre
4 cuillerées à soupe d'eau

• Préparez le caramel. Réunissez l'eau et le sucre dans une petite casserole, faites chauffer à feu vif en remuant de temps en temps la casserole, comme si vous vouliez faire des ronds. Surtout, ne plongez aucun ustensile dans la casserole… L'eau va s'évaporer et, petit à petit, le sirop va se colorer, prendre une couleur caramel blond, puis brun clair. L'odeur doit être agréable ; si une odeur de brûlé survient et que le caramel vire au brun foncé, très foncé, jetez-le et recommencez. Versez ensuite le caramel dans le fond du moule. Attrapez le bord du moule avec un torchon et répartissez le caramel dans le fond. Attention à ne pas vous brûler ! Laissez refroidir.

• Préparez la crème. Mettez le lait à bouillir avec la gousse de vanille fendue en deux et laissez infuser quelques minutes. Dans un saladier, mélangez les œufs entiers avec le sucre. Versez progressivement le lait bouillant sur la préparation précédente, en remuant avec un fouet (les œufs ne doivent pas coaguler). Filtrez la crème au travers d'un chinois (petite passoire à grille très fine), retirez la gousse de vanille et récupérez les petites graines noires à l'intérieur pour les mettre dans la crème. Versez la préparation dans le moule.

• Préchauffez le four à 180 °C. Déposez une feuille de papier sulfurisé dans le fond d'un plat à gratin. Posez le moule dans le plat et versez de l'eau bouillante à mi-hauteur. Faites cuire la crème dans ce bain-marie pendant 35 à 40 minutes. Vérifiez la cuisson en piquant la pointe d'un couteau au cœur de la crème : aucune trace ne doit apparaître (sinon, prolongez la cuisson de quelques minutes). Retirez du four, laissez refroidir, puis mettez au frais pendant 2 heures.

• Au moment de servir, décollez la crème en longeant délicatement la paroi du moule à l'aide d'un couteau. Posez un plat sur le dessus et renversez le moule : la crème va se décoller, et le caramel se répartira uniformément.

Vous pouvez aussi utiliser de petits moules individuels.

Boisson conseillée : Vieux Rivesalte, Quart de Chaume.

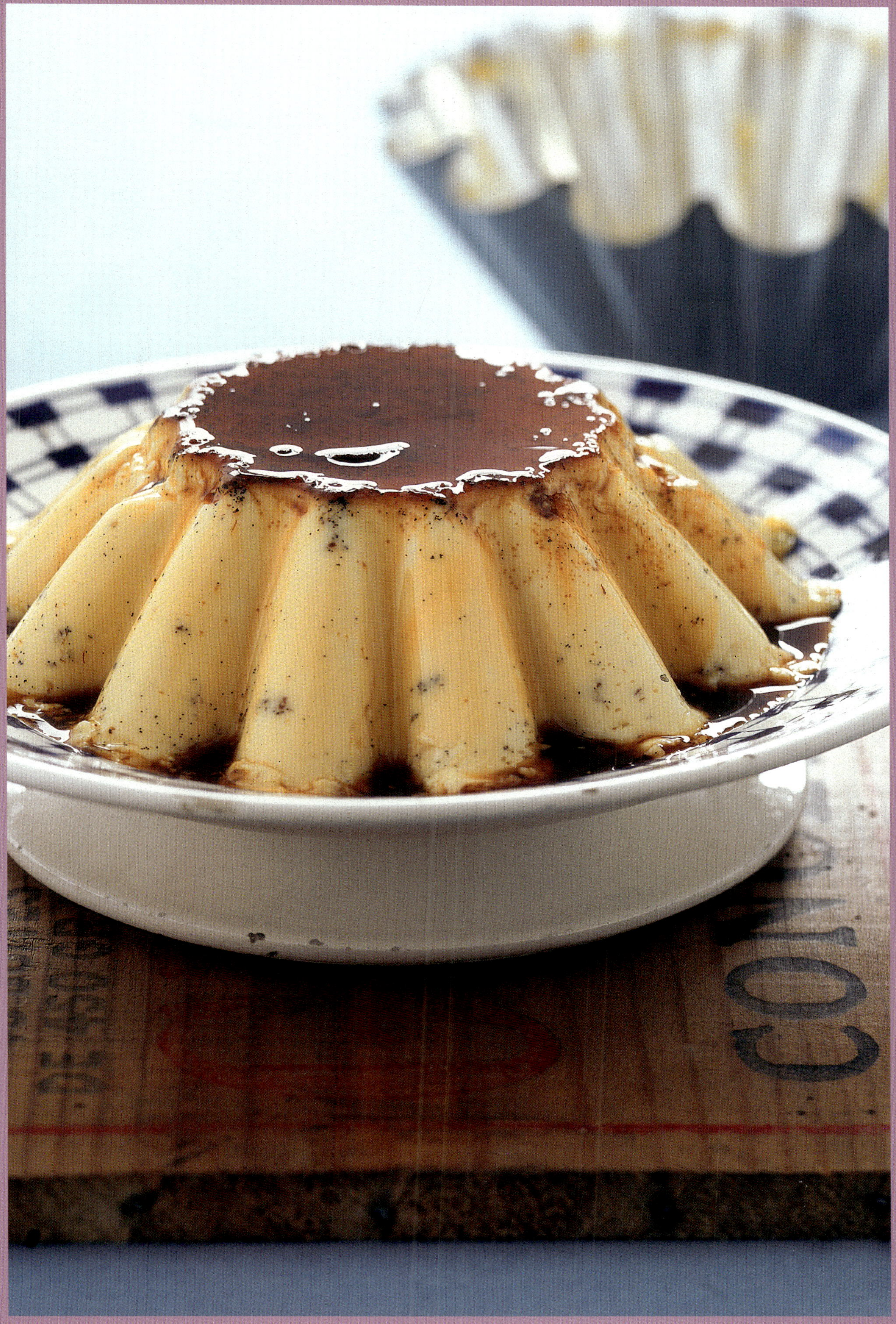

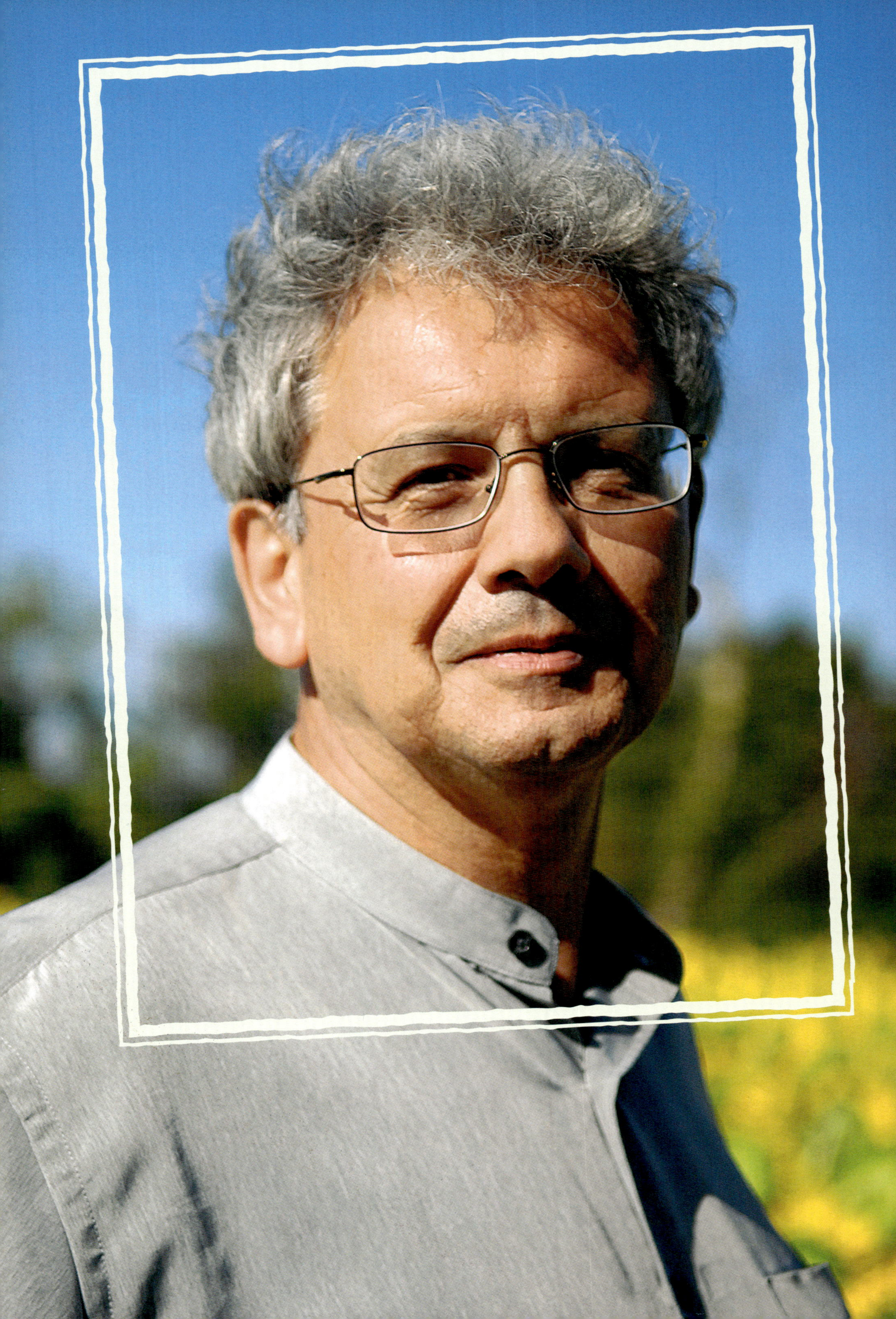

Jean-Paul

Le grand-père

Si j'étais... une couleur,

je serais le vert clair des jeunes pousses
qui symbolisent la nature, l'espoir et la vie.

Si j'étais... une odeur,

je serais celle du basilic, qui donne à tous les plats méditerranéens
une saveur incomparable.

Si j'étais... une saveur,

je serais celle du vinaigre pour que mon acidité relève le quotidien.

Si j'étais... un ustensile,

je serais un presse-purée pour préparer une nourriture
qui peut être donnée aux plus faibles.

Si j'étais... un souvenir gourmand,

je serais une salade de fruits frais comme savait si bien la préparer Maman.

Si j'étais... un péché mignon,

je serais une tarte aux pommes...
parce que c'est tout simplement mon dessert préféré.

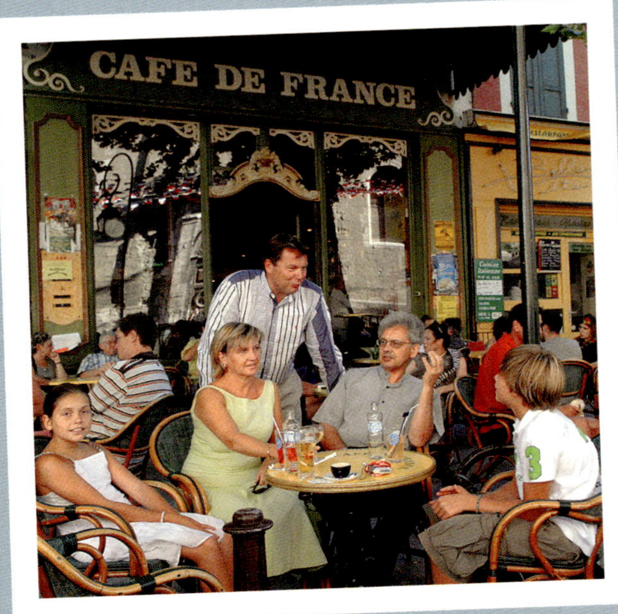

À servir sur du pain grillé ou avec des petits légumes crus, ces tapenades sentent bon la Provence. À déguster sans modération à l'ombre d'un olivier !

Tapenade aux trois couleurs

Préparation : 20 minutes Pour 6 personnes

125 g d'olives noires dénoyautées
125 g d'olives vertes dénoyautées
2 gousses d'ail
100 g de miettes de thon
100 g de câpres
100 g d'anchois
8 cuillerées à soupe d'huile d'olive
250 g de tomates confites ou séchées
100 g de pignons de pin
thym
1 bouquet de basilic
poivre

- Pelez et hachez une gousse d'ail et coupez-la en deux. Égouttez le thon et les câpres.
- Mixez une demi-gousse d'ail, le thon, la moitié des câpres et 2 cuillerées à soupe d'huile d'olive avec les olives vertes égouttées. Poivrez, ajoutez un peu de thym et versez la tapenade verte dans un ravier. Décorez avec une olive verte.
- Mixez l'autre demi-gousse d'ail, les anchois, le reste des câpres et 2 cuillerées à soupe d'huile d'olive avec les olives noires égouttées. Poivrez, ajoutez un peu de thym et versez la tapenade noire dans un deuxième ravier. Décorez avec une olive noire.
- Épluchez la deuxième gousse d'ail. Mixez-la avec les tomates, les pignons, le basilic et 4 cuillerées à soupe d'huile d'olive. Poivrez, puis versez la tapenade rouge dans un troisième ravier. Décorez d'une feuille de basilic.
- Servez ces tapenades avec de petits croûtons grillés ou des légumes crus (radis, concombre, chou-fleur, endives, tomates-cerises...).

Boisson conseillée : Côte de Provence rosé.

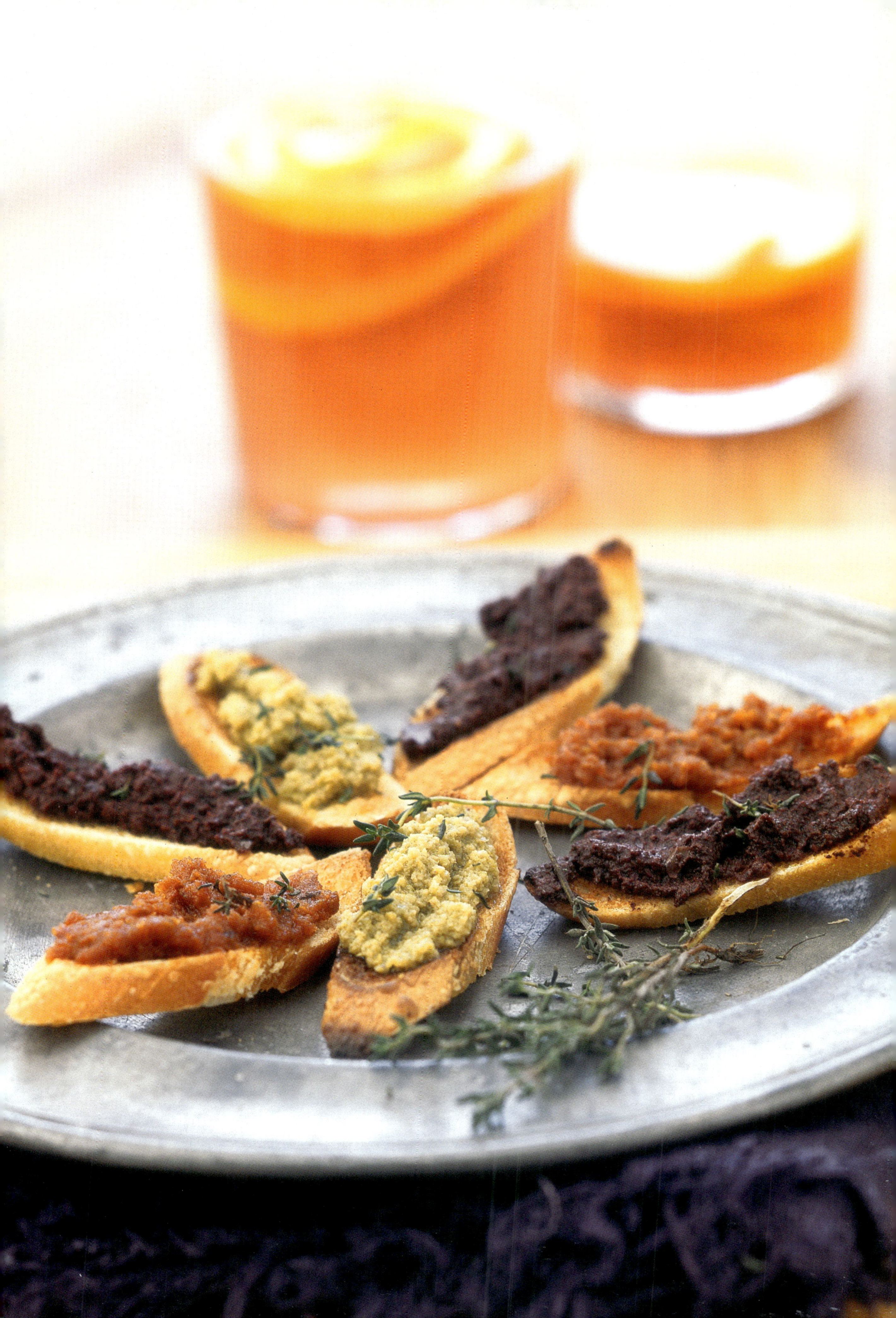

La véritable pissaladière est une pâte à pain à l'huile d'olive, sur laquelle on étend une compote d'oignon additionnée de pissalat avant de la décorer de filets d'anchois et d'olives noires de Nice. Mais le pissalat étant un petit poisson qui se pêche uniquement la nuit en Méditerranée et que l'on trouve donc assez rarement, même à Nice, je vous propose une pissaladière sans pissalat, comme la font la plupart des gens, sauf que vous et moi savons maintenant pourquoi...

Pissaladière sans pissalat

Préparation : 30 minutes Cuisson : 30 minutes Pour 4 personnes

Pour la pâte à pain
250 g de farine
1/2 sachet de levure
1 pincée de sel
10 cl d'huile
10 cl d'eau bouillante
thym
poivre

Pour la garniture
2 kg d'oignons
huile d'olive
3 cuillerées à soupe d'eau
50 g d'olives noires de Nice
(« caillettes »)
12 filets d'anchois
thym
sel, poivre

- Préparez la pâte. Mélangez les ingrédients dans l'ordre donné et ramassez la pâte en boule. Réservez au frais pendant que vous préparez la garniture. Si vous manquez de temps, vous pouvez commander la pâte à pain chez le boulanger.
- Pelez les oignons et coupez-les en rondelles de 5 mm d'épaisseur. Déposez-les dans une cocotte avec 5 cuillerées à soupe d'huile d'olive, l'eau et une pincée de sel. Couvrez et laissez mijoter 20 à 30 minutes. Les oignons doivent confire sans colorer. En fin de cuisson, ôtez le couvercle pour faire évaporer le maximum de jus. Poivrez et laissez refroidir.
- Étalez la pâte en un disque plat d'environ 5 mm d'épaisseur. Déposez les oignons dessus, égalisez, saupoudrez de thym et faites des croisillons avec les anchois. Répartissez les olives, arrosez d'un filet d'huile d'olive et enfournez 25 à 30 minutes. Dégustez chaud, tiède ou froid.

Boissons conseillées : blanc de Cassis ou de Beullet.

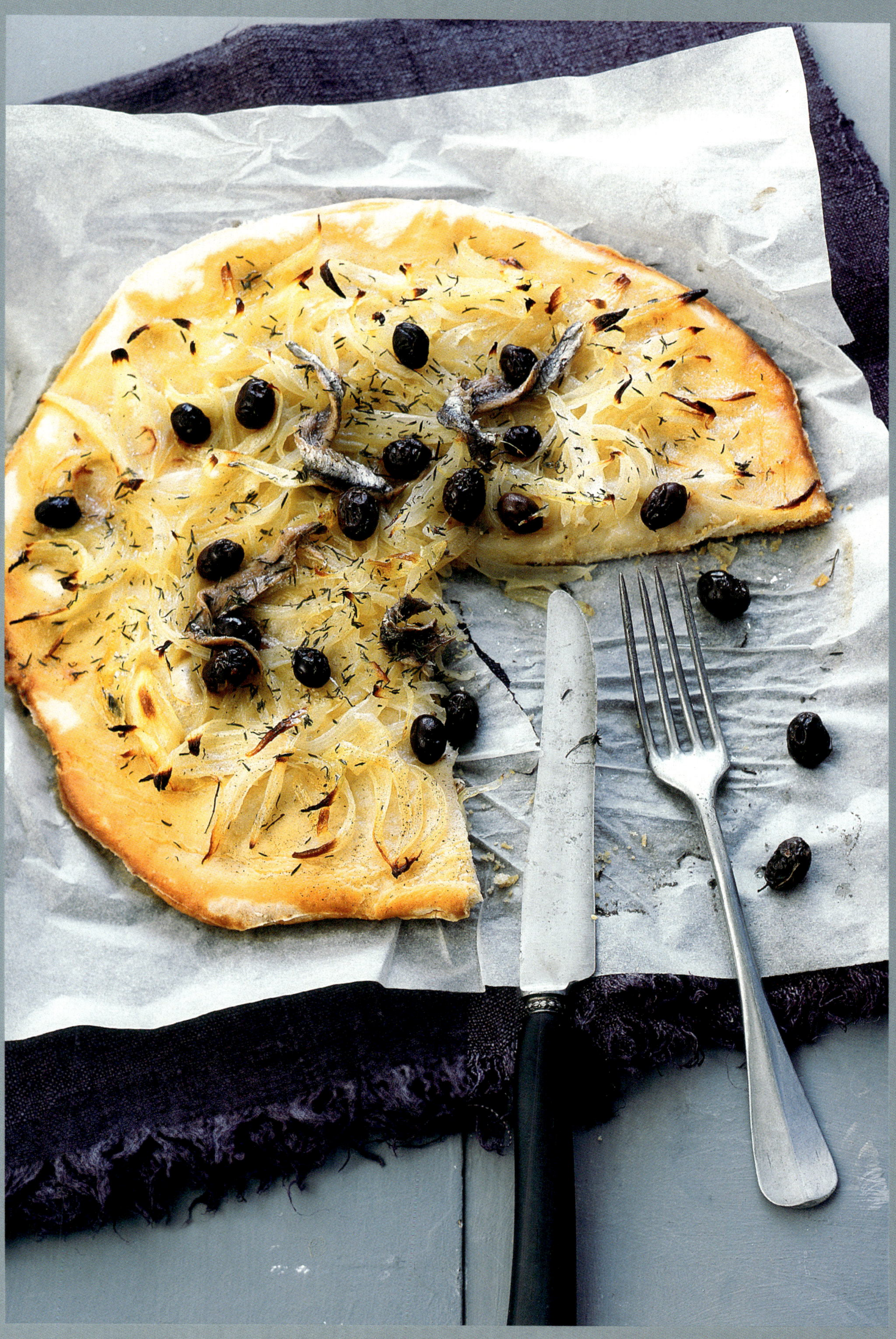

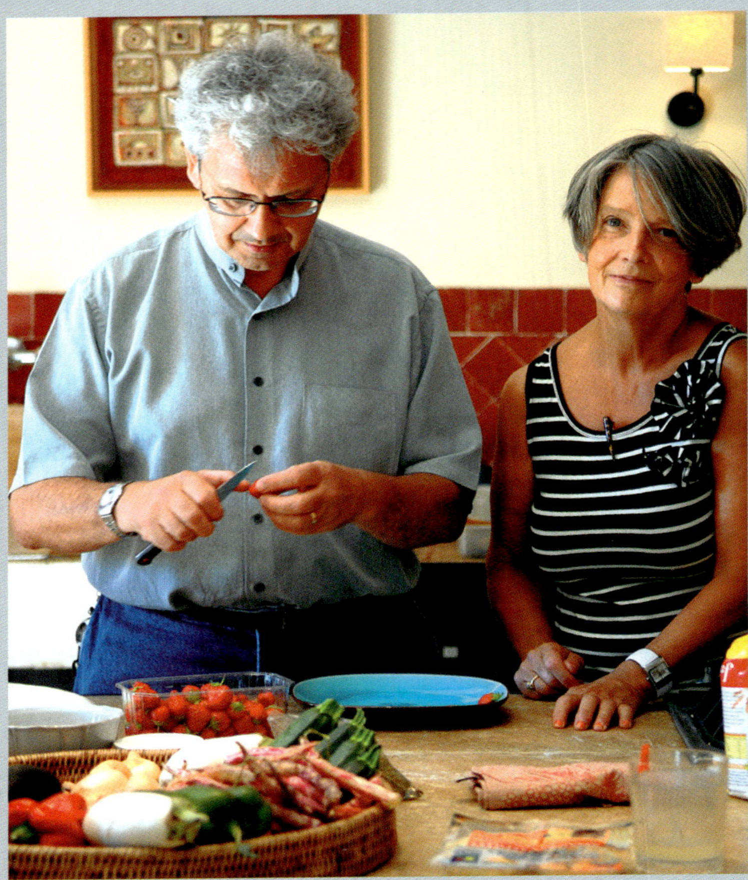

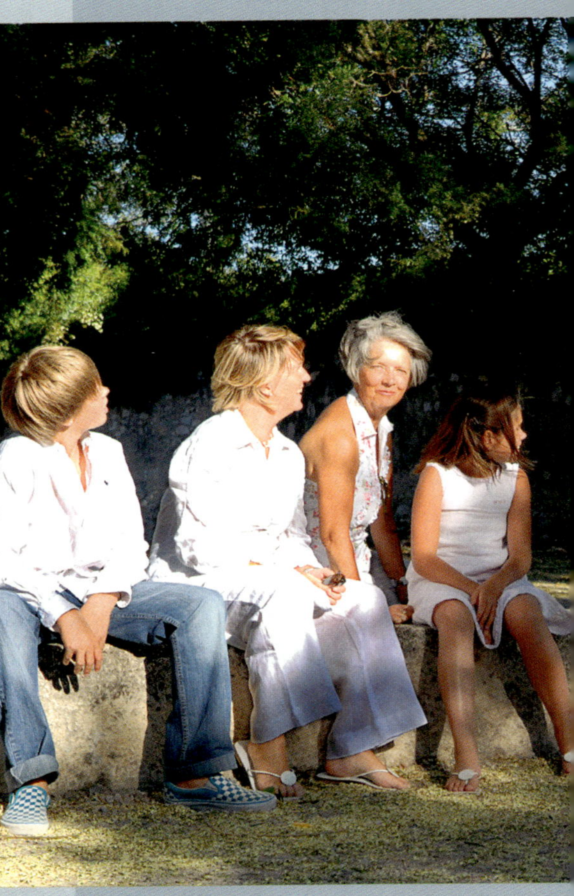

Ratatouille poêlée minute à la fleur de thym et au basilic

Préparation : 30 minutes

Cuisson : 20 minutes

Pour 4 personnes

1 tomate
1 poivron rouge
1 poivron vert
1 poivron jaune
1 courgette
1 aubergine
1 petit bocal de coulis de tomate
50 g d'échalotes
1 oignon
2 gousses d'ail
5 feuilles de basilic
10 cl d'huile d'olive
fleur de thym
sel, poivre blanc

Comment parler de la Provence sans évoquer la ratatouille que cuisinait mon père le plus simplement du monde avec les légumes de son jardin.

- Lavez et taillez tous les légumes en petit dés. Versez l'huile d'olive dans une poêle, puis ajoutez l'échalote pelée et hachée et les gousses d'ail en chemise (avec leur peau), légèrement écrasées avec le plat du couteau. Assaisonnez de sel et de poivre et faites suer sans laisser colorer.
- Ajoutez les légumes et faites compoter doucement pendant 15 à 20 minutes, tout en remuant.
- Liez la ratatouille avec le coulis de tomate, ajoutez un peu de fleur de thym et le basilic, laissez cuire encore une dizaine de minutes. Servez chaud, tiède ou froid.

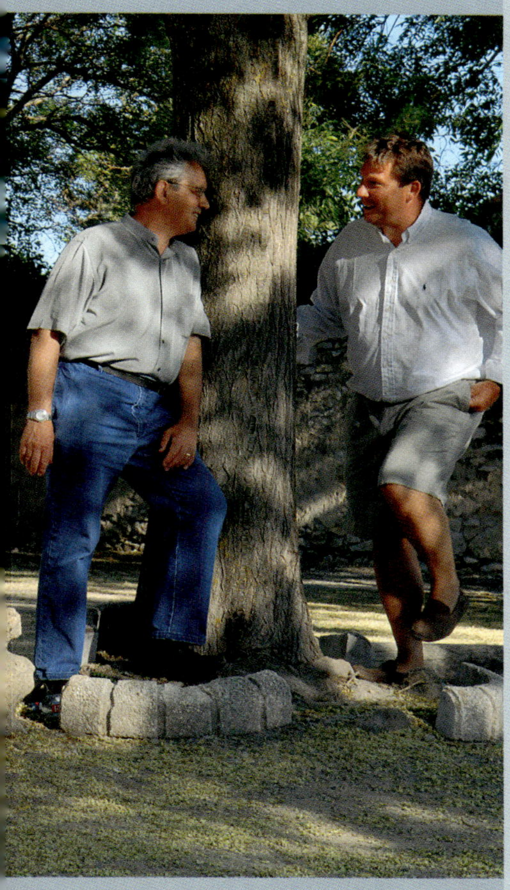

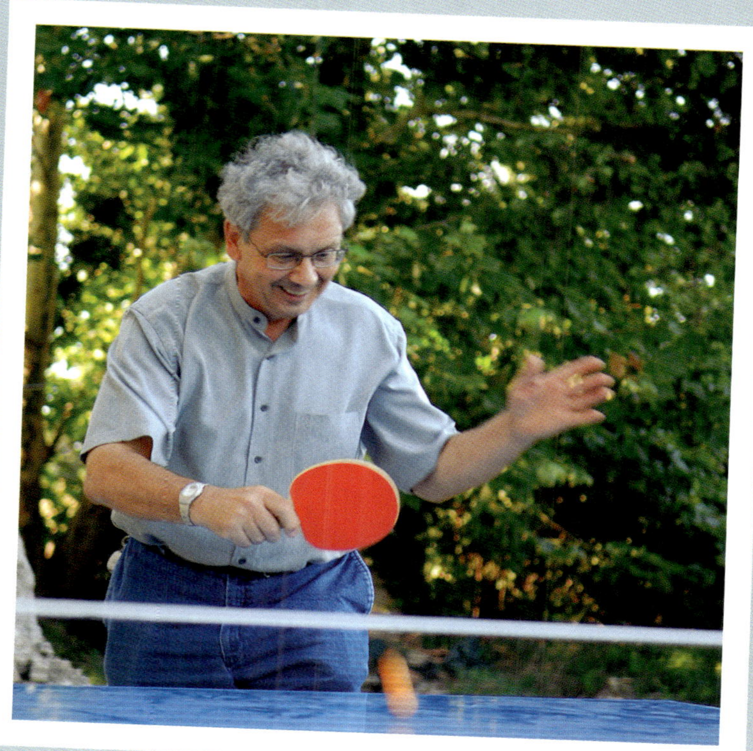

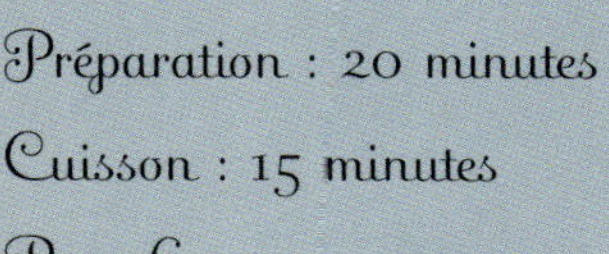

Préparation : 20 minutes

Cuisson : 15 minutes

Pour 6 personnes

Brochettes du pêcheur à l'aïoli

Typiquement méditerranéen, l'aïoli accompagnait autrefois en Provence le traditionnel plat de poisson du vendredi. Pour ma part, j'ai un peu adapté cette sauce classique en y incorporant une pointe de moutarde et une autre de safran.

Pour les brochettes

200 g de filet de lotte
200 g de filet de saumon
16 grosses crevettes

Pour l'aïoli

1 jaune d'œuf
2 gousses d'ail
1/2 cuillerée à café de moutarde forte
20 cl d'huile d'olive vierge pas trop forte (ou moitié huile d'olive et moitié huile de colza)
le jus de 1/2 citron
1 pointe de safran
sel, poivre de Cayenne

- Préparez l'aïoli. Dans un petit saladier, mélangez le jaune d'œuf, la moutarde, une goutte d'eau, du sel, du poivre de Cayenne, une pointe de safran et les gousses d'ail pelées et hachées. Montez l'aïoli à la main ou au mixeur en incorporant lentement la moitié de l'huile.
- Ajoutez le jus de citron et éventuellement une goutte d'eau, rectifiez l'assaisonnement et incorporez le reste de l'huile d'olive.
- Préparez les brochettes du pêcheur. Coupez les poissons en morceaux de taille identique, enfilez-les sur des piques en bois, en intercalant les crevettes. Faites cuire au barbecue et servez avec la sauce aïoli.

Ce plat est un hymne à la Provence, à déguster l'hiver quand le mistral soufle. La daube est un plat coloré et parfumé qui mijote sur le coin du feu et embaume toute la maison.

Daube à la provençale

Préparation : 30 minutes Marinade : 3 heures Cuisson : 2 h 30 Pour 6 personnes

1,500 kg de bœuf à cuisson longue (paleron ou jumeau)
5 cl d'huile d'olive
50 g de beurre
1 oignon émincé
400 g de coulis de tomate
branches de thym frais
et feuilles de laurier pour la décoration
quelques olives noires ou vertes
sel, poivre

Pour la marinade
60 cl de rosé de Provence
4 gousses d'ail épluchées
3 branches de thym
2 feuilles de laurier
1 carotte épluchée
et coupée en rondelles
1 oignon émincé

- Préparez la marinade en mettant tous les ingrédients dans un saladier. Ajoutez les morceaux de bœuf coupés en gros cubes, mélangez et recouvrez avec du film alimentaire. Laissez mariner de 3 à 6 heures au réfrigérateur.
- Filtrez la marinade et conservez tous les ingrédients : la viande et l'oignon d'une part, la marinade, le thym et le laurier d'autre part.
- Dans une cocotte de préférence en fonte, mettez le beurre à fondre avec l'huile d'olive. Ajoutez la viande et l'oignon de la marinade, faites-les dorer sur toutes leurs faces. Ajoutez l'autre oignon émincé, mélangez avec une cuillère en bois.
- Quand la viande et les oignons ont une belle coloration, versez la marinade, avec le thym et le laurier, ajoutez le coulis de tomate et 15 cl d'eau ; salez, poivrez, couvrez la cocotte et laissez mijoter 2 h 30 à feu très doux (ou au four à 150 °C). Surveillez régulièrement et mélangez de temps en temps.
- Servez dans la cocotte, après avoir décoré de feuilles de laurier et de thym frais et parsemé de quelques olives.

Si vous trouvez que la sauce est trop réduite, ajoutez un peu d'eau ; si au contraire elle est trop liquide, ôtez le couvercle pour laisser évaporer. Ce plat est délicieux réchauffé.

Boissons conseillées : rosé de Provence, rosé de Bandol Château d'OTT.

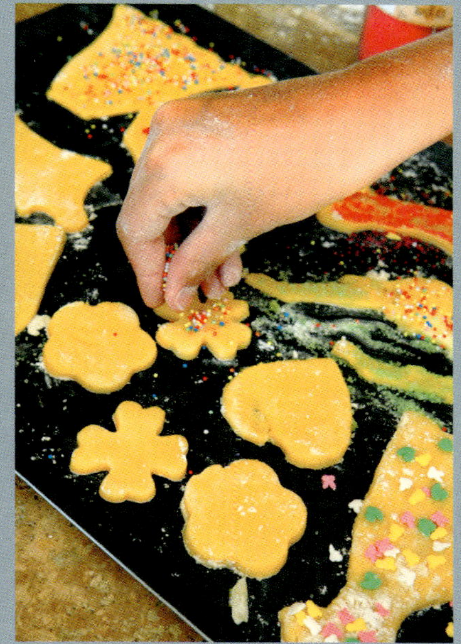
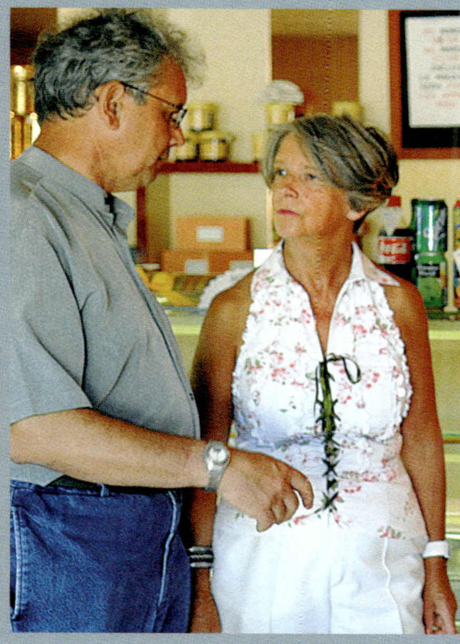
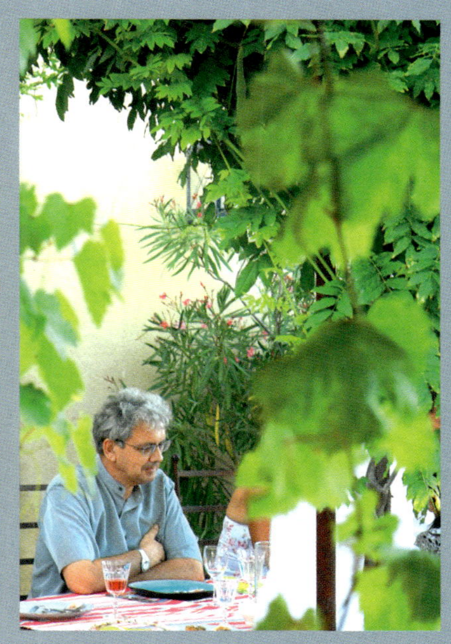

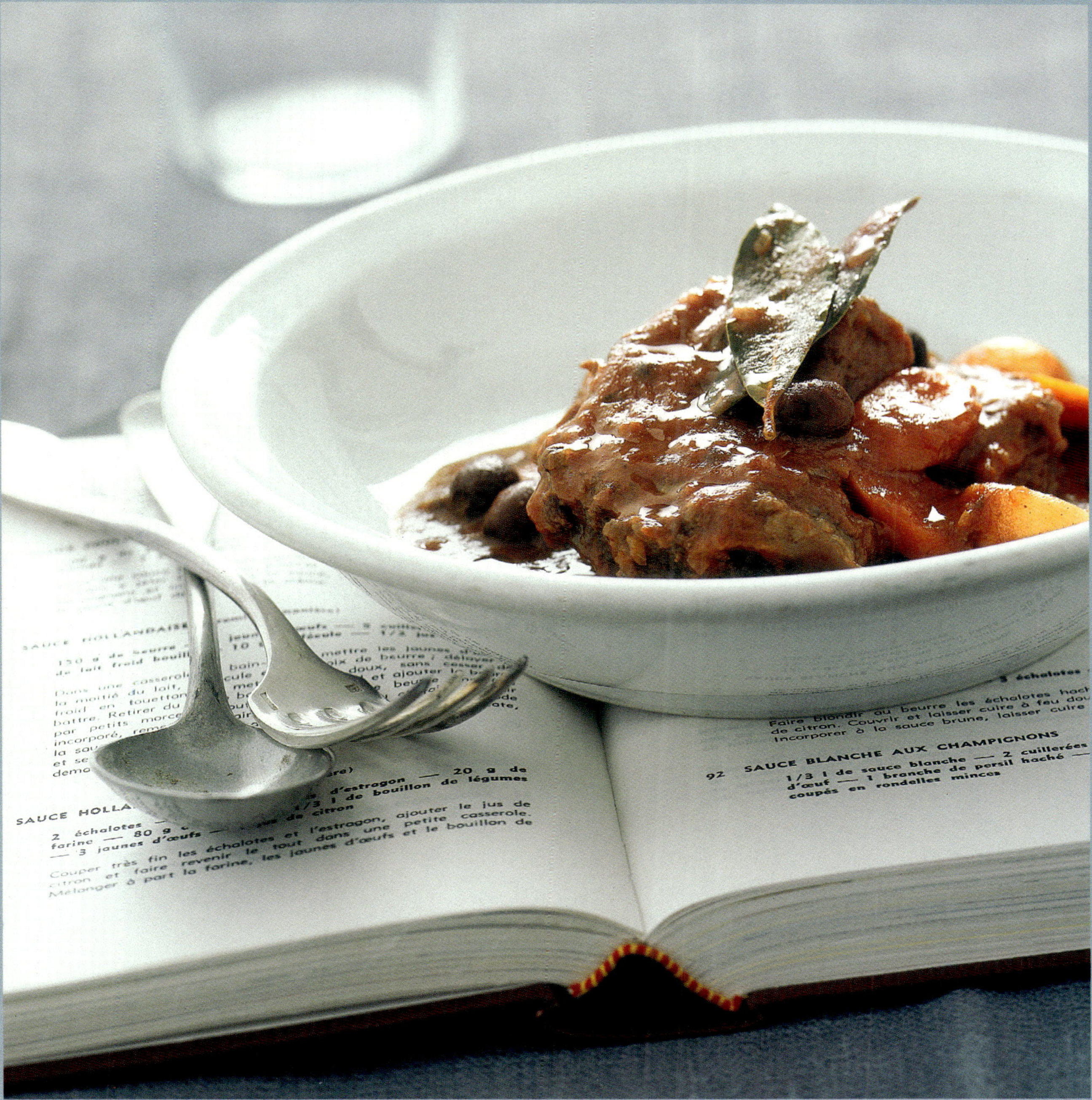

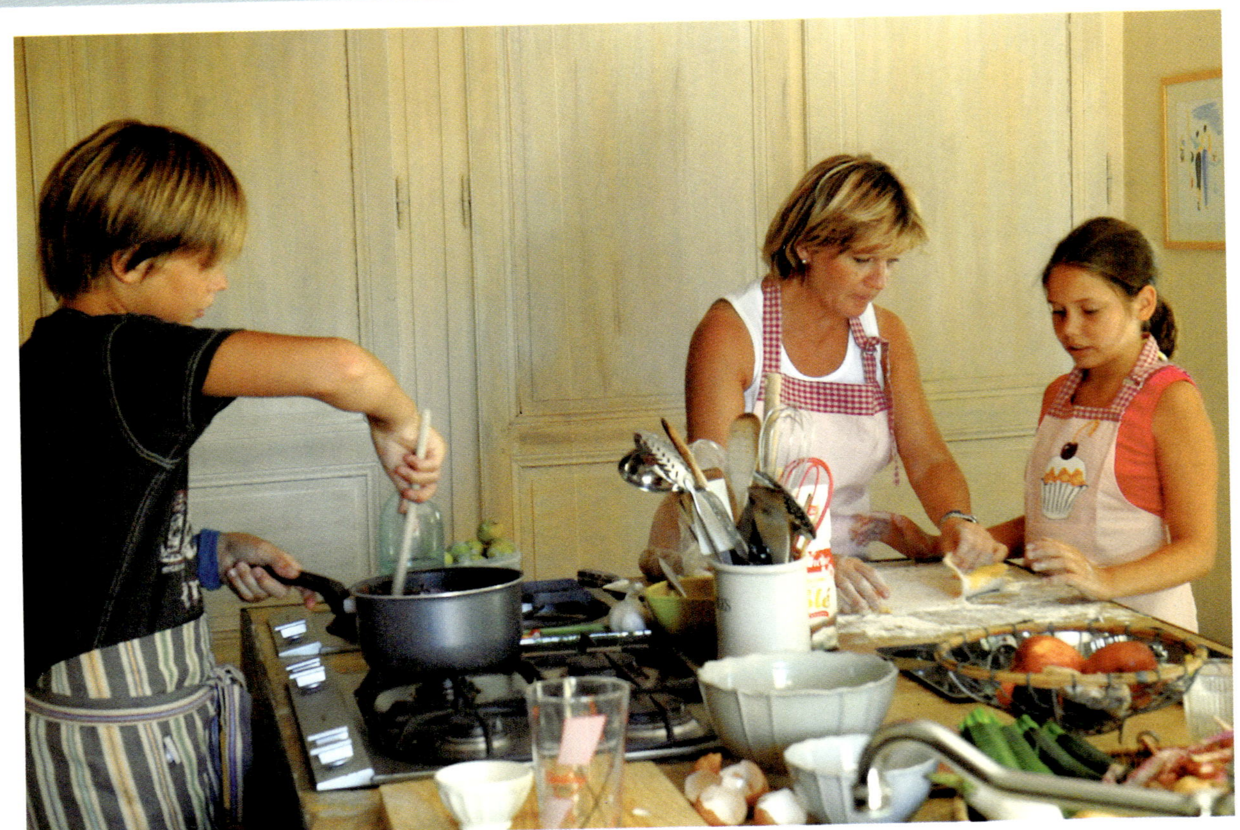

La pompe à l'huile fait partie des treize desserts du Noël provençal. Nous la préférons en portions individuelles, plus faciles à déguster. J'ai appris à tous mes petits-enfants à la préparer, et quand ils se lancent, je les regarde faire avec bienveillance et fierté.

Pompe à l'huile

Préparation : 10 minutes Cuisson : 35 minutes Pour 6 personnes

300 g de farine,
plus 20 g pour le plan de travail
100 g de sucre
1 tasse à café d'huile d'olive
1/2 tasse à café de fleur d'oranger
1/2 tasse à café de lait condensé non sucré
le zeste de 1 citron ou de 1 orange
beurre ou huile

- Mélangez la farine et le sucre, ajoutez l'huile d'olive, la fleur d'oranger, le lait et le zeste d'agrume.
- Préchauffez le four à 150 °C. Étalez la pâte sur le plan de travail fariné. À l'aide d'un emporte-pièce ou tout simplement d'un verre, découpez des petits ronds de pâte. Percez-y 4 trous pour les décorer. Faites cuire 35 minutes au four sur une pâque graissée, en surveillant la cuisson, car les biscuits brunissent très vite. Laissez refroidir.

Boisson conseillée : liqueur de verveine.

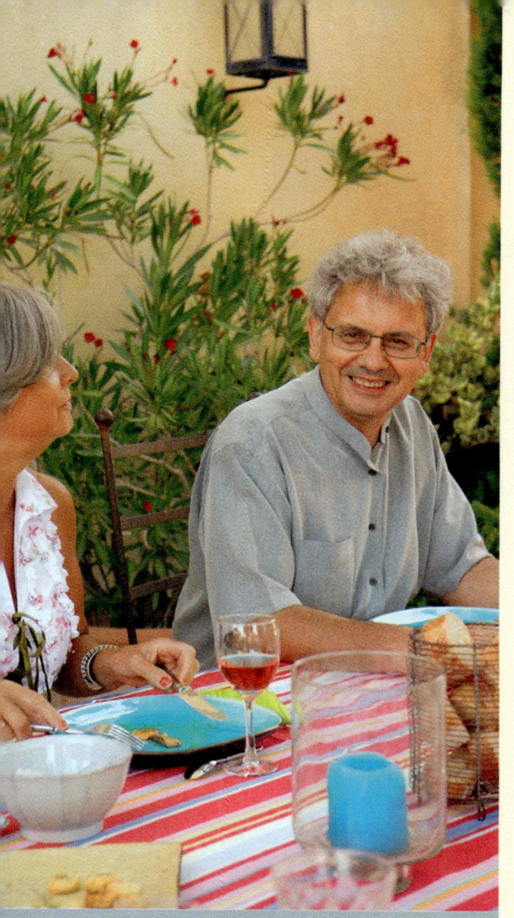

Tarte aux nectarines et à la crème de calisson

J'ai découvert la crème de calisson à Aix-en-Provence à la boutique du Roy René. Lors de nos nombreux passages en Provence, j'en profite toujours pour « faire le plein » de ces friandises, que nous dégustons seules ou dans des recettes que nous inventons, comme celle-ci.

Préparation : 1 heure
Réfrigération : 2 heures
Cuisson : 30 minutes
Pour 8 personnes

Pour la pâte à tarte

150 g de beurre
1/2 gousse de vanille
90 g de sucre glace
25 g de poudre d'amande
1 pincée de fleur de sel
1 œuf entier
250 g de farine

Pour la garniture

4 nectarines
50 g d'amandes émondées
1 cuillerée à café de sucre en poudre
1/2 pot de crème de calisson

Pour la crème à l'amande

5 cl de kirsch
150 g de sucre
75 g de poudre d'amande
2 œufs
2 jaunes d'œufs
20 cl de crème liquide

- Préparez la pâte. À l'aide d'un robot, malaxez le beurre en pommade ; ajoutez la vanille, le sucre glace, la poudre d'amande, le sel, l'œuf et enfin la farine. Travaillez la pâte. Mettez au frais pendant 2 heures.
- Préparez la crème. Fouettez les œufs entiers, les jaunes et le sucre jusqu'à ce que le mélange pâlisse. Incorporez la poudre d'amande, la crème liquide et le kirsch.
- Lavez et dénoyautez les nectarines, coupez-les en quartiers. Préchauffez le four à 180 °C.
- Étalez la pâte, chemisez-en un moule à tarte, piquez le fond avec les dents d'une fourchette, puis recouvrez de crème de calisson. Rangez les fruits dessus, nappez de crème à l'amande. Faites cuire au four pendant 35 minutes.
- Sortez la tarte du four et laissez tiédir 15 minutes. Pendant ce temps, grillez les amandes émondées avec le sucre dans une poêle, mélangez, laissez dorer à feu doux, jusqu'à ce que le mélange caramélise. Éparpillez sur la tarte après avoir laissé refroidir.

Si vous ne trouvez pas de crème de calisson, remplacez par 50 g de poudre d'amande.

Boisson conseillée : Coteau du Layon.

Ce cake, qui marie le goût du vrai chocolat noir et celui de la vanille, est un réel délice. Personne ne lui résiste !

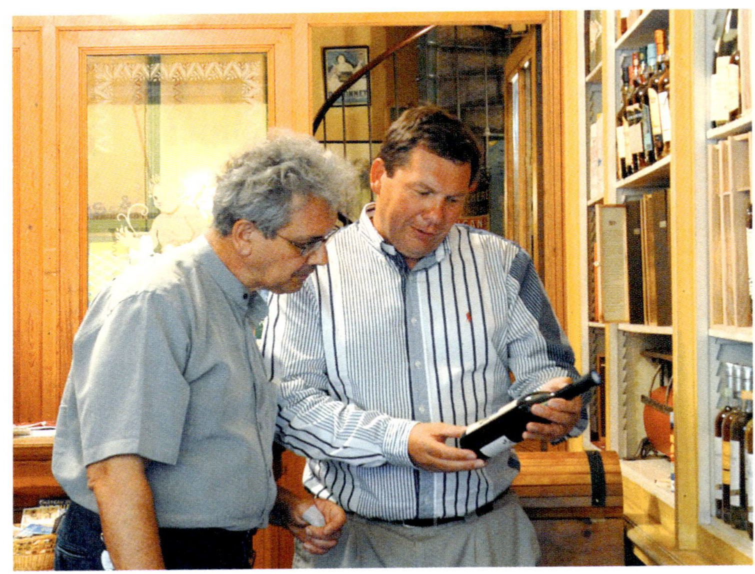

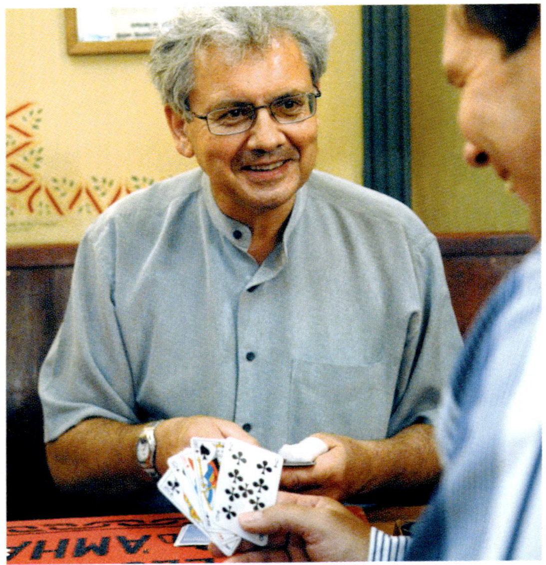

Cake marbré aux deux chocolats

Préparation : 30 minutes Cuisson : 45 minutes Pour 6 personnes

200 g de chocolat noir
100 g de chocolat au lait
170 g de beurre fondu
30 g de beurre
les graines d'une gousse de vanille
ou de la poudre de vanille
175 g de sucre en poudre
3 gros œufs
225 g de farine de blé
1/2 cuillerée à café de levure chimique

- Beurrez le moule à cake. Préchauffez le four à 180 °C. Dans une petite casserole, faites fondre à feu doux le chocolat noir avec 30 g de beurre, mélangez pour obtenir une pâte brillante et lisse.
- Battez le sucre et les œufs entiers dans une jatte, puis versez 170 g de beurre fondu, les graines de vanille (ou la poudre de vanille), la farine et la levure chimique ; mélangez l'ensemble, afin d'obtenir une pâte homogène.
- Déposez une couche de pâte au fond du moule, puis recouvrez d'une couche de chocolat fondu à l'aide d'une cuillère à soupe. Lissez bien. Ajoutez une deuxième couche de pâte à la vanille, versez dessus le reste du chocolat noir fondu et terminez par une troisième couche de pâte à la vanille.
- Déposez les morceaux de chocolat au lait concassés sur le dessus du cake et mettez au four 45 minutes. Vérifiez la cuisson en enfonçant la pointe d'un couteau : si elle ressort sèche, c'est que le cake est cuit ; dans le cas contraire, prolongez la cuisson de quelques minutes.

Démoulez sur une grille et dégustez tiède ou froid.

Boissons conseillées : thé, café, chocolat chaud, vieux rhum cubain ou d'Haïti.

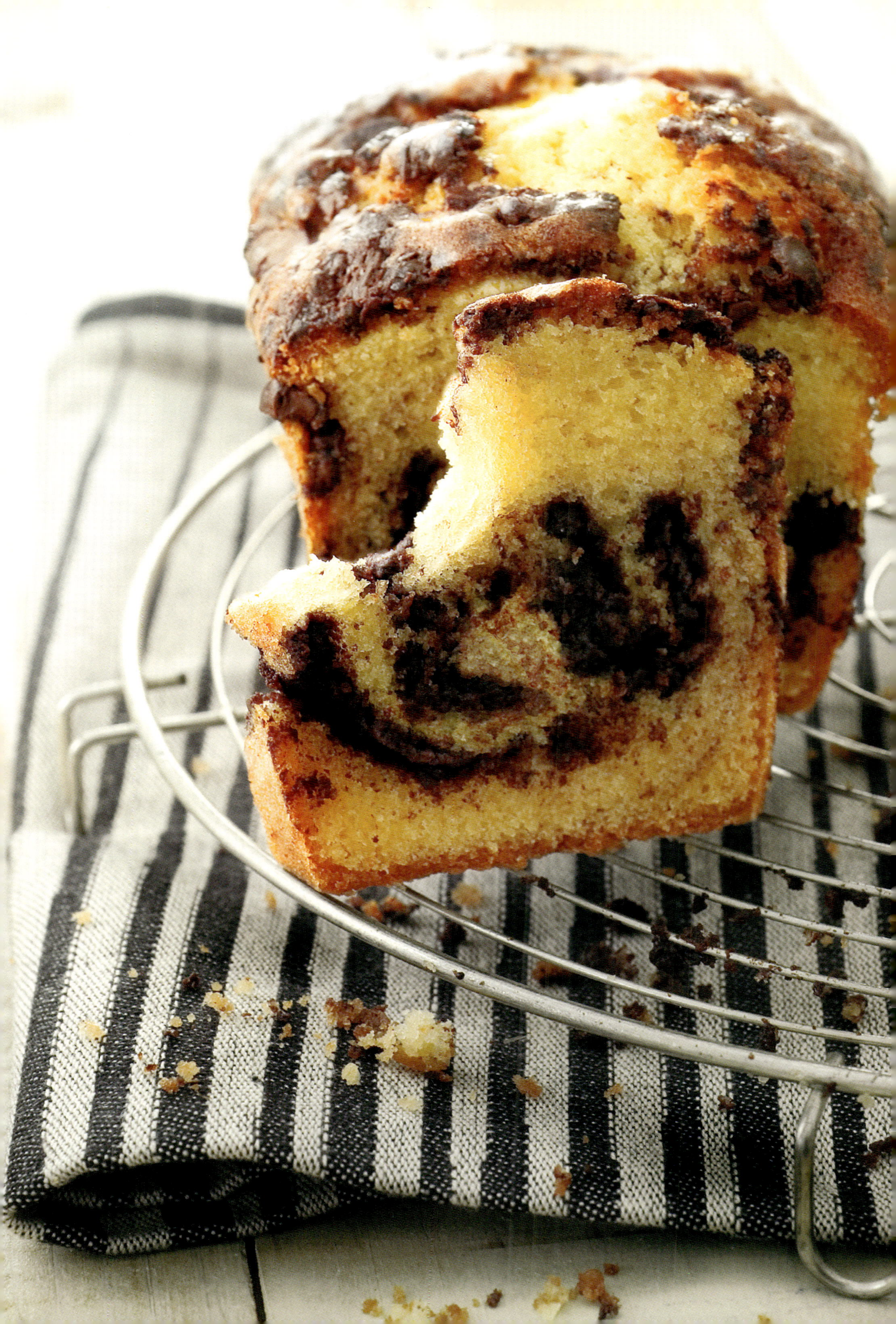

Index des recettes

Carnet d'adresses

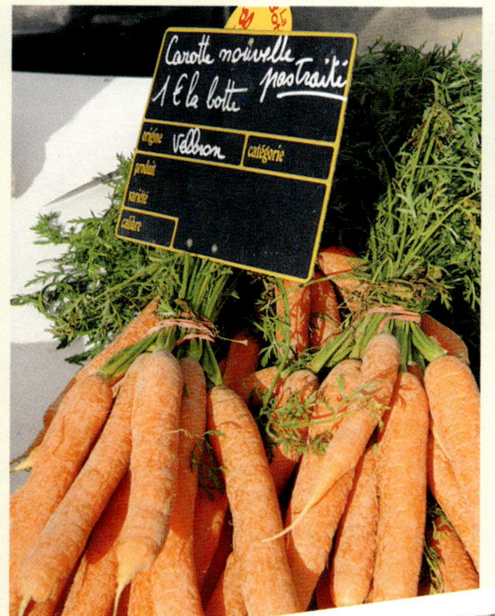

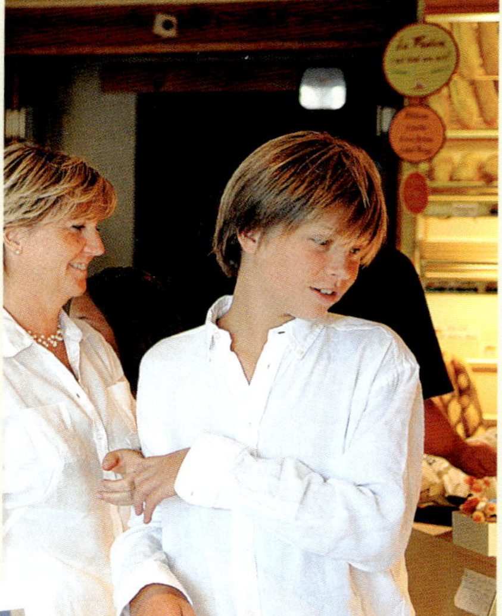

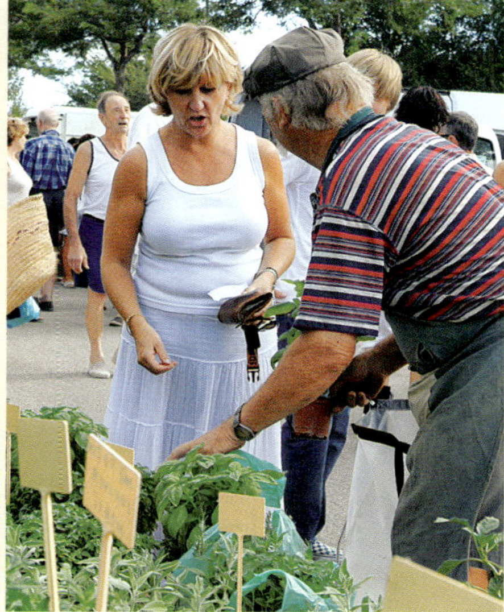

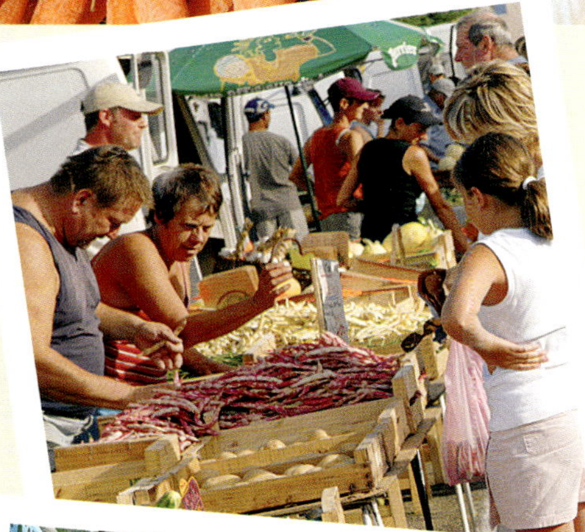

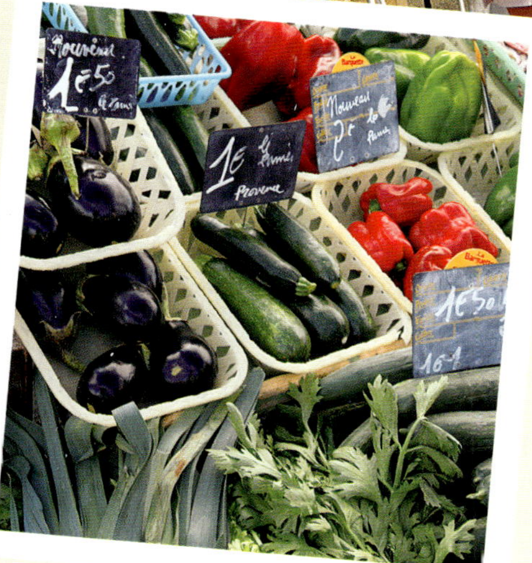

• **Homard de Chausey**
Philippe Thevenin
« le Fort »
50400 Les Îles Chausey
Tél. : 02 33 90 73 86

• **Truffe de Bourgogne**
Mr Beaucamp
27, rue de la Salle
89290 Nangis-Quenne
Tél. : 03 86 40 35 30
Fax : 03 86 40 27 21
Internet :
beaucamp.f@wanadoo.fr

• **La pâte à Calisson**
Confiserie du Roy René
rue Guillaume-du-Vair
13290 Aix-en-Provence
Tél. : 04 42 39 29 89
Internet : royrene@calisson.com

• **Le Repaire de Bacchus**
Jean-Benoît Dupouy
60, rue de Poissy
78100 Saint-Germain-en-Laye
Tél. : 01 30 61 74 92

• **Caveau de la Tour de l'Isle**
12, rue de la République
84 800 Isle-sur-la-Sorgue

• **Marché de Saint-Germain-en-Laye**

Place du marché :
le mardi, vendredi
et dimanche matin

Place de la Gare :
le mercredi et le samedi matin

Boucherie :
Gérard Delobre
(spécialités viande d'agneau,
veau fermier et bœuf)

Fruits et légumes :
Gérard Parisot
(demander Gérard,
André ou Didier)

Crème fraîche, beurre
et œufs de Normandie :
Bruno Margeot
(spécialités : crème crue,
fromages de Normandie,
œufs de ferme, beurre)

Dans la même collection :

La cuisine indienne, La cuisine italienne, La cuisine thaïlandaise, La cuisine antillaise.

À paraître : La cuisine mexicaine, La cuisine marocaine

Merci…

à Corinne pour sa confiance en me proposant l'écriture de ce projet. À Serge pour ses conseils avisés et sa patience. À Jean-Marc pour son œil de pro et sa grande gentillesse pendant les séances photos. À toute l'équipe de Solar et à toutes les personnes qui ont participé à la réussite de ce projet.

à Jean-Benoît pour ses précieux conseils œnologiques, aux 3 fées Agnès, Pascale et Frédérique, à Patrick, unique et irremplaçable, à Arthur et Zoé mes cuisiniers en herbe... (je suis fière de vous !), à Trish et Lucy (the best friends !), à ma chère Maman et à Mamie Nickie, à Jean-Paul notre Grand-Père Provençal, à Puce, à Papy pour ses crêpes, à Alix, Christine, Clément, Françoise, Ghislaine, Pascale, Philippine, Tina, Valérie, à Monsieur et Madame Bagros, à toutes celles et ceux qui partagent ma passion et ma gourmandise, à tous ceux et celles que je ne peux citer ou que j'oublie...
Véronique (www.coachingfactory.fr)

Natacha Arnoult, styliste culinaire, remercie chaleureusement : Jeannine Cros (textiles anciens), 11 rue d'Assas, 75006 Paris (Tél. : 01 45 48 00 67), Farrow and Ball (peintures et papiers peints), 50 rue de l'Université, 75007 Paris (Tél. : 01 45 44 47 94), Édition Compagnie (assiettes), 6 passage Josset, 75011 Paris (Tél. : 01 43 57 30 44).

Directrice littéraire : Corinne Césano

Secrétaire d'édition : Serge Gras

Collaboration éditoriale : Julie Guilleminot

Responsable artistique : Vu Thi

Création graphique et réalisation : Guylaine Moi

Fabrication : Denis Lanson

Photogravure : Point 4

ISBN : 978-2-263-04275-1
Code éditeur : S04275

Dépôt légal : mars 2007
Imprimé en Espagne par Graficas Estella

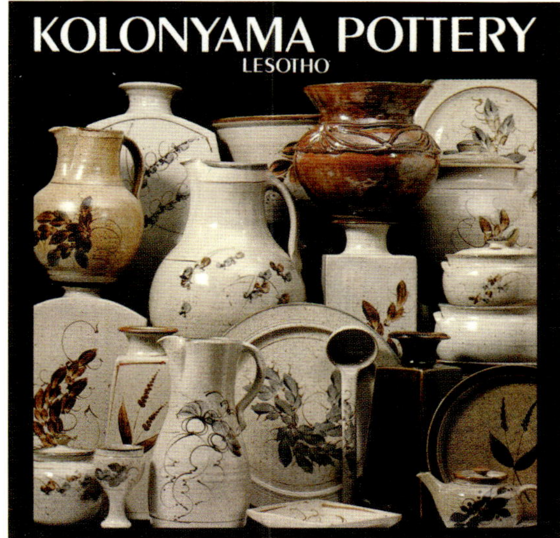

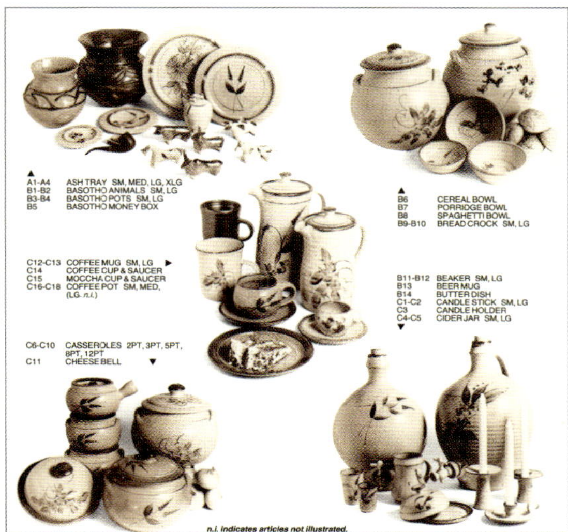

Kolonyama Pottery catalogue, 1980s | Provenance: Joe Finch

WILSON, Dave

Another 'Winchcombite', Wilson worked at Kolonyama from October 1979 to 1988. Wilson was introduced to Kolonyama by Graham Taylor, who had been at the same college as him. He worked as potter, decorator and glazer. He rejoined Winchcombe Pottery in about 1999 and currently still works there.[167]

Unidentified staff

[Surname unknown], Joseph

Of mixed Basotho/Indian origins, Joseph was employed by Joe Finch. He was a talented young man who learnt to throw very quickly. He left Kolonyama in 1971 and first worked at the new Maseru Pottery before joining the police force.

[Surname unknown], Josephina

Josephina worked under Milway and Taylor as a glaze technician.

[Surname unknown], Majolani (deceased)

Majolani started as 'tea lady' and cleaner but then went on to slab work, including slab dishes and lamp bases. He died before Taylor arrived.

[Surname unknown], Malefi

Malefi was employed as a clay assistant and wedged clay, and worked under Milway and Taylor.

[Surname unknown], Rosaline

Employed by Milway as a glaze worker, Rosaline had left prior to Taylor's arrival.

[Surname unknown], Sina (aka Alice)

Responsible for washing and cleaning, Sina worked under Milway and Taylor.

[Surname unknown], Mathabiso

Mathabiso worked under Taylor.

Le Hi Potteries (1935–1941)

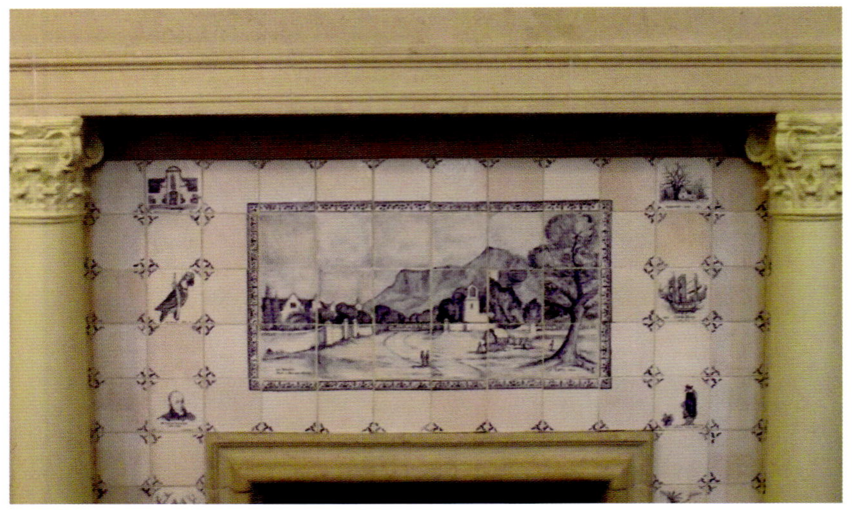

Leta Hill | Hearth tiles, Stellenbosch Council Chamber, ca.1941 | Photograph by Laura du Toit

Location

Le Hi Potteries was located in Church Street, Cape Town.

Name

The name Le Hi is an abbreviation of Leta Hill's name but also resonates with the name of a previous tenant, Sam Lee, who ran a laundry on the pottery's premises.

Founder

Elizabeth Maude Hill (née Redford), known as Leta Hill.

Staff

The artist John Dronsfield (1900–1951) assisted Hill with certain tile panels (Kerrod 2010:47). Given the magnitude of her production range, it is likely that Hill employed decorators and other assistants.

Wares manufactured

The studio produced door furniture (finger plates, door knobs, key plates) with floral decorations, masks, beer mugs, vases, animal and bird ornaments, fruit dishes, candle sticks, tea strainers, decanter labels, sets of buttons and ashtrays. Hill also produced 'Leta Hill Houses' in the manner of Staffordshire houses and castles. These ornaments were faithful reproductions of Cape colonial architecture, and Hill ensured that the original moulds were destroyed after production. Similar in style, Hill produced cheese or butter dishes that took the form of replicas of vernacular cottages and gabled homes (including Karoo-, Malay- and Cape Dutch-style dwellings).

The pottery is perhaps best known for its hand-decorated tiles depicting maps, flora, fauna, landscapes, architecture and street scenes. Cape Dutch homesteads were her leit-motif and the buildings she depicted include Groot Constantia, the Drostdy of Graaff-Reinet, Groote Schuur, Hohenort and Haslemere (located in the Cape Company Gardens). Sets of four or six individual tiles, depicting a homestead, were popular. Often individual tiles or tile sets were set into stinkwood frames, table tops and trays. Some tile designs were executed in a highly controlled manner, while others, such as those depicting Malay figures, were done in a far looser style. Hill created sets of tiles for bathrooms and kitchens; the latter decorated with an image of a cook's head or various fruit. Clients commissioned tiles inscribed with house names. She also produced round and oval panels decorated with floral studies as well as wares that resemble English jazz wares of the 1930s.

Production methods

While a potter's wheel was used, most wares were moulded or cast. It appears that the tiles she decorated were commercial blanks.

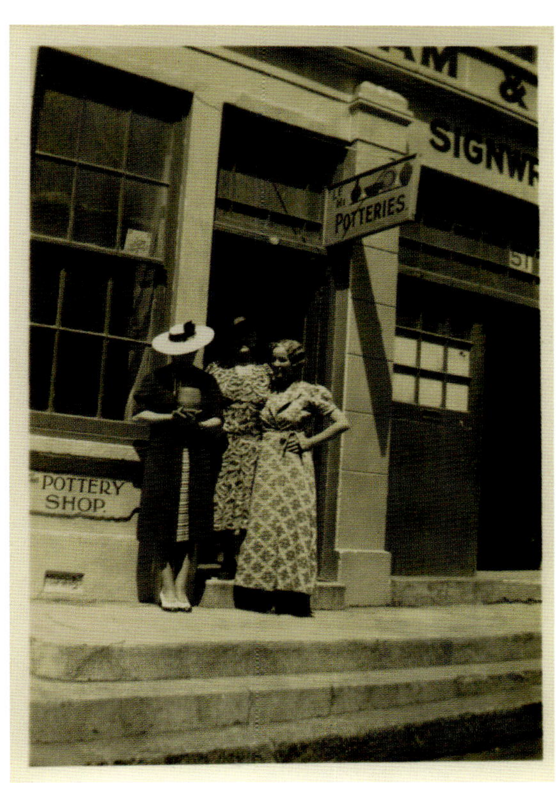

Exterior of Le Hi Potteries, Cape Town | Provenance: SHC Iziko| SACHM89/95 | Scan by Lailah Hisham

Brief history of the pottery

Compared to other contemporary tile operations, Le Hi Potteries was a small and relatively insignificant operation but was extremely well-known in its heyday, through its extensive exposure in the Cape press. Leta Hill's spouse, William Henry Roland Hill, held a senior position at the *Cape Argus*, and as a result Hill obtained the status of a minor Cape Town celebrity. She was frequently included in the 'society' pages, and the pottery was often featured in exhibition reviews and articles on the arts. Le Hi also appeared in at least one contemporary building and engineering journal, which encouraged the use of tiles and compared Le Hi's produts with the decorative tiles of Holland and the European Latin countries.

Most of her domestic ware and home furnishings have disappeared, and thus Le Hi is currently synonymous with tiles depicting local maps and other indigenous imagery, characterised by delicate and meticulous brushwork, in the manner of a miniature painting. The enterprise had a distinctly Cape bias and thus Cape-based niche market. There are no stylistic differences within her oeuvre, compared to the tiles of the Ceramic Studio and Linnware, where a more collective approach was evident in larger tile panels. Hill was clearly responsible for all the designs and her detailed, illustrative, decorative style is distinctive. Hill's tiles offer us a vision of idyllic Cape architectural landmarks and flora, and assist in the construction of an enhanced local identity, one that was being proliferated in other local visual arts. However, her pottery offered clients an economy of means, that was no doubt lacking when compared to other art forms such as contemporary painting.

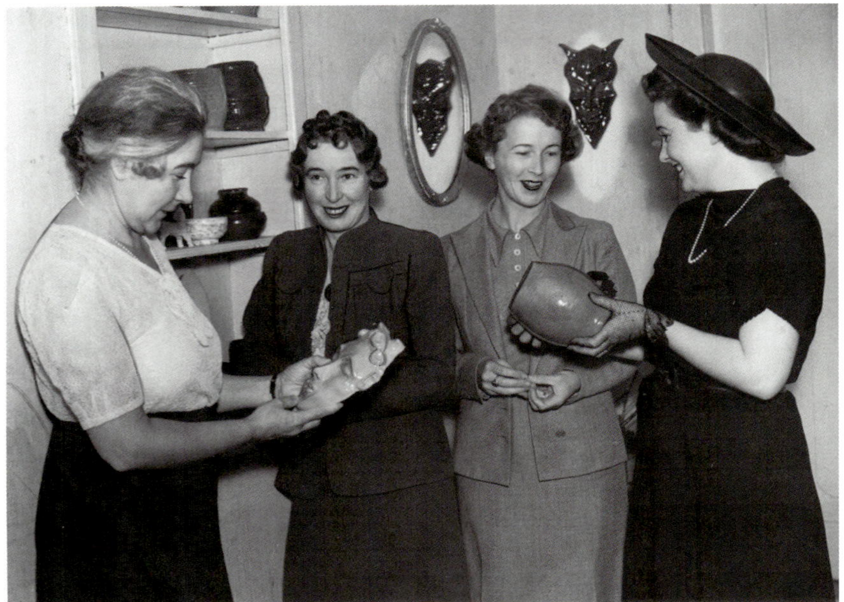

Leta Hill entertaining friends at the Le Hi Potteries | Provenance: SHC Iziko | SACHM89/96 | Additional information: This image appeared in an undated newspaper cutting with the following caption, 'Leta Hill (second from left) entertained several friends to morning tea at her attractive new pottery studio in Church Street, on Wednesday morning. Admiring some of the exhibits are, left to right, Mrs M. Overbeek, Mrs Rodney Malcolmson and Mrs T.C.U. Fanshawe.' | Note: The mask in Mrs Overbeek's hand is illustrated on p. 195. | Scan by Lailah Hisham

Hill was associated with some of the most important avant-garde Cape Town artists, such as the painter Ruth Prowse (1883–1967), who was photographed visiting her exhibitions in 1949, and whose exhibition of paintings was reviewed in the same press articles. In addition, Hill's pottery was displayed at exhibitions of other contemporary artists, such as Gregoire Boonzaier (1909–2005). Despite her association with prominent artists, Hill, like the artists of the Ceramic Studio, rallied for the creation of a cohesive alliance between the arts and industry. As a critic lyrically noted, '... what she has done is light a flaming torch that should give the lead to industry's acceptance of art as a basic factor in the design of tomorrow' (Anon. 1945:s.n.).

While Hill's oeuvre appears rather insipid and conventional by contemporary standards, it was exciting and fresh in her generation. Cape Town residents had very little previous experience of locally produced pottery or tiles. Her work is described as having 'a friendly warmth that encourages covetousness, and is lacking in the frigid aloofness and serenity of the days of Greek classicism' (Rayner 1941:s.n.). A contemporary reviewer aptly describes Hill as 'creating a living record in clay, of morsels of our history, that someday may be recognised as Africana' (Mills 1949:s.n.). The significance of the archival aspect of her work was evident as early as 1949, when Hill noted that many of the buildings she depicted on her tiles in Cape Town's old Malay Quarter had been demolished by the apartheid government. Indeed, Leta Hill, together with the Transvaal-based Ceramic Studio, consolidated a genre of Africana within local ceramics, and jointly influenced generations of subsequent artists.

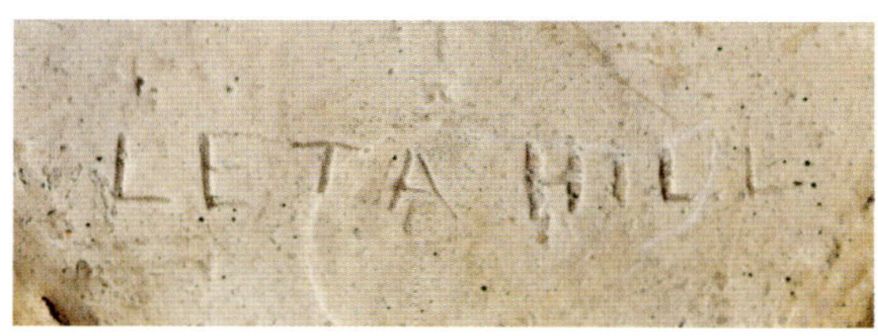

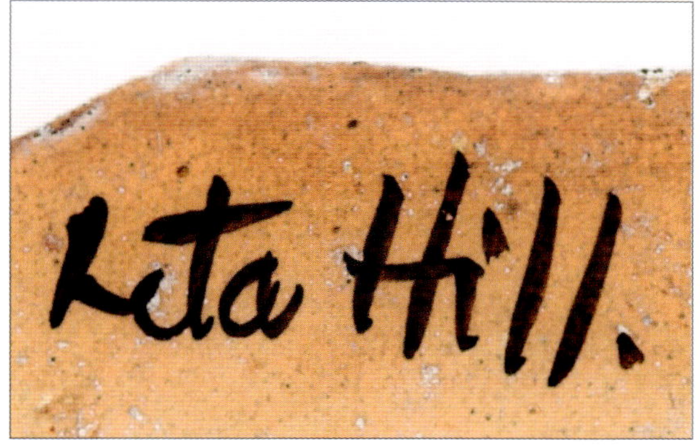

TOP: Leta Hill | Maker's mark | Relief moulded name, 'LETA HILL' | Photograph by Natalie Field

ABOVE BOTTOM: Leta Hill | Maker's mark | Hand-painted marking, 'Leta Hill' | Photograph by Natalie Field

Marks

Tiles are generally signed 'L.H.' or 'Leta Hill' on the face. Alternatively, they were signed on the base, with the artist's painted signature, or with a cast or stamped signature. Sculptures and utilitarian items have similar painted markings on their bases. Exceptionally, wares were stamped with a square seal that containec her initials.

Exhibitions and commissions

The boundaries between the personal wares of Leta Hill and the production wares of Le Hi Potteries are blurred and the exhibitions are thus listed together:

1949 The Leta Hill Pottery held a solo exhibition of 60 lots (200 objects) at the SA Association of the Arts Gallery, Cape Town. Hill exhibited wares that resemb e English jazz wares of the 1930s.

1947 Hill was commissioned to make dinner services for the use of the English Royal family (King George VI, Queen Elizabeth and the Princesses Elizabeth and Margaret) during their visit to Government House. Other objects, such as candlesticks, mugs, jars, bowls, jugs and tiles were lent to Government House to decorate the suites occupied by the Royal Family.

1945 Argus Gallery, Cape Town. The exhibition included a series of watercolour paintings, and over 70 pottery wares. One of Hill's largest works, a set of 35 tiles, covering nearly nine square feet (approx. 1 sq m), representing the Atlantic Charter map of the Cape, was commissioned by Lady Ina Oppenheimer, and was to be set in a teak table after the war (its current location is unknown). Oppenheimer also commissioned Hill to produce three tile panels for the bathrooms of her new Muizenberg home. They were decorated with fish, sea plants and shells.

1938 Hill was commissioned by the architect Jan Zeger Schuurmans Stekhoven (1895–1956) to produce tile panels of marine life for the new aquarium in Sea Point with 'many decorative effects and attractive colours. Purity of design is one of this artist's characteristics' (Money 1940). The aquarium has been extenisevly renovated and the tiles are no longer extant.[168]

1939 Le Hi Potteries submitted tiles decorated with Cape Dutch buildings for an exhibition of the Natal Society of Artists.

1930s In the late 1930s, Hill was commissioned by the architects Charles Perciva Walgate (1886–1972) and Lancelot Andrew Elsworth (1891–1971) to produce a series of tiles for the grate of the banquet hall of the Stellenbosch Council Chamber, inaugurated in 1941. The large central panel resembles a Bowler painting and depicts Die Braak, the Stellenbosch Town Square. It is surrounded by individual tiles, most of which are decorated with small geometric patterns in the corner. However, some of the surrounding tiles contain hand-painted Africana motifs of historic figures, homes or ships. Hill produced approximately 150 tiles for this project.

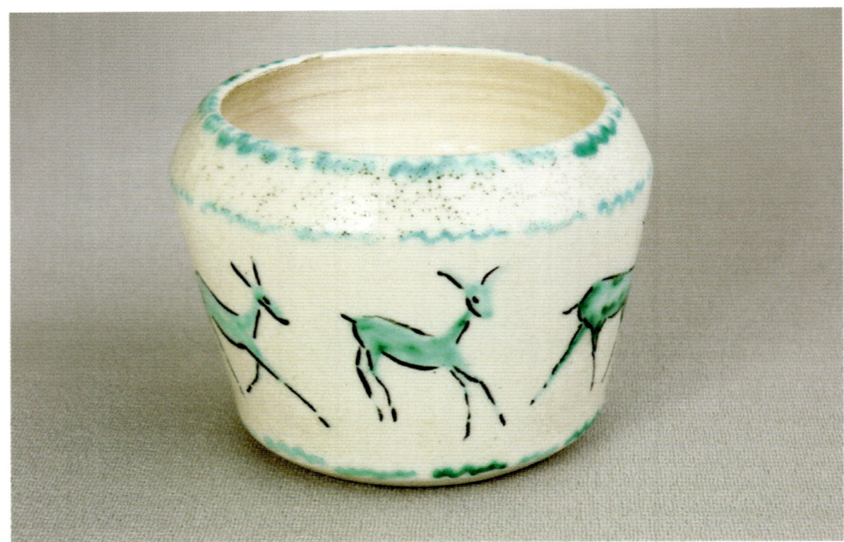

Leta Hill | Bowl or vase decorated with frieze of green antelope | 85x110mm | Provenance: SHC Iziko | 75/326 | Marks: painted marks on the base, 'Leta Hill' | Additional information: stylised antelope recall San parietal art | Photograph by Natalie Field

In addition, the Governor General's wife, Mrs E G Jansen, commissioned finger plates and other door furniture for Westbrooke[169] and Mrs J H Sims commissioned a tile panel of Kronendal, a well-known Hout Bay home.

Biography

HILL, Elizabeth Maude (aka Leta) (née Redford) (Mrs William Henry Rowland Hill) (d.1973)

Trained as a primary school teacher at the Grahamstown training college where she studied Art, in 1925 Hill was appointed to SACS Junior School, Cape Town in 1925. Simultaneously, Hill enrolled at the Michaelis School of Fine Art, University of Cape Town. Subsequently she went to London for a course in pottery at the London School of Arts and Crafts. Upon her return to Cape Town in approximately 1935, she continued making pottery with Mrs Grace Wheatley, who had established a pottery studio at Michaelis. When Wheatley returned to London in 1937, Hill took over the pottery department.[170] Hill extensively researched local clays and used those from Stellenbosch and Gordon's Bay (which fired to a rich brown), Simon's Town (pure white), Wellington (burgundy-brown), Ceres (red-brown with a dense body that was watertight when fired) and Koelenhof (purple-brown).

Hill established Le Hi Potteries in Cape Town in 1939 and became well-known for her hand-decorated tiles depicting Cape Dutch homesteads and other South African imagery. The artist closed the pottery in late 1941, but continued to work from a studio in her Oranjezicht home. Hill was active in the South African Association of the Arts, Cape Town, exhibiting regularly in their gallery and serving as a committee member in 1946.

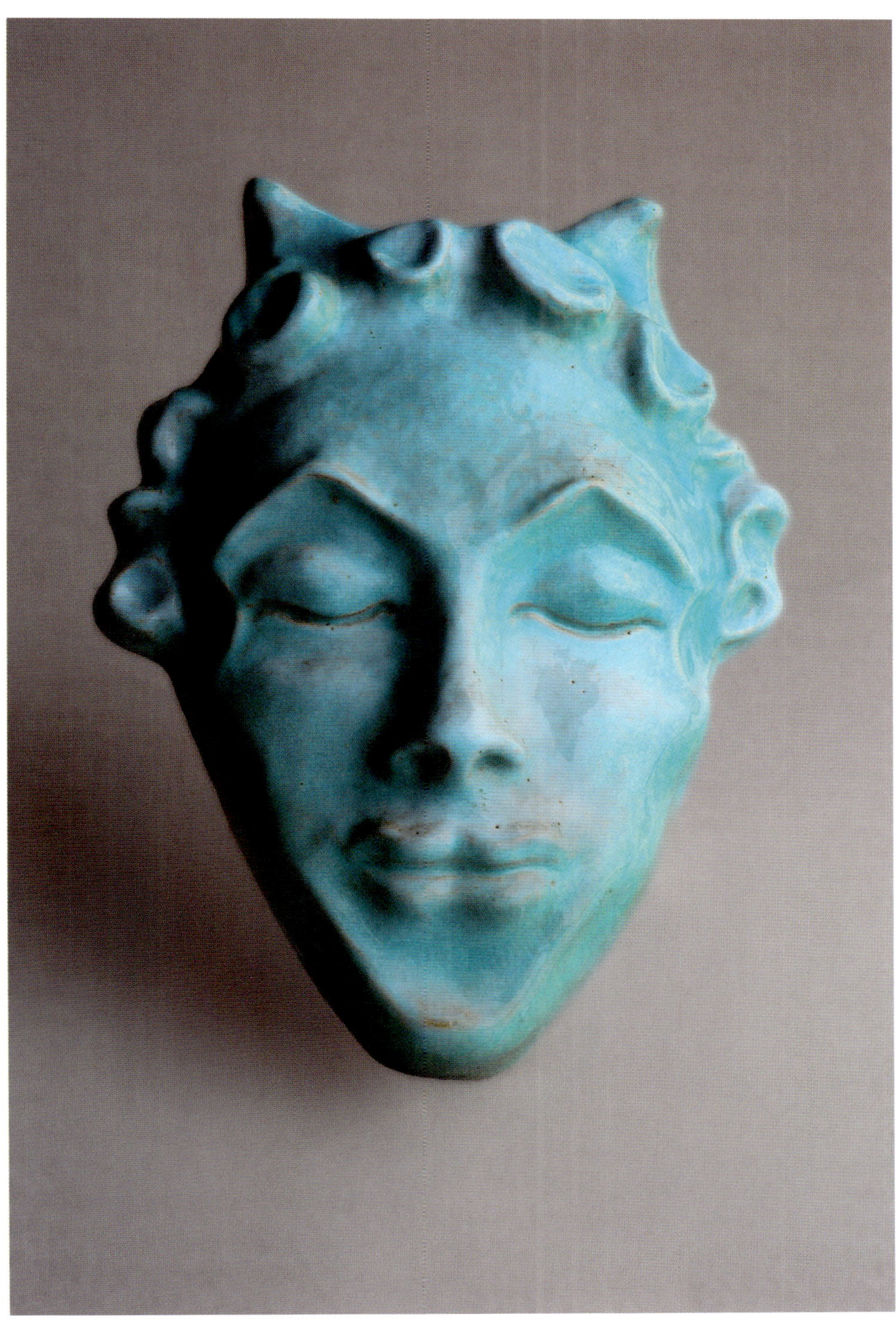

Leta Hill | Mask glazed with turquoise glaze | 200x156x65mm | Provenance: SHC Iziko | 75/291 | Marks: base unglazed, brown pairted marks,' Leta Hill', stamped mark, 'Leta Hill' | Additional information: This mask is depicted in an image of Leta Hill entertaining friends at the Le Hi Potteries, p.192. | Photograph by Natalie Field

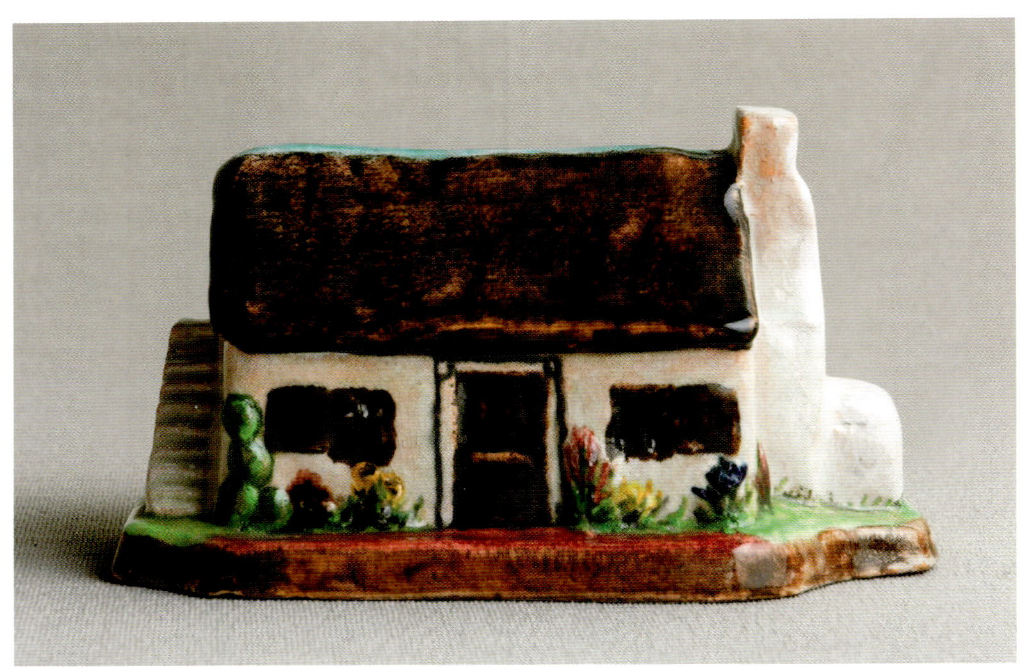

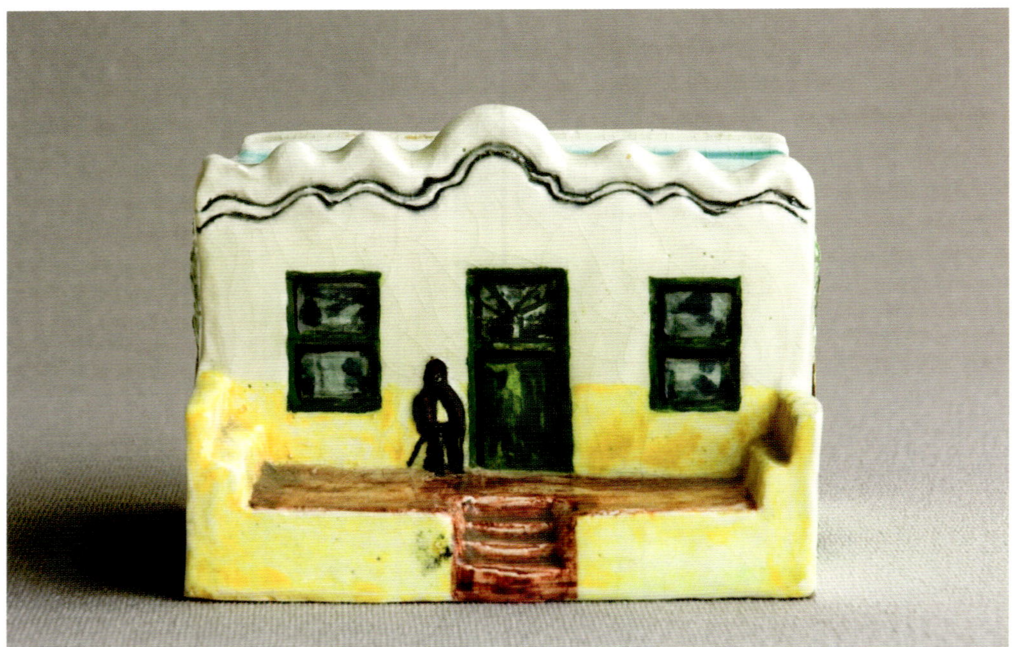

TOP: Leta Hill | Staffordshire cottage, ceramic model of Karoo cottage (ca.1950) | 90x140mm | Provenance: SHC Iziko | 84/599 | marks: painted marks in the interior, 'Karoo Huis' | Photograph by Natalie Field | Courtesy of Graham Taylor

BOTTOM: Leta Hill | Staffordshire cottage, ceramic model of Cape Malay cottage (ca.1950) | 75x103x101mm | Provenance: SHC Iziko | 84/596 | Marks: painted marks in the interior, 'Malay Huis. Cape Town. Leta Hill 1950' | Additional information: this house is most probably the building in which the Iziko Bo-Kaap Museum is housed today. It is the only remaining building in the area which has an undulating parapet. | Photograph by Natalie Field

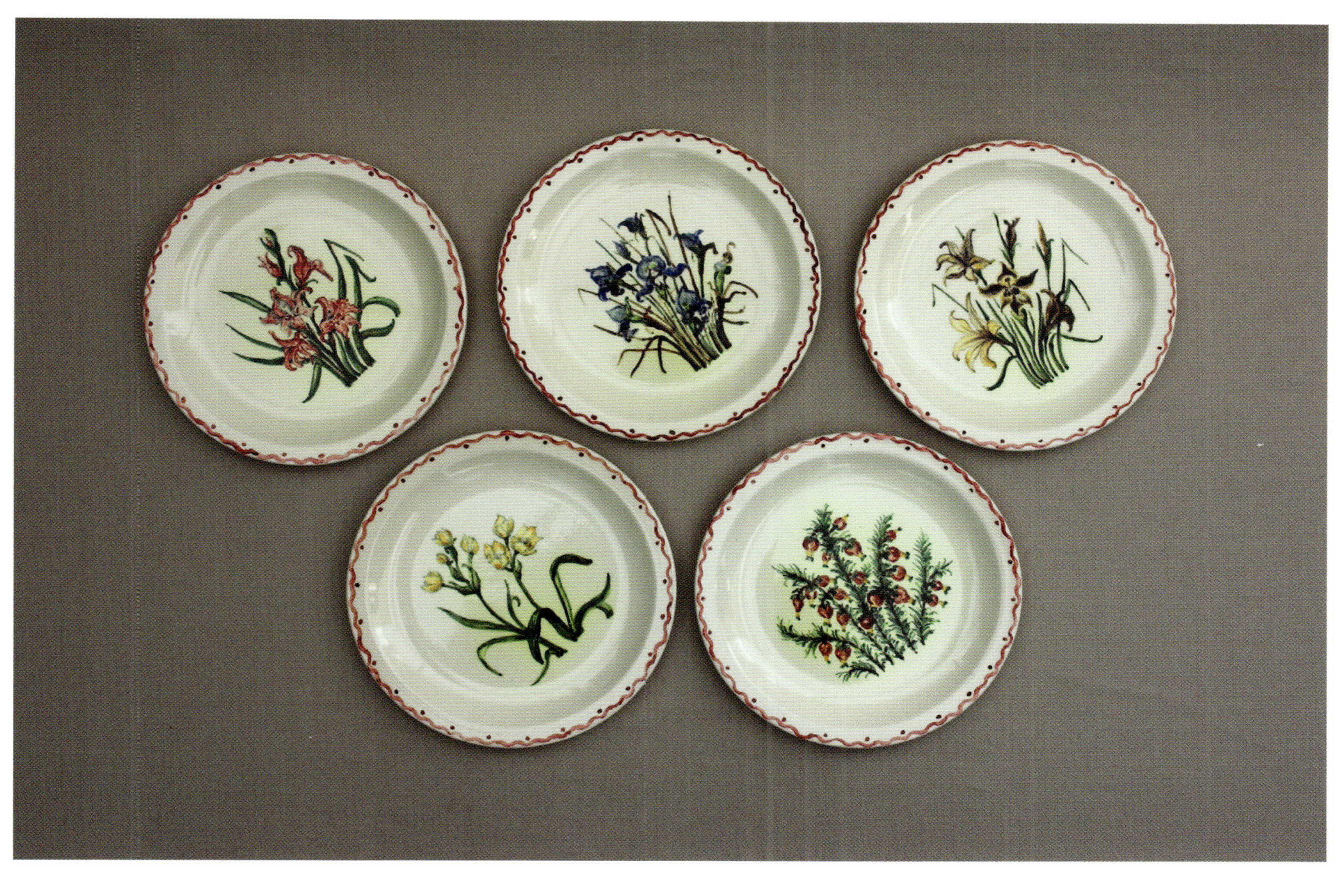

Leta Hill | Set of five small plates decorated with indigenous flowers | 137mm diameter | Provenance: SHC Iziko | 75/273a-f | Marks: painted marks on the back, 'Leta Hill 1949' | Photograph by Natalie Field

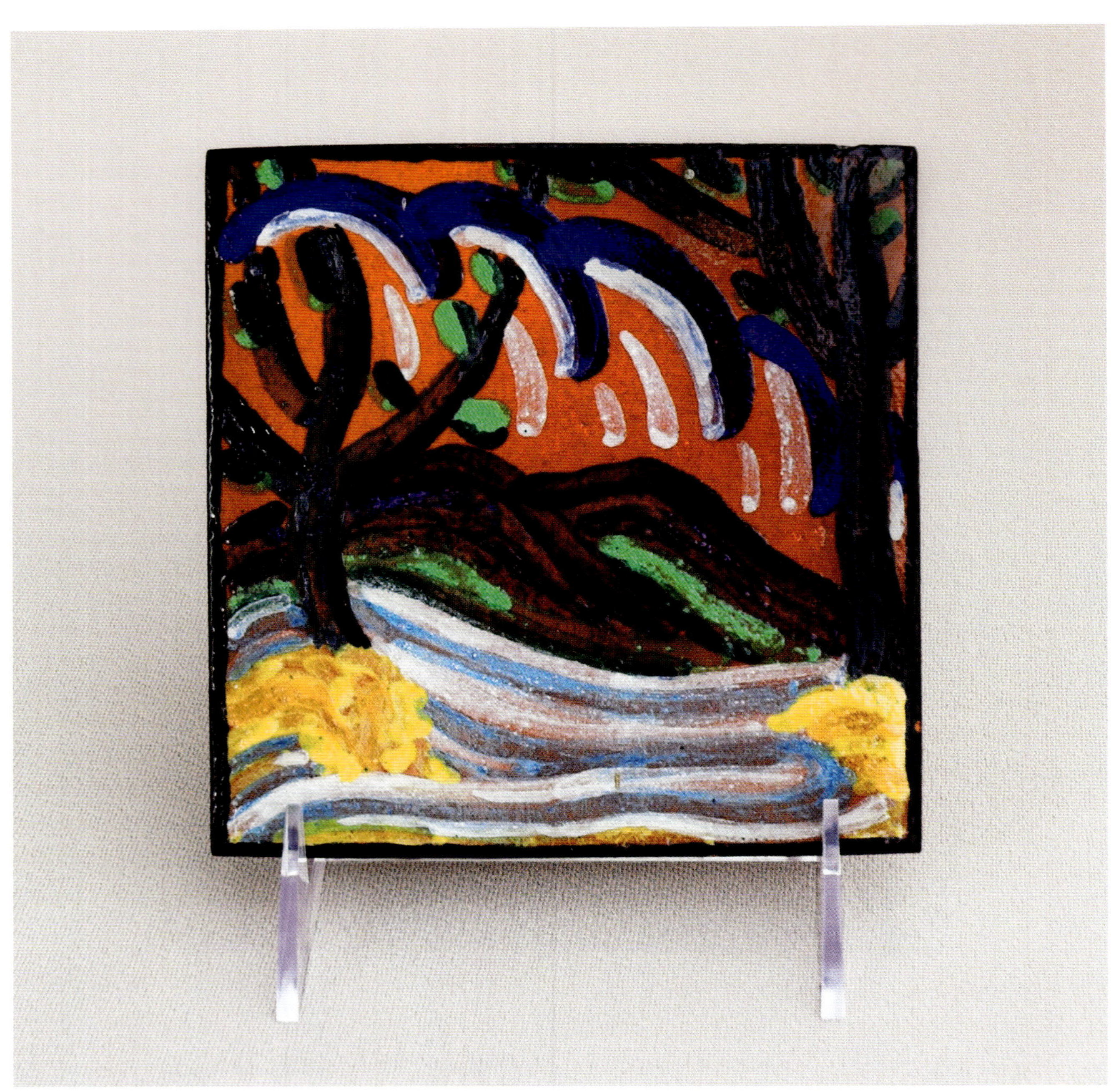

Leta Hill | Tile, earthenware, decorated with a polychrome, expressive landscape (1949) | 127x129mm | Provenance: SHC Iziko | 75/325a | Marks: painted marks on the back, 'Leta Hill' | Photograph by Natalie Field

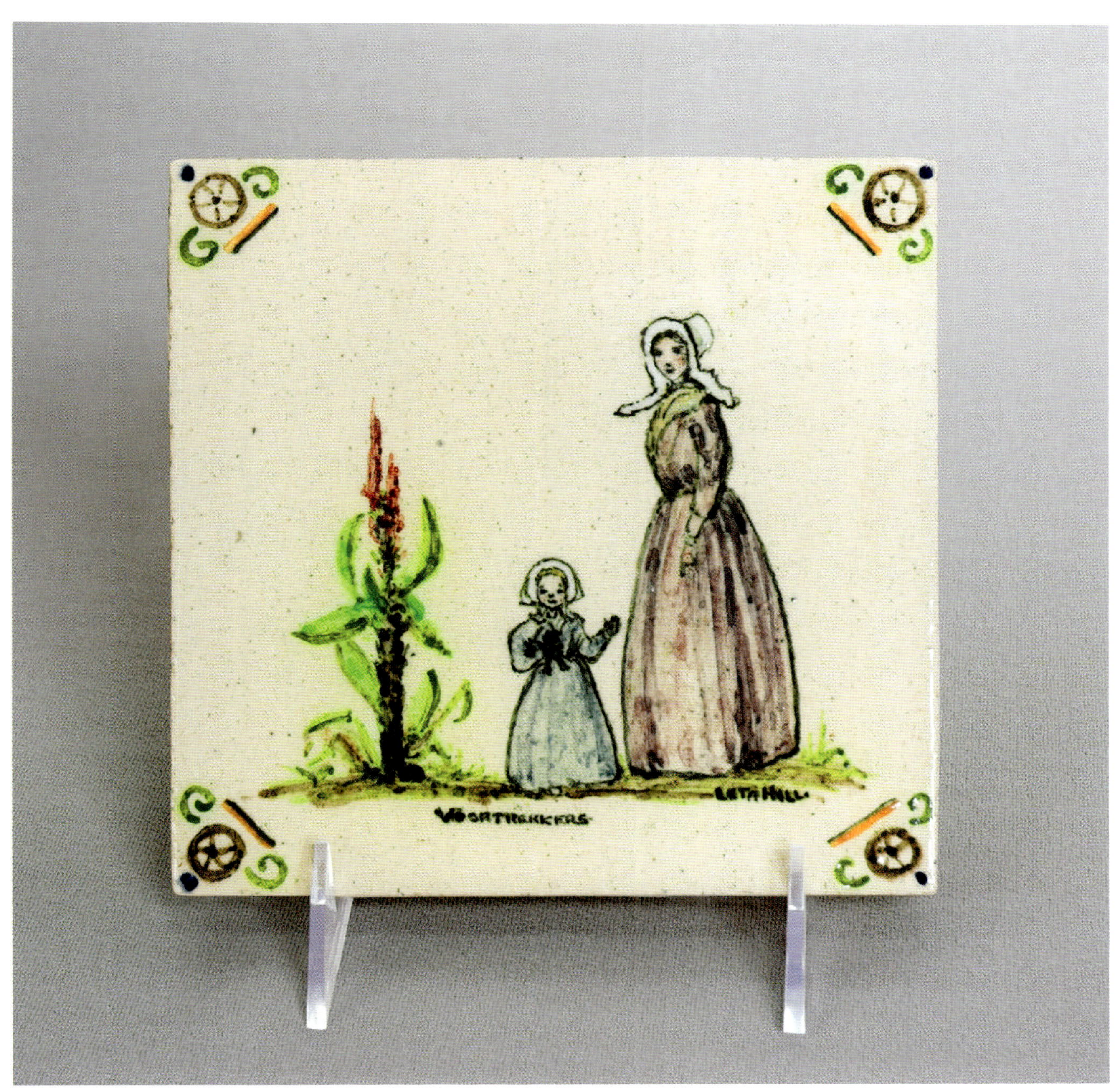

Leta Hill | Tile decorated with Voortrekker woman and child (ca.1940) | 155x155mm | Provenance: SHC Iziko | 75/301 | Marks: painted marks on the front: 'Voortrekkers – Leta Hill' | Photograph by Natalie Field

Liebermann Pottery and Tiles (1955–present)

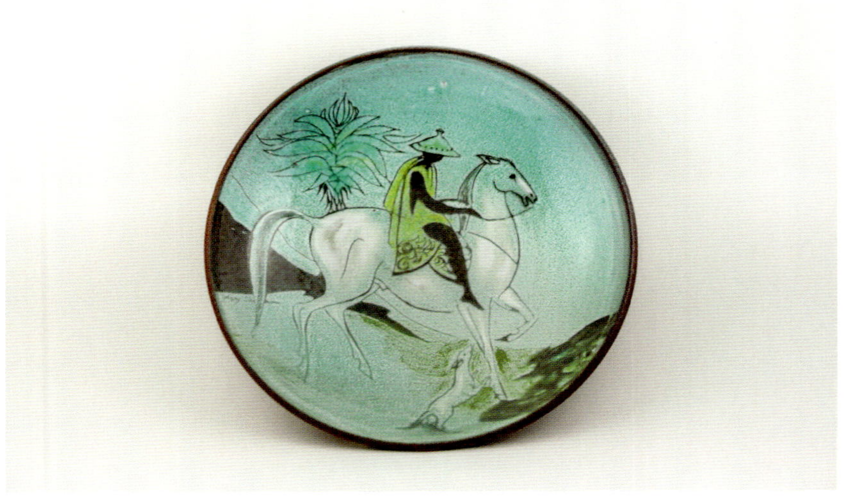

Chelsea Pottery | Landscape with Basotho horse-rider | 275x68mm | Provenance: Wendy Gers | Marks: unglazed terracotta base with hand-painted black glaze markings, 'Chelsea' and 'yin-yang' logo | Photograph by Damien Artus

Location

Liebermann Pottery and Tiles was initiated in the home of Sammy and Mary Liebermann at the 'The Stable' in Kelvin, Johannesburg from where they operated for ten years. Eventually the operation required industrial premises and in 1966 they acquired the factory of Silwood Ceramics, located in Kramerville near Johannesburg. In 1978 the firm moved to larger premises in Wynberg. The Liebermanns also had a shop, 'Liebermann Pottery', in Sandton City, which sold their wares, and those of Kolonyama and Izandla.

Founders and managers

1955–1984 Sammy and Mary Liebermann
1984–1988 Adrian Jaspan
1988 Adriaan Turgel

Staff

Over the years Liebermann has employed numerous apprentices and staff members. In the 1970s, when the pottery was at its peak, it had a total of 60 staff, including 12 potters. Among others, Liebermann employed the following people: Bilha Abramowitz, Makonya Alcock, Mike Anderson, Martha Baloyi, Anne-Marie Berry, Amy Bondonga, Modechai Brodie, Kansamy (aka Robert or Bob) Chetty, Alvina Chilate, Rosten Chorn, Michel Dangereaux, Thulani Dube, Janet Durbach, Elsje Gutridge, Fine Hadebe, Caroline Mary Haenggi-Nicholson, Leah Henarein, Patricia Hlope, Sue Hope Bailey, Pauline (aka Polly) Horwitz, Baba Issac, Madga Jascinska, Adrian Jaspan, Lisa Köter, Oliver Köter, Peter Kroll, Louise Lazarus, Bila Leganyane, Camina Leganyane, Dinah Leganyane, France Legwabe, Annette Lewis Barr, Ann Liebermann, Bertie Liebermann, Mary Liebermann, Ray Liebermann, Simon Liebermann, Joseph Madisha, John Mahlabane, Wilson Mahlabane, Chrisitina Maimane,

Freddy Makamu, Nikolaus Maredu, David Matabula, Richard Matabula, Shedrack Matabula, July Matjebe, Mary Matonza, Don McLellan, Jonas Mello, Merriam Meshesh, Sue Meyer, Matthews Milebi, Kainus Mkhari, Silas Modiba, Thando Modisha, Dolly Mofokeng, Onicca Molepo, Philemon Morotoba, Fran Mortimer, Bongikosi Mota, Grace Motopeng, Patch Mpofu, Nikolas Mpokeng, Petrus Mulauczi, Wison Mzumba, Patrick Aswindini Netshuha, Steve Wilson Ngobeni, Sam Ngwenya, Lucien Nkomo, Joseph Nyembe, Knox Raolane, One-and-six Raolane, Janet Roberts, Alison Rosten, John Sachs, Kim Sacks, Olita Seottlo, Aaron Shoniwa, Shelly Sibeko, Herman A J Smit, Agnes Sutton, Jane Tshabalala, Adriaan Turgel, Ricca Turgel, Andy Vanderlinde, Andrew Walford, Bruce Walford, David Walford, Caroline Waterkein, Erica White, Chris Morgan Wilson, Joke and Like Witkamp, and Jeremy Zinn. Staff whose surnames are not recalled include Corlia, Cheryl, Jerry, Joyce, Margareth, Mzie, Rachel and Sophia.

Wares manufactured

It is likely that Liebermann Pottery produced the largest range of ceramic products in any single South African factory. They are renowned for their decorated tiles and tile panels and wheel-thrown earthenware crockery, including jugs, condiment and cruet sets, egg cups, crockery, tea- and coffee-sets, sugar and jam pots, butter jars, lidded casseroles, and serving and salad bowls. Sculptures and fancy goods such as ashtrays, candle-holders, clock faces, ceramic jewellery, ceramic curtains, nativity sets and piggy banks were manufactured on a small scale. The company also undertook commissions for tiles panels and other items.

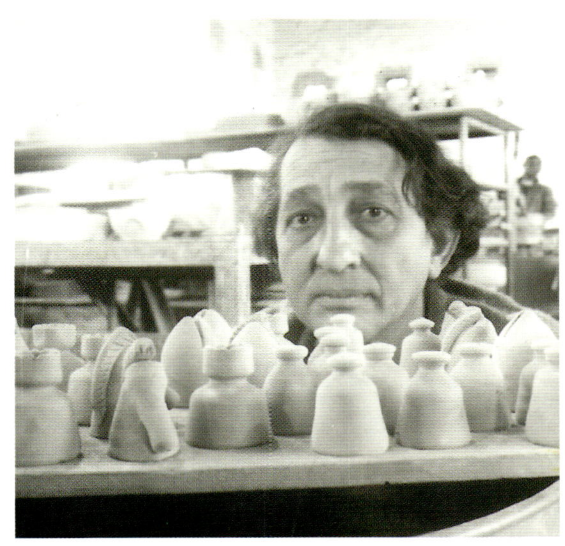

Liebermann Pottery | Sammy Liebermann in front of an unfinished, partial chess set | Provenance: Lisa Liebermann, ex Mary Liebermann | Scan by Adriaan Turgel

Production methods

A variety of production methods were employed, including hand-throwing, moulding, jiggers and jolleys.[171] The tile department decorated industrial blanks obtained from Pilkington or Johnson.

Brief history of the pottery

Chelsea Pottery

Sammy and Mary Liebermann were both members of a potters' cooperative in London called Chelsea Pottery. When they moved to South Africa in 1954, they continued producing wares under the name of Chelsea Pottery until 1955. These were signed 'Chelsea Pottery S.A.', often accompanied by the studio's 'yin-yang' incised or painted mark. Some pottery from this period was also signed 'Mary Liebermann'.

Liebermann Pottery and Tiles

The Liebermanns produced both domestic ware and tiles from the beginning. Mary was responsible for the tile department, and later also supervised the production of novelties[172] and fancy goods, small and large sculptures and ornaments, and special commissions.[173]

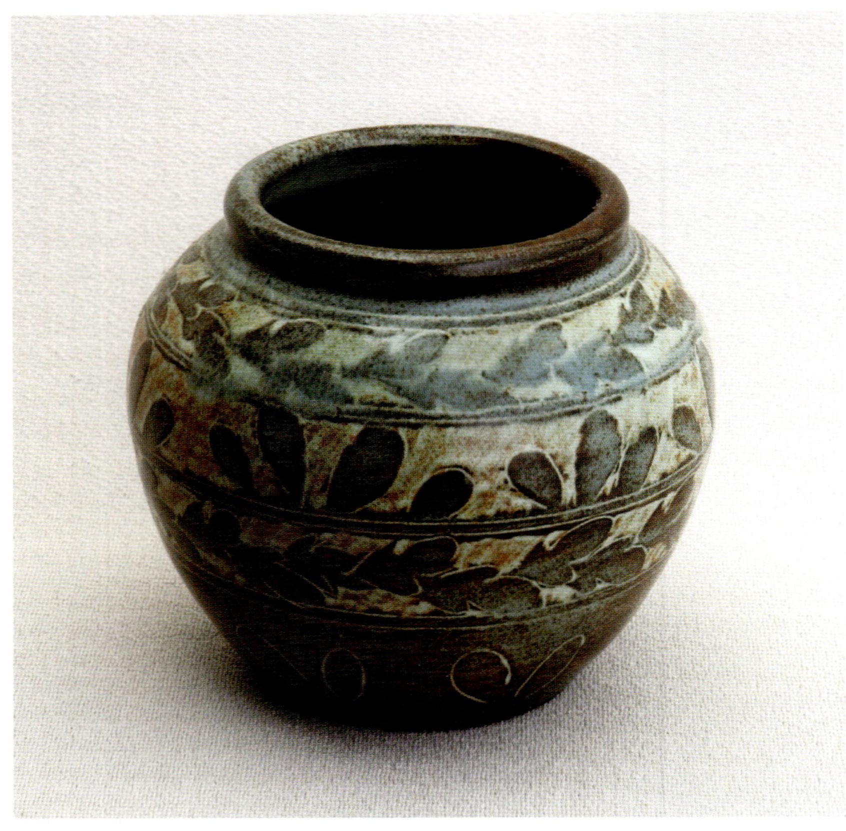

Liebermann Pottery | Vase | 100x78x68mm | Provenance: Douglas van der Horst | Mark: impressed 'L' mark | Photograph by Natalie Field

Initially, while operating from their home, all Liebermann domestic ware was handmade, and Mary's first decorated tiles were commercial quarry tiles. However, when they acquired Silwood Ceramics in 1966, they also acquired moulds and used them for a brief while, but soon discontinued this practice as they didn't fit the Liebermanns' aesthetic vision. Lisa Liebermann explains:

> My sister Anne, only four years old at the time, thought the [Silwood Ceramics] vases were beautiful, but Mary [Liebermann] was thankful to throw out the worn moulds – after all, they had bought Silwood Ceramics for its space and its kilns, not because they wanted to produce what she described as slip-cast 'kitsch' (Liebermann 2005:chapter 7).

From 1958 Sammy concentrated on dinner services, while Mary produced modelled tile panels and decorated quarry tiles. Initially Sammy Liebermann used earthenware clay exclusively, but later introduced stoneware clay to the earthenware body to improve the strength and durability of the wares. Sammy originally mixed his own glazes but later employed a technician to improve the glazes and resolve other technical problems. Almost all their clay and glaze components were locally obtained, and they claimed to produce a product that was 97 per cent South African!

In the late 1960s, with the technical assistance of Herman A J Smit, the company consolidated its expertise and started manufacturing on a large scale. Despite its industrial expansion, the factory retained the character of a pottery studio, with an emphasis on the handcrafted nature of its production. During this period, staff wore different coloured overalls that indicated their proficiency. Catalogues were artistically illustrated with calligraphy decorations and were printed on quality paper. Liebermann aimed to produce authentic handcrafted domestic ware, which was aesthetically pleasing, durable and functional. In order to enhance the handcrafted aspect of the wares, Sammy Liebermann encouraged the workers to leave finger rings on thrown vessels. He believed pottery should feature natural curves and display the intrinsic characteristic of clay – plasticity and subtlety. He loved cooking and understood the essential link between the physical form of his crockery and the production, presentation and consumption of food, the washing up of the crockery, and the freezing of home-cooked meals. He repudiated harsh corners and rigid lines and endeavoured to create harmonious delicate forms. He insisted that a corner may never be sharper than the pad of one's finger. Liebermann was responsible for quality control and personally inspected one in every ten items produced. He insisted that wares not exceed 6.5mm in thickness.

Inspired by Japanese pottery, Liebermann believed that the colour of one's crockery should enhance the appeal of one's food, and thus used mainly soft, earthy colours, avoiding bright colours. Originally the domestic ware was produced in three colours, known as peacock-blue, Scottish honey (a shade of yellow-ochre, referred to by staff as 'Scott') and chestnut-brown.[174] Subsequently a light blue, an off-white, dull (mink) brown and a grey were introduced. The slightly speckled glaze finish meant that no two items of the service were exactly alike. Sammy Liebermann championed their limited palette and maintained a strict uniformity of colour as a form of loyalty to his customers. He argued that most international potteries changed their colours after two years, and that this practice compromised customers. Liebermann crockery was thus sold individually so that people could gradually acquire a full set and easily replace broken items, a practice that was greatly appreciated.

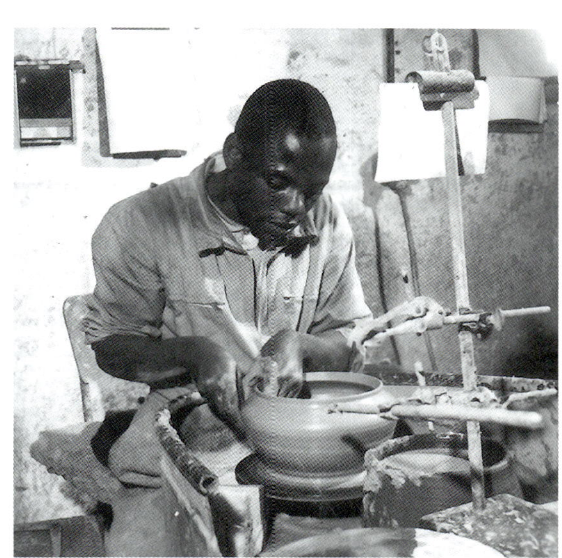

Liebermann Pottery | Patrick Aswindini Netshuha throwing | Provenance: Lisa Liebermann, ex Mary Liebermann | Scan by Adriaan Turgel

Mary Liebermann headed the tile department and, like the pottery section, it started off as a small-scale operation, but expanded rapidly. Initially each item was hand decorated, mainly by incising the designs through an opaque white glaze on a dark ground and then applying coloured reactive glazes with a brush. Some form of mechanisation was clearly necessary, not only to increase production but also to avoid the health hazards associated with sgraffito. Mary thus started experimenting with silk screens, adjusting the mesh gauge to suit the consistency of the glazes and also trying out different glaze carriers, glycerine finally being chosen as the most suitable medium. Michel Dangereaux, a French potter who had worked in Vallauris at Picasso's former studio, had joined the company and assisted with these experiments, helping Mary to correct the tension of the screens, the thickness of the glaze application, and the register for multiple-colour printing. While sgraffito and hand painting continued to be used for a proportion of Liebermann tiles, especially one-off projects such as house names, commemorative tiles, and mural commissions, the standard range of designs for which the company became so well known were all screen printed. However, because the process still involved an extraordinary amount of handwork, each tile produced by this method was unique.

A wide variety of different decorative images were applied to tiles. For kitchens and dining areas the company offered panels portraying medieval feasts and harvests, rustic farm scenes and domestic animals, as well as single-tile designs depicting kitchen utensils, fruit, vegetables, grains and herbs. Underwater scenes with mermaids and similar mythological creatures, as well as individual tiles and small panels showing fish, shells and other marine animals, were intended for bathrooms, patios and swimming pool areas. The country's landscapes, birdlife, flora, folklore, mining history and vernacular architecture all served as the inspiration for designs. The tiles in the 'Signs of the Zodiac' series were popular as gifts, being sold framed with a printed horoscope pasted onto the back.

During the period 1979–1985, tiles became a highly important aspect of the business, accounting for about 30 per cent of the firm's annual turnover, and at one stage large consignments were exported to America.

Liebermann sold its pottery through their on-site show room, through Klaus Wasserthal, Pretoria, the up-market department store Garlicks and Greatermans as well as other craft galleries. Tiles were also sold through building merchants, gift shops, architects, interior designers and decorators. Standard tile panels consisted of 2 to 18 tiles.

The pottery undertook numerous commissions for hand-painted tile panels for public and private buildings and even for boats! Original motifs included home and street names and numbers, family history, heraldry and children's playroom scenes. One of the more unusual commissions was to provide tiles with numbers for the 85-kilometre Fish River water tunnel. Tiles were placed at intervals as distance markers inside the tunnel to prevent workers on the project becoming disoriented.

Mary Liebermann, Magda Jascinska, Michel Dangereaux, Polly Horwitz, Elsje Gutridge and Anne-Marie Berry worked in the tile section, designing and creating tiles according to their own styles and interests. Jascinska, a Polish immigrant, contributed numerous designs for tiles that featured Central and Eastern European peasants.[175] Various other artists, including Leah Henarein, stayed for shorter periods. Liebermann, Berry and Jascinska were the most prominant in terms of designs and the length of time they worked there.

Liebermann Pottery became one of the largest family-run ceramic enterprises in southern Africa in the 1970s. In the late 1970s it expanded its operations to the Western Cape and established a warehouse in Muizenberg. The warehouse was managed by Sammy Liebermann's brother and

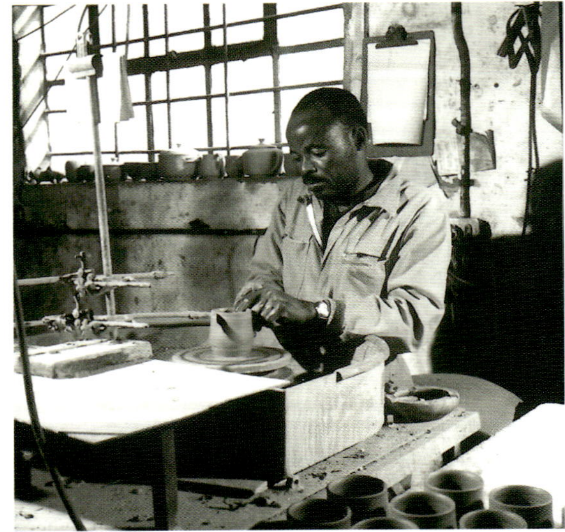

Liebermann Pottery | Lucian Nkomo | Provenance: Lisa Liebermann, ex Mary Liebermann | Scan by Adriaan Turgel

sister-in-law, Bertie and Ray Liebermann. In 1977 the company employed over 90 staff, including 15 throwers. The scale of its operations meant that it was constantly plagued with the consequences of apartheid labour legislation that prohibited the free circulation of African staff members. In the mid-1970s it considered opening another factory in Estcourt, but this never materialised. In the mid-1980s Sammy Liebermann considered moving the pottery to Brits to take advantage of the benefits offered by the government's policy of economic decentralisation. However, housing could not be provided for their skilled workers. According to Sammy Liebermann:

> A day or two later a representative of the Ministry of Planning called to say housing was available but by then our workers, who come from many different ethnic groups, had lost faith in the move ... They decided they would rather stay here as they feared uncertainty and also that non-Tswanas would be discriminated against ([No author] 1980s).

Liebermann Pottery is significant because it trained and employed hundreds of talented and creative people over a period of three decades. Sammy Liebermann always accepted new potters if they seemed motivated to learn the profession. In exchange for pottery tuition (and often accommodation), Sammy demanded that apprentices undertook certain duties, such as administrative work or delivery services. Sammy had a philosophy of learning 'from the floor up', whereby all new pottery interns spent their first two weeks sweeping the floors and observing the production processes. Over the years, numerous people learnt the trade and moved on, some became independent artist potters, and others went in new directions. Among others, apprentice potters included Madeline Anderson, Mordechai Brodie, Rosten Chorn, Carey Farrakaris, Piet Grobbelaar, Mike Kamstra, Lisa Meinhart, John Rosewane, John Sachs, Ricca Turgel, the brothers Andrew and Bruce Walford, and Caroline Waterkein.

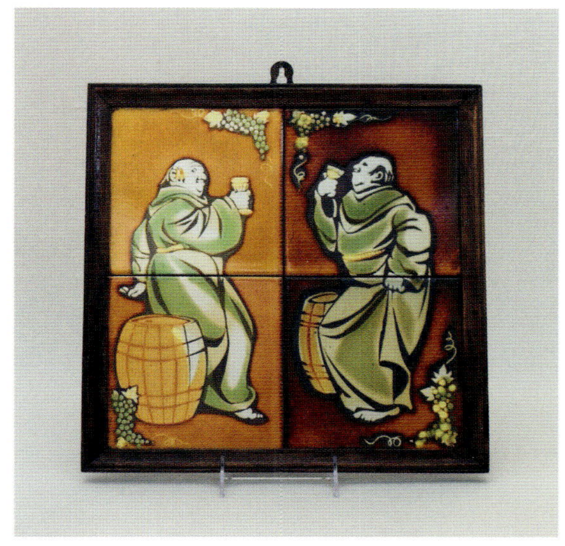

Liebermann Pottery | Tile panel | Image of pair of friars with chalice and barrel | 340x340x18mm (individual tiles 150mm²) | Provenance: Carol Birch | Photograph by Natalie Field

The Liebermanns treated their staff exceptionally well and all former employees attest to the privilege of working in that environment. Virtually all the Liebermann children and the large extended Liebermann family (including the Turgels and Horwitzes) worked for the pottery. Similarly, other extended families, such as the Raolanes, Nkomos and Leganyanes, worked there for multiple generations. The pottery was an environment of mutual respect, and staff were encouraged to engage in the work that made them happiest. Staff took advantage of this liberty, and there was a regular rotation of staff in all sections, including the administrative, pottery and sales departments. Some staff even chose to work in different departments on different days of the week! This liberty is unique among South African potteries and one that was, and still is, cherished by the few remaining staff.

Berry describes the studio:

> When there was a break for food or tea, we would gather around a kettle, squatting on old car seats and talk, about anything and everything from Arthur Rackham [the English book illustrator] to Plato to the Rivonia Treason Trial to best bread recipes. Anarchists and failed Maths teachers, illegal job seekers and pregnant cats all found refuge and flourished there. Sammy ran this small factory along anthropological rather than business lines but it worked and during those years there was an extraordinary flowering of talent and exuberance.[176]

The company's philanthropy extended beyond the pottery and it supported local charities with the production of special pieces for charity raffles and auctions. In the 1970s it produced a tile mural depicting iguanas for the Learn Fund. Sammy was also extensively involved in the Association of Potters and was invited to judge various competitions, such as the 1973 Brickor Ceramic Art Competition.

The unexpected death of Sammy Liebermann in March 1984 left the pottery staff shocked and destabilised. Liebermann's son-in-law, Adrian Jaspan, took over the direction of the company between 1984 and 1988. It was a tough period and the pottery experienced many difficulties, including drug abuse among employees, aggressive, disruptive trade unions and the negative economic effect of international trade sanctions against South Africa. In addition, there was a shift in public taste away from rustic domestic ware. The pottery experienced a severe decline in production and sales. Thus, at the end of 1988, Mary Liebermann approached her nephew Adriaan Turgel about the management of the company. Turgel volunteered to take over immediately, and in 1993 he bought the company.

Turgel made various changes to the structure of the business, including retrenching various senior staff and not replacing staff when they left. He made changes to the thickness of some vessels, changed the length of handles on casseroles and other items, and discontinued many standard products that were no longer economically viable. He presently manages the company. The Liebermann Gallery no longer exists and the pottery has changed focus. Liebermann Pottery no longer makes tiles, but produces a small quantity of crockery and flower pots. Over the previous decade the business has shrunk considerably in size. In 2002 it employed approximately 30 people and currently employ less than 20 elderly staff. Today it primarily retails imported Asian (mostly Chinese) ceramics and also sells clay. In 2010 Liebermann Pottery was struck off the register of South African companies.[177]

In conclusion, Sammy and Mary created something of a Liebermann dynasty in South African ceramics. The pottery trained hundreds of potters, and inculcated an awareness and appreciation of handmade domestic ware, fancy goods and tiles in generations of South African consumers. For those

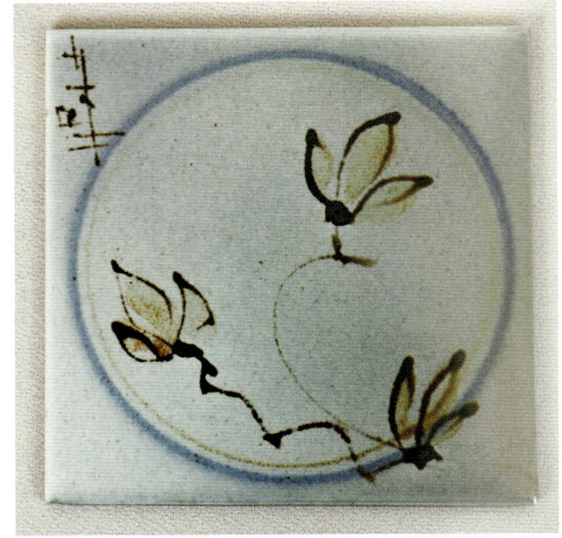

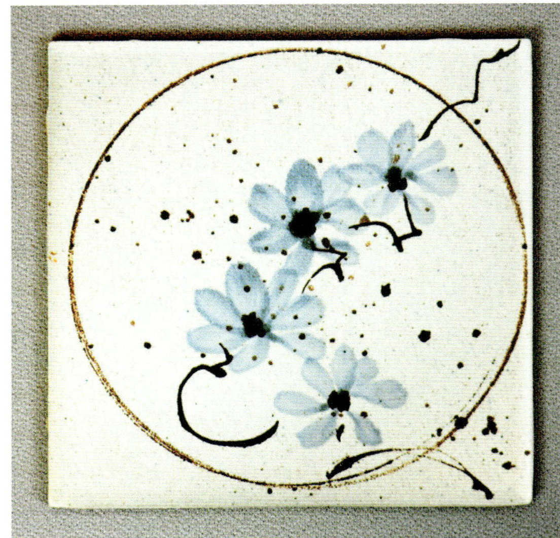

Liebermann Pottery | Tile | Pair of tiles decorated with Japanese inspired vignette | Provenance: Wendy Gers ex. Liebermann Pottery | Additional information: artist, Erica White | Photographs by Natalie Field

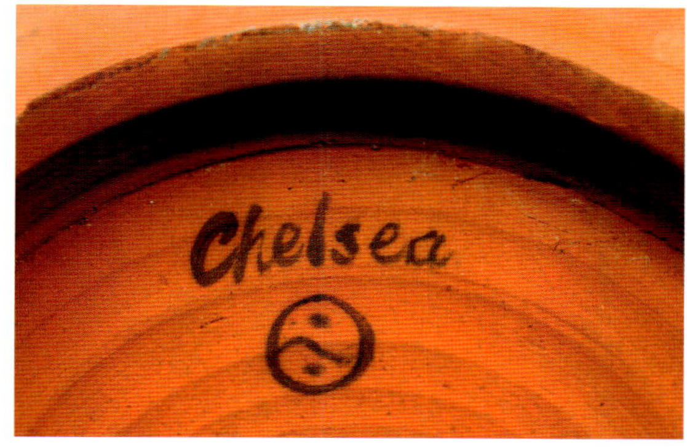

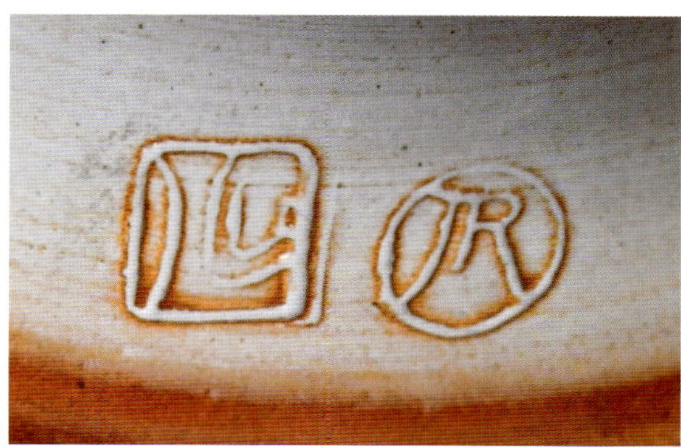

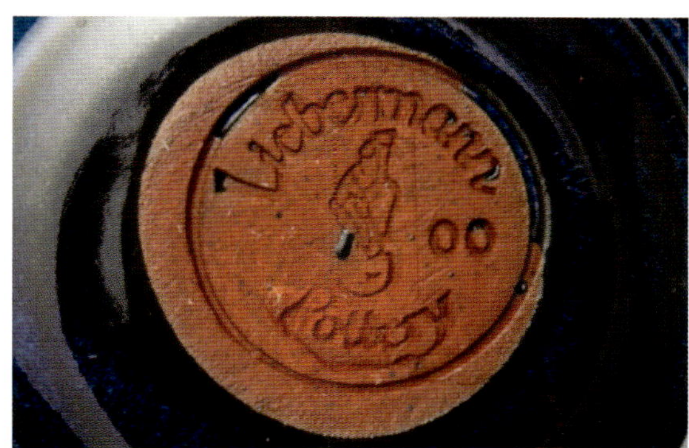

TOP: Chelsea Pottery | Maker's mark | Hand-painted black glaze markings, 'Chelsea' and 'yin-yang' logo | Provenance: Wendy Gers | Photograph by Damien Artus

ABOVE MIDDLE: Liebermann Pottery | Pair of stamped maker's marks | Provenance: Douglas van der Horst | Additional information: second stamped mark, 'JR' refers to artist, Janet Roberts. This mark is on the pottery bell illusrated on p.213 | Photograph by Natalie Field

ABOVE BOTTOM: Liebermann Pottery | Maker's mark | 2000 | Photograph by Natalie Field

people associated with the pottery, their overwhelming memory is of the great professional liberty and personal enrichment that was central to Liebermann Pottery. Berry reminisces:

> ... the years I spent working alongside Mary were a rich and rewarding apprenticeship. Not only did I learn a craft but acquired new ways of seeing, analysing, taking inspiration from nature and the material cultures of many sources and translating it into, not great art but a beautiful decorative element ... which, being fired clay, endures a long time.[178]

Marks

- Most tiles, domestic ware and fancy goods are unmarked.
- Some wares bear sgraffito marks, 'Liebermann Pottery'.
- Some wares are marked with an underglaze stamping machine. However the machine was frequently out of order.
- Various different handheld stamps, e.g. 'Handmade Liebermann', 'Liebermann Pottery' or various versions of a Liebermann logo (depicting a potter seated at a wheel image).
- Special seals were used to mark the bases of small objects, such as teacups. One such stamp featured a solitary 'L' next to a bowl.
- A rubber date stamp was sometimes used for objects that were too small to bear the Liebermann stamp or seal.
- Some wares were marked with a stamp that recorded the year of creation. However, these stamps frequently disappeared and their use appears to be rather random.
- Some artistic wares contain an additional mark of their creator, e.g. Janet Roberts who used a circular seal containing her initials.
- Stickers were also used during certain periods, including an oval-shaped, red sticker with 'Liebermann' printed in silver. Another rectangular sticker said: 'Hand Crafted. Liebermann Pottery. High fired. Oven, microwave, freezer and dishwasher safe'.

Select exhibitions and commissions

1985	South African Breweries, Rosslyn, Chamdor (Krugersdorp) and Spartan. Tile murals.
1983–1984	Southern Sun Hotels, including Johannesburg, Muizenburg, Beacon Island (Plettenberg Bay), Drakensberg and Hluhluwe. Tile murals.
1977	Klaus Wasserthal Gallery, Pretoria. Exhibition of pottery and tiles, and demonstrations.
1975–1976	Ohlsson's Brewery, Newlands, Cape Town. This tile mural is 12m in diameter and consists of four panels that recount the history of beer production. The first panel shows harvesting grain and hops, the second depicts a medieval monastic brewery, the third depicts

Van Riebeeck with his beer cargo, and the last depicts the original buildings on the site of the current brewery.

1975 Barclay's Square, Pretoria. Exhibition of pottery and tiles.

1975 Botswana House and Anglo American offices, Gaborone, Botswana. Tile murals.

1975 Barclays Bank Services building, Selby, Johannesburg. Tile murals depicting the history of banking and other financial themes. These are 5.5x3.5 m and took six weeks to complete.

1975 Barclays Bank, Bramley, Johannesburg. A series of seven panels for the reception area of this branch.

1972 SA Association of the Arts, Pretoria. An exhibition that included a chess set by Sammy Liebermann, handmade panels and tiles by Mary Liebermann, tiles by Gutridge and Dangereaux, ceramic curtains by Hurwitz and silk-screened tiles by Berry.

1970–1971 320 West Street, Durban. A tile mural depicting the history of Durban.

1969 Art and Craft Show, Florence, Italy. Exhibition of ceramic wares.

1969 47th Padova Show, Italy. Exhibition of ceramic wares.

1969 Messina Trade Fair, Italy. Exhibition of ceramic wares.

1969 'Fiera del Mediterraneo', Palermo, Sicily. Exhibition of ceramic wares.

1969 'Fiera del Levante,' Bari, Italy. Exhibition of ceramic wares.

1968–1969 Hyde Park Shopping Centre, Johannesburg. Relief mural.

1968 Barclays Bank, Greyville, Durban. Tile mural of horse racing.

1967–1968 KWV headquarters, London. Tile mural.

1967 Tile panel for Safmarine. This depicted the original Cape Dutch home, Morgenster, Somerset West. It consisted of over 40 tiles.

1965–1967 The Garden Room, Brenthurst, Johannesburg. Tile mural.

1964 Building Centre, Pretoria. Exhibition of domestic ware, tiles and figurines.

1960 KWV headquarters, Stellenbosch. Tile mural.

Biographies

ABRAMOWITZ, Bilha (née Turgel) (b.1958)

Abramowitz works as a general assistant at Liebermann Pottery.

ALCOCK, Makonya

Alcock was employed as a general assistant for approximately three years from 1989 or 1990.

ANDERSON, Madeline

Anderson was an apprentice and later a potter at Liebermann.

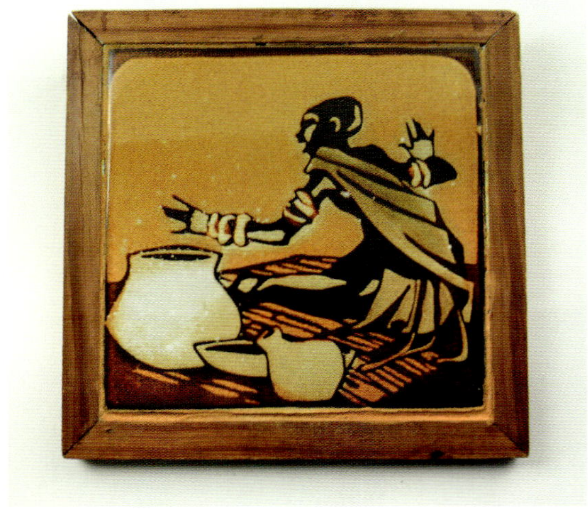

Liebermann Pottery | Tile | African Mythology series of framed tiles 'black magic, and white' | 190mm² | Provenance: Wendy Gers | Additional information: artist Mary Liebermann | Photograph by Natalie Field

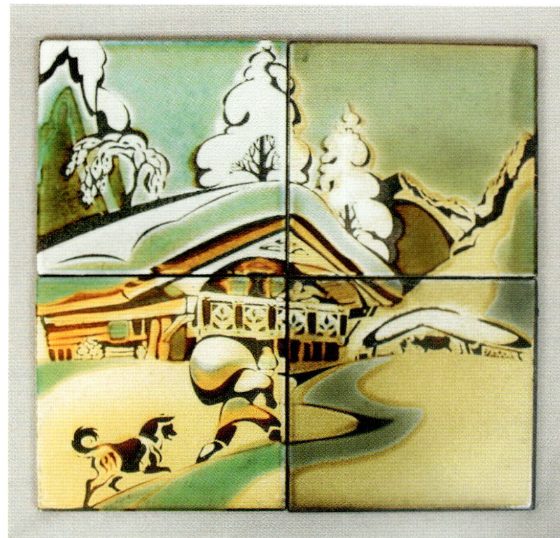

Liebermann Pottery | Tile panel depicting a landscape with peasant, dog and Alpine cottage | Composed of four tiles | Provenance: Liebermann Pottery | Photograph by Natalie Field

BALOYI, Martha (b.1945)
The resident historian at Liebermann, Baloyi was responsible for glazing and grading. She commenced working for the pottery in 1970 and still works part-time, sorting the finished works.

BERRY, Anne-Marie (née Lieser) (Mrs Maresch, Mrs Archdeacon) (aka Anno) (b.1948)
Born of German-Mauritian ancestry, Berry studied at the University of the Witwatersrand, the University of Cape Town and Hamburg University. She also worked at the Montezuma Craft Village in New Mexico. She married David B Berry, a well-known kiln-maker, renowned for his distinctive red-and-white electric kilns. He produced over 6 000 kilns for private and corporate use in southern Africa.

Berry was employed by Liebermann from 1969 to 1979 as a tile designer who excelled in figurative and animal images. Berry and Mary Liebermann frequently collaborated, and in time their individual styles blended together. She also undertook administrative work 'involving African workers and their complex and laborious dealings with the apartheid bureaucracy of the time and its oppressive labour laws' (Berry 1998).

From 1980 to 1997 she worked at Mapepe Craft at Henley-on-Klip. In the late 1980s and early 1990s Berry also worked for Peter Kroll's company, Designer Tiles, where she designed tile panels for various southern African SOS Children's Villages and training centres, including the Aldeia de Crianças, Lubango, Angola (1996); Hermann Gmeiner Primary School, Maseru, Lesotho (1996); Pietermaritzburg (1996); Mthatha, Transkei (1998); Windhoek, Namibia (1998); Renosterspruit Training Centre (1999); Port Elizabeth (1998/1999); Tsumeb, Namibia (1999); and Ennerdale, Johannesburg (2000).

Berry illustrated textbooks for African children. In the late 1980s, 1990s and early 2000s she produced figurative sculptures inspired by African anthropology, which she studied through the University of South Africa. She has works in private collections in South Africa, America, France and England.

BONDONGA, Amy
Bondonga was employed by Liebermann as a tile decorator for approximately a year.

CHILATE, Alvina
Chilate was employed by Liebermann from approximately 1986 to December 2007 as a jigger.

CHORN, Rosten (1954–2005)
Rosten Chorn worked at Liebermann in the early 1970s. He subsequently worked as a professional potter for a number of years. Chorn qualified as a

clinical psychologist in 1993 in South Africa, and in 1996 he immigrated to the UK where he was employed by the NHS. Within a few years he was appointed Head of Psychology for Learning Disabilities at the North-East London Mental Health Trust.

DANGEREAUX, Michel
A French potter who had worked in Picasso's former studio at Vallauris, assisted Liebermann with technical aspects of tile production. He helped Mary Liebermann to correct the tension of the silk screens, the thickness of the glaze application, and the register for multiple-colour printing. He produced hand-painted works and exhibited with the studio in 1972. He lived at the Liebermanns' Kelvin homestead, and departed in approximately 1983.

DUBE, Thulani
Originally from Zimbabwe, Dube worked as a sales representative under Turgel.

GROBBELAAR, Piet (b. ca.1938)
Born in the Free State, Grobbelaar studied pottery with Miss Luckoff at the Bloemfontein Technical College, and worked as a potter at Liebermann from approximately 1954 to the 1970s. Grobbelaar took advantage of Sammy Liebermann's vision of multi-tasking and, in addition to his work as a thrower, he landscaped the garden, planting exotic species at the Kelvin homestead. He had a solo exhibition at Gallery 101, Johannesburg in December 1966, and participated in its Christmas stock exhibition in 1967 where he exhibited tea services, tableware, lamp bases, urns and brandy jars.

GUTRIDGE, Elsje
Gutridge was employed by Liebermann Pottery and Tiles in the 1970s. She assisted with the coordination of the tile department and sales, and also made decorative tiles.

HADEBE, Fine (aka Fire)
Hadebe was employed by Liebermann Pottery and Tiles as a potter from approximately 1968. He could throw particularly fine wares, and was usually responsible for throwing and assembling teapots. Hadebe also assisted Mary in the throwing of complex and specialised forms for various commissions.

HAENGGI, Caroline Mary (née Nicholson) (b.1946)
Born in Clocolan, Free State, Caroline Nicholson studied ceramics at the Natal Technical College from 1963 to 1964. She worked at Liebermann from January 1965 until March 1968 on the production line, creating her own works after-hours. During this period she participated in the Brickor competition exhibition, Pretoria, and in an exhibition of birds at Gallery 101.[179] In 1968 she married Fernand F Haenggi, a well-known art dealer and initiator of the Pelmama

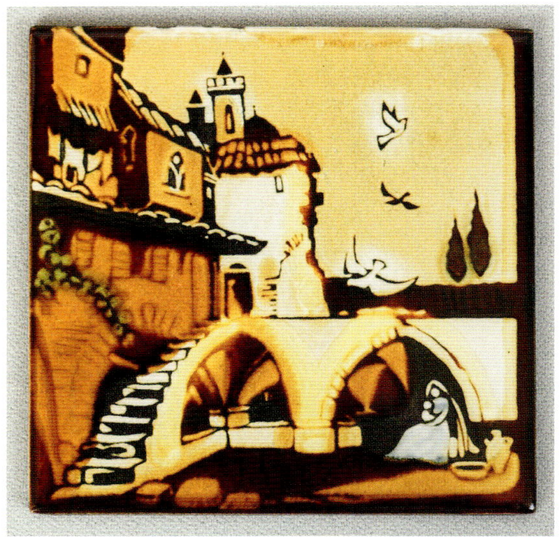

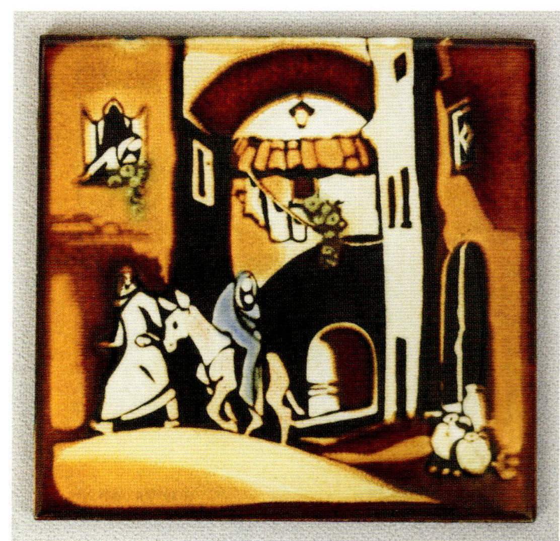

Liebermann Pottery | Tiles from the Nativity series | 155mm2 | Provenance: Wendy Gers ex. Liebermann Pottery | Additional information: artist, Mary Liebermann | Photograph by Natalie Field

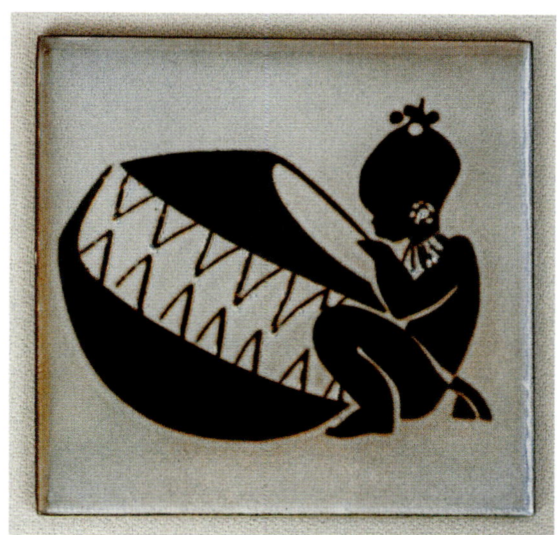

Liebermann Pottery | Tile | African child and large pot | 155mm2 | Provenance: Wendy Gers, ex Liebermann Pottery | Photograph by Natalie Field

Collection and the former Pelmama Academy, Soweto. In 1993 the Haenggi family moved to Switzerland, Fernand's home country. The greater portion of their collection, the Pelmama Permanent Art Collection was donated to art museums throughout South Africa. A significant part of the Haenggi collection was donated to the Oliewenhuis Art Museum, and ceramics from the Gertrude Agranat Bequest and the Pelmama Collection were donated to the Pretoria Art Museum in 2006.[180] Caroline resumed her pottery activities in 2004 and has been a member of the Clubschule Migros in Basel, Switzerland, since 1997.

HENAREIN, Leah

A fine art graduate from Tel Aviv, Henarein worked in the tile department and was responsible for developing an innovative series of brightly coloured tiles, featuring patterns and stripes in industrial glazes. She worked in the pottery for a year in 1988, then with Simon Liebermann in the shop for another year.

HLOPE, Patricia

Hlope worked at Liebermann from 1986 to 1989.

HOPE BAILEY, Sue

Hope Bailey obtained a National Diploma in Fine Arts from the Johannesburg Technikon and joined Liebermann Pottery in 1981, working as a designer and decorator in the tile department, specialising in naïve images of children fishing, swinging and watering flowers. She is currently employed by The King's School, Linbro Park, Johannesburg.

HORWITZ, Pauline (Polly) (ca.1914–ca.1993)

Sammy Liebermann's oldest sister Polly was employed by Liebermann and was responsible for managing the vibrant 'seconds' shop that was initially run from a garage in Kelvin. She also produced ceramic jewellery and ceramic curtains. Horwitz was known as the 'Vera Lynn' of the pottery, after the popular World War II entertainer and vocalist. Having had no children, she devoted her life to her bead necklaces, beautiful clothes and paintings.

ISSAC, Baba (d.1985/86)

Baba Issac was employed as a kiln packer. He also mixed clay and packed fired works for transport. He worked at Liebermann from the 1950s to the early 1980s.

JASCINSKA, Magda

Jascinska obtained a master's degree in garden sculpture and ceramics in Poland. She commenced working for Liebermann in 1969, and still works occasionally for the firm. Many of her designs reflected the folk-art traditions of her homeland. She also undertook the majority of small special orders, including house names and numbers, and small plates commemorating a baby's date of birth. She is also recalled for her fortune telling, which she undertook in her tea break to supplement her income.

JASPAN, Adrian

Jaspan was married to Ann Liebermann and worked at Liebermann as a director from 1983 to 1988. Upon his departure Adriaan Turgel took over as director.

KÖTER, Oliver (b.1965)

Köter worked at Liebermann from 1989 to 1991 upon the completion of his military service. He was a mould-maker and was responsible for general maintenance. In 1991 he helped Mary Liebermann to construct giant earthenware insects with legs of metal, which he welded. He also assisted with slip-casting and the sculpture of Christmas figurines. Adriaan Turgel nicknamed him 'Umlumgisi', meaning 'the one who fixes things'.

KROLL, Peter (1944–2003)

Born in 1944 in Landsberg, Kroll studied ceramic engineering in Hoehr-Grenzhausen, Germany. He immigrated to South Africa in 1966 and worked for Ferro, Johannesburg and was subsequently employed as a director of Liebermann from 1969 to 1972. In 1972 he established Kettenhofen Kroll, with Rudolf Kettenhofen. In 1975 he established Designer Tiles in Germiston. This factory produced approximately 35 different designs of rustic handmade tiles, some of which were designed and decorated by Asnath Matinketja, Manrico Guisardi, Anne-Marie Berry and Magda Jascinska. Their tiles decorated numerous chain stores, including Fruit and Veg City, King Pie, Red Pepper, Wimpy and Pannerotti's restaurants. Designer Tiles also makes swimming pool tiles and coping tiles.

LAZARUS, Louise

Lazarus worked with Mary Liebermann at Liebermann in the late 1960s. She made sculptures and fountains.

LEGANYANE, Bila

The daughter of Dinah, Bila has been employed at Liebermann as a jigger operator since 1994.

LEGANYANE, Camina

The daughter of Dinah, Camina was employed at Liebermann as an administrator from 2001 to 2005. She presently works as a teacher.

LEGANYANE, Dinah

Dinah Leganyane was employed as a general assistant at Marrakesh Ware and later worked for Liebermann.

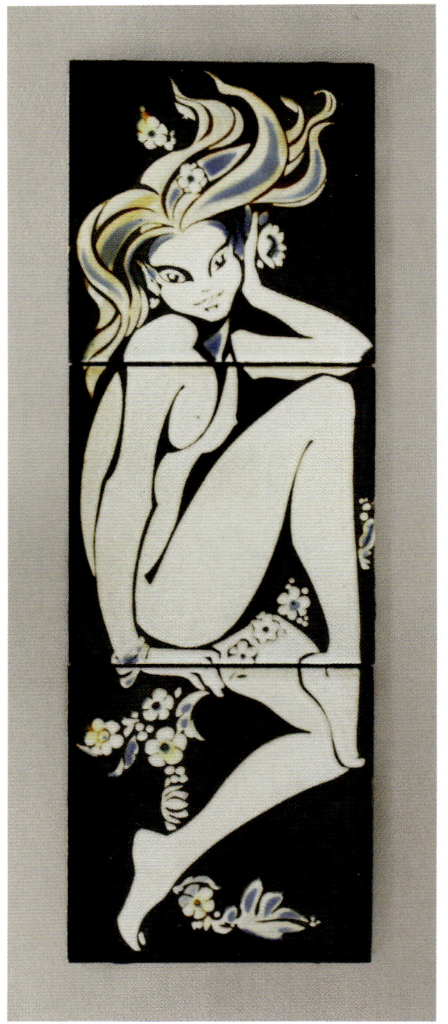

Liebermann Pottery | Tile panel depicting a nymph | 150mm^2 | Provenance: Jan Middeljans | Photograph by Natalie Field

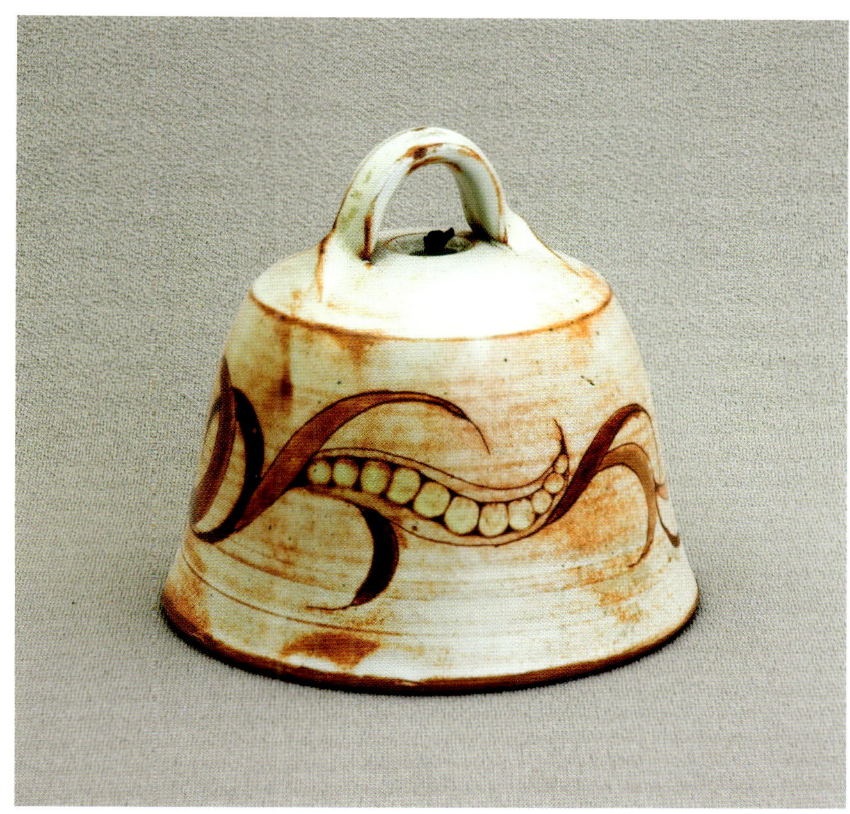

Liebermann Pottery | Bell | 105x114mm | Provenance: Douglas van der Horst | Additional information: artist, Janet Roberts, maker's marks illustrated on p.207 | Photograph by Natalie Field

LEGWABE, France
Legwabe was employed as a potter and turner for Liebermann from 1974 to 1997.

LEWIS BAR, Annette
Lewis Bar worked as a potter at Liebermann in the 1960s. In 1971 she opened the Potters Shop in Rivonia, Johannesburg, which, among other items, stocked Liebermann products.

LIEBERMANN, Adam (b.1955)
Adam Liebermann was the second child of Mary and Sammy Liebermann. Like his siblings, he was a pupil potter and later helped with the electrical installations of the Wynberg pottery.

LIEBERMANN, Anne (b.1957)
Anne Liebermann, the third child of Mary and Sammy Liebermann, studied pottery with Barbara Robinson, the mother-in-law of Bruce Walford. She later worked at the tile department of Liebermann, specialising in Chinese-style painted images of birds and fish. After the death of Sammy Liebermann in 1984, Anne assisted her husband, Adrian Jaspan manage the business until 1992, when Mary Liebermann offered it to her nephew, Adriaan Turgel.

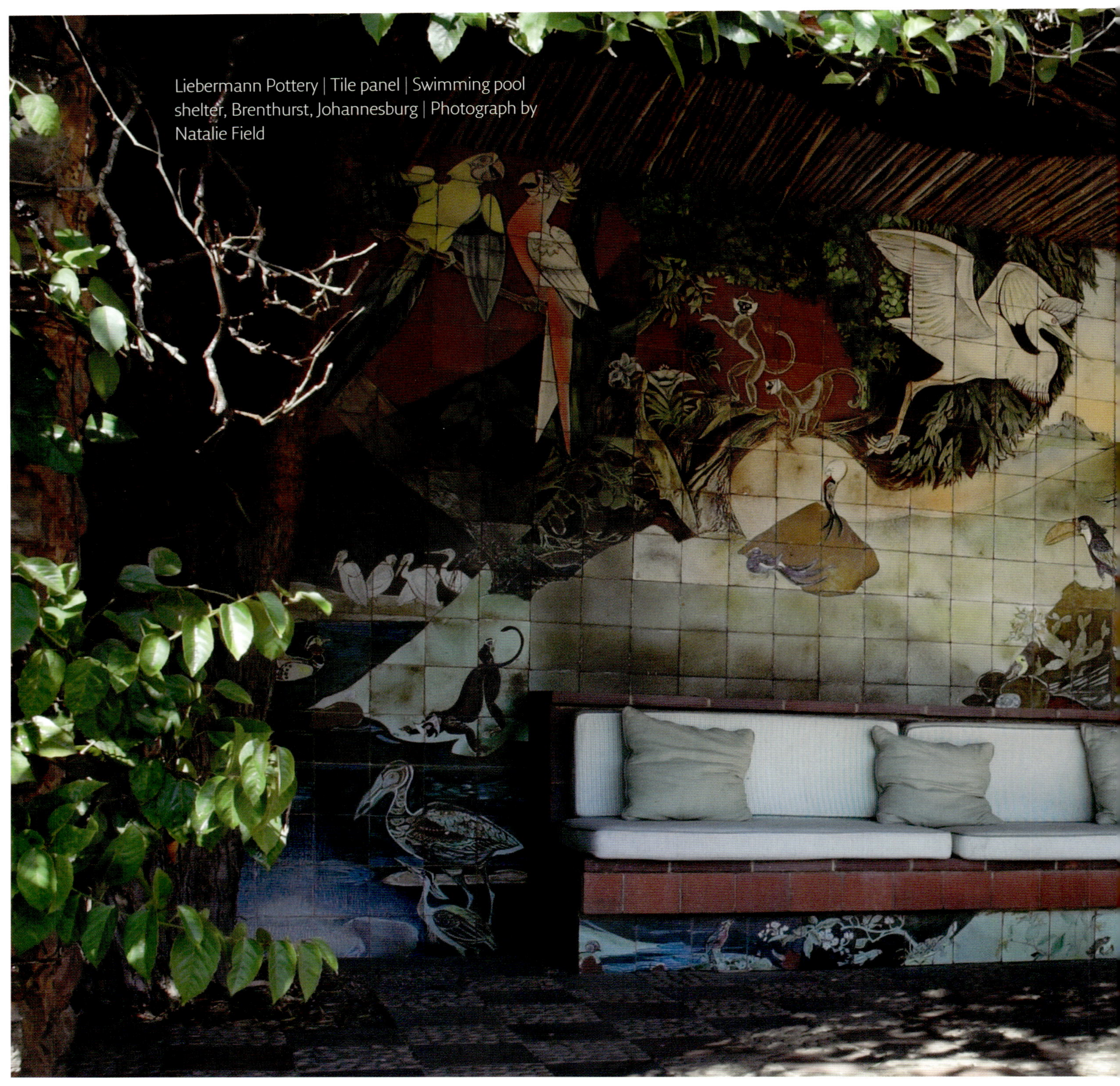

Liebermann Pottery | Tile panel | Swimming pool shelter, Brenthurst, Johannesburg | Photograph by Natalie Field

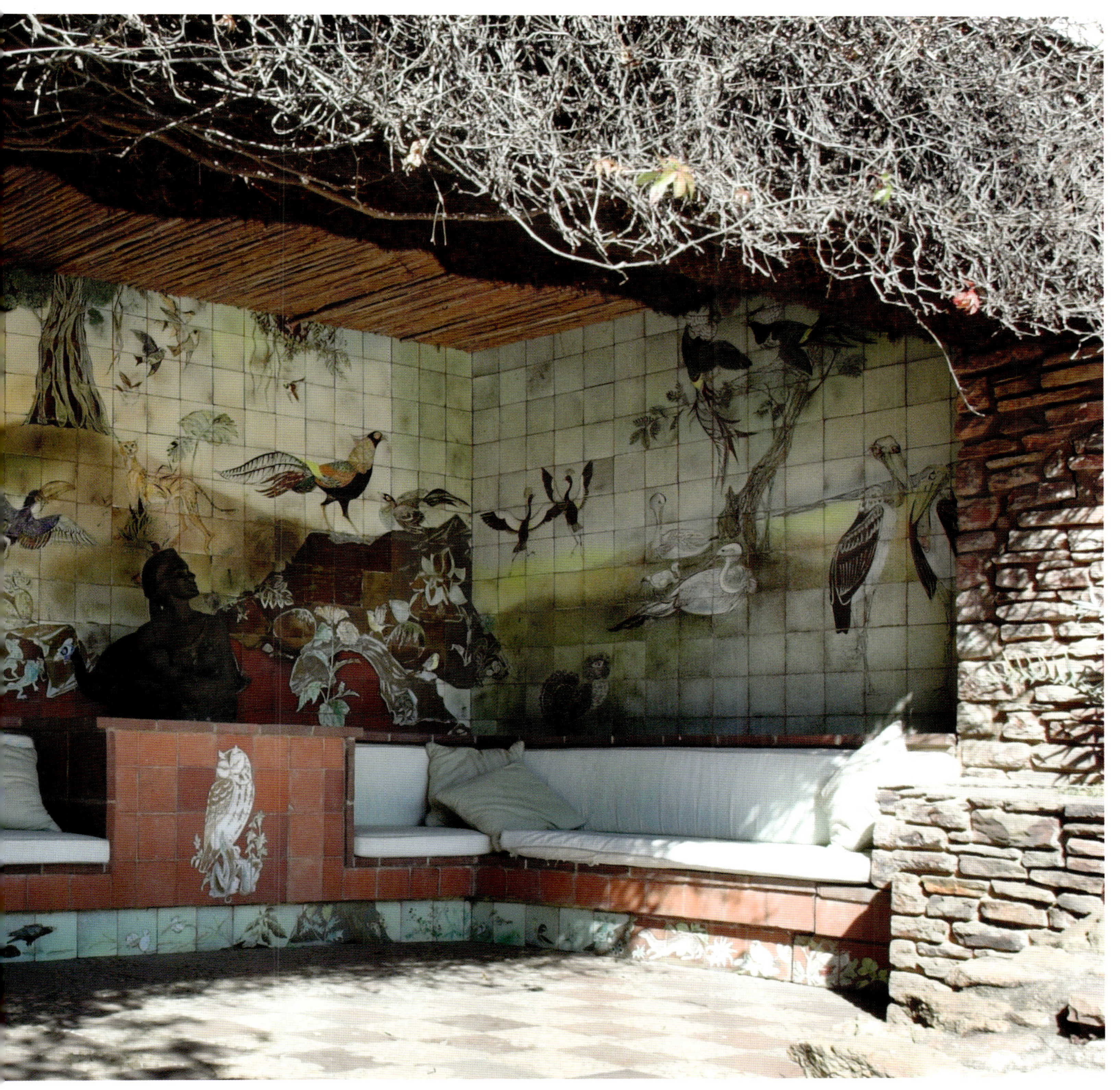

LIEBERMANN, Bertie (deceased)

Bertie Liebermann, Sammy Liebermann's brother, was employed as a warehouse manager at Liebermann. He was married to Ray Liebermann.

LIEBERMANN, Lisa (b.1969)

The last child of Sammy and Mary Liebermann, Lisa grew up with the pottery and as a teenager she recalls helping in the studio. She worked in the pottery intermittently from 1988 to 1990. She met her former husband Oliver Köter in 1985 when he came with his mother for pottery lessons, which were held in the courtyard of the former Liebermann Pottery. She currently manages her own pottery, Olisa Pottery and Tiles, in Plettenberg Bay.

LIEBERMANN, Mary (née Stonehouse) (1929–2007)

Mary Liebermann was born in Rugeley, Staffordshire, into a family connected with the ceramics industry; her grandfather was a glaze chemist. She studied at the Wolverhampton College of Art in the late 1940s and subsequently spent two years at the Central School of Arts and Crafts in London. The renowned Dora Billington, who was then teaching pottery at the Central School, had been very friendly with Mary's mother at the Hanley School of Art and Mary attended some of her classes although she was actually specialising in book production and illustration. The famous illustrator, painter, author and poet Mervyn Peake (1911–1968) was one of her tutors. After leaving the Central School with a diploma in book production, she obtained a secure but not very interesting job with a firm of lithographic printers.

She met Sammy Liebermann in London and in 1953 joined Chelsea Pottery, a communal workshop for potters that had been established by David Rawnsley[181] in 1952. After their marriage in November 1953 the couple visited South Africa and decided to settle there permanently. From humble origins in 1955, they established a thriving pottery and tile manufacturing business. Mary was responsible for tile production and was assisted by two devoted designers, Anne-Marie Berry and Magda Jascinska. In addition to the overall management of the department, she was a tile designer and her distinctive style recalls the expressive lines, flowering reverse curves and interlaced patterns of the Art Nouveau movement. She also made hundreds of sculptures and sgraffito plates, with masterfully viscous glazes.

In addition to an active professional life, Mary also had a full family life. She and Sammy had five children: Simon, Adam, Anne, Mathew and Lisa.

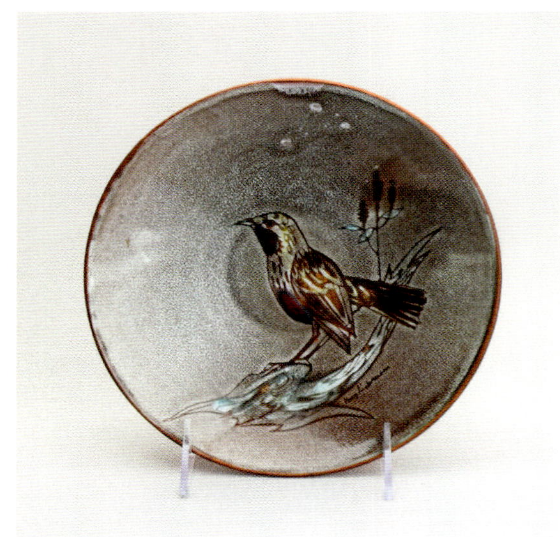

Chelsea Pottery | Plate with bird (pink-throated long-claw) | 193x43mm | Provenance: Douglas van der Horst | Marks: Signed 'Mary Liebermann' under branch. Incised mark on base, 'Chelsea Pottery S.A.' Chelsea yin-yang incised mark | Photograph by Natalie Field

LIEBERMANN, Mathew Lieber (1960–1981)

Mathew Liebermann, the fourth child of Mary and Sammy Liebermann, was a pupil potter and later worked at Liebermann. He was interested in electricity and assisted with the electrical wiring of the Wynberg factory. He was studying to become a sound engineer, and died in a tragic motorbike accident. It was rumoured that he was killed as a result of his association with the then banned ANC.

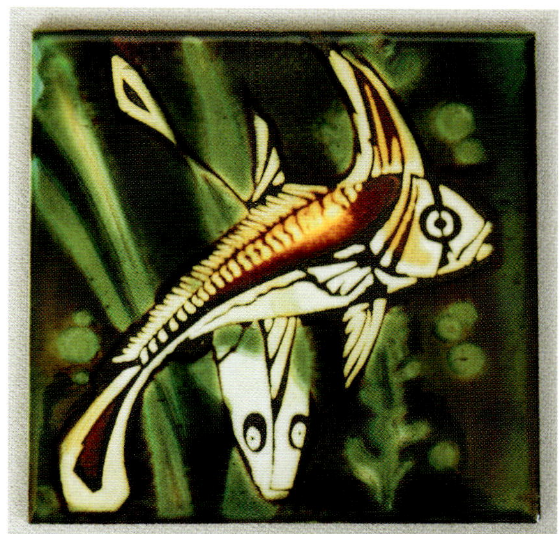

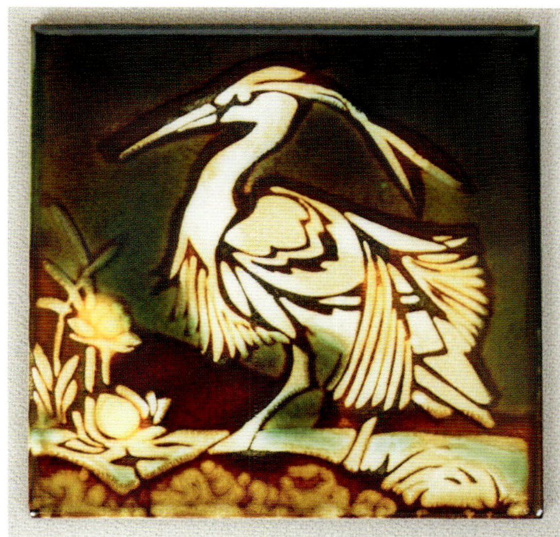

Liebermann Pottery | Tiles from the exotic pond life series - Pair of Koi and a Heron | 155mm² | Provenance: Wendy Gers, ex Liebermann | Photograph by Natalie Field

LIEBERMANN, Ray (deceased)

Ray Liebermann, the wife of Bertie Liebermann, was employed as the sales manager of the company's warehouse in Muizenberg, Cape Town. She was an extremely competent financial administrator.

LIEBERMANN, Sammy (1920–1984)

Sammy Liebermann was born in Johannesburg in 1920 into a family of Lithuanian Jewish immigrants. He studied at the University of the Witwatersrand, where he majored in Greek and Latin, and served in the air force during World War II. In 1949 Liebermann travelled to England to study law at Gray's Inn, and taught in London for two years. Lieberman inherited his father's interest in clay (Lieber Liebermann, Sammy's father, quarried kaolin clay for use in whitewash and insecticides) and was unhappy in his legal studies. A visit to Lucie Rie and Hans Coper's studio reignited his interest and imagination, and he was taught how to wedge clay by Rie.

Liebermann abandoned his legal career and joined Chelsea Pottery, a communal studio established and directed by David and Mary Rawnsley, as a 'Boy-Friday', scrubbing floors, working as a general assistant and later managing the pottery briefly. The studio was founded on the philosophy of a medieval craftsmen's guild. He met his future wife, Mary, who was employed as a designer from 1952.

In 1953 the couple returned to South Africa and the following year established a pottery in a former stable in Kelvin, near Johannesburg. Rawnsley had given Liebermann a letter inviting him to open up a Chelsea Pottery in South Africa; however, after a few months Liebermann decided that his own name was more fitting. The Kelvin homestead, composed of numerous houses, stables, outbuildings, barns and cultivated fields, accommodated all the extended Liebermann family and their enterprises. Referred to as The Old Pottery for many years, their first project was making flower pots for Bertie Liebermann, who ran a nursery at the homestead. They subsequently diversified, making crockery, tiles and ornaments. They worked here for ten years before relocating to larger premises in Kramerville, Johannesburg.

Liebermann loved cooking and believed that the colour of one's crockery should enhance the appeal of one's food, and thus preferred muted glaze tones. His pieces are characterised by a search for harmonious proportions between the foot, midpoint and lip of a form. He insisted on soft curves and lines and avoided corners or harsh angles.

Liebermann was devoted to promoting ceramics, and in 1973 was elected the first chairman of APSA. He served on various APSA committees in the 1970s. Lisa Liebermann recalls that:

> early APSA meetings were held in our house in Kelvin. Potters from all over would bring their special pieces for what would become an annual APSA Exhibition. At one of the early, or possibly even the first of these exhibitions,

my brother Simon – about six at the time – took serious exception to losing in the attention stakes to pottery, and to demonstrate his feelings, he took all of one lady's ceramic offerings and dropped them down the bore-hole (2005:Chapter 6).

Sammy's open and enthusiastic character resulted in a vast network of friends in the ceramic industry. He was a patient and enthusiastic teacher, as described by Andrew Walford, 'Sammy, no matter how busy we were, would always make time to help and teach you' (Guassardo 1988:21). His training of hundreds of potters is perhaps his greatest contribution to South African pottery. The tragic death of his son Mathew in 1981 led to a profound depression. The strain of managing the pottery in a highly charged political environment compounded his illness, and Liebermann committed suicide in 1984.[182]

LIEBERMANN, Simon Jan (b.1954)
Simon Liebermann, the first child of Mary and Sammy Liebermann, was a pupil potter and later a potter in the family business. He obtained his BA degree from the University of Cape Town in 1978, and managed the pottery sales department and the Liebermann shop at Sandton City until 1983. He currently lives in England.

MADISHA, Joseph (deceased)
Madisha was a potter at Liebermann. He subsequently set up his own pottery in Alexandra Township.

MAHLABANE, John
Mahlabane was a turner at Liebermann.

MAHLABANE, Wilson
A potter employed by Liebermann, Mahlabane made large vases and other items on the potter's wheel in the late 1960s.

MAIMANE, Christina
Maimane was a glazer and decorator at Liebermann from 1969 to 2002.

MAKAMU, Freddy
Makamu was employed as a turner at Liebermann from 1974 to 1991 (or 1992).

MANHARDT, Lisa
Manhardt worked at Liebermann in the 1960s. She lived with the Liebermanns in the Kelvin homestead.

MAREDI, Nikolaus
Maredi was the foreman and helped in production. He is presently the sales manager at Liebermann. He started in the late 1950s or early 1960s.

Liebermann Pottery | Tile of St Francis of Assisi | 155mm^2 | Provenance: Wendy Gers, ex Liebermann | Photograph by Natalie Field

MATABULA, David
David Matabula worked from 1986 to 1997 as a jigger operator at Liebermann.

MATABULA, Shedrack
Shedrack Matabula was employed as a storeman at Liebermann from 1993 to 1997.

MATJEBE, July (d. ca.2002)
Matjebe was employed as a turner at Liebermann from the 1960s to 2001.

MATONZA, Mary
Matonza assisted Magda Jasinska with tile decoration and presently works as a general assistant, cleaning and unpacking imported Asian wares at Liebermann. She has worked there from 1980 to the present.

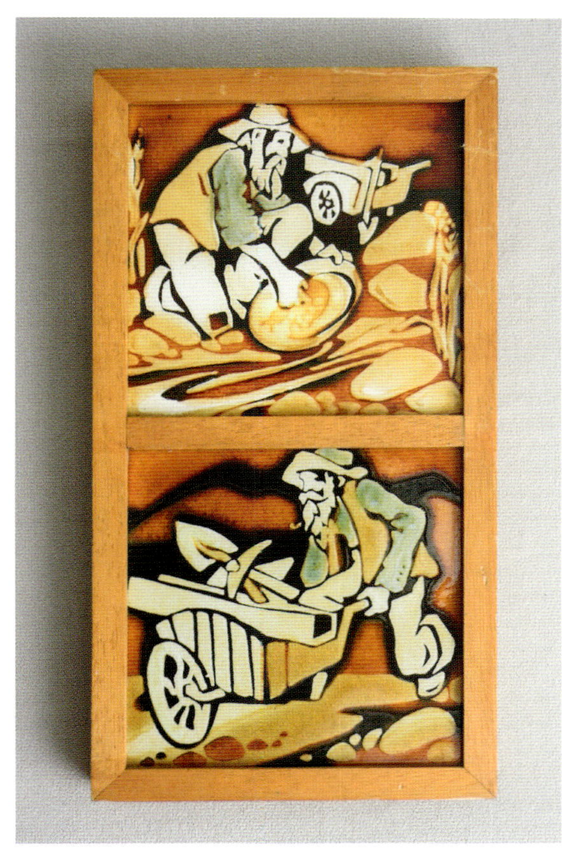
Liebermann Pottery | Framed pair of tiles showing gold prospectors | Provenance: Douglas van der Horst | Photograph by Natalie Field

McLELLAN, Don
McLellan worked at Liebermann (dates unknown).

MELLO, Jonas (d. ca.1992)
Mello worked at Liebermann as a turner, and also assisted with stamping and quality control. He was employed from the late 1950s or early 1960s until his death.

MESHESH, Merriam
Meshesh worked as a studio assistant in the mid- to late 1960s and was responsible for ensuring that throwers always had a container of clay balls, each of an identical weight. She lived in Alexandra Township.

MEYER, Sue
Meyer worked for the pottery in the 1980s. She is an acclaimed glass artist and lives in Cape Town.

MILEBI, Matthews
Milebi, worked as a potter at Liebermann. He also worked in the tile department.

MKHARI, Kainus
Mkhari worked as a thrower at Liebermann from 1972 to 1982.

MODIBA, Elias (d.1996)
From 1977 to 1995 Modiba was the head of the glazing section at Liebermann. He was also responsible for welding and repairing kilns.

MODISHA, Thando
Modisha studied ceramics for a year at the Pretoria Technikon. She worked from 1996 to 2001/2002 as a glaze technician at Liebermann.

MOFOKENG, Dolly
According to press reports, Dolly assembled up to 1 500 items per day. She also worked as a decorator, incising the Liebermann 'creole' design on wares.

MOLEPO, Onicca
Molepo was employed at Liebermann from 1993 to 2000.

MOROTOBA, Philemon
Morotoba was one of the first potters trained by Sammy Liebermann in the original pottery at the Kelvin homestead.

MORTIMER, Fran
Mortimer was a thrower at Liebermann in the 1960s. She learnt pottery in England in the early 1960s. In the 1970s Mortimer taught pinch pottery and glaze-making from her studio in Bryanston. Lindsay Scott joined her as a fellow teacher in the late 1970s.

MOTA, Bonginkosi (aka Ephraim)
Originally from Swaziland, Mota was a glaze sprayer in the 1980s. He was a charismatic shop steward during the strikes of the late 1980s.

MOTOPENG, Grace
From 1970 Motopeng assisted with glazing and decorating, and currently prepares orders at Liebermann.

MPOFU, Patch (b.1949)
Born near Brits, of Sotho and Matabele origins. Patch was adopted at the age of five by a South African family of British origin. He studied in Leribi, Lesotho, where his adoptive father worked for De Beers. Patch loved making clay animals as a child and after high school joined Liebermann Pottery. Patch was trained by Sammy Liebermann in the 1970s and worked as the lead designer in the domestic ware department for a few years. At Liebermanns he was renowned for his perfect English accent. In May 1974 he went to London and worked as a thrower at Briglin Pottery for six years and left when it closed down. Mpofu then retrained as a medical theatre practitioner, and currently exercises this profession. Margaret Thatcher bought one of Mpofu's pots at Briglin.

MPOKENG, Nikolas (aka Big Nick)
Mpokeng worked for Liebermann from 1971 to 1993. Initially, he was responsible for mixing glazes, but advanced rapidly and soon took over as production manager. He currently owns a taxi business.

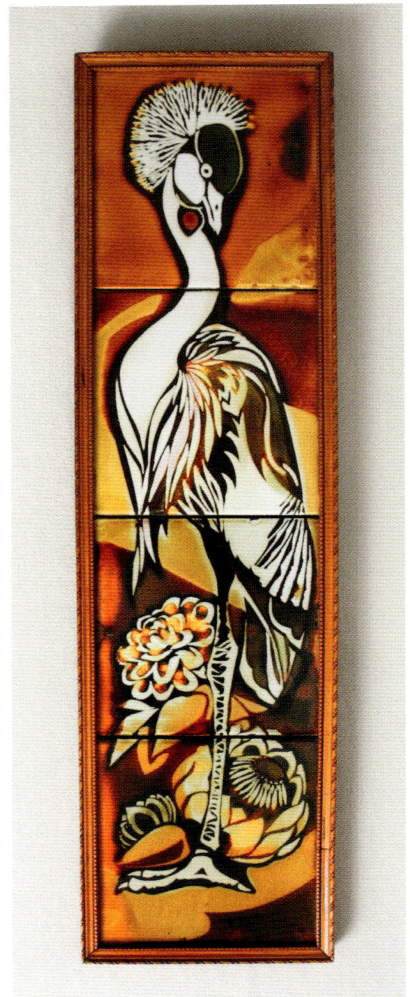

Liebermann Pottery | Tile panel depicting a crane | Provenance: Douglas van der Horst | Photograph by Natalie Field

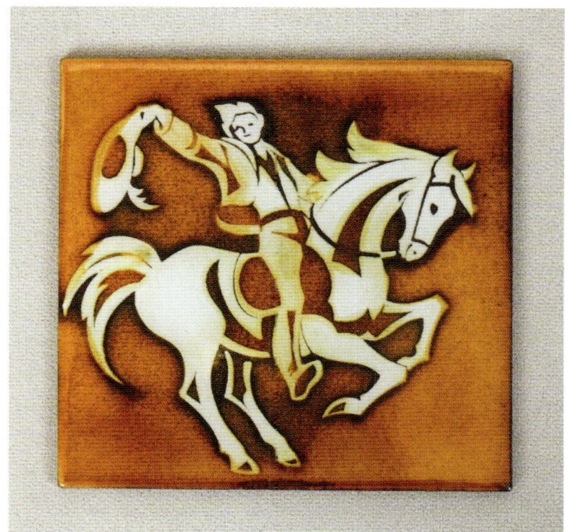

Liebermann Pottery | Tile | Cowboy on rearing horse | 155mm² | Provenance: Wendy Gers, ex Lieberman | Additional information: artist, Mary Lieberman | Photograph by Natalie Field

MULAUDZI, Petrus

Mulaudzi was a turner, driver, glazer and general assistant at Liebermann from 1972 to 1998/1999.

MZUMBA, Wison

Mzumba, a Malawian, was a potter at Liebermann from the late 1950s or 1960s to the 1980s.

NETSHUHA, Patrick Aswindini (b.1965)

Netshuha worked in various divisions of Liebermann including the stamping, clay manufacturing and jigging sections. He also worked as a mechanic, driver and repairman from 1985 to 2006.

NGOBENI, Steve Wilson

Ngobeni was employed at Liebermann Pottery and Tiles in 1985, where he presently works as a jigger, mould-maker and turner.

NGWENYA, Sam

Ngwenya was a potter at at Liebermann Pottery and Tiles from the early 1970s to 1990.

NKOMO, Lucien, Margaret, Miriam and Alice

Lucien Nkomo, of Malawian origin, was one of the most competent and prolific potters at Liebermann, able to throw 900 cups per day. He worked from the late 1950s or early 1960s until approximately 1995.

Nkomo was married to Margaret, who worked in the pottery, applying handles and decorating wares. Their daughters Miriam and Alice also worked for the pottery. Miriam, the elder daughter, started in the early 1970s and worked until 1979/1980. Alice worked from 1975/1976 to 1979/1980.

NYEMBE, Joseph

Nyembe was responsible for loading the tile kilns and supervising the firing. He was employed from 1972 and continues to work there. He replaced Michel Dangereaux.

RAOLANE, Knox

Raolane was employed at Liebermann from 1993 to 2006 as a manager.

RAOLANE, One-and-six

The father of Knox Raolane, One-and-six was employed at Liebermann from approximately 1955 to 1995. He worked in the pottery, and for many years also grew vegetables at the Kelvin homestead.

ROBERTS, Janet (d.2006)
Roberts received one year of ceramics training in England. She worked at Liebermann in the late 1960s and early 1970s as a design assistant in the domestic ware section.

ROSTEN, Alison
From 1975 to approximately 1980 Rosten worked as pupil potter at Liebermann Pottery and Tiles. She assisted with quality control and also supplied production figures to Sammy Liebermann.

SACHS, John (b. 1954)
Sachs undertook an apprenticeship at Liebermann, Johannesburg between 1975 and 1976. Between 1976 and 1986 he managed Mapepe Craft Pottery. In 1978 Sachs Joined the Transkei Development Corporation as a senior manager for Craft Industries. He then worked as a senior craft development manager for Mzamba Village Market from 1989 to 1995. The Village hosted 150 crafters and exported crafts to Canada, UK, USA and Australia.

Sachs moved to Cape Town in 1995 and consulted to the Working for Water programme in developing secondary industries from alien vegetation. Sachs has also worked as a project manager for La Repose Resort near Port Elizabeth (2008 to the present); the Nelson Mandela Museum, Mvezo (1998 to present); Bulhoek Massacre Site, Queenstown; Karoo National Park Interpretive Centre, Beaufort West; Interpretive Centre, Stilbaai; Cango Caves Interpretive Centre, Oudtshoorn (1998–2000); the Overberg Community Partnership, Overberg (1995–1998); Kleinplasie Museum, Worcester (1996); Working for Water project (1996–1999); tourist resort developers in Upington and Colesberg (1998); and Guga Isitheba Cultural Centre, Langa (1995).

Sachs is one of the founder members of the CCDI (Cape Craft and Design Institute). Sachs has worked as a design consultant to Woolworths from 1998 to present. From 2001 to present Sachs has operated Red Seal Design and Manufacturing Studio, Barrydale. He has consulted for the O R Tambo Memorial and Narrative Centre, Ekurhuleni and the J L Dube Memorial Site, Inanda.

SACKS, Kim (b.1956)
Born in Johannesburg, Sacks took pottery classes at a local recreation centre in 1969. Sacks subsequently joined Liebermann Pottery as an apprentice and potter in 1973. According to Sacks:

> Sammy taught me the hard lessons of throwing when I was 17: [I] used to catch 6 buses a day to get to and from his factory in Kramerville ... I would spend the whole morning throwing jug after jug – and he would come and sweep his hand through them, scrunch them, one on top of the other

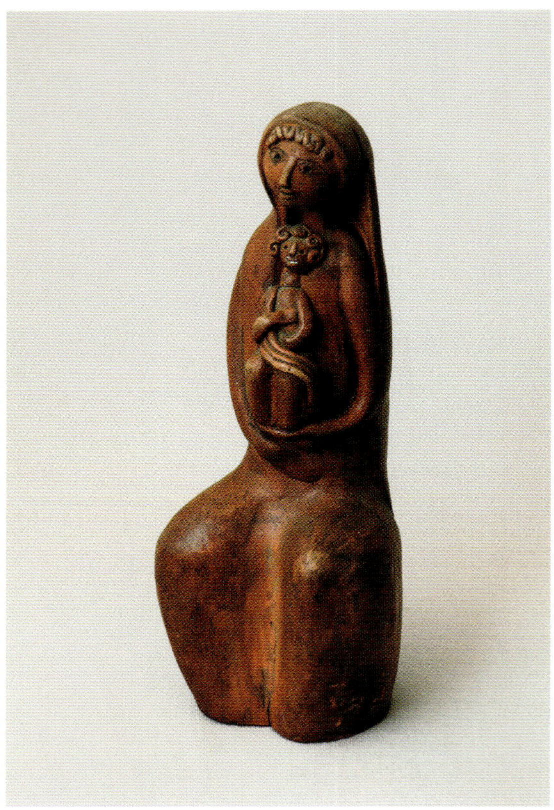

Liebermann | Statuette of madonna and child | 155x70mm | Provenance: Liebermann Pottery & Tiles | Additional information: artist, Mary Lieberman | Photograph by Natalie Field

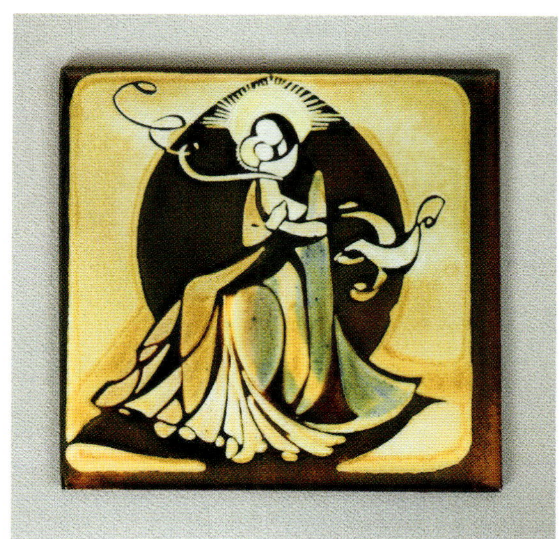

Liebermann Pottery | Madonna and child | 155mm² | Provenance: Wendy Gers, ex Liebermann | Additional information: artist, Mary Liebermann |Photograph by Natalie Field

> – and tell me to make another tableful ... those were the days ... I would still catch 6 buses – to anywhere I needed to – to grow another branch to my tree ... thank you Sammy.[183]

From 1974 to 1975 Sacks studied textile design part-time while doing her final years at high school at the Johannesburg Art School. She did this as she was both passionate about textiles and ceramics – and was undecided about her future profession. In 1978 she was awarded a bursary to study at the Danish School of Craft and Design in Copenhagen where she obtained her master's qualification in 1981. Sacks subsequently travelled extensively in the Americas, Asia and Europe, the Middle East and on the African continent. When she returned to South Africa in 1986, she established her own workshop and founded the Kim Sacks School of Ceramics, training some of South Africa's most prominent ceramic artists like Deborah Bell, Anthony Shapiro, Paul de Jongh, Lisa Firer, Loren Kaplan, Carolyn Heydenrych, Ozolo Ntshali, Zenzani Mazibuko, Caroline Schultz Viera and Jabu Nene.

In 1986 she opened the Kim Sacks Gallery which specialises in contemporary South African and African design, craft, folk and 'tribal' art. Sacks founded and operated a community-based ceramic collective Ntshali-Ware in Yeoville from 1996 to 2007. The original members of this collective comprised seven decorators from Ardmore Pottery, including Ozolo Ntshalitshali (Bonny's sister), Zenzani Mazibuko, Vusi Ntshalishali, to name but a few. The collective became a space for a group of rural woman to support one another and develop skills. Samke Ntshali, Josephine Ghesa (b.1958), Zanele Nala (1979–2006) and Jabu Nala (b.1969), the daughters of Nesta Nala (1940–2005) worked with this group of women. The name Ntshali-Ware was soon abandoned as artists created and exhibited in their own names. This group was also responsible for training many other migrant women in Yeoville.

Sacks currently works as gallery owner, curator and ceramicist. She has won various prizes, including the Corobrik National Award in 1989 (joint winner), 'Colours in the '90s' Southern Transvaal Regional Exhibition 1990 (joint winner), and a merit award at the 2002 Vita Craft Awards, Johannesburg for a collaborative work with Joseph Msomi. Her works are found in numerous public and private collections, including: the Pretoria Art Museum; the Nelson Mandela Metropolitan Art Museum, Port Elizabeth; the Tatham Art Gallery, Pietermaritzburg; and the Johannesburg Art Gallery. Sacks has been featured in numerous journal articles including *Ceramics Art & Perception*, Issue 14 and in several books: Moira Vincentelli's book *Women Potters: Transforming Traditions on Traditional Women Potters* mentioned Sacks in connection with her role with traditional potters in South Africa; Glenda Mentis mentioned Sacks in her unpublished 1997 MAFA thesis, 'A Critical Survey of Ardmore Ceramics 1985–96'; and Sacks was included in Wilma Cruise's book, *Contemporary Ceramics in South Africa* (1991).

Between 2003 and 2008 Sacks exhibited on an ongoing basis in her gallery in Johannesburg as well as in many local exhibitions including: the First APSA National Exhibition, Association of Arts Gallery, Pretoria, 1973; 'Corobrik Clay & Fibre Exhibition', Pretoria Art Museum, 1986; 'Edges', Goodman Gallery, 1992; international exhibitions such as Gallery Besson, London, in 1998; and in the 2001 'Bowled Over' exhibition of South African Craft at the Oxo Gallery, Oxo Tower Wharf, London.

SEOTTLO, Olita

Seottlo applied handles at Liebermann. She has worked for the pottery from 1973 to 2006. She currently helps occasionally with teapots.

SHONIWA, Aaron

Shoniwa, a Zimbabwean with two degrees from English universities, worked as a glaze technician at Liebermann from 1989 to 1999.

SIBEKO, Shelly

From 1985–1990 Sibeko worked at Liebermann.

SMIT, Herman A J

Smit was originally a master potter at Olifantsfontein. He was subsequently employed by Silwood Ceramics in 1951 as a potter and mould-maker. When Liebermann took over Silwood, he continued in their employ in the capacity of production manager. Smit was later associated with SA Art Potteries. In his free time he manufactured electric kilns.

SUTTON, Agnes

Sutton worked at Liebermann in the 1960s. She worked in both the administrative and production departments.

TSHABALALA, Gladys

Tshabalala worked in the glazing section in about 1982.

TSHABALALA, Jane (d.2006)

Tshabalala applied handles and assembled teapots at Liebermann. She also did carving and engraving on unglazed wares. She worked at the pottery from 1968 to 1999/2000, and occasionally thereafter until her death.

TURGEL, Adriaan (b.1954)

Born in Johannesburg to Donald and Menucha (aka Phyllis) Turgel, Adriaan spent much of his childhood in potteries. His parents operated an enterprise that made Marrakesh ware and his maternal uncle and aunt, Sammy and Mary Liebermann, founded Liebermann Pottery and Tiles.

In 1970 Turgel studied ceramics at the Camden Art Centre, London. He subsequently studied for a BA in anthropology at the University of the

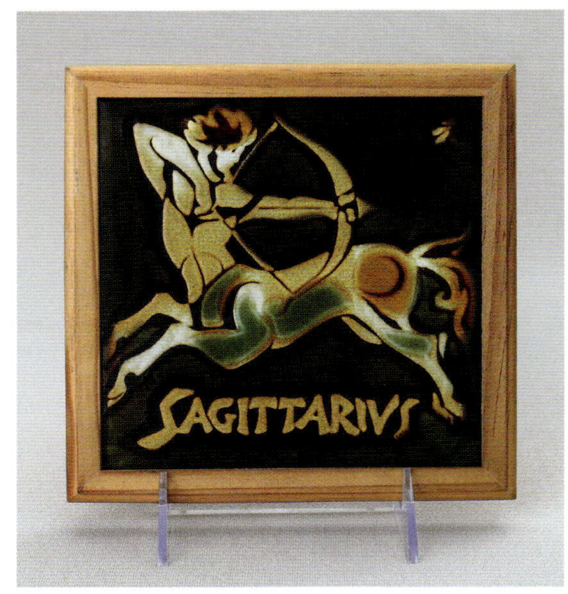

Liebermann Pottery | Framed tile with Sagittarius, sign of Zodiac | 150mm² | Provenance: Jan Middeljans | Additional information: back of frame has info on Sagittarius | Photograph by Natalie Field

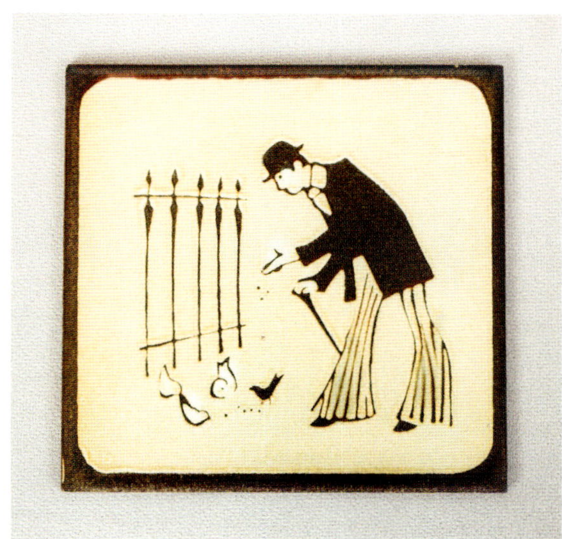

Liebermann Pottery | Madonna and child | 155mm² | Provenance: Wendy Gers, ex Liebermann | Additional information: artist, Mary Liebermann |Photograph by Natalie Field

Witwatersrand (ca.1985). In 1988 he began working for the SA Council of Churches on a community housing and urban development project called the Crown Mines Community Trust. He worked closely with the United Nations, lobbying in New York.

In 1989 Turgel took over from Adrian Jaspan as the director of Liebermann. Turgel reorientated the company, retrenched various management staff and adopted a policy of not replacing staff when they left. In 2002 the pottery employed approximately 30 people. The pottery currently sells clay and imported Asian pots to supplement its income. Turgel also made some changes to production, as various standards had dropped since Sammy Liebermann's death. Turgel was concerned about the heaviness of various items, and made changes to the thickness of some vessels, as well as the length of handles on casseroles and other items.[184]

TURGEL, Ricca (née Keifer) (b.1954)

Born in Bildstock, Germany, Keifer was the production manager at Liebermann from early 1982 to 1985. She worked as a sculptor and produced numerous one-off stoneware modelled items. Keifer also decorated tiles with oriental motifs and assisted with bookkeeping including sales analysis. She also did lots of glaze testing, in conjunction with the CSIR. Keifer was the second wife of the late Donald Turgel. She currently manages a textile project in the Eastern Cape.[185]

ULLMANN, Ernest (1900–1975)

Ullmann gave advice and made glazed quarry tiles at Liebermann.

VANDERLINDE, Andy

Vanderlinde was responsible for maintenance in the 1980s.

VEIRA, Carlos (d. ca.1995)

Veira was a mould-maker at Liebermann. He worked from 1984/85 until his death in 1995/96.

WALFORD, Andrew (b.1942)

Walford's parents immigrated to South Africa in 1947. He studied briefly at the Durban Art School and worked in his holidays at the Walsh-Marais studio near Durban. The studio, which was run by A Walsh and C Marais, manufactured teapots and slip-cast ornaments like Siamese cats. In 1959 he became an apprentice potter at Liebermann, and worked there for approximately 18 months. Upon gaining valuable experience under Sammy Liebermann, Walford left and in 1961 purchased the Walsh-Marais studio, and reorientated the pottery. Among other items, he produced reduction stoneware.

In 1964 Walford immigrated to Europe; in England he met Bernard Leach, Michael Cardew and Lucy Rie, the foremost exponents of the 'Anglo-Oriental' tradition in England. He also met Shoji Hamada in Japan, and he later worked briefly at Gustavsberg with Stig Lindberg and Lisa Larsen. In 1965 he started a studio near Freiberg, Germany, and a year later was invited to teach at the Hamburg Academy of Art.

In 1967 Walford returned to KwaZulu-Natal, where he established himself as an independent studio potter. In the early 1970s Walford was involved with the establishment of the Natal branch of APSA. Walford is a prominent South African potter, has exhibited extensively nationally and internationally, and his works are in numerous public and private collections.[186]

WALFORD, Bruce (b.1951)
The older brother of Andrew, Bruce joined the pottery at the age of 15. His mother was a painter and he introduced the pottery to oriental brushes. He lived briefly at the Liebermann's Kelvin homestead.

WATERKEIN, Caroline
In 1974 Waterkein was employed by Liebermann as a design assistant in the domestic ware section. She also assisted with quality control until her departure in 1980. She designed the 'Caroline candle holder'.

WHITE, Erica (née Lieser)
The sister of Anne-Marie Berry, Erica worked at Liebermann and lived in the Liebermann homestead at Kelvin. She worked in the tile department, and often did intricate brushwork with oxides onto thin matt glaze. She was employed for a few years from 1983.

WILSON, Chris Morgan
Wilson was a potter at Liebermann in the 1970s.

WITKAMP, Joke and Like
These two sisters, originally from Holland, were employed in the tile department of Liebermann in the 1960s. They made a relief mural, which was designed by Giuseppe Cattaneo, for the Hyde Park Shopping Centre, Johannesburg.

ZINN, Jeremy (b.1955)
Zinn was born in Cape Town and studied ceramics for a year at the West Surrey College of Art and Design in 1977, before being apprenticed to Hym Rabinowitz from 1978 to 1981. He worked very briefly at Liebermann Pottery in 1981, then with Gillian Bickell, and for three months at Mapepe Craft, Henley-on-Klip. Zinn subsequently worked with Chris Green producing earthenware flower pots and other wares at Tim Morris's studio. Zinn returned to Cape Town and did some brief work with Rabinowitz in 1982 before establishing a small pottery while also teaching at the Cape Town Art Centre in Green Point common.

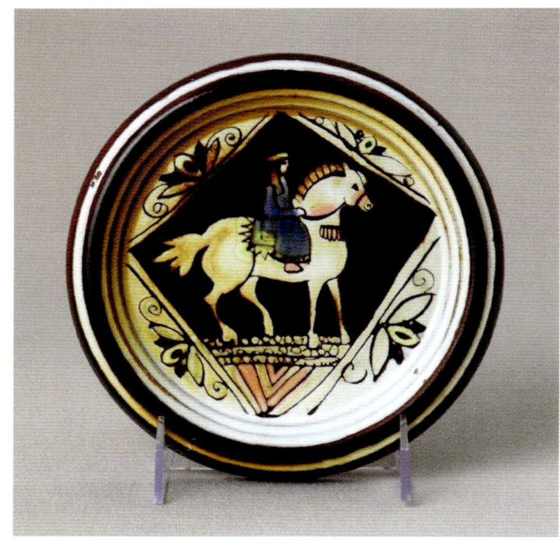

Liebermann Pottery | Charger decorated with a woman on a horse and floral detail | 170x20mm | Provenance: DNMCH | HG 55960 | Marks: unglazed terracotta base | Additional information: c.1960 | Photograph by Natalie Field

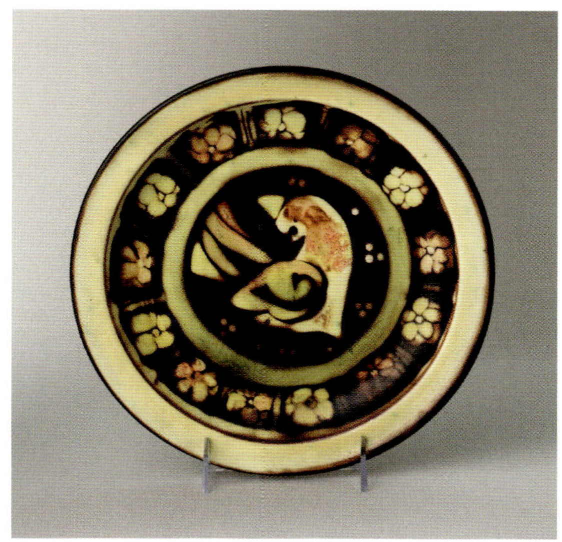

Liebermann Pottery | Charger decorated with a stylised cockerel in central roundel with floral border | 251x37mm | Provenance: DNMCH | HG 55947 | Marks: Pale yellow glazed base with wire attached to back with glue; impressed stamp, L, faintly visible under glaze | Photograph by Natalie Field

In 1985 Zinn left the arts and joined the family business, Pest and Hygiene Services, and is currently its managing director.

Unidentified staff

[Surname unknown], Cheryl

Cheryl worked at Liebermann in the 1960s.

[Surname unknown], Corlia

Corlia worked at Liebermann in the 1960s.

[Surname unknown], Jerry

Employed as a fettler in the mid- to late 1960s, Jerry lived in Alexandra Township.

[Surname unknown], Joyce

Of Chinese extraction, Joyce worked in the tile department from approximately 1985 to 1986.

[Surname unknown], Margareth

Margareth was employed as a decorator in the pottery department in the mid- to late 1960s.

[Surname unknown], Mzie

Originally from Zimbabwe, Mzie worked in the tile department for two or three years under Turgel.

[Surname unknown], Rachel

Rachel worked as a decorator in the pottery department in the mid- to late 1960s.

[Surname unknown], Sophia

Sophia was employed as an assistant in the pottery department in the mid- to late 1960s.

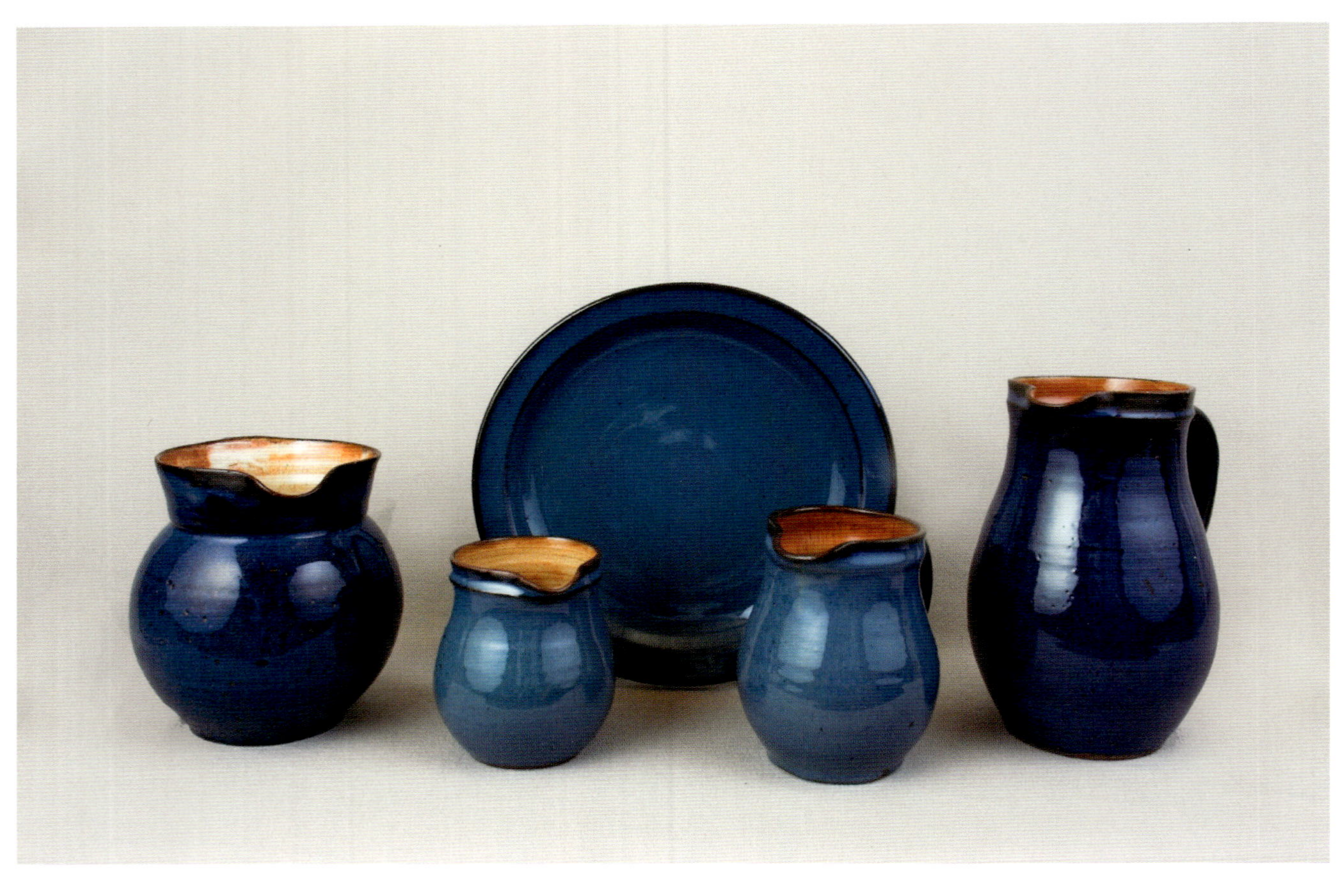

Liebermann Pottery | Set of four jugs and a dinner plate | Plate 257x30mm | Provenance: Liebermann Pottery | Unmarked | Photograph by Natalie Field

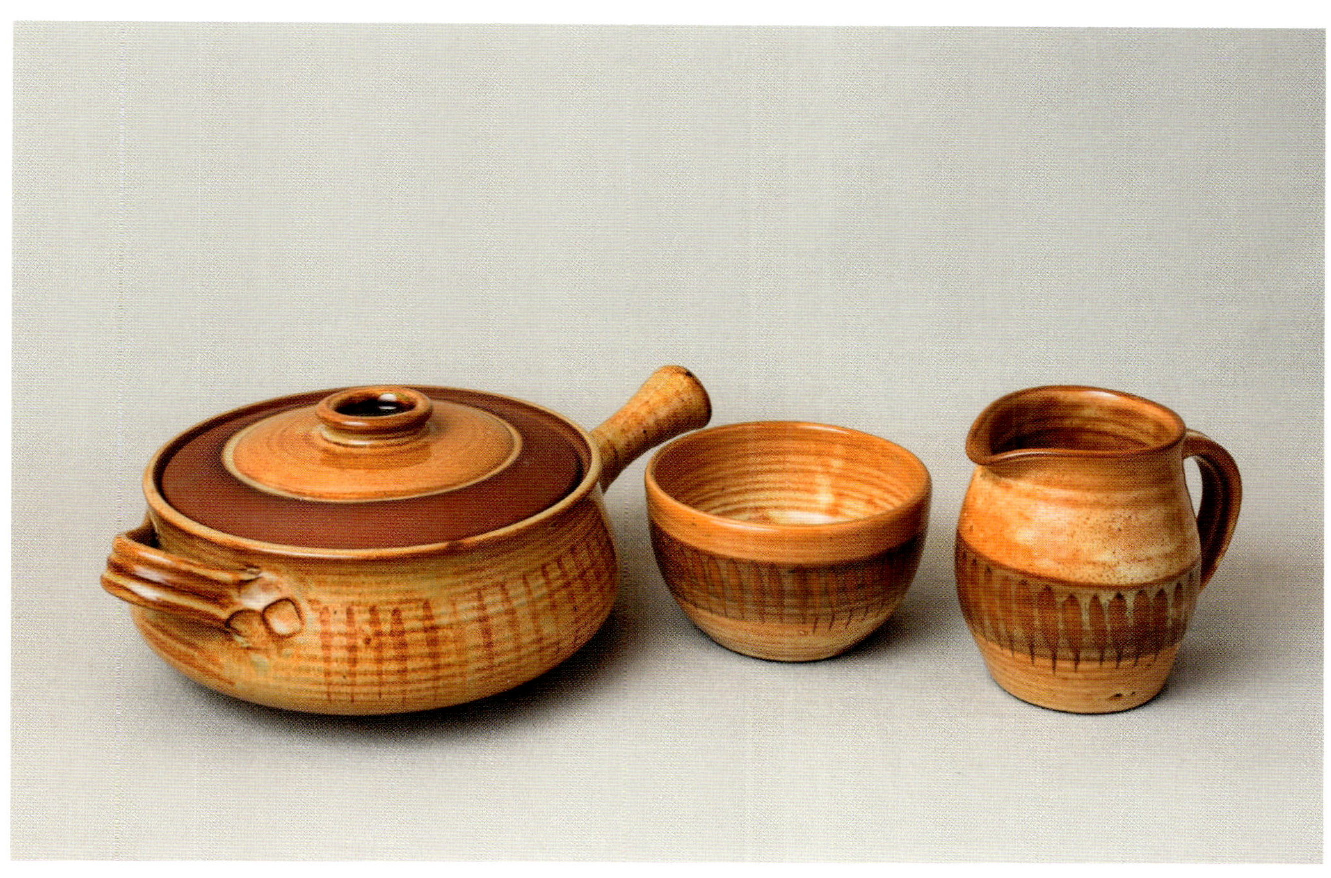

Liebermann Pottery | Casserole, bowl and jug | Jug 115x80x67mm | Provenance: Liebermann Pottery | Marks: casserole base has impressed stamp from 1970s; bowl is marked with a 'L' and a pot stamp; jug is unmarked | Photograph by Natalie Field

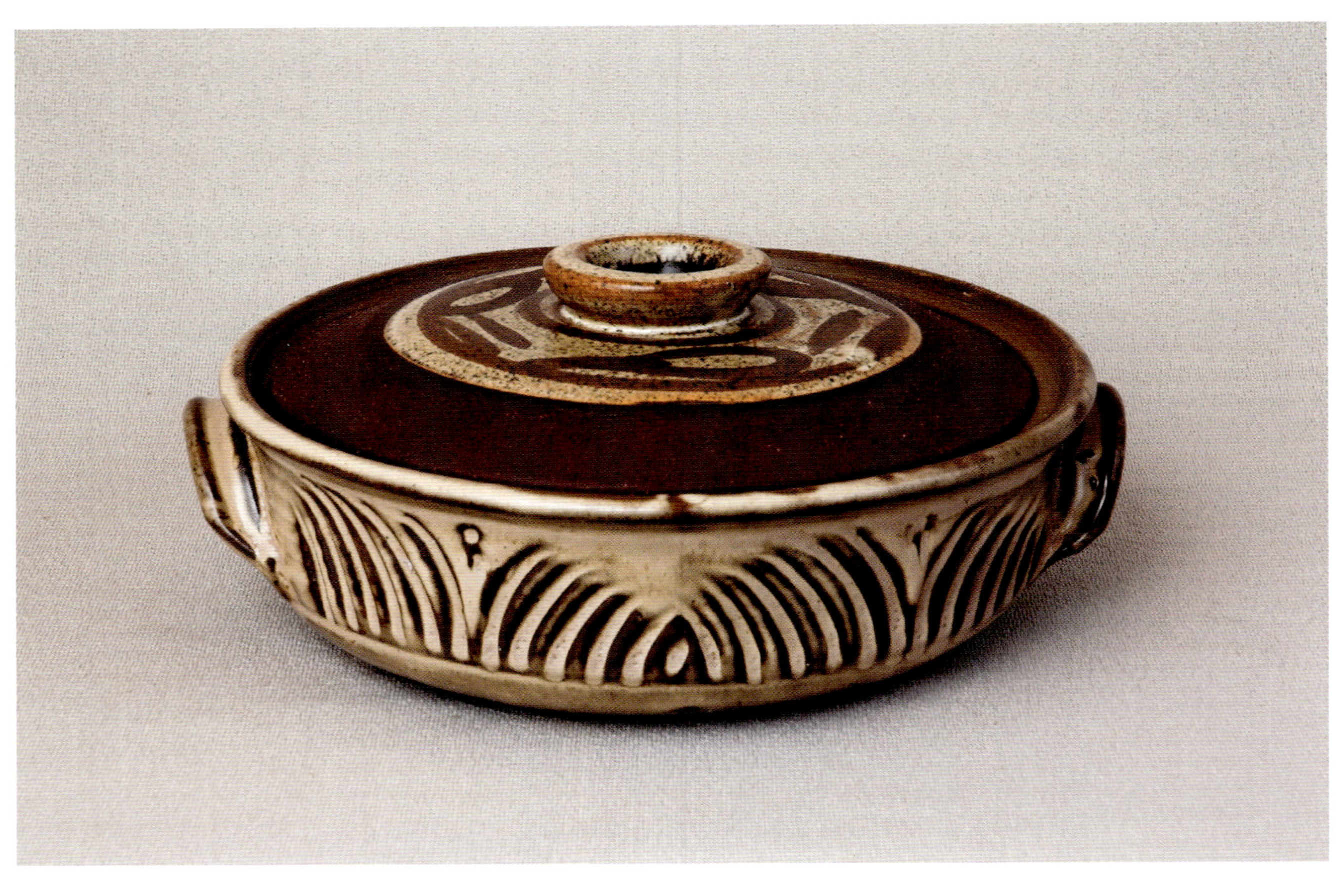

Liebermann Pottery | Casserole with incised decoration on sides | 82x180x125mm | Provenance: Liebermann Pottery | Marks: unmarked glazed base | Photograph by Natalie Field

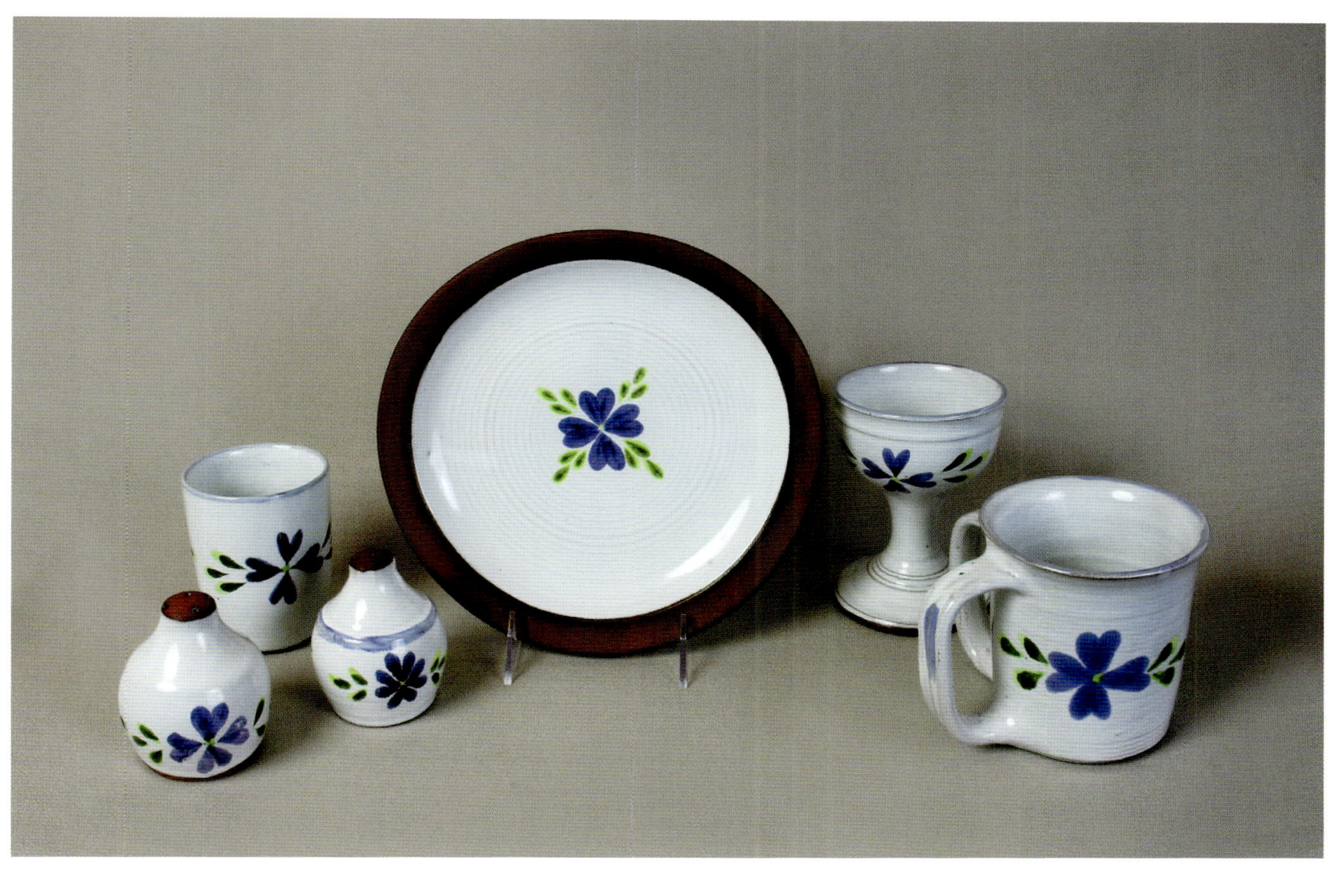

Liebermann Pottery | Group of white domestic wares with blue and green floral motifs | Salt cellar 90x22x55mm; pepper cellar 90x23x58mm; cup 100x80x58mm; plate 247x257mm; goblet 135x100x92mm; jewish cup 101x101x80mm | Provenance: Liebermann Pottery | Marks: all unmarked except cup and jewish cup which have 'Liebermann 00' impressed stamp | Photograph by Natalie Field

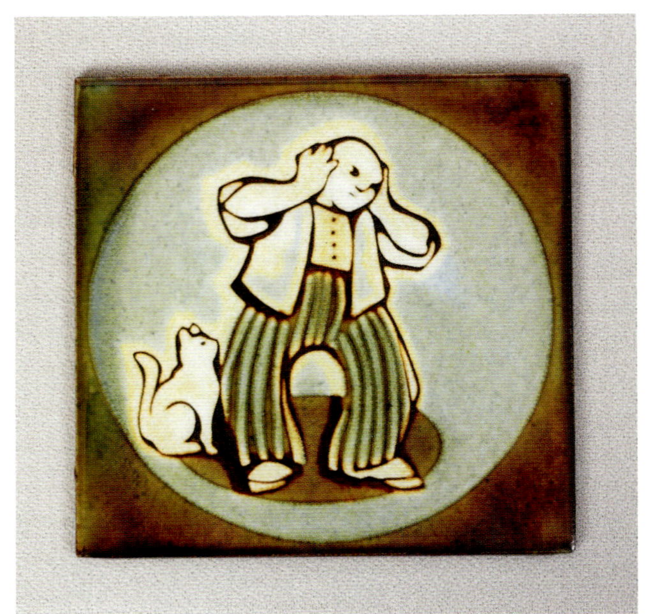
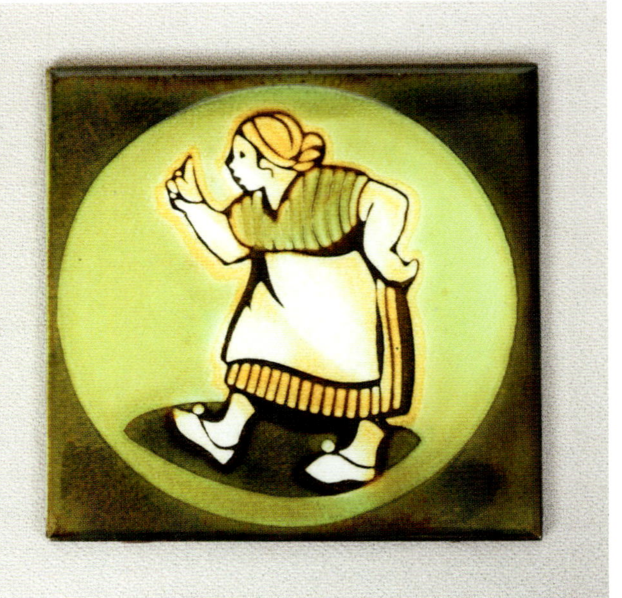
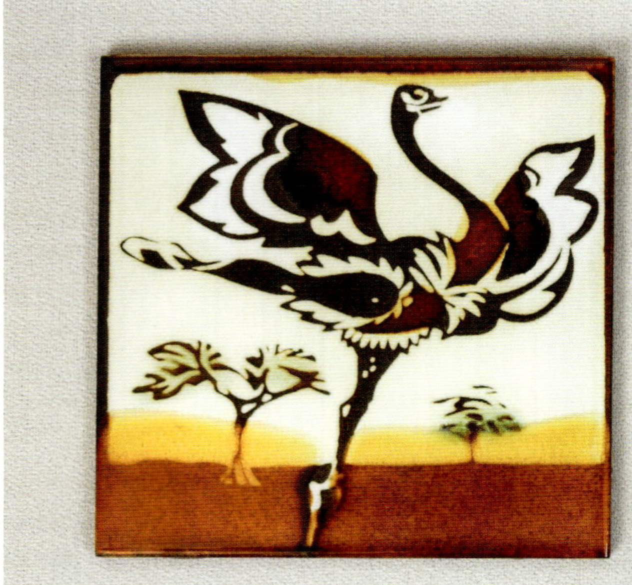
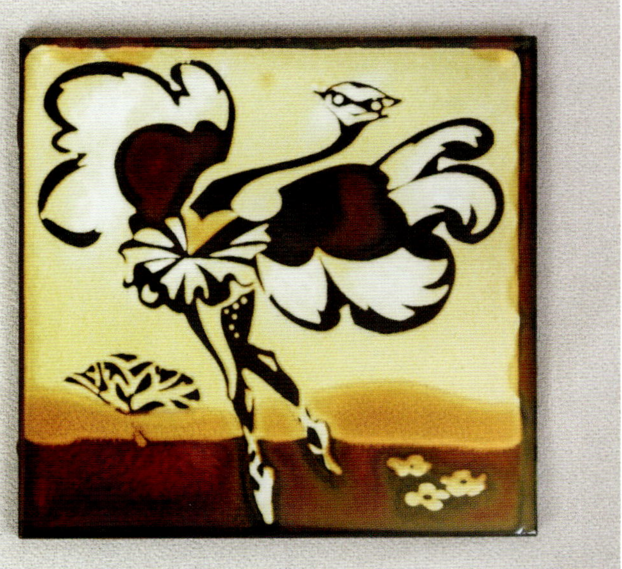

TOP: Liebermann Pottery | Tile set | Pair of 'scolding peasants' | 155mm² | Provenance: Wendy Gers, ex Liebermann | Additional information: artist, Magda Jasinska | Photograph by Natalie Field

BOTTOM: Liebermann Pottery | Tile set | Pair of 'dancing ostriches' | 155mm² | Provenance: Wendy Gers, ex Liebermann | Photograph by Natalie Field

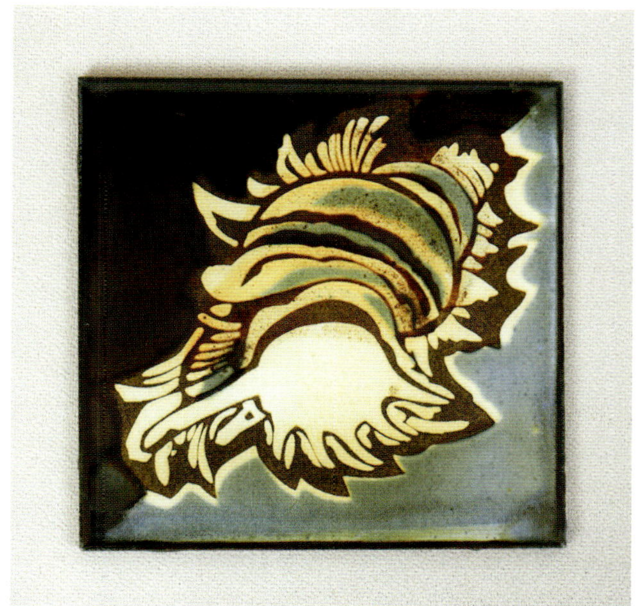
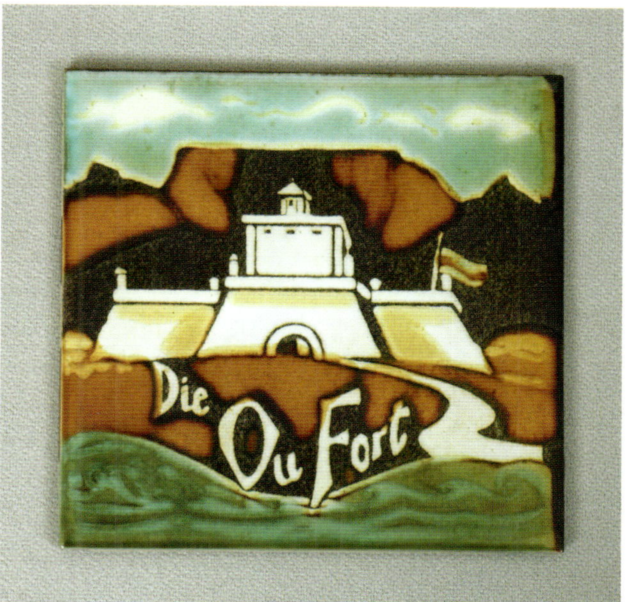

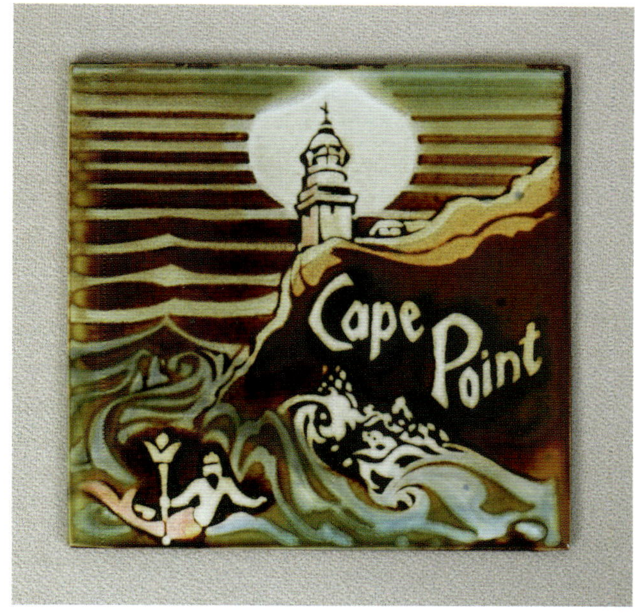

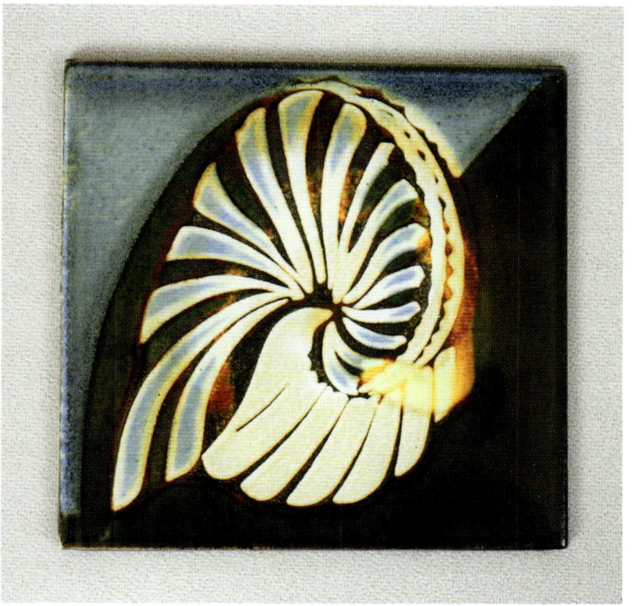

TOP LEFT: Liebermann Pottery | Tile from Marine Life Series – Chicoreus torrefactus | 155mm² | Provenance: Wendy Gers, ex Liebermann | Photograph by Natalie Field

TOP RIGHT: Liebermann Pottery | Tile from Cape Town Series – View of the Cape Town Castle, with subtitle, 'Die Ou Fort' | 155mm² | Provenance: Wendy Gers, ex Liebermann | Photograph by Natalie Field

BOTTOM LEFT: Liebermann Pottery | Tile from Cape Town Series – Landscape with Cape Point | 155mm² | Provenance: Wendy Gers, ex Liebermann | Photograph by Natalie Field

BOTTOM RIGHT: Liebermann Pottery | Tile from Marine Life Series – Nautilus shell | 155mm² | Provenance: Wendy Gers, ex Liebermann | Photograph by Natalie Field

Lucky Bean Farm (1974–ca.1983)

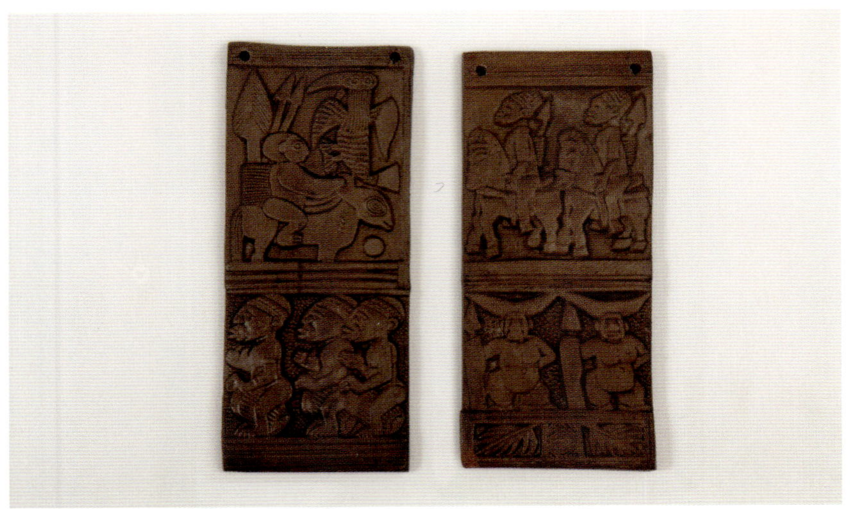

Lucky Bean Farm Pottery | African Mythology Series | 140x100mm | Provenance: Wendy Gers | Photograph by Micha Birch Hannemann

Location

Elandslaagte near Ladysmith in KwaZulu-Natal.

Founders

John Edwards (1929–1989) and Valmai Olsen Edwards established Lucky Bean Farm. While it was a joint venture, by the late 1970s Valmai ran the pottery as John was occupied with the farm, building pottery wheels and his teaching activities.

Staff

The pottery employed three women assistants, Kathazile Ngwenya, Gogo Ngwenya and Thembisile Zungu, who were involved with the finishing of unfired and fired tiles as well as their packing.

Wares manufactured

Lucky Bean's main products were highly original decorative tiles and tile murals depicting mythological motifs for the tourist industry. In 1982 it produced 25 000 stoneware tiles.

Production methods

Press-moulded tiles were made from locally dug clay, which was improved by the addition of various elements, including kaolin and fireclay. Most tiles were dipped in melted brown shoe polish to achieve a special decorative effect. Certain tile designs were modified and cast in bronze.

Brief history of the pottery

Lucky Bean's most popular product was its zodiac tiles. These were sold in tourist shops and were much appreciated as they were small and relatively strong. The eccentric compositions combined elements of Western astrology with motifs derived from a medley of pan-African and South American material culture. For example, the Virgo tile included the word '*tokolosh*' and a stylised zombie head as well as reproductions of a trio of Akua'ba fertility dolls produced by the Ashanti in Ghana.

The pottery received many large, prestigious commissions to decorate foyers and shops of Natal Parks Board buildings, including its headquarters in Pietermaritzburg.[187] Sadly, all these impressive tile murals have been destroyed. Wares were also sold through prominent outlets including Helen de Leeuw in the Carlton Centre, Johannesburg and the Yellow-Door Gallery, Cape Town. The pottery also had agents in America and Italy (Vermeulen 1984:332, 381–390).

Marks

A variety of different marks were incorporated into the designs of the tiles. Articles were marked on the upper surface with a circular motif that includes modified alphabetic symbols that resemble VE, IJ and BL, among others.

Biographies

EDWARDS, John (1929–1989)

John Edwards, a fifth generation potter, was born and educated in England. He graduated from the North Staffordshire Technical College with a qualification in factory administration and glaze chemistry, and in 1952 was employed by Drostdy Ware as a works chemist. He remained there for approximately 18 months before establishing his own factory to produce slip-cast vessels. During this period he also taught ceramics part-time at Rhodes University.

From 1957 to 1967 Edwards taught pottery at the Johannesburg Technical College, where his pupil numbers rose from 30 to a 100 with a waiting list of 500.[188] He also taught at the Braamfontein Recreation Centre. Edwards was a master technician and was extremely generous with his knowledge and made a significant contribution to the nascent ceramics industry and art pottery sector of the 1950s and 1960s. Prominent potters such as the Hoets family (including Dilys, Lesley-Ann, Digby and Garth), Thelma Marcuson, Charlotte Katzen, Debbie Klein, Joyce Keyser, Dina Katz and Wendy Goldblatt were his former students.[189] He manufactured pottery wheels, made and repaired kilns, and undertook various consulting jobs, including assisting with the construction of a massive kiln at Riverside Pottery.

From 1967 Edwards ran a private pottery school from his home in Johannesburg, before moving to Elandslaagte in KwaZulu-Natal, where he and his wife, Valmai Olsen Edwards (1934–2010) opened Lucky Bean Farm in 1974. Edwards established another private pottery school in Ladysmith, built pottery wheels and also farmed.

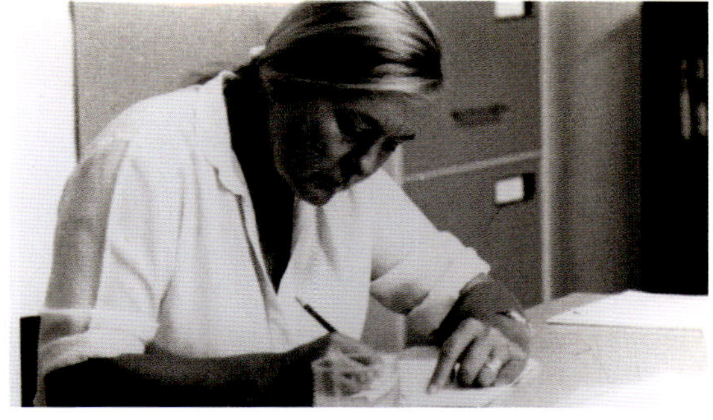

Valmai Edwards | Scans & photos: Thomas Vermeulen, 1983 | Vermeulen, T.F. 1983. *Die Potterbakkerskuns van Natal met spesiale verwysing na die mees invloedryke pottebakkers buite die provinsie se grense*. Unpublished MA Thesis. University of Natal.

OLSEN EDWARDS, Valmai (1934–2011)

Born in Durban, she studied art at the School of Art and Design in Johannesburg and in 1953 won the 'Best Student of the Year' award. Olsen Edwards worked for a year with a display company before establishing her own design studio in Johannesburg, where she focused on illustration, cartoons and covers for magazines and LP records. Clients included her father's company, which commissioned her to illustrate advertisements for the Zero Freezer, a paraffin deep-freezer for farmers. For years, *Personality* magazine commissioned her to illustrate full-page women's fiction stories in the late 1960s. Olsen Edwards also worked as a cartoonist for the *Argus* newspaper group for 16 years.

Olsen Edwards married John Edwards in 1961 and made the gradual transition from paper to clay. The couple established a pottery at their home in Fairview, Johannesburg, where Valmai taught modelling and John taught wheel work. Many of their pupils were actors and the classes were as professional as they were social! Students included Dilys Hoets (the mother of Digby, Lesley Anne and Garth), Digby Hoets (potter), Christine Suzman (artist) and Penny Gawith (potter). She exhibited clay works at the Adler Fielding Gallery in Johannesburg on several occasions and in numerous other leading craft galleries. While teaching from Fairview, Valmai met Ria and Boet Cronjé, sheep-farmers from Ladysmith, who required a designer for their company, Tactile Handcrafts, which manufactured hand-knotted rugs and carpets. In 1972 Olsen Edwards was appointed to this position. John and Valmai bought 'Lucky Bean' farm at Elandslaagte in 1973, to which they relocated so that Valmai could work more closely with the Cronjés. The couple sold their Fairview pottery to Digby Hoets.[190]

Valmai produced approximately 30 designs for earthenware tiles under the nomenclature of Lucky Bean Farm.[191] Tactile Handcrafts rugs and carpets were

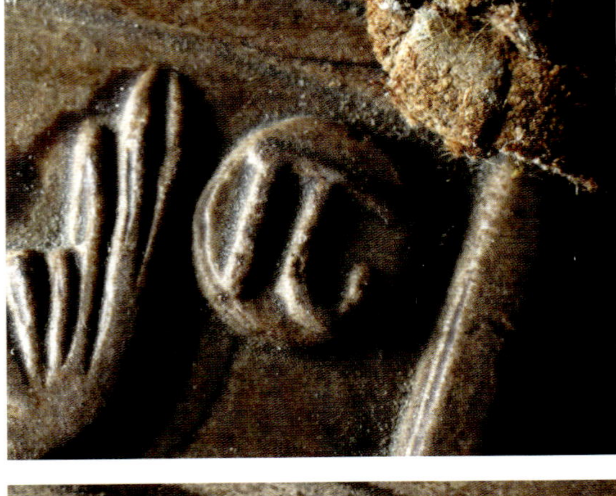

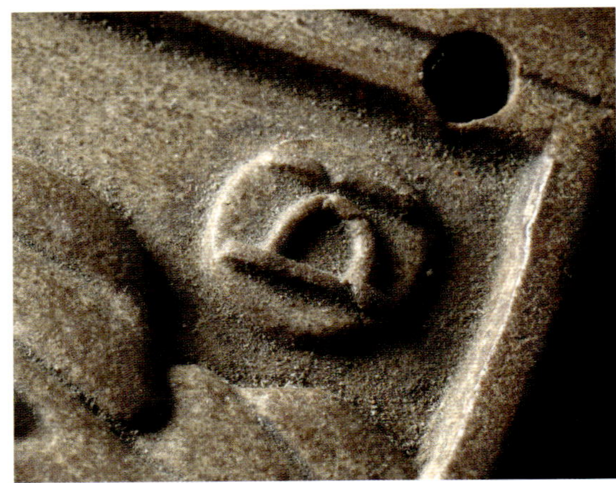

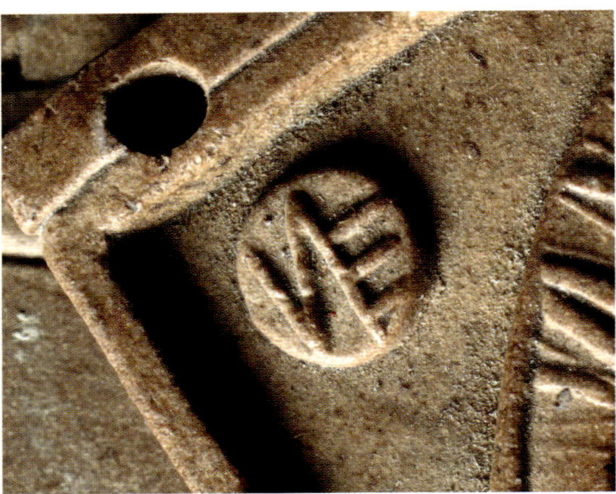

Lucky Bean Farm Pottery | Various markings on 'Jurassic Park' tile series | 140x100mm | Provenance: SHC Iziko | Photograph by Carina Beyer

exhibited at the Linda Goodman Gallery, Johannesburg; the SA Association of the Arts, Pretoria; Helen de Leeuw Gallery, Johannesburg; and other major galleries in Durban, Cape Town and Namibia. Valmai was commissioned by architects to design the floor and wall rugs for many of South Africa's banks, building societies, insurance companies and hotels. Interior decorators commissioned her to produce accent rugs for private homes in South Africa and abroad. The rugs and carpets were also exhibited and sold in Norway, Germany, America, Belgium, England, Japan, Austria and Australia. Tactile carpets are in the permanent collection of the Talana Museum, Dundee. In 1982 Valmai received the South African Design Institute's Shell Design Award for her carpet and rug designs.

In 1983 Valmai joined Kei Carpets as the principal designer. The Ciskei-based company was part of a community development project that produced hand-knotted, karakul wool carpets that were sold in craft galleries, including Christoff-Dekor, Stellenbosch, in 1988. Upon completion of this project she re-established her own design and craft studio, Bushpig & Afrikan [sic] Story. In 1991, with her partner Stephen Hornby and Brian Stonebanks, she established a fabric-printing business called Bushpig Fabrics in Knysna, Western Cape. The company sold screen-printed items, including wall hangings, tablecloths, runners, napkins, placemats, cushion covers and T-shirts produced at a factory in Rheenendal near Knysna. During this period she decorated ceramic plates,[192] painted 'woodscapes' of local wildlife on indigenous wood, and wrote and illustrated a book of African stories. Upon the unexpected death of Hornby, Valmai sold Bushpig Fabrics to Gail Honiball-Nockels and retired. She died in Port Elizabeth in early 2012.[193]

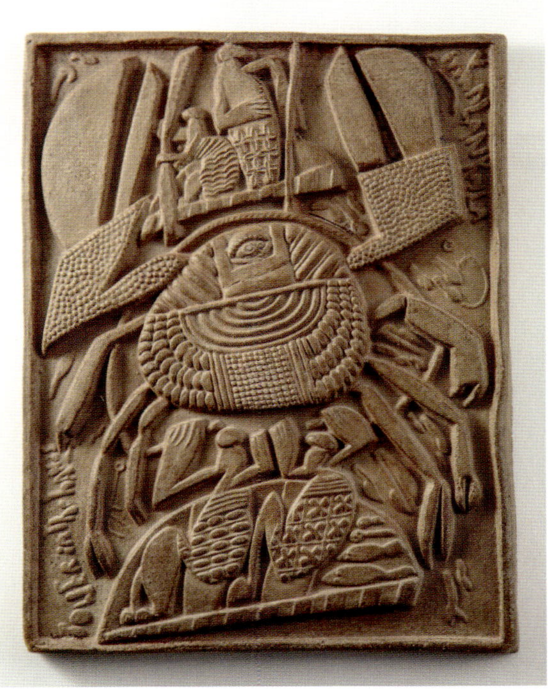

Lucky Bean Farm Pottery | Tile | Zodiac Series – Cancer | 147x1[illegible]7mm | Provenance: Wendy Gers, ex Thomas Vermeulen | Photograph by Damien Artus

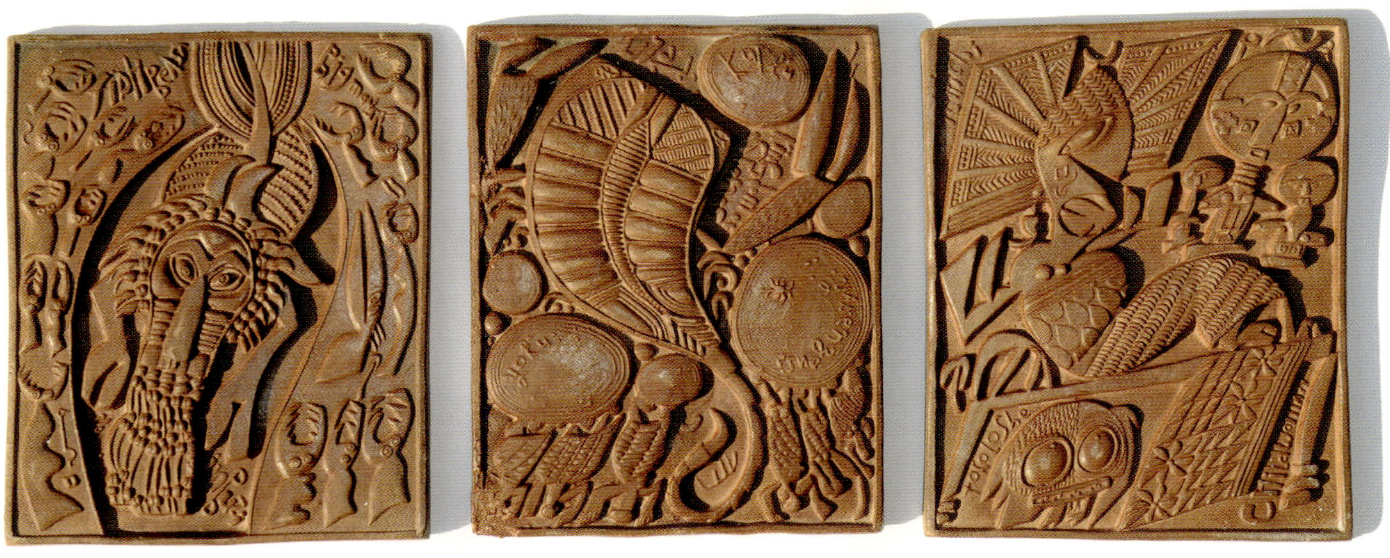

Lucky Bean Farm Pottery | Tiles | Zodiac Series – Leo, Scorpio & Gemini | 115x150mm | Provenance: Thomas Vermeulen | Photograph by Thomas Vermeulen

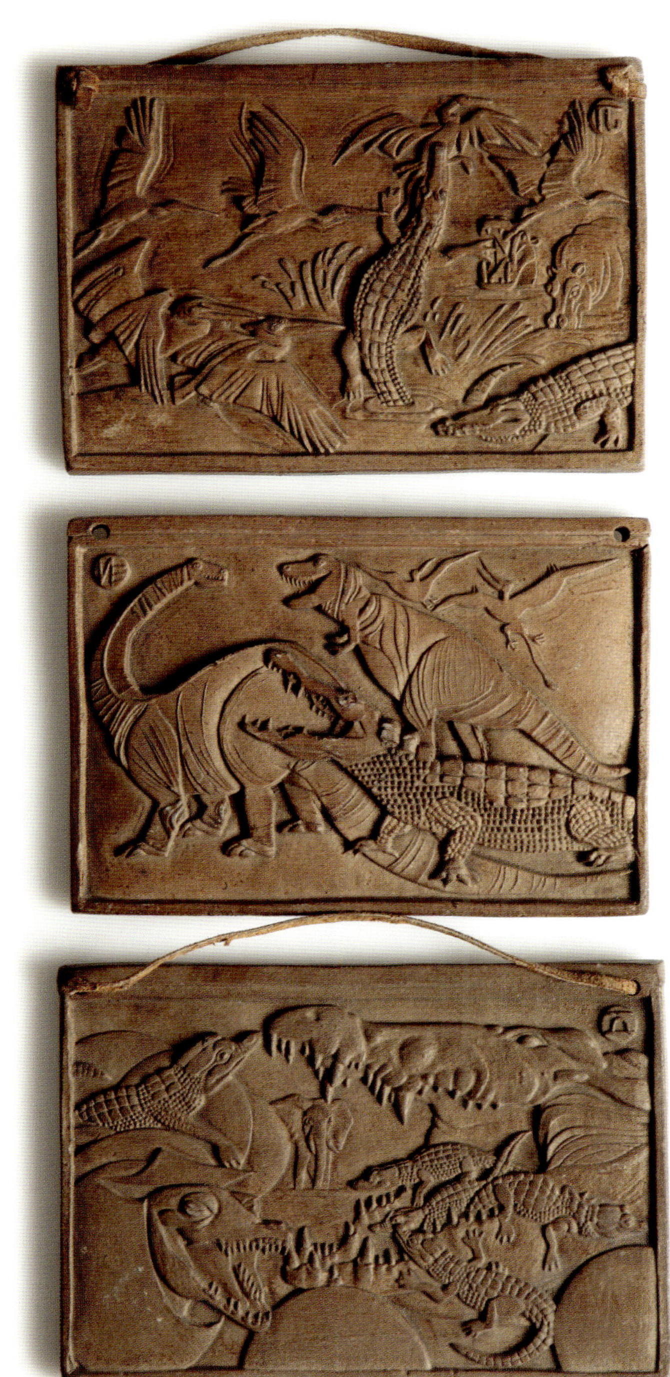

Lucky Bean Farm Pottery | Three tiles from 'Jurassic Park series | 140x100mm each | Provenance: SHC Iziko | From top to bottom SH2011/214, 215 & 216 | Photograph by Carina Beyer

Mantenga Craft Pottery, Swaziland (1976–1989)

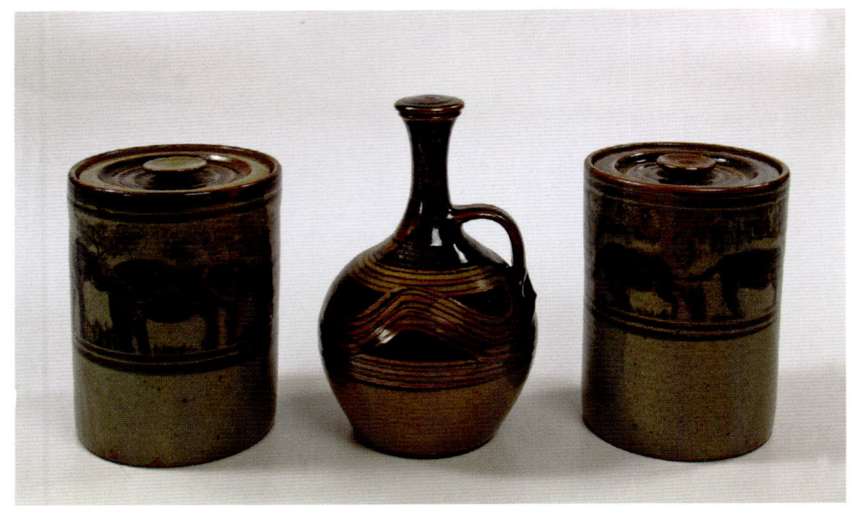

Mantenga Craft Pottery | Two storage jars and a water flask | Storage jars 350x200m; water flask 400x180mm | Provenance: Dr Helen Mentis | Marks: storage jars both signed 'Austin' and stamped above the base; water flask stamped above base and has Mantenga sticker on neck | Photograph by Micha Birch Hannemann

Location

Situated at the entrance to the Mantenga Falls in the Ezulwini Valley, Swaziland.

Founders

The Mantenga Craft Centre was a development project set up by EDESA (Economic Development Bank for Equatorial and Southern Africa).[194]

Managers

1976–1977 Bill van Gilder
1978 Chris Green
1979–1981 Mordechai Brodie
1981–1989 Aaron Msibi

Staff

Bill van Gilder's initial staff came from SEDCO, and key staff included thrower Austin Hleza, Sibongo (aka Sipho) Gumede, Aaron Msibi and Joel Msibi. Other staff included Elliot Dlamini, Sam Gingidza, Elliot Mabaso, Sipho Nzamande and Jobe Mavuso. Unidentified staff included Nelia and Ben.

Wares manufactured

- Mantenga initially produced finely thrown wood-fired earthenware decorated with extensive stamped decoration. Planters of all sizes were the training pieces and soon the range expanded to include water-coolers, bottles, storage jars, sculptures, slab-built bottles, masks and hundreds of beads for use in the macramés that were made at the craft centre.
- As the throwers' ability improved, Van Gilder introduced a range of

tableware including tea sets, casseroles, bowls and platters. These were glazed in a clear transparent glaze. Wares were also dipped into a cream slip that was then combed. Van Gilder introduced various decorative options, including an iron-banded decorative trim, a leaf motif and combed patterns. Geometric friezes were produced using a sponge stamp.

- From June 1977 Mantenga's new standard stoneware dinner services were glazed in a pale grey or rich green celadon. The product range expanded to include other utility wares such as bowls, platters, casseroles, baking dishes, beakers, wine goblets, coffee mugs and pots, tea sets, water jugs and cookie jars. Some of the items decorated by Chris Green feature Oriental-style brushwork, especially a leaf pattern. Green's leaf pattern is discernible as he was left-handed, and the lines flow from left to right, while the leaves by Van Gilder and Brodie were painted from the right.
- Mantenga also produced 'special' pieces, including larger items, decorative bottles, platters, bread crocks and individually decorated pieces by Austin Hleza. Under Brodie 'special' pieces included one-off bowls and large jugs, up to about 30cm high, large vases and other free-standing pieces (quirky, humorous and expressive sculptures). This mixed production of basic dinnerware and individual pieces continued until the late 1980s.
- Glaze colours and shapes changed in the latter years. Brodie experimented with cobalt and other glazes, but abandoned these as he felt they were not very successful. He also introduced ovenproof ware and less formal ware.

Brief history of the pottery

The Mantenga Craft Centre included a pottery, weaving studio, textile design workshop, silversmithing department, screen-printing studio and macramé workshop. It was one of several projects established to develop craftwork and business skills throughout EDESA's operational zone.[195] Swaziland was perceived as an ideal host for the various craft development projects because, according to Green, 'this country was still one where traditions of craftsmanship ran strong and people would proudly use handmade items.'[196] EDESA management employed acclaimed international designers and craftspeople to train local Swazis and establish a top-class craft centre. The emphasis was on quality and commercial success and the managers of the different divisions worked closely together to develop the centre.

The original intention was for the pottery to create distinctive and original wares. Bill van Gilder produced earthenware that broke with the dominant style of English stoneware made so successfully at Kolonyama and numerous other small individual studios. The crisp new style, high-quality and earthy African 'look' of all the Mantenga products was, in conjunction with intense advertising and marketing, the core of EDESA's approach.

From the outset, individually decorated pieces made by Austin Hleza, such as large bread crocks, large bottles and wide platters, were very popular. Under Van Gilder, Hleza transferred some of his linocut motifs to sgraffito decoration.

The reduction glazes brought a rich and dynamic feel to them. Hleza was a key thrower of the standard production ware, and could thus only devote a limited part of his time to creating original wares. He produced his 'specials' on Saturdays, when there were many visitors to the studio.

In June 1977, after 18 months, EDESA management decided to change their production range from earthenware to stoneware. Production was overhauled, and Van Gilder developed a range of products that featured new shapes and glazes. Mantenga entered into a highly competitive southern African stoneware pottery market. The change in production necessitated a new clay body and kiln for the higher temperatures of stoneware. At the same time as the move to stoneware, Van Gilder's contract expired and he indicated his desire to return to the United States. Chris Green, who had worked under Van Gilder at Kolonyama, was appointed. The new production was already underway when Green arrived at Mantenga.

Green's tenure began with a host of complex technical and managerial challenges. Staff went on strike over previously promised bonuses and there was general confusion about the shift to stoneware. Furthermore, their supplier altered the stoneware's composition without informing customers, resulting in massive losses from cracked ware, which set production back three months. Green resolved these problems and during the winter of 1978 organised a set of reciprocal visits for Kolonyama and Mantenga staff.[197]

The Mantenga Craft Centre grew substantially and Johannes Gaston, the Mantenga silversmith, produced a catalogue of standard production ware in early 1978.[198] Despite requests to prolong his tenure, Green departed in December 1978 when his contract expired.[199] Mantenga Pottery's new manager, Mordechai Brodie, reorganised marketing and sales, moving wares from art and craft galleries to venues that accommodated broader audiences. Brodie undertook numerous sales trips by road to 'touristy' towns in South Africa. This resulted in a new way of selling Mantenga ware.

Brodie was not an experienced production potter, nor was he too familiar with reduction firing, and over time the quality of the wares diminished.[200] Brodie encouraged Austin Hleza to produce individual pieces independently, and submitted some of these, including a sculpture of a seated man with a bowl and elaborately decorated wine carafes and beer-pots, to an APSA exhibition. Mantenga twice exhibited wares at the annual APSA exhibition and also had exhibitions in KwaZulu-Natal and Cape Town.

Brodie's activity in the studio diminished over time and he reflected later that his aims were to 'develop people' and sales networks, not to 'be a potter' per se.[201] In 1982 he was transferred from the pottery and became sales and marketing manager for the centre, leaving the pottery in the hands of Aaron Msibi. That same year Brodie started the first of his African Magic chain of shops in South Africa, which sold a range of crafts from the region, including Mantenga.

The mid- and late 1980s saw a shift in fashion from Anglo-Oriental pottery to bright polychromatic earthenware. This, together with management

TOP: Mantenga Craft Pottery | Maker's mark | Sticker | Micha Birch Hannemann

MIDDLE: Mantenga Craft Pottery | Maker's mark | Stamp | Micha Birch Hannemann

BOTTOM: Mantenga Craft Pottery | Maker's mark | Stamp and incised signature, 'Austin' | Micha Birch Hannemann

problems, resulted in the ultimate demise of Mantenga Pottery in the late 1980s. While the Mantenga Craft Centre continues to sell crafts from Swaziland and other parts of Africa, little remains of the ambitious, perhaps utopian, dream of the 1970s.

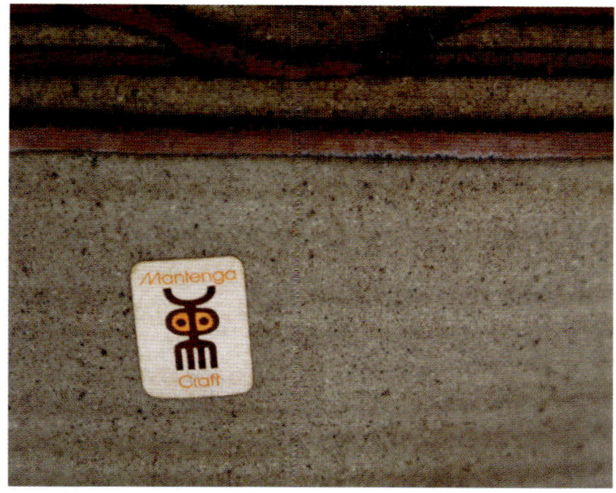

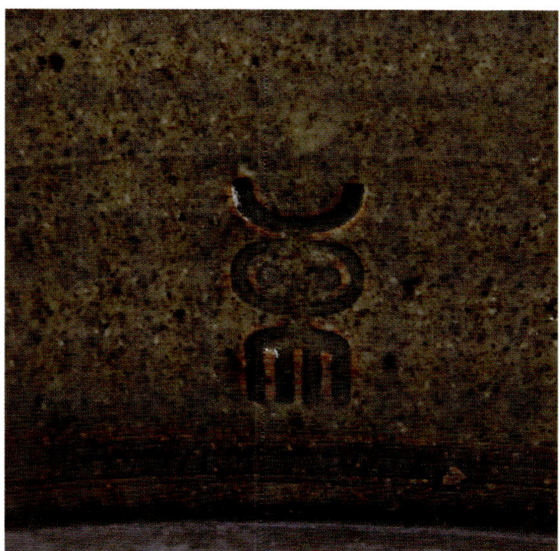

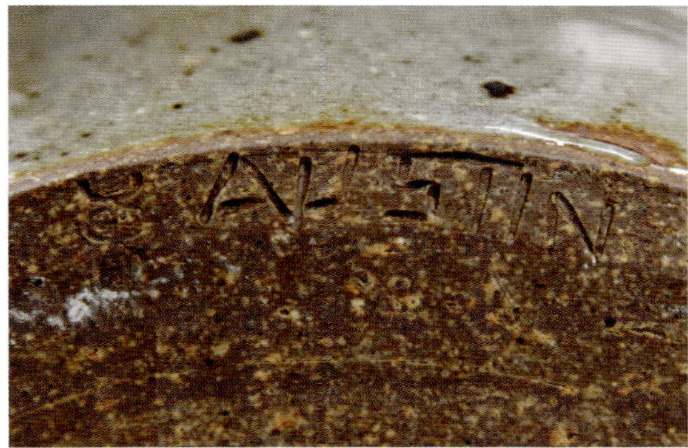

Marks

- Mantenga's seemingly 'African' mark is derived from the signet ring of Peter Hayes. He designed the logo which appears stamped on the base of pots as well as on stickers. Other departments also used the logo and on labels and printed tickets.
- The stamp was not always in use. Some wares were merely signed by potters, most notably Austin Hleza, who signed his first name or just his last name.

Select exhibitions

1978	Milner Park, Johannesburg (represented Mantenga Handicraft Centre).
1983	Indingilizi Gallery, Mbabane, Swaziland (three-person exhibition with Kirk Creed and Bill Gossman).
1984	UN, Pietermaritzburg (Corobrik Collection of Ceramics); Total Gallery Johannesburg (Artists in Swaziland).
1985	Johannesburg College of Education (solo); Cape Town Triennial; FUBA (solo). Africana Museum in Progress, Johannesburg (Tributaries).
1985–1986	NSA, Durban. Irma Stern Museum, Cape Town; Market Gallery (Out of Africa).
1986	Standard Bank National Arts Festival, Grahamstown; WITS (Standard Bank Foundation Collection of African Art); Market Gallery (two-person exhibition with Nelson Mukhuba); Africana Museum in Progress, Johannesburg (Jubilee Exhibition of the Institute for the Study of Man in Africa).
1987	Karen McKerron Gallery, Sandton; Swaziland Theatre Club; Standard Bank National Arts Festival, Grahamstown, (VhaVenda Sculpture); JAG (Vita Art Now).
1988	UNISA (Clay+). Craft Gallery Johannesburg (solo); Potchefstroom Museum (two-person exhibition with Barry Douglas); Beuster Skolimowski Gallery, Pretoria (two-person exhibition with Barry Douglas); Gallery 5, Kimberley (two-person exhibition with Barry Douglas); Chicago Art Caravan, Chicago, (SAFTO exhibit); Export Mart, World Trade Centre, Taipei; Klerksdorp Museum (group); SAAA, Pretoria (VhaVenda/Shangaan Wood Sculpture); JAG (Vita Art Now); SANG (Wood).

Collections

Irma Stern Museum, Cape Town; SANG (several pieces); University of Cape Town African Studies Department; UNISA, Pretoria; Corobrik Permanent Collection, PAM; Johannesburg Art Gallery and the University of the Witwatersrand, Johannesburg.

Biographies

BRODIE, Mordechai (b.1952)

Born in Port Elizabeth, Brodie graduated from the University of the Witwatersrand in 1973 with a BA in philosophy. During his studies he made his first contact with sangomas. From 1974 to 1977 he undertook theological studies in a rabbinic college in Israel.

Brodie was apprenticed by Sammy Liebermann from 1977 to 1978. He spent most of his first few months learning to throw pots. Then he learnt to develop glazes, studied ceramic chemistry, and became peripherally involved in production management. He was also given various 'office' tasks such as production flow analyses and, in the Liebermann tradition, occasionally washed Sammy's car and did other odd jobs.

From late 1978 until late 1981 Brodie was employed as the manager of the Mantenga Craft Centre in Swaziland. His initial job and primary responsibility was to develop and run the pottery, oversee pottery production and manage around 15 staff. When he arrived the pottery had numerous problems, including an unsuitable clay body, poor sales and unmotivated potters. As soon as the pottery was 'back on track', Brodie gradually withdrew from everyday production and became involved in product development and marketing, while still overseeing the technical side. He also became involved in design and marketing of all the handicrafts from Mantenga, and in the early 1980s its wares were supplied throughout South Africa via craft and gift shops. Brodie left Mantenga in 1984 to work full-time for his African Magic project in South Africa, which he had begun in 1982.

Brodie's link with southern African ceramics continued on a smaller scale through the African Magic shops he established in Yeoville, Johannesburg, and in Plettenberg Bay in the Cape. These outlets sold traditional and contemporary southern African art and craft to museums and other collectors. On seeing a few 'traditional' pots from isolated potters in Venda and Gazankulu painted with enamel paints, he encouraged the (mostly) women to experiment and add more painted pots to their range. Brodie sometimes took tins of paint to the more remote regions where these were difficult and expensive to obtain. He also took photographs and books showing various contemporary and traditional potters at work. In some ways, this input influenced and encouraged dialogue and creativity among the women.

Brodie believed that this encouraged the continuation of traditional crafts and the dignity of both the practitioners and the cultures within which their crafts were practised. After closing African Magic in 1994, Brodie began his

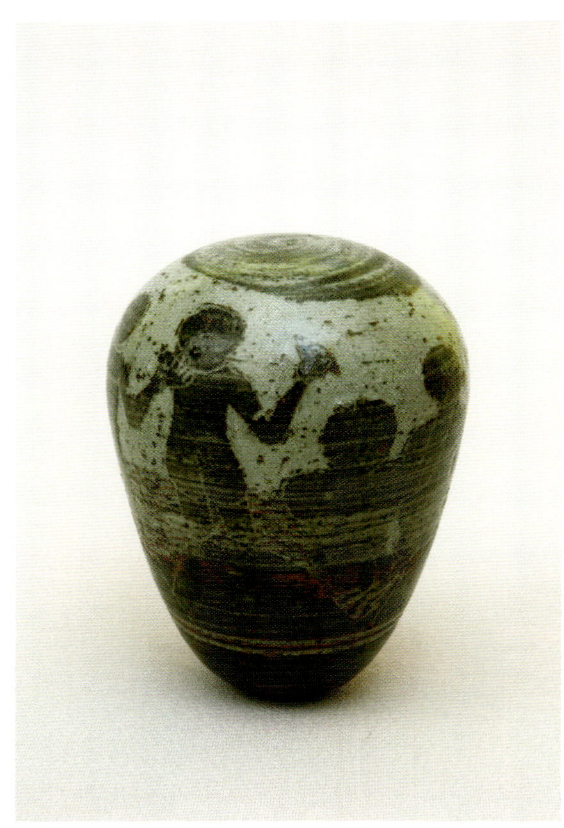

Mantenga Craft Pottery | Egg form decorated with sgraffito images of people viewed from behind, standing in water amid large boulder, waving and looking into the distance | 162x120x36mm | Provenance: Jan Middeljans | Marks: signed 'Austin' | Photograph by Natalie Field

current work as a teacher and archetypal psychotherapist, and practices in Cape Town and Knysna.

DLAMINI, Elliot
Elliot Dlamini was responsible for firing the kiln at Mantenga.

GINGIDZA, Sam
Gingidza helped with glazing and also modelled small animals.

GREEN, Christopher (aka Chris) (b.1953)
Born in Johannesburg, Green studied at the University of the Witwatersrand from 1972 to 1975. During his studies Green had informal lessons with Tim Morris, John Edwards (Lucky Bean Farm) and Digby Hoets. After his BA degree, Green worked at Kolonyama from January to March 1976. He then joined the Tim Morris studio pottery. Esias Bosch invited Green to replace Bill van Gilder, who was leaving Mantenga and Green went to Swaziland at the end of 1977 and spent three weeks training with Van Gilder. From 1978 to 1979 Green managed Mantenga Pottery with his wife, Julie.

In 1979 Green set up his own workshop in Johannesburg. Between 1996 and 1997 he worked for David Schlapobersky making washbasins. He played an active part in APSA and was on the APSA Transvaal committee, serving as a regional judge and guest national selector. He was one of the inspirations behind the popular APSA 'Clay Days', hosted many workshops around the country and taught as a guest lecturer at the Wits Technikon. Green left the pottery industry in the late 1990s and currently works as a management consultant and tour guide.

GUMEDE, iSibongo (aka Sipho)
Gumede was a thrower who originally trained at the Pottery Development Centre, Mbabane. He worked as a potter and as foreman in the early years of the pottery's existence.

HLEZA, Austin (1949–1998)
Austin Hleza was born in Mpuluzi, Swaziland. As a child, Hleza was introduced to local pottery by his grandmother and made his own toys from clay. Hleza completed his junior certificate at Mater Dolorosa in Swaziland and then trained for two years at the SEDCO Pottery Development Centre, Mbabane. During this time he attended art classes in the evening, studying drawing and painting.

From 1973 to 1975 Hleza worked as a clerk at the post office and then briefly on a gold mine in Kinross in the Eastern Transvaal. In 1976 he returned to Swaziland and worked as a production potter and assistant manager in the ceramics department at Mantenga. During this period Hleza was featured in a photo essay that demonstrated the making of a teapot (*Sgraffiti* 15, 1977). Hleza also worked part-time as a sculptor for Faragher's Pottery, where he was remembered as being a capable thrower. According to Brodie:

> Around that time he [Hleza] made the first of his later-signature 'funny vehicles' and I recall showing one of those ... at some show. It was on the basis of this work that I urged him to produce individual pieces whenever the demands in the studio allowed. Afterwards, I encouraged him to set up his own studio.[202]

In 1982 Hleza left Mantenga and set up his own ceramic sculpture workshop in the back of a craft shop run by Jenny Thorn in the Malkerns area, Swaziland. He became renowned for his articulated clay vehicles (motor bikes, cars, tractors and buses) populated by expressive figurines. These original vehicles won him an important APSA prize. According to Cruise, the vehicles were his personal protest at the increase in traffic in Swaziland (Cruise 1991:112) but Mordechai Brodie disagrees:

> My personal view of the story about Austin's ceramics being a 'social protest against the increase of traffic in Swaziland' or some other ironic commentary on life, is that this is a story that was invented after his pieces caught the popular imagination. In the many times we spoke about creating, producing, exhibiting and selling art, such conversations never came up. In those days, we were concerned with technical production and more especially with how to sell more to earn more money to pay the rent. But I don't wish to stand against the construction of myth, urban or otherwise. I have experienced this 'fictionalising' of art, helping to develop a 'story' to better promote the artist, in every other field of craft and art and I have no problem with that.[203]

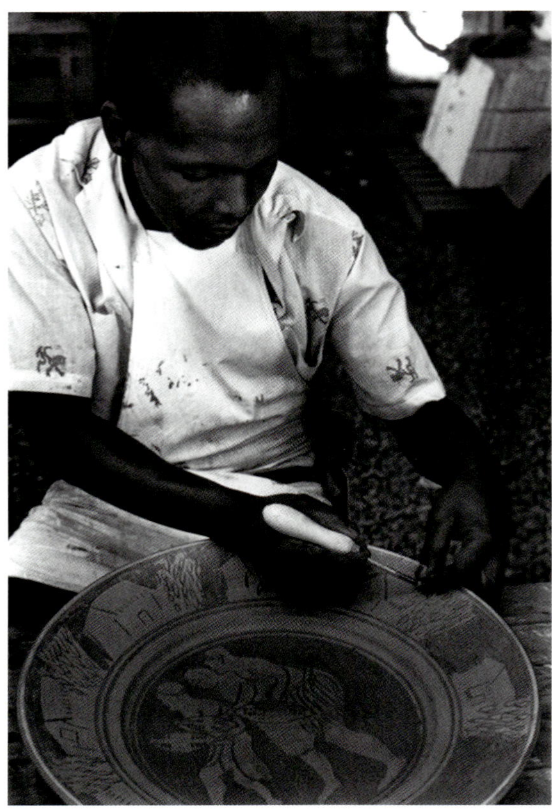

Mantenga Craft Pottery | Austin Hleza | c.1978 | Photograph and scan by Johannes Gaston

Hleza later moved his studio nearer to Mantenga and sold his ceramics and linocuts from African Magic, operated by former Mantenga manager, Brodie. In 1987 Hleza returned to SEDCO and shortly thereafter obtained a post as a lecturer at the National Handicraft Centre (informally known as the Chinese Handicraft Centre). Hleza's skill was recognised internationally and he conducted a workshop at the Durbanville Cultural Centre in 1987. During 1988 he worked periodically at Barry Douglas's pottery studio in Johannesburg and befriended various artists working at the Katlehong Art Centre, including Bhekisani Manyoni.[204] Hleza participated in a Thupelo International Artists' Workshop in 1989. In the early 1990s Hleza set up a workshop and gallery on the main road from Manzini to Mbabane in Swaziland.

A traditionalist at heart, Hleza explored the tension between 'traditional' rural and modern urban Swazi society with a sense of humour. His talent was recognised by prominent art critics in South Africa, who invited him to participate in various prestigious exhibitions and festivals. A posthumous exhibition, 'A Tribute to Swazi Artist, Austin Hleza', was held by the Alliance Française in Mbabane, Swaziland in 2005. This toured South Africa (Johannesburg, Durban and Cape Town) and Maputo, Mozambique in 2006.

MABASO, Elliot
Mabaso was charged with firing the kiln, as well as preparing the fuel at Mantenga.

MSIBI, Aaron
Aaron Msibi was employed from the outset of the pottery and was soon promoted to the post of foreman. He was very ambitious and when Brodie arrived Msibi was a 'nominal foreman-manager'. Upon Brodie's departure, Msibi managed the pottery from 1981 to 1989. Brodie insists that Msibi was an adequate manager and a capable but unexceptional potter. However, he was incapable of dealing with technical problems, product design or marketing, as he had no training or skill in these matters. Msibi later worked as a production potter for Bundu Potteries in Middelburg, South Africa, until about 2004.

MSIBI, Joel
Msibi was initially trained as a potter at the SEDCO Pottery Development Centre. He was recruited to work at Mantenga by Bill van Gilder.

NZAMANDE, Sipho
A thrower under Van Gilder, he was featured in *Sgraffiti* magazine (no 15, 1977) demonstrating how to throw goblets.

VAN GILDER, Bill (b.1951)
Born in Ithaca, New York, Van Gilder worked as an apprentice at various potteries, including the Byron Temple Pottery, New Jersey (1967–1969); the Terrybaun Pottery, Ireland (1970); the Coxwold Pottery, UK (1971); and the Quay Pottery (Colin Pearson), UK (1972–1973). He graduated as a studio potter from the Harrow School of Art, London in 1973, where he met Toff Milway. Van Gilder managed Kolonyama from 1973 to 1976. He subsequently established Mantenga Pottery in Swaziland for EDESA.

Upon his departure from Swaziland, Van Gilder established the Van Gilder Pottery in Pensylvania (1978–1986). He then relocated to Maryland where he has run the Van Gilder Pottery and Craft Gallery since 1986.

Van Gilder has always believed in sharing his knowledge, and while in Lesotho, he developed a reputation for hosting outstanding workshops. He continues to deliver workshops and seminars throughout the USA and around the world and was the creator and host of the 'DIY Pottery' television series. Since 2001, he has written a 'teaching techniques' column in *Clay Times*. In 2000 he established the Frederick Pottery School in Maryland, which he presently directs. From 1999 to 2006 Van Gilder was a faculty member at the Art League School, Virginia. He also owns and operates 'Van Gilder ClayTools'.

Van Gilder has written numerous articles and co-authored the monograph *Wheel-Thrown Pottery: An Illustrated Guide of Basic Techniques*, 2006. His work is exhibited and held in collections worldwide. It has been featured in ceramic periodicals including *Clay Times, Ceramics Monthly, Ceramic Review* (UK), *Ceramic Arts* (China), *Sgraffito* (South Africa), and in books, including *500 Teapots and High Fire Glazes* (Lark Books), *Salt Glazing* (A&C Black, London) and *The Art of American Ceramics* (Krause Books), among others.[205] He has participated in many exhibitions, including Wood Fired, NCECA, Louisville, KY 2007; The English Connection, Mary Baldwin College, VA, 2006; Alabama Clay Conference Invitational, AL 2004; and Six Maryland Potters, MD. Travelling exhibition, 1999.

Unidentified staff

[Surname unknown], Ben

Ben mixed clay in a bakers' dough mixer during Green's tenure.

[Surname unknown], Nelia

Nelia prepared clay for the throwers in balls of suitable sizes during Green's tenure.

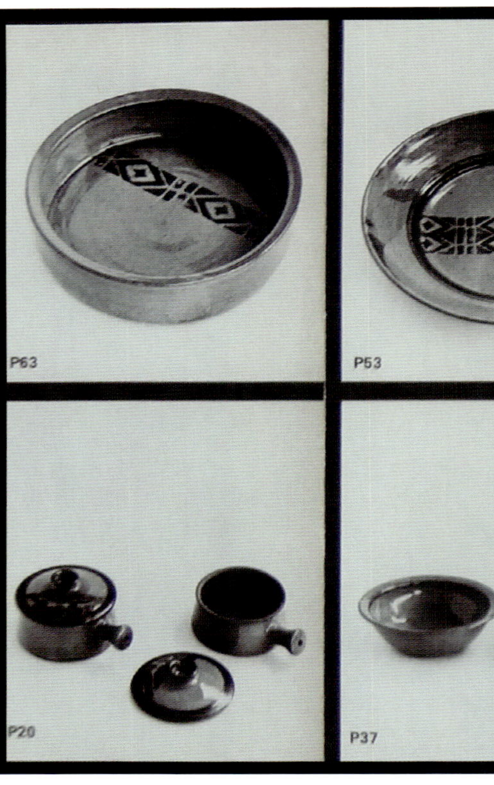

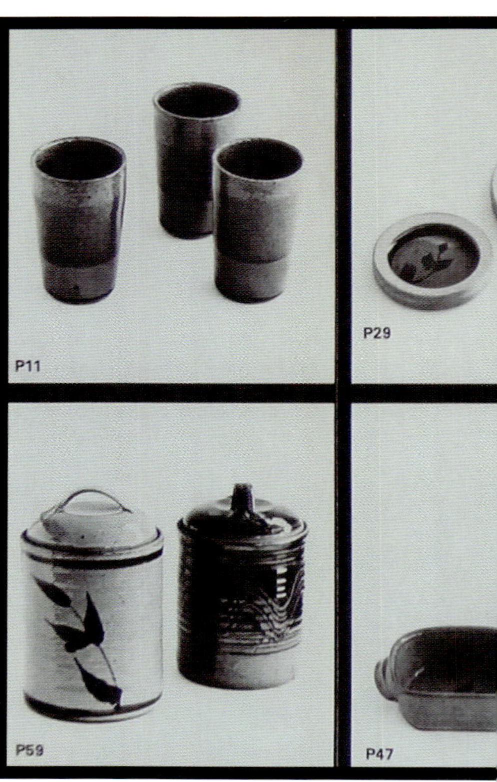

Mantenga Craft Pottery | Catalogue | Photograph and scan by Johannes Gaston

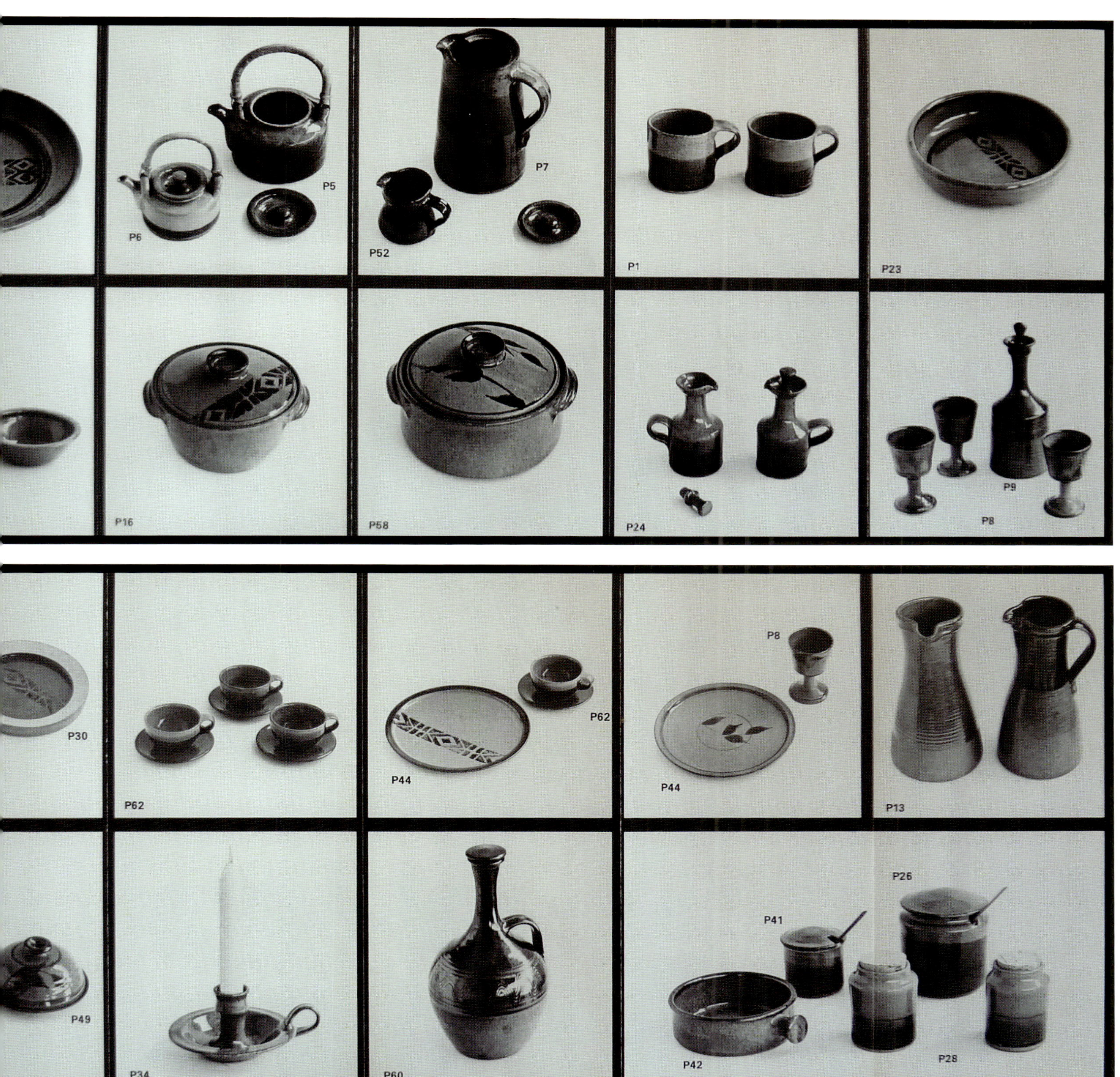
P5
P6
P7
P52
P1
P23
P16
P58
P24
P9
P8
P30
P62
P62
P44
P8
P44
P13
P49
P34
P60
P26
P41
P42
P28

Marrakesh Ware (1956–1961)

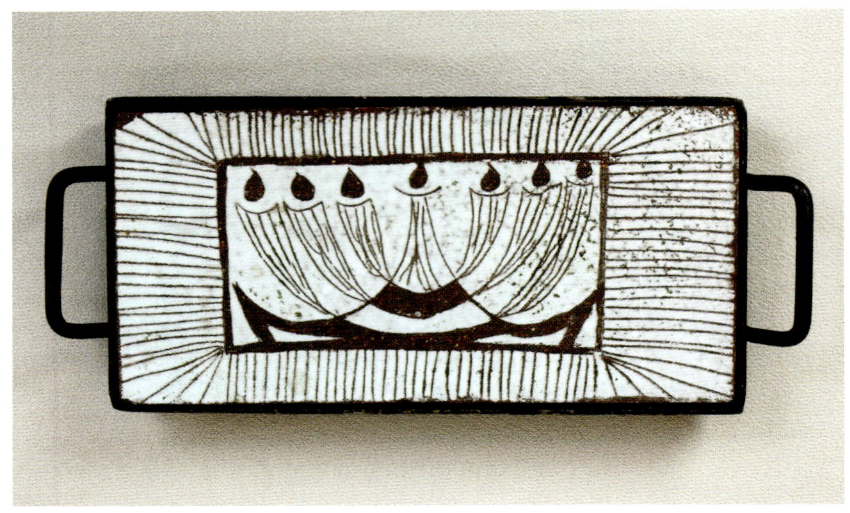

Marrakesh Ware | Menorah tile panel in metal stand | 230x115x15mm | Provenance: Adriaan Turgel | Marks: unmarked | Photograph by Natalie Field

Location

Marrakesh ware was established in the back garden of Donald and Phyllis Turgel's home in Kew, Johannesburg.

Name

According to Phyllis Turgel, the word Marrakesh means 'red clay' in Arabic. Marrakesh Wares' red earthenware recalled the town of Marrakesh's ancient walls of terracotta clay.[206]

Founders

Donald Turgel (1921–1999), his wife Phyllis (aka Menucha) Turgel (née Liebermann) (b. ca.1915–2005) and Denis Morgan Blewett (1931–2011).

Staff

The studio employed two or three assistants, including Dinah Leganyane, who was also a domestic worker for the Turgels.

Wares manufactured

A wide variety of glazed and unglazed wares were produced: glazed platters and chargers, unglazed sculptural planters, decorated quarry tiles, candle holders, *kalabashes*, which were large rounded earthy vases, and small dishes (known humorously as hemlock dishes).

Production methods

The pottery produced hand-built coiled or pinched vessels, press-moulded platters and thown articles.

Brief history of the pottery

Marrakesh Ware was founded by three friends, who had met in Casablanca and subsequently travelled together and lived in Morocco and other North African countries. They learnt pottery from a local teacher in Fez, and studied Berber and Bedouin pottery. The trio shared all aspects of production. Donald, an architect by profession, made moulds and handmade items. He had a disabled hand, which enabled him to make delicate small pots with unique forms. Phyllis threw items on the wheel and decorated and glazed wares. Denis Blewett assisted with various aspects of production and the packing of the kilns.

Inspired by Bedouin and other North African elements, the bulk of their wares appear to have been decorated bowls and platters with zigzags and other angular or organic linear patterns predominating. Other platters were decorated with stylised images of cockerels, peacocks, bulls, fish and leaves. Quarry tiles were decorated individually or incorporated into tile panels with white glaze and sgraffito or resist decoration. These were often incorporated into tables, walls (a shop sign) or buildings (St Michael All Angels Church in Elgin features a large tiled cornerstone).

The studio was awarded a gold medal at the 1957 Rand Easter Show. It caused a sensation as it was displayed in a Bedouin tent outside the main exhibition halls. On weekends the Turgels sold pottery from their Bedouin tent, installed on Rivonia Road, Johannesburg. In an interview with the author, Menucha insisted that the wares were very amateur and crude, but when marketed as *artistic* were successful. While this may be true, they were charmingly whimsical and display a unique creative energy, sensitivity and a passion for the essential tactile nature of the medium.

Marks

Some wares had a mark that resembled the hand of Fatima.

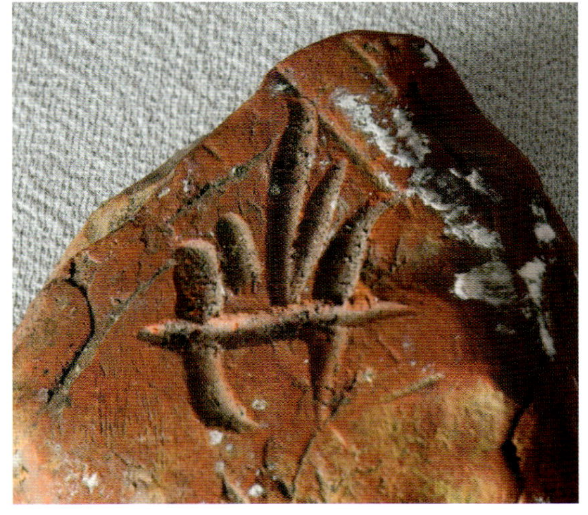

Marrakesh Ware | Maker's mark | Photograph by Natalie Field

Biographies

BLEWETT, Denis Morgan (1931–2011)

Blewett was born in Timmins, Canada. After a childhood and adolescence spent in Canada, Cornwall, Zambia and South Africa, Blewett returned to the UK in 1952 and worked briefly in Yorkshire before hitchhiking through the UK, France, Spain, Algeria and Morocco. Here he met Donald and Menucha Turgel in Casablanca and learnt pottery. A vintage car enthusiast, Blewett and the Turgels toured extensively, camping in the desert.

Blewett subsequently worked briefly on a ship to Walvis Bay en route back to Zambia to finish an apprenticeship there. A year later, at about the age of 23, he reunited with the Turgels in Johannesburg and got involved with Marrakesh Ware. Blewett left South Africa again in 1957 and hiked to Dar es Salaam, Tanzania. He then returned to the UK, where he met and married Eileen Mallory in 1960. Between 1969 and 1979 Blewett worked for Consolidated Pneumatic in Zambia, Kenya, the UK, South Africa and Canada, before settling in South Africa in 1980 where he was employed by CAMEC. During this period he carved wooden masks, ornaments and walking sticks.

Blewett retired to Port Shepstone in 1986 and started making pottery again. His greatest joy was that all the clay and ingredients, including glazes were from his immediate environment, the only 'foreign' elements were the cones he used in the kiln! He relocated to Johannesburg in 2003 and stopped making pottery. After battling cancer, Blewett passed away in Johannesburg in 2011.[208]

TURGEL, Donald (1921–1999)

Turgel was born in London and trained as an architect. He co-founded Marrakesh Ware with his wife Menucha and Denis Blewett. In 1959 Donald ceased to make pottery when he returned to architecture and established a highly successful practice, designing private homes and churches of various denominations.

TURGEL, Phyllis (aka Menucha) (née Liebermann) (b. ca.1915–2005)

Phyllis studied Art at the Johannesburg Art School. Her subjects included wood-carving and pottery, which was taught by an English potter, Grace Brown. However, her earliest contact with clay stemmed from her youth in Zebediela near Potgietersrus, where her father Lieber Liebermann mined kaolin.

Turgel was invited by her brother Sammy Liebermann to work in his new pottery in the early 1950s, but the environment did not fit her mode of expression and she and her husband Donald set up their own operation in the back of their home. In 1959 Donald returned to architecture. Phyllis continued at the studio briefly, before closing the pottery as Donald needed the space for his practice. Simultaneously they were informed that municipal zoning did not allow them to fire a kiln in their residential area. She is remembered for her humour, when asked by a friend what she did about warping, she is reputed to have replied, 'Warping ... what [would] I do without it!'[207]

In the 1960s Turgel starting designing and making clothing and accessories, and called this enterprise Marrakesh Studio. Lisa Liebermann recalls her designer clothes: 'She clothed all her children in the most enviable styles. She combined African and Jewish with a touch of Victorian. She would wear long beaded skirts and aprons and a turban on her head' (2005:chapter 6). In the 1970s Turgel travelled to Israel, connected with an orthodox Jewish group in Jerusalem, and changed her name to Menucha. Turgel had seven children: Mya, Ixe, Adriaan, Grecka, Bihla, Zara and Camina. Many of her descendents continue to have connections with the pottery industry. Adriaan manages Liebermann Pottery, Grecka married the potter Neville Burde and Bihla works part-time for Liebermann Pottery.

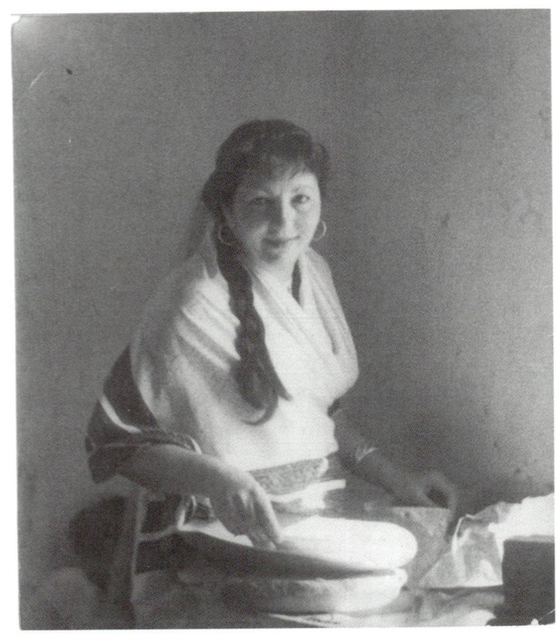

Marrakesh Ware | Phyllis Turgel | Provenance: Adriaan Turgel | Scan by Adriaan Turgel

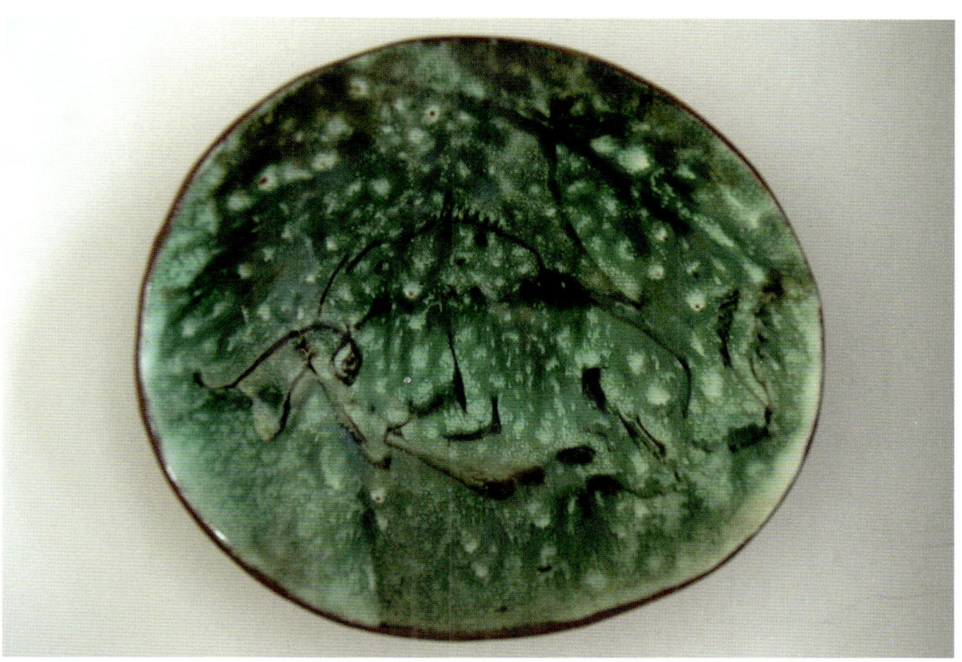

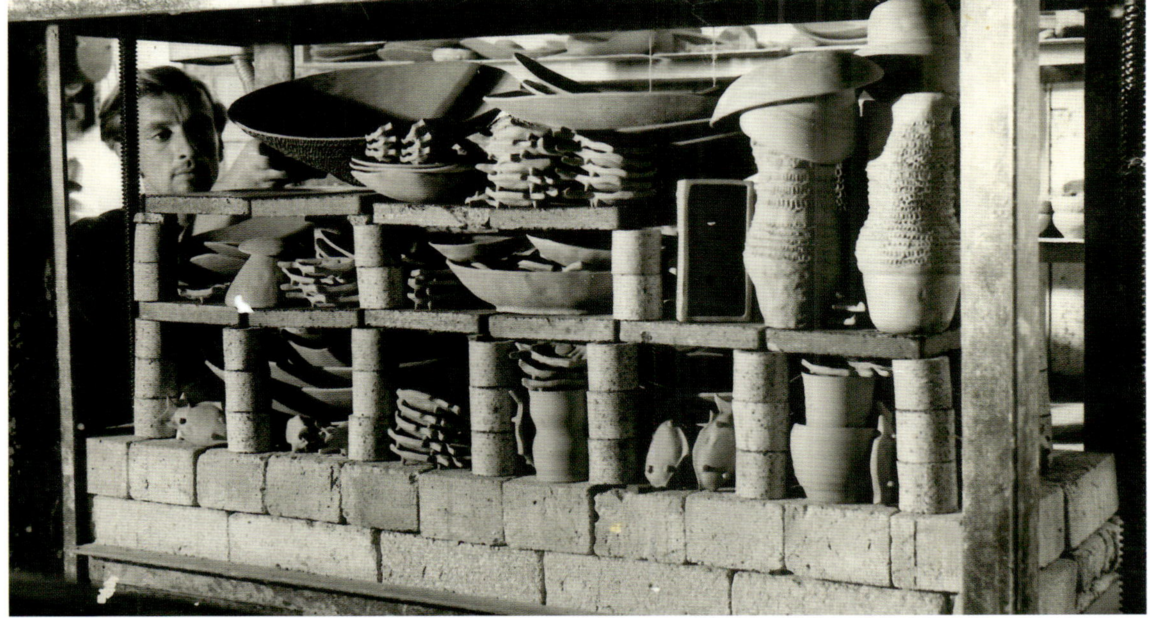

TOP: Marrakesh Ware | Charger depicting a stylised bull | 145x150mm | Provenance: Eileen Blewett | Marks: unmarked | Photograph by Denis Blewett

BOTTOM: Marrakesh Ware | Denis Morgan Blewett | Provenance: Adriaan Turgel, ex Phyllis Turgel | Scan by Adriaan Turgel

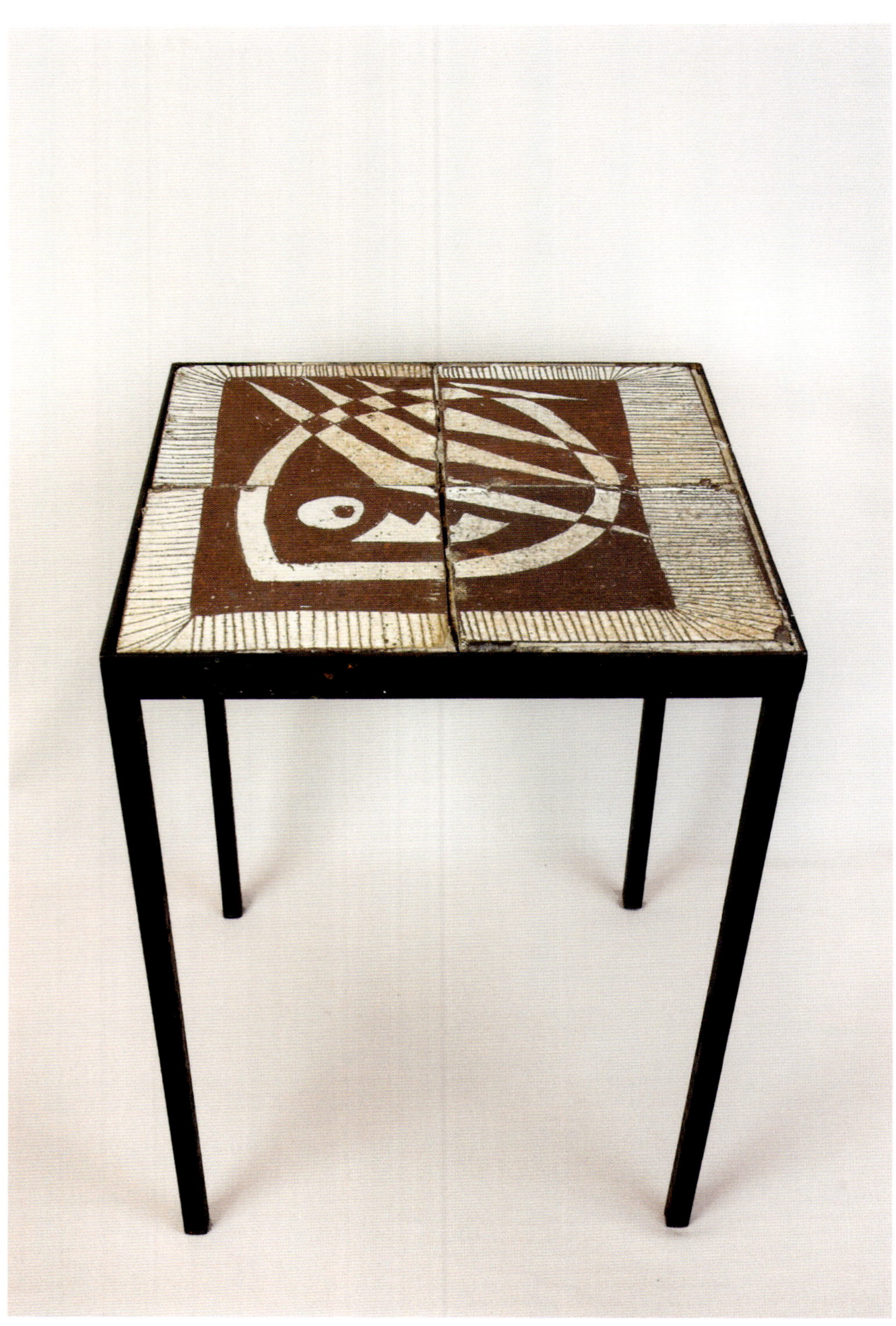

Marrakesh Ware | Table with fish | 360x360x460mm | Provenance: Adriaan Turgel | Marks: unmarked | Photograph by Natalie Field

Milton Pottery Company/Pretoria Potteries (1915–1929)

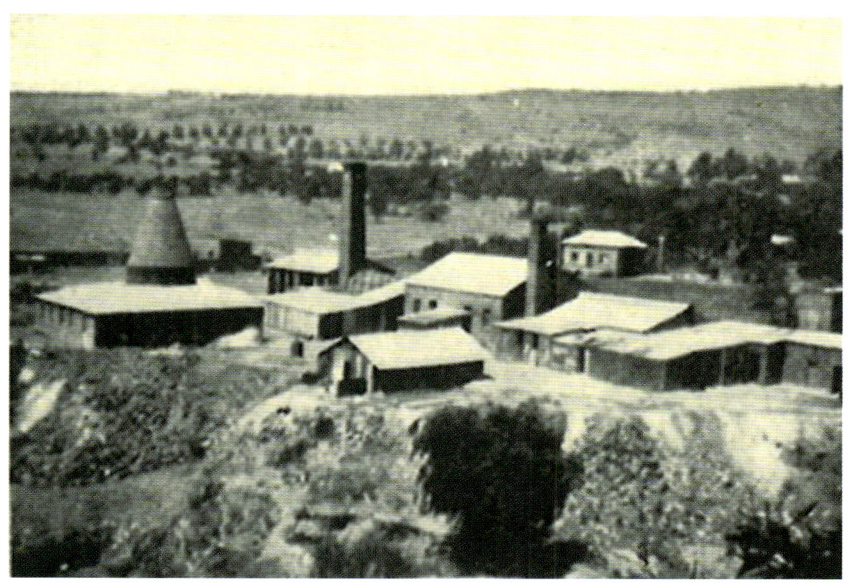

The Milton Pottery Company was established in 1915 in Pretoria and, for some years manufactured Rockingham and Samian teapots based on models from Trent Pottery, England. By 1926 the pottery had changed its name to Pretoria Potteries.[209] In 1929 Albert Walker of Globe Potteries acquired the pottery. It was subsequently managed by his sons Joseph and Albert Walker.

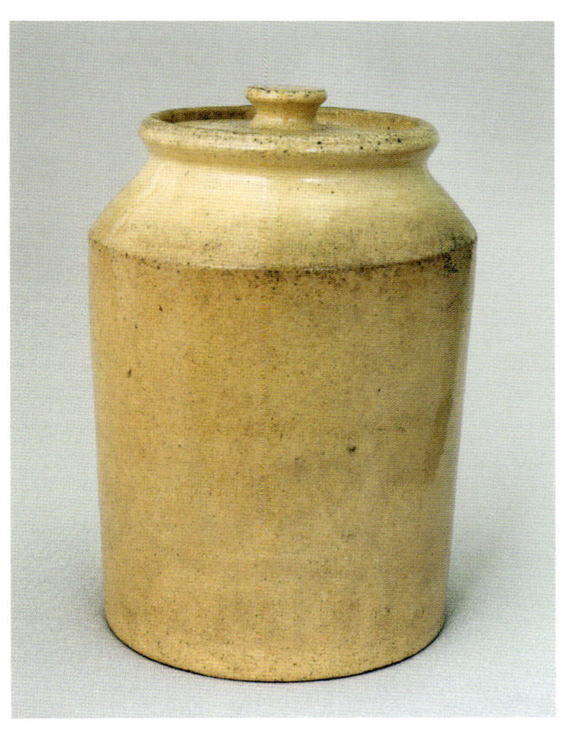

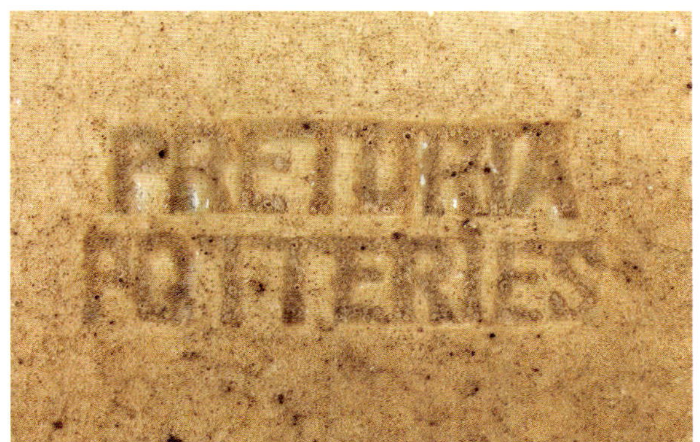

TOP: Milton Pottery Company, Pretoria | Provenance: Macmillan, A. c.1935. Environs of the Golden City and Pretoria. *Cape Times*: Cape Town. p. 387 | Scan by William Martinson

ABOVE: Pretoria Potteries | Maker's mark | Stamp | Photograph by Natalie Field

LEFT: Pretoria Potteries | Large lidded jar | 280x135x167mm | Provenance: De Kamper and Welman Collection | Marks: impressed stamp | Photograph by Natalie Field

Rand Ceramics Industries (ca.1920s–1955)

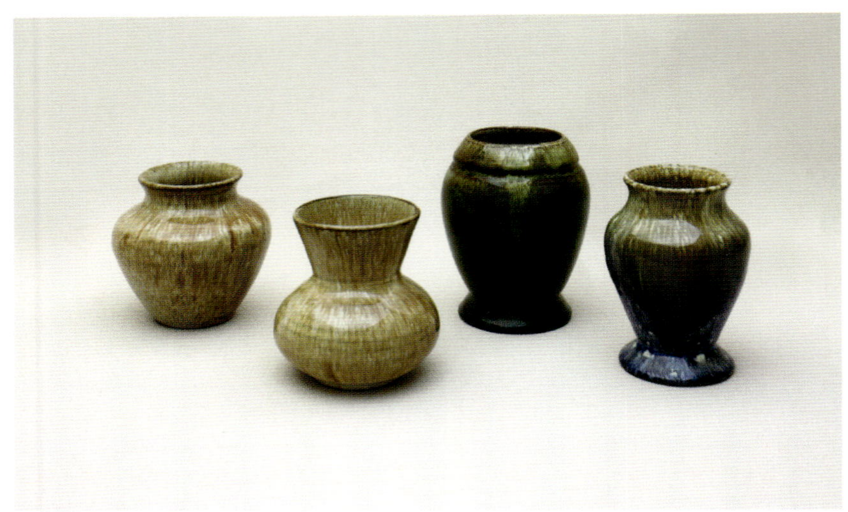

Rand Ceramics | Group of small vases | Small vases 100mm; tall vase 120mm | Providence: Douglas van der Horst | Marks: base glazed with transparent glaze; from left: impressed numbers, visible under the glaze on the bases, 3428, 3426, 3619, 3445 | Photograph by Natalie Field

Location

Johannesburg

Founder

H B Hammerschlag

Wares manufactured

The company manufactured a wide variety of vases and bowls, and tall vessels to be used as planters or umbrella holders. Wares were expertly glazed with two or more glazes. Some of its products resemble items made by Globe and Linnware in terms of their 'classical' forms, but the glazes, for the most part are richer and more transluscent.

Production methods

The bulk of the wares appear to have been wheel-thrown.

Brief history of the pottery

There is very little archival information about this pioneer pottery, yet wares yield some information. Many articles reveal an evidence of excessive glaze viscosity and glaze speckling,[210] which suggest that wares were produced in a coal-burning, down-draught kiln of a brick factory. These outdoor kilns were very susceptible to the elements, resulting in a lack of control during the glaze firing process.

Marks

Wares are marked with a number that is stamped or engraved under the glaze on their bases. Some items bear an oval black-and-silver 'Rand Ceramics' factory sticker incorporating the image of a teapot.

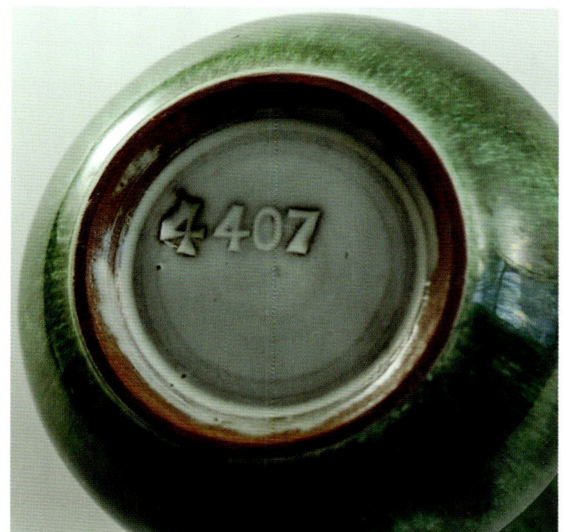

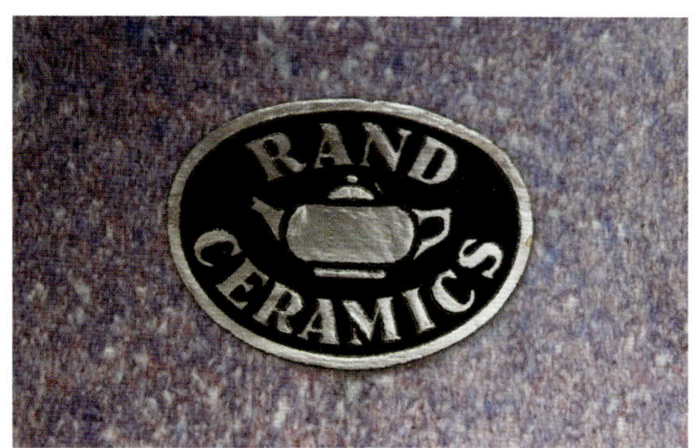

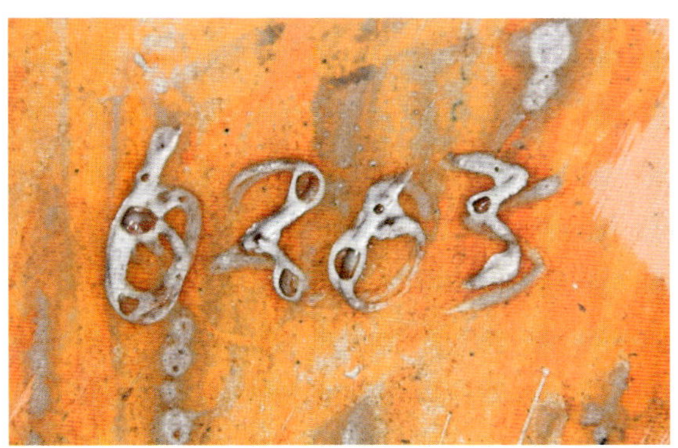

TOP: Rand Ceramics | Maker's mark | Impressed numbers '4407', visible under white glaze base | Photograph by Damien Artus

MIDDLE: Rand Ceramics | Maker's mark | Sticker | Silver and black with teapot logo and 'Rand Ceramics' | Photograph by Natalie Field

BOTTOM: Rand Ceramics | Maker's mark | Sgraffito numbers, '6283' | Photograph by Natalie Field

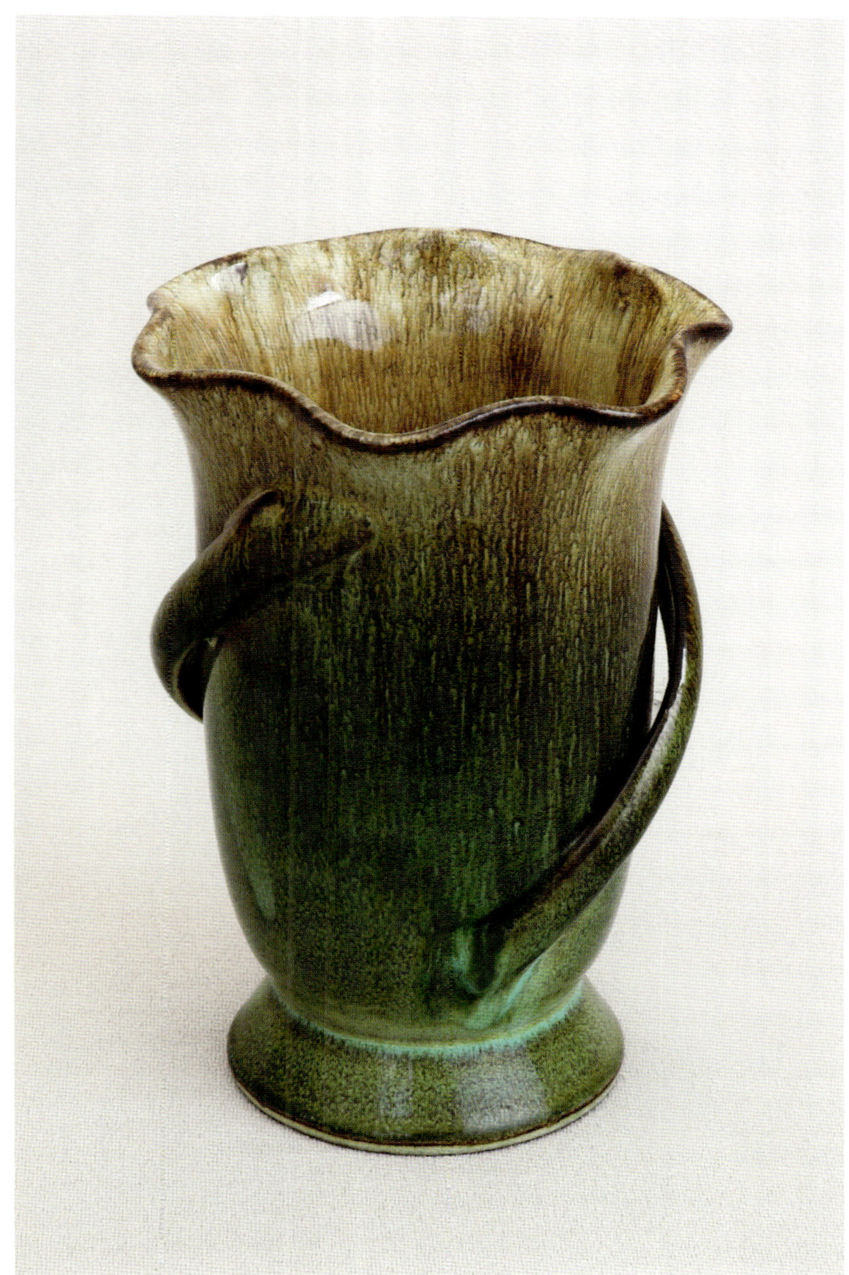

Rand Ceramics | Green vase with fluted lip and fine diagonal decorative handles | 175x120x85mm | Provenance: Douglas van der Horst | Marks: base glazed with transparent glaze; impressed number, '496', visible under glaze | Photograph by Natalie Field

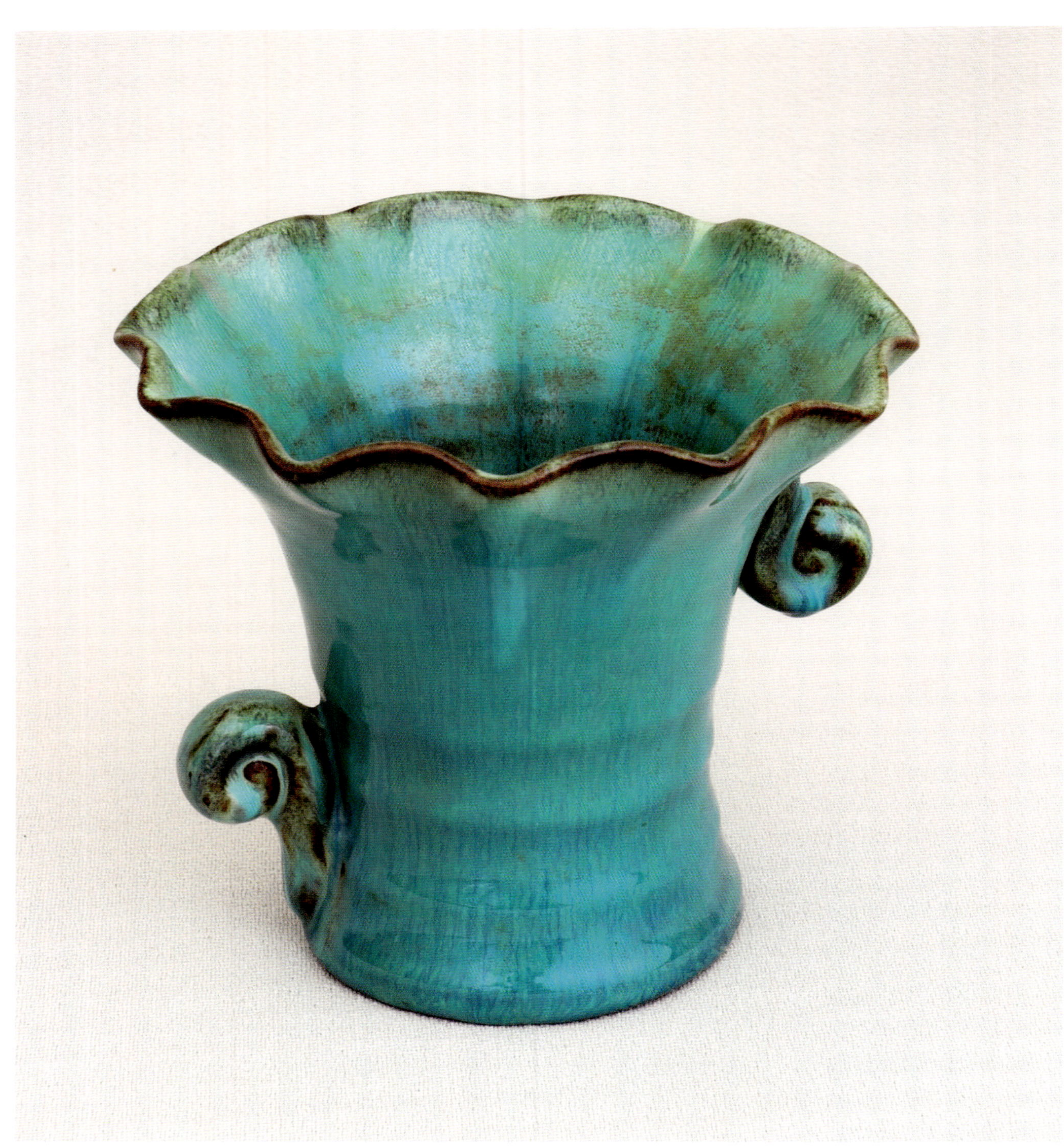

Rand Ceramics | Turquoise vase with fluted lip and small ornamental handles | 140x150x90mm | Provenance: Douglas van der Horst | Marks: base glazed with transparent glaze; impressed number, '6458', visible under glaze | Photograph by Natalie Field

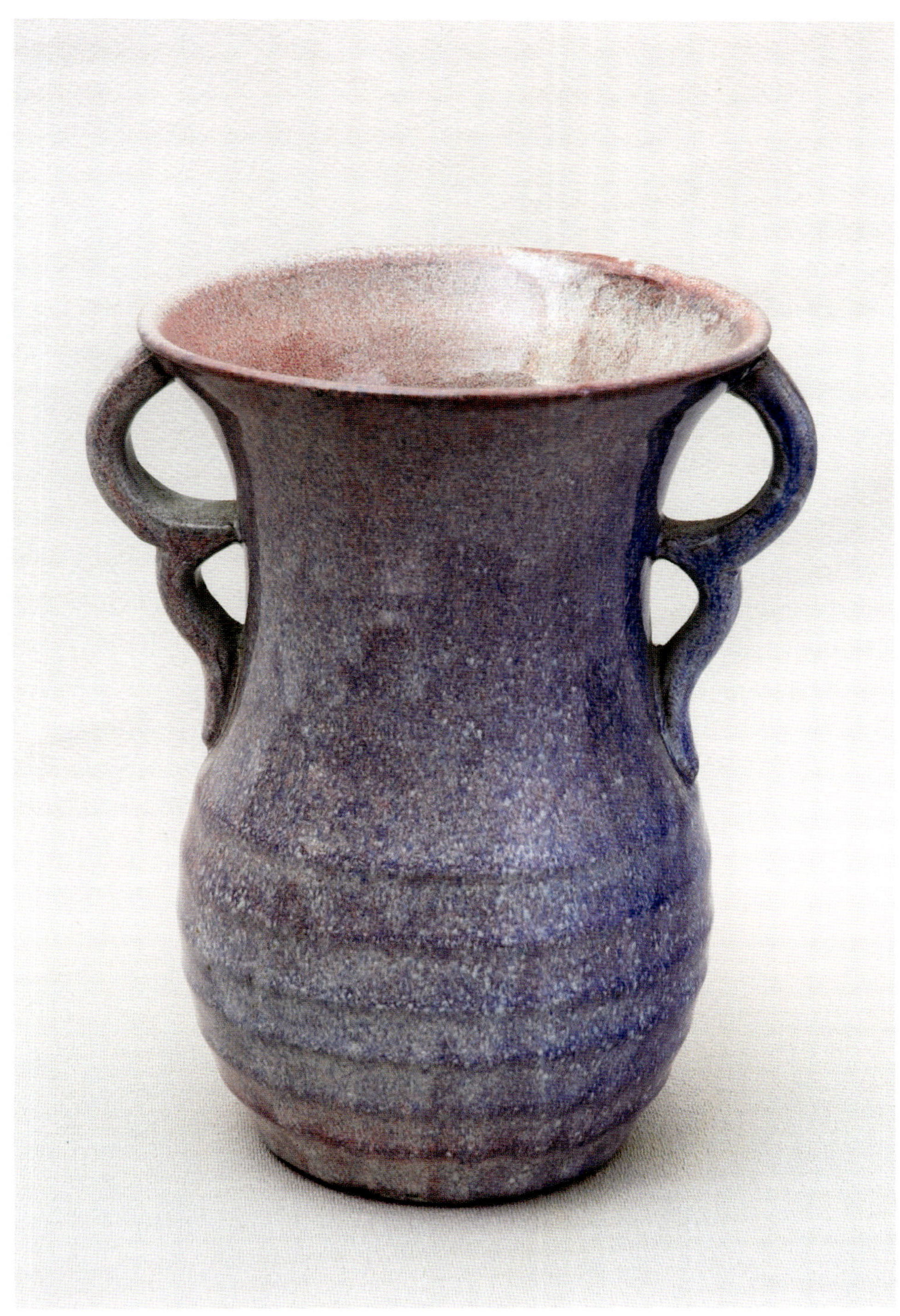

Rand Ceramics | Mauve vase with ribbed belly and elaborate double handles | 215x150x85mm | Provenance: Douglas van der Horst | Marks: Rand Ceramics sticker and impressed marking on the base, '10325' | Photograph by Natalie Field

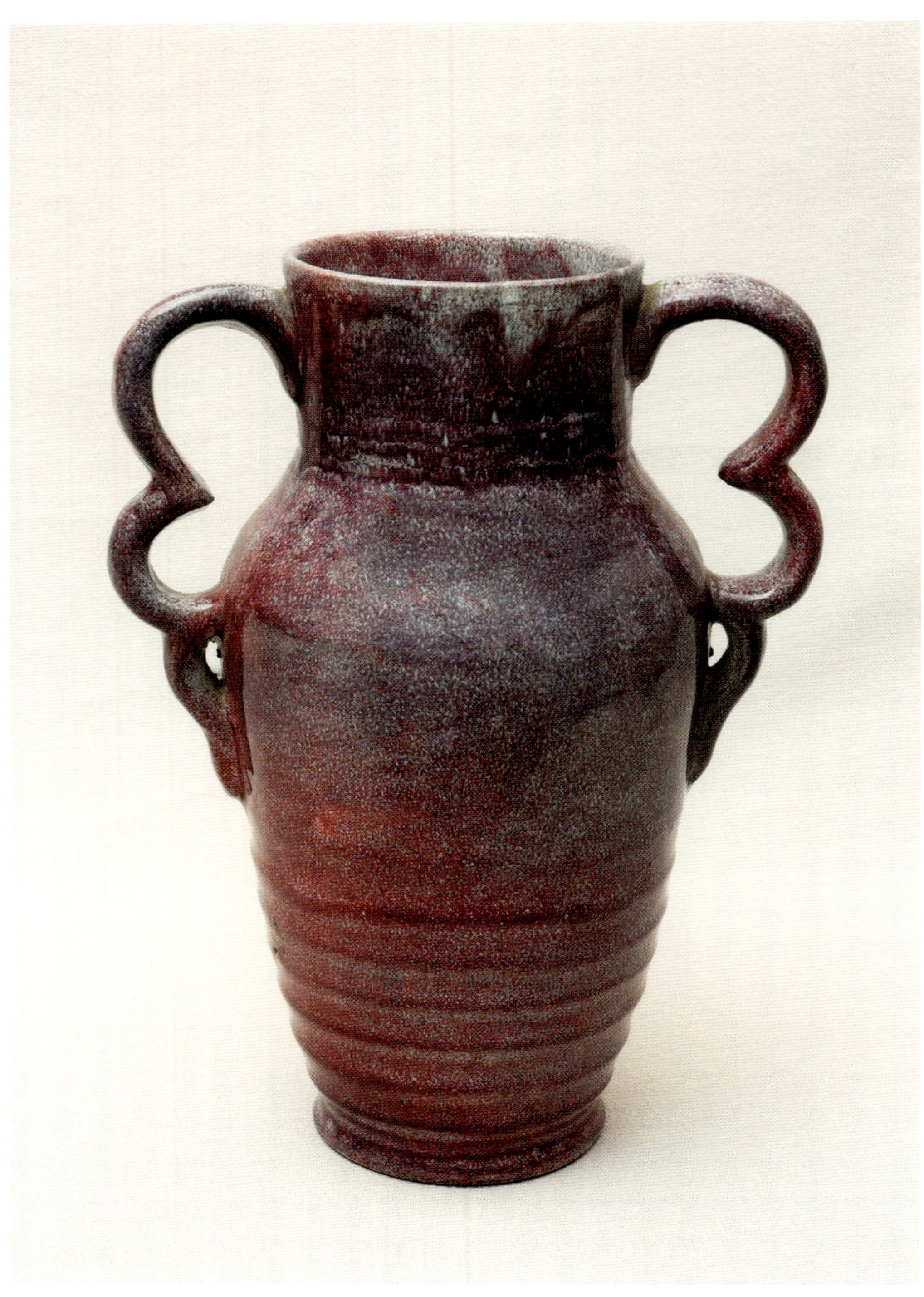

Rand Ceramics | Mauve vase with ribbed lover belly and elaborate heart-shaped double handles | 290x100x90mm | Provenance: Douglas van der Horst | Marks: base glazed with transparent glaze; impressed number '13302' visible under glaze | Photograph by Natalie Field

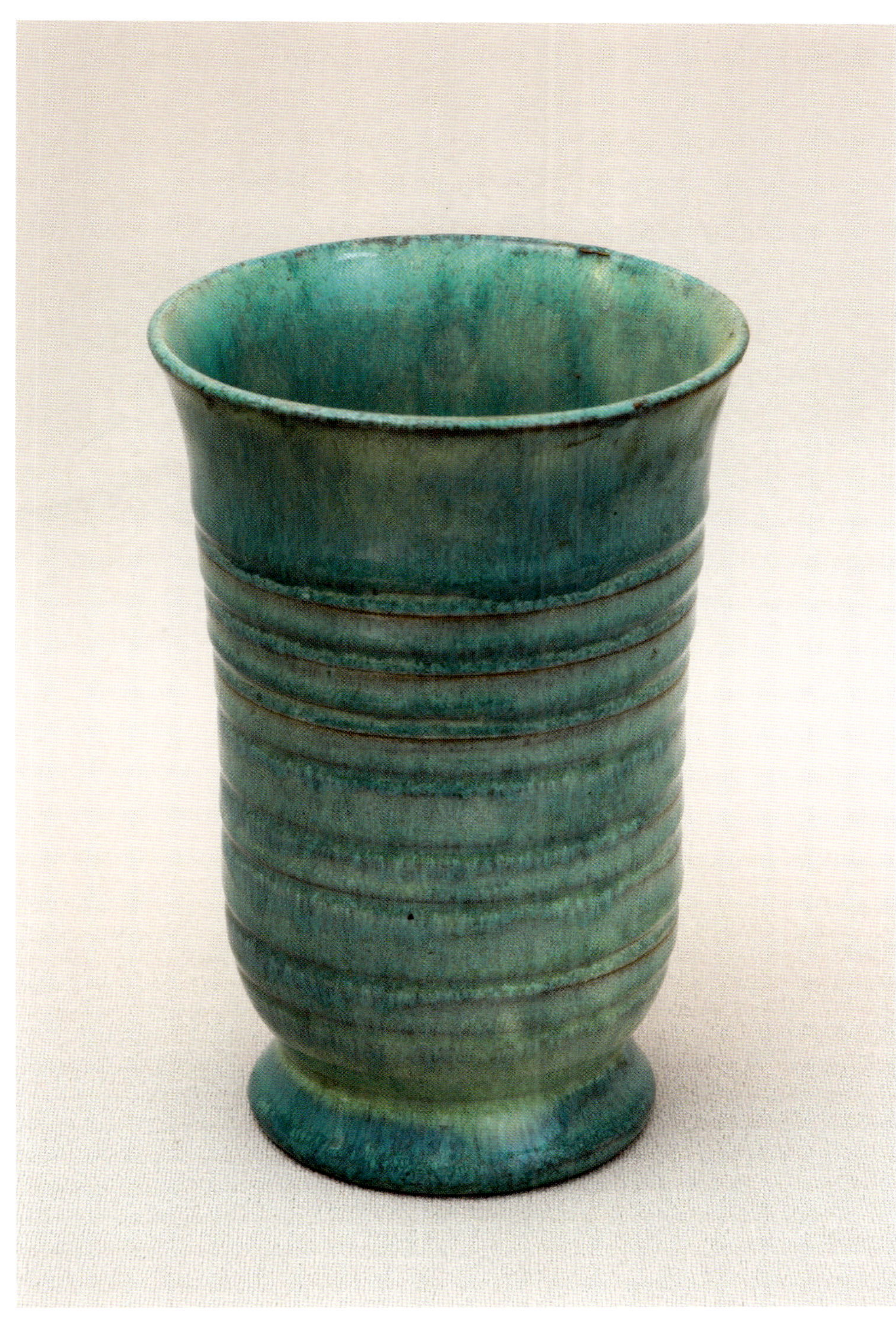

Rand Ceramics | Turquoise vase with ribbed body | 165x105x75mm | Provenance: Douglas van der Horst | Marks: base glazed with transparent glaze; impressed number, '5609', visible under glaze | Photograph by Natalie Field

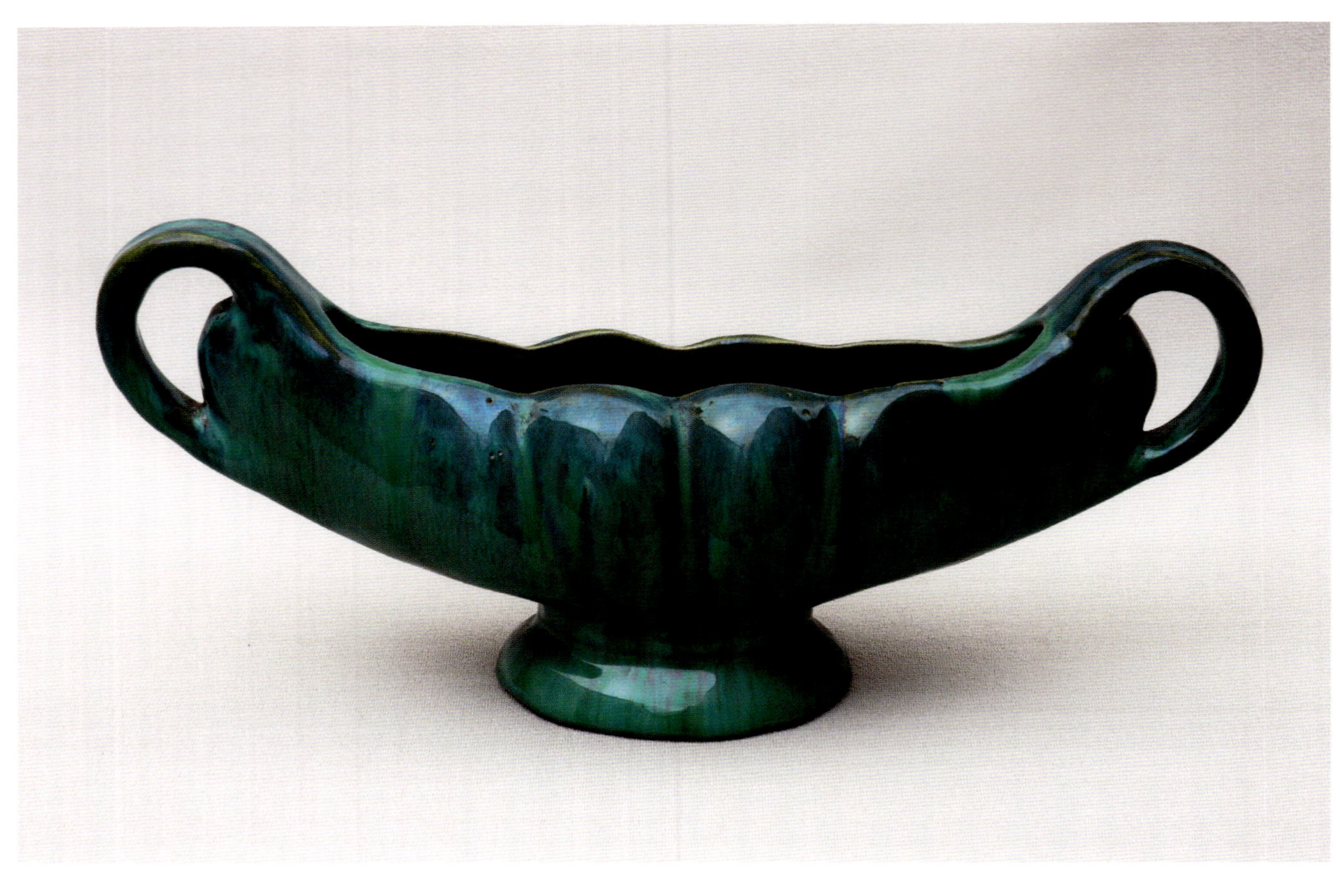

Rand Ceramics | Turquoise kylix gondola vase | Provenance: Douglas van der Horst | Marks: base glazed with transparent glaze; impressed number, '1080', visible under glaze | Photograph by Natalie Field

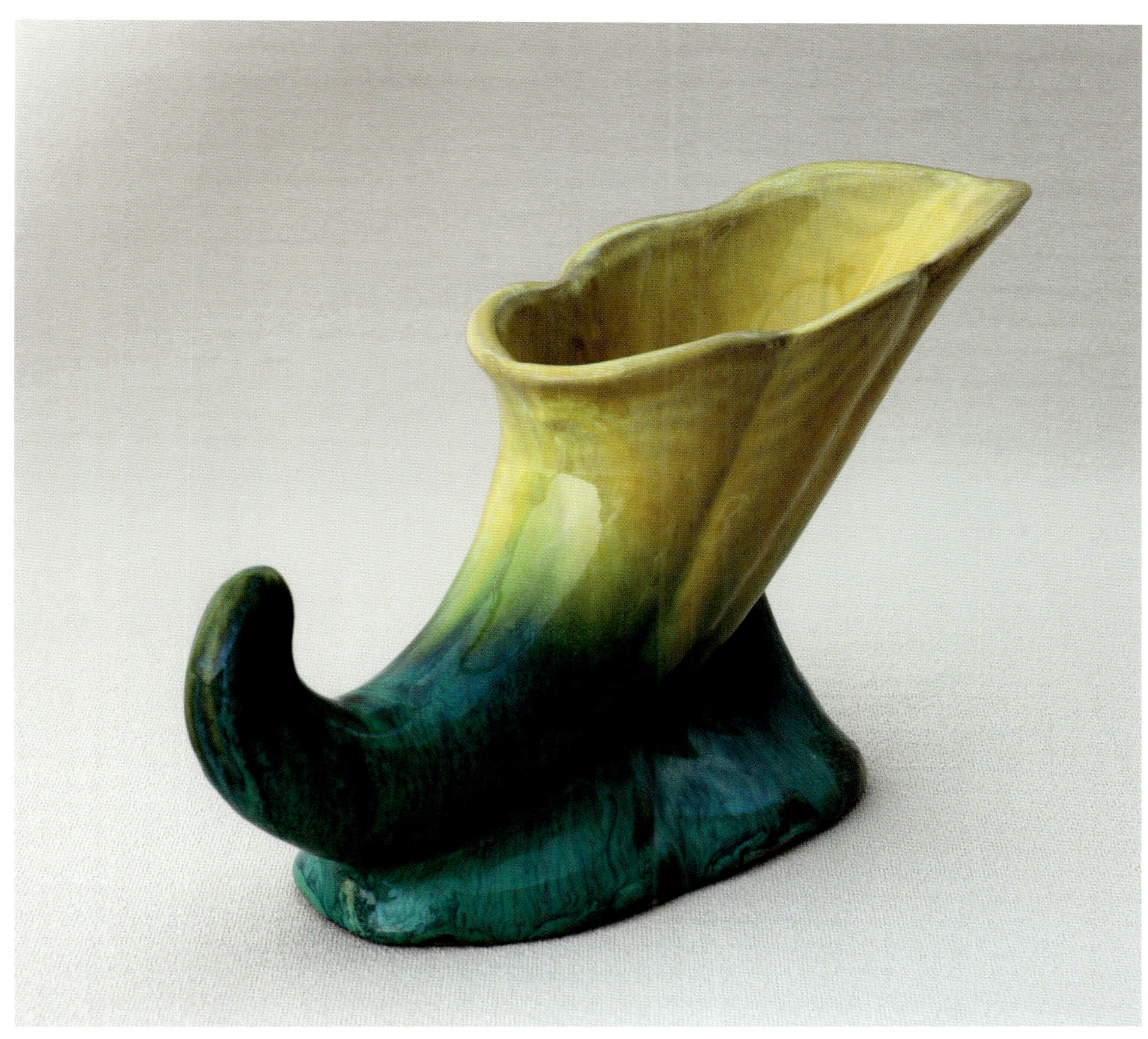

Rand ceramics | Yellow and turquoise pedestal vase in the form of a horn | Provenance: Douglas van der Horst | Marks: base glazed with transparent glaze; impressed number, '1865', visible under glaze | Additional information: grey clay body visible on rim | Photograph by Natalie Field

Rorke's Drift (1968–present)

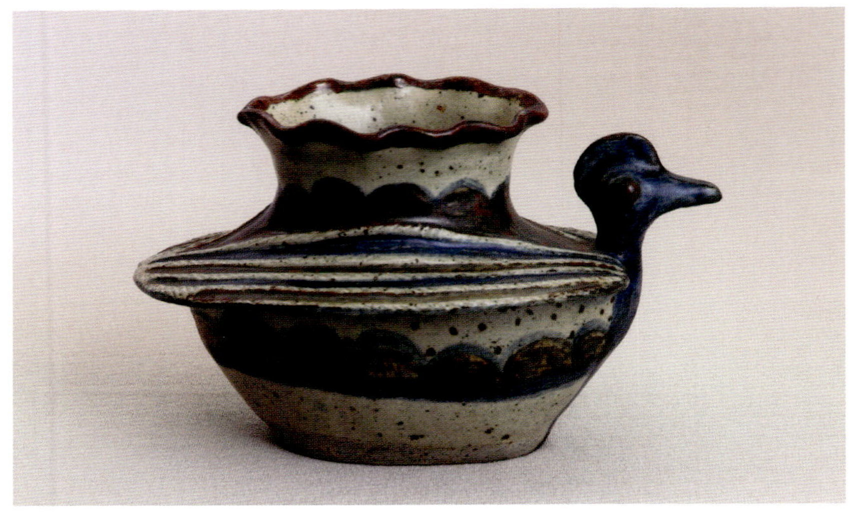

Rorke's Drift | Hand-built stoneware vase with fluted lip and body in the form of a stylised guinea fowl, with a bird's head | 145x210x140mm | Provenance: TAG | 721/83 | Marks: unglazed base with dark brown [oxide] marks, 'Elizabeth Mbatha S.162. 82' and Rorke's Drift leaf logo | Photograph by Natalie Field

Location

Rorke's Drift ceramic studio is housed in the Arts and Crafts Centre of the Evangelical Lutheran Church of Southern Africa (ELCSA) at eShiyane, near Dundee, KwaZulu-Natal. The ceramic studio is part of a larger art and craft project that included a fine art school (renowned for its graphic works) and textile studios (that included fabric printing and sewing workshops as well as a famous tapestry and rug workshop), which were established in 1962.

Name

Rorke's Drift is the historical site of the battle between British colonial forces and Zulu warriors following the Battle of Isandlwana in 1879. The British forces withstood the attack, and it proved to be the historical turning point that finally brought the Zulu kingdom under British colonial control.

Founders and managers

The ceramic studio at Rorke's Drift was founded in 1966 by Kirstin Olsson, who ran the workshop alone on a largely experimental basis. It was properly established by the Danish artist Peter Tybjerg in 1968. Upon his departure in 1969, a Danish couple, Anne and Ole Nielsen, took over as coordinators and ran the department from May 1969 to September 1970. Gordon Mbatha has coordinated the pottery workshop from 1970 to the present.

Staff

Isaiah Buthelezi, Euriel Damane, Peder Gowenius, Ulla Gowenius,Thamasqua (Thami) Rutherford Jali, Miriam Khumalo, Christopher Khuzwayo, Lindumusa Mabaso, Bhekisani Manyoni, Elizabeth Mbatha, Enval Mbatha, Gordon Mbatha, Judith Mkhabela, Gideon Mkhize, Phineas Mkhize, Dinah Molefe, Ivy Molefe, Lephinah Molefe, Loviniah Molefe, Nestah Molefe, Ole Nielsen,

Caiphas Nxumalo, Victor Shabangu, David Sibisi, Florence Sibisi, Jabulisiwe Sibisi, Joel Sibisi, Peter Tybjerg, Marietjie van der Merwe, Aaron Xulu, Ephraim Ziqubu, and Ivy Zulu. Marietjie van der Merwe assisted on a regular basis from 1971 until her death.

Wares manufactured

Under Nielsen, Rorke's Drift produced original, unique pieces and sculptures, decorated with coloured slips.[211] From late 1970 a simple glaze was used for the inside of pots, consisting of beer bottles that were crushed in an old maize grinder and made viscous by the addition of wallpaper glue.[212] Rorke's Drift produced an unusual variety of utilitarian wares, including crockery, tea services, mugs, vases and bowls. Wares recall both indigenous traditions as well as distinctly European forms. The indigenous forms are rooted in Zulu and Sotho pottery traditions, e.g. the large, coiled *izinkamba* (beer pots) serve as vases and decorative wares.

Rorke's Drift artists depicted images of Zulu history, local culture and biblical images, which were often used metaphorically to make socio-political comments on issues of deprivation, redemption and social justice. Similar political statements were also made in the other workshops (such as printmaking and tapestry), indicating an ideological cohesion among the staff and resident artists (Hosking 2005:31).

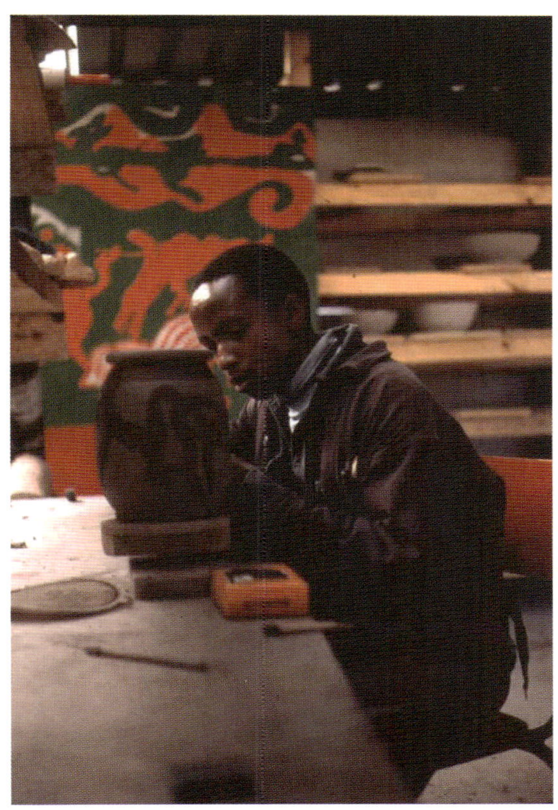

Rorke's Drift | Gordon Mbatha decorating, 1969 | Scan and photograph by Ole Nielsen

Production methods

Wares are hand-built by coiling or are thrown on the potter's wheel, while some items combine both techniques. There is a strong gender division, with the men doing the throwing and the women building vessels manually via the coiling method. Women currently decorate wares that have been thrown by men.

Brief history of the pottery

Established in 1962, the Arts and Craft Centre of Rorke's Drift was initially coordinated by Peder and Ulla Gowenius, who were appointed by Bishop Helge Fosseus and the ELCSA, in conjunction with the Swedish artist and teacher Bertha Hansson. The centre initially offered an art and craft adviser's course (to train artists to work in occupational therapy activities for churches or hospitals) and a weaving workshop. Until the late 1970s the centre was run by Swedish teachers, and from 1964 to 1968 various advisers and artists (including the weaver Allina Ndebele and the graphic artist Azaria Mbatha) were sent to study in Sweden.

The year 1968 was a particularly important one in the life of Rorke's Drift – it saw the founding of the ceramic studio, the textile studio and the fine art school. During this bleak historical period, when apartheid institutions denied formal artistic training to Africans, the centre trained many distinguished artists, including Azaria Mbatha (b.1941), John Muafangejo (1943–1987), Dan

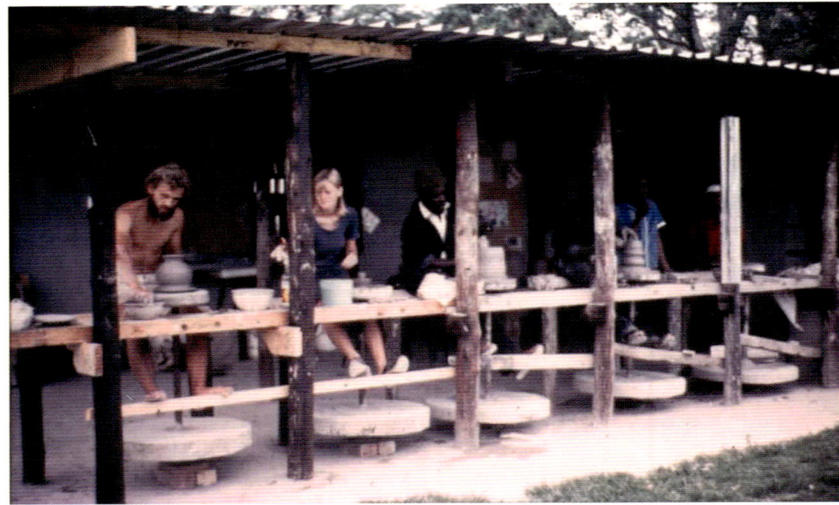

Rorke's Drift | Ole and Anne Nielsen, Caiphas Nxumalo, 1969 | Scan and photograph by Ole Nielsen

Rakgoathe (1937–2004), Bongiwe Dlhomo (one of the centre's few women artists) (b.1956), Musiweyixhwala Tabete, Cyprian Shilakoe (b.1946), Caiphas Nxumalo (c.1940–2002), Vuminkosi Zulu (1948–1996), Eric Mbatha (b.1948) and Tony Nkotsi (b.1955). Aware of the indigenous ceramic traditions practised by local women, the Scandanavian staff intended to offer them a venue to produce wares that incorporated aspects of the local vernacular, as well as to train them in European studio practices. The ultimate goal was financial self-sufficiency, and wares produced were designed to find markets in Sweden and South Africa.

Peter Tybjerg built the original coal-fired kiln and recruited Dinah Molefe, an accomplished maker of beer pots from the adjacent Nqutu district. Gordon Mbatha (trained in the weaving workshop), Joel Sibisi and Ephraim Ziqubu were simultaneously trained by Tybjerg as throwers. Dinah's daughter Lephinah and relatives Ivy and Nestah followed shortly thereafter. These six ceramicists formed a central team at Rorke's Drift.

Technical difficulties hampered the early development of the pottery, caused by local clay problems and routine firing hiccups. Early earthenware items manufactured under Tybjerg are simpler and often more overtly 'European' in form. These hand-built and thrown wares were decorated with various earth-coloured slips and oxides, and often not glazed. Coloured slips included black, deep red (made from iron oxide) and various shades of yellow ochre. The result was an earthy body with a matt finish. Some wares from this period also feature a certain fluorescence as a result of the addition of salt to the kiln to act as a 'fixative'. Under Nielsen the studio experimented with various home-made glazes using crushed beer bottles.

In 1971 Marietjie van der Merwe was appointed the studio consultant. She served as a technical adviser[213] and mentor to the pottery until her death in 1992. Her husband H W van der Merwe (1924–2001), Emeritus Honorary

Professor, University of Cape Town, also served on the Rorke's Drift Board. In the mid-1970s Marietjie van der Merwe organised a one-month training course for Gordon Mbatha, Ephraim Ziqubu and Joel Sibisi with Hyme Rabinowitz in Cape Town.

Glazed stoneware items produced under Van der Merwe's supervision are very expressive and sometimes feature more complex combinations of hand-built and thrown forms. Many hand-built wares were decorated with bas-relief geometric patterns and sculptural additions known as *amasumpa* (warts). The decorative chevron motif, which was frequently applied to Rorke's Drift wares, is a common feature in indigenous crafts, including beadwork, carving, basketry and ceramics.

The change from earthenware to stoneware was undertaken for various reasons. Peder Gowenius insisted that 'traditional' African crafts would not sell in Sweden as the market there was saturated with Mexican crafts, which included earthenware and maiolica vessels (Cruise 2005:134). The austere palette of Rorke's Drift ceramic wares was in sharp contrast to the vibrant and colourful tapestries, as well as the works produced by numerous artists in the printmaking workshop. This deliberate choice was probably influenced by the Mexican factor, although it is also rooted in the sobriety of the Konstfackskolan in Sweden, where many of the initial teachers had trained. The Konstfackskolan promoted a Bauhaus functionalism and austerity in design and decoration. Furthermore, Peder Gowenius insisted that 'usefulness' should apply to all activities of the centre. The austere palette of the pottery has echoes in traditional Nguni earthenware, which are characterised by terracotta, brown or blackened vessels with black and/or blue smoke marks. This sobriety of colour had the additional benefit of being relatively easily understood by a local market, familiar with the palette of many contemporary South African potteries operating within the Anglo-Oriental tradition.

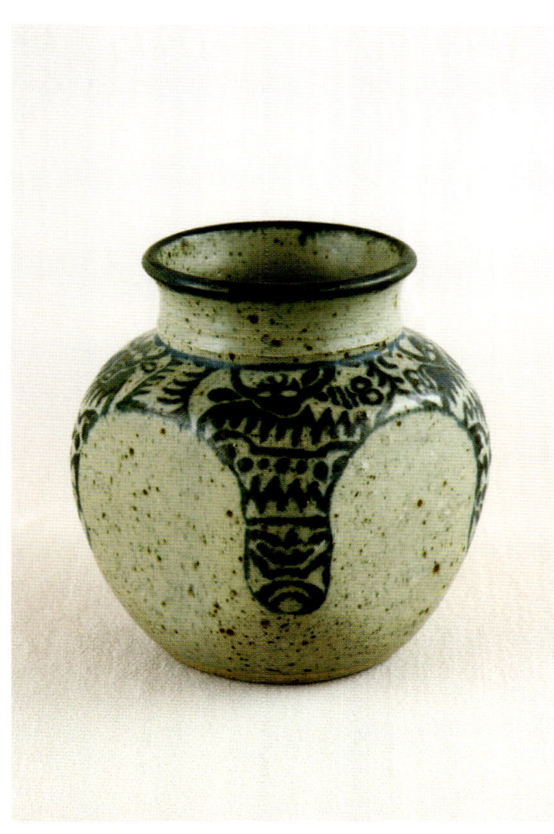

Rorke's Drift | Hand-built stoneware vase with cattle images | 178x113mm | Provenance: SHC Iziko | 94/215 | Marks: unglazed base with dark brown [oxide] marks, 'Ephraim Ziqubu, U.110. TT' and Rorke's Drift leaf logo | Photograph by Natalie Field

While the pottery of Rorke's Drift thus reflected contemporary chromatic tendencies, the majority of the forms break radically from the modernist canon, as well as with the wares produced at the time by numerous potteries. While the studio indeed made severe, classical modernist shapes, a significant percentage of their wares engage in a far more complex and expressive dialogue. The formal variety of wares is significant and should not be disregarded: some items are highly decorated, ornamental, almost bordering on the naïve; other wares are whimsical and humorous; others are eloquent and sophisticated; yet others are complex creations composed of stacked forms and sculptural elements.

The majority of the thrown wares produced by the male potters were decorated with figurative, animal or zoomorphic motifs. These motifs were derived from a variety of sources, including indigenous mythology, oral history and biblical stories. These figurative motifs were initially painted onto the wares, usually in black slip. However, after 1972, when Mbatha and Sibisi were trained in printmaking, incised decorative images became the hallmark of Rorke's Drift thrown wares. These sgraffito marks clearly echo the linocut carving technique taught at the fine art school (Clark and Wagner 1974:144–148,166–168, Vermeulen 1984:317–329).

Rorke's Drift's characteristic attribution of an artist's signature on the base of an article is of central importance. This practice occurs infrequently in southern African commercial and production pottery and is certainly not a feature of other contemporary rural potteries. It may be seen as a distinctly Nordic feature but the signature of pottery by African artists had an awesome significance during this period of grand apartheid. It was a bold political statement. Indeed Rorke's Drift was a hotbed of political activity and subject to frequent police raids, harassment and intimidation. This level of political activism resulted in various staff being expelled from South Africa, including the Goweniuses.

While partially based on traditional African forms Rorke's Drift pottery was designed and intended for Western consumption. It was sold in art and craft galleries in Scandinavia, South Africa (e.g. the African Life Centre, Durban and Devcraft, Johannesburg) and in the Rorke's Drift Shop. It was also sold by local civil liberty groups such as the Black Sash, the African Art Centre (Durban) and the South African Institute of Race Relations, which shared a similar political agenda. The pottery also participated in exhibitions in local art museums, but this was problematic as a result of the antagonistic relationship between Rorke's Drift and the State, and by extension the Swedish staff were suspicious of various public institutions.

Rorke's Drift is unique in its articulation of a very specific aesthetic – namely that of an Afro-Nordic union. The Scandinavian teachers, as well as Marietjie van der Merwe, were schooled in a very specific Nordic or northern European modernist aesthetic that favoured highly designed, refined, sensual and restrained forms. The Nordic legacy was that of simplicity, functionality, brevity and sobriety. This is evident in virtually every aspect of the pottery – from the sober matt finish to the extremely plastic qualities of jug and casserole handles, and the spouts and walls of vases. The stacked and joined forms of tall vases reveal aspects of late modernist northern European ceramic design, although contemporary European forms were seldom as original. While Nordic elements may be ascertained, the overall stylistic configuration is a *panache* of non-European and especially pan-African elements.

Marietjie van der Merwe introduced the potters to images of wares produced by Pueblo Indians from New Mexico, and especially to a book on Nigerian pottery. The Nigerian forms and decorative schemata particularly influented the women hand-builders. The exposure to these various pottery traditions resulted in a 'stacking' of formal and decorative components, as seen on numerous *ukhamba*. The vessels' surfaces became 'crowded' with sculptural detail (especially with bands of *amasumpa*), interlaced with painted geometric motifs, perhaps influenced by Nigerian or Pueblo traditions. The

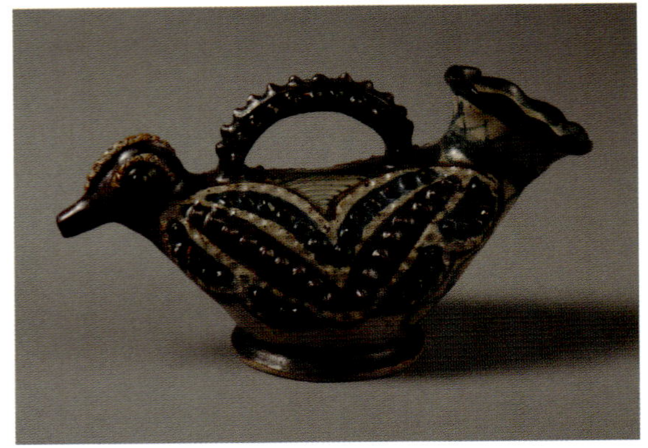

Rorke's Drift | Hand-built stoneware bird-shaped vessel with handle |128x90x230mm | Provenance: WHAG, ex Christine Ross-Watt, 2009 | 4120 | Marks: unglazed base with [oxide] markings, 'Elizabeth Mbatha' Rorke's Drift leaf logo, and 'y.126.83 ' | Photograph by Russell Scott

works produced by the male throwers, in turn, display an innovative synthesis of Zulu narrative effervescence with formal decorative techniques gleaned from the printmaking workshop. This is particularly evident in the use of sgraffito decoration on an area that has been coated with black slip. Until the late 1970s, there was considerable fluidity within the various divisions at Rorke's Drift, and students moved between the textile, weaving and printmaking workshops (Hobbs and Rankin 2003:63).

In recent years the centre has struggled to survive, and the pottery is presently semi-operational, producing a very limited output. This is a reflection on a lack of institutional leadership, as the centre's director from 2006, Christiane Voith, departed in 2013 and has not been replaced. Despite its current situation, Rorke's Drift is a highly significant cultural landmark within the South African applied arts sector. Its programme was highly original and courageous given the political context. The evolution of the ceramic studio evokes a unique marriage of numerous elements – a Zulu narrative tradition, the formal design traditions of northern Europe, and Pueblo and Nigerian formal and decorative elements. Its oeuvre is charged with a sense of nuanced hybridity – that clearly laid the foundation for subsequent African potters, such as the Ardmore studio, where colourful (and occasionally extravagant) eclectic borrowing is the cornerstone of their oeuvre. The pottery almost single-handedly championed the recognition of African potters in South Africa. Though recognised as a highly significant aspect of South African artistic patrimony and collected by most major South African art museums, it has never generated much income for the potters themselves, who continue to struggle financially.

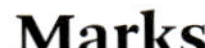

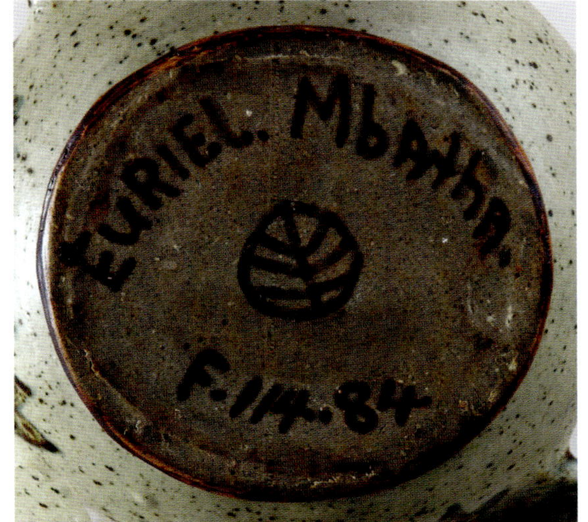

Rorke's Drift | Maker's mark | Unglazed base, 'Euriel Mbatha. F.114.84.' and Rorke's Drift leaf logo | Photograph by Natalie Field

Marks

- The bases of all items are marked with the Rorke's Drift logo, a leaf that symbolises the tree of life.
- Works are also usually signed with an artist's name (often applied by a third person) and also assigned a three-part number. This normally contains a letter and then two sets of numbers, e.g. 'V-3-86'. The letter indicates the number of the firing in the year; the first number is the piece number of the firing; and the second number refers to the year. This numeric registration system corresponds to the internal accounting system, which allocates funds to artists for sold items. Despite efforts to the contrary, the numbering system is completely eccentric, containing duplicates and other errors.[214]
- These identifying marks are usually hand-painted in a matt brown slip or oxide.
- Variations of the above mark scheme occur. The earliest works from ca.1968–1969 were marked with an incised tree of life. During the period 1968 to 1970, some stamps were used erratically.
- From the 1990s to the present, a black marker is often used to mark wares.

Select exhibitions[215]

2012 All Fired Up: Conversations between Kiln and Collection; DAG.
2011 Meeting the Makers: Contemporary Craft of KwaZulu-Natal; TAG.
2010 Carpets, tapestries, ceramics, hand printed fabrics and accessories. ELC Art and Craft Centre, Rorke's Drift; WHAG.
2003 & 2004 Veterans of KwaZulu-Natal: Artists from the 1970s & 1980s; DAG & Margate Art Gallery, 2003; TAG, Carnegie Art Gallery, New Castle & TEACH Museum, Empangeni 2004.
1998 Ubumba; TAG and DAG.
1989 Rugs, Tapestries and Pottery made at the ELC Art and Craft Centre, Rorke's Drift; WHAG.
1987 Rorke's Drift Fine Art School in Retrospect, TAG.
1987 African Perspectives: Symbolism and Religion, University of Zululand.
1985 Afrikansk Konst, Gothenburg, Sweden.
1983 Carpets, Rugs, Ceramics and Printed Fabrics from the ELC Art and Craft Centre, Rorke's Drift; WHAG.
1981 The Cape Gallery, Cape Town.
1975 Art South Africa Today exhibition, which formed part of the Fifteenth Republic Festival. Rorke's Drift works are separated (with many other craft and 'naive' works) from 'progressive' mainstream art and placed in a specially devised marginal category.
1975 ELC Art & Craft Centre, Rorke's Drift; WHAG.
1974 38th International Arts and Crafts Fair, Florence, Italy.
1974 Third Brickor Ceramic Art Exhibition.
1973 Art from KwaZulu, SANG.
1972 KwaZulu Art of Rorke's Drift, SANG.
1970 Sculpture and ceramics from Rorke's Drift. DAG. In purchasing Rorke's Drift works, DAG became the first museum to actively acquire the work of African artists.
1970 Untitled exhibition. PAM. All the works on this exhibition were purchased by Gallery 101, Johannesburg.
1970 Sculpture and Ceramics from Rorke's Drift; DAG.
1970 NMMAM.
1968 Art and Craft from Rorke's Drift, DAG and TAG.

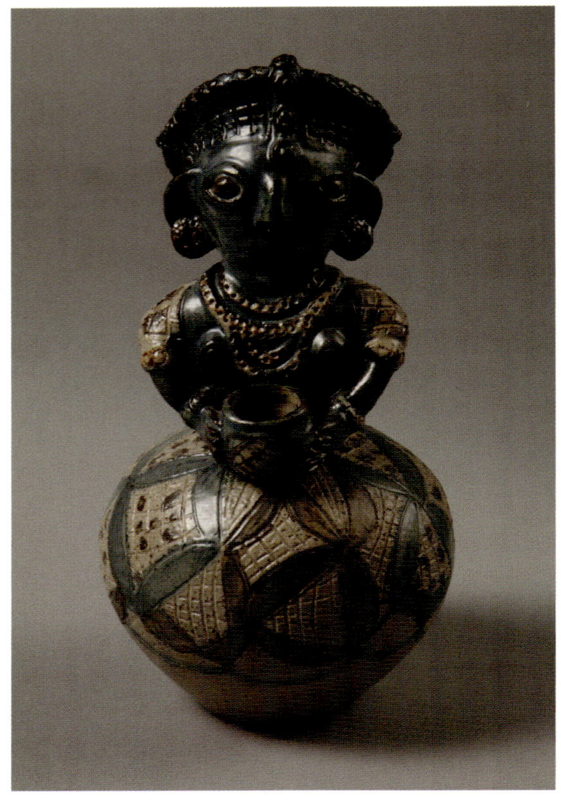

Rorke's Drift | Hand-built stoneware woman figurine holding a bowl | 277x143mm | Provenance: WHAG ex Rorke's Drift | 3904 | Marks: unglazed base with faint [oxide] markings, 'Elizabeth Mbatha,' Rorke's Drift leaf logo, and 'W.106-89' | Photograph by Russell Scott

Biographies

BUTHELEZI, Isaiah (b.1952)

Buthelezi worked at Rorke's Drift Pottery from 1977–1980. His works are in the collection of WHAG.

DAMANN, Euriel (née Mbatha) (aka Damane, aka Dammann) (b.1952)

Damann, who also marked works in her maiden name, worked in the hand-building section. Trained in 1980 by Dinah Molefe, she is the sister of Gordon

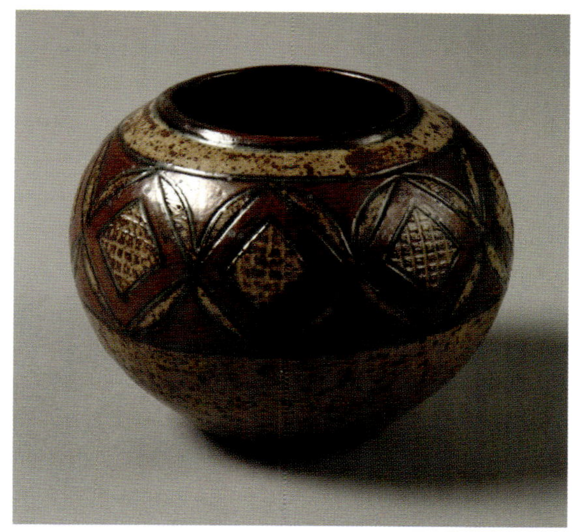

Rorke's Drift | Hand-built stoneware pot in the form of an *Ukhamba* | 123x152mm | Provenance: WHAG ex Rorke's Drift | 3901 | Marks: unglazed base with faint [oxide] markings, 'Euriel Damman', Rorke's Drift leaf logo, and 'T-55-88' | Photograph by Russell Scott

Mbatha. Damann's work, Vessel, 1984 was previously on permanent display in the ceramics room at Slave Lodge, is currently being exhibited on Fired, SHC Iziko. Her work has also been displayed on the APSA National Exhibition (1986) NMMAM; Rugs, Tapestries and Pottery made at the ELC Art & Craft Centre (1989); Jabulisa; Carpets, Rugs, Ceramics and Printed Fabrics (2010), WHAG; and All Fired Up Conversations between Kiln and Collection, DAG. Four vessels and a vase are currently exhibited on Fired, SHC Iziko. Collections of her work include the DAG, Jumuna Collection, NMMAM, SHC Iziko, South African Heritage Resources Agency, TAG and WHAG.

GOWENIUS, Peder (b.1936)
Born in Gårdsby, Sweden, Gowinius studied art education and printmaking at Konstfackskolan, Stockholm. Upon his graduation in 1961 he was recruited by the Church of Sweden Mission to work at the Ceza Mission Hospital in South Africa. He and his wife Ulla initially trained female students to work as art and craft advisers offering convalescents occupational therapy and weaving. The following year the couple established the art and craft centre at Rorke's Drift under the auspices of the Evangelical Lutheran Church of Southern Africa. In 1963 they relocated the centre to the current Rorke's Drift site. As rector, he coordinated exhibitions at galleries in several countries, including the Moderna Museet in Stockholm, 1966, and managed the art and craft centre and Rorke's Drift until 1968. After escalating pressure from the security branch of the South African police,[216] he and Ulla moved to the 'independent' state of Lesotho.

In 1968 they established Thabana li Mele in Lesotho, a community arts project that resembled Rorke's Drift in its focus on empowering local communities. In 1970 the couple fled from Lesotho and the project was closed for many years. In 1973 they established a cooperative craft project, Lentswe-La-Odi, near Serowe, Botswana, where they taught local Batswana to spin, dye and weave, and manage their cooperative. They left Botswana in 1978, but over the years have continued to visit and work with southern African artists and craftspeople.

GOWENIUS, Ulla (née Kylberg) (1925–2005)
Born in Kylberg, Sweden, she studied textiles at Konstfackskolan, Stockholm, where she met Peder Gowenius. She worked at Rorke's Drift from 1961 to 1968, where she taught spinning and weaving. The weaving workshop was central to the institution's success: financial reports up to 1971 indicate that the substantial profits generated by the weaving section financed other sections. The tapestries include geometric patterns and images of contemporary life, historical scenes, folklore and biblical stories, and have been exhibited internationally, including at the National Museums of Stockholm and Copenhagen, and the Malmo Museum of Modern Art, Sweden.

Upon retirement, the couple returned to Peder's childhood village, Gårdsby near Växjö. Here Ulla continued to produce textiles, including an altar carpet for Växjö Cathedral, until her death in 2005.

JALI, Thamsanqa (Thami) Rutherford (b.1955)
Jali was born Durban, and is a painter, sculptor and a graphic artist. He studied at the Rorke's Drift Art Centre from 1981–1982 and later specialized in ceramics at the Natal Technikon, 1983–1984. Jali has participated in several group exhibitions in SA and aboard, including the Zabalaza Festival, London, 1990 and the New Dehli Triennale, India, 1997. Between 2004 and 2007 he returned to Rorke's Drift to teach and assist with a project to resuscitate the ceramic studio. He has had three solo exhibitions; Ungqofo Ulalele, Menzi Mchunu Gallery, BAT Centre, Durban, 1998; Transformation, at the same venue in 2007, and 'Restless Spirit Thamsanqa (Thami) Rutherford Jali' which was shown at the DAG and TAG in 2014. The latter included some of his ceramics from Rorke's Drift.

KHUMALO, Miriam (b.1951) (aka Mirriam)
Khumalo worked in the hand-building section at Rorke's Drift Pottery between 1970 and 1974.

KHUZWAYO, Christopher
Khuzwayo was employed as a thrower at Rorke's Drift.

MABASO, Lindumusa (b.1956)
A thrower at Rorke's Drift, Mabaso joined in approximately 1975 as a clay mixer, and is still employed in the Pottery. He was taught to throw by Gordon Mbatha and Joel Sibisi. His work was exhibited on Rugs, Tapestries and Pottery made at the ELC Art & Craft Centre; All Fired Up: Conversations between Kiln and Collection; and his Vessel, 1989 is currently exhibited on Fired, SHC Iziko. His work is in numerous public and private collections including the Bernstein Collection, University of KwaZulu-Natal; DAG; the Jumuna Collection; PAM; the Gertrude Agranat Bequest of the Pelmama Permanent Art Collection (also housed at PAM), SHC Iziko; the South African Heritage Resources Agency and WHAG.

MANYONI, Bhekisani (b.1945)
Manyoni was among the first throwers trained at Rorke's Drift and studied at the Fine Art School from 1960–1963. He was a close friend and fishing partner of Ole Nielsen, and he accompanied the Nielsens to Swaziland to set up Mbabane Ceramic Training Centre. Manyoni lived with the Nielsens in Mbabane and helped teach the students. In Swaziland he spent most of his time carving wooden sculptures, and sold them to the expatriates and tourists. Manyoni stayed on in Swaziland when the Nielsens left in 1972. In Swaziland, Manyoni befriended Austin Hleza and taught him graphics (Meyer 1987:6). His work is in public collections including the TAG and DAG and was included in Ubumba and All Fired Up .

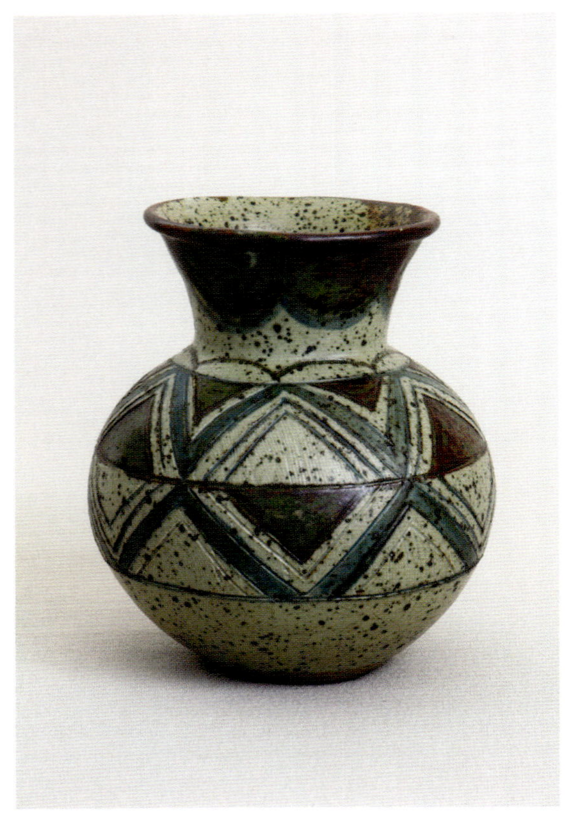

Rorke's Drift | Hand-built stoneware vase in form of an 'Uphiso' | 200x118x65mm | Provenance: TAG | 719/83 | Marks: unglazed base with dark brown [oxide] marks, 'Elizabeth Mbatha L.21. 82' and Rorke's Drift leaf logo | Photograph by Natalie Field

MBATHA, Elizabeth (b.1950)
Currently employed as a hand-builder at Rorke's Drift, Elizabeth joined the pottery in 1980. She was trained by Dinah Molefe and Lephina Molefe, and is the wife of Gordon Mbatha. Works by Mbatha have been included in numerous exhibitions including Rugs, Tapestries and Pottery made at the ELC Art & Craft Centre; No Man's Land; Ubumba; Veterans of KwaZulu-Natal: Artists from the 1970s & 1980s; Jabulisa, and Carpets, tapestries, ceramics, hand printed fabrics and accessories [from the] ELC Art & Craft Centre. Her work is in numerous collections including the Bernstein Collection, University of KwaZulu-Natal; DAG; Jumuna Collection; NMMAM; Rorke's Drift Collection TAG and WHAG.

MBATHA, Enval
Enval Mbatha worked as a thrower until 2009. Several of his works are in the collection of the South African Heritage Resources Agency.

MBATHA, Gordon (b.1948)
Gordon Mbatha joined the weaving centre in 1965 and was the first male to join the pottery in 1968. He was trained as a thrower by Peter Tybjerg. Mbatha served as the head potter at Rorke's Drift and was also the general foreman and supervisor, responsible for firing and glazing. He attended a graphics course at Rorke's Drift from 1970 to 1972, and in the mid-1970s he participated in a one-month training period under Hyme Rabinowitz in Cape Town. Mbatha left Rorke's Drift in 1998, returned in 2004, and is still working there. Over the years his linocuts and ceramics have been exhibited extensively. Mbatha's work has been shown in numerous exhibitions, including Ubumba; Veterans of KwaZulu-Natal: Artists from the 1970s & 1980s; Meeting the Makers: Contemporary Craft of KwaZulu-Natal; and All Fired Up: Conversations between Kiln and Collection. He is represented in various public and private collections including the Bernstein Collection, University of KwaZulu-Natal; DAG; SHC Iziko; NMMAM and TAG.

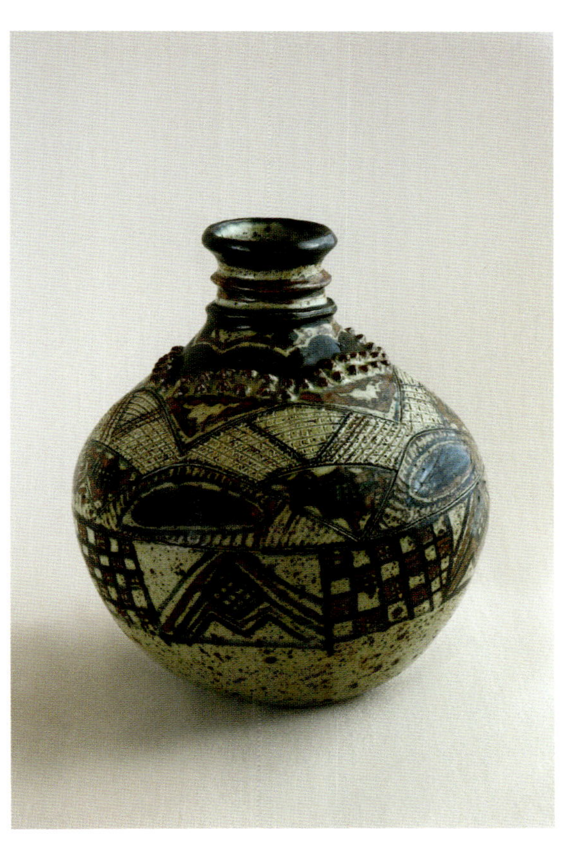

Rorke's Drift | Vase | 286x78mm | Provenance: SHC Iziko | 94/217 | Marks: unglazed base with [oxide] marks, 'Ivy Molefe, B 71 74' and Rorke's Drift leaf logo | Photograph by Natalie Field

MKHABELA, Judith (d.2005)
Mkhabela began as a weaver at Rorke's Drift and subsequently worked as a hand-builder in 1975 and 1976. Her date of departure is unknown, but she did not stay for more than two or three years. It is possible that she may have developed the bird form of vessel that became a key item in the pottery's repertoire. Mkhabela's work outside this institution is also significant. She was a talented independent potter (making *ukhamba*) and sculptor. Mkhabela is known for her sculptures of elephants and pigs that were sold through Rorke's Drift and Vukani Arts and Craft Cooperative, Mahlabatini. She was assisted by her sister and her daughter, Buyisiwe, and cooperated with another local woman potter, Martha Msiya, for a 15-year period. Mkhabela is acknowledged as an innovator and leader of a group of women potters who worked in extremely isolated and difficult conditions.

MKHIZE, Gideon (1939–2008)

A senior thrower at Rorke's Drift, Mhkize joined the Pottery in 1978 and worked until 2008. Works by Mkhize are in the collection of the SHC Iziko; the South African Heritage Resources Agency and WHAG.

MKHIZE, I

Worked at Rorke's Drift in the early 1980s. His work is found in the Jumuna Collection.

MKHIZE, Phineas

Worked at Rorke's Drift in the 1980s. His work was featured on the exhibition, Rugs, Tapestries and Pottery made at the ELC Art & Craft Centre, Rorke's Drift (1989).

MOLEFE, Dinah (1927–2011)

Of Sotho origin and originally from the Nqutu district of KwaZulu-Natal, Molefe was one of the first potters in the hand-building section at Rorke's Drift. She was already an accomplished *umsamo* potter when she joined in 1968. She retired from Rorke's Drift in 1983.

For over 20 years she produced some of the most original South African pottery. Molefe exhibited at the 1970 exhibition, 'Sculpture and Ceramics from Rorke's Drift', DAG and in 1974 at the 38th International Arts and Crafts Fair, Florence, Italy. She won a prize at the Third Brickor Ceramic Art Competition, 1974. Her work is in numerous private collections in the Durban Art Gallery and at Rorke's Drift.

Her work was included on the exhibition, Veterans of KwaZulu-Natal: Artists from the 1970s & 1980s. Her Gourd-shaped vase, 1978 (SH2011/32) is currently on display in Fired, SHC Iziko. Molefe's work is in numerous collections including the Bernstein Collection, University of KwaZulu-Natal; Rust-en-Vrede Gallery & Clay Museum, Durbanville; DAG; DNMCH; PAM and SHC Iziko.

MOLEFE, Ivy (b.1923)

Molefe worked at Rorke's Drift between 1971 and 1984. Her work, Vessel, 1974 (SACHM94/217) was on permanent display in the ceramics room at the Slave Lodge in Cape Town. Public collections that contain her work include the SHC Iziko, DNMCH and the Bernstein Collection, University of KwaZulu-Natal.

MOLEFE, Lephinah (b.1926)

Lephinah Molefe was employed as a hand-builder at Rorke's Drift. She is the daughter of Dinah Molefe. She left the pottery in 1974 and returned in 1983.

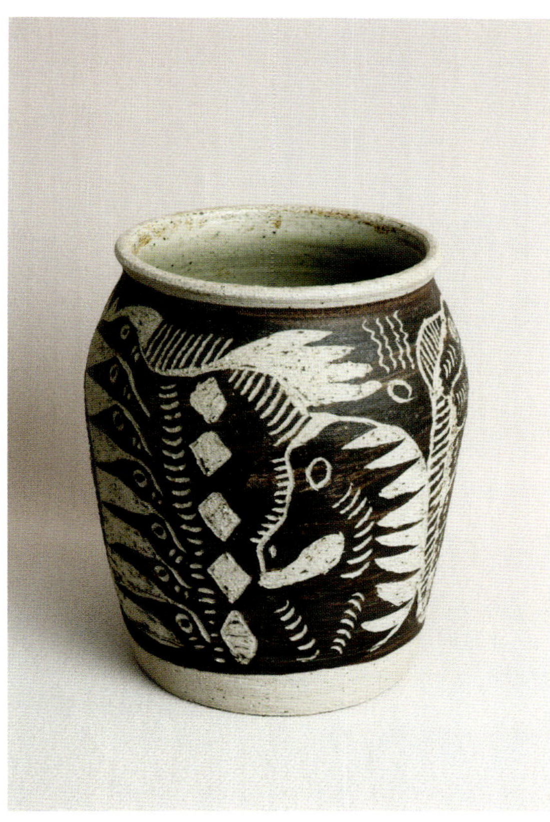

Rorke's Drift | Stoneware vase thrown form with stylised horse motifs painted in oxide | 183x127x116mm | Provenance: Prof. Mark Watson | Marks: unglazed base with [oxide] marks, 'Joel Sibisi' and Rorke's Drift leaf logo | Photograph by Natalie Field

MOLEFE, Loviniah (b.1945) (aka MOLIFE, Lephiniah; MOLEFE, Lovenia and MOLEFE, Lephinah)

Molefe worked at Rorke's Drift between 1970 and approximately 1980. Her work was included in Ubumba, and her Vessel, 1972 (SH2004/9) is currently on display on Fired, SHC Iziko. Public collections that contain her work include the Jumuna Collection; SHC Iziko and TAG.

MOLEFE, Nesta (aka Nester)

Worked at Rorke's Drift briefly in the early 1970s. Molefe's work can be found in the Jumuna Collection and the TAG.

MOLEFE, Nestah (b.1928)

Nestah Molefe was employed at Rorke's Drift from 1974 to 1984.

NIELSEN, Ole (b.1946)

Ole Nielsen was born in Denmark and studied at the Academy of Art, Aarhus and the School of Art and Craft, Copenhagen. After his graduation Nielsen and his wife, Anne, joined Rorke's Drift and worked there from late 1969 to 1970, being employed by the Ministry of Foreign Affairs in Denmark to assist with the establishment of the pottery. Prior to their arrival another Danish couple, Peter Tyberg and Kirsten Ernst, had worked at Rorke's Drift for a year but little of their efforts remained when the Nielsens arrived. They built a workshop from asbestos sheets on a pole framework, and worked with the kick wheels that Tyberg had constructed.

In 1970 Nielsen met Peter Simkin, an adviser to the Swazi government in charge of SEDCO. Simkin invited the Nielsens to work in Swaziland, and made the request to the Danida, the Danish NGO responsible for their mission. According to Nielsen:

> They [the Danish Ministry of Foreign Affairs] forgot to tell us that we were expected to be missionaries as well as pottery teachers. We were supposed to go to church each day before work [at Rorke's Drift], but did not, and as I refused to check on whether the students had been, I was seen as a bad influence. The irony of the whole thing was that I did not belong to any church. The missionaries were shocked when I told them.
>
> Whenever we had a disagreement it was because 'you don't believe in Jesus'. We associated with people outside the mission – South Africans, both white and black. We had monthly dinners with our students. We even attended heathen weddings in Zululand.

Peter Simkin asked us to come to Swaziland and the Swedish bishop agreed to a transfer 'as we cannot afford conflict within the mission'. After our first meeting at SEDCO Peter Simkin ended by saying 'and you are allowed to go to church if you want' – and I knew that I would get on with him.[217]

In 1970 the Nielsens established the Mbabane Ceramic Training Centre and fired the first glazed pottery in Swaziland. The centre aimed to train Swazis in technical and practical ceramic skills and help them establish their own businesses. In 1971, six months before leaving Swaziland, Nielsen and his successor Breznick became good friends.

In 1972 the Nielsens left Swaziland and established his own pottery in Newtown Kells, Ireland. He produced mainly salt-glazed stoneware, and domestic and sculptural items. Due to the political instability in Ireland, in 1977 they sold the pottery and immigrated to Australia. On the way to Australia, Nielsen visited Tonda Breznik, in Bangkok, where he was based. Nielsen then worked in Nepal from 1978 to 1979 as a ceramic expert for the ILO.

After Nepal, Nielsen returned to Australia and opened his own workshop in Beaumont, producing wood-fired and salt-glazed stoneware. In 1984 the Nielsens separated and Ole went to France, where he stayed with Tonda and Claire Breznik in Ferney-Voltaire. From 1985 to 1986 Nielsen worked as a United Nations volunteer in Duala, Cameroon, teaching pottery. In 1986 Nielsen established his own workshop in Longeray, France, where he mainly made porcelain wares. From 1989 to 1991 Nielsen worked as Ceramic Adviser for the ILO in Bangladesh. From 1991 to 1995 he taught part-time and started a workshop in Sogndal, Norway, where he made stoneware and some stone sculpture. Nielsen returned to Australia in 1995 and started a new workshop, making one-off stoneware. He gradually moved from pottery to sculpture in wood, stone and bronze, and now works as a sculptor.

Nielsen regularly exhibited at The Bock Gallery in Kangaroo Valley, NSW, Australia between 1995 and 2003. Other significant exhibitions in which he has participated include the International Exhibition, Vallauris, France; the International Exhibition, Faenza, Italy; the Ulster Museum, Belfast, Ireland, 1976; and the Craft Expo, Sydney in 1982. In 1975 he was awarded a gold medal at the International Exhibition, Faenza, Italy and the first prize by the Royal Dublin Society, Ireland.

Nielsen's work is in many important public collections, including the Faenza Museum, Italy; the Australian Industrial Development Corporation (Australian Capital Territory); the New South Wales Premier's Department; the Commonwealth Banking Corporation, Sydney; the Art Gallery of Western Australia; and private collections in Europe, Australia and the USA.

NXUMALO, Caiphas (aka Caiaphas) (c.1940 – 2002)

Born in the Msinga district, Nxumalo was among the most senior of the male artists at Rorke's Drift. He was a sculptor, potter and also produced linocuts prints. Nxumalo had a great technical mind and was very inventive. It is claimed that he devised a petrol-fuelled mechanical weaving loom (Hobbs and Rankin 2003:222). Nxumalo left Rorke's Drift and set up a workshop near Pomeroy. His workshop was subsequently burned by jealous neighbours. Exhibitions include Art and Craft from Rorke's Drift, DAG, 1968; Sculpture and Ceramics from Rorke's Drift, DAG, 1970; KwaZulu Art of Rorke's Drift, SANG, 1972; Rorke's Drift Fine Art School in Retrospect, TAG 1987; African Perspectives: Symbolism and Religion, University of Zululand, 1987 and 1910–2010: Pierneef to Gugulective SANG, 2010. His works are in various collections including SANG and the University of Fort Hare Gallery.

SHABANGU, Victor (b.1954)
Shabangu joined the pottery in 2007.

SIBISI, David
David Sibisi worked in the pottery in the mid-1970s.

SIBISI, Florence (b.1954)
Florence from 1990 Sibisi was employed as a hand-builder at Rorke's Drift Pottery. She was trained by Elizabeth Mbatha and Euriel Damman. She is the sister-in-law of Joel Sibisi.

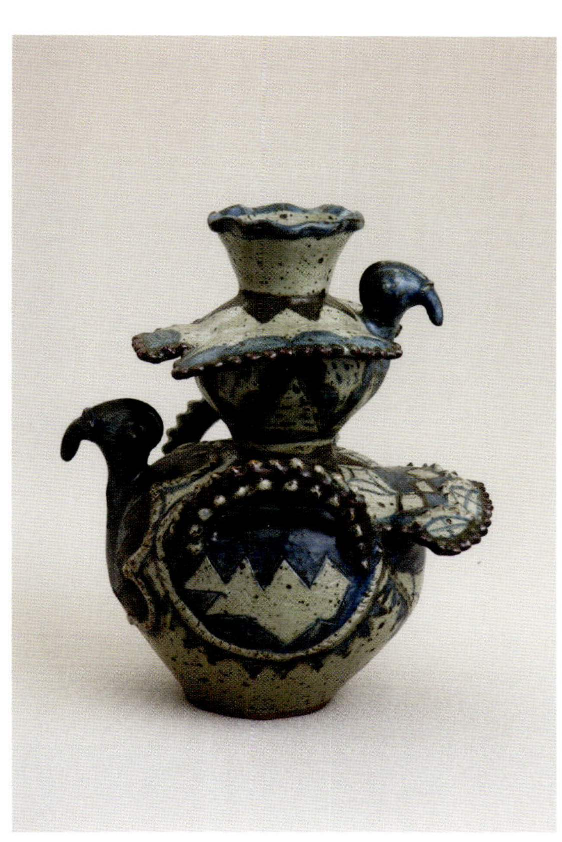

Rorke's Drift | Hand-built stoneware sculptural double tiered vase with two birds | 240x70x65mm | Provenance: TAG | 720/83 | Marks: unglazed base with [oxide] marks, 'Elizabeth Mbatha T.55. 55. 82' and Rorke's Drift leaf logo | Photograph by Natalie Field

SIBISI, Jabuliswe (b.1967)
Jabuliswe Sibisi joined Rorke's Drift in 2008.

SIBISI, Joel (b.1945)
Born at Rorke s Drift, KwaZulu-Natal Sibisi joined the ELC Arts and Crafts Centre in early 1969 and in 1972 he was awarded a diploma in Fine Art. He was trained to throw by Peter Tybjerg. In the mid-1970s he participated in a one-month training period under Hyme Rabinowitz in Cape Town. Sibisi was a senior thrower and pottery workshop co-supervisor at Rorke's Drift. He retired in approximately 2008.

Sibisi is renowned for his strong sculptural forms, but is also a graphic artist. He regularly assists the other studios with designs for tapestries and fabrics. His work has been exhibited at the Gencor Art Gallery, Johannesburg in 1993, and on Ubumba and Jabulisa. Sibisi's Bottle-shaped vase (1997SH2008/2) is currently displayed on the exhibition, Fired, SHC Iziko. Collections that contain his work include the Bernstein Collection, University of KwaZulu-Natal; DAG; the Jumuna Collection; SANG and TAG.

TYBJERG, Peter (b.1944)
Born in Iceland, Tybjerg left school at the age of 15 and worked as a farm assistant until he was apprenticed as a fitter, which he completed in 1964. In his spare time he made potter's wheels and kilns for his friends. In 1964, Tybjerg saw an exhibition of ceramics by Pablo Picasso in Antibes, and this had a decisive influence on the subsequent years he spent investigating ceramics as a mode of sculptural expression from his studio in Hindsholm, Denmark. In 1967, he exhibited at the Artists' Autumn Exhibition held in the Free Exhibition Building in Copenhagen.

In 1968 Tybjerg worked at Rorke's Drift, where he constructed a ceramics workshop. In 1969 he undertook a study tour of Swaziland, Zimbabwe, Mozambique and Lesotho. He subsequently analysed clay deposits in Swaziland.

Upon returning to Denmark, Tybjerg worked as an independent potter, consultant and lecturer in Studio Ceramics. From 1973 to 1976 he served as a member of the Board of Directors at Kerteminde Kunstforening, Toldboden, Denmark, and from 1976 to 1978 he was a member of the Board of Directors at Danske Kunsthåndværkeres Landsorganisation, Denmark. Since 1996 he has worked a potter from his studio in Assens, Denmark.

Tybjerg has undertaken various public commissions, including in the University of Odense, Denmark; Prairie Peace Park, World Peace Center, Nebraska (1993); and the lobby of an office building in Al Khobar, Saudi Arabia. He has participated in numerous international exhibitions at galleries including the Keramikmuseet Grimmerhus, Middelfart, Denmark, 1998; the Northern Arizona Art Museum, 1993; the Röhsska Kunstslöjdmuseum, Göteborg, Sweden, 1991; the Keramikmuseum Het Prinsessenhof, Leuvarden, Holland, 1984; and the Berkeley Art Center, California, 1983. Between 1982 and 1997, Tybjerg was awarded various grants and prizes from Danish cultural organisations including the Kulturministeriets Designfond, Denmark in 1997.

VAN DER MERWE, Elizabeth Maria (aka Marietjie) (née Botha) (1935–1992)

Van der Merwe was born in 1935 in Zimbabwe. In 1956 she was awarded a teacher's diploma in music and an organist's diploma from the University of Stellenbosch. Her marriage to the sociologist Hendrik Willem van der Merwe in 1957 afforded her further opportunities to travel, study and teach. In 1963 she was awarded her BA in art, then an MA in design, specialising in ceramics, from the University of California, Los Angeles. She worked closely with the American potter Laura Anderson.

In 1963 Van der Merwe returned to South Africa and settled in Grahamstown and later in Cape Town. From 1963 to 1971 she taught ceramics part-time at Rhodes University and at the University of Natal where she was also external examiner in Ceramics. In later years she taught at the Frank Joubert Art Centre in Cape Town and the Cape Town Teachers Training College.

Van der Merwe held her first solo exhibition in Cape Town in 1966. In 1969 she studied at Chicago Art Institute for one year and in 1971 and was appointed a studio consultant at the Rorke's Drift pottery workshop. Here, she made numerous technical changes, including building a new kiln, introducing new raw materials, original designs and decorative schemes. In 1986 she taught raku and spent a year in a Resident Artist programme at Wood Brooke College, England. She also attended conferences in North Carolina and South Dakota.

She designed and supervised the construction of several kilns and wrote articles on her work. She initially worked in stoneware, but in the 1980s

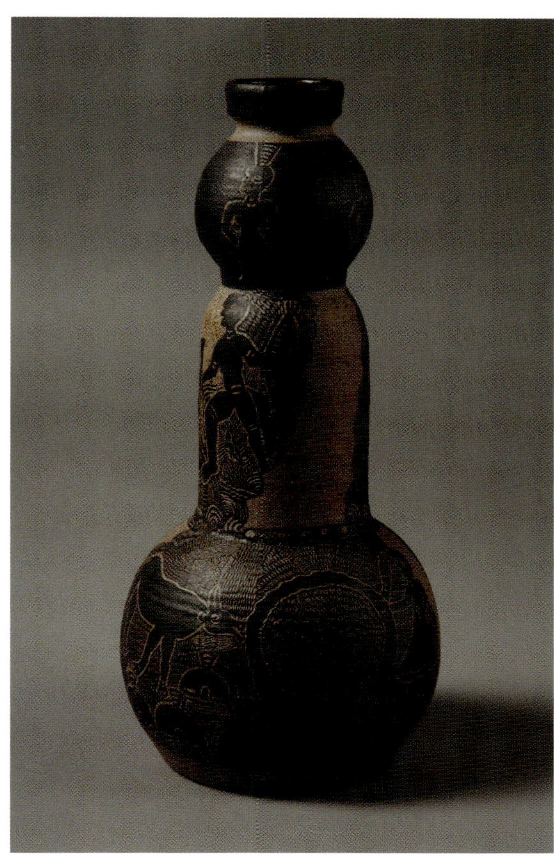

Rorke's Drift | Thrown stoneware vase with painted and incised motifs | 387x174mm | Provenance: WHAG ex Rorke's Drift 3905 | Marks: unglazed base with [oxide] markings, 'L. Mabaso', Rorke's Drift leaf logo, and 'V-11-89' | Photograph by Russell Scott

changed to porcelain. Most of her later pieces were done in very fine vitreous porcelain on the wheel. She retired in the late 1980s as a result of health problems.

Perhaps her most important contribution to South African ceramics was her teaching, technical assistance and mentoring of South African potters.

Van der Merwe has participated in numerous national and international exhibitions including a joint exhibition with Katherine Glenday, The Cameo, Stellenbosch, 1985; and 'Weavings Rorke's Drift and Ceramics - South African Potters', Gallery International, Cape Town, 1979. The previous year and she exhibited 136 stoneware and porcelain works at the same gallery on a joint exhibition with Sonja Gerlings. Van der Merwe exhibited on the 39th International Fair, Florence, Italy, 1975; at 'International Ceramics 1972', Victoria and Albert Museum, London, 1972, and in the USA.

XULU, Aaron (b.1964)

This artist worked briefly at Rorke's Drift as a thrower.

ZIQUBU, Ephraim (1948–2011)

Ziqubu was a senior thrower at Rorke's Drift. He joined in early 1969 and was trained to throw by Peter Tybjerg. In the mid-1970s he participated in a one month training period under Hyme Rabinowitz in Cape Town. Shortly thereafter, Ziqubu left the Pottery to work at Katlehong, but appears to have returned relatively frequently over the years, including between 2007 and 2008.

Nielsen claimed that despite the fact that Ziqubu was illiterate and only spoke Zulu, he was an incredible talented potter and draughtsman. Ziqubu made preliminary drawing on rectangular A4 paper and then skillfully transformed these design onto a round plates.[218] His work was included in All Fired Up... and one of his jugs from 1974 (HG 52645) is currently on display at the DNMCH in the exhibition Objects telling stories: Visual links. For many years his Vessel, 1977 (SACHM94/215) was on permanent display in the ceramics room at the Slave Lodge in Cape Town. His works are found in the Bernstein Collection, University of KwaZulu-Natal, DAG, DNMCH, PAM, SANG, SHC Iziko and TAG.

ZULU, Ivy

Zulu works in the hand-building section at Rorke's Drift.

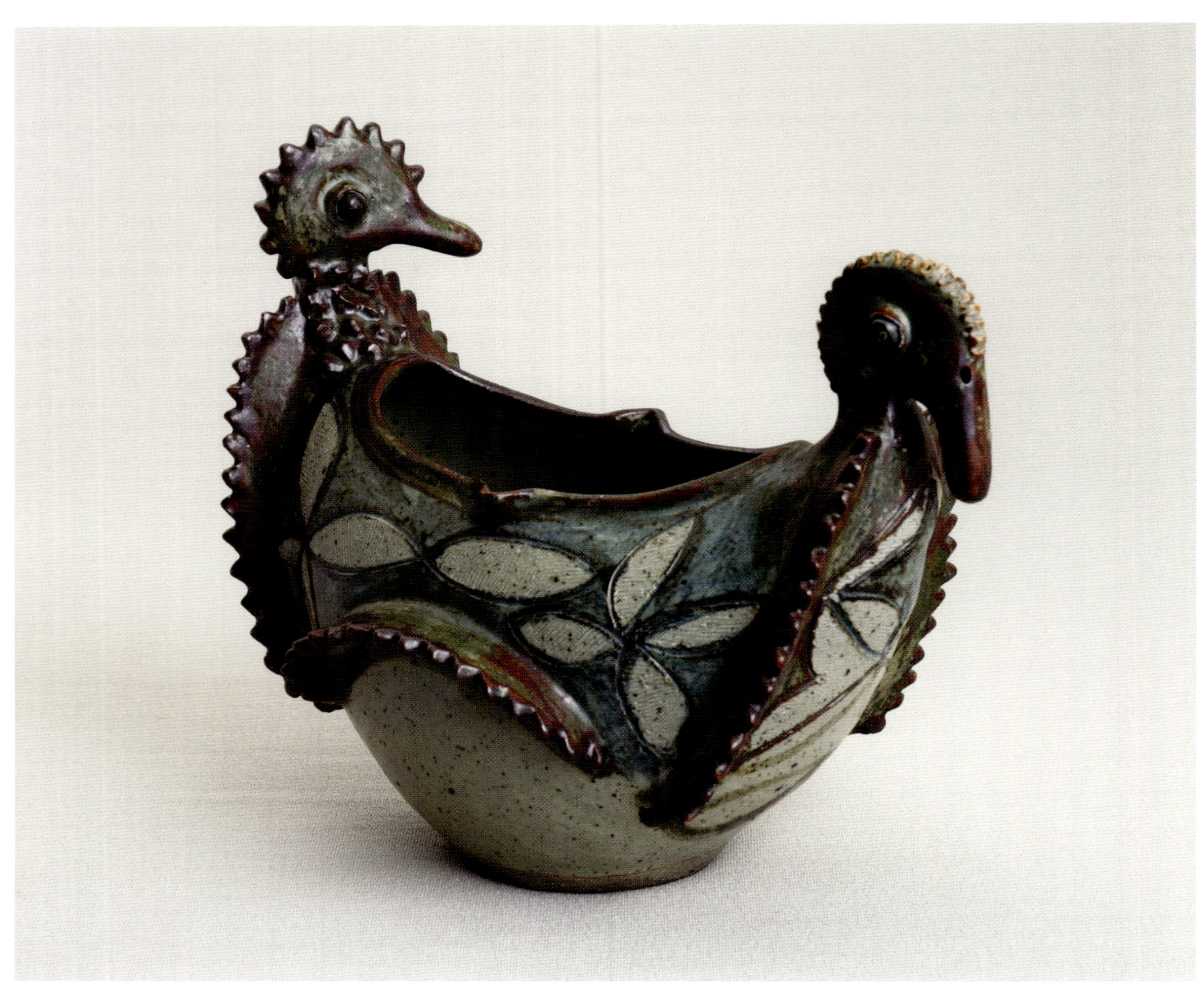

Rorke's Drift | Hand-built stoneware bowl with two bird-head handles | 230x220x170mm | Provenance: TAG | 852/82 | Marks: unglazed base with dark brown [oxide] marks, 'Elizabeth Mbatha T. 80 46' and Rorke's Drift leaf logo | Photograph by Natalie Field

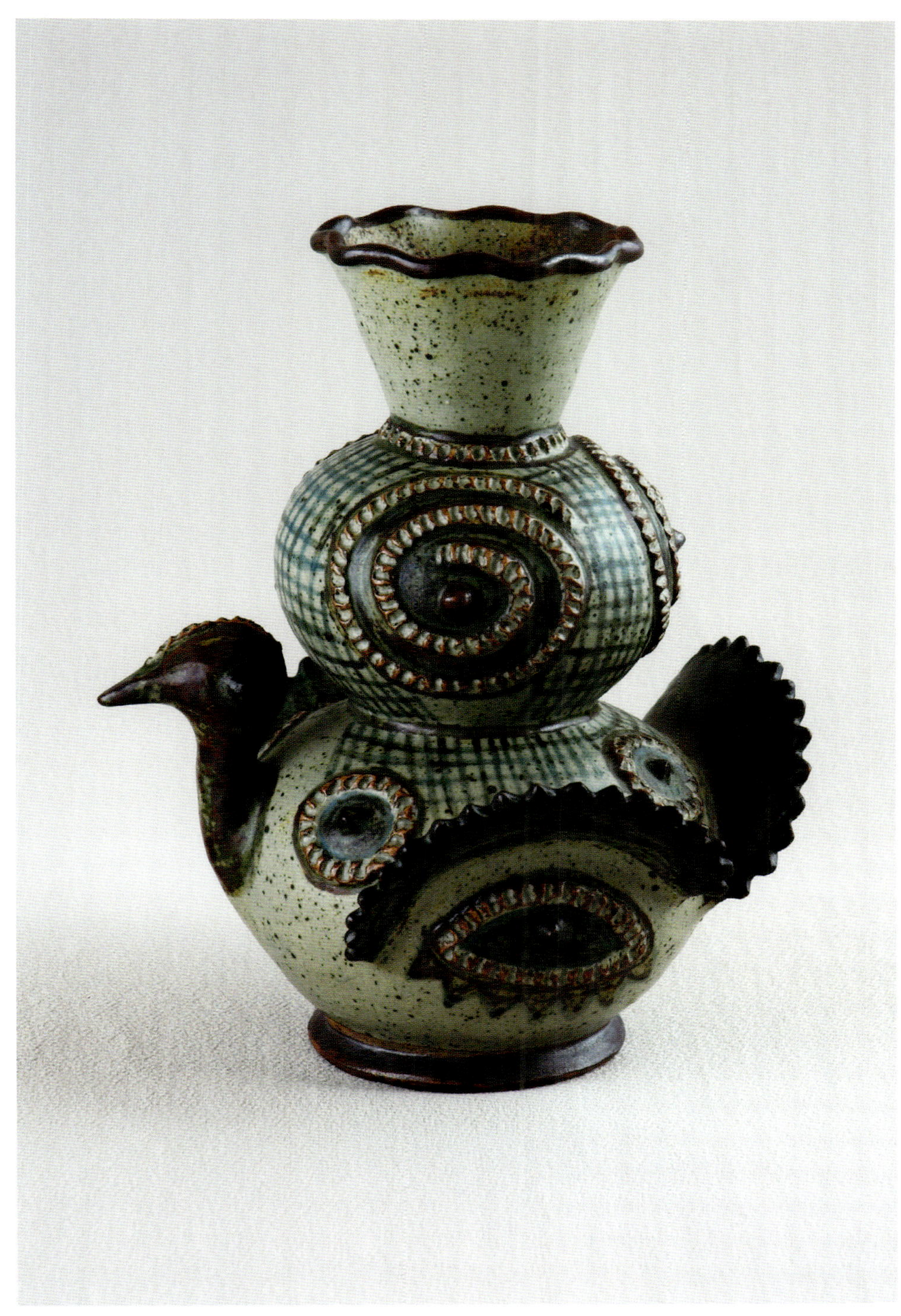

Rorke's Drift | Hand-built stoneware vase with bird head | 233x82mm | Provenance: SHC Iziko | 94/216 | Marks: unglazed base with [oxide] marks, 'Euriel Mbatha. F.114.84.' and Rorke's Drift leaf logo | Photograph by Natalie Field

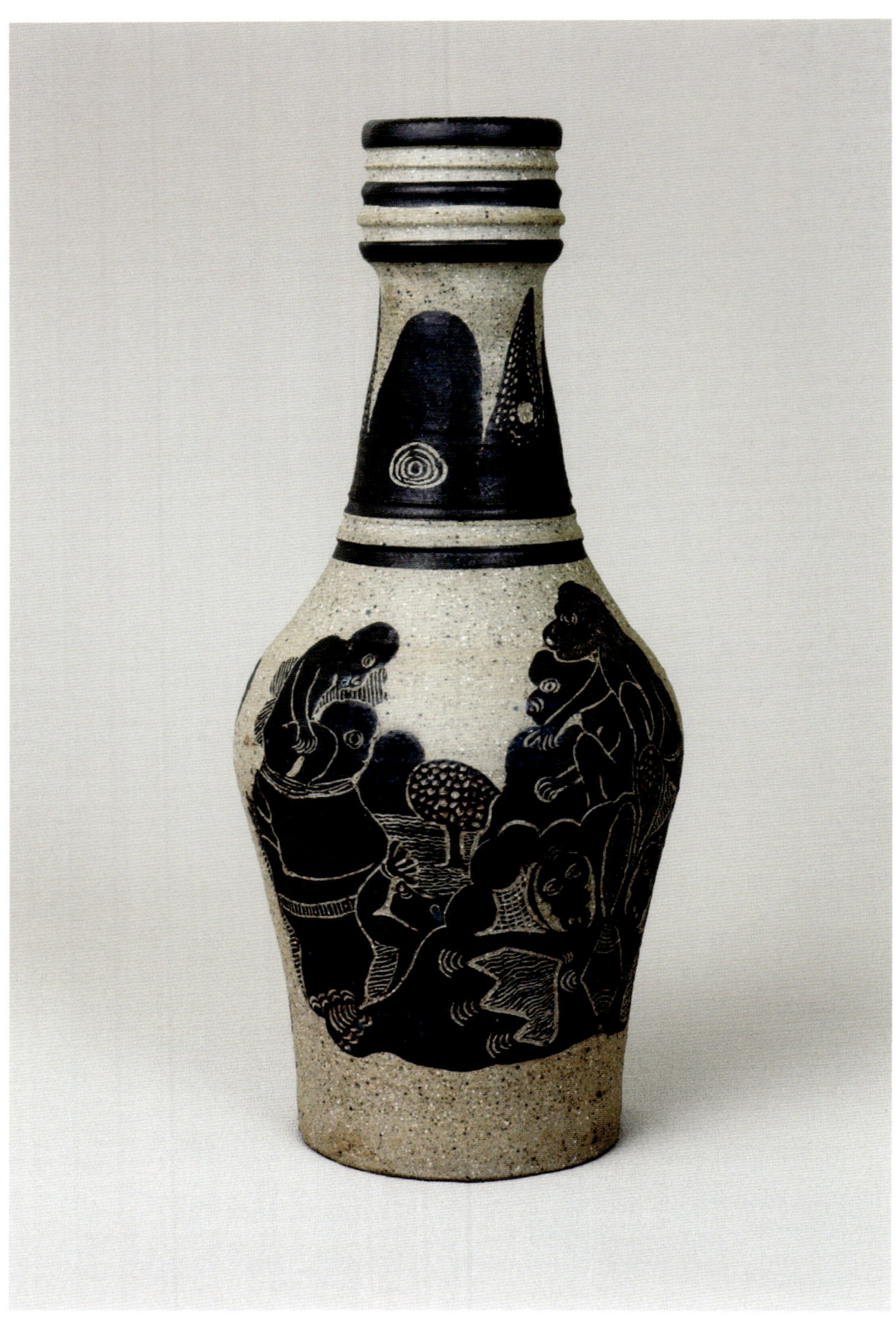

Rorke's Drift | Thrown stoneware bottle-shaped vase | Decorated with painted dark brown oxide | Motifs also features incised sgraffito details | 377x70x112mm | Provenance: TAG | 854/87 | Marks: unglazed base with dark brown [oxide] marks, 'J. Sibisi. V-3- 86' and Rorke's Drift leaf logo | Photograph by Natalie Field

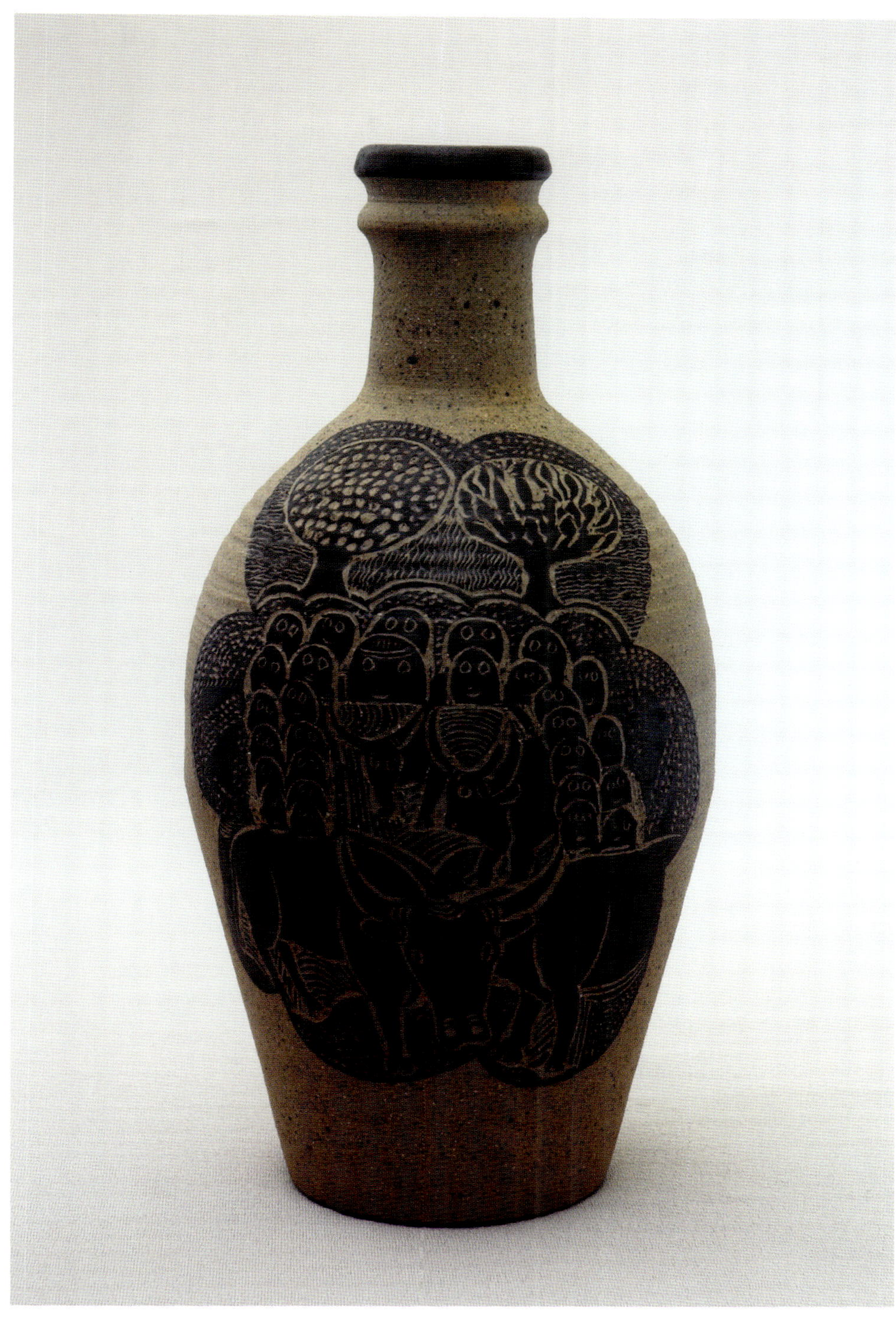

Rorke's Drift | Thrown stoneware bottle-shaped vase decorated with painted and incised motifs of cattle in dark brown oxide | 330x55x90mm | Provenance: TAG | Marks: unglazed base with dark brown [oxide] marks, 'J. Sibisi. Z-22- 867 and Rorke's Drift leaf logo | Additional information: exhibited on Ubumba (TAG, DAG 1998) and Jabulisa 2006 (TAG, etc.) | Photograph by Natalie Field

Silwood Ceramics (1950–1962)

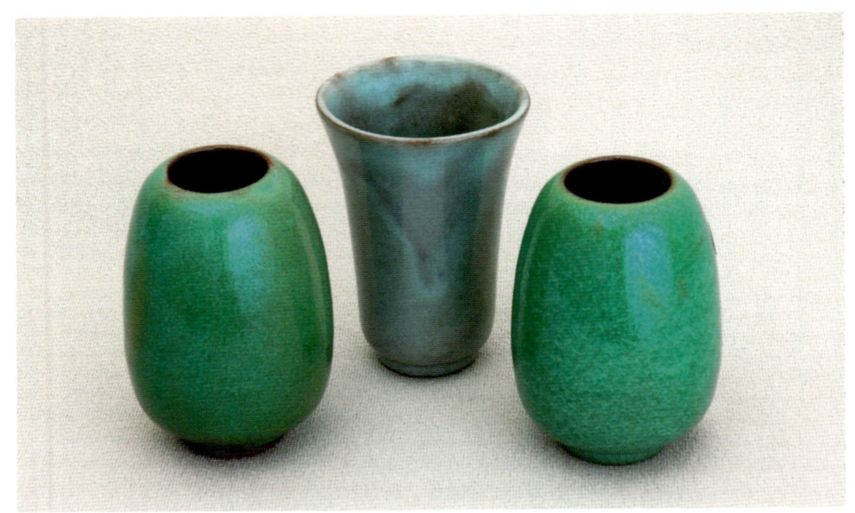

Silwood Ceramics was founded by Dr G H B Lovell,[219] his wife Mrs B M Lovell[220] and their friend J B Livesey[221] in 1950 in a small building, formerly used for growing mushrooms, in Silwood Road, Bramley, Johannesburg. In 1951 the enterprise moved to industrial premises in Kramerville, Johannesburg.

Silwood manufactured artistic pottery, particularly miniatures, some of which feature metal fittings, such as tankards, cruet and condiment sets. It initially used terracotta clay, but later replaced it with white-bodied clay. G H B Lovell designed the vast majority of Silwood's wares. In 1951 the artist Eduardo Villa designed a few items. Wares were cast in moulds or formed on the potter's wheel. Mr Herman A J Smit, an experienced potter, was employed by Silwood Ceramics in 1951 as a potter and mould-maker. Most wares were glazed in a single colour, and were not decorated. The wares did not have any characteristic factory marks, but the name 'Silwood Ware' was printed on a sticker attached to the item.

In 1955 Lovell became disabled and was forced to relinquish his position to Livesey. The pottery was acquired by Flora Ann Pottery in 1962. In 1965 Flora Ann/Silwood was acquired by Liebermann Pottery and Tiles. At this time the pottery was producing slip-cast vases that were decorated with decals of the English countryside and were sold by African traders.

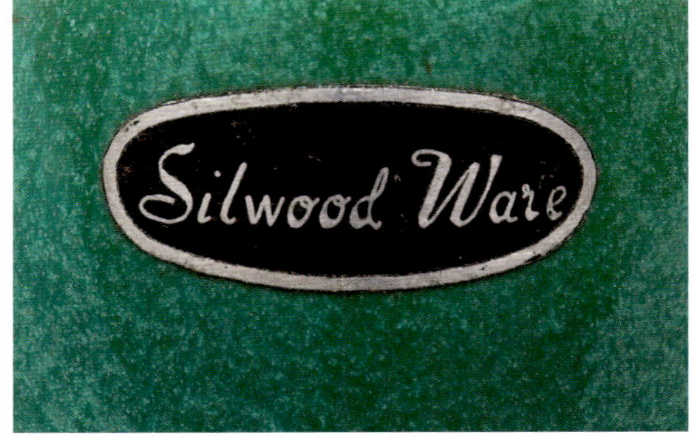

TOP: Silwood Ware | Three small vases | From left: 87x25x33mm; 88x57x28mm, 87x25x33mm | Provenance: Douglas van der Horst | Marks: first and third are marked with sticker, Silwood Ware | Photograph by Natalie Field

LEFT: Silwood Ware | Maker's mark | Sticker | Black with silver text, 'Silwood Ware' | Photograph by Natalie Field

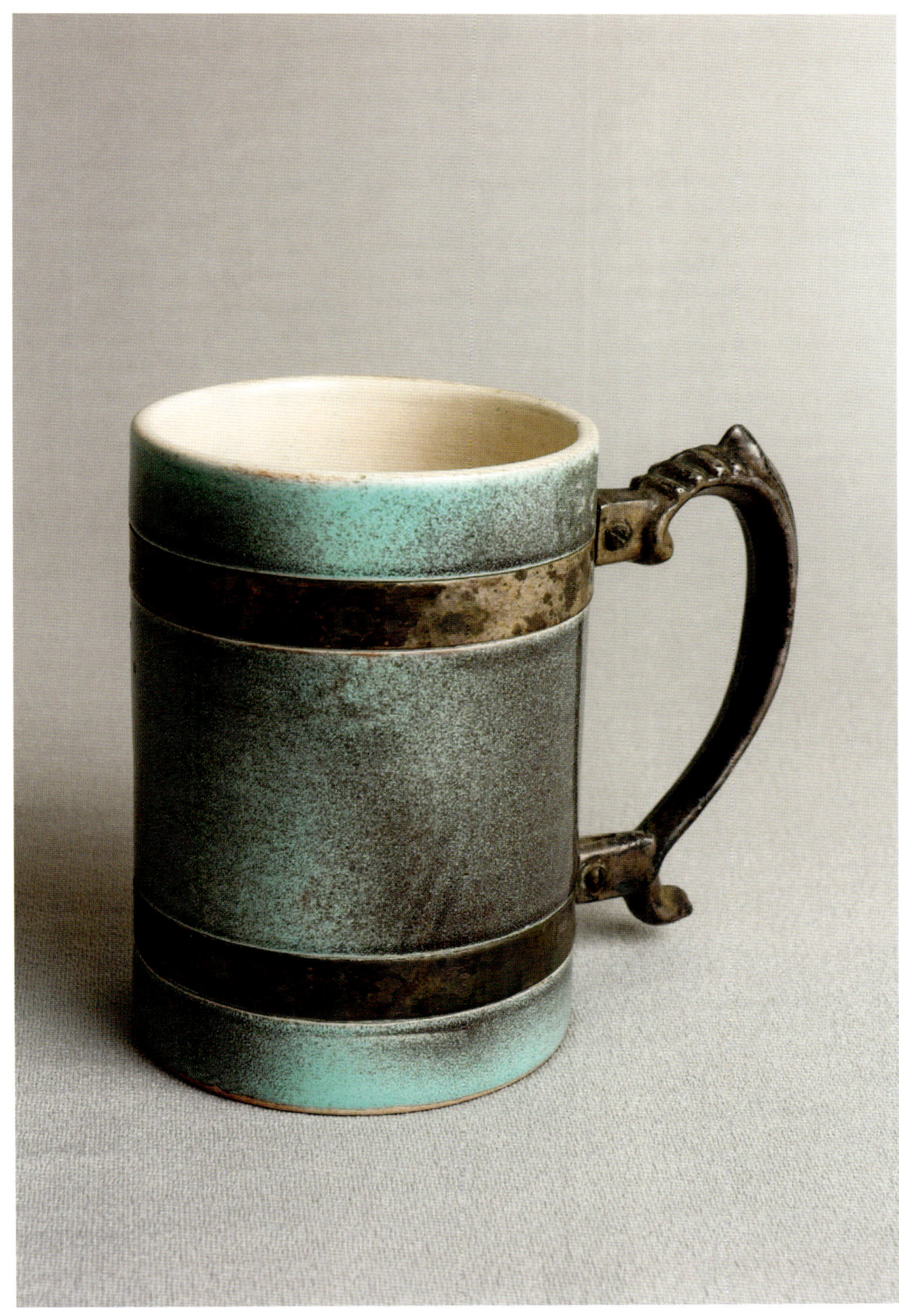

Silwood Ware | Tankard with turquoise glaze and metal handle | 132x90x90mm | Provenance: TAG | Accession number: 2433/06 | Marks: glazed base, black-and-silver sticker, 'Silwood Ware' | Photograph by Natalie Field

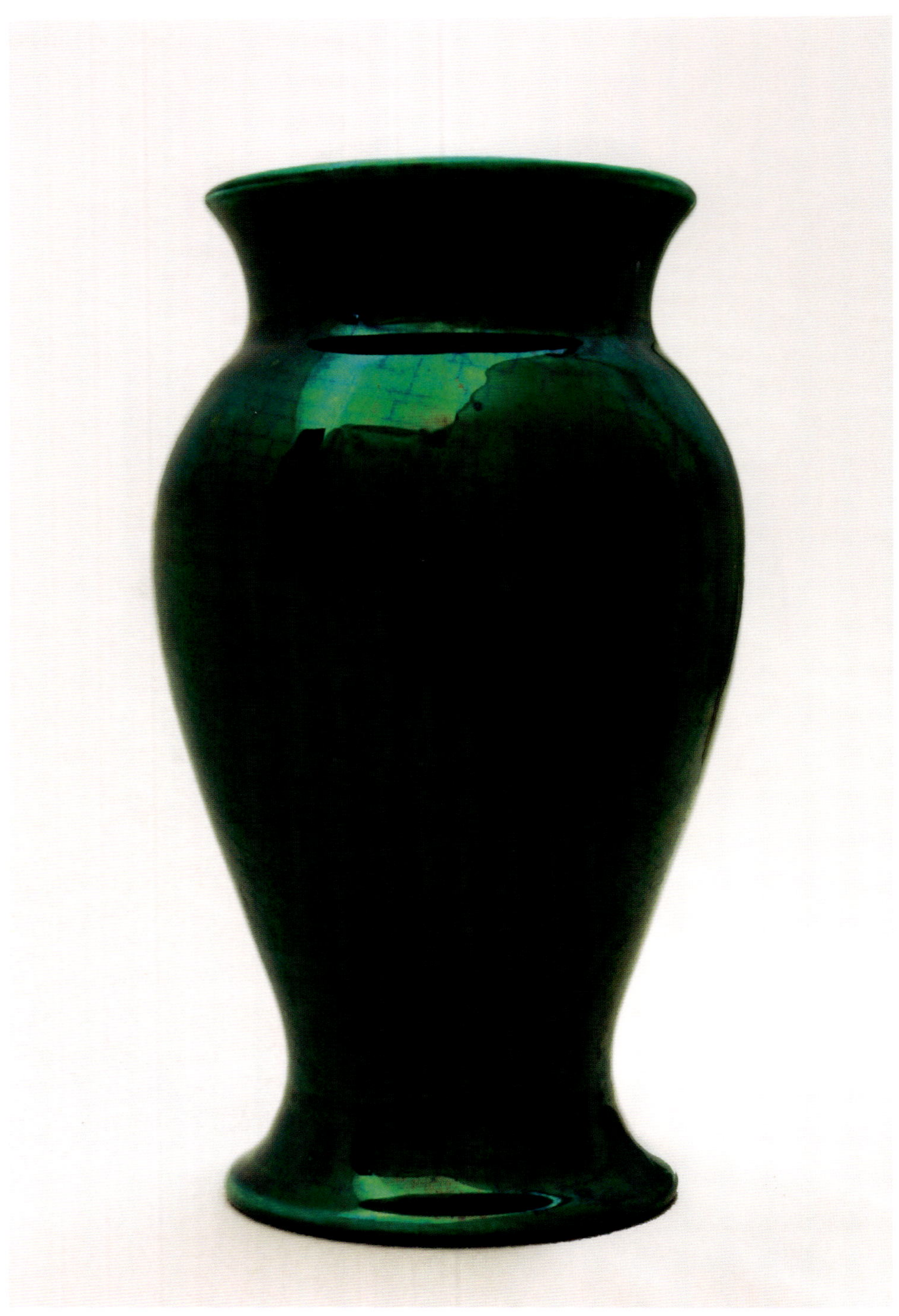

Silwood Ware | Green vase | 235x108x100mm | Provenance: Douglas van der Horst | Marks: printed 'Silwood' mark on base, 'Silwood Ware' sticker on shoulder | Photograph by Natalie Field

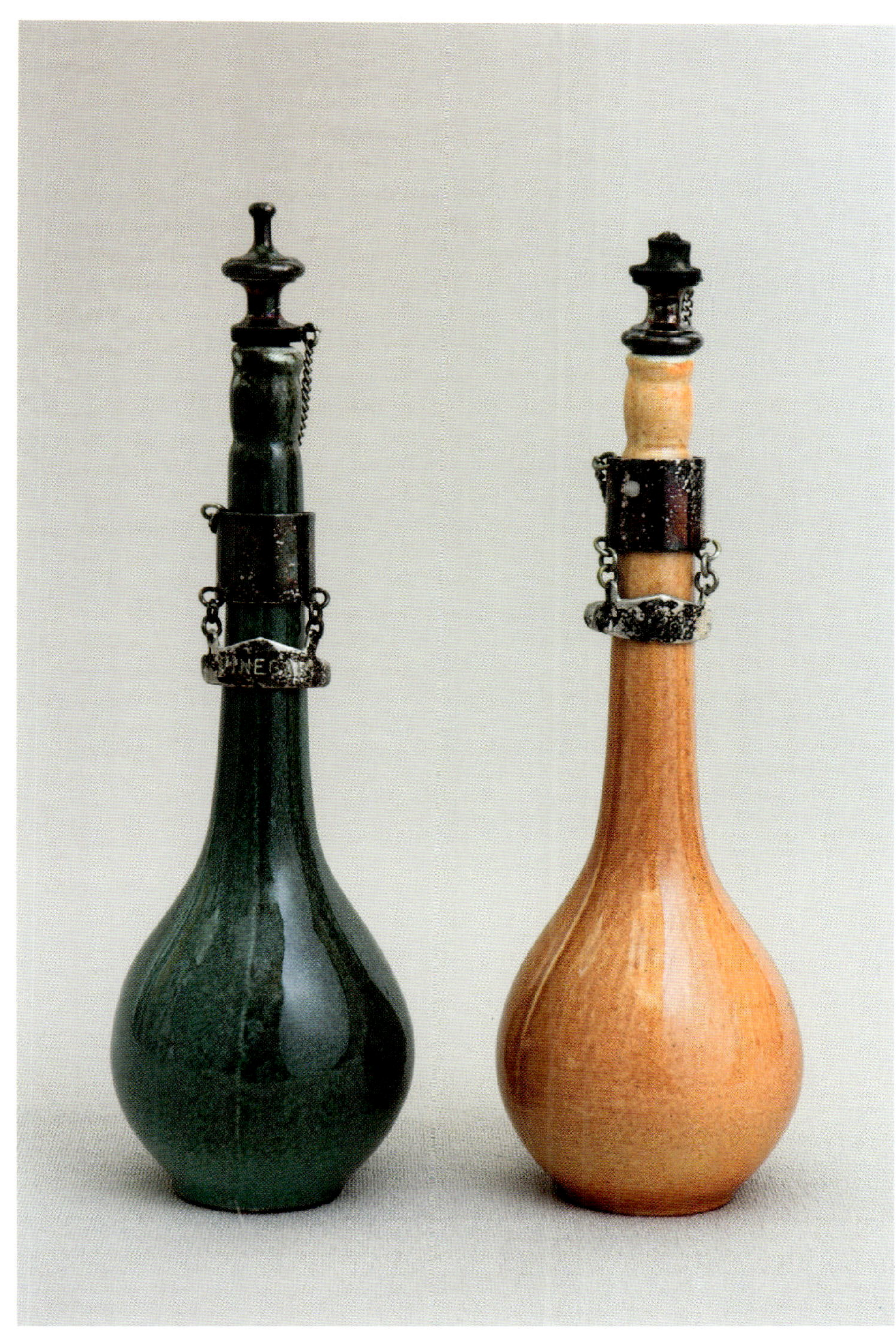

Silwood Ware | Set of cruets with metal [possibly pewter] fittings | 230x15x37mm | Provenance: TAG | orange 2419/06 | Marks: orange glazed base with black-and-silver sticker marked, 'Silwood Ware', green glazed base with black-and-silver sticker marked, 'Silwood Ware' | Photograph by Natalie Field

South African Glazing Company, Boksburg East Potteries, Lucia Ware and Joy China (1945–late 1950s)

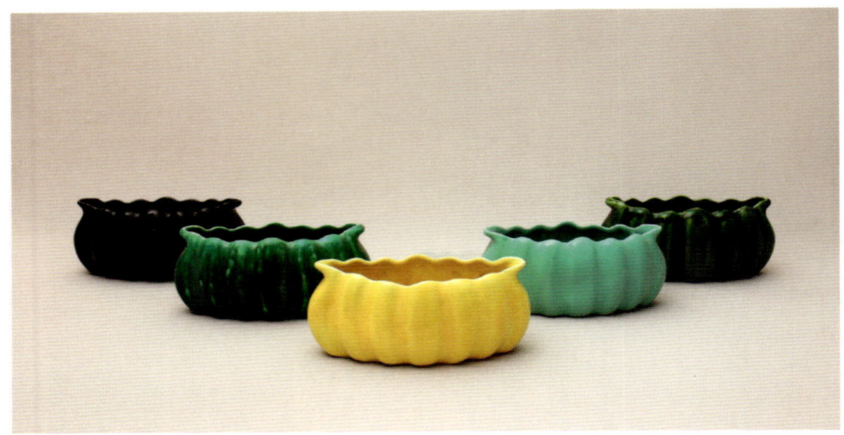

Lucia Ware & Joy China | Set of five scalloped vases | 80x165x145x55mm | Provenance: Douglas van der Horst | Marks: from left back: [black] unmarked [green] embossed mark 'Joy-China KO56' [yellow] embossed mark 'Lucia 3301' [blue] embossed mark 'Lucia 3301' [dark green] embossed mark 'Lucia Ware 486' | Photograph by Natalie Field

Location

Boksburg, Gauteng

Founders and managers

The South African Glazing Company (SAG) was established in 1945 to sell processed minerals for clays and glazes. SAG established a subsidiary, Boksburg East Potteries (BEP) that same year, directed by Leslie Lulofs, Krige and Hoseck. Archival documents from 1959 indicate that Lulofs became the managing director.

Staff

Certain decorators are identified by their initials marked on the bases of wares including CH, BN, MP, PH, JHK, TWR, J, JLK, SG, TUP, DPJ, RvM and TvN.

Wares manufactured

SAG initially manufactured ceramic wall tiles and electrical porcelain (ceramic insulators for railway and telephone lines). From 1947 it produced a limited amount of white 'fancy goods' such as slip-cast crockery and miniature vases. From 1950, they started producing domestic teapots, milk jugs, egg cups and several other utility articles (Thornton 1973:13, 14). An extensive range of glaze colours was used, including gold. BEP initially manufactured only white teapots and jugs. The pottery later made a small quantity of hand-decorated 'artistic' wares, including vases in the shape of a gondola and a conch shell. Lucia Ware predominantly manufactured monochromatic ornaments and vases. These articles were often produced in a variety of different sizes, e.g. the fish, an elaborate shoe and antelope ornaments, so that 'family' compositions could be formed. A limited range of stock glaze colours was used on these articles. Lucia Ware also produced some more complex wares, including imitation Delft vases and tankards and some other intricate hand-decorated wares. These pseudo-Delft vases bear typical Dutch landscapes with windmills, canals and

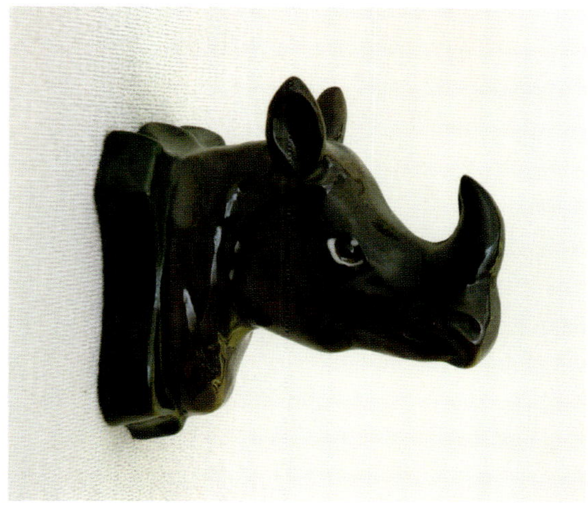

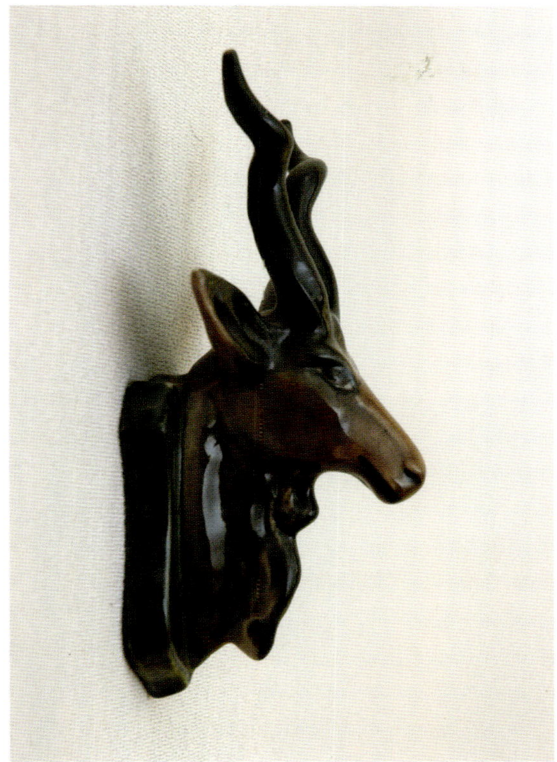

Lucia Ware | Ornaments in the form of a trophy rhino and kudu head | rhino: 65x67x78mm kudu: 145[including horns]x55x60mm | Provenance: Jan Middeljans | Marks: base glazed with transparent glaze with embossed mould marks, 'Lucia 3322' (rhino) and 'Lucia 3320' (kudu) | Photographs by Natalie Field

small sailing boats. In the mid-1950s Lucia Ware produced a rather fine series of small trophy heads of indigenous animals, including a springbok, buffalo, hippo, lion, rhino and kudu. The skilfully cast and painted ornaments were packed in attractive packaging with a transparent lid, and were marketed as ideal souvenirs for tourists. Lucia Ware produced some other relatively skilfully modelled, hand-painted ornaments and figurines including a camel, a wall hanging containing a boy pirate, a hornbill, a canary on a branch, a young girl with an elaborate layered dress, a provocatively posed oriental dancer and a seated young girl holding a dog. It also made a limited quantity of hand-decorated wares for corporate clients, e.g. Blumberg and Kleinman commissioned articles decorated with the image of a leaping springbok in the African bushveld (illustration p.371). Hand-decorated wares often include the initials of the decorator. The quality of draughtsmanship of many of the decorators ranges from entertainingly naïve to extremely poor.

Production methods

BEP and Lucia wares were slip-cast. Some Lucia items are crudely modelled on Crown Devon, Royal Doulton, Wedgewood and Beswick originals. Both potteries struggled with technical problems and a lack of quality control is evident. Lucia Ware and Joy China display a regrettably high percentage of poorly finished wares. Crude mould seams, glaze flaws (such as bubbles or uneven cover), excessively heavy forms and numerous other imperfections are common features of Lucia Ware.

Brief history of the pottery

SAG and BEP both produced domestic ware, although SAG also produced industrial wares. According to a 1954 report of the Cape Chamber of Commerce, BEP exclusively manufactured white teapots and jugs. However, over time this changed, and BEP also produced vases and domestic wares (known as BEP Ware).

BEP was divided into at least two subsidiaries, Lucia Ware and Joy China, both producing domestic and decorative wares. Lucia Ware was especially prolific, and by 1953 its adverts claimed that the pottery produced over 400 different designs – a significant achievement so soon after its establishment! Indeed, this variety of different designs was made possible by the fact that moulds were shared between the companies, with the result that the same item may be found with different company marks.[222] Vermont, BEP Ware, Lucia Ware and Joy China share similar mould number fonts and mould numbers. Some Vermont wares resemble Lucia and BEP items, while other items are far more refined, being competently manufactured and decorated. The author is aware of an article bearing a BEP mark and a Vermont sticker, suggesting an association between the two companies.

Various informants proclaim different demises for Boksburg East Potteries. According to Perold, the company was taken over by, and incorporated into,

SA Glazing, the parent company. Middeljans argues that Lucia Ware was taken over by Maiolica Pottery, Johannesburg, and that its moulds were recycled by Maiolica Pottery. He adds that Maiolica also took over Faiarte Potteries, Rustenburg, and that Faiarte moulds occasionally bear the name Lucia and feature mould numbers that surpass 10 000.[223] Regardless of the finer details of its demise, the company became a veritable institution on the cultural landscape, with a large and loyal customer base. It became *the* major mass producer of popular pottery, especially vases and ornaments. By enabling a large proportion of South Africans to decorate their home with inexpensive and popular ornaments, BEP and Lucia Ware's colourful cornucopia offered many the possibility of creating an illusion of a certain sophistication, luxury, belongingness, adventure and cultural identity.

Marks

South African Glazing Company

While most wares are unmarked, some have a sticker and others contain a dual mark, 'S.A. Glazing and Lucia Ware'. Some items were simply marked SAG.

BEP

- BEP ware has different moulded marks on the base, including 'Bep ware', 'BEP' or 'B.E.P.' Some BEP ware has additional marks, which may be mould numbers, e.g. 'MP028', '4600', '5014 16'.
- Rare artistic BEP ware specimens include a cast mark and an additional 'hand-painted' glaze mark.
- Some BEP is marked with a black-and-silver sticker in the form of an inverted triangle, 'VITREOUS CHINA BEP WARE'.

Lucia Ware

- Lucia Ware is marked on the base by bas-relief moulded lettering, 'Lucia Ware' or 'Lucia'. Most Lucia ware has a moulded number, e.g. '2502/06'.
- Some Lucia ware has additional painted marks, such as numerical elements, the initials of a decorator or the name of the commissioning agent, e.g. 'JHK Hand painted for Blumberg and Kleinman', 'Delftsblue [sic] Handpainted 224 TWR.'
- At least two different Lucia stickers were used to indicate provenance.
- Some wares display both BEP and Lucia marks.
- Some wares display both SAG and Lucia marks.

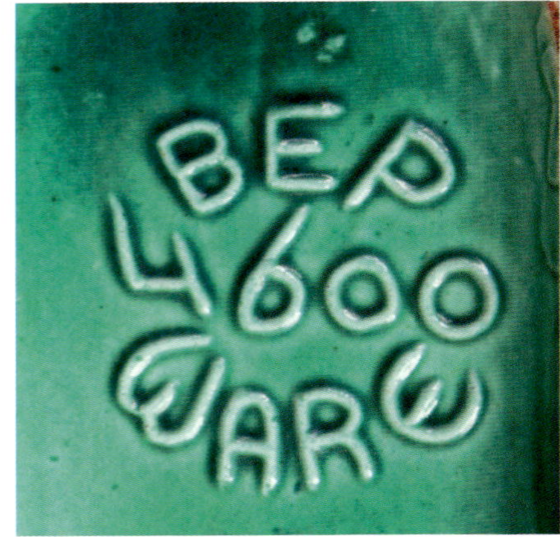

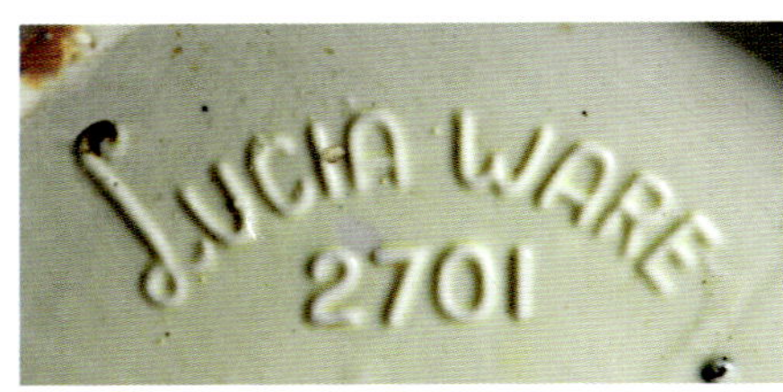

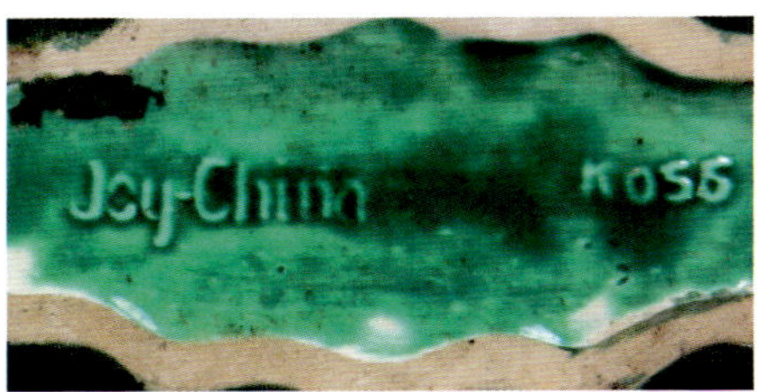

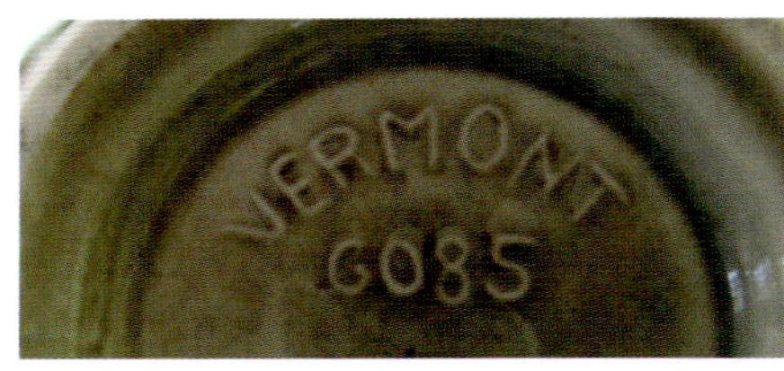

TOP: BEP Ware | Maker's mark | Raised relief moulded letters, 'Bep Ware 4600' | Photograph by Natalie Field

SECOND FROM TOP: Lucia Ware | Maker's marks | Raised relief moulded letters, 'Lucia Ware 2701' | Photograph by Natalie Field

SECOND FROM BOTTOM: Joy China | Maker's marks | Raised relief moulded letters, 'Joy China K 056' | Photograph by Natalie Field

BOTTOM: Vermont | Maker's mark | Raised relief moulded letters, 'Vermont G180' | Photograph by Natalie Field

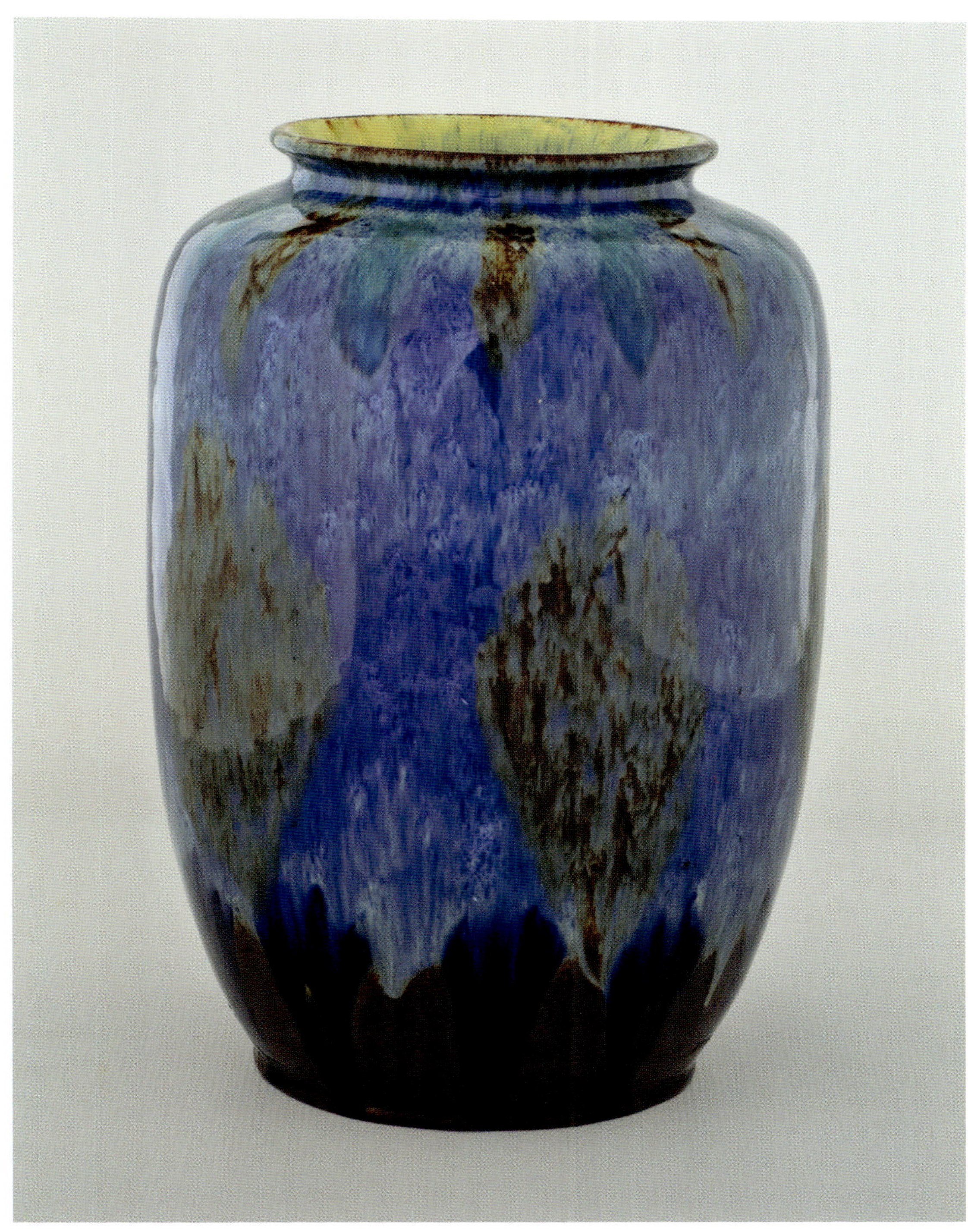

Lucia Ware | Vase | H 341 Height, Diam 230, Width of lip 152 diam, Width of lip 152 diam Provenance: TAG | 2030/oc | Marks: Relief inscription under the glaze on cream base: 'Lucia Ware' in semi-circle | Photograph by Roger O'Neil, © TAG

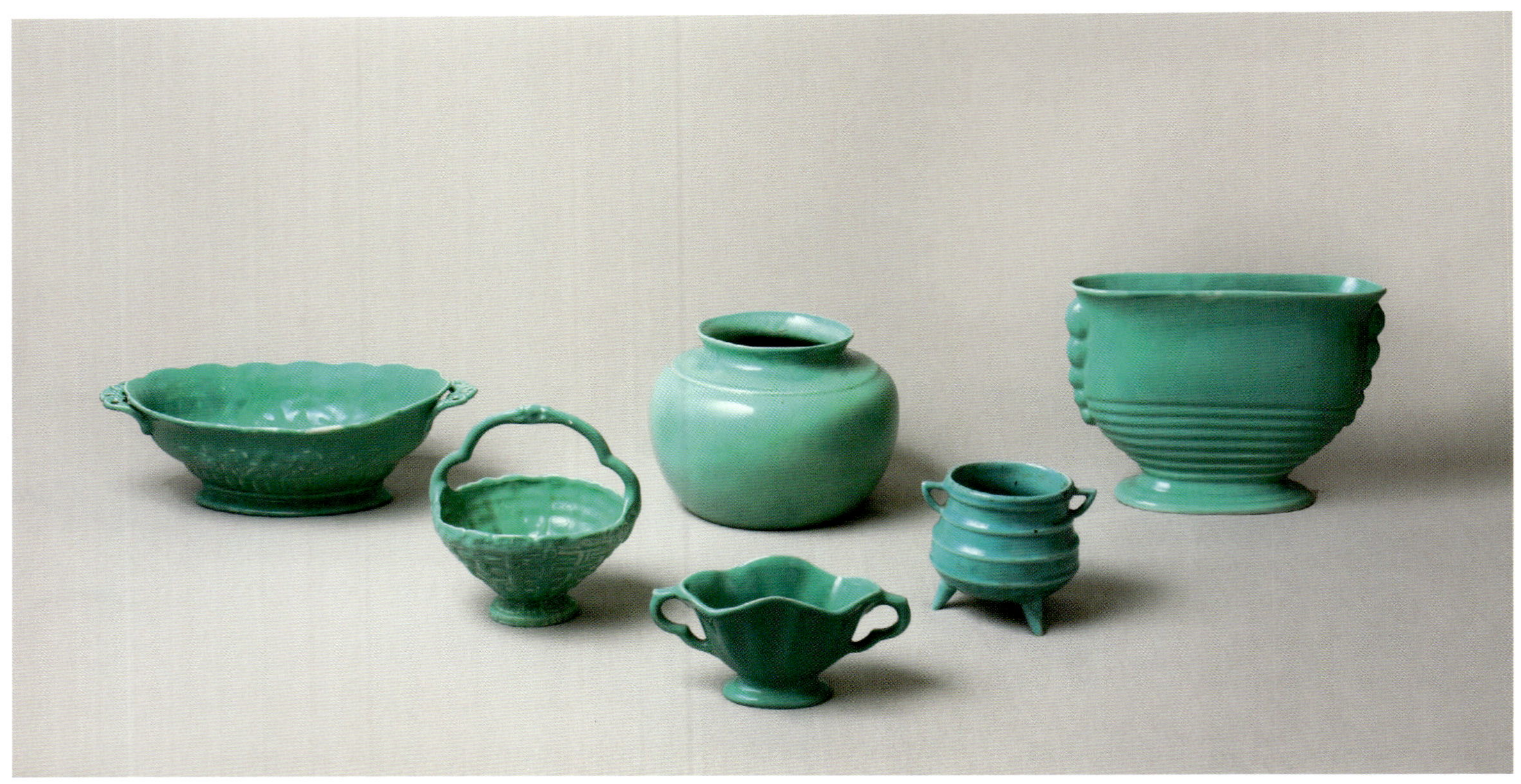

Lucia Ware | Group of six turquoise glazed vases and ornaments | Front: small vase with handles 84x124x75x65x50mm; 2nd row from left: small basket 164x125x140x60mm; three-legged cooking pot 105x85mm; back row: large open basket form 105x254x175mm; rounded vase 150x125x133mm; flat vase with ornamental handles 190x250xrimx81x160x95mm | Provenance: TAG | 2521/06; 2506/06; 24806/06; 2471/06; 2506/06; 2508/06; 2478/06 | Marks: turquoise glazed base with embossed mould marks beneath the glaze, 'Lucia 2504'; 2nd row from left: small basket, turquoise glazed base with impressed mould marks beneath the glaze, 'Lucia Ware, 380'; three-legged cooking pot, turquoise glazed base with embossed mould marks beneath the glaze, 3103; back row: large open basket form, turquoise glazed base with embossed mould marks beneath the glaze, 'Lucia 8402'; flat vase with ornamental handles, turquoise glazed base with indistinct embossed mould marks beneath the glaze, resembling 'Lucia' and four digits; flat vase with ornamental handles, turquoise glazed base with embossed mould marks beneath the glaze, 'Lucia Ware 9903' | Photograph by Natalie Field

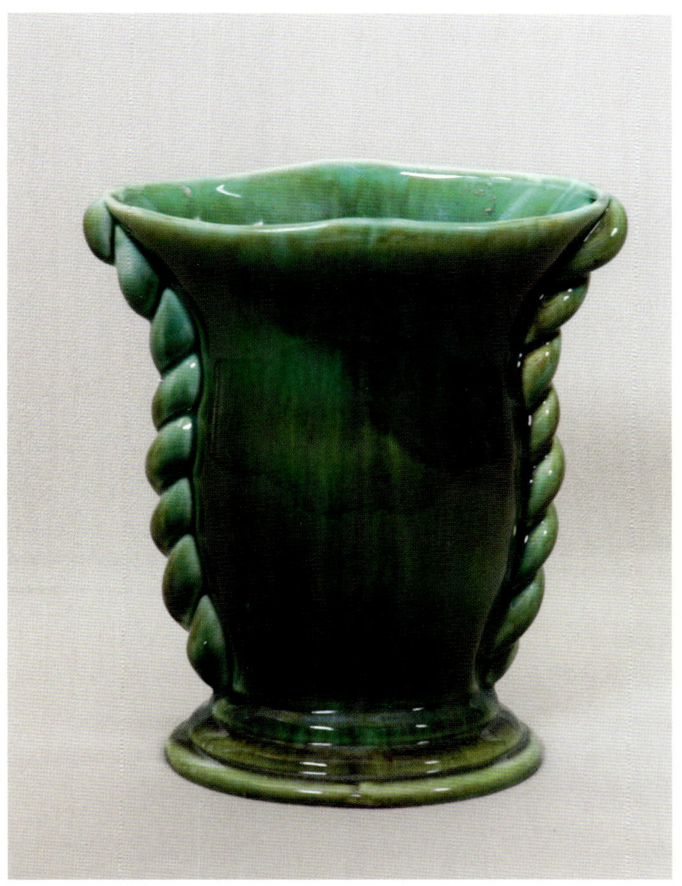

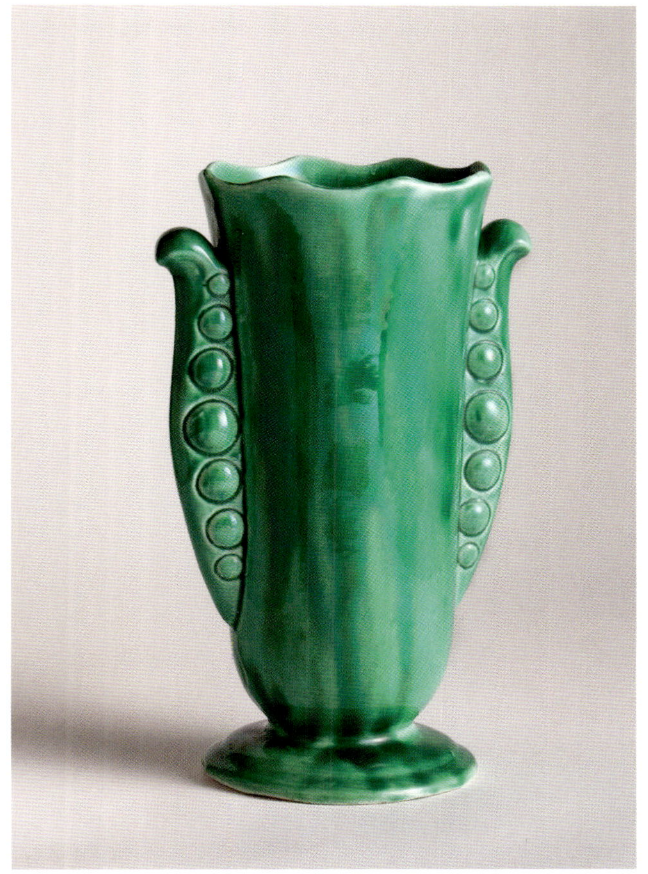

LEFT: Joy China | Large vase with twisted cord-like handles 253x205x128x157x127mm | Provenance: TAG | 2512/06 | Marks: green glazed base with embossed mould marks beneath the glaze, 'Joy China K071' | Additional information: Mould seams and glaze bubbles evident | Photograph by Natalie Field

RIGHT: Joy China | Green vase with ornamental handles that resemble pea pods | 270x120x117mm | Provenance: Wendy Gers | Marks: green glazed base, relief cast markings, 'Joy China K 095' | Photograph by Damien Artus

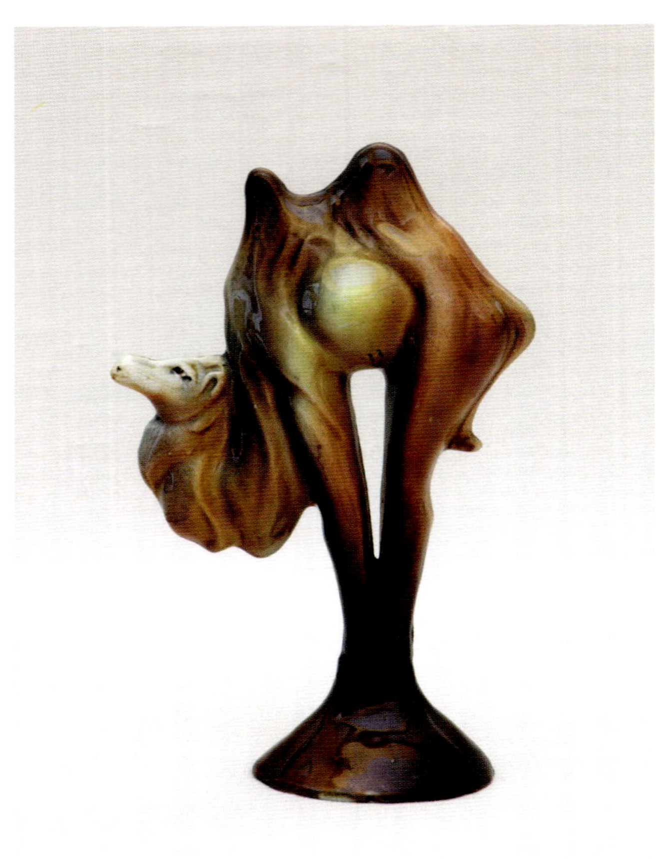

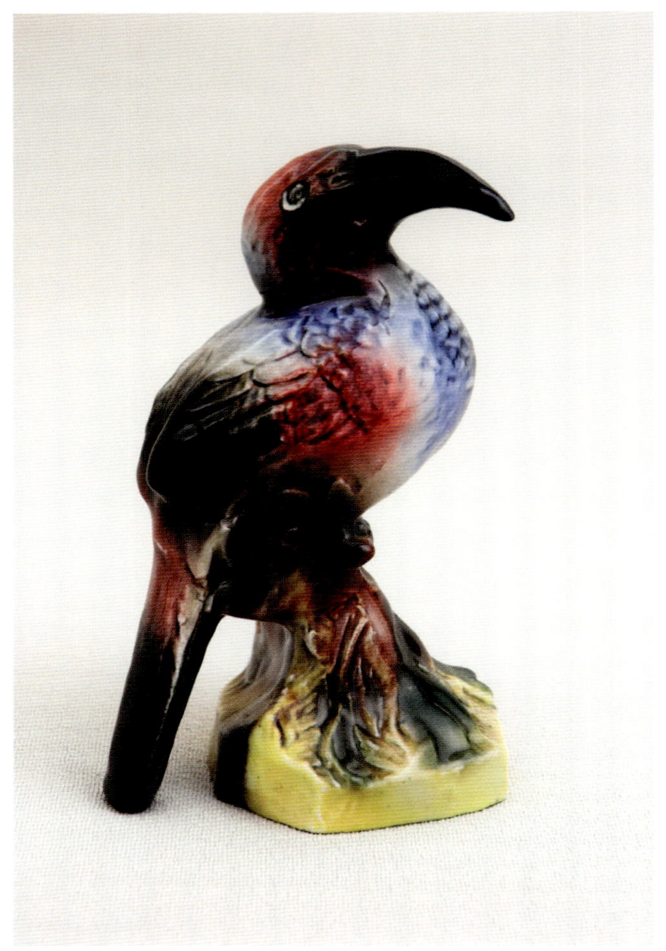

LEFT: Lucia Ware | Camel ornament | 260x170x85x905mm | Provenance: TAG | 2505/06 | Marks; transparent glazed base with embossed mould marks under the glaze, 'Lucia 6602' | Additional information: ornament very heavy and has numerous glaze bubbles | Photograph by Natalie Field

RIGHT: Lucia Ware | Ornament in the form of a hornbill, item sprayed with multiple colours of glaze, eyes also delicately hand painted | 150x90x88mm | Provenance: TAG | 2499/06 | Marks: transparent glazed base with embossed mould marks under the glaze, 'Lucia 6011' | Additional information: decoration very labour intensive | Photograph by Natalie Field

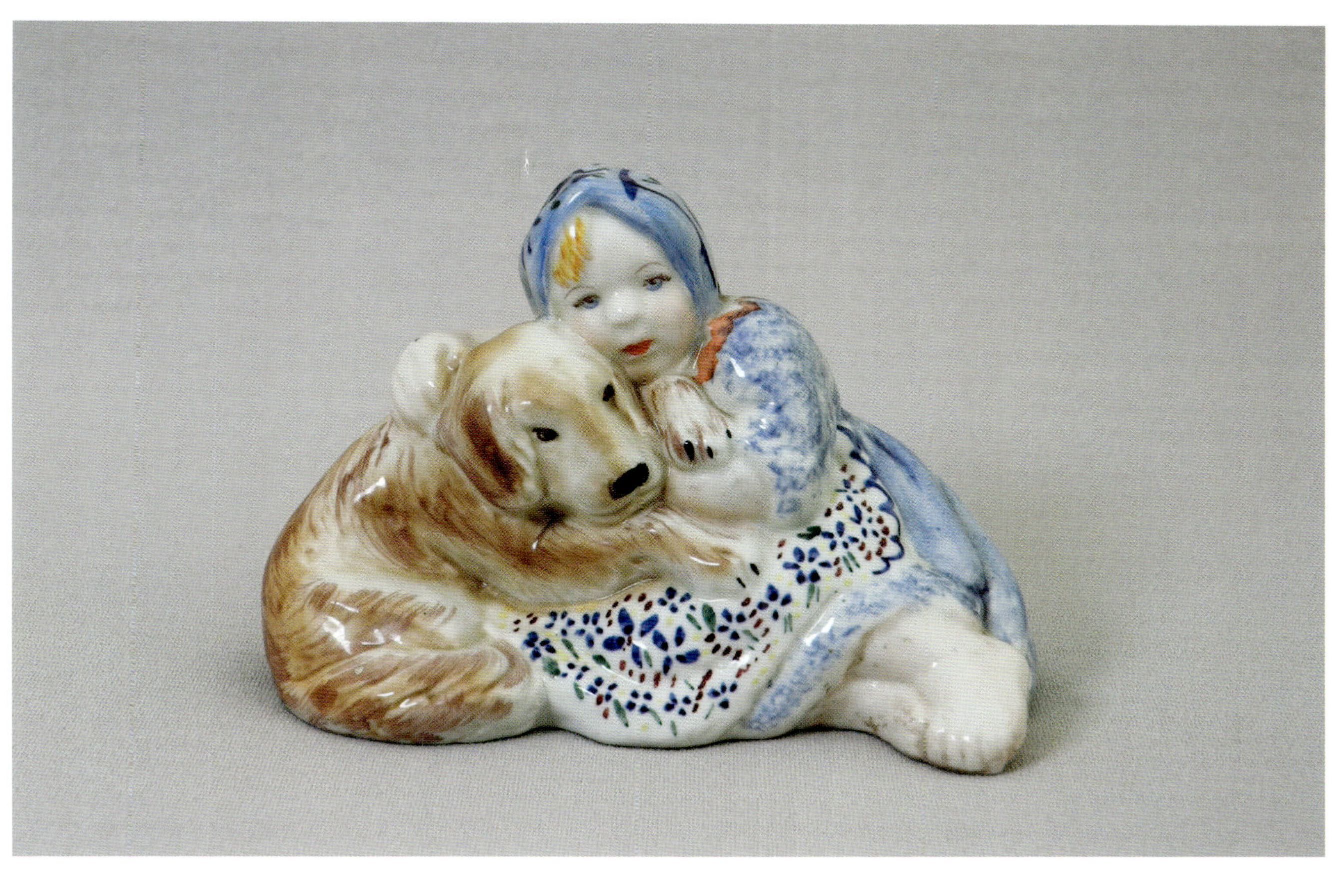

Lucia Ware | Ornament of a seated girl holding a dog | 150x175x90mm | Provenance: De Kamper and Welman Collection | Marks: unglazed white base with embossed mould marks, 'Lucia Ware 1014' | Photograph by Natalie Field

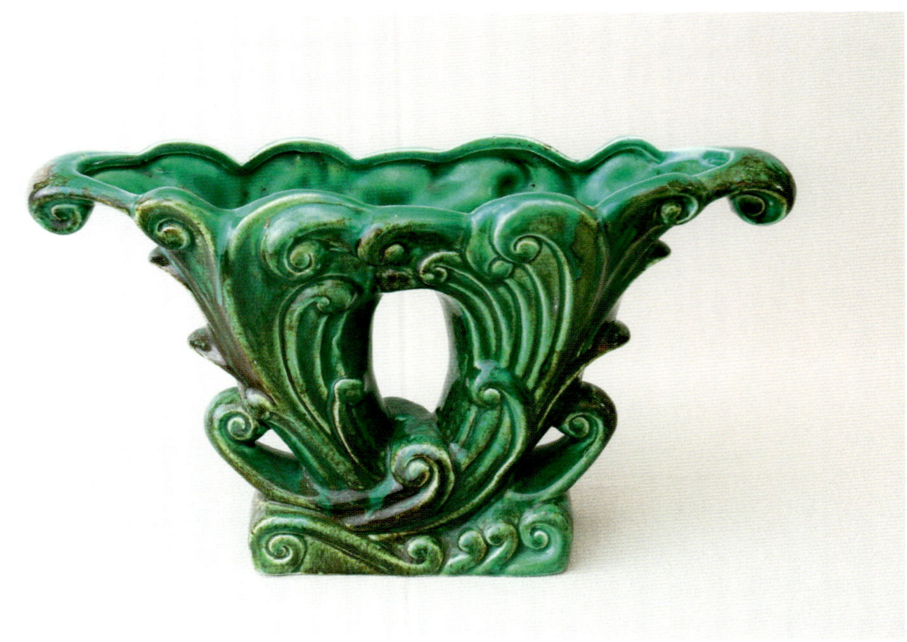

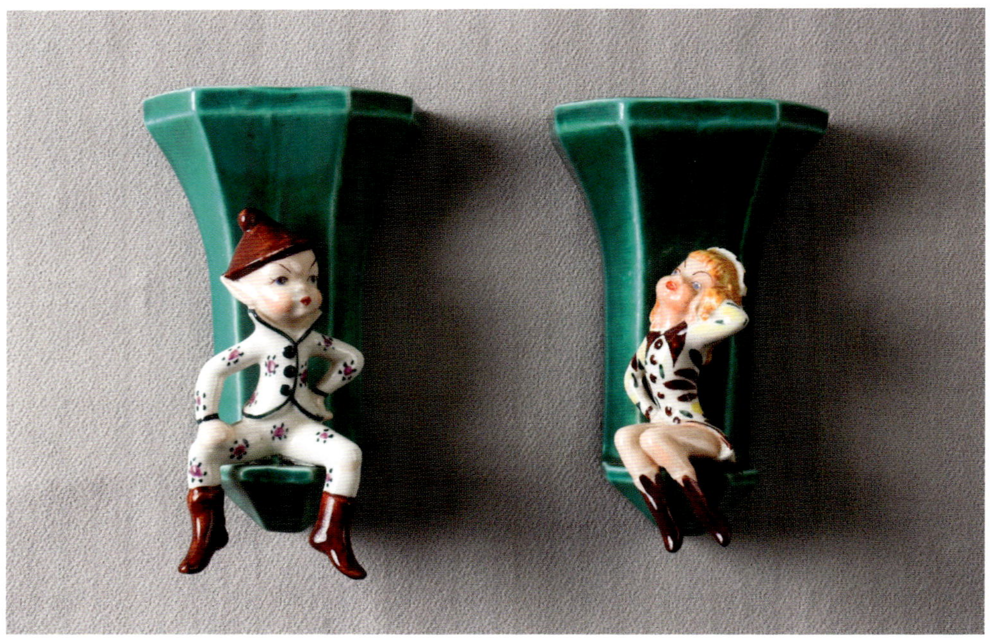

TOP: Vermont | Vase with elaborate moulded swirling decorated elements | 195x322x100mm | Provenance: Prof. Mark Watson | Marks: moulded, embossed marks, 'Vermont, G180' | Photograph by Natalie Field

BOTTOM: Lucia Ware | Pair of wall pocket vases with male and female pixie figurines on their bases | 160x97x72mm | Provenance: TAG | male pixie 2513/06; female pixie 2511/06 | Marks: green glazed base with embossed mould marks under the glaze, 'Lucia 7004'; Red pencil marks, 'A226 L/A' | Photograph by Natalie Field

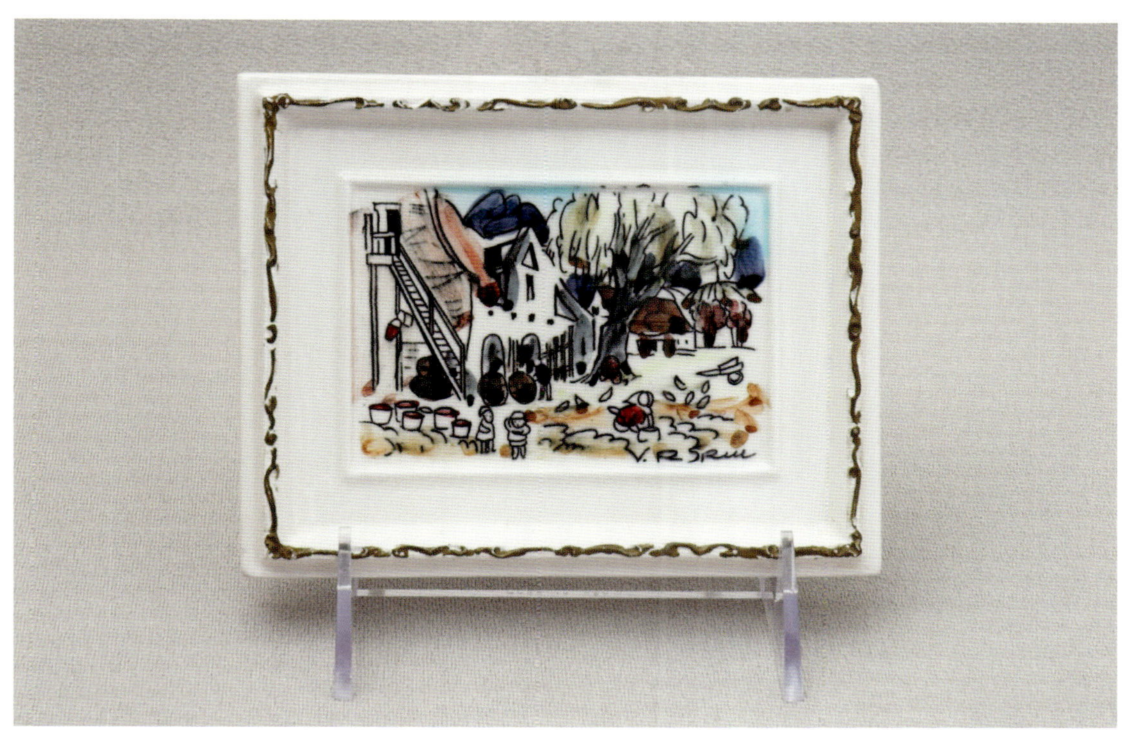

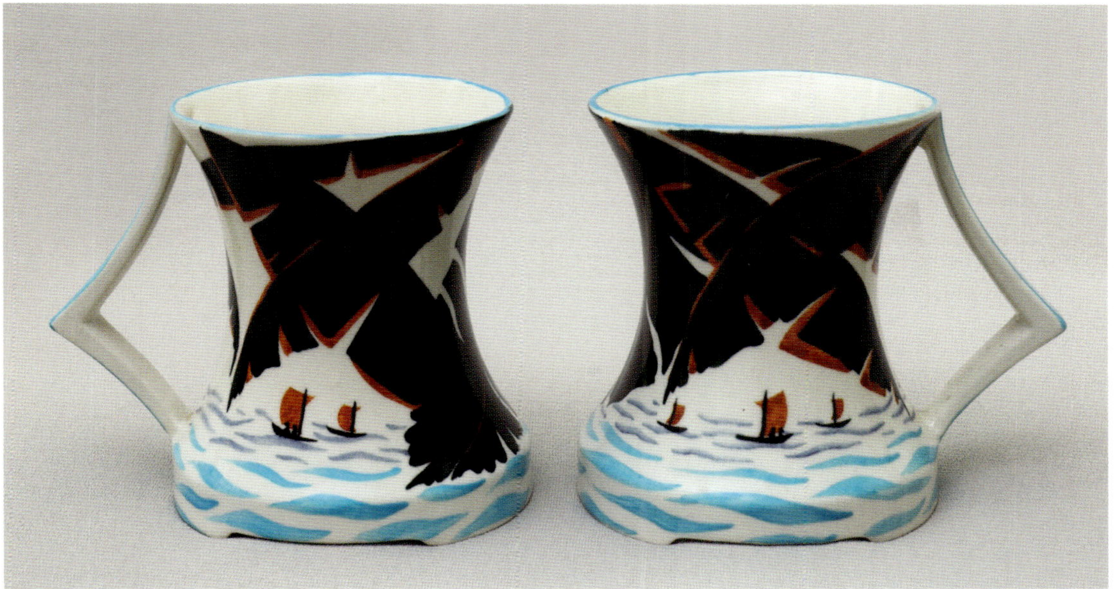

TOP: Vermont | Plaque showing Cape-Dutch farm scene | 110x135x13mm | Provenance: Douglas van der Horst | Photograph by Natalie Field

BOTTOM: BEP Ware | Pair of Tankards with 'jazz' motifs of palm ocean, boats and banana palm fronds 147x117x130mm | Provenance: De Kamper and Welman Collection | Marks: both items have the same markings – white base with transparent glaze and embossed mould number 4804, black painted marking, 'Hand Painted B.E.P.' | Photograph by Natalie Field

Thaba Bosigo, Lesotho (1972–ca.1981)

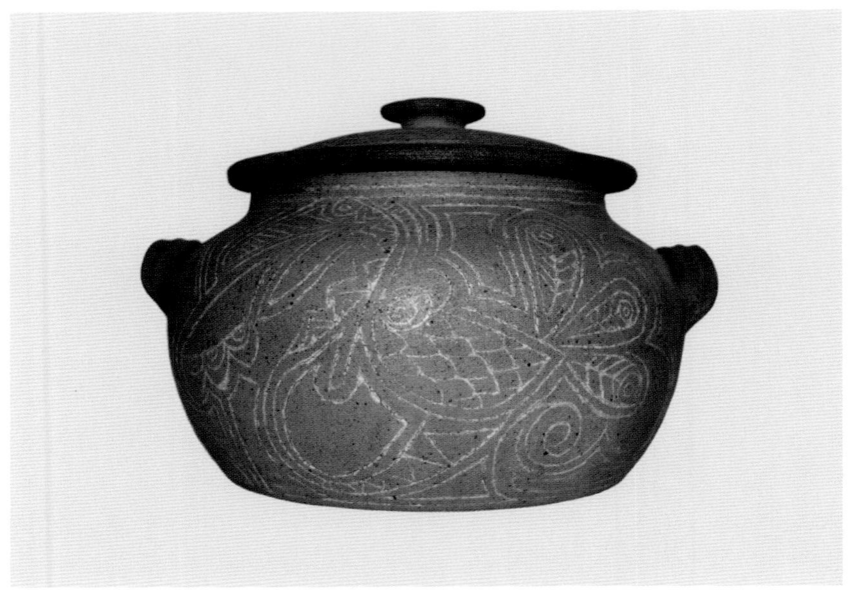

Thaba Bosigo | Casserole with sgrafitti decoration | 230x280mm | Provenance: Peter Hayes | Marks: no marks | Photograph by Peter Hayes

Name

The name of the pottery is associated with a venerated Basotho heritage site and national monument. The Thaba Bosigo mountain was used as a fortress in times of war, especially against Boer invasions. The virtually impenetrable fortress could accommodate the entire Basotho nation, and is widely referred to as the birth place of the Basotho nation.

Location

20 km east of the Maseru district, Lesotho

Founders and managers

In February 1971 the pottery was established by Geoffrey Whiting in conjunction with the Lesotho National Development Corporation (LNDC).[224] As a result of personal problems, Whiting returned to England within a year.[225] The LNDC subsequently invited Peter Hayes to re-establish it in 1972, and he worked there until 1974. Hayes was replaced by Barbara Hudson from 1979 to 1980. The pottery was then managed briefly by an unidentified American Peace Corps volunteer. When she left the pottery dwindled and finally closed.

Staff

The pottery grew to become a fairly large concern, and in 1974 employed 28 unnamed locals. Under Hudson the pottery employed approximately 20 Basotho women. Both Hayes and Hudson struggled to recall the names of their staff. Hayes recalled Gilbert (general foreman), Elizabeth (a thrower), and the physically handicapped employees, Julius and Mpeli. Hudson could only recall Reggie (general foreman).

Wares manufactured

Thaba Bosigo made an extremely wide variety of wares. Standardised utilitarian items were generally glazed and decorated in the Anglo-Oriental style and included beer tankards, wine carafes with tumblers or goblets, jugs, ashtrays, tea and coffee services, kettles, breakfast wares, large storage jars, oven dishes, lamp bases, a variety of different pierced candle holders, pizza dishes and different size casseroles. The pottery also made numerous decorative items that reflect a more avant-garde, contemporary, abstract, modernist idiom, including elegant tapered pots, jars and vases with extremely fine necks, and a highly popular Madonna-and-Child figurine. Thaba Bosigo also produced hand-carved tiles, and received a large commission for tiles for the coffee shop of the Hilton Hotel, Maseru in ca.1978.

Most significantly, the pottery produced wares that attempted to embrace local Basotho traditions. One of the more important ranges of items, the hybridised *Letima*[226] pot, was derived from the local form of mural decoration applied to the exterior of Basotho dwellings.[227] The pottery produced 'warrior' pots and lamp bases decorated with a wide band of simplified and naïve sgraffito images of war scenes. Hayes and his staff developed various small sculptural wares that depict *tokoloshes*, as well as figurines based on Basotho fertility dolls. Staff used various mythological motifs including a bird-woman, which was carved onto platters.

Hayes worked with various independent Basotho collaborators. Tsitso Mohapi used to fire his sculptures in the Thaba Bosigo kiln and sold his wares in its shop. Herd-boys made traditional cattle and other animals, to which pottery staff attached small bowls. These were sold as candle holders and were extremely popular.

Thaba Bosigo | Figurine | 265x80mm | Provenance: Douglas van der Horst | Marks: hollow base with gold sticker, 'Thaba Bosigo Ceramics, Kingdom of Lesotho,' with bull logo | Photograph by Natalie Field

Production methods

Everything was made in stoneware clay that came from Cape Town. A variety of production methods were employed, including coiling, slabbing, throwing and casting. Slabbed and coiled pots were usually assembled with thrown necks. Almost all the wares were glazed.[228]

Brief history of the pottery

The pottery was developed by the Lesotho National Development Corporation (LNDC) as part of its post-independence drive to develop a craft infrastructure in Lesotho. Hayes tells of his arrival in January 1972 with his wife, Joan, their infant son and three-month-old daughter:

> The Lesotho National Development Corporation ... booked us into the local hotel/brothel! And handed me a huge bundle of keys, which turned out to be the keys of a long-abandoned brewery with attached living quarters on a so-called industrial estate. The place was huge and long forgotten, with an inch of red dust completely covering everything. When I eventually

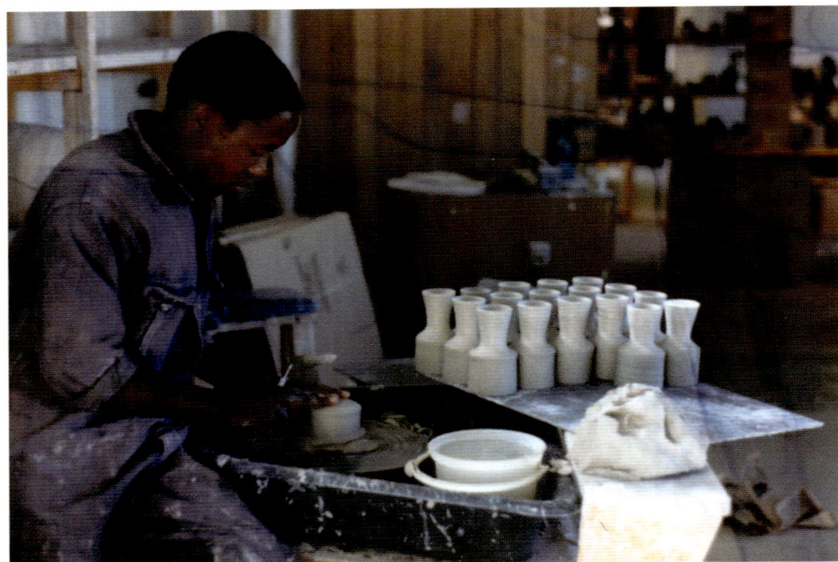

Thaba Bosigo | Unidentified thrower | Provenance: Peter Hayes | Photograph by Peter Hayes

> managed to open the sliding doors, various things scuttled away. At this time, I thought what the hell have I let myself and my family in for. The only thing I was sure of, I had the return air tickets to London if everything went wrong (Hayes 2009).

Hayes discovered that the abandoned pottery contained unpacked potters' wheels that were still in their original crates and 3 000 fire bricks that Whiting had ordered from the United Kingdom. Whiting had intended to build a gas-fired kiln but had not started this undertaking. Hayes also intended to build, but ran into opposition from the LNDC, and eventually a 60-foot (18-metre) electic kiln was purchased from the renowned South African kiln specialist, Dave Berry. Hayes later built a kiln using the remaining bricks and purchased another 100-foot (30.5-metre) electric kiln.

Thaba Bosigo made an extremely wide variety of wares, and Hayes continually experimented, creating and testing new products. This constant experimentation meant that there was a considerable fluidity with regard to Hayes's personal artistic pieces and standard production wares. Over time things settled down as staff members specialised in certain techniques or in making certain products. From about 1974 a dependable production range was standardised.

Hayes recalls the recruitment of staff:

> I started Thaba Bosigo Ceramics by asking the local radio to announce that I was looking for local potters. Early next morning when I pushed open the bedroom curtains, I was greeted by a sea of faces, all encamped on the grass, awaiting silently to be interviewed. It took three days for everybody to be seen (Hayes 2009).

Initially the staff was predominantly male but Hayes soon recognised that female employees were far more reliable and competant as pottery is traditionally a woman's domain in Lesotho.[229]

> I chose my team, built a kiln, made a clay filter press from an old wine press, taught people how to throw a pot and slowly but steadily we started producing quite nice work. In eighteen months we were a team of twenty eight strong. We had six throwers, five lady potters from the mountains making large burnished pots, four hefty lads preparing the clay, glazers, kiln stackers, etc. as well as my counterpart Gilbert. The general idea was to get the place up and running and into a profit, and for myself to slowly back out (Hayes 2009).

The intention of all the LNDC (and the TNDC) craft projects was that they should be self-sustaining after a period of apprenticeship. Hayes received R1 500 and the premises rent-free for the first year. His goal was that his manager Gilbert should take over, but this did not materialise, and Gilbert later went on to become the manager of the Lesotho Brickworks. Hayes left the pottery in 1974 and its quality dwindled.[230]

Saddened by the fate of the pottery, Peter Hayes, then a craft adviser, organised financial assistance from international aid agencies. The new manager, Barbara Hudson, a friend of Hayes, operated the pottery from 1979 to 1980. She claimed that it was still producing Hayes's original designs and traditional pots made by a Basotho potter known as Agnes. Under Hudson, the pottery employed approximately 20 female and two male staff members. Hudson organised exhibitions in Cape Town and Bloemfontein, but numerous problems were experienced, including theft and strikes over the dismissal of a staff member suspected of theft. The pottery received some large orders but the staff refused to work overtime or weekends to meet the orders. They also experienced problems with seconds, which were being sold in the showroom. Hudson wanted the Basotho manager and foreman, Reggie, to take over when she departed, but this proved impossible.

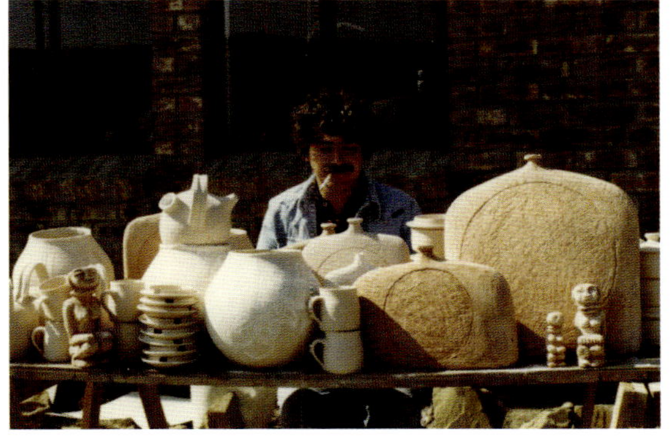

Thaba Bosigo | Peter Hayes decorating pottery | Provenance: Peter Hayes | Photograph by Peter Hayes

Thaba Bosigo was often perceived as producing 'poor man's Kolonyama'. However, this is entirely false as the enterprise was far more complex. Unlike Kolonyama, it was extremely open to multiple diverse stylistic and cultural forms, including contemporary modernist,[231] Anglo-Orientalist vernacular and local Basotho forms. Hayes's delicate balancing act between marketable items and a drive to create more distinctly Basotho wares, contributed to a lively southern African debate concerning African identity and became part of a dynamic new visual idiom within the region.

Marks

- Most wares are unmarked.
- Some have a gold sticker on the bases with 'Thaba Bosigo' and an African bull.
- A few have a stamped logo showing a person with a large shield.

Biographies

HAYES, Peter (b.1946)

Hayes was born in Birmingham, England, and studied ceramic sculpture in Birmingham. He re-established Thaba Bosigo in 1972.

Hayes subsequently spent many years as an NGO adviser. From 1974–1978 he was employed as the Pan-African crafts adviser to EDESA. From 1979–1982 he worked as a production development adviser to the Commonwealth Secretariat in Lesotho. In 1984 he was an adviser on the development of ceramics for the Commonwealth Fund for Technical Cooperation in Nepal, India, Japan and South Korea.

In 1985 Hayes returned to Britain and worked as a craft adviser for South West Arts. He held this position until 1987, when he entered the contemporary art scene. His installations frequently incorporated sculptural elements. Hayes exhibits internationally and his works are found in many public collections, including the Scottish National Gallery, Edinburgh; the Museum of Modern Art, Kingston, Jamaica; the Gardener Collection, Toronto; the Museum of Modern Art, Brussels, Belgium; the Silber Collection, California; and the J B Speed Museum, Louisville, Kentucky, USA.

Hayes has undertaken numerous public and private commissions. These include the following sculptures: The Foyer, Hanover Street, London (2005); Raku Water Sculpture, Rufford Country Park, Nottinghamshire (2004); Bronze Family Group, Jerwood Foundation, Whitney Sculpture Park (2002); Six Totems, Shackleton House, London (2002); Mounted Pebbles, GlaxoSmithKline, London (2001); Seated Bronze Figures, Prior Centre Oxfordshire (2001); and Four Figures, Taiwan Bank, Taipei (1998).[232]

HUDSON, Barbara (b.1940)

Hudson, a self-trained potter, was heavily inspired by Leach's *A Potter's Book* and later undertook ceramics classes at Red Roof School, Norton, Stockton-on-Tees. Her late husband Tony Hudson was a good friend of Peter Hayes. The couple received an invitation from Hayes to assist with Thaba Bosigo and in 1979 they travelled to Lesotho, where he worked as a painter and she managed the pottery for a year. Upon her return to England she established African Connection, an art and craft gallery in St Ives, Cornwall, which sold 'traditional' pots from Lesotho, among other objects. The gallery is currently run by her family.[233]

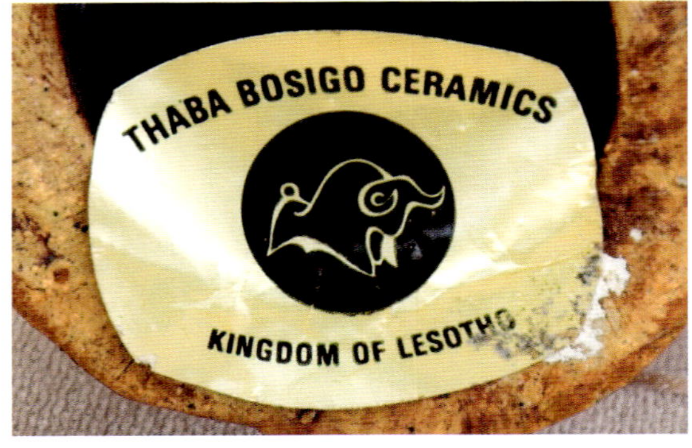

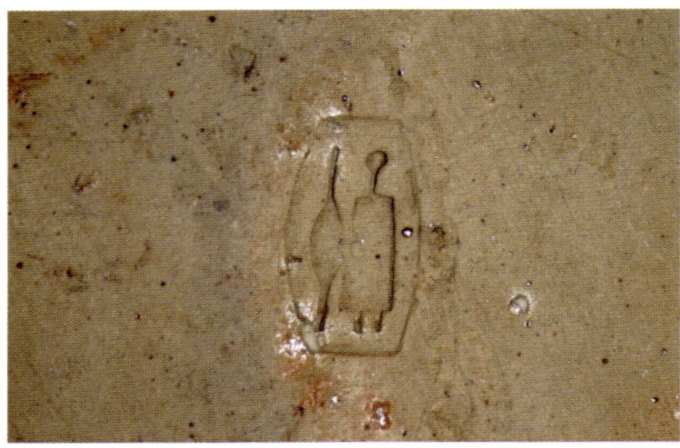

TOP: Thaba Bosigo | Maker's mark | Gold foil sticker with black bull logo and text, 'Thaba Bosigo Ceramics, Kingdom of Lesotho' | Photograph by Natalie Field

ABOVE BOTTOM: Thaba Bosigo | Maker's mark | Stamp | Provenance: Peter Hayes | Photograph by Peter Hayes

WHITING, Geoffrey (1919–1988)

Geoffrey Whiting was born in Stocksfield, Northumberland. He initially studied at the Birmingham School of Architecture (1930s) but developed a passion for ceramics when he came into contact with village potters while on army service in India during World War II. He spent six-and-a-half years in India learning to make simple unglazed domestic earthenware.

Later, Whiting was deeply inspired by Leach's *A Potter's Book* and became a devout disciple of the Anglo-Oriental tradition. In ca.1952 Whiting established his first pottery workshop attached to the Adult Education College at Avoncroft, Worcestershire. From ca.1964–65 he taught at Stoke-on-Trent College of Art with Derek Emms. He mass produced pots for the domestic market, as well as single items for the collector, specialising in high temperature stoneware and porcelain. Whiting, like so many Anglo-Oriental potters, shared a pioneering instinct, and an altruistic desire to work with others, to share and teach.[234] A farewell note appeared in *Ceramic Review* that claimed that:

> After nearly twenty years of potting in this country, Geoffrey feels the need to continue against a different background and in conditions of more anonymity. He says, 'it will be a wonderful opportunity and a great privilege to work once more with unsophisticated people, and such a relief to get away from all the ghastly High Art thinking which bedevils pottery training in Art Colleges in this country, and the minds of those responsible for it (Henry 1971:2).

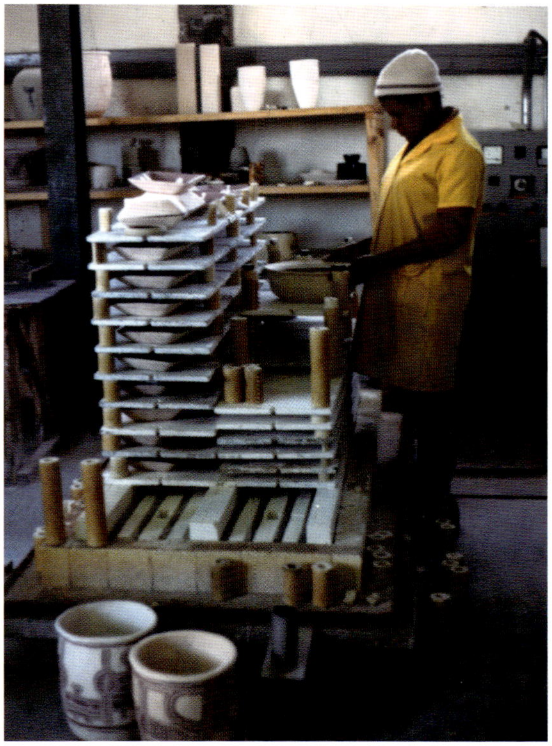

Thus, in 1971 he travelled to Lesotho to establish a pottery for the LNDC. As a result of personal problems (alcoholism and depression), the pottery was not a viable proposition under his management and it closed shortly thereafter. In extremely poor health, Whiting collapsed at Heathrow airport upon his return (Whiting 2004:39).

While his period in Lesotho was brief and essentially unsuccessful, it was extremely influential in terms of his personal development. As soon as he regained his health, he wrote a seminal essay for *Ceramic Review* that argued for the importance of production workshop training for potters and protested against a studio approach. He wrote extensively on the importance of production throwing of standard wares, of the value of repetition throwing, and the need to focus on useful objects. He claimed that:

> ... repetition production, provided it is not carried too far, engenders a self-discipline in the workmanship and a humility towards clay which I doubt can be acquired in any other manner. It is also the only way of gaining real insight into form. No potter who has thrown a shape to the same superficial measurements, many hundreds of times, over a period of years, and has seen the shape change, either voluntarily or involuntarily, will fail to understand this' (Whiting 1994).

Thaba Bosigo | Unidentified staff member cleaning pots and stacking them onto kiln dolly | Provenance: Peter Hayes | Photograph by Peter Hayes

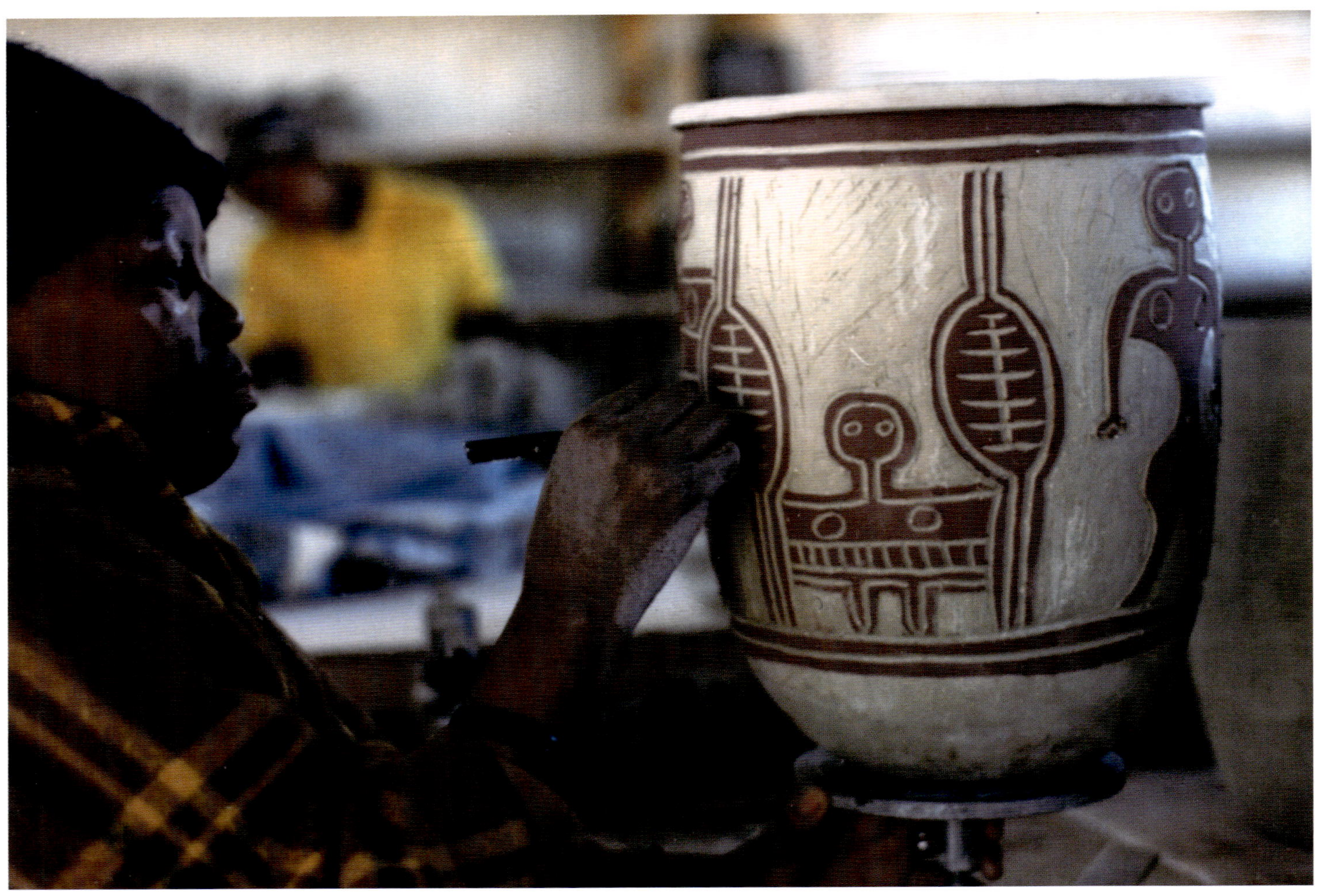

Thaba Bosigo | Unidentified staff member decorating a vase with 'letima' motifs | Provenance: Peter Hayes | Photograph by Peter Hayes

This article had a profound effect on many potters, and ultimately led to the establishment of the Dartington Pottery Workshop in Kent.[235] In 1972 he established a new studio at St Augustine's Pottery, Canterbury which he ran until his death in 1988. Whiting also taught from this studio. While at Canterbury he taught at Kings School. From ca.1974 to 1976 Whiting taught at Medway College of Art and Design with Colin Pearson. He was an important teacher, and his students include Edmund de Waal (b.1964); Jack Kenny; the renowned Indian potter Mansimran 'Mini' Singh (b.1939); and Henry Sandon, a prominent English lecturer, broadcaster and ceramics expert. Whiting contributed to many ceramics journals and exhibited widely. Commissioned works included candlesticks for Canterbury Cathedral, among other ecclesiastical wares.

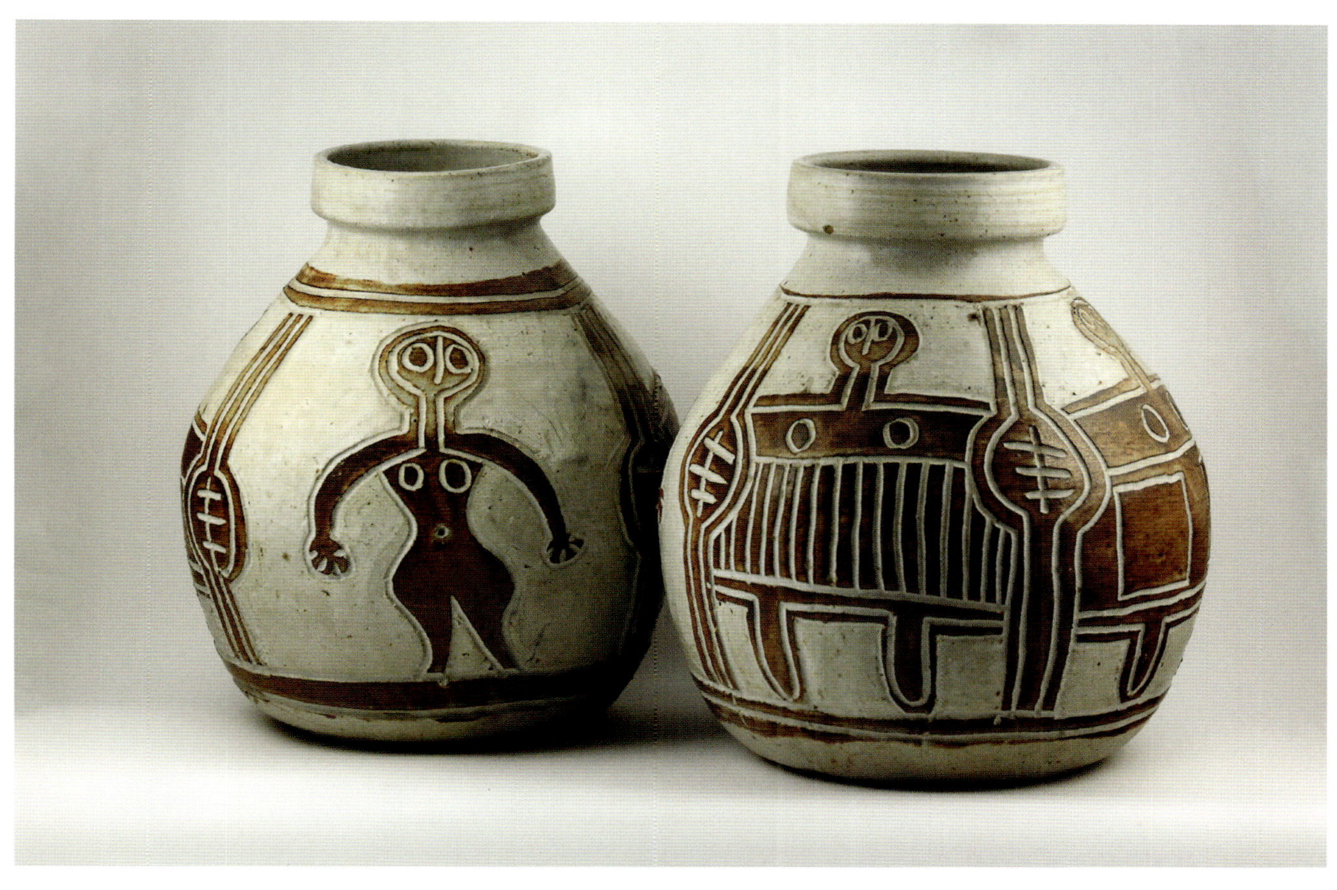

Thaba Bosigo | Pair of lamp bases decorated with 'Letima' motifs | 300x120x165mm | Provenance: Wendy Gers | Marks: unmarked, unglazed bases | Photograph by Damien Artus

Thamaga Pottery, Botswana (1973–present)

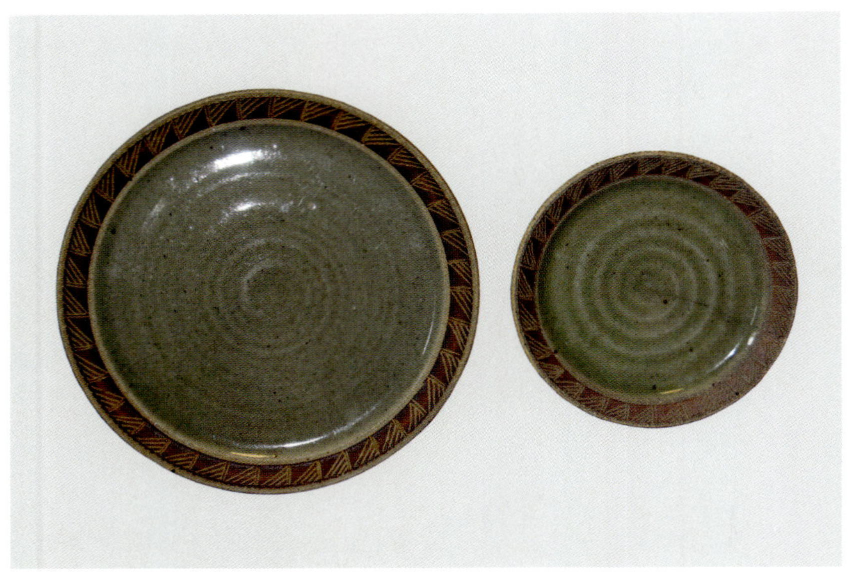

Thamaga Pottery | Dinner and side plate | dinner plate 250mm; side plate 170mm | Provenance: Sietze Praamsma | Photograph by Sietze Praamsma

Location

The pottery is located at the Botswelelo Centre, Thamaga, Botswana.

Founder

Father Julian James Black established the pottery.

Staff

Over the years, the Botswelelo Centre has been assisted by numerous foreign volunteers. A Canadian, Anita Hutchings, was the first potter at Thamaga. In 1973 she was recruited as a volunteer through the CUSO (Canadian University Services Overseas) programme. Hutchings was replaced in August 1975 by her friend Bodil Pearson, a fellow Canadian, who worked as a volunteer for two years. Hutchings and Pearson worked together between August and December 1975, Hutchings focusing on building and the technical aspects of pottery and Pearson on training and management.

Upon Pearson's departure, Saskia and Sietze Praamsma worked as volunteers from 1977 to 1980. They were the last of the CUSO volunteers, although another Canadian potter, Nicholas Falgiatore later worked at the pottery. Other potters included Louise Holso and an English potter called Jack. A British NGO called War of Poverty assisted in the 1980s and early 1990s.

Pottery workers included Teko Dikgobe, Metsiyame Dikobe, Mosiane Ikobe, Molebe Kebonang, Moswarakgosi Kebotsamang, Mmanko Moeng, Tsitsipane Monageng, Taki Sepakile, Motobedi Tshipi, Radiau Tshipi, Khusi [surname unknown], Mmapula [surname unknown], Morwesi [surname unknown], Olebogeng [surname unknown], Rra [first name unknown], Rra Sejabodile (potter), Sereko [surname unknown], Setlhoko [surname unknown] and

Setsipane [surname unknown]. Mma [first name unknown] Mompati worked worked briefly as a manager under Pearson. Moraka Poshoko, a South African potter, who formerly worked at Serowe Pottery, was recruited by Praamsma in 1978 and trained to be a manager.

There were originally 12 potters and there are now 20, the majority being senior women. Most of the original potters have left, and only Taki Sepakile and Motobedi Tshipe remain.

Botlalo Keipeile started working at the pottery in 1995 as an administrator. Donna Neseyif, from the UK, was the financial and administrative manager from 1996 to 1999. When she left, Keipeile took over as financial and administrative manager. Dagmar Hanisch assisted Keipeile with the financial and administrative management of the pottery from 2000 to 2002. Keipeile currently manages the operation.

Wares manufactured

The pottery originally made coiled non-utilitarian earthenware items based on traditional Tswana pottery forms. The original production consisted of small hand-built pots that resembled vases. However, the market was limited to ex-patriots as the villagers could not afford these wares. In 1974 Hutchings expanded the product range significantly and commenced the production of wheel-thrown stoneware dinner services. Under Pearson the production range expanded further and consisted of 16 articles. In the early years, many utilitarian wares were decorated by a frieze of incisions in an iron band around the outside of the wares. The geometric sgraffito decorative motifs are derived from decorative friezes applied to the floor, exterior walls and the compound walls of traditional dwellings. Hutchings introduced celadon and tenmoku glazes. A white glaze was applied to the inner surfaces of functional items.

From the outset the pottery made ornamental animals, including cattle, zebra, giraffe, elephants, buffalo and monkeys. These animals were inspired by an indigenous practice of making terracotta animals. The pottery also made original figurines.

Under the Praamsmas the pottery produced reduction-fired stoneware, including dinner, tea and coffee services, glazed in celadon green and dark brown. The plates had a glazed body with an unglazed rim featuring incised patterns. Coffee mugs had unglazed exteriors with glazed rims.

In the 1980s the pottery became renowned for its bowls, platters and goblets, which featured a hazy-blue glaze (derived from the application of cobalt oxide under a transparent glaze).

Production methods

Originally a wood-fired kiln was used, but as wood is a scarce and valuable commodity in Botswana, the pottery's consumption was a source of conflict with local villagers. In 1976, when the pottery was rebuilt, the kiln was replaced by a diesel kiln, capable of producing stoneware.[236] All machinery, technical material and clay were imported from South Africa. While local clay is abundant, it requires purification, and this service is not yet available.

Brief history of the pottery

Father Julian Black established the pottery project in Thamaga in 1973 as part of a rural development initiative. There were almost no employment opportunities for local women, and many elderly folk were abandoned as one of the only employment opportunities for men were as migrant labourers on South African mines. Black intended to develop the pottery and sewing workshops to re-establish some social balance in the community.

Anita Hutchings, the first CUSO volunteer potter, undertook an extensive study tour of South African potteries in 1973 and concluded that:

> rather than producing one-of-a-kind touristy items (of which there were many being made, though only in fragile earthenware rather than durable stoneware), we would be better off producing dinnerware that had an 'African' orientation – something that I did not see anywhere on the market. The only dinnerware being produced was of an English, Western flavour and, though it was very popular, I felt that a totally different design would fill a gap in the market.
>
> My rationale for wanting to do this was that I knew that it would be possible to set up the pottery and to teach people how to make the pots, but that the marketing would always be a problem. I felt that if we created something which the market truly wanted then the problem would be resolved as people, including shopkeepers from Johannesburg (and please remember that Apartheid was in full swing at the time), would come to Thamaga Pottery. Also, hardly anyone buys just one item of dinnerware – they buy multiple pieces and whole sets...[237]

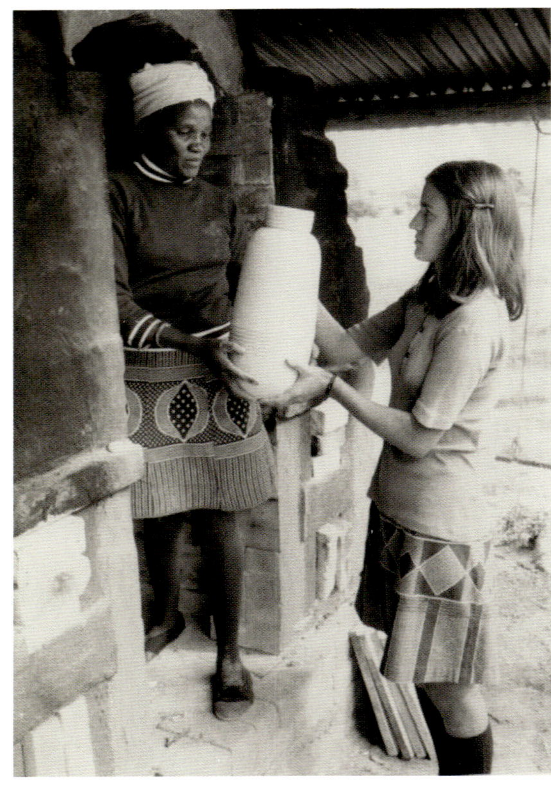

Thamaga Pottery | Anita Hutchings and Mma Mompati, April 1977 | Provenance: Dorte Deans | Photograph by Bodil Pearson

Less than a year after the pottery's establishment, and shortly after Bodil Pearson's arrival, the clay huts that housed Thamaga Pottery collapsed after torrential rains in April 1975. A decision was taken to rebuild, and the Board of Directors decided to use the opportunity to improve operations, and to refocus and reconceptualise the entire ethos of the pottery. Shortly thereafter, Hutchings approached potters in South Africa and Lesotho on a fact-finding mission. She essentially required technical and marketing assistance and visited, among other potteries, Kolonyama and Thaba Bosigo. She was concerned about the proposed new premises for the pottery. The difficulties were compounded by its isolation; there was no electricity and only one phone at the post office.

In 1975 Toff Milway (Kolonyama) and Peter Hayes (Thaba Bosigo) visited Thamaga. Milway stayed on for a while and helped build a new pottery (including the workshop buildings and the kiln) on an imposing granite slab in the bush. The new site was across the local river outside Thamaga. Villagers donated their labour, as well as raw materials and the vehicles needed for transporting the building materials. The new pottery was built out of locally produced concrete blocks. Upon the reconstruction of Thamaga, funds were obtained to train local potters in production wares. The pottery was small in scale, initially employing only six people. However, the pottery has expanded over time.

Thamaga wares were sold from a shop in the Botswelelo Centre and in Helen de Leeuw's gallery in Hyde Park, Johannesburg. In approximately 1975, sales to South Africa were discontinued, as the pottery found that it could survive on local trade.

The Botswelelo Centre evolved quickly and by 1975 numerous ambitious plans were underway to set up a sorghum grinder, a cement block and brick plant, a vegetable garden, a small nursery, and an interest-free financial service for the local villagers. According to Hutchings: 'Inherent in all these plans is the education in development needed to upgrade a subsistence economy, the working from within a community in creating the realisation that an easier, more fulfilling life was possible without too much difficulty.' (1975:13). The following year the pottery won first prize at the prestigious Gaborone Trade Fair. By 1977 the centre had become a community-driven enterprise, and was controlled by a board of directors.

From 1977 to 1980 the Praamsmas worked at Thamaga. When they arrived the Botswelelo project consisted of a production pottery producing high-fired stoneware, a small textile factory producing clothing for both local and tourist consumption and a small concrete block manufacturing operation. The centre employed approximately 25 people full-time, and was the largest income-generating project in the area.

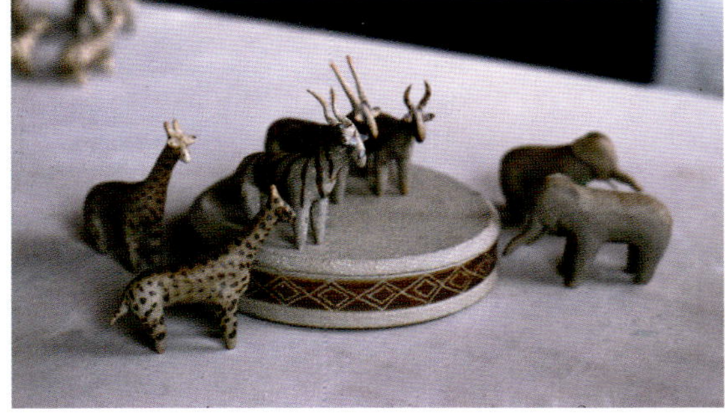

Thamaga Pottery | Animal figurines 1977 | Provenance: Dorte Deans | Photograph by Bodil Pearson

Sietze Praamsma was charged with upgrading pottery skills and managing the pottery operation. He solved a number of technical problems,[238] and when Father Julian departed in 1982, Sietze's job description expanded to include the business management of the whole centre. As centre manager, Sietze undertook various important projects. Together with Saskia, he trained local managers for all the workshops and employed more workers. The couple also established a restaurant. The road through Thamaga was one of the gateways to the cattle posts of the Kalahari Desert, and there was a lot of passing traffic. The building design was based on traditional Setswana architecture. They also founded a retail outlet for the products of the centre, and for traditional crafts that were locally produced, including baskets, toys and furniture.

The Praamsmas organised workshops where local traditional potters demonstrated their techniques. Sietze notes:

> Our aim was to create an understanding with the younger generation of the value of their elders' traditions (as wherever Western progress was happening, a general tendency to discard old tech as useless was common).

> This collaboration was exciting, but I cannot really say that it was very succesful![239]

Some of the experimental pots[240] that were made by the Thamaga potters were exhibited on the Botswelelo Centre exhibition in the Botswana National Gallery in December 1979. Another noteworthy project was the spontaneous production of animals, especially cattle, which often became collectors' items. They were made by the male potters, who often had extensive discussions regarding the cattle that passed by the pottery to and from the Kalahari cattle posts.

By 1980 the centre had a reasonably functional administration, had started to generate a decent living wage for an increasing number of people and was independent of outside financial support. According to Praamsma, '... the greatest challenge was to convince people that the centre belonged to them and that they didn't need outsiders (like me) to run it...'[241] The Praamsmas achieved a certain level of sustainability in the pottery by recruiting and training a local pottery manager. The existing glazes were improved and new glazes and slips were introduced. Sietze worked with the Botswana Geological Survey to locate materials for use in the pottery. He also improved the existing clay bodies, developed new bodies and glazes from local materials, and designed and built equipment, such as potters' wheels, drying racks and clay-processing systems. The pottery workshop was expanded with a large throwing room, a section for hand-building projects, a large kiln room with drying facilities and a 120-cubic-foot (3½-cubic-metre) walk-in downdraft kiln with false floor.

After the Praamsma's departure, isolation and a lack of local technical expertise plagued the pottery, and it frequently needed outside assistance. It experienced problems with poor clay quality, which resulted in a costly firing time of 39 hours. In 1980 Chris Green visited the pottery, and advised a change to Ndebele clay and the addition of ceramic fibre, and their firing time was reduced to less than ten hours. In the mid-1980s the managers of the pottery and the centre absconded with money, and the centre closed down for some years. It was re-opened and in the late 1980s and in the early 1990s British volunteers assisted with marketing and business management. From 2006 to 2008, The African Development Foundation (ADF) assisted the pottery financially.

In the 1990s Thamaga Pottery prioritised the production of high-quality dinnerware and pots, and obtained important commissions from some of Botswana's leading hotels, including the Gabarone Hotel and the Mafenya Tlala Hotel, Molepolole. Despite occasional commissions, the pottery continues to struggle financially and the remaining staff members are elderly. The pottery cannot attract young recruits as a result of the meagre current salaries.

Since the 1970s Thamaga has regularly participated in various annual exhibitions hosted by the Botswana National Museum. It also regularly

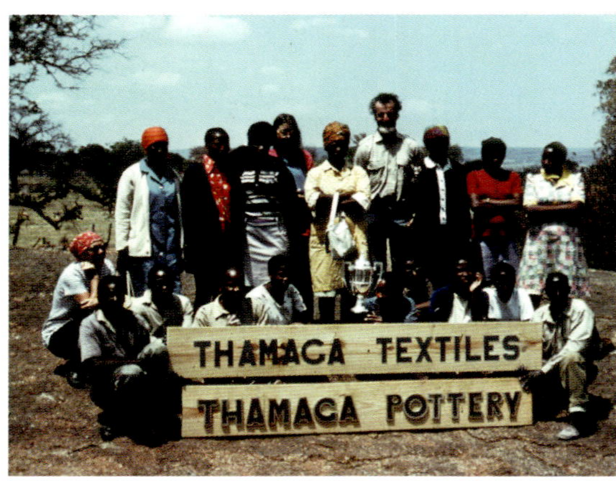

Thamaga Pottery and Textiles Staff | October 1976 | Provenance: Dorte Deans | Photograph by Bodil Pearson

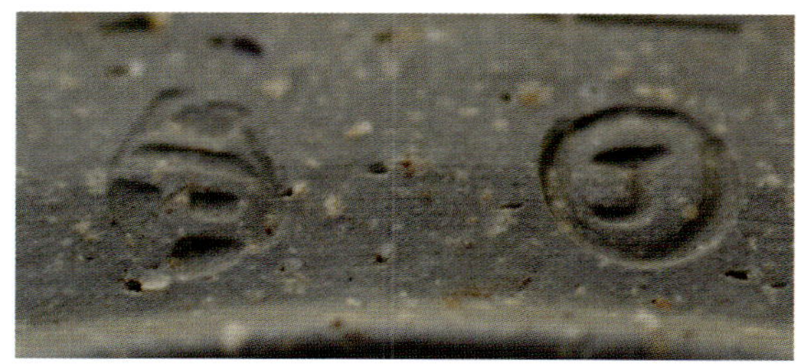

Thamaga Pottery | Two stamps | The first stamp identifies the pottery, the second identifies the thrower (J) | Provenance: Sietze Praamsma | Photograph by Sietze Praamsma

participated in trade fairs such as 'Craft, Art and Basketry', Global Expo, and Consumer Affairs and Women's Affairs, Gaborone.

For many years Thamaga Pottery was a benchmark standard for a successful CUSO project, as it was considered to represent the use of appropriate technology in a third-world setting. While NGOs have played an important role, it is essential to note that Thamaga is one of the few southern African potteries that have managed to survive successive generations of changes in fashion and taste. Perhaps this is because it strikes a chord with locals and foreigners, who realise that Thamaga pottery is quintessentially a revised and updated version of an inherently ancient local tradition and is an important local cultural landmark.

Marks

- 'Thamaga' or 'Thamaga Botswana' is incised underneath all vessels.
- During the Praamsmas' time the pottery used a couple of stamps bearing the initials TP. An additional stamp was occasionally used to indicate the initials of the potter, e.g. 'J' or 'P'. It was sometimes accompanied by other stamps including, 'Made in Botswana' (illus. Kerrod 2010:197) and the initials of the potter, e.g. 'J'.
- After the Praamsmas, a metallic foil sticker was used that indicated 'Thamaga Pottery, Botswana' (illus.Kerrod 2010).

Biographies

BLACK, Julian James (b.1936)

Born in Ballycastle, Northern Ireland, Black entered the Congregation of the Passion seminary in Crossgar at a young age. After a novitiate period of one year, Black studied for his three-year degree in theology in Dublin and undertook six months of training in mission orientation in 1962.

In 1963 Black arrived in Botswana and after an initial three months in Ramotswa to learn Setswana, was dispatched to various mission stations to replace missionaries on sabbatical, and this exposure drew his attention to the desperate fate of the elderly, abandoned by their children, who had migrated to urban centres or to South Africa in search of employment. This awareness prompted Black to seek further training, and from 1968 to 1969 he studied social leadership in the University of St Francis Xavier, Nova Scotia, Canada.

In 1974 Father Black established the Botswelelo Centre in Thamaga, which initially included a pottery and later a textiles workshop, shop and restaurant. Black jokes that 'divine providence' brought Anita Hutchings to work as a volunteer for CUSO in Botswana. Black and Hutchings built the pottery together, starting with the cement bricks. Black worked as the business manager while Hutchings took care of production, which he continued until 1982, working alongside the various volunteers and local Tswana staff.

From 1982 to 1985 Black worked at the Sedibeng Mission in Molepolole, where he designed and built a mission that combined Batswana architectural

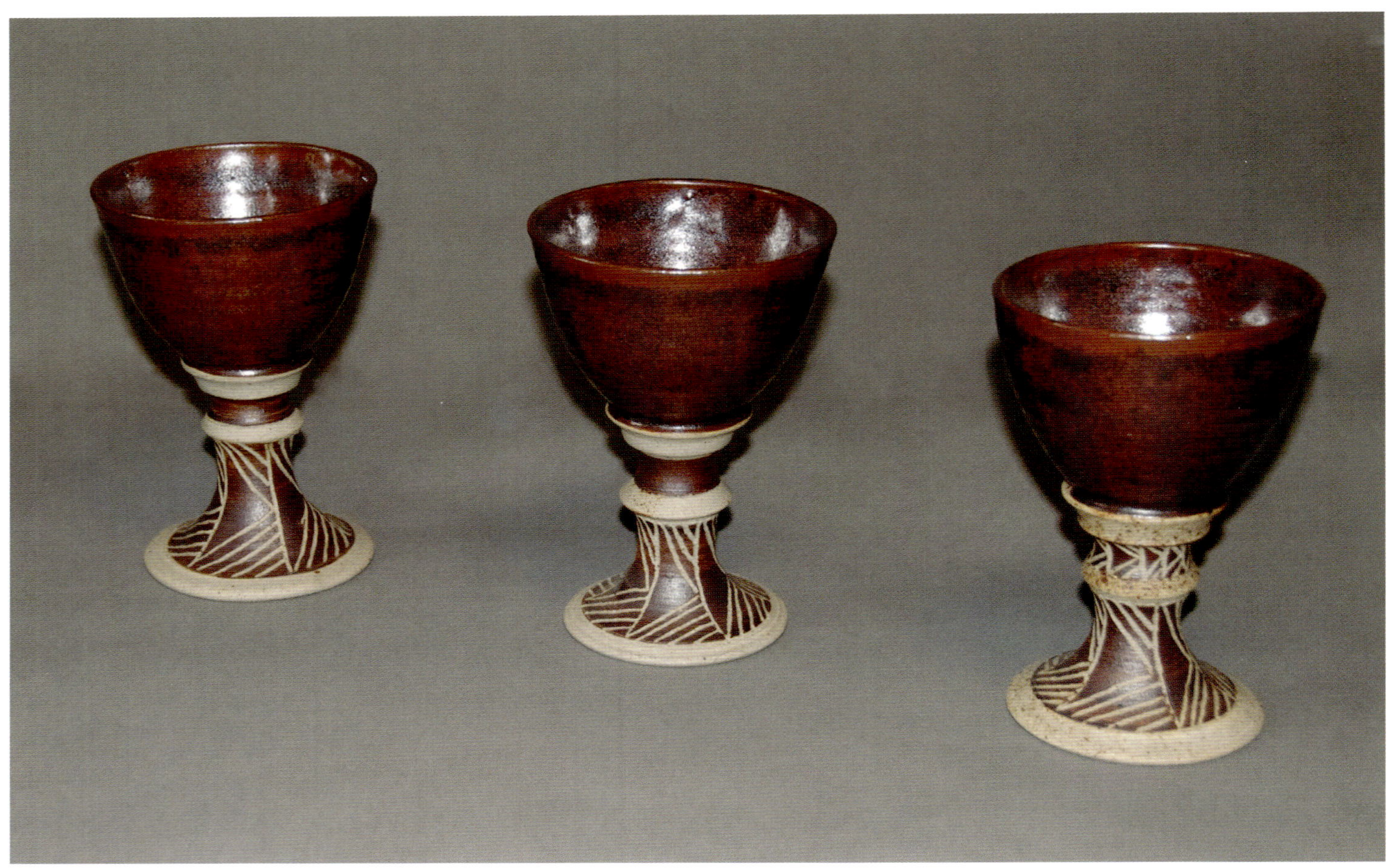

Thamaga Pottery | Goblets | 150mm | Provenance: Sietze Praamsma | Photograph by Sietze Praamsma

elements with modern building materials. Black subsequently worked at the Forest Hills Meditation Centre near Gaborone, then spent three years at the Tsabong Catholic Mission in the Kalahari Desert, working at various outstations with the Basarwa. He returned to Ireland in 2002 for a year of sabbatical. Black subsequently returned to his work with the Basarwa. He remained in the desert until 2006, when he retired to Forest Hills, where he currently resides.[242]

HANISCH, Dagmar

Born in Germany, Hanisch worked as an administrator and organiser at Thamaga Pottery from 2000 to 2002, posted there by the German Development Agency (DED). Dagmar was paired with a local counterpart who revealed she was HIV positive. She became her partner's 'treatment buddy', which helped her understand what living with the virus meant in Botswana. Dagmar and her colleague helped Thamaga set up an HIV counselling centre, and Dagmar enrolled for the post-graduate diploma in HIV/AIDS Management at the University of Stellenbosch. She is currently employed as technical adviser to the Apparel Lesotho Alliance to Fight Aids (ALAFA).

HUTCHINGS, Anita (née Komarica) (b.1950)

Born in Mramorak, Yugoslavia (now Serbia), Hutchings studied from 1970 to 1973 at Sheridan College, Canada, and graduated with a diploma in ceramics.

Hutchings and Father Julian Black established the Thamaga Pottery in Botswana to create employment in the village. Hutchings first spent a couple of months living in another village with a Motswana family, taking private Setswana lessons in order to be able to communicate with the prospective potters. She also travelled around southern Africa, visiting many potteries to learn what was being produced, what items were popular, and to locate galleries and craft dealers. She worked at the pottery from August 1973 to February 1976.

She worked at the pottery from August 1973 to February 1976 as a potter and trainer. Upon her return to Canada, Hutchings established the Anita Hamilton Pottery at White Lake, Ontario, which she operated until 1988. From 1993 to 2000 she served as a councillor on the Arnprior Town Council, Ontario. From 2001 until her retirement in 2005 she was employed as the executive director of the Galilee Retreat and Conference Centre, Ontario.

KEIPEILE, Botlalo (b.1964)

Born in Thamaga, Keipeile joined the pottery in 1995. She took over from Donna Neseyif as manager in 1999. She is currently employed in this capacity.

MOMPATI, [first name unknown]

Mompati, formerly a school teacher, worked briefly at the pottery. Pearson had hoped to train her as a manager. However, her husband didn't like her working away from home and she was forced to resign.[243]

NESEYIF, Donna

Born in the United Kingdom, Neseyif worked as the manager at Thamaga from 1996 to 1999.

PEARSON, Bodil (née Nederstrom) (1923–1993)

Born in Copenhagen, Pearson and her husband Preben Erichsen and their two daughters immigrated to Montreal, where Erichsen and his business partner established a modern Danish furniture store. Pearson was surprised by the lack of good modern design in Canada and became interested in making light fixtures. She produced original handmade lights with wicker, raffia and similar materials, for which she won a Canadian design award in 1957. In 1958 the family moved to Hamilton, Ontario, and opened Erichsen's. Their marriage ended in 1963 and she later married Norman Pearson.

A friendship with Bunn Smith, a Mohawk potter, prompted Pearson to start making pottery, beginning with night courses in the Department of Art at McMaster University in Hamilton. Pearson continued her studies completing a three-year ceramic programme at Sheridan College in 1971 and establishing her own studio in Dundas Valley, near Hamilton.

At Sheridan, Pearson befriended Anita Hutchings who later invited her to visit Thamaga, in the hope that Pearson would continue the project when her term lapsed. Pearson was enchanted with Botswana, and returned a year later to head the CUSO project. She worked at Thamaga Pottery from 1975 to 1977.

Thamaga was fairly well established when Pearson arrived. In July 1975 the rainy season was particularly wet and the adobe pottery building collapsed. Pearson apparently ran into the melting building to retrieve records, and insisted the men evacuate the equipment before the roof gave way.

Pearson and Black obtained some funds and acquired a press to make concrete blocks for a new pottery, with assistance from some Kolonyama potters who acted as technical advisers. The new pottery was relocated to the outskirts of the village, on the site of the original wood-fired kiln that Hutchings had built. The kiln was located on a large flat outcrop of rock, as the ash from the chimney was a fire hazard in this parched region. Pearson converted the kiln to oil as the wood that was previously used as kiln fuel was a scarce commodity in the near-desert region. The new pottery building was stuccoed to cover up their inexperienced cement block work, and to blend in with the environment. Pearson's second challenge was the redesign of production. With Hutching's input, she set the pottery on a course of producing a broad range of domestic stoneware, including bowls, plates, mugs, planters and candle holders.

Pearson, then in her early 50s, struggled with a lack of technical support and materials. She had problems with both the supply of kiln oil and local clay, and had to rely on imports from South Africa, which upset her greatly. Tired by the ruthless heat, and the enormous physical challenges, she warned CUSO that she was 'wearing out' and that they should find a replacement. That took most of 1976, and by the time she handed the project over to the Praamsmas, Thamaga Pottery was operating successfully.

In 1977, after attending folk schools in rural Denmark, she considered relocating permanently, but returned to Dundas, Canada, in August 1978. Pearson continued to work as a potter, with a deep commitment to community projects. With three potter friends she co-founded the Beyond the Valley Studio Tour in 1981, an annual crafters 'open studio' programme. She was also a founding member of the Hamilton and Region Potters' Guild, which is still a thriving organisation.

In 1989, at the age of 65, tired by the great physicality of pottery, she decided to peruse her interest in textiles. She renovated her pottery studio, set up several looms and began a very successful body of work in woven garments.

Scott Barnim, a close friend who rented a pottery studio from Pearson from 1976 to 1993, recalls:

> Bodil was often involved on the periphery of women's issue projects, and was a woman that younger women gravitated to – there was often company in the house. She was always thankful that she had friends that

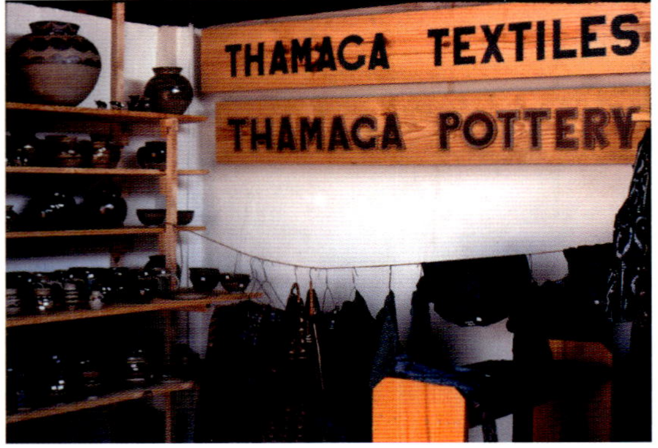

View of Thamaga Gallery | Provenance: Dorte Deans | Photograph by Bodil Pearson

> were younger than her, as she couldn't imagine her old age so rich with new ideas and energy without all of us around.[244]

Pearson planned to return to Thamaga, as she missed her friend Father Julian Black and longed to see the village, the desert, and how things had changed at the pottery with the introduction of electricity and electric kilns. In the early 1990s Pearson discovered that she had mesothelioma lung cancer, an illness acquired from working with asbestos boards in Thamaga. At a time before the danger of asbestos was understood, most of the construction and production materials were made of it, including kiln backing boards and cold insulation, throwing bats and ware boards (used as a base for modelling, drying, decorating and glazing). Before she passed away, Pearson contacted Father Julian Black to ensure that all asbestos was safely removed from Thamaga.

Pearson has works in The Potters' Guild of Hamilton and Region permanent collection, Burlington Arts Centre permanent collection, and in many private collections.

PRAAMSMA, Saskia (née Schierbeek) (b.1944)

Born in Amsterdam, Saskia Praamsma studied French at the Sorbonne from 1963 to 1964 and then art and design at the Rietveld Akademie, Amsterdam from 1965 to 1966. Praamsma was then apprenticed in the Hannie Mein Production Pottery, Amsterdam, from 1966 to 1967. In 1967 she married Sietse Praamsma in Amsterdam. The couple then immigrated to America, where from 1967 to 1973 Saskia studied ceramics and sculpture at the University of Wisconsin. She subsequently furthered her studies and worked in the Pottery department at the Sheridan School of Design, Canada, from 1973 to 1974.

Under the auspices of CUSO she and her husband Sietse worked as co-managers of the Botswelelo Centre in Botswana. Saskia supervised the pottery and textile workshops, the retail store and the restaurant from 1977 to 1980, and worked with the potters to develop their own pottery designs, based on the traditional Setswana motifs. With Sietze she organised a workshop with a local potter, who showed the workers in the centre how to make and fire traditional Setswana beer pots. The objective was to inculcate the value of traditional crafts. They trained a number of women to become throwers as traditionally these pots were hand-built by them. The potter's wheel at the Botswelelo Centre was seen as a machine of the future. Consequently throwing attained more status than hand-building and without any proactive advocacy automatically became a man's job.

Upon her return to Canada in 1981 she joined the Clayton Clay Works, Ontario as a potter and teacher, a position she still holds. She co-founded the Almonte Potters' Guild in 2002, where she currently works as the technician, business manager and instructor of adult, teenage and children's classes. From May 2007 to January 2008 the couple worked for the Turquoise Mountain Foundation in Afghanistan. During this time they oversaw the establishment of the new school, including the building of the facility, the formulation of the curriculum, the teaching of classes, the selection of new students and the establishment of sound practices.

Praamsma produces hand-built textured stoneware vessels and sculptures. Many are inspired by architecture elements.

In 1992 she had a solo exhibition at the Atrium Gallery, Nepean, Canada. Praamsma has participated in numerous group exhibitions including 'Ambiguity', White Shop Gallery, Ottawa (2008); Mississippi Arts Connection, Almonte (1990); Amaryllis Artists Cooperative, Carleton Place (1988); two-person show at Nepean Visual Arts Centre, Nepean (1985); and 'A Gathering of Friends', Harbourfront, Toronto (1975). From 1984 to 1986 and 1998 to 2008 she has participated in Ottawa Potters' Guild Exhibitions, in 2005, 2006 and 2008 she participated in the '260 Fingers' Exhibition in the Glebe Community Centre, Ottawa. Praamsma participated in the 'Thamaga Pottery Exhibition' at the National Art Gallery of Botswana in 1979, and two pots were purchased by the Gallery for its permanent collection. She has won various awards, notably from the Ottawa Potters' Guild exhibitions, including Juror's Choice Prizes in 1985, 2004 and 2005, and an honourable mention at the 2008 show.

PRAAMSMA, Sietse (b.1936)

Born in Zeist, Netherlands, Sietse Praamsma was awarded a bachelor's degree in geology at the University of Amsterdam. From 1967 to 1973 he studied ceramics at the University of Wisconsin, Madison, where he worked as a pottery technician in the ceramics department and studied X-ray mineralogy, specialising in clay minerals. This enabled him to make a seamless transition to ceramics, at least with regard to the clay and glaze chemistry. During this period he was a member of the Cat's Cradle Craft Cooperative (pottery, macramé), participated in a rural cooperative pottery studio experiment and built a catenary arch down-draft kiln and a raku kiln. He worked as a pottery technician at the Sheridan School of Design, Canada, from 1973 to 1977. He taught kiln-building and worked with Angela Fina. Together with Saskia, he co-founded the Harbourfront Crafts Studios, an important institution in the artistic life of Toronto. He subsequently became the programme director.

From 1977 to 1980 he worked with Saskia at Thamaga, Botswana, as a CUSO volunteer to contribute to the development of the Botswelelo Centre. Sietze was initially hired as a pottery teacher and adviser to manage the production pottery and to solve a number of technical problems. After Father Julian retired, his job description expanded rapidly to include the business management of the whole centre.

From 1980 to the present, Praamsma has been associated with the Nepean Visual Arts Centre, Ottawa. Working initially as a pottery technician, he later became the coordinator and programme director of the centre. He is a member of the executive of the Ottawa Potters' Guild and the Clayton Clay Works studio. Praamsma currently works primarily as a technical documentary writer.

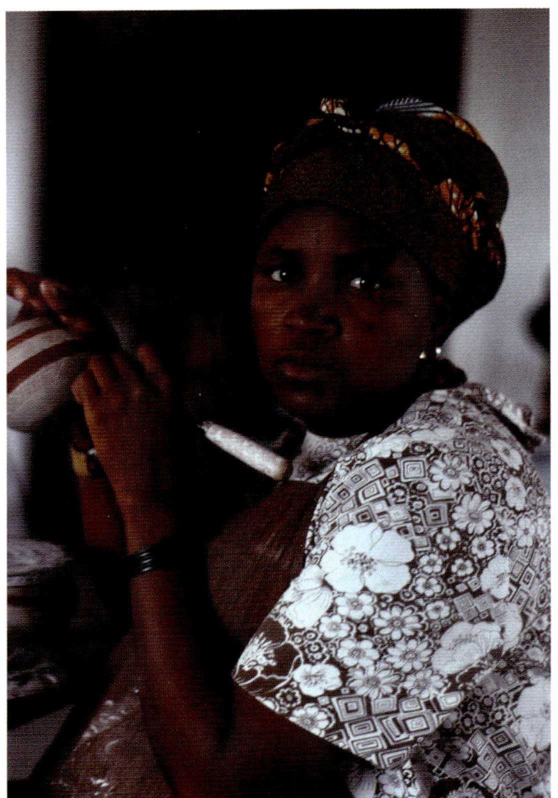

Thamaga Pottery | Setlhoko making miniature traditional pots, April 1977 | Provenance: Dorte Dean | Photograph by Bodil Pearson

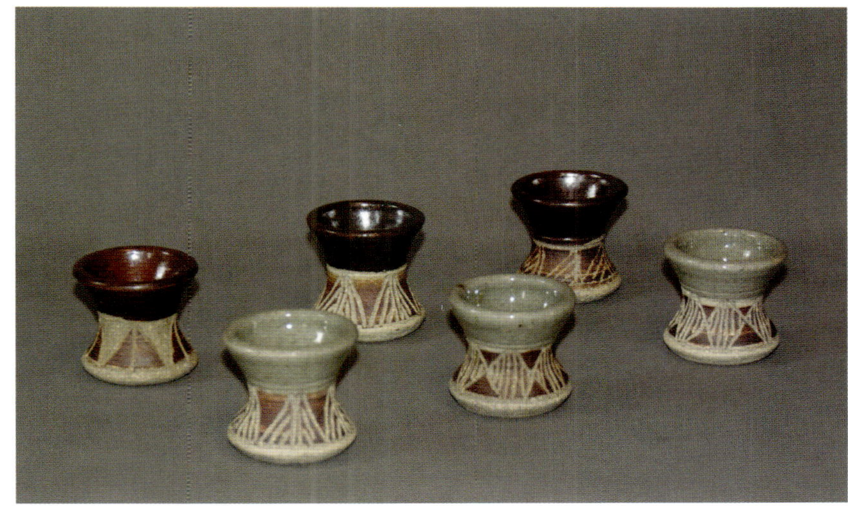

Thamaga Pottery | Egg cups | 60mm | Provenance: Sietze Praamsma | Photograph by Sietze Praamsma

SEPAKILE, Taki (b.1952)
Born in Thamaga, Sepakile started working at the pottery in 1974. She is still employed as a thrower and a potter.

SEREKO, [first name unknown]
Rra Sereko prepared the clay for everyone, and made animals including cows, elephants, giraffe, antelope and baboons. According to Pearson he had six children and spent almost all his earnings on school fees.[245]

TSHIPI, Motobedi (b.1935)
Born in Thamaga, Tshipi joined the pottery in 1975 and helped build the workshop after the original building was destroyed by rain. He is still employed by Thamaga and works as a thrower and with hand-built wares and assists with many other aspects of the business. According to Pearson, 'Motebele [sic] had a natural aptitude for throwing, being persistent and meticulous in all his work. He also had a fine feeling for form'.[246] According to Praamsma, he always worked in a white shirt, and managed to keep it perfectly clean![247]

Unidentified staff

[Surname unknown], Khusi
According to Pearson, Khusi was one of the 'old' potters, who made mugs, beer steins, sugar sets and candle holders. She was also responsible for glazing. As a single mother, she suffered social marginalisation and often brought her toddler, Moffat, to the pottery as child care was unavailable.[248]

[Surname unknown], Mmapula
Under Pearson, Mmapula made highly personalised figurines, some with humorous names such as 'Ashley' and 'Dandy'.

[Surname unknown], Setlhoko
Trained as a decorator by the Praamsmas, she also made miniature traditional pots, which were popular tourist items.

[Surname unknown], Setsipane
Under Pearson, Setsipane learned to stack and fire the kiln.

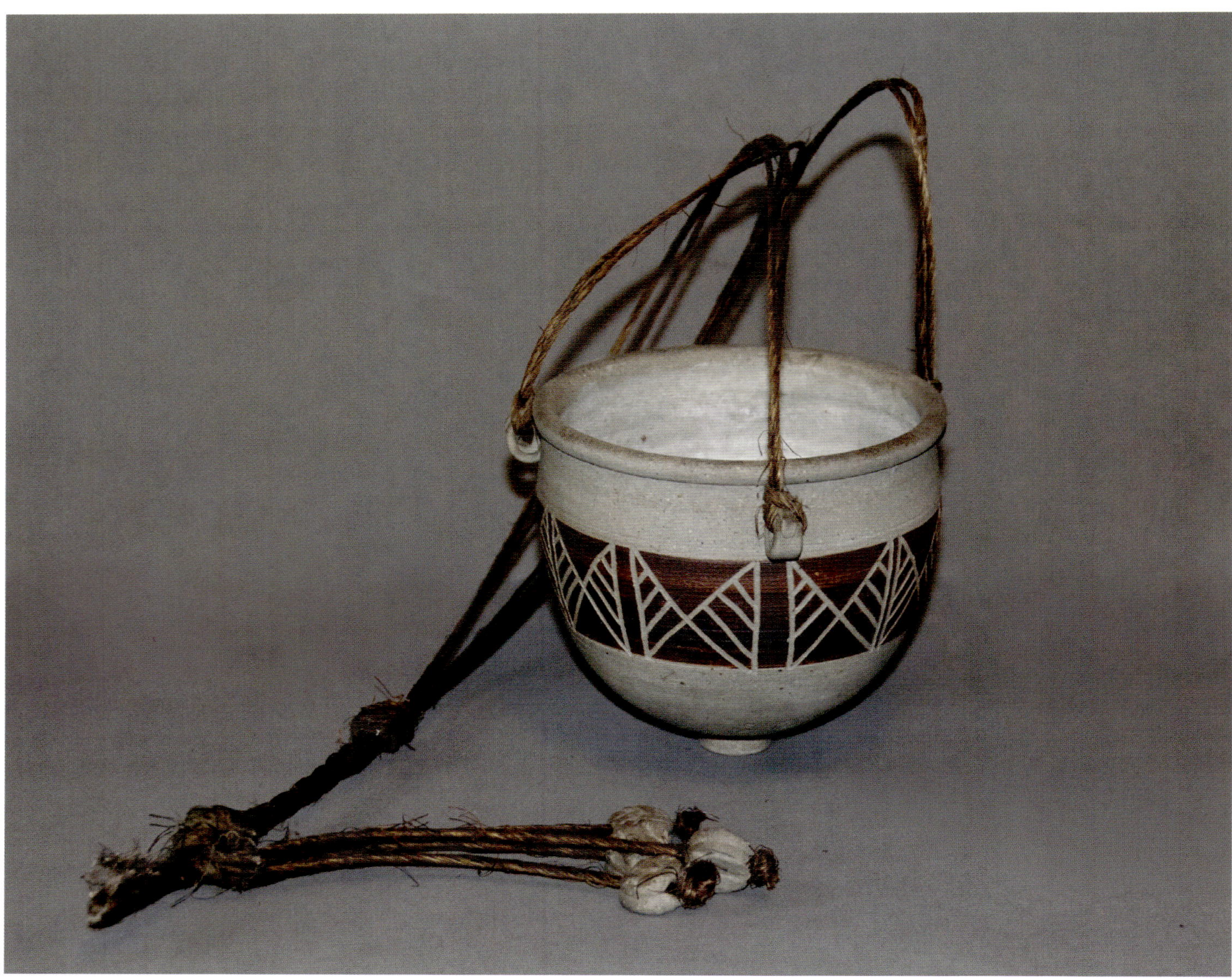

Thamaga Pottery | Hanging planter | 115x115mm | Provenance: Sietze Praamsma | Photograph by Sietze Praamsma

The Old Jar Pottery (1953–1984)

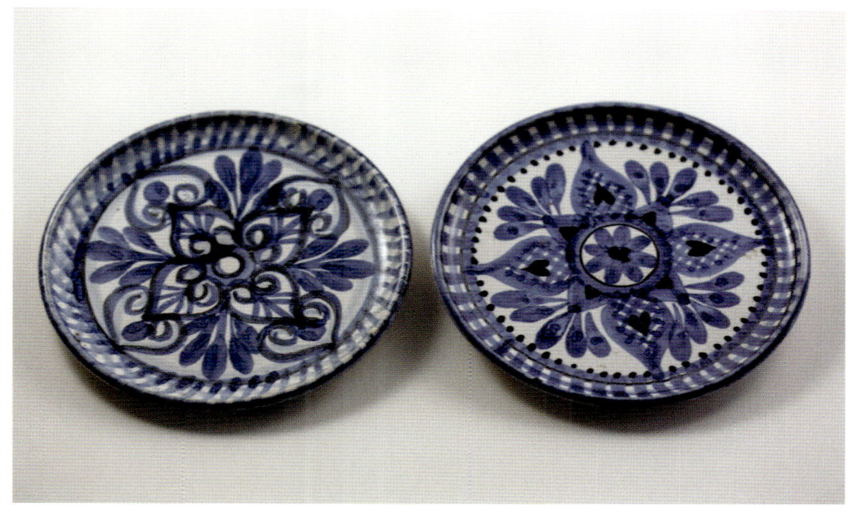

The Old Jar | Pair of small ornamental plates | 130x15mm | Provenance: Wendy Gers | Marks: both unglazed bases have an oval black-and-white sticker, 'The Old Jar Potteries Benoni' and black hand-written markings, '177 R.S.A.' | Photograph by Damien Artus

Location

29 Elston Ave, Benoni

Name

The Old Jar Pottery (TOJ) was named after De Olde Kruyk, a Dutch pottery located in Milsbeek, near the German border, where the founder Henk Jacobs did his apprenticeship. TOJ pottery made maiolica wares in the same style as Jacobs's alma mater in the late 1940s. In subsequent years De Olde Kruyk changed its decorative repertoire, but TOJ remained faithful to its original formula.

Founders

In 1953 Jacobs founded The Old Jar Pottery with Jaap Allenson (d.2004) who had previously been associated with the Benoni brickworks. Allenson left the pottery in 1953 and 1954 and Jacobs went into partnership with Herry Duys, another Dutch immigrant and colleague he had met while working at Boksburg East Potteries. Duys was responsible for marketing and sales, while Jacobs was the artist responsible for the production and running of the business. In 1963 Jacobs sold his share of the business to Duys and returned to Holland in 1964.

Staff

When Nilant surveyed the pottery in the late 1950s, it employed three professional (European) and seven non-professional (African) staff members. In the mid-1960s the staff had grown to include approximately 15 workers and four decorators. By the early 1970s the labour force had grown to 30, including nine white and 21 African, Indian and coloured staff members. Initially all the decorators were Dutch women immigrants. The original two decorators were Margreet (aka Greetjie or Gre) de Kok and Joni Hogewind. De Kok was initially employed as a decorator in 1957 but soon became the general manager. Other decorators included Vanessa Halcutt, Sally Julsing, Mrs Man Kramers and Wendy Williamson. Louis le Sueur worked for a year at the pottery in 1959. By 1979 all the Dutch decorators had been replaced by African and coloured women.

Over the years, TOJ employed approximately five potters, including two Indian potters, Jeram Bhana and Kansamy (aka Robert or Bob Chetty). Pieter Malele was capable of throwing 40 cups an hour and was employed for many years. Like Liebermann Pottery, the management supported the staff and families of employees, and the spouses, siblings and relatives of various workers were employed.

Wares manufactured

Initially the pottery manufactured bowls for the florist industry. However, as a result of competition from Japanese rivals, it introduced the hand-decorated maiolica-style pottery for which it is renowned. All the wares feature a painted decoration, with a characteristic white background onto which a limited range of colours was applied. The Old Jar manufactured a wide range of domestic crockery, including tea and coffee sets, vases, oven to tableware, and fancy goods such as beer mugs, ashtrays, planters, ornamental oxen and horses, decorated tiles, commemorative plates, chargers and lamp bases. TOJ undertook a few commissions, among them an ashtray for Associated Lead Manufacturers.[249] In the 1970s it produced a range of 260 different items and in the early 1980s this range was reduced to 120 items.

Production methods

Initially the majority of the wares were hand-thrown, turned and hand-decorated. Jiggers and jolleys were introduced by Duys in 1964. The handles of milk jugs, tea cups and other vessels were slip-cast.

Brief history of the pottery

The Old Jar was initially located in the premises of a small bakery. Like so many potteries, it started with minimal infrastructure and equipment. The potter's wheels and other equipment were made by the founder, Jacobs. He was a skilled potter who observed a niche in the market for well-crafted, handmade domestic ware in the maiolica style. The pottery grew rapidly, and in 1980 was producing 32 000 items annually. Artists were given freedom to develop a variety of maiolica-style motifs, although their relatively uniform palette serves to identify TOJ ceramics. Blue painting on a white background was dominant in the early years as cobalt oxide was an easy-to-use, stable colouring agent. Early pieces are characterised by delicate chromatic nuances and abundant, fine-detailed brushwork. Although blue and white (with outlines in black) dominated the early pottery, the colour was enhanced with a light grey/blue permitting more shading and decorative potential. The background was not pure white,

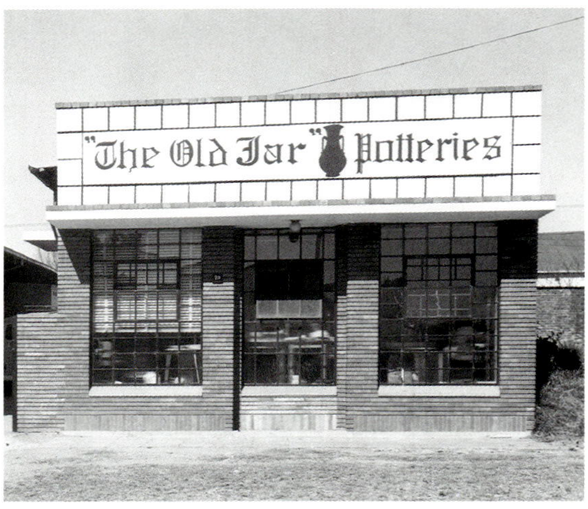

TOJ Potteries, Benoni | Provenance: Herry Duys | Scan by Corine Meyer, DNMCH

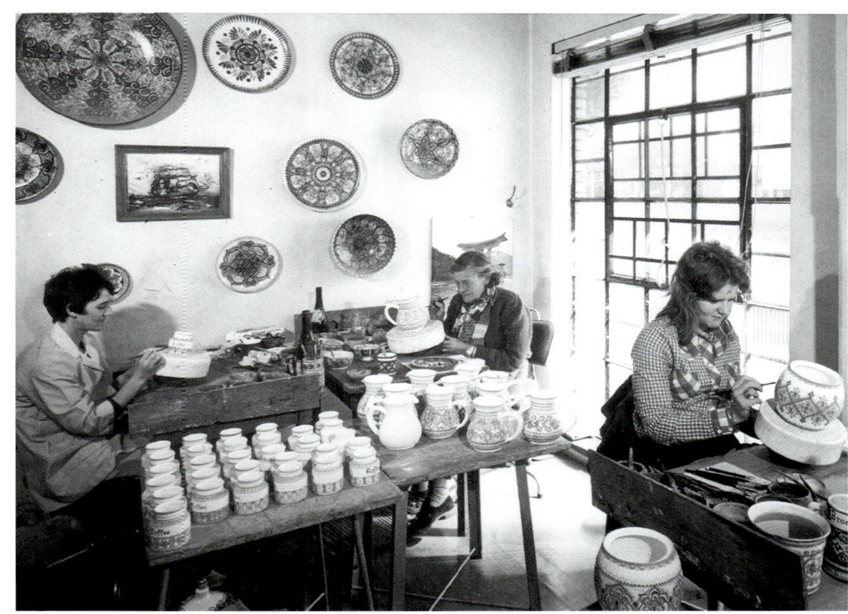

The Old Jar | Unidentified decorators | Provenance: Herry Duys | Scan by Corine Meyer, DNMCH

but had a soft b uish/greyish appearance. The decoration of later examples is characterised by brighter colours that appear to be flat in comparison to earlier wares. Later pieces generally have less decoration and simplified patterns.[250]

Over the years, TOJ struggled to obtain a reliable source of clay. Jacobs developed its clay body, using clay from Garsfontein, Pretoria, which was mixed with kaolin, ball clay and silica. Thus, early TOJ wares have a dark red, porous, soft clay body. Upon his return to Holland, Jacobs exported Dutch clay to South Africa, suitable for the production of oven-to-table ware. Later artefacts have a light-coloured red body, which was less porous. Sometimes a white clay body was used. Every five years glazes were imported from De Plasmolen in the Netherlands. This factor no doubt ensured the conformity of their palette.

Wares were sold at the Rand Easter Show and at most major craft shops in South Africa. The company often struggled to meet local demand, and thus never entered the export market.

Herry Duys was a gifted manager and expert at marketing. He organised TOJ's first major publicity event, which was held on Shrove Tuesday in 1961. The studio attracted headlines when it invited various prominent South African artists, including Walter Battiss, Guiseppe Cattaneo, Anna Vorster, Dirk Meerkotter and Gordon Vorster to participate in 'a clay spree' (Loxton 1961). These artists decorated vases and clowned around, to the great enjoyment of the press and other guests.

Photos of TOJ reveal that the work space was skilfully designed, clean, light, well ventilated, spacious and extremely well organised, with customised trolleys for moving trays of pottery and mobile platforms for moving green wares onto the drying shelves on the mezzanine level. Visiting British researcher and consultant David Thornton commented: 'If I once could adequately describe a factory as being a "happy factory" this is indeed one' (Thornton 1973:124, 125).

The factory closed in approximately 1984 as a result of the importation of cheap mass-produced Taiwanese wares that looked similar to TOJ wares.[251] The pottery is significant in that it survived three decades without making many significant changes to the essential design of its products. The colourful wares satisfied customers because they were offered artefacts that were neither too modern nor too old-fashioned. The decoration, which combined floral and geometric motifs, was appealingly feminine, but not too sentimental. It offered a hint of the exotic, with its maiolica references to North African, Moorish and Italian pottery, yet was comfortingly local, with the majority of their wares signed with a patriotic 'Hand Made in South Africa' or 'R.S.A.' This home-grown maiolica tradition became a 'classic' in South Africa, enduring may decades of changing fashions in the pottery industry.

Marks

TOJ wares are identified by a variety of marks. An approximate chronological order has been established, and known dates are indicated in brackets. However, it is important to note that some marks overlapped or were used simultaneously.

- Sgraffito mark, 'Jacobs' (1953).
- Glazed base with a black (or occasionally a dark blue) hand-painted marks, 'TOJ' or 'T.O.J.; HANDMADE' or 'HANDPAINTED' (from approximately 1959). Many wares include additional hand-painted marks such as a one-, two- or three-digit reference number. This number referred to the sales catalogue.
- Some wares include the initials of decorators, for example 'JH', 'MK', 'HI', 'EL' (or 'ER') and 'TV' (late 1950s/early 1960s).
- Gilt oval-shaped sticker with embossed text (late 1950s/early 1960s).
- Black sticker with silver text, 'The Old Jar Benoni' (late 1960s).
- Unglazed base with impressed logo; impressed place name 'BENONI' and black painted marks, 'T.O.J.' (1960s).
- Glazed base with painted marks, 'Handmade', or 'Handmade in S.A.' or 'HANDMADE IN R.S.A.' (late 1960s/1970s).
- Some smaller wares had abbreviated marks, such as 'RSA' or 'R.S.A.' and a one- or two-digit number.
- Other small items had no marks (1970s/1980s).
- Transparent sticker with blue oval, 'The Old Jar Potteries, Benoni' (1980s).
- Gilt sticker in the shape of an inverted triangle with illustration of a large pot, 'The Old Jar, Benoni' (date unknown) (illus. Kerrod 2010:198).
- Cast raised marks, 'T.O.J.' which were accompanied by a cast mould number, for example 'A17' (date unknown) (illus. Kerrod 2010).

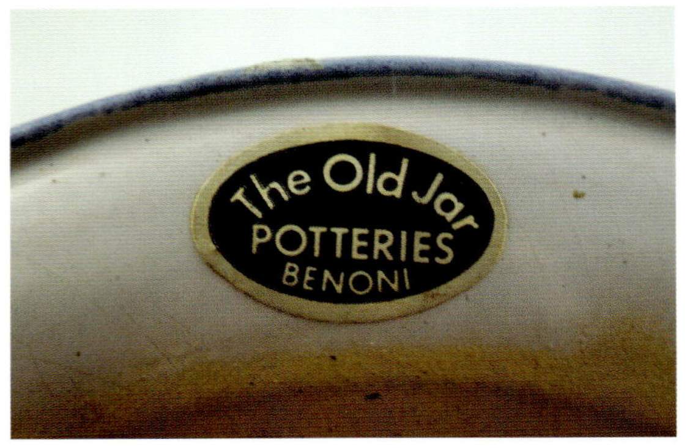

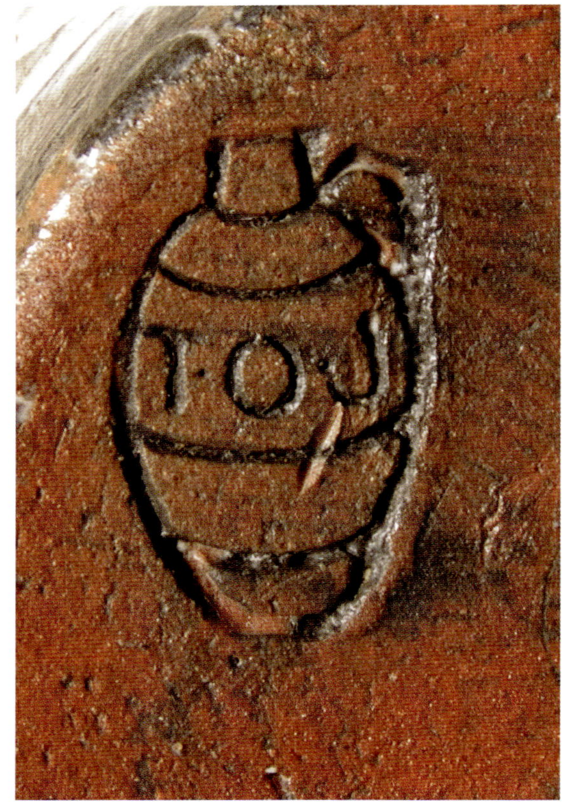

TOP: The Old Jar | Maker's mark | Sticker, black and white | Photograph by Damien Artus

BOTTOM: The Old Jar | Maker's mark | Stamp | Photograph by Natalie Field

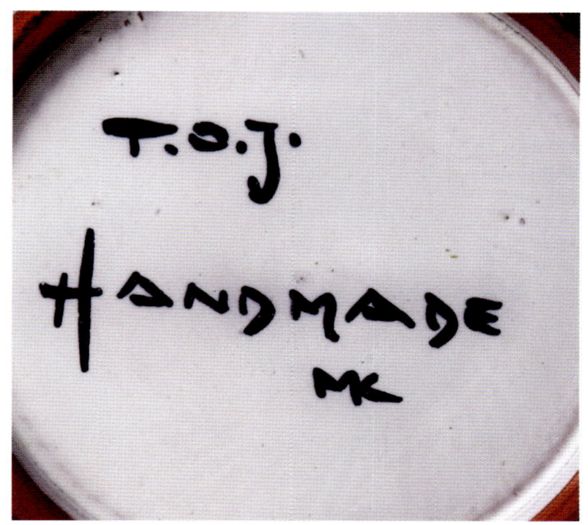

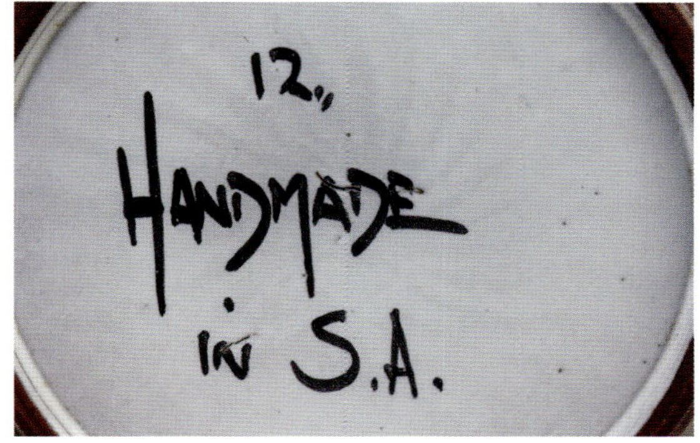

TOP: The Old Jar | Maker's mark | Black painted glaze marks, 'T.O.J. HANDMADE' with initials 'MK' (Margreet de Kok) | Photograph by Natalie Field

BOTTOM: The Old Jar | Maker's mark | Black painted glaze marks, '12., Handmade in S.A.' | Photograph by Natalie Field

Biographies

BHANA, Jeram

Bhana studied painting in India and was employed as a potter by Duys after their meeting at the Divine Life Society. He eventually became the second thrower, after Chetty. Duys invited Bhana to move to Benoni, where he lived for 12 years.

CHETTY, Kansamy (aka Robert or Bob Chetty)

Chetty worked as a thrower at Globe Potteries in the 1950s and at Riverside Pottery Works in the 1960s. He was subsequently employed by Dykor and then worked as a master potter at TOJ for over 20 years. Initially he worked with Jacobs, then for a period he was the sole potter. At TOJ Chetty was subsequently assisted by Bhana. In the 1970s, Chetty worked at Liebermann Pottery.

DE KOK, Margreet (Greetjie) (deceased)

De Kok was employed as a decorator in 1957. The wares that she decorated were signed with her initials. De Kok subsequently became the manager of the pottery.

DUYS, Herry (1922–2008)

Born in Bussum, Holland, Duys studied at Deventer Agricultural High School, and then at Tropical Agricultural Engineering. As a result of the lack of professional opportunities after World War II, Duys departed for Australia and the former Dutch New Guinea (now known as Irian Jaya/West Papua), where he worked as a labourer, installing telephone poles in tea plantations. Malaria and dysentery resulted in his repatriation. He subsequently married and the couple joined Duys's eldest brother in South Africa in the early years.

Duys was employed at SA Glazing as a sales representative. After meeting Jacobs, the pair decided to set up their own pottery and in 1953 they acquired a site in Benoni and commenced operations. Duys was responsible for sales, marketing and administration. In 1984 he sold his share of the business to Duys and returned to Holland in 1964. In 1984 Duys sold the business to David and Sheila Chambers, and retired.

HALCUTT, Vanessa

Halcutt was employed by TOJ as a decorator from ca.1971 to 1980.

HOGEWIND, Joni (d.2011)

Miss Hogewind, a Dutch artist, was employed as a decorator by TOJ from 1959 to mid-1961, when she went back to the Netherlands. There she married a potter, Han Cornelissens. They established a pottery in a small historical village, Bronkhorst.

JACOBS, Henk W M (b.1924)
Jacobs was born in Amsterdam. He studied ceramics at De Plasmolen, and from 1946 to 1947 he was apprenticed to Olde Kruyk in Milsbeek and the Art Academy in Arnhem. He came to South Africa in 1952 as a result of a lack of professional opportunities in Holland after the war and was employed at SA Glazing by another Hollander, Leslie Lulofs. Jacobs co-founded The Old Jar Potteries in 1953. He was the original potter at TOJ and continued to make wares until 1964, when he returned to Holland.

In the early years he did all the decoration himself, but soon employed decorators. He would paint an eighth of the surface and the decorators were obliged to complete the wares. Jacobs continued to work as a studio potter in Gennep, Noord-Limburg, Holland, until the early 1990s when he retired. Wares produced in his pottery 'De Champignon' are marked with a mushroom.[252]

JULSING, Sally (deceased)
Julsing, a Dutch immigrant, was employed as a decorator by TOJ.

KRAMERS, Man (deceased)
Mrs Kramers, a Dutch immigrant, was employed as a decorator by TOJ.

LE SUEUR, Louis (b.1942)
Born in Pretoria, Le Sueur studied at The Old Jar Pottery in Benoni in 1959 before continuing his formal studies in 1966 at the Johannesburg College of Art, where he majored in drawing and sculpture. He became a professional sculptor, working primarily in bronze. Le Sueur has lived in South Africa, Zimbabwe, America and Namibia and currently resides in the United Kingdom. He has undertaken various prestigious commissions and has works in South African institutions including the Pelmama Permanent Art Collection of PAM and Oliewenhuis Art Museum, Bloemfontein, as well as in various international collections.[253]

MALELE, Pieter
Malele was the foreman; a skilled technician and thrower, he was capable of throwing 40 cups an hour. Malele was one of the longest-serving employees of TOJ.

WILLIAMSON, Wendy
Williamson was employed as a decorator by TOJ.

Unidentified staff

[Surname unknown], Ellen
Ellen was employed as a decorator by TOJ.

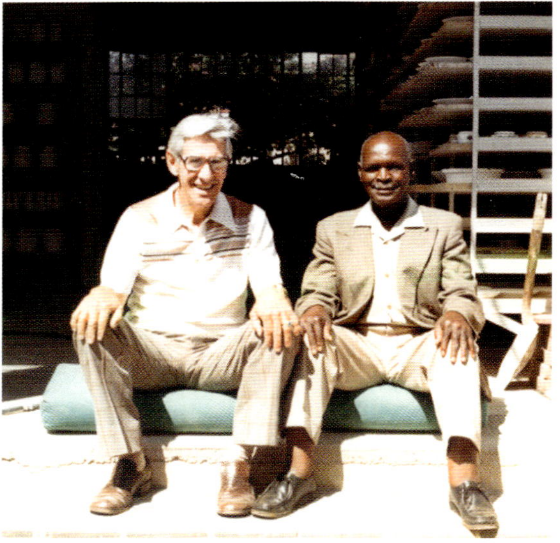

The Old Jar | Herry Duys & Pieter Malele | Provenance: Heery Duys | Scan by Corine Meyer, DNMCH

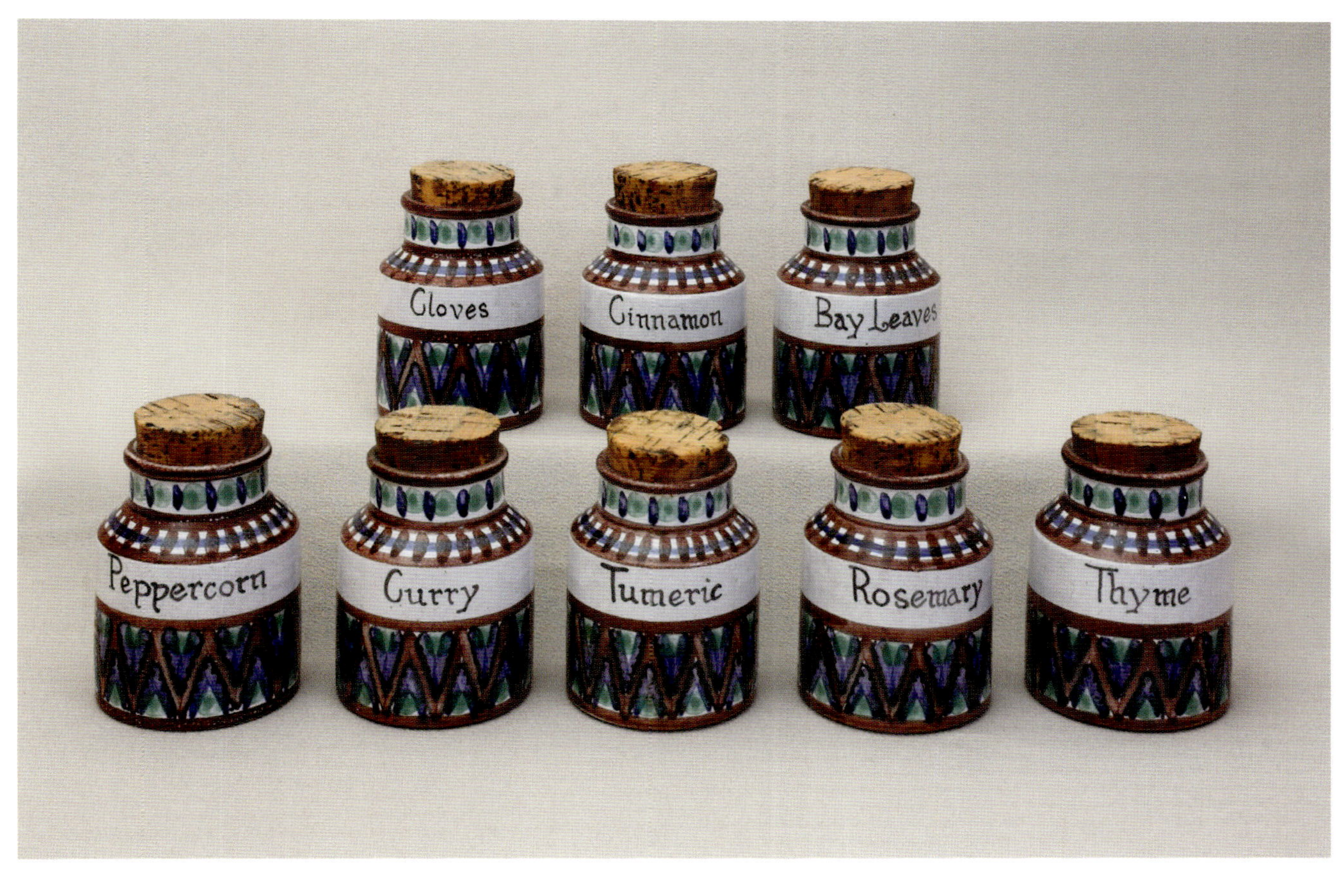

The Old Jar | Set of herb and spice jars | 100x55x76mm | Provenance: Douglas van der Horst | Marks: unglazed terracotta base with black painted markings, '20 Hand made in S.A.' | Photograph by Natalie Field

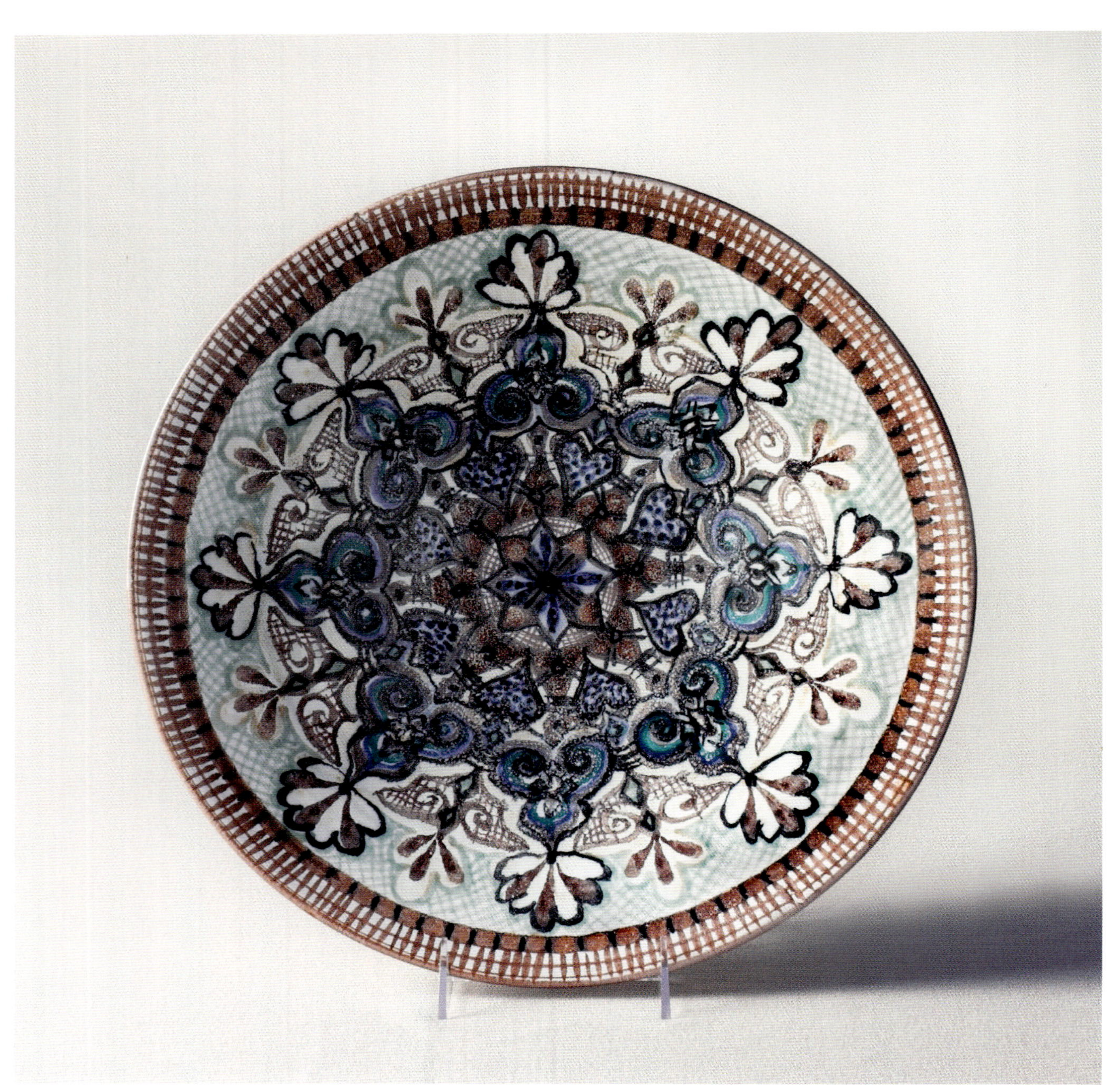

The Old Jar | Large charger with mandala majolica decoration | 370x30mm | Provenance: Gordon Radowsky | Marks: base glazed with T.O.J. S.A. S. impressed TOJ stamp | Photograph by Natalie Field

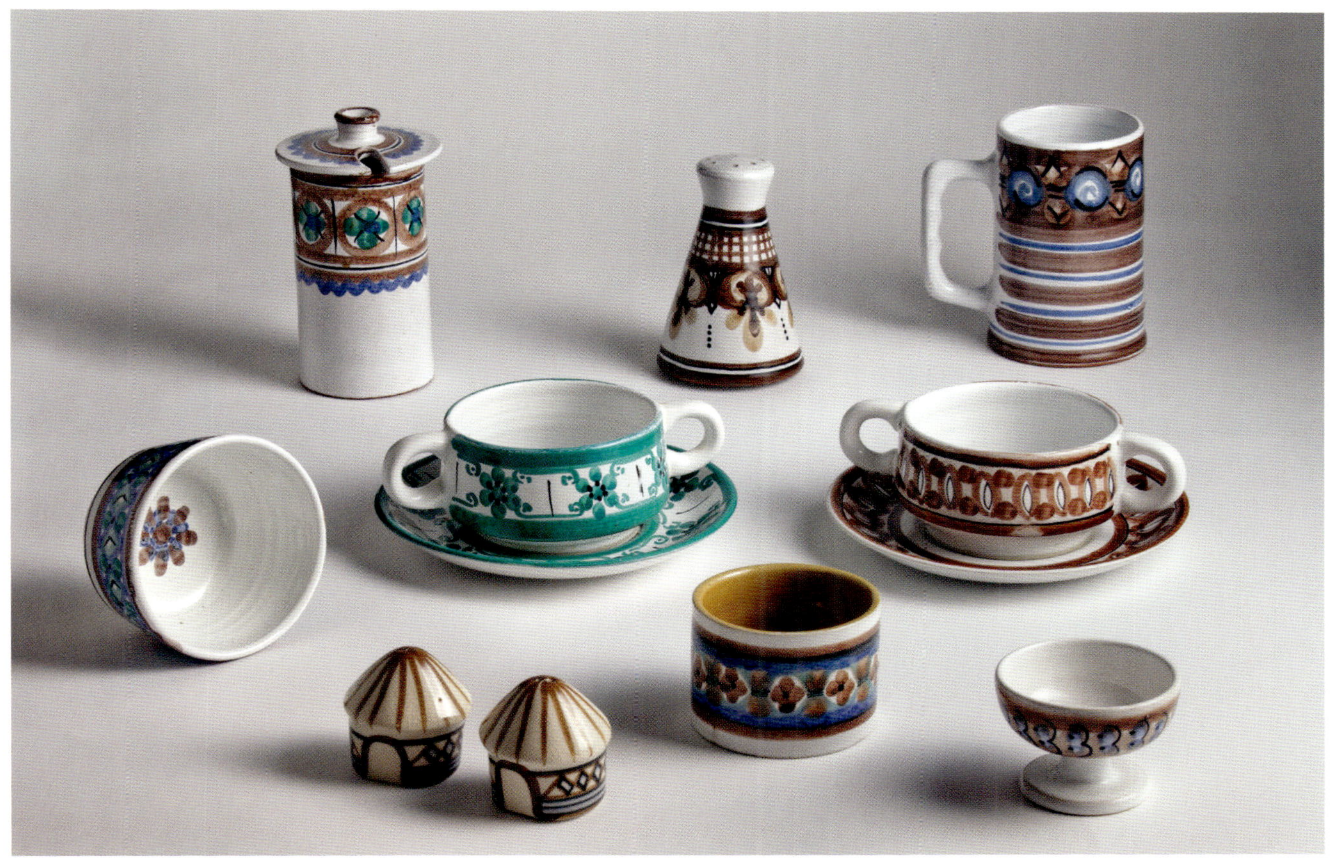

The Old Jar | Diverse domestic ware | salt cellar 125x46x80; mug 137x85x90mm; pair of soup bowls 65x105x180x85mm; pair of saucers for soup bowls 22x180mm; cylindrical storage jar 170x72x75mm; cylindrical storage jar lid 35x95mm; small ramekin salt and pepper cellars in the shape of a hut 65x47mm; miniature goblet 57x78x55mm; bowl 65x109x80mm | Provenance: Wendy Gers | Marks: salt cellar glazed white base with hand-painted black glaze markings, 'SA 186'; mug glazed white base with hand-painted black glaze markings, '125 RSA'; soup bowls glazed white base with hand-painted black glaze markings, '209'; salt and pepper cellars in the shape of a hut unmarked; miniature goblet glazed white base with hand-painted black glaze markings '17'; miniature goblet glazed white base with hand-painted black glaze markings, '161 R.S.A' | Photograph by Damien Artus

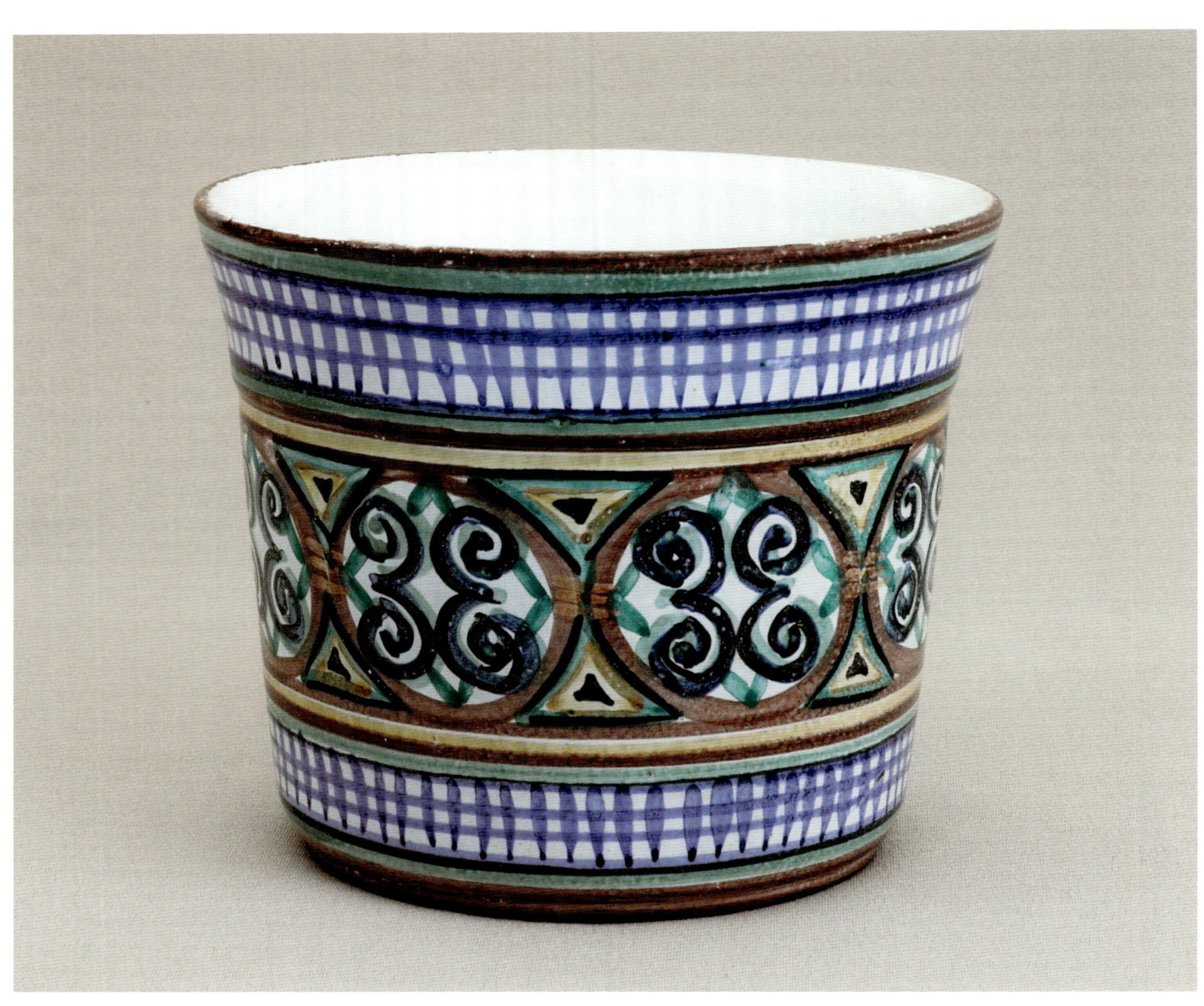

The Old Jar | Large vase | 205x232x170mm | Provenance: TAG | 2738/07 | Marks: glazed white base with black glaze marks, '12., Handmade in S.A.' | Photograph by Natalie Field

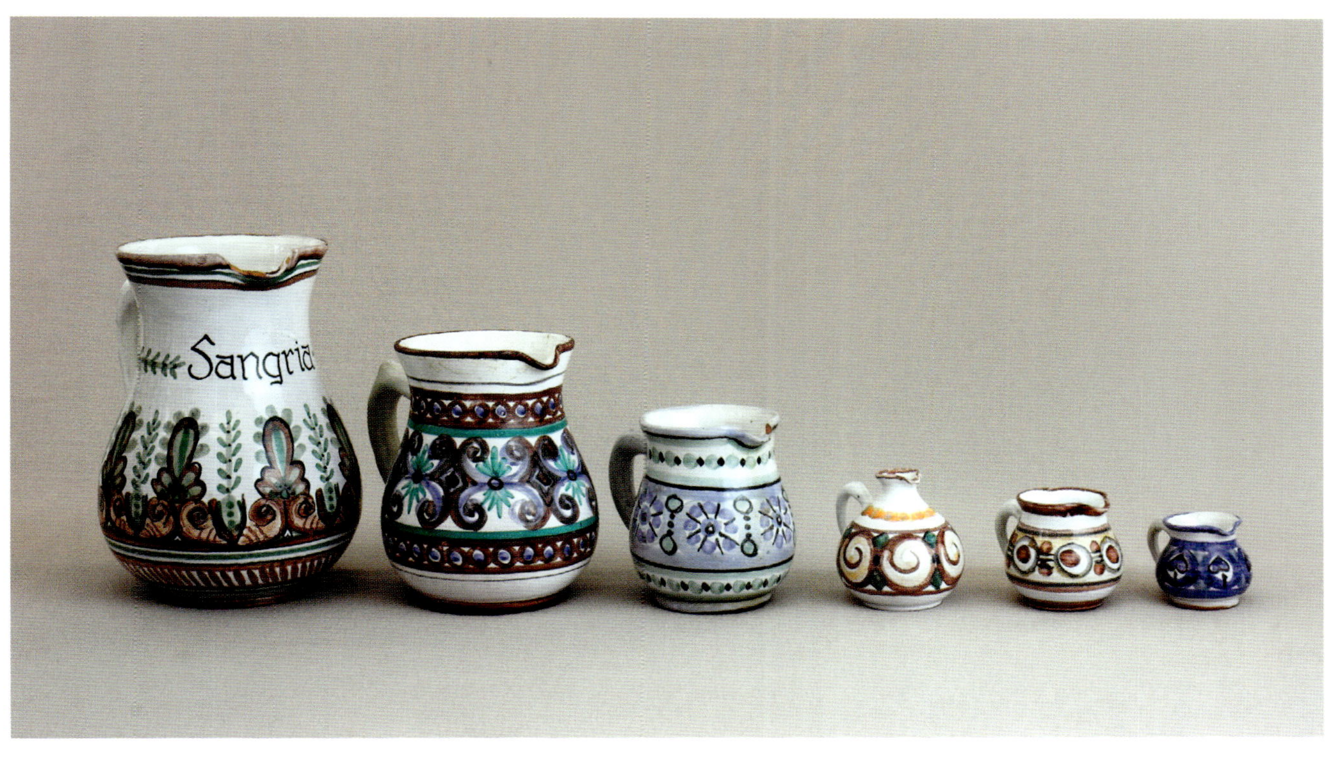

The Old Jar | Group of six jugs | From left: 225x130x95mm; 166x105x95mm; 120x80x66mm; 85x25x45mm; 69x55x43mm; 54x46x40mm | Provenance: TAG | From left: 2742/07; 2734/02; 2741/07; 2723/07; 2722/07; 2721/07 | Marks from left: white glazed base with black painted markings, 'R.S.A. 66.'; white glazed base with black painted markings, '40 Handmade in S.A.'; white glazed base with black painted markings, 'Handmade in SA. 39'; white glazed base with black painted markings, 'R.S.A. 175'; white glazed base with black painted markings, 'Handmade in SA 37'; white glazed base with black painted markings, '36' | Photograph by Natalie Field

Vereeniging Brick and Tile Company (VBTC) (1903–1909)

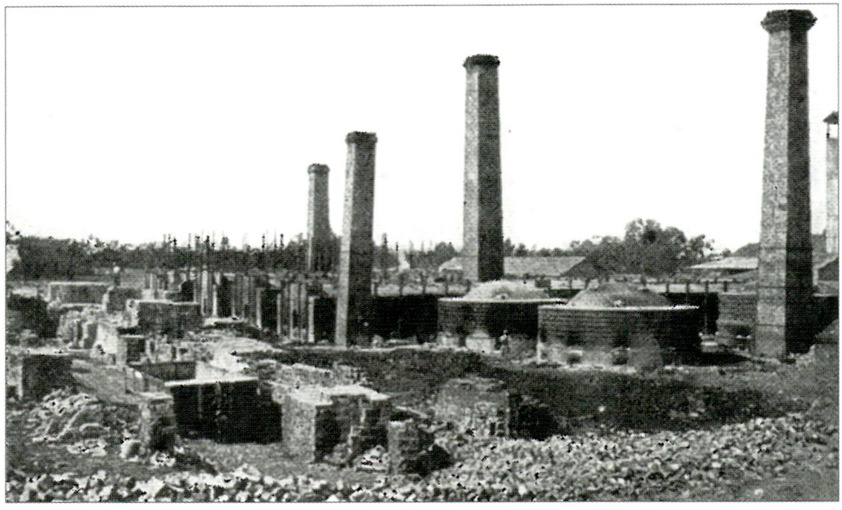

In 1890 fire-clay deposits were found under the coal seams of Bedworth Colliery, owned by the financier and manufacturing mogul Sammy Marks (1843–1920).[254] By 1894 the coal mining company produced fire-clay bricks[255] and domestic bricks[256] as a secondary activity. Marks realised the potential of establishing a pottery, and in approximately 1903 the company's managing director, A H Rogers, imported artistic craftsmen from Staffordshire. The Vereeniging Brick and Tile Company (VBTC) made 'ornamental vases and other choice pottery' to the design of the famous architect Sir Herbert Baker (1862–1946) (Leigh 1968:s.n.).

There are currently no known examples of the VBTC's artistic wares.[257] However, by 1909 the VBTC abandoned its production of artistic wares in favour of the relatively more lucrative production of bricks and industrial wares, including planters and storage jars.[258] Baker's support of the VBTC was also associated with his specification of their roofing tiles on the railway station (1908) and later the Union Government Buildings (1910) in Pretoria. These orders undoubtedly confirmed the quality of locally produced wares and stimulated the growth of this sector.

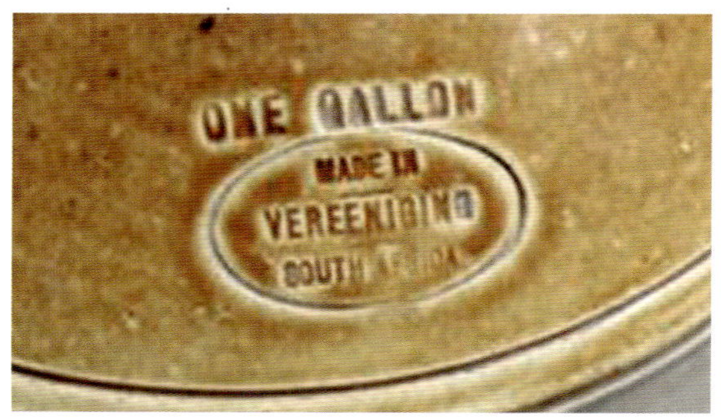

TOP: Vereeniging Brick and Tile Company | SA Who's Who 1926. p. 618 | Scan by William Martinson

LEFT: Vereeniging Brick and Tile Company | Impressed maker's mark on the shoulder of a stoneware gallon bottle: 'One Gallon' above an oval stamp containing, 'Made in Vereeniging South Africa' | Provenance: Jan Middeljans | Photograph by Natalie Field

Zaalberg Potterij (1951–1983)

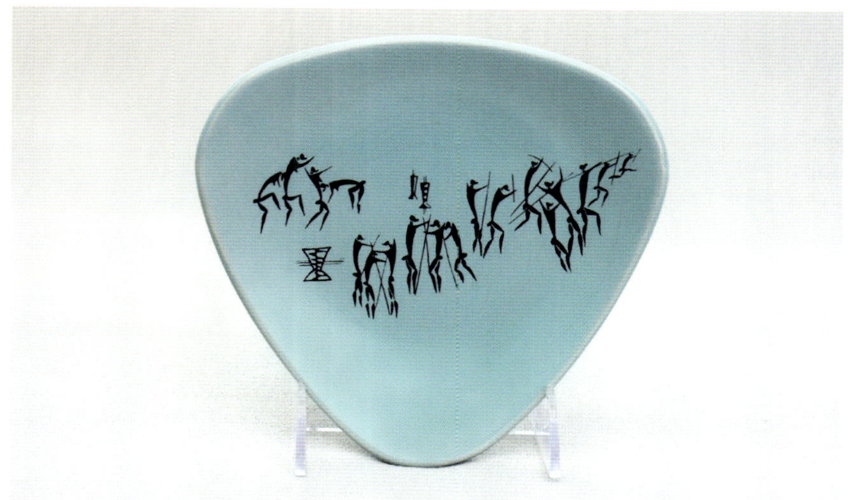

Zaalberg Potterij | Charger | Pale blue glazed form decorated with a transfer of San motifs | 170x170x25mm | Provenance: TAG | 2398/06 | Marks: glazed base with two transfers, black transfer 'With compliments Beare Bros. Durban.' indistinct light brown transfer, 'Zaalberg Potterij' below round logo | Photograph by Natalie Field

Location

Parow East, near Cape Town

Name

Various formulations of the name were used, including Zaalberg Pottery, Zaalberg Potteries and Zaalberg Potterij. The latter seems to be the preferred official form.

Founder

Maarten Zaalberg founded Zaalberg Potterij in the early 1950s. In later years he appointed L A Steens (chairman), S J Ewijk van der Bijl (director) and A M V Stapper (secretary).

Staff

He was initially assisted by Nicola Canosa, Sophy Bodenstein (née Louw) and Fransie Lombardt. Zaalberg claimed that he designed all the items made by the pottery. The pottery also employed various unnamed decorators who are known by the initials K,[259] CK[260] and/or GR.

Wares manufactured

Zaalberg Potterij produced a wide range of inexpensive utilitarian wares including tea and coffee sets, dinner services, sets of snack bowls, soup bowls with lids and handles, condiment sets (salt, pepper, mustard, oil and vinegar), two-toned hors d'oeuvres sets on wooden bases, table bells, lidded cheese dishes, lidded jam pots, ashtrays, piggy-banks, fruit bowls, cool drink sets (with a jug and beaker), candle holders and ice buckets with cane handles. A wide variety of vases and pedestal bowls for florists, wall plaques, decorative tiles, ornaments, planters with or without saucers and ovenware were also

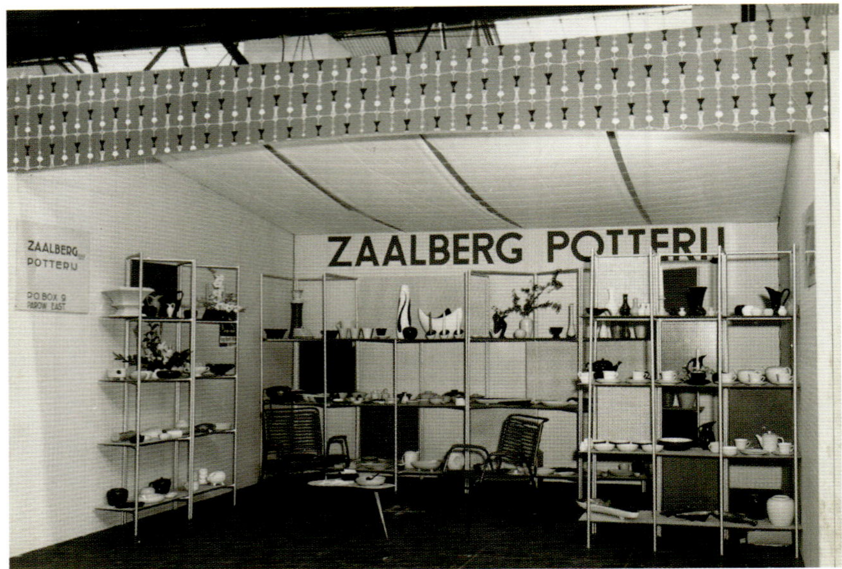

Zaalberg Potterij | Exhibition stand at an unknown trade fair | Provenance: Zaalberg Archives, SHC Iziko | SACHM 90/606 | Marks: photo marked on verso, 'Anson Press, PO Box 5944 JHB, Photo 900.' | Scan by Lailah Hisham

produced. These brightly coloured monochrome wares were available in yellow, mauve, pale turquoise, celadon, black and grey. They recall American table services of the mid-1930s, (such as 'Fiesta' by F H Read [1880–1942]) which were reproduced in pastel shades in Holland after the war (Bogaers 1988:17).

In the 1950s and 1960s the pottery also produced some artistic vessels decorated with stylised sgraffito images of San parietal art. These vessels included large triangular bowls, lidded casseroles, vases, planters, mugs and tankards, ashtrays, candle holders, plates, bowls and chargers. Zaalberg also produced a smaller quantity of wares decorated with sgraffito motifs of African figures, dressed in stylised blankets. Another artistic range of wares, primarily bottles and vases, was decorated with stylised Zulu and San shields. There is a wide variety of stylistic variations in the execution of the designs and this is probably due to the individual styles of the respective decorators. Many of these forms resemble those that were fashionable in contemporary Holland, including the 'Black Princess' service that was manufactured by Regina in 1955. These Dutch designs had their roots in Swedish design of the 1930s (Bogaers 1988:44).

From the late 1950s the pottery produced pierced cylindrical lampshades, which were replaced in the early 1970s by a far more elaborate baroque form with steep undulating curves. It also produced garden lights composed of a stacked column of joined squat thrown pots. The final pot was pierced to allow the light to illuminate the garden. By 1962 the pottery had produced over 250 different products.

From the early 1960s Zaalberg Potterij manufactured large amounts of advertising wares with silk-screened transfers of corporate logos. Among others, corporate clients included automobile manufacturers,[261] banks,[262] large industrial concerns[263] and various smaller businesses and organisations.[264]

Zaalberg Potterij also produced square and rectangular wall tiles that featured decorative elements that recall celestial bodies, such as suns, moons and stars. Most feature a raised or depressed central circular element, surrounded by concentric rings. The company also made matching tiles and door knobs. Tiles were manufactured in three sizes[265] and were modular. The tiles were attached to asbestos panels in order to facilitate the installation of large decorative murals. They were made in a variety of colours including orange, olive-green, deep turquoise, blue and black, and all feature a metallic glaze with yellow, orange, red and brown highlights.

Production methods

Maarten Zaalberg initially used a potter's wheel and produced and decorated all items by hand in the early years. However, in subsequent years, slip-casting and mechanical production methods such as jiggers and jolleys were introduced to improve efficiency. For standard industrial ware, less time-consuming means of decorating wares were introduced, including transfers.

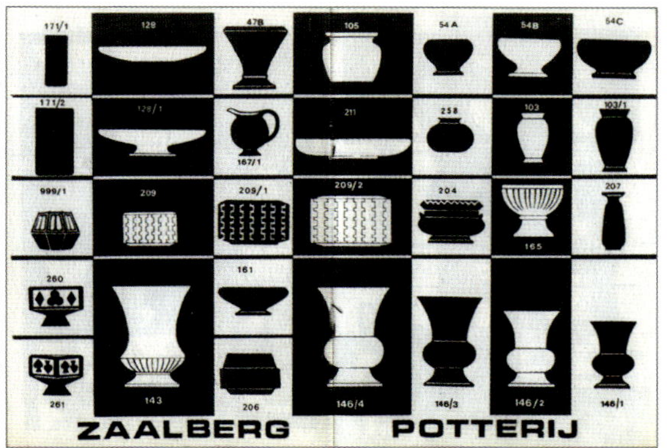

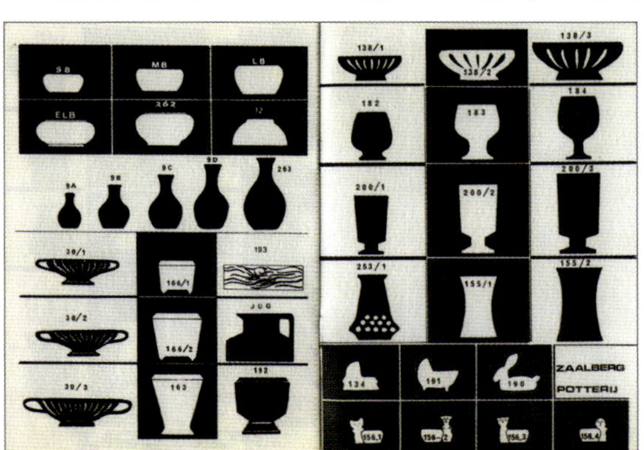

Zaalberg Potterij | Catalogue 1973, p. 4, 5, 6, 7 | Provenance: Zaalberg Archives, SHC Iziko | SACHM 90/606 | Scan by Lailah Hisham

Brief history of the pottery

In 1951 Zaalberg immigrated to South Africa and spent one year conducting intense technical investigations before opening his first pottery in the garage of his home. Shortly thereafter he established Zaalberg Potterij as a local branch of Zaalberg Potterij, Holland. The association of the two potteries appears to have been primarily for publicity, intended to impress prospective clients with the European connection. In 1952 Zaalberg commenced stoneware production. These early works are highly significant as they are the first documented production of stoneware in South Africa, and predate Hilda Ditchburn (née Rose) (1917–1986) of the University of Natal, who built her stoneware kiln in 1954, and was previously considered the pioneer of this medium (Calder 2012:60). However, Zaalberg's stoneware was not appreciated by the local market, and after a few years of hard work and no visible financial benefits, Zaalberg decided to open a factory and mass-produce objects. He taught himself to make moulds, and converted the kiln to earthenware.

Zaalberg was initially assisted by Sofie Bodenstein (née Louw) and Fransie Lombardt. By the mid-1950s the pottery employed about 19 staff members. In the early years he faced great technical difficulties, as clay was not easily available, and glazes, kilns and equipment had to be imported. Wares were predominantly sold in South Africa, but some were also exported to the former Rhodesia and other Central African countries. By the mid-1970s Zaalberg Potterij was obtainable in a number of exclusive department stores and craft shops, including Stuttafords, Garlicks, John Orr's, Binnehuis Interiors and Gift Horse, Pretoria.

As a foreigner, Zaalberg overcame many obstacles in his early years, including language. In 1956 he explained to Dr FGE Nilant:

> In the begin we have tried to make specially artistic ware, like I was used to in Holland. This was very hard as the people do not understand here yet the meaning of modern or really pottery. We have changed a bit, and made our colours a bit stronger and on the other hand try to make the shapes as simple as possible. Just by a simple shape and a glazing without decor, one can achieve interesting nice things [sic] (Zaalberg 1956).

While the vast majority of Zaalberg's wares were commercially or aesthetically motivated, some quirky exceptions exist. One particularly interesting plate reflects Zaalberg's sense of humour over the ludicrous idiosyncrasies of the Nationalist government of the late 1960s. This plate is decorated with transfers of the old South African flag and an Afrikaans newspaper clipping of a new law being passed requiring permission from a special parliamentary committee to use images of national emblems such as the flag and coat of arms. It claimed that anyone who violated this law would be prosecuted. According to Esther Esmyol, curator, SHC Iziko, this plate was frequently included as a prank in large consignments.

Zaalberg was a man torn between two worlds. He earned his livelihood mass producing bright popular ceramics, yet was an ardent supporter of the Anglo-Oriental tradition. He crusaded this aesthetic sensibility within the Cape Potters Association and, for many people, Zaalberg '... represented one of a group of South African potters who are to our country what Leach and Cardew were to England: the first generation of studio potters that paved the way for our generation ...' (Hayward Fell 1989:4). Constantly faced with the need to compromise his sense of taste and style and design for a mass market, Zaalberg explained that 'Some [designs] have to be made, because there is a market for it' (Zaalberg 1956).

Marks

Standard undecorated industrial ware was generally unmarked.

- A large variety of transfers were used on commercial wares. These included numerous variations of the Zaalberg name, e.g. 'Zaalberg Pottery Parow', 'Zaalberg Potterij', 'Zaalberg Pottery South Africa', 'Zaalberg Handpainted'.
- A transfer depicting a chequered incomplete shield, with 'Zaalberg, South Africa' adjacent to the shield, was used on some wares decorated with 'bushman' motifs in the late 1950s.
- Two different circular logos were frequently used. The first, used in the late 1950s, contains three segments containing the letters Z, S and A. The second logo consisting of three concentric circles containing variations of the pottery's name was used in the late 1960s and early 1970s. An additional external curved tangent was added to this logo in the 1980s.
- Some wares were marked with a gold sticker that contained 'Zaalberg Potterij, Parrow' in a circular logo.

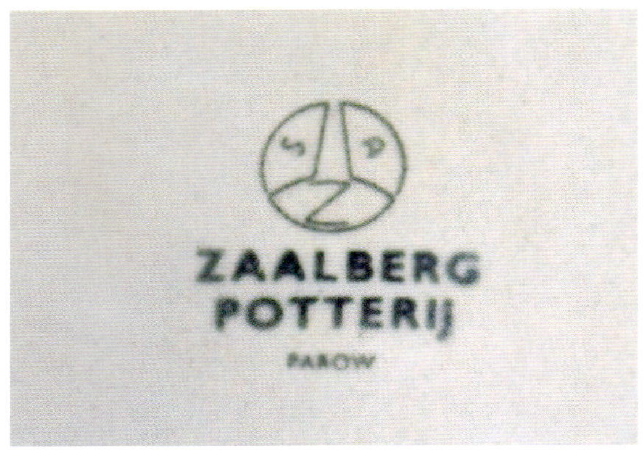

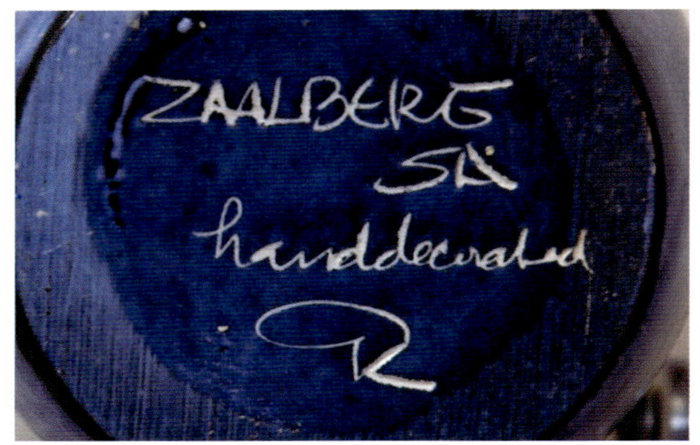

TOP: Zaalberg Potterij | Maker's mark | Glaze stamp, segmented circle containing 'ZSA' above inscription, 'Zaalberg Potterij Parrow' | Additional information: circa 1950s | Photograph by Natalie Field

BOTTOM: Zaalberg Potterij | Maker's mark | Hand engraved inscription in blue glaze on base, 'Zaalberg SA hand-decorated GR' | Additional information: circa 1950s | Photograph by Natalie Field

- Some wares from the 1950s and 1960s have sgraffito marks on their bases, such as 'Zaalberg Pottery. South Africa', 'Zaalberg, S.A.', 'Zaalberg Potterij, Parow', 'Studio Zaalberg', 'Zaalberg Potterij South Africa', or 'Z.S.A.' Frequently, wares that have a sgraffito mark on the base were a little more refined than standard industrial wares.
- Certain wares have hand-painted marks, e.g. 'Zaalberg Handpainted SA'.
- Zaalberg used a glaze stamp mark, 'Zaalberg Potterij, Parrow.' He also impressed a 'Z' insignia stamp on the side near the base of some of his personal wares. In the late 1970s his personal works bore a stamped mark, 'MZ'.

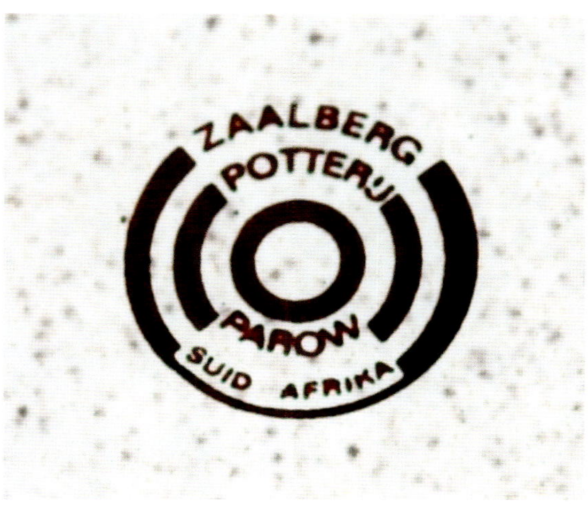

TOP: Zaalberg Potterij | Maker's mark | Brown transfer with three concentric rings, 'Zaalberg Potterij Parrow Suid Afrika' | Additional information: circa 1980s | Photograph by Natalie Field

Select exhibitions and commissions

1953	Exhibition of 'Zaalberg Pottery' and pottery demonstrations by Zaalberg, Garlicks, Cape Town.
1953	Exhibition and pottery demonstration for the Theatrical Garden Party, De Waal Park, Cape Town.
ca.1953	Exhibition of 'Zaalberg Pottery' and pottery demonstrations by Zaalberg, Binnehuis Interiors, Cape Town.
1955	'Exhibition of South African Ceramics', Stuttafords, Cape Town. The exhibition was sponsored by the Pottery Manufacturers Association of South Africa and the 'Buy South African' campaign.
1959 & 1967	The Cape Show, Goodwood, Cape Town.
1975	'Zaalberg Potteries' exhibition and pottery demonstration, Stuttafords, Cape Town.

Zaalberg Potterij received commissions for tile panels including Braby House, Cape Town, and in approximately 1973 was commissioned to produce all the ceramics for use in and on the Cabana Beach Hotel, Umhlanga Rocks. This included tile panels for lift interiors and the lift landings, bedroom and corridor lamp-shades, dressing table panels, vanity counter aprons, doorknobs, door-panels, room numbers, stair tiles, ashtrays and candle holders.

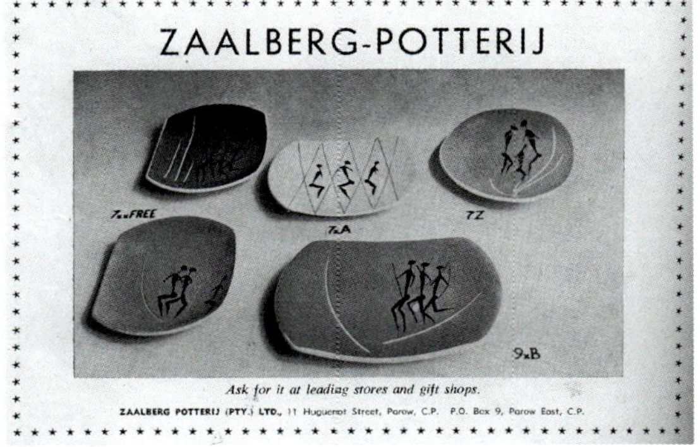

Zaalberg Potterij | Advert | *House and Home in Southern Africa* magazine, June and July 1958 p. 44 | Provenance: Zaalberg Archives, SHC Iziko | SACHM 90/606 | Scan by Lailah Hisham

Biographies

BODENSTEIN, Sophy (née Louw)

The daughter of a prominent architect from Paarl, Sophy Louw studied Fine Art at the University of Cape Town, and also obtained a certificate in pottery. She and a friend subsequently established a small studio and imported a one-and-a-half-tonne kiln from England. In 1948/1949, when she travelled to Britain to work with Bernard Leach in Cornwall, Louw and her father visited Zaalberg Potterij in Holland on their way to and from Cornwall. Via his friendship with the Louws, Zaalberg immigrated to South Africa. Bodenstein worked at the pottery until late 1953, when she got married and moved to a farm in the Transvaal near the Bechuanaland (now Botswana) border.

LOMBARDT, Fransie

Lombardt was employed by Zaalberg Potterij in the early years.

ZAALBERG, Maarten (1924–1989)

Maarten Zaalberg was born in Leiderdorp and came from an entrepreneurial family associated with the ceramic industry in the Netherlands.

His grandfather was a coppersmith. His father, Herman Zaalberg Sr (1880–1958) was employed as a sculptor in a ceramics factory in Leiden, but later resigned to establish his own pottery known as Aardewerkfabriek De Rijn in the Netherlands. It was operational from 1918 to World War II and produced vases and flowerpots. In the 1920s Zaalberg's oldest brother, Meindert (1907–1989) joined the family venture and they changed the name to Potterij Zaalberg. The pottery produced thrown tableware. The firm was a member of BKI, the Dutch association for art in industry in the mid- to late 1920s (Bogaers 1988:13). In response to the war regulation whereby 90 per cent of Dutch production was reserved for Germany, Potterij Zaalberg remodelled its kiln and produced salt-glazed pots for bottling and preserving food. During the war the pottery also produced innovative multifunctional items that served as both lids and plates, thereby economising on ration tickets (Bogaers 1988:20).

Maarten Zaalberg studied sculpture and modelling at the Akademie vir Beeldende Kunsten, The Hague from 1940 to 1945, and then worked in his father's pottery, which had become a leader in the field of Dutch artistic pottery, specialising in articles associated with the florist industry. Asian floral arrangement traditions were popular in Holland with many contemporary Dutch firms, including Groeneveld and Mobach potteries, also producing wares inspired by Chinese and Japanese prototypes (Bogaers 1988:59). These austere wares, in conjuction with his reading of Leach's *A Potter's Book*, informed the artistic sensibilities of the young Zaalberg when he arrived in South Africa in 1951 to start a local branch of Zaalberg Potterij. Indeed, his archive contained copies of glaze recipes from Leach's book as well as newspaper cuttings from South African and Dutch newspapers about Michael Cardew (1901–1983).

Zaalberg initially made artistic stoneware pottery, but soon re-orientated his pottery to manufacture popular mass-produced earthenware. From 1968 Zaalberg was able to return to making artistic pottery, when he built a large studio next to his Durbanville home. This was coincidently the year that Meindert Zaalberg was honoured with a major retrospective exhibition at the Museum Boijmans Van Beuningen, Rotterdam.

In 1982, when he retired from Zaalberg Potterij, Maarten Zaalberg rededicated himself to creating unique artistic wares. His talent was recognised nationally and he was awarded various important public and private commissions, including large sculptural tile murals for public buildings such as airports.

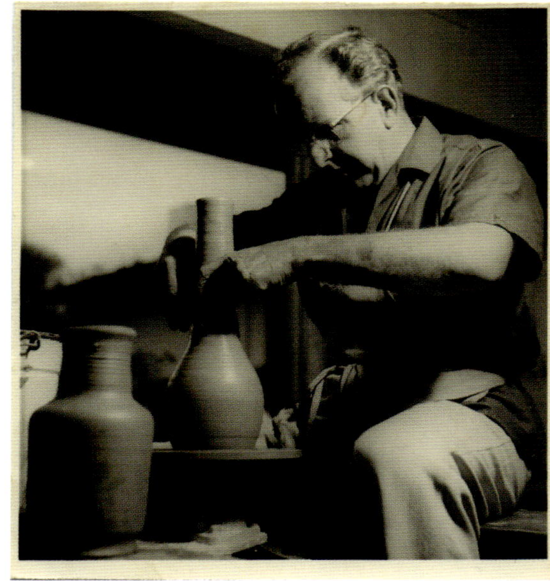

Zaalberg throwing on the potter's wheel | Provenance: Zaalberg Archives, SHC Iziko | SACHM 90/607 | Scan by Lailah Hisham

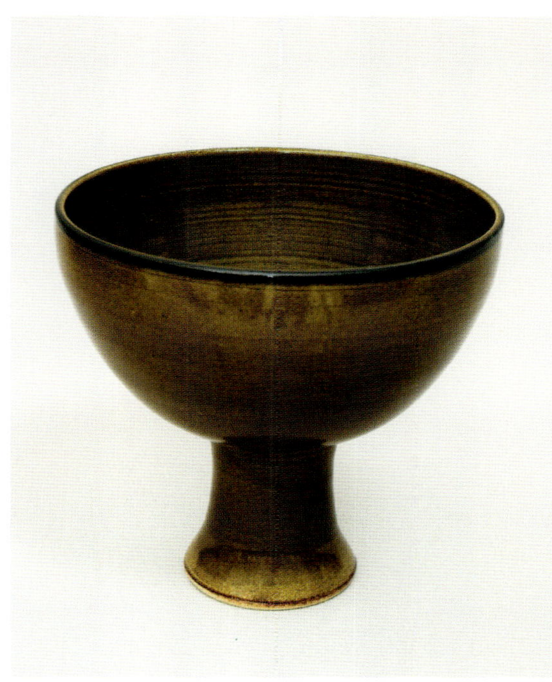

Zaalberg, M | Large chalice, or 'coupe'-shaped bowl, glazed with greenish-brown glaze, exterior mouth-rim dark brown or black | 190x196x84mm | Provenance: SHC Iziko | 90/722 | Marks: impressed 'z' within a circle on side of bowl, near stem | Photograph by Natalie Field

In his personal work, Zaalberg was a purist at heart, making restrained wheel-thrown stoneware vessels such as vases, bowls and pots featuring exquisite glazes. He limited decoration to the natural flow of glazes and slips, which had been applied with a wooden spoon. One of Zaalberg's preferred forms was the pedestal-coupe, inspired by Chinese prototypes from the Ming and Manchu dynasties. In his personal archives, the author found an undated illustrated article on Chinese ceramics in the collection of the Victoria and Albert Museum, London. The 'coupe' form that became something of a hallmark of Zaalberg was prominently illustrated in the article.

Zaalberg was an important contributor to local ceramics and played a pivotal role in APSA. He was a strong regional chairman (ca.1974–1979) and national chairman (1987–1988) of APSA, and was often invited to be part of the judging panel of various APSA exhibitions. In this capacity Zaalberg hosted a workshop for the Potters Association of Namibia in 1988, shortly before he resigned from active service in APSA. He was a founder member of the South African Ceramics Awards and was instrumental in establishing the Clay Museum at Rust-en-Vrede, Durbanville in 1986 and was chairman of its committee. In 1987 Zaalberg led a study trip to Japan. In 1988 he opened the ceramics gallery at the former South African Cultural History Museum (now part of Iziko Museums of Cape Town) and was the subject of a retrospective exhibition, 'Maarten Zaalberg: 50 Years of Clay, Water and Fire' at the Dorp Street Gallery, Stellenbosch and the Beuster-Skolimowski Gallery, Pretoria.

Maarten Zaalberg died in 1989 in Cape Town. His widow bequeathed his estate to Iziko. Various commercial and artistic works, as well as the contents of his studio and library are preserved for research and display purposes.

Zaalberg participated in numerous exhibitions, both as an individual artist and as a part of Zaalberg Potterij. Exhibitions included 'Maarten Zaalberg, Potter and Charles Kinnear, Ikebana' Beuster-Skolimowski Gallery, Pretoria, 1982; '30 years in South Africa', the Yellow Door Gallery, Cape Town, 1981; and Maarten Zaalberg and Ikebana artist Gert Hume, Edrich Gallery, Stellenbosch, 1979. His works are in numerous public and private collections, including the CM, SHC Iziko, DNMCH, TAG and NMMAM.

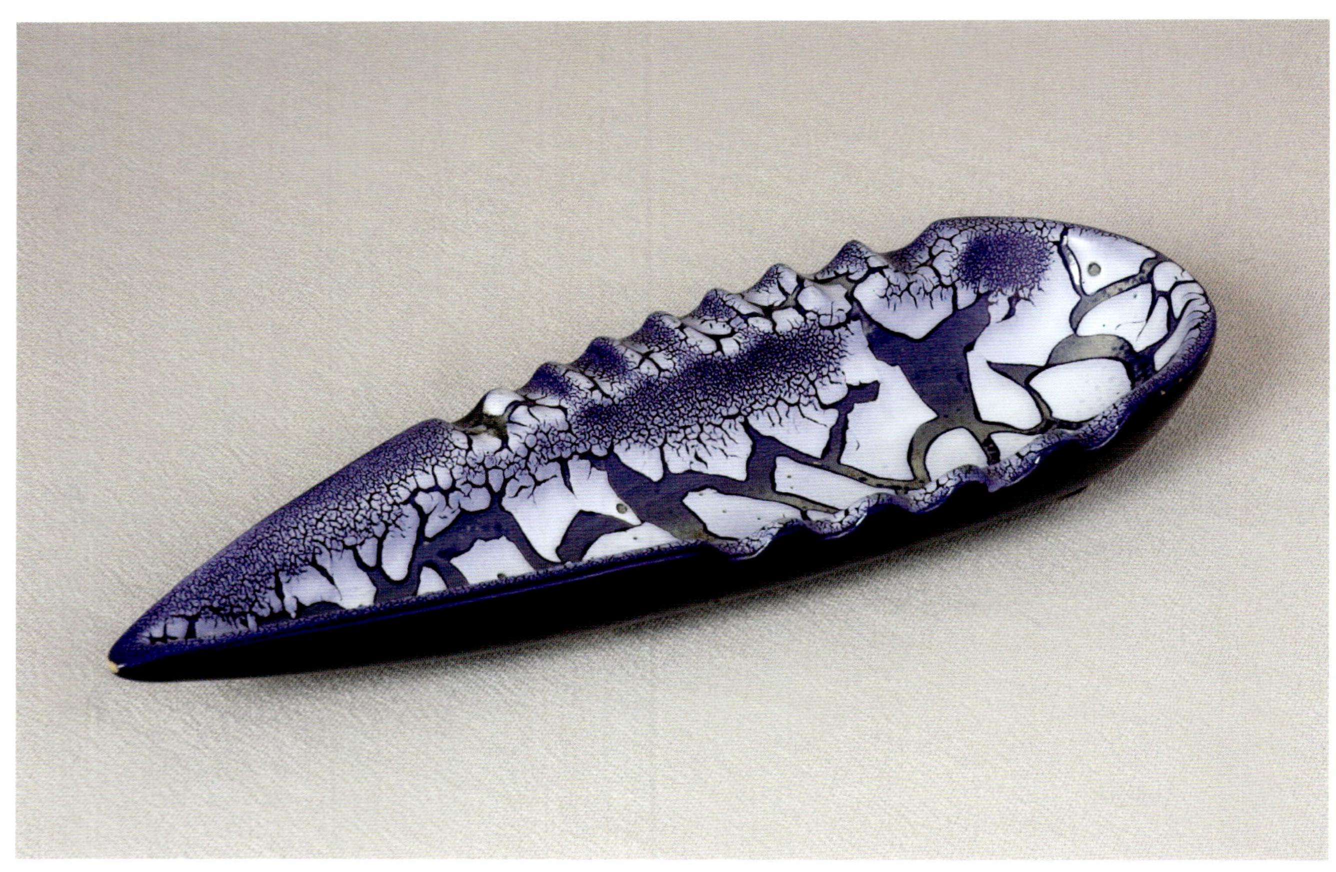

Zaalberg Potterij | Flat elongated ashtray with one round end, and one pointed end, exterior covered with glossy deep blue glaze, interior covered with an off-white glaze that has crazed | 275x35mm | Provenance: SHC Iziko | 91-83 | Photograph by Natalie Field

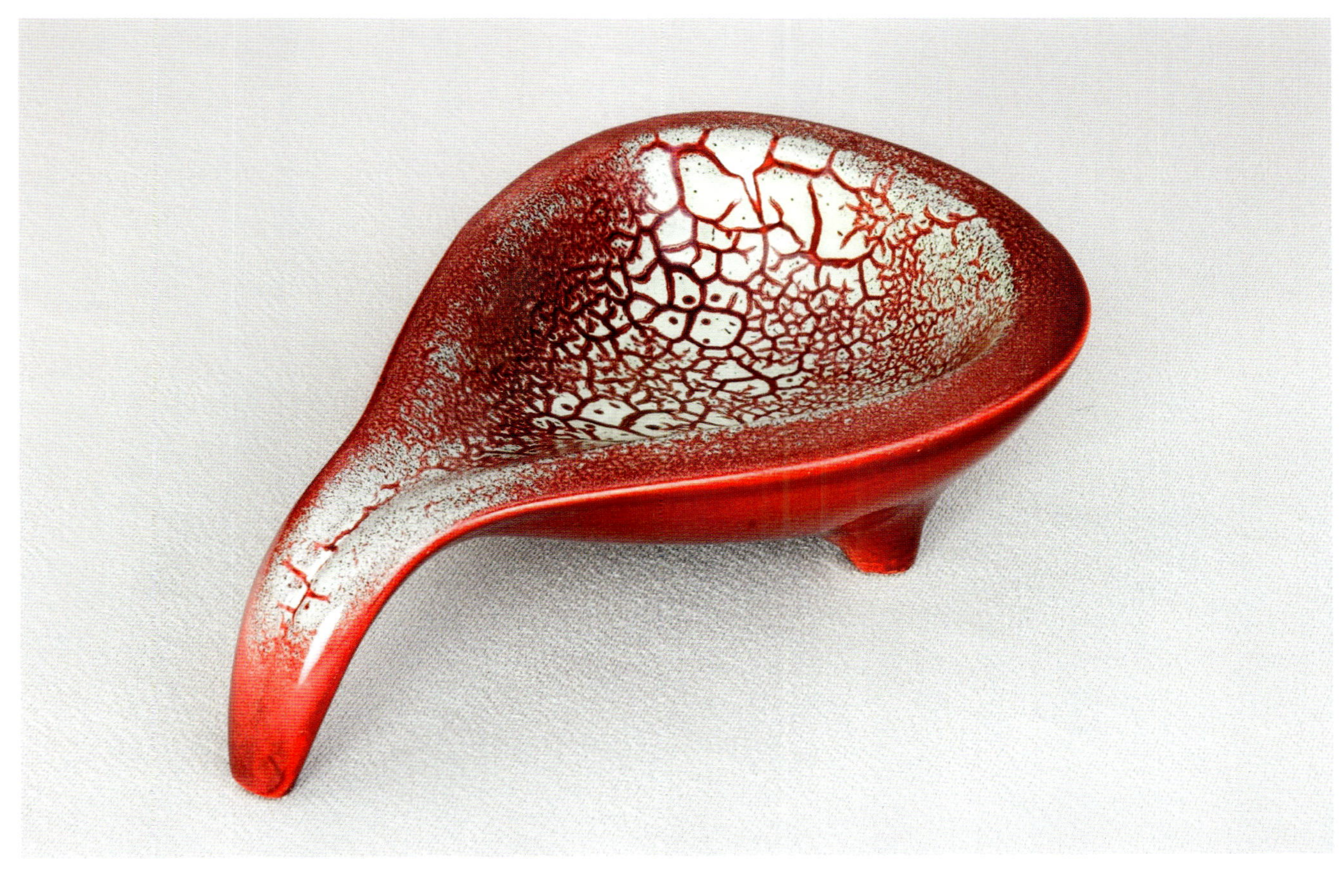

Zaalberg Potterij | Bowl | Exterior of bowl glazed with ox-blood red glaze, interior features crazed off-white glaze against red background, triangular with rounded corners | 56x125x182mm | Provenance: SHC Iziko | 92/187 | Marks: 'Zalberg Potterij Parrow' | Photograph by Natalie Field

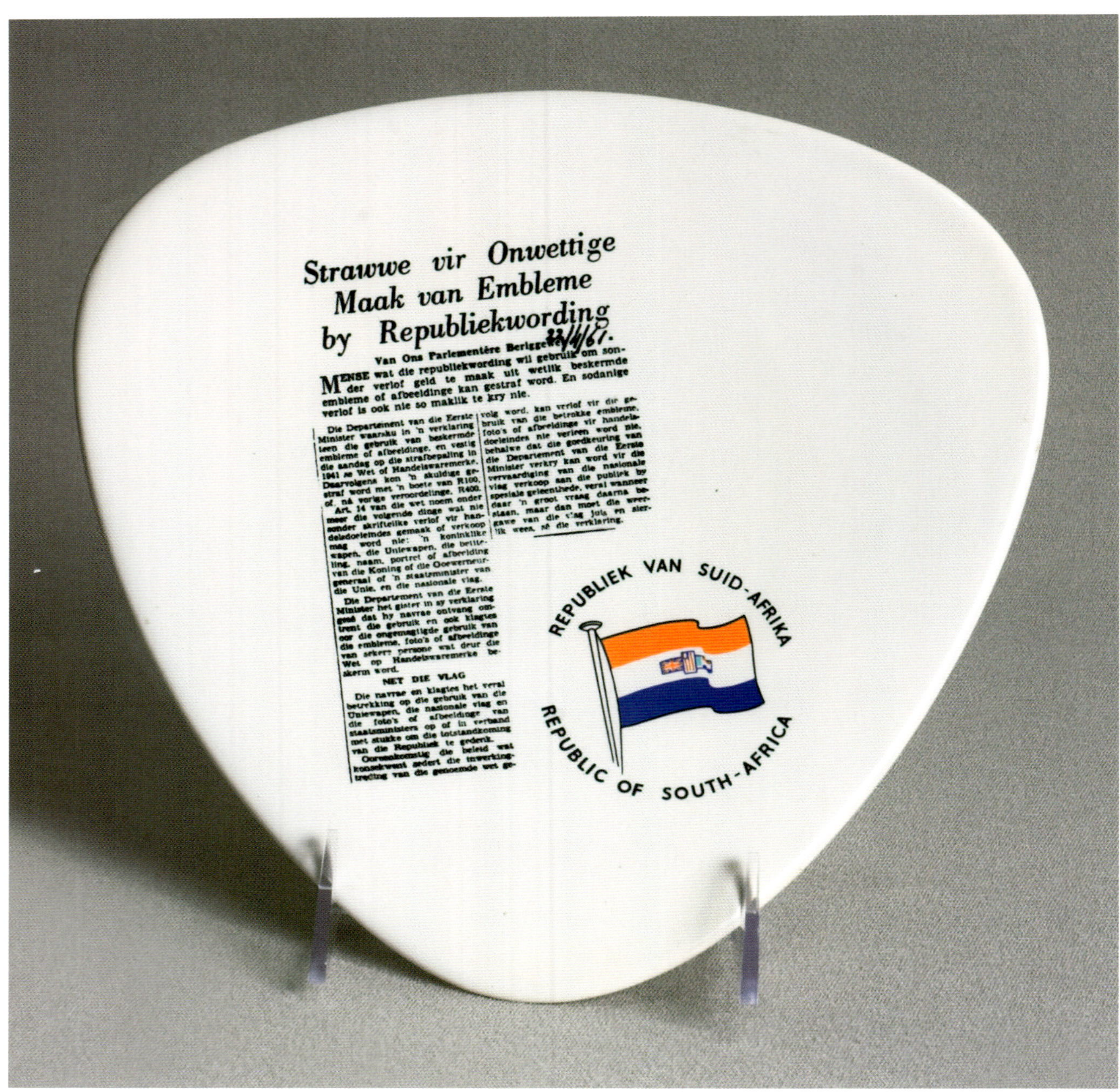

Zaalberg Potterij | Plate with newspaper cutting and flag [cutting from Die Burger 22/4/61 | 220mm | Provenance: SHC Iziko | Accession number: 89/54 | Marks: 'Zaalberg Potterij, Parrow,' with logo ZSA in circle, date of origin, c. 1961 | Photograph by Natalie Field

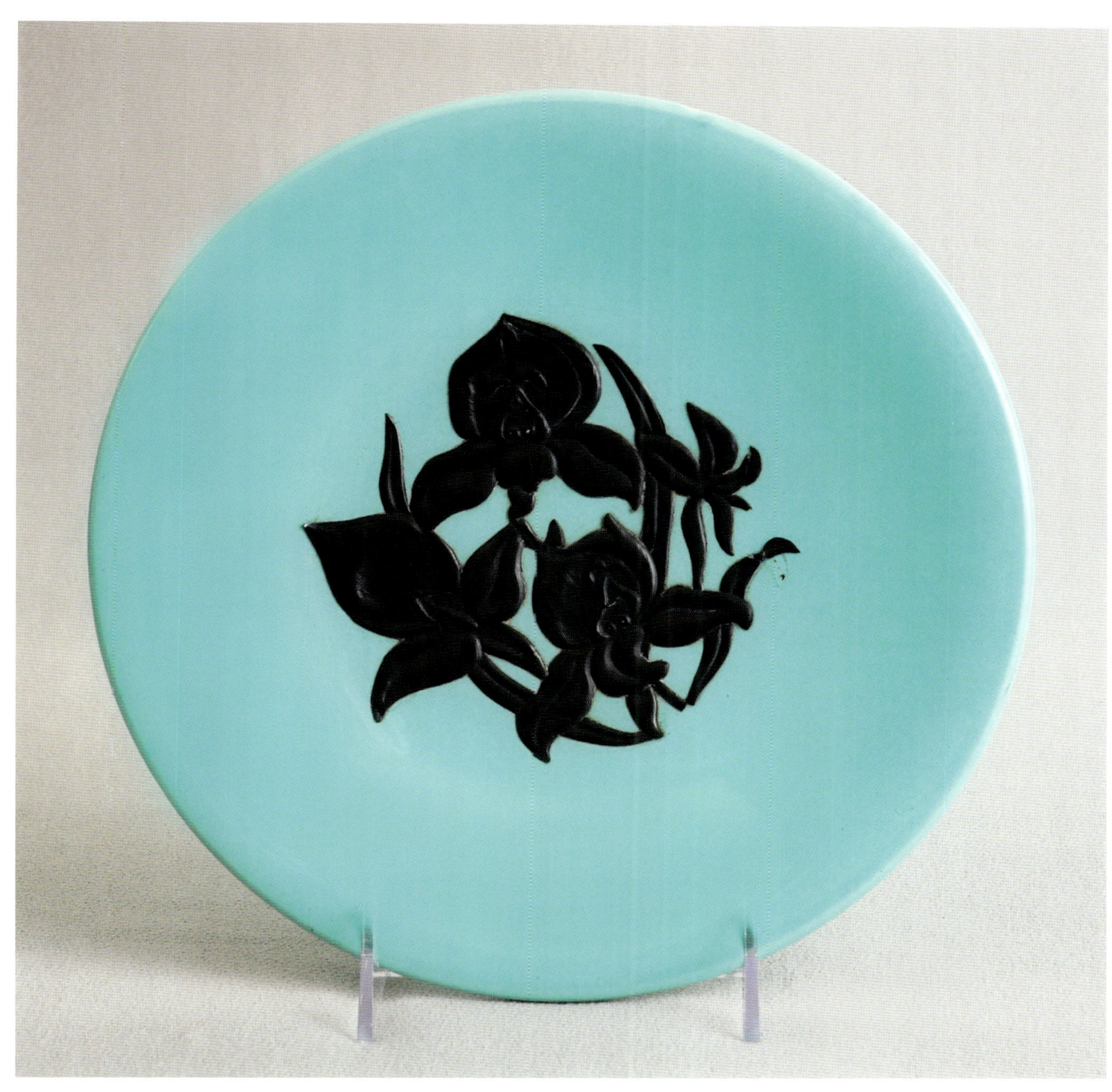

Zaalberg Potterij | Plate | Blue glazed plate with applied moulded pewter decoration of red disas | 24x235x111mm | Provenance: TAG | 2399/06 Marks: blue glazed base with blue glazed stamp 'Zaalberg Potterij, Parrow' | Photograph by Natalie Field

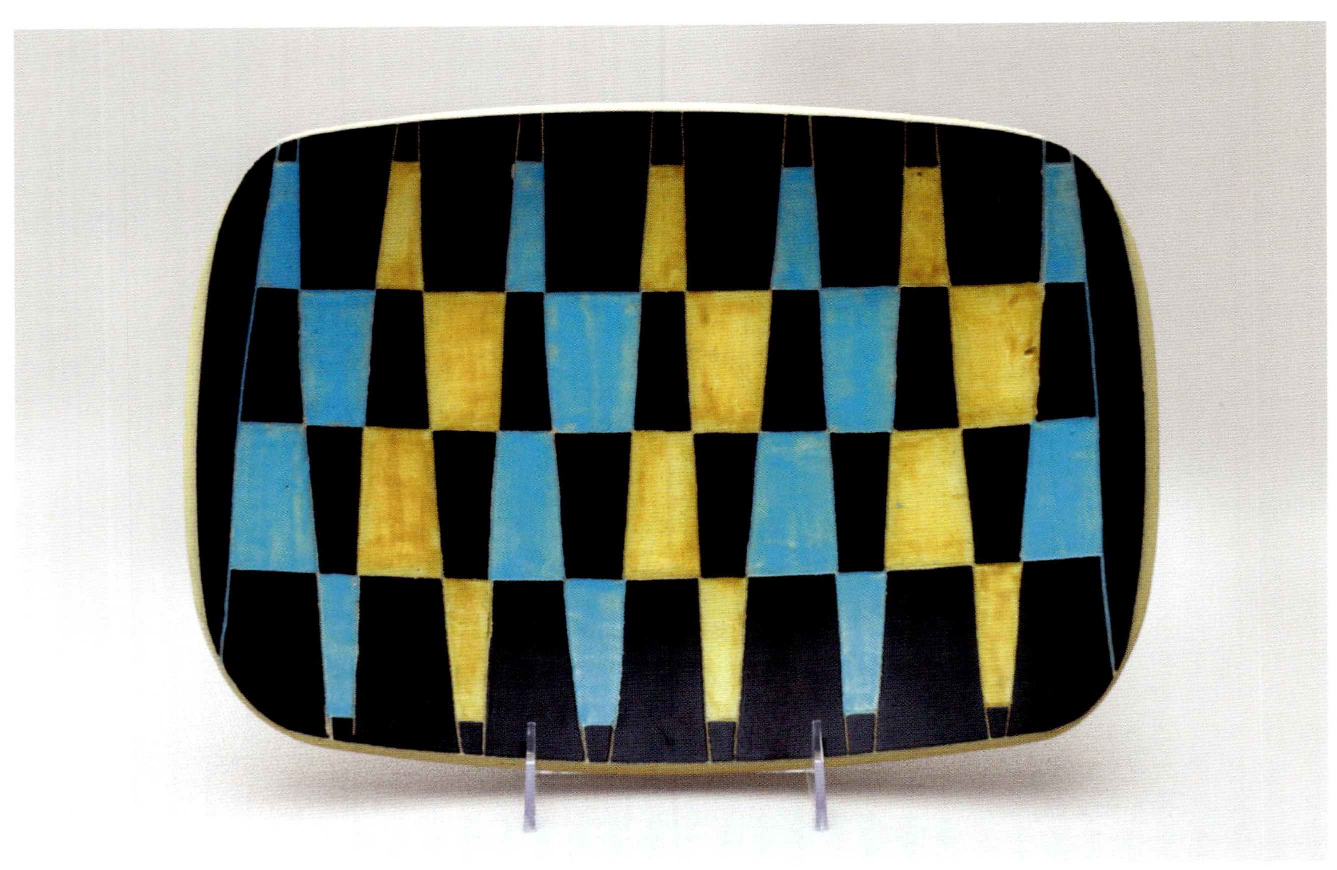

Zaalberg Potterij | Charger | Chequered sgraffito decoration with abstract yellow and blue forms | 235x32x40mm | Provenance: DNMCH | MJ 78 | Marks: white glazed base with blue marks, 'Zaalberg SA' | Photograph by Natalie Field

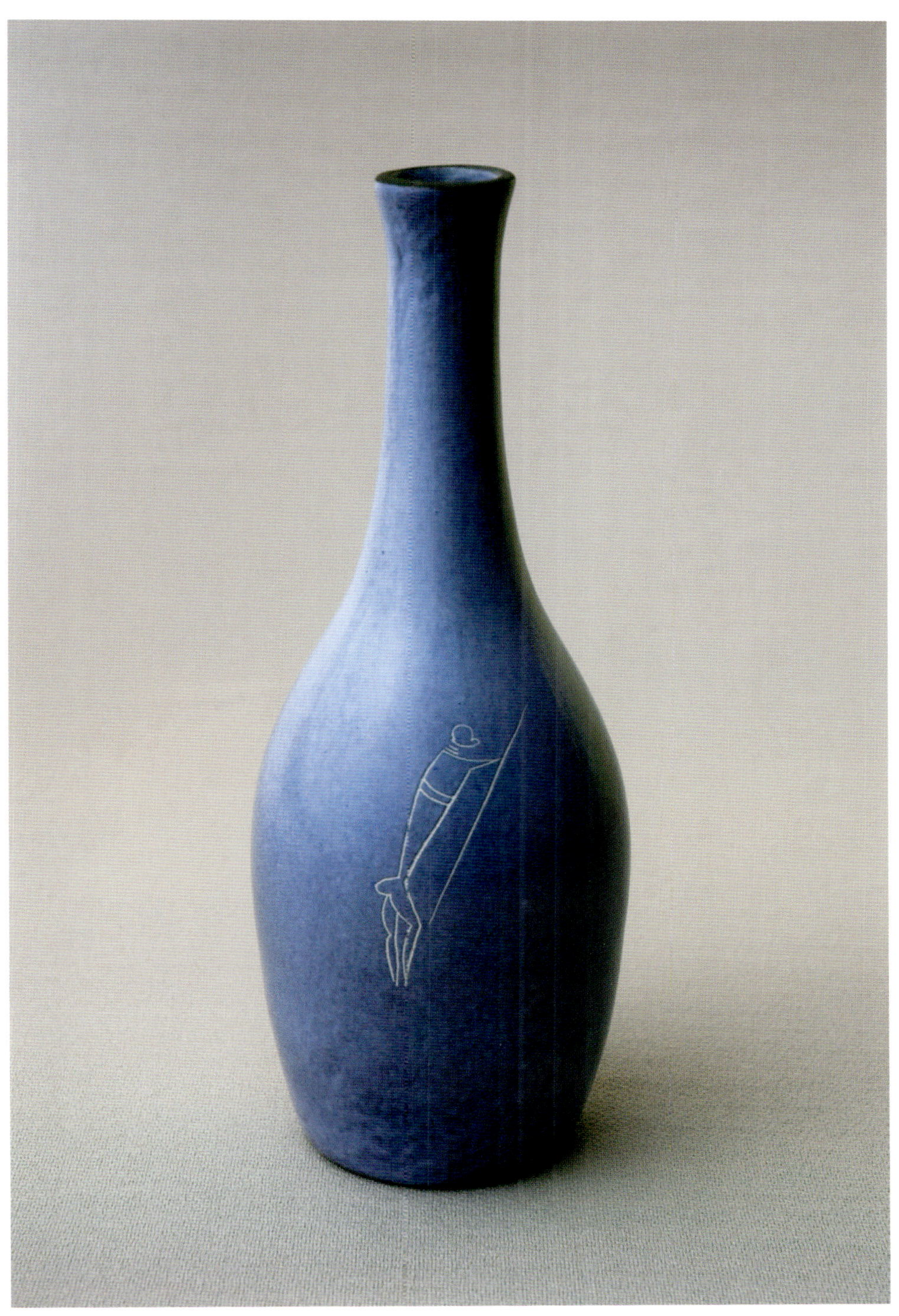

Zaalberg Potterij | Blue vase with sgraffito images of stylised bushmen art | 250x30x65mm | Provenance: Jan Middeljans | Marks: blue glazed base with incised markings, 'Zaalberg SA, hand-painted GR' | Additional information: base illustrated p.334 | Photograph by Natalie Field

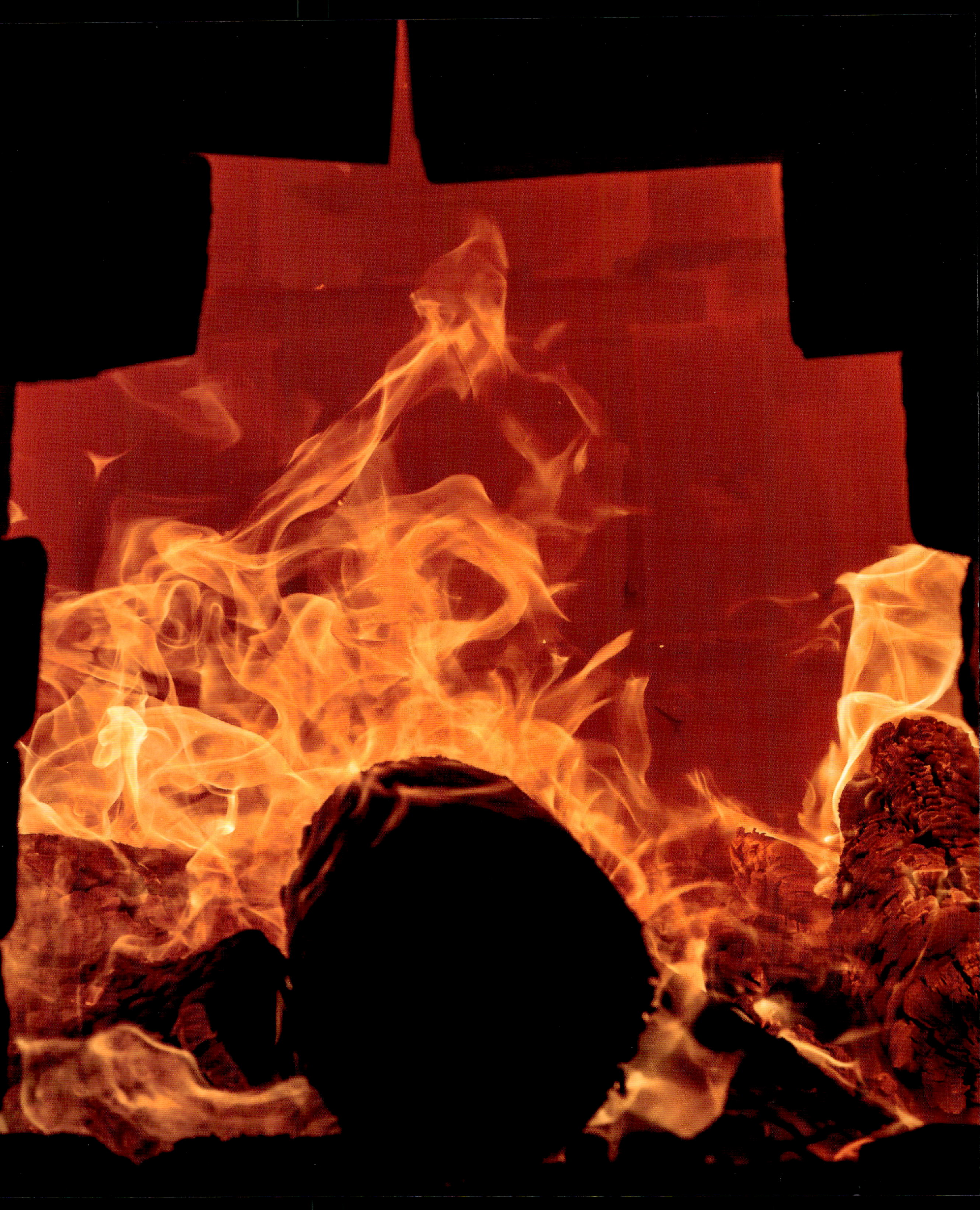

Glossary[266]

Africana Forms or images of, or pertaining to, Africa.

Ash glaze A glaze made with ground ash, usually wood ash and sometimes mixed with other materials.

Ball clay A sedimentary clay that is plastic in quality and has the capacity to withstand high firing temperatures.

Bisque / bisqueware (or biscuit) Pots that have been given a preliminary firing to render them hard enough for further work such as decoration and glazing. The higher the temperature of the bisque firing, the harder the pot will be, resulting in reduced reaction between glaze and body in the final firing.

Body The substance from which a pot is made. A mixture of one or more clays and other elements to produce a material suitable for shaping and firing.

Bone china China-made white and translucent by the addition of a minimum of 25 per cent calcined animal bone ash to the clay body.

Bottle kiln A large kiln, wide at the bottom and narrow at the top like a bottle.

Burnish To smooth the surface of a pot by rubbing with a hard object to give a finish with a polished effect.

Cast To produce shapes by pouring fluid clay into moulds. The 'negative' moulds usually consist of plaster of Paris, and are made from a 'positive' so that when they wear out, new ones can be made.

China Unspecific modern popular term for decorative and utilitarian ceramic wares that were usually made of porcelain.

Celadon A pale grey or blue-green glaze that was popular on Chinese export wares from the Sung and Ming dynasties.

China clay A clay body that is characterised by the addition of calcined animal bone to the body.

Clay A mixture of water and powder from decomposed feldspar. Clay is the potter's basic material. When moist it is soft and plastic; when fired it becomes permanently hard.

Cobalt oxide Used to produce a blue colour in glazes.

Coiling A piece of clay rolled like a rope, used in making pottery. The rounded section welds to itself when fired to make a solid form.

Cone Cones are test pieces inserted in the kiln to indicate to the potter when a certain temperature has been reached. They are made of various glaze materials of known melting point.

Crackle Cracks in the glaze formed intentionally as a decorative feature (see also Crazing).

LEFT: Untitled | Detail of kiln interior during firing | Photograph by Richard Yates

Crazing A fine network of cracks in the glaze usually caused by uneven contraction and expansion of the body and the glaze during changes of temperature. In some pottery this is a design feature rather than a fault (see Crackle), but in earthenware pots the cracks can allow moisture to penetrate the porous body leading to further damage.

Creamware Cream-coloured English earthenware of the second half of the eighteenth century and its European imitations. The technique was perfected in Staffordshire, England, between 1740 and 1750. English creamware was exported internationally from the late eighteenth century. It was produced for nearly a century.

Della Robbia style Wares manufactured in the manner of the Della Robbia Pottery (1894–1906) of Conrad Dressler and Harold Rathbone. The pottery, based near Liverpool, specialised in tiles, but also made architectural ware, relief plaques and decorative domestic ware. Its oeuvre was inspired by the work of the Florentine sculptor Luca della Robbia and his family. The pottery had lustrous lead glazes and often used patterns of interweaving plants, heraldic and Islamic motifs. Rathbone's designs reflected the ideals of the contemporary Arts and Crafts Movement. Goods were sold at prestigious outlets such as Liberty & Co, and were exhibited worldwide.

Double-glazing A glaze technique whereby an object is initially dipped into a white opaque glaze before being sprayed with a transparent glaze mixed with either an oxide-like copper oxide (to obtain a green finish), cobalt oxide (to obtain a blue finish) or manganese oxide (to obtain a mauve finish).

Earthenware A low-fired clay body that is porous when unglazed. Glazed earthenware pottery is fired to a temperature of approximately 1 100°C. Earthenware clays are usually available in red or white. Earthenware is softer and more easily damaged than stoneware.

Enamel Coloured glazes that are fired to a low temperature.

Engobe This term is most often used to describe coloured slips. It is a wet fluid made from clay, oxide and water, often used for decoration or for covering the base of a coloured body of greenwear or leather-hard pieces before bisque firing.

Faience The name given to the French tin-glazed earthenware developed from Italian maiolica. The term is also used for tin-glazed earthenware products from Germany and Scandinavia. The British equivalent of faience is delftware, the Dutch equivalent is delft. Faience was first produced in any quantity in France from the late sixteenth century.

Feldspar A crystalline substance found in granite.

Fettle The removal of unwanted blemishes, seams and flash from nearly dry pots before glazing and firing.

Fireclay A type of clay that is capable of withstanding the high temperatures of a furnace or kiln. Fireclay was formerly used to make facing bricks, drainage pipes and gullies. Fireclay bricks are yellowish or whiteish.

Firing The controlled heat treatment of ceramic ware in a kiln or furnace for a specific time during the process of manufacture to develop certain desired properties.

Flatware Plates, saucers, trays.

Foot The base of a pot.

Glaze A vitreous substance used to decorate pottery to render it impermeable to moisture.

Glaze firing The last firing of a pot when the glaze is applied.

Hand-building Constructing pots from pre-made parts. The components might be moulded, coiled or fashioned by hand.

Hollow ware Cups, jugs, bowls, etc.

Impressed (design or mark) Stamped into the leather-hard clay with a tool or die.

Incised (design) A design or pattern cut into the clay with a sharp tool.

Incised (mark) Maker's name, monogram or mark cut into the clay with a pointed tool.

Jigger A mould or profile used when uniform shapes have to be made repetitively on the wheel (see also Jiggering, Jolley and Jolleying).

Jiggering Jiggering is a method of making plates and flatware by pressing bats of clay onto a plaster mould that forms the top surface of the piece. The back is formed by a metal profile that is lowered onto the clay as it turns.

Jolley Mould or profile used when uniform shapes have to be made repetitively on the wheel (see also Jolleying and Jigger).

Jolleying Jolleying is similar to jiggering but used for hollow ware (mugs, cups, certain vases and tankards), where the plaster mould forms the outside against which clay is pressed.

Kaolin White clay made from pegmatite, also known as China clay.

Kiln The oven in which pots are fired. Kilns can be fired by wood, coal, oil, gas or electricity.

Kiln props Kiln furniture includes refractory posts, props and shelves used for stacking pottery in the kiln for firing.

Kommetjie A small open bowl that was used by the early Dutch and German settlers as a standard industrial and domestic measure.

Lead glaze A clear glaze containing a lead component.

Maiolica Tin-glazed earthenware, also known as delft in Holland and faience in France.

Manganese oxide Used to produce a purple or brown colour in glazes.

Mould A concave shape made from plaster of Paris for slip-casting. Also the die used for press-moulding.

Pipkin A long-handled earthenware cooking pot with a flat or tripod base and a pouring spout. Once used in open-hearth cooking, much like saucepans are today.

Plastic (adj) Capable of being formed into a shape or moulded.

Porcelain A hard, fine, white, glossy and translucent material made from china clay, feldspar and silica. Porcelain is fired at high temperatures, between 1 330°C and 1 500°C.

Pouncing technique Decorative images were reproduced on ceramic wares by applying a card or paper template that was perforated with fine holes that indicated the design. Carbon dust was then brushed over, and a network of dots resulted. These dots guided the decorator who subsequently painted an image over them. The carbon dots burnt away in the firing.

Pugmill A machine to used to homogenise plastic claybodies. It is similar in operation to a domestic food mincer. The clay is put in at the top and comes out of the mouth at the bottom in the form of slices or wedges.

Raku Low-fired, Japanese, lead-glazed earthenware. Raku is Japanese for 'enjoyment' and this type of pottery is traditionally used in Japan for the tea ceremony.

Reduction Firing in a reducing atmosphere. This is when there is insufficient air for the flame to burn off its carbon content. The result is a smoky atmosphere (of unoxidised carbon and hydrogen), which extracts oxygen molecules from the surface of wares, altering the appearance of clay and glaze.

Refractory This refers to the quality of a material to retain its strength at high temperatures. Refractory materials are used to make kiln furniture, crucibles and linings for furnaces, kilns and incinerators.

Saggar A fire-clay box used to protect pottery while it is being fired.

Salt glaze A thin glaze produced by the reaction, at elevated temperature, between the ceramic body surface and salt fumes produced in the kiln atmosphere by throwing salt into the kiln. The vapourised salt produces a fine 'orange-peel' texture to the surface of the pot.

Samian ware Expensive tableware, distinctive for its red/orange colouring and pressed decoration, it was found extensively in the Roman empire.

Scutcheon The shield around a keyhole or a finger plate or similar flat protective covering on a door or wall.

Sgraffito The technique of scratching through a coating of slip to reveal the contrasting colour beneath.

Silk screen printing A technique to reproduce multicolour designs on tiles and flat surfaces. Ceramic inks are available from suppliers or can be mixed from stain pigments and oil or glycerine bases. Screens may be printed 'on contact' or 'off contact'. The latter gives a sharper image.

Slabbing / slab-building A building technique where flat sheets of clay are formed and joined.

Slip (engobe) A slip is a suspension of clay and mineral particles in a water medium. It has a creamy consistency and is used for decorating and joining, and as a material for casting. Slip is applied over the surface of a leather-hard vessel for decorating and joining purposes. It is also used to change the colour of a vessel but may be used to reduce the permeability of food and drinking vessels by partially sealing the surface. Slips are applied in a viscous state by dipping, pouring or painting. They are not well absorbed by the clay body and are easily distinguished as a separate layer on the surface. Slip may also be used as a glaze and can be glossy or matt and any colour or texture. Slip is also used for casting items in moulds.

Slip decoration The application of slip to a pot. This can take the form of an all-over or partial coating, or a trailed, feathered, combed or brushed design.

Slip-trailing Method of decoration where slip is trailed onto a pot through a fine nozzle. It is a technique akin to icing a cake, and is sometimes used to build up plastic features on the surface of a vessel.

Slipware Slip-decorated earthenware pottery.

Spur marks The marks left by the stilts used to support pottery in the kiln, usually seen as three dots in the form of an equilateral triangle.

Stoneware All ceramic wear fired between 1 100°C and 1 300°C. Stoneware is inherently non-porous, vitreous or semi-vitreous, not translucent, and is more durable than earthenware.

Tenmoku A Japanese name for a Chinese glaze containing iron oxide. Tenmoku glazes are characterised by their black to reddish-brown colour, which is lighter where the glaze is thinner and darker where it is thicker.

Terracotta Red earthenware, usually unglazed.

Throw To make a vessel on a potter's wheel. The wheel revolves and maintains a fairly constant speed as would a flywheel. The clay is thrown onto the centre of the wheel and the potter shapes it by hand to the desired form.

Tin-glaze White opaque glaze containing tin oxide.

Transfer printing Method of decoration where a pattern or picture is printed onto the gelatin coating of paper and then, when wet, is slid onto the surface of a pot. The gelatin can be sensitised with silver halide allowing the same process to be used photographically.

Transparent glaze A glaze that transmits light clearly.

Underglaze decoration A decoration applied to a bisque or once-fired pot for subsequent covering with a transparent glaze.

Wall pocket A vase, usually with a flat back, that has a hole or holes for fixing to a wall.

Wax-resist Wax applied to a pot to prevent adhesion of slip or glaze and to produce a decorative effect.

Wedging A method of kneading clay to make it homogenous by cutting and rolling.

Wheel A heavy horizontal wheel onto which clay is thrown and shaped. The weight of the wheel gives momentum to preserve continuity of speed. Potter's wheels can be powered by the potter's foot, an assistant or electricity.

RIGHT: Untitled | Inspecting a kiln during firing | Photograph by Richard Yates

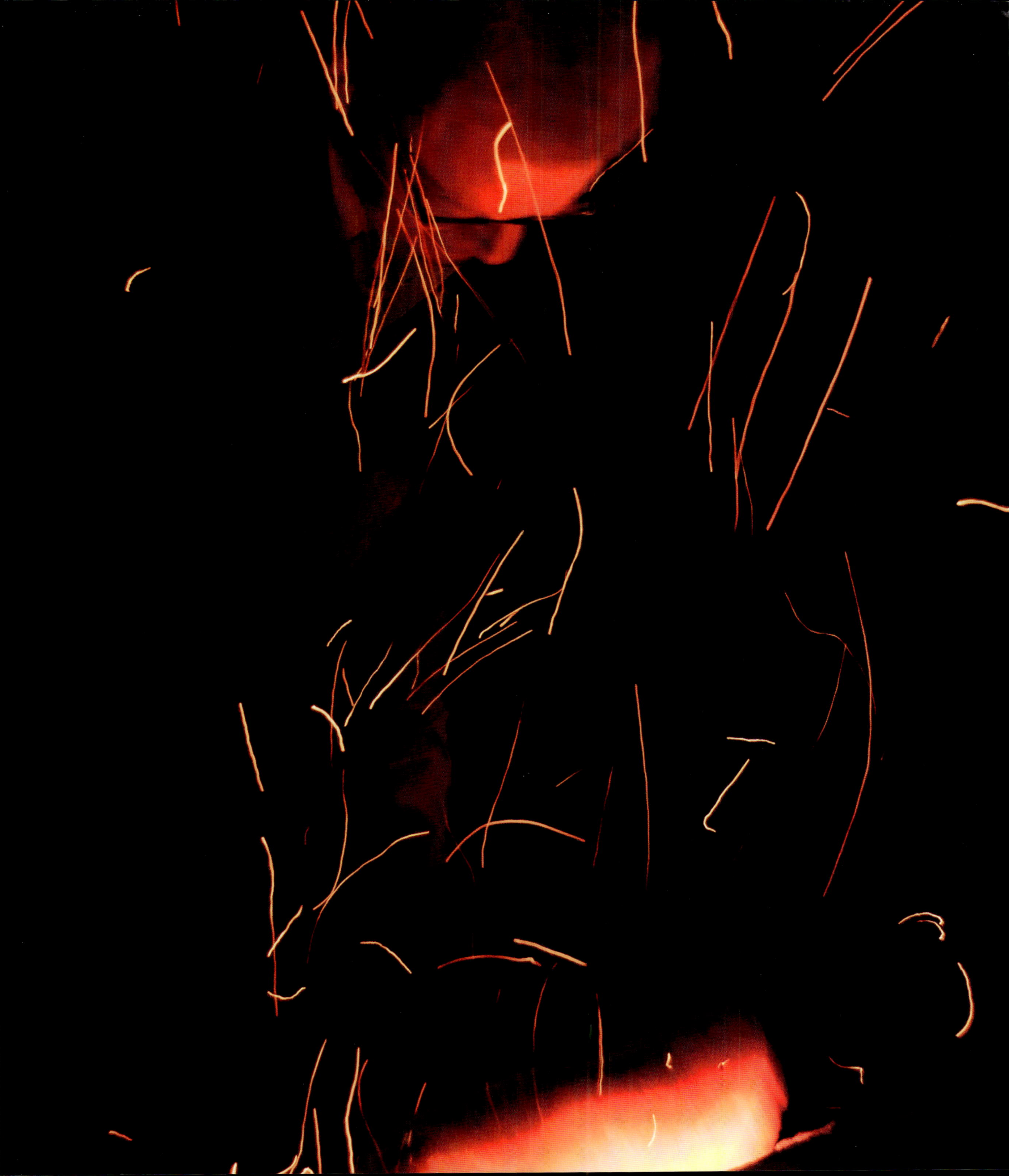

Acknowledgements

Heartfelt thanks are due to the sponsors, Corobrik, Brenthurst Trust, Oppenheimer Memorial Trust and Jacana Media.

Douglas van der Horst, Dr Melanie Hillebrand, Natalie Field, Micha Birch Hanneman, Damien Artus, Fernand Haenggi, Kobie Venter and William Martinson deserve special mention.

Numerous individuals have contributed to my research into South African potteries. They include:

Academics

Armstrong, Juliet (late) – Centre for Visual Art, UKZN
Basson, Dr Eunice – Dept. of Art History, UNISA, Pretoria
Calder, Ian – Centre for Visual Art, UKZN
De Kamper, Gerard – University of Pretoria
Duffey, Prof. Alex – University of Pretoria
Klose, Dr Jane – formerly at Department of Archaeology, UCT
Leeb-du Toit, Dr Juliette – formerly at Centre for Visual Art, UKZN
Malan, Dr Antonia – Department of Archaeology, UCT
Perrill, Dr Elizabeth – University of North Carolina at Greensboro, USA
Smith, Dr Benjamin – formerly at Rock Art Research Institute, University of the Witwatersrand
Steele, John – Walter Sisulu University, East London

Museum & heritage professionals

Addleson, Jill – formerly at DAG
Abrahams-Willis, Dr Gabeba – formerly at the SHC Iziko
Andrea Lewis – SANG
Bayliss, Dr Paul – Absa Collection
Bell, Brendan – TAG
Bester, Rory – Reserve Bank Collection, Johannesburg
Beyer, Carina – Iziko SACH
Clark, Bryony – TAG
Davidson, Dr Patricia – formerly at Iziko SAM
De Waal, Dr Lydia – University Museum, Stellenbosch University
Du Preez, Hannele – PAM
Du Preez, Leon – Ann Bryant Art Gallery, East London
Esmyol, Esther – SHC Iziko
Geldenhuys, Carolina – Roodepoort Museum
Geustyn, Melanie – National Library of South Africa
Herselman, Deon – Rupert Museum, Stellenbosch
Hillebrand, Dr Melanie – NMMAM
Hisham, Lailah – SHC Isiko
Hundt, Stefan – Sanlam Art Collection, Bellville, Cape Town
Kolby-Hardy, Patty – formerly at the Natale Labia Museum, SANG

Kuijers, Arie – Johannes Stegmann Art Gallery, University of the Free State
Le Roux, Ester – Oliewenhuis Art Museum, Bloemfontein
Letts, Alba – formerly at the Roodepoort Museum
Malan, Linda – Oliewenhuis Art Museum, Bloemfontein
Meyer, Corine – DNMCH
Middeljans, Jan – DNMCH
Ouzman, Sven – Iziko SAM
Pretorius, Ann – WHAG
Proud, Hayden – SANG
Ross, Monica – CM
Siebert, Kim – formerly at SANG
Starkey, Anthony – Durban University of Technology
Stockenström, Rika – WHAG
Stretton, Jenny – DAG
Taggert, Emma – NMMAM
Trehaven, Rose – formerly No. 7 Castle Hill Museum, Port Elizabeth
Van Eeden, Jeanne – University of Pretoria
Venter, Kobie – TAG
Vos, Hennie – Stellenbosch Museum
Wall, Diana – MA
Way-Jones, Fleur – formerly at the Albany Museum, Grahamstown

Ceramics dealers & collectors

Berlyn, Clive, Ann and Jo – Mthatha, Transkei
Birch Hannemann, Micha – Johannesburg
Bird, Flo – Johannesburg
Burr, Geoff – Cape Town
Cloete-Hopkins, Nicky & Dudley – Cape Town
De Kamper, Gerard – Pretoria
Dold, Mary-Rose (late) – Port Elizabeth
Fiori, Antonio – Knysna
Fornali, Tony & Hazel – Johannesburg
Greenberg, Susan Anne – Alberobello, Italy
Hartley-Wiley, Chris – Cambridge, England
Hudson-Reed, Marge & Derek – Pietermaritzburg
Millin, Peter (late) – Pietermaritzburg
Newman, Clive (late) – Port Elizabeth and Grahamstown
O'Hagan, Tony – Knysna
Radowsky, Gordon – Cape Town
Van Gass, Elsa – Parys
Wassenaar, Mies – Pietermaritzburg
Watson, Prof. Mark – Port Elizabeth
Welman, Nick – Pretoria

Van Gass, Elsa – Parys
Welz, Stephen – Johannesburg
Xafis, Lucy – Johannesburg

Pottery staff, independent researchers & others

Anderson, Gill – Howick, KwaZulu-Natal
Anderson, Gillian – Halesworth, Suffolk, England
Bandtock, Judith – Lewes, Surrey, England
Barnim, Scott – Dundas, Ontario, Canada
Bell, Lilian – Cajarc, France
Black, Father Julian James – Gaborone, Botswana
Boerner, Fred – Johannesburg
Brodie, Mordechai – Knysna
Blewett, Denis Morgan II – Johannesburg
Burkhalter, Elsbeth – Johannesburg
Christie, Penny – Cape Town
Claassens, Lissa – Hout Bay, Cape Town
Corda, Sr Maria – Mariannhill Convent, KwaZulu-Natal
Dare, Yvonne – Cape Town
Deans, Dorte – Hamilton, Ontario, Canada
De Jongh, Paul – McGregor, Western Cape
De Klerk, Gail – Johannesburg
De Lange, Deon – Johannesburg
Du Toit, Laura – Stellenbosch
Duys, Herry (late) – Johannesburg
Eichhoff, Hilmar – Grahamstown
Faragher, Joe (late) – Cape Town
Faragher, Lynette – London
Faragher, Mary – Cape Town
Faragher, Ruth – Johannesburg
Faragher, Tamsin – Cape Town
Finch, Joe & Trudi – Tanygroes, Wales
Finch, Mike – Winchcombe Pottery, England
Finch, Ray (late) – Winchombe Pottery, England
Fornali, Tony – Johannesburg
Gaston, Johannes – Minnetonka, MN, USA
Garrett, Ian – Swellendam
Gers, Craig and Bronwyn – Johannesburg
Gers, Mervyn – Cape Town
Gill, Michael – formerly of Sherborne, Dorset, England
Green, Chris – Johannesburg
Grivainis, Veikla – Cape Town
Haenggi, Fernand F – Basel, Switzerland
Hamilton, Anita – Arnprior, Ontario, Canada

Hayes, Peter and Joan – Bath, England
Hayward Fell, Carol – Durban
Heymans, Riana – Pretoria
Hoentsch, Jürgen – Cape Town
Holding, Janet – Knysna
Hull, Janet – Johannesburg
Jacobs, Henk – Gennep, Holland
Kirk, Angelique – Cape Town
Kroll, Peter (late) – Johannesburg
Lastovica, Ethleen – Cape Town
Lecoultre Brejnik, Anne-Belle – Geneva, Switzerland
Lehmkuhl, Colleen – Johannesburg
Liebenberg, Nico – Cape Town
Liebermann, Mary (late) – Cape Town
Liebermann Koter, Lisa – Plettenberg Bay
Locke, Hester (late) & Eugene (late) – Port Alfred
Mabena, Timothy – Pretoria
Malherbe, Leonie – Durban
Marais, Ann – Cape Town
Marot, France & Renée – Umhlanga Rocks
Martinson, William – East London
Masuku, Meshack – Port Edward
Millar, Alan – Johannesburg
Mills, Natalie – Port Elizabeth
Milway, Toff – Conderton, England
Molefi, Nicodemus – Johannesburg
Murray, Nathan Jeff – Champaign, IL., USA
Mzantsi, Bongani – Mthatha, Transkei
Ncoyini, Mathemba – Mthatha, Transkei
Ndugane, Richard – Mthatha, Transkei
Ngubo, Keslina – Mthatha, Transkei
Nielsen, Ole – Kangaroo Valley, NSW, Australia
Newdigate, John – Swellendam
Ngubo, Keslina – Mthatha, Transkei
Olsen, Glenn – Port Elizabeth
Pais, Jannora – Betty's Bay, Western Cape
Paule, Sr Mary – Mthatha, Transkei
Perold, Marie & 'Pierre' I A (late) – Pretoria
Piriou, Nicole – Valenciennes, France
Praamsma, Sietsa & Saskia – Clayton, Ontario, Canada
Prinsley, Marian – Norwich, Norfolk, England
Rabinowitz, Jenifer & Hyme (late) – Cape Town
Ringdahl, Peter – Johannesburg
Sachs, John – Barrydale

Sacks, Kim – Johannesburg
Schließler, Albrecht – Krugersdorp
Schlapobersky, David & Felicity Potter – Swellendam
Scott, Lindsay – Lidgetton, KwaZulu-Natal
Scott Deetz, Patricia – Williamsburg, Virginia, USA
Sekokotoana, Matsoana – Maseru, Lesotho
Sellschop, Susan – Johannesburg
Shain, Morrie – Johannesburg
Shirley, John – Johannesburg
Sihlali, Durant (late) – Johannesburg
Sinclair Bolton, Catherine – Johannesburg
Steele-Gray, Norman (late) – Kenton-on-Sea
Takis, George – Wellington
Taylor, Graham & Lynda – Rothbury, Northumberland, England
Thage, Abram – Pretoria
Thronton, David (late) – Stoke on Trent, England
Turgel, Adriaan – Johannesburg
Turgel, Menucha (late) – Johannesburg
Turgel, Ricca – (formerly) Johannesburg
Van der Riet, Karen – Centurion, Gauteng
Van der Walt, Clementina – Cape Town
Van Gilder, Bill – Gapland, Maryland, USA
Venter, Spies – Johannesburg
Vermeulen, Thomas – Pietermaritzburg
Walford, Leanda & Andrew – Shongweni, KwaZulu-Natal
Walters, David – Franschhoek
Watt, Ronnie – Johannesburg
Wheeler, Ron – Gloucestershire, England
Wilson, Dave – Winchcombe Pottery, England.
Witkin, Isaac – Vermont, USA
Yates, Richard – Salem, Oregon, USA
Zettler, Martha – (formerly) Durban

Endnotes

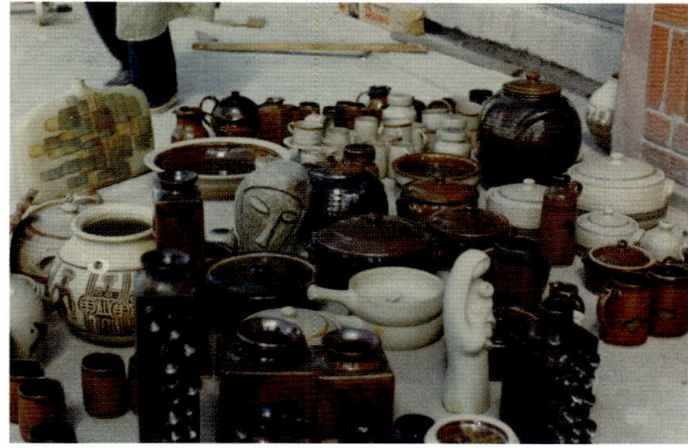

Thaba Bosigo | Display of production pottery and Peter Hayes' personal works | Provenance: Peter Hayes | Photograph by Joan Hayes

1 The term is commonly used in military strategy and history, and refers to the process of advancing and destroying an opposition's property. This usage is not intended here.

2 The term pottery is as slippery as its muddy origins and has multiple uses. A pottery is a studio, workshop or factory that produces earthenware, stoneware or porcelain wares. The term pottery is also used to refer to decorative, artistic and utilitarian wares produced by potters. In this latter sense, the term pottery is equivalent to the term ceramics.

3 The ceramic industry in southern Africa is riddled with contradictions and it is frequently difficult to distinguish between individual potters' artistic wares and industrial wares. Some individual potters promoted their wares as handmade individual pieces, but in fact employed assistants and replicated wares on a semi-industrial scale. On the other hand, many ceramic artists, including Mary Liebermann (Lieberman Pottery and Tiles), Valmai Olson (Lucky Bean Pottery), Lindsay Scott (Lzandla), Mordechai Brodie (Mantenga Falls Pottery), Austin Hleza, Bill van Gilder, Joe Faragher, Maarten Zaalberg and Toff Milway who were involved in production potteries, clearly distinguished between their commercial wares and their individual creations. This was achieved by signing certain 'special' wares with a different or additional signature or stamp, and by entering these individual pieces in art exhibitions. This is a standard studio practice among many significant British and European potteries, and is associated with famous potters such as William Staite Murray (1881–1962), Bernard Leach (1887–1979), Michael Cardew and Ray Finch (1914–2012). In Sweden and Denmark the early twentieth century witnessed the deployment of artists and designers in factories such as Gustavsberg and Rorstrand, Sweden, and Royal Copenhagen Porcelain, Denmark. They designed commercial products as well as their own studio lines. Artistic, 'personal', 'one-off' or limited edition wares were more costly than standard production items, thus providing an important revenue source for the artists.

4 The term production pottery is used among potters to describe a pottery, pottery workshop or small factory that produces set 'lines' of work. The emphasis is on an efficient high-output production rather than unique or original wares. Despite the emphasis on productivity, the pottery may be high quality and original. Synonymous with commercial pottery, it does not have any negative connotations, and may or may not be art pottery.

5 Studio potters are philosophically or stylistically associated with the Anglo-Oriental tradition of Bernard Leach, Shoji Hamada (1894–1978) and Michael Cardew. Some studio potters operated alone, while others established small collaborative studios. Studio potters generally produce unique items or small series, usually with all stages of manufacture carried out by one individual. In South Africa, key adherents of this tradition include Andrew Walford, Hyme Rabinowitz and Esias Bosch.

6 Tile manufacturers included Union Ceramics, Meyerton, which was established in 1947 and taken over by Pilkingtons in 1955 and Johnson Tiles (Pty) Ltd (Thornton 1973 14,104).

7 Archival records attest to the proliferation of numerous clay quarries in the nineteenth century, including in Fort Beaufort (1844), Grahamstown, Diep River (1890) and Bathurst (1893). Early twentieth century brick works included the Kempton Park Brick and Tile, Coronation Brick (Pty) Ltd; Vereeniging Tile and Brick Company (Thornton 1973:121, Nilant [1956], Stadsraad van Kempton Park 1978:55); Colonial Brick Company, Cape Town; Boksburg Brick & Fireclay; H.J. Brandt Brickmaker, New Muckleneuk, Pretoria; Groenkloof Brick, Tiles and Pottery, Pretoria; Economic Fireclay Works, Boksburg; Primrose Brick Works, Germiston; Lemmon and Mutch Brickfield and Quarry, East Rand the West Springs Brick & Fireclay Works and Maritzburg Stoneware, Tile and Pottery Company, Pietermaritzburg. (The latter is discussed in endnote 20).

8 Sanitary whiteware manufacturers included Vaal Potteries Ltd, Meyerton, Shanks and Co. (South Africa) (Pty) Ltd., Olifantsfontein and Twyfords (South Africa) (Pty) Ltd., Alberton. The latter two companies were established in 1962.

9 Industrial Ceramics was operational in the mid-1950s.

10 Ceramic Industries, Factreton Township, Cape Town, under the trusteeship of P Guicherit, erected a factory in 1946 to manufacture glazed tiles, electrical elements and insulators.

11 Kempton Park Pottery (Pty) Ltd (establised 1928) appeared mainly to produce planters and garden pots (Stadsraad van Kempton Park 1978:55).

12 Among the earliest producers of glazed stoneware storage bottles in South Africa was the Vereeniging Brick and Tile Company. In 1914, due to shortages experienced as a result of the onset of World War I, the pottery modified its production and prioritised acid-resistant wares, including glazed stoneware storage bottles and containers, which were marked with an oval stamp, 'Made in Vereeniging South Africa'. In 1937 the pottery commenced the manufacture of silica bricks. It possessed 19 kilns with a capacity of 750 000 bricks per month and supplied many local municipalities and public bodies with bricks. The company is extant, operating as part of the investment group Vereeniging Refractories (Pty) Limited, trading as Verref.

13 Commercial tiles were produced by Dykor, John & Tina Dunn of Wall Clad Tiles near Roodepoort in the 1970s and 1980s. Peter Kroll produced tiles at Kettenhofen Kroll in the early 1970s, and later at Designer Tiles in Germiston from the mid-1970s to 2003.

14 Within South Africa the following potteries operated in the period under consideration: A G Gillies (manufacturers of Bell Ware), Meyerton, Gauteng; Alicia Floral Ware, Bergvlei; Alwyn Potteries, Pretoria and later White River; Arcangeli Pottery, Kempton Park; Argilla Pottery, Pretoria; SA Art Potteries, Kempton Park, Johannesburg; Barry Douglas Pottery, Bramley, Johannesburg; Bitou Crafts, Knysna; Canosa Pottery, Hammerskraal and later Babalegi; Canosa Pottery, Paarl; Ceramex, Isithebe, KwaZulu-Natal; Continental China, Kuils River, Cape Town; Cresset House, Halfway House, Gauteng; Delta, Durban; Edgeware Ceramics, Pinetown; Elwood Pottery, Garsfontein; Faiarte Ceramics, Angola and Rustenburg; Figula Ceramics, Honeydew, Johannesburg; Floral Bone China, Pinetown; Gillimeads Stone Ware, Gauteng; Gray Ceramics (producers of G.C. Ware), Olifantsfontein; Huguenot Porcelain, Rosslyn; Innes Ware, location unknown; Kai Potteries, Cape Town; Kempton Park Potteries, Johannesburg; Lanes Ceramics, Durbanville and Wellington; Majolica Pottery, Maraisburg, Roodepoort; Mapepe Craft, Henley on Klip; National Ceramics Industries, Lawleys, Germiston (manufacturers of 'Wychwood Ware'); National Ceramics Industries, Germiston; Old Nick Pottery, Plettenberg Bay; Old Pont Pottery, Port Edward; Oranje Pottery, Viljoenskroon; Riverside Pottery Works, Silverton, Pretoria; Sherwood Pottery, Cape Town; Silwood Ceramics, Bergvlei, Gauteng; Transvaal Ceramics, Johannesburg (manufacturers of 'Felicitas' ceramics); and Vaal Potteries, Meyerton, Johannesburg.

Botswana was host to Boiteko Pottery Centre, Serowe; Lentswe-La-Odi Pottery, Lentswe-La-Odi; and Letsopa Pottery, Letsopa. Thabana-Li-Mele Handicraft Centre operated briefly in Lesotho. The Mbabane Pottery Development Centre, Mbabane operated in Swaziland. Zimbabwe was home to many artistic and commercial potteries, including Mutapo Pottery, Harare; Mzilikazi Arts and Crafts Centre, Bulawayo; Norbel Potteries, Bulawayo; Sitra, Bromley; The Studio, location unknown; and Willsgrove Pottery, Bulawayo. Lourenço Marques Pottery operated in Mozambique near the South African border. Malindi Pottery (1978–1999) was located in the Mangochi District of Malawi.

15 For example, feldspar is found in abundance in the Limpopo province, silica at Delmas and calcite at Umzimkulu. Various clay bodies are found all over the country, including deposits of Wallace and Palmer clays in Grahamstown,

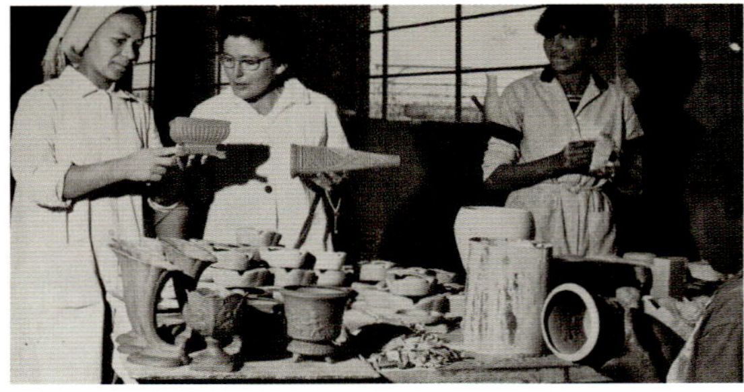

Arcangeli Pottery, c.1976 | Kempton Park Town Council 1976, Kempton Park: Transvaal, Johannesburg: Felstar p. 35 | Scan by Jan Middeljans

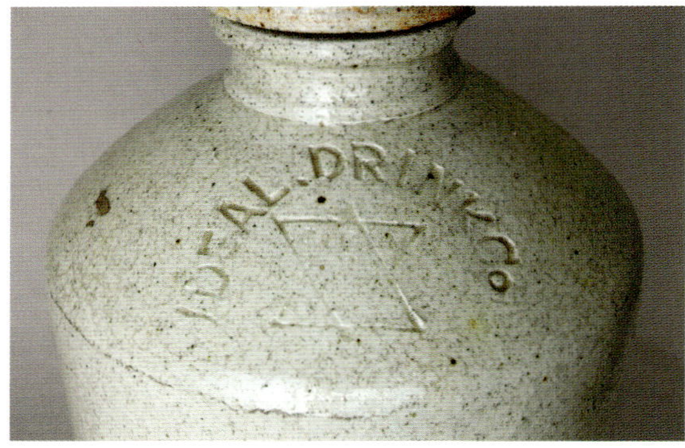

Conrand | Stoneware flask with scalloped lid | Ideal Drinking Co | 340x70x175mm | Provenance: De Kamper and Welman Collection | Marks: stamped marks, 'Ideal Drinking Co.' Star of David has C, R, B, P ... Co Ltd.' initials evident [L] missing | Photograph by Natalie Field

weathered kaolinitic shale clay from Garsfontein (near Pretoria), China clay in the Cape and ball clays in Lawleys (Johannesburg), Grahamstown and Kraaifontein.

16 Records of dock dues on clay and manganese for export (1906) and consolidated harbour and railway taxes for the export of China clay (1908) are lodged in the Cape archives.

17 My sincere thanks to Clementina van der Walt for her useful comments on this point.

18 The colour, shape and form of a plate or bowl may affect the cook's choice of ingredients. One is reluctant to find spinach or other green vegetables appetising when served on green dinner plates, like those made by Linnware.

19 The significance of establishing a reliable local source of building and flooring materials cannot be overestimated. Early settlements were infested with vermin, which made tunnels in the beaten clay floors of domestic and public buildings. The introduction of fired floor tiles was an essential step in the drive to improve public sanitation.

20 The first concise account of the production of glazed domestic pottery in KwaZulu-Natal concerns E R C Most, a prospector with Pietermaritzburg Stoneware, Tile and Pottery Company. He previously worked as manager for the Fernwood Brick and Tile Company, Cape Town. With the assistance of his wife, Most undertook extensive investigation of local clay samples. He claimed that the composition of Natal clay was completely different to English clays, and it was necessary to 'discover' suitable glazes and enamels. After two years of experimentation, he was convinced of the suitability of Pietermaritzburg clay for manufacturing crockery. Most boasted that he had made 'household pottery equal to the imported article'. His basins and small bowls (bearing decoration on their sides) were 'fit to stand alongside anything of the kind in the china shops in town'. He claimed that there was a great scope for profit in the local manufacture of pottery. Prices were inflated by breakages that occurred during their importation (at sea and in the port) and subsequent transport. Furthermore, the cost of railage from Durban to Pietermaritzburg could add an additional 50–75 per cent to the price. In 1905, while working for the Pietermaritzburg Stoneware, Tile and Pottery Company, Most attempted to establish a crockery factory in Pietermaritzburg. He submitted applications for financial assistance to various local government departments, including that of the prime minister of KwaZulu-Natal. A lack of subsequent archival documents and examples of wares suggest that his attempt to establish a crockery factory in Pietermaritzburg were unsuccessful.

21 Records concerning ERC Most. 1905. Doc Nr NAB191002346, Batch no 4235004000, Depot NAB, Source PM, Vol: 52, System 01, Ref.: 1905/147, Part 1.

22 'Colonial cringe', also referred to as 'cultural cringe', is an antipodean expression that was invented by the Australian cultural theorist, A A Phillips in the late 1940s and early 1950s to allude to a colonial inferiority complex or deference attitude to the presumed superior culture, heritage and institutions of the British metropole (Ashcroft 1989:2–12).

23 For further information consult Lastovica 2000 and Smit 1981.

24 Adams studied at the Hanley School of Art and the Royal College of Art, and after graduation was appointed to the post of lecturer at the Royal College of Art, London. His wife, Truda Adams (née Gertrude Sharp) was also an ARCA. From 1915 to 1921 Adams was the first head of The School of Art, Durban, where he established a pottery department. Truda also taught and assisted at the school. Despite the brevity of their tenure, the couple played a vital role in the development of ceramics in South Africa, both artistic and industrial, and John played an active role in the local artistic community. He served as a member of the Advisery Committee of the Durban Art Gallery, and was president of the Natal Society of Artists (NSA, Durban), regularly participating in their exhibitions. He organised Winter School lectures and public forums. Public commissions undertaken by the couple include the War Memorial at St Mary's Church, Greyville, Durban (1920).

25 The Durban Art School later became the Natal Technical College, was subsequently renamed the Natal Technikon and is currently part of the Durban University of Technology.

26 From 1928 to 1933, Armstrong was principal of the Art School at the Johannesburg Technical College.

27 It is noted that at this time South African society was fractured by apartheid and women of colour were excluded from these economic privileges.

28 Author's interview with Norman Steele-Gray, Kenton-on-Sea, 16 November 1996.

29 Former British prime minister, Harold Macmillan in his famous speech in Cape Town, 1960.

30 The former Rhodesia was involved in a lengthy and bloody civil war, the Zimbabwe War of Liberation, which ended white minority rule (1964–1978).

31 Mozambique was devastated by a vicious spiral of wars. The War of independence (1964–1974) was followed by the horrific Mozambican Civil War (1977–1992). The ruling party, the Front for Liberation of Mozambique (FRELIMO), was violently opposed from 1977 by the Rhodesian-funded (later South African-funded) Mozambique Resistance Movement (RENAMO). Over 900 000 died in fighting and from starvation, five million civilians were displaced, many were made amputees by landmines. Mozambique's first multi-party elections were held in 1994.

32 From 1966 Zambia, Angola and South West Africa (Namibia) were involved in ongoing military skirmishes with the South African Defence Force.

33 In Angola colonial economic development did not translate into social development for natives. The Portuguese regime encouraged white immigration, especially after 1950, which intensified racial antagonisms. As decolonisation progressed elsewhere in Africa, Portugal rejected independence and treated its African colonies as overseas provinces. Three main opposition groups launched a struggle for independence in the the early 1960s, including the Popular Movement for the Liberation of Angola (MPLA), the National Front for the Liberation of Angola (FNLA), and the National Union for the Total Independence of Angola (UNITA). The 1974 coup d'etat in Portugal established a military government that promptly ceased the war and agreed to hand over power to a coalition of the three movements. Ideological differences between the three movements eventually led to armed conflict. The intervention of troops from South Africa on behalf of UNITA, Zairean troops on behalf of the FNLA and Cuban troops for the MPLA in 1975 internationalised the conflict. After Angolan independence (1975), warfare intensified, especially in Ovamboland.

34 International aid agencies that established or assisted potteries in the 1960s and 1970s included the American Peace Corps and The Canadian University Services Overseas (CUSO). In later years War on Want, a British NGO, sponsored Serowe's Boiteko Trust.

35 Religious fraternities that established potteries in the 1960s and 1970s included the Evangelical Lutheran Church (Rorke's Drift), and various Catholic missions and orders, including the Catholic order of the Nuns of Precious Blood (Ikhwezi Lokusa) and the men's order, the Passionists (Thamaga).

36 Local development authorities that established potteries in the 1960s and 1970s included the Transkei Development Corporation (TDC) (Izandla), the Lesotho National Development Corporation (LNDC) (Thaba Bosigo), and the Housing and Community Services Department of the Bulawayo City Council (Mzilikazi).

37 Potteries in Lesotho included the commercial operation Kolonyama near Tetateyaneng and two CED (Community Economic Development Enterprise) initiatives namely Thaba Bosigo, Maseru, and Thabana Li Mele Pottery.

38 Swaziland potteries included Faragher's Pottery, Mbabane; Mantenga Craft Pottery, Mantenga Handcraft Centre, near Ezulwini; and the Mbabane Pottery Development Centre, Mbabane. All three potteries had strong philanthrophic and developmental aims.

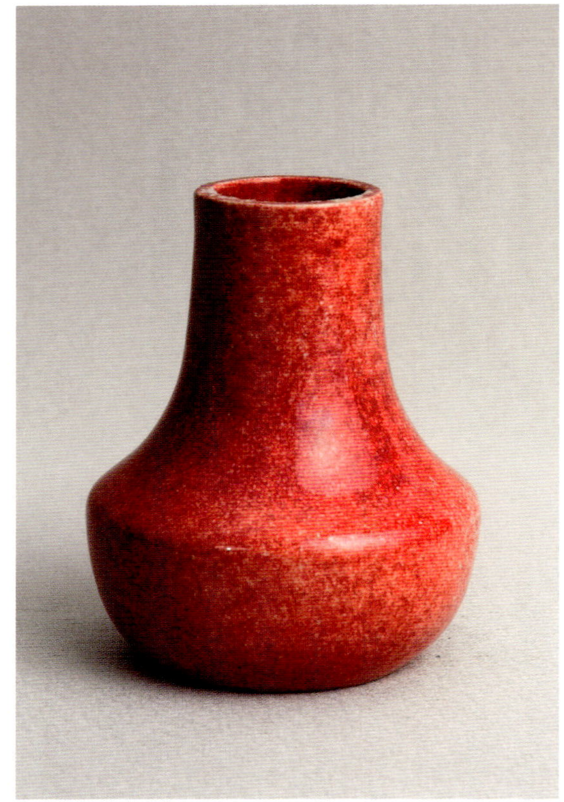

Armstrong, F W | Vase, specked pink glaze | 157x43x58mm | Provenance: Clive Newman | Marks: impressed mould mark below pale pink glaze, VAG, hand-painted marks, 'FWA GT 1923, F.W. Armstrong' | Photograph by Natalie Field

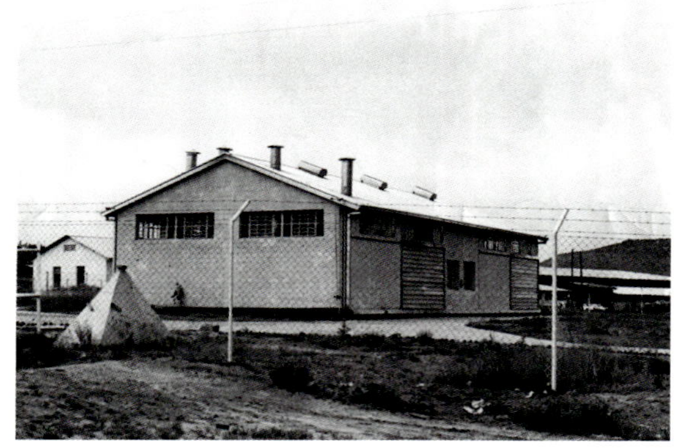

Thaba Bosigo | New premises | Provenance: David Whiting ex Geoffrey Whiting | Photograph by Geoffrey Whiting

39 CED Potteries in Botswana included Lentswe-La-Odi Pottery near Serowe and Thamaga Pottery near Gaborone.

40 My thanks to Ian Calder for drawing my attention to Heckroodt's work.

41 In 1902 Conrand was established by Cullinan for brick-making on his newly acquired clay-rich farm in Olifantsfontein. Upon the discovery of white-firing clay below the red-brick clay, Cullinan extended operations to include industrial ceramics and domestic ware. The following year, his application to mine the clay was approved and Cullinan appeared set to embark upon a new industrial adventure. However, the outbreak of the Anglo-Boer War delayed his plans. Finally in 1907 Conrand produced industrial sanitary whiteware (urinals, baths, lavatories, basins and pedestals, wall and floor tiles), bricks, earthenware pipes, fireclay goods, stoneware bottles, ink bottles, salt-glazed bricks, crucibles and liners for the gold industry, and drainage and sewage pipes. Conrand's industrial stoneware (including stock and gallon jars) is marked with the same star stamp, containing the initials 'C.R.B.P. & L. Co. Ltd.', but in most cases the stamp was applied while the clay was wet, creating a relief impression. Some industrial stoneware is marked with an impressed stamp, 'Cullinan Olifantsfontein TVL'. Other industrial stoneware is marked with an impressed stamp of a horizontally elongated diamond containing the company's initials. The company also produced white stoneware bottles for the 'Ideal Drinking Co'. In the mid-1940s, Conrand manufactured insulators. Its production facilities included clay quarries, brickfields and a massive factory complex punctuated with distinctive towering bottle kilns. Nearby, Cullinan constructed a residential compound with staff housing for the English staff and a hostel for Boer orphans. The government contributed a school building for the orphans and Cullinan constructed sports and recreation facilities.

42 During the economic boom of the Transvaal gold rush Cullinan was a building contractor, but soon became a construction magnate, politician and gold speculator. Upon the discovery of the Premier diamond fields in 1898, he founded the Premier Diamond Mining Company, on whose property the world's largest diamond was found in 1905. He is renowned for giving his name to this, the largest rough gem-quality diamond, that measured 3 106 carats (621 g).

43 A list of initial English technical staff include: Kelly, H (oven-builder), Edwards, WHV (engineer's fitter), Jones, W L (potter's joiner), Alcock, J (tile-maker), Alcock, L (warehouse hand), Perry, G (potter's warehouse man), Pointon, G H (mould-maker), Budd, G (pottery fireman), Stuart, H W (sanitary wares presser), Pointon, T (saggar-maker), Taylor, W (i) (potter's oven odd man), Ware, H (engineer's fitter), Taylor, M A Mrs (paintress), Taylor, W (ii) (general), Hall, J (slip-maker), Hall, E Mrs (transferer), Hughes, A S (tile-maker).

44 The set is part of the collection of the DNMCH, Pretoria. It contains 21 of the original dinner plates, among other items.The wares all have a gold insignia containing the initials 'LB' and are all marked with a glaze stamp in the form of a Star of David containing the initials 'C.R.B.P. and L. Co. Ltd'.

45 *Die Volkstem* newspaper reported an excursion in 1909 to Olifantsfontein, whereby Cullinan chartered a train for 200 Volksraad members from Pretoria station. After a tour of the factory, delegates were taken to Cullinan's home for coffee and speeches.

46 Transvaal Pottery's early clients included Worthington Bros, Cleveland and Rossouw Bros, Zeerust.

47 This mismatched jug is part of the Louis Botha dinner service, DNMCH, Pretoria.

48 For further information on Stainbank, consult Liebenberg-Barkhuizen 1998, Hillebrand 1989, Hillebrand 1986, Heymans 1989 and Hillebrand 1991. Stainbank's studio is recreated in the Voortrekker Museum, Pietermaritzburg.

49 I am grateful to Jan Middeljans and William Martinson for sharing this information.

50 Both Linnware and the Ceramic Studio used earthenware clays but the clay body of the Ceramic Studio is generally paler and less dense than that of Linnware.

51 Thelma Newlands-Currie recalled the special quality of the earlier handmade tiles that were slip-cast in wooden moulds and contrasted radically with the mechanically finished factory-made blanks that were used subsequently (Hillebrand [1991]:17,18).

52 For further information see www.art-archives-southafrica.ch/BYRD.htm, accessed on 12 August 2014.

53 Author's interview with Riana Heymans, Researcher, Voortrekker Monument Museum, Pretoria. 14 November 1997.

54 For further information on Mayer, see Basson 2006.

55 This is disputed by Liebenberg-Barkhuizen, who claims she was born in Liverpool (2003:2).

56 Author's electronic correspondence with Avril Wolfe-Coote, Johannesburg, concerning her grandmother, Barbara Dorrington (née Kelly), 21 & 26 September 2011.

57 A complete dinner service consisted of a dozen soup, dinner, side and pudding plates, three meat plates in different sizes, two vegetable dishes with covers and two sauce boats with stands. A complete tea set had a dozen cups, saucers and cake plates, two bread and butter plates, a slop or sugar basin and a cream jug (Hillebrand [1991]:27).

58 Email correspondence with Jannora Pais concerning her late aunt, Inez Sprenger de Rover, 1 March 2012.

59 In the late 1970s, Hans Kumpf designed six transfers of indigenous African wildlife, including a giraffe, a lion, a zebra, a leopard, a waterbuck and an elephant.

60 The author is aware of examples of souvenir wares bearing the following marks: 'Kruger National Park', '[Valley of] 1000 Hills', 'Willem Pretorius Game Reserve', 'Addo Elephant Park', 'Royal Natal National Park Hotel', 'Port Elizabeth Museum' and 'Durban Oceanarium'. The transfers were imported from Germany.

61 The term 'uranium' also reflected the fact that some yellow glazes used to contain uranium as a core element. Uranium had various other contemporary associations, e.g. with nuclear armament, space exploration and the 'space race' that began in the 1950s. Furthermore, uranium was associated with the development of nuclear power and electricity. In the 1950s, uranium was a significant export commodity in South Africa, such that in 1958 record sales of South African uranium were forecast. The colour (and the name) of the wares conveyed ideas of technological triumph and cosmopolitanism and possibly invested the owner with similar attributes of status and contemporaneity.

62 My thanks to Mark Watson for this insight.

63 Trent Potteries (later Crescent Potteries), Stoke-on-Trent. www.thepotteries.org/potworks_wk/138.htm, accessed on 6 January 2013.

64 Author's interview with Durant Sihlali in Johannesburg, 15 November 1997.

65 Otto Schließler was trained at the Academy of Art in Karlsruhe and was a 'master student' of Professor Hermann Volz. He concluded his studies in 1912 and then taught evening classes at the Karlsruhe 'Trade School'. Between 1914 and 1918 he was a soldier in World War I, after which he set up a studio in a castle in Schwetzingen. In 1920 he married Gertrude Körner, a painter and sculptor from Wiesbaden. She supported him financially and he enjoyed recognition and had several large exhibitions. In 1922, in Wiesbaden, Schließler was awarded the Ernest Ludwig prize. In 1927 he was awarded the first prize at an exhibition presented by the ministry of Culture in Baden, Germany. In 1928 he won the gold medal at the German Exhibition in Düsseldorf.

66 Author's interview with Morrie Shain in Johannesburg, 1 July 1997.

67 These dates, obtained during an interview with Sihlali in 1997, vary considerbaly from those supplied by Rankin (1989:163), who claimed that Sihlali worked for Atlanta between 1965 and 1970.

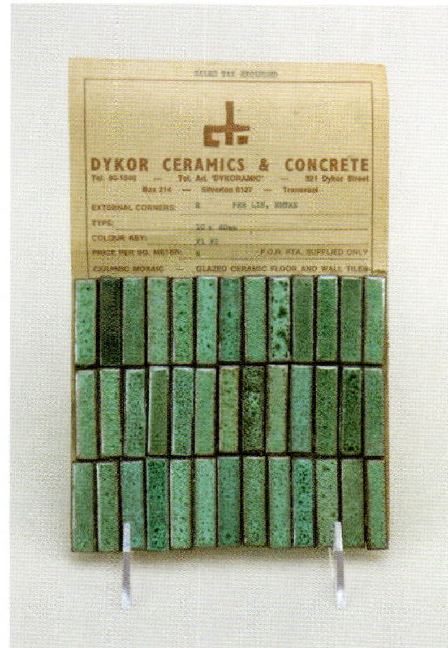

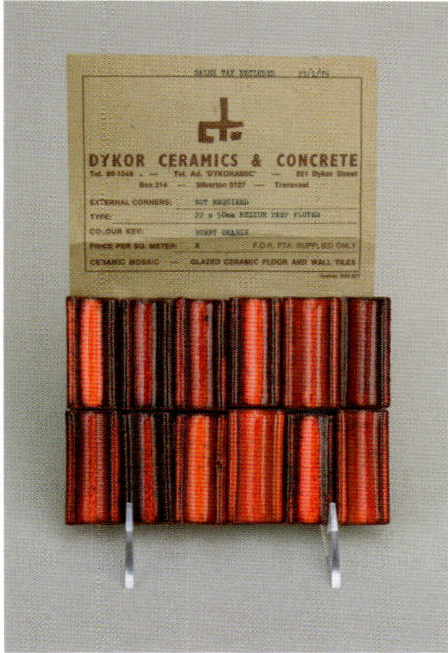

TOP: Dykor Ceramics and Concrete | Tile samples | 10x40mm | Provenance: Jan Middeljans | Photograph by Natalie Field

BOTTOM: Dykor Ceramics and Concrete | Tile samples | 10x40mm | Provenance: Jan Middeljans | Photograph by Natalie Field

68 See Richards 1997:81-97, Sarrazin (ed.) 1994, and Rankin 1989 for further information on Sihlali.

69 Herman Wald, a Hungarian, was a sculptor of busts, animals, figures and Biblical scenes. Mediums used by Wald included bronze, marble, wood, fiberglass and terracotta. He studied from 1924 to 1928 at the Budapest Academy, Hungary, from 1928 to 1931 at the School of Arts and Crafts, Vienna, in 1931 in Berlin and from 1932 to 1933 in Paris and London. Wald undertook numerous public commissions. His sculptures are represented in various local and international collections (Ogilvie 1988:728,9).

70 Author's correspondence with Isaac Witkin in Vermont, United States of America, 31 March 1997.

71 Author's telephonic communication with I A Perold, Pretoria, 5 March 2002a.

72 Perold's original kiln was supplied by a leading ceramic technician and University of Pretoria academic, Dr Hysteck.

73 Author's interview with I A Perold, Pretoria, 6 September 2004.

74 The only known exception being the Fauna and Flora Exhibition, Brakpan, 1956.

75 Dykor's mosaic tiles were rolled in a press and cut in a die. The original dimensions were 1x4cm and 2x4cm. They were rectangular and glazed in red, 'cereal', 'gun-metal' grey, orange, and pale grey-green (celadon). One of the early characteristic tiles had a pair of parallel ribs descending the length of the tile. The other characteristic early tile, called 'knobbly', had a slightly different profile, with a set of parallel ribs, the initial on the edge and the other in the centre of the tile. The tiles were either laid with the ribs aligned, or, more often, they were staggered to achieve an interesting textured surface. In later years Dykor introduced a number of different-sized tiles including 3x5cm and 4x5cm. Tile mosaics were used in many different applications, including bathrooms and swimming pools.

76 Author's correspondence with I A Perold, Pretoria, 25 September 2002b.

77 Polley's Arcade Pretoria was designed by the prominent architect Norman Eaton and inaugurated in ca.1959.

78 Author's interview with I A Perold, Pretoria, 6 September 2004.

79 Perold was handsome and loved women. His four wives were: (1) Anna Margaretha Susanna Perold (née Kok), known as Rita. Married ca.1953, divorced in 1958. He had two children with her, Braam and Ingrid; (2) Margrietha Elizabeth Perold (née Snyman), known as Grita. The couple were married for eight years and had no children. Snyman had a daughter, Grechen, from her first marriage. Louis Wilsenach married Grechen; (3) Dirkje Perold (née de Vries), known as De. The couple were married in ca.1970 and divorced in 1972. Their son, Izak Abraham Francois Perold died in 1971; (4) Marie-Josee Perold (née de Wit), known as Marie. The couple married in 1982 and the marriage lasted until Perold's death, 24 years later. They had no children.

80 Telephonic interview with Oscar Hisrch, Pretoria, 5 September 2008.

81 Interview with Marie Perold, Pretoria, 2 September 2008.

82 Interview with Abram Thage, Pretoria, 30 August 2008.

83 Telephonic interview with Louis Wilsenach, Muldersdrift, 5 September 2008 and email correspondence with Louis Wilsenach, Muldersdrift, 8 and 12 November 2008.

84 Faragher, J. 2002. Interviews with Joe Faragher, Cape Town, 16 April & 21 September 2002. Telephonic interview with Joe Faragher, Cape Town, 15 June 2006.

85 Email correspondence with Lynette Faragher, Australia, 27 March 2012.

86 Telephonic interview with Lynette Faragher, London, 21 June 2006. Telephonic interview and email correspondence with Lynette Faragher, London, 15 and 17 June 2009.

87 Telephonic interview and email correspondence with Meshack Masuku, Port Elizabeth. 23 February & 26 June 2002.

88 Perold indicated 1946 as the year of Globe's sale. However, archival records indicate that Robert Leggat was a mental patient and his estate was filed in 1944, so it must have been slightly earlier (author's interview with I A Perold, Pretoria, 6 September 2004).

89 Author's telephonic communication with I A Perold, Pretoria, 5 March 2002.

90 Author's correspondence with I A Perold, Pretoria, 25 September 2002.

91 Down-draught, coal-fired kilns were extremely susceptible to the elements. If the wind conditions changed, an entire kiln batch could be ruined. Another problem caused by these kilns was the limited glaze palette they supported.

92 Research has only uncovered one commercial exhibition. In 1923/24 Globe was awarded a gold medal at the Pretoria Show (Rayner 1941).

93 Most of the women decorators employed by Drostdy Ware were white, with the notable exception of Susan Douglas, who was coloured.

94 Various decorative and domestic chargers, plates and tiles, which included those depicting 'bushman' motifs, were hand-painted.

95 A second generation of tiles, domestic and decorative wares were decorated by means of hand-coloured transfers, and included images of native studies, wildlife and indigenous flora. The designs for the native studies and indigenous flora appear to have been executed by France Marot, while the wildlife designs were commissioned from Hans Kumpf.

96 Subsequent tiles, domestic and decorative wares were decorated with simple home-made screen-printed transfers, e.g. native studies designed by Leila Simpson.

97 A later 'generation' of tiles was decorated with imported, commercially manufactured colourful screen-printed-on-glaze transfers of images such as vintage cars. These multi-coloured screen-printed transfers were probably imported and it's likely that these wares were produced after Continental China took over Grahamstown Pottery.

98 Archival records attest that permission was granted for the use of royal titles, prefixes and images (photographs), provided that the item was not used 'in such a way as to give the impression that the product or firm concerned had received Royal custom' (TAB Doc No 601210850000, Depot SAB, Source GG, Type Leer, Vol: 2212, system 01, Ref: 78/201, Part A).

99 Way Jones, F [1994]. Unpublished typed notes on the South African Ceramics Industry. Albany Museum, Grahamstown.

100 Author's interview with Hester Locke, Port Alfred, 16 November 1996.

101 These breweries included Chandler, Castle, Stag, Ohlsson's, Simba, Windhoek Brewery (Namibia), Tusker Breweries (Kenya) and Northern Rhodesian Breweries. Steele-Gray in this interview with the author in 1996 boasted that Grahamstown Pottery manufactured tankards, jugs and ashtrays for every white-owned brewery in southern Africa.

102 Tied houses were hotels with bars that were in a contractual agreement with the SAB. This contract precluded the sale of beers manufactured by SAB's competitors.

103 Author's interview with Norman Steele-Gray, Kenton-on-Sea, 11 February 1998.

104 Grahamstown Pottery's technical staff were transferred to other branches of Continental China in Rosslyn (near Pretoria) and Blackheath (near Cape Town). The tunnel kilns and other equipment were moved to Blackheath.

105 'Native studies' produced by Drostdy Ware predominantly depict indigenous women in a rural, 'tribal' setting, as if the subjects were frozen in a pre-colonial era. There are few attempts to contextualise the subject historically, economically or geographically. The artists ignored urban and 'township' environs, denied cross-cultural dimensions, and omitted the political and social transitions occurring in contemporary African society. They also ignored their own presence, as white people in South Africa. Drostdy Ware offered the spectator an image of Africa that was not racked by the social realities of poverty, violence or disease. Images

Globe Potteries, Ltd.

Dam Street, New Muckleneuk,

PRETORIA.

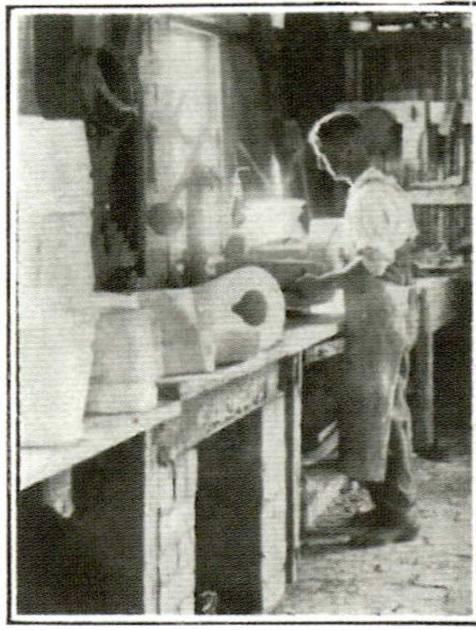

MOULD MAKING.

GOLD MEDALLISTS

PRETORIA SHOWS

1923-1924.

Manufacturers of All Kinds of Pottery.

Prices on Application.

Write for our Illustrated Catalogue.

Globe Advert | *Die Boervrou*, January 1923 | Scan by Jan Middeljans

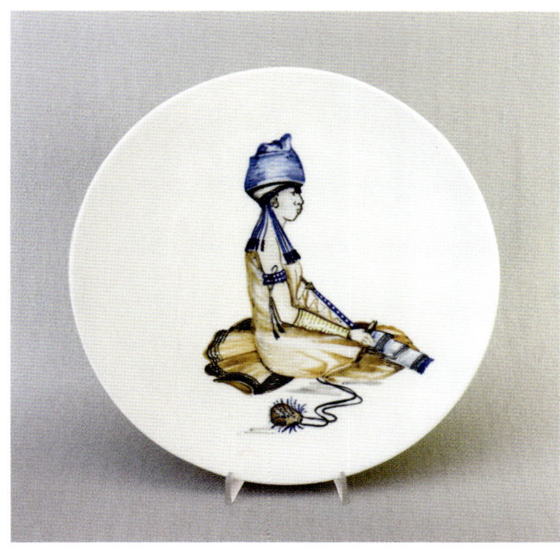

Drostdy Ware | Xhosa woman | 264x34mm | Provenance: Prof. Mark Watson | Marks: stamp 'Drostdy' black hand-written text, 'France Marot. / Hand painted JTB [unclear] / Xhosa woman, Eastern Cape Province. Drostdy Ware. Made in South Africa. | Photograph by Natalie Field

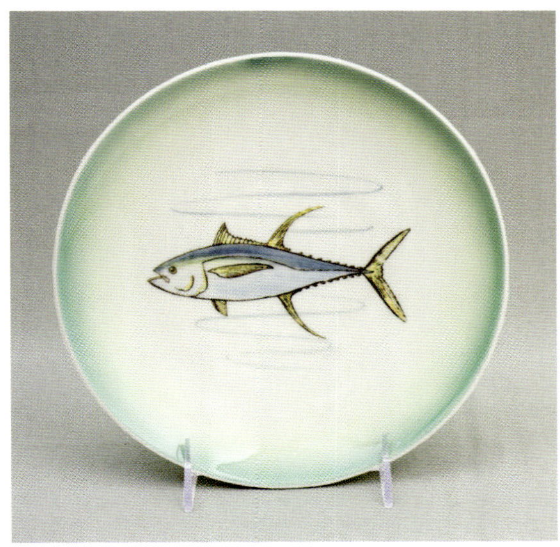

Drostdy Ware | Plate depicting a yellow-fin tune | 213x28mm | Provenance: Clive Newman | Marks: impressed stamp, 'Drostdy' hand-painted, 'Yellow Fin Tuna', printed glaze stamp, 'Drostdy Ware, Made in South Africa' | Photograph by Natalie Field

were influenced by conventions regarding picturesque qualities, and potentially controversial subjects were avoided. The labels on the back of many of Drostdy's works depicting women indicate that the subjects represented a variety of 'tribal' or linguistic groupings, such as the Zulu, Ndebele, Pondo [sic] and Xhosa. In these works the ethnicity of the subject was revealed through various supposedly distinctive cultural traits, including costume, adornments and hairstyles, e.g. a Pondo woman was identified by her long wavy hair, a Ndebele woman by her bracelets and a Zulu woman by her *isicholo* or *inhloko*. It is noted that contemporary theorists view as problematic any attempts to classify people using ethnicity as a parameter and argue that ethnicity is a fictional construct involving social engineering (Clifford 1988:10). Ethnic identity [sic] is essentially 'mixed, relational and inventive' (Clifford 1988:10). Drostdy's native studies convey not merely an ideological distortion convenient to a dominant group, but a densely imbricated arrangement of imagery that constituted a distinct binary other.

106 This mug commemorated the Rhodesian UDI of 1965. It depicts the country's former prime minister Ian Smith on the one side and the credo of Rhodesian independence on the other.

107 Copies of Drostdy's coronation orb are found in Museum Africa and the Ditsong National Cultural History Museum in Pretoria.

108 Many of the series of Port Elizabeth buildings were sponsored by United Cement Industries (Pty) Ltd., Port Elizabeth, which used these plates as corporate gifts. Most were decorated with hand-coloured transfers. Other Port Elizabeth buildings in this series include the African Life Building, Barclays Bank, the F C Sturrock Building, the Johannesburg Building Society, the Old Mutual building and the Bird Street laboratories of the University of Port Elizabeth.

109 The Department of Ichthyology at Rhodes University commissioned a series of wares decorated with illustrations of South African marine fish. See adjacent illustration.

110 The South African Motor Assemblers and Distributors (SAMAD) produced Studebaker cars at their factory in Uitenhage between 1948 and 1965. Drostdy produced a series of four plates that were decorated with transfers of various Studebakers.

111 [No author] 'Pottery pioneer tells the story of S.A.'s luxury industry'. *The Star*, 25 January 1955.

112 See Schoonraad, M. & E. 1989:89–95 for further information on Connolly.

113 From 1924 to 1928 Andersen studied under Alfred Martin at the Natal Technical Art School. He studied ceramics at the Natal Technical Art School from 1938 and taught ceramics at the Durban Tech from 1942 to 1944 (Berman 1983:36,37; Ogilvie 1988:13,14).

114 Author's interview with France and Renée Marot, Durban, 18 April 1998 and author's interview with France Marot, Durban, 29 December 1996.

115 Author's interview with Hester Locke, Port Alfred, 5 September 1997.

116 Author's interview with Norman Steele-Gray, Port Elizabeth, 14 February 1997, and author's interview with Norman Steele-Gray, Kenton-on-Sea, 16 November 1996.

117 Born in Sandwick, Orkney, Kirkness arrived in South Africa in 1879. Initially engaged in building operations in the Natal Colony, Kirkness moved to the Orange Free State Republic in 1880 and subsequently to the Transvaal in 1885. Eventually he made his headquarters in the Kirkness Building, Pretoria. Kirkness was a member of the Pretoria Municipal Council for many years and served as mayor.

118 Author's interview with I A Perold, Pretoria, 6 September 2004.

119 The author is aware of three articles bearing this mark. One example is unnumbered and the other two examples are numbered 43 & 44. These low numbers may suggest that it was manufactured in the early years of Hamburger Pottery

or perhaps when Hamburger was based at Grahamstown Potteries between approximately 1939 and 1948.

120 Small light blue horse. Hamburger impressed stamp mark under right front hoof. Impressed stamp 'N. Bates', under left front hoof. Douglas van der Horst.

121 Most of Hamburger's domestic ware features matt glazes and either slip-trailed, sgraffito or wax-resist decoration. These techniques were effectively used on both white and terracotta clays. Hamburger's trademark glaze colours are white, grey, yellow, light and dark blue, green, turquoise, brown and a colour Hamburger termed red honey.

122 Hamburger's aloof nature and outsider status has been commented on by various informants who were his former students at Rhodes University, including Hylton Nel and Mary-Rose Dold.

123 Hamburger and Rie fled Nazi persecution in continental Europe, both arriving in London in 1938. It is not known whether they met or if Hamburger was aware of her work.

124 Marguèrite Friedlaender Wildenhain (1896–1985) was born in Lyon, France and attended the Berlin School for Applied Arts from 1917 to 1919 and the Weimar Bauhaus from 1919 to 1925, where she was the first of only seven ceramic students, and the only woman in the group. Wildenhain received her master's degree in 1926 from Halle Saale. She worked as a ceramics teacher and porcelain designer in Germany before she was expelled from her teaching position on anti-Semitic grounds. She briefly moved to Holland before emigrating to the United States of America in 1940. Wildenhain settled north of San Francisco where she founded Pond Farm, a celebrated artist colony and school. She lived, worked and taught at Pond Farm for the rest of her life, retiring in 1980. Wildenhain became one of the most influential potters of her time.

125 Interview with Joe Faragher, Cape Town, 16 April 2002.

126 Interview with Sr Mary Paule, Ikhwezi Lokusa, Mthatha, 24 February 2002.

127 Telephonic interview with Mathemba Ncoyini, Ikhwezi Lokusa, Mthatha, 19 September 2011.

128 Interview with John Steele, East London, 23 February 2002.

129 Interview with Joe Faragher, Cape Town, 21 September 2004.

130 Interview with Angelique Kirk, Cape Town, 13 April 2002.

131 Interview with Lindsay Scott, Hillfold Pottery, Lidgetton, KwaZulu-Natal, 1 March 2002.

132 Interview with Michael Gill, Sherborne, Dorset, England, 17 August 2004.

133 Wares were fired to 1400ºC for over 24 hours on a weekly cycle, in one of two six-metre cubic kilns. These trolley kilns burnt a mixture of diesel and sump oil. Gill replaced the original kiln with a new envelope electric kiln.

134 Interview with Clive Berlyn and Richard Ndungane, Mthatha, 1 April, 2002.

135 Personal observation, visit to Izandla pottery, 2008.

136 Department of Trade & Industry. 2010. Registrar of Companies - Cipro Publication No. 201056, Notice No. 25. Deregistrations.p.831. www.cipro.co.za/info_library/Publications/CipPub201056_25_CO.pdf, accessed 10 September 2012.

137 Interview with Gill, Sherborne, Dorset, England, 17 August 2004.

138 Mason cited in Moon 2008. *Across the Ditch: Australian Ceramics in the Post War Period*, www.damonmoon.com/articles/across-the-ditch.html, accessed on 26 September 2011.

139 Interview with Gill, Sherborne, Dorset, England, 17 August 2004.

140 Correspondence with Leonie Malherbe, Durban, 13 May 2002.

141 Correspondence with Keslina Ngubo, Mthatha, 30 April 2006.

142 I am grateful to Juliette Leeb-du Toit, Pietermaritzburg, who shared this information with me in 1998.

143 Author's interview with Veikla Grivainis, Pinelands, Cape Town, 13 January 1998.

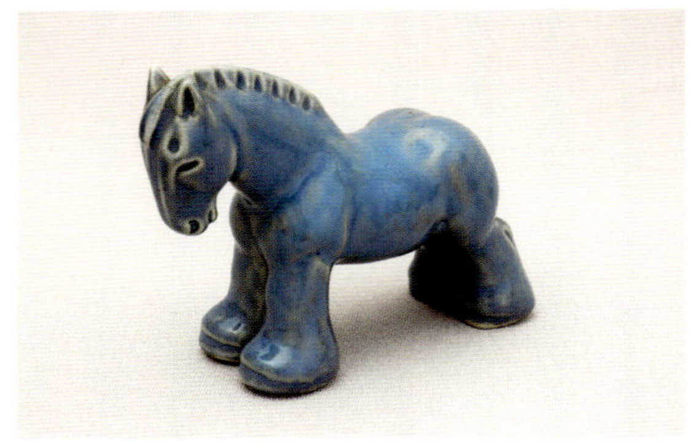

Hamburger's Pottery | Ornament | Small light blue 'cart' horse | 100x135mm | Provenance: Douglas van der Horst | Marks: Hamburger impressed stamp mark, 'GH', under right front hoof, impressed stamp, 'N. Bates', under front left hoof | Photograph by Natalie Field

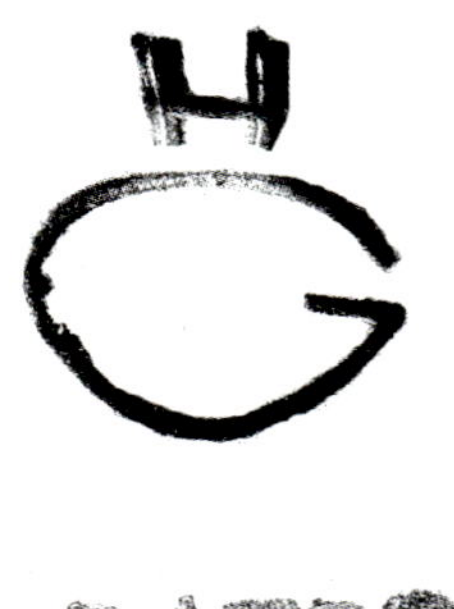

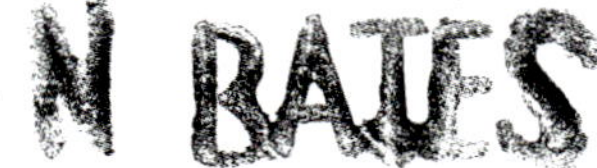

Hamburger's Pottery | Digital rendering of impressed stamped mark under right front left hoof of ornamental cart horse, 'GH' 'N.Bates' | Provenance: Douglas van der Horst

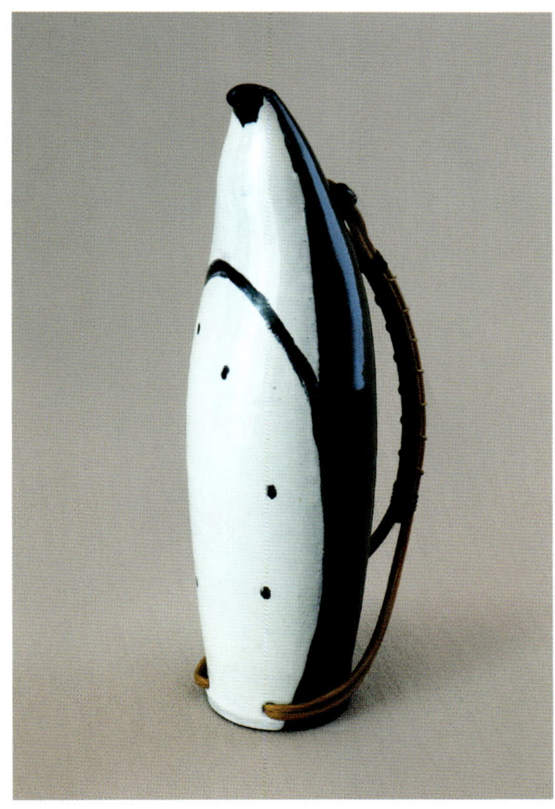

Kalahari | Penguin jug | 380x23mm | Provenance: SHC Iziko | 90/75 | Marks: painted mark: 'Kalahari' | Photograph by Natalie Field

144 The Kalahari Studio manufactured an ashtray and a small plate bearing the KWV initials. The KWV (Ko-operatiewe Wijnbouwers-Vereeniging), one of the largest wine cooperatives in the world has its headquarters in Paarl.

145 Certificate of Registration of a trademark. 17 February. 1954. Caspareuthus, A. Department of Labour, Cape Town.

146 Information Officer for Cultural Affairs, State Information Office, Department of External Affairs. 1956. Letter to Mr and Mrs Klopcanovs, 13 September 1956.

147 Professor Wilhelm Kåge (1869–1960) was an important Swedish artist, ceramicist and designer. Kåge was responsible for pioneering and promoting the use of 'modern' and 'democratic' designs. In the 1930s he designed numerous 'oven-to-table' sets, including 'Praktika' and 'Pyro'. His 'Liljeblå' or 'Set for the working class' remained in production until 1940. 'Praktika' of 1933 was functional, austere, and consisted of multi-purpose forms and stacking pieces. By 1937 Kåge's designs had moved away from the austerity of modernist purism to more organic plastic shapes, as typified by his set of 'Soft shapes' (Hannah 1986:59,82).

148 RV Cullinan, the director of the company, lobbied the Immigration Selection Board of the Department of the Interior to speed up the appointment of Vestman. Within a month the entrance permit was granted and Vestman's appointment was confirmed.

149 Winchcombe Pottery, an old country pottery that had closed in World War I, was reopened by Michael Cardew in 1926. Ray Finch joined Winchcombe in 1936 and spent most of his life working there.

150 Author's electronic correspondence with Lissa Claassens, Hout Bay, 16 April 2012.

151 Initially a 20-tonne load of dry raw clay arrived by rail at Ficksburg. Later, an 18-tonne truck would annually deliver clay from Brackenfell. The clay was wind-dried, then raked and crushed with a garden roller. It was then shovelled into a blunger, processed and stored in an underground reservoir.

152 The LNDC was established by an act of Parliament in 1967 and was mandated to initiate, promote and facilitate the development of manufacturing and processing industries, mining and commerce in a manner calculated to raise the level of income and employment in Lesotho.

153 The clay-processing shed was followed by two throwing rooms and then by a room with the bisque kiln. There was no intermediate drying room as bisque wares dried outside. The bisque-fired wares then moved on to the waxing room, followed by the glaze room and finally to the glaze kiln room, which housed the already-mentioned large oil-fired kiln. In later years, the glaze room also housed a 36-cubic-foot (1-cubic-metre) kiln that was used for salt-glazing. Once glazed, the wares proceded to the stock and packing rooms. A final selection of wares was displayed in the showroom.

154 Joe Finch built the first large oil-fired kiln, which measured over 100 cubic feet (2.8 cubic metres). He used locally produced fire bricks, with kiln props and shelves imported from England. It was based on the Winchcombe kiln, and was originally used for both bisque and glaze firings. Finch supervised the manufacture of a pug mill by a local engineer according to plans sent out by his father, Ray Finch. Joe Finch purchased a filter press from Tim Morris in Johannesburg and built a manual blunger, which was operated by Lesole Motanyane and Philemon Koloko. When needed, clay was air pressured into the filter press and accessed. The clay-making operation was improved by Ray Finch, who introduced drying tables for the clay, which had previously been left outside on the floor to dry. Joe and Trudi Finch spent a year in South Africa, not three years as claimed by Ray Finch.

155 Finch built one of the wheels, a second was donated by Oxfam, two came from England and one from South Africa.

156 The original kiln, built by Finch was rebuilt by Van Gilder. Later, Milway had an electric one constructed. Milway used Finch's original oil-fired kiln for bisque wares. Van Gilder's kiln was later replaced by Dave Wilson, who rebuilt a 150-cubic-foot

(4.2-cubic-metre) trolley kiln in its place. Wilson's kiln was subsequently replaced by Taylor, who built a 180-cubic-foot (5-cubic-metre) diesel-fired trolley kiln.

157 At the Fourth APSA National Exhibition, a three-pint (1½-litre) casserole was awarded a certificate of Distinction. Similarly, a plate by Milway was awarded a prize in the functional hand-building section.

158 These private galleries included Gallery 101 (1970), Gallery 21 (1975), and the Potters House in Johannesburg; the Yellow Door Gallery, the Potter's Shop and Craft Corner in Cape Town; and The Lookout Gallery in Plettenberg Bay. Wares were also sold through trade fairs such as Design for Living in Cape Town and the Rand Easter Show.

159 Over the years, Dare had acquired several other businesses in KwaZulu-Natal. He was often away on business trips, sorting out various pressing management problems.

160 Author's correspondence with Judith Bandtock, Lewes, Surrey, England, 15 & 24 November 2004.

161 Author's correspondence with Yvonne Dare, Cape Town, 7 & 20 November 2004.

162 Author's correspondence with Joe Finch,Tanygroes, Wales, 15 November 2012.

163 Interview with Michael Finch, Winchcombe Pottery, England, 18 August 2004.

164 Interview with Ray Finch, Winchcombe Pottery, England, 18 August 2004.

165 Interview with Toff Milway, Conderton, England, 18 August 2004.

166 Author's correspondence with Graham Taylor, Crown Studio, Rothbury, England, 2 April 2012.

167 Interview with Dave Wilson, Winchcombe Pottery, England, 18 August 2004.

168 My grateful thanks to William Martinson who specially visited the aquarium in 2012 to verify this.

169 In 1828 Judge Sir William Westbrooke Burton bought Onder Schuur, a small south-east portion of Rhodes's homestead Groote Schuur. It has subsequently been renamed Genadendal. It is believed that all Hill's door furniture was later replaced during the redecoration of the building.

170 Calder's claim that Hilda Ditchburn, who taught at the Department of Fine Art at the University of Natal, Pietermaritzburg from 1946–1981 was the first Ceramics lecturer in South Africa is thus false (Calder 2012:59). Hill replaced Mrs Grace Wheatley, who had established a pottery studio at Michaelis. The dates of the inception of Pottery department at Rhodes University are unknown, and may predate Michaelis.

171 In its heyday, Liebermann Pottery had approximately 20 electric pottery wheels, jiggers and jolleys on which workers produced different domestic items according to their individual expertise. From the 1980s, jiggers were used to produce approximately 1 500 plates per machine per day. The foot rim was added manually. A number of electric kilns were built by the Liebermanns. The potters produced between 400 and 1 000 thrown items per day. The dimensions and forms of the thrown items were all carefully standardised, and based on prototypes developed by Sammy. In the late 1970s the pottery produced approximately 8 000 handmade pieces each week. These were all inspected by Sammy Liebermann.

172 Liebermann Pottery produced numerous novelty items, such as sculptural planters known as '*blom meide*' figurines. This item consisted of a thrown tube body with the torsos of an African adult and infant emerging. The adult figurine supported a small bowl on her head, which was used as a planter. Another novelty was 'Candelly', an elephant with an opening for a candlestick in its back. Liebermann also produced garden fountains in numerous different forms, including a wall fountain in the form of a sculptural, abstract mask.

173 Mary Liebermann accepted private commissions for unique sculptures, including figures, masks and decorative pieces such as fountains, fantastic animals and gargoyles. Sammy Liebermann occasionally undertook sculptural works, e.g. in 1972 he exhibited a chess set at an exhibition sponsored by the Northern Transvaal

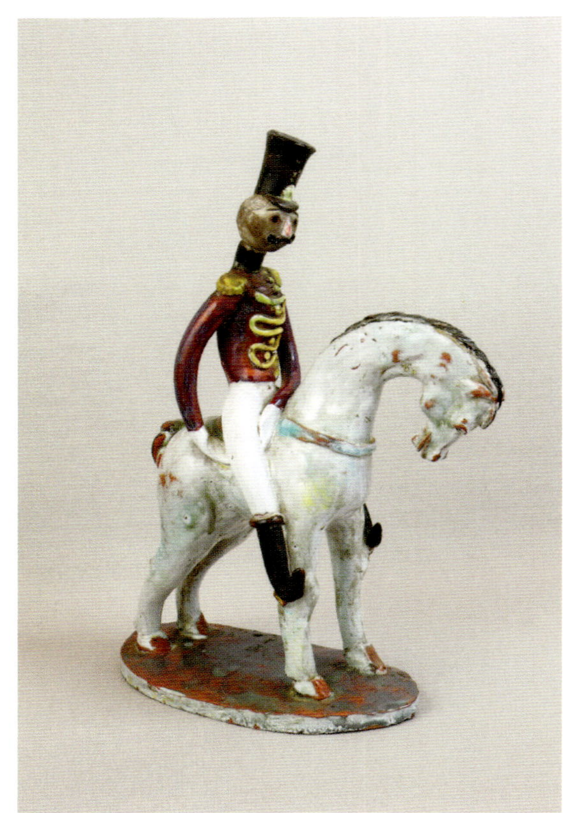

Liebermann Pottery | Statuette of a soldier on horse | Unique piece by Mary Liebermann | 362x230x111mm | Provenance: Liebermann Pottery | Marks: unmarked, unglazed base | Photograph by Natalie Field

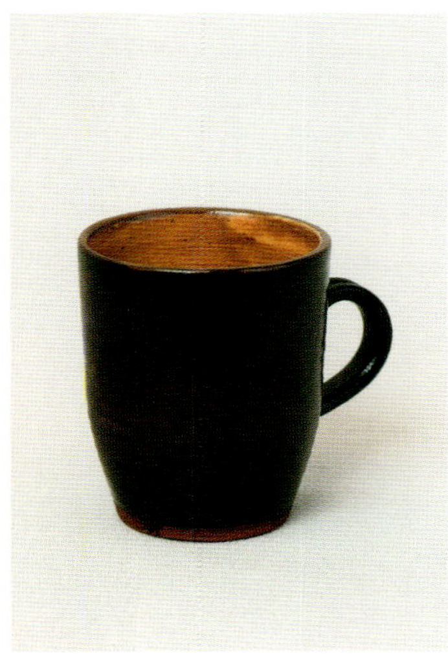

Liebermann Pottery | Coffee mug | 80x95x60mm | Provenance: Liebermann Pottery | Marks: glazed brown base with small resist stamp of potter, Turgel era | Photograph by Natalie Field

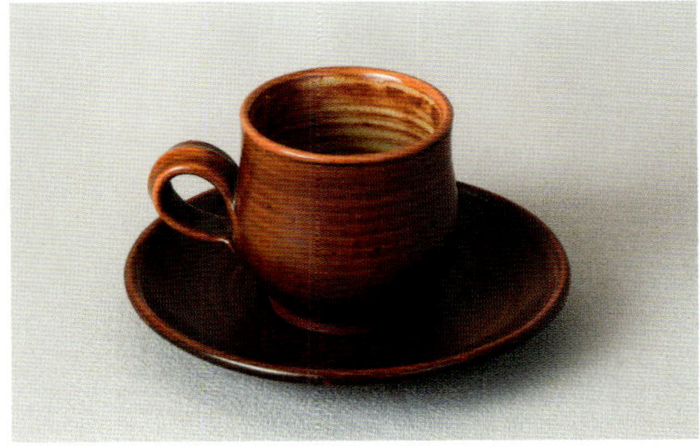

Liebermann Pottery | Dark brown 'Lucien' tea cup and saucer | Cup 77x73x55mm; saucer 152x25mm | Provenance: Liebermann Pottery | Marks: cup base unmarked, saucer has faint stamp under glaze | Photograph by Natalie Field

branch of the SA Association of the Arts, Pretoria. Over the years the pottery undertook hundreds of personal sculptural commissions of a humble nature. Mary made 'tiles and fountains and little bits for people's homes' as she 'share[d] their pleasure in getting things just right' (Women's Page Reporter 1968:s.n.).

174 Liebermann's chestnut colouring, the tonal qualities of the glazes, the oven-proof clay body and the emphasis on practical forms recalls Arabia's highly influential 'Ruska' range. The Finnish pottery manufacturer Arabia exported this range to South Africa and numerous other countries from the 1960s to the 1980s. Designed by Ulla Procopé-Nyman (1921–1968), Ruska wares were oven- and dishwasher-proof.

175 European peasant folk scenes occurred on various other European wares, including those designed by Birger Kaipainen for the Arabia Pottery, Finland, in the mid-1940s and the 'Karneval' range of Stig Lindberg for the Gustavsberg Pottery, Sweden.

176 Thanks to Anne-Marie Berry for providing most of the information about the methods of decorating Liebermann tiles in a letter to Douglas van der Horst dated 8 September 1998.

177 Department of Trade & Industry. 2010. Registrar of Companies – Cipro Publication No. 201056, Notice No. 25. Deregistrations.p.78. www.cipro.co.za/info_library/Publications/CipPub201056_25_CO.pdf, accessed 10 September 2012.

178 Letter from Anne-Marie Berry to Douglas van der Horst, 8 September 1998, p.2.

179 Haenggi's correspondence with the author on 7 November 2011.

180 The Gertrude Agranat Bequest includes many of South Africa's leading studio potters and other international wares. Highlights include Kim Sacks, David Schlapobersky, Tim Morris, Andrew Walford, Digby Hoets, Chris Patten, The Old Jar Pottery, Rorke's Drift, Dirk Meerkotter and the grande dame of British studio pottery, Lucie Rie.

181 David Willingham Rawnsley was a British architect and engineer. He worked as an art film director during the 1930s and 1940s. After the war he established a pottery in Paris. In 1952 David and his wife Mary founded Chelsea Pottery in London. It was styled as an 'open studio' – a place where any potter could come to work and learn. The pottery was run on a 'club' basis, as had been the Paris pottery. In 1959 the Rawnsleys established the Bahamas Chelsea Pottery in Nassau. After a couple of years David moved on to open yet another pottery, this time in Mexico. On a solo trip to Capri in the early seventies Rawnsley died of a heart attack.

Chelsea pottery produced a wide range of handmade, highly decorated earthenware ceramics. They were decorated with sgraffito incisions and sophisticated coloured glazes – a technique that has been referred to as 'inlay and overlay'. In the 1960s and 1970s Chelsea Pottery became very popular with the rich and famous and obtained large orders from American department stores, including Lord & Taylor and Neiman Marcus.

182 According to Liebermann's obituary in *Ceramix*, July/September 1990, p. 6, he died of a heart attack. His daughter, Lisa Liebermann Köter, among other Liebermann family members and close friends have stated to the author that his cause of death was suicide.

183 Sacks's correspondence with the author on 25 August 2011 on South African Pottery History's Facebook group.

184 Interview with Adriaan Turgel, Johannesburg, 5 February 2002 and telephonic interviews with Adriaan Turgel, Johannesburg, 22 & 29 May 2008.

185 Interview with Rika Turgel, Johannesburg, 7 February 2002.

186 Email correspondence with Andrew Walford, Shongweni, 24 March 2006.

187 The main tile panel at the Natal Parks Board headquarters included elements of the life cycle of the crocodile (Vermeulen 1984:388).

188 Email correspondence with Thomas Vermeulen, Pietermaritzburg, 19 June 2012.

189 Correspondence with Digby Hoets, Carlswald, Johannesburg, via Facebook group, South African Pottery History, 18 November 2011.

190 Digby Hoets subsequently taught John's wheel-work students until 1976. Lesley-Ann Hoets, Digby's sister, taught Valmai's hand-work classes until she moved to Cape Town in 1975 (email correspondence with Penny and Digby Hoets, Carlswald, Johannesburg. 22 & 24 November 2011).

191 Kerrod claimed that Olsen Edwards also produced tiles under the name Stone Pottery (Kerrod 2010:50,191). The author (in conjunction with various collectors and museum curators) is not aware of any such tiles, and when clarification of this claim was requested, Kerrod did not respond.

192 It is likely that during this period Olsen Edwards painted detailed studies of animals and landscapes on commercial glazed plates, e.g. she painted a pair of cats on a plate made by Continental China. Bidorbuy ID: 6730356. www.bidorbuy.co.za/item/6730356/Kitty_Cats_Plate.html, accessed on 29 September 2011.

193 Email correspondence with Glenn Olsen, Port Elizabeth, 16, 17 & 21 October, 2 & 14 November 2011, and 11 June 2012.

194 The South African industrialist, Dr Anton Rupert was central to the establishment in 1972 of a private development bank known as EDESA (Economic Development Bank for Equatorial and Southern Africa) which was registered in Luxembourg with a capital of $20 million. EDESA was established for the purpose of making available private capital investment in development projects in the independent and developing states and adjacent islands of Equatorial and Southern Africa. The Southern African operational headquarters of the bank were in Swaziland (Venter 1974:31).

195 In Swaziland there were three main EDESA projects: the Mantenga Craft Centre, a second carpet weaving factory in Mbabane and a beekeeping and honey project. The main EDESA stakeholders were the Rembrandt Group, General Motors and Mitsubishi.

196 Email correspondence with Chris Green, Johannesburg, 5 and 9 January, 8 June, 3 August 2012.

197 Interview with Chris Green, Johannesburg, 2 & 6 August 2012.

198 Email correspondence with Johannes Gaston, 26 & 27 June and 2 & 3 August 2012.

199 Green notes that his decision to leave Mantenga at the end of the year was determined by the inability of his wife, a school teacher, to obtain a work permit (email correspondence with Chris Green, Johannesburg. 8, 11, 13, 15 & 22 November 2004).

200 According to Green, 'the carefully fired reduction celadons and rich tenmokus were not so much in evidence and the reduction effects gave way to neutral atmosphere firings, the glazes became simpler in appearance' (email cprrespondence with Chris Green, 10 August 2012).

201 Author's email correspondence with Mordechai Brodie, 20, 23, 25 & 30 November 2008.

202 Author's email correspondence with Mordechai Brodie, 8 June 2008 & 5 & 9 January 2009.

203 Brodie 2009.

204 Sue Meyer (1987:6) is incorrect in her claim that Manyoni taught graphics to Hleza, as he was already a capable draughtsman and designer by the time he visited the Katlehong Art Centre.

205 Author's correspondence with Bill van Gilder, Gapland, Md, USA, 26 March, 2012.

206 Interview with Menucha Turgel, Johannesburg, 6 February 2002.

207 Interview with Mary Liebermann, Cape Town, 12 February 2002.

208 Email correspondence with Denis Morgan Blewett II, Johannesburg, 12 & 16 September 2012.

209 The pottery is listed in Methley 1926:21.

210 The wares of Rand Ceramics Industries frequently either stuck to the kiln shelf or, if they were fired on stilts, the glaze flowed below the level of the base. This problem

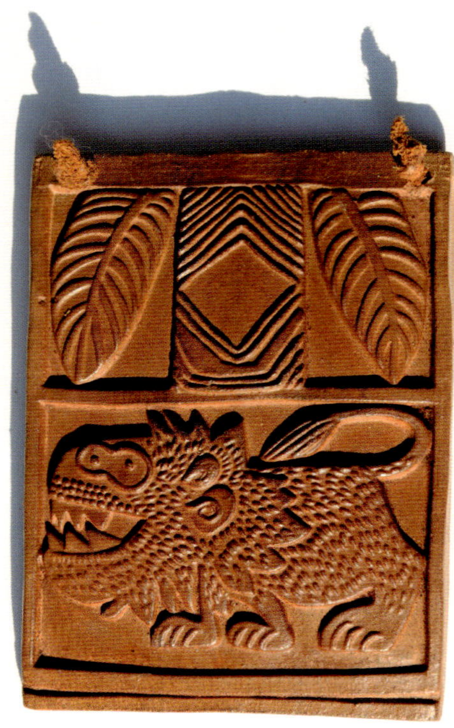

Lucky Bean Farm Pottery | 'Amulet' tile with leather thong for hanging | Earthenware | Decorated with a lion | 65x90mm | Provenance: Thomas Vermeulen | Photograph by Thomas Vermeulen

was remedied by grinding away the excess glaze flow. The same phenomenon is also evident on numerous Linnware and Globe pieces. The glaze speckling was probably caused by cinders settling on the glazes in the final phase of the cooling process.

211 Works in the collection of DAG that feature these coloured slips are fading significantly according to Jenny Stretton (personal communication with Jenny Stretton, Curator, DAG, 29 July 2012).

212 Email correspondence with Nielson, 25 November 2008.

213 In the early 1970s Van der Merwe introduced firing schedules, stoneware clay and a feldspathic glaze that served to soften the hard dry appearance and improve the glaze's strength. She also designed and supervised the construction of a new drip-fed oil kiln.

214 Email correspondence with Voith, 12 October 2012.

215 It is noted that Rorke's Drift generally organised exhibitions of works for the entire centre, and not for specific individuals or departments. Furthermore, the Rorke's Drift archives lack documentation concerning individual potters and exhibitions (Voith email, 2012).

216 Email correspondence with P Gowenius, 4, 7 & 17 March 2010.

217 Email correspondence with Nielsen, 25 November 2008.

218 Nielsen 2008.

219 Dr G H B Lovell was born and raised in England. He was employed as the chief chemist at Josiah Wedgwood and Co, Stoke-on-Trent, for five years. Thereafter he worked for four years as a research officer at the British Refractories Research Association. Dr Lovell held several degrees and taught at the University of the Witwatersrand. He founded Silwood Ware and later Alicia Floral China. In 1955 Lovell was accidentally shot in the head and incapacitated.

220 Mrs B M Lovell, the wife of G H B Lovell, had no formal training in ceramics, but worked as a decorator for Silwood Ware and later at Alicia Floral China.

221 J B Livesey was born in England and was experienced in the electrical industry before he was stationed in South Africa as a pilot by the Royal Air Force during World War II. After the war he returned to South Africa and joined Silwood Ceramics.

222 My thanks to Jan Middeljans for drawing my attention to a pair of nearly identical wall pockets. One is marked 'S.A. Glazing Boksburg, 603' and the other is marked 'Lucia'.

223 Middeljans, J. 2010. Maiolica Pottery. Unpublished research notes. Middeljans, J. 2008. South African Glazing Co (Pty) Ltd Boksburg East Pottery. Unpublished research notes.

224 Dr Anton Rupert, the South African industrialist, who was honorary industrial adviser to the Lesotho government, initiated the Lesotho National Development Corporation (LNDC). Wynand van Graan, one of Rupert's senior executives, was seconded to the post of managing director of the corporation.The LNDC claimed that it brought direct foreign investment to Lesotho of more than Rl4.5 million, and has an income from its own commercial activities of more than R800 000 a year, which it re-invested in Lesotho, creating an impressive list of industries, including a 250-room hotel, a national airline, an assembly plant for tractors, a weaving factory, a clothing factory, a light-fitting factory, a diamond cutting and polishing factory, a jewellery workshop, two potteries and a candle factory (Venter 1974:31).

225 Interview with Finch, Winchombe Pottery, England, 18 August 2004.

226 In Lesotho and neighbouring South Africa, Sotho women developed a tradition of decorating the walls of their houses with geometric patterns, *litema*. The walls are first plastered with a mixture of mud and dung, and often coloured with natural dyes. While the mud is still wet, the women engrave the walls, using their forefingers. Their art is seasonal: the sun dries and cracks it, and the rain washes it away. The entire village is redecorated before special celebrations, including

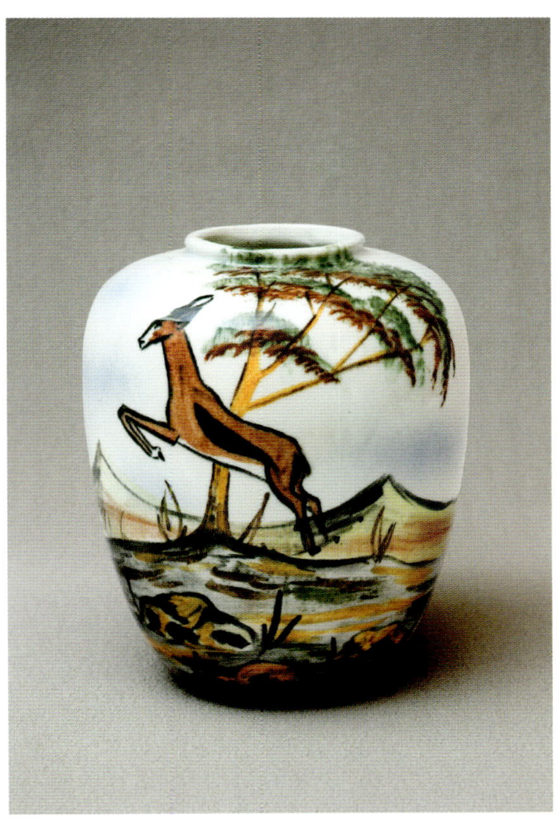

Lucia Ware | Vase with hand-painted image of leaping springbok and landscape | 163x57x65mm | Provenance: Prof. Mark Watson | Marks: Raised mark, 'Lucia Ware, 209' and hand-painted markings, 'JHK Hand painted for Blumberg and Kleinman. Silver foil 'Lucia Ware' sticker attached to back of vase | Photograph by Natalie Field

engagement parties and weddings. Symmetry is a basic feature of the *litema* patterns, which are normally built up from squares and use two tones.

227 Letima pots were decorated, when leather-hard, with the application of sgraffito decoration onto a coating of iron slip. A white matt glaze was then applied.

228 Hayes was responsible for the glaze manufacture and five basic glazes were used: 1) Tenmoku glaze that was a broken brown and very glossy (as a result of a high iron content); 2) speckled white glaze; 3) transparent oatmeal glaze that was similar to a celadon green; 4) transparent green glaze that was used over a Tenmoku glaze; wax resist decorations were used with the Tenmoku glaze; and 5) the last glaze was a rich deep transparent brown with crazing, which was made from crushed beer bottles.

229 After approximately nine months of employment, a Lesotho company was legally required to issue an employee with an employment certificate, which allowed their holders to work legally in South Africa. The Basotho men thus all departed as soon as they acquired their certificates. They earned significantly higher wages in South Africa. Hayes claimed that his best paid staff member earned approximately 60c per day, whereas in South Africa he could easily earn between 80c and R1 per day.

230 Interview with Peter Hayes, Bath, England, 19 August 2004.

231 Clark and Wagner presented Thaba Bosigo as producing essentially modernist wares (1974:168). Their understanding of pottery's production is somewhat biased and superficial.

232 Author's interview with Peter and Joan Hayes. Bath, England, 11 October 2009.

233 Author's telephonic interview with Barbara Hudson, St Ives, England, 25 July 2009.

234 Author's telephonic interview with David Whiting, son of the late Geoffrey Whiting, 16 July 2009.

235 Whiting, D, interview 2009.

236 The new kiln also had the advantage of diminishing the losses caused by the hazards of wood firing, such as crud damage and the rough spots caused by unfluxed ashes.

237 Hutchings's email correspondence with the author, 2 November 2009.

238 The existing oil-fired catenary arch kiln, which had originally been built for firing with wood, had a bad temperature distribution and one of the two glazes did not work properly. The Thamaga clay (originally imported from RSA) was modified with additions of local materials (ant hills, coloured earths such as ochre and umber-like materials) and was fired at Cone 10 and did not need glazing in order to become waterproof. A hammer mill was acquired for the processing of local raw materials including clay, sand and granite (Author's telephonic interview with Saskia Praamsma, Canada, 4 November 2009).

239 Praamsma interview 2009.

240 These pots were not glazed, but slips (engobes and terra sigillata) were used for decoration.

241 Praasma interview 2009.

242 Telephonic interview with Father Julian Black, Botswana, 8 July 2009 and email correspondence, 31 July 2009.

243 Pearson, B. 1978. Unpublished typed notes for CUSO Slide Show of Thamaga Pottery. Courtesy of Dorte Deans, Canada. p.4.

244 Barnim, S. 2009. Email correspondence with the author concerning Bodil Pearson. 5 February 2009, 11 February 2009, 17 February 2009 and 8 June 2009.

245 Pearson, B. 1978. Unpublished typed notes for CUSO Slide Show of Thamaga Pottery. Courtesy of Dorte Deans, Canada. p.4.

246 Pearson 1978, p.3.

247 Praamsma, S. 2009; Ibid.

248 Pearson ca.1978:3,4.

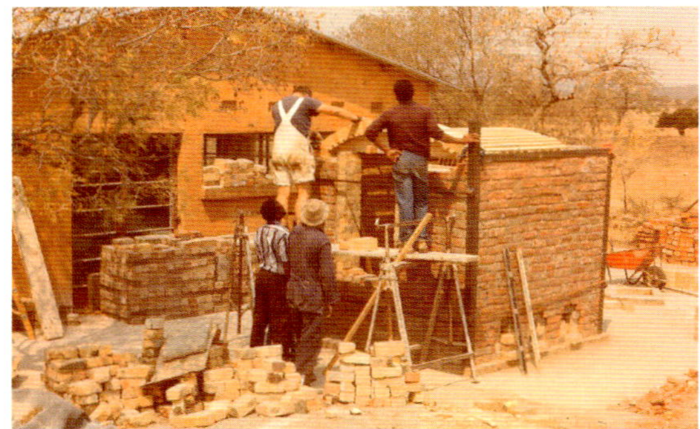

Thamaga Pottery | Sietze Praamsma and staff building kiln c.1979 | Provenance: Sietze Praamsma | Photograph by Saskia Praamsma | Scan by Sietze Praamsma

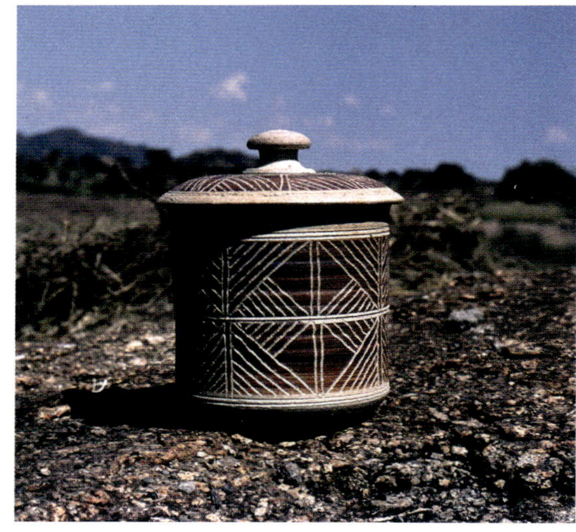

Thamaga Pottery | Lidded jar in the veld | Provenance: Dorte Deans | Photograph by Bodil Pearson

249 The Old Jar ashtray with painted floral maiolica decoration and embossed symbol in the centre. 40 H, 165 diam rim, 140 diam base.Tatham Art Gallery Collection. Accession number 2739/07. White glazed base with black glazed mark, 'Hand made for Associated Lead Mnfrs.'

250 Author's email correspondence with Corine Meyer, Ditsong NCHM, 6 March 2012.

251 Author's telephonic interview with Herry Duys, Johannesburg, 24 July 2005.

252 Author's telephonic interview with Henk Jacobs, Holland, 24 July 2005 and 8 March 2006.

253 My sincere thanks to F H Haenggi for informing me that Louis Le Sueur studied at the Old Jar Pottery in Benoni in 1959. (Email correspondence with F H Haenggi, Switzerland, 12 April 2012).

254 The Bedworth Colliery was owned by the Vereeniging Estates Limited until 1903, when the Vereeniging Brick and Tile Company Limited (VBTC) was formally established.

255 The fire-clay bricks were supplied to the Cape Government Railways to line the fire-boxes of locomotives.

256 These domestic bricks were dispatched to the diamond mines and township of Kimberley.

257 The only known examples of VBTC wares are simple, rustic, undecorated glazed earthenware casseroles and braziers, and can be found in Coll: Sammy Marks House Museum, DNMCH.

258 The Vereeniging Brick and Tile Company (VTBC) primarily produced building bricks, paving and Klompje bricks, salt-glazed stoneware pipes, fire, building and paving bricks, sanitary fittings, agricultural drainage tiles, floor and roof tiles, insulators, acid-proof wares, and wine and acid jars.

259 The anonymous 'K' was responsible for producing an elegant wheel-thrown earthenware bottle with streaky yellow-ochre and brown matt glaze in the 1950s [Acc. No. 90/719. Iziko SACH].

260 CK was responsible for decorating a large elongated bowl with sgraffitto images of San art in the 1950s or 1960s.

261 Automobile manufacturers included Volkswagen, Opel, Chevrolet, Nissan, Mazda and Leyland.

262 Banks included Barclays Bank, Allied, Nedbank and the SA Permanent Building Society.

263 Large manufacturing concerns included Philips, Firestone, Mobil, Caltex, Kroneburg, Windhoek Beer, Hansa Beer, PG Glass, Motorcraft, Oshkosh, Rothmans Cigarettes, Svenmill, Bears Furniture Stores, IBS, Induna, Sasko, Epol and Barlow's.

264 These included Meltonwold (The Oasis of the Karoo), the National Sea Rescue Institute (NSRI); Hamlet Hotel; NG Kerk, Kroonstasd-Sud; AE Motor Spares; Afmec Crane Hire; The Pharmaceutical Society of South Africa; Hamilton Sports Club; Grey ands Ostrich Farm; 1969 SADC Hockey Festival, Windhoek; and DF Malan Airport.

265 Zaalberg's tile sizes were 78mm square, 156mm square and 156x78mm.

266 The bulk of these references were obtained from the website www.studiopottery.com Other terms were obtained from www.digitalfire.com, www.tulane.edu/~kidder/Anth%20461/ceramic%20terms.html and www.ceramicartsdaily.org.

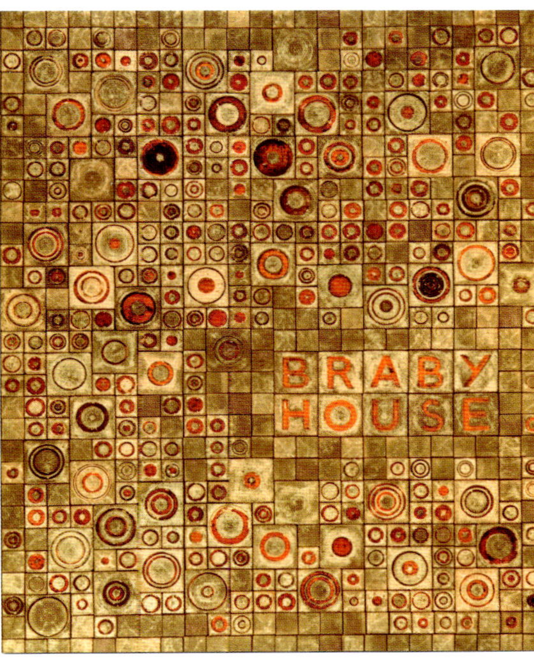

Zaalberg Potterij | Tile mural, Braby House | Provenance: Zaalberg Archives, SHC Iziko | SACHM 90/607 | Scan by Lailah Hisham

Bibliography

Monographs, journals and theses

Abrahams, G. 1994. Coarse Earthenware of the VOC Period: 18th-century pottery excavated from the Grand Parade at the Cape. *Annals of the South African Cultural History Museum*. 6 (1):5–14.

Abrahams, G. 1996. Foodways of the mid-eighteenth century Cape: Archaeological ceramics from the Grand Parade in central Cape Town. (PhD. Thesis).

Abrahams-Willis, G., 1998. Archaeology and Local Cuisine: Signatures of the Cape around 1750. Annals of the South African Cultural History Museum. 10.

Anderson, G. 1976. Kolonyama Workshop Number 2. *Sgraffiti*. 10:10,11.

Ashcroft, B. 1989. Place and displacement. In Ashcroft, B., G. Griffiths & H. Tiffin (eds.). *The Empire Writes Back: Theory and Practice in Post-Colonial Literatures*. London & New York: Routledge. pp.2–12.

Basson, E.L. 2006. Pottering around in Africa: Erich Mayer's search for an indigenous South African style as exemplified in his ceramic designs. *De Arte*. 74:3–19.

Calder, I. 2012. Continuity and Change: Ceramics at the Centre for Visual Art, UKZN PMB. In Stretton, J. (ed.) *All Fired Up: Conversations between Kiln and Collection*. Durban: Durban Art Gallery, pp.59–64.

Chase, J. 1842. *The Cape of Good Hope and the Eastern Province of Algoa Bay*. London: Pelham Richardson.

Clark, G. & Wagner, L. 1974. *Potters of Southern Africa*. Cape Town: Struik.

Clifford, J. 1988. *The Predicament of Culture: Twentieth-century Ethnography, Literature and Art*, First ed. Cambridge, Mass.: Harvard University Press.

Cruise, W. 1991. *Contemporary Ceramics in South Africa*. Cape Town: Struik.

Donaldson, K. (ed.) 1926. *South African Who's Who (Social and Business) 1925–1926*. Cape Town: Ken Donaldson.

Donaldson, K. (ed.) 1937. *South African Who's Who (Social & Business) 1937*. Cape Town: Ken Donaldson.

Donaldson, K. (ed.) 1955. *South African Who's Who 1955*. Johannesburg: Ken Donaldson.

Duffey, A.E. 1986. Afrikana Keramiek. *Suid-Afrikaanse Tydskrif vir Kunsgeskiedenis*. 1(3 and 4):37–42.

Edwards, D. 1895. *The General Directory of South Africa for 1894–95*. Cape Town: Dennis Edwards.

Francis Harrison, C.W. (ed.) 1903. *Natal: an Illustrated Official Railway Guide and Handbook of General Information*. London: Payne Jennings.

Gers, W. 1998. Latvian Immigrants Negotiating a South African Identity. Negotiating Identities. Proceedings of the 14th Annual Conference of the South African Association of Art Historians, 15–17 July 1998, University of South Africa, Pretoria.

Gers, W. 1998. *South African Studio Ceramics: A selection from the 1950s*. Port Elizabeth: King George VI Art Gallery.

Gers, W. 2000. South African Studio Ceramics, ca.1950s: the Kalahari Studio, Drostdy Ware and Crescent Potteries. Unpublished master's thesis, University of Natal, Pietermaritzburg.

Hall, A.W.H. 1936. *Report on Economic Conditions in South Africa, October 1935*. London: His Majesty's Stationery Office, p.22.

Heymans, J.A. 1989. Pottebakkerswerk in Suid-Afrika met spesifieke verwysing na die werk wat vanaf 1925 tot 1952 by Olifantsfontein gedoen is. Unpublished master's thesis, University of Pretoria.

Heysteck, H. 1973. Clays for the S.A. Potter. *Sgraffiti*. 1:5.

Hobart Houghton, D. 1964. *The South African Economy*. Cape Town: Oxford University Press.

Jones, J. 2007. *Studio Pottery in Britain 1900–2005*. London: A & C Black.

Kannemeyer, M. 1951. Dr Mikrill's Notebook. *Africana Notes and News*. VIII:55–59.

Kerrod, J. 2010. *Southern African Ceramics, their Marks, Monograms & Signatures*. [Cape Town]: BOE.

Kirby, P.R. 1958. James Hancock, China painter. *Africana Notes and News* 13(1):2–10.
Klose, J.E. 1997. Analysis of ceramic assemblage from four Cape historical sites dating from the late seventeenth century to the mid-nineteenth century. Unpublished master's thesis, University of Cape Town.
Klose, J.E. & Malan, A. 1993. *Ceramics of the Southwestern Cape, 1650-1850: a guide to the analysis and interpretation of ceramic assemblage from archaeological sites.* Cape Town: Historical Archaeological Group, University of Cape Town.
Konczacki, Z.A. 1967. *Public Finance and Economic Development in Natal, 1893–1910.* Durham, N.C.: Duke University Press.
Laidler, P.W. 1927. *A Tavern of the Ocean: being a social and historical sketch of Cape Town from its earliest days.* Cape Town: Maskew Miller.
Lastovica, E. 2000. *An Illustrated Guide [to] Ginger Beer Bottles for South African Collectors.* Wynberg, Cape Town: Gaffer.
Leigh, R. L. 1968. *Vereeniging.* Johannesburg: Courier-Gazette.
Liebenberg, B.J & S.B. Spies. (eds). 1993. *South Africa in the 20th Century.* Pretoria: J.L. van Schaik.
Macmillan, A. ca.1935. *Environs of the Golden City and Pretoria.* Cape Town: Cape Times Limited.
Malan, A. & Klose, J. 2000. The ceramic signature of the Cape in the nineteenth century, with particular reference to the Tennant Street site, Cape Town. *The South African Archaeological Bulletin* 55(171):49–59.
Malan, A. & Klose, J. 2003. Nineteenth century ceramics in Cape Town, South Africa. In S. Lawrence (ed.), *Archaeologies of the British: explorations of identity in Great Britain and its colonies 1600–1945.* London: Routledge, pp.191–210.
Martinson, W. & Fisher, R. Lexicon: Vereeniging tiles. www.artefacts.co.za/main/Buildings/style_det.php?styleid=1224, consulted 18 February 2012.
Miller, D. Materials analysis of archaeological ceramics in Southern Africa. *South African Archaeological Bulletin* 46:12–18.
Mitford-Barberton, I. 1968. *Some frontier families: Biographical sketches of 100 Eastern Province families before 1840.* Cape Town: Human & Rousseau.
Nel, K. 2000. African Art FromThe Egon Guenther Family Collection. Sotheby's Auction Catalogue. Reproduced on the Rand African Art website, www.randafricanart.com/Egon_Guenther_Interview.html, accessed 6 July 2009.
Nilant, F.G.E. 1963. *Contemporary Pottery in South Africa.* Cape Town: Balkema.
Perrill, E. 2012. (un)Earthing History: Ceramics at the Durban Art Gallery. In Durban Art Gallery. *All Fired Up: Conversations netween Kiln and Collection.* Durban: Durban Art Gallery.
Preziosi, D.A. 1998. *The Art of Art History: A Critical Anthology.* Oxford: OUP.
Rosenthal, E. 1961. *Tankards and Traditions.* Cape Town: Howard Timmins.
Schoonraad, M. & Schoonraad, E. 1989. *Companion to South African Cartoonists.* Johannesburg: AD Donker.
South African Bureau of Standards 1961. Pottery Testing: Help for a growing Industry. *South African Standards Bulletin* 15:26–28.
Stadsraad van Kempton Park. 1978 *Spieëlbeeld van die Verleede: Kempton Park 1903–1978.* Kempton Park: Stadsraad.
Thornton, K.L. 1990. South African Pottery. Unpublished dissertation, H.N.D. Studio Ceramics, Derbyshire College of Education, England.
Thornton, R.D. 1973. A survey of the South African ceramics industry. Unpublished M.Phil. Thesis, Leeds University.
Trotter, A.F. 1900. *Old Colonial Houses of the Cape of Good Hope.* London: Batsford.
Vermeulen, T.F. 1984. Die Potterbakkerskuns van Natal met spesiale verwysing na die mees invloedryke pottebakkers buite die provinsie se grense. Unpublished MA Thesis, University of Natal.
Vos, H. 1979. Kaapse Kookpotte. *Stellenbossiania.* 2:4.

Watt, R. 2012. Red-hot roots. Art At Work Today. *National Ceramics Quarterly* 100:12–17.
Winer, M. & Deetz, J. 1990. The transformation of British Culture in Eastern Cape, 1820–1860. *Social Dynamics.* 16(1):55–75.
Woodward, C.S. 1974. *Oriental ceramics at the Cape of Good Hope, 1652–1795.* Cape Town: A.A. Balkema.
Zaalberg, M. (ed) 1985. *1985 Yearbook of South African Ceramics.* Cape Town: Perskor.

Archival records

1950. Certificate of Registration of Kalahari Studio. 1 September. Klopcanovs Archives.
Adams, J. 1916.The possibilities of pottery manufacture in Natal. Publisher: [Durban]: Natal Society for the Advancement of Science and Art (Durban, South Africa). National Art Library, London. General Collection 96.HH Box X, Normal -122086.
Boshoff, S. ca.1976. Liebermann – Sy Pottebakkery. Unpublished essay for Art History III, University of Pretoria. NA UP.
Cape Town Chamber of Commerce, 1954–1955. Doc No:KAB 194373557, Batch No 23034041000, Depot KAB, Source: CC, Type: Leer, Vol: 3/4/1/31. System: 01, Ref: E/300/4/2, Part:1.
Cooper, H.W.A. (Secretary of J.C. Smuts). 1955. Letter of thanks to Alexander Klopcanovs for pieces of pottery presented at the Witwatersrand Agricultural Show. Klopcanovs Estate.
Cullinan, R.V. 1947. Letter to Major General I. P. de Villiers, Chairman, Immigrant Selection Board, Department of the Interior. 15 Sept. TAB Doc No 601210850000, Depot SAB, Source GG, Type Leer, Vol: 2212, system 01, Ref: 78/201, Part A.
Export of China clay: consolidated harbour and railway taxes (1908). Doc Nr 194058539, Batch no 509640089000, Depot KAB, Source T, Vol: 109, System 01, Ref.: 1207, Part 1.
Frank, A. 1987. Unpublished correspondence between Mrs Rose Trehaven, Curator, No. 7 Castle Hill Museum, Port Elizabeth, and Audrey Frank, Durban, 9 August. Courtesy of R. Trehaven.
Glenday, K. 1990. Marietjie van der Merwe: Past Award Winner Corobrik. *Ceramix and Craft South Africa.* pp.6,7. Archival collection of Marietjie van der Merwe's personal papers found in BC 1148 The HW Van Der Merwe Papers, Manuscripts & Archives: University of Cape Town Libraries.
Hill, L. 1945. Pottery [Exhibition Catalogue]. Cape Town: Tip Top. L. Hill File, Ceramics Archives. SHC Izikollliquid case. The Old Jar Pottery Company (Pty.) Ltd. Versus Russ-Electric Furnaces South Africa (Pty.) Ltd. 1966. Doc No: TAB 496861517, Batch No 817230110000, Depot TAB, Source: WLD, Type: Leer, Vol: 0. System: 01, Ref: 4610/1966, Part:1.
Liebermann, S. 1975. Letter. 4 Oct. Collection of Douglas van der Horst, Cape Town.
Lovell, B.M. 1959. Letter from Silwood Ceramics to F.G.E. Nilant. 21 Jan. NA UP.
Mills, G.M. 1949. Die kuns van die pottebakker: 'n besoek aan Leta Hill. *Die Naweek.* 31 March. L. Hill File, Ceramics Archives, SHC Iziko.
Mines and Minerals Board 1903. Permission asked by Messrs. Baumann and Gilfillan on behalf of The Consolidated Rand Brick, Pottery & Lime Company to extract clay from claims nos 576, 587 and 186 on the farm Vogelfontein. Transvaal Archives. Doc. No. TAB496890321. Batch No. 606950860000. Vol 3, ref. Drk374/03, part 1.
Money, A.M.C. 1940. Erdewerk. *Die Naweek.* 7 November. L. Hill File, Ceramics Archives, SHC Iziko.
Muirhead, J.M. 1959a. Letter from The Ceramic Industries Association of the Transvaal Chamber of Industries to Dr F.G.E. Nilant. 10 March. NA UP.
Muirhead, J.M. 1959b. Letter to members of the Ceramic Industries Association of South Africa. 28 April.
Muirhead, J.M. 1960. Letter from The Ceramic Industries Association of the Transvaal Chamber of Industries to Dr F.G.E. Nilant. 12 Feb. NA UP.
Nilant, F.G.E. 1956. [List of] Pottery factories in South Africa in the 1950s. NA UP.

Nilant, F.G.E. 1958. Circular letter to all potteries and ceramic manufacturers. 8 December. NA UP.
Nilant, F.G.E. 1958. Ons Pottebakkers Verdien Steun. *Die Transvaler.* 21 October. NA UP.
Nilant, F.G.E. 1960. Steun Gevra vir Pottebakkers. *Die Transvaler.* 29 January. NA UP.
Nilant, F.G.E. 1962. Unpublished research notes on Crescent Potteries. NA UP.
Nilant, F.G.E. 1962. Unpublished research notes on the Kalahari Studio. NA UP.
[No author] 1939. Interesting People. *The Pictorial.* p. 39. L. Hill File, Ceramics Archives, SHC Iziko.
[No author] 1939.The Decoration in Modern Planning. *Architect Builder & Engineer.* p. 31. L. Hill File, Ceramics Archives, SHC Iziko.
[No author] 1957 A visit to the home of ... Drostdy Ware, Grahamstown Potteries Limited, Grahamstown, C.P. [sic] [Grahamstown Pottery]: [Grahamstown].
[No author] 1959a. Potters cannot face Jap. competition. [sic] *Sunday Times.* 10 May. N UP.
[No author] 1959b. Pottebakkersbedryf 'Regering Blaas Nuwe Lewe In'. *Die Vaderland.* 8 October. NA UP.
[No author] 1970s. Pot-bakkery kry stoot in Transkei. Unmarked newspaper cutting concerning Izandla, courtesy of A. Kirk.
[No author] 1972. Potter's craft. *The Pretoria News.* 11 September. NA UP.
[No author] 1975. Their pictures on the wall... *The Star.* 18 November. NA UP.
[No author] 1976. Story of beer told in 12 metres of ceramic panels. *The Argus.* 4 May. NA UP.
[No author] 1978. Hand-made tiles. *S.A. Digest.* 15 December. NA UP.
[No author] 1978. Pottery studio started on 'less than a shoe-string'. *The Star.* 26 September. NA UP.
[No author] 1980s. Sammy decided that his law studies could go to pot. Unknown newspaper. No date. NA UP.
Raad van Handel en Nywerheid. 1958. Letter to Dr F.G.E. Nilant. 12 November. NA UP.
Rayner, P. 1941. What is a Potter? *Trek.* 19 July. L. Hill File, Ceramics Archives, SHC Iziko.
Records concerning E.R.C. Most. (1905). Doc Nr NAB191002346, Batch no 4235004000, Depot NAB, Source PM, Vol: 52, System 01, Ref.: 1905/147, Part 1.
Records of Dock dues on Clay and Manganese for export (1906). Doc Nr 194054433, Batch no 509230079000, Depot KAB, Source T, Vol: 995, System 01, Ref.: 3370, Part 1.
Rosenthal, E. 1960. Consolidated Rand Brick Pottery & Lime Co. Minutes of Board Meetings, 1947–1960. SA Library, TT Manuscript MSC 32.
SA Association of the Arts. 1946. Minutes of a Meeting of the Ceramic Exhibition Committee, SA Association of the Arts, Cape Town, 19 November. L. Hill File, Ceramics Archives SHC Iziko.
Steele-Gray, N. 1955. Reply to F.G.E. Nilant's Questionnaire on Pottery in South Africa. NA UP.
Strydom, M. 1974. Liebermann Pottebakkery. Unpublished Honours Thesis, University of Pretoria. NA UP.
Van der Merwe, H.J. 1962. Letter from the Ceramic Industries Association of the Transvaal Chamber of Industries to Dr F.G.E. Nilant. 1 June. NA UP.
Van Zyl, A. 1972. Liebermanns se werk hier te sien. *Hoofstad.* 8 January. NA UP.
[Women's Page Reporter]. 1968. Art and the potter. *The Star.* 19 March. NA UP.
Zaalberg, M. 1956. Letter to F.G.E. Nilant. NA UP.

South African Art and History – general texts

Alexander, F.L. 1962. *Art in South Africa: Painting, Sculpture and Graphic Work since 1900.* Cape Town: A.A. Balkema.
Andersen, J. & A.R. Goliath. (eds) 1989. *South African Art News Index: 1983–1988.* Cape Town: South African National Gallery.
Arnold, M. 1996. *Women and Art in South Africa.* Cape Town: David Philip.

Ashton, H. 1967. *The Basuto: A Social Study of Traditional and Modern Lesotho*. Second Edn. London: OUP.
Berman, E. 1975. *The Story of South African Painting*. Cape Town: A.A. Balkema.
Berman, E. 1983. *Art and Artists of South Africa. An illustrated Biographical Dictionary and Historical Survey of Painters, Sculptors and Graphic Artists since 1875*. Cape Town: A.A. Balkema.
Berman, E. 1996. *Art and Artists of South Africa*. Halfway House: Southern. Third edition.
Brown, J.A. 1978. *South African Art*. Cape Town: Macdonald.
De Jager, E.J. 1973. *Contemporary African Art in South Africa*. Cape Town: Struik.
De Kok, V. 1960. *Our Heritage/Ons Erfenis*. Cape Town: Nasionale Boekhandel Bpk.
Denbow, J.R. & Thebe, P.C. 2006. *Culture and Customs of Botswana*. Westport, Conn.: Greenwood.
Fransen, H. 1982. *Three Centuries of South African Art*. Johannesburg: A.D. Donker.
Gaskin, L.J.P. 1965. *A Biography of African Art*. London: International African Institute.
Harmsen, F. 1985. *Looking at South African Art: A guide to the Study and Appreciation of Art*. Pretoria: J.L. van Schaik.
Hillebrand, M. 1986. *Art and Architecture in Natal*. Unpublished PhD. Thesis, University of Natal, Pietermaritzburg.
Jeppe, H. 1963. *South African Artists. 1900–1962*. Johannesburg: Afrikaanse Pers-boekhandel.
Johannesburg Art Gallery. 1988. *The Neglected Tradition: Towards a New History of South African Art (1930–1988)*. Johannesburg: Johannesburg Art Gallery.
Levinsohn, R. 1984. *Art and Craft of Southern Africa*. Craighall: Delta.
Lissoos, S. 1986. *Johannesburg Art and Artists: Selections from a Century*. Johannesburg: Johannesburg Art Gallery.
McClelland, L. & L. Alexander (eds) 1985. *Women Artists in South Africa*. Cape Town: South African National Gallery.
Miles, E. 1997. *Land and Lives: a story of early black artists*. Cape Town: Human and Rousseau.
Nettleton, A. & D. Hammond-Tooke (eds) 1989. *African Art in Southern Africa: From Tradition to Township*. Johannesburg: A.D. Donker.
Nienaber, P.J. 1951. *Skone Kunste in Suid Afrika*. Johannesburg: Afrikaanse Pers-boekhandel. Deel 1.
Nilant, F.G.E. & Schoonraad, M. 1976. *Biografie: Suid Afrikaanse Kunstenaars*. No. 3. Pretoria: University of Pretoria.
Ogilvie, G. 1988. *The Dictionary of South African Painters and Sculptors*. Johannesburg: Everard Read.
Ramsay, J. & Morton, B. & F. 1996. *Historical Dictionary of Botswana*. London: Scarecrow Press.
Rankin, E. & Miles, E. 1989. The role of the missions in art education in South Africa. South African Association of Art Historians 5th Annual Conference. Durban: University of Natal, pp.74–81.
Stevenson, M & Viljoen, D. 1999. *Southern African Art, 1850–1990*. Johannesburg: B.C.I. Fine Art.
[W.H.K.] 1934. *The Arts of South Africa*. Durban: Knox.
Williams, S. 2006. *Colour Bar: The Truimph of Seretse Khama and his Nation*. London: Penguin.

Individual potteries

Conrand: Transvaal Pottery, the Ceramic Studio and Linnware

Anon. 1938. *The South African Woman's Who's Who*. Biographies: Johannesburg. pp.54, 358, 398.
Cartwright, A.P. 1977. *Diamonds and Clay*. Cape Town: Purnell. pp.87, 88.
Gers, W. 1999. South African pottery studios: The Ceramic Studio and Linnware. *Reflections of Yesteryear* 1(5).

Grice, J. 1951. The Potter's Ancient Craft: From a layman to laymen. *Iscor News* 16: 292–297, 304.
Hillebrand, M. 1989. *Mary Stainbank Retrospective Exhibition.* [No place]: [s.n.]
Hillebrand, M. 1991. *The Women of Olifantsfontein: South African Studio Ceramics.* Cape Town: South African National Gallery.
Liebenberg-Barkhuizen, E. 1998. 'Self' and 'other': Some portraits by Mary Stainbank. In: B. Bell & I. Calder (eds.). *Umbumba: Aspects of indigenous ceramics in KwaZulu-Natal.* Pietermaritzburg: Tatham Art Gallery.
Liebenberg-Barkhuizen, E. 2002.The Iconography of the 'indigene' in Mary Stainbank's sculpture ca.1920–1940. Unpublished doctoral thesis, University of South Africa.
Liebenberg-Barkhuizen, E. 2003. Mary Stainbank, Modernism and the Spirit of Africa. Paper presented to the History and African Studies Seminar in the McIntyre Library, University of KwaZulu-Natal, 8 April 2003. www.history.ukzn.ac.za/node/559. Consulted 10 December 2008.
Methley, J. 1926. The Development of Pottery making in South Africa. *The Common Room Magazine.* Summer: 21–25.
[No author] 1955. *Centenary Exhibition of S.A. Crafts.* [Catalogue]. 23 August–9 September 1955.
Ringdahl, P 1991. Early Transvaal Pottery at Olifantsfontein 1907–1955 – An Historic Presentation. *Ceramix and Craft South Africa.* January, February, March. pp.9, 10.
SA Association of the Arts. 1954. *Arts and Crafts Exhibition* [Catalogue]. 22 June–5 July 1954.
Thornton, R.D. 1973. A survey of the South African ceramics industry. Unpublished M.Phil. Thesis, Leeds University. pp.12, 13.
Van der Horst, D. 1996. Tiles on the Veld: a Pioneering South African Ceramics Enterprise. *Glazed Expressions* 33(Autumn):1–2.
Van der Horst, D. 1999. The Decorative Tiles of Olifantsfontein. Part 1. *Cape Chronicle.* 3(3):1, 3–4.
Van der Horst, D. 1999. The Decorative Tiles of Olifantsfontein. Part 2. *Cape Chronicle.* 3(4): 3–4.

Crescent Potteries

Crescent Potteries. [ca.1959] [Catalogue of] African Ceramics. [Johannesburg].
De Wet 2012. 'Lawyer "hijacks" art treasure.' M&G Online. 13 July. www.mg.co.za/article/2012-07-12-sowetos-great-art-rip-off/ Consulted on 1 September 2013.
Gers, W. ca.1998 SA Pottery: South African pottery studios: Crescent Potteries. *Reflections of Yesteryear* 1(2):12–14.
Kuhn, J. 1974. *Twelve shades of black.* Cape Town: Don Nelson.
[No author] 1958. Here's Africa – in clay. *The South African Exporter.* Sept, pp.14, 15.
[No author] 1958a. Demand for South Africa's Uranium. *The South African Exporter.* Sept, p.15.
[No author][No date] *Otto Schließler: Zeichnungen eines Bildhauers.* [Translated into English by Vivian Trobek. 28 July 1997].
Richards, C. 1997. Cross Purposes: Durant Sihlali's art of allegory. In: Geers, K. (ed). *Contemporary South African Art: The Gencor Collection.* Johannesburg: Jonathan Ball, pp.81–97.
Sarrazin, M. (ed). 1994. *Durant Sihlali: Mural Retrospective. 1960–1994.* Johannesburg: The Artist's Press.
Rankin, E. 1989. *Images of Wood – Aspects of the History of Sculpture in 20th Century South Africa.* Johannesburg: Johannesburg Art Gallery, p.163.

Dykor Ceramic Studio

Viviers, A. 2008. Architectour. *VISI.* 39:199–222.

Globe Potteries

Bosch, A. & De Waal, J. 1988. *Esias Bosch*. Cape Town: Struik Winchester, p.22.

[Harlequin Gallery] [s.n.] Information on Douglas Portway, www.studio-pots.com/DouglasPortway.htm.

Methley, J. 1926. The Development of Pottery making in South Africa. *The Common Room Magazine*. Summer:22.

Modern British Artists. 2005. Information on Douglas Portway. Consulted on 20 May 2007. www.modernbritishartists.co.uk/portway_index.htm. Consulted on 20 May 2007.

Grahamstown Pottery and Hamburger's Pottery

Drostdy ware [Catalogue] ca.1950. African ceramics from the colourful continent. [s.n.].

Gers, W. 1997. Images of gender and the 'other' on the domestic ceramics of Drostdy Ware. *Proceedings of the 1997 Conference of South African Art Historians Association*. Stellenbosch: University of Stellenbosch.

Gers, W. 1998a. SA Pottery: South African pottery studios: Grahamstown Pottery, Drostdy Ware. *Reflections of Yesteryear*. 1(1): 18–20.

Gers, W. 2000b. South African pottery studios: Hamburger's Pottery. *Reflections of Yesteryear* 1(12).

[No author] 1953. Twenty-fold expansion in five years. *The South African Exporter*. pp.25–28.

[No author] 1955 Pottery the world is ordering. *Grahamstown – the Spirit of Progress; 1820–1955*. Johannesburg: Municipal Public Relations Bureau.

[No author] 1962. Industry with its roots in history. *Eastern Province Herald*. 3:11.

[No author] 1963. An old craft becomes a young industry. *The Caltex Circle*. 4(2):15–17.

P.H.W. [Boshoff]. 1950. S.A. Applied Arts on View. *Cape Times*. 6 February.

Groenkloof Brick, Tile and Pottery Works

Donaldson, K. 1927. *South African Who's Who (Social and Business): 1927–1928*. Cape Town: Ken Donaldson. p.168.

Duffey, A.E. 2005. *A Commemorative Tale of Two Cities: Ceramics and Glass wares celebrating Pretoria and Johannesburg. [Exhibition Catalogue]*. Pretoria: University of Pretoria.

Ikhwezi Lokusa

Riddle, G. 2006. Training in the Ikhwezi Lokusa Project. In: ILO. 2007. *People with disabilities: Pathways to decent work: Report of a tripartite workshop, Pretoria, South Africa, 19–21 September 2006*. Geneva. www.ilo.org/wcmsp5/groups/public/---ed_emp/---ifp_skills/documents/publication/wcms_107787.pdf. Accessed 15 October 2009.

[No author] 1988. Ikhwezi Lokusa Pottery. *Daily Dispatch*. 6 May.

Steele, J. 1988. Ikhwezi Lokusa Pottery. *Ceramix*. 4:26–29.

Izandla

Gill, M. CV obtained from the Cornwall Artists web site, www.cornwallartists.org/cornwall-artists/michael-gill. Accessed 15 July 2010.

Rich, P.B. (ed). 1996. *Reaction and Renewal in South Africa*. Palgrave: USA.

Kalahari Studio

Albrecht, E. 1949. Klei in die hand van die potterbakker: twee immigrante skep 'n nuwe standaard in ons land. *Sarie Marais*, 21 December, pp.7, 8, 9, 16.

Birstowe, A. 1999. Kalahari Ware's comeback after 40 years in the wilderness. *Sunday Times*. (Gauteng Metro Section). 7 Feb.

Cheales, R. 1969. An artist with a gossamer touch. *The Star*. 1 July.

Cumming, F 1973. Meetings with Peninsula artists. *The Natal Witness.* 4 Apr.
Dubow, N. 1963. Pieter Wenning Gallery: First Art show is mixed bag. *The Cape Argus.* 10 January.
Gers, W. 1998b. SA Pottery: South African pottery studios: the Kalahari Ware Studio. *Reflections of Yesteryear.* 1(2):12–14.
Gers, W. 1998f. The Kalahari Studio. Stephan Welz and Co. In Association with Sotheby's. Decorative and Fine Arts [Catalogue for Auction to be held in] Cape Town, 20 October 1998. [Cape Town]: [Stephan Welz and Co. In Association with Sotheby's.] pp.25.
Kettering, K. 1998. Domesticating Uzbeks: Central Asians in Soviet decorative art of the twenties and thirties.
[No author] 1950. S.A. Applied Arts on View. *Cape Times.* 6 February.
[No author] 1953. Ceramics for U.S. *The Cape Times.* 25 August.
[No author] 1955. *Centenary Exhibition of S.A. Crafts* [Catalogue]. 23 August–9 September.
[No author] 1955. Klei uit die Kaapse strate is hul kos. *Die Huisgenoot.* 10 October, pp.39, 40.
[No author] 1961. Ceramic artist's unusual house. *The Cape Times.* 12 July.
[No author] 1962. Artist's ceramic castle amid the tall pines. *The Cape Argus.* 21 December.
[No author] 1964a. The economy of line. *Rand Daily Mail.* 10 October.
[No author] 1964b. Art in Industry. *South African Panorama.* November:20–21.
Reinhardt, M. 1961. Potters place art first: Indigenous theme in ceramics. *Data.* December:6.
[Siebert, K. & Hardy, P.] 1992. Kalahari ware. *National Ceramics Quarterly.* 21(September):16.
[Smithsonian Institution] 1953. [Catalogue of the] *Fourth Annual International Exhibition of Ceramic Arts: Pottery, Enamel, Ceramic Sculpture, Stained Glass. 1–28 Sept. 1953.* Washington DC: Smithsonian Institution.
South African Association of the Arts 1954. *Arts and Crafts Exhibition* [Catalogue]. 22 June–5 July
Stephan Welz and Co. In Association with Sotheby's 1998. Decorative and Fine Arts [Catalogue for Auction to be held in] Cape Town, 20 Oct. 1998. [Cape Town]: [Stephan Welz and Co. In Association with Sotheby's.] pp.25–30.
Stephan Welz and Co. In Association with Sotheby's 1999. Decorative and Fine Arts [Catalogue for Auction of held in] Cape Town, 11, 12 October 1999. [Cape Town]: [Stephan Welz and Co. In Association with Sotheby's.] p.95.
Winder, H.E. 1976a. Must be seen to be believed. *Rand Daily Mail.* 14 September.
Winder, H.E. 1976b. Strength, humour, colour and excitement. *Rand Daily Mail.* 30 November.

Kolonyama Pottery, Lesotho

Barnett, R. 1976. Kolonyama – Potter's Paradise. *The Garden & Home.* Dec.
Finch, J. [undated]. CV. From www.potteryandpaintings.co.uk/index.htm. Consulted 10 March 2012.
Finch, T. [undated]. CV. From www.potteryandpaintings.co.uk/paintings.htm Consulted 10 March 2012.
Hale, A. 1994. NEVAC (National Electronic and Video Archive of the Crafts) interview with Ray Finch, owner of Winchcombe Pottery, Gloucestershire, 9 April 1994, NEVAC no. AC 77. Transcription typed up by Janine Partington 03 Apr.2000. pp. 58-60. www.interpretingceramics.com/issue001/finch/finch.htm, Consulted 6 March 2012.

Liebermann Pottery and Tiles

Berry, A. 1988. David B. Berry and the Ultimate Electric Kiln. *Ceramix and Craft: Southern Africa.* January:11.
Guassardo, M. 1988. In conversation with Andrew Walford. *National Ceramics Quarterly* 3:22.

Liebermann, L. 2005. Sammy Liebermann: his life, his work & his family. Unpublished manuscript, www.olisa9.wix.com/lisalieb#!book, accessed 2 June 2012.
[No author] History of Chelsea Pottery, www.studiopottery.com/cgi-bin/mp.cgi?item=52%20(Jan%202007), accessed 8 July 2008.
[No author] History of David Rawnsley and Chelsea Pottery, www.antonymaitland.com/hanbry01.htm#_Toc174202200, accessed 8 July 2008.
Silove, Y. 1988. Anne-Marie Berry. *Ceramix and Craft: Southern Africa.* July:23.
Van der Horst, D. 1998. Liebermann Tiles. *Glazed Expressions.* 37:1–3.

Mantenga Craft Pottery, Swaziland

Meyer, S. 1987. Profile: Speelman Mhlangu and notes on the Katlehong Art Centre. *Ceramix.* 2:6.
Venter, D. (ed.) 1974. *International Relations in Southern Africa.* Braamfontein: The South African Institute of International Affairs.

Marrakesh Pottery

Sinton-Hewett, J.J. 1957. Marrakesh in Johannesburg. *SA Panorama.* Oct. (s.n.)

Rorke's Drift Pottery

Battiss, W. 1977. ELC Art and Craft Centre at Rorke's Drift. *African Arts.* 11(1):38–42.
Calder, I. 1999. The inception of Rorke's Drift Pottery Workshop: tradition and innovation. South African Association of Art Historians, Proceedings of the Fifteenth Annual Conference, 1999, University of Natal. Pietermaritzburg, pp.39–51.
Cruise, W. 2005. Breaking the Mould: Women Ceramicists in KwaZulu-Natal. In Arnold, M. & B. Schmahmann (eds.). *Between Union and Liberation: Women Artists in South Africa, 1910-1944.* Aldershot: Ashgate. pp.132–151.
Du Plessis, L. 2007. Marietjie van der Merwe: ceramics 1960–1988. Unpublished Master of Art in Fine Arts dissertation, University of KwaZulu-Natal, Pietermaritzburg.
Hobbs, P. & Rankin, E. 2003. *Twenty Years of Printmaking in South Africa: Rorke's Drift: Empowering Prints.* Cape Town: Double Storey Books.
Hosking, S. 2005. Tradition and innovation: Rorke's Drift ceramics in the collection of the Durban Art Gallery, KwaZulu-Natal. Unpublished Master of Art in Fine Arts dissertation, University of KwaZulu-Natal, Pietermaritzburg.
Le Roux, P. 1998. Rorke's Drift pottery. In: B. Bell & I. Calder (eds.). *UBUMBA: aspects of indigenous ceramics in KwaZulu-Natal.* Pietermaritzburg: Tatham Art Gallery.
Maggs,T. & Ward, V. 2011. Judith Mkhabela, an inspirational potter from KwaZulu-Natal. *Southern African Humanities* 23: 151–71.
Offringa, D. 1988. Die Evangeliese Lutherse Kerk Kuns en Handwerksentrum, Rorke's Drift. Unpublished MA dissertation, University of Pretoria. Pretoria.
Rankin, E. & Hobbs, P. 1999. Imprinting Primitivism: Perceptions and Preconceptions of Printmaking at Rorke's Drift. *Mots Pluriels* 12, www/arts.uwa.edu.au/MotsPluriels/MP1299r&h.html. Consulted 10 January 2009.
University of Cape Town. Curriculum Vitae of M. van der Merwe. University of Cape Town Web Site. www.lib.uct.ac.za/mss/index.php?html=/mss/newaids/BC1148.HTM&msscollid=42. Consulted 14 June 2007.
Younge, G. 1988. *Art of the South African Townships.* London: Thames & Hudson.

South African Glazing Company, Boksburg East Potteries, Lucia Ware & Joy China

Gers, W. ca.2000.South African pottery studios: Lucia Ware. *Reflections of Yesteryear.* 1(11).

Thaba Bosigo Pottery, Lesotho

Hayes, P. 2009. Peter Hayes. Overview. Milestones. Step 2 – Africa. www.peterhayes-ceramics.uk.com. Consulted 3 October 2012.

Henry, P. 197- . Craftsmen Potters Association: News of Members. Geoffrey Whiting. *Ceramic Review*. 8 (March/April):2.

Van Gilder, B. 1973. Use of Slips on Pottery. *Sgraffitti*. 2(November):10, 11.

Van Gilder, B. 1974. Glazes. *Sgraffitti*. 3(March): 8, 9.

Whiting, D. 2004. Geoffrey Whiting 1919–1988. *Studio Pottery* 11(Oct/Nov):35–41.

Whiting, G. & Cooper, E. 1989. *Geoffrey Whiting, potter: A Retrospective Exhibition*. Aberystwyth: Aberystwyth Arts Centre, Wales.

Venter, D. (ed.) 1974. *International Relations in Southern Africa*. Braamfontein: The South African Institute of International Affairs.

Thamaga Pottery, Botswana

Anon. Biography of Saskia Praamsma. www.almontepottersguild.com/instructors.htm. Consulted 10 November 2008.

Grant, S. 2005. Craft: of weaving, pottery and basketry. Mmegi on-line newspaper. www.mmegi.bw/2005/May/Friday20/684896920820.html. Consulted 22 November 2008.

Hutchings, A. 1975. Build it up – with concrete blocks. *Sgraffiti*. 8:13, 14.

Mokgoabone, K. 2005. Promoting Thamaga's underprivileged. Mmegi on-line newspaper. www.mmegi.bw/2005/September/Friday23/4914123841122.html, Consulted 20 November 2008.

The Old Jar Pottery

Gidish, L. 1980. Potters' old-style craftsmanship alive and well. *The Star*. 3 September.

Loxton, A. 1961. Artists go on a 'clay spree': Instead of painting, they made pottery. *Sunday Times*. 26 March.

Salberg, B. 1981. The *Benoni City Times* talks to... Potter, Henry Duys. [sic] *Benoni City Times en Oosrandse Nuus*. 20 February.

Zaalberg Potterij

Bogaers, M. 1988. *Made in Holland: Dutch domestic pottery 1945–1988*. 's-Hertogenbosch: Het Kruithuis.

Gers, W. 2000a. South African pottery studios: Zaalberg Pottery. *Reflections of Yesteryear*. 2(1).

Guassardo, M. 1988. Service above Self' Maarten Zaalberg – philanthropist and potter. *National Ceramics Quarterly*. 5(October):14–18.

Hayward Fell, C 1989. Letter to the Editor. *The Cape Potter*. 48 (December):4.

Holme, R. & K. Frost (eds) 1956. *Decorative Art 1955–56*. London: The Studio.

Lurssen, N. 1979. The Modest Master. *Weekend Argus*. 14 July. Zaalberg File, IZIKO Ceramics Archives, Cape Town.

Zaalberg, M. (ed) 1985. *1985 Yearbook of South African Ceramics*. Cape Town: Perskor.

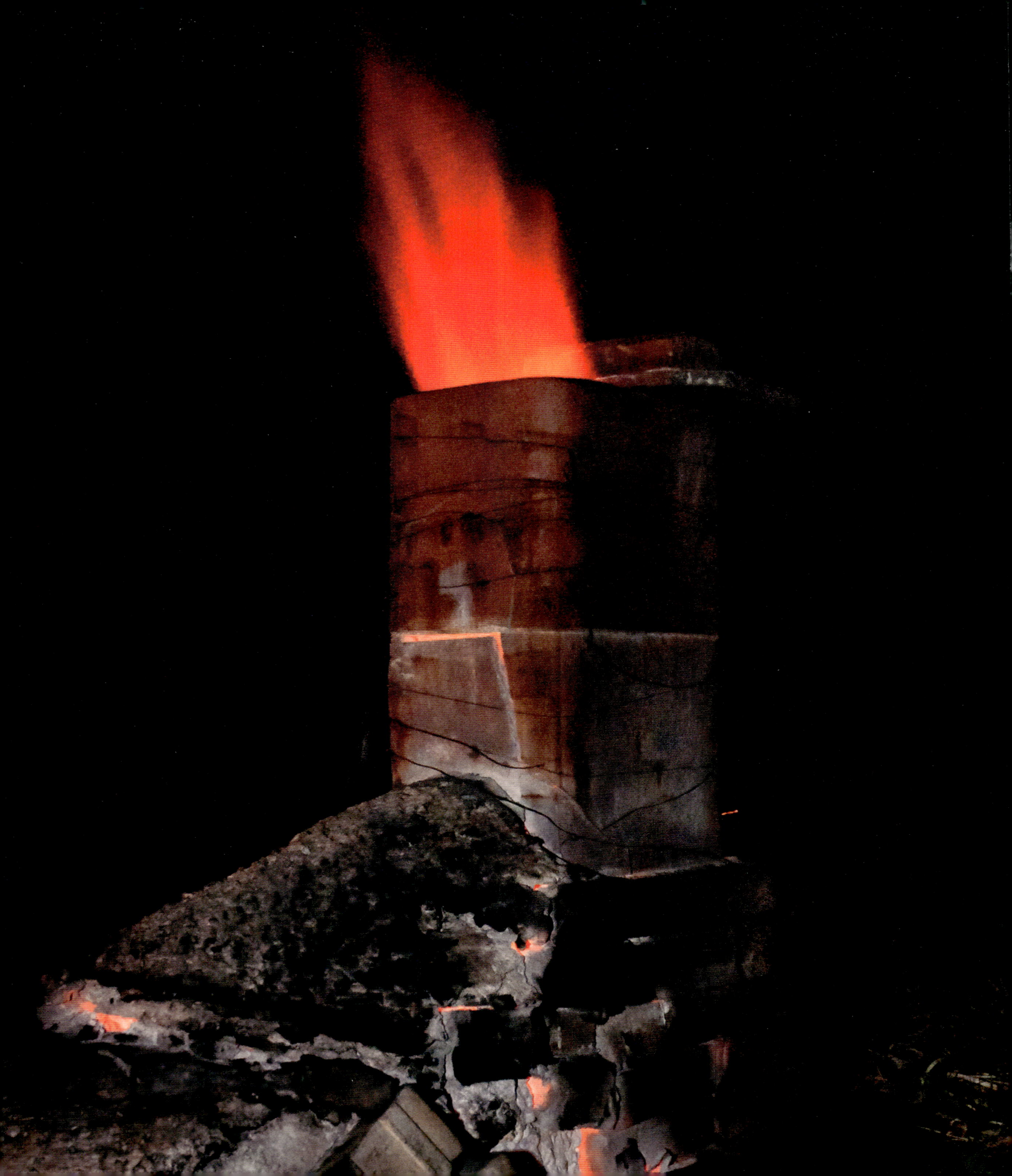

Index

Numbers in bold are main entries for each pottery or biographical entries for individuals.
Numbers in italics refer to photographs.

Untitled | Kiln chimney during firing | Photograph by Richard Yates

C

N